1990 MLA
International Bibliography
of Books and Articles
on the Modern Languages
and Literatures

VOLUME IV: GENERAL LITERATURE AND

RELATED TOPICS

PUBLISHED BY

The Modern Language Association of America

This is Volume IV of five volumes of the 1990 *MLA International Bibliography*. The five volumes are collected in a cumulative edition for libraries.

ISBN 0-87352-637-6

© 1991 by The Modern Language Association of America,
10 Astor Place, New York, NY 10003-6981

Guide for Users of the
1990 MLA International Bibliography

The *MLA Bibliography* provides a classified listing and subject index for books and articles published on modern languages, literatures, folklore, and linguistics. It is compiled by the staff of the Center for Bibliographical Services at MLA headquarters in New York City with the cooperation of more than two hundred contributing bibliographers in the United States and abroad.

The *Bibliography* is published in five volumes: Volume I, British Isles, British Commonwealth, English Caribbean, and American Literatures; Volume II, European, Asian, African, and Latin American Literatures; Volume III, Linguistics; Volume IV, General Literature and Related Topics; and Volume V, Folklore.

Individual paperbound volumes include author and subject indexes. Library editions are available in three different combinations: all five volumes with author and subject indexes; all five volumes with author index only; and Volumes I, II, and III with author index only.

The *Bibliography*, published annually, is available from the Member and Customer Services Office, MLA, 10 Astor Place, New York, NY 10003-6981.

Although the staff and contributors make every effort to cover all publications pertinent to the *Bibliography*, omissions do occur. To make certain that publications are listed in the *Bibliography*, authors are urged to send offprints of articles and copies of books for citation in subsequent volumes to the Center for Bibliographical Services, MLA, 10 Astor Place, New York, NY 10003-6981. Since the contents of documents listed in the *Bibliography* are indexed for subject access, it is mandatory that the document be included with notification of publication. Authors unable to send a copy of a monograph to be indexed must at least submit photocopies of the title page, verso of the title page, and table of contents page, as well as all pagination information, for the document to be eligible for listing.

Subject Scope

Works on literature transmitted orally, in print, or in audiovisual media and on human language, including both natural languages and invented languages that exhibit the characteristics of human language (e.g., sign language for the deaf, Esperanto, computer-programming languages), are listed. Works limited to pedagogy, even as it relates to the teaching of language, literature, composition, and related subjects, are excluded. Works on subjects such as aesthetics, human behavior, communication, and information processes are included only if they treat human language or literature. There are no historical-period restrictions on language coverage; for literature, works exclusively on classical Greek and Latin literatures are excluded since those literatures are covered in *L'année philologique*.

Document Scope

1. *Nationality and language.* There are no restrictions concerning either the place of origin or publication or the original language of works.

2. *Form.* Critical works on literature, language, and folklore are included. There is no restriction on the organization, format, or purpose of these works. Articles from journals, monographs, and collections—including working papers, conference papers, and proceedings—and indexes, bibliographies, catalogs, handbooks, dictionaries, and other types of reference works are listed. Literary works and translations are generally excluded unless they are newly discovered or rare works or editions that are accompanied by new critical or bibliographical apparatus or that are based on a newly established authoritative text. Reviews of literary and scholarly works are not included as these are covered in such indexes as *Book Review Index* and *Index to Book Reviews in the Humanities*; review articles that survey a number of scholarly works or that make an independent contribution to scholarship are included. Letters to editors, obituary notices, and the like are excluded unless they make a significant contribution to literary, linguistic, or folklore scholarship. Unpublished doctoral dissertations are not included, but citations to *Dissertation Abstracts International* are listed.

3. *Level.* Works of interest to scholars are included whether they are written for a scholarly or a more general audience, provided that the content or its treatment places them within the scope of the *Bibliography*. Master's theses, guides that are essentially plot summaries, and other apprentice or simplified works are excluded.

4. *Physical medium.* There is no restriction on the physical type or medium of works. Books, book articles, and articles from periodicals are the most frequently listed materials. Other media include films, sound recordings, microforms, and machine-readable materials.

5. *Status.* Only published items are listed. In general, only new publications are included; revised editions of previously published works are considered as new works. Reprints are excluded unless they are of significant literary or scholarly works that have been unavailable to the scholarly community. There is no restriction concerning availability or accessibility of the published items; however, only items that have been seen by a bibliographer are included.

6. *Date.* The *Bibliography* covers publications issued during 1990 and materials issued earlier that were not included in previous bibliographies.

Sources

The basis for compilation of the *Bibliography* is the Master List of Periodicals. Any regularly published journal or series that prints items on literature, language, or folklore either exclusively or frequently is eligible for inclusion on the Master List. Editors of journals or series not currently on the Master List are invited to submit sample copies to the Center for Bibliographical Services for possible inclusion. The Master List printed in the *Bibliography* is drawn from the *MLA Directory of Periodicals*, which provides comprehensive information about the journals and series.

Monographs, collections, and items from journals peripheral to literature and language are included insofar as is possible. Authors, publishers, and editors are invited to send offprints of articles and copies of books to the Center for Bibliographical Services.

Although all items listed in the *Bibliography* have been seen, they are not all owned by the Modern Language Association or housed in any single collection. The *Bibliography* records the existence of items but does not provide physical access to them.

Descriptors and Indexing

The *Bibliography* uses the Contextual Indexing and Faceted Taxonomic Access System (CIFT). The classified sequence and the subject index both depend on subject analysis of cited documents by MLA staff and contributors in terms of an ordered sequence of facets—fundamental categories of information relevant to the study of literature, linguistics, and folklore. A computer system developed at the MLA is used to input, edit, arrange, and format entries and indexes.

In indexing an item for the *Bibliography*, the indexers use terms that describe its content. These descriptors, based on the document author's own wording, are assigned to facets pertinent to that item, and these facets control its classification and provide subject access to it in the index.

Several general principles govern the assigning of descriptors. Descriptors are usually specific terms; appropriate cross-references are provided to similar or related terms in the index. Descriptors define the explicit content: for example, authors are not identified as belonging to groups unless their group identification is a subject treated, and methodological approaches are specified only when they are discussed and/or clearly applied. Finally, descriptors are assigned for an item if, and only if, users seeking information on the topic indicated by a descriptor would be likely to want to retrieve the item.

A thesaurus is used to standardize and control the terms used in the *Bibliography*. To reflect the changing needs and interests of the scholarly community, the thesaurus undergoes constant revision.

Classified Section

In the classified arrangement, general items precede specific ones: documents on literature, language, or folklore in general are listed before documents limited to particular literatures, languages, or regions; documents on genres used by many authors precede documents on individual authors.

Each item is entered only once in the classified sequence of any volume of the *Bibliography*, in the place where it would most likely be sought. Additional access through other relevant subjects is provided in the subject index. This index also contains all cross-references; there are no cross-references in the classified listing. Users are reminded, therefore, never to limit their search either to the classified section or to the index section. A document discussing the treatment of the self by three authors, for instance, will be listed in the classified section once under the first author discussed. Reference to the other authors will be found in the subject index only. The document described in the following index entry was listed under "Forster, E. M." in the "English literature/1900–1999" section of the classified sequence.

LAWRENCE, D. H. (1885–1930)

English literature. Novel. 1900–1999.
Forster, E. M. *Where Angels Fear to Tread*. Treatment of Italy compared to LAWRENCE, D. H.: *The Lost Girl*. I:4176.

The same entry will also be found in the subject index under the lead term "Italy."

Entries in the classified section exhibit a maximum three-level structure. Main headings characterize a document in terms of its main focus; second and third levels further define and narrow the classification, as in the following samples:

NATIONAL LITERATURES

American literature/1800–1899

HAWTHORNE, NATHANIEL (1804–1864)
Novel/The Blithedale Romance (1852)

LINGUISTICS

Indo-European languages. Germanic languages. West Germanic languages. English language

ENGLISH LANGUAGE (MODERN)
Syntax/Subject

GENERAL LITERATURE

Genres

FICTION
Science Fiction

FOLKLORE

Folk literature

FOLK POETRY
Folk song/Asia

As an aid to users, all descriptors not used in classification are printed in a gloss following the citation. Subject-index descriptors are preceded by a dagger as in the following:

[1265] Reynolds, Larry. "The Renfrew Ballad of 'Young Conway'." *CFMJ*. 1988; 16: 43–48. [Fr. sum.; incl. texts. †Renfrew. Treatment of Conway, Michael. Variants.]

Thus a user looking under a particular author will have, in one place, both the citation and the index terms for all items classed primarily under that author. The index will have to be checked for secondary references. The inclusion of the descriptors assigned to the document will assist the user in determining the content of the document cited. Often other information pertaining to the document being cited is also included, such as "Eng. sum., 42." Such information can be distinguished from descriptor strings by the presence of the dagger.

Volumes I & II (National Literatures)

The arrangement of these volumes is based on the concept of national literatures, using the combined considerations of geography and language. The macro arrangement is by geographical region, with individual literatures within those regions arranged alphabetically. Whenever possible, the regions are also listed alphabetically. When the national designation and the language of the literature are not logically linked or when there are two or more languages prominently used within a given country, access to the language is given in the index. Thus, all Indian literature will be found in one place regardless of its language; all items on Hindi language literature will be found in one place in the index. The same is true for Latin language literature and Celtic language literatures. Materials on Irish Gaelic literature will be classified within the Irish literature section; checking the index under Irish Gaelic language literature will yield all items on literature written in Irish Gaelic.

In general, subject authors have been placed within the national literature with which they are most closely associated. If a user is unable to locate a particular author, the subject index should be consulted, because it includes every author listed in the classified sequence.

Authors' names have been cited in their fullest forms unless an author is better known by another form of the name. References to and from pseudonyms and other forms of names will be found in the subject index.

Titles of works produced by subject authors are listed in their original language when that information is available. If the title in its original language could not be verified by press time, the title was listed in the form given in the document being cited. Similarly, when genre designations for particular works could not be verified, genre descriptions were taken from the document being cited.

Genre designations in Volumes I and II follow accepted English-language scholarly usage. A subgenre term will follow the primary designation when the work discussed in an indexed item is treated specifically as an example of that subgenre: for example, *Paradise Lost* discussed as an epic poem will be classified as "poetry: epic poetry." Story-length works of modern short fiction are generally classified under the genre designation "short story." However, to accommodate the broader terminology used to describe such fiction throughout world literature, the term "fiction" is also used, with a subgenre designation when truly appropriate. The subgenre terms used in either situation are accessible through the subject indexes of Volumes I and II.

Volume III (Linguistics)

Items on the history and theory of linguistics appear immediately after linguistic items of a general nature. Next are the broad linguistic topics, arranged alphabetically (e.g., Comparative Linguistics, Diachronic Linguistics), followed by the sections for specific languages. The arrangement of specific languages is patterned after that set forth in C. F. Voegelin and F. M. Voegelin, *Classification and Index of the World's Languages* (1977). The *Bibliography* differs from Voegelin and Voegelin in that it sometimes treats as languages what the Voegelins term dialects.

Volume IV (General Literature and Related Topics)

Items in this volume do not concern specific national literatures; they pertain to the study of literature in general, bibliographical studies, literary theory and criticism, genres, figures of speech, literary forms, and themes. Each of these topics may be subclassified once or twice. Thus, under Bibliographical one might find "manuscripts—manuscript editing" or under Genres, "biography—hagiography." Studies of film are in this volume, although many also appear in the national literatures volumes.

Volume V (Folklore)

Items of general interest to folklorists are listed first. The main body of folklore materials is arranged according to folklore types or genres. Each major heading may have up to two levels of subclassification. Thus, under folk literature may be found "folk poetry—epic poetry" and "folk narrative—folk tale" or under material culture, "folk art—embroidery," "folk craft—furniture," or "technology—agriculture." All these are further subdivided by the place under consideration. In the classified section, places will not be defined more closely than by country; more specific places (e.g., New York City or Southern India) may be found in the index.

Citation Format

Citations are presented in a format that is based on specifications of the American National Standards Institute (ANSI). All document authors are listed with the last name first; if an entry has more than one author, the names are separated by semicolons. Article titles appear in roman type within quotation marks; book titles are in italics. Publication information for journals follows this order: journal acronym or title, year, month, day, volume, issue, and pagination. Whether all or some of these identifying elements appear depends on the journal.

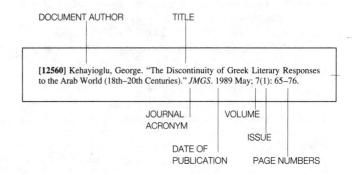

The order of publication information for books is: place, publisher, year, pages, series name, and series number.

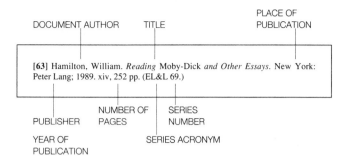

Citations to articles published within collections of essays by diverse hands include the full publication information for the collection in which the articles appeared, as in the following sample:

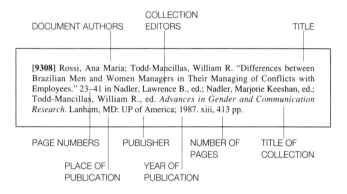

Citations for works in other media follow similar patterns.

If a journal or series cited is included on the Master List, it is referred to by an acronym. The acronym listing follows this guide.

Citations appear in their original language if they were published in the Roman alphabet. Other citations are converted to the Roman alphabet according to the Library of Congress system.

Subject Index

The subject index provides access to names of persons, languages, groups, genres, stylistic and structural features, themes, sources, influences, processes, theories, and other related topics. Most important, it contains all intravolume cross-references. Subject descriptors are listed in an alphabetical, context-preserving index generated by CIFT. The indexing is contextual in that each descriptor used as a heading is followed by a display of other descriptors assigned to documents in conjunction with it. The contextual subheadings enable a user to judge the probable relevance of items before looking up the citations in the classified listing.

Entries in the subject index exhibit a three-level structure:

1. The main heading (in uppercase letters) consists of a single descriptor. The main heading is repeated (in uppercase letters) in its original place in a subheading to indicate its role in the entry.

2. The primary subheading (in boldface type) consists of descriptors representing literatures, languages, performance media, folklore types, places, genres, periods, and major linguistic aspects.

3. The secondary subheading (in roman type) consists of descriptors from all other facets. It is followed by numbers referring to citations in the classified sequence. In the combined subject index to all

five volumes of the *Bibliography*, a number enclosed in parentheses refers to the same citation as a preceding number in the same index entry. Such citations are listed in more than one volume of the *Bibliography* and thus have more than one reference number. Citation numbers in the combined subject index are preceded by roman numerals to indicate the volume to which the number refers.

Punctuation conventions help indicate relations among descriptors: periods separate facets, semicolons appear between independent descriptors within a facet, and colons connect descriptors having a hierarchical whole-part, genus-species, entity-aspect, object-process type of conceptual relationship or relate an author to a work used as a cross-reference (e.g., French language: French Canadian dialect; Wordsworth, William: *The Prelude*).

Examples of index entries are:

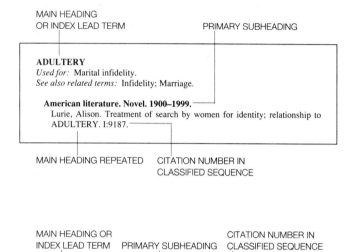

The subject index also contains references to related, narrower, and preferred terms. Users will note some unevenness in the inclusion of such references. These terms are generated by the system used to control the indexing vocabulary, and that thesaurus system is a work in progress that is updated daily. Users working with the individual volumes of the *Bibliography* will sometimes notice a term, not followed by index entries, that does not seem related to the area being covered in that particular discipline. Thus "FOLK BELIEF SYSTEMS, *See also narrower term:* Magic" might appear as a heading in one of the national literature volumes because, for instance, there are references to magic as a theme in that particular volume and because "folk belief systems" is the broader term for magic. Since indexing is done once to accommodate all five volumes of the *Bibliography*, such instances are unavoidable. Similarly, users will notice that a reference to a nonpreferred term followed by a use reference may appear near the reference to the preferred term. Proximity of such terms has not been a criterion for their printing or not printing, since the file that produces the printed *Bibliography* is also used for online searching, where such references are mandatory.

In some cases, so many related or narrower terms are needed to represent correctly a subject term that listing them becomes cumbersome. Users will notice, therefore, such terms are treated less specifically than others, as in the following examples:

MYTH
See also: entries for myths of specific countries, areas, or peoples by consulting the index under the adjectival form of the country, area, or people.

TRANSLATION
See also: entries under headings for specific language translation, e.g., English language translation, French language translation, etc.

Documents that apply specific approaches are likewise too numerous to list in the printed *Bibliography*, but they will be available in the computer-searchable version. Users are alerted to the existence of such terms by messages like the following:

FEMINIST APPROACH
See also related terms: Feminism; Feminist literary theory and criticism; Women; Women writers.
Documents applying specific approaches are so numerous that access to them is provided only in the electronic versions of the *Bibliography*.

Search Strategies

To do a thorough search one should check both the classified section and the index. A user searching a topic within the traditional framework of the *Bibliography* (e.g., author and work) will probably want to start in the classified portion. The index, however, cannot be ignored, for it may contain pertinent references that have been classed elsewhere. In the index, under the subject authors' names, there will be notations indicating where the author is to be found in the classified section (e.g., "*See also classified section:* 1567 ff.").

Users interested in themes, genres, and other topics that cross literary boundaries will want to begin their search in the index. When a search includes two or more concepts, the user should begin searching under the less common one. Since headings under each lead heading in the index are subarranged by literature or language, genre, period, literary author, major linguistic aspect, etc., the user will find it more efficient to begin searching for concepts other than these. For example, if the user is looking for items that concern methods of characterization used by James Joyce, it is better to look under "CHARACTERIZATION" before "JOYCE, JAMES." Under the former heading the items on Joyce will be drawn together under the subheading "Irish literature. 1900–1999. Joyce, James"; listings under the heading for Joyce are not sorted by literary technique.

The user should be aware that the subject index does not always provide direct access. Literature and language descriptors, date spans used to divide literatures, and other terms that form the primary basis for classification cannot necessarily be used for index access. The user should go to the classified section for such broad topics. Although these descriptors do appear in the index, they contain general referrals to the classified listing or items in which they represent secondary concerns, because only the first descriptor assigned in each facet is considered in classifying the item; other descriptors are accessible only through the index. Thus, if a work discusses both folk tale and myth, folk tale is used in classification; myth must be searched in the index.

Electronic Retrieval

The *Bibliography* is available for online searching through DIALOG Information Services and through the H. W. Wilson Company's WILSONLINE. MLA Online via DIALOG consists of annual bibliographies for the years 1963–90; via WILSONLINE, bibliographical years 1981–90 are available. Both files are updated monthly from December through June and again in October. Online users can search both files using free-text searching or on the basis of classification headings, document authors, and other elements of the citation. Beginning with the 1981 *Bibliography*, subject-index descriptors and document language can be used in retrieval.

The 415,000 citations in the 1981–90 volumes of the *Bibliography* are also available on CD-ROM through Wilson's WILSONDISC program. The *Bibliography* on WILSONDISC is searchable using classification headings, document authors, subject-index descriptors, document language, and other elements in addition to free-text searching. The Wilson Company has based its CD-ROM software on the premise that not all users will be experienced in search techniques, and its menu-driven software, offering a choice of searching strategies, greatly enhances novices' use of the file. The WILSONDISC version of the *Bibliography* is updated on a quarterly basis.

Related Publication

The *MLA Directory of Periodicals*, published biennially as a companion to the *Bibliography*, contains current publication information for journals and series on the MLA Master List of Periodicals. The data, collected by the MLA staff and the network of bibliographers, are sent periodically to the editors of the journals and series for verification. Data range from such information as when the publication began to the restrictions placed on contributors. Entries in the *Directory* are arranged alphabetically by title and are supplemented by indexes to the languages in which the periodicals publish, to editorial personnel and sponsoring organizations, and to subjects covered by the periodicals listed.

The *Directory* is available from the Member and Customer Services Office, MLA, 10 Astor Place, New York, NY 10003-6981.

Editorial Staff

Computer Center Staff

The editorial staff thanks Jeffrey Grossman of the University of Texas, Austin; Szilvia E. Szmuk of St. John's University; and the staffs of the Sprague Library at Montclair State College and the Bobst Library at New York University for their invaluable cooperation and consideration. It also extends its appreciation to Judith Altreuter, Anne Yanagi, Stephen R. Ingle, and Kerime B. Toksu for their assistance in the production of the *Bibliography*.

The production of Volume V, Folklore, was assisted by a grant from the American Folklore Society, with additional support from Indiana University, Bloomington.

Contributors to the *MLA International Bibliography* for 1990

Festschriften and Other Analyzed Collections

Brigitte La Presto, Pikeville College, Section Head
Willard Fox III, University of Southwestern Louisiana,
   Assistant Section Head
Robert Acker, University of Montana
Russell Burrows, Northwest College
John R. Burt, Bowling Green State University
Federico Chalupa, Bowling Green State University
Patricia Coward, Bowling Green State University
Elsa Gutmann, Bowling Green State University
Terry Hansen, Lindsey Wilson College
James L. Harner, Texas A&M University
James L. Karpen, Maharishi International University
Kevin P. Mulcahy, Rutgers University
Christine D. Tomei, Allegheny College
Phillip J. Wolfe, Allegheny College

Assistant Bibliographers:

Tracy A. Crouch, Purdue University
Deepika B. Karle, Bowling Green State University
Judith M. Mulcahy, Lindsey Wilson College

General Literature and Related Topics

S. K. Aithal, Indian Institute of Technology, Kanpur
Stephen H. Dill, University of South Dakota
Elaine A. Franco, University of California, Davis
James R. Kelly, George Washington University
Lawrence H. Maddock
Peter Milward, SJ, Sophia University
Mary Ann O'Donnell, Manhattan College
Robert Ross, University of Texas, Austin

English Literature

Rosemarie A. Battaglia, Michigan State University
Ann Willardson Engar, University of Utah
Margaret Loftus Ranald, Queens College
Sara Jayne Steen, Montana State University
Michael Wentworth, University of North Carolina, Wilmington

American Literature

S. L. Clark, Rice University
Pattie Cowell, Colorado State University
William Gargan, Brooklyn College
Joan Stockard, Wellesley College
Jeffrey Walker, Oklahoma State University

Celtic Studies

James J. Blake, Nassau Community College, Section Head

Medieval and Neo-Latin Studies

Paul G. Remley, University of Washington, Seattle

Folklore

James R. Dow, Iowa State University, Co–Section Head
Michael Taft, Saskatoon, SK, Co–Section Head*
Alla Abramovich-Goman, Indiana University, Bloomington
Linda Adams, Indiana University, Bloomington
Amy Craver, Indiana University, Bloomington
David Gay, Indiana University, Bloomington
Henni Ilomäki, Suomalaisen Kirjallisuuden Seura, Helsinki
Doreen Klassen, Indiana University, Bloomington
Kenneth D. Pimple, Indiana University, Bloomington
Gerald L. Pocius, Memorial University of Newfoundland
Guntis Smidchens, Indiana University, Bloomington
Moira L. Smith, Indiana University, Bloomington**
Vickie West, Indiana University, Bloomington
Clover Williams, Indiana University, Bloomington
John B. Wolford, Indiana University, Bloomington

*The work of Michael Taft was aided by a grant from the American Folklore Society.

**Under the auspices of the MLA-IU Cooperative Folklore Bibliography Project.

General Romance and Minor Romance Literatures (Provençal, Catalan, etc.)

Christian Bonnet, Angoulême, France
Heidi Siller-Runggaldier, University of Innsbruck

French Literature

William Wrage, Ohio University, Section Head
Ruth B. Antosh, State University of New York, Fredonia
Larry S. Crist, Vanderbilt University
Mary Donaldson-Evans, University of Delaware
Gary M. Godfrey, Weber State University
Aleksandra Gruzinska, Arizona State University
Charles J. Stivale, Wayne State University
Michael Vincent, Wichita State University

Italian Literature

Thomas L. Cooksey, Armstrong State College
Augustus A. Mastri, University of Louisville
Koraljka J. Ramphall, University of California, Davis

Spanish Literature

Oliver T. Myers, University of Wisconsin, Milwaukee, Section Head
Leonardo C. De Morelos, Black Mountain, NC,
   Section Head Emeritus
Brian J. Dendle, University of Kentucky
David William Foster, Arizona State University
Dennis A. Klein, University of South Dakota
Ernest E. Norden, Baylor University
Rosa E. Penna, Universidad Católica Argentina
Duane Rhoades, University of Wyoming
L. Teresa Valdivieso, Arizona State University

Portuguese and Brazilian Literature

Gregory McNab, University of Rhode Island, Section Head
John M. Parker, University of Aveiro, Portugal

Romanian Literature

Ştefan Stoenescu, Cornell University, Section Head
Marcel Cornis-Pop, Virginia Commonwealth University
Thomas Amherst Perry, East Texas State University
Liliana Zancu, Millersville University

German Literature

William N. Hughes, Michigan State University, Section Head

MASTER LIST OF PERIODICALS IN ACRONYM ORDER

The Master List of Periodicals contains the acronyms and titles for all journals and series in the *MLA Directory of Periodicals* file. These titles have been identified as being of primary interest to scholars in language, literature, linguistics, and folklore. Although every attempt is made to screen these titles annually for documents of interest to users of the *Bibliography,* each title is not necessarily represented by citations in each year's *Bibliography.*

Asterisks precede the acronyms of journals and series that are represented in this *Bibliography.* Only documents within the scope of the *Bibliography* have been indexed.

AA   American Anthropologist
*AAA   Archivio per l'Alto Adige: Rivista di Studi Alpini
AAASH   Acta Antiqua Academiae Scientiarum Hungaricae
AAD   Afroasiatic Dialects
AAF   Anglo-American Forum
A&A   Anglica et Americana
A&CS   Area and Culture Studies (Tokyo, Japan)
A&E   Anglistik & Englischunterricht
AArmL   Annual of Armenian Linguistics (Cleveland, OH)
AAS   Asian and African Studies
*AASF   Annales Academiae Scientiarum Fennicae. Dissertations Humanarum Litterarum
*AASFB   Annales Academiae Scientiarum Fennicae/Suomalaisen Tiedeakatemian Toimituksia
*AAWG   Abhandlungen der Akademie der Wissenschaften in Göttingen: Philologisch-Historische Klasse; Folge 3
AB   Acta Baltica
*ABäG   Amsterdamer Beiträge zur Älteren Germanistik
*ABalzac   L'Année Balzacienne
Abbia: Revue Culturelle Camerounaise/Cameroon Cultural Revue
ABC   American Book Collector
*ABI   Academie e Biblioteche d'Italia
ABK   Aachener Beiträge zur Komparatistik
*ABLS   The Albert Bates Lord Studies in Oral Tradition
*ABnG   Amsterdamer Beiträge zur Neueren Germanistik
ABORI   Annals of the Bhandarkar Oriental Research Institute
ABPR   The African Book Publishing Record
*ABR   American Benedictine Review
Abr-Nahrain
*ABS   Acta Baltico-Slavica: Archaeologia, Historia, Etnographia, et Linguarum Scientia (Warsaw, Poland)
*ABSt   A/B: Auto/Biography Studies
ACar   Analecta Cartusiana (Salzburg, Austria)
*ACCP   Arquivos do Centro Cultural Português (Paris, France)
ACer   Anales Cervantinos
*ACF   Annali di Ca' Foscari: Rivista della Facoltà di Lingue e Letterature Straniere dell'Università di Venezia
ACiL   Amsterdam Studies in the Theory and History of Linguistic Science I: Amsterdam Classics in Linguistics 1800-1925
ACist   Analecta Cisterciensia
ACLALSB   ACLALS Bulletin
*ACM   The Aligarh Critical Miscellany
Acme: Annali della Facoltà di Lettere e Filosofia
ACP   Amitié Charles Péguy: Bulletin d'Informations et de Recherches
ACS   Australian-Canadian Studies: A Journal for the Humanities & Social Sciences
Acta (Binghamton, NY)
ActaA   Acta Asiatica: Bulletin of the Institute of Eastern Culture
*ActaG   Acta Germanica: Jahrbuch des Südafrikanischen Germanistenverbandes (Frankfurt, FRG)
*ActaLit   Acta Literaria
ActN   L'Action Nationale
ActSem   Actes Semiotiques
Actualidades: Consejo Nacional de la Cultura, Centro de Estudios Latinoamericanos "Romulo Gallegos"/Caracas, Venezuela
Adam   ADAM International Review
*ADEB   ADE Bulletin
*ADFLB   ADFL Bulletin
AdI   Annali d'Italianistica
AdLB   Brahmavidya, The Adyar Library Bulletin
*AdM   Annales du Midi: Revue de la France Méridionale
ADML   Automatic Documentation and Mathematical Linguistics

ADPh   Német Filológiai Tanulmányok/Arbeiten zur Deutschen Philologie
*ADS   Australasian Drama Studies
*AdTb   Altdeutsche Textbibliothek
AdUA   Annales de l'Université d'Abidjan: Serie D: Lettres
ADz   Akadēmiskā Dzīve
*AEASH   Acta Ethnographica Academiae Scientiarum Hungaricae
AEB   Analytical & Enumerative Bibliography
AEFil   Anuario de Estudios Filologicos
Aegyptus: Rivista Italiana di Egittologia e di Papirologia
AEM   Archeion Euvoikōn Meletōn
AES   Abstracts of English Studies
*Aevum: Rassegna di Scienze Storiche, Linguistiche, Filologiche
*AF   Anglistische Forschungen
AfB   Africana Bulletin
AFH   Archivum Franciscanum Historicum
AFIMS   The American Film Institute Monograph Series
AFLFP   Annali della Facoltà di Lettere e Filosofia dell'Università di Perugia
AFLFUM   Annali della Facoltà di Lettere e Filosofia dell'Università di Macerata
AFLSHY   Annales de la Faculté des Lettres et Sciences Humaines de Yaoundé
AFLToul   Annales Publiées par la Faculté des Lettres et Sciences Humaines de Toulouse
AFolk   Les Archives de Folklore: Documents et Etudes sur les Moeurs, Coutumes, Croyances, Légendes, Contes, Chansons, Langue et Arts Populaires
AfrA   African Arts
AfrF   Afrika Focus
Africa: Rivista Trimestrale di Studi e Documentazione (Rome, Italy)
AfricaL   Africa: Journal of the International African Institute/Revue de l'Institut Africain International (Manchester, England)
AfricanM   African Musicology
AfricaR   Africa Report
AfrL   Africana Linguistica (Tervuren, Belgium)
AfrLit   American University Studies XVIII: African Literature
AfrLJ   Africana Journal: A Bibliographic Library Journal and Review Quarterly
*AfrM   Africana Marburgensia
AfrN   African Notes: Journal of the Institute of African Studies
*AfrS   African Studies (Johannesburg, S. Africa)
AfrSR   The African Studies Review
Afr-T   Africa-Tervuren
AfrWS   African Writers Series
*AFS   Asian Folklore Studies
AGald   Anales Galdosianos
AGB   Archiv für Geschichte des Buchwesens
*Agenda
*AGI   Archivio Glottologico Italiano
*Agora: A Journal in the Humanities and Social Sciences
AGP   Archiv für Geschichte der Philosophie
AHDLMA   Archives d'Histoire Doctrinale et Littéraire du Moyen Âge
AHR   Afro-Hispanic Review
*AI   American Imago: A Psychoanalytic Journal for Culture, Science, and the Arts
*Aidai (Brooklyn, NY)
AIEO   Annales de l'Institut d'Etudes Occitanes
*AILAR   AILA Review
AiolikaG   Aiolika Grammata
*AION-SO   Annali Istituto Universitario Orientale, Napoli, Sezione Orientale

AION-SR Annali Istituto Universitario Orientale, Napoli, Sezione Romanza

AION-SS Annali Istituto Orientale, Napoli, Seminario di Studi dell-'Europa Orientale

AIPHOS Annuaire de l'Institut de Philologie et d'Histoire Orientales et Slaves

AIQ American Indian Quarterly

AIV Atti del R. Istituto Veneto di Scienze, Lettere ed Arti. Venezia. Classe di Scienze Morali e Lettere

AJ The Age of Johnson: A Scholarly Annual

AJES The Aligarh Journal of English Studies

AJFS Australian Journal of French Studies

AJGLL American Journal of Germanic Linguistics and Literatures

AJL Australian Journal of Linguistics: Journal of the Australian Linguistic Society

AJS The American Journal of Semiotics

AKG Archiv für Kulturgeschichte

AKML Abhandlungen zur Kunst-, Musik- und Literaturwissenschaft

Akzente: Zeitschrift für Literatur

AL American Literature: A Journal of Literary History, Criticism, and Bibliography

ALA L'Afrique Littéraire

Alaluz: Revista de Poesia, Narracion y Ensayo

AL&C African Languages and Cultures

ALASH Acta Linguistica Academiae Scientiarum Hungaricae

Alcance: Revista Literaria

ALCGP Annali del Liceo Classico "G. Garibaldi" di Palermo

ALE Anales de Literatura Española

ALEC Anales de la Literatura Española Contemporánea

Alfa: Revista de Lingüística

Alföld: Irodalmi Művelődési és Kritikai Folyóirat

ALH Acta Linguistica Hafniensia: International Journal of General Linguistics

ALHis Anales de Literatura Hispanoamericana

Alighieri L'Alighieri: Rassegna Bibliografica Dantesca

ALIL Anuar de Lingvistică şi Istorie Literară

ALing Analecta Linguistica: Informational Bulletin of Linguistics

ALitASH Acta Litteraria Academiae Scientiarum Hungaricae

AlJ Alemannisches Jahrbuch

AllaB Alla Bottega: Rivista di Cultura ed Arte

Allegorica

ALM Archives des Lettres Modernes: Etudes de Critique et d'Histoire Littéraire

ALMA Archivum Latinitatis Medii Aevi (Bulletin du Cange)

AlP Altro Polo: A Volume of Italian Studies

ALR American Literary Realism, 1870-1910

ALS Australian Literary Studies

ALT African Literature Today

AMCF American Material Culture and Folklife: Masters of Material Culture

Américas

Amérindia: Revue d'Ethnolinguistique Amérindienne

AmerP American Poetry

AmerS American Studies

Ameryka: A Ukrainian Catholic Daily (Philadelphia, PA)

AmEx The American Examiner: A Forum of Ideas

AmLH American Literary History

AmLit American University Studies XXIV: American Literature

AmLS American Literary Scholarship: An Annual

AmP American Psychologist

AmRev The Americas Review: A Review of Hispanic Literature and Art of the USA

AMSAP AMS Ars Poetica

AmSeph The American Sephardi: Journal of the Sephardic Studies Program of Yeshiva University

AMSML AMS Studies in Modern Literature

AMSR AMS Studies in the Renaissance

AMSS AMS Studies in the Eighteenth Century

AMSSC AMS Studies in the Seventeenth Century

AMSSE AMS Studies in the Emblem

AMSSMA AMS Studies in the Middle Ages

AMSSN AMS Studies in the Nineteenth Century

Amst Amerikastudien/American Studies

Amstel Amstelodamum: Maandblad voor de Kennis van Amsterdam. Orgaan van Het Genootschap Amstelodamum

AmStudies American Studies/Amerikastudien: A Monograph Series

AMus Asian Music: Journal of the Society for Asian Music

AN Acta Neophilologica (Ljubljana, Yugoslavia)

AnA Anuari d'Anglès

Anais: An International Journal

Analysis: Quaderni di Anglistica

Anatolica: Annuaire International pour les Civilisations de l'Asie Antérieure

AnBol Analecta Bollandiana

AnBret Annales de Bretagne et des Pays de l'Ouest

AnCNT L'Anello Che Non Tiene: Journal of Modern Literature

ANF Arkiv för Nordisk Filologi/Archives for Scandinavian Philology

Angelicum: Periodicum Trimestre Pontificae Studiorum Universitatis a Sancto Thoma Aquinate in Urbe

Angles Angles on the English Speaking World

Anglia: Zeitschrift für Englische Philologie

AnL Anthropological Linguistics

ANLMSF Atti della Accademia Nazionale dei Lincei. Rendiconti della Classe di Scienze Morali, Storiche e Filologiche

ANQ: A Quarterly Journal of Short Articles, Notes, and Reviews

AnSch Annals of Scholarship: Studies of the Humanities and Social Sciences [Formerly *Annals of Scholarship: Metastudies of the Humanities and Social Sciences*]

ANSDSL Australian and New Zealand Studies in German Language and Literature/Australisch-Neuseeländische Studien zur Deutschen Sprache und Literatur

AnST Analecta Sacra Tarraconensia: Revista de Ciencias Historico-Eclesiasticas Balmesiana

ÁNT Általános Nyelvészeti Tanulmányok

AntC L'Antiquité Classique

Anthropologica

Anthropos: International Review of Ethnology and Linguistics

AntigR The Antigonish Review

Antípodas: Journal of Hispanic Studies of the University of Auckland

Antipodes: A North American Journal of Australian Literature

Antonianum

AntQ Anthropological Quarterly

ANTS Anglo-Norman Text Society

AnUS Annual of Urdu Studies

ANYAS Annals of the New York Academy of Sciences

ANZSC Australian and New Zealand Studies in Canada

AOASH Acta Orientalia Academiae Scientiarum Hungaricae

AÖAW Anzeiger der Philosophisch-Historischen Klasse der Österreichischen Akademie der Wissenschaften

AODNS Acta Orientalia (Societates Orientales Danica, Fennica, Norvegica, Svecica) (Copenhagen, Denmark)

AP Aurea Parma: Rivista di Lettere, Arte e Storia

APK Aufsätze zur Portugiesischen Kulturgeschichte (Subseries of Portugiesische Forschungen der Görresgesellschaft)

AppalJ Appalachian Journal: A Regional Studies Review

AppLing Applied Linguistics (Oxford, England)

APR The American Poetry Review

APSL Amsterdamer Publikationen zur Sprache und Literatur

APsy Applied Psycholinguistics (New York, NY)

ApTS Approaches to Translation Studies

AQ American Quarterly

AR The Antioch Review

ArAA Arbeiten aus Anglistik und Amerikanistik

Arabica: Revue d'Etudes Arabes

Arabiyya Al-'Arabiyya: Journal of the American Association of Teachers of Arabic

ARAL Annual Review of Applied Linguistics

ARB Africana Research Bulletin

*Arbor: Ciencia, Pensamiento y Cultura

Arc   L'Arc (Aix-en-Provence, France)

*Arcadia: Zeitschrift für Vergleichende Literaturwissenschaft

Archiginnasio   L'Archiginnasio: Bolletino della Biblioteca Comunale di Bologna

*Archiv   Archiv für das Studium der Neueren Sprachen und Literaturen

Archīvs: Raksti par Latviskām Problēmām (Melbourne, Australia)

ARCS   The Annual Report on Cultural Science

ARG   Archiv für Reformationsgeschichte

Ariel: A Review of Arts and Letters in Israel (Jerusalem, Israel)

*ArielE   Ariel: A Review of International English Literature (Calgary, Canada)

ArielK   Ariel (Lexington, KY)

ARIPUC   Annual Report of the Institute of Phonetics, University of Copenhagen

*ArmD   Armchair Detective: A Quarterly Journal Devoted to the Appreciation of Mystery, Detective, and Suspense Fiction

*ArO   Archív Orientální: Quarterly Journal of African, Asian, and Latin-American Studies

*ArQ   Arizona Quarterly

*ARS   Augustan Reprint Society

ARSCJ   Association for Recorded Sound Collections Journal

ArsL   Ars Lyrica: Journal of Lyrica, Society for Word-Music Relations

*ArthI   Arthurian Interpretations

*Arv: Scandinavian Yearbook of Folklore

*AS   American Speech: A Quarterly of Linguistic Usage

ASBFC   Archivio Storico di Belluno, Feltre e Cadore

*ASch   The American Scholar

*ASE   Anglo-Saxon England

ASEA   Asiatische Studien/Etudes Asiatiques: Zeitschrift der Schweizerischen Gesellschaft für Asienkunde/Revue de la Société Suisse d'Etudes Asiatiques

ASEES   Australian Slavonic & East European Studies

ASEL   Acta Semiotica et Lingvistica: International Review of Semiotics and Linguistics (São Paulo, Brazil)

Asemka: A Literary Journal of the University of Cape Coast

ASGM   Atti del Sodalizio Glottologico Milanese (Milan, Italy)

ASI   Archivio Storico Italiano

ASILO   Adalbert Stifter Institut des Landes Oberösterreich: Vierteljahresschrift

ASInt   American Studies International

ASL   Archivio Storico Lombardo

*AsMj   Asia Major

*ASNSP   Annali della Scuola Normale Superiore di Pisa: Classe di Lettere e Filosofia

*Assaph: Studies in the Theatre

Assays: Critical Approaches to Medieval and Renaissance Texts

Assur

*Astrado   L'Astrado: Revisto Bilengo de Prouvènço

Astraea   Collection Astraea

AŞUI   Analele Ştiintifice ale Universităţii "Al.I. Cuza" din Iaşi (Serie nouă), e. Lingvistică

ASWL   Authoritative Studies in World Literature

*ATAS   American Translators Association Series

Atenea: Revista de Ciencia, Arte y Literatura de la Universidad de Concepción

Athēna: Syngramma Periodikon tēs en Athēnais Epistēmonikēs Hetaireias

*Athenaeum: Studi Periodici di Letteratura e Storia dell'Antichità

Athēnaïka: Periodikē Ekdosis tou Syllogou ton Athenaion

*ATJ   Asian Theatre Journal

Atlantis: A Women's Studies Journal/Journal d'Etudes sur la Femme

*ATQ   American Transcendental Quarterly

*AtS   Approaches to Semiotics

AÜ   Afrika und Übersee: Sprachen-Kulturen

AuA   Anglistik und Amerikanistik

AUC   Anales de la Universidad de Chile

AuE   Arheoloǧija un Etnogrāfija

Augustinianum

Augustinus: Quarterly Review of The Fathers Augustinian Recollects

*AUMLA: Journal of the Australasian Universities Language and Literature Association: A Journal of Literary Criticism and Linguistics

*AUNS   Al'manakh Ukraïns'koho Narodnoho Soiuzu (Jersey City, NJ)

*Aurora: Jahrbuch der Eichendorff Gesellschaft

AUS-AG&R   Acta Universitatis Szegediensis de Attila József Nominatae: Acta Romanica

AUS-AHLH   Acta Universitatis Szegediensis de Attila József Nominatae: Acta Historiae Litterarum Hungaricarum

Ausblick: Zeitschrift für Deutsch-Skandinavische Beziehungen

AUS-E&L   Acta Universitatis Szegediensis de Attila József Nominatae: Sectio Ethnographica et Linguistica/Néprajz és Nyelvtudomány/Volkskunde und Sprachwissenschaft

*AusFolk   Australian Folklore: A Journal of Folklore Studies

AusPl   Australian Playwrights

Aut Aut: Rivista di Filosofia e di Cultura

*AUUSAU   Acta Universitatis Upsaliensis, Studia Anglistica Upsaliensia

AUUSGU   Acta Universitatis Upsaliensis, Studia Germanistica Upsaliensia

*AUUSRU   Acta Universitatis Upsaliensis, Studia Romanica Upsaliensia

AUUSlU   Acta Universitatis Upsaliensis, Studia Slavica Upsaliensia

*AUUSSU   Acta Universitatis Upsaliensis, Studia Semitica Upsaliensia

AUUUSH   Acta Universitatis Umensis, Umeå Studies in the Humanities

AV   Ateneo Veneto: Rivista di Scienze, Lettere ed Arti

AvC   Avalon to Camelot

*AvG   Avant Garde: Revue Interdisciplinaire et Internationale des Arts et Littératures du XXe Siècle/Interdisciplinary and International Review of Literature and Arts of the 20th Century

*AzSL   Abhandlungen zur Sprache und Literatur

*Aztlán: A Journal of Chicano Studies

BAA   Braunschweiger Anglistische Arbeiten

*BAAG   Bulletin des Amis d'André Gide

*Babel: International Journal of Translation

*BAC   Boletín de la Academia Colombiana

*BACLA   Bulletin de l'ACLA/Bulletin of the CAAL

BADL   Bonner Arbeiten zur Deutschen Literatur

BAFAS   Bibliotheca Afroasiatica

BAGB   Bulletin de l'Association Guillaume Budé

BALCAM   Bulletin de l'ALCAM: Revue de Linguistique Camerounaise

Balcanica: Annuaire de l'Institut des Etudes Balkaniques

*BALF   Black American Literature Forum

BALI   Bollettino dell'Atlante Linguistico Italiano

BALit   Biblioteka Analiz Literackich

BALM   Bollettino dell'Atlante Linguistico Mediterraneo

BalSt   Balkan Studies

*Baltistica: Baltų Kalbų Tyrinėjimai (Vilnius, U.S.S.R.)

*B&L   Brain and Language

BAnglia   Buchreihe der Anglia

BANLE   Boletín de la Academia Norteamericana de la Lengua Española

BAR   Bulletin de l'Association des Amis de Rabelais et de La Devinière

BARLLF   Bulletin de l'Académie Royale de Langue et de Littérature Françaises

BArn   Bibliotheca Arnamagnæana

Baroque: Revue Internationale

Barroco (Minas Gerais, Brazil)

BAS   Bochumer Anglistische Studien

BASL   Bochumer Arbeiten zur Sprach- und Literaturwissenschaft

BaumB   The Baum Bugle (Lakemont, GA)

BAWS   Bayerische Akademie der Wissenschaften. Philosophisch-Historische Klasse, Sitzungsberichte

*Bazmavep   Revue Bazmavep: Hayagitakan-Banasirakan-Grakan Handēs/Revue d'Etudes Arméniennes

*BB   Bulletin of Bibliography

*BBA   Berliner Byzantinistische Arbeiten

*BBaud   Bulletin Baudelairien

*BBCS   Bulletin of the Board of Celtic Studies/Bwletin y Bwrdd Gwybodau Celtaidd (Cardiff, Wales)

*BBH   Books in Bosnia and Herzegovina: A Yugoslav Literary Journal
BBib   Beschreibende Bibliographien
*BBMP   Boletín de la Biblioteca de Menéndez Pelayo
BBN   Berliner Beiträge zur Namenforschung
BBr   Books at Brown
BBSIA   Bulletin Bibliographique de la Société Internationale Arthurienne
*BC   The Book Collector
BCB   Boletin Cultural y Bibliografico (Bogotá, Colombia)
BCDI   Bollettino della Carta dei Dialetti Italiani
*BCH   Bulletin de Correspondance Hellénique
*BCILA   Bulletin de la Commission Interuniversitaire Suisse de Linguistique Appliquée
*BCILL   Bibliothèque des Cahiers de l'Institut de Linguistique de Louvain
*BCom   Bulletin of the Comediantes
*BCSM   Bulletin of the Cantigueiros de Santa Maria
*BCSV   Bollettino del Centro di Studi Vichiani
BDBU   Bulletin of Daito Bunka University: The Humanities
*BdF   Boletim de Filologia
BDLM   Bibliographien zur Deutschen Literatur des Mittelalters
*BDM   Bollettino della Domus Mazziniana (Pisa, Italy)
BDP   Beiträge zur Deutschen Philologie
BDVA   Beiträge zur Deutschen Volks- und Altertumskunde
*BE   Bŭlgarski Ezik: Organ na Instituta za Bŭlgarski Ezik pri Bŭlgarskata Akademiia na Naukite (Sofia, Bulgaria)
BEAD   Bati Edebiyatlari Arastirma Dergisi (Ankara, Turkey)
*Béaloideas: The Journal of the Folklore of Ireland Society
*BEDS   Beiträge zur Erforschung der Deutschen Sprache
*Belfagor: Rassegna di Varia Umanità
*BelL   Belaruskaia Linhvistyka
Bellmansstudier   Bellmansstudier Utg. av Bellmanssällskapet
BEP&S   Bulletin d'Etudes Parnassiennes et Symbolistes
Bergomum: Bollettino della Civica Biblioteca
*Bestia: Yearbook of the Beast Fable Society
*BêteN   Bête Noire
*BEV   Bulletin des Etudes Valéryennes
BEz   Balkansko Ezikoznanie/Linguistique Balkanique
*BF   Books from Finland
*BFFGL   Boletín de la Fundación Federico García Lorca
BFil   Boletín de Filología (Santiago, Chile)
BForum   Book Forum: An International Transdisciplinary Quarterly
BG   Bungaku
BGDSL   Beiträge zur Geschichte der Deutschen Sprache und Literatur
BGPTM   Beiträge zur Geschichte der Philosophie und Theologie des Mittelalters
*BGU   Bluegrass Unlimited
BH   Bulletin Hispanique
BHe   Baltische Hefte
BHEA   Biblioteca Hispanoamericana y Española de Amsterdam
BHF   Bonner Historische Forschungen
*BHR   Bibliothèque d'Humanisme et Renaissance
*BHS   Bulletin of Hispanic Studies
BhV   Bharatiya Vidya
*BI   Books at Iowa
*BibA   Biblical Archaeologist
*Biblio 17
Bibliofilia: Rivista di Storia del Libro e di Bibliografia
Biblioteca   Biblioteca/The Library: Quarterly Bulletin for Librarianship
Bibliotheck   The Bibliotheck: A Scottish Journal of Bibliography and Allied Topics
*BIEA   Boletín del Instituto de Estudios Asturianos
*Biḳoret u-Parshanut: Ketav-'et le-Sifrut, Lashon, Historiah ve-Esteṭiḳah (Ramat Gan, Israel)
BILC   Boletim do Istituto Luís de Camões (Macau, Asia)
*Biography: An Interdisciplinary Quarterly
BiP   Biuletyn Polonistyczny: Kwartalnik
BIPG   Bulletin de l'Institut de Phonétique de Grenoble

BIS   Browning Institute Studies: An Annual of Victorian Literary and Cultural History
BISDSL   Britische und Irische Studien zur Deutschen Sprache und Literatur
Bitzaron: Quarterly Review of Hebrew Letters/Riv'on Sifrut, Hagut, Meḥkar
BJA   British Journal of Aesthetics
BJDC   British Journal of Disorders of Communication
*BJECS   British Journal for Eighteenth-Century Studies
*BJL   Belgian Journal of Linguistics
*BJP   British Journal of Psychology
*BJRL   Bulletin of the John Rylands University Library of Manchester
BlackI   Black Images: A Critical Quarterly on Black Arts and Culture
BlackIC   Black i: A Canadian Journal of Black Expression
*Blake: An Illustrated Quarterly
BLBI   Bulletin des Leo Baeck Instituts
BLcp   Bulletin du Laboratoire de la Communication Parlée
BLE   Bulletin de Littérature Ecclésiastique
*BLJ   The British Library Journal
BLL   Belaruskaia Litaratura
BLM   Bonniers Litterära Magasin
*Bloch-Almanach: Eine Veröffentlichung des Ernst-Bloch-Archivs der Stadtbibliothek Ludwigshafen
*BLR   Bodleian Library Record
BMFEA   Bulletin of the Museum of Far Eastern Antiquities
BMM   Belaruskaia Mova: Mizhvuzaŭski Zbornik
*BMP   Bulletin Marcel Proust [Formerly Bulletin de la Société des Amis de Marcel Proust et des Amis de Combray]
BMSLP   Boletim Mensal da Sociedade de Língua Portuguêsa
BN   Beiträge zur Namenforschung
BN&R   Botswana Notes and Records
BNJ   Byzantinisch-Neugriechische Jahrbücher: Internationales Wissenschaftliches Organ
*BNL   Beiträge zur neueren Literaturgeschichte
BO   Black Orpheus: Journal of African and Afro-American Literature
*Bokvännen
*BoundaryII   Boundary 2: An International Journal of Literature and Culture
BP   Banasthali Patrika
BPN   The Barbara Pym Newsletter
*BPS   Bulletin of the Psychonomic Society
BPTJ   Biuletyn Polskiego Towarzystwa Językoznawczego/Bulletin de la Société Polonaise de Linguistique
BRAE   Boletín de la Real Academia Española
BrechtJ   Brecht-Yearbook
*BrenS   Brenner-Studien
BRev   Boston Review
BRG   Blätter der Rilke-Gesellschaft
BRIES   Bibliothèque Russe de l'Institut d'Etudes Slaves
Brotéria
BRP   Beiträge zur Romanischen Philologie (Berlin, FRG)
BRQ   Book Research Quarterly
BR/RB   The Bilingual Review/La Revista Bilingüe
BRT   Behavior Research and Therapy: An International Multi-Disciplinary Journal
BRTS   Biblioteca della Ricerca: Testi Stranieri
BSAM   Bulletin de la Société des Amis de Montaigne
*BSAPLF   Bulletin de la Société Américaine de Philosophie de Langue Française
*BSci   Behavioral Science
BSDSL   Basler Studien zur Deutschen Sprache und Literatur
BSE   Brno Studies in English
BSEAA   Bulletin de la Société d'Etudes Anglo-Américaines des XVII et XVIII Siècles
BSIS   Bulletin of the Society for Italian Studies: A Journal for Teachers of Italian in Higher Education
*BSJ   The Baker Street Journal: An Irregular Quarterly of Sherlockiana
BSl   Byzantinoslavica: Revue Internationale des Etudes Byzantines

BslBzl Brasil/Brazil: Revista de Literatura Brasileira/A Journal of Brazilian Literature

BSLP Bulletin de la Société de Linguistique de Paris

BSNotes Browning Society Notes

BSOAS Bulletin of the School of Oriental and African Studies

BSTG Bulletin de la Société Théophile Gautier

BStu Bunyan Studies: John Bunyan and His Times

BTLV Bijdragen tot de Taal-, Land- en Volkenkunde

BTMG Blätter der Thomas Mann Gesellschaft

BU Blues Unlimited

BuR Bucknell Review: A Scholarly Journal of Letters, Arts and Sciences

BWR Black Warrior Review

BWVACET The Bulletin of the West Virginia Association of College English Teachers

ByronJ The Byron Journal

BYUS Brigham Young University Studies

Byzantion: Revue Internationale des Etudes Byzantines

BZ Byzantinische Zeitschrift

BZCP Buchreihe der Zeitschrift für Celtische Philologie

BzNH Bizantion—Nea Hellas

BZRP Beihefte zur Zeitschrift für Romanische Philologie

CA Cuadernos Americanos

CACM Communications of the ACM

CACP Cahiers de l'Amitié Charles Péguy

CahiersE Cahiers Elisabéthains: Etudes sur la Pré-Renaissance et la Renaissance Anglaises

CahiersS Cahiers Staëliens

CAIEF Cahiers de l'Association Internationale des Etudes Françaises

CAld Cuadernos de Aldeeu

Caliban (Toulouse, France)

Calibano (Rome, Italy)

Callaloo: An Afro-American and African Journal of Arts and Letters

CalR Calcutta Review

CALS Cambridge Applied Linguistics Series

CalSS California Slavic Studies

CamObsc Camera Obscura: A Journal of Feminism and Film Theory

C&L Christianity and Literature

C&T Culture & Tradition

CanL Canadian Literature

CAnn The Carlyle Annual

CanPo Canadian Poetry: Studies, Documents, Reviews

CanRom Canadiana Romanica

CAnth Current Anthropology: A World Journal of the Human Sciences

ČaR Čakavska Rič

CARA: Actes du Centre Aixois de Recherches Anglaises

CARB Cahiers des Amis de Robert Brasillach

Carrell The Carrell: Journal of the Friends of the University of Miami Library (Coral Gables, FL)

CarSP The Carlyle Society Papers

Carte Carte Segrete: Rivista Trimestrale di Letteratura ed Arte

CarteI Carte Italiane: A Journal of Italian Studies

CArts Critical Arts: A Journal of Cultural Studies

CasaA Casa de las Américas

CAsJ Central Asiatic Journal: International Periodical for the Languages, Literature, History and Archeology of Central Asia

CASS Canadian-American Slavic Studies

Castilla: Boletín del Departamento de Literatura Española

CathSt Cather Studies

CAtI Contemporary Approaches to Ibsen

CaudaP Cauda Pavonis: Studies in Hermeticism

CBAA A Current Bibliography on African Affairs

CBunH Chūgoku Bungaku Hō

CCC College Composition and Communication

CCCist Cîteaux Commentarii Cistercienses (Brecht, Belgium)

CCFCSP Canadian Centre for Folk Culture Studies Papers: Canadian Museum of Civilization Mercury Series

CCIEP Courrier du Centre International d'Études Poétiques

CCM Cahiers de Civilisation Médiévale (Xe-XIIe Siècles)

CComp Chinese Comparatist

CCon Cahiers Confrontation

CCR The Claflin College Review

CCRev Comparative Civilizations Review

CCrit Comparative Criticism: A Yearbook

CCTEP Conference of College Teachers of English Studies

CCur Cross Currents: A Yearbook of Central European Culture

CCV Cahiers Charles V

CD Child Development

CDCP Comparative Drama Conference Papers

CdD La Ciudad de Dios: Revista Agustiniana

CdDLSL Cahiers du Département des Langues et des Sciences du Langage

CdDS Cahiers du Dix-septième: An Interdisciplinary Journal

CdF Cuadernos de Filología (Valencia, Spain)

CdIL Cahiers de l'Institut de Linguistique de Louvain

CdL Cahiers de Lexicologie

CdP Cuadernos de Poética

CE College English

CEA CEA Critic: An Official Journal of the College English Association

CEAfr Cahiers d'Etudes Africaines

CEAL Critical Essays on American Literature

CE&S Commonwealth Essays and Studies

CEBL Critical Essays on British Literature

CEc Corps Ecrit

CEd Communication Education

CEG Cuadernos de Estudios Gallegos

CEGe Cahiers d'Etudes Germaniques

CEL Cadernos de Estudos Lingüísticos

Celestinesca: Boletín Informativo Internacional

CelfanR Revue Celfan/Celfan Review

Celtica

CEM Cahiers d'Etudes Médiévales

CEMC Centro de Estudios Mayas-Cuadernos

CEML Critical Essays in Modern Literature

Cenobio: Rivista Trimestrale di Cultura

CentR The Centennial Review (E. Lansing, MI)

CEP Conference on Editorial Problems. University of Toronto

CER Cahiers d'Etudes Romanes

Cervantes: Bulletin of the Cervantes Society of America

CeS Cultura e Scuola

CEStudies Canadian Ethnic Studies/Etudes Ethniques au Canada

CEWL Critical Essays on World Literature

CFC Cuadernos de Filología Clásica

CFMA Classiques Français du Moyen Âge

CFMB Canadian Folk Music Bulletin

CFMJ Canadian Folk Music Journal

CFolc Cadernos de Folclore

CFS Cahiers Ferdinand de Saussure: Revue de Linguistique Générale

CGFT Critical Guides to French Texts

CGGT Critical Guides to German Texts

CGN Cahiers Gérard de Nerval

CGP Carleton Germanic Papers

CGST Critical Guides to Spanish Texts

CH Crítica Hispánica

CHA Cuadernos Hispanoamericanos: Revista Mensual de Cultura Hispanica

Chasqui: Revista de Literatura Latinoamericana

ChauR The Chaucer Review: A Journal of Medieval Studies and Literary Criticism

ChC Chinese Culture: A Quarterly Review

CHelv Colloquium Helveticum: Cahiers Suisses de Littérature Comparée/Schweizer Hefte für Allgemeine und Vergleichende Litteraturwissenschaft/Quaderni Svizzeri di Letteratura Generale e Comparata

ChibaR Chiba Review

ChildL Children's Literature: An International Journal, Inc. Annual of the Modern Language Association Division on Children's Literature and the Children's Literature Association

ChinL   Chinese Literature
ChiR   Chicago Review
Chiricú
*ChLB   Charles Lamb Bulletin
*ChLC   Challenging the Literary Canon
*Chloe: Beihefte zum Daphnis
CHLSSF   Commentationes Humanarum Litterarum Societatis Scientiarum Fennicae
*ChrE   Chronique d'Egypte
CHum   Computers and the Humanities
*CIBS   Communications from the International Brecht Society
*CICIM: Revue pour le Cinéma Français
*CIEFLB   Central Institute of English and Foreign Languages Bulletin
CIF   Cuadernos de Investigación Filológica
CIFM   Contributi dell'Istituto di Filologia Moderna. Ser. Ital. 1. Univ. Cattolica del Sacro Cuore
*CILT   Amsterdam Studies in the Theory and History of Linguistic Science IV: Current Issues in Linguistic Theory
CimR   Cimarron Review
*Cineaste: America's Leading Magazine on the Art and Politics of the Cinema
CinJ   Cinema Journal
CiP   Amsterdam Studies in the Theory and History of Linguistic Science II: Classics in Psycholinguistics
*Círculo: Revista de Cultura
*CIRRI   Centre Interuniversitaire de Recherche sur la Renaissance Italienne
CIS   Cahiers Internationaux de Symbolisme
*Cithara: Essays in the Judaeo-Christian Tradition
CJ   The Classical Journal
CJAfS   Caribbean Journal of African Studies
*CJAS   Canadian Journal of African Studies/Revue Canadienne des Etudes Africaines
CJC   Cahiers Jean Cocteau
CJG   Cahiers Jean Giraudoux
CJIS   Canadian Journal of Irish Studies
*CJItS   Canadian Journal of Italian Studies
*CJL   Canadian Journal of Linguistics/Revue Canadienne de Linguistique
*CJNS   Canadian Journal of Netherlandic Studies/Revue Canadienne d'Etudes Néerlandaises
CJPhil   Canadian Journal of Philosophy
CJVŠ   Cizí Jazyky ve Škole
*CL   Comparative Literature (Eugene, OR)
ČL   Česká Literatura: Časopis pro Literární Vědu
CLAJ   College Language Association Journal
CLAO   Cahiers de Linguistique—Asie Orientale
*CLAQ   Children's Literature Association Quarterly
Classic   The New Classic (Benoni, South Africa)
*ClassQ   The Classical Quarterly
*ClaudelS   Claudel Studies
*CLC   Columbia Library Columns
*CLEAR   Chinese Literature: Essays, Articles, Reviews
ČLid   Český Lid: Národopisný Časopis
CLing   Cercetări de Lingvistică
Clio: Rivista Trimestrale di Studi Storici (Rome, Italy)
*ClioI   CLIO: A Journal of Literature, History, and the Philosophy of History
*CLL   Creole Language Library
*CLO   Cahiers Linguistiques d'Ottawa
*ClQ   Colby Quarterly [Formerly Colby Library Quarterly]
CLS   Comparative Literature Studies
CLTL   Cadernos de Lingüística e Teoria da Literatura
*CLTT   Child Language Teaching and Therapy
*Clues: A Journal of Detection
*CMat   Critical Matrix: Princeton Working Papers in Women's Studies
CMC   Crosscurrents/Modern Critiques
*CMCS   Cambridge Medieval Celtic Studies

CMEALL   The Cooper Monographs on English and American Language and Literature
ČMF   Časopis pro Moderní Filologii
*CMHLB   Cahiers du Monde Hispanique et Luso-Brésilien/Caravelle
*CML   Classical and Modern Literature: A Quarterly (Terre Haute, IN)
*CMLR   Canadian Modern Language Review/La Revue Canadienne des Langues Vivantes
CMo   Creative Moment
*CMRLFC   Collection Monographique Rodopi en Littérature Française Contemporaine
*CMRS   Cahiers du Monde Russe et Soviétique
CN   Cultura Neolatina
*CNat   Les Cahiers Naturalistes
CNIE   Commonwealth Novel in English
CNLR   Council on National Literatures/World Report
CoA   The Coat of Arms: A Heraldic Quarterly Magazine
*CogLi   Cognitive Linguistics
*CogN   Cognitive Neuropsychology
*Cognition: International Journal of Cognitive Science
Collections (Newark, DE)
*CollG   Colloquia Germanica, Internationale Zeitschrift für Germanische Sprach- und Literaturwissenschaft
*CollL   College Literature
Colóquio   Colóquio/Letras
Comhar
Comitatus: A Journal of Medieval and Renaissance Studies
*ComM   Communication Monographs
*Commentary
Commonweal
*Comparatist   The Comparatist: Journal of the Southern Comparative Literature Association
*CompD   Comparative Drama
Compendia: Computer Generated Aids to Literary and Linguistic Research
*CompJ   The Computer Journal
*CompL   American University Studies III: Comparative Literature
*CompLing   Computational Linguistics
ComQ   Commonwealth Quarterly
Comunità: Rivista di Informazione Culturale
Conch   The Conch: A Sociological Journal of African Cultures and Literatures
Confluencia: Revista Hispánica de Cultura y Literatura
*ConL   Contemporary Literature
ConLit   Convorbiri Literare
*Conradian   The Conradian
Conradiana: A Journal of Joseph Conrad Studies
*Constructions
Contemporanul
*ContempR   Contemporary Review (London, England)
*Continuum: Problems in French Literature from the Late Renaissance to the Early Enlightenment
*Contrastes: Revue de l'Association pour le Développement des Etudes Contrastives
Coranto: Journal of the Friends of the Libraries, University of Southern California
Corona: Marking the Edges of Many Circles
*Corónica   La Corónica: Spanish Medieval Language and Literature Journal and Newsletter
*Costerus: Essays in English and American Language and Literature
Co-textes
*Courier   Syracuse University Library Associates Courier
Cowrie: A Chinese Journal of Comparative Literature
CPA   Culture Populaire Albanaise
*CPALS   Carleton Papers in Applied Language Studies
CPe   Castrum Peregrini
*CPsy   Cognitive Psychology
*CQ   The Cambridge Quarterly
CR   The Critical Review (Canberra, Australia)
CRB   Cahiers Renaud-Barrault

CRCL   Canadian Review of Comparative Literature/Revue Canadienne de Littérature Comparée

*CREDIF   Bulletin Bibliographique du C.R.E.D.I.F. (Centre de Recherche et d'Etude pour la Diffusion du Français Service de Documentation)

*CREL   Cahiers Roumains d'Etudes Littéraires: Revue Trimestrielle de Critique, d'Esthétique et d'Histoire Littéraires

*CRev   The Chesterton Review: The Journal of the Chesterton Society

CRevAS   Canadian Review of American Studies

CRevB   Conch Review of Books: A Literary Supplement on Africa

CrF   Creative Forum: A Quarterly Journal of Contemporary Writing

Crisol

*Cristallo: Rassegna di Varia Umanità (Bolzano, Italy)

*Crit   Critique: Studies in Contemporary Fiction

*CritI   Critical Inquiry

*Criticism: A Quarterly for Literature and the Arts (Detroit, MI)

*Criticón

Critique: Revue Générale des Publications Françaises et Etrangères (Paris, France)

CritLett   Critica Letteraria

*CritQ   Critical Quarterly

CritSt   Critical Studies: A Journal of Critical Theory, Literature and Culture

*CritT   Critical Texts: A Review of Theory and Criticism

CritTh   Critical Theory: Interdisciplinary Approaches to Language, Discourse and Ideology

CRLN   The Comparative Romance Linguistics Newsletter

Croatica: Prinosi Proučavanju Hrvatske Književnosti

*Crosscurrents

*CRR   Cincinnati Romance Review

*CrSurv   Critical Survey

*CRUX: A Journal on the Teaching of English

*CSALC   Cambridge Studies in American Literature and Culture

CSci   Cognitive Science: A Multidisciplinary Journal of Artificial Intelligence, Linguistics, Neuroscience, Philosophy, Psychology

CSF   Cambridge Studies in French

CSG   Cambridge Studies in German

*CSGLL   Canadian Studies in German Language and Literature

*CSiL   Copenhagen Studies in Language [Formerly CEBAL: Copenhagen School of Economics and Business Administration. Language Department Publications]

CSJP   Cahiers Saint-John Perse

*CSL   Cambridge Studies in Linguistics

*CSLAIL   Cambridge Studies in Latin American and Iberian Literature

*CSLBull   Bulletin of the New York C. S. Lewis Society

*CSLing   Current Studies in Linguistics

CSP   Canadian Slavonic Papers: An Inter-Disciplinary Quarterly Devoted to the Soviet Union and Eastern Europe

CSR   Christian Scholar's Review

ČsR   Československá Rusistika

CSRL   Cambridge Studies in Russian Literature

*CSW   Cahiers Simone Weil

*CSWL   Contributions to the Study of World Literature

*CT   Ciencia Tomista: Publicación Cuatrimestral del Centro de Estudios Teológicos de San Esteban

*CTC   Cuadernos de Teatro Clásico

CTR   Canadian Theatre Review

CulL   Cultura Ludens

Cultura (Milan, Italy)

*CUNYF   CUNYForum: Papers in Linguistics

CUWPL   Columbia University Working Papers in Linguistics

CuyahogaR   Cuyahoga Review

*CV   Città di Vita: Bimestrale di Religione Arte e Scienza

*CVE   Cahiers Victoriens et Edouardiens: Revue du Centre d'Etudes et de Recherches Victoriennes et Edouardiennes de l'Université Paul Valéry, Montpellier

CWLM   Chung-wai Literary Monthly: Publicación Cuatrimestral del Centro di Estudios Teológicos de San Esteban

CWPL   Cornell Working Papers in Linguistics

*Cycnos

Dactylus

*Dada   Dada/Surrealism

Dædalus: Journal of the American Academy of Arts and Sciences

DAEM   Deutsches Archiv für Erforschung des Mittelalters

*DaF   Deutsch als Fremdsprache: Zeitschrift für Theorie und Praxis des Deutschunterrichts für Auslaender

*DAI   Dissertation Abstracts International

DanF   Danske Folkemål

*Dansk Udsyn (Askov, Denmark)

*Daphnis: Zeitschrift für Mittlere Deutsche Literatur

DASDJ   Deutsche Akademie für Sprache und Dichtung, Darmstadt. Jahrbuch

*Daugava: Literaturno-Khudozhestvennyĭ i Obshchestvenno-Politicheski ĭ Ezhemesiachnyĭ Zhurnal Soiuza Sovetskikh Pisateleĭ Latvii

*DC   Dutch Crossing: A Journal of Low Countries Studies

DDG   Deutsche Dialektgeographie/Dialektographie

DDJ   Deutsches Dante-Jahrbuch

DdW   Les Dialectes de Wallonie

*Degrés: Revue de Synthèse à Orientation Sémiologique

Delo: Mesecni Knjizevni Casopis (Belgrade, Yugoslavia)

DeltaES   Delta: Revue du Centre d'Etudes et de Recherche sur les Ecrivains du Sud aux Etats-Unis (Montpellier, France)

*DevB   Devil's Box

*DFS   Dalhousie French Studies

*DHA   Diálogos Hispánicos de Amsterdam

*DHLR   The D. H. Lawrence Review

*DHS   Dix-Huitième Siècle

*Diachronica: International Journal for Historical Linguistics/Revue Internationale pour la Linguistique Historique/Internationale Zeitschrift für Historische Linguistik

*Diacritics: A Review of Contemporary Criticism

Dialoghi: Rivista Bimestrale di Letteratura Arti Scienze

*Dialogi: Mesečnik za Vprašanja Kulturnega in Javnega Življenja

*Dialogue: Canadian Philosophical Review/Revue Canadienne de Philosophie

*DialogW   Dialog: Miesięcznik Poświęcony Dramaturgii Współczesnej: Teatralnej, Filmowej, Radiowej, Telewizyjnej (Warsaw, Poland)

*Dickensian   The Dickensian

*DicS   Dickinson Studies: Emily Dickinson (1830-86), U.S. Poet

*Dictionaries: Journal of the Dictionary Society of North America

DidS   Diderot Studies

*Dieciocho: Hispanic Enlightenment, Aesthetics, and Literary Theory

Differentia: Review of Italian Thought

*DilR   Diliman Review (Quezon City, Philippines)

Dimension: Contemporary German Arts and Letters

*Diogenes

Dionysos: The Literature and Intoxication TriQuarterly

Dires: Revue du Centre d'Etudes Freudiennes

*Discourse: Journal for Theoretical Studies in Media and Culture

*Discurso: Revista de Estudios Iberoamericanos [Supersedes Discurso Literario: Revista de Temas Hispánicos]

Dispatch   The Dispatch

*Dispositio: Revista Hispánica de Semiótica Literaria

DL   Deus Loci: The Lawrence Durrell Quarterly

*DLB   Dictionary of Literary Biography

*DLE   Documents sur l'Espéranto

DLN   Doris Lessing Newsletter

DM   The Dublin Magazine

DMLS   Durham Modern Languages Series

DMT   Durham Medieval Texts

Dnipro: Literaturno-Khudozhniĭ ta Hromads'ko-Politychnyĭ Zhurnal

DNR   Dime Novel Roundup: A Magazine Devoted to the Collecting, Preservation and Literature of the Old-Time Dime and Nickel Novels, Libraries and Popular Story Papers

DocCRLLI   Documents du Centre de Recherche de Langue et Littérature Italiennes

Dolphin   The Dolphin: Publications of the English Department, University of Aarhus

DownR   Downside Review: A Quarterly of Catholic Thought
*DP   Developmental Psychology
*DPPNGL   Data Papers in Papua New Guinea Languages
DPr   Discourse Processes: A Multidisciplinary Journal
*DQ   Denver Quarterly
*DQR   Dutch Quarterly Review of Anglo-American Letters
DQu   Dickens Quarterly
DR   Dalhousie Review
Dramma: Mensile dello Spettacolo (Turin, Italy)
*DruzhN   Druzhba Narodov: Ezhemesiachnyĭ Literaturno-Khudozhestvennyĭ i Obshchestvenno-Politicheskiĭ Zhurnal
*DS   Danske Studier
*DSA   Dickens Studies Annual: Essays on Victorian Fiction
*DSARDS   Dante Studies, with the Annual Report of the Dante Society
DSec   Degré Second: Studies in French Literature
DSFNS   Deutsch-Slawische Forschungen zur Namenkunde und Siedlungsgeschichte
*DSGW   Deutsche Shakespeare-Gesellschaft West: Jahrbuch
DSLL   Duquesne Studies in Language and Literature
*DSp   Deutsche Sprache: Zeitschrift für Theorie, Praxis, Dokumentation
DSS   Dix-Septième Siècle
*DS/SD   Discours Social/Social Discourse: The International Research Papers in Comparative Literature
DSt   Deutsche Studien
DStudies   Dostoevsky Studies: Journal of the International Dostoevsky Society
DT   Divus Thomas: Commentarium de Philosophia et Theologia
DTM   Deutsche Texte des Mittelalters
*DU   Der Deutschunterricht: Beiträge zu Seiner Praxis und Wissenschaftlichen Grundlegung
*DUJ   Durham University Journal
Duklja (Prešov, Czechoslovakia)
*DVLG   Deutsche Vierteljahrsschrift für Literaturwissenschaft und Geistesgeschichte
DWB   Dietsche Warande en Belfort: Tijdschrift voor Letterkunde en Geesteleven
DzD   Dzejas Diena
*EA   Etudes Anglaises: Grande-Bretagne, Etats-Unis
EAA   Estudos Anglo-Americanos (São Paulo, Brazil)
*EAL   Early American Literature
*E&H   Ear and Hearing: Official Journal of the American Auditory Society
E&S   Essays and Studies (London, England)
*EAS   Essays in Arts and Sciences
EBSK   Erlanger Beiträge zur Sprach- und Kunstwissenschaft
EBT   Les Etudes Balkaniques Tchécoslovaques
*EC   Etudes Celtiques
ECAMML   The Edward C. Armstrong Monographs on Medieval Literature
ECB   Estudos de Castelo Branco: Revista de História e Cultura
*ECent   The Eighteenth Century: Theory and Interpretation
*ECF   Eighteenth-Century Fiction
ECl   Les Etudes Classiques
*ECLife   Eighteenth-Century Life
ECM   Estudios de Cultura Maya: Publicación Periódica del Centro de Estudios Mayas
ECN   Estudios de Cultura Náhuatl (Mexico City, Mexico)
Eco: Revista de la Cultura de Occidente
*ECr   L'Esprit Créateur
*ECS   Eighteenth-Century Studies (Cincinnati, OH)
*ECW   Essays on Canadian Writing
EDAMMS   Early Drama, Art, and Music Monograph Series
EDAMRef   Early Drama, Art, and Music Reference Series
EDAMRvw   The Early Drama, Art, and Music Review
EdArn   Editiones Arnamagnæanæ
*Edda: Nordisk Tidsskrift for Litteraturforskning/Scandinavian Journal of Literary Research
Edebiyât: A Journal of Comparative and Middle Eastern Literatures
*EdF   Erträge der Forschung

EDH   Essays by Divers Hands
Editio: Internationales Jahrbuch für Editionswissenschaft/International Yearbook of Scholarly Editing/Revue Internationale des Sciences de l'Edition Critique
*EdL   Etudes de Lettres
EDLA   Estudios de Lingüística Aplicada
EdLing   Estudios de Lingüística
*EdN   Editors' Notes
*EdO   Edad de Oro
EDoc   Esperanto Documents
*EDS   English Dance and Song
EEPSAPT   Epistēmonikē Epetērida Philosophikēs Scholēs Aristoteleiou Panepistēmiou Thessalonikēs
EES   Explorations in Ethnic Studies: The Journal of the National Association for Ethnic Studies
*EEsc   Estudis Escènics: Quaderns de l'Institut del Teatre de la Diputació de Barcelona
EETS   Early English Text Society
EF   Etudes Françaises
*EFG   Erlanger Forschungen A: Geisteswissenschaften
*EFil   Estudios Filológicos
EFL   Essays in French Literature (Nedlands, Western Australia)
EFLL   Essays in Foreign Languages and Literature
EFO   Etudes Finno-Ougriennes
*EG   Etudes Germaniques
*EGA   Etudes Germano-Africaines: Revue Annuelle de Germanistique Africaine Jahresschrift für Afrikanische Germanistik/Annual Review of German Studies in Africa
EGN   Ellen Glasgow Newsletter
EHBS   Epetēris Hetaireias Byzantinōn Spoudōn
*EI   Etudes Irlandaises: Revue Française d'Histoire, Civilisation et Littérature de l'Irelande
*EIC   Essays in Criticism: A Quarterly Journal of Literary Criticism (Oxford, England)
EIDOS: The International Prosody Bulletin
*EigoS   Eigo Seinen
Éigse: A Journal of Irish Studies
EinA   English in Africa
EiP   Essays in Poetics: The Journal of the British Neo-Formalist School
*EIRC   Explorations in Renaissance Culture
*Éire   Éire-Ireland: A Journal of Irish Studies (St. Paul, MN)
*EiT   Essays in Theatre
EJ   The English Journal (Urbana, IL)
EKEEK   Epetēris tou Kentrou Epistēmonikon Ereunōn Kyprou
EKEHL   Epetēris tou Kentrou Ereunēs tēs Hellēnikēs Laographias
*ELA   Etudes de Linguistique Appliquée
*EL&L   American University Studies IV: English Language and Literature
ELawr   Etudes Lawrenciennes
Elementa: Schriften zur Philosophie und ihrer Problemgeschichte
*ELet   Esperienze Letterarie: Rivista Trimestrale di Critica e Cultura
*ELF   Etudes Littéraires Françaises
*ELH
ELing   Etudes Linguistiques: Revue du Département de Linguistique de l'Université de Niamey
ELit   Etudes Littéraires
ElizS   Elizabethan & Renaissance Studies (Salzburg, Austria)
ELkT   Epitheōrēsē Logou kai Technēs
ELLF   Etudes de Langue et Littérature Françaises
*ELLS   English Literature and Language (Tokyo, Japan)
*ELN   English Language Notes (Boulder, CO)
*ELR   English Literary Renaissance
*ELS   English Literary Studies Monograph Series
ELSt   Exeter Linguistic Studies
*ELT   English Literature in Transition (1880-1920)
*ELWIU   Essays in Literature (Macomb, IL)
Emblematica: An Interdisciplinary Journal of Emblem Studies
*Emérita: Revista de Lingüística y Filología Clásica (Madrid, Spain)
EMong   Cahiers d'Etudes Mongoles et Siberiennes

*EmSA   Emakeele Seltsi Aastaraamat
Enclitic
Encomia: Bibliographical Bulletin of the International Courtly Literature
    Society
*Encounter (London, England)
*Encyclia: The Journal of the Utah Academy of Sciences, Arts, and Letters
*EngLing   English Linguistics: Journal of the English Linguistics Society
    of Japan (Tokyo, Japan)
English: The Journal of the English Association (London, England)
*EngR   English Record
*Ensayistas   Los Ensayistas: Georgia Series on Hispanic Thought
*EnT   English Today: The International Review of the English Language
Envoi: A Review Journal of Medieval Literature
*EOMC   Estudios de Asia y Africa (Mexico City, Mexico)
*EONR   The Eugene O'Neill Review
Eos.: Commentarii Societatis Philologae Polonorum (Wrocław, Poland)
*EP   Etudes Philosophiques
*EPA   Estudos Portugueses e Africanos
*EPC   El Popola Ĉinio
ĖpH   Ėpeirōtikē Hestia
*Epos: Revista de Filología
EPP   Estonian Papers in Phonetics
EPSS   Ezra Pound Scholarship Series
Equivalences: Revue de l'Institut Supérieur de Traduction et d'Interprètes
    de Bruxelles
Equivalencias   Equivalencias/Equivalences
ER   Etudes Rabelaisiennes
*Eranos: Acta Philologica Suecana
ErasmusE   Erasmus in English
ERBr   Etudes Romanes de Brno
Ériu
ERP   English Renaissance Prose
ERUO   Etudes Romanes de l'Université d'Odense
*ES   English Studies: A Journal of English Language and Literature
    (Lisse, Netherlands)
ESA   English Studies in Africa: A Journal of the Humanities (Johannes-
    burg, South Africa)
*ESC   English Studies in Canada
*Escritura: Revista de Teoría y Crítica Literarias
ESef   Estudios Sefardíes
ESELL   Tohoku Gakuin University Review: Essays and Studies in Eng-
    lish Language and Literature [Tohoku Gakuin Daigaku Ronshu, Eigo-
    Eibungaku] (Sendai, Japan)
ESJ   European Studies Journal
ESMSLCC   The Edward Sapir Monograph Series in Language, Culture,
    and Cognition
*EspA   Español Actual
*EspDok   Esperanto-Dokumentoj
*Esperanto (Rotterdam, Netherlands)
*Esprit (Paris, France)
*ESQ: A Journal of the American Renaissance
ESRS   Emporia State Research Studies
ESt   Erlanger Studien
*Estreno: Cuadernos del Teatro Español Contemporáneo
*ETC.: A Review of General Semantics
*EtCr   Etudes Créoles
*ETh   Elizabethan Theatre
EthF   Ethnologia Fennica/Finnish Studies in Ethnology (Helsinki, Fin-
    land)
*EthnoE   Ethnologia Europaea
EthnoF   Ethnologie Française: Revue Trimestrielle de la Société d'Eth-
    nologie Française
*Ethnographia   A Magyar Néprajzi Társaság Folyóirata
*Ethnology: An International Journal of Cultural and Social Anthropology
    (Pittsburgh, PA)
*Ethnomusicology: Journal of the Society for Ethnomusicology
*Ethology
EthS   Ethnologia Slavica
*EthSc   Ethnologia Scandinavica: A Journal for Nordic Ethnology

*EtIE   Etudes Indo-Européennes
EtR   Etudes Romandes/Swiss-French Studies (Wolfville, Canada)
*Etudes (Paris, France)
*Euphorion: Zeitschrift für Literaturgeschichte (Heidelberg, FRG)
*EurH   Europäische   Hochschulschriften/Publications   Universitaire
    Européennes/European University Studies
Europe: Revue Littéraire Mensuelle
Eutopias: Teorías/Historia/Discurso
*EuWN   Eudora Welty Newsletter
*EW   East-West Film Journal
*EWhR   Edith Wharton Review [Formerly Edith Wharton Newsletter]
*EWNS   Evelyn Waugh Newsletter and Studies [Supersedes Evelyn
    Waugh Newsletter]
*EWW   English World-Wide: A Journal of Varieties of English
*Exemplaria: A Journal of Theory in Medieval and Renaissance Studies
*Expl   Explicator
Explor   Exploration (San Diego, CA)
*ExplorSp   Explorations: Special Series
ExTL   Explicación de Textos Literarios
*Extrapolation: A Journal of Science Fiction and Fantasy
Fabu   Fabula (Villeneuve d'Ascq, France)
*Fabula: Zeitschrift für Erzählforschung/Journal of Folktale Studies/Re-
    vue d'Etudes sur le Conte Populaire
Fachsprache (Vienna, Austria)
FaN   Le Français au Nigéria
Fataburen: Nordiska Museets och Skansens Årsbok
*FauxT   Faux Titre: Etudes de Langue et Littérature Françaises
FB   Fontane Blätter
FBG   Frankfurter Beiträge zur Germanistik
*FBS   Franco-British Studies: Journal of the British Institute in Paris
*FCB   The Flannery O'Connor Bulletin
*FCS   Fifteenth-Century Studies
FD   Filosofs'ka Dumka: Naukovo-Teoretychnyĭ Zhurnal
FDHRS   Freies Deutsches Hochstift: Reihe der Schriften
*FdL   Forum der Letteren: Tijdschrift voor Taal- en Letterkunde
FE   France-Eurafrique: La Tribune Libre des Deux Continents
*FFC   Folklore Fellows' Communications
*FForum   Folklore Forum
*FGADL   Forschungen zur Geschichte der Älteren Deutschen Literatur
FGO   Forschungen zur Geschichte Oberösterreichs
FH   Die Neue Gesellschaft/Frankfurter Hefte: Zeitschrift für Demok-
    ratie und Sozialismus
*FHP   Fort Hare Papers (Alice, Republic of Ciskei, South Africa)
*FI   Forum Italicum
*Field: Contemporary Poetry and Poetics
*FilmC   Film Criticism
*FilmQ   Film Quarterly
*Filología (Buenos Aires, Argentina)
*FirstL   First Language
FIZ   Farhang-e Irān Zamin: Revue des Etudes Iranologiques
*FJ   The Faulkner Journal
FJS   Fu Jen Studies: Literature & Linguistics (Taipei)
FK   Filológiai Közlöny
FLits   Foreign Literatures
Florilegium: Carleton University Annual Papers on Late Antiquity and
    the Middle Ages
*FLS   French Literature Series (Columbia, SC)
FLTR   Foreign Language Teaching and Research: A Quarterly of For-
    eign Languages and Cultures
*FM   Le Français Moderne: Revue de Linguistique Française
FMAS   Frühmittelalterliche Studien
*FMJ   Folk Music Journal (London, England)
*FMLS   Forum for Modern Language Studies
*FMonde   Le Français dans le Monde
*FN   Filologicheskie Nauki
*FNS   Frank Norris Studies
FoK   Folk og Kultur: Årbog for Dansk Etnologi og Folkemindeviden-
    skab

*FoL   Folk Life: Journal of Ethnological Studies (Cardiff, Wales)

*FoLi   Folia Linguistica: Acta Societatis Linguisticae Europaeae

FoliaO   Folia Orientalia (Cracow, Poland)

Folio: Essays on Foreign Languages and Literatures

FolkAn   Folklife Annual

*FolkH   The Folklore Historian: Journal of the Folklore and History Section of the American Folklore Society

*Folklore (London, England)

FolkloreC   Folklore: English Monthly Devoted to the Cause of Indian Folklore Society

*FolkS   Folklore Suisse/Folclore Svizzero: Bulletin de la Société Suisse des Traditions Populaires/Bolletino della Società Svizzera per le Tradizioni Populari

ForL   Forum Linguisticum (Bern, Switzerland)

*ForLing   Forum Linguisticum (Lake Bluff, IL)

Formations

ForoL   Foro Literario: Revista de Literatura y Lenguaje

*ForumHL   Forum Homosexualität und Literatur (Siegen, FRG)

*ForumS   Forum: A Ukrainian Review (Scranton, PA)

ForumZ   Forum (Zagreb, Yugoslavia)

*FoS   Foundations of Semiotics

*Foundation: The Review of Science Fiction

Foxfire

*FPhon   Folia Phoniatrica: International Journal of Phoniatrics, Speech Therapy and Communication Pathology

*FPVRV   Forschungen zu Paul Valéry—Recherches Valéryennes

*FR   The French Review: Journal of the American Association of Teachers of French

*Francofonia: Studi e Ricerche Sulle Letterature di Lingua Francese

*FranS   Franciscan Studies

Fremdsprachen: Zeitschrift für Theorie und Praxis der Sprachmittlung

*FrF   French Forum

*FrFM   French Forum Monographs

*FRG&C   Focus on Robert Graves and His Contemporaries

*FrH   Französisch Heute

*FrL   La France Latine

Fróðskaparrit: Annales Societatis Scientiarum Faeroensis (Tórshavn, Faroe Islands)

FrontenacR   Revue Frontenac Review

*Frontiers: A Journal of Women Studies

FrSt   Franziskanische Studien

*FS   French Studies: A Quarterly Review

*FSB   French Studies Bulletin: A Quarterly Supplement

*FSSA   French Studies in Southern Africa

*FSt   Feminist Studies

FT   Finsk Tidskrift

*FUF   Finnisch-Ugrische Forschungen: Zeitschrift für Finnisch-Ugrische Sprach- und Volkskunde

FurmS   Furman Studies

FWC   A Finnegans Wake Circular

FZPT   Freiburger Zeitschrift für Philosophie und Theologie

GA   Germanistische Abhandlungen

*GAf   Genève-Afrique

*GAG   Göppinger Arbeiten zur Germanistik

GAGL   Groninger Arbeiten zur Germanistischen Linguistik

*GaiS   Gai Saber: Revista de l'Escòla Occitana (Toulouse, France)

*GaR   The Georgia Review

Gardar: Årsbok för Samfundet Sverige-Island i Lund-Malmö

GB   Grazer Beiträge: Zeitschrift für die Klassische Altertumswissenschaft

GCBI   Godisnjak Centar za Balkanoloska Ispitivanja (Sarajevo, Yugoslavia)

GCFI   Giornale Critico della Filosofia Italiana

*GCY   German-Canadian Yearbook/Deutschkanadisches Jahrbuch

GdG   Grundlagen der Germanistik

GEFR   The George Eliot Fellowship Review

*GEGHLN   The George Eliot-George Henry Lewes Newsletter

*Genders

*GenL   American University Studies XIX: General Literature

Genre (Norman, OK)

*Geolinguistics: Journal of the American Society of Geolinguistics

*Germanistik: Internationales Referatenorgan mit Bibliographischen Hinweisen

GerSR   German Studies Review

*Gestos: Teoria y Practica del Teatro Hispanico

Gestus: The Electronic Journal of Brechtian Studies [Full text available online through EIES, NWI, COSY (Canada)]

*GettR   The Gettysburg Review

GezellianaK   Gezelliana: Kroniek van de Gezellestudie

GGF   Göteborger Germanistische Forschungen

*GHJ   George Herbert Journal

Gids   De Gids

*GIF   Giornale Italiano di Filologia

*GissingN   The Gissing Newsletter

*GJ   Gutenberg-Jahrbuch

*GK   Gengo Kenkyū: Journal of the Linguistic Society of Japan

*GL   General Linguistics (Binghamton, NY)

*GL&L   German Life and Letters

*GliA   Gli Annali Università per Stranieri

*GLL   American University Studies I: Germanic Languages and Literature

GLLM   German Language and Literature Monographs

*GLML   Garland Library of Medieval Literature

*Glotta: Zeitschrift für Griechische und Lateinische Sprache

*GlottaC   Glotta: Organo de Difusión Lingüística

*Glottodidactica: An International Journal of Applied Linguistics (Poznań, Poland)

GLS   Grazer Linguistische Studien

GlyphT   Glyph Textual Studies

*GMit   Germanistische Mitteilungen: Zeitschrift für Deutsche Sprache, Literatur und Kultur in Wissenschaft und Praxis

*GMT   Garland Medieval Texts

*GN   Germanic Notes

Gnomon: Kritische Zeitschrift für die Gesamte Klassische Altertumswissenschaft

*Goethe   Goethe-Jahrbuch

GoldK   Di Goldene Keyt

GothSE   Gothenburg Studies in English

*GPQ   Great Plains Quarterly

GQ   The German Quarterly

*GR   Germanic Review

Gradiva: International Journal of Italian Literature

*GrandS   Grand Street

Grani: Zhurnal Literatury, Iskusstva, Nauki i Obshchestvenno-Politicheskoĭ Mysli

Gratia: Bamberger Schriften zur Renaissanceforschung

*Greyfriar: Siena Studies in Literature

*Grial: Revista Galega de Cultura (Vigo, Spain)

Griot: Official Journal of the Southern Conference on Afro-American Studies, Inc.

*GRLH   Garland Reference Library of the Humanities

*GRM   Germanisch-Romanische Monatsschrift

Grundzüge

GSA   Germanic Studies in America

*GSJ   Gaskell Society Journal

GSlav   Germano-Slavica: A Canadian Journal of Germanic and Slavic Comparative Studies

*GSLI   Giornale Storico della Letteratura Italiana

*GSLS   Georgia State Literary Studies

*GSNA   Goethe Yearbook: Publications of the Goethe Society of North America

*GSS   George Sand Studies

*GStud   Grundtvig-Studier

*GTS   Germanistische Texte und Studien (Hildesheim, FRG)

GURT   Georgetown University Round Table on Languages and Linguistics

*Gymnasium: Zeitschrift für Kultur der Antike und Humanistische Bildung

HA   Handēs Amsōreay: Zeitschrift für Armenische Philologie
Haiku   Haiku Review
HAR   Hebrew Annual Review
Hasifrut   Ha-Sifrut/Literature: Ti'uriah—Po'etiḵah—Sifrut 'Ivrit—Sifrut Hashva'atit/Theory—Poetics—Hebrew and Comparative Literature
HBK   Hoppo Bunka Kenkyu: Bulletin of the Institute for the Study of North Eurasian Cultures, Hokkaido University
HBl   Hofmannsthal Blätter
HBR   Heidelberger Beiträge zur Romanistik
HBSÅ   Hjalmar Bergman Samfundet Årsbok (Stockholm, Sweden)
*HC   The Hollins Critic
HCompL   Hebrew Linguistics: A Journal for Hebrew Formal, Computational, Applied Linguistics, and Modern Hebrew
*HD   Human Development
*HDNews   H. D. Newsletter
*HEAS   Harvard East Asian Monographs
*HEI   History of European Ideas
*HeineJ   Heine Jahrbuch
Helikon: Világirodalmi Figyelő (Budapest, Hungary)
Hellenika (Bochum, FRG)
HellēnikaS   Hellēnika: Philologikon, Historikon kai Laographikon Periodikon Syngramma
Hermaea: Germanistische Forschungen
*Hermes: Zeitschrift für Klassische Philologie
HES   Harvard English Studies
HF   Heidelberger Forschungen
*HisJ   Hispanic Journal (Indiana, PA)
*Hispam   Hispamerica: Revista de Literatura
*Hispania: A Journal Devoted to the Interests of the Teaching of Spanish and Portuguese
*Hispano   Hispanófila (Chapel Hill, NC)
*HispIss   Hispanic Issues
HJA&S   Hitotsubashi Journal of Arts & Sciences
HJAS   Harvard Journal of Asiatic Studies
*HJb   Hebbel-Jahrbuch
*HJR   The Henry James Review (Baton Rouge, LA)
HK   Heritage of the Great Plains
*HL   Historiographia Linguistica: International Journal for the History of the Language Sciences/Revue Internationale pour l'Histoire des Sciences du Langage/Internationale Zeitschrift für die Geschichte der Sprachwissenschaften
*HLB   Harvard Library Bulletin
*HLing   Hispanic Linguistics
*HLQ   Huntington Library Quarterly: A Journal for the History and Interpretation of English and American Civilization
*HLS   Historiska och Litteraturhistoriska Studier (Helsinki, Finland)
*HN   The Hemingway Review
*HofP   Horns of Plenty: Malcolm Cowley and his Generation
HöJb   Hölderlin-Jahrbuch
Homme   L'Homme: Revue Française d'Anthropologie
Hor Yezh
*Horen   Die Horen: Zeitschrift für Literatur, Kunst und Kritik
*Horisont   Kulturtidskriften HORISONT: Organ för Svenska Österbottens Litteraturförening
*Horizontes: Revista de la Universidad Católica de Puerto Rico
HPEN   The Hungarian P.E.N./Le P.E.N. Hongrois
HPLR   High Plains Literary Review
HPS   Hamburger Philologische Studien
*HQ   The Hopkins Quarterly
*HR   Hispanic Review
HRD   Hamburger Romanistische Dissertationen
HS   Humanities in the South: Newsletter of the Southern Humanities Council
HSCL   Harvard Studies in Comparative Literature
*HSE   Hungarian Studies in English (Debrecen, Hungary)
HSELL   Hiroshima Studies in English Language and Literature
*HSHL   Historische Sprachforschung/Historical Linguistics
HSJ   Housman Society Journal

*HSL   University of Hartford Studies in Literature: A Journal of Interdisciplinary Criticism
HSR   Hungarian Studies Review
*HSRL   Harvard Studies in Romance Languages
*HSt   Hamlet Studies: An International Journal of Research on The Tragedie of Hamlet, Prince of Denmarke *(New Delhi, India)*
HStudien   Hispanistische Studien
HT   Historisk Tidskrift (Stockholm, Sweden)
HTR   Harvard Theological Review
*HudR   The Hudson Review
*HumanS   Human Studies: A Journal for Philosophy and the Social Sciences
*HumB   Humanitas: Rivista bimestrale di Cultura (Brescia, Italy)
*HumLov   Humanistica Lovaniensia: Journal of Neo-Latin Studies (Louvain, Belgium)
*Humor: International Journal of Humor Research
*HUS   Harvard Ukrainian Studies
HUSL   Hebrew University Studies in Literature and the Arts
HymnM   Hymnologiske Meddelelser: Tidsskrift om Salmer
HZM   Handelingen van de Koninklijke Zuidnederlandse Maatschappij voor Taal- en Letterkunde en Geschiedenis
*IAN   Izvestiia Akademii Nauk S.S.S.R., Seriia Literatury i Iazyka (Moscow, U.S.S.R.)
I&L   Ideologies and Literature: Journal of Hispanic and Lusophone Discourse Analysis
IAS   Irish Arts Series
*IASL   Internationales Archiv für Sozialgeschichte der Deutschen Literatur
IASOP   Institute of African Studies, Occasional Publications (Ibadan, Nigeria)
*IAT   Izvestiia Akademii Nauk Turkmenskoï SSR, Seriia Obshchestvennykh Nauk
IBD   Infant Behavior and Development: An International and Interdisciplinary Journal
Ibero   Iberoromania: Zeitschrift für die Iberoromanischen Sprachen und Literaturen in Europa und Amerika/Revista Dedicada a las Lenguas y Literaturas Iberorrománicas de Europa y América
*IBK   Innsbrucker Beiträge zur Kulturwissenschaft: Germanistische Reihe
*IBLA: Revue de l'Institut des Belles Lettres Arabes
*IBP   Italian Books and Periodicals: Cultural and Bibliographic Review
*I/C   Information/Communication
ICarbS (Carbondale, IL)
ID   Italia Dialettale: Rivista di Dialettologia Italiana
*Idc   L'Intermédiaire des Casanovistes (Rome, Italy)
*IdD   Ilha do Desterro: A Journal of Language and Literature
*IdF   Impulse der Forschung
Idiomatica: Veröffentlichungen der Tübinger Arbeitsstelle 'Sprache in Südwestdeutschland'
IEY   Iowa English Bulletin
*IF   Indogermanische Forschungen: Zeitschrift für Indogermanistik und Allgemeine Sprachwissenschaft
IFr   Italia Francescana
*IFR   International Fiction Review
*IFRev   International Folklore Review: Folklore Studies from Overseas
*IG   L'Information Grammaticale
IHS   Irish Historical Studies
*IIJ   Indo-Iranian Journal
*IJAL   International Journal of American Linguistics
IJDL   International Journal of Dravidian Linguistics
*IJL   Indian Journal of Linguistics/Praci-Bhasha-Vijnan
*IJLex   International Journal of Lexicography [Incorporates *The EURALEX Bulletin*]
*IJMES   International Journal of Middle East Studies
IJOAL   Indian Journal of Applied Linguistics
*IJPP   Interpretation: A Journal of Political Philosophy
*IJRS   International Journal of Rumanian Studies (Amsterdam, Netherlands)
*IJŠ   Inostrannye Iazyki v Shkole

IJSL International Journal of the Sociology of Language
IJSLP International Journal of Slavic Linguistics and Poetics
IJT International Journal of Translation
IK Irodalomtörténeti Közlemények
IKw Inmun Kwahak: The Journal of Humanities
IL L'Information Littéraire: Revue Paraissant Cinq Fois par An
ILing Initiation à la Linguistique
ILL Publications de l'Institut de Langue et Littérature d'Oc
ILML Istituto Lombardo, Accademia di Scienze e Lettere, Memorie
ILR The Indian Literary Review: A Tri-Quarterly of Indian Literature
ILRL Istituto Lombardo, Accademia di Scienze e Lettere, Rendiconti della Classe di Lettere
Imágenes: Publicación Semestral de Teoría, Técnica, Crítica y Educación Acerca de la Imagen en Movimiento
Imagine: International Chicano Poetry Journal
Imprévue (Montpellier, France)
IMU Italia Medioevale e Umanistica
Incipit (Buenos Aires, Argentina)
IndH Indian Horizons
IndL Indian Literature
IndLing Indian Linguistics: Journal of the Linguistic Society of India
Indonesia (Ithaca, NY)
Infini L'Infini
InG In Geardagum: Essays on Old and Middle English Language and Literature
Inklings: Jahrbuch für Literatur und Ästhetik
InLi Incontri Linguistici
InozF Inozemna Filolohiia
Insula: Revista de Letras y Ciencias Humanas
Interface: Journal of Applied Linguistics / Tijdschrift voor Toegepaste Linguïstiek
Interplay: Proceedings of Colloquia in Comparative Literature and the Arts
Interprete L'Interprete (Ravenna, Italy)
Inti: Revista de Literatura Hispánica
IonC Index on Censorship
IowaR The Iowa Review
IPAJ Journal of the International Phonetic Association
IPEN The Indian P.E.N.
Ipotesi Ipotesi 80: Rivista Quadrimestrale di Cultura
IQ Italian Quarterly
IqR Iqbal Review: Journal of the Iqbal Academy Pakistan
IRAL International Review of Applied Linguistics in Language Teaching
Iran: Journal of the British Institute of Persian Studies
IranS Iranian Studies: Journal of the Society for Iranian Studies
Irian: Bulletin of Irian Jaya
Iris (Montpellier, France)
IrishSt Irish Studies
IrisW Iris: Graduate Journal of French Critical Studies
IRLI Italianistica: Rivista di Letteratura Italiana
IrodalF Irodalomtörténeti Füzetek
Irodalom Irodalomtörténet: History of Literature (Budapest, Hungary)
Ironwood
IS Italian Studies (Leeds, England)
ISh The Independent Shavian
Islam Der Islam: Zeitschrift für Geschichte und Kultur des Islamischen Orients
ISLR Issues in Second Language Research
ISlSt Irish Slavonic Studies
ISSJ International Social Science Journal
ItalAm Italian Americana
Italianist The Italianist: Journal of the Department of Italian Studies, University of Reading
Italica
ItalienischZ Italienisch: Zeitschrift für Italienische Sprache und Literatur
ItB It Beaken: Tydskrift fan de Fryske Akademy
ItC Italian Culture (Hamilton, Ontario)

ItF Italyan Filolojisi / Filologia Italiana
ITL: Review of Applied Linguistics
IUB Indiana University Bookman
IUPUAS Indiana University Uralic and Altaic Series
IUR Irish University Review: A Journal of Irish Studies
Izraz: Časopis za Književnu i Umjetničku Kritiku (Sarajevo, Yugoslavia)
JAAC Journal of Aesthetics and Art Criticism
JAAL Journal of Afroasiatic Languages
JAAR Journal of the American Academy of Religion
Jabberwocky: The Journal of the Lewis Carroll Society
JAC Journal of Advanced Composition
JACult Journal of American Culture
JAF Journal of American Folklore
JALL Journal of African Languages and Linguistics (Leiden, Netherlands)
JAmS Journal of American Studies
JAOS Journal of the American Oriental Society
JAP Journal of Abnormal Psychology
JAPLA Journal of the Atlantic Provinces Linguistic Association / Revue de l'Association de Linguistique des Provinces Atlantiques
JapQ Japan Quarterly
JAR Journal of Anthropological Research
JARAAS Journal of the American Romanian Academy of Arts and Sciences
JArabL Journal of Arabic Literature
JAS Journal of the Acoustical Society of America
JASAT Journal of the American Studies Association of Texas
JASB Journal of the Asiatic Society of Bombay
JAsiat Journal Asiatique
JASt Journal of Asian Studies
JATJ Journal of the Association of Teachers of Japanese
JBalS Journal of Baltic Studies
JBeckS Journal of Beckett Studies
JByelS Journal of Byelorussian Studies
JC Journal of Communication (New York, NY)
JCF Journal of Canadian Fiction
JCG Journal of Cultural Geography
JCHAS Journal of the Cork Historical and Archaeological Society
JChinL Journal of Chinese Linguistics (Berkeley, CA)
JChinP Journal of Chinese Philosophy
JChL Journal of Child Language
JChSt Journal of Chinese Studies
JCL The Journal of Commonwealth Literature
JCLA Journal of Comparative Literature and Aesthetics
JCLS Jyväskylä Cross-Language Studies
JCLTA Journal of the Chinese Language Teachers Association
JCM The Journal of Country Music
JCP Journal of Canadian Poetry
JCS Journal of Croatian Studies: Annual Review of the Croatian Academy of America, Inc.
JCSJ John Clare Society Journal
JCSR Journal of Canadian Studies / Revue d'Etudes Canadiennes
JCSt Journal of Caribbean Studies
JCunS Journal of Cuneiform Studies
JD Journal of Documentation
JDECU Journal of the Department of English (Calcutta Univ.)
JDHLS D. H. Lawrence: The Journal of the D. H. Lawrence Society
JDJ John Donne Journal: Studies in the Age of Donne
JDN James Dickey Newsletter
JDS Jacobean Drama Studies
JDSG Jahrbuch der Deutschen Schiller-Gesellschaft
JEFL Journal of English and Foreign Languages
JEGP Journal of English and Germanic Philology
JEI Journal of the English Institute
JELL The Journal of English Language and Literature
JELL-CB Journal of the English Language and Literature (Chungbuk Branch, English Language and Literature Assn. of Korea)
JEn Journal of English
JEngL Journal of English Linguistics

JEngS   Journal of English Studies
*JENS   Journal of the Eighteen Nineties Society
*JEP   Journal of Evolutionary Psychology
*JES   Journal of European Studies
*JEthS   The Journal of Ethnic Studies
*JExPH   Journal of Experimental Psychology: Human Perception and Performance
*JExPLMC   Journal of Experimental Psychology: Learning, Memory, and Cognition
*Jezik: Časopis za Kulturu Hrvatskoga Književnog Jezika (Zagreb, Yugoslavia)
*JF   Južnoslovenski Filolog
*JFDH   Jahrbuch des Freien Deutschen Hochstifts (Tübingen, FRG)
JFL   Jahrbuch für Fränkische Landesforschung
*JFR   Journal of Folklore Research (Bloomington, IN)
*JGa   Jaunā Gaita
*JGE: The Journal of General Education
JGG   Jahrbuch der Grillparzer-Gesellschaft
JGJRI   Journal of the Ganganatha Jha Kendriya Sanskrit Vidyapeetha
JH   Journal of Humanities
JHD   Journal of the Hellenic Diaspora
JHI   Journal of the History of Ideas
*JHP   Journal of Hispanic Philology (Tallahassee, FL)
*JIES   Journal of Indo-European Studies
JIG   Jahrbuch für Internationale Germanistik
*JIGA   Jahrbuch für Internationale Germanistik: Reihe A: Kongressberichte
*JIL   Journal of Irish Literature
JILS   Journal of Interdisciplinary Literary Studies/Cuadernos Interdisciplinarios de Estudios Literarios
JIP   Journal of Indian Philosophy
*JiS   Jezik in Slovstvo (Ljubljana, Yugoslavia)
JISHS   Illinois Historical Journal
JIWE   The Journal of Indian Writing in English
JJCL   Jadavpur Journal of Comparative Literature
*JJPG   Jahrbuch der Jean-Paul-Gesellschaft
*JJQ   James Joyce Quarterly
JJS   The Journal of Japanese Studies
JKMG   Jahrbuch der Karl-May-Gesellschaft
*JKSA   Journal of the Kafka Society of America
JKSUA   Journal of King Saud University, Arts
JKWJC   Journal of Kyoritsu Women's Junior College
*JL   Journal of Linguistics (Cambridge, England)
JLAL   Journal of Latin American Lore
*JLD   Journal of Learning Disabilities
JLDS   Journal of the Lancashire Dialect Society
*JLN   Jack London Newsletter
JLS   Journal of Literary Semantics
*JLSP   Journal of Language and Social Psychology
*JLSTL   Journal of Literary Studies/Tydskrif Vir Literatuurwetenskap
JMAS   The Journal of Modern African Studies
*JMemL   Journal of Memory and Language
*JMGS   Journal of Modern Greek Studies
*JML   Journal of Modern Literature
JMLing   Journal of Mayan Linguistics
*JMMD   Journal of Multilingual and Multicultural Development
*JMMLA   The Journal of the Midwest Modern Language Association
*JMRS   Journal of Medieval and Renaissance Studies
JMSUB   Journal of the Maharaja Sayajirao University of Baroda
JNB   Journal of Nonverbal Behavior
*JNES   Journal of Near Eastern Studies (Chicago, IL)
*JNMD   Journal of Nervous and Mental Disease
JNPH   Journal of Newspaper and Periodical History
*JNT   Journal of Narrative Technique
JNWSL   Journal of Northwest Semitic Languages
JÖBG   Jahrbuch der Österreichischen Byzantinistik
*JOCI   Journal of Communication Inquiry
*JoHS   Journal of Hellenic Studies
*JOIB   Journal of the Oriental Institute (Baroda, India)

Jolan: Journal of the Linguistic Association of Nigeria
JoS   Journal of Semantics: An International Journal for the Interdisciplinary Study of the Semantics of Natural Language (Oxford, England)
*JP   Journal of Philosophy
*JPC   Journal of Popular Culture
*JPCL   Journal of Pidgin and Creole Languages
*JPFT   Journal of Popular Film and Television
*JPhon   Journal of Phonetics
*JPL   Journal of Philosophical Logic
JPNP   Journal de Psychologie Normale et Pathologique
*JPol   Język Polski
*JPrag   Journal of Pragmatics: An Interdisciplinary Bi-monthly of Language Studies
*JPRS   The Journal of Pre-Raphaelite and Aesthetic Studies
*JPS   Journal of the Polynesian Society (Auckland, New Zealand)
*JPSP   Journal of Personality and Social Psychology: Attitudes and Social Cognition Section
*JPsyR   Journal of Psycholinguistic Research
*JQ   Journalism Quarterly
JRAS   Journal of the Royal Asiatic Society of Great Britain and Ireland
JRASM   Journal of the Malaysian Branch of the Royal Asiatic Society
*JRG   Jahrbuch der Raabe-Gesellschaft
*JRMMRA   Journal of the Rocky Mountain Medieval and Renaissance Association
*JRR   Jean Rhys Review
*JRS   Journal of Russian Studies
JRSAI   Journal of the Royal Society of Antiquaries of Ireland
*JRStud   Journal of Ritual Studies
JRUL   Journal of the Rutgers University Libraries
*JS   Journal des Savants
*JSA   Joyce Studies Annual
*JSBSA   Journal of the Society of Basque Studies in America
JSem   Journal for Semitics/Tydskrif vir Semitistiek
JSGLL   Japanese Studies in German Language and Literature
*JSHD   Journal of Speech and Hearing Disorders
*JSHR   Journal of Speech and Hearing Research
JSK   Jahrbuch der Sammlung Kippenberg (Düsseldorf, FRG)
JSL   Journal of the School of Languages
JSoAL   Journal of South Asian Literature
*JSS   Journal of Semitic Studies
JSSB   Journal of the Siam Society (Bangkok, Thailand)
*JSSE   Journal of the Short Story in English
JSSR   Journal for the Scientific Study of Religion (Akron, OH)
*JSw   Journal of the Southwest
JTamS   Journal of Tamil Studies
Judaism: A Quarterly Journal of Jewish Life and Thought
*JUkGS   Journal of Ukrainian Studies
JV   Jahrbuch für Volksliedforschung
JWAL   Journal of West African Languages
JWB   Jahrbuch der Wittheit zu Bremen
JWCI   Journal of the Warburg and Courtauld Institutes
*JWGV   Jahrbuch des Wiener Goethe-Vereins
*JWMS   The Journal of the William Morris Society
*Kadmos: Zeitschrift für Vor- und Frühgriechische Epigraphik
KAL   Kyushu American Literature (Fukuoka, Japan)
*Kalbotyra: Lietuvos TSR Aukštųjų Mokyklų Mokslo Darbai (Vilnius, U.S.S.R.)
Kalki: Studies in James Branch Cabell
Kanava
Káñina: Revista de Artes y Letras de la Universidad de Costa Rica
KanoS   Kano Studies: Journal of Saharan and Sudanic Research (Ibadan, Nigeria)
*KanQ   Kansas Quarterly
KAr   Kansatieteellinen Arkisto
*Karogs (Riga, U.S.S.R.)
KASL   Kasseler Arbeiten zur Sprache und Literatur: Anglistik-Germanistik-Romanistik
KB   Kulturos Barai

KBCJ Jaarboek Koninklijke Belgische Commissie voor Volkskunde, Vlaamse Afdeling

KBGL Kopenhagener Beiträge zur Germanistischen Linguistik

*KDSL Konzepte der Sprach- und Literaturwissenschaft

KDVS Kongelige Danske Videnskabernes Selskab. Historisk-Filosofiske Meddelelser (Copenhagen, Denmark)

*KeK Keiryō Kokugogaku/Mathematical Linguistics

KerC Kerkyraïka Chronika

KFQ Keystone Folklore

*KGad Kritikas Gadagrāmata (Riga, Latvian S.S.R., U.S.S.R.)

*KGGJ Klaus-Groth-Gesellschaft Jahresgabe

KGUAS Kwansei Gakuin University Annual Studies

Kiabàrà: Journal of the Humanities

Kierunki

KiJ Književnost i Jezik

Kiswahili

KJ The Kipling Journal

*KjK Keel ja Kirjandus (Tallinn, Estonian S.S.R., U.S.S.R.)

KL Kypriakos Logos

**Klasgids: By die Studie van die Afrikaanse Taal en Letterkunde*

*KN Kwartalnik Neofilologiczny (Warsaw, Poland)

Knji Književnost

KnjiK Književna Kritika: Časopis za Estetiku Književnosti

KnjiNov Književne Novine: List za Knjizevnost i Kulturu (Belgrade, Yugoslavia)

KnjIst Književna Istorija

**Knygotyra: Lietuvos TSR Aukštųjų Mokyklų Mokslo Darbai* (Vilnius, U.S.S.R.)

Kodikas Kodikas/Code/Ars semeiotica

*KoJ Korea Journal

Kontekst: Literary Theory Studies

KopGS Kopenhagener Germanistische Studien

*Kortárs Kortárs: Irodalmi és Kritikai Folyóirat

Korunk (Bucarest, Romania)

KP Kritika Phylla: Periodike Ekdose Logotechias Kai Genikes Paideas

*KPR Kentucky Philological Review

KPS Korespondence Pomembnih Slovencev

KQ Koreana Quarterly

*KR The Kenyon Review

KRA Kölner Romanistische Arbeiten

Kredsen: Teologi, æstetik, filosofo. Medlemsblad for Studenterkredsen i København, Odense og Aarhus (Aarhus, Denmark)

*KRev The Kentucky Review

Kritik: Tidsskrift for Litteratur, Forskning, Undervisning (Copenhagen, Denmark)

*KRQ Romance Quarterly

KSDL Kieler Studien zur Deutschen Literaturgeschichte

*KSGT Kleine Schriften der Gesellschaft für Theatergeschichte

*KSJ Keats-Shelley Journal: Keats, Shelley, Byron, Hunt, and Their Circles

KSl Kul'tura Slova

*KSMB Keats-Shelley Review

KSV Kirjallisuudentutkijain Seuran Vuosikirja (Helsinki, Finland)

KSVK Kalevalaseuran Vuosikirja

Kuka: Journal of Creative and Critical Writing (Zaria, Nigeria)

*KuKl Kultur og Klasse

KuL Kunst und Literatur: Zeitschrift für Fragen der Aesthetik und Kunsttheorie

*KulturaP Kultura: Szkice, Opowiadania, Sprawozdania (Paris, France)

*Kunapipi

KVHAA Kungliga Vitterhets Historie och Antikvitets Akademiens Handlingar Filologisk-Filosofiska Serien

*KVNS Korrespondenzblatt des Vereins für Niederdeutsche Sprachforschung

KyS Kypriakai Spoudai

LA Linguistica Antverpiensia

LA&LD Language Acquisition & Language Disorders

*LAcq Language Acquisition: A Journal of Developmental Linguistics

LAf Linguistique Africaine

*LAILJ Latin American Indian Literatures Journal: A Review of American Indian Texts and Studies

*LAkt Linguistik Aktuell

*LAL Library of Arabic Linguistics

*LAlb Les Lettres Albanaises: Revue Littéraire et Artistique

LaLit Louisiana Literature: A Review of Literature and Humanities

*LALR Latin American Literary Review

LAmer Letteratura d'America: Rivista Trimestrale

LAMR Latin American Music Review/Revista de Música Latinoamericana

**L&B* Literature and Belief

**L&C* Language & Communication: An Interdisciplinary Journal

**L&Comp* Language and Computers: Studies in Practical Linguistics

**L&E* Linguistics and Education: An International Research Journal

**Landfall: A New Zealand Quarterly*

**L&LC* Literary and Linguistic Computing: Journal of the Association for Literary and Linguistic Computing

**L&LifeA* Literature and Life: American Writers

**L&LifeB* Literature and Life: British Writers

**L&LifeM* Literature and Life: Mystery Writers

L&LifeW Literature and Life: World Writers

**L&LinM* Language and Linguistics in Melanesia: Journal of the Linguistic Society of Papua New Guinea

**L&M* Literature and Medicine

**L&P* Literature and Psychology (Teaneck, NJ)

**L&S* Language and Speech

**L&Soc* Langage et Société

**L&T* Literature & Theology: An Interdisciplinary Journal of Theory and Criticism

**L&U* The Lion and the Unicorn: A Critical Journal of Children's Literature

*Langages (Paris, France)

**Lang&C* Language and Culture (Hokkaido Univ.)

**Lang&H* Le Langage et l'Homme

Lang&S Language and Style: An International Journal

LangF Language Forum

*LangQ The Language Quarterly (Tampa, FL)

*LangR Language Research

*LangS Language Sciences

LangT Language Testing

**Language: Journal of the Linguistic Society of America*

**Langues&L* Revue Langues et Linguistique

*LanM Les Langues Modernes

*LArb Linguistische Arbeiten

*LArm Literaturnaia Armeniia: Ezhemesiachnyĭ Literaturno-Khudozhestvennyĭ i Obshchestvenno-Politicheskiĭ Zhurnal

LAS Living Author Series

Latinitas: Commentarii Linguae Latinae Excolendae

Latomus: Revue d'Etudes Latines

*LATR Latin American Theatre Review

*Laurels

*LB Leuvense Bijdragen: Tijdschrift voor Germaanse Filologie

LBib Linguistica Biblica: Interdisziplinäre Zeitschrift für Theologie und Linguistik

*LBl Living Blues: A Journal of the Black American Blues Tradition

LBR Luso-Brazilian Review

**LC&C* Language, Culture, and Curriculum

LCC Léachtaí Cholm Cille

*LCP Language and Cognitive Processes

LCRC Literature and Contemporary Revolutionary Culture: Journal of the Society of Contemporary Hispanic and Lusophone Revolutionary Literatures

*LCrit The Literary Criterion (Mysore, India)

*LCUT Library Chronicle of the University of Texas

LD Lituanistikos Darbai: Lituanistikos Instituto Metraštis

*LDant Lectura Dantis: A Forum for Dante Research and Interpretation

LdC Lletra de Canvi

*LdD Letras de Deusto

*LdProv Il Lettore di Provincia

LE   Linguistica Extranea
*LEA   Lingüística Española Actual
LE&W   Literature East and West
LeedsSE   Leeds Studies in English
*Legacy: A Journal of Nineteenth-Century American Women Writers
*Lendemains: Etudes Comparées sur la France/Vergleichende Frankreichforschung
*LengM   Lenguas Modernas
Lenguaje (Cali, Colombia)
*LeS   Lingua e Stile: Trimestrale di Linguistica e Critica Letteraria (Bologna, Italy)
*Leshonenu   Leshonenu/Lěšonénu: A Journal for the Study of the Hebrew Language and Cognate Subjects/Ketav-'Et le-Ḥeqer ha-Lashon ha-'Ivrit ve-ha-Teḥumim ha-Semukhim Lah
*LetC   Letture Classensi
*LetP   Letras Peninsulares
Letterato: Periodico di Attualità e Cultura
*Letture: Libro e Spettacolo/Mensile di Studi e Rassegne
*Lexicographica: International Annual for Lexicography/Revue Internationale de Lexicographie/Internationales Jahrbuch für Lexikographie
*LexicographicaS   Lexicographica; Series Maior
Lexique (Villeneuve d'Ascq, France)
Lexis: Revista de Lingüística y Literatura
LF   Listy Filologické
*LFC   Letteratura Francese Contemporanea le Correnti d'Avanguardia: Berenice
*LFem   Letras Femeninas
*LFoiro   Literatura Foiro: Kultura Revuo en Esperanto
*LFQ   Literature/Film Quarterly
*LFr   Langue Française
*LFront   Literaturen Front: Organ na Sŭiuza na Bŭlgarskite Pisateli (Sofia, Bulgaria)
*LG   Literaturnaia Gazeta
*LGF   Lunder Germanistische Forschungen
LGJ   Lost Generation Journal
LHRev   The Langston Hughes Review
LHY   Literary Half-Yearly
*LI   Lettere Italiane
*Lib&C   Libraries & Culture: A Journal of Library History
Liberté (Montréal, Canada)
Librarium: Zeitschrift der Schweizerischen Bibliophilen-Gesellschaft/Revue de la Société Suisse des Bibliophiles
*Library   The Library: A Quarterly Journal of Bibliography
Libri: International Library Review (Copenhagen, Denmark)
LIC   Letteratura Italiana Contemporaneo: Rivista Quadrimestrale di Studi Sul Novecento
Licorne   La Licorne
*LiLi: Zeitschrift für Literaturwissenschaft und Linguistik
*LiMen   Literatūra ir Menas
*LimR   Limba Română
*Ling   American University Studies XIII: Linguistics
*LingA   Linguistic Analysis
*LingAb   Linguistics Abstracts
Ling&L   Língua e Literatura: Revista dos Departamentos de Letras da Faculdade de Filosofia, Letras e Ciêncas Humanas da Universidade de São Paulo
*Ling&P   Linguistics and Philosophy: An International Journal
*LingB   Linguistische Berichte
*LingI   Linguistic Inquiry
*LingInv   Lingvisticæ Investigationes: Revue Internationale de Linguistique Française et de Linguistique Générale
*Lingua: International Review of General Linguistics
*Linguist   The Linguist
*Linguistica (Ljubljana, Yugoslavia)
*Linguistics: An Interdisciplinary Journal of the Language Sciences
*Linguistique   La Linguistique: Revue de la Société Internationale de Linguistique Fonctionnelle/Journal of the International Society of Functional Linguistics (Paris, France)
LiNQ: (Literature in North Queensland)

*LinS   Language in Society (Oxford, England)
LIS   Lingvisticæ Investigationes: Supplementa: Studies in French & General Linguistics/Etudes en Linguistique Française et Générale
LiSa   Litteratur og Samfund
*LISL   Amsterdam Studies in the Theory and History of Linguistic Science V: Library and Information Sources in Linguistics
*Lit   Littérature (Paris, France)
*LIT   Lit: Literature Interpretation Theory
LitAS   Literatur als Sprache: Literaturtheorie—Interpretation—Sprachkritik
LitC   Literatura Chilena: Creación y Crítica
LitE   The Literary Endeavour: A Quarterly Journal Devoted to English Studies
*Literatura (Budapest, Hungary)
Literatūra: Lietuvos TSR Aukštųjų Mokyklų Mokslo Darbai (Vilnius, U.S.S.R.)
LitLeks   Literarni Leksikon
LitM   Literární Měsíčník
*LitR   The Literary Review: An International Journal of Contemporary Writing (Madison, NJ)
*Litt   Littératures (Toulouse, France)
Litteraria: Teoria Literatury. Metodologia. Kultura. Humanistyka
*Lituanus: Baltic States Quarterly of Arts & Sciences
*Livstegn: Journal of the Norwegian Association for Semiotic Studies
*LJb   Lutherjahrbuch
*LJGG   Literaturwissenschaftliches Jahrbuch im Auftrage der Görres-Gesellschaft
LJH   Legon Journal of the Humanities (Legon, Ghana)
*LJHum   Lamar Journal of the Humanities
*LKK   Lietuvių Kalbotyros Klausimai
*LL   Language Learning: A Journal of Applied Linguistics
LLa   Leshonenu La'Am: Kuntresim 'Amamiyyim le-'Inyane Lashon/-Popular Journal of Language
Llên Cymru
LLNL   Les Langues Néo-Latines: Bulletin Trimestriel de la Société de Langues Néo-Latines
*LLSEE   Linguistic and Literary Studies in Eastern Europe
*LLud   Literatura Ludowa
*LMAD   Lietuvos TSR Mokslų Akademijos Darbai. A Serija (Vilnius, U.S.S.R.)
LMC   Literature, Meaning, Culture
*LMex   Literatura Mexicana
LMHS   Liverpool Monographs in Hispanic Studies
LMi   Literaturna Misŭl (Sofia, Bulgaria)
LN   Lingua Nostra
*LO   Literaturnoe Obozrenie: Organ Soiuza Pisateleĭ SSSR
Logophile: The Cambridge Journal of Words and Language
LoomingE   Looming: Eesti Kirjanike Liidu Kuukiri (Tallinn, U.S.S.R.)
*Lore&L   Lore and Language
LOS   Literary Onomastics Studies
*LP   Lingua Posnaniensis: Czasopismo Poświecone Językoznawstwu Porównawczemu i Ogólnemu
LPFMRD   Lingvisticheskie Problemy Funktsional'nogo Modelirovaniia Rechevoĭ Deiatel'nosti
*LPLP   Language Problems and Language Planning/Lingvaj Problemoj kaj Lingvo-Planado
*LQ   Lettres Québécoises
*LR   Les Lettres Romanes
*LRB   London Review of Books
*LRN   Literary Research: A Journal of Scholarly Method and Technique
*LSE   Lund Studies in English
LSil   Linguistica Silesiana
*LSlov   Le Livre Slovène (Ljubljana, Yugoslavia)
*LSoc   Language in Society (Charlottesville, VA)
*LSp   Lebende Sprachen: Zeitschrift für Fremde Sprachen in Wissenschaft und Praxis
LSPd   Literary Studies in Poland/Etudes Littéraires en Pologne
LSS   Leyte-Samar Studies
*LSt   Lovecraft Studies

LT   Levende Talen
*LTBA   Linguistics of the Tibeto-Burman Area
*LTeach   Language Teaching: The International Abstracting Journal for Language Teachers and Applied Linguists
LTM   Leeds Texts and Monographs
Luc   Luceafărul (Bucharest, Romania)
Lud: Organ Polskiego Towarzystwa Ludoznawczego/Organe de la Société Polonaise d'Ethnologie
LuG   Literatur und Geschichte: Eine Schriftenreihe
*LuK   Literatur und Kritik (Vienna, Austria)
*LuM   Literatura un Māksla
*LUral   Linguistica Uralica [Formerly Sovetskoe Finno-Ugrovedenie/-Soviet Finno-Ugric Studies/Sowjetische Finnisch-ugrische Sprachwissennschaft/La Linguistique Finno-ougrienne Soviétique]
*Luther: Zeitschrift der Luther-Gesellschaft
*LV&C   Language Variation and Change
*LVKJ   Latviešu Valodas Kultūras Jautājumi
*LWU   Literatur in Wissenschaft und Unterricht (Kiel, FRG)
LY   Lessing Yearbook/Jahrbuch
*LyC   Lenguaje y Ciencias
Lyrikvännen (Stockholm, Sweden)
LZ   Literaturen Zbor: Spisanie na Sojuzot na Društavata za Makedonski Jazik i Literatura na SR Makedonija
*LZAV   Latvijas PSR Zinātņu Akadēmijas Vēstis (Riga, U.S.S.R.)
*MA   Le Moyen Âge: Revue Historique
*Maatstaf
*MachT   Machine Translation
MACLCL   Memórias da Academia das Ciências de Lisboa, Classe de Letras
MacR   Macedonian Review: History, Culture, Literature, Arts
*MÆ   Medium Ævum
Magazine (Abington, PA)
MagN   Magyar Nyelvőr
Maia: Rivista di Letterature Classiche
Makedonika
*MAL   Modern Austrian Literature
Maladosts': Literaturno-Mastatski i Hramadska-Palitychny Chasopis
Maledicta: The International Journal of Verbal Aggression
*Mallorn: The Journal of the Tolkien Society
Mana
M&C   Memory & Cognition
M&H   Medievalia et Humanistica: Studies in Medieval and Renaissance Culture
*M&L   Music and Letters
M&N   Man and Nature/L'Homme et La Nature: Proceedings of the Canadian Society for Eighteenth-Century Studies/Actes de la Société Canadienne d'Etude du Dix-Huitième Siècle
M&PS   Man and Poet Series
*M&SA   Metaphor and Symbolic Activity
*ManQ   The Mankind Quarterly
*Manuscripta (St. Louis, MO)
Manuscriptum: Revistă Trimestrială Editată de Muzeul Literaturii Române
MAPS   Memoirs of the American Philosophical Society
*MARev   Mid-American Review
*Marges
Marginalien: Zeitschrift für Buchkunst und Bibliophilie
Marianum
*Markers: The Journal of the Association for Gravestone Studies
MarkhamR   Markham Review
*MarM   Marbacher Magazin
MASO   Meijerbergs Arkiv för Svensk Ordforskning
*Matatu: Zeitschrift für afrikanische Kultur und Gesellschaft
MAWAR   MAWA Review
Mawazo: The Makerere Journal of the Faculties of Arts and Social Sciences
MayR   The Maynooth Review/Reiviú Mhá Nuad: A Journal of the Arts
MBG   Marburger Beiträge zur Germanistik

MBMRF   Münchener Beiträge zur Mediävistik u. Renaissance-Forschung
MCh   Mikrasiatiki Chronika
*MCL   Modern Chinese Literature
McNR   McNeese Review
MCRel   Mythes, Croyances et Religions dans le Monde Anglo-Saxon
MCul   Material Culture: Journal of the Pioneer American Society
McWPL   McGill Working Papers in Linguistics/Cahiers Linguistiques de McGill
*MD   Modern Drama
MDAM   Majalle(h)-ye Dāneshkade(h)-ye Adabiyyāt-e va Olume-e Ensanie-e Danashga(h)-e Ferdowsi
*MDOG   Mitteilungen der Deutschen Orient-Gesellschaft zu Berlin
*MEAH   Miscelanea de Estudios Arabes y Hebraicos: II. Filologia Hebrea, Biblia y Judaismo
*Meanjin
Meddelelser
*Mediaevalia: A Journal of Mediaeval Studies
Medien   Medien in Forschung + Unterricht: Series A
MedLR   Mediterranean Language Review
*MedR   Medioevo Romanzo
*MELUS: The Journal of the Society for the Study of the Multi-Ethnic Literature of the United States
*Menckeniana: A Quarterly Review
*Merkur: Deutsche Zeitschrift für Europäisches Denken
*MertAn   The Merton Annual: Studies in Thomas Merton, Religion, Culture, Literature and Social Concerns
*Mester
MET   Middle English Texts
*Meta: Journal des Traducteurs/Translators' Journal
*METh   Medieval English Theatre
METhMST   Medieval English Theatre Modern-Spelling Texts
*Metmenys
MF   Makedonski Folklor/Le Folklore Macédonien: Spisanie na Institutot za Folklor "Marko Cepenkov," Skopje/Revue de l'Institut de Folklore "Marko Cepenkov" de Skopjé
MFCG   Mitteilungen und Forschungsbeiträge der Cusanus-Gesellschaft
MFra   Le Moyen Français
*MFS   Modern Fiction Studies
*MFSJ   Missouri Folklore Society Journal
MGB   Münchener Germanistische Beiträge
*MGS   Michigan Germanic Studies
*MGSL   Minas Gerais, Suplemento Literário
MGStu   Modern German Studies
*MGv   Molodaia Gvardiia: Ezhemesiachnyǐ Literaturno-Khudozhestvennyǐ i Obshchestvenno-Politicheskiǐ Zhurnal
*MH   Museum Helveticum: Schweizerische Zeitschrift für Klassische Altertumswissenschaft/Revue Suisse pour l'Etude de l'Antiquité Classique/Rivista svizzera di Filologia Classica
MHG   Mitteilungen der E.T.A. Hoffmann-Gesellschaft-Bamberg e.V.
*MHL   Modern Hebrew Literature
*MHRADS   Modern Humanities Research Association Texts and Dissertations Series
MichA   Michigan Academician
*Midamerica: The Yearbook of the Society for the Study of Midwestern Literature
*MidF   Midwestern Folklore
*MidSF   Mid-America Folklore
*MiltonQ   Milton Quarterly
MiltonS   Milton Studies
Mimesis: Untersuchungen zu den Romanischen Literaturen der Neuzeit/Recherches sur les Littératures Romanes depuis la Renaissance
*Mind: A Quarterly Review of Philosophy
MinnR   The Minnesota Review
Minos: Revista de Filologia Egea (Salamanca, Spain)
Miorița: A Journal of Romanian Studies
MiscMed   Miscellanea Mediaevalia
*MissFR   Mississippi Folklore Register

*MissQ Mississippi Quarterly: The Journal of Southern Culture

*MissR The Missouri Review

MitJ Mittellateinisches Jahrbuch: Internationale Zeitschrift für Mediävistik/International Journal of Medieval Studies/Revue Internationale des Etudes Médiévales/Rivista Internazionale di Studi Medievali

MJ Makedonski Jazik

MJCL&L Meerut Journal of Comparative Literature and Language

*MK Magyar Könyvszemle: Könyvtörténeti Folyóirat/Revue pour l'Histoire du Livre et de la Presse

MKNAL Mededelingen der Koninklijke Nederlandse Akademie van Wetenschappen, Afdeling Letterkunde, Nieuwe Reeks

MKS Mon-Khmer Studies

*ML Modern Languages: Journal of the Modern Language Association (London, England)

*Mladika (Trieste, Italy)

MLing Modèles Linguistiques

MLit Miesięcznik Literacki (Warsaw, Poland)

MLJ The Modern Language Journal

*MLN (Baltimore, MD)

*MLNew The Malcolm Lowry Review

*MLQ Modern Language Quarterly

*MLR The Modern Language Review

*MLS Modern Language Studies

*MM Maal og Minne

*MMisc Midwestern Miscellany

MML Monographs in Modern Languages

MMLA Majallat Majma' al-Lughah al-'Arabīyah (Cairo, United Arab Republic)

*MN Monumenta Nipponica

MNCDN Mededelingen van de Nijmeegse Centrale voor Dialect- en Naamkunde

*Mnemosyne: Bibliotheca Classica Batava

MnēmosynēA Mnēmosynē: Etēsion Periodikon tēs Hetaireias Historikōn Spoudōn epi tou Neōterou Hellēnismou (Athens, Greece)

MNy Magyar Nyelv

MNyj Magyar Nyelvjárások

*ModA Modern Age: A Quarterly Review

Modellanalysen: Literatur

Mogućnosti: Književnost, Umjetnost, Kulturni Problemi

MOII Metodika Obuchenia Inostrannym Iazykam: Romanskoe i Germanskoe Iazykoznanie (Minsk)

*Monatshefte: Für Deutschen Unterricht, Deutsche Sprache und Literatur

*MontS Montaigne Studies: An Interdisciplinary Forum

Moon 13th Moon: A Feminist Literary Magazine

*MOR Mount Olive Review

*Moreana: Bulletin Thomas More

Morphé: Semiótica y Lingüística

*Mosaic: A Journal for the Interdisciplinary Study of Literature

*Mostovi

Motif: International Review of Research in Folklore & Literature [Formerly Motif: International Newsletter of Research in Folklore & Literature]

*Mov Movoznavstvo: Naukovo-Teoretychnyĭ Zhurnal Viddilennia Literatury, Movy i Mystetstvoznavstva Akademiĭ Nauk Ukraïns'oĭ RSR (Kiev, U.S.S.R.)

*Moznayim: Yarḥon Agudat ha-Soferim ha-'Ivrim be-Medinat Yiśrael/-Monthly of the Association of Hebrew Writers in Israel (Tel Aviv, Israel)

*MP Modern Philology: A Journal Devoted to Research in Medieval and Modern Literature

MPhP Mediaevalia Philosophica Polonorum

MPR The Mervyn Peake Review

*MQ Midwest Quarterly: A Journal of Contemporary Thought (Pittsburg, KS)

*MQR Michigan Quarterly Review

*MR Massachusetts Review: A Quarterly of Literature, the Arts and Public Affairs (Amherst, MA)

MRD Memoirs of the Research Department of the Tōyō Bunko (Tokyo, Japan)

MRDE Medieval & Renaissance Drama in England: An Annual Gathering of Research, Criticism and Reviews

MRMS Medieval and Renaissance Monograph Series

MRom Marche Romane

*MRRM Monographic Review/Revista Monográfica

*MRS Michigan Romance Studies

*MRTS Medieval & Renaissance Texts & Studies

*MS Mediaeval Studies (Toronto, Canada)

MSAS Monographs in International Studies, Africa Series

*MSB Mongolian Studies: Journal of the Mongolia Society

MSC Michigan Slavic Contributions

MScan Mediaeval Scandinavia

*MSE Massachusetts Studies in English

*MSEx Melville Society Extracts

MSFL Metodologia delle Scienze e Filosofia del Linguaggio

MSFO Mémoires de la Société Finno-Ougrienne (Helsinki, Finland)

MSH Michigan Studies in the Humanities

*MSI Moody Street Irregulars: A Jack Kerouac Magazine

MSNH Mémoires de la Société Néophilologique de Helsinki

MSpr Moderna Språk (Stockholm, Sweden)

*MSR Mélanges de Science Religieuse

MSS Manuscripts

MStrR The Mickle Street Review

MSzA Mainzer Studien zur Amerikanistik: Eine Europäische Hochschulreihe

MSzS Münchener Studien zur Sprachwissenschaft

*MTJ Mark Twain Journal

*MTUDLM Münchener Texte und Untersuchungen zur Deutschen Literatur des Mittelalters

*MuK Maske und Kothurn: Internationale Beiträge zur Theaterwissenschaft

*Multilingua: Journal of Interlanguage Communication

*MultM Multilingual Matters

Muse The Muse: Literary Journal of the English Association at Nsukka

MuseumsJ Museums Journal

MusilS Musil Studien

*Muttersprache: Zeitschrift zur Pflege und Erforschung der Deutschen Sprache

MW The Muslim World (Hartford, CT)

*MysticsQ Mystics Quarterly

*Mythlore: A Journal of J. R. R. Tolkien, C. S. Lewis, Charles Williams, General Fantasy and Mythic Studies

*Nabokovian The Nabokovian

NAc New Accents

NADS Newsletter of the American Dialect Society

*NAk Národopisné Aktuality

*Names: Journal of the American Name Society

*N&Q Notes and Queries

*N&T Now and Then

NArg Nuovi Argomenti

NAS Norwegian-American Studies

NatP Nationalities Papers

*NB Namn och Bygd: Tidskrift för Nordisk Ortnamnsforskning/Journal for Nordic Place-Name Research

NBL Neue Beiträge zur Literaturwissenschaft

*NCarF North Carolina Folklore Journal

*NCC Nineteenth-Century Contexts

NCF Nineteenth-Century Literature

*NCFS Nineteenth-Century French Studies

*NCHR North Carolina Historical Review

*NConL Notes on Contemporary Literature

*NCP Nineteenth Century Prose

*NCS Nineteenth-Century Studies (Charleston, SC)

*NCStud Nineteenth-Century Studies (Ann Arbor, MI)

NCTR Nineteenth Century Theatre

NDAT Nashriyye(h)-ye Dāneshkade(h)-ye Adabiyyāt va Olum-e Ensāni-ye Tabriz

*NDH Neue Deutsche Hefte

NdL Neudrucke Deutscher Literaturwerke: Neue Folge

*NDQ   North Dakota Quarterly

*NdW   Niederdeutsches Wort: Beiträge zur Niederdeutschen Philologie

NegCap   Negative Capability

Neman: Literaturno-Khudozhestvennyĭ i Obshchestvenno-Politicheskiĭ Zhurnal (Minsk, U.S.S.R.)

Nëntori: Organ i Lidhjes së Shkrimtarëve dhe Artistëve të Shqipërisë (Tiranë, Albania)

Neohelicon: Acta Comparationis Litterarum Universarum

*Neophil   Neophilologus (Groningen, Netherlands)

*NEQ   The New England Quarterly: A Historical Review of New England Life and Letters

*NER   New England Review and Bread Loaf Quarterly

NETJ   New England Theatre Journal

Neurolinguistik: Zeitschrift für Aphasieforschung und -therapie

Neva (Leningrad, U.S.S.R.)

*NewC   The New Criterion

*NewComp   New Comparison: A Journal of Comparative and General Literary Studies

NewL   New Letters: A Magazine of Fine Writing

NewS   New Scholar: An Americanist Review

Newsboy

NF   Nigerian Field: The International Field Studies Journal of West Africa

NFJ   Nordfriesisches Jahrbuch

*NFS   Nottingham French Studies

NG   Neue Germanistik (Minneapolis, MN)

*NGC   New German Critique: An Interdisciplinary Journal of German Studies

*NGR   New German Review: A Journal of Germanic Studies

*NGS   New German Studies

*NH   New Historicism: Studies in Cultural Poetics

*NHLS   North-Holland Linguistic Series

*NHQ   The New Hungarian Quarterly

*NHR   The Nathaniel Hawthorne Review

*NietzscheS   Nietzsche Studien: Internationales Jahrbuch für die Nietzsche-Forschung

Nigrizia: Fatti e Problemi del Mondo Nero

*NIK   Nyelv-és Irodalomtudományi Közlemények

Nivel

NJ   Niederdeutsches Jahrbuch: Jahrbuch des Vereins für Niederdeutsche Sprachforschung

*NJe   Naš Jezik (Belgrade, Yugoslavia)

NJF   New Jersey Folklife

*NJL   Nordic Journal of Linguistics

NK   Nyelvtudományi Közlemények

*Nku   Naamkunde

NLÅ   Norsk Litterær Årbok (Oslo, Norway)

*NL&LT   Natural Language & Linguistic Theory

NLauR   New Laurel Review

NLCHAIBS   The Newberry Library Center for the History of the American Indian Bibliographical Series

*NLH   New Literary History: A Journal of Theory and Interpretation

*NLib   Notre Librairie: Revue du Livre: Afrique, Caraïbes, Océan Indien

*NLing   Notes on Linguistics

*NLitsR   New Literatures Review

NLWJ   The National Library of Wales Journal/Cylchgrawn Llyfrgell Genedlaethol Cymru

*NM   Neuphilologische Mitteilungen: Bulletin de la Société Néophilologique/Bulletin of the Modern Language Society

NMHR   New Mexico Humanities Review

*NMIL   Notes on Modern Irish Literature

NMS   Nottingham Medieval Studies

NMW   Notes on Mississippi Writers

Noaj: Revista Literaria

NoEF   Northeast Folklore

Nomina: A Journal of Name Studies Relating to Great Britain and Ireland

*NOQ   Northwest Ohio Quarterly

*NOR   New Orleans Review

Nordelbingen: Beiträge zur Kunst und Kulturgeschichte

*Norsklrrn   Norsklæraren/Norsklæreren: Tidsskrift for Språk og Litteratur

Norte: Revista Hispano Americana

*NOT   Notes on Translation

Novel: A Forum on Fiction (Providence, RI)

*NovM   Novyi Mir: Literaturno-Khudozhestvennyĭ i Obshchestvenno-Politicheskiĭ Zhurnal

NovŽ   Novyĭ Zhurnal/The New Review (New York, NY)

NOWELE: North-Western European Language Evolution

Nowi Dni

NP   Nea Poreia

NR   The Nassau Review: The Journal of Nassau Community College Devoted to Arts, Letters, and Sciences

*NŘeč   Naše Řeč

*NRF   Nouvelle Revue Française

*NRFH   Nueva Revista de Filología Hispánica (Mexico City, Mexico)

NRL   Nouvelles de la République des Lettres

*NRO   Nouvelle Revue d'Onomastique

*NRP   Nueva Revista del Pacífico

*NRs   Neue Rundschau

NRSS   Nouvelle Revue du XVIe Siècle

*NS   Die Neueren Sprachen

NSAA   Neue Studien zur Anglistik und Amerikanistik

NSammlung   Neue Sammlung: Vierteljahres-Zeitschrift für Erziehung und Gesellschaft

*NsM   Neusprachliche Mitteilungen aus Wissenschaft und Praxis

*NSov   Nash Sovremennik: Literaturno-Khudozhestvennyĭ i Obshchestvenno-Politicheskiĭ Zhurnal

NSSVD   Naučni Sastanak Slavista u Vukove Dane (Belgrade, Yugoslavia)

NStv   Narodno Stvaralaštvo. Folklor

NTBB   Nordisk Tidskrift för Bok- och Biblioteksväsen

*NTE   Narodna Tvorchist' ta Etnohrafiia

*NTg   De Nieuwe Taalgids: Tijdschrift voor Neerlandici

*NTQ   New Theatre Quarterly

NUm   Narodna Umjetnost (Zagreb, Yugoslavia)

Numen: International Review for the History of Religions

*NVS   New Vico Studies

*NwFolk   Northwest Folklore

NWGB   New Writers Group Bulletin (Lusaka, Zambia)

NWi   North Wind: Journal of the George MacDonald Society

NWR   Northwest Review

*NWRev   The New Welsh Review

NYLF   New York Literary Forum

NYRB   The New York Review of Books

NyS   Nydanske Studier & Almen Kommunikationsteori

NYSNDL   New Yorker Studien zur Neueren Deutschen Literaturgeschichte

NysS   Nysvenska Studier: Tidskrift för Svensk Stil- och Språkforskning

NZJFS   New Zealand Journal of French Studies

*NZSJ   New Zealand Slavonic Journal

*O&C   Oeuvres & Critiques: Revue Internationale d'Etude de la Réception Critique d'Etude des Oeuvres Littéraires de Langue Française

ÖAS   Österreich in Amerikanischer Sicht: Das Österreichbild im Amerikanischen Schulunterricht

*OB   Ord och Bild

Oberon: Magazine for the Study of English and American Literature (Tokyo, Japan)

Obsidian II: Black Literature in Review

Oceania

*OcL   Oceanic Linguistics

Odra (Wrocław, Poland)

Odù: A Journal of West African Studies

*Oduma   Oduma Magazine

Ody   Odyssey: A Journal of the Humanities

OE   Oriens Extremus: Zeitschrift für Sprache, Kunst und Kultur der Länder des Fernen Ostens

OEM   Oxford English Monographs

*OENews   Old English Newsletter

OG   Orientalia Gandensia (Ghent, Belgium)

Ogam: Tradition Celtique

*OGE   Ons Geestelijk Erf: Driemaandelijks Tijdschrift voor de Geschiedenis van de Vroomheid in de Nederlanden (Antwerp, Belgium)

OGK   Onsei Gakkai Kaihô [Bulletin of the Phonetic Society of Japan]

ÖGL   Österreich in Geschichte und Literatur (mit Geographie)

OGS   Oxford German Studies

*OhR   The Ohio Review

*Ojáncano: Revista de Literatura Española

OJES   Osmania Journal of English Studies

Okike: An African Journal of New Writing

*Okt   Oktiabr': Literaturno-Khudozhestvennyĭ i Obshchestvenno-Politicheskiĭ Zhurnal

*OL   Orbis Litterarum: International Review of Literary Studies

*Olifant: A Publication of the Société Rencesvals, American-Canadian Branch

OLP   Orientalia Lovaniensia Periodica

OLR   The Oxford Literary Review

OLSP   Oceanic Linguistics Special Publications

OM   Objets et Mondes: La Revue du Musée de l'Homme

OMLLM   Oxford Modern Languages and Literature Monographs

ON   The Old Northwest: A Journal of Regional Life and Letters

*Onoma: Bibliographical and Information Bulletin

*Onomastica: Pismo Poświęcone Nazewnictwu Geograficznemu i Osobowemu

*OnomasticaC   Onomastica Canadiana (Ottawa, Canada)

OnomJug   Onomastica Jugoslavica

OnsE   Ons Erfdeel: Algemeen-Nederlands Tweemaandelijks Cultureel Tijdschrift

*OntarioR   Ontario Review

OPLing   Occasional Papers on Linguistics (Carbondale, IL)

OPLLL   Occasional Papers in Language, Literature and Linguistics

OralH   Oral History: The Journal of the Oral History Society

OrGoth   Orientalia Gothoburgensia

*Orizont: Revista a Uniunii Scriitorilor din Republica Socialista România

Orpheus: Rivista di Umanità Classica e Cristiana

OS   Orientalia Suecana (Uppsala, Sweden)

*Osamayor: Graduate Student Review

*OSP   Oxford Slavonic Papers

Osteuropa: Zeitschrift für Gegenwartsfragen des Ostens

ÖstO   Österreichische Osthefte: Zeitschrift des Österreichischen Ost- und Südosteuropa Instituts

OT   Oral Tradition

*OTM   Old Time Music

*OUÅ   Ortnamnssällskapets i Uppsala Årsskrift

OUSE   Odense University Studies in English

*Overland (Melbourne, Australia)

*ÖZV   Österreichische Zeitschrift für Volkskunde

PA   Présence Africaine: Revue Culturelle du Monde Noir/Cultural Review of the Negro World

*PAAS   Proceedings of the American Antiquarian Society

*PAC   Papers of the Algonquian Conference/Actes du Congrès des Algonquistes

PADS   Publication of the American Dialect Society

*PAFS   Publications of the American Folklore Society

*Paideia: Rivista Letteraria di Informazione Bibliografica (Brescia, Italy)

PaideiaFS   Paideia (Buffalo, NY)

Paideuma: A Journal Devoted to Ezra Pound Scholarship (Orono, ME)

PaideumaM   Paideuma: Mitteilungen zur Kulturkunde (Stuttgart, FRG)

Paintbrush: A Journal of Poetry, Translations, and Letters

Palabra   La Palabra: Revista de Literatura Chicana (Tempe, AZ)

*Palacio   El Palacio: Magazine of the Museum of New Mexico

*Palaestra: Untersuchungen aus der Deutschen, Englischen, und Scandinavischen Philologie (Göttingen, FRG)

Palaestra: Rivista di Cultura ed Arte (Maddaloni, Italy)

*Palimpsest

*PAMWS   Proceedings of the Annual Meeting of the Western Society for French History

*P&B   Pragmatics & Beyond: New Series

*P&L   Philosophy and Literature

*P&P   Perception & Psychophysics

*P&R   Philosophy and Rhetoric

PANPJ   Prace Językoznawcze

PANPKS   Prace Komisji Słowianoznawstwa

PAPA   Publications of the Arkansas Philological Association

PAPS   Proceedings of the American Philosophical Society Held at Philadelphia for Promoting Useful Knowledge

*PAR   Performing Arts Resources

Parabola: The Magazine of Myth and Tradition

ParadeS   Parade Sauvage

Paragone: Rivista Mensile di Arte Figurativa e Letteratura

*Paragraph: A Journal of Modern Critical Theory

Parergon: Bulletin of the Australian and New Zealand Association for Medieval and Renaissance Studies

Parnasso (Helsinki, Finland)

ParnassosL   Parnassos Literary Journal (Athens, Greece)

*Parnassus: Poetry in Review

*PArtsJ   Performing Arts Journal

PASAA: A Journal of Language Teaching and Learning in Thailand

PaSlow   Pamiętnik Słowiański

PaT   Pamiętnik Teatralny: Kwartalnik Poświęcony Historii I Krytyce Teatru

*Paunch

PAus   Poetry Australia

PAusL   Papers in Australian Linguistics (Subseries of Pacific Linguistics. Series A: Occasional Papers)

PAWNL   Papers in Western Austronesian Linguistics (Subseries of Pacific Linguistics. Series A: Occasional Papers)

*PBA   Proceedings of the British Academy

*PBH   Patma-Banasirakan Handes: Istoriko-Filologičeskiĭ Zhurnal

*PBML   Prague Bulletin of Mathematical Linguistics

PBSA   Papers of the Bibliographical Society of America

*PBSC   Papers of the Bibliographical Society of Canada/Cahiers de la Société Bibliographique du Canada

PCLS   Proceedings of the Comparative Literature Symposium (Lubbock, TX)

*PCP   Pacific Coast Philology

PCS   Papers in Comparative Studies

PD   Poetic Drama & Poetic Theory

*PdD   Probleme der Dichtung

*PeakeSt   Peake Studies

PE&W   Philosophy East and West: A Quarterly of Asian and Comparative Thought

*PEGS   Publications of the English Goethe Society

*Pensée   La Pensée: Revue du Rationalisme Moderne

Pequod: A Journal of Contemporary Literature and Literary Criticism

Pergalé (Vilnius, U.S.S.R.)

Peritia: Journal of the Medieval Academy of Ireland

*Persuasions: Journal of the Jane Austen Society of North America

*PF   Pennsylvania Folklife

*PForschA   Potsdamer Forschungen: Wissenschaftliche Schriftenreihe der Pädagogischen Hochschule "Karl Liebknecht" Potsdam, Reihe A

*PFr   Présence Francophone: Revue Internationale de Langue et de Littérature

*PFSCL   Papers on French Seventeenth Century Literature

*PG   Paroles Gelées: UCLA French Studies

*PH   La Palabra y el Hombre: Revista de la Universidad Veracruzana

*Philobiblon: Eine Vierteljahrsschrift für Buch- und Graphiksammler

*PHist   Printing History (New York, NY)

*PhoenixC   Phoenix: The Journal of the Classical Association of Canada/Revue de la Société Canadienne des Etudes Classiques

PhoenixK   Phoenix (Seoul, Korea)

*Phonai: Lautbibliothek der Deutschen Sprache

*Phonetica: International Journal of Speech Science

PhoneticaS   Phonetica Saraviensia: Veröffentlichungen des Instituts für Phonetik

*Phonology (Cambridge, England)

PhP Philologikē Protochronia
* *PhQ* The Philosophical Quarterly
* *PhR* Philosophical Review
* *PhS* Philosophical Studies: An International Journal for Philosophy in the Analytic Tradition
PhSR Philippine Sociological Review
* *PHT* Personhistorisk Tidskrift
PHum Przegląd Humanistyczny
Phylon: The Atlanta University Review of Race and Culture
PIMÉ Petőfi Irodalmi Múzeum Évkönyve
* *PIMSST* Pontifical Institute of Mediaeval Studies, Studies and Texts
PintR The Pinter Review
* *PJ* Poradnik Językowy (Warsaw, Poland)
* *PJGG* Philosophisches Jahrbuch der Görres-Gesellschaft (Freiburg, FRG)
* *PJL* Philippine Journal of Linguistics
PK Philologikē Kypros
PKJ Prace Komisji Językoznawstwa
* *PKn* Primerjalna Književnost
* *PKy* Pneumatikē Kypros
PL Pamiętnik Literacki: Czasopismo Kwartalne Poświęcone Historii i Krytyce Literatury Polskiej
Plamŭk: Mesechno Spisanie za Literatura, Izkustvo i Publitsistika
Plaza: Revista de Literatura
PLG Probleme de Lingvistică Generală
* *PLL* Papers on Language and Literature: A Journal for Scholars and Critics of Language and Literature
Ploughshares
PLPLS-LHS Proceedings of the Leeds Philosophical and Literary Society, Literary & Historical Section
* *Plural: Revista Cultural de Excelsior*
PM Pembroke Magazine
* *PmdnS* Postmodern Studies
PMHB Pennsylvania Magazine of History and Biography
PMHS Proceedings of the Massachusetts Historical Society
* *PMLA: Publications of the Modern Language Association of America*
PMPA Publications of the Missouri Philological Association
* *PMS* Perceptual and Motor Skills
* *PNotes* Pynchon Notes
PNR PN Review
Po&sie Po&sie
* *PoeS* Poe Studies
Poesía (Valencia, Venezuela)
* *Poetica: Zeitschrift für Sprach- und Literaturwissenschaft* (Amsterdam, Netherlands)
* *PoeticsJ* Poetics: Journal for Empirical Research on Literature, the Media and the Arts
Poétique: Revue de Théorie et d'Analyse Littéraires
* *PoetryR* Poetry Review (London, England)
* *Poeziia* (Kiev, U.S.S.R.)
* *Poezja* (Warsaw, Poland)
Polonica
PolP Polish Perspectives
* *PolR* The Polish Review
Polymia
POMPA Publications of the Mississippi Philological Assn.
* *Ponte* Il Ponte: Rivista Mensile de Politica e Letteratura Fondata da Piero Calamandrei
Portico Il Portico: Biblioteca di Lettere e Arti
PostB Postilla Bohemica/Postylla Bohemica: Vierteljahresschrift der Konstanzer Hus-Gesellschaft e.V.
* *PostS* Post Script: Essays in Film and the Humanities
* *PoT* Poetics Today
* *PP* Philologica Pragensia
PPCL Papers in Pidgin and Creole Linguistics (Subseries of Pacific Linguistics. Series A: Occasional Papers)
PPhL Papers in Philippine Linguistics (Subseries of Pacific Linguistics. Series A: Occasional Papers)
PPJ Prilozi Proučavanju Jezika

* *PPMRC* Proceedings of the PMR Conference: Annual Publication of the International Patristic, Mediaeval and Renaissance Conference
* *PPol* Il Pensiero Politico: Rivista di Storia delle Idee Politiche e Sociali
* *PPR* Philosophy and Phenomenological Research: A Quarterly Journal
PPS Publications of the Philological Society
* *PQ* Philological Quarterly (Iowa City, IA)
* *PQCS* Philippine Quarterly of Culture and Society
PR Partisan Review
PRAN Proust Research Association Newsletter
PraPol Prace Polonistyczne
Prapor: Literaturno-Khudozhniĭ ta Hromads'ko-Politychnyĭ Zhurnal (Kharkov, U.S.S.R.)
Praxis: A Journal of Culture and Criticism
Precisely
* *Prépub* (Pré)publications (Aarhus, Denmark)
* *Pre/Text: A Journal of Rhetorical Theory*
* *Pretexts: Studies in Writing and Culture*
* *PRev* The Powys Review
PRF Publications Romanes et Françaises
Prilozi Prilozi za Književnost, Jezik, Istoriju i Folklor
Prismal/Cabral: Revista de Literatura Hispánica/Caderno Afro-Brasileiro Asiático Lusitano
* *Problemi: Periodico Quadrimestrale di Cultura*
* *Probus: International Journal of Latin and Romance Languages*
* *Profession*
* *ProL* Pro Lingua
Proměny
* *Prooftexts: A Journal of Jewish Literary History*
Prospects: An Annual Journal of American Cultural Studies
* *Proteus: A Journal of Ideas*
* *ProverbiumY* Proverbium: Yearbook of International Proverb Scholarship (Burlington, VT)
PSCL Papers and Studies in Contrastive Linguistics
PSEAL Papers in South East Asian Linguistics (Subseries of Pacific Linguistics. Series A: Occasional Papers)
PSEKUT Paar Sammukest Eesti Kirjanduse Uurimise Teed
* *PSem* Problemata Semiotica
* *PSM* Philippine Studies (Manila, Philippines)
PSP Papers in Slavic Philology
PSSEAS Monographs in International Studies, Southeast Asia Series. Ohio University Center for International Studies
* *PSt* Prose Studies: History, Theory, Criticism (London, England)
PStud Portuguese Studies
* *PsyB* Psychological Bulletin
* *Psychiatry: Interpersonal and Biological Processes*
PsychologR Psychological Review
* *PSzL* Polska Sztuka Ludowa
PText Papiere zur Textlinguistik/Papers in Textlinguistics
* *PTFS* Publications of the Texas Folklore Society
PTRSC Proceedings & Transactions Royal Society of Canada
PU Problemi di Ulisse
PubHist Publishing History: The Social, Economic and Literary History of Book, Newspaper and Magazine Publishing
* *PULC* Princeton University Library Chronicle
* *PUMRL* Purdue University Monographs in Romance Languages (Amsterdam, Netherlands)
PURBA Panjab University Research Bulletin (Arts)
PuW Poesie und Wissenschaft
* *PVR* Platte Valley Review
PWS The Poet's Workshop Series
* *PZKA* Philologus: Zeitschrift für Klassische Philologie
* *PzL* Papiere zur Linguistik
Qanṭara Al- Qanṭara: Revista de Estudios Arabes
QDLLSM Quaderni del Dipartimento di Lingue e Letterature Straniere Moderne, Universita di Genova
QFG Quaderni di Filologia Germanica della Facoltà di Lettere e Filosofia dell'Università di Bologna
QFSK Quellen und Forschungen zur Sprach- und Kulturgeschichte der Germanischen Völker

*QI   Quaderni d'Italianistica: Official Journal of the Canadian Society for Italian Studies

*QIA   Quaderni Ibero-Americani: Attualità Culturale nella Penisola Iberica e America Latina

*QJS   The Quarterly Journal of Speech

QL   La Quinzaine Littéraire

QLing   Quantitative Linguistics

QLit   Le Québec Littéraire

QLL   Quaderni di Lingue e Letterature

QP   Quaderni Portoghesi (Pisa, Italy)

*QPar   Qui Parle: A Journal of Literary and Critical Studies

*QQ   Queen's Quarterly

QRFV   Quarterly Review of Film and Video

*QSem   Quaderni di Semantica: Rivista Internazionale di Semantica Teorica e Applicata/An International Journal of Theoretical and Applied Semantics (Bologna, Italy)

QSGLL   Queensland Studies in German Language and Literature

*Qu   Quadrant (Montpellier, France)

*Quadrant (Victoria, Australia)

*Quest   New Quest (Pune, India)

*Quimera: Revista de Literatura

*RA   Romanistische Arbeitshefte (Tübingen, FRG)

RAAD   Revue de l'Académie Arabe de Damas

Rad   Rad Jugoslavenske Akademije Znanosti i Umjetnosti

*RAdL   Revista Argentina de Lingüística

RadT   Radical Teacher: A Newsjournal of Socialist Theory and Practice

Raduga

*RAEI   Revista Alicantina de Estudios Ingleses

*Raft: A Journal of Armenian Poetry and Criticism

*RagL   Il Ragguaglio Librario: Rassegna Mensile Bibliografica Culturale

*RAIP   Rapport d'Activités de l'Institut de Phonétique

RaJAH   The Rackham Journal of the Arts and Humanities (Univ. of Michigan)

RAL   Research in African Literatures

*RALS   Resources for American Literary Study

*RAMR   Revue André Malraux Review

*R&L   Religion and Literature (Notre Dame, IN)

RANNAM   Recherches Anglaises et Nord-Américaines

*RAQL   Revue Québécoise de Linguistique Théorique et Appliquée

*Raritan: A Quarterly Review

*Raz SAZU   Razprave Razreda za Filološke in Literarne vede Slovenske Akademije Znanosti in Umetnosti

Razgledi: Spisanie za Literatura Umetnost i Kultura

RB   Revue Bénédictine

RBL   Revista Brasileira de Lingüística

RBLL   Revista Brasileira de Língua e Literatura

*RBML   Rare Books & Manuscripts Librarianship

*RBPH   Revue Belge de Philologie et d'Histoire/Belgisch Tijdschrift voor Filologie en Geschiedenis

*RBSL   Regensburger Beiträge zur Deutschen Sprach- und Literaturwissenschaft. Reihe B: Untersuchungen (Bern, Switzerland)

*RC   Ruperto Carola: Heidelberger Universitätshefte

RCCM   Rivista di Cultura Classica e Medievale

*RCEH   Revista Canadiense de Estudios Hispánicos

RCEI   Revista Canaria de Estudios Ingleses

*RCF   The Review of Contemporary Fiction

*RChL   Revista Chilena de Literatura

*RCLL   Revista de Critica Literaria Latinoamericana

RCrit   Le Ragioni Critiche: Rivista di Studi Linguistici e Letterari

*RcRt   Romantic Reassessment

*RCSCSPL   Russian, Croatian and Serbian, Czech and Slovak, Polish Literature (Amsterdam, Netherlands)

*RD   La Rivista Dalmatica

*RdE   Rivista di Estetica

RdH   Revista de História

*RDLet   Revista de Letras

*RdLing   Rivista di Linguistica

RdSO   Rivista degli Studi Orientali

*RdT   Revista de Teatro

*RDTP   Revista de Dialectología y Tradiciones Populares

*RdVV   Reihe der Villa Vigoni: Deutsch-Italienische Studien

*RE   Revue d'Esthétique

REA   Revue des Etudes Augustiniennes

Reader: Essays in Reader-Oriented Theory, Criticism, and Pedagogy

REAL   RE Arts & Letters: A Liberal Arts Forum

*REALB   REAL: The Yearbook of Research in English and American Literature (Tübingen, FRG)

RealM   Realtà del Mezzogiorno: Mensile di Politica Economia Cultura

*REAnc   Revue des Etudes Anciennes

*ReapprC   Reappraisals: Canadian Writers

REArmNS   Revue des Etudes Arméniennes

RechA   Recherches Augustiniennes

RechSR   Recherches de Science Religieuse

RECIFS   Recherches et Etudes Comparatistes Ibéro-Francophes de la Sorbonne Nouvelle

RecL   Recovering Literature: A Journal of Contextualist Criticism

*RECTR   Restoration and 18th Century Theatre Research

RedL   Red Letters: A Journal of Cultural Politics

*REE   Revista de Estudios Extremeños

*REEDN   Records of Early English Drama Newsletter

REF   Revista de Etnografie şi Folclor

*REG   Revue des Etudes Grecques

*REH   Revista de Estudios Hispánicos (Poughkeepsie, NY)

REH-PR   Revista de Estudios Hispánicos (Río Piedras, Puerto Rico)

*REI   Revue des Etudes Italiennes

*Reinardus: Yearbook of the International Reynard Society/Annuaire de la Société Internationale Renardienne

*REIsl   Revue des Etudes Islamiques

RELat   Revue des Etudes Latines

*RELC   RELC Journal: A Journal of Language Teaching and Research in Southeast Asia

*Ren&R   Renaissance and Reformation/Renaissance et Réforme

*Renascence: Essays on Value in Literature

RenB   The Renaissance Bulletin

*RenD   Renaissance Drama

Renditions: A Chinese-English Translation Magazine

*RenM   Renaissance Monographs

*RenP   Renaissance Papers

*RenQ   Renaissance Quarterly

*RenSt   Renaissance Studies: Journal of the Society for Renaissance Studies

*RePL   Revue Pierre Loti

*Representations

*RES   Review of English Studies: A Quarterly Journal of English Literature and the English Language

*REspL   Revista Española de Lingüística

*Restant: Tijdschrift voor Recente Semiotische Teorievorming en de Analyse van Teksten/Review for Semiotic Theories and the Analysis of Texts

*Restoration: Studies in English Literary Culture, 1660-1700

*Rev   Review (Blacksburg, VA)

RevI   Revista/Review Interamericana

*Review: Latin American Literature and Arts (New York, NY)

RevIMA   RIMA: Review of Indonesian and Malaysian Affairs

Revisor

*RevPL   Revue de Phonétique Appliquée

*RevR   Revue Romane

*RF   Romanische Forschungen

RFE   Revista de Filología Española

*RFEA   Revue Française d'Etudes Américaines

*RFNS   Rivista di Filosofia Neo-Scolastica

RFULL   Revista de Filología de la Universidad de La Laguna

RG   Revue Générale

*RGad   Raiņa Gadagrāmata (Riga, U.S.S.R.)

*RGer   Recherches Germaniques

*RGL   Reihe Germanistische Linguistik

RHE   Revue d'Histoire Ecclésiastique

Rhetorica: A Journal of the History of Rhetoric

RhetRev   Rhetoric Review
RHistM   Römische Historische Mitteilungen
RHL   Revue d'Histoire Littéraire de la France
RHM   Revista Hispánica Moderna
RHT   Revue d'Histoire du Théâtre
RhV   Rheinische Vierteljahrsblätter
RI   Revista Iberoamericana
RIB   Revista Interamericana de Bibliografía/Inter-American Review of Bibliography
RIber   Rassegna Iberistica
RID   Rivista Italiana di Dialettologia: Scuola Società Territorio
RIJAZUZ   Radovi Instituta Jugoslavenske Akademije Znanosti i Umjetnosti u Zadru
RIL   Rendiconti dell'Istituto Lombardo Accademia di Scienze e Lettere
RILA   Rassegna Italiana di Linguistica Applicata
Rinascimento: Rivista dell'Istituto Nazionale di Studi sul Rinascimento
RíoPla   Río de la Plata: Culturas
RIPh   Revue Internationale de Philosophie (Brussels, Belgium)
Riscontri: Rivista Trimestrale di Cultura e di Attualità
RITL   Revista de Istorie şi Teorie Literară
RJ   Romanistisches Jahrbuch
RJN   Robinson Jeffers Newsletter
RJR   Russkiĭ Iazyk za Rubezhom
RJŠ   Russkiĭ Iazyk v Shkole: Metodicheskiĭ Zhurnal
RJV   Rheinisches Jahrbuch für Volkskunde
RKH   Rocznik Komisji Historycznoliterackiej
RKJ   Rozprawy Komisji Językowej
RL   Revista de Literatura
RL&LR   Romance Linguistics & Literature Review
RL&LS   Romance Languages and Linguistics Series
RLC   Revue de Littérature Comparée
RLet   Revista Letras (Paraná, Brazil)
RLetras   República de las Letras
RLI   Rassegna della Letteratura Italiana
RLiR   Revue de Linguistique Romane
RLit   Russkaia Literatura: Istoriko-Literaturnyĭ Zhurnal (Leningrad, U.S.S.R.)
RLJ   Russian Language Journal
RLL   American University Studies II: Romance Languages and Literature
RLM   La Revue des Lettres Modernes: Histoire des Idées et des Littératures
RLMC   Rivista di Letterature Moderne e Comparate (Pisa, Italy)
RLR   Revue des Langues Romanes
RLS   Regional Language Studies (St. John's, Newfoundland)
RLT   Russian Literature Triquarterly
RLTA   RLA: Revista de Lingüística Teórica y Aplicada
RM   Rowohlts Monographien
RMM   Revue de Métaphysique et de Morale
RMP   Rheinisches Museum für Philologie
RMR   Rocky Mountain Review of Language and Literature
RMS   Renaissance & Modern Studies
RMSt   Reading Medieval Studies
RNI   Research Notes (Ibadan, Nigeria)
RNL   Review of National Literatures
RO   Revista de Occidente
RocO   Rocznik Orientalistyczny (Warsaw, Poland)
RoHum   Roczniki Humanistyczne (Lublin, Poland)
ROLIG   Rolig-Papir
RoLit   România Literară: Săptămânal de Literatură şi Artă Editat de Uniunea Scriitorilor din Republica Socialistă România
Romania: Revue Consacrée à l'Etude des Langues et des Littératures Romanes
Romantisme: Revue du Dix-Neuvième Siècle
Romantist   The Romantist
RomG   Romanica Gandensia
RomGoth   Romanica Gothoburgensia
RomLi   Romance Linguistics [Croon Helm Romance Linguistics]
RomN   Romance Notes

RomSl   Romanoslavica
ROO   Room of One's Own: A Feminist Journal of Literature and Criticism
RoR   Romanian Review
RORD   Research Opportunities in Renaissance Drama
RoSlaw   Rocznik Slawistyczny/Revue Slavistique
RPF   Revista Portuguesa de Filologia
RPFilos   Revista Portuguesa de Filosofia
RPh   Romance Philology
RPLHA   Revue de Philologie de Littérature et d'Histoire Anciennes
RPLit   Res Publica Litterarum: Studies in the Classical Tradition
RPML   Rodopi Perspectives on Modern Literature
RPsych   Reading Psychology: An International Quarterly
RQ   Riverside Quarterly
RQCAK   Römische Quartalschrift für Christliche Altertumskunde und Kirchengeschichte
RQdL   Revue Québécoise de Linguistique
RR   Romanic Review
RRL   Revue Roumaine de Linguistique [Incorporates *Cahiers de Linguistique Théorique et Appliquée*]
RRQ   Reading Research Quarterly
RSBN   Rivista di Studi Bizantini e Neoellenici
RSCl   Rivista di Studi Classici
RSH   Revue des Sciences Humaines
RSI   Rivista Storica Italiana
RSieg   Reihe Siegen: Beiträge zur Literatur-, Sprach- und Medienwissenschaft
RSItal   Rivista di Studi Italiani
RSl   Ricerche Slavistiche (Rome, Italy)
RsLI   Recherches sur l'Imaginaire
RSLR   Rivista di Storia e Letteratura Religiosa
RSQ   Rhetoric Society Quarterly
RSR   Rassegna Storica del Risorgimento
RSSI   Recherches Sémiotiques/Semiotic Inquiry
RSV   Revista Signos: Estudios de Lengua y Literatura
RTAM   Recherches de Théologie Ancienne et Médiévale
RThom   Revue Thomiste: Revue Doctrinale de Théologie et de Philosophie
RTSS   Revue Tunisienne de Sciences Sociales
RTT   Research in Text Theory/Untersuchungen zur Texttheorie
RuchL   Ruch Literacki
RUSEng   Rajasthan University Studies in English
RusF   Russkiĭ Fol'klor: Materialy i Issledovaniia
RuskN   Ruskin Newsletter
RusLing   Russian Linguistics: International Journal for the Study of the Russian Language
RusR   The Russian Review: An American Quarterly Devoted to Russia Past and Present
RusRe   Russkaia Rech': Nauchno-Populiarnyĭ Zhurnal
RVC   Roman 20-50: Revue d'Etude du Roman du XXe Siècle
RyF   Razón y Fe: Revista Hispanoamericana de Cultura
RZSF   Radovi Zavoda za Slavensku Filologiju
SAA   Schweizer Anglistische Arbeiten
SAC   Studies in the Age of Chaucer: The Yearbook of the New Chaucer Society
SacE   Sacris Erudiri: Jaarboek voor Godsdienstwetenschappen
SAD   Studies in American Drama, 1945-Present
SAF   Studies in American Fiction
SAG   Stuttgarter Arbeiten zur Germanistik
Saga-Book (London, England)
SagaS   Saga och Sed. Kungl. Gustav Adolfs Akademiens Årsbok
SAGE: A Scholarly Journal on Black Women
SagetriebIO   Sagetrieb: A Journal Devoted to Poets in the Imagist/Objectivist Tradition
Saggi   Saggi e Ricerche di Letteratura Francese
SAH   Svenska Akademiens Handlingar
SAHQ   Swedish-American Historical Quarterly
SAIL   Studies in American Indian Literature: The Journal of the Association for the Study of American Indian Literature

*SAJAL   South African Journal of African Languages/Suid-Afrikaanse Tydskrif vir Afrikatale (Pretoria, South Africa)
*SAJL   Studies in American Jewish Literature
*SAL   Studies in African Linguistics
*SAlb   Studia Albanica (Tirana, Albania)
*SALit   Chu-Shikoku Studies in American Literature
*Salmagundi
Samlaren: Tidskrift för Svensk Litteraturvetenskaplig Forskning
*Samtiden: Tidsskrift for Politikk, Litteratur og Samfunnsspørsmål
Sananjalka: Suomen Kielen Seuran Vuosikirja
*S&I   Sprache und Information: Beiträge zur Philologischen und Linguistischen Datenverarbeitung, Informatik, und Informationswissenschaft
*S&K   Sprache & Kognition: Zeitschrift für Sprach- und Kognitionspsychologie und ihre Grenzgebiete
*S&S   Syntax and Semantics
S&W   South & West: An International Literary Magazine
SAnt   Suomen Antropologi/Antropologi i Finland
SAP   Studia Anglica Posnaniensia: An International Review of English Studies
Sapienza: Rivista di Filosofia e di Teologia
*SAQ   South Atlantic Quarterly
*SAR   Studies in the American Renaissance
SARE   Southeast Asian Review of English (Kuala Lumpur, Malaysia)
SARev   South Asian Review
SArt   Speculum Artium (Ravenna, Italy)
*SaS   Slovo a Slovesnost
SATF   Société des Anciens Textes Français
*SATJ   South African Theatre Journal
SAV   Schweizerisches Archiv für Volkskunde
Savacou: A Journal of the Caribbean Artists Movement (Jamaica, West Indies)
Savremenik: Mesečni Književni Casopis
*SB   Studies in Bibliography: Papers of the Bibliographical Society of the University of Virginia
SBHC   Studies in Browning and His Circle: A Journal of Criticism, History, and Bibliography
*SBLL   Selected Bibliographies in Language and Literature
*SBN   Saul Bellow Journal
*SBoc   Studi sul Boccaccio
*SBR   Swedish Book Review
*SC   Stendhal Club: Revue Internationale d'Etudes Stendhaliennes. Nouvelle Série. Revue Trimestrielle
*Scan   Scandinavica: An International Journal of Scandinavian Studies
ScanR   Scandinavian Review
*ScEc   Science et Esprit
*SCen   The Seventeenth Century
Scena: Časopis za Pozorišnu Umetnost
*SCFS   Seventeenth-Century French Studies
SCh   Sources Chrétiennes
*Schatzkammer   Schatzkammer der Deutschen Sprachlehre, Dichtung und Geschichte
Schlesien: Arts, Science, Folklore
*SchP   Scholarly Publishing: A Journal for Authors and Publishers
*ScI   Scripta Islandica: Isländska Sällskapets Årsbok
*SCJ   The Sixteenth Century Journal
*SCL   Studies in Canadian Literature
SCLing   Siouan and Caddoan Linguistics
*SCLit   Studies in Comparative Literature
ScLJ   Scottish Literary Journal: A Review of Studies in Scottish Language and Literature
SCN   Seventeenth-Century News
*ScotL   Scottish Language
SCR   South Carolina Review
*SCr   Strumenti Critici: Rivista Quadrimestrale di Cultura e Critica Letteraria
*Screen (Glasgow, Scotland)
*SCRev   South Central Review: The Journal of the South Central Modern Language Association

*Scriblerian   The Scriblerian and the Kit Cats: A Newsjournal Devoted to Pope, Swift, and Their Circle
*Scripsi
Scriptorium: Revue Internationale des Etudes Relatives aux Manuscrits-/International Review of Manuscript Studies
*ScS   Scottish Studies (Edinburgh, Scotland)
SCSSL   Semiosis: Seminario de Semiótica, Teoría, Análsis
SCUL   Soundings: Collections of the University Library, University of California, Santa Barbara
*SD   Studi Danteschi
SdG   Studii de Gramatică
*SDi   Slovenské Divadlo: Revue Dramatických Umení
*SDL   Studies in Descriptive Linguistics
SDR   South Dakota Review
SDv   Sprache und Datenverarbeitung: International Journal for Language Data Processing
SE   Slovenski Etnograf
SEA   Studies in English and American (Budapest, Hungary)
*SEALLC   Studies in English and American Literature, Linguistics, and Culture
*SECC   Studies in Eighteenth-Century Culture
*SECL   Studies in English and Comparative Literature
SECOLASA   SECOLAS Annals: Southeastern Council on Latin American Studies
*SECOLB   The SECOL Review: Southeastern Conference on Linguistics
*SEEA   Slavic and East European Arts
*SEEJ   Slavic and East European Journal
*SEER   The Slavonic and East European Review
*Sefarad: Revista de Estudios Hebraicos, Sefardies y de Oriente Proximo
Seges: Textes et Etudes Philologiques et Littéraires Publiés par la Faculté des Lettres de l'Université de Fribourg Suisse
*SEL: Studies in English Literature, 1500-1900
*Selecta: Journal of the Pacific Northwest Council on Foreign Languages
*SELit   Studies in English Literature (Tokyo, Japan)
*SELL   Studies in English Language and Literature (Kyushu University)
*SELL-SG   Studies in English Language and Literature (Seinan Gakuin University)
SemCross   Semiotic Crossroads
*Seminar: A Journal of Germanic Studies
*Semiosis: Internationale Zeitschrift für Semiotik und Ästhetik
Semiotext(e)
Semiotica: Journal of the International Association for Semiotic Studies/Revue de l'Association Internationale de Sémiotique
Semitics (Pretoria, South Africa)
SeN   Seara Nova
Senara: Revista de Filoloxía
Septemvri: Mesechno Spisanie za Khudozhestvena Literatura, Kritika i Obshtestveni Vŭprosi (Sofia, Bulgaria)
SerL   Serie Linguistica (Brasilia, Brazil)
Serpe: Rivista Letteraria
SES   Sophia English Studies
SeSL   Studi e Saggi Linguistici
Seven: An Anglo-American Literary Review
*SEzik   Săpostavitelno Ezikoznanie/Sopostavitel'noe Jazykoznanie/-Contrastive Linguistics (Sofia, Bulgaria)
SF&R   Scholars' Facsimiles & Reprints
SFC   Science Fiction Chronicle: The Monthly Science Fiction & Fantasy News Magazine (New York, NY)
SFen   Studia Fennica: Review of Finnish Linguistics and Ethnology
SFI   Studi di Filologia Italiana: Bollettino Annuale dell'Accademia della Crusca
*SFic   Science Fiction: A Review of Speculative Literature
*SFil   Studime Filologjike (Tirana, Albania)
*SFIS   Stanford French and Italian Studies
SFNL   Shakespeare on Film Newsletter
*SFolk   Southern Folklore
*SFR   Stanford French Review
*SFr   Studi Francesi

*SFran Studi Francescani: Trimestrale di vita culturale e religiosa a cura dei Frati Minori d'Italia

*SFS Science-Fiction Studies

SFT Studi di Filologia Tedesca

SGAK Studien zur Germanistik, Anglistik und Komparatistik

SGerS Stanford German Studies

SGF Stockholmer Germanistische Forschungen

SGG Studia Germanica Gandensia

SGh Studia Ghisleriana (Pavia, Italy)

*SGLLC Studies in German Literature, Linguistics, and Culture

*SGoldoniani Studi Goldoniani

SGS Scottish Gaelic Studies

SGT Schriften der Gesellschaft für Theatergeschichte

SGym Siculorum Gymnasium

SH Studia Hibernica (Dublin, Ireland)

*ShakB Shakespeare Bulletin

*ShakS Shakespeare Studies (New York, NY)

Shavian The Shavian: The Journal of Bernard Shaw

ShawR Shaw: The Annual of Bernard Shaw Studies

*Shenandoah

*Shiron

ShJE Shakespeare-Jahrbuch (Weimar, FRG)

ShJW Jahrbuch der Deutschen Shakespeare-Gesellschaft West (Bochum, FRG)

*SHL Amsterdam Studies in the Theory and History of the Language Sciences III: Studies in the History of the Language Sciences

ShLR Shoin Literary Review

*ShN The Shakespeare Newsletter

SHnd The Single Hound: The Poetry and Image of Emily Dickinson

SHR Southern Humanities Review

*ShS Shakespeare Survey: An Annual Survey of Shakespeare Studies and Production

*ShSA Shakespeare in Southern Africa: Journal of the Shakespeare Society of Southern Africa

*ShStud Shakespeare Studies (Tokyo, Japan)

*SHum Scripta Humanistica

SHUR Sacred Heart University Review

*ShY Shakespeare Yearbook

*SIAA Studi d'Italianistica Nell'Africa Australe/Italian Studies in Southern Africa

*SIcon Studies in Iconography

*Sig Sigma: Revue de Centre d'Etudes Linguistiques d'Aix

SIGLA Studies in Generative Linguistic Analysis

*Siglo Siglo XX/20th Century

*Signature: A Journal of Theory and Canadian Literature

*Signs: Journal of Women in Culture and Society

Sìlarus: Rassegna Bimestrale di Cultura

SILTA Studi Italiani di Linguistica Teorica ed Applicata

*SILUTAPL Summer Institute of Linguistics and the University of Texas at Arlington Publications in Linguistics

SiM Studies in Medievalism

*SiML Studies in Modern Literature

*Sing Out Sing Out!: The Folk Song Magazine

SINSU Skrifter Utgivna av Institutionen för Nordiska Språk vid Uppsala Universitet

*Sipario: Il Mensile Italiano dello Spettacolo

*SiPC Studies in Popular Culture

*SIPL Studies in Philippine Linguistics

*SIR Studies in Romanticism (Boston, MA)

SIs Studi Ispanici (Pisa, Italy)

*SiTZ Sprache im Technischen Zeitalter [Includes supplement Literatur im Technischen Zeitalter]

SJ Silliman Journal

SJL Southwest Journal of Linguistics

*SJS San José Studies

SjV Sirp ja Vasar

Skandinavistik: Zeitschrift für Sprache, Literatur und Kultur der Nordischen Länder

*SKDS Studien zum Kleinen Deutschen Sprachatlas

SkGgD Sammlung Kurzer Grammatiken Germanischer Dialekte

*Skírnir: Tímarit Hins Íslenska Bókmenntafélags (Reykjavik, Iceland)

SKS Suomalaisen Kirjallisuuden Seuran Toimituksia (Helsinki, Finland)

*SL Studia Linguistica (Lund, Sweden)

SL&L Studies in Language and Literature

*SL&Li American University Studies XII: Slavic Languages and Literature

*SLang Studies in Language: International Journal Sponsored by the Foundation "Foundations of Language"

*SLAPC Studies in Latin American Popular Culture

*SlavH Slavica Helvetica

*Slavia: Časopis pro Slovanskou Filologii

*SlavO Slavica Othiniensia

*SlavR Slavic Review: American Quarterly of Soviet and East European Studies

SlavS Slavistički Studii: Spisanie za Rusistika, Polonistika i Bohemistika

*SLCS Studies in Language Companion Series (Amsterdam, Netherlands)

*SLD Studia Litteraria (Debrecen, Hungary)

*SLF Skrifter Utgivna av Svenska Litteratursällskapet i Finland

SlfÅ Svensklärarföreningens Årsskrift

SLIA Studi di Letteratura Ispano-Americana

*SLitI Studies in the Literary Imagination

*SLJ Southern Literary Journal

SLL Studies in Language Learning: An Interdisciplinary Review of Language Acquisition, Language Pedagogy, Stylistics and Language Planning

SLog Studia Logica: An International Journal for Symbolic Logic

SlOr Slavia Orientalis

Slovakia (Middletown, PA)

SlovLit Slovenská Literatúra: Revue Pre Literárnu Vedu (Bratislava, Czechoslovakia)

SlovN Slovenský Národopis

*Slovo: Časopis Staroslavenskog Zavoda u Zagrebu

SlovP Slovenské Pohl'ady na Literatúru a Umenie (Bratislava, Czechoslovakia)

*SlovS Slovene Studies: Journal of the Society for Slovene Studies

*SLP Serie Lingüística Peruana (Lima, Peru)

*SlR Slavistična Revija (Ljubljana, Yugoslavia)

SLRAAA Sprache und Literatur: Regensburger Arbeiten zur Anglistik und Amerikanistik (Bern, Switzerland)

*SLRe Second Language Research

*SlReč Slovenská Reč: Časopis Pre Výskum Slovenského Jazyka (Bratislava, Czechoslovakia)

SLRev Stanford Literature Review

*SLRJ Saint Louis University Research Journal of the Graduate School of Arts and Sciences

*SLS Sign Language Studies

*SLSc Studies in the Linguistic Sciences

*SLSF Svenska Landsmål och Svenskt Folkliv (Uppsala, Sweden)

SM Sammlung Metzler

SMC Studies in Medieval Culture (Kalamazoo, MI)

SMEA Studi Micenei ed Egeo-Anatolici

SMed Studi Medievali

*SMELL Studies in Medieval English Language and Literature

*SMGL Studies in Modern German Literature

SMS Studier i Modern Språkvetenskap

SMus Studia Musicologica Academiae Scientiarum Hungaricae (Budapest, Hungary)

SMV Studi Mediolatini e Volgari

SMy Studia Mystica

*SN Studia Neophilologica: A Journal of Germanic and Romance Languages and Literature

SNew Sidney Newsletter (Waterloo, Canada)

*SNNTS Studies in the Novel (Denton, TX)

*SNov Studi Novecenteschi: Revista Semestrale di Storia della Letteratura Italiana Contemporanea (Padua, Italy)

SNS Slovo na Storozhi

SNSS Skrifter Utgivna av Svenska Språknämnden

SO Symbolae Osloenses

SOÅ Sydsvenska Ortnamnssällskapets Årsskrift/The Annual Journal of the South Swedish Place-Name Society

SoAR South Atlantic Review

SÖAW Sitzungsberichte der Österreichischen Akademie der Wissenschaften in Wien, Philosophisch-Historische Klasse

Sociocriticism

Socioling Sociolinguistics (Dordrecht, Netherlands)

Sodobnost (Ljubljana, Yugoslavia)

SOF Südost-Forschungen

SoK Sprog og Kultur (Aarhus, Denmark)

SophiaT Sophia (Tokyo, Japan)

SoQ The Southern Quarterly: A Journal of the Arts in the South (Hattiesburg, MS)

SoR The Southern Review (Baton Rouge, LA)

SoRA Southern Review: Literary and Interdisciplinary Essays (Adelaide, Australia)

SoS Syn og Segn: Norsk Tidsskrift

SoSt Southern Studies: An Interdisciplinary Journal of the South

Soundings: An Interdisciplinary Journal

Southerly: A Review of Australian Literature (Sydney, Australia)

SovEt Sovetskaia Ètnografiia

SovH Sovetish Heymland/Sovetskaia Rodina: Ezhemesiachnyĭ Literaturno-Khudozhestvennyĭ Zhurnal

SovL Soviet Literature

SovR Soviet Review: A Journal of Translations

Sovremenost: Spisanie za Literatura, Umetnost i Opštestveni Prašanja

SovT Sovetskaia Tiurkologiia

SP Studies in Philology

SPAN: Journal of the South Pacific Association for Commonwealth Literature and Language Studies

SPCT Studi e Problemi di Critica Testuale

Speculum: A Journal of Medieval Studies

SPEI Selected Papers from the English Institute (New York, NY)

Spektator: Tijdschrift voor Neerlandistiek (Dordrecht, Netherlands)

SPELL Swiss Papers in English Language and Literature

SPFA Bulletin de la Société des Professeurs Français en Amérique

SPh Studia Phonetica

Sphinx The Sphinx: A Magazine of Literature and Society

SPIL: (Stellenbosch Papers in Linguistics)

Spirit: A Magazine of Poetry

SPKFLC:SS Selected Proceedings of the Kentucky Foreign Language Conference: Slavic Section

SpL Spiegel der Letteren: Tijdschrift voor Nederlandse Literatuurgeschiedenis en voor Literatuurwetenschap

SpM Spicilegio Moderno: Letteratura, Lingua, Idee

Sprachdienst Der Sprachdienst

Sprache Die Sprache: Zeitschrift für Sprachwissenschaft

Sprachkunst: Beiträge zur Literaturwissenschaft

Sprachmittler Der Sprachmittler: Informationshefte des Sprachendienstes der Bundeswehr

SprachstrukA Sprachstrukturen, Reihe A: Historische Sprachstrukturen

Sprachwiss Sprachwissenschaft

Språkvård: Tidskrift Utgiven av Svenska Språknämnden

Spr&Spr Sprachpflege und Sprachkultur: Zeitschrift für Gutes Deutsch [Formerly *Sprachpflege: Zeithschrift für Gutes Deutsch*]

SpRi Spunti e Ricerche: Rivista d'Italianistica

Spsp Sprachspiegel: Schweizerische Zeitschrift für die deutsche Muttersprache

SPsy Social Psychology Quarterly

SPWVSRA Selected Papers from the West Virginia Shakespeare and Renaissance Association

SQ Shakespeare Quarterly

SR Sewanee Review

SRC Studies in Religion/Sciences Religieuses: Revue Canadienne/A Canadian Journal

SRIELA Selected Reports in Ethnomusicology

SRL Studies in Romance Languages

SRo Studi Romani: Rivista Trimestrale dell'Istituto Nazionale di Studi Romani

SS Scandinavian Studies

SSAA Salzburger Studien zur Anglistik und Amerikanistik

SSASH Studia Slavica Academiae Scientiarum Hungaricae

SSAWL Sitzungsberichte der Sächsischen Akademie der Wissenschaften zu Leipzig

SSBL Stockholm Studies in Baltic Languages

SSCP SUNY Series in Cultural Perspectives

SSe Studi Secenteschi

SSEL Stockholm Studies in English

SSEng Sydney Studies in English

SSF Studies in Short Fiction

SSFin Studia Slavica Finlandensia

SSG Schriften der Theodor-Storm-Gesellschaft

SSGL Studies in Slavic and General Linguistics

SSI Social Science Information/Information sur les Sciences Sociales

SSl Scando-Slavica (Copenhagen, Denmark)

SSL Studies in Scottish Literature (Columbia, SC)

SSLA Studies in Second Language Acquisition

SSLit Soviet Studies in Literature

SSLP Studies in Slavic Literature and Poetics

SSLS Studies in the Sciences of Language Series

SSLSN Skrifter Utgivna av Svenska Litteratursällskapet. Studier i Nordisk Filologi

SSMLN Society for the Study of Midwestern Literature Newsletter

SSO Studier fra Sprog- og Oldtidsforskning

SSR Scottish Slavonic Review

SSRL Stockholm Studies in Russian Literature

SSpF Studies in Speculative Fiction

SSt Spenser Studies: A Renaissance Poetry Annual

SStud Swift Studies: The Annual of the Ehrenpreis Center

ST Studi Tassiani

StAH Studies in American Humor

StAS Studia Anthroponymica Scandinavica: Tidskrift för Nordisk Personnamnsforskning

Stasinos: The Bulletin of the Greek Philologists

StBoT Studien zu den Boğazköy-Texten (Wiesbaden, FRG)

StC Studia Celtica

StCL Studii și Cercetări Lingvistice

StCS Studies in Contemporary Satire: A Creative and Critical Journal

Steaua

StES Steinbeck Essays Series

STFM Société des Textes Français Modernes

StG Studi Germanici

Stgr Studia Grammatica

StGrI Studi di Grammatica Italiana

StH-LPS Studies in the Humanities: Literature-Politics-Society (New York, NY)

StHum Studies in the Humanities (Indiana, PA)

StII Studien zur Indologie und Iranistik

StIL Studi dell'Istituto Linguistico

StIR Stanford Italian Review

StIS Studies in Interactional Sociolinguistics

StIsl Studia Islamica

StLF Studi di Letteratura Francese

STLing Studien zur Theoretischen Linguistik

StLM Studien zur Literatur der Moderne

StM Studia Monastica

StMed Studia Mediewistyczne

StMS Steinbeck Monograph Series

StQ Steinbeck Quarterly

STr Studi Trentini di Scienze Storiche

Stremljenja: Časopis za Književnost i Umetnost (Priština, Yugoslavia)

Strindbergiana

STS Scottish Text Society

STSL Studien und Texte zur Sozialgeschichte der Literatur

StSS Stanford Slavic Studies

StTCL Studies in Twentieth Century Literature

StudiaI Studia Iranica
Studiekamraten: Tidskrift för det Fria Bildningsarbetet
Studies: An Irish Quarterly Review (Dublin, Ireland)
StudIsl Studia Islandica: Íslenzk Fræði
Studium (Rome, Italy)
StuSta Studia Staropolskie
Stvaranje: Časopis za Književnost i Kulturu
StWF Studies in Weird Fiction
Style (DeKalb, IL)
SubStance: A Review of Theory and Literary Criticism
SuD Sprache und Dichtung
Sudetenland
SüdoA Südostdeutsches Archiv
SuF Sinn und Form: Beiträge zur Literatur
SULI Skrifter Utgivna av Litteraturvetenskapliga Institutionen vid Uppsala Universitet
SULLA Studi Urbinati, Serie B3: Linguistica, Letteratura, Arte
Sumlen: Årsbok för Vis- och Folkmusikforskning
Survey: A Journal of East & West Studies
SUS Susquehanna University Studies (Selinsgrove, PA)
SUVSL Skrifter Utgivna av Vetenskaps-Societeten i Lund
SV Schweizer Volkskunde: Korrespondenzblatt der Schweizerischen Gesellschaft für Volkskunde
Svantevit: Dansk Tidsskrift for Slavistik
SVDI Serie de Vocabularios y Diccionarios Indigenas "Mariano Silva y Aceves"
SVEC Studies on Voltaire and the Eighteenth Century
Svoboda: Ukrainian Daily
SWR Southwest Review
SXX Secolul 20
Symposium: A Quarterly Journal in Modern Foreign Literatures
Synthese: An International Journal for Epistemology, Methodology and Philosophy of Science
Synthesis: Bulletin du Comité National de Littérature Comparée de la République Socialiste de Roumanie (Bucharest, Romania)
Syria: Revue d'Art Orientale et d'Archéologie
SZ Stimmen der Zeit
SzDL Studien zur Deutschen Literatur
SzEP Studien zur Englischen Philologie
Szinház: Theatre, Theoretical and Critical Journal of Theatrical Arts
SzNU Sbornik za Narodni Umotvoreniia i Narodopis
TA Theatre Annual
TAH The American Hispanist
TAI T. A. Informations: Revue Internationale du Traitement Automatique du Langage
Talisman: A Journal of Contemporary Poetry and Poetics
Tamarack: Journal of the Edna St. Vincent Millay Society
T&D Testi e Discorsi: Strumenti Linguistici e Letterari
T&K Text & Kontext
T&T Tools & Tillage: A Journal on the History of the Implements of Cultivation and Other Agricultural Processes
Tarbiz: A Quarterly for Jewish Studies
Target: International Journal of Translation Studies
TASJ The Transactions of the Asiatic Society of Japan
TCBS Transactions of the Cambridge Bibliographical Society
TCEL Thought Currents in English Literature
TCHN Twayne's Critical History of the Novel
TCHPS Twayne's Critical History of Poetry Series
TCHSS Twayne's Critical History of the Short Story
TCL Twentieth Century Literature: A Scholarly and Critical Journal
TCrit Texto Crítico
TCW Turn-of-the-Century Women
TDRev TDR: The Drama Review: A Journal of Performance Studies
TE Teología Espiritual
Te Reo: Journal of the Linguistic Society of New Zealand
Teanga: Iris Chumann na Teangeolaíochta Feidhmí/Journal of the Irish Association for Applied Linguistics
Teangeolas
TEAS Twayne's English Authors Series

Temenos: Studies in Comparative Religion Presented by Scholars in Denmark, Finland, Norway and Sweden
Tenggara
TENSO: Bulletin of the Societe Guilhem IX
TESOLQ TESOL Quarterly
TeT Taal en Tongval
TexasR The Texas Review
TexP Textual Practice
Text: Transactions of the Society for Textual Scholarship
Textus: Annual of the Hebrew University Bible Project
TFSB Tennessee Folklore Society Bulletin
TGSI Transactions of the Gaelic Society of Inverness
Thalia: Studies in Literary Humor
ThD Themes in Drama
Theater (New Haven, CT)
TheatreS Theatre Studies
Theatron: Studien zur Geschichte und Theorie der Dramatischen Künste
Theoria: A Journal of Studies in the Arts, Humanities and Social Sciences (Natal, S. Africa)
Thēsaurismata
Thesaurus: Boletín del Instituto Caro y Cuervo
THeth Texte der Hethiter
THIC Theatre History in Canada/Histoire du Théâtre au Canada
ThirdR Third Rail: A Review of International Arts & Literature
THJ The Thomas Hardy Journal
THJCS Tsing Hua Journal of Chinese Studies
ThMS Thomas-Mann-Studien
Thought: A Review of Culture and Idea
ThR Theatre Research International
THR Travaux d'Humanisme et Renaissance
ThS Theatre Survey: The American Journal of Theatre History
THSC Transactions of the Honourable Society of Cymmrodorion
THStud Theatre History Studies
THY The Thomas Hardy Yearbook
TICOJ Transactions of the International Conference of Orientalists in Japan
Tinta
Tirade
TiS Topics in Sociolinguistics
TJ Theatre Journal
TkR Tamkang Review: A Quarterly of Comparative Studies between Chinese and Foreign Literatures
TLA Trabalhos em Linguistica Aplicada
Tlalocan: Revista de Fuentes para el Conocimiento de las Culturas Indigenas de México (Mexico City, Mexico)
TLF Textes Littéraires Français
TLG Travaux de Linguistique: Publications du Service de Linguistique Française de l'Université de l'Etat à Gand (Ghent, Belgium)
TLit Teoría Literária: Texto y Teoría
TLQ Travaux de Linguistique Quantitative
TLQue Travaux de Linguistique Québécoise
TLR The Linguistic Review
TLS [London] Times Literary Supplement
TM Temps Modernes
TMJ Thomas Mann Jahrbuch
TMS Twayne's Masterwork Studies
TN Theatre Notebook: A Journal of the History and Technique of the British Theatre
TNCIS Twayne's New Critical Introductions to Shakespeare
TNTL Tijdschrift voor Nederlandse Taal- en Letterkunde (Leiden, Netherlands)
TODRL Trudy Otdela Drevnerusskoĭ Literatury
Tōhōgaku: Eastern Studies
Topic: A Journal of the Liberal Arts (Washington, PA)
Torre La Torre: Revista de la Universidad de Puerto Rico
TPA T'oung Pao: Revue Internationale de Sinologie
TPAS Texas Pan American Series
TPB Tennessee Philological Bulletin: Proceedings of the Annual Meeting of the Tennessee Philological Association

TPQ   Text and Performance Quarterly
*TPS   Transactions of the Philological Society (Oxford, England)
Tradisjon: Tidsskrift for Folkeminnevitskap
Traditio: Studies in Ancient and Medieval History, Thought, and Religion
Tradition: A Journal of Orthodox Jewish Thought
*TraLiPhi   Travaux de Linguistique et de Philologie
*TraLit   Travaux de Littérature
Translation (New York, NY)
* *Travessia*
*TRB   The Tennyson Research Bulletin
*TrCIEREC   Travaux du CIEREC (Centre Interdisciplinaire d'Etudes et de Recherches sur l'Expression Contemporaine)
Tréteaux: Bulletin de la Société Internationale pour l'Etude du Théâtre Médiéval Section Française
*TRev   Translation Review
Trimestre (Chieti, Italy)
TriQ   TriQuarterly (Evanston, IL)
Tristania: A Journal Devoted to Tristan Studies
Triveni: Journal of Indian Renaissance
Trivium (Dyfed, Wales)
TrM   Traditional Music
* *Tropismes*
Tropos
*TrP   Translation Perspectives
TS   Tijdschrift voor Skandinavistiek (Amsterdam, Netherlands)
TSB   Thoreau Society Bulletin
TSDL   Tübinger Studien zur Deutschen Literatur
TSJSNW   Transactions of the Samuel Johnson Society of the Northwest
*TSLang   Typological Studies in Language
TSLit   Trierer Studien zur Literatur
*TSLL   Texas Studies in Literature and Language
TSM   Texte des Späten Mittelalters und der Frühen Neuzeit
TSMon   Tennyson Society Monographs
*TSO   Teatro del Siglo de Oro: Ediciones Críticas
*TSOL   Teatro del Siglo de Oro: Estudios de Literatura
TSRLL   Tulane Studies in Romance Languages and Literature
TSSF   Twayne's Studies in Short Fiction
*TStL   Tennessee Studies in Literature
*TSWL   Tulsa Studies in Women's Literature
*TTR   TTR: Traduction, Terminologie, Rédaction: Etudes Sur le Texte et Ses Transformations
TTrA   Textes et Traitement Automatique
TUBWPL   Technische Universität Berlin Arbeitspapiere zur Linguistik/Working Papers in Linguistics
*TuK   Text + Kritik: Zeitschrift für Literatur
Tulimuld: Eesti Kirjanduse ja Kultuuri Ajakiri
TUSAS   Twayne's United States Authors Series
TvG   Tydskrif vir Geesteswetenskappe
*TvL   Tydskrif vir Letterkunde
*Tw   Twórczość
TWA   Transactions of the Wisconsin Academy of Sciences, Arts, and Letters
*TWAS   Twayne's World Authors Series
TWN   The Thomas Wolfe Review
TWo   Third Woman
TWP   Trondheim Workingpapers
*TYDS   Transactions of the Yorkshire Dialect Society (Leeds Univ.)
*TZ   Zapiski Russkoi Akademicheskoi Gruppy v S.Sh.A./Transactions of the Association of Russian-American Scholars in the U.S.A.
TzF   Texte zur Forschung
*TZI   Traditiones: Zbornik Inštituta za Slovensko Narodopisje
*TZS   TheaterZeitSchrift: Beiträge zu Theater, Medien, Kulturpolitik
*UAJ   Ural-Altaische Jahrbücher/Ural-Altaic Yearbook: Internationale Zeitschrift für Nord-Eurasien
UAM   Uniwersytet im. Adama Mickiewicza w Poznaniu: Seria Filologia Angielska
*UCAL   Understanding Contemporary American Literature
UCLAOPL   UCLA Occasional Papers in Linguistics

UCPFS   University of California Publications, Folklore and Mythology Studies
*UCPL   University of California Publications in Linguistics
UCPMP   University of California Publications in Modern Philology
*UCrow   The Upstart Crow
*UDL   Untersuchungen zur Deutschen Literaturgeschichte
*UdLH   Universidad de La Habana
*UDR   University of Dayton Review
*UeL   Uomini e Libri: Periodico Bimestrale di Critica ed Informazione Letteraria
*UES   Unisa English Studies: Journal of the Department of English
*UF   Ulster Folklife
Ufahamu: Journal of the African Activist Association
*UFMH   University of Florida Monographs, Humanities Series
ÚÍ   Új Írás: Irodalmi, Művészeti és Kritikai Folyóirat
*UKPHS   University of Kansas Humanistic Studies
UkrI   Ukraïns'kyï Istoryk
UkrK   Ukraïns'ka Knyha: Ukrainian Bibliographic Quarterly
UkrMov   Ukraïns'ke Movoznavstvo: Mizhvidomchyï Naukovyï Zbirnyk
UkrR   The Ukrainian Review: A Quarterly Journal Devoted to the Study of the Ukraine
UlbR   Ulbandus Review: A Journal of Slavic Languages and Literatures
ULR   University of Leeds Review
ULULA: Graduate Studies in Romance Languages
ULz   Ukraïns'ke Literaturoznavstvo: Mizhvidomchyï Respublikans'kyï Zbirnyk
*UMELAL   Understanding Modern European and Latin American Literature
Umma: A Magazine of Original Writing
*UMSE   University of Mississippi Studies in English
UNCSCL   University of North Carolina Studies in Comparative Literature
*UNCSGLL   University of North Carolina Studies in the Germanic Languages and Literatures
UNCSRLL   North Carolina Studies in Romance Languages and Literatures
Unilit (Secunderabad, India)
Unitas: A Quarterly for the Arts and Sciences (Manila, Philippines)
Univ   Universitas: Zeitschrift für Wissenschaft, Kunst und Literatur (Stuttgart, FRG)
UNS   University of Nebraska Studies
UP   Die Unterrichtspraxis
*UPAL   Utrechtse Publikaties voor Algemene Literatuurwetenschap/Utrecht Publications in General and Comparative Literature
UPMFF   University of Pennsylvania Monographs in Folklore and Folklife
UPSSA   University of Pennsylvania Studies on South Asia
*UQ   Ukrainian Quarterly: Journal of East European and Asian Affairs
Urbe: Rivista Romana di Storia, Arte, Lettere, Costumanze (Rome, Italy)
URP   Untersuchungen zur Romanischen Philologie
*USLL   Utah Studies in Literature and Linguistics
USPFFLCH   Universidade de São Paulo Faculdade de Filosofia, Letras e Ciências Humanas
USSE   The University of Saga Studies in English
UTDEMS   University of Tulsa Monograph Series
*UTFS   University of Toronto Romance Series
*UTIS   University of Toronto Italian Studies
*UTQ   University of Toronto Quarterly: A Canadian Journal of the Humanities
*UW   Us Wurk: Tydskrift foar Frisistyk
Vagant
Vagartha: Critical Quarterly of Indian Literature
*VANB   Vestsi Akadémii Navuk BSSR
*V&I   Voix et Images: Littérature Québécoise
* *Varaviksne*
VC   Virginia Cavalcade
*VChrist   Vetera Christianorum
VCom   The Visionary Company: A Magazine of the Twenties

VDASD   Veröffentlichungen der Deutschen Akademie für Sprache und Dichtung

VEAW   Varieties of English Around the World

* *Veltro*   Il Veltro: Rivista della Civiltà Italiana

* *Ventanal: Revista de Creación y Crítica*

* *Verba: Anuario Galego de Filoloxía*

* *Verbatim: The Language Quarterly*

* *Verri*   Il Verri: Rivista di Letteratura

* *Versus: Quaderni di Studi Semiotici*

  Vértice: Revista de Cultura e Arte (Coimbra, Portugal)

* *VFR*   Victorian Fiction Research Guides

VGIEMTP   Veröffentlichungen des Grabmann Instituts zur Erforschung der Mittelalterlichen Theologie und Philosophie

* *Viator: Medieval and Renaissance Studies*

VIDV   Veröffentlichungen zur Volkskunde und Kulturgeschichte

VigC   Vigiliae Christianae: A Review of Early Christian Life and Language

* *VIJ: Victorians Institute Journal*

VIndJ   Vishveshvaranand Indological Journal

* *Vinduet* (Oslo, Norway)

* *Vir*   Virittäjä: Journal de Kotikielen Seura

ViR   Viaţa Românească (Bucharest, Romania)

Vitchyzna: Literaturno-Khudozhniĭ ta Hromads'ko-Politychnyĭ Misiachnyk (Kiev, U.S.S.R.)

Vivarium: An International Journal for the Philosophy and Intellectual Life of the Middle Ages and Renaissance

* *VJa*   Voprosy Iazykoznaniia (Moscow, U.S.S.R.)

VKR   Voprosy Kul'tury Rechi

VLang   Visible Language: The Quarterly Concerned with All That Is Involved in Our Being Literate

VlG   De Vlaamse Gids

* *VLit*   Voprosy Literatury

* *VLT*   The Velvet Light Trap: Review of Literature

* *VLU*   Vestnik Leningradskogo Universiteta. Seriia 2, Istoriia, Iazykoznanie, Literaturovedenie

* *VMU*   Vestnik Moskovskogo Universiteta. Seriia 9, Filologiia

* *VN*   Victorian Newsletter

VOEI   Veröffentlichungen der Abteilung für Slavische Sprachen und Literaturen des Osteuropa-Instituts (Slavisches Seminar) an der Freien Universität Berlin

* *Volkskunde: Driemaandelijks Tijdschrift voor de Studie van het Volksleven* (Antwerp, Belgium)

* *VP*   Victorian Poetry

* *VPR*   Victorian Periodicals Review

VQR   Virginia Quarterly Review: A National Journal of Literature and Discussion (Richmond, VA)

* *VR*   Vox Romanica: Annales Helvetici Explorandis Linguis Romanicis Destinati

* *VRev*   Victorian Review: The Journal of the Victorian Studies Association of Western Canada

VRL   Voprosy Russkoĭ Literatury: Respublikanskiĭ Mezhvedomstvennyĭ Nauchnyĭ Sbornik

* *VS*   Victorian Studies: A Journal of the Humanities, Arts and Sciences

* *Vsesvit: Literaturno-Mystets'kyĭ ta Hromads'ko-Politychnyĭ Zhurnal*

VSF   Vinaver Studies in French

VSLÅ   Vetenskaps-Societeten i Lund Årsbok

* *Vuelta*

VULT   Voprosy Uzbekskogo Iazyka i Literatury

vwa   [vwa]

* *VWM*   Virginia Woolf Miscellany

VyV   Verdad y Vida: Revista de las Ciencias del Espíritu (Madrid, Spain)

* *VyzSh*   Vyzvol'nyĭ Shliakh/Liberation Path

* *WADL*   Wiener Arbeiten zur Deutschen Literatur

* *Waiguoyu*

WAJML   West African Journal of Modern Languages/Revue Ouest-Africaine des Langues Vivantes

* *WAL*   Western American Literature

* *WAn*   Wide Angle: A Film Quarterly of Theory, Criticism, and Practice

* *W&D*   Works and Days: Essays in the Socio-Historical Dimensions of Literature and the Arts

* *W&I*   Word & Image: A Journal of Verbal/Visual Enquiry (London, England)

W&L   Women & Literature

* *W&Lang*   Women and Language

* *W&P*   Women & Performance: A Journal of Feminist Theory

* *WascanaR*   Wascana Review

* *WB*   Weimarer Beiträge: Zeitschrift für Literaturwissenschaft, Ästhetik und Kulturtheorie

WBEP   Wiener Beiträge zur Englischen Philologie

WBN   Wolfenbütteler Barock-Nachrichten

* *WC*   The Wordsworth Circle

* *WCPMN*   Willa Cather Pioneer Memorial Newsletter

WCSJ   Wilkie Collins Society Journal

* *WCWR*   William Carlos Williams Review

* *WdF*   Wege der Forschung

WdL   Wirkung der Literatur

WE   The Winesburg Eagle: The Official Publication of the Sherwood Anderson Society

* *The Wellsian: The Journal of the H. G. Wells Society*

* *Westerly: A Quarterly Review*

* *WF*   Western Folklore

* *WGCR*   West Georgia College Review

WGY   Women in German Yearbook: Feminist Studies and German Culture

WHR   Western Humanities Review

WI   Die Welt des Islams: Internationale Zeitschrift für die Geschichte des Islams in der Neuzeit

* *WIRS*   Western Illinois Regional Studies

* *WL&A*   War, Literature, and the Arts

WLG   Wiener Linguistische Gazette

* *WLT*   World Literature Today: A Literary Quarterly of the University of Oklahoma

* *WLWE*   World Literature Written in English

* *WMQ*   The William and Mary Quarterly: A Magazine of Early American History and Culture

* *WO*   Die Welt des Orients: Wissenschaftliche Beiträge zur Kunde des Morgenlandes

WolfenbüttelerB   Wolfenbütteler Beiträge: Aus den Schätzen der Herzog August Bibliothek

* *Word*   WORD: Journal of the International Linguistic Association

* *WPL*   Working Papers in Linguistics (Columbus, OH)

WPLU   Working Papers (Lund University Department of Linguistics)

WPo   Winterthur Portfolio: A Journal of American Material Culture

* *WPP*   UCLA Working Papers in Phonetics

WPSILUNDS   Work Papers of the Summer Institute of Linguistics, University of North Dakota Session

WS   Women's Studies: An Interdisciplinary Journal

WSA   Wolfenbütteler Studien zur Aufklärung

* *WSaR*   The Wicazo SA Review: A Journal of Indian Studies

WSJ   Wiener Slavistisches Jahrbuch

* *WSJour*   The Wallace Stevens Journal: A Publication of the Wallace Stevens Society

* *WSl*   Die Welt der Slaven: Halbjahresschrift für Slavistik (Munich, FRG)

* *WSlA*   Wiener Slawistischer Almanach

* *WStu*   Weber Studies: An Interdisciplinary Humanities Journal

WT   Wetenschappelijke Tijdingen op het Gebied van de Geschiedenis van de Vlaamse Beweging

* *WVUPP*   West Virginia University Philological Papers

* *WWays*   Word Ways: The Journal of Recreational Linguistics

* *WWort*   Wirkendes Wort: Deutsche Sprache und Literatur in Forschung und Lehre

* *WWQR*   Walt Whitman Quarterly Review

* *WWS*   Western Writers Series (Boise State University)

WZBL   Wissenschaftliche Zeitschrift der Brandenburgischen Landeshochschule [Formerly *Wissenschaftliche Zeitschrift der Pädagogischen Hochschule "Karl Liebknecht" Potsdam*]

WZKS   Wiener Zeitschrift für die Kunde Südasiens und Archiv für In-
dische Philosophie (Vienna, Austria)

WZUB   Wissenschaftliche Zeitschrift der Humboldt-Universität zu Berlin. Gesellschaftswissenschaftliche Reihe

WZUG   Wissenschaftliche Zeitschrift der Ernst Moritz Arndt-Univer-
sität Greifswald: Gesellschaftswissenschaftliche Reihe

WZUH   Wissenschaftliche Zeitschrift der Martin-Luther Universität
Halle-Wittenberg. Gesellschafts- und Sprachwissenschaftliche Reihe

WZUJ   Wissenschaftliche Zeitschrift der Friedrich-Schiller-Universität
Jena. Gesellschaftswissenschaftliche Reihe

WZUL   Wissenschaftliche Zeitschrift der Karl-Marx-Universität Leipzig. Gesellschaftswissenschaftliche Reihe

WZUR   Wissenschaftliche Zeitschrift der Wilhelm-Pieck-Universität
Rostock. Gesellschaftswissenschaftliche Reihe

XUS   Xavier Review

Y Traethodydd (Caernarvon, Wales)

YA   Yed'a-'Am/Yeda-Am: Bamah le-Folḳlor Yehudi/Journal of the Israel Folklore Society

YAlm   Yerushalaymer Almanakh

YBPS   Yearbook of the British Pirandello Society

YCC   Yearbook of Comparative Criticism

YCGL   Yearbook of Comparative and General Literature

YeA   Yeats Annual

Yeats: An Annual of Critical and Textual Studies

YER   Yeats Eliot Review: A Journal of Criticism and Scholarship

YES   Yearbook of English Studies

YFS   Yale French Studies

Yiddish (Flushing, NY)

YIS   Yearbook of Italian Studies: A Publication of the Italian Cultural
Institute

YJC   The Yale Journal of Criticism: Interpretation in the Humanities

YK   Yiddishe Kultur

YLS   The Yearbook of Langland Studies

YR   The Yale Review

YRS   Yearbook of Romanian Studies: A Publication of the Romanian
Studies Association of America

YTELSA   Yearbook of the Estonian Learned Society in America

YTM   Yearbook for Traditional Music

YULG   Yale University Library Gazette

YWES   Year's Work in English Studies

YWMLS   The Year's Work in Modern Language Studies

Z: Filmtidsskrift

ŽA   Živa Antika

Z-A   Zaïre-Afrique

ZAA   Zeitschrift für Anglistik und Amerikanistik

ZAH   Zeitschrift für Althebraistik

ZAL   Zeitschrift für Arabische Linguistik

Zambezia: The Journal of the University of Zimbabwe

Zapisy (Rutherford, NJ)

ZAVA   Zeitschrift für Assyriologie und Vorderasiatische Archäologie

ZB   Zeitschrift für Balkanologie

ZbirP   Zbirnyk Prats' Naukovoï Shevchenkivs'koï Konferentsiï

ZCP   Zeitschrift für Celtische Philologie

ZD   Zielsprache Deutsch: Zeitschrift für Unterrichtsmethodik und An-
gewandte Sprachwissenschaft

ZDA   Zeitschrift für Deutsches Altertum und Deutsche Literatur

ZDFALP   Z Dziejów Form Artystycznych W Literaturze Polskiej

ZDL   Zeitschrift für Dialektologie und Linguistik

ZDMG   Zeitschrift der Deutschen Morgenländischen Gesellschaft

ZDP   Zeitschrift für Deutsche Philologie (Berlin, FRG)

Zeta: Rivista Internazionale di Poesia (Udine, Italy)

ZfK   Zeitschrift für Katalanistik: Revista d'Estudis Catalans

ZFL   Zbornik za Filologiju i Lingvistiku

ZFSL   Zeitschrift für Französische Sprache und Literatur

ZG   Zeitschrift für Germanistik

ZGL   Zeitschrift für Germanistische Linguistik

Zhovten': Literaturno-Mystets'kyĭ ta Hromads'ko-Politychnyĭ Zhurnal

ZIK   Zbornik Istorije Književnosti

Život: Časopis za Književnost i Kulturu

ZKJ   Zbornik za Književnost i Jezik

ŽLit   Życie Literackie

Znak: Miesięcznik (Cracow, Poland)

Znamenje (Ljubljana, Yugoslavia)

*Znamia: Literaturno-Khudozhestvennyĭ i Obshchestvenno-Politicheskiĭ
Zhurnal* (Moscow, U.S.S.R.)

ZNHF   The Zora Neale Hurston Forum

ZOF   Zeitschrift für Ostforschung: Länder und Völker im Östlichen
Mitteleuropa

ZPSK   Zeitschrift für Phonetik, Sprachwissenschaft und Kommunika-
tionsforschung

ZR   Zadarska Revija: Časopis za Kulturu i Društvena Pitanja

ZRL   Zagadnienia Rodzajów Literackich: Woprosy Literaturnych Żan-
rov/Les Problèmes des Genres Littéraires

ZRP   Zeitschrift für Romanische Philologie

ZS   Zeitschrift für Slawistik

ZSP   Zeitschrift für Slavische Philologie

ZV   Zeitschrift für Volkskunde: Halbjahreschrift der Deutschen Ges. f.
Volkskunde

Zvezda (Leningrad, U.S.S.R.)

ZzS   Zbornik za Slavistiku

1990 MLA

International Bibliography

of Books and Articles

on the Modern Languages

and Literatures

VOLUME IV: GENERAL LITERATURE AND
RELATED TOPICS

Guide to Classified Listings

The classification structure of the *MLA International Bibliography* accommodates all areas of literary study. This guide to the classified listings includes classification headings for topics of general literary interest. The numbers following the headings refer to the first bibliographical entry number listed under a particular heading. Headings under which no books, articles, or other documents appear are omitted from this guide. Users wishing to locate documents on more specific topics or concepts are directed to the Subject Index that accompanies this volume.

1990 MLA

International Bibliography

of Books and Articles

on the Modern Languages

and Literatures

[1] "First International Conference of the International Society for the Study of European Ideas: Turning Points in History: 'Comparative History of European Revolutions' (in Celebration of the Bicentenary of the French Revolution), 'Nietzsche's Influence on Contemporary Thought,' 'Popular and Elite Culture': International Conference, 26-30 September 1988, RAI Congress Centre, Amsterdam." *HEI.* 1989; 11. [Spec. iss. †And popular literature.]

[2] "Literature & the Historical Process." *Perspectives on Contemporary Literature.* 1988; 14. [Spec. iss. †Relationship to history.]

[3] "Mekomam U Ma'amadam shel Haiyur VeHatziur BeSifrut HaYeladim." *Be'emmet.* 1989 Spring; 3: 181-191. [†For children. Illustration.]

[4] "Rethinking Female Authorship: Literary Traditions and National Contexts." *CMat.* 1986 Spring; 2(1-3). [Spec. iss. †By women writers.]

[5] Ackley, Katherine Anne, ed. *Women and Violence in Literature: An Essay Collection.* New York: Garland; 1990. xxi, 325 pp. (GRLH 1271.) [Incl. introd. †By women writers.]

[6] Afzal, Mohammad. "Creativity in the Art of Writing and Sciences." *Quest.* 1990 Sept.-Oct.; 83: 279-286. [†And science. Creativity.]

[7] Aïtmatov, Chingiz. "Literatura—zhizn' moia: Zakon vsemirnogo tiagoteniia." *LG.* 1989 Apr. 26; 17 [5239]: 7.

[8] Aldridge, A. Owen. "Literature and the Study of Man." 41-63 in Dennis, Philip, ed.; Aycock, Wendell, ed. *Literature and Anthropology.* Lubbock: Texas Tech UP; 1989. ix, 227 pp. (SCLit 20.) [See also *Jour. of Eng. Lang. & Lit.* 1989; 35(1): 57-82. †Relationship to anthropology.]

[9] Andringa, Els, ed.; Viehoff, Reinhold, ed. "Literary Understanding." *PoeticsJ.* 1990 June; 19(3). [Spec. iss.; introd., 221-230. †Relationship to reader.]

[10] Bal, Mieke. "De-Disciplining the Eye." *CritI.* 1990 Spring; 16(3): 506-531. [†Role of the real; relationship to reading; textuality.]

[11] Baldick, Chris. *The Concise Oxford Dictionary of Literary Terms.* Oxford: Oxford UP; 1990. x, 243 pp. [†Dictionary of literary terms.]

[12] Barnes, Hazel E., ed.; Calder, William M., III, ed.; Schmidt, Hugo, ed. *Studies in Comparison.* New York: Peter Lang; 1989. 493 pp. (USLL 28.) [†Comparative approach.]

[13] Barricelli, Jean-Pierre. "The Quest for Values." 86-93 in Barricelli, Jean-Pierre, ed.; Gibaldi, Joseph, ed.; Lauter, Estella, ed. *Teaching Literature and Other Arts.* New York: Mod. Lang. Assn. of Amer.; 1990. vi, 183 pp. (Options for Teaching 10.) [†And art. Pedagogical approach.]

[14] Barricelli, Jean-Pierre, ed.; Gibaldi, Joseph, ed.; Lauter, Estella, ed. *Teaching Literature and Other Arts.* New York: Mod. Lang. Assn. of Amer.; 1990. vi, 183 pp. (Options for Teaching 10.) [Incl. introd. †Relationship to arts. Pedagogical approach.]

[15] Bart, Rolan; Stambolova, Albena, tr. "Smŭrtta na Avtora." *LFront.* 1990 May 17; 20: 8. [†Role of writer.]

[16] Bartmiński, Jerzy. "Opozycja ustności i literackości a współczesny folklor." *LLud.* 1989 Jan.-Feb.; 33(1): 3-12. [Eng. sum. †Compared to oral tradition.]

[17] Bauer, Roger, ed.; Fokkema, Douwe, ed.; Graat, Michael de, ed.; Boening, John, ed.; Gillespie, Gerald, ed.; Moog-Grünewald, Maria, ed.; Nemoianu, Virgil, ed.; Ricapito, Joseph, ed.; Schmeling, Manfred, ed.; Thüsen, Joachim von der, ed.; Uhlig, Claus, ed. *Proceedings of the XIIth Congress of the International Comparative Literature Association/Actes du XIIe congrès de l'Association Internationale de Littérature Comparée: München 1988 Munich, II: Space and Boundaries in Literature/Espace et frontières dans la littérature.* In Five Volumes/En cinq volumes. Munich: Iudicium; 1990. 606 pp. (Proceedings of the Congress of the International Comparative Literature Association 12: 2.) [†Treatment of space; boundary.]

[18] Bauer, Roger, ed.; Fokkema, Douwe, ed.; Graat, Michael de, asst. ed.; Wimmer, Ruprecht, asst.; Goppel, Thomas, greeting. *Proceedings of the XIIth Congress of the International Comparative Literature Association/Actes du XIIe congrès de l'Association Internationale de Littérature Comparée: München 1988 Munich, I: Plenary Sessions/Séances plénières; Colloquium Munich/Colloque Munich.* In Five Vols./En cinq vols. Munich: Iudicium; 1990. 251 pp. (Proceedings of the Congress of the International Comparative Literature Association 12: 1.) [Incl. fwd.]

[19] Bauer, Roger, ed.; Fokkema, Douwe, ed.; Graat, Michael de, asst. ed.; Kaiser, Gerhard, asst.; Rinner, Fridrun, asst.; Wertheimer, Jürgen, asst. *Proceedings of the XIIth Congress of the International Comparative Literature Association/Actes du XIIe congrès de l'Association Internationale de Littérature Comparée: München 1988 Munich, IV: Space and Boundaries of Literature/Espace et frontières de la littérature.* Munich: Iudicium; 1990. 651 pp. (Proceedings of the Congress of the International Comparative Literature Association 12: 4.) [†Role of space.]

[20] Bauer, Roger, ed.; Fokkema, Douwe, ed.; Graat, Michael de, asst. ed.; Aldridge, A. Owen, asst.; Higonnet, Margaret, asst.; Klein, Holger M., asst.; Meisami, Julie Scott, asst.; Rigney, Ann, asst.; Ronen, Ruth, asst.; Sondrup, Steven P., asst.; Templeton, Joan, asst.; Walker, Janet A., asst. *Proceedings of the XIIth Congress of the International Comparative Literature Association/Actes du XIIe congrès de l'Association Internationale de Littérature Comparée: München 1988 Munich, III: Space and Boundaries in Literature (Continuation)/Espace et frontières dans la littérature (suite).* Workshops: China and the West; Medieval Islamic Literature; The Feminist Redefinition of Literary Space. Munich: Iudicium; 1990. 509 pp. (Proceedings of the Congress of the International Comparative Literature Association 12: 3.) [†Role of space.]

[21] Bauer, Roger, ed.; Fokkema, Douwe, ed.; Graat, Michael de, asst. ed.; Fischer-Lichte, Erika, asst.; Garstin, Marguerite, asst.; Ibsch, Elrud, asst.; Stackelberg, Jürgen von, asst. *Proceedings of the XIIth Congress of the International Comparative Literature Association/Actes du XIIe congrès de l'Association Internationale de Littérature Comparée: München 1988 Munich, V: Space and Boundaries in Literary Theory and Criticism/Espace et frontières dans la critique et la théorie littéraire; Space and Boundaries in the Teaching of General and Comparative Literature/Espace et frontières dans l'enseignement de la littérature générale et comparée.* In Five Vols./En cinq vols. Munich: Iudicium; 1990. 415 pp. (Proceedings of the Congress of the International Comparative Literature Association 12: 5.)

[22] Ben, Menachem. *Ein Shira Bilti Muvenet, Ve Ma'amarim Aherim.* Tel Aviv: Yaton Golan/Prose; 1989. 159 pp.

[23] Benson, Ciarán. "Art and Language in Middle Childhood: A Question of Translation." *W&I.* 1986 Apr.-June; 2(2): 123-140. [†For children. Illustration; relationship to realism.]

[24] Bernheimer, Charles, ed.; Kahane, Claire, ed. *In Dora's Case: Freud—Hysteria—Feminism.* New York: Columbia UP; 1990. xiv, 344 pp. (Gender and Culture.) [Rev. ed.; incl. introd. †Treatment of feminism; hysteria. Psychoanalytic approach. Theories of Freud, Sigmund.]

[25] Bersani, Leo. *The Culture of Redemption.* Cambridge: Harvard UP; 1990. 232 pp. [†1800-1999. Relationship to redemption.]

[26] Biletzky, J. Ch. *Mifqashim MeHaSuq HaSifruti.* Tel Aviv: Daniella Di-Nur; 1988. 116 pp.

[27] ———. *Otzarot Yiddish.* Tel Aviv: Papyrus, Tel Aviv Univ.; 1989. 173 pp. [†Yiddish language literature.]

[28] Blain, Virginia, ed.; Clements, Patricia, ed.; Grundy, Isobel, ed. *The Feminist Companion to Literature in English: Women Writers from the Middle Ages to the Present.* New Haven: Yale UP; 1990. xvi, 1231 pp. [†By women writers. English language literature. Handbook.]

[29] Bonnefoy, Yves; Naughton, John, tr. "Lifting Our Eyes from the Page." *CritI.* 1990 Summer; 16(4): 794-806. [Tr. of art. from *Nouvelle Revue de Psychanalyse.* 1988 Spring. †On reading; relationship to interruption.]

[30] Boyarin, Daniel. "Old Wine in New Bottles: Intertextuality and Midrash." *PoT.* 1987; 8(3-4): 539-556. [†Intertextuality in Midrash.]

[31] Brémond, Claude, introd. "Perspectives sur la thématique." *SCr.* 1989 May; 4(2 [60]). [Spec. iss.; incl. introd. †Thematization.]

[32] Browne, Ray B. "Redefining Literature." *JPC.* 1989 Winter; 23(3): 11-21.

[33] Brulotte, Gaétan. "Le Métier du risque." *Beffroi.* 1990 Dec.-1991 Mar.; 13: 61-68. [†Writer as profession; relationship to risk.]

[34] Bruner, Jerome. *Acts of Meaning.* Cambridge: Harvard UP; 1990. xvii, 179 pp. (Jerusalem-Harvard Lectures.) [†Role of narrative; relationship to meaning; language; autobiography. Psychological approach.]

[35] Čačinovič-Puhovski, Nadežda. "Odgovor na pitanje 'postojili ženska poetika/ estetika'." *Izraz.* 1990 Feb.-Mar.; 34(2-3): 186-193. [†By women writers. Poetics; relationship to gender.]

[36] Cardy, Michael. "La Découverte du beau au sein de la laideur: Essai d'esthétique comparée." 33-40 in Valdés, Mario J., ed. *Toward a Theory of Comparative Literature: Selected Papers Presented in the Division of Theory of Literature at the XIth International Comparative Literature Congress.* New York: Peter Lang; 1990. 275 pp. (Proceedings of the International Comparative Literature Association 11: 3.) [†Aesthetics.]

[37] Cargas, Harry James. "The Christian as Scholar—the Humanist as Christian: An Interview with Walter Ong." *Crosscurrents.* 1990 Spring; 40(1): 96-108. [†Role of Christian scholars. Interview with Ong, Walter J.

[38] Carlevaro, Tazio. "La ignorata kuzo." *LFoiro.* 1990 Oct.; 21(127): 43-46. [†Ido language poetry.]

[39] Casement, William. "Literature, Irrationality, and the Prospect of Didacticism." *JGE.* 1986; 37(4): 261-279. [†Relationship to didacticism.]

[40] Caws, Mary Ann. "Perception in Literature and Art." 25-29 in Barricelli, Jean-Pierre, ed.; Gibaldi, Joseph, ed.; Lauter, Estella, ed. *Teaching Literature and Other Arts.* New York: Mod. Lang. Assn. of Amer.; 1990. vi, 183 pp. (Options for Teaching 10.) [†Perception compared to visual arts. Pedagogical approach.]

[41] Clark, Mark Andrew. "The Difficulty in Saying 'I': Identifying, Analyzing, and Critiquing Voices of Self, Difference and Discourse in College Students' Reading and Writing about Literature." *DAI.* 1990 Nov.; 51(5): 1536A. [†Role of the self in interpretation by college students. Pedagogical approach. Dissertation abstract.]

[42] Clarke, Bruce, ed.; Aycock, Wendell, ed. *The Body and the Text: Comparative Essays in Literature and Medicine.* Lubbock: Texas Tech UP; 1990. ix, 221 pp. (SCLit 22.) [Incl. introd. †Relationship to medicine.]

[43] Clüver, Claus. "The Comparative Study of the Arts." 16-24 in Barricelli, Jean-Pierre, ed.; Gibaldi, Joseph, ed.; Lauter, Estella, ed. *Teaching Literature and Other Arts.* New York: Mod. Lang. Assn. of Amer.; 1990. vi, 183 pp. (Options for Teaching 10.) [†Relationship to art. Pedagogical approach.]

[44] Coelho, Jacinto do Prado. "Apontamentos sobre Literaturas Marginais." *BdF.* 1983; 28(1-4): 329-332. [†Marginal literature.]

[45] Cohen, Adir. *Temurot beSifrut Yeladim.* Haifa: Ah; 1988. 256 pp. [†For children.]

[46] Cohn, Jan. "Redefining Literature." *JPC.* 1989 Winter; 23(3): 23-29.

[47] Colley, Ann C. *The Search for Synthesis in Literature and Art: The Paradox of Space.* Athens: U of Georgia P; 1990. x, 175 pp. [Illus. †And art. Role of space.]

[48] Cornea, Paul. "Le Système de la littérature et les frontières du littéraire." 595-601 in Bauer, Roger, ed.; Fokkema, Douwe, ed.; Graat, Michael de, asst. ed.; Kaiser, Gerhard, asst.; Rinner, Fridrun, asst.; Wertheimer, Jürgen, asst. *Proceedings of the XIIth Congress of the International Comparative Literature Association/Actes du XIIe congrès de l'Association Internationale de Littérature Comparée: München 1988 Munich, IV: Space and Boundaries of Literature/Espace et frontières de la littérature.* Munich: Iudicium; 1990. 651 pp. (Proceedings of the Congress of the International Comparative Literature Association 12: 4.)

[49] Coulet, Henri. "Perspectives de la SATOR." 153-156 in Boursier, Nicole, ed.; Trott, David, ed. *La Naissance du roman en France.* Paris: Papers on Fr. Seventeenth Cent. Lit.; 1990. 156 pp. (Biblio 17 54.) [†Topos.]

[50] Craige, Betty Jean. "Twentieth-Century Ideas in Literature and Painting." 116-121 in Barricelli, Jean-Pierre, ed.; Gibaldi, Joseph, ed.; Lauter, Estella, ed. *Teaching Literature and Other Arts.* New York: Mod. Lang. Assn. of Amer.; 1990. vi, 183 pp. (Options for Teaching 10.) [†1900-1999. And painting. Pedagogical approach.]

[51] Davis, Geoffrey V., ed.; Maes-Jelinek, Hena, ed. *Crisis and Creativity in the New Literatures in English: Cross/Cultures.* Amsterdam: Rodopi; 1990. xii, 529 pp. (Readings in the Post/Colonial Literatures in English 1.) [Incl. introd. †By postcolonial writers. English language literature. 1900-1999.]

[52] Dawidoff, Robert. "History ... But." *NLH.* 1990 Winter; 21(2): 395-406. [†Narrative; relationship to history.]

[53] Delbanco, Nicholas, ed. *Speaking of Writing: Selected Hopwood Lectures.* Ann Arbor: U of Michigan P; 1990. 393 pp. [Incl. introd. †Creative process.]

[54] Demers, Patricia. "Catechisms: Whatsoever a Christian Child Ought to Know." 41-48 in Gannon, Susan R., ed.; Thompson, Ruth Anne, ed. *Cross-Culturalism in Children's Literature: Selected Papers from the Children's Literature Association, Carleton University, Ottawa, Canada, May 14-17, 1987.* New York: Pace Univ.; 1988. i, 116 pp. [†For children. Didacticism; relationship to catechism.]

[55] Dennis, Philip, ed.; Aycock, Wendell, ed. *Literature and Anthropology.* Lubbock: Texas Tech UP; 1989. ix, 227 pp. (SCLit 20.) [Incl. introd. & pref. †Relationship to anthropology.]

[56] Dev, Amiya. "International Space and International Boundaries in International Literary Reception." 364-369 in Bauer, Roger, ed.; Fokkema, Douwe, ed.; Graat, Michael de, asst. ed.; Kaiser, Gerhard, asst.; Rinner, Fridrun, asst.; Wertheimer, Jürgen, asst. *Proceedings of the XIIth Congress of the International Comparative Literature Association/Actes du XIIe congrès de l'Association Internationale de Littérature Comparée: München 1988 Munich, IV: Space and Boundaries of Literature/Espace et frontières de la littérature.* Munich: Iudicium; 1990. 651 pp. (Proceedings of the Congress of the International Comparative Literature Association 12: 4.)

[57] D'haen, Theo, ed. "Verbal/Visual Crossings 1880-1980." *Restant.* 1990; 18(1). [Spec. iss.; incl. introd. †Visual imagery; relationship to the verbal.]

[58] Diego, Fernando de. "Recenzoj kaj recenzantoj." *Fonto.* 1990 May; 10(113): 5-8. [†Esperanto language literature.]

[59] Dittmar, Linda. "Literature as Art: Sequencing Learning in the Core Curriculum." 78-85 in Barricelli, Jean-Pierre, ed.; Gibaldi, Joseph, ed.; Lauter, Estella, ed. *Teaching Literature and Other Arts.* New York: Mod. Lang. Assn. of Amer.; 1990. vi, 183 pp. (Options for Teaching 10.) [†And art. Pedagogical approach.]

[60] Donoghue, Denis. "I Have Never Been Able to Tell a Story." *New York Times Book Review.* 1990 Sept. 2: 11, 26. [†Relationship to storytelling.]

[61] Dorrestein, Renate; Boeke, Wanda, tr. "'Make Way for What People Say': Notes on Gender and Writing." *FSt.* 1988 Summer; 14(2): 337-348. [†Writing; relationship to feminism.]

[62] Dreifuss-Kattan, Esther. "Cancer and Creativity: Cancer Stories: A Psychooncological and Psychoanalytic Study of the 'Cancer Literature' Seen in Autobiographic, Fictional and Poetic Accounts Written by Cancer Patients and Its Relation to Loss, Mourning, Dying and Creativity and Its Clinical Implications." *DAI.* 1990 Dec.; 51(6): 3127B. [†By patient with cancer. Relationship to art therapy. Treatment of mourning; creativity. Psychoanalytic approach. Dissertation abstract.]

[63] Dudek, Louis. "The Idea of Art." *CanL.* 1990 Autumn; 126: 50-64. [†Relationship to aesthetics.]

[64] Dupuy, Jean-Pierre. "Self-Reference in Literature." *PoeticsJ.* 1989 Dec.; 18(6): 491-515. [†Self-reflexiveness.]

[65] Easley, Jesse J. "Literature and Architecture: Spatial Form and Composition." 46-53 in Barricelli, Jean-Pierre, ed.; Gibaldi, Joseph, ed.; Lauter, Estella, ed. *Teaching Literature and Other Arts.* New York: Mod. Lang. Assn. of Amer.; 1990. vi, 183 pp. (Options for Teaching 10.) [†Spatial form; composition compared to architecture. Pedagogical approach.]

[66] Elliott, Dyan. "The Historian and Her Past." *Exemplaria.* 1990 Fall; 2(2): 706-711. [†Middle Ages. Treatment of marriage; relationship to abstinence from sexual intercourse.]

[67] Ertl, Istvan. "Eŭropo kaj esperanta literaturo." *Bulgara Esperantisto.* 1990 Apr.; 59(4): 25-27. [†Esperanto language literature.]

[68] Escal, Françoise. "Entretien." *RSH.* 1987 Jan.-Mar.; 76(205 [1]): 131-144. [†Role of text in musical composition. Interview with Boucourechliev, André.]

[69] ———. "Entretien." *RSH.* 1987 Jan.-Mar.; 76(205 [1]): 145-153. [†Role of text in musical adaptation. Interview with Henry, Pierre.]

[70] Faucheux, Michel; Walker, R. Scott, tr. "Literature and Disenchantment." *Diogenes.* 1989 Winter; 148: 42-60. [†Relationship to disenchantment.]

[71] Feldman, Carol Fleisher; Bruner, Jerome; Renderer, Bobbi; Spitzer, Sally. "Narrative Comprehension." 1-78 in Britton, Bruce K., ed.; Pellegrini, A. D., ed. *Narrative Thought and Narrative Language.* Hillsdale, NJ: Erlbaum; 1990. viii, 278 pp. [†Narrative; relationship to cognitive processes.]

[72] Fisch, Harold. "Character as Linguistic Sign." *NLH.* 1990 Spring; 21(3): 593-606. [†Characterization.]

[73] Fortini, Franco; Rumble, Patrick, tr. "Opus servile." *QI.* 1990 Spring; 11(1): 5-12. [†Text; relationship to culture.]

[74] Foster, Dennis A. *Confession and Complicity in Narrative.* Cambridge: Cambridge UP; 1987. ix, 146 pp. [†Confession in narrative.]

[75] Freihow, Halfdan W. "Om alvor, underholdning og litteratur." *Vinduet.* 1990; 44(3): 2-8. [†1900-1999. As entertainment.]

[76] Frenzel, Elisabeth. *Motive der Weltliteratur: Ein Lexikon dichtungsgeschichtlicher Längsschnitte.* Stuttgart: Kröner; 1988. 907 pp. (Kröners Taschenausgabe 301.) [3rd rev. ed.]

[77] Frey, Charles; Griffith, John. *The Literary Heritage of Childhood: An Appraisal of Children's Classics in the Western Tradition.* New York: Greenwood; 1987. x, 244 pp. (CSWL 20.) [†For children.]

[78] Friedman, Susan Stanford, ed. "[1989 International Conference on Narrative.]" *JNT.* 1990 Spring; 20(2). [Spec. iss.; incl. introd. †Narrative.]

[79] Gadamer, Hans-Georg; Norton, Roger C., tr. "Hearing—Seeing—Reading." *L&C.* 1990; 10(1): 87-92. [†Relationship to reading.]

[80] Gadamer, Hans-Georg; Schmidt, Dennis J., tr. "Culture and the Word." *TrP.* 1990; 5: 11-23. [Tr. from *Lob der Theorie.* †Language; relationship to culture.]

[81] Gannon, Susan R., ed.; Thompson, Ruth Anne, ed. *The Child and the Family: Selected Papers from the 1988 International Conference of the Children's Literature Association, College of Charleston, Charleston, South Carolina, May 19-22, 1988.* New York: Pace Univ.; 1989. 86 pp. [†For children.]

[82] ———. *Cross-Culturalism in Children's Literature: Selected Papers from the Children's Literature Association, Carleton University, Ottawa, Canada, May 14-17, 1987.* New York: Pace Univ.; 1988. i, 116 pp. [Incl. introd. †For children.]

[83] Gans, Eric. "The Past and Future of Generative Anthropology: Reflections on the Departmental Colloquium." *PG.* 1990; 8: 35-41. [†Relationship to generative anthropology.]

[84] Genette, Gérard. "Romances sans paroles." *RSH.* 1987 Jan.-Mar.; 76(205 [1]): 113-120. [†Role of text in musical composition.]

[85] Geppert, Hans Vilmar, ed. *Grosse Werke der Literatur.* Augsburg: Augsburg; 1990.

[86] Gérard, Albert. "Literature, Language, Nation and the Commonwealth." 93-101 in Davis, Geoffrey V., ed.; Maes-Jelinek, Hena, ed. *Crisis and Creativity in the New Literatures in English: Cross/Cultures.* Amsterdam: Rodopi; 1990. xii, 529 pp. (Readings in the Post/Colonial Literatures in English 1.) [†By postcolonial writers. English language literature. 1900-1999. Relationship to marginality.]

[87] Gnisci, Armando. "Evénement, liaison, rendez-vous." 615-620 in Bauer, Roger, ed.; Fokkema, Douwe, ed.; Graat, Michael de, asst. ed.; Kaiser, Gerhard, asst.; Rinner, Fridrun, asst.; Wertheimer, Jürgen, asst. *Proceedings of the XIIth Congress of the International Comparative Literature Association/Actes du XIIe congrès de l'Association Internationale de Littérature Comparée: München 1988 Munich, IV: Space and Boundaries of Literature/Espace et frontières de la littérature.* Munich:

Iudicium; 1990. 651 pp. (Proceedings of the Congress of the International Comparative Literature Association 12: 4.)

[88] Goldberg, Jonathan. "On the One Hand …." 77-99 in Bender, John, ed.; Wellbery, David E., ed. *The Ends of Rhetoric: History, Theory, Practice.* Stanford: Stanford UP; 1990. xiv, 238 pp. [†Psychology of writer.

[89] Goldsmith, Evelyn. "Learning from Illustrations: Factors in the Design of Illustrated Educational Books for Middle School Children." *W&I.* 1986 Apr.-June; 2(2): 111-121. [†For children. Illustration; relationship to comprehension. Semiotic approach.]

[90] Golomb, Harai. "Is the Grass across the Boundary between Music and Literature Greener?" 524-529 in Bauer, Roger, ed.; Fokkema, Douwe, ed.; Graat, Michael de, asst. ed.; Kaiser, Gerhard, asst.; Rinner, Fridrun, asst.; Wertheimer, Jürgen, asst. *Proceedings of the XIIth Congress of the International Comparative Literature Association/Actes du XIIe congrès de l'Association Internationale de Littérature Comparée: München 1988 Munich, IV: Space and Boundaries of Literature/Espace et frontières de la littérature.* Munich: Iudicium; 1990. 651 pp. (Proceedings of the Congress of the International Comparative Literature Association 12: 4.) [†Relationship to music.]

[91] Gossman, Lionel. *Between History and Literature.* Cambridge: Harvard UP; 1990. 412 pp. [†Relationship to history. Theories of Thierry, Augustin; Michelet, Jules.]

[92] Green, Jon D. "Determining Valid Interart Analogies." 8-15 in Barricelli, Jean-Pierre, ed.; Gibaldi, Joseph, ed.; Lauter, Estella, ed. *Teaching Literature and Other Arts.* New York: Mod. Lang. Assn. of Amer.; 1990. vi, 183 pp. (Options for Teaching 10.) [†Relationship to art. Pedagogical approach.]

[93] Gregor, D. B. *La Valeur culturelle de l'espéranto.* Rotterdam: Universala Esperanto-Asocio; 1983. 15 pp. (DLE 13F.) [†Esperanto language literature.]

[94] Hamilton, John Maxwell. "The Mistakes in This Essay Are My Own." *New York Times Book Review.* 1990 Apr. 15; 1, 25-26. [†Creative process.]

[95] Harris, Wilson. "Oedipus and the Middle Passage." 9-21 in Davis, Geoffrey V., ed.; Maes-Jelinek, Hena, ed. *Crisis and Creativity in the New Literatures in English: Cross/Cultures.* Amsterdam: Rodopi; 1990. xii, 529 pp. (Readings in the Post/ Colonial Literatures in English 1.) [†By postcolonial writers. English language literature. 1900-1999. Treatment of oppression.]

[96] Hayles, N. Katherine. *Chaos Bound: Orderly Disorder in Contemporary Literature and Science.* Ithaca: Cornell UP; 1990. xvi, 309 pp. [†Relationship to order; chaos; study example: Adams, Henry Brooks: *The Education of Henry Adams;* Lessing, Doris: *The Golden Notebook;* Lem, Stanisław.]

[97] Higonnet, Margaret, coordinator & introd. "Groupe de travail: 'La Redéfinition féministe de l'espace littéraire'/Workshop: 'The Feminist Redefinition of Literary Space'." 465-504 in Bauer, Roger, ed.; Fokkema, Douwe, ed.; Graat, Michael de, asst. ed.; Aldridge, A. Owen, asst.; Higonnet, Margaret, asst.; Klein, Holger M., asst.; Meisami, Julie Scott, asst.; Rigney, Ann, asst.; Ronen, Ruth, asst.; Sondrup, Steven P., asst.; Templeton, Joan, asst.; Walker, Janet A., asst. *Proceedings of the XIIth Congress of the International Comparative Literature Association/Actes du XIIe congrès de l'Association Internationale de Littérature Comparée: München 1988 Munich, III: Space and Boundaries in Literature (Continuation)/Espace et frontières dans la littérature (suite).* Munich: Iudicium; 1990. 509 pp. (Proceedings of the Congress of the International Comparative Literature Association 12: 3.) [Spec. sect.; incl. introd. †Role of space. Feminist approach.]

[98] Hollindale, Peter, ed. "Children's Art and Literature." *W&I.* 1986 Apr.-June; 2(2). [Spec. iss.; incl. introd. †For children. Relationship to visual arts.]

[99] Hunt, Peter. "Cross-Culturalism and Inter-Generational Communication in Children's Literature." 37-40 in Gannon, Susan R., ed.; Thompson, Ruth Anne, ed. *Cross-Culturalism in Children's Literature: Selected Papers from the Children's Literature Association, Carleton University, Ottawa, Canada, May 14-17, 1987.* New York: Pace Univ.; 1988. i, 116 pp. [†For children. Treatment of adult-child relations. Reader-response approach.]

[100] Huse, Nancy L., ed.; Alberghene, Janice M., ed. "Children's Humor: Subversion or Socialization?" *CLAQ.* 1990 Fall; 15(3): 114. [Spec. sect.; incl. introd. †For children. Humor.]

[101] Iser, Wolfgang. "Fictionalizing: The Anthropological Dimension of Literary Fictions." *NLH.* 1990 Autumn; 21(4): 939-955. [†Fictionality; relationship to anthropology.]

[102] Iveković, Rada, introd. "Ženska poetika?" *Izraz.* 1990 Feb.-Mar.; 34(2-3). [Spec. iss.; incl. introd. †By women writers.]

[103] Jameson, Fredric; Jonsson, Stefan, tr. "Tredje världens litteratur i den multinationella kapitalismens era." *OB.* 1989; 4: 44-69. [†In Third World. 1900-1999. Marxist approach.]

[104] Johansen, Jørgen Dines. "The Triple Status of a Fictional Universe of Discourse." 77-82 in Bauer, Roger, ed.; Fokkema, Douwe, ed.; Graat, Michael de, asst. ed.; Fischer-Lichte, Erika, asst.; Garstin, Marguerite, asst.; Ibsch, Elrud, asst.; Stackelberg, Jürgen von, asst. *Proceedings of the XIIth Congress of the International Comparative Literature Association/Actes du XIIe congrès de l'Association Internationale de Littérature Comparée: München 1988 Munich, V: Space and Boundaries in Literary Theory and Criticism/Espace et frontières dans la critique et la théorie littéraire; Space and Boundaries in the Teaching of General and Comparative Literature/Espace et frontières dans l'enseignement de la littérature générale et comparée.* Munich: Iudicium; 1990. 415 pp. (Proceedings of the Congress of the International Comparative Literature Association 12: 5.) [†Discourse.]

[105] Johnson, Penelope D. "False Dichotomies." *Exemplaria.* 1990 Fall; 2(2): 689-692. [†Role of women; relationship to history; literature in Middle Ages.]

[106] Jones, Anne Hudson. "Literature and Medicine: Traditions and Innovations." 11-24 in Clarke, Bruce, ed.; Aycock, Wendell, ed. *The Body and the Text: Comparative Essays in Literature and Medicine.* Lubbock: Texas Tech UP; 1990. ix, 221 pp. (SCLit 22.) [†Relationship to medicine.]

[107] Jones, Libby Falk, ed.; Goodwin, Sarah Webster, ed.; Pfaelzer, Jean, response; Elshtain, Jean Bethke, response. *Feminism, Utopia, and Narrative.* Knoxville: U of Tennessee P; 1990. x, 222 pp. (TStL 32.) [†By women writers. Relationship to feminism; utopia.]

[108] Jost, François, ed.; Friedman, Melvin J., asst. ed. *Aesthetics and the Literature of Ideas: Essays in Honor of A. Owen Aldridge.* Newark: U of Delaware P; 1990. 290 pp. [Incl. introd. †Festschrift for Aldridge, Alfred Owen.]

[109] Jousse, Marcel; Sienaert, Edgard, tr.; Whitaker, Richard, tr. *The Oral Style.* New York: Garland; 1990. xxviii, 266 pp. (ABLS 6; GRLH 1352.) [†Oral style.]

[110] Kachru, Braj B. *The Alchemy of English: The Spread, Functions, and Models of Non-Native Englishes.* Urbana: U of Illinois P; 1990. ix, 200 pp. [†English language literature. 1900-1999. Relationship to colonialism.]

[111] Kaminker, Jean Pierre. "Le Canon de la Méduse: Analyse d'un cas de lecture." 415-421 in Deledalle, Gérard, ed. *Semiotics and Pragmatics.* Amsterdam: Benjamins; 1989. 467 pp. (FoS 18.) [†Sign. Theories of Blot, Jean-Yves: *La Méduse, chronique d'un naufrage ordinaire.*]

[112] Kaplan, E. Ann. "Women, Morality, and Social Change from a Discourse Analysis Perspective." 347-361 in Eisenberg, Nancy, ed.; Reykowski, J., ed.; Staub, E., ed. *Social and Moral Values: Individual and Societal Perspectives.* New York: Erlbaum; 1989. 376 pp. [†Treatment of women; relationship to moral values.]

[113] Kennedy, DayAnn M.; Spangler, Stella S.; Vanderwerf, Mary Ann. *Science & Technology in Fact and Fiction: A Guide to Children's Books.* New York: Bowker; 1990. xii, 319 pp. [†For children. Treatment of science; technology. Reference guide.]

[114] Kernan, Alvin. *The Death of Literature.* New Haven: Yale UP; 1990. ix, 230 pp.

[115] Kittler, Friedrich. "Literatur und Psychotechnik." *MAL.* 1990; 23(2): 99-110. [†1900-1999. Relationship to film; recordings.]

[116] Klaus, Meredith. "Narrative Voice in Books for Young People on Medieval History and Culture." 396-404 in Otten, Charlotte F., ed.; Schmidt, Gary D., ed. *The Voice of the Narrator in Children's Literature: Insights from Writers and Critics.* New York: Greenwood; 1989. xviii, 414 pp. (CSWL 28.) [†For children. English language literature. 1900-1999. Narrative voice. Treatment of Middle Ages.]

[117] Klerk, W. A. de. "Letterkunde as geskiedenis—die oorvloediger geskiedenis." *TvL.* 1990 Feb.; 28(1): 1-11. [†Relationship to history.]

[118] Kramer, Lawrence. *Music as Cultural Practice, 1800-1900.* Berkeley: U of California P; 1990. xv, 226 pp. [†1800-1899. Relationship to music.]

[119] Lamarque, Peter. "Narrative and Invention: The Limits of Fictionality." 131-153 in Nash, Cristopher, ed. *Narrative in Culture: The Uses of Storytelling in the Sciences, Philosophy, and Literature.* London: Routledge; 1990. xvi, 228 pp. (Warwick Studies in Philosophy and Literature.) [†Role of fictionality in narrative; relationship to logic; epistemology.]

[120] Lancashire, Ian. "Discovering Literary *Topoi* by Computer." 139-151 in Boursier, Nicole, ed.; Trott, David, ed. *La Naissance du roman en France.* Paris: Papers on Fr. Seventeenth Cent. Lit.; 1990. 156 pp. (Biblio 17 54.) [†Role of topos; relationship to application of computer.]

[121] Lang, George. "Periphery as Paradigm: Creole Literatures and the Polysystem." *PoT.* 1987; 8(3-4): 529-537. [†In creole languages. Application of polysystem theory.]

[122] Lastinger, Valérie Cretaux. "Littérature féminine et écriture enfantine: Quelques implications de la critique féministe." *DAI.* 1990 Mar.; 50(9): 2919A. [†For children. Study example: Ségur, Sophie, comtesse de. Feminist approach. Dissertation abstract.]

[123] Lenz, Millicent. *Nuclear Age Literature for Youth: The Quest for a Life-Affirming Ethic.* Chicago: Amer. Lib. Assn.; 1990. xli, 315 pp. [†For adolescents. Relationship to nuclear age.]

[124] Lindenberger, Herbert. *The History in Literature: On Value, Genre, Institutions.* New York: Columbia UP; 1990. xix, 269 pp. [†Role of history; relationship to genre; values; institution.]

[125] Link, Franz, ed. *Paradeigmata: Literarische Typologie des Alten Testaments, I: Von den Anfängen bis zum 19. Jahrhundert; II: 20. Jahrhundert.* Berlin: Duncker & Humblot; 1989. 945 pp. (Schriften zur Literaturwissenschaft 5.) [Incl. introd. †Sources in Old Testament.]

[126] Lubin, Orly. "Bordering Reality: Character as Juncture between Text and Extra-Text." *DAI.* 1990 Oct.; 51(4): 1221A-1222A. [†Text; relationship to extratextuality. Dissertation abstract.]

[127] Lynch, Enrique. "O Xénero Fragmentario." *Grial.* 1990 Apr.-June; 28(106): 165-168. [†Fragment.]

[128] Macaskill, Brian Kenneth. "Framing Value in Literature: Style and Ideology." *DAI.* 1990 Feb.; 50(8): 2500A. [†Framing; relationship to style; ideology. Dissertation abstract.]

[129] Magnusson, Magnus, ed.; Goring, Rosemary, ed. *Cambridge Biographical Dictionary.* Cambridge: Cambridge UP; 1990. xii, 1604 pp.

[130] Marder, Elissa. "Human, None Too Human: Readings in Literature, Psychoanalysis and Film." *DAI.* 1990 Aug.; 51(2): 519A. [†Treatment of nonhuman figures; relationship to humanism. Dissertation abstract.]

[131] Marino, Adrian. "'Literatura europeană,' azi." *Transilvania.* 1990; 19(1): 24-30. [†1900-1999. World literature; relationship to European literature.]

[132] ——. "Literature and Ideology in the Republic of Letters." 214-224 in Jost, François, ed.; Friedman, Melvin J., asst. ed. *Aesthetics and the Literature of Ideas: Essays in Honor of A. Owen Aldridge*. Newark: U of Delaware P; 1990. 290 pp. [†Role of republic of letters.]

[133] Martindale, Colin. *The Clockwork Muse: The Predictability of Artistic Change*. New York: Basic; 1990. xiv, 411 pp. [†Role of creativity; relationship to novelty. Psychological approach.

[134] Massé, Michelle A. "Gothic Repetition: Husbands, Horrors, and Things That Go Bump in the Night." *Signs*. 1990 Summer; 15(4): 679-709. [†Gothicism.]

[135] Mazzella, Anthony J. "Adaptations of Literature into Other Arts." 61-67 in Barricelli, Jean-Pierre, ed.; Gibaldi, Joseph, ed.; Lauter, Estella, ed. *Teaching Literature and Other Arts*. New York: Mod. Lang. Assn. of Amer.; 1990. vi, 183 pp. (Options for Teaching 10.) [†Adaptation into art. Pedagogical approach.]

[136] Miĥalkov, Georgi. "Ĉu ĝi ekzistas?" *Bulgara Esperantisto*. 1989 Nov.; 58(11): 2-3. [†Esperanto language literature.]

[137] Miner, Earl. "Common, Proper, and Improper Place." 95-100 in Bauer, Roger, ed.; Fokkema, Douwe, ed.; Graat, Michael de, asst. ed.; Aldridge, A. Owen, asst.; Higonnet, Margaret, asst.; Klein, Holger M., asst.; Meisami, Julie Scott, asst.; Rigney, Ann, asst.; Ronen, Ruth, asst.; Sondrup, Steven P., asst.; Templeton, Joan, asst.; Walker, Janet A., asst. *Proceedings of the XIIth Congress of the International Comparative Literature Association/Actes du XIIe congrès de l'Association Internationale de Littérature Comparée: München 1988 Munich, III: Space and Boundaries in Literature (Continuation)/Espace et frontières dans la littérature (suite)*. Munich: Iudicium; 1990. 509 pp. (Proceedings of the Congress of the International Comparative Literature Association 12: 3.) [†Role of space; relationship to setting.]

[138] Mirollo, James V. "The History of Western Culture: Literature and Art." 70-77 in Barricelli, Jean-Pierre, ed.; Gibaldi, Joseph, ed.; Lauter, Estella, ed. *Teaching Literature and Other Arts*. New York: Mod. Lang. Assn. of Amer.; 1990. vi, 183 pp. (Options for Teaching 10.) [†And art in Western world. Pedagogical approach.]

[139] Mitchell, W. J. T. "Against Comparison: Teaching Literature and the Visual Arts." 30-37 in Barricelli, Jean-Pierre, ed.; Gibaldi, Joseph, ed.; Lauter, Estella, ed. *Teaching Literature and Other Arts*. New York: Mod. Lang. Assn. of Amer.; 1990. vi, 183 pp. (Options for Teaching 10.) [†And visual arts. Pedagogical approach.]

[140] Mitosek, Zofia. "Langage littéraire, langage commun: Frontières ou identité?" 602-606 in Bauer, Roger, ed.; Fokkema, Douwe, ed.; Graat, Michael de, asst. ed.; Kaiser, Gerhard, asst.; Rinner, Fridrun, asst.; Wertheimer, Jürgen, asst. *Proceedings of the XIIth Congress of the International Comparative Literature Association/Actes du XIIe congrès de l'Association Internationale de Littérature Comparée: München 1988 Munich, IV: Space and Boundaries of Literature/Espace et frontières de la littérature*. Munich: Iudicium; 1990. 651 pp. (Proceedings of the Congress of the International Comparative Literature Association 12: 4.) [†Literary language compared to spoken language.]

[141] Moebius, William. "Introduction to Picturebook Codes." *W&I*. 1986 Apr.-June; 2(2): 141-158. [†For children. Use of code in picture books.]

[142] Molino, Jean. "Thèses sur le langage, le discours, la littérature et le symbolique." *ZFSL*. 1990; 100: 154-167. [†Textual analysis.]

[143] Monroe, William. "Performing Persons: A Locus of Connection for Medicine and Literature." 25-40 in Clarke, Bruce, ed.; Aycock, Wendell, ed. *The Body and the Text: Comparative Essays in Literature and Medicine*. Lubbock: Texas Tech UP; 1990. ix, 221 pp. (SCLit 22.) [†Narrative; rhetoric; relationship to medicine; study example: Percy, Walker: *Lancelot*; *The Moviegoer*.]

[144] Mortensen, Peter Leslie. "Authority, Discourse, Community." *DAI*. 1990 Jan.; 50(7): 2042A. [†Authority in discourse; relationship to community. Dissertation abstract.]

[145] Moser, Walter. "Expérimentation fictionnelle et fiction expérimentale: Des frontières mouvantes entre science et littérature." 567-577 in Bauer, Roger, ed.; Fokkema, Douwe, ed.; Graat, Michael de, asst. ed.; Kaiser, Gerhard, asst.; Rinner, Fridrun, asst.; Wertheimer, Jürgen, asst. *Proceedings of the XIIth Congress of the International Comparative Literature Association/Actes du XIIe congrès de l'Association Internationale de Littérature Comparée: München 1988 Munich, IV: Space and Boundaries of Literature/Espace et frontières de la littérature*. Munich: Iudicium; 1990. 651 pp. (Proceedings of the Congress of the International Comparative Literature Association 12: 4.) [†Relationship to science. Application of theories of Mach, Ernst: *Erkenntnis und Irrtum*; Vaihinger, Hans.]

[146] Mullane, Janet, ed.; Wilson, Robert Thomas, ed.; DuBlanc, Robin, assoc. ed. *Nineteenth-Century Literature Criticism, XXII: Excerpts from Criticism of the Works of Novelists, Poets, Playwrights, Short Story Writers, Philosophers, and Other Creative Writers Who Died between 1800 and 1899, from the First Published Critical Appraisals to Current Evaluations*. Detroit: Gale; 1989. xv, 585 pp. [Illus. †1700-1899. Treatment in criticism.]

[147] Mullane, Janet, ed.; Wilson, Robert Thomas, ed.; DuBlanc, Robin, assoc. ed. *Nineteenth-Century Literature Criticism, XXIII: Excerpts from Criticism of the Works of Novelists, Poets, Playwrights, Short Story Writers, Philosphers, and Other Creative Writers Who Died between 1800 and 1899, from the First Published Critical Appraisals to Current Evaluations*. Detroit: Gale; 1989. xv, 564 pp. [Illus. †1700-1899. Treatment in criticism.]

[148] ——. *Nineteenth-Century Literature Criticism, XXI: Excerpts from Criticism of the Works of Novelists, Poets, Playwrights, Short Story Writers, Philosophers, and Other Creative Writers Who Died between 1800 and 1899, from the First Published Critical Appraisals to Current Evaluations*. Detroit: Gale; 1989. xiv, 613 pp. [Illus. †1700-1899. Treatment in criticism.]

[149] Mullane, Janet, ed.; Wilson, Robert Thomas, ed.; Abbey, Cherie D., assoc. ed.; Ligotti, Thomas, assoc. ed. *Nineteenth-Century Literature Criticism XXVI: Excerpts from Criticism of the Works of Novelists, Poets, Playwrights, Short Story Writers, Philosophers, and Other Creative Writers Who Died between 1800 and 1899, from the First Published Critical Appraisals to Current Evaluations*. Detroit: Gale; 1990. xv, 511 pp. [Illus. †1700-1899. Treatment in criticism.]

[150] Murray, Jacqueline, ed. "A Symposium on Women, History, and Literature: Theory and Methodology." *Exemplaria*. 1990 Fall; 2(2): 687-715. [Spec. sect.; incl. introd. & replies. †Middle Ages and Renaissance. Treatment of women. Panel discussion.]

[151] Myatt, Rosalind. "The Child and the Story: The Search for Identity." *DAI*. 1990 Aug.; 51(2): 466A. [†For children. Psychoanalytic approach. Dissertation abstract.]

[152] Nagy, Gregory. "The Crisis of Performance." 43-59 in Bender, John, ed.; Wellbery, David E., ed. *The Ends of Rhetoric: History, Theory, Practice*. Stanford: Stanford UP; 1990. xiv, 238 pp. [†Performance of oral tradition.]

[153] Nash, Cristopher, ed. *Narrative in Culture: The Uses of Storytelling in the Sciences, Philosophy, and Literature*. London: Routledge; 1990. xvi, 228 pp. (Warwick Studies in Philosophy and Literature.) [†Narrative; relationship to fiction; scientific discourse.]

[154] Nuessel, Frank. "Defining the Cultural Characteristics of Esperanto Literature." *Geolinguistics*. 1990; 16: 107-117. [†Esperanto language literature.]

[155] Nussbaum, Martha C. *Love's Knowledge: Essays on Philosophy and Literature*. New York: Oxford UP; 1990. xiv, 403 pp. [†Relationship to moral philosophy; love.]

[156] Nyirö, Lajos. "Le Mot, la structure et l'oeuvre littéraire." *CASS*. 1988; 22(1-4): 147-155. [†Role of word; relationship to structure.]

[157] Ofek, Uriel. *Sifrut HaYeladim HaIvrit: 1900-1948, I & II*. Tel Aviv: Dviv; 1988. 334 + 721 pp. [†For children (1900-1948). Hebrew language literature.]

[158] Ong, Walter J. *Fighting for Life: Contest, Sexuality, and Consciousness*. Amherst: U of Massachusetts P; 1981. 231 pp. [†Orality.]

[159] ——. *Interfaces of the Word: Studies in the Evolution of Consciousness and Culture*. Ithaca: Cornell UP; 1982. 352 pp. [Rpt. of 1977 ed. †On written language; relationship to narrative voice; closure; oral tradition.]

[160] Ong, Walter J.; Scatasta, Gino, tr.; Barilli, Renato, introd. *Interfacce della parola*. Bologna: Mulino; 1989. 359 pp. [†Word.]

[161] Ortega, José. "Los gitanos y la literatura." *CHA*. 1990 July; 481: 91-100. [†Treatment of Gypsies.]

[162] Otten, Charlotte F., ed.; Schmidt, Gary D., ed. *The Voice of the Narrator in Children's Literature: Insights from Writers and Critics*. New York: Greenwood; 1989. xviii, 414 pp. (CSWL 28.) [Illus.]

[163] Oudvorst, A. F. van. "Intellectuelen en de wereld na 1945." *Maatstaf*. 1989; 8-9: 38-51. [†Role of intellectuals; relationship to politics (1945-1990).]

[164] Oz, Amos. "Lama Likro Sifrut?" *Moznayim*. 1989; 63(5-6): 43-45.

[165] Pál, József. "A propos de quelques aspects de l'étude comparée des œuvres littératures et des œuvres d'art plastique." 518-523 in Bauer, Roger, ed.; Fokkema, Douwe, ed.; Graat, Michael de, asst. ed.; Kaiser, Gerhard, asst.; Rinner, Fridrun, asst.; Wertheimer, Jürgen, asst. *Proceedings of the XIIth Congress of the International Comparative Literature Association/Actes du XIIe congrès de l'Association Internationale de Littérature Comparée: München 1988 Munich, IV: Space and Boundaries of Literature/Espace et frontières de la littérature*. Munich: Iudicium; 1990. 651 pp. (Proceedings of the Congress of the International Comparative Literature Association 12: 4.) [†Relationship to visual arts.]

[166] Paulson, William. "Closing the Circle: Science and Literature, and the Passion of Matter." *NER*. 1990 Summer; 12(4): 512-526. [†Treatment of science.]

[167] Peterfreund, Stuart, ed. *Literature and Science: Theory & Practice*. Boston: Northeastern UP; 1990. vi, 248 pp. [Incl. introd. †Relationship to science.]

[168] Pointon, Marcia. "Aesthetic and Commodity: An Examination of the Function of the Verbal in J. M. W. Turner's Artistic Practice." 76-94 in Marwick, Arthur, ed. *The Arts, Literature, and Society*. London: Routledge; 1990. xii, 332 pp. [Illus.; incl. letters. †Language; relationship to imagery in painting by Turner, Joseph Mallord William.]

[169] Ponimonsky, Genya; Tal, Leah. "MiKoreh? Ma Koreh? Eikh Koreh? Ha'adafot VeHergelim BiKriat 'Sifrut Yafah' BeKerev Talmidim." *Be'emmet*. 1987 Winter; 1: 73-86.

[170] Posner, Richard A. *Law and Literature: A Misunderstood Relation*. Cambridge: Harvard UP; 1988. xi, 371 pp. [†Relationship to law.]

[171] Pribic, Rado. *Nobel Laureates in Literature: A Biographical Dictionary*. New York: Garland; 1990. xxiv, 473 pp. (GRLH 849.) [†By recipients of Nobel Prize in Literature (1901-1988). Biographical dictionary.]

[172] Prince, Gerald. "L'alternarré." *SCr*. 1989 May; 4(2 [60]): 223-231. [†Narrative; relationship to narratee.]

[173] ——. "Remarques sur le *topos* et sur le dénarré." 113-122 in Boursier, Nicole, ed.; Trott, David, ed. *La Naissance du roman en France*. Paris: Papers on Fr. Seventeenth Cent. Lit.; 1990. 156 pp. (Biblio 17 54.) [†Topos; relationship to *dénarré*.]

[174] Privat, Edmond; Mayer, Herbert, pref. *Pri Esperanta literaturo*. Vienna: Pro Esperanto; 1990. 28 pp. [3d ed. of 1912 pub. †Esperanto language literature.]

[175] Rastier, François. "Microsémantique et thématique." *SCr*. 1989 May; 4(2 [60]): 151-162. [†Thematic structure; relationship to semantics.]

[176] Ravazzoli, Flavia. "La nozione di 'figura': Intersezioni tra linguistica, retorica e semiotica." *SCr*. 1989 Sept.; 4(3 [61]): 325-336. [†Figures; relationship to rhetoric; semiotics.]

[177] Richler, Mordecai. "Just Find a Million Readers and Success Will Surely Follow." *New York Times Book Review*. 1990 June 10: 3, 41.

 SEE SUBJECT INDEX FOR CROSS-REFERENCES

[178] Ricoeur, Paul. "Mimesis, Reference and Refiguration in *Time and Narrative*." *Scripsi*. 1989 Aug.; 5(4): 91-102. [†Temporality in narrative.]

[179] Riggan, William. "The Neustadt International Prize for Literature: Jurors and Candidates." *WLT*. 1990 Winter; 64(1): 38-53. [†Neustadt International Prize for Literature (1990).

[180] Rodrigues Corréa, Glauco. "Kio estas Esperanta literaturo?" *Gazeto*. 1990 June 15; 5(5 [29]): 20-22. [†Esperanto language literature.]

[181] Rollin, Roger. "'Words, Words, Words …': On Redefining Literature." *JPC*. 1989 Winter; 23(3): 1-10.

[182] Romano, Carlin. "Part-Time Love: What's Existentialism Got To Do With It?" *Village Voice Literary Supplement*. 1990 Oct.; 89: 27-28. [†Relationship to existentialism.]

[183] Roth, Michael S., introd. "History and …." *NLH*. 1990 Winter; 21(2). [Spec. iss. †Relationship to history.]

[184] Schorske, Carl E. "History and the Study of Culture." *NLH*. 1990 Winter; 21(2): 407-420. [†Relationship to cultural history; historiography. Sources in Herodotus.]

[185] Seixo, Maria Alzira, ed. *Os Estudios Literários: (Entre) Ciência e Hermenêutica: Actas do I Congresso da APLC, I*. Lisbon: Reprografia da A. E. F. L. L.; 1990. [†Relationship to science; hermeneutics.]

[186] Selig, Karl-Ludwig, ed.; Sears, Elizabeth, ed. *The Verbal and the Visual: Essays in Honor of William Sebastian Heckscher*. New York: Italica; 1990. xiv, 255 pp. [Incl. fwd. †And visual arts. Festschrift for Heckscher, Wilhelm Sebastian.]

[187] Senick, Gerard J., ed.; Hug, Melissa Reiff, assoc. ed. *Children's Literature Review, XVI: Excerpts from Reviews, Criticism, and Commentary on Books for Children and Young People*. Detroit: Gale; 1989. xii, 261 pp. [Illus. †For children. Treatment in criticism.]

[188] Sherman, Laurie, ed.; Jones, Michael W., assoc. ed.; Lazzari, Marie, assoc. ed.; Ligotti, Thomas, assoc. ed.; McClellan, Michelle L., assoc. ed.; Prosyniuk, Joann, assoc. ed. *Nineteenth-Century Literature Criticism, XXVIII: Topics Volume: Excerpts from Criticism of Various Topics in Nineteenth-Century Literature, including Literary and Critical Movements, Prominent Themes and Genres, Anniversary Celebrations, and Surveys of National Literatures*. Detroit: Gale; 1990. xv, 505 pp. [Illus. †1800-1899. Treatment in criticism.]

[189] Shipps, Anthony W. *The Quote Sleuth: A Manual for the Tracer of Lost Quotations*. Urbana: U of Illinois P; 1990. xi, 194 pp. [†Quotation. Reference guide.]

[190] Showalter, Elaine. *Sexual Anarchy: Gender and Culture at the* fin de siècle. New York: Viking; 1990. xii, 242 pp. [†1800-1999. Role of gender; relationship to culture.]

[191] Slemon, Stephen. "Unsettling the Empire: Resistance Theory for the Second World." *WLWE*. 1990 Autumn; 30(2): 30-41. [†Postcolonial literature.]

[192] Solomon, J. Fisher. "Between Determinism and Indeterminism: Notes toward a Potentialist Metaphysics." *SubStance*. 1988; 17(1 [55]): 18-32. [†Relationship to determinism; uncertainty.]

[193] Spaethling, Robert. "Literature and Music." 54-60 in Barricelli, Jean-Pierre, ed.; Gibaldi, Joseph, ed.; Lauter, Estella, ed. *Teaching Literature and Other Arts*. New York: Mod. Lang. Assn. of Amer.; 1990. vi, 183 pp. (Options for Teaching 10.) [†Relationship to music. Pedagogical approach.]

[194] Stanton, Edward F. "Treason or Trampoline? Translation and Teaching." 620-624 in Fernández Jiménez, Juan, ed.; Labrador Herraiz, José J., ed.; Valdivieso, L. Teresa, ed.; Morón Arroyo, Ciriaco, pref. *Estudios en homenaje a Enrique Ruiz-Fornells*. Erie, PA: Asociación de Licenciados & Doctores Españoles en Estados Unidos; 1990. xxvi, 706 pp. (Homenajes 1.) [†On translation; relationship to teaching.]

[195] Steig, Michael. "Why Bettelheim: A Comment on the Use of Psychological Theories in CriticismCriticism." *ChildL*. 1990; 18: 125-126. [†For children. Sources in *Märchen*. Theories of Bettelheim, Bruno: *The Uses of Enchantment*.]

[196] Steiner, Wendy. "Literature and Painting." 40-45 in Barricelli, Jean-Pierre, ed.; Gibaldi, Joseph, ed.; Lauter, Estella, ed. *Teaching Literature and Other Arts*. New York: Mod. Lang. Assn. of Amer.; 1990. vi, 183 pp. (Options for Teaching 10.) [†Temporality; spatiality compared to painting. Pedagogical approach.]

[197] Stocchi, Manlio Pastore. "Letteratura e non letteratura (frammento di un seminario sulla storia letteraria)." *LI*. 1990 Jan.-Mar.; 42(1): 8-25.

[198] Suleiman, Susan Rubin. *Subversive Intent: Gender, Politics, and the Avant-Garde*. Cambridge: Harvard UP; 1990. 272 pp. [†Feminist literature. Treatment of gender; relationship to politics; avant-garde.]

[199] Taylor, Mary Agnes, ed. "Humor in Children's Literature." *StAH*. 1986-1987 Winter; 5(4): 223-319. [Spec. sect.; illus. †For children. Humor.]

[200] Thierse, Wolfgang. "'Das Ganze aber ist das, was Anfang, Mitte und Ende hat': Problemgeschichtliche Beobachtungen zur Geschichte des Werkbegriffs." *WB*. 1990; 36(2): 240-264.

[201] Tomiyama, Takao. "Dainamaito wo Nagero: Seikimatsu Bungaku to Anâkizumu." *EigoS*. n.d.; 135: 8-11. [†1800-1899: *fin de siècle*. Relationship to anarchism.]

[202] Tremper, Ellen. "Felt Presence: Narrative Tone in Information Books for Children." 389-395 in Otten, Charlotte F., ed.; Schmidt, Gary D., ed. *The Voice of the Narrator in Children's Literature: Insights from Writers and Critics*. New York: Greenwood; 1989. xviii, 414 pp. (CSWL 28.) [†For children. English language literature. 1900-1999. Narrative voice.]

[203] Turner, Edith. "The Literary Roots of Victor Turner's Anthropology." 163-169 in Ashley, Kathleen M., ed. *Victor Turner and the Construction of Cultural Criticism*. Bloomington: Indiana UP; 1990. xxii, 185 pp. (Between Literature and Anthropology.) [†Influence on theories of Turner, Victor Witter.]

[204] Tyler, Carole-Anne. "Female Impersonation." *DAI*. 1990 Feb.; 50(8): 2504A. [†Treatment of female impersonation; relationship to feminism; poststructuralism. Dissertation abstract.]

[205] Vajda, György M. "The Marginal Revolt: Problems of Marginality in Contemporary Literature." 217-222 in Bauer, Roger, ed.; Fokkema, Douwe, ed.; Graat, Michael de, asst. ed.; Kaiser, Gerhard, asst.; Rinner, Fridrun, asst.; Wertheimer, Jürgen, asst. *Proceedings of the XIIth Congress of the International Comparative Literature Association/Actes du XIIe congrès de l'Association Internationale de Littérature Comparée: München 1988 Munich, IV: Space and Boundaries of Literature/Espace et frontières de la littérature*. Munich: Iudicium; 1990. 651 pp. (Proceedings of the Congress of the International Comparative Literature Association 12: 4.) [†Marginality.]

[206] Vasil'ev, Igor'. "Dvukhgolosnaia fuga: Konstantin Rudakov: Grafika i illiustratsiia." *LO*. 1990; 3: 75-77. [†Illustration by Rudakov, Konstantin Ivanovich.]

[207] Webb, Robert L. "'Apocalyptic': Observations on a Slippery Term." *JNES*. 1990 Apr.; 49(2): 115-126. [†Apocalyptic literature; relationship to Dead Sea scrolls.]

[208] Weinberger, Miriam. "Bibliotherapia VeShimusheiha BeSifrut Yeladim VeNoar." *Be'emmet*. 1989 Spring; 3: 159-169. [†For children; young adults. Role of bibliotherapy.]

[209] Wiercińska, Janina. "Ilustracja w książce literackiej polskiego oświecenia." *RoHum*. 1987; 35(4): 167-181. [Illus. †Illustration in Poland (1700-1899).]

[210] Williams, Raymond L.; Vélez, Margarita, tr. "Entrevista a Walter J. Ong, S.J." *Revista de Estudios Colombianos*. 1987; 4: 71-72. [†Orality. Interview with Ong, Walter J.]

[211] Wilson, Katharina M., ed.; Warnke, Frank J., ed. *Women Writers of the Seventeenth Century*. Athens: U of Georgia P; 1989. xxiii, 545 pp. [Incl. introd. †By women writers. 1600-1699. Includes biobibliographical information.]

[212] Winner, Irene Portis. "How Ethnic Texts Speak." *CASS*. 1988; 22(1-4): 173-187. [†Communication in ethnic text.]

[213] Woodcock, John. "Teaching Literature and Medicine: Theoretical, Curricular, and Classroom Perspectives." 41-54 in Clarke, Bruce, ed.; Aycock, Wendell, ed. *The Body and the Text: Comparative Essays in Literature and Medicine*. Lubbock: Texas Tech UP; 1990. ix, 221 pp. (SCLit 22.) [†And medicine. Pedagogical approach.]

[214] Worthington, Pepper, introd. "Special Issue: Great Literature: What, Why, and Who Creates It?" *MOR*. 1990 Spring; 4. [Spec. iss.]

Bibliography

[215] Adams, Gillian; Anderson, Celia; DeLuca, Geraldine; Gellert, James; Hunt, Peter; Shaner, Mary; Wilson, Anita. "The Year's Work in Children's Literature Studies: 1988." *CLAQ*. 1990 Summer; 15(2): 58-107. [†For children. (1988).]

[216] Borck, Jim Springer, ed. *The Eighteenth Century: A Current Bibliography N.S. 11—for 1985*. New York: AMS; 1990. viii, 738 pp. [†1700-1799. (1985).]

[217] Cohen, Selma Jeanne, comp.; Barricelli, Jean-Pierre, comp.; Clüver, Claus, comp. & ed.; Faris, Wendy, comp.; Flanigan, C. Clifford, comp.; Kelly, James R., comp.; Reynolds, John J., comp.; Scher, Steven P., comp. & contrib. ed.; Wallace, Robert K., comp. "1987 Bibliography on the Relations of Literature and Other Arts." *YCGL*. 1987; 36: 205-248. [†Relationship to art. (1987).]

[218] Krömer, Tilman, ed. "Germanistik: Internationales Referatenorgan mit bibliographischen Hinweisen." *Germanistik*. 1989; 30(1). 1989; 30(2). 1989; 30(3). 1989; 30(4). 1990; 31(1). 1990; 31(2). 1990; 31(3). 1990; 31(4).

[219] Reinhold, Meyer, ed.; Hanawalt, Emily Albu, ed.; Barkey, Sandra Jamie, ed. "Bibliography of the Classical Tradition for 1987." *CML*. 1990 Spring; 10(3): 183-286. [Incl. pref. †Relationship to classical literature. (1987).]

[220] Thompson, George Austin, Jr. "An Annotated Bibliography of Reference Materials in Comparative and World Literature." *DAI*. 1990 Mar.; 50(9): 2890A. [†Dissertation abstract.]

Film

[221] "Zelenye rostki v zloveshcheĭ teni: Evgeniĭ Evtushenko o svoem fil'me 'Pokhorony Stalina'." *LG*. 1990 Mar. 28; 13 [5287]: 3. [†On Evtushenko, Evgeniĭ Aleksandrovich: *Pokhorony Stalina*. Interview.]

[222] Acland, Charles R. "Tampering with the Inventory: Colorization and Popular Histories." *WAn*. 1990 Apr.; 12(2): 12-20. [†Role of colorization.]

[223] Adkins, Joan F. "Sacrifice and Dehumanization in Plievier's *Stalingrad*." *WL&A*. 1990 Spring; 2(1): 1-22. [†Treatment of World War II; relationship to sacrifice in Plievier, Theodor: *Stalingrad*.]

[224] Aguinaga, Raúl de; Dube, Renu; Fraser, Diane; Ortuño, Michelle. "The Ideological Instances in *Scarface*." *Sociocriticism*. 1989; 5(1 [9]): 109-112. [†Treatment of power in Hawks, Howard: *Scarface*.]

[225] Allen, Robert C. "From Exhibition to Reception: Reflections on the Audience in Film History." *Screen*. 1990 Winter; 31(4): 347-356. [†Role of audience in film history; relationship to exhibition. Reception study.]

[226] Alm, Richard. "Bryllupsfesten: Landdryg 'folkekomedie'." *Z*. 1989; 30(4): 12. [†On Wam, Svend and Vennerød, Petter: *Bryllupsfesten*.]

[227] Ambrosini, R.; Matera, V.; Sanfilippo, M. "*Tony Goes to Hollywood*: Gli italo-americani e il cinema." *Veltro*. 1990 May-Aug.; 34(3-4): 373-387. [It., Fr., & Eng. sums. †Treatment of Italian Americans.]

[228] Arbitman, Roman. "Otvety mognut byt' raznymi: Po stranitsam zhurnala 'Iskusstvo Kino'." *LO*. 1990; 10: 61-65. [†Treatment in *Iskusstvo Kino*.]

[229] Armour, Robert A. "Biograph and the Invention of Movie Reviews and Screenwriting." *SiPC*. 1989; 12(2): 61-69. [†And screenplay; film review; relationship to American Biograph Company; study example: Woods, Frank E.; Griffith, D. W.]

[230] ——. "Comic Strips, Theatre, and Early Narrative Films 1895-1904." *SiPC*. 1987; 10(1): 14-26. [†And comic strip; theater; relationship to popular culture (1895-1903).

[231] Arnold, Alison. "Popular Film Song in India: A Case of Mass-Market Musical Eclecticism." *Popular Music*. 1988 May; 7(2): 177-188. [†In India. Role of folk song.]

[232] Balio, Tino. "When Is an Independent Producer Independent? The Case of United Artists after 1948." *VLT*. 1986; 22: 53-64. [Illus. †By independent filmmakers. Relationship to film industry; study example: United Artists Corporation. Film history.]

[233] Banka, Michael. "Interview on Elm Street: An Interview with Wes Craven." *Cineaste*. 1990; 17(3): 22-25. [†Interview with Craven, Wes.]

[234] Bargainnier, Earl F. "The Sahara of the 1920's: Popular Images of *Araby*." *SiPC*. 1985; 8(1): 37-45. [†And fiction. Treatment of Middle East.]

[235] Barr, Charles. "A Letter from Charles Barr." *VLT*. 1985 Summer; 21: 5-7. [On *Film Quarterly*. 1963 Summer; 16(4): 4-24. †On wide-screen. CinemaScope.]

[236] Barry, Thomas F. "The Weight of Angels: Peter Handke and *Der Himmel über Berlin*." *MAL*. 1990; 23(3-4): 53-64. [†Role of Handke, Peter in Wenders, Wim: *Der Himmel über Berlin*.]

[237] Batchan, Alexander. "The 'Alienation' of Slava Tsukerman." 15-34 in Petrie, Graham, ed.; Dwyer, Ruth, ed. *Before the Wall Came Down: Soviet and East European Filmmakers Working in the West*. Lanham, MD: UP of America; 1990. 249 pp. [Discussion, 45-47. †On Tsukerman, Slava: *Liquid Sky*. Interview.]

[238] ——. "Andrei Plakhov on the Work of the Conflicts Commission." *WAn*. 1990 Oct.; 12(4): 76-80. [†In U.S.S.R. Interview with Plakhov, Andreí.]

[239] Bates, Milton J. "Men, Women, and Vietnam." 27-63 in Gilman, Owen W., Jr., ed.; Smith, Lorrie, ed. *America Rediscovered: Critical Essays on Literature and Film of the Vietnam War*. New York: Garland; 1990. xix, 386 pp. (GRLH 986.) [†Treatment of Vietnam War; male-female relations in Kasdan, Lawrence: *The Big Chill* compared to Mason, Bobbie Ann: *In Country*.]

[240] Bates, Peter. "Lost and Found." *Cineaste*. 1990; 17(4): 56-57. [†On McNaughton, John: *Henry: Portrait of a Serial Killer*.]

[241] Bathrick, David, ed.; Rentschler, Eric, ed. "Special Issue on Weimar Mass Culture." *NGC*. 1990 Fall; 51. [Spec. iss.; incl. introd. †In Germany (1918-1933).]

[242] Bazin, André; Jones, Catherine, tr.; Neupert, Richard, tr. "Three Essays on Widescreen." *VLT*. 1985 Summer; 21: 8-16. [Tr. of *Esprit*. 1953 Oct.-Nov.; 207-208: 672-683; *Cahiers du Cinéma*. 1954 Jan.; 31: 43; & *Cahiers du Cinéma*. 1955 June; 48: 45-47. †On wide-screen. CinemaScope compared to Cinerama.]

[243] Becker, Jens P., ed. *Filme*. Heidelberg: Winter; 1988. 206 pp. (Anglistik und Englischunterricht 36.) [Incl. introd.]

[244] Beebe, John. "The Notorious Postwar Psyche." *JPFT*. 1990 Spring; 18(1): 28-35. [†Treatment of mother; relationship to Nazism in postwar period in Hitchcock, Alfred: *Notorious*. Application of theories of Jung, Carl Gustav.]

[245] Beledian, Krikor. "Der stumme Film der Rede: In Memoriam Sergej Paradschanow." *Horen*. 1990; 35(4 [160]): 178-185. [†On Paradzhanov, Sergeí: *Saiat Nova*.]

[246] Bellamy, Michael. "Carnival and Carnage: Falling Like Rock Stars and Second Lieutenants." 10-26 in Gilman, Owen W., Jr., ed.; Smith, Lorrie, ed. *America Rediscovered: Critical Essays on Literature and Film of the Vietnam War*. New York: Garland; 1990. xix, 386 pp. (GRLH 986.) [†Treatment of Vietnam War in Carradine, David: *Americana*.]

[247] Bellour, Raymond; Polan, Dana, tr. "Believing in the Cinema." 98-109 in Kaplan, E. Ann, ed.; Bellour, Raymond, afterword; Rosolato, Guy, afterword. *Psychoanalysis & Cinema*. London: Routledge; 1990. xi, 249 pp. (AFI Film Readers.) [†Role of Tourneur, Jacques.]

[248] Bender, Felicia. "Mothers of Invention: The Rise and Fall and Rise of Women Film Directors." *PVR*. 1990 Winter; 18(1): 61-68. [†In Hollywood by women filmmakers.]

[249] Benson, Peter. "Screening Desire." *Screen*. 1990 Winter; 31(4): 377-389. [Incl. photogs. †Treatment of desire in Seidelman, Susan: *Desperately Seeking Susan*. Psychoanalytic approach.]

[250] Bergstrom, Janet. "Psychological Explanation in the Films of Lang and Pabst." 163-180 in Kaplan, E. Ann, ed.; Bellour, Raymond, afterword; Rosolato, Guy, afterword. *Psychoanalysis & Cinema*. London: Routledge; 1990. xi, 249 pp. (AFI Film Readers.) [†By Lang, Fritz; Pabst, Georg Wilhelm. Psychoanalytic approach.]

[251] Bergstrom, Janet, ed.; Doane, Mary Ann, ed. "The Spectatrix." *CamObsc*. 1989 Sept.; 20-21. [Spec. iss.; incl. introd. †Female spectator.]

[252] Bernstein, Matthew. "Fritz Lang, Incorporated." *VLT*. 1986; 22: 33-52. [Illus. †By Lang, Fritz; relationship to independent filmmakers; film studios. Film history.]

[253] Bernstein, Matthew, ed. "American Widescreen." *VLT*. 1985 Summer; 21. [Spec. iss.; incl. introd. & bibliog. †On wide-screen.]

[254] Bernstein, Matthew, ed. & introd. "Hollywood Independents." *VLT*. 1986; 22. [Incl. photos. †By independent filmmakers. Film history.]

[255] Berry, Chris; He, Xiujun. "Leftist Chinese Cinema of the Thirties." *Cineaste*. 1990; 17(3): 36-37. [†In China (1930-1939). Treatment of the Left.]

[256] Bertolina, Gian Carlo. "Mario Monicelli e la commedia come riflessione sociale." *Letture*. 1990 May; 45(467): 391-402. [†By Monicelli, Mario.]

[257] Beylie, Claude; Sturm, Georges. "La Cinémathèque universitaire." *CICIM*. 1989 May; 26: 86-94. [Rpt. from *CinémAction*. 1987; 45. †In France. Role of Cinémathèque universitaire; relationship to archives.]

[258] Biesty, Patrick. "The Myth of the Playful Dancer." *SiPC*. 1990; 13(1): 73-88. [†Treatment of dancer; relationship to play; American dream.]

[259] Bini, Luigi. "I fratelli Taviani: Cinema fra ideologia e fantasia, I & II." *Letture*. 1990 Feb.; 45(464): 105-118. 1990 Mar.; 45(465): 199-212. [†By Taviani, Paolo and Taviani, Vittorio.]

[260] ——. "Il 'Decalogo' di K. Kieslowski: Dieci storie de vita." *Letture*. 1990 Nov.; 45(471): 781-796. [†On Kieslowski, Krzysztof: *Dekalog*.]

[261] Blaetz, Robin J. "Strategies of Containment: Joan of Arc in Film." *DAI*. 1990 Mar.; 50(9): 2680A. [†Treatment of Jeanne d'Arc, Saint. Dissertation abstract.]

[262] Blomkvist, Mårten. "Riktiga och 'naturliga' filmdjur." *OB*. 1989; 3: 76-77. [†Treatment of animals; relationship to sympathy; sentimentality in Annaud, Jean-Jacques: *L'Ours* compared to Disney, Walt.]

[263] Blum-Reid, Sylvie. "The Voice-Over in *India Song* by Marguerite Duras." *Journal of Durassian Studies*. 1989 Fall; 1: 35-45. [†Voice-over narration in Duras, Marguerite: *India Song*.]

[264] Blythe, Martin. "The Romance of Maoriland: Ethnography Tourism in New Zealand Films." *EW*. 1990 June; 4(2): 90-110. [†In New Zealand. Treatment of tourism; ethnography; relationship to Maori in McDonald, James.]

[265] Bordwell, David. "Widescreen Aesthetics and Mise en Scène Criticism." *VLT*. 1985 Summer; 21: 18-25. [Incl. photos. †On wide-screen. *Mise en scène*. Application of theories of Bazin, André.]

[266] Borstein, Yigal. "Panim Kisdeh-Krav: HaHistoria HaKolnoit shel HaPanim HaYisraelim." *Moznayim*. 1989; 63(5-6): 84-95. [†Treatment of Israeli history.]

[267] Bourdette, Robert E., Jr. "Rereading *The Deer Hunter*: Michael Cimino's Deliberate American Epic." 165-188 in Gilman, Owen W., Jr., ed.; Smith, Lorrie, ed. *America Rediscovered: Critical Essays on Literature and Film of the Vietnam War*. New York: Garland; 1990. xix, 386 pp. (GRLH 986.) [†Role of historical context in Cimino, Michael: *The Deer Hunter*.]

[268] Bower, Anne L. "Tyranny, Telling, Learning: Teaching the Female Student." *WVUPP*. 1990; 36: 38-45. [†Treatment of student-teacher interaction in Gilbert, Lewis: *Educating Rita* compared to Spark, Muriel: *The Prime of Miss Jean Brodie*; Shaw, George Bernard: *Pygmalion*; Ionesco, Eugène: *La Leçon*.]

[269] Brashinsky, Michael. "The Ant Hill in the Year of the Dragon." *NOR*. 1990 Spring; 17(1): 74-78. [Illus. †In U.S.S.R. Relationship to *perestroïka*.]

[270] Bredella, Lothar. "How to Cope with Evil? References to the Holocaust in American Films of the 1970s and 1980s." 51-92 in Freese, Peter, ed. *Germany and German Thought in American Literature and Cultural Criticism*. Essen: Blaue Eule; 1990. (Arbeiten zur Amerikanistik 6.) [†In United States (1970-1989). Treatment of the Holocaust.]

[271] Brians, Paul. "Nuclear Family/Nuclear War." *PLL*. 1990 Winter; 26(1): 134-142. [†Treatment of nuclear war; relationship to female point of view in Littman, Lynne: *Testament* compared to McCloy, Helen: *The Last Day*; Merril, Judith: *Shadow on the Hearth*.]

[272] Brill, Lesley. "*The Misfits* and the Idea of John Huston's Films." *Proteus*. 1990 Fall; 7(2): 9-17. [†On Huston, John: *The Misfits*.]

[273] Budra, Paul. "Rambo in the Garden: The POW Film as Pastoral." *LFQ*. 1990; 18(3): 188-192. [†Role of pastoralism in Kotcheff, Ted: *First Blood* compared to Cosmatos, George Pan: *Rambo II*; Mulcahy, Russell: *Rambo III*.]

[274] Bueno, Eva; Oviedo, José; Varona, Michael. "*Scarface*: The Erasure of Society and the Narrative of Prophecy." *Sociocriticism*. 1989; 5(1 [9]): 113-117. [†Treatment of prophecy; fatalism in Hawks, Howard: *Scarface*.]

[275] Burch, Noël; Brewster, Ben, ed. & tr. *Life to Those Shadows*. Berkeley: U of California P; 1990. 317 pp. [†Language. Film history.]

[276] Burke, Frank. "Federico Fellini: From Representation to Signification." *RLA: Romance Languages Annual*. 1989; 1: 34-40. [†Representation; relationship to signification in Fellini, Federico.]

[277] Burzlaff, Werner. "Phanéoscopies du film." 359-371 in Deledalle, Gérard, ed. *Semiotics and Pragmatics*. Amsterdam: Benjamins; 1989. 467 pp. (FoS 18.) [†Speech acts. Application of theories of Peirce, Charles Sanders.]

[278] Byg, Barton. "What Might Have Been: DEFA Films of the Past and the Future of German Cinema." *Cineaste*. 1990; 17(4): 9-15. [†In East Germany.]

[279] Callejas, Bernardo. "Con Fernando Solanas: 'Relanzar la hermosa y necesaria idea de una cinematografía latinoamericana'." *UdLH*. 1989 Sept.-Dec.; 236: 215-224. [†Interview with Solanas, Fernando G.]

[280] Cameron, Deborah. "Discourses of Desire: Liberals, Feminists, and the Politics of Pornography in the 1980s." *AmLH*. 1990 Winter; 2(4): 784-798. [†As pornography; relationship to feminism. Review article.]

[281] Carbine, Mary. "The Finest Outside the Loop': Motion Picture Exhibition in Chicago's Black Metropolis, 1905-1928." *CamObsc*. 1990 May; 23: 9-41. [†In Chicago (1905-1928). Relationship to exhibition in African American neighborhoods.]

[282] Cardullo, Bert. "Some Notes on Classic Films." *NOR*. 1990 Summer; 17(2): 5-13. [Illus.]

[283] Castiglia, Christopher. "Rebel without a Closet." 207-221 in Boone, Joseph A., ed.; Cadden, Michael, ed. *Engendering Men: The Question of Male Feminist Criticism*. New York: Routledge; 1990. vi, 333 pp. [†Treatment of homosexuality in Ray, Nicholas: *Rebel without a Cause* compared to Cates, Gilbert: *Consenting Adult*.]

[284] Caughie, John; Frith, Simon. "The British Film Institute: Re-Tooling the Culture Industry." *Screen*. 1990 Summer; 31(2): 214-222. [See also MacCabe, below. †In Great Britain. Role of British Film Institute.]

SEE SUBJECT INDEX FOR CROSS-REFERENCES

[285] Cavell, Stanley. "Postscript (1989): To Whom It May Concern." *CritI*. 1990 Winter; 16(2): 248-289. [On Sedgwick, Eve Kosofsky. "The Beast in the Closet: James and the Writing of Homosexual Panic." in *Sex, Politics, and Science in the Nineteenth-Century Novel*. †Treatment of homosexuality in Ophüls, Max: *Letter from an Unknown Woman* compared to James, Henry, Jr.: "The Beast in the Jungle."]

[286] ——. "Ugly Duckling, Funny Butterfly: Bette Davis and *Now, Voyager*." *CritI*. 1990 Winter; 16(2): 213-289. [Illus. †Treatment of women; relationship to marriage in Rapper, Irving: *Now, Voyager*.]

[287] Cesare, Tony. "Pasolini's Theorem." *FilmC*. 1989 Fall; 14(1): 22-25. [†Treatment of the sacred in Pasolini, Pier Paolo: *Teorema*.]

[288] Chow, Rey. "Silent Is the Ancient Plain: Music, Filmmaking, and the Conception of Reform in China's New Cinema." *Discourse*. 1990 Spring-Summer; 12(2): 82-109. [†In China. Treatment of reform in Ch'en K'ai-ko: *Huang t'u-ti*; *Ta yueh ping*; *Hai-tzu wang*.]

[289] Christensen, Julie. "Fathers and Sons at the Georgian Film Studio." *WAn*. 1990 Oct.; 12(4): 48-60. [†In Georgian S.S.R. Treatment of youth.]

[290] Christensen, Peter G. "Eisenstein's *Ivan the Terrible* and Shakespeare's Historical Plays." *SEEA*. 1990 Winter; 6(2): 124-138. [†Treatment of Russian history in Ĕĭzenshteĭn, Sergeĭ Mikhaĭlovich: *Ivan Groznyĭ*. Sources in Shakespeare, William.]

[291] ——. "The Representation of the Late Eighteenth Century in the von Baky/Kästner *Baron Münchhausen*: The Old Regime and Its Links to the Third Reich." *GL&L*. 1990 Oct.; 44(1): 13-24. [†Treatment of aristocracy; relationship to Third Reich in Baky, Josef von: *Münchhausen*; Kästner, Erich: *Baron Münchhausen*.]

[292] ——. "Skolimowski's *The Lightship* and Conrad." 85-101 in Petrie, Graham, ed.; Dwyer, Ruth, ed. *Before the Wall Came Down: Soviet and East European Filmmakers Working in the West*. Lanham, MD: UP of America; 1990. 249 pp. [Discussion, 139-142. †On Skolimowski, Jerzy: *The Lightship* compared to Conrad, Joseph: *Victory*.]

[293] Clark, Danae A. "Actor's Labor and the Politics of Subjectivity: Hollywood in the 1930s." *DAI*. 1990 Aug.; 51(2): 320A. [†In Hollywood (1933). Role of actors as workers; relationship to subjectivity. Dissertation abstract.]

[294] Clover, Carol J., ed.; Rogin, Michael, ed. "Entertaining History: American Cinema and Popular Culture." *Representations*. 1990 Winter; 29: 1-123. [Spec. sect. †In United States. Relationship to popular culture.]

[295] Coates, Paul. "Exile and Identity: Kieslowski and His Contemporaries." 103-114 in Petrie, Graham, ed.; Dwyer, Ruth, ed. *Before the Wall Came Down: Soviet and East European Filmmakers Working in the West*. Lanham, MD: UP of America; 1990. 249 pp. [Discussion, 139-142. †By Kieslowski, Krzysztof; relationship to exile.]

[296] Cobbs, John L. "*Alien* as an Abortion Parable." *LFQ*. 1990; 18(3): 198-201. [†Treatment of sexuality; abortion in Scott, Ridley: *Alien*.]

[297] Cohen, Keith. "Pleasures of Voicing: Oral Intermittences in Two Films by Alain Resnais." *ECr*. 1990 Summer; 30(2): 58-67. [†Voice in Resnais, Alain: *L'Année dernière à Marienbad*; *Hiroshima mon amour*.]

[298] Colvile, Georgiana. "Children Being Filmed by Truffaut." *FR*. 1990 Feb.; 63(3): 444-451. [†Treatment of children in Truffaut, François: *Les Quatre Cents Coups*; *L'Enfant sauvage*; *L'Argent de poche*. Theories of Freud, Sigmund.]

[299] Conley, Tom. "Tirez sur le PP." *ECr*. 1990 Summer; 30(2): 26-37. [In Eng. †By Truffaut, François: *Tirez sur le pianiste*.]

[300] Conley, Verena Andermatt. "A Fraying of Voices: Jean-Luc Godard's *Prénom Carmen*." *ECr*. 1990 Summer; 30(2): 68-80. [†On Godard, Jean-Luc: *Prénom Carmen*.]

[301] Conlon, James. "Making Love, Not War: The Soldier Male in *Top Gun* and *Coming Home*." *JPFT*. 1990 Spring; 18(1): 18-27. [†Treatment of masculinity; relationship to love; war in Ashby, Hal: *Coming Home*; Scott, Tony: *Top Gun*.]

[302] Cormack, Michael James. "Ideology and Cinematographic Style in Hollywood Films of the Thirties." *DAI*. 1990 Dec.; 51(6): 1809A. [†In Hollywood (1930-1939). Style; relationship to semiotics; ideology. Dissertation abstract.]

[303] Cormier, Raymond. "The Metaphorical Window in Truffaut's *Small Change*." *FR*. 1990 Feb.; 63(3): 452-463. [†On Truffaut, François: *L'Argent de poche* as pedagogical tool.]

[304] Costanzo, Angelo, ed.; Custer, Elizabeth Penn, introd. "Film Career of John Huston." *Proteus*. 1990 Fall; 7(2). [Spec. iss. †By Huston, John.]

[305] Craik, Philip Lee. "Musical Theory and Practice in the Stage, Film, and Non-Theatre Collaborative Works of Bertolt Brecht and Hanns Eisler, 1930-1956." *DAI*. 1990 June; 50(12): 3796A. [†Collaboration between Brecht, Bertolt and Eisler, Hanns. Dissertation abstract.]

[306] Cro, Stelio. "Il resto è letteratura: I film di Alain Resnais." *LFC*. 1987 July; 20: 13-25. [†By Resnais, Alain.]

[307] Crowdus, Gary. "Keeping Alive the Memory of the Holocaust: An Interview with Costa-Gavras." *Cineaste*. 1990; 17(3): 4-7. [†Interview with Costa-Gavras, Constantin.]

[308] Cubitt, Sean, ed. "Over the Borderlines: Questioning National Identities." *Screen*. 1989 Autumn; 30(4). [Spec. iss.; incl. introd. †Relationship to national identity.]

[309] Damnjanović, Milan. "Film, teorija filma, estetika filma." *Izraz*. 1990 Feb.-Mar.; 34(2-3): 357-372. [†And film theory and criticism.]

[310] de Lauretis, Teresa. "Guerrilla in the Midst: Women's Cinema in the 80's." *Screen*. 1990 Spring; 31(1): 6-25. [Incl. photos. †Alternative film by women filmmakers for women.]

[311] De Santi, Gualtiero. "Il principio d'avventura dell'immagine." *SULLA*. 1986; 59: 141-155. [†In Italy (1945-1950). Theories of Barthes, Roland.]

[312] De Santis, Giuseppe; Lawton, Ben, introd. & tr.; Lawton, Lorraine, introd. & tr. "Birth, Development, and Death of Neorealism." *RLA: Romance Languages Annual*. 1989; 1: 2-6. [†Neorealism.]

[313] Decock, Jean. "Entretien avec Louis Malle: Un Cinéma du regard." *FR*. 1990 Mar.; 63(4): 671-678. [†By Malle, Louis. Interview.]

[314] deCordova, Richard. "Ethnography and Exhibition: The Child Audience, the Hays Office and Saturday Matinees." *CamObsc*. 1990 May; 23: 91-106. [†For children (1920-1939). Relationship to ethnography. Reception study.]

[315] ——. *Picture Personalities: The Emergence of the Star System in America*. Urbana: U of Illinois P; 1990. x, 160 pp. [†In United States (1907-1922). Role of star system.]

[316] Denisoff, R. Serge; Romanowski, William D. "The Pentagon's Top Guns: Movies and Music." *JACult*. 1989 Fall; 12(3): 67-78. [†Treatment of war; role of United States Department of Defense.]

[317] DeRose, David J. "A Dual Perspective: First-Person Narrative in Vietnam Film and Drama." 109-119 in Gilman, Owen W., Jr., ed.; Smith, Lorrie, ed. *America Rediscovered: Critical Essays on Literature and Film of the Vietnam War*. New York: Garland; 1990. xix, 386 pp. (GRLH 986.) [†Narrative voice. Treatment of Vietnam War compared to Rabe, David: *Sticks and Bones*; *Streamers*; *The Basic Training of Pavlo Hummel*.]

[318] Dick, Bernard F. *Anatomy of Film*. New York: St. Martin's; 1990. xiv, 273 pp. [2nd ed.]

[319] Dickerson, Gary Edward. "Images of America in Baseball Films." *DAI*. 1990 May; 50(11): 3387A. [†(1929-1984). Treatment of baseball in United States. Dissertation abstract.]

[320] Dixon, Wheeler Winston. *Archetypes of the Heavy in Classical Hollywood Cinema*. Bowling Green: Popular; 1990. 243 pp. [†Treatment of stock characters in Hollywood film.]

[321] ——. "Film and Literature: The Narrative Connection." *Thousand Oaks Journal*. 1987 Fall; 1(1): 35-38. [†Narrative.]

[322] Dowell, Pat. "Black Rain: Hollywood Goes Japan Bashing." *Cineaste*. 1990; 17(3): 8-10. [†Treatment of Japan in Scott, Ridley: *Black Rain*.]

[323] Draper, Ellen. "'Controversy Has Probably Destroyed Forever the Context': *The Miracle* and Movie Censorship in America in the Fifties." *VLT*. 1990 Spring; 25: 69-79. [†On Rossellini, Roberto: *Il miracolo*; relationship to censorship.]

[324] Durovicova, Natasa. "Auditioning for America: Method, Madness and Banality in *Anna*." 115-123 in Petrie, Graham, ed.; Dwyer, Ruth, ed. *Before the Wall Came Down: Soviet and East European Filmmakers Working in the West*. Lanham, MD: UP of America; 1990. 249 pp. [Discussion, 139-142. †On Bogajewicz, Jurek: *Anna*.]

[325] Dyer, Richard. "Less and More Than Women and Men: Lesbian and Gay Cinema in Weimar Germany." *NGC*. 1990 Fall; 51: 5-60. [†In Germany (1918-1933). Treatment of homosexuals.]

[326] Eagle, Herbert. "The Indexicality of *Little Vera* and the End of Socialist Realism." *WAn*. 1990 Oct.; 12(4): 26-37. [†Socialist realism in Pichul, Vasiliĭ: *Malen'kaia Vera*.]

[327] Edwardson, Mickie. "Patterns in Choosing Oscar-Winning Best Pictures." *JPFT*. 1990 Winter; 17(4): 130-138. [Incl. photos & tables. †Academy of Motion Picture Arts and Sciences awards.]

[328] Ehrlich, Linda C. "The Artist's Desire: Eight Films of Mizoguchi Kenji." *DAI*. 1990 Jan.; 50(7): 1829A. [†Treatment of artist in Mizoguchi Kenji. Dissertation abstract.]

[329] ——. "The Artist's Desire: Reflections on the Films of Mizoguchi Kenji." *EW*. 1990 June; 4(2): 1-13. [†Treatment of artist; relationship to desire in Mizoguchi Kenji.]

[330] Emery, Michael James. "U. S. Horror: Gothicism in the Work of William Faulkner, Thomas Pynchon, and Stanley Kubrick." *DAI*. 1990 Apr.; 50(10): 3227A. [†Treatment of Gothicism in Kubrick, Stanley compared to Faulkner, William: "A Rose for Emily"; *As I Lay Dying*; *Sanctuary*; Pynchon, Thomas: *V.*; *Gravity's Rainbow*; *The Crying of Lot 49*. Dissertation abstract.]

[331] Engel, Leonard. "Irony and Sentiment in *Prizzi's Honor*: Shades of Spade in the '80's." *Proteus*. 1990 Fall; 7(2): 18-21. [†Irony; relationship to sentimentality in Huston, John: *Prizzi's Honor*.]

[332] Feldstein, Richard. "Displaced Feminine Representation in Woody Allen's Cinema." 69-86 in Barr, Marleen S., ed.; Feldstein, Richard, ed. *Discontented Discourses: Feminism/Textual Intervention/Psychoanalysis*. Urbana: U of Illinois P; 1989. 250 pp. [†Treatment of female characters; phallocentrism in Allen, Woody. Feminist approach.]

[333] Fiedler, Leslie A. "Mythicizing the Unspeakable." *JAF*. 1990 Oct.-Dec.; 103(410): 390-399. [†Treatment of hero of Vietnam War; relationship to mythification.]

[334] Finney, Brian. "Suture in Literary Analysis." *LIT*. 1990 Nov.; 2(2): 131-144. [†Narrative technique; relationship to suture; focalization compared to Joyce, James: *A Portrait of the Artist as a Young Man*.]

[335] Finslo, Yngve. *Helt i sin tid: På eventyr in kinømorket*. Oslo: LNU/Cappelen; 1990. 155 pp. [†Treatment of hero.]

[336] Flitterman-Lewis, Sandy. *To Desire Differently: Feminism and the French Cinema*. Urbana: U of Illinois P; 1990. xii, 340 pp. [†In France by women filmmakers. Feminism in Dulac, Germaine; Epstein, Marie; Varda, Agnès.]

[337] Fragola, Anthony. "Surrealism Revisited: Style and Technique in Robbe-Grillet's *La Belle Captive* and *Eden and After*." *Symposium*. 1989-1990 Winter; 43(4): 260-273. [†By Robbe-Grillet, Alain: *La Belle Captive*; *L'Eden et après*. Sources in Surrealism.]

[338] Fraterrigo, Vincenzo. "La breve stagione del Neorealismo cinematografico italiano." *Journal: A Collection of Articles and Essays* (Hankuk Univ. of Foreign Studies, Seoul). 1989; 22: 471-485. [†In Italy. Neorealism.

[339] Frith, Simon. "[Popular Culture]." *Screen*. 1990 Summer; 31(2): 231-235. [On 1989 Bibliog. IV.996; 1989 Bibliog. I.7634; & Shiach, Morag. *Discourse on Popular Culture*. †Relationship to popular culture. Review article.]

[340] Fuchs, Daniel. "Strictly Movie." *Commentary*. 1989 Sept.; 88(3): 38-46. [†Screenplay by Fuchs, Daniel. Creative process.]

[341] Fuentes, Víctor. "Galdós en Buñuel: Sobre una simbiosis creadora." 515-522 in *Actas del Tercer Congreso Internacional de Estudios Galdosianos, II*. Las Palmas: Excmo. Cabildo Insular de Gran Canaria; 1990. 569 pp. [†By Buñuel, Luis. Sources in Pérez Galdós, Benito.]

[342] Fuller, Graham. "A Second Look." *Cineaste*. 1990; 17(4): 58-59. [†On Coppola, Francis Ford: *One from the Heart*.]

[343] Gabbard, Krin; Gabbard, Glen O. "Play It Again, Sigmund: Psychoanalysis and the Classical Hollywood Text." *JPFT*. 1990 Spring; 18(1): 7-17. [†Role of politics; myth in Curtiz, Michael: *Casablanca*. Psychoanalytic approach.]

[344] Gaines, Jane. "From Elephants to Lux Soap: The Programming and 'Flow' of Early Motion Picture Exploitation." *VLT*. 1990 Spring; 25: 29-43. [†Role of film star; relationship to advertising.]

[345] Gassen, Heiner. "Howard Vernon." *CICIM*. 1989 May; 26: 74-85. [Incl. photos. †Role of Vernon, Howard in Melville, Jean-Pierre: *Le Silence de la mer*; Lang, Fritz: *Die tausend Augen des Dr. Mabuse*. Includes discussion with Vernon.]

[346] George, Cynthia. "From Innocence to Grandeur: The Costumes of 'Gone with the Wind'." *LCUT*. 1986; 36: 33-55. [Illus. †Costume by Plunkett, Walter in Fleming, Victor: *Gone with the Wind*; relationship to Selznick, David O.]

[347] Gieri, Manuela. "The Pirandellian Mode in European Cinema: Luigi Pirandello and Federico Fellini." *DAI*. 1990 Jan.; 50(7): 1829A. [†Role of Fellini, Federico; Pirandello, Luigi. Dissertation abstract.]

[348] Gillespie, Gerald. "Savage Places Revisited: Conrad's *Heart of Darkness* and Coppola's *Apocalypse Now*." *Comparatist*. 1985 May; 9: 69-88. [†On Coppola, Francis Ford: *Apocalypse Now*. Sources in Conrad, Joseph: "Heart of Darkness."]

[349] Ginsberg, Terri. "Nazis and Drifters: The Containment of Radical (Sexual) Knowledge in Two Italian Neorealist Films." *Journal of the History of Sexuality*. 1990 Oct.; 1(2): 241-261. [†Treatment of sexuality; relationship to Nazism in Rossellini, Roberto: *Roma, città aperta*; Visconti, Luchino: *Ossessione*.]

[350] Goldberg, Marianne. "The Body, Discourse, and *The Man Who Envied Women*." *W&P*. 1987-1988; 3(2 [6]): 97-102. [†Narrative discourse. Treatment of female body in Rainer, Yvonne: *The Man Who Envied Women*.]

[351] Gomery, Douglas. "Thinking about Motion Picture Exhibition." *VLT*. 1990 Spring; 25: 3-11.

[352] Goulding, Daniel J. "The Films of Dusan Makavejev: Between East and West." 143-156 in Petrie, Graham, ed.; Dwyer, Ruth, ed. *Before the Wall Came Down: Soviet and East European Filmmakers Working in the West*. Lanham, MD: UP of America; 1990. 249 pp. [Discussion, 177-181. †By Makavejev, Dušan.]

[353] Green, Debra Louise. "The Divided I/Eye: Problems of Subjectivity in the Novels and Films of Marguerite Duras." *DAI*. 1989 Summer; 50(2): Item 687C. [†Subjectivity in Duras, Marguerite. Narratological approach. Dissertation abstract.]

[354] Green, Shelley Rae. "Radical Juxtaposition: The Films of Yvonne Rainer." *DAI*. 1990 Sept.; 51(3): 661A. [†By Rainer, Yvonne.]

[355] Greenberg, Harvey Roy, ed. "Psychoanalysis and Cinema." *JPFT*. 1990 Spring; 18(1). [Spec. iss.; incl. introd. †Relationship to psychoanalysis.]

[356] Griggers, Catherine Joan. "Reinventing the Popular: Inscriptions of the Feminine Subject in Postmodern Genres." *DAI*. 1990 Sept.; 51(3): 1024A. [†Treatment of female figures in DePalma, Brian: *Body Double*; Lynch, David: *Blue Velvet* compared to Acker, Kathy: *Don Quixote, Which Was a Dream*.]

[357] Grobel, Lawrence. "'We Were All John's Children'." *Proteus*. 1990 Fall; 7(2): 5-8. [†By Huston, John.]

[358] Gross, Robert. "Kane and Able: Welles's Film and Hampton's Screenplay." 79-94 in Gross, Robert, ed. *Christopher Hampton: A Casebook*. New York: Garland; 1990. xvii, 146 pp. (GRLH 989; Casebooks on Modern Dramatists 4.) [†Treatment of detection in Welles, Orson: *Citizen Kane* compared to Hampton, Christopher: *Able's Will*.]

[359] Grossi, Edoardo G. "Eisenstein e il progetto di 'Regissura'." *SULLA*. 1984; 57: 219-251. [†On Ėĭzenshteĭn, Sergeĭ Mikhaĭlovich: *Rezhissura*.]

[360] Grunberg, Slawomir. "A Polish Filmmaker in the United States." 125-131 in Petrie, Graham, ed.; Dwyer, Ruth, ed. *Before the Wall Came Down: Soviet and East European Filmmakers Working in the West*. Lanham, MD: UP of America; 1990. 249 pp. [Discussion, 139-142. †By Polish filmmakers.]

[361] Guerrero, Edward Villaluz. "The Ideology and Politics of Black Representation in U. S. Narrative Cinema." *DAI*. 1990 Nov.; 51(5): 1420A-1421A. [†Representation of African Americans; slavery. Dissertation abstract.]

[362] Haffner, Pierre. "Auf der Suche nach dem Kino in den Städten Schwarzafrikas." *CICIM*. 1989 Nov.; 27-28: 6-16. [Incl. photos. †In urban areas of black Africa.]

[363] ———. "Das Vorbild: Paulin Soumanou Vieyra." *CICIM*. 1989 Nov.; 27-28: 93-116. [Incl. photos. †By Vieyra, Paulin Soumanou.]

[364] ———. "Der Handel mit Filmen." *CICIM*. 1989 Nov.; 27-28: 17-23. [Incl. photos. †In black Africa. Role of film industry.]

[365] ———. "Der Held: Ababacar Samb-Makharam." *CICIM*. 1989 Nov.; 27-28: 117-134. [Incl. photos. †Interview with Samb-Makharam, Ababacar.]

[366] ———. "Der Widerstandskämpfer: Sembène Ousmane." *CICIM*. 1989 Nov.; 27-28: 76-92. [Incl. photos. †By Sembène Ousmane.]

[367] ———. "Die Chronik des Bösen." *CICIM*. 1989 Nov.; 27-28: 135-169. [Incl. photos. †Treatment of evil at Journées Cinématographiques de Carthage in Tunis (1988).]

[368] ———. "Die Gründerstädte des Films." *CICIM*. 1989 Nov.; 27-28: 47-58. [Incl. photos. †In black Africa. Relationship to urban areas.]

[369] ———. "Ein Handwerk, um das Leben zu verändern." *CICIM*. 1989 Nov.; 27-28: 170-187. [Incl. photos. †In black Africa. Production; relationship to neocolonialism.]

[370] ———. "Eine kleine Geographie des schwarzafrikanischen Kinos." *CICIM*. 1989 Nov.; 27-28: 24-34. [†In black Africa.]

[371] ———. "Eine nationale Schule: Der Niger." *CICIM*. 1989 Nov.; 27-28: 35-46. [Incl. photos. †In Niger.]

[372] ———. "Zur Ästhetik des schwarzafrikanischen Kinos." *CICIM*. 1989 Nov.; 27-28: 59-75. [Incl. photos. †In black Africa. Aesthetics.]

[373] Haffner, Pierre, ed.; Bartsch, Karola, tr.; Daigfuss, Elisabeth, tr.; Gassen, Heiner, tr.; Restorff, Brigitta, tr. "Kino in Schwarzafrika." *CICIM*. 1989 Nov.; 27-28. [Spec. iss.; incl. introd. †In black Africa.]

[374] Hagopian, Kevin. "Declarations of Independence: A History of Cagney Productions." *VLT*. 1986; 22: 16-32. [Incl. photos. †By independent filmmakers. Relationship to film studios; role of Cagney, James (1941-1948). Film history.]

[375] Hains, Maryellen. "Beauty and the Beast: 20th Century Romance?" *Merveilles & Contes*. 1989 May; 3(1): 75-83. [†On Cocteau, Jean: *La Belle et la bête* compared to McKinley, Robin: *Beauty*; romance novel; folk tale.]

[376] Hake, Sabine. "Architectural Hi/stories: Fritz Lang and *The Nibelungs*." *WAn*. 1990 July; 12(3): 38-57. [Illus. †Mise en scène; narrative; relationship to fascism in Lang, Fritz: *Siegfried*; *Kriemhilds Rache*.]

[377] ———. "Chaplin Reception in Weimar Germany." *NGC*. 1990 Fall; 51: 87-111. [†Role of Chaplin, Charles Spencer. Reception study: reception in Germany (1918-1933).]

[378] ———. "'Pardon, ich such den Autor dieses Films!': Zu Fritz von Unruhs *Phaea*." 171-184 in Koopmann, Helmut, ed.; Muenzer, Clark, ed. *Wegbereiter der Moderne*. Tübingen: Niemeyer; 1990. viii, 208 pp. [†Treatment of artist; relationship to mass media in Unruh, Fritz von: *Phaea*.]

[379] Hall, Kenneth E. *Guillermo Cabrera Infante and the Cinema*. Newark, DE: Juan de la Cuesta; 1989. xxiii, 240 pp. (Hispanic Monographs: Estudios de Literatura Latinoamericana "Irving A. Leonard" 3.) [†And film theory and criticism; role of Cabrera Infante, Guillermo.]

[380] Hall, Michael L. "*Jesus Christ, Superstar* and Medieval Drama: Anachronism and Humor." 111-115 in Emmerson, Richard K., ed.; Kolve, V. A., introd. *Approaches to Teaching Medieval English Drama*. New York: Mod. Lang. Assn. of Amer.; 1990. xvii, 182 pp. (Approaches to Teaching World Literature 29.) [†On Rice, Tim: *Jesus Christ Superstar*; relationship to English drama (1100-1499). Pedagogical approach.]

[381] Hanche, Øivind. "Penga eller livet—en Nordsjø-tragedie." *Z*. 1989; 30(4): 10-11. [†On Cole, Tristan de Vere: *Dykket*.]

[382] Hansen, Miriam. "Adventures of Goldilocks: Spectatorship, Consumerism and Public Life." *CamObsc*. 1990 Jan.; 22: 51-71. [†Treatment of women; relationship to consumerism. Film history.]

[383] Hansen, Miriam, ed. "Special Issue on Alexander Kluge." *NGC*. 1990 Winter; 49. [Spec. iss.; incl. introd. †By Kluge, Alexander.]

[384] Haralovich, Mary Beth. "The Proletarian Woman's Film of the 1930s: Contending with Censorship and Entertainment." *Screen*. 1990 Summer; 31(2): 172-187. [Incl. photos. †(1930-1939). Treatment of working women in Beaumont, Harry: *Our Blushing Brides* compared to Bacon, Lloyd: *Marked Woman*.]

[385] ———. "The Sexual Politics of *The Marriage of Maria Braun*." *WAn*. 1990 Jan.; 12(1): 6-16. [Illus. †Treatment of sexual identity; relationship to economics in Fassbinder, Rainer Werner: *Die Ehe der Maria Braun*.]

[386] Hardt, Ursula. "Erich Pommer: Film Producer for Germany." *DAI*. 1990 May; 50(11): 3387A. [†In Germany. Role of Pommer, Erich. Dissertation abstract.]

[387] Harty, Kevin J. "Film Treatments of the Legend of King Arthur." 278-290 in Lagorio, Valerie M., ed.; Day, Mildred Leake, ed. *King Arthur through the Ages, II*. New York: Garland; 1990. xvi, 335 pp. (GRLH 1301.) [†Treatment of Arthurian legend.]

[388] Haskell, Molly. "John Huston's Heart of Light and Darkness." *Proteus*. 1990 Fall; 7(2): 1-4. [†Treatment of women in Huston, John.]

[389] Hawkins, Harriett. *Classics and Trash: Traditions and Taboos in High Literature and Popular Modern Genres*. Toronto: U of Toronto P; 1990. xix, 219 pp. [†And English literature; American literature; popular fiction.]

[390] Heil, Jerry. "Isaak Babel and His Film Work." *RCSCSPL*. 1990 Apr. 1; 27(3): 289-416. [Monog. iss. †Screenplay by Babel', Isaak Ėmmanuilovich.]

[391] Henderson, Lisa Helen. "Cinematic Competence and Directorial Persona in Film School: A Study of Socialization and Cultural Production." *DAI*. 1990 Nov.; 51(5): 1421A. [†Ethnographic approach. Dissertation abstract.]

[392] Hernández García, Lissette. "Críticas sobre cine y teatro cubano: Arturo Arias Polo." *PH*. 1990 July-Sept.; 75: 195-206. [†In Cuba. Interview with Arias Polo, Arturo.]

SEE SUBJECT INDEX FOR CROSS-REFERENCES

[393] Higginbotham, Virginia. "Feminism and Buñuel: Points of Contact." *RLA: Romance Languages Annual*. 1989; 1: 464-467. [†Treatment of female characters; relationship to feminism in Buñuel, Luis.]

[394] Higson, Andrew. "The Concept of National Cinema." *Screen*. 1989 Autumn; 30(4): 36-46. [†Relationship to national identity.]

[395] Hill, John. "[Cinema and Society]." *Screen*. 1990 Summer; 31(2): 223-230. [†In Great Britain (1909-1972). Role of censorship. Review article.]

[396] Horne, Philip. "Henry Hill and Laura Palmer." *LRB*. 1990 Dec. 20; 12(24): 20-21. [†And television. On Lynch, David: *Twin Peaks*; *Blue Velvet*; Scorsese, Martin: *GoodFellas*; relationship to *film noir*.]

[397] Horton, Andrew. "Filmmaking in the Middle: From Belgrade to Beverly Hills: A Cautionary Tale." 157-167 in Petrie, Graham, ed.; Dwyer, Ruth, ed. *Before the Wall Came Down: Soviet and East European Filmmakers Working in the West*. Lanham, MD: UP of America; 1990. 249 pp. [Discussion, 177-181. †By Yugoslavian filmmakers. Relationship to Hollywood.]

[398] Horton, Andrew, introd. "Soviet Cinema Comes of Age." *NOR*. 1990 Spring; 17(1): 73-93. [Spec. sect.; illus. †In U.S.S.R.]

[399] Hwong, Lucia. "Political Commitment in Filmmaking: Oliver Stone." *ThirdR*. 1988; 9: 34-36. [†Relationship to politics. Interview with Stone, Oliver.]

[400] Iacono, Gianfranco. "Ambiguità de 'L'attimo fuggente': Dal vitalismo libertario all'occultismo." *Vita e Pensiero: Mensile di Cultura dell' Universitá Cattolica*. 1990 Apr.; 73(4): 281-292. [†Treatment of nihilism in Weir, Peter: *Dead Poets Society*.]

[401] Iversen, Gunnar. "Den levende fortiden: Om Martin Asphaugs film *En håndfull tid*." *Z*. 1989; 30(4): 6-7. [†On Asphaug, Martin: *En håndfull tid*.]

[402] ——. "Drømmer og dilettant: Om filmpioneren Peter Lykke-Seest." *Z*. 1989; 30(4): 38-42. [†By Lykke-Seest, Peter.]

[403] ——. "Portrett av en usynlig mann: Om Bjørn Breigutu og hans filmer." *Z*. 1989; 29(3): 52-56. [†By Breigutu, Bjørn.]

[404] Jacobs, Lea. "Reformers and Spectators: The Film Education Movement in the Thirties." *CamObsc*. 1990 Jan.; 22: 29-49. [†Film education (1930-1939).]

[405] Jacobs, Lea, ed.; Petro, Patrice, ed. "Feminism and Film History." *CamObsc*. 1990 Jan.; 22. [Spec. iss. †Relationship to feminism.]

[406] Jacobson, Denise Brooke. "Regional Film: A Resistance to Cultural Dominance." *DAI*. 1990 Jan.; 50(7): 1829A-1830A. [†In United States (1978-1988). Regionalism. Dissertation abstract.]

[407] Jaehne, Karen. "CEO and Cinderella: Interview with Dolly Parton." *Cineaste*. 1990; 17(4): 16-19. [†Interview with Parton, Dolly.]

[408] Jameson, Fredric. *Signatures of the Visible*. New York: Routledge; 1990. 254 pp. [†Treatment of history; relationship to postmodernist literary theory and criticism.]

[409] Jenkins, Henry. "'If I Could Speak with Your Sound': Fan Music, Textual Proximity, and Liminal Identification." *CamObsc*. 1990 May; 23: 149-175. [†Role of song by fans; relationship to Meyer, Nicholas: *Star Trek II: The Wrath of Khan*.]

[410] Johnson, Vida T. "The Films of Andrei Konchalovsky." 35-43 in Petrie, Graham, ed.; Dwyer, Ruth, ed. *Before the Wall Came Down: Soviet and East European Filmmakers Working in the West*. Lanham, MD: UP of America; 1990. 249 pp. [Discussion, 45-47. †By Mikhalkov-Konchalovskiĭ, Andreĭ Sergeevich.]

[411] Johnston, Claire. "Femininity and the Masquerade: *Anne of the Indies*." 64-72 in Kaplan, E. Ann, ed.; Bellour, Raymond, afterword; Rosolato, Guy, afterword. *Psychoanalysis & Cinema*. London: Routledge; 1990. xi, 249 pp. (AFI Film Readers.) [†Treatment of femininity; relationship to masquerade in Tourneur, Jacques: *Anne of the Indies*.]

[412] Joo, Jinsook. "Constraints on Korean National Film: The Intersection of History, Politics and Economics in Cultural Production." *DAI*. 1990 Dec.; 51(6): 1816A. [†In Korea (1987-1988). Dissertation abstract.]

[413] Kaige, Chen. "Breaking the Circle: The Cinema and Cultural Change in China." *Cineaste*. 1990; 17(3): 28-31. [†In China. Treatment of cultural change; relationship to Fifth Generation.]

[414] Kaitting, Mary Lou. "Parody in Cinema." 95-103 in Thomson, Clive, ed. *Essays on Parody*. Toronto: Victoria Univ.; 1986. 103 pp. (Monographs, Working Papers and Prepublications of The Toronto Semiotic Circle 4.) [†Parody.]

[415] Kanzog, Klaus; Ormrod, John, tr.; Weisstein, Ulrich, introd. "German Philology and the Analysis of Film." *YCGL*. 1988; 37: 145-152.

[416] Kaplan, E. Ann. "Consuming Images: The Images and Its Rhetoric in American and Cultural Studies." 39-68 in *Screen and Monitor: A Critical Investigation of Image Culture*. Taipai, Taiwan: Fu Jen UP; 1990. [†Imagery.]

[417] ——. "Discourses of the Mother in Postmodern Film and Culture." *Westerly*. 1989 Dec.; 34(4): 24-34. [†Treatment of motherhood; relationship to Postmodernism.]

[418] ——. "Motherhood and Representation: From Postwar Freudian Figurations to Postmodernism." 128-142 in Kaplan, E. Ann, ed.; Bellour, Raymond, afterword; Rosolato, Guy, afterword. *Psychoanalysis & Cinema*. London: Routledge; 1990. xi, 249 pp. (AFI Film Readers.) [†Treatment of motherhood. Psycholanalytic approach.]

[419] ——. "Sex, Work and Motherhood: The Impossible Triangle." *Journal of Sex Research*. 1990 Aug.; 27(3): 409-425. [†Treatment of sexuality; relationship to motherhood.]

[420] Kaplan, E. Ann, ed.; Bellour, Raymond, afterword; Rosolato, Guy, afterword. *Psychoanalysis & Cinema*. London: Routledge; 1990. xi, 249 pp. (AFI Film Readers.) [Incl. introd. †Relationship to psychoanalysis.]

[421] Karriker, Alexandra Heidi. "Patterns of Spirituality in Tarkovsky's Later Films." 183-201 in Petrie, Graham, ed.; Dwyer, Ruth, ed. *Before the Wall Came Down: Soviet and East European Filmmakers Working in the West*. Lanham, MD: UP of Ameri-

ca; 1990. 249 pp. [Discussion, 223-228. †Treatment of spirituality in Tarkovskiĭ, Andreĭ A.]

[422] Kear, Lynn. "Attitudes toward Popular Film, Learning, and Education: A Survey of Undergraduate College Students." *DAI*. 1990 May; 50(11): 3387A. [†Attitudes of college students. Pedagogical approach. Dissertation abstract.]

[423] Keller, Virginia Lin. "Multiple Points of View: Dialectics of Film Narration." *DAI*. 1990 Sept.; 51(3): 661A. [†Dialectics of narration. Dissertation abstract.]

[424] Kepley, Vance, Jr., ed. "Contemporary Soviet Cinema." *WAn*. 1990 Oct.; 12(4). [Spec.; incl. introd. †In U.S.S.R.]

[425] Kinder, Marsha. "The Subversive Potential of the Pseudo-Iterative." *FilmQ*. 1989-1990 Winter; 43(2): 3-16. [†Iterative narrative in Ford, John: *How Green Was My Valley* compared to Stevens, George Cooper: *A Place in the Sun*; De Sica, Vittorio: *Umberto D.*; Olmi, Ermanno: *Il posto*. Application of theories of Genette, Gérard.]

[426] Kirby, Lynne Elizabeth. "The Railroad and the Cinema, 1895-1929: Institutions, Aesthetics and Gender." *DAI*. 1990 Apr.; 50(10): 3091A-3902A. [†Treatment of train. Dissertation abstract.]

[427] Kirihara, Donald Paul. "Style and Tradition in Four Films by Kenji Mizoguchi." *DAI*. 1990 Mar.; 50(9): 2680A. [†(1930-1939). Narration in Mizoguchi Kenji. Dissertation abstract.]

[428] Kline, T. Jefferson, ed. "The Film and the Book." *ECr*. 1990 Summer; 30(2). [Spec. iss. †Relationship to French literature (1900-1999).]

[429] Knapp, Elise; Glen, Robert. "Milos Forman." *ECLife*. 1990 May; 14(2): 98-107. [†On Forman, Miloš: *Valmont*. Interview.]

[430] Korson, Tom. "The Beat Generation: An American Dream." *MSI*. 1989-1990 Winter; 22-23: 17. [†1900-1999. Treatment of Beat Generation in Forman, Janet: *The Beat Generation: An American Dream*.]

[431] Kosta, Barbara Kujundzich. "Personal Histories: Autobiography and Female Identity in Contemporary German Literature and Film." *DAI*. 1990 Apr.; 50(10): 3242A. [†Treatment of the self; female identity in Sanders-Brahms, Helma: *Deutschland, bleiche Mutter*; Brückner, Jutta: *Hungerjahre* compared to Wolf, Christa: *Kindheitsmuster*; Rehmann, Ruth: *Der Mann auf der Kanzel*. Dissertation abstract.]

[432] Kreuzer, Helmut, introd. "Weltkriege in Literatur und Film." *LiLi*. 1989; 19(75). [Spec. iss. †In Germany. And German literature. Treatment of World War I; World War II.]

[433] Kristensen, Bjørn Sverre. "Musikk til film—noen innfallsvinkler." *Z*. 1989; 30(4): 26-29. [†Role of music.]

[434] Krzemiński, Ireneusz. "Dekalog, Kieślowski i Bog." *DialogW*. 1990 July; 35(7 [406]): 123-127. [†Treatment of God; Christianity in Kieslowski, Krzysztof: *Dekalog*.]

[435] Kuberski, Philip. "Hardcopy: The Remains of the Cold War." *ArQ*. 1990 Summer; 46(2): 55-71. [†Relationship to Cold War; technology.]

[436] Kuhn, Annette, ed.; Radstone, Susannah, ed. *The Women's Companion to International Film*. London: Virago; 1990. xvi, 464 pp. [†By women filmmakers. Handbook.]

[437] La Piana, Siobhan. "Homosociality and the Postmodern Twin." *Constructions*. 1990: 15-33. [†Treatment of twins in Greenaway, Peter: *A Zed and Two Noughts* compared to Barth, John: "Petition"; Calvino, Italo: *Il visconte dimezzato*; Schwob, Marcel: *Les Sans-Gueules*. Feminist approach.]

[438] Lacy, Norris J. "Arthurian Film and the Tyranny of Tradition." *ArthI*. 1989 Fall; 4(1): 75-85. [†1900-1999. Treatment of Arthur in Boorman, John: *Excalibur*; Rohmer, Eric: *Perceval le Gallois*; Romero, George A.: *Knightriders*.]

[439] Langner-Burns, Heidi M. "The Image of Journalists in American Film and Fiction from 1975 to 1987: An Application of Leo Löwenthal's Model." *DAI*. 1990 June; 50(12): 3993A. [†In United States (1975-1987). And American fiction. Treatment of journalists. Application of theories of Lowenthal, Leo. Dissertation abstract.]

[440] Larsen, Kevin S. "*Tirano Banderas y Aguirre, der Zorn Gottes*: Diapositivas en un *continuum* cinematográfico." 376-382 in Fernández Jiménez, Juan, ed.; Labrador Herraiz, José J., ed.; Valdivieso, L. Teresa, ed.; Morón Arroyo, Ciriaco, pref. *Estudios en homenaje a Enrique Ruiz-Fornells*. Erie, PA: Asociación de Licenciados & Doctores Españoles en Estados Unidos; 1990. xxvi, 706 pp. (Homenajes 1.) [†Cinematic technique in Herzog, Werner: *Aguirre, der Zorn Gottes* compared to Valle-Inclán, Ramón María del: *Tirano Banderas*.]

[441] Lary, Nikita. "Eisenstein's (Anti-)Theatrical Art, from Kino-Fist to Kino-Tragedy." *SEEA*. 1990 Winter; 6(2): 88-123. [†And theater. Role of Ĕĭzenshteĭn, Sergeĭ Mikhaĭlovich.]

[442] Lavery, David. "Departure of the Body Snatchers: Or, The Confessions of a Carbon Chauvinist." *HudR*. 1986 Autumn; 39(3): 383-404. [†Treatment of denial of human body in Siegel, Don: *Invasion of the Body Snatchers*; Kaufman, Philip: *Invasion of the Body Snatchers*.]

[443] Lawton, Anna. "Soviet Cinema Four Years Later." *WAn*. 1990 Oct.; 12(4): 8-25. [†In U.S.S.R. Role of *perestroĭka*; relationship to Goskino.]

[444] Lawton, Ben. "'Remember, You Can't Live without Rossellini!'." 181-193 in Matteo, Sante, ed.; Noble, Cinzia Donatelli, ed.; Sowell, Madison U., ed. *Italian Echoes in the Rocky Mountains*. Provo, UT: David M. Kennedy Center for Internat. Studies & Amer. Assn. for It. Studies; 1990. xiv, 226 pp. [†On Rossellini, Roberto: *Roma, città aperta*.]

[445] Leach, Jim. "'Hideousness and Beauty': A Reading of Tarkovsky's *The Sacrifice*." 203-214 in Petrie, Graham, ed.; Dwyer, Ruth, ed. *Before the Wall Came Down: Soviet and East European Filmmakers Working in the West*. Lanham, MD:

UP of America; 1990. 249 pp. [Discussion, 223-228. †Representation in Tarkovskiĭ, Andreĭ A.: *Offret*.]

[446] Leibman, Nina Clare. "It's a Family Problem: The Representation of the American Family in Film and Television, 1954-1963." *DAI*. 1990 Oct.; 51(4): 1026A. [†And television in United States (1954-1963). Treatment of family. Dissertation abstract.]

[447] Leitch, Thomas M. "Twice Told Tales: The Rhetoric of the Remake." *LFQ*. 1990; 18(3): 138-148.

[448] Lellis, George. "Misplaced Mistrust: A Dissenting View of Milos Forman's *Amadeus*." 49-62 in Petrie, Graham, ed.; Dwyer, Ruth, ed. *Before the Wall Came Down: Soviet and East European Filmmakers Working in the West*. Lanham, MD: UP of America; 1990. 249 pp. [Discussion, 79-84. †On Forman, Miloš: *Amadeus*.]

[449] Lent, John A. *The Asian Film Industry*. Austin: U of Texas P; 1990. x, 309 pp. (Texas Film Studies Series.) [†In Asia.]

[450] Leto, Giovanni. "L'arco di Federico Fellini." *Belfagor*. 1990 May 31; 45(3 [267]): 327-332. [†By Fellini, Federico.]

[451] Leutrat, Jean-Louis; Liandrat-Guigues, Suzanne. "Le Sphinx." *ECr*. 1990 Summer; 30(2): 81-91. [†Treatment of postcards in Godard, Jean-Luc: *Les Carabiniers* compared to Simon, Claude: *Histoire*.]

[452] Linderman, Deborah. "Cinematic Abreaction: Tourneur's *Cat People*." 73-97 in Kaplan, E. Ann, ed.; Bellour, Raymond, afterword; Rosolato, Guy, afterword. *Psychoanalysis & Cinema*. London: Routledge; 1990. xi, 249 pp. (AFI Film Readers.) [†Cinematic technique in Tourneur, Jacques: *Cat People*. Psychoanalytic approach.]

[453] Lindroth, James. "Down the Yellow Brick Road: Two Dorothys and the Journey of Initiation in Dream and Nightmare." *LFQ*. 1990; 18(3): 160-166. [†Treatment of dream; relationship to initiation in Fleming, Victor: *The Wizard of Oz* compared to Lynch, David: *Blue Velvet*. Psychoanalytic approach.]

[454] Loiseau, Jean-Claude. "La saga de Indiana." *PH*. 1990 Jan.-Mar.; 73: 139-165. [†Characterization in Spielberg, Steven: *Indiana Jones: The Last Crusade*.]

[455] Lorch, Maristella, introd. "Rossellini in America." 169-193 in Matteo, Sante, ed.; Noble, Cinzia Donatelli, ed.; Sowell, Madison U., ed. *Italian Echoes in the Rocky Mountains*. Provo, UT: David M. Kennedy Center for Internat. Studies & Amer. Assn. for It. Studies; 1990. xiv, 226 pp. [Spec. sect. †By Rossellini, Roberto.]

[456] Lourdeaux, Lee. *Italian and Irish Filmmakers in America*. Philadelphia: Temple UP; 1990. xi, 288 pp. [†By Ford, John; Capra, Frank; Coppola, Francis Ford; Scorsese, Martin.]

[457] Løvø, Stein Åsmund; Dreyer, Lisbeth. "Mannen som tok Amanda for harde livet." *Z*. 1989; 30(4): 24-25. [†On Endresen, Sigve: *For harde livet*.]

[458] Lowry, Ed; Polan, Dana, introd. "Dimension Pictures: Portrait of a 70's Independent." *VLT*. 1986; 22: 65-74. [Illus. †By independent filmmakers (1970-1979). Study example: Dimension Pictures.]

[459] Loy, R. Philip. "Saints or Scoundrels: Images of Mormons in Literature and Film about the American West." *JASAT*. 1990 Oct.; 21: 57-74. [†And American literature. Treatment of Mormons in Western United States.]

[460] Luckhurst, Roger. "Shut(ting) the Fuck Up: Narrating *Blue Velvet* in the Postmodernist Frame." *BêteN*. 1989 Autumn-1990 Spring; 8-9: 170-182. [†Narrative; relationship to Postmodernism in Lynch, David: *Blue Velvet*.]

[461] Lundemo, Trond. "Nordens filmhåp flagger ut." *Z*. 1989; 23(3): 6-9. [†In Norway. Interview with Kaurismäki, Aki and Kaurismäki, Mika.]

[462] Lyndina, Ėl'ga. "'Eto byli my ...'." *LO*. 1990; 9: 69-74. [†Interview with Abdrashitov, Vadim.]

[463] Lynn, Kenneth S. "The Torment of D. W. Griffith." *ASch*. 1990 Spring; 59(2): 255-264. [†Role of Griffith, D. W.]

[464] MacCabe, Colin. "British Film Institute: A Response." *Screen*. 1990 Autumn; 31(3): 322-323. [Replies to Caughie & Frith, above. †In Great Britain. Role of British Film Institute.]

[465] Maccubbin, Robert. "Christopher Hampton." *ECLife*. 1990 May; 14(2): 81-89. [†On Frears, Stephen: *Dangerous Liaisons*. Interview with Hampton, Christopher.]

[466] ——. "Glenn Close." *ECLife*. 1990 May; 14(2): 67-74. [†On Frears, Stephen: *Dangerous Liaisons*. Interview with Close, Glenn.]

[467] ——. "Stephen Frears." *ECLife*. 1990 May; 14(2): 75-80. [†On Frears, Stephen: *Dangerous Liaisons*. Interview.]

[468] ——. "Stuart Craig." *ECLife*. 1990 May; 14(2): 90-97. [†On Frears, Stephen: *Dangerous Liaisons*. Interview with Craig, Stuart.]

[469] MacCurdy, Marian. "Bitch or Goddess: Polarized Images of Women in Arthurian Literature and Films." *PVR*. 1990 Winter; 18(1): 3-24. [†Treatment of women in Boorman, John: *Excalibur* compared to Malory, Sir Thomas: *Le Morte Darthur*.]

[470] MacDonald, Scott. "Ernie Gehr: Camera Obscura/Lens/Filmstrip." *FilmQ*. 1990 Summer; 43(4): 10-16. [†Use of camera in Gehr, Ernie: *Morning*; *Serene Velocity*; *Eureka*.]

[471] MacFadden, Patrick. "Remarks on the Polish Session." 133-137 in Petrie, Graham, ed.; Dwyer, Ruth, ed. *Before the Wall Came Down: Soviet and East European Filmmakers Working in the West*. Lanham, MD: UP of America; 1990. 249 pp. [Discussion, 139-142. †By Polish filmmakers.]

[472] MacKinnon, Kenneth. *Misogyny in the Movies: The DePalma Question*. Newark: U of Delaware P; 1990. London: Associated UPs; 1990. 224 pp. [†Role of misogyny in DePalma, Brian.]

[473] Macklin, Jenny. "'Chariots of Fire'—an Approach." *CRUX*. 1990 May; 24(2): 18-29. [†On Hudson, Hugh: *Chariots of Fire*; relationship to teaching.]

[474] Mahieu, José A. "Imágenes del pasado: Panorama histórico del cine argentino en los años 30." *CHA*. 1990 July; 481: 81-90. [†In Argentina (1930-1939).]

[475] ——. "Las migraciones de cineastas españoles." *CHA*. 1989 Nov.-Dec.; 473-474: 29-44. [†In Spain.]

[476] Mahieu, José Agustín. "Diez años de cine latinoamericano." *CHA*. 1990 Oct.; 484: 39-48. [†In Latin America.]

[477] Makolkina, Anna. "A Nostalgic Vision of Tarkovsky's *Nostalgia*." 215-221 in Petrie, Graham, ed.; Dwyer, Ruth, ed. *Before the Wall Came Down: Soviet and East European Filmmakers Working in the West*. Lanham, MD: UP of America; 1990. 249 pp. [Discussion, 223-228. †Treatment of loss of humanism; home in Tarkovskiĭ, Andreĭ A.: *Nostalghia*.]

[478] Maltby, Richard. "*The King of Kings* and the Czar of All the Rushes: The Propriety of the Christ Story." *Screen*. 1990 Summer; 31(2): 188-213. [Incl. photos. †Role of religious groups; relationship to DeMille, Cecil B.: *King of Kings*.]

[479] Mann, Karen B. "Narrative Entanglements: *The Terminator*." *FilmQ*. 1989-1990 Winter; 43(2): 17-27. [†Narrative technique in Cameron, James: *The Terminator*. Application of theories of Genette, Gérard.]

[480] Marchetti, Bianca Maria; Niccolini, Daniela. "Per una definizione della struttura stilistica del realismo di Roberto Rossellini." *SULLA*. 1981-1982; 55: 239-257. [†Style; relationship to realism in Rossellini, Roberto: *Roma, città aperta*. Application of theories of Metz, Christian.]

[481] Marcus, Millicent. "Bertolucci's *Last Emperor* and the Case for National Cinema." *RLA: Romance Languages Annual*. 1989; 1: 45-51. [†Role of Italian identity in Bertolucci, Bernardo: *The Last Emperor*.]

[482] Marrone, Gaetana. "L'attualità di *Francesco*: Incontro con Liliana Cavani." *AnCNT*. 1990 Fall; 2(2): 43-55. [†By Cavani, Liliana: *Francesco*. Interview.]

[483] ——. "Narratività e storia in *Interno berlinese* di Liliana Cavani." *RLA: Romance Languages Annual*. 1989; 1: 52-55. [†Narrative; relationship to history in Cavani, Liliana: *Interno berlinese*.]

[484] Mart'ianova, I. A. "Vozmozhnye podkhody k izucheniiu kompozitsionno-sintaksicheskogo svoeobraziia teksta kinostsenariia." *FN*. 1990; 4: 109-115. [†Relationship to screenplay. Linguistic approach.]

[485] Martin, Andrew. "Vietnam and Melodramatic Representation." *EW*. 1990 June; 4(2): 54-67. [†And television. Melodrama. Treatment of Vietnam War in Ashby, Hal: *Coming Home*; *China Beach*.]

[486] Mayne, Judith. *The Woman at the Keyhole: Feminism and Women's Cinema*. Bloomington: Indiana UP; 1990. x, 260 pp. (Theories of Representation and Difference.) [†By women filmmakers. Relationship to feminism.]

[487] McCann, Graham. *Woody Allen: New Yorker*. London: Polity; 1990. viii, 267 pp. [†Treatment of Jewish identity in Allen, Woody.]

[488] McCreadie, Marsha; Jaehne, Karen. "Great Belles of Fire: Southern Women on the Screen." *Cineaste*. 1990; 17(4): 20-21, 64. [†Treatment of women in Southern United States.]

[489] McMullen, Wayne Joseph. "A Rhetorical Analysis of Peter Weir's 'Witness'." *DAI*. 1990 Apr.; 50(10): 3092A. [†Rhetoric in Weir, Peter: *Witness*. Dissertation abstract.]

[490] Medhurst, Andy. "[Charlie Chaplin]." *Screen*. 1990 Winter; 31(4): 458-461. [On Maland, Charles J. *Chaplin and American Culture: The Evolution of a Star Image* & Clausius, Claudia. *The Gentlemen Is a Tramp: Charlie Chaplin's Comedy*. †Role of Chaplin, Charles Spencer. Review article.]

[491] Membrez, Nancy J. "'Llévame al cine, Mamá': The Cinematograph in Spain 1896-1920." *RLA: Romance Languages Annual*. 1989; 1: 540-547. [†In Spain (1896-1920).]

[492] Metress, Christopher. "'Hopeless Tatters': The American Movie Tradition and Vietnam in Stephen Wright's *Meditations in Green*." *StHum*. 1989 Dec.; 16(2): 111-120. [†In United States. Treatment of Vietnam War compared to treatment in Wright, Stephen: *Meditations in Green*.]

[493] Middleton, Andrew S. "The Films of Andy Warhol and Paul Morrissey." *DAI*. 1990 Jan.; 50(7): 1830A. [†(1963-1988). By Warhol, Andy; Morrissey, Paul. Dissertation abstract.]

[494] Miller, D. A. "Anal *Rope*." *Representations*. 1990 Fall; 32: 114-133. [†On Hitchcock, Alfred: *Rope*.]

[495] Miller, John M. "'Frankly My Dear I Just—Don't—Care': Val Lewton and Censorship at Selznick International Pictures." *LCUT*. 1986; 36: 11-31. [†Role of censorship in Fleming, Victor: *Gone with the Wind*; relationship to Lewton, Val; Selznick, David O.]

[496] Miranda, Julio E. "El nuevo cine venezolano." *CHA*. 1990 July; 481: 49-60. [†In Venezuela.]

[497] ——. "Retrato de habaneras: Notas sobre cierto cine cubano de los ochenta." *CHA*. 1990 Feb.; 476: 35-44. [†In Cuba (1980-1989).]

[498] Miró, Pilar; Amell, Alma, tr. "Ten Years of Spanish Cinema." 38-46 in Amell, Samuel, ed.; Amell, Alma, tr. *Literature, the Arts, and Democracy: Spain in the Eighties*. Cranbury, NJ: Fairleigh Dickinson UP; 1990. 144 pp. [†In Spain.]

[499] Mirza, Candace. "The Collective Spirit of Revolt: An Historical Reading of *Holiday*." *WAn*. 1990 July; 12(3): 98-116. [Illus. †Role of collaboration in Cukor, George: *Holiday*; relationship to studio system in Hollywood (1935-1939).]

[500] Mitchell, Tony. "The Construction and Reception of Anna Magnani in Italy and the English-Speaking World, 1945-1988." *FilmC*. 1989 Fall; 14(1): 2-21. [†In Italy. Role of Magnani, Anna.]

[501] Mizejewski, Linda. "Sally Bowles: Fascism, Female Spectacle, and the Politics of Looking." *DAI*. 1990 May; 50(11): 3388A. [†And theater. Treatment of Bowles,

Sally (character); relationship to spectator. Feminist approach. Dissertation abstract.]

[502] Moon, Michael; Sedgwick, Eve Kosofsky. "Divinity: A Dossier: A Performance Piece: A Little-Understood Emotion." *Discourse*. 1990-1991 Fall-Winter; 13(1): 12-39. [Incl. photos. †Treatment of transvestism; homosexuality in Waters, John: *Pink Flamingos*; *Polyester*.

[503] Muraire, André. "Le Mythe rural dans le cinéma américain: Variations sur populisme, socialisme et utopie." 27-49 in *Mythes ruraux et urbains dans la culture américaine*. Aix-en-Provence: Univ. de Provence; 1990. 204 pp. (Groupe de Recherche et d'Etudes Nord-Américaines (G.R.E.N.A.).) [†In United States (1930-1990). Treatment of American myth.]

[504] Murray, Bruce. *Film and the German Left in the Weimar Republic: From Caligari to Kuhle Wampe*. Austin: U of Texas P; 1990. x, 293 pp. [†In Germany. Relationship to the Left in Weimar Republic.]

[505] Nandy, Ashis. "Satyajit Ray's Secret Guide." *EW*. 1990 June; 4(2): 14-37. [†Treatment of divided self in Ray, Satyajit compared to Wells, H. G.; Rushdie, Salman.]

[506] Naremore, James. *The Magic World of Orson Welles*. Dallas: Southern Methodist UP; 1989. xvi, 310 pp. [†By Welles, Orson.]

[507] Neupert, Richard. "*L'Immortelle*: The ciné-roman and the ciné-lecteur." *FLS*. 1990; 17: 35-42. [†On Robbe-Grillet, Alain: *L'Immortelle* compared to novel; relationship to audience. Narratological approach.]

[508] ———. "The Musical Score as Closure Device in *The 400 Blows*." *FilmC*. 1989 Fall; 14(1): 26-32. [†Role of music in Truffaut, François: *Les Quatre Cents Coups*.]

[509] Ning, Ma. "New Chinese Cinema: A Critical Account of the Fifth Generation." *Cineaste*. 1990; 17(3): 32-35. [†In China. Role of Fifth Generation.]

[510] Noa, Pedro. "Ultimo encuentro con Oscar Valdés." *Gaceta de Cuba*. 1990 July: 30-31. [†In Cuba. Interview with Valdés, Oscar.]

[511] Nolte, Rüdiger. "Der stete Klassizismus—zur Abhängigkeit von Blick und Ideal (The Constant Classicism—on the Dependency of View and Ideal)." *DAI*. 1989 Fall; 50(3): Item 1608C. [†Dissertation abstract.]

[512] Novak, Glenn D.; Breen, Myles P. "Anti-Melodramatic Realism and Narrative Ambiguity in Peter Weir's *Picnic at Hanging Rock*." *WGCR*. 1990 May; 20: 1-14. [†Narrative form; ambiguity; relationship to melodrama in Weir, Peter: *Picnic at Hanging Rock*.]

[513] Nowell-Smith, Geoffrey. "On History and the Cinema." *Screen*. 1990 Summer; 31(2): 160-171. [†Treatment of history; relationship to war; television.]

[514] O'Healy, Áine. "Oedipus Adrift: Unravelling Patriarchy in Antonioni's *Identificazione di una donna*." *RLA: Romance Languages Annual*. 1989; 1: 56-61. [†Treatment of protagonist; relationship to myth of Oedipus in Antonioni, Michelangelo: *Identificazione di una donna*.]

[515] Ohmer, Susan. "Female Spectatorship and Women's Magazines: Hollywood, Good Housekeeping, and World War II." *VLT*. 1990 Spring; 25: 53-68. [Illus. †Female spectator; relationship to magazines for women.]

[516] Palmer, William J. "Symbolic Nihilism in *Platoon*." 256-274 in Gilman, Owen W., Jr., ed.; Smith, Lorrie, ed. *America Rediscovered: Critical Essays on Literature and Film of the Vietnam War*. New York: Garland; 1990. xix, 386 pp. (GRLH 986.) [†Treatment of Vietnam War; relationship to nihilism in Stone, Oliver: *Platoon*.]

[517] Peary, Gerald. "Hollywood in Yugoslavia." 169-175 in Petrie, Graham, ed.; Dwyer, Ruth, ed. *Before the Wall Came Down: Soviet and East European Filmmakers Working in the West*. Lanham, MD: UP of America; 1990. 249 pp. [Discussion, 177-181. †In Hollywood. Reception study: reception in Yugoslavia.]

[518] Peckham, Linda. "Not Speaking with Language/Speaking with No Language: Leslie Thornton's *Adynata*." 181-187 in Kaplan, E. Ann, ed.; Bellour, Raymond, afterword; Rosolato, Guy, afterword. *Psychoanalysis & Cinema*. London: Routledge; 1990. xi, 249 pp. (AFI Film Readers.) [†On Thornton, Leslie: *Adynata*.]

[519] Pellow, C. Kenneth. "*Blue Velvet* Once More." *LFQ*. 1990; 18(3): 173-178. [†Narrative technique; relationship to irrationality in Lynch, David: *Blue Velvet*.]

[520] Peña, Richard. "Borges and the New Latin American Cinema." 229-243 in Aizenberg, Edna, ed. *Borges and His Successors: The Borgesian Impact on Literature and the Arts*. Columbia: U of Missouri P; 1990. xii, 296 pp. [Illus. †In Chile. Role of Ruiz, Raúl. Sources in Borges, Jorge Luis.]

[521] Perkins, Eric. "Renewing the African American Cinema: The Films of Spike Lee." *Cineaste*. 1990; 17(4): 4-8. [†Treatment of African American community in Lee, Spike: *She's Gotta Have It*; *School Daze*; *Do the Right Thing*.]

[522] Petric, Vlada. "Tarkovsky's Dream Imagery." *FilmQ*. 1989-1990 Winter; 43(2): 28-34. [†Dream imagery in Tarkovskiĭ, Andreĭ A.: *Zerkalo*; *Stalker*.]

[523] Petrie, Graham, ed.; Dwyer, Ruth, ed. *Before the Wall Came Down: Soviet and East European Filmmakers Working in the West*. Proc. of Conf. Held at McMaster Univ., Hamilton, Ont. on Mar. 10-11, 1989. Lanham, MD: UP of America; 1990. 249 pp. [Incl. introd. †By Eastern European filmmakers in United States; Europe.]

[524] Petro, Patrice. "Feminism and Film History." *CamObsc*. 1990 Jan.; 22: 9-26. [†Feminism; relationship to film history.]

[525] Pflaum, Hans Günther; Picht, Robert, ed.; Helt, Richard C., tr.; Richter, Roland, tr. *Germany on Film: Theme and Content in the Cinema of the Federal Republic of Germany*. Detroit: Wayne State UP; 1990. 157 pp. [†In Germany. Theme; relationship to symbolism.]

[526] Pick, Zuzana M. "The Dialectical Wanderings of Exile." *Screen*. 1989 Autumn; 30(4): 48-64. [Incl. photos. †Role of exile; relationship to cultural identity; study example: Ruiz, Raúl: *Les Trois Couronnes du matelot*; Solanas, Fernando E.: *Tangos—L'Exil de Gardel*.]

[527] Pickowicz, Paul G. "Popular Cinema and Political Thought in Post-Mao China: Reflections on Official Pronouncements, Film, and the Film Audience." 37-53 in Link, Perry, ed.; Madsen, Richard, ed.; Pickowicz, Paul G., ed. *Unofficial China: Popular Culture and Thought in the People's Republic*. Boulder: Westview; 1989. xii, 238 pp. [†In China.]

[528] Piemonti, Anita. "Sul tradimento in amore: Un film, un libro." *Belfagor*. 1990 Nov.; 45(6 [270]): 687-695. [†Treatment of betrayal in Allen, Woody: *Crimes and Misdemeanors* compared to Matt, Peter von: *Liebesverrat: Die Treulosen in der Literatur*.]

[529] Pierce, Constance. "Language-Silence-Laughter: The Silent Film and the 'Eccentric' Modernist Writer." *SubStance*. 1987; 16(1 [52]): 59-75. [†Silent film; relationship to Modernism.]

[530] Pietrasik, Zdzislaw. "Applause for a Donkey: An Interview with Krzysztof Zanussi." *PArtsJ*. 1990; 12(2-3 [35-36]): 21-28. [†Interview with Zanussi, Krzysztof.]

[531] Pinsker, Sanford. "Woody Allen's Lovably Anxious *Schlemiels*." *StAH*. 1986 Summer-Fall; 5(2-3): 177-189. [†Treatment of schlemiel in Allen, Woody.]

[532] Poague, Leland. "Figures of Narration in *Le Crime de Monsieur Lange*." *NOR*. 1990 Summer; 17(2): 22-36. [†Narration in Renoir, Jean: *Le Crime de M. Lange*.]

[533] Popovici, Alina. "The Mirror Image." *RoR*. 1990; 44(2-3): 75-80. [†In Romania.]

[534] Portuges, Catherine. "Between Worlds: Re-Placing Hungarian Cinema." 63-70 in Petrie, Graham, ed.; Dwyer, Ruth, ed. *Before the Wall Came Down: Soviet and East European Filmmakers Working in the West*. Lanham, MD: UP of America; 1990. 249 pp. [Discussion, 79-84. †By Hungarian filmmakers.]

[535] Preston, Janet L. "Dantean Imagery in *Blue Velvet*." *LFQ*. 1990; 18(3): 167-172. [†Imagery in Lynch, David: *Blue Velvet* compared to Dante: *La Divina Commedia*.]

[536] Rabinovitz, Lauren. "Temptations of Pleasure: Nickelodeons, Amusement Parks, and the Sights of Female Sexuality." *CamObsc*. 1990 May; 23: 71-88. [†In Chicago (1906-1908). And nickelodeon; amusement park as cultural space; relationship to sexuality of women.]

[537] Rainer, Yvonne. "Some Ruminations around the Cinematic Antidotes to the Oedipal Net(les) While Playing with De Lauraedipus Mulvey: Or, He May Be Off Screen, But …." 188-197 in Kaplan, E. Ann, ed.; Bellour, Raymond, afterword; Rosolato, Guy, afterword. *Psychoanalysis & Cinema*. London: Routledge; 1990. xi, 249 pp. (AFI Film Readers.)

[538] Rentschler, Eric. "Remembering Not to Forget: A Retrospective Reading of Kluge's *Brutality in Stone*." *NGC*. 1990 Winter; 49: 23-41. [†On Kluge, Alexander and Schamoni, Peter: *Brutalität im Stein*; relationship to film during Third Reich.]

[539] ———. "The Triumph of Male Will: *Münchhausen* (1943)." *FilmQ*. 1990 Spring; 43(3): 14-23. [†Role of fantasy; relationship to masculinity in Baky, Josef von: *Münchhausen*.]

[540] Respall Fina, Raimundo, prol. *Letra y solfa, I: Crónicas sobre cine (1951-1959)*. Madrid: Mondadori; 1990. 242 pp. [†Edition of film review (1951-1959) by Carpentier, Alejo.]

[541] Reynaud, Berenice; Rainer, Yvonne; Fusco, Coco, rejoinder. "Responses to Coco Fusco's 'Fantasies of Oppositionality'." *Screen*. 1989 Summer; 30(3): 79-99. [Replies to *Screen*. 1988 Autumn; 29(4). †Treatment of sexism; colonialism.]

[542] Ringnalda, Donald. "Unlearning to Remember Vietnam." 64-74 in Gilman, Owen W., Jr., ed.; Smith, Lorrie, ed. *America Rediscovered: Critical Essays on Literature and Film of the Vietnam War*. New York: Garland; 1990. xix, 386 pp. (GRLH 986.) [†Treatment of Vietnam War; relationship to historical fact in Stone, Oliver: *Platoon* compared to Herr, Michael: *Dispatches*.]

[543] Ríos, Alejandro. "Spike Lee: *Hacer lo correcto*." *Gaceta de Cuba*. 1990 Mar.: 6-7. [†By African American filmmakers. On Lee, Spike: *Do the Right Thing*. Interview.]

[544] Rivette, Jacques; Gassen, Heiner, ed. & tr.; Göttler, Fritz, ed. & tr. "Jacques Rivette: Schriften fürs Kino." *CICIM*. 1989 Jan.; 24-25: 8-183. [Monog. iss.; incl. photos.]

[545] Rodríguez, Aleida Anselma. "Arqueología de Omagua y Dorado." *DAI*. 1990 Nov.; 51(5): 1628A-1629A. [†Treatment of expedition in Herzog, Werner: *Aguirre, der Zorn Gottes*. Dissertation abstract.]

[546] Rogin, Michael. "'Make My Day!': Spectacle as Amnesia in Imperial Politics." *Representations*. 1990 Winter; 29: 99-123. [†In United States. Relationship to spectacle; imperialism.]

[547] Ropars-Wuilleumier, Marie-Claire. "Les Deux Yeux de la chouette: Note sur l'intervalle du cinéma et de la littérature chez Alain Robbe-Grillet." *ECr*. 1990 Summer; 30(2): 38-46. [†By Robbe-Grillet, Alain.]

[548] Rosen, Miriam. "Isabelle Adjani: The Actress as Political Activist." *Cineaste*. 1990; 17(4): 22-24. [†Role of Adjani, Isabelle; relationship to politics.]

[549] Rosen, Philip. "Disjunction and Ideology in a Preclassical Film: *A Policeman's Tour of the World*." *WAn*. 1990 July; 12(3): 20-36. [Illus. †*Mise en scène*; narrative in Velle, Gaston: *Tour du monde d'un policier*.]

[550] Ross, Andrew. "Ballots, Bullets, or Batmen: Can Cultural Studies Do the Right Thing?" *Screen*. 1990 Spring; 31(1): 26-44. [Illus. †Treatment of racism in Lee, Spike: *Do the Right Thing* compared to Burton, Tim: *Batman*; *Batman: The Dark Knight* by Miller, Frank.]

[551] Ross, Bruce. "Nostalgia and the Child 'Topoi': Metaphors of Disruption and Transcendence in the Work of Joseph Brodsky, Marc Chagall and Andrei Tarkovsky." *Analecta Husserliana*. 1990; 28: 307-323. [†Treatment of childhood; nostalgia; relationship to homeland in Tarkovskiĭ, Andreĭ A.: *Ivanovo detstvo*; *Nostalghia*; *Offret* compared to Brodskiĭ, Iosif Aleksandrovich; Chagall, Marc.]

[552] Rossellini, Ingrid. "Rossellini and the Adventure of Life: Reminiscences." 175-180 in Matteo, Sante, ed.; Noble, Cinzia Donatelli, ed.; Sowell, Madison U., ed. *Italian Echoes in the Rocky Mountains.* Provo, UT: David M. Kennedy Center for Internat. Studies & Amer. Assn. for It. Studies; 1990. xiv, 226 pp. [†By Rossellini, Roberto. Reminiscence.]

[553] Rossello, Nicola. "Alain Robbe-Grillet dalla letteratura a un cinema di ricerca." *Letture.* 1990 June-July; 45(468): 487-498. [†By Robbe-Grillet, Alain.]

[554] Rouch, Jean. "Ein anderes Universum: Jean Rouch erzählt, III." *CICIM.* 1989 May; 26: 21-25. [Incl. photos. †Treatment of Africa in Rouch, Jean Pierre.]

[555] ——. "In Afrika zum Film: Jean Rouch erzählt, II." *CICIM.* 1989 May; 26: 12-14. [Incl. photos. †Treatment of Africa in Rouch, Jean Pierre.]

[556] ——. "Le Renard fou et le maitre pale." *CICIM.* 1989 May; 26: 26-49. [Incl. photos. †Treatment of Africa in Rouch, Jean Pierre.]

[557] ——. "Unsterblicher Sigui: Jean Rouch erzählt, IV." *CICIM.* 1989 May; 26: 50-55. [Incl. photos. †Treatment of Africa in Rouch, Jean Pierre.]

[558] ——. "Wirklichkeit und Imagination: Jean Rouch erzählt, I." *CICIM.* 1989 May; 26: 9-11.

[559] Roudaut, Jean. "Les Cuisines mystérieuses." *NRF.* 1990 Oct.; 453: 68-73. [†On Greenaway, Peter: *The Cook, the Thief, His Wife and Her Lover.*]

[560] Routt, William D. "The Menace." *SubStance.* 1988; 17(1 [55]): 69-76. [†Treatment in Medved, Harry and Dreyfuss, Randy: *The Fifty Worst Films of All Time.*]

[561] Royer, Michelle. "Une Traversée du féminin: Les Films de Marguerite Duras." *DAI.* 1990 Nov.; 51(5): 1421A. [†By Duras, Marguerite; relationship to feminism; psychoanalysis. Dissertation abstract.]

[562] Russell, Catherine Jean. "Narrative Mortality: Death and Closure in International Postwar Cinema." *DAI.* 1990 Oct.; 51(4): 1026A-1027A. [†Treatment of death. Dissertation abstract.]

[563] Said, Salim. "Man and Revolutionary Crisis in Indonesian Film." *EW.* 1990 June; 4(2): 111-129. [†In Indonesia. Treatment of revolution.]

[564] Sanaker, John Kristian. "*Jesus fra Montréal:* Mangfold, motsetninger og messias." *Z.* 1989; 30(4): 14-15. [†On Arcand, Denys: *Jésus de Montréal.*]

[565] Sanderson, Jim. "Old Corrals: Texas According to 80s Films and TV and Texas according to Larry McMurtry." *JACult.* 1990 Summer; 13(2): 63-73. [†And television (1980-1989). Treatment of Texas compared to treatment in McMurtry, Larry.]

[566] Santner, Eric L. *Stranded Objects: Mourning, Memory, and Film in Postwar Germany.* Ithaca: Cornell UP; 1990. xiv, 200 pp. [†In West Germany. Treatment of mourning; memory; relationship to Third Reich; study example: Syberberg, Hans Jürgen: *Hitler, ein Film aus Deutschland*; Reitz, Edgar: *Heimat.*]

[567] Schaeffer, Eric. "The Sinking of David O. Selznick's 'Titanic'." *LCUT.* 1986; 36: 57-73. [†Treatment of Titanic; relationship to Hitchcock, Alfred; Selznick, David O.]

[568] Scheiner, Georganne J. "Are These Our Daughters? The Image of Female Adolescence in Film, 1920-1970." *DAI.* 1990 Oct.; 51(4): 1364A. [†In United States (1920-1970). Treatment of adolescent females. Dissertation abstract.]

[569] Schneider, Irving. "Deus ex Animo: Or, Why a Doc?" *JPFT.* 1990 Spring; 18(1): 36-39. [†Treatment of psychiatrist; study example: Wiene, Robert: *Das Kabinett des Doktor Caligari*; Robson, Mark: *Home of the Brave*; Hitchcock, Alfred: *Psycho*; Meyer, Russ: *The Immoral Mr. Teas.*]

[570] Schulte-Sasse, Linda. "A Nazi History: The Paradox of Female 'Genius' in Pabst's Neuberin Film *Komödianten* (1941)." *NGC.* 1990 Spring-Summer; 50: 57-84. [†Treatment of genius of women; relationship to Nazism in Pabst, Georg Wilhelm: *Komödianten.*]

[571] Schwartz, Leonard. "Impressions of Robert Bresson." *ThirdR.* 1988; 9: 40-41. [†By Bresson, Robert.]

[572] Seelye, John. "Moby-Kong." *CollL.* 1990; 17(1): 33-40. [†Intertextuality in Cooper, Merian C.: *King Kong.*]

[573] Segovia, Raquel. "'El jardín de las delicias' de Carlos Saura." *DAI.* 1990 Dec.; 51(6): 1810A. [†Treatment of Spanish history in Saura, Carlos: *El jardín de las delicias.* Dissertation abstract.]

[574] Shattuc, Jane Morris. "R. W. Fassbinder's 'Berlin Alexanderplatz': The Clash of the Art Cinema with Popular Culture." *DAI.* 1990 Mar.; 50(9): 2680A-2681A. [†On Fassbinder, Rainer Werner: *Berlin Alexanderplatz*; relationship to television in West Germany. Dissertation abstract.]

[575] Shattuc, Jane, ed. "The Other Fassbinder." *WAn.* 1990 Jan.; 12(1). [Spec. iss.; incl. introd.; illus. †By Fassbinder, Rainer Werner.]

[576] Shchepotinnik, Peter. "With *perestroika,* without Tarkovsky." *NOR.* 1990 Spring; 17(1): 79-83. [Illus. †In U.S.S.R. (1986-1989). Relationship to *perestroika.*]

[577] Sievers, Heiko. "'Ici souffrit le pauvre Antoine Doinel': Ein Graffito François Truffauts als Paradigma seiner 'biographie imaginaire'." *Lendemains.* 1988; 13(50): 101-108. [Fr. sum. †On Truffaut, François: *Les Quatre Cents Coups* as imaginary biography.]

[578] Silverman, Kaja. "Historical Trauma and Male Subjectivity." 110-127 in Kaplan, E. Ann, ed.; Bellour, Raymond, afterword; Rosolato, Guy, afterword. *Psychoanalysis & Cinema.* London: Routledge; 1990. xi, 249 pp. (AFI Film Readers.) [†Relationship to subjectivity in men. Psychoanalytic approach.]

[579] Simmons, Kenith L. "Professor Immanuel Rath and Fetishes of Power: Sternberg's *Der Blaue Engel.*" *WVUPP.* 1990; 36: 46-52. [†Treatment of women; relationship to sexuality; fetishism in Sternberg, Josef von: *Der blaue Engel.*]

[580] ——. "Reconstructing the Code: Subjectivity in Two Films by Hollis Frampton." *NOR.* 1990 Spring; 17(1): 55-59. [†Subjectivity in Frampton, Hollis: *(nostalgia)*; *Zorns Lemma.*]

[581] Sims, Jethro Michael. "Ernest Lehman, Alfred Hitchcock, 'North by Northwest': A Case Study of Narrative Elaboration in Hollywood Filmmaking." *DAI.* 1990 Dec.; 51(6): 1810A. [†In Hollywood. Narrative; relationship to authorship in Hitchcock, Alfred: *North by Northwest*; role of screenplay by Lehman, Ernest Paul. Dissertation abstract.]

[582] Singer, Armand E. "Don Juan Goes to the Movies." *WVUPP.* 1990; 36: 9-15. [†Treatment of Don Juan.]

[583] Skådinn, Harald. "Fra teater til Tarkovskij—og tilbake." *Z.* 1989; 29(3): 18-20. [†In Norway. Interview with Edwall, Allan.]

[584] Skirball, Sheba F.; Bauer, Yehuda, introd. *Films of the Holocaust: An Annotated Filmography of Collections in Israel.* Garland: New York; 1990. xxix, 273 pp. (Garland Filmographies 2; Garland Reference Library of Social Science 463.) [†Treatment of the Holocaust. Catalogue of archives in Israel; relationship to Steven Spielberg Jewish Film Archive.]

[585] Sklar, Robert. "Chinese Cinema after Tienanmen?" *Cineaste.* 1990; 17(3): 35. [†In China. Relationship to massacre in Tiananmen Square.]

[586] Sklar, Robert; Jones, Jacquie; Muwakkil, Salim; Davis, Zeinabu Irene; Musser, Charles; Kennedy, Lisa. "What Is the Right Thing? A Critical Symposium on Spike Lee's *Do the Right Thing.*" *Cineaste.* 1990; 17(4): 32-39. [†On Lee, Spike: *Do the Right Thing.*]

[587] Slotkin, Richard. "The Continuity of Forms: Myth and Genre in Warner Brothers' *The Charge of the Light Brigade.*" *Representations.* 1990 Winter; 29: 1-23. [†Role of myth; genre; relationship to history in Curtiz, Michael: *The Charge of the Light Brigade.*]

[588] Smal', Vatslaŭ. "Ne saperniki, a siabry: Prablemy ŭzaemaŭplyvu belaruskaĭ litaratury i kino, I & II." *Belaruskaia Mova i Litaratura u Shkok.* 1990 Jan.; 1: 67-71. 1990 Feb.; 2: 61-64. [†Relationship to Belorussian literature.]

[589] Smith, Lorrie. "Disarming the War Story." 87-99 in Gilman, Owen W., Jr., ed.; Smith, Lorrie, ed. *America Rediscovered: Critical Essays on Literature and Film of the Vietnam War.* New York: Garland; 1990. xix, 386 pp. (GRLH 986.) [†Treatment of Vietnam War; relationship to language.]

[590] Smith, Murray. "Technological Determination, Aesthetic Resistance or *A Cottage on Dartmoor*: Goat-Gland Talkie or Masterpiece?" *WAn.* 1990 July; 12(3): 80-97. [Illus. †Use of sound in Asquith, Anthony: *A Cottage on Dartmoor*; relationship to film history.]

[591] Smith, Roch C. "Generating the Erotic Dream Machine: Robbe-Grillet's *L'Eden et après* and *La Belle Captive.*" *FR.* 1990 Feb.; 63(3): 492-502. [†Intertextuality relationship to painting in Robbe-Grillet, Alain: *L'Eden et après*; *La Belle Captive.*]

[592] Sobolewski, Tadeusz. "Ruski i Szwed." *DialogW.* 1990 Sept.; 35(9 [408]): 80-84. [†On Tarkovskiĭ, Andreĭ A.: *Offret*; relationship to Josephson, Erland: *En natt i den svenska sommaren.*]

[593] Spellerberg, James. "CinemaScope and Ideology." *VLT.* 1985 Summer; 21: 26-34. [Incl. photos. †On wide-screen. CinemaScope; relationship to ideology. Application of theories of Bazin, André.]

[594] Spergel, Mark Jonathan. "Rouben Mamoulian: Reinventing Reality—His Art and His Life." *DAI.* 1990 Nov.; 51(5): 1446A. [†And theater in United States. Role of Mamoulian, Rouben. Dissertation abstract.]

[595] Spigel, Lynn, ed. "Popular Culture and Reception Studies." *CamObsc.* 1990 May; 23. [Spec. iss.; incl. introd.]

[596] Spoto, Donald. *Madcap: The Life of Preston Sturges.* Boston: Little, Brown; 1990. xiii, 288 pp. [†By Sturges, Preston.]

[597] Sterba, Wendy E. "The Representation of the Prostitute in Contemporary German and English Language Film." *DAI.* 1990 June; 50(12): 3770A. [†English language literature; German language literature. Treatment of prostitute. Dissertation abstract.]

[598] Stishova, Elena; Meany, John, tr.; Kepley, Vance, Jr., tr. "Passions over *Commissar.*" *WAn.* 1990 Oct.; 12(4): 62-75. [†Role of censorship; relationship to Askol'dov, Aleksandr: *Kommissar.*]

[599] Stoianovich, Ivan. "Ne biakhme geroi, no ...: Po povod edna godishina." *LFront.* 1990 Mar. 1; 9: 3. [†In Bulgaria.]

[600] Stone, Mirto Golo. "The Feminist Critic and Salomé: On Cavani's *The Night Porter.*" *RLA: Romance Languages Annual.* 1989; 1: 41-44. [†Treatment of feminism in Cavani, Liliana: *Il portiere di notte.*]

[601] Straayer, Chris. "The She-Man: Postmodern Bi-Sexed Performance in Film and Video." *Screen.* 1990 Autumn; 31(3): 262-280. [Incl. photos. †And video art; music video. Role of sexuality; relationship to Postmodernism. Imagery.]

[602] Strike, William Norman. "Distance and Voice in the Writing of Marguerite Duras: From Narration to Expression." *DAI.* 1990 Mar.; 50(9): 2893A. [†Narrative distance; narrative voice in Duras, Marguerite. Dissertation abstract.]

[603] Sullivan, Henry W. "Paul, John and *Broad Street.*" *Popular Music.* 1987 Oct.; 6(3): 327-338. [†Role of Lennon, John and McCartney, Paul in Webb, Peter: *Give My Regards to Broad Street.* Application of theories of Lacan, Jacques.]

[604] Svendsen, Trond Olav. "Ola Solums *Landstrykere*: Knapper og glansbilder." *Z.* 1989; 30(4): 8-9. [†On Solum, Ola: *Landstrykere.*]

[605] Swart, Stanley L. "Neutralization Theory in Popular Film: A Criminological Perspective on *Save the Tiger.*" *SiPC.* 1985; 8(1): 79-85. [†Treatment of criminal in Avildsen, John Guilbert: *Save the Tiger.*]

[606] Szpakowska, Małgorzata. "Kieślowski: Jedenaste jest tajemnicą." *DialogW.* 1990 Dec.; 35(12 [411]): 114-118. [†By Kieslowski, Krzysztof.]

[607] Taylor, Helen. *Scarlett's Women: Gone With the Wind and Its Female Fans.* New Brunswick: Rutgers UP; 1989. 275 pp. [†On Fleming, Victor: *Gone with the Wind.*]

[608] Testa, Bart. "Reflections on Makavejev: The Art Film and Transgression." 229-245 in Petrie, Graham, ed.; Dwyer, Ruth, ed. *Before the Wall Came Down: Soviet and East European Filmmakers Working in the West.* Lanham, MD: UP of America; 1990. 249 pp. [†On Makavejev, Dušan: *Sweet Movie.*]

[609] Thomas, François. "4 Interviews zu *I Want to Go Home.*" *CICIM.* 1990 Mar.; 29: 104-118. [Incl. photogs. †On Resnais, Alain: *I Want to Go Home.* Interview with Benson, Laura; Leterrier, Catherine; van Damme, Charlie; Laureux, Jean-Claude.]

[610] Thompson, Kristin. "*Parade:* A Review of an Unreleased Film." *VLT.* 1986; 22: 75-83. [Illus. †On Tati, Jacques: *Parade.*]

[611] Thomsen, Christian Braad. "Der doppelte Mensch." *TuK.* 1989 July; 103: 3-9. [†Role of Fassbinder, Rainer Werner.]

[612] Thomsen, Christian Braad; Burns, Joseph, tr. "The Doubled Individual." *WAn.* 1990 Jan.; 12(1): 60-65. [Tr. of *Kritik.* 1989 July; 103: 3-9; illus. †Treatment of the double in Fassbinder, Rainer Werner.]

[613] Triggs, Jeffery Alan. "The Faustian Theme in Fassbinder's *The Marriage of Maria Braun.*" *StHum.* 1989 June; 16(1): 24-32. [†Treatment of Braun, Maria (character) in Fassbinder, Rainer Werner: *Die Ehe der Maria Braun;* relationship to Faust in Goethe, Johann Wolfgang von: *Faust.*]

[614] Troncale, Joseph. "Kozintsev's *Odna.*" *SEEA.* 1990 Winter; 6(2): 139-147. [†On Kozintsev, Grigoriĭ Mikhaĭlovich and Trauberg, Leonid Zakharovich: *Odna.*]

[615] Tsivian, Yuri, comp.; Usai, Paolo Cherchi, ed.; Codelli, Lorenzo, ed.; Montanaro, Carlo, ed.; Robinson, David, ed. *Silent Witnesses: Russian Films 1908-1919/ Testimoni silenziosi: Film russi 1908-1919.* London: British Film Inst./Edizioni Biblioteca dell'Immagine; 1989. 621 pp. [†In Russian Empire (1908-1919). Film guide.]

[616] Twomey, John E. "From Eisenstein to Prime Time: The Film and Television Design Career of Nikolai Soloviov." 71-77 in Petrie, Graham, ed.; Dwyer, Ruth, ed. *Before the Wall Came Down: Soviet and East European Filmmakers Working in the West.* Lanham, MD: UP of America; 1990. 249 pp. [Discussion, 79-84. †And television. Scene design by Solov'ev, Nikolaĭ.]

[617] Uhrmeister, Beate. "'It Was Indeed a German Hollywood Film': Fassbinder-Rezeption in den USA: Notizen zu einem produktiven Missverständnis." *TuK.* 1989 July; 103: 80-85. [†By Fassbinder, Rainer Werner. Reception study: reception in United States.]

[618] Ukadike, Nwachukwu Frank. "Black African Cinema." *DAI.* 1990 Aug.; 51(2): 321A. [†By black Africans. Relationship to oral tradition. Dissertation abstract.]

[619] Valicha, Kishore. "Indian Cinema: Mahesh Bhatt's *Arth*—a Textual Analysis." *Quest.* 1990 Mar.-Apr.; 80: 107-113. [†On Bhatt, Mahesh: *Arth.*]

[620] ——. "Repetitiveness as a Structuring Principle in Indian Cinema: Some Considerations." *Quest.* 1990 Sept.-Oct.; 83: 299-301. [†In India. Repetition.]

[621] van Nypelseer-Wolfowicz, Jacqueline. "L'Enseignement de la littérature de scénario." 195-200 in Bauer, Roger, ed.; Fokkema, Douwe, ed.; Graat, Michael de, asst. ed.; Fischer-Lichte, Erika, asst.; Garstin, Marguerite, asst.; Ibsch, Elrud, asst.; Stackelberg, Jürgen von, asst. *Proceedings of the XIIth Congress of the International Comparative Literature Association/Actes du XIIe congrès de l'Association Internationale de Littérature Comparée: München 1988 Munich, V: Space and Boundaries in Literary Theory and Criticism/Espace et frontières dans la critique et la théorie littéraire; Space and Boundaries in the Teaching of General and Comparative Literature/Espace et frontières dans l'enseignement de la littérature générale et comparée.* Munich: Iudicium; 1990. 415 pp. (Proceedings of the Congress of the International Comparative Literature Association 12: 5.) [†And television. Role of screenplay; television drama. Pedagogical approach.]

[622] Van Wert, William F. "Psychoanalysis and Con Games: *House of Games.*" *FilmQ.* 1990 Summer; 43(4): 2-10. [†Treatment of psychoanalysis; confidence game; relationship to male-female relations in Mamet, David: *House of Games.*]

[623] Vasudevan, Ravi. "Indian Commercial Cinema." *Screen.* 1990 Winter; 31(4): 446-453. [†In India in Hindi language. Role of commercialism.]

[624] Viano, Maurizio. "Theorein." *RLA: Romance Languages Annual.* 1989; 1: 62-69. [†Signification. Treatment of passion in Pasolini, Pier Paolo: *Teorema.*]

[625] Vincendeau, Ginette. "[Feminism and French Cinema]." *Screen.* 1990 Winter; 31(4): 454-457. [On Flitterman-Lewis, Sandy. †In France by women filmmakers. Role of feminism. Review article.]

[626] ——. "Melodramatic Realism: On Some French Women's Films in the 1930s." *Screen.* 1989 Summer; 30(3): 51-65. [Incl. photos. †In France (1930-1939). For women. Realism; relationship to melodrama.]

[627] Viry-Babel, Roger. "Momentaufnahme: *La Marseillaise* oder Die verklärte Revolution." *CICIM.* 1990 Mar.; 29: 119-135. [Incl. photos. †On Renoir, Jean: *La Marseillaise.*]

[628] Viswanathan, Jacqueline. "Approche pédagogique d'un classique du cinéma québécois: *Mon oncle Antoine.*" *FR.* 1990 Apr.; 63(5): 849-858. [†On Jutra, Claude: *Mon oncle Antoine.* Pedagogical approach.]

[629] Vitti, Antonio. "Dal *Messia* rosselliniano al Cristo delle tentazioni." *RLA: Romance Languages Annual.* 1989; 1: 70-74. [†Treatment of Christ in Rossellini, Roberto: *Messia* compared to Scorsese, Martin: *The Last Temptation of Christ.*]

[630] Von Gunden, Kenneth Ray. "Five Postmodern *Auteurs:* Coppola, Lucas, DePalma, Spielberg, and Scorsese." *DAI.* 1990 Aug.; 51(2): 321A. [†Postmodernism in Coppola, Francis Ford; Lucas, George; DePalma, Brian; Spielberg, Steven; Scorsese, Martin. Dissertation abstract.]

[631] Voser, Silvia, ed.; Beatt, Cynthia, ed.; Daigfuss, Elisabeth, tr.; Gassen, Heiner, tr.; Restorff, Brigitta, tr. "Jean Rouch." *CICIM.* 1989 May; 26. [Spec. iss.; incl. introd. †By Rouch, Jean Pierre.]

[632] Waldman, Diane. "'What Do Those Birds in Hollywood Have That I Don't?': Early Filmmaking in Colorado." *VLT.* 1986; 22: 3-15. [Incl. photos. †By independent filmmakers in Colorado (1897-1928). Film history.]

[633] Walker, Janet. "Couching Resistance: Women, Film, and Postwar Psychoanalytic Theory." 143-162 in Kaplan, E. Ann, ed.; Bellour, Raymond, afterword; Rosolato, Guy, afterword. *Psychoanalysis & Cinema.* London: Routledge; 1990. xi, 249 pp. (AFI Film Readers.) [†Treatment of women; relationship to psychoanalytic literary theory and criticism.]

[634] Waller, Gregory A. "Situating Motion Pictures in the Prenickelodeon Period: Lexington, Kentucky." *VLT.* 1990 Spring; 25: 12-28. [Illus. †In United States: Lexington (Kentucky) (1897-1906).]

[635] Waller, Marguerite. "Neither an 'I' nor an 'Eye': The Gaze in Fellini's *Giulietta degli spiriti.*" *RLA: Romance Languages Annual.* 1989; 1: 75-80. [†Treatment of gaze of female protagonist in Fellini, Federico: *Giulietta degli spiriti.*]

[636] ——. "Whose *Dolce vita* Is This Anyhow? The Language of Fellini's Cinema." *QI.* 1990 Spring; 11(1): 127-135. [†Cinematic technique; relationship to autobiography in Fellini, Federico: *La dolce vita.*]

[637] Warchol, Tomasz. "The Rebel Figure in Miloš Forman's American Films." *NOR.* 1990 Spring; 17(1): 64-71. [†Treatment of rebel in Forman, Miloš.]

[638] Wead, George, introd. "[David O. Selznick]." *LCUT.* 1986; 36. [Spec. iss. †Role of Selznick, David O. as producer.]

[639] Weldon, Michael J. "Mondo Bongo: A Guide to Beat 'Sploitation Flicks." *MSI.* 1989-1990 Winter; 22-23: 21-22. [Rpt. from *Hightimes.* 1987 Apr. †Treatment of Beat Generation.]

[640] Werner, Gösta. "Fritz Lang and Goebbels: Myth and Facts." *FilmQ.* 1990 Spring; 43(3): 24-27. [†Role of Goebbels, Joseph in censorship of Lang, Fritz: *Das Testament des Dr. Mabuse.*]

[641] Werner, Gösta; Gunnemark, Erik, tr. "James Joyce and Sergej Eisenstein." *JJQ.* 1990 Spring; 27(3): 491-507. [†Role of Eĭzenshteĭn, Sergeĭ Mikhaĭlovich; relationship to Joyce, James.]

[642] West, Dennis. "Confronting the Crisis in Mexican Cinema." *Inti.* 1989 Spring-Fall; 29-30: 215-217. [†In Mexico.]

[643] Westbrook, Max. "The Night John Wayne Danced with Shirley Temple." *WAL.* 1990 Aug.; 25(2): 157-169. [†Treatment of hero in Ford, John: *Fort Apache.*]

[644] Whillock, David Everett. "Narrative Structure in *Apocalypse Now.*" 225-237 in Gilman, Owen W., Jr., ed.; Smith, Lorrie, ed. *America Rediscovered: Critical Essays on Literature and Film of the Vietnam War.* New York: Garland; 1990. xix, 386 pp. (GRLH 986.) [†Narrative structure. Treatment of Vietnam War in Coppola, Francis Ford: *Apocalypse Now.* Application of theories of Lévi-Strauss, Claude.]

[645] Whynot, Chris. "Canadian Film: In Search of a Future." *QQ.* 1988 Summer; 95(2): 403-413. [†In Canada.]

[646] Wider, Todd. "The Positive Image of the Physician in American Cinema during the 1930s." *JPFT.* 1990 Winter; 17(4): 139-152. [†In United States (1930-1939). Treatment of doctor. Includes filmography.]

[647] Wiese, Ingrid. "Timer i regi." *Z.* 1989; 30(4): 34-37. [†By Mikhalkov-Konchalovskiĭ, Nikita.]

[648] ——. "Timer med skuespillerne." *Z.* 1989; 29(3): 48-51. [†By Mikhalkov-Konchalovskiĭ, Nikita.]

[649] Wild, Florianne. "*Ecriture* and Cinematic Practice in Agnès Varda's *Sans toit ni loi.*" *ECr.* 1990 Summer; 30(2): 92-104. [†On Varda, Agnès: *Sans toit ni loi.*]

[650] Williams, Alan. "Pirandello at the Movies: L'Herbier, Chenal, and the Late Mattia Pascal." *ECr.* 1990 Summer; 30(2): 14-25. [†In France. Sources in Pirandello, Luigi.]

[651] Williams, John. "Bill Gunn (1929-1989): Black Independent Filmmaker, Scenarist, Playwright, Novelist: A Critical Index of the Collected Film, Dramatic, and Literary Works." *Obsidian II.* 1990 Summer; 5(2): 115-147. [†Role of Gunn, Bill. Index.]

[652] Willis, Susan. "*Fantasia:* Walt Disney's Los Angeles Suite." *Diacritics.* 1987 Summer; 17(2): 83-96. [†On Disney, Walt: *Fantasia.*]

[653] Wolfe, Charles. "Vitaphone Shorts and *The Jazz Singer.*" *WAn.* 1990 July; 12(3): 58-78. [Illus. †Use of sound in Crosland, Alan: *The Jazz Singer* compared to use of Vitaphone in short film.]

[654] Woods, Roy. "Siegfried Lenz's *Ein Kriegsende:* Text and Film." *NGS.* 1988-1989; 15(3): 207-224. [†On Lenz, Siegfried: *Ein Kriegsende.*]

[655] Wurzer, Wilhelm; Silverman, Hugh J. "Filming: Inscriptions of *Denken.*" 173-186 in Silverman, Hugh J., ed. *Postmodernism—Philosophy and the Arts.* New York: Routledge; 1990. vi, 319 pp. (Continental Philosophy 3.) [†Relationship to Postmodernism.]

[656] Wurzer, Wilhelm S. *Filming and Judgment: Between Heidegger and Adorno.* Atlantic Highlands, NJ: Humanities; 1990. xviii, 149 pp. (Philosophy and Literary Theory.) [†Cinematic technique; relationship to judgment. Theories of Heidegger, Martin; Adorno, Theodor W.]

[657] Wyatt, Ernest; Rowden, Ginny. "John Huston's Obsessive Characters." *Proteus.* 1990 Fall; 7(2): 34-41. [†Characterization; relationship to obsession in Huston, John.]

[658] Wyatt, Justin. "The Economics of High Concept: Economic and Aesthetic Change in Contemporary American Film." *DAI.* 1990 Mar.; 50(9): 2681A. [†In United States. Dissertation abstract.]

[659] Yates, Jessica. "The Other 50th Anniversary." *Mythlore*. 1990 Spring; 16(3 [61]): 47-50. [†Naming of dwarf in Disney, Walt: *Snow White and the Seven Dwarfs*; relationship to Tolkien, J. R. R.]

[660] Zappulla Muscarà, Sarah. "Giovanni Verga e il cinema." *SIAA*. 1990; 3(3): 39-50. [Eng. sum. †On Verga, Giovanni as screenwriter.]

[661] Zhang, Yingjin. "Ideology of the Body in *Red Sorghum*: National Allegory, National Roots, and Third Cinema." *EW*. 1990 June; 4(2): 38-53. [†In China. Treatment of human body; relationship to ideology in Chang I-mo: *Hung kao-liang*. Application of theories of Jameson, Fredric; Bakhtin, Mikhail Mikhaĭlovich.]

[662] Zika, Damouré. "Mystérieux et dommage d'affaires." *CICIM*. 1989 May; 26: 15-20. [Incl. photographs. †Treatment of Africa in Rouch, Jean Pierre.]

[663] Zimmerman, Patricia R. "*Demon Lover Diary*: Deconstructing Sex, Class, and Cultural Power in Documentary." *Genders*. 1990 July; 8: 91-109. [†Treatment of social class; sexuality in DeMott, Joel: *Demon Lover Diary*.]

[664] Žižek, Slavoj. "How the Non-Duped Err." *QPar*. 1990 Fall; 4(1): 1-20. [†Role of the other in Hitchcock, Alfred.]

Bibliography

[665] "Filmographie Jean Rouch." *CICIM*. 1989 May; 26: 62-71. [†By Rouch, Jean Pierre.]

[666] Combs, James. *American Political Movies: An Annotated Filmography of Feature Films*. New York: Garland; 1990. xiii, 173 pp. (GRLH 970; Filmographies 1.) [†In United States. Treatment of politics. Filmography.]

[667] Dixon, Wheeler, ed.; Everson, William K., introd. *Producers Releasing Corporation: A Comprehensive Filmography and History*. Jefferson, NC: McFarland; 1986. vii, 151 pp.

[668] Drew, Bernard A. *Motion Picture Series and Sequels: A Reference Guide*. New York: Garland; 1990. 412 pp. (GRLH 1186.) [Illus. †Serial film.]

[669] Kolb, W. M. "*Blade Runner*: An Annotated Bibliography." *LFQ*. 1990; 18(1): 19-64. [†On Scott, Ridley: *Blade Runner*.]

[670] Paul, Barbara Dotts. *The Germans after World War II: An English-Language Bibliography*. Boston: Hall; 1990. xviii, 190 pp. [†(1945-1989). Treatment of Germans.]

[671] Streible, Dan, ed. "The Literature of Film Exhibition: A Bibliography." *VLT*. 1990 Spring; 25: 80-119.

FILM ADAPTATION

[672] Andrew, Dudley. "The Impact of the Novel on French Cinema of the 30s." *ECr*. 1990 Summer; 30(2): 3-13. [†Of French cinema (1930-1939).]

[673] Apostolidès, Jean-Marie. "*Pinocchio*: Or, A Masculine Upbringing." *Merveilles & Contes*. 1988 Dec.; 2(2): 75-86. [†Of Lorenzini, Carlo: *Le avventure di Pinocchio* compared to folk tale.]

[674] Aste, Mario. "*Padre padrone* and the 'Sardinian Question': From Ledda's Novel to the Tavianis' Film." *RLA: Romance Languages Annual*. 1989; 1: 27-33. [†Treatment of Sardinia in film adaptation of Ledda, Gavino: *Padre padrone* by Taviani, Paolo and Taviani, Vittorio.]

[675] Bachorski, Hans-Jürgen. "Viele bunte Bilder, aber schlichte Gedanken: Annauds Verfilmung von Ecos Roman 'Der Name der Rose'." *LiLi*. 1988; 18(72): 107-115. [†Of Eco, Umberto: *Il nome della rosa* by Annaud, Jean-Jacques.]

[676] Barbour, Sarah. "Where Is the Woman in This Text? Marguerite Duras and *Le Navire Night* 'Histoire d'images noires'." *Journal of Durassian Studies*. 1989 Fall; 1: 1-33. [†Treatment of gender in Duras, Marguerite: *Le Navire Night* compared to prose version.]

[677] Berg, Charles Ramírez. "'The Third Man''s Third Man: David O. Selznick's Contribution to 'The Third Man'." *LCUT*. 1986; 36: 93-113. [†Role of Selznick, David O. in film adaptation of Greene, Graham: *The Third Man* by Reed, Sir Carol.]

[678] Boling, Becky. "From *Beso* to *Beso*: Puig's Experiments with Genre." *Symposium*. 1990 Summer; 44(2): 75-87. [†Of Puig, Manuel: *El beso de la mujer araña* compared to dramatic adaptation.]

[679] Brami, Joseph. "Mme de Merteuil, Juliette, and the Men: Notes for a Reading of Vadim's *Liaisons dangereuses 1960*." *ECLife*. 1990 May; 14(2): 56-66. [†Treatment of libertinism; women in film adaptation of Laclos, Pierre Ambroise François Choderlos de: *Les Liaisons dangereuses* by Vadim, Roger.]

[680] Brüggemann, Heinz. "*Berlin Alexanderplatz* oder 'Franz, Mieze, Reinhold, Tod und Teufel'? R. W. Fassbinders filmische Lektüre des Romans von Alfred Döblin: Polemik gegen einen melodramatischen Widerruf der ästhetischen Moderne." *TuK*. 1989 July; 103: 51-65. [†Modernism in film adaptation of Döblin, Alfred: *Berlin Alexanderplatz* by Fassbinder, Rainer Werner.]

[681] Carson, John F. "John Huston's *The Dead*: An Irish Encomium." *Proteus*. 1990 Fall; 7(2): 26-29. [†Of Joyce, James: "The Dead" by Huston, John.]

[682] Conroy, Peter V., Jr. "*Amadeus* on Stage and Screen." *PostS*. 1989-1990 Fall-Winter; 9(1-2): 25-37. [Illus. †Of Shaffer, Peter: *Amadeus* by Forman, Miloš.]

[683] Cripps, Thomas. "*Native Son*, Film and Book: A Few Thoughts on a 'Classic'." *MissQ*. 1989 Fall; 42(4): 425-427. [†Of Wright, Richard: *Native Son* by Freedman, Jerrold.]

[684] Cuesta, Mercedes. "'Los santos inocentes,' reflexiones y críticas de la prensa." *Ventanal*. 1984; 8: 139-147. [†Of Delibes, Miguel: *Los santos inocentes* by Camus, Mario. Reception study: reception in France.]

[685] Daly, Brenda O. "An Unfilmable Conclusion: Joyce Carol Oates at the Movies." *JPC*. 1989 Winter; 23(3): 101-114. [†Treatment of violence against women in Cho-

pra, Joyce: *Smooth Talk* as film adaptation of Oates, Joyce Carol: "Where Are You Going, Where Have You Been?"]

[686] Davis, Paul. *The Lives and Times of Ebenezer Scrooge*. New Haven: Yale UP; 1990. x, 283 pp. [†Treatment of Scrooge, Ebenezer (character) in Dickens, Charles: *A Christmas Carol* compared to television adaptation; theatrical production; cartoons.]

[687] Dean, Thomas K. "The Critical Reception of Erich von Stroheim's *Greed*." *FNS*. 1989 Spring; 9: 7-11. [†On Stroheim, Erich von: *Greed* as film adaptation of Norris, Frank: *McTeague*. Reception study.]

[688] Deats, Sara M. "Polanski's *Macbeth*: A Contemporary Tragedy." *SiPC*. 1986; 9(1): 84-93. [†Of Shakespeare, William: *Macbeth* by Polanski, Roman.]

[689] Deveny, Thomas. "From Page to Screen: Contemporary Spanish Narratives of the Spanish Civil War." 129-138 in Pérez, Janet, ed.; Aycock, Wendell, ed. *The Spanish Civil War in Literature*. Lubbock: Texas Tech UP; 1990. 178 pp. (SCLit 21.) [†Treatment of Spanish Civil War in film adaptation of Spanish novel (1900-1999).]

[690] Dixon, Wheeler. "The 'Performing Self' in Filmed Shakespearean Drama." *ShakB*. 1987 July-Aug.: 18-19. [†Of Shakespeare, William; relationship to formality; distance.]

[691] Dixon, Wheeler Winston. "The Films of *Frankenstein*." 166-179 in Behrendt, Stephen C., ed. *Approaches to Teaching Shelley's* Frankenstein. New York: Mod. Lang. Assn. of Amer.; 1990. x, 190 pp. [†Of Shelley, Mary Wollstonecraft: *Frankenstein*. Pedagogical approach.]

[692] ——. "Notes on the Cinematic Interpretations of the Works of H. P. Lovecraft." *LSt*. 1990 Fall; 22-23: 3-9. [†Of Lovecraft, Howard Phillips.]

[693] Dougherty, Dru. "*La colmena* en dos discursos: Novela y cine." *Insula*. 1990 Feb.-Mar.; 45(518-519): 19-21. [†Of Cela Trulock, Camilo José: *La colmena*.]

[694] Elsaesser, Thomas. "*Berlin Alexanderplatz*: Franz Biberkopf /S/ Exchanges." *WAn*. 1990 Jan.; 12(1): 30-43. [Illus. †Treatment of identity; relationship to substitution; exchange in film adaptation of Döblin, Alfred: *Berlin Alexanderplatz* by Fassbinder, Rainer Werner.]

[695] Eversberg, Gerd. "Der erste 'Pole Poppenspäler'-Film." *Mitteilungen aus dem Storm-Haus*. 1990; 2: 14-20. [†Of Storm, Theodor: *Pole Poppenspäler* by Oertel, Curt.]

[696] Fareniaux, Louisette. "Yourcenar-Delvaux: Le Projet alchimique." *RVC*. 1990 May; 9: 109-115. [†Of Yourcenar, Marguerite: *L'Œuvre au noir* by Delvaux, André.]

[697] Fenton, Jill Rubinson, ed.; Waugh, Charles G., ed.; Russo, Jane, ed.; Greenberg, Martin H., ed. *Women Writers from Page to Screen*. New York: Garland; 1990. xiii, 483 pp. (GRLH 687.) [†(1920-1984). Of women writers in England and United States. Handbook.]

[698] French, Warren. "*The Red Pony* as Story Cycle and Film." 71-84 in Benson, Jackson J., ed. *The Short Novels of John Steinbeck: Critical Essays with a Checklist to Steinbeck Criticism*. Durham: Duke UP; 1990. x, 349 pp. [†Of Steinbeck, John: "The Red Pony."]

[699] Frizler, Paul. "John Huston's Film of James Joyce's 'The Dead'." *Proteus*. 1990 Fall; 7(2): 22-25. [†Of Joyce, James: "The Dead" by Huston, John.]

[700] Grant, Barry Keith. "When Worlds Collide: *The Cool World*." *LFQ*. 1990; 18(3): 179-187. [†Narrative technique in film adaptation of Miller, Warren: *The Cool World* by Clarke, Shirley.]

[701] Haag, Achim. "'Er hat immer diese Sehnsucht nach Liebe gehabt, und deswegen war er böse': Franz Biberkopf und Reinhold: Die Kontrahenten der Seelenkämpfe R. W. Fassbinders." *TuK*. 1989 July; 103: 35-50. [†Role of autobiography in film adaptation of Döblin, Alfred: *Berlin Alexanderplatz* by Fassbinder, Rainer Werner.]

[702] Haase, Donald P. "Is Seeing Believing? Proverbs and the Film Adaptation of a Fairy Tale." *ProverbiumY*. 1990; 7: 89-104. [†Use of proverb; *Märchen* in Jordan, Neil and Carter, Angela: *The Company of Wolves*.]

[703] Hartigan, Karelisa V. "Artemis in South Australia: Classical Allusions in *Picnic at Hanging Rock*." *CML*. 1990 Fall; 11(1): 93-98. [†Classical allusion in film adaptation of Lindsay, Joan: *Picnic at Hanging Rock* by Weir, Peter.]

[704] Haskell, Molly. "Is It Time to Trust Hollywood?" *New York Times Book Review*. 1990 Jan. 28: 1, 36-37. [†By filmmakers in Hollywood.]

[705] Hoare, Stephanie Alison. "Melodrama and Innovation: Literary Adaptation in Contemporary Chinese Film." *DAI*. 1990 Mar.; 50(9): 2901A. [†Of Chinese fiction. Dissertation abstract.]

[706] Holmer, Joan Ozark. "'O, What Learning Is!': Some Pedagogical Practices for *Romeo and Juliet*." *SQ*. 1990 Summer; 41(2): 187-194. [†Of Shakespeare, William: *Romeo and Juliet*. Pedagogical approach.]

[707] Knapp, Elise F.; Glen, Robert. "'The Energy of Evil Has Diminished': Less Dangerous Liaisons." *ECLife*. 1990 May; 14(2): 41-48. [†Of Laclos, Pierre Ambroise François Choderlos de: *Les Liaisons dangereuses* by Forman, Miloš; Frears, Stephen; relationship to Hampton, Christopher: *Les Liaisons dangereuses*.]

[708] Knapp, Elise F., introd.; Glen, Robert, introd. "Film Forum: *Les Liaisons dangereuses* (1959, 1988, & 1989)." *ECLife*. 1990 May; 14(2): 39-107. [Spec. sect. †And dramatic adaptation of Laclos, Pierre Ambroise François Choderlos de: *Les Liaisons dangereuses*.]

[709] Kunz, Don. "Oliver Stone's Film Adaptation of *Born on the Fourth of July*: Redefining Masculine Heroism." *WL&A*. 1990 Fall; 2(2): 1-25. [†Of Kovic, Ron: *Born on the Fourth of July* by Stone, Oliver.]

[710] Leparulo, William E. "From Theater to Film: Bellocchio's and Pirandello's '*Enrico IV*'." *CJItS*. 1990; 13(40-41): 69-74. [†Of Pirandello, Luigi: *Enrico IV* by Bellocchio, Marco.]

SEE SUBJECT INDEX FOR CROSS-REFERENCES

[711] Lovell, Terry. "Landscapes and Stories in 1960s British Realism." *Screen*. 1990 Winter; 31(4): 357-376. [Incl. photos. †And television in Great Britain (1959-1963). Realism; relationship to working class life in film adaptation; television adaptation of drama; fiction.]

[712] Maggitti, Vincenzo. "Dis/adattamento: *The French Lieutenant's Woman*." 123-147 in Izzo, Donatello, ed. *Il racconto allo specchio: Mise en abyme e tradizione narrativa*. Rome: Nuova Arnica; 1990. 173 pp. (Testi e Studi 2.) [†Treatment of reality; relationship to fiction in film adaptation of Fowles, John: *The French Lieutenant's Woman* by Reisz, Karel.

[713] Margolis, Harriet E. "Lost Baggage: Or, The Hollywood Sidetrack." 160-165 in Behrendt, Stephen C., ed. *Approaches to Teaching Shelley's* Frankenstein. New York: Mod. Lang. Assn. of Amer.; 1990. x, 190 pp. [†Of Shelley, Mary Wollstonecraft: *Frankenstein*. Pedagogical approach.]

[714] Marshall, Scott. "Edith Wharton on Film and Television." *EWhN*. 1990 Spring; 7(1): 15-17. [†And television adaptation of Wharton, Edith.]

[715] Marwick, Arthur, ed. "*Room at the Top*: The Novel and the Film." 249-279 in Marwick, Arthur, ed. *The Arts, Literature, and Society*. London: Routledge; 1990. xii, 332 pp. [Incl. photos. †Of Braine, John: *Room at the Top* by Clayton, Jack.]

[716] Masson, Jean-Claude; Tostado, Conrado, tr. "Tiempo de espectáculos." *Vuelta*. 1990 Mar.; 14(160): 42-45.

[717] McDonald, Keiko I. "Novel into Film: Morita Yoshimitsu's *Sorekara (And Then)*." *PostS*. 1989-1990 Fall-Winter; 9(1-2): 67-81. [Illus. †Of Natsume Sōseki: *Sorekara* by Morita Yoshimitsu.]

[718] Miguel, Casilda de; Fernández, Augusto. "De la literatura al cine: Desarrollo fílmico de una novela de Joseph Conrad." 321-324 in Menchacatorre, Félix, ed. *Ensayos de literatura europea e hispanoamericana*. San Sebastián: Univ. del País Vasco; 1990. xvi, 605 pp. [†On Coppola, Francis Ford: *Apocalypse Now* as film adaptation of Conrad, Joseph: "Heart of Darkness."]

[719] Monegal-Brancós, Antonio. "Luis Buñuel: De la literatura al cine: Una poética del objeto." *DAI*. 1990 Feb.; 50(8): 2513A. [†Treatment of objects as sign in film adaptation by Buñuel, Luis. Dissertation abstract.]

[720] Morrison, Rachela. "*Casablanca* Meets *Star Wars*: The Blakean Dialectics of *Blade Runner*." *LFQ*. 1990; 18(1): 2-10. [†Treatment of antinomy; relationship to human nature in Scott, Ridley: *Blade Runner* as film adaptation of Dick, Philip K.: *Do Androids Dream of Electric Sheep?*]

[721] Nudd, Donna Marie. "*Jane Eyre* and What Adaptors Have Done to Her." *DAI*. 1990 Mar.; 50(9): 2910A. [†Role of gender compared to theatrical adaptation of Brontë, Charlotte: *Jane Eyre*.]

[722] O'Shea, Michael J. "'Raiders and Cinemen Too': Joyce on Video." *James Joyce Literary Supplement*. 1990 Spring; 4(1): 21-23. [†Of Joyce, James: *Ulysses*; *A Portrait of the Artist as a Young Man* by Strick, Joseph compared to Huston, John: *The Dead*; Pearce, Michael: *James Joyce's Women*.]

[723] Pearson, Roberta E.; Uricchio, William. "How Many Times Shall Caesar Bleed in Sport: Shakespeare and the Cultural Debate about Moving Pictures." *Screen*. 1990 Autumn; 31(3): 243-261. [†Of Shakespeare, William: *Julius Caesar* by Vitagraph Company of America (1908).]

[724] Perlmutter, Ruth. "Can a Man Know a Woman? *The Malady of Death* by Marguerite Duras and Its Film Adaptation by Peter Handke." *Journal of Durassian Studies*. 1989 Fall; 1: 70-97. [†Treatment of male-female relations in film adaptation of Duras, Marguerite: *La Maladie de la mort* by Handke, Peter.]

[725] Pilkington, Ace G. "Screening Shakespeare." *DAI*. 1990 July; 51(1): 3A. [†And television adaptation. Role of videotape in criticism of adaptation of Shakespeare, William. Dissertation abstract.]

[726] Rapf, Joanna E. "'A Larger Thing': John Michael Hayes and *The Children's Hour*." *PostS*. 1989-1990 Fall-Winter; 9(1-2): 38-52. [Illus. †Of Hellman, Lillian: *The Children's Hour* by Wyler, William; role of Hayes, John Michael.]

[727] Renzi, Thomas Charles. "H. G. Wells: Six Scientific Romances Adapted for Film." *DAI*. 1990 June; 50(12): 3938A. [†Of Wells, H. G. Dissertation abstract.]

[728] Rogero, Anito; Sopeña Balordi, A. Emma. "Analyse des renforcements affectifs et des changements de niveau de la langue dans la traduction en espagnol de 'Zazie dans le métro': L'Adaptation cinématographique et son doublage en espagnol." *Contrastes*. 1988 Dec.; 17: 39-60. [Eng. sum. †Role of dubbing in Spanish language translation in film adaptation of Queneau, Raymond: *Zazie dans le métro*.]

[729] Santoro, Patricia Jane. "Novel into Film: The Case of 'La familia de Pascual Duarte' and 'Los santos inocentes'." *DAI*. 1990 Jan.; 50(7): 2079A. [†Of Cela Trulock, Camilo José: *La familia de Pascual Duarte* by Franco, Ricardo compared to adaptation of Delibes, Miguel: *Los santos inocentes* by Camus, Mario. Dissertation abstract.]

[730] Simmonds, Roy S. "Steinbeck's *The Pearl*: Legend, Film, Novel." 173-184 in Benson, Jackson J., ed. *The Short Novels of John Steinbeck: Critical Essays with a Checklist to Steinbeck Criticism*. Durham: Duke UP; 1990. x, 349 pp. [†Of Steinbeck, John: *The Pearl*.]

[731] Singer, Robert Lewis. "The Faust Film Adaptation: A Study in the Interrelationship between Literature and Film." *DAI*. 1990 Mar.; 50(9): 2890A. [†Treatment of Faust. Dissertation abstract.]

[732] Singerman, Alan J. "Variations on a Denouement: *Les Liaisons dangereuses* on Film." *ECLife*. 1990 May; 14(2): 49-55. [†Denouement in film adaptation of Laclos, Pierre Ambroise François Choderlos de: *Les Liaisons dangereuses*.]

[733] Slade, Joseph W. "Romanticizing Cybernetics in Ridley Scott's *Blade Runner*." *LFQ*. 1990; 18(1): 11-18. [†Treatment of cybernetics in Scott, Ridley: *Blade Runner* as film adaptation of Dick, Philip K.: *Do Androids Dream of Electric Sheep?*]

[734] Slott, Kathryn. "From Agent of Destruction to Object of Desire: The Cinematic Transformation of Stevens Brown in *Les Fous de Bassan*." *Québec Studies*. 1989 Fall-1990 Winter; 9: 17-28. [Fr. sum. †Treatment of Brown, Stevens (character) in film adaptation of Hébert, Anne: *Les Fous de Bassan* by Simoneau, Yves.]

[735] Smith, Ronald L. *Poe in the Media: Screen, Songs, and Spoken Word Recordings*. New York: Garland; 1990. x, 226 pp. (GRLH 1272.) [†And musical adaptation; radio adaptation; recordings of Poe, Edgar Allan. Catalogue.]

[736] Taves, Brian. "On the Set of *A Study in Scarlet*." *ArmD*. 1989 Spring; 22(2): 142-148. [†Of Conan Doyle, Sir Arthur: *A Study in Scarlet* by Marin, Edwin L.]

[737] Thurm, Brigitte. "Wer traf sich in Travers? Geschichte im psychologischen Drama." *WB*. 1990; 36(3): 512-517. [†Treatment of French Revolution in film adaptation of Hofmann, Fritz: "Treffen in Travers" by Knauf, Thomas; Gwisdek, Michael.]

[738] Uricchio, William; Pearson, Roberta E. "Dante's Inferno and Caesar's Ghost: Intertextuality and Conditions of Reception in Early American Cinema." *JOCI*. 1990 Summer; 14(2): 71-85. [†Of Shakespeare, William: *Julius Caesar* compared to *Francesca da Rimini* by Vitagraph Company of America as film adaptation of Dante: *La Divina Commedia: Inferno*. Reception study.]

[739] Varela, Antonio. "Reading and Viewing *Los santos inocentes*." *RLA: Romance Languages Annual*. 1989; 1: 639-644. [†Of Delibes, Miguel: *Los santos inocentes* by Camus, Mario.]

[740] Vick, Christina. "Cinematic Aspects and Film Adaptations of Selected Works of Thomas Hardy." *DAI*. 1990 Nov.; 51(5): 1623A. [†Of Hardy, Thomas. Dissertation abstract.]

[741] Zeffirelli, Franco. "Filming Shakespeare." 239-270 in Loney, Glenn, ed. *Staging Shakespeare: Seminars on Production Problems*. New York: Garland; 1990. xviii, 278 pp. (GRLH 798.) [Illus. †Of Shakespeare, William: *Romeo and Juliet* by Zeffirelli, Franco. Includes interview.]

[742] Zito, Marina. "Appunti sulle trascrizioni cinematografiche di Luchino Visconti." *AION-SR*. 1989 July; 31(2): 449-456. [†Of Tomasi di Lampedusa, Giuseppe: *Il gattopardo*; Mann, Thomas: *Der Tod in Venedig* by Visconti, Luchino.]

Bibliography

[743] Berchenko, Pablo. "Miguel Delibes frente a la crítica y el cine: Bibliografía crítica y filmografía." *Ventanal*. 1984; 8: 148-178. [†Of Delibes, Miguel.]

FILM GENRES

[744] Abel, Richard. "Scenes from Domestic Life in Early French Cinema." *Screen*. 1989 Summer; 30(3): 4-28. [†Melodrama in France (1905-1907). By Pathé Frères.]

[745] Allan, Blaine. "Musical Cinema, Music Video, Music Television." *FilmQ*. 1990 Spring; 43(3): 2-14. [†Musical film. And music video; music television.]

[746] Bacon-Smith, Camille M. "Enterprising Women: Television, Folklore, and Community." *DAI*. 1990 Jan.; 50(7): 2194A. [†Science fiction film. And television; relationship to women as fans. Ethnography. Dissertation abstract.]

[747] Benamou, Catherine. "Redefining Documentary in the Revolution: An Interview with Paolo Martin of the El Salvador Film and Television Unit." *Cineaste*. 1990; 17(3): 11-17. [†Documentary film. Interview with Martín, Paolo.]

[748] Buckner, Noel; Dore, Mary; Paskin, David; Sills, Sam. "History Is Made at Night: The Case for the Good Fight." *Cineaste*. 1990; 17(3): 18-21. [†Documentary film. Treatment of Abraham Lincoln Battalion in Buckner, Noel and Dore, Mary and Paskin, David and Sills, Sam: *The Good Fight*.]

[749] Cardullo, Bert. "Viet Nam Revisted." *HudR*. 1987 Autumn; 40(3): 458-464. [†War film. Treatment of Vietnam War in Post, Ted: *Go Tell the Spartans*; Stone, Oliver: *Platoon*.]

[750] Cohan, Carley; Crowdus, Gary. "Reflections on *Roger & Me*, Michael Moore, and His Critics." *Cineaste*. 1990; 17(4): 25-30. [†Documentary film. On Moore, Michael: *Roger and Me*.]

[751] Conquest, John. *Trouble Is Their Business: Private Eyes in Fiction, Film and Television, 1927-1988*. New York: Garland; 1990. liii, 497 pp. (GRLH 1151.) [†Detective film. And television; hard-boiled detective fiction. Treatment of private eye. Reference guide.]

[752] Cooper, Douglas W. "The Lovely Load: An Archetype of the Horror Film." *SiPC*. 1990; 13(1): 17-26. [Illus. †Horror film. Treatment of archetypes of monsters carrying beautiful woman.]

[753] Cormier, Raymond. "The Closed Society and Its Friends: Plato's *Republic* and Lucas's *THX-1138*." *LFQ*. 1990; 18(3): 193-197. [†Science fiction film. Treatment of totalitarianism in Lucas, George: *THX-1138* compared to Plato: *Politeia*.]

[754] Crafton, Donald. *Emile Cohl, Caricature, and Film*. Princeton: Princeton UP; 1990. xxvi, 404 pp. [†Animated film in France. Biography of Cohl, Emile.]

[755] Creed, Barbara. "[Horror Movies]." *Screen*. 1990 Summer; 31(2): 236-242. [On Tudor, Andrew. *Monsters and Mad Scientists: A Cultural History of the Horror Movies*. †Horror film. Review article.]

[756] ——. "Phallic Panic: Male Hysteria and *Dead Ringers*." *Screen*. 1990 Summer; 31(2): 125-146. [†Horror film. Treatment of women; womb; relationship to the grotesque; hysteria of men in Cronenberg, David: *Dead Ringers*. Application of theories of Freud, Sigmund.]

[757] Doane, Mary Ann. "Melodrama, Temporality, Recognition: American and Russian Silent Cinema." *EW*. 1990 June; 4(2): 69-89. [†Silent film in United States and Russian S.F.S.R. Melodrama; relationship to temporality. Theories of Benjamin, Walter.]

[758] Dobrotworsky, Sergei; Dobrotworsky, Ekaterina, tr. "The Most Avant-Garde of All Parallel Ones." *NOR*. 1990 Spring; 17(1): 84-87. [Illus. †Avant-garde film in U.S.S.R.]

[759] Fraser, Harry L.; Dixon, Wheeler W., ed.; Fraser, Audrey Brown, ed. *I Went That-a-Way: The Memoirs of A Western Film Director*. Metuchen, NJ: Scarecrow; 1990. ix, 147 pp. [†American Western film. Reminiscence.]

[760] Fuchs, Cynthia J. "'Vietnam and Sexual Violence': The Movie." 120-133 in Gilman, Owen W., Jr., ed.; Smith, Lorrie. ed. *America Rediscovered: Critical Essays on Literature and Film of the Vietnam War*. New York: Garland; 1990. xix, 386 pp. (GRLH 986.) [†War film. Treatment of Vietnam War; relationship to sex; violence.]

[761] Garrett, Greg. "*Let There Be Light* and Huston's *film noir*." *Proteus*. 1990 Fall; 7(2): 30-33. [†Documentary film. Relationship to *film noir* in Huston, John: *Let There Be Light*.]

[762] George, Russell. "Some Spatial Characteristics of the Hollywood Cartoon." *Screen*. 1990 Autumn; 31(3): 296-321. [Illus. †Animated film. Spatiality.]

[763] Gilman, Owen W., Jr., ed.; Smith, Lorrie. ed. *America Rediscovered: Critical Essays on Literature and Film of the Vietnam War*. New York: Garland; 1990. xix, 386 pp. (GRLH 986.) [Incl. introd. †War film. Treatment of Vietnam War.]

[764] Goodhall, Jane R. "Aliens." *SoRA*. 1990 Mar.; 23(1): 73-82. [†Horror film. On Cameron, James: *Aliens*. Feminist approach.]

[765] Goodland, Giles. "Dylan Thomas and Film." *NWRev*. 1990 Summer; 3(1 [9]): 17-22. [Incl. photos. †Documentary film. Role of Thomas, Dylan: *Deaths and Entrances* in Eldridge, John: *Wales—Green Mountain Black Mountain*; *Our Country*.]

[766] Gripsrud, Jostein. "De *fryktinngytende* bilder." *Z*. 1989; 29(3): 10-17. 1989; 29(4): 16-23. [†Horror film.]

[767] Hairston, Robert Burl. "An Examination of the Nonverbal Communication in Three Noir Films: 'The Postman Always Rings Twice,' 'The Big Sleep,' and 'Murder My Sweet' in the Original and Remake Versions." *DAI*. 1990 June; 50(12): 3770A. [†*Film noir*. Nonverbal communication in Garnett, Tay: *The Postman Always Rings Twice*; Hawks, Howard: *The Big Sleep*; Dmytryk, Edward: *Murder, My Sweet* compared to remakes by Rafelson, Bob; Winner, Michael; Richards, Dick. Dissertation abstract.]

[768] Hall, Jeanne Lynn. "Refracting Reality: The Early Films of Robert Drew & Associates." *DAI*. 1990 July; 51(1): 2A. [†Documentary film for television. *Cinéma vérité* in film by Drew Associates. Dissertation abstract.]

[769] Hickethier, Knut. "Krieg im Film—nicht nur ein Genre: Anmerkungen zur neueren Kriegsfilm-Diskussion." *LiLi*. 1989; 19(75): 39-53. [Eng. sum. †War film in Germany (1950-1959).]

[770] Horton, Andrew. "'Nothing Worth Living For': Soviet Youth and the Documentary Movement." *WAn*. 1990 Oct.; 12(4): 38-46. [†Documentary film in U.S.S.R. Treatment of youth; relationship to *glasnost'*.]

[771] House, Rebecca R. "Night of the Soul: American *film noir*." *SiPC*. 1986; 9(1): 61-83. [†*Film noir*.]

[772] Hutchings, Peter Ward. "The British Horror Film: An Investigation of British Horror Production in Its National Context." *DAI*. 1990 Aug.; 51(2): 320A. [†Horror film in Great Britain (1956-1973). Relationship to national culture. Dissertation abstract.]

[773] James, David E. "Rock and Roll in Representations of the Invasion of Vietnam." *Representations*. 1990 Winter; 29: 78-98. [†In United States. War film. Treatment of Vietnam War; relationship to rock and roll music compared to Herr, Michael: *Dispatches*.]

[774] Jenkins, Henry Guy, III. "'What Made Pistachio Nuts?': Anarchistic Comedy and the Vaudeville Aesthetic." *DAI*. 1990 July; 51(1): 3A. [†Comic film in United States. Relationship to vaudeville. Dissertation abstract.]

[775] Kahn, Lorraine Susan. "Cinematic Collaborations: Production System and Film Structure in Documentary." *DAI*. 1990 Dec.; 51(6): 1809A-1810A. [†Documentary film. Collaboration. Dissertation abstract.]

[776] Kapsis, Robert E. "Hitchcock in the James Bond Era." *SiPC*. 1988; 11(1): 64-79. [†Spy film. Role of Bond, James (character) compared to film by Hitchcock, Alfred.]

[777] Kassabian, Anahid. "[Music in Film]." *Screen*. 1990 Spring; 31(1): 119-124. [On Gorbman, Claudia. *Unheard Melodies: Narrative Film Music* & Altman, Rick. *The American Film Musical*. †Musical film. Review article.]

[778] Keeton, Patricia Ludeman. "Generic Interaction and Social Class Representation in the Hollywood Collective Struggle Film." *DAI*. 1990 Aug.; 51(2): 320A-321A. [†Political film in Hollywood (1970-1987). Treatment of working class; relationship to violence; collective struggle. Dissertation abstract.]

[779] Khlebarov, Ivan. "Film za Stefan Stambolov." *Rodoliubie*. 1990; 2(86): 64-65. [Incl. photos. †Documentary film on Cholakov, Georgi and Ovcharov, Svetoslav: *Stefan Stambolov—süzidateliat i süsipateliat*. Interview.]

[780] Landon, Philip J. "From Cowboy to Organization Man: The Hollywood War Hero, 1940-1955." *SiPC*. 1989; 12(1): 28-41. [†War film (1940-1955). Treatment of hero.]

[781] Langman, Larry; Ebner, David. *Encyclopedia of American Spy Films*. New York: Garland; 1990. xix, 443 pp. (GRLH 1187.) [†Spy film in United States. Encyclopedia.]

[782] Luckett, Perry D. "The Black Soldier in Vietnam War Literature and Film." *WL&A*. 1989-1990; 1(2): 1-27. [†War film. Treatment of African American soldiers; relationship to Vietnam War.]

[783] Lyndina, Ėl'ga. "In the Orbits of the Future." *SovL*. 1988; 12 [489]: 148-154. [†Science fiction film in U.S.S.R.]

[784] Mandziuk, Roseann Marie. "History in Her Own Image: The Rhetorical Functions of Women's Documentary Film for the Contemporary Women's Movement." *DAI*. 1990 Aug.; 51(2): 344A. [†Documentary film (1970-1985) by women filmmakers. Treatment of women. Dissertation abstract.]

[785] Marsh, John L. "Dick Powell and the Landmark Musicals of 1923." *SiPC*. 1986; 9(1): 51-60. [†Musical film. Role of Powell, Dick.]

[786] McReynolds, Douglas J.; Lips, Barbara J. "Taking Care of Things: Evolution in the Treatment of a Western Theme, 1947-1957." *LFQ*. 1990; 18(3): 202-208. [†American Western film (1947-1957). Treatment of patriarchy in Zinnemann, Fred: *High Noon* compared to Mann, Anthony: *The Tin Star*.]

[787] Mellencamp, Patricia. *Indiscretions: Avant-Garde Film, Video, & Feminism*. Bloomington: Indiana UP; 1990. xix, 234 pp. [†Avant-garde film and video art. Relationship to feminism.]

[788] Merrill, Robert. "Altman's *McCabe and Mrs. Miller* as a Classic Western." *NOR*. 1990 Summer; 17(2): 79-86. [Illus. †American Western film. Treatment of frontier in Altman, Robert: *McCabe and Mrs. Miller*.]

[789] Neale, Steve. "Questions of Genre." *Screen*. 1990 Spring; 31(1): 45-66.

[790] Newfield, Denise; Peskin, Stanley. "*Chariots Of Fire* and Docudrama." *CRUX*. 1990 Feb.; 24(1): 16-21. [†Docudrama. On Hudson, Hugh: *Chariots of Fire*.]

[791] Ophuls, Marcel. "Marcel Ophuls: Söldner des Dokumentarfilms." *CICIM*. 1990 Mar.; 29: 6-103. [Incl. photos. †Documentary film. By Ophüls, Marcel. Includes interview.]

[792] Penley, Constance. "Time Travel, Primal Scene, and the Critical Dystopia." 33-49 in Tagg, John, ed. *The Cultural Politics of "Postmodernism"*. Binghamton: Dept. of Art Hist., State Univ. of New York; 1989. xii, 112 pp. (Current Debates in Art History 1.) [See also 1988 Bibliog. IV.801. †Science fiction film. Treatment of time travel; primal scene; dystopia in Cameron, James: *The Terminator*.]

[793] Plantinga, Carl Rendit. "A Theory of Representation in the Documentary Film." *DAI*. 1990 July; 51(1): 3A. [†Documentary film. Representation. Dissertation abstract.]

[794] Poplovsky, Vitali; Andreev, Natasha, tr. "Waiting for Comedy: A Glance at the Development of Soviet Film Laughter." *NOR*. 1990 Spring; 17(1): 88-93. [†Comic film in U.S.S.R.]

[795] Reimers, Karl Friedrich. "'Hände am Werk—ein Lied von deutscher Arbeit' (1935): Volkskundliche 'Ästhetikreferenzen' im nationalsozialistischen Dokumentarfilm: Ein Hinweis." 219-224 in Gerndt, Helge, ed. *Volkskunde und Nationalsozialismus: Referate und Diskussion einer Tagung*. Munich: Münchner Vereinigung für Volkskunde; 1987. 333 pp. (Münchner Beiträge zur Volkskunde 7.) [†Documentary film in Germany during Third Reich.]

[796] Rentschler, Eric. "Mountains and Modernity: Relocating the *Bergfilm*." *NGC*. 1990 Fall; 51: 137-161. [†In Germany. Mountain film; relationship to modernity; Nazism.]

[797] Richardson, Carl. "Autopsy: An Element of Realism in *Film Noir*." *DAI*. 1990 Sept.; 51(3): 661A-662A. [†*Film noir*. Realism. Dissertation abstract.]

[798] Roof, Gayle. "Context as Instability: Aspects of Object Presentation in Luis Buñuel's Avant-Garde Works." 257-267 in Paolini, Gilbert, ed. *La Chispa '89: Selected Proceedings*. New Orleans: Tulane Univ.; 1989. 418 pp. [†Avant-garde film. Treatment of objects in Buñuel, Luis.]

[799] Roof, Gayle Elaine. "Luis Buñuel's Avant-Garde Artistic Production: Toward a Poetics of Synthesis." *DAI*. 1990 Nov.; 51(5): 1633A. [†Avant-garde film. Role of Buñuel, Luis. Dissertation abstract.]

[800] Rosen, Miriam. "The Architecture of Documentary Filmmaking." *Cineaste*. 1990; 17(3): 48-50. [†Documentary film in Israel. Interview with Gitai, Amos.]

[801] Ross, Andrew. "Cowboys, Cadillacs, and Cosmonauts: Families, Film Genres, and Technocultures." 87-101 in Boone, Joseph A., ed.; Cadden, Michael, ed. *Engendering Men: The Question of Male Feminist Criticism*. New York: Routledge; 1990. vi, 333 pp. [†American Western film. Treatment of nuclear family.]

[802] Sanjek, David. "Fans' Notes: The Horror Film Fanzine." *LFQ*. 1990; 18(3): 150-159. [†Horror film. Relationship to fan magazines.]

[803] Schlüpmann, Heide. "Melodrama and Social Drama in the Early German Cinema." *CamObsc*. 1990 Jan.; 22: 73-87. [†In Germany (1910-1914). Melodrama; social drama.]

[804] Shattuc, Jane. "R. W. Fassbinder's Confessional Melodrama: Towards Historicizing Melodrama within the Art Cinema." *WAn*. 1990 Jan.; 12(1): 44-59. [Illus. †Melodrama in Fassbinder, Rainer Werner.]

[805] Singer, Ben. "Female Power in the Serial-Queen Melodrama: The Etiology of an Anomaly." *CamObsc*. 1990 Jan.; 22: 91-129. [†Melodrama. Treatment of heroine.]

[806] Sjögren, Olle. "Lekmannen i skrattspegeln: En kulturpsykologisk analys av tio manliga filmkomiker (The (P)layman in the Funny Mirror: A Psychocultural Analysis of Ten Leading American Film Comedians)." *DAI*. 1990 Summer; 51(2): Item 706C. [†Comic film. Dissertation abstract.]

[807] Sobchack, Vivian. "'Surge and Splendor': A Phenomenology of the Hollywood Historical Epic." *Representations*. 1990 Winter; 29: 24-49. [†Epic film. Treatment of history.]

[808] Tullos, Allen; Patterson, Daniel W.; Davenport, Tom. "*A Singing Stream: A Black Family Chronicle*: Background, Commentary, and Transcription of the Film." *NCarF*. 1989 Winter-Spring; 36(1): 1-61. [Monog. iss. †Documentary film. Treatment of gospel music in Davenport, Tom: *A Singing Stream*.]

[809] Vasudevan, Ravi. "The Melodramatic Mode and the Commercial Hindi Cinema: Notes on Film History, Narrative and Performance in the 1950s." *Screen*. 1989 Summer; 30(3): 29-50. [Incl. photos. †Melodrama in India in Hindi language (1950-1959).]

[810] Vincendeau, Ginette, ed. "Indian and European Melodrama." *Screen*. 1989 Summer; 30(3). [Spec. iss.; incl. introd. & photos. †Melodrama.]

[811] Welebit, Diane. "The Simple Life." *Americana*. 1987 Sept.-Oct.; 15(4): 37-39. [†Documentary film. Treatment of Shakers in Burns, Ken and Burns, Amy Stechler.

[812] Welsh, Jim, ed. "Cult Movies, Genre Films." *LFQ*. 1990; 18(3). [Spec. iss.]

[813] Wilkening, Thomas. "Krieg ohne Ende: Die Indochina-Aggression der USA im amerikanischen Spielfilm." *WB*. 1990; 36(3): 419-433. [†War film. Treatment of Vietnam War.]

[814] Wintersole, Margaret. "The British Hero in Feature Films of World War II." *SiPC*. 1989; 12(2): 79-88. [†War film in England during World War II. Treatment of hero.]

[815] Yilbar-Sertöz, Z. Tülin. "Issues in Documentary Practice: With a Focus on Turkey." *DAI*. 1990 Feb.; 50(8): 2309A. [†Documentary film in Turkey. Dissertation abstract.]

[816] Zubiri, Nancy. "Basque-American Documentary Film Nears Completion: Saga of the Basque Pioneer in America." *JSBSA*. 1990; 10: 57-62. [†Documentary film. Treatment of Basques in United States in Bordagaray, Stanley George, Jr.: *Amerikanuak: The Basques of the American West*.]

Bibliography

[817] Whillock, David Everett. "The Fictive American Vietnam War Film: A Filmography." 303-312 in Gilman, Owen W., Jr., ed.; Smith, Lorrie, ed. *America Rediscovered: Critical Essays on Literature and Film of the Vietnam War*. New York: Garland; 1990. xix, 386 pp. (GRLH 986.) [†War film. Treatment of Vietnam War.]

FILM THEORY AND CRITICISM

[818] Allen, Richard William. "Representation, Meaning, and Experience in the Cinema: A Critical Study of Contemporary Film Theory." *DAI*. 1990 Apr.; 50(10): 3091A. [†Dissertation abstract.]

[819] Arnold, Robert F. "Film Space/Audience Space: Notes Toward a Theory of Spectatorship." *VLT*. 1990 Spring; 25: 44-52. [†Spectator. Theories of Bazin, André; Comolli, Jean-Louis.]

[820] Berenstein, Rhona. "As Canadian as Possible: The Female Spectator and the Canadian Context." *CamObsc*. 1989 Sept.; 20-21: 40-52. [†In Canada. Female spectator.]

[821] Borgheggiani, Pier Antonio. "La riscoperta di Ricciotto Canudo." *Paideia*. 1986 Jan.-Apr.; 41(1-2): 51-60. [†Theories of Canudo, Ricciotto.]

[822] Brunette, Peter; Wills, David. *Screen/play: Derrida and Film Theory*. Princeton: Princeton UP; 1989. xi, 210 pp. [†Theories of Derrida, Jacques.]

[823] Bruno, Giuliana. "The Image (and the) Movement: An Overview of Italian Feminist Research." *CamObsc*. 1989 Sept.; 20-21: 28-39. [†Relationship to feminism in Italy.]

[824] Buckland, Warren. "Critique of Poor Reason." *Screen*. 1989 Autumn; 30(4): 80-103. [On Carroll, Noel. *Mystifying Movies: Fads and Fallacies in Contemporary Film Theory*. †Review article.]

[825] Creed, Barbara. "Medusa in the Land of Oz: The Female Spectator in Australia." *CamObsc*. 1989 Sept.; 20-21: 53-67. [†In Australia. Female spectator.]

[826] Doane, Mary Ann. "Remembering Women: Psychical and Historical Constructions in Film Theory." 46-63 in Kaplan, E. Ann, ed.; Bellour, Raymond, afterword; Rosolato, Guy, afterword. *Psychoanalysis & Cinema*. London: Routledge; 1990. xi, 249 pp. (AFI Film Readers.) [†Feminist film theory and criticism. Psychoanalytic approach.]

[827] Friedberg, Anne. "A Denial of Difference: Theories of Cinematic Identification." 36-45 in Kaplan, E. Ann, ed.; Bellour, Raymond, afterword; Rosolato, Guy, afterword. *Psychoanalysis & Cinema*. London: Routledge; 1990. xi, 249 pp. (AFI Film Readers.) [†Feminist film theory and criticism.]

[828] Grant, Michael. "[Psychoanalysis and Film Theory]." *Screen*. 1990 Autumn; 31(3): 341-345. [On Thompson, Kristin. *Breaking the Glass Armor*. †Relationship to psychoanalysis. Review article.]

[829] Gunning, Tom. "Film History and Film Analysis: The Individual Film in the Course of Time." *WAn*. 1990 July; 12(3): 4-19. [Illus. †Film history.]

[830] Gunning, Tom, ed. "The Place of Film Analysis in Film History." *WAn*. 1990 July; 12(3). [Spec. iss. †Relationship to film history.]

[831] Hartsough, Denise. "Cine-Feminism Renegotiated: Fassbinder's *Ali* as Interventionist Cinema." *WAn*. 1990 Jan.; 12(1): 18-29. [Illus. †Feminist film theory and criticism and psychoanalytic film theory and criticism; applied to Fassbinder, Rainer Werner: *Angst essen Seele auf*.]

[832] Hickethier, Knut. "Theorieanfänge: Anmerkungen zur Theorie sozialistischer Film- und Fernsehkunst." *TZS*. 1988 Summer; 2(24): 104-108. [†In East Germany. And television theory; relationship to socialism.]

[833] Koch, Gertrud. "Rudolf Arnheim: The Materialist of Aesthetic Illusion—Gestalt Theory and Reviewer's Practice." *NGC*. 1990 Fall; 51: 164-178. [†(1918-1933). Theories of Arnheim, Rudolf; relationship to Gestalt theory.]

[834] Matich, Rosemary L. "Functional Criticism: Cinematic Space/Time Theory and Phenomenology." *DAI*. 1990 July; 51(1): 11A. [†Spatiotemporal relations; relationship to phenomenology. Application of theories of Heidegger, Martin; Merleau-Ponty, Maurice. Dissertation abstract.]

[835] Mulvey, Laura. "Afterthoughts on 'Visual Pleasure and Narrative Cinema' Inspired by *Duel in the Sun*." 24-35 in Kaplan, E. Ann, ed.; Bellour, Raymond, afterword; Rosolato, Guy, afterword. *Psychoanalysis & Cinema*. London: Routledge; 1990. xi, 249 pp. (AFI Film Readers.) [†Feminist film theory and criticism. Applied to Vidor, King: *Duel in the Sun*.]

[836] ——. "British Feminist Film Theory's Female Spectators: Presence and Absence." *CamObsc*. 1989 Sept.; 20-21: 68-81. [†In Great Britain. Relationship to feminism; female spectator.]

[837] Paeck, Joachim. "Filmwissenschaftliche Zwischenbilanz: Anmerkungen zu Geschichte und Struktur der Filmwissenschaft in Deutschland (BRD und DDR)." *TZS*. 1988 Summer; 2(24): 84-92. [†In Germany (1912-1933, 1945-1988).]

[838] Russell, Catherine. "Past Pleasures: New Film Histories." *QQ*. 1990 Spring; 97(1): 88-101. [†Film history in United States; Germany. Review article.]

[839] Slater, Thomas J. "Considering the Active Viewer: The Basis for Seeing Film's Liberating Impact on Language." *Style*. 1989 Winter; 23(4): 545-565. [†Relationship to phenomenology. Theories of Carroll, Noel E.]

[840] Von der Fehr, Drude. "The Cinematic Sign and Its Female Spectator." *Livstegn*. 1989; 7(2): 152-160. [†Sign; relationship to female spectator; feminist literary theory and criticism; semiotic literary theory and criticism.]

[841] Wark, McKenzie. "The Logistics of Perception." *Meanjin*. 1990 Autumn; 49(1): 95-101. [†Perception in film; relationship to militarism. Theories of Virilio, Paul: *Guerre et cinéma*.]

[842] Weiss, Allen S. "Subject Construction and Spectatorial Identification: A Revision of Contemporary Film Theory." *DAI*. 1990 Aug.; 51(2): 321A. [†Spectator; relationship to self-identity. Dissertation abstract.]

[843] Welle, John P. "Delio Tessa and Greta Garbo: Notes on the Poet as Film Critic." *AnCNT*. 1990 Fall; 2(2): 33-41. [†Theories of Tessa, Delio.]

Opera

[844] Studwell, William E.; Hamilton, David A. *Opera Plot Index: A Guide to Locating Plots and Descriptions of Operas, Operettas, and Other Works of the Musical Theater, and Associated Material*. New York: Garland; 1990. xxi, 466 pp. (GRLH 1099.) [†And operetta; musical theater. Plot. Index.]

Radio

[845] Ricci, Connie. "The Lone Ranger Rides Again." 115-120 in Abernethy, Francis Edward, ed. *The Bounty of Texas*. Denton: U of North Texas P; 1990. 232 pp. (PTFS 49.) [†And television. Treatment of Lone Ranger as hero.]

Television

[846] Agüero, Luis. "La telenovela: ¿De la degeneración al género?" *Gaceta de Cuba*. 1990 June: 9. [†Soap opera in Brazil.]

[847] Allan, Blaine. "The State of the State of the Art of TV." *QQ*. 1988 Summer; 95(2): 318-329. [†In Canada.]

[848] Allen, Boo. "A Study of Evelyn Waugh's 'Brideshead Revisited' as Compared to the Telefilm Version." *DAI*. 1990 Nov.; 51(5): 1617A. [†Television adaptation of Waugh, Evelyn: *Brideshead Revisited*. Dissertation abstract.]

[849] Auster, Albert. "The Missiles of October: A Case Study of Television Docudrama and Modern Memory." *JPFT*. 1990 Winter; 17(4): 164-172. [†Docudrama. Role of memory; relationship to fact.]

[850] Beaud, Paul. "La Nonchalance et le sérieux: Sur les médias et le temps." *Degrés*. 1989 Spring; 57: f1-f21. [†Role of temporality. Theories of Hoggart, Richard.]

[851] Benn, Linda. "White Noise: The Long, Sad Story of TV Criticism." *Village Voice Literary Supplement*. 1990 Dec.; 91: 14-16. [†Treatment in criticism.]

[852] Bertens, Hans. "Sjef van Oekel, Fred Hachee, and the Question of Postmodernism." 15-22 in Westerweel, Bart, ed.; D'haen, Theo, ed. *Something Understood: Studies in Anglo-Dutch Literary Translation*. Amsterdam: Rodopi; 1990. 335 pp. (DQR: Studies in Literature 5.) [†In Netherlands. Role of Postmodernism in *Sjef van Oekel*; *Fred Hachee*.]

[853] Best, Steven; Kellner, Douglas. "(Re)Watching Television: Notes toward a Political Criticism." *Diacritics*. 1987 Summer; 17(2): 97-113. [On Gitlin, Todd, ed. *Watching Television*. †Treatment in postmodernist literary theory and criticism. Review article.]

[854] Bettetini, Gianfranco, R.A.I. "Télévision et sémiotiques." *Degrés*. 1989 Spring; 57: b1-b13. [†Relationship to semiotic literary theory and criticism.]

[855] Birbaumer, Ulf, ed. "Fernsehunterhaltung: Analysemethoden und Werkstattberichte." *MuK*. 1986; 32(3-4). [Spec. iss. †And film. Relationship to mass culture.]

[856] Blaney, Martin. "'Dry and Boring': Reflections on Television Entertainment in Great Britain and West Germany." *TZS*. 1988-1989 Winter; 4(26): 83-88. [†In Great Britain and West Germany. Relationship to entertainment.]

[857] Boddy, William. "Alternative Television in the United States." *Screen*. 1990 Spring; 31(1): 91-101. [Incl. photos. †Alternative television in United States.]

[858] Boehrer, Bruce Thomas. "Great Prince's Donatives: MTV Video and the Jacobean Court Masque." *SiPC*. 1988; 11(2): 1-21. [†Music television. Discourse; relationship to power compared to masque for royal court of Jacobean period.]

[859] Bordaz, Robert. "Pierre-Aimé Touchard à la R.T.F." *RHT*. 1990 Jan.-June; 42(1-2 [165-166]): 67-68. [†Role of Touchard, Pierre-Aimé at Radiodiffusion-Télévision Française.]

[860] Brunsdon, Charlotte. "Problems with Quality." *Screen*. 1990 Spring; 31(1): 67-90. [Incl. photos. †In Great Britain. Role of quality; relationship to television studies; film studies.

[861] Coelho, Luiz Antonio. "Toward a Taxonomy of Reflexive Structures for American Television." *DAI*. 1990 Oct.; 51(4): 1035A. [†In United States. Reflexivity. Dissertation abstract.]

[862] Cubitt, Sean. "Video Art and Colonialism: An Other and Its Others." *Screen*. 1989 Autumn; 30(4): 66-79. [Incl. photos. †On video art.]

[863] Donald, James. "[Television and Discourse]." *Screen*. 1990 Spring; 31(1): 113-118. [On 1987 Bibliog. IV.806 & Fiske, John. *Television Culture*. †Relationship to culture studies. Review article.]

[864] Espínola, Adriano. "Cultura Brasileira Contemporânea: Da Utopia à Nostalgia." *BslBzl*. 1990; 3(3): 5-17. [Eng. sum. †And radio in Brazil.]

[865] Fackler, Mark; Darling, Stephen. "Forgiveness on Prime-Time Television: A Case Study: *Hill Street Blues*." *SiPC*. 1987; 10(1): 64-73. [†Treatment of forgiveness in *Hill Street Blues*. Sources in religion.]

[866] Finlay, Marike. "The Represidency: A Critical Review of the Representational Model's Epistemological Incapacity to Name Ideology: Toward a Social Discursive Approach." *DS/SD*. 1988 Winter; 1(1): 23-58. [†Role of representation; relationship to social discourse; ideology; study example: inauguration (1981) of Reagan, Ronald.]

[867] Fiske, John. "Popular Narrative and Commercial Television." *CamObsc*. 1990 May; 23: 133-147. [†Role of cultural dominance; relationship to commercialism; popular culture. Application of theories of Bourdieu, Pierre.]

[868] Gardner, Joann. "Self-Referentiality in Art: A Look at Three Television Situation-Comedies of the 1950s." *SiPC*. 1988; 11(1): 35-50. [†Situation comedy. Self-reflexivity in *The George Burns and Gracie Allen Show*; *I Love Lucy*; *The Jack Benny Show*.]

[869] Glynn, Kevin. "Tabloid Television's Transgressive Aesthetic: *A Current Affair* and the 'Shows That Taste Forgot'." *WAn*. 1990 Apr.; 12(2): 22-44. [Incl. photos. †Tabloid television; study example: *A Current Affair*.]

[870] Hallenberger, Gerd. "Fernseh-Spiele: Über den Wert und Unwert von Game Shows und Quizsendungen." *TZS*. 1988-1989 Winter; 4(26): 17-30. [Incl. photos. †Game show; quiz show.]

[871] Hanson, Cynthia A. "The Women of China Beach." *JPFT*. 1990 Winter; 17(4): 154-163. [Incl. photographs. †Treatment of women in *China Beach*.]

[872] Helbo, A[ndré], introd. "Signes des médias." *Degrés*. 1989 Spring; 57. [Spec. iss. †And mass media. Semiotic approach.]

[873] Henderson, Heather. "The Well Made Pray: Evangelism and the TV Stage." *Theater*. 1987 Fall-Winter; 19(1): 35-44. [†In United States. Role of evangelism.]

[874] Hickethier, Knut. "Unterhaltung ist Lebensmittel: Zu den Dramaturgien der Fernsehunterhaltung—und ihrer Kritik." *TZS*. 1988-1989 Winter; 4(26): 5-16. [†Role of entertainment; relationship to criticism.]

[875] Hill, George; Raglin, Lorraine; Johnson, Chas Floyd; Cash, Rosalind, fwd. *Black Women in Television: An Illustrated History and Bibliography*. New York: Garland; 1990. xii, 168 pp. (GRLH 1228.) [Illus. †Role of black women.]

[876] Hilmes, Michelle. "Where Everybody Knows Your Name: *Cheers* and the Mediation of Cultures." *WAn*. 1990 Apr.; 12(2): 64-73. [†Role of culture in *Cheers*.]

[877] Hunter, Mead. "While You Were Out." *Theater*. 1987 Fall-Winter; 19(1): 45-49. [†In United States. Wrestling as paratheater.]

[878] Igel, Regine. "RAI oder CANALE 5: Wer wäscht weisser? Sponsoring im italienischen Fernsehen." *TZS*. 1988-1989 Winter; 4(26): 89-94. [†In Italy. Role of advertisers.]

[879] Inglis, Fred. "Degrees of Freedom: Narratives on the Page and the Television Screen." *W&I*. 1986 Apr.-June; 2(2): 186-194. [†Narrative.]

[880] Jaehne, Karen. "Home Video." *Cineaste*. 1990; 17(4): 60-61. [†Home video in Italy.]

[881] Jarvik, Laurence. "'It's Only a Movie': The Television Docu-Drama and Social Issue Movie as the American Marketplace of Ideas." *SiPC*. 1988; 11(1): 80-96. [†Docudrama and movie of the week. Treatment of social problems.]

[882] Kepley, Vance, Jr. "The Weaver Years at NBC." *WAn*. 1990 Apr.; 12(2): 46-63. [Incl. photos. †Role of Weaver, Sylvester Laflin; relationship to National Broadcasting Company.]

[883] Kilborn, Richard. "'They Don't Speak Proper English': A New Look at the Dubbing and Subtitling Debate." *JMMD*. 1989; 10(5): 421-434. [†Subtitles; dubbing.]

[884] King, Scott Benjamin. "Sonny's Virtues: The Gender Negotiations of *Miami Vice*." *Screen*. 1990 Autumn; 31(3): 281-295. [†Role of sex roles in *Miami Vice*.]

[885] Kircher, Cassie. "The Disruption of Glamour: Gender and MTV." *PVR*. 1990 Winter; 18(1): 40-47. [†Music television. Treatment of men; women; glamour; sexuality.]

[886] Kurz, Ingrid. "Overcoming Language Barriers in European Television." 168-175 in Bowen, David, ed.; Bowen, Margareta, ed. *Interpreting—Yesterday, Today and Tomorrow*. Binghamton: State U of New York P; 1990. 183 pp. (ATAS 4.) [†And radio in Europe. Role of translator; interpreter.]

[887] Laboissonniere, Barbara Rose. "A Study of Rock Music Videos as the Poetry of Secondary Orality." *DAI*. 1990 May; 50(11): 3590A. [†Music video as oral poetry. Dissertation abstract.]

[888] LaFia, Christine. "'Superwoman' in Television Situation Comedies of the 1980s." *SiPC*. 1988; 11(2): 78-90. [†Situation comedy (1980-1985). Treatment of women as superwoman.]

[889] Landbeck, Hanne. "Der Werbespot als Mikrokosmos der Fernsehunterhaltung." *TZS*. 1988-1989 Winter; 4(26): 58-70. [Incl. photos. †Role of advertising as entertainment.]

[890] Lasky, Kathryn. "The Newspaper Critics of American Television." *DAI*. 1990 Apr.; 50(10): 3097A-3098A. [†Television criticism in newspapers. Dissertation abstract.]

[891] Latourette, Debra Jane. "Doctor Who Meets Vladimir Propp: A Comparative Narrative Analysis of Myth/Folktale and the Television Science Fiction Genre." *DAI*. 1990 Dec.; 51(6): 1817A. [†On *Doctor Who*; relationship to science fiction. Application of theories of Propp, Vladimir Iakovlevich. Dissertation abstract.]

[892] Lawrence, Amy. "The Aesthetics of the Image: The Hanging of Colonel Higgins: A CBS NewsBreak." *WAn*. 1990 Apr.; 12(2): 6-11. [†Treatment of death in news.]

[893] Livingstone, Sonia M. "Interpreting a Television Narrative: How Different Viewers See a Story." *JC*. 1990 Winter; 40(1): 72-85. [†Relationship to television viewer.]

[894] Lovell, Alan. "That Was the Workshops That Was." *Screen*. 1990 Spring; 31(1): 102-112. [†In Great Britain. Role of television workshop.]

[895] MacKirdy, Cailean. "Television Studies: An Interdisciplinary Approach." *DAI*. 1990 Apr.; 50(10): 3098A. [†Dissertation abstract.]

[896] Marranca, Bonnie. "The Century Turning International Events." *PArtsJ*. 1990; 12(2-3 [35-36]): 66-74. [†Role of image; representation; relationship to revolution in Central Europe (1989).]

[897] Meyers, Ric. "The Woman of *Mystery*." *ArmD*. 1990 Summer; 23(3): 325-335. [†On *Mystery* (television program). Interview with Eaton, Rebecca.]

[898] Mikos, Lothar. "Luxus, Prunk und Protzerei: Verdinglichter Lebensstil in Fernsehserien." *TZS*. 1988-1989 Winter; 4(26): 37-50. [†Serial drama. Representation of luxury; relationship to television viewer.]

[899] Mintz, Lawrence E. "Ideology in the Television Situation Comedy." *SiPC*. 1985; 8(2): 42-51. [†Situation comedy. Role of ideology.]

[900] Morley, David; Robins, Kevin. "Spaces of Identity: Communications Technologies and the Reconfiguration of Europe." *Screen*. 1989 Autumn; 30(4): 10-34. [†In Europe. Role of cultural identity.]

[901] Müller, Roswitha. "From Public to Private: Television in the Federal Republic of Germany." *NGC*. 1990 Spring-Summer; 50: 41-55. [†In West Germany.]

[902] Nehamas, Alexander. "Serious Watching." *SAQ*. 1990 Winter; 89(1): 157-180.

[903] Osterholm, J. Roger. "Michener's *Space*, the Novel and Miniseries: A Study in Popular Culture." *JPC*. 1989 Winter; 23(3): 51-64. [†Television adaptation of Michener, James A.: *Space*; relationship to popular culture.]

[904] Penn, Ray. "What Designing Women Do Ordain: The Women's Ordination Movement Comes to Prime Time." *SiPC*. 1990; 13(1): 89-102. [†Treatment of ordination of women in *Designing Women*.]

[905] Preussner, Arnold W. "Countergenre and Performance: *Twelfth Night*." 16-25 in Jones, Dennis M., ed. *A Humanist's Legacy: Essays in Honor of John Christian Bale*. Decorah, IA: Luther Coll.; 1990. 100 pp. [†Role of genre; relationship to television adaptation of Shakespeare, William: *Twelfth Night* compared to theatrical production.]

[906] Probyn, Elspeth. "New Traditionalism and Post-Feminism: TV Does the Home." *Screen*. 1990 Summer; 31(2): 147-159. [Incl. photos. †Treatment of women in home; relationship to feminism.]

[907] Quinn, David James. "Television Advertising and Myth." *DAI*. 1990 Oct.; 51(4): 1035A-1036A. [†Advertising; relationship to myth. Dissertation abstract.]

[908] Radner, Hilary. "Quality Television and Feminine Narcissism: The Shrew and the Covergirl." *Genders*. 1990 July; 8: 110-128. [†Treatment of femininity; narcissism in *Moonlighting* as television adaptation of Shakespeare, William: *The Taming of the Shrew*. Feminist approach.]

[909] Rogers, Deborah D. "Guiding Blight: The Soap Opera and the Eighteenth-Century Novel." *CentR*. 1990 Winter; 34(1): 73-91. [†Soap opera. Treatment of family; sexuality; patriarchy compared to English novel (1700-1799).]

[910] Rollins, Peter C. "Historical Interpretation or Ambush Journalism? CBS vs Westmoreland in *The Uncounted Enemy: A Vietnam Deception* (1982)." *WL&A*. 1990 Spring; 2(1): 23-61. [†Treatment of deception of the public; relationship to Vietnam War in Crile, George: *The Uncounted Enemy: A Vietnam Deception*.]

[911] Romm, Tsilia. "The Stereotype of the Female Detective Hero on Television: A Ten Year Perspective." *SiPC*. 1986; 9(1): 94-102. [†(1970-1979). Treatment of women detectives.]

[912] Rowe, Kathleen K. "Roseanne: Unruly Woman as Domestic Goddess." *Screen*. 1990 Winter; 31(4): 408-419. [†Treatment of disorder in housekeeping by women in *Roseanne* compared to *Married ... with Children*.]

[913] Rutsky, R. L. "Visible Sins, Vicarious Pleasures: Style and Vice in *Miami Vice*." *SubStance*. 1988; 17(1 [55]): 77-82. [†Treatment of law; relationship to style in *Miami Vice*.]

[914] Scheffer, Bernd. "Fernsehen ist das Fernsehen der 'Anderen': Annäherung und Distanz zwischen Fernsehunterhaltung und Medienwissenschaft." *TZS*. 1988-1989 Winter; 4(26): 71-82. [†Role of entertainment; relationship to mass media studies.]

[915] Schenk, Michael. "Realität und Fiktion: Verändern Serien die Vorstellungen von der Realität?" *TZS*. 1988-1989 Winter; 4(26): 51-57. [†Role of advertising as entertainment.]

SEE SUBJECT INDEX FOR CROSS-REFERENCES

[916] Schenkewitz, Jan. "Videopop: Musik als strukturbildendes Element einer Gattung." *TZS*. 1988-1989 Winter; 4(26): 104-109. [†Music video. Role of music; relationship to genre.]

[917] Schwab, David Philip. "Shakespeare Designed for Television: Lessons from 'The BBC TV Shakespeare' Series, 1978-1985." *DAI*. 1990 Feb.; 50(8): 2502A. [†Scene design in television adaptation of Shakespeare, William by British Broadcasting Corporation (1978-1985). Dissertation abstract.]

[918] Seitz, Brian. "The Televised and the Untelevised: Keeping an Eye on/off the Tube." 187-206 in Silverman, Hugh J., ed. *Postmodernism—Philosophy and the Arts*. New York: Routledge; 1990. vi, 319 pp. (Continental Philosophy 3.) [†Relationship to Postmodernism.]

[919] Suleman, Saleh. "Representations of Gender in Prime-Time Television: A Textual Analysis of Drama Series of Pakistan Television." *DAI*. 1990 Nov.; 51(5): 1431A. [†In Pakistan (1985-1989). Treatment of gender; relationship to Pakistani society in *Dewareen*; *Tanhaiyan*. Dissertation abstract.]

[920] Wilson, Tony. "Reading the Postmodernist Image: A 'Cognitive Mapping'." *Screen*. 1990 Winter; 31(4): 390-407. [Incl. photos. †Imagery; relationship to cognitive representation; Postmodernism. Application of theories of Jameson, Fredric.]

[921] Worland, Eric John. "The Other Living-Room War: Evolving Cold War Imagery in Popular TV Programs of the Vietnam Era, 1960-75." *DAI*. 1990 June; 50(12): 3770A. [†In United States (1960-1975). Imagery of Cold War in treatment of Vietnam War. Dissertation abstract.]

[922] Wulff, Hans-Jürgen. "Saal- und Studiopublikum: Überlegungen zu einer fernsehspezifischen Funktionsrolle." *TZS*. 1988-1989 Winter; 4(26): 31-36. [†Role of studio audience.]

[923] Yeager, Gertrude. "*Angel Malo* ['Bad Angel'], a Chilean *telenovela*." *SLAPC*. 1990; 9: 249-262. [†Soap opera. On *Angel Malo*.]

Theater

[924] "Streettheatre versus Festival: International Federation for Theatre Research (FIRT/IFTR), Professors Conference, Vienna, 31.8.-3.9.1988." *MuK*. 1987; 33(1-2). [Spec. iss. †Street theater.]

[925] Alberts, David. "A Critical Analysis of the Historical and Theoretical Issues of Modern MimeMime." *DAI*. 1990 Feb.; 50(8): 2305A. [†Pantomime. Dissertation abstract.]

[926] Allen, Robert C. "'The Leg Business': Transgression and Containment in American Burlesque." *CamObsc*. 1990 May; 23: 43-68. [†Popular theater. Role of burlesque; relationship to sexuality; female body.]

[927] Alter, Jean; Rojas, Mario A., tr. "Hacia una gramática teatral: Signos primarios, signos naturales, significado." *Dispositio*. 1988; 13(33-35): 51-70. [†Role of sign theory; referentiality.]

[928] Banning, Yvonne. "Language in the Theatre: Mediating Realities in an Audience." *SATJ*. 1990 May; 4(1): 12-37. [†Language; relationship to audience.]

[929] Barba, Eugenio; Fowler, Richard, tr. "Four Spectators." *TDRev*. 1990 Spring; 34(1 [125]): 96-101. [†Role of director; spectator.]

[930] Beleva, Belka. "El mia teatra sperto." *Bulgara Esperantisto*. 1989 Nov.; 58(11): 4-5. [†Esperanto language literature.]

[931] Bouissac, Paul. "Espace performatif et espace médiatisé: La Déconstruction du spectacle de cirque dans les représentations télévisées." *Degrés*. 1989 Spring; 57: d1-d21. [†Circus on television. Semiotic approach.]

[932] Carlson, Marvin. *Theatre Semiotics: Signs of Life*. Bloomington: Indiana UP; 1990. xviii, 125 pp. [†Social function; role of audience. Semiotic approach.]

[933] ——. *Theories of the Theatre: A Historical and Critical Survey, from the Greeks to the Present*. Ithaca: Cornell UP; 1989. 528 pp. [Rpt. of 1984 ed.]

[934] Cohen-Stratyner, Barbara Naomi, ed. "Arts and Access: Management Issues for Performing Arts Collections." *PAR*. 1990; 15: 1-102. [Spec. iss. †1900-1999.]

[935] Constantinidis, Stratos E. "Illusion in Theater: The Sign/Stimulus Equivalence." *PoT*. 1987; 8(2): 245-260. [†Illusion; relationship to audience response.]

[936] De Marinis, Marco. "Dallo spettatore modello allo spettatore reale: Processi cognitivi nella ricezione teatrale." *Versus*. 1989 Jan.-May; 52-53: 81-98. [†Relationship to spectator. Application of reception theory; frame theory.]

[937] De Toro, Fernando. "Toward a Specification of Theatre Discourse." *Versus*. 1989 Sept.-Dec.; 54: 3-20. [†Relationship to discourse. Semiotic approach. Theories of Ubersfeld, Anne.]

[938] Donington, Robert. *Opera and Its Symbols: The Unity of Words, Music, and Staging*. New Haven: Yale UP; 1990. viii, 248 pp. [†Opera. Symbolism in word; music; staging.]

[939] Fischer-Lichte, Erika. "Theatre in Search of a Universal Language." 131-138 in Bauer, Roger, ed.; Fokkema, Douwe, ed.; Graat, Michael de, asst. ed.; Fischer-Lichte, Erika, asst.; Garstin, Marguerite, asst.; Ibsch, Elrud, asst.; Stackelberg, Jürgen von, asst. *Proceedings of the XIIth Congress of the International Comparative Literature Association/Actes du XIIe congrès de l'Association Internationale de Littérature Comparée: München 1988 Munich, V: Space and Boundaries in Literary Theory and Criticism/Espace et frontières dans la critique et la théorie littéraire; Space and Boundaries in the Teaching of General and Comparative Literature/Espace et frontières dans l'enseignement de la littérature générale et comparée*. Munich: Iudicium; 1990. 415 pp. (Proceedings of the Congress of the International Comparative Literature Association 12: 5.) [†Role of Brook, Peter; Suzuki Tadashi.]

[940] Fischer-Lichte, Erika; Rojas, Mario A., tr. "Hacia una comprensión del teatro: Algunas perspectivas de la semiótica del teatro." *Dispositio*. 1988; 13(33-35): 1-28. [†Relationship to semiotics.]

[941] Fitzpatrick, Tim. "Models of Visual and Auditory Interaction in Performance." *Gestos*. 1990 Apr.; 5(9): 9-22. [†Treatment in performance theory; relationship to the aural; the visual.]

[942] Gevisser, Mark. "Gay Theater Today." *Theater*. 1990 Summer-Fall; 21(3): 46-51. [Illus. †Treatment of homosexuality.]

[943] Huppertz, Karel J. "Spiegelungen der theatralischen Volkskultur." *MuK*. 1987; 33(1-2): 61-67. [†Relationship to laughter; popular culture. Theories of Bakhtin, Mikhail Mikhaïlovich; Eco, Umberto; Fo, Dario.]

[944] Janoff, Barbara Letofsky. "The Legend Impersonated in Solo Performance: The History, Development, and Functions of a Contemporary Dramatic Form." *DAI*. 1990 Sept.; 51(3): 683A. [†Impersonation in solo performance. Dissertation abstract.]

[945] Kowzan, Tadeusz; Ferguson, Jeanne, tr. "The Semiology of the Theater: Twenty-Three Centuries or Twenty-Two Years?" *Diogenes*. 1990 Spring; 149: 84-104. [†Semiotic approach.]

[946] Kruger, ⌐oren. "Staging Boundaries: Institutional Limits to Legitimate Theatre." 423-429 in Bauer, Roger, ed.; Fokkema, Douwe, ed.; Graat, Michael de, asst. ed.; Kaiser, Gerhard, asst.; Rinner, Fridrun, asst.; Wertheimer, Jürgen, asst. *Proceedings of the XIIth Congress of the International Comparative Literature Association/Actes du XIIe congrès de l'Association Internationale de Littérature Comparée: München 1988 Munich, IV: Space and Boundaries of Literature/Espace et frontières de la littérature*. Munich: Iudicium; 1990. 651 pp. (Proceedings of the Congress of the International Comparative Literature Association 12: 4.) [†And drama.]

[947] Lazarowicz, Klaus. "Analogien und Differenzen zwischen szenischer Agitation, Kollusion und Konzelebration." *MuK*. 1987; 33(1-2): 41-50. [†Street theater.]

[948] Lengsted, Jørn. "Is Street Theatre Theatre?" *MuK*. 1987; 33(1-2): 9-13. [†Street theater.]

[949] McGlynn, Fred. "Postmodernism and Theater." 137-154 in Silverman, Hugh J., ed. *Postmodernism—Philosophy and the Arts*. New York: Routledge; 1990. vi, 319 pp. (Continental Philosophy 3.) [†Treatment of the absurd; secularity; relationship to Postmodernism.]

[950] Miller, Judith Graves. "Theatricalizations of the French Revolution." *Theater*. 1989-1990 Winter-Spring; 21(1-2): 10-16. [Illus. †1900-1999. Treatment of French Revolution.]

[951] Naversen, Ronald Arthur. "The Scenographer as Camoufleur." *DAI*. 1990 Dec.; 51(6): 1833A-1834A. [†Scenography; relationship to camouflage; war. Dissertation abstract.]

[952] Newlin, Jeanne T. "The Harvard Theatre Collection: Ever New Crossroads." *THStud*. 1990; 10: 213-228. [Illus. †Role of Harvard Theatre Collection.]

[953] O'Dair, Sharon. "Justifying Subsidizing: Or, Literature and Social Process." *CentR*. 1990 Fall; 34(4): 595-603. [†Role in society; relationship to government subsidies.]

[954] Pavis, Patrice. "Etudes théâtrales." 95-107 in Angenot, Marc, ed.; Bessière, Jean, ed.; Fokkema, Douwe, ed.; Kushner, Eva, ed. *Théorie littéraire*. Paris: PU de France; 1989. 395 pp.

[955] Peeters, Frank. "The Historiography of Written Fiction with Special Reference to Theater History." 237-245 in Valdés, Mario J., ed. *Toward a Theory of Comparative Literature: Selected Papers Presented in the Division of Theory of Literature at the XIth International Comparative Literature Congress*. New York: Peter Lang; 1990. 275 pp. (Proceedings of the International Comparative Literature Association 11: 3.) [†Theater history; relationship to literary history.]

[956] Pineault, Wallace John. "Industrial Theatre: The Businessman's Broadway." *DAI*. 1990 Feb.; 50(8): 2307A-2308A. [†Industrial theater. Dissertation abstract.]

[957] Pradier, Jean-Marie. "Towards a Biological Theory of the Body in Performance." *NTQ*. 1990 Feb.; 6(21): 86-98. [†Role of biology; human body; relationship to performance.]

[958] Prinz, Jessica. "'Always Two Things Switching': Laurie Anderson's Alterity." 150-174 in Perloff, Marjorie, ed.; Davis, Robert Con, fwd.; Schleifer, Ronald, fwd. *Postmodern Genres*. Norman: U of Oklahoma P; 1989. xx, 276 pp. (Oklahoma Project for Discourse and Theory.) [See also 1988 Bibliog. IV.973. †Visual imagery; relationship to text; Postmodernism in performance art by Anderson, Laurie.]

[959] Quinn, Michael L. "Celebrity and the Semiotics of Acting." *NTQ*. 1990 May; 6(22): 154-161. [†Role of acting; relationship to celebrity. Semiotic approach. Application of theories of Prague School of Linguistics.]

[960] Roach, Joseph R. "Darwin's Passion: The Language of Expression on Nature's Stage." *Discourse*. 1990-1991 Fall-Winter; 13(1): 40-58. [Illus. †Representation of nature in theatrical production; relationship to Realist movement and Naturalism. Theories of Darwin, Charles Robert; Le Brun, Charles.]

[961] Rojas, Mario, ed. "Semiótica del teatro." *Dispositio*. 1988; 13(33-35). [Spec. iss.; incl. introd. †Semiotic approach.]

[962] Rovit, Rebecca Laughlin. "The Marionette as an Ideal in Acting: Dualism Resolved in Craig's *Übermarionette*, Meyerhold's Biomechanics, and Schlemmer's Stage Workshop." *DAI*. 1990 Feb.; 50(8): 2308A. [†Marionettes; relationship to performance theory. Theories of Craig, Edward Gordon: "The Actor and the Übermarionette"; Meĭerkhol'd, Vsevolod Émil'evich; Schlemmer, Oskar; Kleist, Heinrich von: "Über das Marionettentheater." Dissertation abstract.]

[963] Russell-Parks, Shelley McKnight. "A Phenomenological Analysis of the Actor's Perceptions during the Creative Act." *DAI*. 1990 July; 51(1): 24A. [†Acting. Phenomenological approach. Dissertation abstract.]

[964] Salosaari, Kari. "Perusteita näyttelijäntyön semiotiikkaan, I osa: Teatterin kieli ja näyttelijä merkityksen tuottajana (Fundamentals in the Semiotics of the Player's Craft. I: The Language of the Theatre and the Player as the Agent of Signification)." *DAI*. 1990 Summer; 51(2): Item 718C. [†Role of actors. Semiotic approach. Application of theories of Greimas, Algirdas Julien. Dissertation abstract.]

[965] Schechter, Joel, ed.; Robinson, Marc, ed. "New Writing." *Theater*. 1990 Summer-Fall; 21(3). [Spec. iss.; illus.

[966] ——. "Theater and Revolution." *Theater*. 1989-1990 Winter-Spring; 21(1-2). [Spec. iss.; illus. †Treatment of revolution.]

[967] Schindler, Otto G. "Die Fachbibliothek für Theaterwissenschaft an der Universität Wien: Neue Räume, neue Dienste, neue Perspektiven." *Mitteilungen der Vereinigung Österreichischer Bibliothekare* (Vienna). 1989; 42(4): 113-120. [†Role of Fachbibliothek für Theaterwissenschaft at Universität Wien.]

[968] Schmitt, Natalie Crohn. "Theorizing about Performance: Why Now?" *NTQ*. 1990 Aug.; 6(23): 231-234. [†Role of theater theory applied to performance compared to science; quantum theory applied to nature.]

[969] Schramm, Helmar. "Theatralität und Öffentlichkeit: Vorstudien zur Begriffsgeschichte von 'Theater'." *WB*. 1990; 36(2): 223-239. [†Historical approach.]

[970] Segre, Cesare. "Semiótica y teatro." *RILCE: Revista de Filología Hispánica* (Univ. de Navarra). 1990; 6(2): 327-336. [†Application of semiotics.]

[971] Shoham, Chaim. *Theatron UDrama Mehapsim Kahal*. Tel Aviv: Or Am; 1989. 159 pp. [†And drama.]

[972] Siegfried, Walter. "Nativity as Living Picture: The Christmas Crib at Andechs." *NTQ*. 1990 Nov.; 6(24): 379-394. [†Passion play. Interview with Stephan, Brother.]

[973] Stewart, Tommie Harris. "The Acting Theories and Techniques of Frank Silvera in His 'Theatre of Being'." *DAI*. 1990 Apr.; 50(10): 3109A. [†Acting. Theories of Silvera, Frank. Dissertation abstract.]

[974] Sullivan, Esther Beth. "Emplotment: A Feminist Analysis of Narrative Onstage." *DAI*. 1990 Apr.; 50(10): 3109A. [†Emplotment; relationship to narrative. Feminist approach. Dissertation abstract.]

[975] Suvin, Darko. "Approach to Topoanalysis and to the Paradigmatics of Dramaturgic Space." *PoT*. 1987; 8(2): 311-334. [†Role of space.]

[976] Tordera, Antonio. "El paso del tiempo: Variaciones sobre teoría del orden teatral." *Dispositio*. 1988; 13(33-35): 129-146. [†Semiotic approach.]

[977] Toro, Alfonso de. "Semiosis teatral postmoderna: Intento de un modelo." *Gestos*. 1990 Apr.; 5(9): 23-51. [†Relationship to Postmodernism.]

[978] Toro, Fernando de. "Semiótica y recepción: Teoría y práctica de la recepción teatral." *Dispositio*. 1988; 13(33-35): 91-114. [†Relationship to text. Semiotic approach.]

[979] Villegas, Juan. "Toward a Model for the History of the Theater." 255-279 in Carroll, David, ed. *The States of "Theory": History, Art, and Critical Discourse*. New York: Columbia UP; 1990. x, 316 pp. (Irvine Studies in the Humanities.) [†Application of New Historicism.]

[980] Wellman, Mac; Jones, Jeffrey M. "New Writing and the Classics: An Exchange." *Theater*. 1990 Summer-Fall; 21(3): 6-15. [†Sources in classical drama.]

[981] Whitehead, Gregory. "The Forensic Theatre: Memory Plays for the Post-Mortem Condition." *PArtsJ*. 1990; 12(2-3 [35-36]): 99-109. [†On catastrophe as theater.]

[982] Wickstrom, Gordon M. "Education for the Theater." *PArtsJ*. 1990; 12(2-3 [35-36]): 155-158. [†Role of theater studies.]

[983] Zivanovic, Judith. "The Rhetorical and Political Foundations of Women's Collaborative Theatre." 209-219 in Redmond, James, pref. *Women in Theatre*. Cambridge: Cambridge UP; 1989. 297 pp. (ThD 11.) [†Collaboration in women's theater groups; relationship to rhetoric; politics. Feminist approach.]

Bibliography

[984] Hadamowsky, Franz. *Bücherkunde deutschsprachiger Theaterliteratur*. Vienna: Böhlau; 1986. 341 pp. (*Maske und Kothurn*, Beihefte 5, 2.) [†Of books in German language (1900-1944).]

[985] ——. *Bücherkunde deutschsprachiger Theaterliteratur, Part I, I: 1750-1899*. Vienna: Böhlau; 1988. 241 pp. (*Maske und Kothurn*, Beihefte 5, 1.) [†Of books in German language (1750-1899).]

[986] Steadman, Susan M. Flierl. "Feminist Dramatic Criticism: Where Are We Now." *W&P*. 1989; 4(2 [8]): 118-148. [†And drama. Of feminist literary theory and criticism.]

Literary movements

Aesthetic movement

[987] Chai, Leon. *Aestheticism: The Religion of Art in Post-Romantic Literature*. New York: Columbia UP; 1990. xiv, 269 pp. [†Relationship to European literature; American literature.]

[988] Small, Ian; Guy, Josephine. "The 'Literary,' Aestheticism and the Founding of English as a Discipline." *ELT*. 1990; 33(4): 443-453. [†Relationship to English studies.]

Avant-garde

[989] Beekman, Klaus. "Die Aktualität der Avantgarde." 113-117 in Drijkoningen, Fernand, ed.; Gevers, Dick, ed. *Anarchia*. Amsterdam: Rodopi; 1989. 123 pp. (AvG 3.) [On Zima, Peter V., ed. and Strutz, Johann, ed. *Europäische Avantgarde* & 1988 Bibliog. II.2610. †Review article.]

[990] Drijkoningen, Fernand, ed.; Gevers, Dick, ed. *Anarchia*. Amsterdam: Rodopi; 1989. 123 pp. (AvG 3.) [Incl. Eng. & Fr. introds. †Relationship to anarchism.]

[991] Kostelanetz, Richard. "'Avant-Garde'." 109-112 in Drijkoningen, Fernand, ed.; Gevers, Dick, ed. *Anarchia*. Amsterdam: Rodopi; 1989. 123 pp. (AvG 3.)

[992] Lawson, Andrew. "Farewell to the Avant-Gardes: Some Notes towards the Definition of a Counter-Culture." *TexP*. 1990 Winter; 4(3): 442-449. [†Relationship to counterculture.]

[993] Nehring, Neil. "What Should the Politics of Cultural Studies Be?" *LIT*. 1990 Mar.; 1(3): 229-237. [†Relationship to mass culture; anarchism. Treatment in criticism.]

[994] Shapir, Maksim. "Chto takoe avangard (v literature)?" *Daugava*. 1990 Oct.; 10(160): 3-6. [†And Modernism.]

[995] van Rossum-Guyon, Françoise. "Entretien avec Julia Kristeva: L'Avant-Garde aujourd'hui." 157-174 in van Rossum-Guyon, Françoise, ed. *Femmes Frauen Women*. Amsterdam: Rodopi; 1990. 182 pp. (AvG 4.) [†Role of women. Interview with Kristeva, Julia.]

[996] van Rossum-Guyon, Françoise, ed. *Femmes Frauen Women*. Amsterdam: Rodopi; 1990. 182 pp. (AvG 4.) [Incl. Fr. introd. †Role of women.]

Enlightenment

[997] Costa, Emilia Viotti da. "The Enlightenment as an Invention: A View from the Periphery." *Dieciocho*. 1990 Spring-Fall; 13(1-2): 4-20.

[998] Luyendijk-Elshout, Antonie. "Of Masks and Mills: The Enlightened Doctor and His Frightened Patient." 186-230 in Rousseau, G. S., ed.; Porter, Roy, introd. *The Languages of Psyche: Mind and Body in Enlightenment Thought*. Berkeley: U of California P; 1990. xix, 480 pp. (Publications from the Clark Library Professorship 12.) [Illus. †Role of medicine; relationship to fear; anxiety.]

[999] Müller, Thomas. *Rhetorik und bürgerliche Identität: Studien zur Rolle der Psychologie in der Frühaufklärung*. Tübingen: Niemeyer; 1990. 162 pp. [†Role of psychology; relationship to bourgeoisie; rhetoric.]

[1000] Popkin, Richard H. "Medicine, Racism, Anti-Semitism: A Dimension of Enlightenment Culture." 405-442 in Rousseau, G. S., ed.; Porter, Roy, introd. *The Languages of Psyche: Mind and Body in Enlightenment Thought*. Berkeley: U of California P; 1990. xix, 480 pp. (Publications from the Clark Library Professorship 12.) [Illus. †Role of anti-Semitism; racism; relationship to medicine.]

[1001] Riehl, Joseph E., ed.; Brantley, Jennifer, asst. ed.; Pittman, Pamela T., asst. ed.; Smith, James, asst. ed. *Explorations: The Age of Enlightenment*. Lafayette, LA: Levy Humanities Ser.; 1987. iv, 86 pp. (ExplorSp 1.)

[1002] Rousseau, G. S., ed.; Porter, Roy, introd. *The Languages of Psyche: Mind and Body in Enlightenment Thought*. Clark Library Lectures 1985-1986. Berkeley: U of California P; 1990. xix, 480 pp. (Publications from the Clark Library Professorship 12.)

Hermetism

[1003] Willard, Thomas S. "Recent Books in Brief." *CaudaP*. 1990 Spring; 9(2): 3-6. [†Review article.]

Humanism

[1004] Southgate, B. C. "'No Other Wisdom'? Humanist Reactions to Science and Scientism in the Seventeenth Century." *SCen*. 1990 Spring; 5(1): 71-92. [†1600-1699. Role of poetry; relationship to science.]

Modernism

[1005] Benstock, Shari. "Expatriate Modernism: Writing on the Cultural Rim." 20-40 in Broe, Mary Lynn, ed.; Ingram, Angela, ed. *Women's Writing in Exile*. Chapel Hill: U of North Carolina P; 1989. xii, 442 pp. [†Relationship to women writers in exile.]

[1006] Caserio, Robert L. "'A Pathos of Uncertain Agency': Paul de Man and Narrative." *JNT*. 1990 Spring; 20(2): 195-209. [†Narrative; relationship to allegory. Treatment in de Man, Paul.]

[1007] di Virgilio, Paul Samuel. "The Mental Labours and Travail of Crossing the Dense Purges of Modernism and Postmodernism." 237-244 in Bauer, Roger, ed.; Fokkema, Douwe, ed.; Graat, Michael de, asst. ed.; Fischer-Lichte, Erika, asst.; Garstin, Marguerite, asst.; Ibsch, Elrud, asst.; Stackelberg, Jürgen von, asst. *Proceedings of the XIIth Congress of the International Comparative Literature Association/Actes du XIIe congrès de l'Association Internationale de Littérature Comparée: München 1988 Munich, V: Space and Boundaries in Literary Theory and Criticism/Espace et frontières dans la critique et la théorie littéraire; Space and Boundaries in the Teaching of General and Comparative Literature/Espace et frontières dans l'enseignement de la littérature générale et comparée*. Munich: Iudicium; 1990. 415 pp. (Proceedings of the Congress of the International Comparative Literature Association 12: 5.) [†And Postmodernism.]

[1008] Eysteinsson, Astradur. *The Concept of Modernism*. Ithaca: Cornell UP; 1990. 265 pp.

[1009] Jarque, Vicente. "A Dispersión da Estética." *Grial*. 1990 Apr.-June; 28(106): 145-153.

[1010] Kirk, Russell. "Obdurate Adversaries of Modernity." *ModA*. 1987 Summer-Fall; 31(3-4): 203-206. [†Antimodernism.]

[1011] Larsen, Neil; Concha, Jaime, fwd.; Millet, Kitty, tr. *Modernism and Hegemony: A Materialist Critique of Aesthetic Agencies*. Minneapolis: U of Minnesota P; 1990. xlvi, 125 pp. (Theory and History of Literature 71.) [†Theories of Adorno, Theodor W.; Marx, Karl.]

   SEE SUBJECT INDEX FOR CROSS-REFERENCES

[1012] Nieli, Russell. "The Cry against Nineveh: Whittaker Chambers and Eric Voegelin on the Crisis of Western Modernity." *ModA*. 1987 Summer-Fall; 31(3-4): 267-274. [†Treatment in Chambers, Whittaker; Voegelin, Eric; relationship to religion; politics.]

[1013] Patrick, James. "Modernity as Gnosis." *ModA*. 1987 Summer-Fall; 31(3-4): 222-233. [†Relationship to Gnosticism.]

[1014] Petersen, Jürgen H. "Anfänge einer literaturwissenschaftlichen Moderne-Forschung in Deutschland." *Arcadia*. 1989; 24(2): 199-208. [On Fülleborn, Ulrich, ed.; Engel, Manfred, ed. *Das neuzeitliche Ich in der Literatur des 18. und 20. Jahrhunderts*; Japp, Uwe. *Literatur und Modernität*; & Bode, Christoph. *Ästhetik der Ambiguität*. †Review article.]

[1015] Regnery, Henry, fwd.; Panichas, George A., introd. "Thirtieth Anniversary Issue: Essays on the Crisis of Modernity." *ModA*. 1987 Summer-Fall; 31(3-4). [Spec. iss.]

[1016] Retallack, Joan. "Post-Scriptum—High Modern." 248-273 in Perloff, Marjorie, ed.; Davis, Robert Con, fwd.; Schleifer, Ronald, fwd. *Postmodern Genres*. Norman: U of Oklahoma P; 1989. xx, 276 pp. (Oklahoma Project for Discourse and Theory.) [See also 1988 Bibliog. IV.1032. †Abstraction; logic in language; relationship to Postmodernism.]

[1017] Riva, Massimo. "1888-1988: Some Remarks on Nihilism and Secularisation." *HEI*. 1989; 11: 979-988. [†And Postmodernism. Role of nihilism. Sources in Nietzsche, Friedrich Wilhelm.]

[1018] Torgovnick, Marianna. *Gone Primitive: Savage Intellects, Modern Lives*. Chicago: U of Chicago P; 1990. xi, 328 pp. [†Relationship to primitivism.]

[1019] Williamson, René. "Reflections of a Political Scientist." *ModA*. 1987 Summer-Fall; 31(3-4): 316-322. [†Relationship to political science; religion; publishing.]

Postmodernism

[1020] Akasofu, Tetsuji. "'Post Modern' no Logos." *EigoS*. n.d.; 134: 532-534. [†Relationship to Logos.]

[1021] Auslander, Philip. "Vito Acconci and the Politics of the Body in Postmodern Performance." 185-195 in Shapiro, Gary, ed. *After the Future: Postmodern Times and Places*. Albany: State U of New York P; 1990. xx, 360 pp. (Contemporary Studies in Philosophy and Literature 2.) [†Study example: Acconci, Vito.]

[1022] Bailey, John. "El postmodernismo y el concepto de autoridad." *RO*. 1990 Sept.; 112: 104-115. [†Relationship to authority; truth.]

[1023] Bennett, David. "Postmodernism and Vision: Ways of Seeing (at) the End of History." 259-279 in D'haen, Theo, ed.; Bertens, Hans, ed. *History and Post-War Writing*. Amsterdam: Rodopi; 1990. 279 pp. (PmdnS 3.) [†Relationship to history. Theories of Owens, Craig; Jameson, Fredric.]

[1024] Bogataj, Matej. "Klin se s klinom izbija." *Sodobnost*. 1990; 38(4): 416-428. 1990; 38(5): 548-557. 1990; 38(6-7): 697-708.

[1025] Borchmeyer, Dieter. "[Postmodernismus]." *Poetica*. 1989; 21(1-2): 201-214. [†Review article.]

[1026] Bywater, William. "The Paranoia of Postmodernism." *P&L*. 1990 Apr.; 14(1): 79-84. [†Relationship to paranoia; study example: Fish, Stanley: *Is There a Text in This Class?* Application of theories of Shapiro, David.]

[1027] Cascardi, Anthony J. "History, Theory, (Post)Modernity." 1-16 in Shapiro, Gary, ed. *After the Future: Postmodern Times and Places*. Albany: State U of New York P; 1990. xx, 360 pp. (Contemporary Studies in Philosophy and Literature 2.) [†Relationship to history.]

[1028] Casey, Edward. "Place, Form, and Identity in Postmodern Architecture and Philosophy: Derrida *avec* Moore, Mies *avec* Kant." 199-211 in Shapiro, Gary, ed. *After the Future: Postmodern Times and Places*. Albany: State U of New York P; 1990. xx, 360 pp. (Contemporary Studies in Philosophy and Literature 2.) [†Relationship to architecture. Theories of Derrida, Jacques; Kant, Immanuel.]

[1029] De Santi, Gualtiero. "Littérature et post-modernisme: La Petre de l'innocence." 550-555 in Bauer, Roger, ed.; Fokkema, Douwe, ed.; Graat, Michael de, asst.; Kaiser, Gerhard, asst.; Rinner, Fridrun, asst.; Wertheimer, Jürgen, asst. *Proceedings of the XIIth Congress of the International Comparative Literature Association/Actes du XIIe congrès de l'Association Internationale de Littérature Comparée: München 1988 Munich, IV: Space and Boundaries of Literature/Espace et frontières de la littérature*. Munich: Iudicium; 1990. 651 pp. (Proceedings of the Congress of the International Comparative Literature Association 12: 4.)

[1030] D'haen, Theo, ed.; Bertens, Hans, ed. *History and Post-War Writing*. Amsterdam: Rodopi; 1990. 279 pp. (PmdnS 3.)

[1031] Engelstad, Carl Fredrik. "Fortid og nærhet." *Kirke og Kultur*. 1989; 94(2): 111-124.

[1032] Eriksen, Trond Berg. "Efter postmodernismen?" *Samtiden*. 1990; 1: 92-104.

[1033] Escobar, Elizam. "El ataúd del *posmodernismo*." *CdP*. 1990 Jan.-Apr.; 7(20): 11-71.

[1034] Faurschou, Gail. "Obsolescence and Desire: Fashion and the Commodity Form." 234-259 in Silverman, Hugh J., ed. *Postmodernism—Philosophy and the Arts*. New York: Routledge; 1990. vi, 319 pp. (Continental Philosophy 3.) [†Relationship to fashion.]

[1035] Fekete, John. "Literary/Cultural Theory, Value, and Post-Modernity." 171-190 in Kreiswirth, Martin, ed.; Cheetham, Mark A., ed. *Theory between the Disciplines: Authority/Vision/Politics*. Ann Arbor: U of Michigan P; 1990. xii, 257 pp.

[1036] Fischer-Lichte, Erika. "Postmoderne: Fortsetzung oder Ende der Moderne? Literatur zwischen Kulturkrise und kulturellem Wandel." *Neohelicon*. 1989; 16(1): 11-27.

[1037] Fuller, Steve. "Does It Pay to Go Postmodern if Your Neighbors Do Not?" 273-284 in Shapiro, Gary, ed. *After the Future: Postmodern Times and Places*. Albany: State U of New York P; 1990. xx, 360 pp. (Contemporary Studies in Philosophy and Literature 2.) [†Relationship to politics.]

[1038] Gebhard, Walter. "Vom Ende des Wissenswillens: Wahrheitsdestruktive Parallelen zwischen dem philosophischen und literarischen Diskurs der 'Postmodernen' und Nietzsches 'Perspektivismus'." *Neohelicon*. 1989; 16(1): 45-86. [†Relationship to Nietzsche, Friedrich Wilhelm.]

[1039] Gilbert, Ron. "Endings." *Meanjin*. 1990 Autumn; 49(1): 43-48. [†And pedagogy; relationship to closure; crisis.]

[1040] Gillespie, Gerald. "Translation, Quotation, Exemplarity, and Intertextuality: Some Case Histories of Postmodern Prose and Poetry: Borges, Barth, Coover, Paz, et al." 31-37 in Seixo, Maria Alzira, ed. *Os Estudios Literários: (Entre) Ciência e Hermenêutica: Actas do I Congresso da APLC, I*. Lisbon: Reprografia da A. E. F. L. L.; 1990. [†Role of writer; relationship to reader; intertextuality.]

[1041] Gould, Timothy. "Aftermaths of the Modern: The Exclusions of Philosophy in Richard Rorty, Jacques Derrida, and Stanley Cavell." 135-153 in Shapiro, Gary, ed. *After the Future: Postmodern Times and Places*. Albany: State U of New York P; 1990. xx, 360 pp. (Contemporary Studies in Philosophy and Literature 2.) [†Relationship to philosophy. Theories of Rorty, Richard; Derrida, Jacques; Cavell, Stanley Louis.]

[1042] Gunleiksrud, Gaute. "Veier til vår tid." *Kirke og Kultur*. 1989; 94(2): 99-109.

[1043] Hoesterey, Ingeborg. "Postmodernisms." *YCGL*. 1988; 37: 161-165. [†Review article.]

[1044] Jiménez Castillo, Jesús. "Postmodernidad: Regreso a lo irracional." *PH*. 1990 Apr.-June; 74: 181-184.

[1045] Johnston, John. "Ideology, Representation, Schizophrenia: Toward a Theory of the Postmodern Subject." 67-95 in Shapiro, Gary, ed. *After the Future: Postmodern Times and Places*. Albany: State U of New York P; 1990. xx, 360 pp. (Contemporary Studies in Philosophy and Literature 2.) [†Linguistic representation; relationship to philosophy; psychology.]

[1046] Khanin, Dmitry. "The Postmodern Posture." *P&L*. 1990 Oct.; 14(2): 239-247. [†Treatment in Kroker, Arthur and Cook, David Bruce: *The Postmodern Scene: Excremental Culture and Hyper-Aesthetics*.]

[1047] Kulcsár Szabó, Ernö. "Klassische Moderne, Avantgarde, Postmoderne: Paradigmen der modernen Literarität angesichts der Krise des ganzheitlichen Denkens." *Neohelicon*. 1989; 16(1): 29-44.

[1048] Kuspit, Donald. "The Contradictory Character of Postmodernism." 53-68 in Silverman, Hugh J., ed. *Postmodernism—Philosophy and the Arts*. New York: Routledge; 1990. vi, 319 pp. (Continental Philosophy 3.)

[1049] Levin, David Michael. "Postmodernism in Dance: Dance, Discourse, Democracy." 207-233 in Silverman, Hugh J., ed. *Postmodernism—Philosophy and the Arts*. New York: Routledge; 1990. vi, 319 pp. (Continental Philosophy 3.) [†Role of dance.]

[1050] Liu, Alan. "Local Transcendence: Cultural Criticism, Postmodernism, and the Romanticism of Detail." *Representations*. 1990 Fall; 32: 75-113. [†Relationship to Romanticism.]

[1051] Milner, Andrew. "Postmodernism and Popular Culture." *Meanjin*. 1990 Autumn; 49(1): 35-42. [†Compared to Modernism. Relationship to popular culture; militarism in Australia.]

[1052] Mukherjee, Arun P. "Whose Post-Colonialism and Whose Postmodernism." *WLWE*. 1990 Autumn; 30(2): 1-9. [†Relationship to postcolonialism.]

[1053] Olkowski-Laetz, Dorothea. "A Postmodern Language in Art." 101-119 in Silverman, Hugh J., ed. *Postmodernism—Philosophy and the Arts*. New York: Routledge; 1990. vi, 319 pp. (Continental Philosophy 3.) [†Relationship to language.]

[1054] O'Neill, John. "Postmodernism and (Post)Marxism." 69-79 in Silverman, Hugh J., ed. *Postmodernism—Philosophy and the Arts*. New York: Routledge; 1990. vi, 319 pp. (Continental Philosophy 3.) [†Relationship to Marxism.]

[1055] ——. "Religion and Postmodernism: The Durkheimian Bond in Bell and Jameson." 285-299 in Shapiro, Gary, ed. *After the Future: Postmodern Times and Places*. Albany: State U of New York P; 1990. xx, 360 pp. (Contemporary Studies in Philosophy and Literature 2.) [†Relationship to religion; politics. Application of theories of Bell, Daniel; Jameson, Fredric.]

[1056] Pfeil, Fred. *Another Tale to Tell: Politics and Narrative in Postmodern Culture*. London: Verso; 1990. vii, 278 pp.

[1057] Robin, Régine. "Bakhtin and Postmodernism: An Unexpected Encounter: Notes on Jean-Paul Goude's 'Marseillaise'." *DS/SD*. 1990 Spring-Summer; 3(1-2): 229-232. [†Role of the carnivalesque; kitsch; relationship to bicentennial of French Revolution in Paris (1989). Application of theories of Bakhtin, Mikhail Mikhaïlovich.]

[1058] Ross, Stephen David. "Power, Discourse, and Technology: The Presence of the Future." 255-272 in Shapiro, Gary, ed. *After the Future: Postmodern Times and Places*. Albany: State U of New York P; 1990. xx, 360 pp. (Contemporary Studies in Philosophy and Literature 2.) [†Relationship to politics.]

[1059] Rubio Carracedo, José. "La ética ante el reto de la postmodernidad." *Arbor*. 1990 Feb.; 135(530): 119-146.

[1060] Schönherr, Ulrich; Daniel, Jamie Owen, tr. "Adorno, *Ritter Gluck*, and the Tradition of the Postmodern." *NGC*. 1989 Fall; 48: 135-154. [†Theories of Adorno, Theodor W.]

[1061] Schrift, Alan D. "The Becoming-Postmodern of Philosophy." 99-113 in Shapiro, Gary, ed. *After the Future: Postmodern Times and Places*. Albany: State U of

New York P; 1990. xx, 360 pp. (Contemporary Studies in Philosophy and Literature 2.) [†Relationship to ontology.]

[1062] Schwind, Klaus. "Verflüchtigung von Satire im Gleich-Wertigen Allerlei? Anmerkungen zu Wirkungspotentialen 'satirischer Texte' unter den Bedingungen der 'Postmoderne' am Beispiel von B. Strauss' 'Kalldewey, Farce'." *Neohelicon*. 1989; 16(1): 129-150. [†Study example: Strauss, Botho: *Kalldewey, Farce.*]

[1063] Scott, Charles E. "Postmodern Language." 33-52 in Silverman, Hugh J., ed. *Postmodernism—Philosophy and the Arts.* New York: Routledge; 1990. vi, 319 pp. (Continental Philosophy 3.) [†Use of language. Application of theories of Nietzsche, Friedrich Wilhelm.]

[1064] Shapiro, Gary, ed. *After the Future: Postmodern Times and Places.* Albany: State U of New York P; 1990. xx, 360 pp. (Contemporary Studies in Philosophy and Literature 2.) [Incl. introd.]

[1065] Shusterman, Richard. "'Ethics and Aesthetics Are One': Postmodernism's Ethics of Taste." 115-134 in Shapiro, Gary, ed. *After the Future: Postmodern Times and Places.* Albany: State U of New York P; 1990. xx, 360 pp. (Contemporary Studies in Philosophy and Literature 2.) [†Relationship to ethics; aesthetics.]

[1066] Silverman, Hugh J., ed. *Postmodernism—Philosophy and the Arts.* New York: Routledge; 1990. vi, 319 pp. (Continental Philosophy 3.) [Incl. introd.]

[1067] Spiridon, Monica. "Poetică și politică." *RoLit.* 1990 Sept. 27; 23(39): 7. [†Relationship to politics. Theories of Hutcheon, Linda.]

[1068] Szabolcsi, Miklós, ed.; Vajda, György M., ed. "Postmodernismus." *Neohelicon.* 1989; 16(1). [Spec. iss.]

[1069] Taylor, Mark C. "Back to the Future." 13-32 in Silverman, Hugh J., ed. *Postmodernism—Philosophy and the Arts.* New York: Routledge; 1990. vi, 319 pp. (Continental Philosophy 3.) [†Relationship to time.]

[1070] Ungvári, Tamás. "The Genesis of the 'Anti-Copernican' Turn." *Neohelicon.* 1989; 16(1): 285-310.

[1071] Watson, Stephen H. "*In Situ*: Beyond the Architectonics of the Modern." 83-100 in Silverman, Hugh J., ed. *Postmodernism—Philosophy and the Arts.* New York: Routledge; 1990. vi, 319 pp. (Continental Philosophy 3.) [†Relationship to architecture.]

[1072] Weiss, Allen S. "Lucid Intervals: Postmodernism and Photography." 155-172 in Silverman, Hugh J., ed. *Postmodernism—Philosophy and the Arts.* New York: Routledge; 1990. vi, 319 pp. (Continental Philosophy 3.) [†Relationship to photography.]

Realist movement

[1073] Jonsson, Stefan. "Realistisk aktivitet." *OB.* 1990; 1: 2-20.

Romanticism

[1074] Burwick, Frederick. "The Dilemma of the 'Mad Rhapsodist' in Romantic Theories of the Imagination." *WC.* 1990 Winter; 21(1): 10-18. [†Theories of imagination; inspiration; relationship to rationality; critical judgment.]

[1075] Carchia, Gianni, ed.; Vercellone, Federico, ed. "Romanticismo e poesia." *RdE.* 1989; 29(31). [Spec. iss.; incl. pref.]

[1076] Garber, Frederick, ed. *Romantic Irony.* Budapest: Akad. Kiadó; 1988. (Comparative History of Literatures in European Languages 8.) [†Romantic irony.]

[1077] Gaull, Marilyn. "Under Romantic Skies: Astronomy and the Poets." *WC.* 1990 Winter; 21(1): 34-41. [†Poetic language; relationship to synecdoche compared to language of astronomy. Application of theories of Newton, Sir Isaac compared to Herschel, Sir William.]

[1078] Genovese, Rino. "L'eredità del romanticismo: Codice dell'arte e codice estetico." *RdE.* 1989; 29(31): 148-162. [†Aesthetics.]

[1079] Gillespie, Gerald. "Cathedral Window Light: Sacral Spaces of Epiphany in Romantic Literature." 283-289 in Bauer, Roger, ed.; Fokkema, Douwe, ed.; Graat, Michael de, ed.; Boening, John, ed.; Gillespie, Gerald, ed.; Moog-Grünewald, Maria, ed.; Nemoianu, Virgil, ed.; Ricapito, Joseph, ed.; Schmeling, Manfred, ed.; Thüsen, Joachim von der, ed.; Uhlig, Claus, ed. *Proceedings of the XIIth Congress of the International Comparative Literature Association/Actes du XIIe congrès de l'Association Internationale de Littérature Comparée: München 1988 Munich, II: Space and Boundaries in Literature/Espace et frontières dans la littérature.* Munich: Iudicium; 1990. 606 pp. (Proceedings of the Congress of the International Comparative Literature Association 12: 2.) [†Treatment of stained-glass window of church as metaphor for epiphany.]

[1080] Hamlin, Cyrus. "Literary History after New Criticism: Paul de Man's Essays on Romanticism." 133-148 in Herman, Luc, ed.; Humbeeck, Kris, ed.; Lernout, Geert, ed. *(Dis)continuities: Essays on Paul de Man.* Amsterdam: Rodopi; 1989. 239 pp. (PmdnS 2.) [†Treatment in de Man, Paul.]

[1081] Hoffmeister, Gerhart, ed. *European Romanticism: Literary Cross-Currents, Modes, and Models.* Detroit: Wayne State UP; 1990. 369 pp. [Incl. pref.]

[1082] Punter, David. *The Romantic Unconscious: A Study in Narcissism and Patriarchy.* New York: New York UP; 1990. x, 200 pp. [†Relationship to patriarchy; narcissism.]

Bibliographical

[1083] Abbott, Craig S. "Goals and Methods in a Traditional Approach to Bibliography and Research." *LRN.* 1987 Spring-Summer; 12(2-3): 95-98.

[1084] Adam, Wolfgang. "Privatbibliotheken im 17. und 18. Jahrhundert: Fortschrittsbericht (1975-1988)." *IASL.* 1990; 15(1): 123-173. [†On personal collections (1600-1799); relationship to literary history. Treatment in criticism (1975-1988).]

[1085] Bieńkowska, Barbara; Chamerska, Halina; Zalewski, Wojciech, ed. & tr.; Payne, Eleanor R., ed. & tr. *Books in Poland: Past and Present.* Wiesbaden: Harrassowitz; 1990. 103 pp. (Publishing, Bibliography, Libraries, and Archives in Russia and Eastern Europe 1.) [†In Poland.]

[1086] Bozeman, Patricia. "264 Catalogues … and Counting: The Leab Awards after Five Years." *RBML.* 1990; 5(2): 85-94. [†Relationship to library exhibition catalogues.]

[1087] Chalmers, John P. "Incunabula in the David Jackson McWilliams Bequest." *LCUT.* 1989; 48: 49-67. [Illus. †Catalogue of incunabula in David Jackson McWilliams Collection at Harry Ransom Humanities Research Center.]

[1088] Cloonan, Michèle Valerie. "Mass Deacidification in the 1990s." *RBML.* 1990; 5(2): 95-103. [†Role of deacidification; relationship to book preservation.]

[1089] Cockx-Indestege, Elly. "Books Printed in the Netherlands in the Fifteenth and Sixteenth Centuries from the Arenberg Collection, Now in the Royal Library of Belgium." 373-393 in Croiset van Uchelen, Ton, ed.; Horst, Koert van der, ed.; Schilder, Günter, ed.; Hesselink, Sebastiaan S., fwd. Theatrum Orbis Librorum: Liber Amicorum *Presented to Nico Israel on the Occasion of His Seventieth Birthday.* Utrecht: HES; 1989. xii, 518 pp. [†1400-1599. Book collecting in Netherlands by Arenberg family; relationship to Bibliothèque Royale Albert Iᵉr.]

[1090] Croiset van Uchelen, Ton, ed.; Horst, Koert van der, ed.; Schilder, Günter, ed.; Hesselink, Sebastiaan S., fwd. Theatrum Orbis Librorum: Liber Amicorum *Presented to Nico Israel on the Occasion of His Seventieth Birthday.* Utrecht: HES; 1989. xii, 518 pp. [Incl. introd. †Festschrift for Israel, Nico.]

[1091] Dickson, Donald C., ed. *George Watson Cole, 1850-1939.* Metuchen, NJ: Scarecrow; 1990. viii, 256 pp. (Great Bibliographers Series 8.) [Prev. pub. material. †Theories of Cole, George Watson.]

[1092] Enright, B. J. "'I Collect and I Preserve': Richard Rawlinson, 1690-1755, and Eighteenth-Century Book Collecting: Portrait of a Bibliophile, XXVIII." *BC.* 1990 Spring; 39(1): 27-54. [Illus. †1700-1799. Book collecting by Rawlinson, Richard.]

[1093] Esposito, Enzo; Solimine, Giovanni; Pizzi, Rino, tr.; Moore, Prentiss, tr. "Bibliographical Studies in Italy since 1945." *Lib&C.* 1990 Summer; 25(3): 433-445. [†In Italy. 1900-1999.]

[1094] Fredeman, William E. "Two Uncollected Bibliographers: Simon Harcourt Nowell-Smith and Michael Trevanion of Erewhon." *BC.* 1989 Winter; 38(4): 464-482. [Illus. †1900-1999. Role of Nowell-Smith, Simon Harcourt; Trevanion, Michael as bibliographer; relationship to book collecting.]

[1095] Graf, Martina. "Johann Joachim Eschenburgs 'Grundriss einer Anleitung zur Bücherkunde' (1792): Ein frühes Dokument einer buchwissenschaftlchen Vorlesung an einer höheren Bildungsanstalt." *GJ.* 1990; 65: 360-379. [Incl. text. †1700-1799. Treatment in Eschenburg, Johann Joachim: "Grundriss einer Anleitung zur Bücherkunde."]

[1096] Hagelin, Ove. "Svenska Läkare Sällskapets bibliotek." *Bokvännen.* 1990; 45(3): 50-60. [†Role of library of Svenska Läkaresällskapet.]

[1097] Hoover, John Neal. "From Eccentric to Sanctified: The Eclectic Exhibition Catalogues of 1989 and the Leab Awards." *RBML.* 1989 Fall; 4(2): 113-120. [†Role of library exhibition catalogues; relationship to exhibition of rare books and manuscripts.]

[1098] Jonsmoen, Ola. "Ha tru på kjærleiken! Om bok, bibliotek og bibliotekarar." *Bok og Bibliotek.* 1990; 1: 10-11. [†Libraries.]

[1099] Kanyar-Becker, Helena. "Fritz Lieb und seine russisch-slavische Bibliothek." 101-116 in Löwenstein, Hans-Jürgen, ed. *Leben mit Büchern: Festschrift für Otto Sagner zum 70. Geburtstag.* Marburg: n.p.; 1990. 189 pp. (Schriften der ABDOSD 1.) [†Personal library of Lieb, Fritz; relationship to Russian literature; Slavic literature.]

[1100] Kuz'min, Evgeniĭ. "Blesk i nishcheta natsional'nykh bibliotek." *LG.* 1990 Feb. 28; 9 [5283]: 3. [†Libraries. Interview with Billington, James H.]

[1101] Le Fontaine, Joseph Raymond. *The Collector's Book Shelf.* Buffalo: Prometheus; 1990. 333 pp. [†Handbook for book collectors.]

[1102] Löwenstein, Hans-Jürgen, ed. *Leben mit Büchern: Festschrift für Otto Sagner zum 70. Geburtstag.* Marburg: n.p.; 1990. 189 pp. (Schriften der ABDOSD 1.) [†Festschrift for Sagner, Otto.]

[1103] Pasternack, Howard. "Online Catalogs and the Retrospective Conversion of Special Collections." *RBML.* 1990; 5(2): 71-76. [†Role of online catalogs; relationship to library collection.]

[1104] Pilette, Roberta; Harris, Carolyn. "It Takes Two to Tango: A Conservator's View of Curator/Conservator Relations." *RBML.* 1989 Fall; 4(2): 103-111. [†Role of curator-conservator relations; relationship to book preservation; rare books.]

[1105] Raguotienė, Genovaitė. "Levo Vladimirovo gyvenimo ir veiklos bruožai." *Knygotyra.* 1988; 15 [22]: 3-12. [Rus. & Eng. sums. †Libraries in Lithuania. Role of Vladimirovas, Levas.]

[1106] Ramsten, Lars. "Mitt findländska bibliotek." *Bokvännen.* 1990; 45(2): 33-36. [†On collection of Ramsten, Lars.]

[1107] Ryan, Michael T. "Shopping Around." *RBML.* 1989 Spring; 4(1): 43-52. [†Role of library collection; relationship to mail-order catalogue.]

[1108] Ryznar, Eliska; Croucher, Murlin; Zalewski, Wojciech, ed. *Books in Czechoslovakia: Past and Present.* Wiesbaden: Harrassowitz; 1989. 103 pp. (Publishing, Bibliography, Libraries, and Archives in Russia and Eastern Europe 2.) [†In Czechoslovakia.]

SEE SUBJECT INDEX FOR CROSS-REFERENCES

[1109] Silver, Joel. "The Lilly Fellowship Program: Training for Rare Book Librarians." *RBML*. 1990; 5(1): 33-38. [†On training of librarians about rare books; manuscripts.]

[1110] Sinkevičius, Klemensas. "Tarybų Lietuvos karių bibliotekinis aptarnavimas Didžiojo Tėvynės karo metais." *Knygotyra*. 1988; 15 [22]: 72-78. [Rus. & Ger. sums. †Libraries in Lithuania (1941-1942); relationship to Soviet army.

[1111] Smiraglia, Edvige. "Donazione di libri sacri alla chiesa di S. Clemente." *VChrist*. 1989; 26(2): 351-360. [†Latin language literature. 700-799. Donation of book to Chiesa di San Clemente. Treatment in epigraph.]

[1112] Staley, Thomas F. "Literary Canons, Literary Studies, and Library Collections: A Retrospective on Collecting Twentieth-Century Writers." *RBML*. 1990; 5(1): 9-21. [†Role of library collection; relationship to canon. Collection study of collection at Harry Ransom Humanities Research Center at University of Texas at Austin.]

[1113] Van Wingen, Peter M. "The Incunabula Collections at the Library of Congress." *RBML*. 1989 Fall; 4(2): 85-100. [†Collection study of collection at Library of Congress.]

[1114] Young, Percy M. "Samuel Hellier: A Collector with a Purpose: Portrait of a Bibliophile, XXVIII." *BC*. 1990 Autumn; 39(3): 350-361. [Illus. †1700-1799. Book collecting by Hellier, Samuel.]

[1115] Zalewski, Wojciech. "Foreigner in American Academic Libraries: Building Polish Collections." 77-100 in Löwenstein, Hans-Jürgen, ed. *Leben mit Büchern: Festschrift für Otto Sagner zum 70. Geburtstag*. Marburg: n.p.; 1990. 189 pp. (Schriften der ABDOSD 1.) [†University libraries in United States; relationship to Polish literature.]

[1116] Zboray, Ronald J. "Archival Standards in Documentary Editing." *SB*. 1990; 43: 34-49. [†Archival standards in documentary editing; use of *Anglo-American Cataloguing Rules II*.]

Bibliography

[1117] Erskine, Elizabeth, ed.; DeMarr, Mary Jean, Amer. ed.; England, D. Gene, Amer. ed. *Annual Bibliography of English Language and Literature for 1986, Volume 61*. London: Mod. Humanities Research Assn.; 1990. xliv, 915 pp. [†In Great Britain; United States.]

[1118] Ivaškevičienė, Genovaitė; Stalnionienė, Eglė. "Levas Vladimirovas: Literatūros rodyklė: 1982-1987." *Knygotyra*. 1988; 15 [22]: 13-23. [†Relationship to libraries; publishing in Lithuania. Treatment in Vladimirovas, Levas.]

ANALYTICAL BIBLIOGRAPHY

[1119] Romani, Valentino. "Della 'bibliografia analitica' e dei suoi primi sviluppi nell'Ottocento italiano." *ABI*. 1989 Apr.-June; 40(2): 44-54. [†In Italy. 1800-1899.]

TEXTUAL CRITICISM

[1120] Gabler, Hans Walter. "Textual Studies and Criticism." *LCUT*. 1990; 20(1-2): 150-165. [Illus. †Textual editing.]

[1121] Tanselle, G. Thomas. "Textual Criticism and Deconstruction." *SB*. 1990; 43: 1-33. [†Role of text compared to role in deconstructionism.]

[1122] Zavala A., Lauro. "Entre autor y lector: La edición anotada." *Gaceta del Fondo de Cultura Económica*. 1990 Oct.; 238: 33-37. [†Role of writer; reader.]

MANUSCRIPTS

[1123] Brumbaugh, Robert S. "Plato Manuscripts: Toward a Completed Inventory." *Manuscripta*. 1990 July; 34(2): 114-121. [†Of Plato. Catalogue.]

[1124] Crews, Kenneth D. "Unpublished Manuscripts and the Right of Fair Use: Copyright Law and the Strategic Management of Information Resources." *RBML*. 1990; 5(2): 61-70. [†Unpublished manuscripts; relationship to copyright law.]

[1125] De Santis, Mario. "Codici, incunaboli e cinquecentine di argomento biblico, patristico e liturgico a Troia e Bovino." *VChrist*. 1985; 22(1): 197-213. [†Latin language literature.]

[1126] D'Ottone, Marina Balsano. "Frammenti in onciale e minuscola romanesca della Biblioteca Vallicelliana." *ABI*. 1989 Apr.-June; 40(2): 55-57. [†In uncial in Biblioteca Vallicelliana.]

[1127] Ferrer, Daniel. "Modo-Post: A Postmodern Reconsideration of the *avant-texte*." 30-36 in Wood, David, ed.; Levinas, Emmanuel, fwd.; Allison, David, tr. of fwd. *Writing the Future*. London: Routledge; 1990. x, 213 pp. (Warwick Studies in Philosophy and Literature.) [†Postmodernist approach.]

[1128] Ganz, David. "The Preconditions for Caroline Minuscule." *Viator*. 1987; 18: 23-44. [†Use of Caroline minuscule. Role of scribe.]

[1129] Kristeller, Paul Oskar. "Auf der Suche nach Handschriften des Mittelalters und der Renaissance." *RC*. 1990 Dec.; 42(82): 17-24. [Tr. of 1988 Bibliog. IV.1129. †Renaissance; humanism.]

[1130] McKitterick, Rosamond. "Carolingian Book Production: Some Problems." *Library*. 1990 Mar.; 12(1): 1-33. [Illus. †Carolingian period.]

[1131] Papazoglou, Georges K. "Un Manuscrit inconnu de Kosinitza." *AnBol*. 1988; 106(3-4): 256-258. [†Relationship to hagiography of Greek saints.]

[1132] Ruggeri, Fausto. "La donazione della biblioteca di mons. Gaetano Oppizzoni al Capitolo Metropolitano di Milano in documenti inediti." *Aevum*. 1990 Sept.-Dec.; 64(3): 445-459. [†In personal library of Oppizzoni, Gaetano.]

[1133] Trahern, Joseph B., Jr., ed. "Year's Work in Old English Studies: 1988." *OENews*. 1989 Fall; 23(1): 43-120. [Spec. sect.; incl. introd. †In England. 400-1099 Old English period.]

Codicology

[1134] Raffaelli, Renato. "Le lettere di modulo maggiore ad inizio di pagina nel Terenzio Bembino (Vat. lat. 3226)." *SULLA*. 1985; 58: 103-114. [Incl. photos. †Latin language literature.]

[1135] Tontini, Alba. "Bipartizioni di versi plautini nel codice Pal. Lat. 1615." *SULLA*. 1987; 60: 101-147. [Incl. facsims. †Latin language literature.]

Illuminated manuscripts

[1136] Armstrong, Lilian. "*Opus Petri*: Renaissance Illuminated Books from Venice and Rome." *Viator*. 1990; 21: 385-412. [Foll. by plates. †In Venice; Rome. Renaissance. Role of Petrus.]

[1137] Backhouse, Janet. "Founders of the Royal Library: Edward IV and Henry VII as Collectors of Illuminated Manuscripts." 23-41 in Williams, Dante, ed. *England in the Fifteenth Century*. Woodbridge, Eng.: Boydell; 1987. xviii, 390 pp. [Incl. list of mss. †1400-1499. Collecting by Edward IV, King of England; Henry VII, King of England.]

[1138] Heck, Christian. "Rapprochement, antagonisme, ou confusion dans le culte des saints: Art et dévotion à Katharinenthal au quatorzième siècle." *Viator*. 1990; 21: 229-238. [Eng. sum., viii. †1300-1399. Relationship to cults of John the Baptist, Saint; John the Apostle, Saint.]

[1139] Heslop, T. A. "The Production of *de luxe* Manuscripts and the Patronage of King Cnut and Queen Emma." *ASE*. 1990; 19: 151-195. [Incl. facsims. †In England. 900-1099. Patronage by Canute I, King of England; Emma, Queen of England.]

[1140] Petzold, Andreas. "Colour Notes in English Romanesque Manuscripts." *BLJ*. 1990 Spring; 16(1): 16-25. [Illus. †In England. 1000-1199.]

[1141] Rogers, Nicholas. "Fitzwilliam Museum MS 3-1979: A Bury St. Edmunds Book of Hours and the Origins of the Bury Style." 229-243 in Williams, Dante, ed. *England in the Fifteenth Century*. Woodbridge, Eng.: Boydell; 1987. xviii, 390 pp. [Illus. †1400-1499. Bury style in Fitzwilliam Museum: MS 3-1979.]

[1142] Tudor-Craig, Pamela. "The Hours of Edward V and William Lord Hastings: British Library Manuscript Additional 54782." 351-369 in Williams, Dante, ed. *England in the Fifteenth Century*. Woodbridge, Eng.: Boydell; 1987. xviii, 390 pp. [Illus. †1400-1499. British Library: MS Additional 54782.]

Manuscript collections

[1143] Formica, Patrizia. "Ancora sulla biblioteca manoscritta di Stazio." *ABI*. 1989 Apr.-June; 40(2): 5-14. [†Of Statius in Biblioteca Vallicelliana.]

[1144] Luckenbill, Dan. "Using dBASE III+ for Finding Aids and a Manuscripts Processing Workflow." *RBML*. 1990; 5(1): 23-31. [†Application of dBASE III+.]

[1145] Ringrose, Jayne. "Making Things Available: The Curator and the Reader." *BC*. 1990 Spring; 39(1): 55-73.

[1146] Romero, Orlando. "Treasures of the History Library, Palace of the Governors." *Palacio*. 1990 Spring-Summer; 95(2): 64-71. [Illus. †At Museum of New Mexico.]

[1147] Rouse, R. H.; Rouse, M. A. "'Potens in Opere et Sermone': Philip, Bishop of Bayeux, and His Books." 315-341 in Bernardo, Aldo S., ed.; Levin, Saul, ed. *The Classics in the Middle Ages*. Binghamton, NY: Medieval & Renaissance Texts & Studies; 1990. 425 pp. (MRTS 69.) [†1100-1199. Of Philippe d'Harcourt, Bishop of Bayeux.]

[1148] Stratford, Jenny. "The Manuscripts of John, Duke of Bedford: Library and Chapel." 329-350 in Williams, Dante, ed. *England in the Fifteenth Century*. Woodbridge, Eng.: Boydell; 1987. xviii, 390 pp. [Illus. †1400-1499. Of John of Lancaster, Duke of Bedford.]

[1149] Zanetti, Ugo. "Un Catalogue des additions coptes de Londres." *AnBol*. 1988; 106(1-2): 171-181. [On Layton, Bentley. *Catalogue of Coptic Literary Manuscripts in the British Library Acquired since the Year 1906*. †In British Library. Review article.]

Manuscript editing

[1150] Flight, Colin. "How Many Stemmata?" *Manuscripta*. 1990 July; 34(2): 122-128. [†Stemma. Application of graph theory.]

[1151] Taylor, P. R. "The Authority of the Codex Carrionis in the MS-Tradition of Valerius Flaccus." *ClassQ*. 1989; 39(2): 451-471. [†Manuscript collation of Valerius Flaccus, Gaius: *Argonautica* by Carrion, Louis.]

PRINTING

[1152] Abdulrazak, Fawzi A. "The Kingdom of the Book: The History of Printing as an Agency of Change in Morocco between 1865-1912." *DAI*. 1990 July; 51(1): 263A-264A. [†In Morocco (1865-1912). Relationship to social change. Dissertation abstract.]

[1153] Allen, Greer. "The Design and Printing of Library Exhibition Catalogues." *RBML*. 1990; 5(2): 77-84. [†Of library exhibition catalogues.]

[1154] Babcock, Robert G. "An Unrecorded Sessa Imprint." *YULG*. 1990 Apr.; 64(3-4): 124-131. [Illus. †In Venice. 1500-1599. Role of Sessa, Giovanni Battista.]

[1155] Berger, Sidney E. "Innovation and Diversity among the Green Family of Printers." *PHist*. 1990; 12(1 [23]): 2-20. [Illus. †In United States (1649-1859).]

[1156] Blouw, Paul Valkema. "Nicolaes Biestkens van Diest, *In Duplo*, 1559-83." 310-331 in Croiset van Uchelen, Ton, ed.; Horst, Koert van der, ed.; Schilder, Günter, ed.; Hesselink, Sebastiaan S., fwd. *Theatrum Orbis Librorum: Liber Amicorum Presented to Nico Israel on the Occasion of His Seventieth Birthday*. Utrecht: HES; 1989. xii, 518 pp. [†(1559-1583). By Biestkens, Nicolaes, the Elder; relationship to Gailliart, Willem.]

[1157] Bohatcová, Mirjam. "Hayd—Haden—Had: Drei Namen eines und desselben Druckers?" *GJ*. 1990; 65: 118-142. [Illus. †In Czechoslovakia. 1500-1599. By Had, Jan.]

[1158] Borsa, Gedeon. "A hazai könyvnyomtatás megalapítása." *MK*. 1989; 105(4): 338-354. [Ger. sum. †In Hungary. 1400-1499.

[1159] Brewer, Fredric. "Mr. Artzt's Western Lever: A Hitherto Unreported Printing Press." *PHist*. 1990; 12(1 [23]): 39-43. [†In Western United States. 1800-1899. Role of Artzt, Charles; relationship to Western Lever Printing Press.]

[1160] Coppens, Christian. "A Monomachia against Alciato: A Hitherto Unknown Pacifist Tract Dedicated to Cardinal Granvelle and Printed by Gillis Coppens of Diest, Antwerp, 1563." *GJ*. 1990; 65: 143-161. [†Latin language literature. 1500-1599. Of monomachia against Alciati, Andrea.]

[1161] Coq, Dominique. "Les 'Politiques éditoriales' des premiers imprimeurs parisiens et lyonnais (1470-1485)." 171-181 in Dunn-Lardeau, Brenda, ed.; Gaiffier, P. Baudoin de, fwd. *Legenda Aurea: Sept siècles de diffusion*. Montréal: Bellarmin; 1986. Paris: Vrin; 1986. 354 pp. (CEM Cahier Spécial 2.) [†In Lyon and Paris (1470-1485). Relationship to Jean de Vignay: *La Légende dorée*.]

[1162] Depas, Rosalind. "The Art of the Book in Munich at the Turn of the Century." 209-213 in Bauer, Roger, ed.; Fokkema, Douwe, ed.; Graat, Michael de, asst. ed.; Wimmer, Ruprecht, asst.; Goppel, Thomas, greeting. *Proceedings of the XIIth Congress of the International Comparative Literature Association/Actes du XIIe congrès de l'Association Internationale de Littérature Comparée: München 1988 Munich, I: Plenary Sessions/Séances plénières; Colloquium Munich/Colloque Munich*. Munich: Iudicium; 1990. 251 pp. (Proceedings of the Congress of the International Comparative Literature Association 12: 1.) [†In Munich (ca. 1900).]

[1163] Eeghen, Isabella H. van. "The Printing-House of Dr. Joan Blaeu behind the New Church." 402-415 in Croiset van Uchelen, Ton, ed.; Horst, Koert van der, ed.; Schilder, Günter, ed.; Hesselink, Sebastiaan S., fwd. Theatrum Orbis Librorum: Liber Amicorum *Presented to Nico Israel on the Occasion of His Seventieth Birthday*. Utrecht: HES; 1989. xii, 518 pp. [†In Amsterdam. 1600-1699. By Blaeu, Joan.]

[1164] Elder, Carol. "Early Printing Offices in Newmarket, Ontario." *PBSC*. 1985; 24: 26-37. [†In Ontario: Newmarket. 1800-1899.]

[1165] Fahy, Conor. "Techniche di stampa cinquecentesche." *ELet*. 1990 Jan.-Mar.; 15(1): 3-16. [Eng., Fr., & Sp., sums. †In Italy. 1500-1599.]

[1166] Feather, John. "Technology and the Book in the Nineteenth Century." *CrSurv*. 1990; 2(1): 5-13. [†In England. 1800-1899.]

[1167] Goldfinch, John. "An Unrecorded Salamanca Incunable." *GJ*. 1990; 65: 84-88. [†In Salamanca. Middle Ages. Of logic textbook.]

[1168] Hellinga, Lotte. "Comments on Paul Needham's Notes." *GJ*. 1990; 65: 65-69. [Replies to Needham, below. †In Germany. 1400-1499. Of Balbi, Giovanni: *Catholicon*.]

[1169] Hunter, David; Nash, N. Frederick. "Composite Books." *BC*. 1990 Winter; 39(4): 504-528. [†Composite books.]

[1170] Kaunas, Domas. "Iš Mažosios Lietuvos ir kaimyninių kraštų knyginių ryšių istorijos." *Knygotyra*. 1988; 15 [22]: 53-67. [Rus. & Ger. sums. †And publishing. In Mažoji Lietuva (1524-1939); relationship to foreign language publishing.]

[1171] Krivatsy, Nati H. "Saint Roch and Exeter: A Note on a Unique *STC* at the Folger." *EIRC*. 1989; 15: 137-144. [†In England (ca. 1510). Of *Short-Title Catalogue*: No. 14077c41 by Faques, Richard.]

[1172] Lefcowitz, Allan B.; Mazzeno, Laurence W. "Sarah Wyman Whitman: Boston's Renaissance Woman." *TCW*. 1990 Summer-Winter; 5(1-2): 26-30. [†Book design by Whitman, Sarah Wyman.]

[1173] Lochhead, Douglas G., introd. "Essays in Canadian Bibliography: Bibliographical Studies in Reprint." *PBSC*. 1984; 23: 30-55. [Spec. sect. †In Canada. 1700-1899.]

[1174] ——. "Essays in Canadian Bibliography: Bibliographical Studies in Reprint." *PBSC*. 1986; 25: 109-138. [Spec. sect. †In Canada and United States. 1800-1899. Role of Mackenzie, William Lyon; relationship to politics.]

[1175] McKenzie, D. F. "Speech-Manuscript-Print." *LCUT*. 1990; 20(1-2): 86-109. [Illus. †Sociological approach.]

[1176] McMullin, B. J. "Press Figures and Concurrent Perfecting: Walker & Greig, Edinburgh, 1817-22." *Library*. 1990 Sept.; 12(3): 236-241. [†Concurrent perfecting by Walker & Greig in Edinburgh (1817-1822).]

[1177] Needham, Paul. "Corrective Notes on the Date of the Catholicon Press." *GJ*. 1990; 65: 46-64. [See also Hellinga, above. †In Germany. 1400-1499. Of Balbi, Giovanni: *Catholicon*.]

[1178] Patterson, Diana. "John Baskerville, Marbler." *Library*. 1990 Sept.; 12(3): 212-221. [Illus. †1700-1799. Marbling by Baskerville, John.]

[1179] Perini, Leandro. "La stampa in Italia nel '500: Firenze e la Toscana." *ELet*. 1990 Apr.-June; 15(2): 17-48. [Eng., Fr., Sp., & Ger. sums. †In Italy. 1500-1599.]

[1180] Rhodes, Dennis E. "Some Unrecorded Sixteenth-Century Coats of Arms." *GJ*. 1990; 65: 174-176. [†1500-1599. Relationship to heraldry.]

[1181] Riley, David W. "'A Definite Claim to Beauty': Some Treasures from the Rylands Private Press Collection." *BJRL*. 1990 Summer; 72(2): 73-88. [Illus. †By private presses. Checklist of collection at John Rylands University Library of Manchester.]

[1182] Robinson, Gwen G. "The Punctator's World: A Discursion, III." *Courier*. 1989 Fall; 24(2): 55-88. [Cont. from *Courier*. 1989 Spring; 24(1): 63-100. †(1400-1550). Punctuation.]

[1183] Röll, Walter. "Die Mainzer Offizin Schöffer und die Drucklegung der 'Römanischen Historie' 1505." *GJ*. 1990; 65: 89-117. [Illus. †In Germany. 1400-1499. Of Latin language literature by Schöffer family.]

[1184] Saxe, Stephen O. "'Franklin' Common Press." *PHist*. 1990; 12(1 [23]): 34-35. [Illus.]

[1185] Schmitz, Wolfgang. "Ein unbekannter Einblattdruck zugunsten der Pariser Minoriten aus dem Jahre 1487/88." *GJ*. 1990; 65: 79-81. [†Of letter (1487-1488).]

[1186] Talman, James J. "The Printing Presses of William Lyon Mackenzie, Prior to 1837." *PBSC*. 1986; 25: 111-115. [†In Canada and United States. 1800-1899. Role of Mackenzie, William Lyon.]

[1187] Taylor, W. Thomas. "Adrian Wilson's *Printing for Theater*." *BI*. 1990 Apr.; 52: 5-11. [Illus. †1900-1999. Role of Wilson, Adrian.]

[1188] Thienen, Gerard van; Knops, Mathieu, tr. "Ein Ablassbrief für Neuhausen (Mainz, Fust und Schöffer, 1461), von Bonaventura Kruitwagen in Nimwegen gefunden." *GJ*. 1990; 65: 70-74. [†Of letters (1461); relationship to Neuhausen. Theories of Kruitwagen, Bonaventura.]

[1189] Van der Bellen, Liana; Page, Alma L.; Murray, Florence B.; Taylor, Andrew; Corley, Nora T.; Jacobsen, Esther; Anson-Cartwright, Hugh; Lochhead, Douglas G. "Marie Tremaine, 1902-1984—a Tribute." *PBSC*. 1984; 23: 13-29. [†In Canada. And bibliography. Role of Tremaine, Marie. Reminiscence.]

Bibliography

[1190] Walters, Gwyn. "Bibliographica: Serial Notes on the Book Arts and History of Printing Represented by Notable Volumes in the Old (Antiquarian) Library at Saint David's University College, Lampeter, II." *Trivium*. 1988 Summer; 23: 107-113. [Illus. †(1503-1767). Of editions of Terence.]

History of printing

[1191] "Reflections on the History of the Book." *BC*. 1990 Spring; 39(1): 9-12, 15-18, 21-24, 26.

[1192] Gerulaitis, Leonardas Vytautas. "Print and the Mind." *FCS*. 1990; 17: 93-103. [†Relationship to literacy.]

[1193] Jaki, Stanley L. "The Modernity of the Middle Ages." *ModA*. 1987 Summer-Fall; 31(3-4): 207-214. [†In Europe. Middle Ages. And universities; relationship to modernity.]

[1194] Roper, Geoffrey. "Arabic Printing in Malta, 1825-1845: Its History and Its Place in the Development of Print Culture in the Arab Middle East." *DAI*. 1989 Summer; 50(2): Item 901C. [†Of Arabic language literature in Malta by English Church Missionary Society (1825-1845). Dissertation abstract.]

[1195] Traister, Daniel. "Reluctant Virgins: The Stigma of Print Revisited." *CIQ*. 1990 June; 26(2): 75-86. [†In England. 1500-1699.]

[1196] Tremaine, Marie. "A Half-Century of Canadian Life and Print, 1751-1800." *PBSC*. 1984; 23: 40-55. [†In Canada (1751-1800).]

[1197] ——. "Early Printing in Canada." *PBSC*. 1984; 23: 32-39. [†In Canada. 1700-1899.]

Binding

[1198] Colin, Georges. "La Fourniture de reliures par l'Officine plantinienne." *GJ*. 1990; 65: 346-359. [Illus. †1500-1599. By Plantin, Christophe.]

[1199] Collins, John. "A Binding by John Williams, c. 1805: English and Foreign Bookbindings 52." *BC*. 1990 Summer; 39(2): 235-237. [Illus. †In London. 1800-1899. By Williams, John.]

[1200] Coppens, Christian. "A 'De Imitatione' for Queen Christina: English and Foreign Bookbindings 53." *BC*. 1990 Winter; 39(4): 529-531. [Illus. †1600-1699.]

[1201] Eck, Reimer. "A Binding by Albertus Magnus, Amsterdam, c. 1670: English and Foreign Bookbindings 51." *BC*. 1990 Spring; 39(1): 74-75. [Illus. †In Amsterdam. 1600-1699. By Magnus, Albert.]

[1202] Foot, Mirjam M. "A Binding by the Scales Binder, *circa* 1456-65." *BLJ*. 1990 Spring; 16(1): 103-106. [Illus. †In London. 1400-1499. By Scales Binder.]

[1203] Greenfield, Jane. "Notable Bindings, I: MS 27." *YULG*. 1990 Apr.; 64(3-4): 172-173. [Illus. †In England. 1300-1499. Study example: *Speculum Humanae Salvationis*; *Meditaciones de Passione Christi*.]

[1204] ——. "Notable Bindings, II: MS 497." *YULG*. 1990 Oct.; 65(1-2): 43-45. [Illus. †In England. 1400-1499. Of Georges d'Esclavonie: *Le Château de virginité*.]

[1205] Hobson, A. R. A. "Note 534: Bindings by Gommar Estienne." *BC*. 1990 Winter; 39(4): 568. [†In France. 1500-1599. By Estienne, Gommar.]

[1206] Sommar, Carl Olov. "Vackra böcker 1989: Från Roslagsskutor till Apollinaire." *Bokvännen*. 1990; 45(2): 37-39. [†And illustration in Sweden (1989).]

[1207] Storm van Leeuwen, Jan. "The Well-Shirted Bookbinding: On Chemise Bindings and *Hülleneinbände*." 277-305 in Croiset van Uchelen, Ton, ed.; Horst, Koert van der, ed.; Schilder, Günter, ed.; Hesselink, Sebastiaan S., fwd. Theatrum Orbis Librorum: Liber Amicorum *Presented to Nico Israel on the Occasion of His Seventieth Birthday*. Utrecht: HES; 1989. xii, 518 pp. [†Chemise binding; wrapper binding.]

[1208] Szirmai, János A. "Ein neu aufgefundenes Beutelbuch in Berlin." *GJ*. 1990; 65: 336-345. [Illus. †1500-1599. Of Latin language literature in girdlebooks.]

[1209] Tulkens, Fl. "La Reliure en Brabant au XVᵉ et XVIᵉ siècle." 306-309 in Croiset van Uchelen, Ton, ed.; Horst, Koert van der, ed.; Schilder, Günter, ed.; Hesselink, Sebastiaan S., fwd. Theatrum Orbis Librorum: Liber Amicorum *Presented to Nico Israel on the Occasion of His Seventieth Birthday*. Utrecht: HES; 1989. xii, 518 pp. [†In Brabant. 1400-1599.]

Illustration

[1210] Borsa, Gedeon. "Eine unbekannte Ausgabe des 'Ordinarius Strigoniensis'." *GJ*. 1990; 65: 82-83. [†Middle Ages. Of *Ordinarius Strigoniensis*.]

[1211] Cockx-Indestege, Elly. "De Passie Delbecq-Schreiber Houtsneden in drukken 1500-1550." *OGE*. 1989 June-Dec.; 63(2-4): 245-278. [Ger. sum.; illus. †On woodcuts of Passion of Christ by Delbecq, Jean Baptiste and Schreiber, Wilhelm Ludwig.]

[1212] Druce, Robert. "Colorless Green Signifieds Sleep Furiously: Reconciling the Image and the Word." *Restant*. 1990; 18(1): 15-44. [Illus. †Visual imagery; language; relationship to signifier.]

[1213] Franz, Gunther. "Die verschollene Gutenbergbibel des Leipziger Buch- und Schriftmuseums und ein Faksimile auf Pergament." *GJ*. 1990; 65: 40-45. [†Middle Ages. Of facsimile of Gutenberg Bible.]

[1214] Hancher, Michael. "Bagpipe and Distaff: Interpreting Dictionary Illustrations." *Dictionaries*. 1988; 10: 93-109. [†Of dictionary.]

[1215] Kuncė, Horste. "Ar reikalingos knygoms iliustracijos?" *Knygotyra*. 1988; 15 [22]: 97-100. [Rus. & Ger. sums.]

[1216] Kuple, Zaiga, ed.; Jēgers, Arvids, ed. *Latviešu bērnu grāmatu grafika: Reprodukciju albums*. Riga: Liesma; 1988. n.pp. [Illus.; incl. Rus., Eng., & Ger. introds. †In Latvian literature for children.]

[1217] Lorenz, Dieter. "Die Verlage von Erich Dreyer und Max Wendt und deren Publikationen mit dreidimensionalen Abbildungen." *GJ*. 1990; 65: 284-296. [†In Germany. 1900-1999. By Dreyer, Erich; Wendt, Max of three-dimensional pictures.]

[1218] Marrow, James H. "Text and Image in Two Fifteenth-Century Dutch Psalters from Delft." *OGE*. 1990 Mar.-Sept.; 64(1-3): 41-52. [Dutch sum.; illus. †In Delft (1450-1475). In Psalter.]

[1219] Pelc, Milan. "Die Illustrationen der südslawischen Reformationsdrucke aus der Uracher Druckerei Hans Ungnads." *GJ*. 1990; 65: 312-335. [Illus. †1500-1599. By Ungnad, Hans, Baron zu Sonneck.]

Paper

[1220] Gröger, Claus. "Papier—vom Aufstieg des Handgeschöpften zum unentbehrlichen Massenprodukt." *IASL*. 1990; 15(1): 184-206.

[1221] Weiss, Wisso. "Symbole und Losungen der Französischen Revolution in der Wasserzeichenkunst." *GJ*. 1990; 65: 17-39. [Illus. †Watermarks (1789-1799); relationship to French Revolution.]

Typography

[1222] Burnett, Kathleen Marie. "Word Becomes Image: Herbert Bayer, Pioneer of a New Vision in Book Design." *DAI*. 1990 July; 51(1): 4A. [†1900-1999. Book design by Bayer, Herbert. Dissertation abstract.]

[1223] Contò, Agostino. "Alle origini della tipografia friulana del Cinquecento." *ELet*. 1990 Apr.-June; 15(2): 49-66. [Eng., Fr., Sp., & Ger. sums. †In Friuli-Venezia Giulia. 1500-1599.]

[1224] Eisenberg, Daniel. "In-House Typesetting on a Tight Budget." *SchP*. 1990 July; 21(4): 205-220.

[1225] Loewenstein, Joseph F. "*Idem*: Italics and the Genetics of Authorship." *JMRS*. 1990 Fall; 20(2): 205-224. [†In Venice (ca. 1500). Italics by Manuzio, Aldo; relationship to copyright.]

[1226] Macchia, André. "Au commencement était la lettre: Louis Jou." *GJ*. 1990; 65: 245-255. [Illus. †1900-1999. By Jou, Louis.]

[1227] Richardson, John, Jr. "Correlated Type Sizes and Names for the Fifteenth through Twentieth Century." *SB*. 1990; 43: 251-272. [Incl. tables. †1400-1999. Role of type size.]

[1228] Schütz, Edmond. "The Oscanian and Vanandian Type-Faces of the Armenian Printing Office in Amsterdam: Christoffel van Dijk—Nicholas Kis of Tótfalu and Their Forerunners." *AOASH*. 1988; 42(2-3): 161-220. [Illus. †In Amsterdam. 1600-1799. Role of Dijk, Christoffel van; Kis, Miklós; relationship to typefaces in Armenian language.]

[1229] Seitz, Wolfgang. "Georg Kress, a *Briefmaler* in Augsburg in the Late Sixteenth and Early Seventeenth Centuries." *GJ*. 1990; 65: 177-204. [Illus. †1500-1699. Role of Kress, Georg as *Briefmaler*.]

[1230] Veneziani, Paolo. "La marca tipografica da Comin da Trino." *GJ*. 1990; 65: 162-173. [†1500-1599. By Comin da Trino of Latin language literature.]

[1231] Walther, Karl Klaus. "Die lithographische Vervielfältigung von Texten in den Ländern des Vorderen und Mittleren Orients." *GJ*. 1990; 65: 223-236. [†In Middle East. 1500-1999. Use of lithography.]

[1232] Weiss, Adrian. "Font Analysis as a Bibliographical Method: The Elizabethan Play-Quarto Printers and Compositors." *SB*. 1990; 43: 95-164. [†In England. 1500-1699. Role of font analysis.]

PUBLISHING

[1233] "Grove Press." *RCF*. 1990 Fall; 10(3). [Spec. iss.; incl. letters from Rosset, Barney; Beckett, Samuel; Girodias, Maurice; Jordan, Fred. †In United States. By Grove Press.]

[1234] Cadioli, Alberto. "Confronti di analisi editoriale (Catalogo Einaudi, 1935-56)." *Problemi*. 1990 Sept.-Dec.; 89: 294-305. [†By Einaudi (1935-1956). Treatment in Turi, Gabriele: *Casa Einaudi: Libri uomini idee oltre il fascismo*.]

[1235] Calder, John. "The Transatlantic Connection." *RCF*. 1990 Fall; 10(3): 143-149. [†In United States. By Grove Press.]

[1236] Diehl, Roberta L. "Electronic Manuscripts: A Low-Risk Approach." *SchP*. 1990 Oct.; 22(1): 29-39. [†Electronic publishing.]

[1237] Fredeman, Jane. "Book Publishing in British Columbia, 1990: More Than a Regional Enterprise." *JCSR*. 1990 Fall; 25(3): 124-138. [Fr. sum. †In Canada: British Columbia.]

[1238] Fredeman, William E. "Thomas Bird Mosher and the Literature of Rapture: A Chapter in the History of American Publishing." *PBSC*. 1987; 26: 27-65. [†In United States. 1800-1899. By Mosher, Thomas Bird.]

[1239] Garrett, George. "American Publishing Now." *SR*. 1988 Summer; 96(3): 516-525. [†In United States.]

[1240] ———. "American Publishing Today." *SR*. 1990 Summer; 98(3): 515-526. [†In United States.]

[1241] Gontarski, S. E. "Dionysus in Publishing: Barney Rosset, Grove Press, and the Making of a Countercanon." *RCF*. 1990 Fall; 10(3): 7-19. [†In United States. By Grove Press; role of Rosset, Barnet Lee, Jr.]

[1242] ———. "Don Allen: Grove's First Editor." *RCF*. 1990 Fall; 10(3): 132-136. [†In United States. By Grove Press. Interview with Allen, Donald Merriam.]

[1243] ———. "Olympia and Grove: An Interview with Maurice Girodias." *RCF*. 1990 Fall; 10(3): 124-127. [†In United States; France. By Grove Press; Olympia Press. Interview with Girodias, Maurice.]

[1244] Hayes, Robert M. "Desktop Publishing: Problems of Control." *SchP*. 1990 Jan.; 21(2): 117-123. [†1900-1999. Desktop publishing.]

[1245] Horowitz, Irving Louis. "The Place of the Festschrift." *SchP*. 1990 Jan.; 21(2): 77-83. [†1900-1999. Of festschrift.]

[1246] Huenefeld, John. *The Huenefeld Guide to Book Publishing*. Bedford, MA: Mills & Sanderson; 1990. xv, 303 pp. [4th rev. ed. †By small publishers.]

[1247] Keeley, Edmund. "The Commerce of Translation." *JMGS*. 1990 Oct.; 8(2): 291-297. [†On English language translation as business.]

[1248] King, Bruce. "*Evergreen Review*, Grove Press, and Jazz." *RCF*. 1990 Fall; 10(3): 162-169. [†In United States. By Grove Press; relationship to *Evergreen Review*; jazz music.]

[1249] Loi, Salvatore. "The Editalia Publishing House." *IBP*. 1987; 30(1-2): 23-24. [†By Editalia.]

[1250] Marowitz, Charles. "Private Communiques/Public Prints." *RCF*. 1990 Fall; 10(3): 170-174. [†In United States. By Grove Press; relationship to *Evergreen Review*.]

[1251] McAllister, Matthew Paul. "Cultural Argument and Organizational Constraint in the Comic Book Industry." *JC*. 1990 Winter; 40(1): 55-71. [†Of comic book; relationship to cultural criticism.]

[1252] Minicucci, Maria Jole. "L'editore Enrico Bemporad, il Gabinetto Vieusseux e la 'Nuova Antologia'." *ABI*. 1989 Jan.-Mar.; 40(1): 11-33. [†In Florence (1890-1920). By Bemporad, Enrico; relationship to Gabinetto Vieusseux; *Nuova Antologia*.]

[1253] Moran, Daniel. *Toward the Century of Words: Johann Cotta and the Politics of the Public Realm in Germany, 1795-1832*. Berkeley: U of California P; 1990. vii, 304 pp. [†Biography of Cotta, Johann Friedrich, Baron von Cottendorf.]

[1254] Münch, Roger. "Der Verleger Johann Friedrich Cotta und die Technik seiner Zeit." *GJ*. 1990; 65: 213-222. [†In Germany. 1700-1799. By Cotta, Johann Friedrich, Baron von Cottendorf.]

[1255] Nichol, Donald W. "On the Use of 'Copy' and 'Copyright': A Scriblerian Coinage?" *Library*. 1990 June; 12(2): 110-120. [†In England. 1700-1799. Role of scribe; relationship to copyright.]

[1256] Oakes, John. "Barnet Rosset and the Art of Combat Publishing: An Interview." *RCF*. 1990 Fall; 10(3): 20-57. [†In United States. By Grove Press. Interview (1981) with Rosset, Barnet Lee, Jr.]

[1257] ———. "The Last Days of Grove." *RCF*. 1990 Fall; 10(3): 175-178. [†In United States. By Grove Press.]

[1258] Petrauskienė, Irena. "Valdovų XVI-XVIII a. privilegijos: Lietuvos spaudos istorijos šaltinis." *Knygotyra*. 1988; 15 [22]: 43-52. [Rus. & Ger. sums. †In Lithuania. 1500-1799.]

[1259] Privat, Jean-Marie. "Les Intermédiaires de lecture." *Pratiques*. 1989 Sept.; 63: 63-101. [†In France. Book distribution; libraries; relationship to social class.]

[1260] Raven, James. "The Noble Brothers and Popular Publishing 1737-89." *Library*. 1990 Dec.; 12(4): 293-343. [†In London. 1700-1799. Role of Noble, Francis; Noble, John.]

[1261] Riggar, T. F.; Matkin, R. E. "Breaking into Academic Print." *SchP*. 1990 Oct.; 22(1): 17-22. [†Scholarly publishing.]

[1262] Robert, Lucie. "Le Livre et l'Etat." *V&I*. 1989 Winter; 14(2 [41]): 183-193. [†In Quebec. 1800-1999. Relationship to state.]

[1263] Röhling, Horst. "Hat es Sinn, Aufsatzsammlungen eines Autors zu drucken?" 189 in Löwenstein, Hans-Jürgen, ed. *Leben mit Büchern: Festschrift für Otto Sagner zum 70. Geburtstag*. Marburg: n.p.; 1990. 189 pp. (Schriften der ABDOSD 1.)

[1264] Rosset, Barney. "On Publishing." *RCF*. 1990 Fall; 10(3): 58-59. [†In United States. By Grove Press.]

[1265] Spadoni, Carl. "The Publishers Press of Montreal." *PBSC*. 1985; 24: 38-50. [†In Montreal (1911-1912). Role of Publishers Press.]

[1266] Springhall, John. "'A Life Story for the People'? Edwin J. Brett and the London 'Low-Life' Penny Dreadfuls of the 1860s." *VS*. 1990 Winter; 33(2): 223-246. [Illus. †In England (1850-1900). By Brett, Edwin John of pulp fiction; penny dreadful.]

[1267] Stetz, Margaret D.; Lasner, Mark Samuels. *England in the 1890s: Literary Publishing at the Bodley Head*. Washington, DC: Georgetown UP; 1990. ix, 94 pp. [Illus. †In England (1890-1900). By Bodley Head.]

[1268] Sutherland, John. "The Making of Codices and Careers." *SchP*. 1990 Jan.; 21(2): 85-91. [Rpt. from *Times Lit. Supp.* 1989 May 26-June 1. †1900-1999. By university presses.]

[1269] Vanasse, André. "L'Exportation de notre littérature: Un Echec?" *LQ*. 1990 Summer; 58: 7-10. [†In Quebec. Exportation.]

[1270] Ward, Anthony; Johnson, Cuthbert. "The Henry Bradshaw Society: Its Birth and First Decade, 1890-1900." *Ephemerides Liturgicae* (Rome). 1990 Mar.-June; 104(2-3): 187-200. [Lat. sum. †Of liturgical books by Henry Bradshaw Society (1891-1900).

[1271] Whiteman, Bruce. "The Early History of the Macmillan Company of Canada, 1905-1921." *PBSC*. 1984; 23: 68-83. [†In Canada (1905-1921). Role of Macmillan Company of Canada.]

[1272] Wilson, E. "Cases for Justus: Preparing a Case Database for a Hypertext Information Retrieval System." *L&LC*. 1990; 5(2): 119-128. [†In England. Relationship to law reports; printing. Application of Justus Project.]

[1273] Zaveckienė, Žiedūnė. "Lietuvos Komunistų partijos 1917-1940 m. spaudos bibliografavimas ir tyrinėjimas." *Knygotyra*. 1988; 15 [22]: 79-84. [Rus. & Eng. sums. †(1917-1940). By Communist Party in Lithuania.]

[1274] Zurbrugg, Nicholas. "'Within a Budding Grove': Pubescent Postmodernism and the Early *Evergreen Review*." *RCF*. 1990 Fall; 10(3): 150-161. [†In United States. By Grove Press; relationship to *Evergreen Review*.]

Bibliography

[1275] Van der Bellen, Liana. "A Checklist of Books and Articles in the Field of the History of the Book and Libraries, I & II." *PBSC*. 1984; 23: 84-99. 1986; 25: 139-152. [†And printing in Canada.]

History of publishing

[1276] Anderson, Patricia Jeanne. "The Printed Image and the Transformation of Popular Culture, 1790-1860." *DAI*. 1990 June; 50(12): 4093A. [†In England (1790-1860). Relationship to popular culture. Dissertation abstract.]

[1277] Chartier, Roger; Pantzer, Katharine, tr. "Histoire de l'édition française." *PHist*. 1990; 12(1 [23]): 36-38. [†In France.]

[1278] Couturier, Maurice. "La Bataille du livre et la naissance du roman anglais." *Cycnos*. 1990; 6: 1-15. [†In England. 1700-1799. Of English novel.]

[1279] Lott, Mare. "Osnovnye cherty istoriografii èstonskoĭ knigi." *Knygotyra*. 1988; 15 [22]: 112-120. [Eng. sum. †In Estonia.]

[1280] Michon, Jacques. "Les Editions de l'Arbre, 1941-1948." *V&I*. 1989 Winter; 14(2 [41]): 194-210. [†In France (1941-1948). By L'Arbre.]

[1281] Sangsue, Daniel. "Démesures du livre." *Romantisme*. 1990; 20(69): 43-59. [†In France. 1800-1899.]

[1282] Žukas, Vladas. "Lietuviškos knygos 400 metų sukakties minėjimas." *Knygotyra*. 1988; 15 [22]: 85-96. [Rus. & Eng. sums. †In Lithuania.]

Book trade

[1283] Åberg, Åke. "Bokköp och bokköpare i Visby 1909-1911." *Bokvännen*. 1990; 45(4): 78-99. 1990; 45(5): 109-120. [†In Sweden: Visby (1909-1911).]

[1284] Ankarcrona, Anita. "Bud på böcker: Bokauktioner i Stockholm, 1782-1801: Traditionen—böckerna—publiken (Bids for Books: Book Auctions in Stockholm, 1782-1801—Tradition, the Books, the Public)." *DAI*. 1990 Spring; 51(1): Item 30C. [†In Stockholm (1782-1801). Book auction. Dissertation abstract.]

[1285] Feldman, Gayle. "The Best-Seller Blues: Hard Lessons from a Cosby Book." *New York Times Book Review*. 1990 June 10: 11, 44-45. [†And marketing.]

[1286] Hetzer, Armin. "Buchhandel und Bibliothekswesen in China." 117-144 in Löwenstein, Hans-Jürgen, ed. *Leben mit Büchern: Festschrift für Otto Sagner zum 70. Geburtstag*. Marburg: n.p.; 1990. 189 pp. (Schriften der ABDOSD.) [†And libraries in China.]

[1287] Houde, Roland; Beaudry, Jacques. "Expression et expansion: L'Offensive littéraire française de l'après-guerre au Québec." *V&I*. 1989 Winter; 14(2 [41]): 237-247. [†In Quebec (1944-1946). Includes catalogue of books by France-Livre.]

[1288] Kaegbein, Paul. "Eine Miszelle über den Buchhandel in Livland." 145-162 in Löwenstein, Hans-Jürgen, ed. *Leben mit Büchern: Festschrift für Otto Sagner zum 70. Geburtstag*. Marburg: n.p.; 1990. 189 pp. (Schriften der ABDOSD 1.) [†In Latvia.]

[1289] Kamiński, Stanisław. "Eine Bemerkung über den Buchhandel im alten Warschau: Buchhändler deutscher Abstammung (17.-19. Jh.)." 162-174 in Löwenstein, Hans-Jürgen, ed. *Leben mit Büchern: Festschrift für Otto Sagner zum 70. Geburtstag*. Marburg: n.p.; 1990. 189 pp. (Schriften der ABDOSD 1.) [†In Warsaw. 1700-1999.]

[1290] Kitson, Jill. "Towards Global Publishing, II." *Meanjin*. 1990 Autumn; 49(1): 67-71. [†In Australia (1989). Relationship to copyright law.]

[1291] Kłossowski, Andrzej; Zalewski, Wojciech. *Sprzedawcy książki polskiej i rosyjskiej na obczyźnie: Od 1918 r. po czasy współczesne: Materiały do historii księgarstwa/Dealers of Polish and Russian Books Active Abroad: 1918 to Present: A Contribution to the History of Book Trade*. Warsaw: Biblioteka Narodowa; 1990. Stanford: Stanford Univ. Libs.; 1990. 193 pp. [Illus. †(1918-1990). Of Polish literature; Russian literature.]

[1292] Löwenstein, Hans-Jürgen. "Karl Ernst von Baer und die Buchhandlung Eggers et Comp. in Petersburg." 175-182 in Löwenstein, Hans-Jürgen, ed. *Leben mit Büchern: Festschrift für Otto Sagner zum 70. Geburtstag*. Marburg: n.p.; 1990. 189 pp. (Schriften der ABDOSD 1.) [†By Baer, Karl Ernst von in St. Petersburg.]

[1293] Martin, Claude; Nadeau, Vincent. "Auteurs et entreprises dans l'édition littéraire contemporaine au Québec." *V&I*. 1989 Winter; 14(2 [41]): 225-236. [†In Quebec. 1900-1999.]

[1294] Mulvihill, Maureen E. "Feminism and the Rare-Book Market." *Scriblerian*. 1989 Autumn; 22(1): 1-5. [†1900-1999. Rare book trade; relationship to English women writers (1600-1799).]

[1295] Radway, Janice. "The Scandal of the Middlebrow: The Book-of-the-Month Club, Class Fracture, and Cultural Authority." *SAQ*. 1990 Fall; 89(4): 703-736. [†Role of Book of the Month Club.]

[1296] Senín, Xabier. "500 Libros Gallegos." *Grial*. 1990 July-Sept.; 28(107): 381-386. [†In Galicia (Spain).]

[1297] Simoni, Anna E. C. "The Hidden Trade-Mark of Laurence Kellam, Printer at Douai." *OGE*. 1990 Mar.-Sept.; 64(1-3): 130-143. [Dutch sum. †Trademark of Kellam, Laurence.]

[1298] Torres Zavaleta, Jorge. "Editors, agentes literarios y editores." *Suplemento Literario La Nación* (Buenos Aires). 1990 Jan. 14: 6. [†In Latin America and Spain.]

[1299] ——. "Peter Weidhaas: De Frankfurt a América Latina." *Suplemento Literario La Nación* (Buenos Aires). 1990 May 20: 6. [†Book fair. Theories of Weidhaas, Peter.]

Editing

[1300] Hellinga, Lotte. "Editing Texts in the First Fifteen Years of Printing." *LCUT*. 1990; 20(1-2): 126-149. [Illus. †1400-1499.]

[1301] Lavagnino, John; Wujastyk, Dominik. "An Overview of EDMAC: A Plain TEX Format for Critical Editions." *TUGboat*. 1990 Nov.; 11(4): 623-643. [†Role of format for critical edition. Application of EDMAC; TEX.]

[1302] Willison, Ian. "Editorial Theory and Practice and the History of the Book." *LCUT*. 1990; 20(1-2): 110-125. [Illus.]

Marketing

[1303] Salord, Philippe. "Edition francophone: L'Esprit pionnier." *Diagonales*. 1988 Apr.; 6: 46-48. [Supp. to *Francais dans le Monde*. 216. †In Africa of French language literature.]

[1304] Weber, Carolyn Jefferson. "A Multidimensional Unfolding Model of Children's Preferences of Literary Style." *DAI*. 1990 Aug.; 51(2): 468A. [†Of literature for children; relationship to reading preference. Dissertation abstract.]

Literary theory and criticism

[1305] Agger, Gunhild. "Aktive lag: Bidrag til K&K's diskussion om litteraturvidenskaben idag." *KuKl*. 1990; 17(4): 29-35. [See also 1989 Bibliog. IV.1452. †In *Kultur og Klasse*.]

[1306] Andringa, Els. "Verbal Data on Literary Understanding: A Proposal for Protocol Analysis on Two Levels." *PoeticsJ*. 1990 June; 19(3): 231-257. [Incl. tr. of story. †On reader response; study example: Schiller, Johann Christoph Friedrich von: "Eine grossmütige Handlung, aus der neusten Geschichte."]

[1307] Angenot, Marc. "Le Réalisme de Lukács." 135-164 in Thomson, Clive, ed. *Georg Lukács et la théorie littéraire contemporaine*. Montreal: Assn. des Professeurs de Fr. des Univ. & Collèges Can.; 1983. 164 pp. [†Realism. Theories of Lukács, György.]

[1308] Angenot, Marc, ed.; Bessière, Jean, ed.; Fokkema, Douwe, ed.; Kushner, Eva, ed. *Théorie littéraire*. Paris: PU de France; 1989. 395 pp. [Incl. bibliog. & index.]

[1309] Armstrong, Paul B. *Conflicting Readings: Variety and Validity in Interpretation*. Chapel Hill: U of North Carolina P; 1990. xiv, 192 pp. [†On interpretation.]

[1310] Ashley, Kathleen M., ed. *Victor Turner and the Construction of Cultural Criticism*. Bloomington: Indiana UP; 1990. xxii, 185 pp. (Between Literature and Anthropology.) [Incl. pref. & introd. †Cultural criticism. Theories of Turner, Victor Witter.]

[1311] Assche, Armand van. "Wat is er aan de hand met de empirische literatuurstudie?" *Spektator*. 1989 May; 18(5): 333-335. [†Role of empiricism.]

[1312] Barsky, Robert F.; Holquist, Michael. "Dialogue: Conversation between Robert F. Barsky and Professor Michael Holquist: Hamden CT, Saturday-Sunday August 18-19, 1990." *DS/SD*. 1990 Spring-Summer; 3(1-2): 1-22. [†Theories of Bakhtin, Mikhail Mikhaĭlovich.]

[1313] Barsky, Robert F., ed.; Holquist, Michael, ed.; Suvin, Darko, fwd.; Angenot, Marc, fr. fwd. "Bakhtin and Otherness." *DS/SD*. 1990 Spring-Summer; 3(1-2). [Spec. iss.; incl. introd. †Theories of Bakhtin, Mikhail Mikhaĭlovich.]

[1314] Barzel, Hillel. *Drakhim BaParshanut HaHadasha—MiTeorya LeMetoda*. Ramat Gan: Bar Ilan Univ.; 1990. 348 pp.

[1315] Bennett, James R. "The Essay in Recent Anthologies of Literary Criticism." *SubStance*. 1989; 18(3 [60]): 105-111. [†Review article.]

[1316] ——. "Intellect Workers and Intellectuals: Critical Theory since the 1960s." 53-63 in Kneupper, Charles W., ed. *Rhetoric and Ideology: Compositions and Criticisms of Power*. Arlington, TX: Rhetoric Society of America; 1989.

[1317] Bennington, Geoffrey. "Towards a Criticism of the Future." 17-29 in Wood, David, ed.; Levinas, Emmanuel, fwd.; Allison, David, tr. of fwd. *Writing the Future*. London: Routledge; 1990. x, 213 pp. (Warwick Studies in Philosophy and Literature.) [†Indeterminacy; relationship to the future. Theories of Derrida, Jacques compared to Kant, Immanuel; Rousseau, Jean-Jacques.]

[1318] Berkhofer, Robert F., Jr. "The Challenge of Poetics to (Normal) Historical Practice." *PoT*. 1988; 9(2): 435-452. [†Applied to historical discourse.]

SEE SUBJECT INDEX FOR CROSS-REFERENCES

[1319] Bernard-Donals, Michael. "'Discourse in Life': Answerability in Language and in the Novel." *SLitI*. 1990 Spring; 23(1): 45-63. [†On novel; relationship to language; society. Theories of Bakhtin, Mikhail Mikhaĭlovich.]

[1320] Bernauer, James W. *Michel Foucault's Force of Flight: Toward an Ethics for Thought*. Atlantic Highlands, NJ: Humanities; 1990. xii, 261 pp. (Contemporary Studies in Philosophy and the Human Sciences.) [†Theories of Foucault, Michel.

[1321] Bernstein, Charles. "Optimism and Critical Excess." *CritI*. 1990 Summer; 16(4): 830-856. [†Radicalism in poetics; relationship to poetry.]

[1322] Bernstein, Michael André. "The Poetics of *ressentiment*." 197-223 in Morson, Gary Saul, ed.; Emerson, Caryl, ed. *Rethinking Bakhtin: Extensions and Challenges*. Evanston: Northwestern UP; 1989. 330 pp. (Northwestern University Press Series in Russian Literature and Theory.) [†On dialogism. Theories of Bakhtin, Mikhail Mikhaĭlovich.]

[1323] Berthoff, Ann E.; Schilb, John, reply; Harkin, Patricia, reply; Swearingen, C. Jan, reply. "How Philosophy Can Help Us." *Pre/Text*. 1988 Spring-Summer; 9(1-2): 61-90. [Incl. rejoinder. †Relationship to philosophy.]

[1324] Bessière, Jean. "Littérature et représentation." 309-324 in Angenot, Marc, ed.; Bessière, Jean, ed.; Fokkema, Douwe, ed.; Kushner, Eva, ed. *Théorie littéraire*. Paris: PU de France; 1989. 395 pp.

[1325] Beugnot, Bernard, ed. "L'Invention critique." *O&C*. 1990; 15(2). [Spec. iss.; incl. fwd.]

[1326] Bizzell, Patricia. "'Cultural Criticism': A Social Approach to Studying Writing." *RhetRev*. 1989 Spring; 7(2): 224-230. [†Cultural criticism; relationship to teaching of writing.]

[1327] Bleich, David, ed.; Caraher, Brian G., ed. "Empiricism and Hermeneutics: The Invention of Facts in the Study of Literature." *PoeticsJ*. 1989 Oct.; 18(4-5). [Spec. iss.; incl. pref. †Relationship to empiricism.]

[1328] Block, Haskell M. "The Use and Abuse of Literary Theory." 25-31 in Valdés, Mario J., ed. *Toward a Theory of Comparative Literature: Selected Papers Presented in the Division of Theory of Literature at the XIth International Comparative Literature Congress*. New York: Peter Lang; 1990. 275 pp. (Proceedings of the International Comparative Literature Association 11: 3.)

[1329] Bloom, James D.; O'Hara, Daniel T., response. "Fellow Travelers: A Canon for Critics." *AmLH*. 1990 Winter; 2(4): 772-783. [†Theories of Burke, Kenneth; Trilling, Lionel. Review article.]

[1330] Booker, M. Keith. "The Critical Condition of Literary Theory." *PLL*. 1990 Spring; 26(2): 289-298. [On 1985 Bibliog. I.3619 (IV.1349); 1989 Bibliog. I.2076; & Cohen, Ralph, ed. *The Future of Literary Theory*. †On crisis of literary theory in academia. Review article.]

[1331] Bottiroli, Giovanni. "Bachtin, la parodia del possibile." *SCr*. 1990 May; 5(2 [63]): 147-166. [†Menippean satire. Theories of Bakhtin, Mikhail Mikhaĭlovich.]

[1332] Bové, Paul A. "A Conversation with William V. Spanos." *BoundaryII*. 1990 Summer; 17(2): 1-39. [†In *Boundary 2*. Relationship to Postmodernism. Interview with Spanos, William V.]

[1333] ——. "The Love of Reading/The Work of Criticism: F. O. Matthiessen and Lionel Trilling." *ConL*. 1990 Fall; 31(3): 373-382. [On Cain, William E. *F. O. Matthiessen and the Politics of Criticism* & O'Hara, Daniel T. *Lionel Trilling: The Work of Literature*. †Theories of Matthiessen, F. O.; Trilling, Lionel. Review article.]

[1334] Boyarin, Daniel. *Intertextuality and the Reading of Midrash*. Bloomington: Indiana UP; 1990. xiii, 161 pp. (Indiana Studies in Biblical Literature.) [†Applied to Midrash; relationship to interpretation; intertextuality.]

[1335] Brantlinger, Patrick. *Crusoe's Footprints: Cultural Studies in Britain and America*. New York: Routledge; 1990. xi, 212 pp. [†Relationship to culture studies. Theories of Thompson, Edward Palmer; Hobsbawm, Eric J.]

[1336] Brill, Rosa. "Con Geoffrey Hartman: Literatura y crítica." *Suplemento Literario La Nación* (Buenos Aires). 1990 Aug. 12: 6. [†Interview with Hartman, Geoffrey H.]

[1337] Brinker, Menachem. *Halm Torat HaSifrut Efsharit?* Tel Aviv: Sifriat Poalim; 1989. 153 pp.

[1338] Broich, Ulrich. "Ways of Marking Intertextuality." 119-129 in Bessière, Jean, ed. *Fiction, texte, narratologie, genre*. New York: Peter Lang; 1989. 238 pp. [†Intertextuality.]

[1339] Brombert, Victor. "Mediating the Work: Or, The Legitimate Aims of Criticism." *PMLA*. 1990 May; 105(3): 391-397.

[1340] Brulotte, Gaétan. "Narratologie du récit dit érotique." *Petite Revue de Philosophie*. 1990 Spring; 11(2): 35-51. [†Narrator; narratee in erotic literature. Theories of Genette, Gérard.]

[1341] Bruns, Gerald L. "Dialogue and the Truth of Skepticism." *R&L*. 1990 Summer-Autumn; 22(2-3): 85-91. [†Skepticism; relationship to ethics. Theories of Cavell, Stanley Louis: *The Claim of Reason* compared to Levinas, Emmanuel: *Totalité et infini; Autrement qu'être*.]

[1342] Bucknell, Brad. "Henry Louis Gates, Jr. and the Theory of 'Signifyin(g)'." *ArielE*. 1990 Jan.; 21(1): 65-84. [†Relationship to signification. Theories of Gates, Henry Louis, Jr.: *The Signifying Monkey*.]

[1343] Bürger, Peter. "The Problem of Aesthetic Value." 23-34 in Collier, Peter, ed.; Geyer-Ryan, Helga, ed. *Literary Theory Today*. Ithaca: Cornell UP; 1990. xii, 249 pp. [†Aesthetics.]

[1344] Burke, John M. "The Death and Return of the Author: Criticism and Subjectivity in Barthes, Foucault and Derrida." *DAI*. 1990 Dec.; 51(6): 2039A. [†Subjectivity in Barthes, Roland; Foucault, Michel; Derrida, Jacques. Dissertation abstract.]

[1345] Busch, Robert. "Bakhtin's 'Problemy tvorchestva Dostoevskogo' and V. V. Vinogradov's 'O khudozhestvennoi proze'—a Dialogic Relationship." *DS/SD*. 1990 Spring-Summer; 3(1-2): 311-324. [†Theories of Bakhtin, Mikhail Mikhaĭlovich: *Problemy poetiki Dostoevkogo* compared to Vinogradov, Viktor Vladimirovich: *O khudozhestvennoĭ proze*.]

[1346] Cain, William. "An Interview with Irving Howe." *AmLH*. 1989 Fall; 1(3): 554-564. [†Interview with Howe, Irving.]

[1347] Capobianco, Michael. "Ensayo preliminar acerca de una teoría matemática de la literatura/Toward a Mathematical Theory of Literature." *Ometeca*. 1989-1990; 1(2)-2(1): 165-219. [In Sp. & Eng. †Relationship to mathematical theory. Treatment of writer; relationship to reader.]

[1348] Carroll, David, ed. *The States of "Theory": History, Art, and Critical Discourse*. New York: Columbia UP; 1990. x, 316 pp. (Irvine Studies in the Humanities.) [Incl. introd.]

[1349] Cassedy, Steven. *Flight from Eden: The Origins of Modern Literary Criticism and Theory*. Berkeley: U of California P; 1990. 253 pp. [†1800-1999. Role of French poets; Russian poets; German poets.]

[1350] Chang, Heesok. "Fascism and Critical Theory." *StiR*. 1990; 8(1-2): 13-33. [†Relationship to fascism.]

[1351] Chanter, Tina. "The Alterity and Immodesty of Time: Death as Future and Eros as Feminine in Levinas." 137-154 in Wood, David, ed.; Levinas, Emmanuel, fwd.; Allison, David, tr. of fwd. *Writing the Future*. London: Routledge; 1990. x, 213 pp. (Warwick Studies in Philosophy and Literature.) [†Role of death in time. Theories of Heidegger, Martin compared to Levinas, Emmanuel.]

[1352] Chase, Cynthia. "Translating Romanticism: Literary Theory as the Criticism of Aesthetics in the Work of Paul de Man." *TexP*. 1990 Winter; 4(3): 349-375. [†Relationship to aesthetics of Romanticism. Theories of de Man, Paul.]

[1353] Chase, Cynthia, ed. "[Paul de Man]." *Diacritics*. 1990 Fall; 20(3). [Spec. iss. †Theories of de Man, Paul.]

[1354] Christensen, Jerome. "From Rhetoric to Corporate Populism: A Romantic Critique of the Academy in an Age of High Gossip." *CritI*. 1990 Winter; 16(2): 438-465. [†In the Academy; relationship to rhetoric. Study example: de Man, Paul.]

[1355] Cmiel, Kenneth. "After Objectivity: What Comes Next in History?" *AmLH*. 1990 Spring; 2(1): 170-181. [†Relationship to history.]

[1356] Cohen, Ed. "Are We (Not) What We Are Becoming? 'Gay Identity,' 'Gay Studies,' and the Disciplining of Knowledge." 161-175 in Boone, Joseph A., ed.; Cadden, Michael, ed. *Engendering Men: The Question of Male Feminist Criticism*. New York: Routledge; 1990. vi, 333 pp. [†Relationship to homosexuality; gay studies.]

[1357] Cohen, Ralph, ed. *The Future of Literary Theory*. Essays by Twenty-Five Leading Crits. & Theorists Chart the Course of Crit. into the 1990s & Beyond. New York: Routledge; 1989. xx, 445 pp. [Incl. introd.]

[1358] Colli, Giangiacomo. "Mimesis as Performance: A Different Approach to the Concept of Imitation." *MuK*. 1987; 33(3-4): 25-31. [†Mimesis. Theories of Aristotle.]

[1359] Collier, Peter, ed.; Geyer-Ryan, Helga, ed. *Literary Theory Today*. Ithaca: Cornell UP; 1990. xii, 249 pp. [Incl. introd.]

[1360] Colomb, Gregory G.; Turner, Mark. "Computers, Literary Theory, and Theory of Meaning." 386-410 in Cohen, Ralph, ed. *The Future of Literary Theory*. New York: Routledge; 1989. xx, 445 pp. [†On meaning; relationship to application of computer.]

[1361] Cook, Deborah. "Reading for Pleasure." *PoT*. 1987; 8(3-4): 557-563. [†On reading; relationship to aesthetics. Theories of Jauss, Hans Robert: *Aesthetische Erfahrung und literarische Hermeneutik* compared to Barthes, Roland: *Le Plaisir du texte*.]

[1362] Cook, Eleanor. "Against Monism: The Canadian Anatomy of Northrop Frye." 283-298 in Lombardo, Agostino, ed. *Ritratto di Northrop Frye*. Rome: Bulzoni; 1989. [†Theories of Frye, Northrop.]

[1363] Cordesse, Gerard; Lebas, Gerard; Le Pellec, Yves. *Langages littéraires: Textes d'anglais*. Toulouse: PU du Mirail; 1990. 141 pp. (Amphi 7.) [†Language.]

[1364] Corngold, Stanley. "Paul de Man on the Contingency of Intention." 27-42 in Herman, Luc, ed.; Humbeeck, Kris, ed.; Lernout, Geert, ed. *(Dis)continuities: Essays on Paul de Man*. Amsterdam: Rodopi; 1989. 239 pp. (PmdnS 2.) [†Role of intention. Theories of de Man, Paul.]

[1365] Coulson, John. "Hans Urs von Balthasar: Bringing Beauty Back to Faith." 218-232 in Jasper, David, ed.; Wright, T. R., ed. *The Critical Spirit and the Will to Believe: Essays in Nineteenth-Century Literature and Religion*. New York: St. Martin's; 1989. xii; 239 pp. [†1800-1899. Faith. Theories of Balthasar, Hans Urs von.]

[1366] Culler, Jonathan. "Anti-Foundational Philology." 49-52 in Ziolkowski, Jan, ed. *On Philology*. University Park: Penn State UP; 1990. 78 pp. [†Especially textual criticism; relationship to philology.]

[1367] ——. "GRIP's Grasp: A Comment." *PoT*. 1988; 9(4): 783-789. [†Role of Group for Research into the Institutionalization and Professionalization of Literary Studies.]

[1368] ——. "La Littérarité." 31-43 in Angenot, Marc, ed.; Bessière, Jean, ed.; Fokkema, Douwe, ed.; Kushner, Eva, ed. *Théorie littéraire*. Paris: PU de France; 1989. 395 pp. [†On literariness; relationship to literary conventions.]

[1369] ——. "Paul de Man's Contribution to Literary Criticism and Theory." 268-278 in Cohen, Ralph, ed. *The Future of Literary Theory*. New York: Routledge; 1989. xx, 445 pp. [†Role of de Man, Paul.]

[1370] ——. "Political Criticism." 192-204 in Wood, David, ed.; Levinas, Emmanuel, fwd.; Allison, David, tr. of fwd. *Writing the Future*. London: Routledge; 1990. x, 213 pp. (Warwick Studies in Philosophy and Literature.) [†Political criticism. Theories of Foucault, Michel; Said, Edward W.]

[1371] Cutrofello, Andrew Fred. "Hegel and Derrida's Conceptions of Textual Interpretation." *DAI*. 1990 Feb.; 50(8): 2518A. [†Interpretation. Theories of Hegel, Georg Wilhelm Friedrich; Derrida, Jacques. Dissertation abstract.]

[1372] Davis, Leonard J. "The Monologic Imagination: M. M. Bakhtin and the Nature of Assertion." *SLitI*. 1990 Spring; 23(1): 29-44. [†On novel; relationship to language. Theories of Bakhtin, Mikhail Mikhaïlovich.]

[1373] Davis, Robert Con, ed.; Finke, Laurie, ed. *Literary Criticism and Theory: The Greeks to the Present*. New York: Longman; 1989. xxi, 952 pp. (Longman English and Humanities Series.) [Incl. introd. †Anthology.]

[1374] de Graef, Ortwin. "Silence to Be Observed: A Trial for Paul de Man's Inexcusable Confessions." 51-73 in Herman, Luc, ed.; Humbeeck, Kris, ed.; Lernout, Geert, ed. *(Dis)continuities: Essays on Paul de Man*. Amsterdam: Rodopi; 1989. 239 pp. (PmdnS 2.) [†Role of de Man, Paul: *Confessions*.]

[1375] de Man, Paul. "Roland Barthes and the Limits of Structuralism." *YFS*. 1990; 77: 177-190. [†Theories of Barthes, Roland.]

[1376] De Schutter, Dirk. "Words Like Stones." 99-110 in Herman, Luc, ed.; Humbeeck, Kris, ed.; Lernout, Geert, ed. *(Dis)continuities: Essays on Paul de Man*. Amsterdam: Rodopi; 1989. 239 pp. (PmdnS 2.) [†Theories of de Man, Paul.]

[1377] Demetz, Peter. "A Conversation with René Wellek." *CCur*. 1990; 9: 135-145. [†Interview with Wellek, René.]

[1378] Derrida, Jacques. "Some Statements and Truisms about Neologisms, Newisms, Postisms, Parasitisms, and Other Small Seismisms." 63-94 in Carroll, David, ed. *The States of "Theory": History, Art, and Critical Discourse*. New York: Columbia UP; 1990. x, 316 pp. (Irvine Studies in the Humanities.)

[1379] Desan, Philippe. "Critical Discussions." *P&L*. 1990 Apr.; 14(1): 142-156. [On Walzer, Michael. *Interpretation and Social Criticism* & Walzer, Michael. *The Company of Critics: Social Criticism and Political Commitment in the Twentieth Century*. †Role of interpretation; relationship to politics; social criticism. Review article.]

[1380] Dhareshwar, Vivek. "The Predicament of Theory." 231-250 in Kreiswirth, Martin, ed.; Cheetham, Mark A., ed. *Theory between the Disciplines: Authority/Vision/Politics*. Ann Arbor: U of Michigan P; 1990. xii, 257 pp.

[1381] Dijkstra, Katinka. "Canonvorming in de literaire communicatie: Indicatoren voor de analyse van de literair-kritische canon." *Spektator*. 1989 Jan.; 18(3): 159-168. [†Role of canon. Empirical approach.]

[1382] Docherty, Thomas. "Anti-Mimesis: The Historicity of Representation." *FMLS*. 1990 July; 26(3): 272-281. [†Representation; relationship to historicity. Treatment in Auerbach, Erich: *Mimesis*; de Man, Paul.]

[1383] Doležel, Lubomír. "Aliens and Visitors in Literary Metalanguage." 265-271 in Bauer, Roger, ed.; Fokkema, Douwe, ed.; Graat, Michael de, asst. ed.; Fischer-Lichte, Erika, asst.; Garstin, Marguerite, asst.; Ibsch, Elrud, asst.; Stackelberg, Jürgen von, asst. *Proceedings of the XIIth Congress of the International Comparative Literature Association/Actes du XIIe congrès de l'Association Internationale de Littérature Comparée: München 1988 Munich, V: Space and Boundaries in Literary Theory and Criticism/Espace et frontières dans la critique et la théorie littéraire; Space and Boundaries in the Teaching of General and Comparative Literature/Espace et frontières dans l'enseignement de la littérature générale et comparée*. Munich: Iudicium; 1990. 415 pp. (Proceedings of the Congress of the International Comparative Literature Association 12: 5.) [†Mimesis; speech acts; relationship to metalanguage.]

[1384] Dorval, Bruce; Dore, John. "The Adolescent's Intimate Other: Comparing Piaget, Freud and Bakhtin in an Analysis of Dialog." *DS/SD*. 1990 Spring-Summer; 3(1-2): 23-56. [†Dialogue; relationship to intersubjectivity. Theories of Bakhtin, Mikhail Mikhaïlovich compared to Piaget, Jean; Freud, Sigmund.]

[1385] Durant, Alan. "[Bakhtin and Film]." *Screen*. 1990 Autumn; 31(3): 334-340. [On Stam, Robert. *Subversive Pleasures: Bakhtin, Cultural Criticism, and Film*. †Relationship to film. Theories of Bakhtin, Mikhail Mikhaïlovich. Review article.]

[1386] Eagleton, Terry. "The Ideology of the Aesthetic." *PoT*. 1988; 9(2): 327-338. [†Aesthetics; relationship to bourgeois society; politics; hegemony.]

[1387] ———. *The Ideology of the Aesthetic*. Oxford: Blackwell; 1990. 426 pp. [†Role of aesthetics; relationship to German philosophy.]

[1388] Easthope, Antony. "The Question of Literary Value." *TexP*. 1990 Winter; 4(3): 376-389. [†Role of literary value.]

[1389] Edmundson, Mark. "Criticism and Class Consciousness." *AmLH*. 1990 Fall; 2(3): 564-579. [†Theories of Barthes, Roland: *Mythologies*.]

[1390] Edwards, Michael. "Writing and Redemption." 129-136 in Wood, David, ed.; Levinas, Emmanuel, fwd.; Allison, David, tr. of fwd. *Writing the Future*. London: Routledge; 1990. x, 213 pp. (Warwick Studies in Philosophy and Literature.) [†Poetics; relationship to Christianity; redemption.]

[1391] Eismann, Wolfgang. "Bericht über das Projekt 'Ethnolinguistisches Wörterbuch der slavischen Altertümer'." 29-40 in Eimermacher, Karl, ed.; Grzybek, Peter, ed.; Witte, Georg, ed. *Issues in Slavic Literary and Cultural Theory*. Bochum: Brockmeyer; 1989. 631 pp. (Evolutionary Cultural Semiotics 21.) [†Relationship to cultural criticism. Application of theories of Propp, Vladimir Iakovlevich.]

[1392] Emerson, Caryl. "Review Essay." *DS/SD*. 1990 Spring-Summer; 3(1-2): 351-356. [On A. F. Eremeev et al., eds. *Estetika M. M. Bakhtina i sovremennost*. †Role of politics; relationship to theories of Bakhtin, Mikhail Mikhaïlovich. Review article.]

[1393] ———. "Russian Orthodoxy and the Early Bakhtin." *R&L*. 1990 Summer-Autumn; 22(2-3): 109-131. [†Role of Bakhtin, Mikhail Mikhaïlovich; relationship to Russian Orthodox Church.]

[1394] Esch, Deborah. "The Work to Come." *Diacritics*. 1990 Fall; 20(3): 28-49. [On de Man, Paul. *Wartime Journalism, 1939-1943* & 1989 Bibliog. IV.1473. †By de Man, Paul. Review article.]

[1395] Fayolle, Roger. "L'Invention terminologique en critique littéraire." *O&C*. 1990; 15(2): 35-50. [†Terminology.]

[1396] Fink-Eitel, Hinrich. "Zwischen Nietzsche und Heidegger: Michel Foucaults 'Sexualität und Wahrheit' im Spiegel neuerer Sekundärliteratur." *PJGG*. 1990; 97(2): 367-390. [†Theories of Foucault, Michel.]

[1397] Finlay, Marike; Robertson, Brian. "Quasi-Direct Discourse in the Psychoanalytic Context: Dialogical Strategy/Strategic Dialogue." *DS/SD*. 1990 Spring-Summer; 3(1-2): 57-81. [†Quasi-direct discourse; relationship to psychotherapy. Theories of Bakhtin, Mikhail Mikhaïlovich.]

[1398] Fischer, Michael. "Perspectivism and Literary Theory Today." *AmLH*. 1990 Fall; 2(3): 528-549. [†Relationship to perspectivism. Review article.]

[1399] Fokkema, Douwe. "Questions épistémologiques." 325-351 in Angenot, Marc, ed.; Bessière, Jean, ed.; Fokkema, Douwe, ed.; Kushner, Eva, ed. *Théorie littéraire*. Paris: PU de France; 1989. 395 pp.

[1400] Franck, D. "Literatuurwetenschappelijke immunologie of: De onderwerping van het onderwerp of: De beveiliging van het subjekt tegen het objekt." *Spektator*. 1989 May; 18(5): 363-364.

[1401] Freiwald, Bina. "Theorist Know Thyself: Foucault, Habermas, and the Unity of Knowledge and Interest." 143-154 in Valdés, Mario J., ed. *Toward a Theory of Comparative Literature: Selected Papers Presented in the Division of Theory of Literature at the XIth International Comparative Literature Congress*. New York: Peter Lang; 1990. 275 pp. (Proceedings of the International Comparative Literature Association 11: 3.) [†Relationship to epistemology of Positivism. Application of theories of Foucault, Michel; Habermas, Jürgen; Lyotard, Jean François.]

[1402] Freundlieb, Dieter. "Semiotic Idealism." *PoT*. 1988; 9(4): 807-841. [†Semiotic idealism. Sources in Kant, Immanuel; Saussure, Ferdinand de.]

[1403] Friggieri, Oliver. "A Critical Approach to Modern Criticism." *Association Internationale des Critiques Littéraires*. 1990; 33: 43-44.

[1404] Galan, F. W. "Bakhtiniada, The Corsican Brothers in the Prague School: Or, The Reciprocity of Reception." *PoT*. 1987; 8(3-4): 565-577. [†Theories of Bakhtin, Mikhail Mikhaïlovich; relationship to Prague School of Linguistics.]

[1405] Gallop, Jane. *Reading Lacan*. Ithaca: Cornell UP; 1985. 198 pp. [†Theories of Lacan, Jacques.]

[1406] Gearhart, Suzanne. "History as Criticism: The Dialogue of History and Literature." *Diacritics*. 1987 Fall; 17(3): 56-65. [On LaCapra, Dominick. *History and Criticism* & 1983 Bibliog. IV.1642. †Relationship to history. Review article.]

[1407] Goodman, Alan H. "Interpreting Art and Literature." *JAAC*. 1990 Summer; 48(3): 205-214.

[1408] Götz, Heinz-Jürgen. "'Erzählen' und 'Erzählung': Zu Paul Ricœurs Gedanke von 'Temps et récit'." *PJGG*. 1990; 97(1): 105-117. [†Narration. Theories of Ricœur, Paul: *Temps et récit*.]

[1409] Graff, Gerald. "The Future of Theory in the Teaching of Literature." 250-267 in Cohen, Ralph, ed. *The Future of Literary Theory*. New York: Routledge; 1989. xx, 445 pp. [†Role in teaching of literature.]

[1410] ———. "Why Theory?" 19-35 in Davis, Lennard J., ed.; Mirabella, M. Bella, ed. *Left Politics and the Literary Profession*. New York: Columbia UP; 1990. xii, 316 pp. (Social Foundations of Aesthetic Forms.) [†Relationship to universities.]

[1411] Grataloup, Nicole. "L'Ecriture théorique: Sujet, langue et travail du texte." *Pensée*. 1990 Mar.-Apr.; 274: 47-61. [†Textuality; subjectivity.]

[1412] Green, Nicholas. "New Developments in Literary Criticism: A Skeptical Reaction." *Hermathena: A Trinity College Dublin Review*. 1987 Summer; 142: 7-12.

[1413] Guattari, Felix; Schiesari, Juliana, tr.; Van Den Abbeele, Georges, tr. "Ritornellos and Existential Affects." *Discourse*. 1990 Spring-Summer; 12(2): 66-81. [†Role of affect; relationship to form; content.]

[1414] Gumbrecht, Hans Ulrich. "(N)on (Literary) Interpretation." *PoeticsJ*. 1989 Oct.; 18(4-5): 375-387. [†Interpretation; relationship to truth.]

[1415] Gunn, Giles. "Beyond Transcendence or Beyond Ideology: The New Problematics of Cultural Criticism in America." *AmLH*. 1990 Spring; 2(1): 1-18.

[1416] Hamilton, A. C. *Northrop Frye: Anatomy of His Criticism*. Toronto: U of Toronto P; 1990. xxii, 294 pp. [†Theories of Frye, Northrop.]

[1417] Hancher, Michael. "Performative Utterance, the Word of God, and the Death of the Author." 27-40 in White, Hugh C., ed. *Speech Act Theory and Biblical Criticism*. Decatur, GA: Scholars; 1988. (Semeia 41.) [†Speech act theory.]

[1418] Hancock, Cassandra Northway. "Synaesthesis in the Criticism of I. A. Richards." *DAI*. 1990 Jan.; 50(7): 2063A. [†Synesthesia. Theories of Richards, I. A. Dissertation abstract.]

[1419] Handelman, Susan. "Ending the Cold War: Literary Theory and the Bibliography and Methods Course." *LRN*. 1987 Spring-Summer; 12(2-3): 115-135. [†Pedagogical approach.]

[1420] ———. "Facing the Other: Levinas, Perelman and Rosenzweig." *R&L*. 1990 Summer-Autumn; 22(2-3): 61-84. [†Relationship to the other; the Holocaust; Judaism. Theories of Levinas, Emmanuel; Perelman, Chaim: *The New Rhetoric*; Rosenzweig, Franz.]

[1421] Harari, Josué V. "Tristes théories." *RSH*. 1989 Apr.-June; 90(214 [2]): 163-176. [†Theories of Lévi-Strauss, Claude; Derrida, Jacques.]

[1422] Harasym, Sarah, ed. *The Post-Colonial Critic: Interviews, Strategies, Dialogues: Gayatri Chakravorty Spivak*. New York: Routledge; 1990. viii, 168 pp. [Incl. note. †Theories of Spivak, Gayatri Chakravorty.]

[1423] Hart, Kevin. "Ricoeur's Distinctions." *Scripsi*. 1989 Aug.; 5(4): 103-125. [†Theories of Ricœur, Paul.]

SEE SUBJECT INDEX FOR CROSS-REFERENCES

[1424] Hauge, Hans. "Paul de Man as Theologian." 163-176 in Herman, Luc, ed.; Humbeeck, Kris, ed.; Lernout, Geert, ed. *(Dis)continuities: Essays on Paul de Man.* Amsterdam: Rodopi; 1989. 239 pp. (PmdnS 2.) [†Role of de Man, Paul; relationship to theology.]

[1425] Hempfer, Klaus W. "Zu einigen Problemen einer Fiktionstheorie." *ZFSL.* 1990; 100: 109-137. [†Fiction.

[1426] Henricksen, Bruce, ed.; Morgan, Thais E., ed. *Reorientations: Critical Theories & Pedagogies.* Urbana: U of Illinois P; 1990. x, 275 pp. [Incl. introd. †Relationship to pedagogy.]

[1427] Hertz, Neil. "Lurid Figures." 100-124 in Bender, John, ed.; Wellbery, David E., ed. *The Ends of Rhetoric: History, Theory, Practice.* Stanford: Stanford UP; 1990. xiv, 238 pp. [†Theories of de Man, Paul.]

[1428] ——. "More Lurid Figures." *Diacritics.* 1990 Fall; 20(3): 2-27. [†Role of textuality. Treatment in de Man, Paul; relationship to Empson, William.]

[1429] Hirschkop, Ken. "Heteroglossia and Civil Society: Bakhtin's Public Square and the Politics of Modernity." *SLitI.* 1990 Spring; 23(1): 65-75. [†On heteroglossia; relationship to society. Theories of Bakhtin, Mikhail Mikhaĭlovich.]

[1430] Hix, H. L. *Morte d'Author: An Autopsy.* Philadelphia: Temple UP; 1990. 254 pp. (Arts and Their Philosophies.) [†Role of authorship.]

[1431] Holquist, Michael; Hawkes, Terence, gen. ed. *Dialogism: Bakhtin and His World.* London: Routledge; 1990. xiii, 204 pp. [Incl. pref. †Theories of Bakhtin, Mikhail Mikhaĭlovich.]

[1432] Hooley, Daniel M. "On Relations between Classical and Contemporary Imitation Theory: Some Hellenistic Suggestions." *CML.* 1990 Fall; 11(1): 77-92. [†Theories of mimesis; relationship to poetic language. Sources in Philodemus.]

[1433] Horn, András. "The Empiricist's Fear of Evaluation." 57-66 in Valdés, Mario J., ed. *Toward a Theory of Comparative Literature: Selected Papers Presented in the Division of Theory of Literature at the XIth International Comparative Literature Congress.* New York: Peter Lang; 1990. 275 pp. (Proceedings of the International Comparative Literature Association 11: 3.) [Role of empiricism; relationship to genre classification.]

[1434] Ibsch, Elrud. "'Facts' in the Empirical Study of Literature: The United States and Germany—a Comparison." *PoeticsJ.* 1989 Oct.; 18(4-5): 389-404. [†In United States compared to Germany. Relationship to empiricism.]

[1435] Ibsch, Elrud, introd. "Groupe de travail: Formation et déformation des concepts dans la théorie littéraire/Workshop: The Formation and Deformation of Concepts in Literary Theory." 251-330 in Bauer, Roger, ed.; Fokkema, Douwe, ed.; Graat, Michael de, asst. ed.; Fischer-Lichte, Erika, asst.; Garstin, Marguerite, asst.; Ibsch, Elrud, asst.; Stackelberg, Jürgen von, asst. *Proceedings of the XIIth Congress of the International Comparative Literature Association/Actes du XIIe congrès de l'Association Internationale de Littérature Comparée: München 1988 Munich, V: Space and Boundaries in Literary Theory and Criticism/Espace et frontières dans la critique et la théorie littéraire; Space and Boundaries in the Teaching of General and Comparative Literature/Espace et frontières dans l'enseignement de la littérature générale et comparée.* Munich: Iudicium; 1990. 415 pp. (Proceedings of the Congress of the International Comparative Literature Association 12: 5.) [Spec. sect.]

[1436] Iser, Wolfgang. "The Aesthetic and the Imaginary." 201-220 in Carroll, David, ed. *The States of "Theory": History, Art, and Critical Discourse.* New York: Columbia UP; 1990. x, 316 pp. (Irvine Studies in the Humanities.) [†Role of imagination; aesthetics.]

[1437] Jachia, Paolo. "La Philosophie du dialogue de M. Bakhtine." *DS/SD.* 1990 Spring-Summer; 3(1-2): 99-107. [†Dialogue. Theories of Bakhtin, Mikhail Mikhaĭlovich.]

[1438] Jacobs, Alan. "The Unnatural Practices of Stanley Fish: A Review Essay." *SoAR.* 1990 Nov.; 55(4): 87-97. [On Fish, Stanley. *Doing What Comes Naturally.* †Review article.]

[1439] Jauss, Hans Robert. "*Historia Calamitatum et Fortunarum Mearum*: Or, A Paradigm Shift in Literary Study." 112-128 in Cohen, Ralph, ed. *The Future of Literary Theory.* New York: Routledge; 1989. xx, 445 pp. [†Relationship to history.]

[1440] Johnson, Barbara. "The Surprise of Otherness: A Note on the Wartime Writings of Paul de Man." 13-22 in Collier, Peter, ed.; Geyer-Ryan, Helga, ed. *Literary Theory Today.* Ithaca: Cornell UP; 1990. xii, 249 pp. [†Role of de Man, Paul.]

[1441] Johnston, John. "Discourse as Event: Foucault, Writing and Literature." *MLN.* 1990 Sept.; 105(4): 800-818. [†Writing. Theories of Foucault, Michel.]

[1442] Juvan, Marko. "Teorije medbesedilnosti." *PKn.* 1990; 13(1): 27-46. [Fr. sum. †Intertextuality.]

[1443] Kálmán, György C. "Boundaries of Interpretive Communities." 105-111 in Bauer, Roger, ed.; Fokkema, Douwe, ed.; Graat, Michael de, asst. ed.; Fischer-Lichte, Erika, asst.; Garstin, Marguerite, asst.; Ibsch, Elrud, asst.; Stackelberg, Jürgen von, asst. *Proceedings of the XIIth Congress of the International Comparative Literature Association/Actes du XIIe congrès de l'Association Internationale de Littérature Comparée: München 1988 Munich, V: Space and Boundaries in Literary Theory and Criticism/Espace et frontières dans la critique et la théorie littéraire; Space and Boundaries in the Teaching of General and Comparative Literature/Espace et frontières dans l'enseignement de la littérature générale et comparée.* Munich: Iudicium; 1990. 415 pp. (Proceedings of the Congress of the International Comparative Literature Association 12: 5.) [†Role of interpretive communities.]

[1444] Kaufmann, David. "The Profession of Theory." *PMLA.* 1990 May; 105(3): 519-530. [†Relationship to politics.]

[1445] Kazuhisa, Takahashi. "Literature, Criticism and Canon: An Interview with Professor Frank Kermode." *Rising Generation.* 1990 Sept. 1; 136(6): 1-10. [†Relationship to canon. Interview with Kermode, Frank.]

[1446] Kellmann, Steven G. "The Macrological Imperative: Pandictic Art." 109-118 in Bessière, Jean, ed. *Fiction, texte, narratologie, genre.* New York: Peter Lang; 1989. 238 pp. [†Intertextuality.]

[1447] Kennedy, Lisa. "Art Ache: The Last Temptation of Julia Kristeva." *Village Voice Literary Supplement.* 1990 Dec.; 91: 15. [†Treatment of depression. Theories of Kristeva, Julia: *Soleil noir, dépression et mélancolie.*]

[1448] Kim, Bohyun. "Piety and Impiety: Two Opposite Attitudes toward Poetic Language." *DAI.* 1990 Feb.; 50(8): 2481A. [†Poetic language. Dissertation abstract.]

[1449] Klein, Richard. "The Future of Nuclear Criticism." *YFS.* 1990; 77: 76-100. [†Relationship to nuclear war.]

[1450] Knudsen, Geir. "Literaturforståelse i rundskrivs form." *Norsklrrn.* 1990; 14(2): 5-12. [†Pedagogical approach. Theories of Nietzsche, Friedrich Wilhelm; Habermas, Jürgen.]

[1451] Krauss, Rosalind. "The Future of an Illusion." 280-290 in Cohen, Ralph, ed. *The Future of Literary Theory.* New York: Routledge; 1989. xx, 445 pp. [†Relationship to art history.]

[1452] Kreiswirth, Martin; Cheetham, Mark A. "'Theory-Mad beyond Redemption' (?)." 1-16 in Kreiswirth, Martin, ed.; Cheetham, Mark A., ed. *Theory between the Disciplines: Authority/Vision/Politics.* Ann Arbor: U of Michigan P; 1990. xii, 257 pp.

[1453] Kreiswirth, Martin, ed.; Cheetham, Mark A., ed. *Theory between the Disciplines: Authority/Vision/Politics.* Ann Arbor: U of Michigan P; 1990. xii, 257 pp. [Incl. introd. †Interdisciplinary approach.]

[1454] Krell, David Farrell. "Beneath the Time of the Line: The Future of Memory." 106-111 in Wood, David, ed.; Levinas, Emmanuel, fwd.; Allison, David, tr. of fwd. *Writing the Future.* London: Routledge; 1990. x, 213 pp. (Warwick Studies in Philosophy and Literature.) [†On memory; relationship to the future. Theories of Heidegger, Martin; Sartre, Jean-Paul.]

[1455] Kress, Gunther. "Critical Discourse Analysis." *ARAL.* 1990; 11: 84-99. [†Relationship to discourse analysis.]

[1456] Krieger, Murray. *A Reopening of Closure: Organicism against Itself.* New York: Columbia UP; 1989. xiv, 125 pp. [†Relationship to organicism.]

[1457] Kruks, Sonia. "Sartre's 'First Ethics' and the Future of Ethics." 181-191 in Wood, David, ed.; Levinas, Emmanuel, fwd.; Allison, David, tr. of fwd. *Writing the Future.* London: Routledge; 1990. x, 213 pp. (Warwick Studies in Philosophy and Literature.) [†Relationship to ethics. Role of theories of Sartre, Jean-Paul: *L'Etre et le néant; Cahiers pour une morale.*]

[1458] Krupat, Arnold. "Criticism and the Canon: Cross-Relations." *Diacritics.* 1987 Summer; 17(2): 3-20. [On Pearce, Roy Harvey. *Gesta Humanorum: Studies in the Historical Mode* & Pearce, Roy Harvey. *The Savages of America: A Study of the Indian and the Idea of Civilization.* †On American literature; American culture; relationship to Native Americans. Review article.]

[1459] Krupnick, Mark. "The Critic and His Connections: The Case of Michael Walzer." *AmLH.* 1989 Fall; 1(3): 689-698. [†Theories of Walzer, Michael: *The Company of Critics; Interpretation and Social Criticism.*]

[1460] Krysinski, Wladimir. "*Subjectum comparationis*: Les Incidences du sujet dans le discours." 235-248 in Angenot, Marc, ed.; Bessière, Jean, ed.; Fokkema, Douwe, ed.; Kushner, Eva, ed. *Théorie littéraire.* Paris: PU de France; 1989. 395 pp. [†On subjectivity.]

[1461] Kühn, Marthinus Johannes. "Literary Theory and the Teaching of Literature." *DAI.* 1990 Dec.; 51(6): 2007A. [†Relationship to teaching of literature. Dissertation abstract.]

[1462] LaCapra, Dominick. *Soundings in Critical Theory.* Ithaca: Cornell UP; 1989. ix, 213 pp.

[1463] Laclau, Ernesto. "Totalitarianism and Moral Indignation." *Diacritics.* 1990 Fall; 20(3): 88-95. [†By de Man, Paul; relationship to anti-Semitism.]

[1464] Lefort, Claude. "Machiavelli: History, Politics, Discourse." 113-124 in Carroll, David, ed. *The States of "Theory": History, Art, and Critical Discourse.* New York: Columbia UP; 1990. x, 316 pp. (Irvine Studies in the Humanities.) [†Relationship to Machiavelli, Niccolò: *Discorsi.*]

[1465] LeGouis, Catherine. "Three Versions of Positivism: Emile Hennequin, Wilhelm Scherer, Apollon Grigoriev." *DAI.* 1990 June; 50(12): 3941A-3942A. [†1800-1899. Role of Hennequin, Emile: *La Critique scientifique;* Scherer, Wilhelm: *Geschichte der deutschen Literatur;* Grigor'ev, Apollon Aleksandrovich. Sources in Positivism. Dissertation abstract.]

[1466] Lentricchia, Frank. "Philosophers of Modernism at Harvard circa 1900." *SAQ.* 1990 Fall; 89(4): 787-834. [†Relationship to Modernism. Theories of Santayana, George; Royce, Josiah; James, William.]

[1467] Lentricchia, Frank; McLaughlin, Thomas. *Critical Terms for Literary Study.* Chicago: U of Chicago P; 1990. vii, 369 pp. [†Handbook of terminology.]

[1468] Levy, Silvano. "Foucault on Magritte on Resemblance." *MLR.* 1990 Jan.; 85(1): 50-56. [†On similarity. Treatment in Foucault, Michel: *Ceci n'est pas une pipe* compared to Magritte, René.]

[1469] Li, Victor. "The Distinction of Literary Theory." 61-76 in Kreiswirth, Martin, ed.; Cheetham, Mark A., ed. *Theory between the Disciplines: Authority/Vision/Politics.* Ann Arbor: U of Michigan P; 1990. xii, 257 pp.

[1470] Lichtenstein, Jacqueline. "Up Close, From Afar: The Subject's Distance from Representation." *QPar.* 1990 Fall; 4(1): 98-116. [†Role of subject; relationship to representation. Application of theories of Pascal, Blaise; Piles, Roger de.]

[1471] Lindenberger, Herbert, ed. "The Politics of Critical Language." *PMLA.* 1990 May; 105(3). [Spec. iss.; incl. introd. †Relationship to politics; ideology.]

[1472] Lodge, David, ed. *After Bakhtin: Essays on Fiction and Criticism*. London: Routledge; 1990. viii, 198 pp. [†And fiction. Theories of Bakhtin, Mikhail Mikhaïlovich.]

[1473] Loriggio, Francesco. "The Question of the Corpus: Ethnicity and Canadian Literature." 53-69 in Moss, John, ed. *Future Indicative: Literary Theory and Canadian Literature*. Ottawa: U of Ottawa P; 1987. 247 pp. (ReapprC 13.) [†In Canada. Role of theme; relationship to ethnic literature.]

[1474] Manning, Frank E. "Victor Turner's Career and Publications." 170-177 in Ashley, Kathleen M., ed. *Victor Turner and the Construction of Cultural Criticism*. Bloomington: Indiana UP; 1990. xxii, 185 pp. (Between Literature and Anthropology.) [†Contributions of Turner, Victor Witter.]

[1475] Mansell, Darrel. "The Difference between a Lump and a Text." *PoT*. 1988; 9(4): 791-805. [†Compared to science.]

[1476] McCloskey, Donald N. "Storytelling in Economics." 5-22 in Nash, Cristopher, ed. *Narrative in Culture: The Uses of Storytelling in the Sciences, Philosophy, and Literature*. London: Routledge; 1990. xvi, 228 pp. (Warwick Studies in Philosophy and Literature.) [†Applied to economics.]

[1477] McGann, Jerome. "How to Read a Book." *LCUT*. 1990; 20(1-2): 12-37. [Illus. †Theories of Adler, Mortimer Jerome: *How to Read a Book*; Pound, Ezra: *ABC of Reading*.]

[1478] ———. "The Third World of Criticism." 85-107 in Levinson, Marjorie, ed. *Rethinking Historicism: Critical Readings in Romantic History*. Oxford: Blackwell; 1989. vi, 149 pp. [†Relationship to Third World literature.]

[1479] Meletinsky, Eleazar; Bessière, Jean. "Sociétés, cultures et faits littéraires." 13-29 in Angenot, Marc, ed.; Bessière, Jean, ed.; Fokkema, Douwe, ed.; Kushner, Eva, ed. *Théorie littéraire*. Paris: PU de France; 1989. 395 pp.

[1480] Mignolo, Walter D. "Fuzzy and Theoretical Domains: An Essay in Conceptual Elucidation." 254-264 in Bauer, Roger, ed.; Fokkema, Douwe, ed.; Graat, Michael de, asst. ed.; Fischer-Lichte, Erika, asst.; Garstin, Marguerite, asst.; Ibsch, Elrud, asst.; Stackelberg, Jürgen von, asst. *Proceedings of the XIIth Congress of the International Comparative Literature Association/Actes du XIIe congrès de l'Association Internationale de Littérature Comparée: München 1988 Munich, V: Space and Boundaries in Literary Theory and Criticism/Espace et frontières dans la critique et la théorie littéraire; Space and Boundaries in the Teaching of General and Comparative Literature/Espace et frontières dans l'enseignement de la littérature générale et comparée*. Munich: Iudicium; 1990. 415 pp. (Proceedings of the Congress of the International Comparative Literature Association 12: 5.)

[1481] Mileur, Jean-Pierre. *The Critical Romance: The Critic as Reader, Writer, Hero*. Madison: U of Wisconsin P; 1990. 234 pp. [†Relationship to romance.]

[1482] Miller, J. Hillis. "The Function of Literary Theory at the Present Time." 102-111 in Cohen, Ralph, ed. *The Future of Literary Theory*. New York: Routledge; 1989. xx, 445 pp.

[1483] Moran, Charles, ed.; Penfield, Elizabeth F., ed. *Conversations: Contemporary Critical Theory and the Teaching of Literature*. Urbana: Nat. Council of Teachers of Eng.; 1990. viii, 237 pp. [Incl. introd. †Relationship to teaching of literature.]

[1484] Morson, Gary Saul; Emerson, Caryl. *Mikhail Bakhtin: Creation of a Prosaics*. Stanford: Stanford UP; 1990. xx, 530 pp. [†Theories of Bakhtin, Mikhail Mikhaïlovich.]

[1485] Morson, Gary Saul, ed.; Emerson, Caryl, ed. *Rethinking Bakhtin: Extensions and Challenges*. Evanston: Northwestern UP; 1989. 330 pp. (Northwestern University Press Series in Russian Literature and Theory.) [Incl. introd.; prev. pub. material. †Role of Bakhtin, Mikhail Mikhaïlovich.]

[1486] Morton, Donald. "Texts of Limits, the Limits of Texts, and the Containment of Politics in Contemporary Critical Theory." *Diacritics*. 1990 Spring; 20(1): 57-75. [†Relationship to politics. Review article.]

[1487] Moser, Dietz-Rüdiger. "Lachkultur des Mittelalters? Michael Bachtin und die Folgen seiner Theorie." *Euphorion*. 1990; 84(1): 89-111. [Illus. †Role of the carnivalesque; relationship to Middle Ages. Theories of Bakhtin, Mikhail Mikhaïlovich.]

[1488] Mowitt, John. "The Coming of the Text: The Text of Publicity." *HEI*. 1989; 11: 573-582. [†Role of text; relationship to cultural context. Theories of Barthes, Roland.]

[1489] Muraškovskij, Julij; Muraškovska, Ingrida. "Kien fluas roj' castalie?" *Survoje*. 1990; 1: 8-14.

[1490] Nancy, Jean-Luc. "Our History." *Diacritics*. 1990 Fall; 20(3): 97-115. [On de Man, Paul. *Wartime Journalism, 1939-1943* & 1989 Bibliog. IV.1473. †By de Man, Paul; relationship to history; politics. Review article.]

[1491] Nash, Cristopher. "Slaughtering the Subject: Literature's Assault on Narrative." 199-218 in Nash, Cristopher, ed. *Narrative in Culture: The Uses of Storytelling in the Sciences, Philosophy, and Literature*. London: Routledge; 1990. xvi, 228 pp. (Warwick Studies in Philosophy and Literature.) [†Role of narrative; relationship to subject in fiction.]

[1492] Naumann, Manfred. "Remarques sur le concept d'institution." 278-284 in Bauer, Roger, ed.; Fokkema, Douwe, ed.; Graat, Michael de, asst. ed.; Fischer-Lichte, Erika, asst.; Garstin, Marguerite, asst.; Ibsch, Elrud, asst.; Stackelberg, Jürgen von, asst. *Proceedings of the XIIth Congress of the International Comparative Literature Association/Actes du XIIe congrès de l'Association Internationale de Littérature Comparée: München 1988 Munich, V: Space and Boundaries in Literary Theory and Criticism/Espace et frontières dans la critique et la théorie littéraire; Space and Boundaries in the Teaching of General and Comparative Literature/Espace et frontières dans l'enseignement de la littérature générale et comparée*. Munich: Iudicium; 1990. 415 pp. (Proceedings of the Congress of the International Comparative Literature Association 12: 5.) [†On literature as institution.]

[1493] Nethersole, Reingard. "From Temporality to Spatiality: Changing Concepts in Literary Criticism." 59-65 in Bauer, Roger, ed.; Fokkema, Douwe, ed.; Graat, Michael de, asst. ed.; Fischer-Lichte, Erika, asst.; Garstin, Marguerite, asst.; Ibsch, Elrud, asst.; Stackelberg, Jürgen von, asst. *Proceedings of the XIIth Congress of the International Comparative Literature Association/Actes du XIIe congrès de l'Association Internationale de Littérature Comparée: München 1988 Munich, V: Space and Boundaries in Literary Theory and Criticism/Espace et frontières dans la critique et la théorie littéraire; Space and Boundaries in the Teaching of General and Comparative Literature/Espace et frontières dans l'enseignement de la littérature générale et comparée*. Munich: Iudicium; 1990. 415 pp. (Proceedings of the Congress of the International Comparative Literature Association 12: 5.) [†Spatial form; relationship to temporal structure.]

[1494] Norris, Christopher. "De Man Unfair to Kierkegaard? An Allegory of (Non)-Reading." 199-239 in Herman, Luc, ed.; Humbeeck, Kris, ed.; Lernout, Geert, ed. *(Dis)continuities: Essays on Paul de Man*. Amsterdam: Rodopi; 1989. 239 pp. (PmdnS 2.) [†Theories of de Man, Paul; relationship to Kierkegaard, Søren.]

[1495] ———. "Right You Are (If You Think So): Stanley Fish and the Rhetoric of Assent." *CL*. 1990 Spring; 42(2): 144-182. [On Fish, Stanley. *Doing What Comes Naturally: Change, Rhetoric and the Practice of Theory in Literary and Legal Studies*. †Role of interpretive conventions in language. Review article.]

[1496] O'Neil, John. "Is There a Class in This Text?" *SCr*. 1990 May; 5(2 [63]): 221-233. [†Interpretive communities; relationship to canon. Treatment in Fish, Stanley: *Is There a Text in This Class?*]

[1497] Owen, Stephen. "Philology's Discontents: Response." 75-79 in Ziolkowski, Jan, ed. *On Philology*. University Park: Penn State UP; 1990. 78 pp. [†Relationship to philology.]

[1498] Papadima, Liviu. "Două metafore epistemice: 'Drumul' şi 'clădirea'." *RITL*. 1989-1990; 37-38(3-4): 73-78.

[1499] Patterson, David. "Laughter and the Alterity of Truth in Bakhtin's Aesthetics." *DS/SD*. 1990 Spring-Summer; 3(1-2): 293-309. [†Role of laughter as aesthetic device; relationship to truth. Theories of Bakhtin, Mikhail Mikhaïlovich.]

[1500] Paul, Lisa. "The New 3 Rs: Repetition, Recollection and Recognition." *CLAQ*. 1990 Summer; 15(2): 55-57. [†Applied to literature for children; relationship to chaos theory.]

[1501] Pavel, Thomas. "Narratives of Ritual and Desire." 64-69 in Ashley, Kathleen M., ed. *Victor Turner and the Construction of Cultural Criticism*. Bloomington: Indiana UP; 1990. xxii, 185 pp. (Between Literature and Anthropology.) [†Theories of Turner, Victor Witter.]

[1502] Pechter, Edward. "Of Ants and Grasshoppers: Two Ways (or More) to Link Texts and Power." *PoT*. 1988; 9(2): 291-306. [†Role of cultural context in interpretation.]

[1503] Pelckmans, Paul. "'Amoureux donc moïques': Kristeva dans l'orbite de Freud." *RSH*. 1986 Jan.-Mar.; 72(201 [1]): 91-101. [†Theories of Kristeva, Julia; relationship to Freud, Sigmund.]

[1504] Perlina, Nina. "Funny Things Are Happening on the Way to the Bakhtin Forum." *SCr*. 1990 Jan.; 5(1 [62]): 1-22. [†Theories of Bakhtin, Mikhail Mikhaïlovich.]

[1505] ———. "Ol'ga Freidenberg's Works and Days." *SCr*. 1990 May; 5(2 [63]): 167-203. [†Theories of Freĭdenberg, Ol'ga Mikhaĭlovna.]

[1506] Peterfreund, Stuart. "Logotomy: Or, Sawing the Language in Half." *ECent*. 1990 Spring; 31(1): 68-80. [On Benjamin, Andrew E.; Cantor, Geoffrey N.; Christie, John R. R. *The Figural and the Literal: Problems of Language in the History of Science and Philosophy 1630-1800*. †Figuration; relationship to literal meaning; study example: scientific language; philosophical language (1630-1800). Review article.]

[1507] Pirog, Gerald. "The Bakhtin Circle's Freud: From Positivism to Hermeneutics." *PoT*. 1987; 8(3-4): 591-610. [†Theories of Bakhtin, Mikhail Mikhaïlovich; relationship to Freud, Sigmund.]

[1508] Ponzio, Augusto. "Bakhtinian Alterity and the Search for Identity in Europe Today." *DS/SD*. 1990 Spring-Summer; 3(1-2): 217-227. [†Otherness; relationship to identity in Europe. Theories of Bakhtin, Mikhail Mikhaïlovich.]

[1509] Procházka, Miroslav. "Two Theories of Literary Development: The Prague School and Bakhtin's Semiotics." 551-569 in Eimermacher, Karl, ed.; Grzybek, Peter, ed.; Witte, Georg, ed. *Issues in Slavic Literary and Cultural Theory*. Bochum: Brockmeyer; 1989. 631 pp. (Evolutionary Cultural Semiotics 21.) [†Theories of Mukařovský, Jan; Vodička, Felix; Bakhtin, Mikhail Mikhaïlovich.]

[1510] Rasula, Jed. "The Poetics of Embodiment: A Theory of Exceptions." *DAI*. 1990 Feb.; 50(8): 2485A-2486A. [†Poetics; relationship to human body; society. Dissertation abstract.]

[1511] Ray, William. *Literary Meaning: From Phenomenology to Deconstruction*. Cambridge, MA: Blackwell; 1984. 300 pp. [†Meaning.]

[1512] Rayan, Krishna. "Literary Theory and Indian Critical Practice." *LCrit*. 1990; 25(1): 24-37. [†In India.]

[1513] Raybin, David. "Aesthetics, Romance, and Turner." 21-41 in Ashley, Kathleen M., ed. *Victor Turner and the Construction of Cultural Criticism*. Bloomington: Indiana UP; 1990. xxii, 185 pp. (Between Literature and Anthropology.) [†Theories of Turner, Victor Witter.]

[1514] Readings, Bill. "Why Is Theory Foreign?" 77-79 in Kreiswirth, Martin, ed.; Cheetham, Mark A., ed. *Theory between the Disciplines: Authority/Vision/Politics*. Ann Arbor: U of Michigan P; 1990. xii, 257 pp.

[1515] Redfield, Marc. "De Man, Schiller, and the Politics of Reception." *Diacritics*. 1990 Fall; 20(3): 50-70. [†By de Man, Paul; relationship to history. Sources in Schiller, Johann Christoph Friedrich von; Kant, Immanuel.]

SEE SUBJECT INDEX FOR CROSS-REFERENCES

[1516] Redfield, Marc W. "Humanizing De Man." *Diacritics*. 1989 Summer; 19(2): 35-53. [On 1987 Bibliog. I.3093 (IV.1739) & Norris, Christopher. *Paul de Man: Deconstruction and the Critique of Aesthetic Ideology*. †Role of de Man, Paul; relationship to humanism. Review article.]

[1517] Riffaterre, Michael. "Fear of Theory." *NLH*. 1990 Autumn; 21(4): 921-938

[1518] Robbins, Bruce. "Falling into Criticism." *AmLH*. 1989 Fall; 1(3): 656-664.

[1519] ——. "The History of Literary Theory: Starting Over." *PoT*. 1988; 9(4): 767-781.

[1520] Roberts, Mathew. "Poetics Hermeneutics Dialogics: Bakhtin and Paul de Man." 115-134 in Morson, Gary Saul, ed.; Emerson, Caryl, ed. *Rethinking Bakhtin: Extensions and Challenges*. Evanston: Northwestern UP; 1989. 330 pp. (Northwestern University Press Series in Russian Literature and Theory.) [†Role of Bakhtin, Mikhail Mikhaĭlovich compared to de Man, Paul.]

[1521] Robin, Régine. "Extension et incertitude de la notion de littérature." 45-49 in Angenot, Marc, ed.; Bessière, Jean, ed.; Fokkema, Douwe, ed.; Kushner, Eva, ed. *Théorie littéraire*. Paris: PU de France; 1989. 395 pp. [†Relationship to canon.]

[1522] Ruprecht, Hans-George. "Conjectures et inférences: Les Universaux de la littérature." 61-77 in Angenot, Marc, ed.; Bessière, Jean, ed.; Fokkema, Douwe, ed.; Kushner, Eva, ed. *Théorie littéraire*. Paris: PU de France; 1989. 395 pp. [†Relationship to universality.]

[1523] Sagovsky, Nicholas. "Von Hügel and the Will to Believe." 206-217 in Jasper, David, ed.; Wright, T. R., ed. *The Critical Spirit and the Will to Believe: Essays in Nineteenth-Century Literature and Religion*. New York: St. Martin's; 1989. xii; 239 pp. [†Treatment of Bible. Theories of Hügel, Friedrich, Freiherr von.]

[1524] Šarčević, Abdulah. "Etika i civilizacija: Problem etike odgovornosti." *Izraz*. 1990 Oct.; 34(10): 355-365. [†Relationship to ethics.]

[1525] Schmidt, Siegfried J. "On the Concept of System and Its Use in Literary Studies." 272-277 in Bauer, Roger, ed.; Fokkema, Douwe, ed.; Graat, Michael de, asst. ed.; Fischer-Lichte, Erika, asst.; Garstin, Marguerite, asst.; Ibsch, Elrud, asst.; Stackelberg, Jürgen von, asst. *Proceedings of the XIIth Congress of the International Comparative Literature Association/Actes du XIIe congrès de l'Association Internationale de Littérature Comparée: München 1988 Munich, V: Space and Boundaries in Literary Theory and Criticism/Espace et frontières dans la critique et la théorie littéraire; Space and Boundaries in the Teaching of General and Comparative Literature/Espace et frontières dans l'enseignement de la littérature générale et comparée*. Munich: Iudicium; 1990. 415 pp. (Proceedings of the Congress of the International Comparative Literature Association 12: 5.) [†On literature as system.]

[1526] ——. "On the Construction of Fiction and the Invention of Facts." *PoeticsJ*. 1989 Oct.; 18(4-5): 319-335. [†Relationship to Constructivism; empiricism.]

[1527] Schultz, Richard Lee. "Prophecy and Quotation: A Methodological Study." *DAI*. 1990 June; 50(12): 3932A. [†On quotation in Old Testament: Isaiah. Diachronic approach. Dissertation abstract.]

[1528] Schulz-Buschhaus, Ulrich. "Typen des Realismus und Typen der Gattungsmischung—eine Postille zu Erich Auerbachs *Mimesis*." *Sprachkunst*. 1989; 20(1): 51-67. [†Mimesis; realism; style. Theories of Auerbach, Erich: *Mimesis*.]

[1529] Schwarz, Daniel R. "The Consolation of Form: The Theoretical and Historical Significance of Frank Kermode's *The Sense of an Ending*." *CentR*. 1984-1985 Fall-Winter; 28-29(4-1): 29-47. [†Theories of Kermode, Frank: *The Sense of an Ending*.]

[1530] ——. "Reading as Moral Activity." *SR*. 1985 Summer; 93(3): 480-485. [†Theories of Booth, Wayne Clayson: *The Rhetoric of Fiction*.]

[1531] Seguin, Robert. "Borders, Contexts, Politics: Mikhail Bakhtin." *Signature*. 1989 Winter; 2: 42-59. [†Dialogism; relationship to context; politics in novel. Theories of Bakhtin, Mikhail Mikhaĭlovich.]

[1532] Shaffer, Elinor S. "The Concept of 'Gap' in Theoretical Discourse." 285-295 in Bauer, Roger, ed.; Fokkema, Douwe, ed.; Graat, Michael de, asst. ed.; Fischer-Lichte, Erika, asst.; Garstin, Marguerite, asst.; Ibsch, Elrud, asst.; Stackelberg, Jürgen von, asst. *Proceedings of the XIIth Congress of the International Comparative Literature Association/Actes du XIIe congrès de l'Association Internationale de Littérature Comparée: München 1988 Munich, V: Space and Boundaries in Literary Theory and Criticism/Espace et frontières dans la critique et la théorie littéraire; Space and Boundaries in the Teaching of General and Comparative Literature/Espace et frontières dans l'enseignement de la littérature générale et comparée*. Munich: Iudicium; 1990. 415 pp. (Proceedings of the Congress of the International Comparative Literature Association 12: 5.) [†Role of gaps.]

[1533] Shaw, Harry E. "With Reference to Austin." *Diacritics*. 1990 Summer; 20(2): 75-92. [On 1988 Bibliog. II.1935. †Role of referent; relationship to realism; study example: Zola, Emile. Application of theories of Austin, J. L. Review article.]

[1534] Shoaf, R. A. "Literary Theory, Medieval Studies, and the Crisis of Difference." 77-92 in Henricksen, Bruce, ed.; Morgan, Thais E., ed. *Reorientations: Critical Theories & Pedagogies*. Urbana: U of Illinois P; 1990. x, 275 pp. [†Relationship to medieval studies.]

[1535] Shumay, David R., ed. "Episodes in the History of Criticism and Theory: Papers from the Fourth Annual Meeting of the GRIP Project." *PoT*. 1988; 9(4). [Spec. iss; incl. introd.]

[1536] Silvers, Anita. "Politics and the Production of Narrative Identities." *P&L*. 1990 Apr.; 14(1): 99-107. [†Relationship to identity. Theories of Novitz, David.]

[1537] Skarpeta, Gi; Lekić, Snežana, tr. "Moja umjenost pisanje romana." *Stvaranje*. 1990 Sept.; 45(9): 925-928. [†Interview with Lévy, Bernard-Henri.]

[1538] Small, Ian; Guy, Josephine. "English in Crisis? (2)." *EIC*. 1990 July; 40(3): 185-197. [Cont. from 1989 Bibliog. IV.1824. †Relationship to English studies.]

[1539] Söderlind, Sylvia. "Back to the Future: Plus or Minus Canadian?" *QQ*. 1989 Autumn; 96(3): 631-638. [On Moss, John. *Future Indicative* & Hutcheon, Linda. *The Canadian Postmodern*. †In Canada. Review article.]

[1540] Solomon, J. Fisher. "Probable Circumstances, Potential Worlds: History, Futurity, and the 'Nuclear Referent'." *PLL*. 1990 Winter; 26(1): 60-72. [†On writing of history; relationship to the future; nuclear war.]

[1541] Spikes, Michael P. "E. D. Hirsch's Misreading of Saul Kripke." *P&L*. 1990 Apr.; 14(1): 85-91. [†On Kripke, Saul A.: *Naming and Necessity*. Treatment in Hirsch, Eric Donald.]

[1542] Spiridon, Monica, coord.; Nemoianu, Virgil; Pavel, Toma; Searle, John R.; Tymieniecka, Ana Teresa. "Teoria literară şi filozofia." *RITL*. 1989-1990; 37-38(3-4): 58-65. [†Relationship to philosophy.]

[1543] Spörk, Ingrid; Nikolić, Danka, tr. "Misao Julije Kristeve." *Izraz*. 1990 Feb.-Mar.; 34(2-3): 340-356. [†Theories of Kristeva, Julia.]

[1544] Stein, A. L. "Literature and Language after the Death of God." *HEI*. 1989; 11: 791-795. [†Relationship to discourse. Application of theories of Foucault, Michel; relationship to Nietzsche, Friedrich Wilhelm.]

[1545] Stengers, Jean. "Paul de Man, a Collaborator?" 43-50 in Herman, Luc, ed.; Humbeeck, Kris, ed.; Lernout, Geert, ed. *(Dis)continuities: Essays on Paul de Man*. Amsterdam: Rodopi; 1989. 239 pp. (PmdnS 2.) [†Role of de Man, Paul.]

[1546] Stern, Frederick C. "Derrida, De Man, Despair: Reading Derrida on De Man's 1940s Essays." *TexP*. 1990 Spring; 4(1): 22-37. [†Role of de Man, Paul; relationship to fascism. Treatment in Derrida, Jacques: "Like the Sound of the Sea Deep within a Shell."]

[1547] Stolz, Peter. "Werk und Wahrheit: Anmerkungen zu Michel Guérins *Qu'est-ce qu'une oeuvre?*" *Lendemains*. 1988; 13(51): 116-121. [On Guérin, Michel. *Qu'est-ce qu'une oeuvre?* †Aesthetics; relationship to language. Review article.]

[1548] Strydom, Leon. "Towards a Typology of Generalizations in Literary Science." 77-86 in Valdés, Mario J., ed. *Toward a Theory of Comparative Literature: Selected Papers Presented in the Division of Theory of Literature at the XIth International Comparative Literature Congress*. New York: Peter Lang; 1990. 275 pp. (Proceedings of the International Comparative Literature Association 11: 3.) [†Role of typology; relationship to comparative literature.]

[1549] Svane, Marie-Louise. "Ballet er ikke forbi." *KuKl*. 1990; 17(4): 21-28. [†Theories of Benjamin, Walter; Larsen, Peter.]

[1550] Svatoň, Vladimír. "Vztah pojmu struktura a sémantické gesto v historické poetice." *Slavia*. 1990; 59(1): 28-34.

[1551] Tamen, Miguel Bénard. "Manners of Interpretation." *DAI*. 1990 Feb.; 50(8): 2482A. [†Interpretation. Dissertation abstract.]

[1552] Thobo-Carlsen, John. "Tekst som læsning: En læsning af Roland Barthes: Écrire la lecture (1970)." *Edda*. 1990; 1: 44-47. [†On Barthes, Roland: *Ecrire la lecture*.]

[1553] Thomas, Brook. "Bringing about Critical Awareness through History in General Education Literature Courses." 219-247 in Henricksen, Bruce, ed.; Morgan, Thais E., ed. *Reorientations: Critical Theories & Pedagogies*. Urbana: U of Illinois P; 1990. x, 275 pp. [†Application in teaching of literature.]

[1554] Thomson, Clive, ed. *Georg Lukács et la théorie littéraire contemporaine*. Montreal: Assn. des Professeurs de Fr. des Univ. & Collèges Can.; 1983. 164 pp. [†Theories of Lukács, György.]

[1555] Thwaites, Tony. "Words in Collision: A Response to John Halperin." *AUMLA*. 1990 May; 73: 193-204. [Replies to 1989 Bibliog. IV.1619. †Role of text. Theories of Foucault, Michel: "Qu'est-ce qu'un auteur?"; *Folie et déraison*; Derrida, Jacques: "La Pharmacie de Platon."]

[1556] Trabant, Jürgen. "Rhythmus versus Zeichen: Zur Poetik von Henri Meschonnic." *ZFSL*. 1990; 100: 193-212. [†Poetics. Theories of Meschonnic, Henri.]

[1557] Turner, Frederick. "'Hyperion to a Satyr': Criticism and Antistructure in the Work of Victor Turner." 147-162 in Ashley, Kathleen M., ed. *Victor Turner and the Construction of Cultural Criticism*. Bloomington: Indiana UP; 1990. xxii, 185 pp. (Between Literature and Anthropology.) [†Relationship to theories of Turner, Victor Witter.]

[1558] Ugolnik, Anthony. "Textual Liturgics: Russian Orthodoxy and Recent Literary Criticism." *R&L*. 1990 Summer-Autumn; 22(2-3): 133-154. [†Text; relationship to liturgy of Russian Orthodox Church. Relationship to theories of Bakhtin, Mikhail Mikhaĭlovich; Florenskiĭ, Pavel Aleksandrovich: *Stolp i utverzhdenie istiny*; Kedrov, Konstantin Aleksandrovich: *Poéticheskiĭ kosmos*.]

[1559] van den Berg, Hubert. "Anarchismus für oder gegen Moderne und Avantgarde? Zur 'anarchistischen Ästhetik' von André Reszler." 85-98 in Drijkoningen, Fernand, ed.; Gevers, Dick, ed. *Anarchia*. Amsterdam: Rodopi; 1989. 123 pp. (AvG 3.) [Eng. & Fr. sums., 122. †Aesthetics; relationship to anarchism. Theories of Reszler, André.]

[1560] Vasilevskiĭ, Andreĭ. "'Tekst,' kontekst i Rolan Bart." *LG*. 1990 Feb. 21; 8 [5282]: 4. [†Relationship to text. Theories of Barthes, Roland.]

[1561] Vuong-Riddick, Thuong. "Lukács et ses critiques." 63-81 in Thomson, Clive, ed. *Georg Lukács et la théorie littéraire contemporaine*. Montreal: Assn. des Professeurs de Fr. des Univ. & Collèges Can.; 1983. 164 pp. [†Theories of Lukács, György.]

[1562] Walder, Dennis, ed. *Literature in the Modern World: Critical Essays and Documents*. Oxford: Oxford UP with Open Univ.; 1990. 384 pp. [Incl. introd.; prev. pub. material.]

[1563] Walker, Ronald G., ed.; Frazer, June M., ed.; Anderson, David R., afterword. *The Cunning Craft: Original Essays on Detective Fiction and Contemporary Literary Theory*. Macomb: Western Illinois Univ.; 1990. vii, 203 pp. (Essays in Literature.) [Incl. introd. †Applied to detective fiction.]

[1564] Wang, Orrin N. C. "Allegories of Praxis: The Reading of Romanticism and Fascism in A. O. Lovejoy and Leo Spitzer." *ClioI.* 1990 Fall; 20(1): 39-51. [†Relationship to fascism; Romanticism. Theories of Lovejoy, Arthur Oncken; Spitzer, Leo.]

[1565] Ward, Patricia A. "Ethics and Recent Literary Theory: The Reader as Moral Agent." *R&L.* 1990 Summer-Autumn; 22(2-3): 21-31. [†Role of reader; relationship to ethics.]

[1566] Watkins, Evan. "Reproduction, Reading, and Resistance." *AmLH.* 1990 Fall; 2(3): 550-563. [†Theories of Bourdieu, Pierre: *La Distinction: Critique sociale du jugement.* Review article.]

[1567] Watson, Stephen. "The Face of the Hibakusha: Levinas and the Trace of Apocalypse." 155-173 in Wood, David, ed.; Levinas, Emmanuel, fwd.; Allison, David, tr. of fwd. *Writing the Future.* London: Routledge; 1990. x, 213 pp. (Warwick Studies in Philosophy and Literature.) [†Role of the apocalypse; relationship to time. Theories of Levinas, Emmanuel: *Totalité et infini.*]

[1568] Webster, Roger. *Studying Literary Theory: An Introduction.* London: Arnold; 1990. 122 pp.

[1569] Wegner, Michael. "Zur Chronotopostheorie Michail Bachtins." 36-42 in Bauer, Roger, ed.; Fokkema, Douwe, ed.; Graat, Michael de, asst. ed.; Fischer-Lichte, Erika, asst.; Garstin, Marguerite, asst.; Ibsch, Elrud, asst.; Stackelberg, Jürgen von, asst. *Proceedings of the XIIth Congress of the International Comparative Literature Association/Actes du XIIe congrès de l'Association Internationale de Littérature Comparée: München 1988 Munich, V: Space and Boundaries in Literary Theory and Criticism/Espace et frontières dans la critique et la théorie littéraire; Space and Boundaries in the Teaching of General and Comparative Literature/Espace et frontières dans l'enseignement de la littérature générale et comparée.* Munich: Iudicium; 1990. 415 pp. (Proceedings of the Congress of the International Comparative Literature Association 12: 5.) [†Chronotope. Theories of Bakhtin, Mikhail Mikhaïlovich.]

[1570] Wellmer, Albrecht. "Metaphysics at the Moment of Its Fall." 35-49 in Collier, Peter, ed.; Geyer-Ryan, Helga, ed. *Literary Theory Today.* Ithaca: Cornell UP; 1990. xii, 249 pp. [†Relationship to metaphysics. Theories of Adorno, Theodor W.]

[1571] West, Rebecca. "Working on Living Writers." *RLA: Romance Languages Annual.* 1989; 1: 216-221. [†Of writer while living.]

[1572] White, Hayden. "'Figuring the Nature of the Times Deceased': Literary Theory and Historical Writing." 19-43 in Cohen, Ralph, ed. *The Future of Literary Theory.* New York: Routledge; 1989. xx, 445 pp. [†Relationship to historiography.]

[1573] ———. "The Rhetoric of Interpretation." *PoT.* 1988; 9(2): 253-274. [†Role of figuration in interpretation in Proust, Marcel: *Sodome et Gomorrhe.* Rhetorical approach.]

[1574] Wilson, Elizabeth. "A Short History of a Border War: Social Science, School Reform, and the Study of Literature." *PoT.* 1988; 9(4): 711-735. [†Relationship to social sciences; progressive education.]

[1575] Wood, David, ed.; Levinas, Emmanuel, fwd.; Allison, David, tr. of fwd. *Writing the Future.* London: Routledge; 1990. x, 213 pp. (Warwick Studies in Philosophy and Literature.) [Incl. introd. †Role of the future; time.]

[1576] Zeeman, Nicolette. "Alterations of Language." *Paragraph.* 1990 July; 13(2): 217-228. [On Minnis, A. J.; Scott, A. B. *Medieval Literary Theory and Criticism c. 1100-c. 1375: The Commentary Tradition.* †Middle Ages. Relationship to textual criticism; Latin language literature. Review article.]

[1577] Ziarek, Krzysztof. "The Language of Praise: Levinas and Marion." *R&L.* 1990 Summer-Autumn; 22(2-3): 93-107. [†Role of the other; language; relationship to ethics; religion. Theories of Levinas, Emmanuel; Marion, Jean-Luc.]

[1578] Ziolkowski, Jan, ed. *On Philology.* University Park: Penn State UP; 1990. 78 pp. [Orig. pub. as *Comparative Literature Studies.* 1990; 27(1). †Relationship to philology.]

[1579] Zumthor, Paul. "L'Imagination critique." *O&C.* 1990; 15(2): 23-34. [†Relationship to imagination.]

Bibliography

[1580] Pinkney, Tony; Minow, Makiko; Knight, Diana. "Literary Theory." *YWES.* 1987; 68: 12-58.

[1581] Ryan, Rory; Ryan, Pamela. "Articles on Literary Aesthetics, Literary Theory and Critical Methodology: A Survey 1988/89." *JDECU.* 1990 Sept.; 28(2): 35-43. [†And aesthetics; critical methodology. (1988-1989).]

DECONSTRUCTIONISM

[1582] Alexander, Natalie. "Presence and Deferral: Derrida's Critique of Husserlian Internal Time-Consciousness (Volumes I and II)." *DAI.* 1990 Feb.; 50(8): 2517A. [†Role of time; consciousness. Treatment in Derrida, Jacques: *La Voix et le phénomène;* relationship to Husserl, Edmund. Dissertation abstract.]

[1583] Allman, John. "Paul de Man, Deconstruction, and Discipleship." *P&L.* 1990 Oct.; 14(2): 324-339. [†Role of discipleship. Study example: de Man, Paul; Johnson, Barbara.]

[1584] Argyros, Alex. "Narratives of the Future: Heidegger and Derrida on Technology." *NOR.* 1990 Summer; 17(2): 53-58. [†Role of language; relationship to technology. Theories of Derrida, Jacques: *De la grammatologie* compared to Heidegger, Martin: "Die Frage nach der Technik."]

[1585] Argyros, Alexander; Flieger, Jerry Aline. "Hartman's Contagious Orbit: Reassessing Aesthetic Criticism." *Diacritics.* 1987 Spring; 17(1): 52-69. [†Relationship to aesthetics. Theories of Hartman, Geoffrey H. Review article.]

[1586] Berezdivin, Ruben. "Drawing: (An) Affecting Nietzsche: With Derrida." 93-107 in Silverman, Hugh J., ed. *Derrida and Deconstruction.* New York: Routledge; 1989. viii, 258 pp. (Continental Philosophy 2.) [†Pathos. Theories of Nietzsche, Friedrich Wilhelm in theories of Derrida, Jacques.]

[1587] Bernet, Rudolf. "On Derrida's 'Introduction' to Husserl's *Origin of Geometry.*" 139-153 in Silverman, Hugh J., ed. *Derrida and Deconstruction.* New York: Routledge; 1989. viii, 258 pp. (Continental Philosophy 2.) [†Applied to Husserl, Edmund: *Erfahrung und Urteil.* On preface by Derrida, Jacques.]

[1588] Bottiroli, Giovanni. "Ritorno al futuro: Dalla grammatologia alla semiotica." *SCr.* 1989 Jan.; 4(1 [59]): 49-83. [†Theories of Derrida, Jacques: *De la grammatologie* compared to Saussure, Ferdinand de: *Cours de linguistique générale.*]

[1589] Bové, Paul A. "Paul de Man: Some Notes on the Critic's Search for Authority against Consensus." *Criticism.* 1990 Spring; 32(2): 149-161. [†Authority of writer; relationship to reader; allegory. Treatment in de Man, Paul: "Rhetoric of Temporality."]

[1590] Brady, Patrick. "Critical Discussions." *P&L.* 1990 Oct.; 14(2): 367-378. [On Hayles, N. Katherine. *Chaos Bound: Orderly Disorder in Contemporary Literature and Science.* †Relationship to chaos theory. Review article.]

[1591] Brogan, Walter. "Plato's *Pharmakon:* Between Two Repetitions." 7-23 in Silverman, Hugh J., ed. *Derrida and Deconstruction.* New York: Routledge; 1989. viii, 258 pp. (Continental Philosophy 2.) [†Theories of Plato: *Pharmakon* in theories of Derrida, Jacques.]

[1592] Caputo, John D. "Mysticism and Transgression: Derrida and Meister Eckhart." 24-39 in Silverman, Hugh J., ed. *Derrida and Deconstruction.* New York: Routledge; 1989. viii, 258 pp. (Continental Philosophy 2.) [†Relationship to mysticism; transgression. Theories of Derrida, Jacques compared to Eckhart, Meister.]

[1593] Caraher, Brian G. "Recovering the Figure of J. L. Austin in Paul de Man's *Allegories of Reading.*" 139-146 in Silverman, Hugh J., ed.; Aylesworth, Gary E., ed. *The Textual Sublime: Deconstruction and Its Differences.* Albany: State U of New York P; 1990. 274 pp. (Contemporary Studies in Philosophy and Literature 1.) [†Theories of de Man, Paul: *Allegories of Reading;* relationship to Austin, J. L.]

[1594] Chaffin, Deborah. "Hegel, Derrida, and the Sign." 77-91 in Silverman, Hugh J., ed. *Derrida and Deconstruction.* New York: Routledge; 1989. viii, 258 pp. (Continental Philosophy 2.) [†Sign; representation. Treatment in Derrida, Jacques: *De la grammatologie* compared to Hegel, Georg Wilhelm Friedrich.]

[1595] Chanter, Tina. "Derrida and Heidegger: The Interlacing of Texts." 61-68 in Silverman, Hugh J., ed.; Aylesworth, Gary E., ed. *The Textual Sublime: Deconstruction and Its Differences.* Albany: State U of New York P; 1990. 274 pp. (Contemporary Studies in Philosophy and Literature 1.) [†Theories of Derrida, Jacques; relationship to Heidegger, Martin.]

[1596] Culler, Jonathan. *On Deconstruction: Theory and Criticism after Structuralism.* Ithaca: Cornell UP; 1990. 307 pp.

[1597] Donato, Eugenio. "Ending/Closure: On Derrida's Margining of Heidegger." 37-51 in Silverman, Hugh J., ed.; Aylesworth, Gary E., ed. *The Textual Sublime: Deconstruction and Its Differences.* Albany: State U of New York P; 1990. 274 pp. (Contemporary Studies in Philosophy and Literature 1.) [See also Wood, below. †Theories of Derrida, Jacques; relationship to Heidegger, Martin.]

[1598] Downing, David B. "Deconstruction's Scruples: The Politics of Enlightened Critique." *Diacritics.* 1987 Fall; 17(3): 66-81. [On Norris, Christopher. *The Contest of Faculties: Philosophy and Theory after Deconstruction* & 1984 Bibliog. IV.1634. †Relationship to politics. Review article.]

[1599] Dupuy, Jean-Pierre; Anspach, Mark, tr. "Tangled Hierarchies: Self-Reference in Philosophy, Anthropology, and Critical Theory." *CCrit.* 1990; 12: 105-123. [†Role of hierarchy; self-reflexiveness; relationship to philosophy; anthropology. Theories of Derrida, Jacques; Dumont, Louis.]

[1600] Easthope, Antony. "Derrida's Epistemology." 207-212 in Silverman, Hugh J., ed.; Aylesworth, Gary E., ed. *The Textual Sublime: Deconstruction and Its Differences.* Albany: State U of New York P; 1990. 274 pp. (Contemporary Studies in Philosophy and Literature 1.) [†Theories of Derrida, Jacques.]

[1601] Felperin, Howard. "The Anxiety of American Deconstruction." 147-161 in Silverman, Hugh J., ed.; Aylesworth, Gary E., ed. *The Textual Sublime: Deconstruction and Its Differences.* Albany: State U of New York P; 1990. 274 pp. (Contemporary Studies in Philosophy and Literature 1.) [†In United States.]

[1602] Fischer, Michael. "Does Deconstruction Make Any Difference?" 23-30 in Silverman, Hugh J., ed.; Aylesworth, Gary E., ed. *The Textual Sublime: Deconstruction and Its Differences.* Albany: State U of New York P; 1990. 274 pp. (Contemporary Studies in Philosophy and Literature 1.) [†Treatment in Norris, Christopher: *Deconstruction: Theory and Practice;* Miller, J. Hillis: "The Function of Rhetorical Study at the Present Time."]

[1603] Flynn, Bernard. "Derrida and Foucault: Madness and Writing." 201-218 in Silverman, Hugh J., ed. *Derrida and Deconstruction.* New York: Routledge; 1989. viii, 258 pp. (Continental Philosophy 2.) [†Theories of Foucault, Michel: *Folie et déraison;* relationship to theories of Derrida, Jacques.]

[1604] Fynsk, Christopher. "The Choice of Deconstruction." 5-12 in Silverman, Hugh J., ed.; Aylesworth, Gary E., ed. *The Textual Sublime: Deconstruction and Its Differences.* Albany: State U of New York P; 1990. 274 pp. (Contemporary Studies in Philosophy and Literature 1.) [†Role of difference.]

[1605] Guetti, Barbara Jones. "Resisting the Aesthetic." *Diacritics.* 1987 Spring; 17(1): 33-45. [On de Man, Paul. *The Resistance to Theory.* †Theories of de Man, Paul. Review article.]

[1606] Handelman, Susan. "Parodic Play and Prophetic Reason: Two Interpretations of Interpretation." *PoT.* 1988; 9(2): 395-423. [†Parodic play; relationship to reason. Theories of Derrida, Jacques compared to Levinas, Emmanuel.]

[1607] Haney, William S., II. "Literature and Consciousness: Beyond Deconstruction." *Discurso*. 1990; 7(2): 365-376. [†Compared to science. Application of theories of Mahesh Yogi, Maharishi.]

[1608] Harvey, Irene E. "Derrida, Kant, and the Performance of Parergonality." 59-76 in Silverman, Hugh J., ed. *Derrida and Deconstruction*. New York: Routledge; 1989. viii, 258 pp. (Continental Philosophy 2.) [†Theories of Kant, Immanuel: *Kritik der Urteilskraft* in theories of Derrida, Jacques: "Parergon."]

[1609] ———. "The *différance* between Derrida and de Man." 73-86 in Silverman, Hugh J., ed.; Aylesworth, Gary E., ed. *The Textual Sublime: Deconstruction and Its Differences*. Albany: State U of New York P; 1990. 274 pp. (Contemporary Studies in Philosophy and Literature 1.) [†Theories of Derrida, Jacques; relationship to de Man, Paul.]

[1610] Hellesnes, Jon. "Rörebud om tidens ände: Om Derrida och det apokalyptiska språket." *OB*. 1990; 3: 71-80. [†Relationship to the apocalypse. Theories of Derrida, Jacques.]

[1611] Heynders, Odile. "Het spel van de tekst: Deconstructie in Nederland." *Spektator*. 1988 July; 17(6): 512-524. [†In Netherlands. Relationship to Postmodernism.]

[1612] Hirsch, David H. "After Alien Gods." *SR*. 1988 Fall; 96(4): 714-724. [†Relationship to Nazism. Theories of Heidegger, Martin; de Man, Paul; Derrida, Jacques.]

[1613] ———. "Paul de Man and the Politics of Deconstruction." *SR*. 1988 Spring; 96(2): 330-338. [†Theories of de Man, Paul; relationship to Nazism.]

[1614] Howells, Christina M. "Derrida and Sartre: Hegel's Death Knell." 169-181 in Silverman, Hugh J., ed. *Derrida and Deconstruction*. New York: Routledge; 1989. viii, 258 pp. (Continental Philosophy 2.) [†Theories of Sartre, Jean-Paul; Hegel, Georg Wilhelm Friedrich; relationship to theories of Derrida, Jacques.]

[1615] Jay, Gregory S. "Paul de Man and the Subject of Literary History." 123-137 in Silverman, Hugh J., ed.; Aylesworth, Gary E., ed. *The Textual Sublime: Deconstruction and Its Differences*. Albany: State U of New York P; 1990. 274 pp. (Contemporary Studies in Philosophy and Literature 1.) [†Relationship to literary history. Theories of de Man, Paul.]

[1616] Judovitz, Dalia. "Derrida and Descartes: Economizing Thought." 40-58 in Silverman, Hugh J., ed. *Derrida and Deconstruction*. New York: Routledge; 1989. viii, 258 pp. (Continental Philosophy 2.) [†Theories of Descartes, René; relationship to theories of Derrida, Jacques: "Cogito et histoire de la folie" compared to theories of Foucault, Michel.]

[1617] Kinczewski, Kathryn. "Is Deconstruction an Alternative?" 13-22 in Silverman, Hugh J., ed.; Aylesworth, Gary E., ed. *The Textual Sublime: Deconstruction and Its Differences*. Albany: State U of New York P; 1990. 274 pp. (Contemporary Studies in Philosophy and Literature 1.) [†Relationship to semiotic literary theory and criticism; hermeneutics.]

[1618] Kofman, Sarah; Kaplan, Caren, tr. "'Ça cloche'." 108-138 in Silverman, Hugh J., ed. *Derrida and Deconstruction*. New York: Routledge; 1989. viii, 258 pp. (Continental Philosophy 2.) [†Theories of Derrida, Jacques compared to Freud, Sigmund.]

[1619] Liiceanu, Gabriel. "An Open Letter to Jacques Derrida." *RoR*. 1990; 44(2-3): 84-90. [†Role of Derrida, Jacques.]

[1620] Lurie, Alison. "Notes on the Language of Poststructuralism." 289-294 in Ricks, Christopher, ed.; Michaels, Leonard, ed. *The State of the Language*. Berkeley: U of California P; 1990. xv, 531 pp. [†Relationship to poststructuralism. Terminology.]

[1621] McKenna, Andrew J. "Deconstruction and the Resistance to Anthropology." *PG*. 1990; 8: 43-48. [†Relationship to generative anthropology. Theories of Derrida, Jacques.]

[1622] Menke, Christoph. "'Absolute Interrogation': Metaphysikkritik und Sinnsubversion bei Jacques Derrida." *PJGG*. 1990; 97(2): 351-366. [†Theories of Derrida, Jacques.]

[1623] Miller, J. Hillis. *Versions of Pygmalion*. Cambridge: Harvard UP; 1990. ix, 263 pp. [†Relationship to Pygmalion.]

[1624] Norris, Christopher. "Limited Think: How Not to Read Derrida." *Diacritics*. 1990 Spring; 20(1): 17-36. [On Derrida, Jacques. *Limited Inc*. & Ellis, John M. *Against Deconstruction*. †Review article.]

[1625] Olson, Gary A. "Jacques Derrida on Rhetoric and Composition: A Conversation." *JAC*. 1990; 10(1): 1-21. [†And rhetorical criticism. Includes interview with Derrida, Jacques.]

[1626] Rapaport, Herman. "Rereading de Man's Readings." *StTCL*. 1990 Winter; 14(1): 109-128. [On Godzich, Wlad, ed.; Waters, Lindsay, ed. *Reading de Man Reading*. †Theories of de Man, Paul: "Rhetoric of Temporality"; *Allegories of Reading*. Review article.]

[1627] Riffaterre, Michael. "Undecidability as Hermeneutic Constraint." 109-124 in Collier, Peter, ed.; Geyer-Ryan, Helga, ed. *Literary Theory Today*. Ithaca: Cornell UP; 1990. xii, 249 pp.

[1628] Rubene, Māra, tr. "Nepakļāvīgais un nesaprotamais Žaks Deridā." *Karogs*. 1990; 8: 149-157. [Introd., 149-151. †Latvian language translation of excerpt from Derrida, Jacques: *De la grammatologie*.]

[1629] Schwartz, Stephen Adam. "The Deconstructive Imperative." *MLN*. 1990 Sept.; 105(4): 857-874. [†Relationship to metaphysics. Theories of Derrida, Jacques.]

[1630] Schwarz, Daniel R. "The Narrative of Paul de Man: Texts, Issues, Significance." *JNT*. 1990 Spring; 20(2): 179-194. [†Theories of de Man, Paul; relationship to anti-Semitism.]

[1631] Shaviro, Steven. "Complicity and Forgetting." *MLN*. 1990 Sept.; 105(4): 819-832. [†Role of writing; relationship to politics. Theories of de Man, Paul.]

[1632] Silverman, Hugh J. "Derrida, Heidegger, and the Time of the Line." 154-168 in Silverman, Hugh J., ed. *Derrida and Deconstruction*. New York: Routledge; 1989. viii, 258 pp. (Continental Philosophy 2.) [†Role of Heidegger, Martin: *Zur Seinsfrage* in theories of Derrida, Jacques.]

[1633] Silverman, Hugh J., ed. *Derrida and Deconstruction*. New York: Routledge; 1989. viii, 258 pp. (Continental Philosophy 2.) [Incl. introd. †Theories of Derrida, Jacques.]

[1634] Silverman, Hugh J., ed.; Aylesworth, Gary E., ed. *The Textual Sublime: Deconstruction and Its Differences*. Albany: State U of New York P; 1990. 274 pp. (Contemporary Studies in Philosophy and Literature 1.) [Incl. introd.]

[1635] Slinn, E. Warwick. "[Critical Discussions]." *P&L*. 1990 Oct.; 14(2): 379-386. [On 1985 Bibliog. II.2843. †Theories of Derrida, Jacques. Review article.]

[1636] Smith, John H. "The Transcendence of the Individual." *Diacritics*. 1989 Summer; 19(2): 80-98. [†And hermeneutics. Role of the individual; relationship to transcendence.]

[1637] Stellardi, Giuseppe. "The Truth in the Shoe: Deconstruction and the Work of Art." *Pretexts*. 1990 Winter; 2(1): 39-51. [†Relationship to art.]

[1638] Tomiyama, Hidetoshi. "Paul de Man no 'Metaphor no Ninshikiron' no Hisan." *EigoS*. n.d.; 134: 574-578. [†Theories of de Man, Paul: "The Epistemology of Metaphor."]

[1639] Trey, George A. "The Philosophical Discourse of Modernity: Habermas's Postmodern Adventure." *Diacritics*. 1989 Summer; 19(2): 67-79. [†Philosophical language; relationship to poetic language. Treatment in Habermas, Jürgen; relationship to theories of Derrida, Jacques.]

[1640] Vaĭnshteĭn, O. "Leopardy v khrame: Dekonstruktsionizm i kul'turnaia traditsiia." *VLit*. 1989 Dec.; 12: 167-199. [†Theories of Derrida, Jacques.]

[1641] Villani, Arnaud. "Poststructuralist Alternatives to Deconstruction." 223-230 in Silverman, Hugh J., ed.; Aylesworth, Gary E., ed. *The Textual Sublime: Deconstruction and Its Differences*. Albany: State U of New York P; 1990. 274 pp. (Contemporary Studies in Philosophy and Literature 1.) [†And poststructuralist literary theory and criticism.]

[1642] Weinstein, Deena; Weinstein, Michael A. "Simmel/Derrida." *Diogenes*. 1990 Summer; 150: 119-141. [†Theories of Derrida, Jacques; Simmel, Georg.]

[1643] Wihl, Gary. "Aesthetic Ideology: Paul de Man's Final Phase." 35-60 in Kreiswirth, Martin, ed.; Cheetham, Mark A., ed. *Theory between the Disciplines: Authority/Vision/Politics*. Ann Arbor: U of Michigan P; 1990. xii, 257 pp. [†Role of de Man, Paul.]

[1644] Wood, David. "The Possibility of Literary Deconstruction: A Reply to Eugenio Donato." 53-59 in Silverman, Hugh J., ed.; Aylesworth, Gary E., ed. *The Textual Sublime: Deconstruction and Its Differences*. Albany: State U of New York P; 1990. 274 pp. (Contemporary Studies in Philosophy and Literature 1.) [Replies to Donato, above. †Theories of Derrida, Jacques; relationship to Heidegger, Martin.]

[1645] Wurzer, Wilhelm S. "The Critical Difference: Adorno's Aesthetic Alternative." 213-221 in Silverman, Hugh J., ed.; Aylesworth, Gary E., ed. *The Textual Sublime: Deconstruction and Its Differences*. Albany: State U of New York P; 1990. 274 pp. (Contemporary Studies in Philosophy and Literature 1.) [†Relationship to aesthetics. Theories of Adorno, Theodor W.]

[1646] Wyschogrod, Edith. "Derrida, Levinas, and Violence." 182-200 in Silverman, Hugh J., ed. *Derrida and Deconstruction*. New York: Routledge; 1989. viii, 258 pp. (Continental Philosophy 2.) [†Relationship to violence. Treatment in Derrida, Jacques compared to Levinas, Emmanuel.]

[1647] Zelechow, Bernard. "Derrida, Deconstructionism and Nietzsche: The Tree of Knowledge and the Tree of Life." *HEI*. 1989; 11: 901-905. [†Theories of Derrida, Jacques; relationship to Nietzsche, Friedrich Wilhelm.]

FEMINIST LITERARY THEORY AND CRITICISM

[1648] Abraham, Julie. "History as Explanation: Writing about Lesbian Writing: Or, 'Are Girls Necessary'." 254-283 in Davis, Lennard J., ed.; Mirabella, M. Bella, ed. *Left Politics and the Literary Profession*. New York: Columbia UP; 1990. xii, 316 pp. (Social Foundations of Aesthetic Forms.)

[1649] Adams, Carol J. *The Sexual Politics of Meat: A Feminist-Vegetarian Critical Theory*. New York: Continuum; 1990. 256 pp. [†Relationship to vegetarianism.]

[1650] Al-Hibri, Azizah Y., ed.; Simons, Margaret A., ed. *Hypatia Reborn: Essays in Feminist Philosophy*. Bloomington: Indiana UP; 1990. vii, 349 pp. [Prev. pub. essays; incl. fwd.]

[1651] Ashcroft, W. D. "Intersecting Marginalities: Post-Colonialism and Feminism." *Kunapipi*. 1989; 11(2): 23-35. [†Relationship to postcolonialism.]

[1652] Ashton-Jones, Evelyn; Thomas, Dene Kay. "Composition, Collaboration, and Women's Ways of Knowing: A Conversation with Mary Belenky." *JAC*. 1990 Fall; 10(2): 275-292. [†Relationship to collaboration in writing.]

[1653] Austin, Gayle. *Feminist Theories for Dramatic Criticism*. Ann Arbor: U of Michigan P; 1990. viii, 139 pp. [†Relationship to drama.]

[1654] Barr, Marleen S., ed.; Feldstein, Richard, ed. *Discontented Discourses: Feminism/Textual Intervention/Psychoanalysis*. Urbana: U of Illinois P; 1989. 250 pp. [Incl. introd.]

[1655] Booker, M. Keith. "The Baby in the Bathwater: Joyce, Gilbert, and Feminist Criticism." *TSLL*. 1990 Fall; 32(3): 446-467. [†On transvestism; study example: Joyce, James: *Ulysses*. Treatment in Gilbert, Sandra M.; Gubar, Susan.]

[1656] Boone, Joseph A. "Of Me(n) and Feminism: Who(se) Is the Sex That Writes?" 11-25 in Boone, Joseph A., ed.; Cadden, Michael, ed. *Engendering Men: The Question of Male Feminist Criticism*. New York: Routledge; 1990. vi, 333 pp. [†By men critics.]

[1657] Boone, Joseph A., ed.; Cadden, Michael, ed. *Engendering Men: The Question of Male Feminist Criticism*. New York: Routledge; 1990. vi, 333 pp. [Incl. introd. †By men critics.]

[1658] Brown, Terry. "Feminism and Psychoanalysis, a Family Affair?" 29-40 in Barr, Marleen S., ed.; Feldstein, Richard, ed. *Discontented Discourses: Feminism/Textual Intervention/Psychoanalysis*. Urbana: U of Illinois P; 1989. 250 pp. [†Relationship to psychoanalysis. Theories of Mitchell, Juliet; Gallop, Jane.]

[1659] Butler, Judith. *Gender Trouble: Feminism and the Subversion of Identity*. New York: Routledge, Chapman and Hall; 1990. xiv, 172 pp.

[1660] Collin, Françoise; Slobodana, Lizdek, tr. "Sadržaj i autor ili Čitanje 'druge žene'." *Izraz*. 1990 Feb.-Mar.; 34(2-3): 275-286.

[1661] Conley, Verena. "Saying 'Yes' to the Other." *DFS*. 1987 Fall-Winter; 13: 92-99. [†Theories of Cixous, Hélène.]

[1662] de Lauretis, Teresa. "Eccentric Subjects: Feminist Theory and Historical Consciousness." *FSt*. 1990 Spring; 16(1): 115-150. [†Relationship to historical consciousness.]

[1663] Donovan, Josephine, ed. *Feminist Literary Criticism: Explorations in Theory*. Lexington: UP of Kentucky; 1989. xxii, 90 pp. [2nd ed. of 1975 Bibliog. I.16; incl. introd.]

[1664] Duarte, Constância Lima. "Literatura Feminina e Crítica Literária." *Travessia*. 1990; 21: 15-23. [†Role of *écriture féminine*.]

[1665] Duyfhuizen, Bernard. "Deconstruction and Feminist Literary Theory II." 174-193 in Kauffman, Linda, ed. *Feminism and Institutions: Dialogues on Feminist Theory*. Cambridge: Blackwell; 1989. viii, 291 pp. [†And deconstructionism.]

[1666] Eifler, Margret. "Postmoderne Feminisierung." *ABnG*. 1989; 29: 1-36. [†Relationship to Postmodernism.]

[1667] Ellis, Kate. "What Is the Matter with Mary Jane? Feminist Criticism in a Time of Diminished Expectations." 103-123 in Davis, Lennard J., ed.; Mirabella, M. Bella, ed. *Left Politics and the Literary Profession*. New York: Columbia UP; 1990. xii, 316 pp. (Social Foundations of Aesthetic Forms.)

[1668] Emig, Janet. "Our Missing Theory." 87-96 in Moran, Charles, ed.; Penfield, Elizabeth F., ed. *Conversations: Contemporary Critical Theory and the Teaching of Literature*. Urbana: Nat. Council of Teachers of Eng.; 1990. viii, 237 pp.

[1669] Ewell, Barbara C. "Empowering Others: Feminist Criticism and the Academy." 43-62 in Henricksen, Bruce, ed.; Morgan, Thais E., ed. *Reorientations: Critical Theories & Pedagogies*. Urbana: U of Illinois P; 1990. x, 275 pp. [†Role in academia.]

[1670] Fraser, Nancy. "The Uses and Abuses of French Discourse Theories for Feminist Politics." *BoundaryII*. 1990 Summer; 17(2): 82-101. [†Relationship to discourse analysis. Theories of Lacan, Jacques; Kristeva, Julia.]

[1671] Gallop, Jane. "Heroic Images: Feminist Criticism, 1972." *AmLH*. 1989 Fall; 1(3): 612-636.

[1672] Gardiner, Judith Kegan. "In the Name of the Mother: Feminism, Psychoanalysis, Methodology." *LIT*. 1990 May; 1(4): 239-252. [†Relationship to psychoanalysis.]

[1673] Gilbert, Sandra M. "Reflections on a (Feminist) Discourse of Discourse: Or, Look, Ma, I'm Talking!" 130-137 in Ricks, Christopher, ed.; Michaels, Leonard, ed. *The State of the Language*. Berkeley: U of California P; 1990. xv, 531 pp.

[1674] Gilbert, Sandra M.; Gubar, Susan. "The Mirror and the Vamp: Reflections on Feminist Criticism." 144-166 in Cohen, Ralph, ed. *The Future of Literary Theory*. New York: Routledge; 1989. xx, 445 pp.

[1675] Grosz, Elizabeth. "Criticism, Feminism, and the Institution." 1-16 in Harasym, Sarah, ed. *The Post-Colonial Critic: Interviews, Strategies, Dialogues: Gayatri Chakravorty Spivak*. New York: Routledge; 1990. viii, 168 pp. [†Theories of Spivak, Gayatri Chakravorty. Includes interview.]

[1676] Hajdukowski-Ahmed, Maroussia. "Ethique de l'altérité, éthique de la différence sexuelle: Bakhtine et les théories féministes." *DS/SD*. 1990 Spring-Summer; 3(1-2): 251-270. [†Dialogism; relationship to difference; otherness. Application of theories of Bakhtin, Mikhail Mikhaïlovich.]

[1677] Heath, Stephen. "The Ethics of Sexual Difference." *Discourse*. 1990 Spring-Summer; 12(2): 128-153. [†And psychoanalytic literary theory and criticism; role of ethics; relationship to sexual difference. Theories of Foucault, Michel; Irigaray, Luce.]

[1678] Hekman, Susan J. *Gender and Knowledge: Elements of a Postmodern Feminism*. Boston: Northeastern UP; 1990. vii, 212 pp. [†Relationship to Postmodernism.]

[1679] Higonnet, Margaret. "Spatial Metaphors in Feminist Literary Theory." 500-504 in Bauer, Roger, ed.; Fokkema, Douwe, ed.; Graat, Michael de, asst. ed.; Aldridge, A. Owen, asst.; Higonnet, Margaret, asst.; Klein, Holger M., asst.; Meisami, Julie Scott, asst.; Rigney, Ann, asst.; Ronen, Ruth, asst.; Sondrup, Steven P., asst.; Templeton, Joan, asst.; Walker, Janet A., asst. *Proceedings of the XIIth Congress of the International Comparative Literature Association/Actes du XIIe congrès de l'Association Internationale de Littérature Comparée*: München 1988 Munich, III: *Space and Boundaries in Literature (Continuation)/Espace et frontières dans la littérature (suite)*. Munich: Iudicium; 1990. 509 pp. (Proceedings of the Congress of the International Comparative Literature Association 12: 3.) [†Spatial metaphor.]

[1680] Holub, Renate. "For the Record: The Non-Language of Italian Feminist Philosophy." *RLA: Romance Languages Annual*. 1989; 1: 133-140. [†In Italy.]

[1681] MacNabb, Elizabeth Ligon. "The Fractured Family: The 'Second Sex' and Its (Dis)Connected Daughters." *DAI*. 1990 Dec.; 51(6): 2010A-2011A. [†(1968-1979). Sources in Beauvoir, Simone de: *Le Deuxième Sexe*. Application of theories of Chodorow, Nancy: *The Reproduction of Mothering*. Dissertation abstract.]

[1682] Marcus, Jane. "Alibis and Legends: The Ethics of Elsewhereness, Gender and Estrangement." 269-294 in Broe, Mary Lynn, ed.; Ingram, Angela, ed. *Women's Writing in Exile*. Chapel Hill: U of North Carolina P; 1989. xii, 442 pp.

[1683] Mauguière, Bénédicte. "Critique littéraire féministe et écriture des femmes au Québec (1970-80)." *FR*. 1990 Mar.; 63(4): 632-641. [†In Quebec (1970-1980).]

[1684] Meese, Elizabeth A. *Extensions: Re-Figuring Feminist Criticism*. Urbana: U of Illinois P; 1990. xi, 206 pp.

[1685] Merchant, Carolyn. "Ecofeminism and Feminist Theory." 100-105 in Diamond, Irene, ed.; Orenstein, Gloria Feman, ed. *Reweaving the World: The Emergence of Ecofeminism*. San Francisco: Sierra Club; 1990. xvi, 320 pp. [†Relationship to ecofeminism.]

[1686] Muchie, Helena. "Not One of the Family: The Repression of the Other Woman in Feminist Theory." 15-28 in Barr, Marleen S., ed.; Feldstein, Richard, ed. *Discontented Discourses: Feminism/Textual Intervention/Psychoanalysis*. Urbana: U of Illinois P; 1989. 250 pp. [†Relationship to psychoanalysis.]

[1687] Newman, Barbara. "On the Ethics of Feminist Historiography." *Exemplaria*. 1990 Fall; 2(2): 702-706. [†Relationship to ethics; historiography.]

[1688] Porter, Catherine. "Translating French Feminism: Luce Irigaray's *Ce sexe qui n'en est pas un*." *TrP*. 1987; 3: 40-52. [†On English language translation of Irigaray, Luce: *Ce sexe qui n'en est pas un*.]

[1689] Ritchie, Joy S. "Confronting the 'Essential' Problem: Reconnecting Feminist Theory and Pedagogy." *JAC*. 1990 Fall; 10(2): 249-273. [†Applied to teaching of literature.]

[1690] Robinson, Lillian S. "Sometimes, Always, Never: Their Women's History and Ours." *NLH*. 1990 Winter; 21(2): 377-393. [†Relationship to history of women; historiography.]

[1691] Russo, Adélaïde. "Le Respect des femmes: Le Retour du père: Quelques réflexions sur le discours philosophique de Sarah Kofman." *DFS*. 1987 Fall-Winter; 13: 105-115. [†Theories of Kofman, Sarah.]

[1692] Sakellaridou, Elizabeth. "The Dead Ends of the Feminist Discourse." *Yearbook of English Studies* (Greece). 1989; 1: 437-451.

[1693] Secrist, Patrice McDermott. "Politics and Scholarship: A Cultural Study of Feminist Academic Journals." *DAI*. 1990 Sept.; 51(3): 903A. [†Role of *Feminist Studies*; *Frontiers*; *Signs*. Dissertation abstract.]

[1694] Showalter, Elaine. "A Criticism of Our Own: Autonomy and Assimilation in Afro-American and Feminist Literary Theory." 347-369 in Cohen, Ralph, ed. *The Future of Literary Theory*. New York: Routledge; 1989. xx, 445 pp. [†And criticism by African American critics.]

[1695] ——. "Feminism and Literature." 179-202 in Collier, Peter, ed.; Geyer-Ryan, Helga, ed. *Literary Theory Today*. Ithaca: Cornell UP; 1990. xii, 249 pp.

[1696] Sørensen, Marianne. "Nye måder." *KuKl*. 1990; 17(4): 36-46.

[1697] Stephenson, Katherine S. "Luce Irigaray: Theoretical and Empirical Approaches to the Representation of Subjectivity and Sexual Difference in Language Use." 412-417 in Prewitt, Terry, ed.; Deely, John, ed.; Haworth, Karen, ed. *Semiotics 1988*. Lanham, MD: UP of America; 1989. [†Subjectivity; relationship to gender. Treatment in Irigaray, Luce.]

[1698] Stimpson, Catharine R. "Woolf's Room, Our Project: The Building of Feminist Criticism." 129-144 in Cohen, Ralph, ed. *The Future of Literary Theory*. New York: Routledge; 1989. xx, 445 pp.

[1699] Straub, Kristina. "Feminist Politics and Post-Modernist Style." *W&D*. 1988 Spring-Fall; 6(1-2 [11-12]): 151-165. [†Style; image; relationship to ideology compared to deconstructionism.]

[1700] Straus, Nina Pelikan. "Rethinking Feminist Humanism." *P&L*. 1990 Oct.; 14(2): 284-303. [†Relationship to humanism. Theories of Nussbaum, Martha Craven: *The Fragility of Goodness: Luck and Ethics in Greek Tragedy and Philosophy*; Gilligan, Carol: *In a Different Voice* compared to Foucault, Michel.]

[1701] Ulmer, Gregory L. "Mystory: The Law of Idiom in Applied Grammatology." 304-323 in Cohen, Ralph, ed. *The Future of Literary Theory*. New York: Routledge; 1989. xx, 445 pp. [†On neologism; relationship to epistemology.]

[1702] Vogel, Nancy. "Gender Differences: Both/And, Not Either/Or." 223-232 in Moran, Charles, ed.; Penfield, Elizabeth F., ed. *Conversations: Contemporary Critical Theory and the Teaching of Literature*. Urbana: Nat. Council of Teachers of Eng.; 1990. viii, 237 pp.

[1703] Vorlicky, Robert. "(In)Visible Alliances: Conflicting 'Chronicles' of Feminism." 275-290 in Boone, Joseph A., ed.; Cadden, Michael, ed. *Engendering Men: The Question of Male Feminist Criticism*. New York: Routledge; 1990. vi, 333 pp.

[1704] Walker, Cheryl. "Feminist Literary Criticism and the Author." *CritI*. 1990 Spring; 16(3): 551-571. [†Role of writer; relationship to poststructuralism.]

[1705] Wallace, Michele. *Invisibility Blues: From Pop to Theory*. London: Verso; 1990. xi, 267 pp. (Haymarket Series.) [†Relationship to African American feminism.]

[1706] Warner, Michael. "Homo-Narcissism: Or, Heterosexuality." 190-206 in Boone, Joseph A., ed.; Cadden, Michael, ed. *Engendering Men: The Question of Male Feminist Criticism*. New York: Routledge; 1990. vi, 333 pp. [†And gay studies. Theories of Freud, Sigmund.]

[1707] Waugh, Patricia. "Reassessing Subjectivity: Modernity, Postmodernity and Feminism in Theory and Aesthetic Practice." *BêteN*. 1989 Autumn-1990 Spring; 8-9: 64-77. [†Relationship to Postmodernism.]

[1708] Wolff, Janet. *Feminine Sentences: Essays on Women and Culture*. Berkeley: U of California P; 1990. 146 pp. [†Role of women; relationship to writing; culture.]

SEE SUBJECT INDEX FOR CROSS-REFERENCES

Bibliography

[1709] Treichler, Paula A. "Language, Feminism, Theory: Entering Decade Three: An Annotated Bibliography." *W&Lang.* 1986 Winter; 10(1): 5-34.

FORMALIST LITERARY THEORY AND CRITICISM

[1710] Jefferson, Ann. "Literariness, Dominance and Violence in Formalist Aesthetics." 125-141 in Collier, Peter, ed.; Geyer-Ryan, Helga, ed. *Literary Theory Today.* Ithaca: Cornell UP; 1990. xii, 249 pp. [†Literariness.]

HERMENEUTICS

[1711] Bernstein, J. M. "Self-Knowledge as Praxis: Narrative and Narration in Psychoanalysis." 51-77 in Nash, Cristopher, ed. *Narrative in Culture: The Uses of Storytelling in the Sciences, Philosophy, and Literature.* London: Routledge; 1990. xvi, 228 pp. (Warwick Studies in Philosophy and Literature.) [†Applied to narrative in psychoanalysis. Application of theories of Habermas, Jürgen.]

[1712] Bollack, Jean. "Zukunft im Vergangenen: Peter Szondis materiale Hermeneutik." *DVLG.* 1990 June; 64(2): 370-390. [Eng. sum. †Theories of Szondi, Peter.]

[1713] Butler, Christopher. "The Future of Theory: Saving the Reader." 229-249 in Cohen, Ralph, ed. *The Future of Literary Theory.* New York: Routledge; 1989. xx, 445 pp. [†Role of humanism.]

[1714] Chiarini, Paolo. "Der 'verborgene' Text: Überlegungen zu einigen hermeneutischen Hypothesen." 37-49 in Baasner, Frank, ed. *Literaturgeschichtsschreibung in Italien und Deutschland: Traditionen und aktuelle Probleme.* Tübingen: Niemeyer; 1989. viii, 197 pp. [†Application of theories of Asor Rosa, Alberto.]

[1715] Dascal, Marcelo. "Hermeneutic Interpretation and Pragmatic Interpretation." *P&R.* 1989; 22(4): 239-259. [†Compared to pragmatics. Theories of Gadamer, Hans-Georg.]

[1716] Davis, Walter A. *Inwardness and Existence: Subjectivity in/and Hegel, Heidegger, Marx, and Freud.* Madison: U of Wisconsin P; 1989. 496 pp. [†Role of subjectivity; relationship to deconstruction; humanism. Theories of Hegel, Georg Wilhelm Friedrich compared to Heidegger, Martin; Marx, Karl; Freud, Sigmund.]

[1717] Demetz, Peter. "Reflections of an Emeritus (To-Be)." *Profession.* 1990: 3-7. [†Relationship to aesthetics.]

[1718] Dennett, Daniel C. "The Interpretation of Texts, People and Other Artifacts." *PPR.* 1990 Fall; 50(supp.): 177-194.

[1719] Gellrich, Jesse M. *The Idea of the Book in the Middle Ages: Language Theory, Mythology, and Fiction.* Ithaca: Cornell UP; 1988. 292 pp. [†And linguistic literary theory and criticism. Middle Ages. Applied to book; relationship to myth; study example: Chaucer, Geoffrey; Dante.]

[1720] Gumbrecht, Hans Ulrich; Mizraji, Margarita N., tr. "Sobre la (no) interpretación (literaria)." *Filología.* 1987; 22(2): 101-117.

[1721] Hoek, Leo. "Chemins battus et chemins détournés: Deux conceptions de l'interprétation." 5-12 in Hoek, Leo H., ed. *L'Interprétation détournée.* Amsterdam: Univ. of Groningen; 1990. 127 pp. (Cahiers de Recherches des Instituts Néerlandais de Langue et de Littératures Françaises (C.R.I.N.).) [†Relationship to context; coherence.]

[1722] Ibsch, Elrud. "Geltungsansprüche an Interpretationen: Der Wandel eines Konzeptes." 304-316 in Bauer, Roger, ed.; Fokkema, Douwe, ed.; Graat, Michael de, asst. ed.; Fischer-Lichte, Erika, asst.; Garstin, Marguerite, asst.; Ibsch, Elrud, asst.; Stackelberg, Jürgen von, asst. *Proceedings of the XIIth Congress of the International Comparative Literature Association/Actes du XIIe congrès de l'Association Internationale de Littérature Comparée: München 1988 Munich, V: Space and Boundaries in Literary Theory and Criticism/Espace et frontières dans la critique et la théorie littéraire; Space and Boundaries in the Teaching of General and Comparative Literature/Espace et frontières dans l'enseignement de la littérature générale et comparée.* Munich: Iudicium; 1990. 415 pp. (Proceedings of the Congress of the International Comparative Literature Association 12: 5.) [†Relationship to scientific method.]

[1723] Jay, Martin. "The Rise of Hermeneutics and the Crisis of Ocularcentrism." *PoT.* 1988; 9(2): 307-326. [†Relationship to visual perception. Theories of Ellul, Jacques.]

[1724] Kibédi Varga, A. "L'Interprétation impossible: Parler d'après une image, peindre d'après un texte." 13-23 in Hoek, Leo H., ed. *L'Interprétation détournée.* Amsterdam: Univ. of Groningen; 1990. 127 pp. (Cahiers de Recherches des Instituts Néerlandais de Langue et de Littératures Françaises (C.R.I.N.).) [†Relationship to the visual.]

[1725] McGuire, Michael. "The Rhetoric of Narrative: A Hermeneutic, Critical Theory." 219-236 in Britton, Bruce K., ed.; Pellegrini, A. D., ed. *Narrative Thought and Narrative Language.* Hillsdale, NJ: Erlbaum; 1990. viii, 278 pp.

[1726] Reagan, Charles. "*La Tâche de l'herméneutique.*" *BSAPLF.* 1989 Fall; 1(3): 13-26. [†Application of theories of Ricœur, Paul: *La Tâche de l'herméneutique.*]

[1727] Schmidt, Dennis J. "Circles—Hermeneutic and Otherwise: On Various Senses of the Future as 'Not Yet.'" 67-77 in Wood, David, ed.; Levinas, Emmanuel, fwd.; Allison, David, tr. of fwd. *Writing the Future.* London: Routledge; 1990. x, 213 pp. (Warwick Studies in Philosophy and Literature.) [†Relationship to the future; circularity. Theories of Heidegger, Martin; Bloch, Ernst; Hegel, Georg Wilhelm Friedrich.]

[1728] Scott, Nathan A., Jr. "Steiner on Interpretation." *R&L.* 1990 Summer-Autumn; 22(2-3): 9-20. [†And deconstruction. Relationship to religion. Theories of Steiner, George.]

[1729] Spay, Joseph Stephen, Jr. "Theological Implications of the Theory of Literature of E. D. Hirsch: A Hermeneutical Model Based on the Concepts of Meaning and Sig-nificance." *DAI.* 1990 Jan.; 50(7): 2090A-2091A. [†Theories of Hirsch, Eric Donald applied to theology. Dissertation abstract.]

[1730] Valdés, Mario. "De l'interprétation." 275-286 in Angenot, Marc, ed.; Bessière, Jean, ed.; Fokkema, Douwe, ed.; Kushner, Eva, ed. *Théorie littéraire.* Paris: PU de France; 1989. 395 pp.

[1731] Valdés, Mario J. "On Interpretation." 296-303 in Bauer, Roger, ed.; Fokkema, Douwe, ed.; Graat, Michael de, asst. ed.; Fischer-Lichte, Erika, asst.; Garstin, Marguerite, asst.; Ibsch, Elrud, asst.; Stackelberg, Jürgen von, asst. *Proceedings of the XIIth Congress of the International Comparative Literature Association/Actes du XIIe congrès de l'Association Internationale de Littérature Comparée: München 1988 Munich, V: Space and Boundaries in Literary Theory and Criticism/Espace et frontières dans la critique et la théorie littéraire; Space and Boundaries in the Teaching of General and Comparative Literature/Espace et frontières dans l'enseignement de la littérature générale et comparée.* Munich: Iudicium; 1990. 415 pp. (Proceedings of the Congress of the International Comparative Literature Association 12: 5.)

[1732] Vattimo, Gianni. "Postmodern Criticism: Postmodern Critique." 57-66 in Wood, David, ed.; Levinas, Emmanuel, fwd.; Allison, David, tr. of fwd. *Writing the Future.* London: Routledge; 1990. x, 213 pp. (Warwick Studies in Philosophy and Literature.) [†Relationship to postmodernist literary theory and criticism. Theories of Heidegger, Martin.]

[1733] Zimmerli, Walther C. "The Emancipation of Rhetorical Elements in Art: From Postmodernity to the Technological Era." 156-167 in Bender, John, ed.; Wellbery, David E., ed. *The Ends of Rhetoric: History, Theory, Practice.* Stanford: Stanford UP; 1990. xiv, 238 pp. [†Relationship to rhetoric. Theories of Gadamer, Hans-Georg.]

LINGUISTIC LITERARY THEORY AND CRITICISM

[1734] Albaladejo, Tomás. "Semántica extensional e intensionalización literaria: El texto narrativo." *Epos.* 1990; 6: 303-314. [†Relationship to semantics; intensionality of narrative.]

[1735] Baiankina, E. G. "O sistemnom podkhode k analizu teksta." *VLU.* 1990 Jan.; 1: 39-44. [Eng. sum. †On discourse analysis.]

[1736] Bartoszynski, Kazimierz. "Research in So-Called Literary Communication." 255-278 in Eimermacher, Karl, ed.; Grzybek, Peter, ed.; Witte, Georg, ed. *Issues in Slavic Literary and Cultural Theory.* Bochum: Brockmeyer; 1989. 631 pp. (Evolutionary Cultural Semiotics 21.) [†Relationship to communication.]

[1737] Blodgett, E. D., ed.; Coward, H. G., ed. *Silence, the Word and the Sacred.* Waterloo: Wilfrid Laurier UP for Calgary Inst. for the Humanities; 1989. xii, 226 pp. [Incl. introd. & fwd.]

[1738] Bono, James J. "Science, Discourse, and Literature: The Role/Rule of Metaphor in Science." 59-89 in Peterfreund, Stuart, ed. *Literature and Science: Theory & Practice.* Boston: Northeastern UP; 1990. vi, 248 pp. [†Metaphor.]

[1739] Bronzwaer, W. "Poëzie en iconiciteit." *FdL.* 1990 June; 31(2): 93-103. [†Iconicity of poetic language. Structuralist approach. Compared to treatment in Pater, W. de and Langendonck, W. van: "Natuurlijkheid van de taal en iconiciteit."]

[1740] Brooke-Rose, Christine. "Ill Locutions." 154-171 in Nash, Cristopher, ed. *Narrative in Culture: The Uses of Storytelling in the Sciences, Philosophy, and Literature.* London: Routledge; 1990. xvi, 228 pp. (Warwick Studies in Philosophy and Literature.) [†Relationship to speech act theory. Theories of Austin, J. L.]

[1741] Carter, Ronald. "Language and Literature." 590-610 in Collinge, N. E., ed. *An Encyclopaedia of Language.* London: Routledge; 1990. xvii, 1011 pp.

[1742] Cueto Pérez, Magdalena. "Epistemología y semiótica: La posibilidad del estudio científico de la literatura." *LEA.* 1990; 12(1): 137-150. [†Compared to semiotic literary theory and criticism; relationship to epistemology; scientific method.]

[1743] Danto, Arthur C. "Beautiful Science and the Future of Criticism." 370-385 in Cohen, Ralph, ed. *The Future of Literary Theory.* New York: Routledge; 1989. xx, 445 pp. [†Applied to scientific discourse; study example: Nathans, Jeremy H.]

[1744] Diaconescu, Ion. "Sintaxa și stilistica." *Limbă și Literatură.* 1990; 1: 11-18.

[1745] Gargesh, Ravinder; Srivastava, R. N., fwd. *Linguistic Perspective on Literary Style.* Delhi: Univ. of Delhi; 1990. 246 pp. [†Style.]

[1746] Hartman, Geoffrey H. "The State of the Art of Criticism." 86-101 in Cohen, Ralph, ed. *The Future of Literary Theory.* New York: Routledge; 1989. xx, 445 pp. [†Role of ambiguity; indeterminacy.]

[1747] Henkel, Jacqueline. "Linguistic Models and Recent Criticism: Transformational-Generative Grammar as Literary Metaphor." *PMLA.* 1990 May; 105(3): 448-463. [†And reader-response theory and criticism. Application of transformational-generative grammar.]

[1748] Hutnyk, John. "Strategy, Identity, Writing." 35-49 in Harasym, Sarah, ed. *The Post-Colonial Critic: Interviews, Strategies, Dialogues: Gayatri Chakravorty Spivak.* New York: Routledge; 1990. viii, 168 pp. [†Theories of Spivak, Gayatri Chakravorty. Includes interview.]

[1749] Ingram, Angela. "Postmarked Calcutta, India." 75-94 in Harasym, Sarah, ed. *The Post-Colonial Critic: Interviews, Strategies, Dialogues: Gayatri Chakravorty Spivak.* New York: Routledge; 1990. viii, 168 pp. [†Theories of Spivak, Gayatri Chakravorty. Includes interview.]

[1750] Kim, Tae-ok. "Linguistic Theories and the Study of Literature: A Cognitive Approach to Literary Communication." *JELL.* 1990 Spring; 36(1): 111-131. [In Korean; Eng. sum. †On communication; relationship to reader response.]

[1751] Lokke, Virgil. "The Naming of the Virgule in the Linguistic/Extralinguistic Binary." 315-331 in Shapiro, Gary, ed. *After the Future: Postmodern Times and Places.* Albany: State U of New York P; 1990. xx, 360 pp. (Contemporary Studies in Philosophy and Literature 2.) [†Role of binary opposition.]

[1752] Mikhal'skaia, A. K. "K sovremennoĭ kontseptsii kul'tury rechi." *FN.* 1990; 5: 50-60. [†Theories of Bakhtin, Mikhail Mikhaĭlovich.]

[1753] Petrilli, Susan. "Dialogue and Chronotopic Otherness: Bakhtin and Welby." *DS/SD.* 1990 Spring-Summer; 3(1-2): 339-350. [†Chronotope; relationship to otherness. Theories of Bakhtin, Mikhail Mikhaĭlovich compared to Welby, Victoria, Lady.

[1754] Rajagopalan, Kanavillil; Arrojo, Rosemary. "Stylistics, Stanley Fish, and Objectified Conventionality: A Rejoinder to Dan Shen." *PoeticsJ.* 1989 Dec.; 18(6): 579-586. [Replies to 1988 Bibliog. III.4191 (IV.1616). †Stylistics; relationship to linguistic conventions. Theories of Fish, Stanley.]

[1755] Reid, Allan. "Who Is Lotman and Why Is Bakhtin Saying Those Nasty Things about Him?" *DS/SD.* 1990 Spring-Summer; 3(1-2): 325-338. [†Theories of Bakhtin, Mikhail Mikhaĭlovich compared to Lotman, Iuriĭ Mikhaĭlovich.]

[1756] Rosiek, Jan. "Source, Writing, (Dis)figuration: Martin Heidegger and Paul de Man." 85-97 in Herman, Luc, ed.; Humbeeck, Kris, ed.; Lernout, Geert, ed. *(Dis)continuities: Essays on Paul de Man.* Amsterdam: Rodopi; 1989. 239 pp. (PmdnS 2.) [†Theories of de Man, Paul; relationship to Heidegger, Martin.]

[1757] Sándor, András. "Poeticity." *PoeticsJ.* 1989 June; 18(3): 299-316. [†Poetic language; relationship to mental model; image; rhythm.]

[1758] Wiebe, Rudy. "The Words of Silence: Past and Present." 13-20 in Blodgett, E. D., ed.; Coward, H. G., ed. *Silence, the Word and the Sacred.* Waterloo: Wilfrid Laurier UP for Calgary Inst. for the Humanities; 1989. xii, 226 pp.

[1759] Zoltán, Szabó. "Stylistic Aspects of Text Semantics." *RRL.* 1989; 34: 141-162. [Iss. combined with *Cahiers de Linguistique Théorique et Appliquée.* 1989 July-Dec.; 26(2). †On style. Application of text linguistics.]

LITERARY HISTORY

[1760] Aarseth, Asbjørn. "Literary Periods and the Hermeneutics of History." 229-236 in Valdés, Mario J., ed. *Toward a Theory of Comparative Literature: Selected Papers Presented in the Division of Theory of Literature at the XIth International Comparative Literature Congress.* New York: Peter Lang; 1990. 275 pp. (Proceedings of the International Comparative Literature Association 11: 3.) [†Relationship to periodization; hermeneutics.]

[1761] Baasner, Frank, ed. *Literaturgeschichtsschreibung in Italien und Deutschland: Traditionen und aktuelle Probleme.* Tübingen: Niemeyer; 1989. viii, 197 pp. [Incl. fwd. †In Germany; Italy.]

[1762] Butler, Marilyn. "Repossessing the Past: The Case for an Open Literary History." 64-84 in Levinson, Marjorie, ed. *Rethinking Historicism: Critical Readings in Romantic History.* Oxford: Blackwell; 1989. vi, 149 pp. [†Relationship to canon.]

[1763] Dineen, M. Joan. "Five Theorists in Search of a Literary Historian: Comments on Douglas Bush's Literary History, *English Literature in the Earlier Seventeenth Century*, in the Perspective of Articles by Hans Ulrich Gumbrecht, Hans Robert Jauss, Claus Uhlig, Robert Weimann, and René Wellek." *LRN.* 1987 Winter; 12(1): 13-21. [†Study example: Bush, Douglas: *English Literature in the Earlier Seventeenth Century.*]

[1764] Doležel, Lubomír. *Occidental Poetics: Tradition and Progress.* Lincoln: U of Nebraska P; 1990. x, 261 pp. [†Poetics.]

[1765] Iser, Wolfgang. "Towards a Literary Anthropology." 208-228 in Cohen, Ralph, ed. *The Future of Literary Theory.* New York: Routledge; 1989. xx, 445 pp.

[1766] Jiménez Ruiz, Juan Luis. "Nuevas claves para una metahistoria simbólica de la historia de la literatura." *Horizontes.* 1988 Oct.-1989 Apr.; 32(63-64): 21-36.

[1767] Kelkar, Ashok R. "Making and Writing Literary History: The Critic's Role." *Quest.* 1990 Mar.-Apr.; 80: 89-95.

[1768] Kemper, Raimund. "Zur öffentlichen Bedeutung der Literaturhistorie." *LB.* 1990 Mar.; 79(1): 25-62.

[1769] Kushner, Eva. "Articulation historique de la littérature." 109-125 in Angenot, Marc, ed.; Bessière, Jean, ed.; Fokkema, Douwe, ed.; Kushner, Eva, ed. *Théorie littéraire.* Paris: PU de France; 1989. 395 pp.

[1770] ——. "From Time Lost to Time Regained: Thoughts on Literary History." 66-76 in Jost, François, ed.; Friedman, Melvin J., asst. ed. *Aesthetics and the Literature of Ideas: Essays in Honor of A. Owen Aldridge.* Newark: U of Delaware P; 1990. 290 pp. [†Role in comparative literature.]

[1771] ——. "Perspectives sur l'histoire littéraire." 28-40 in Bauer, Roger, ed.; Fokkema, Douwe, ed.; Graat, Michael de, asst. ed.; Wimmer, Ruprecht, asst.; Goppel, Thomas, greeting. *Proceedings of the XIIth Congress of the International Comparative Literature Association/Actes du XIIe congrès de l'Association Internationale de Littérature Comparée: München 1988 Munich, I: Plenary Sessions/Séances plénières; Colloquium Munich/Colloque Munich.* Munich: Iudicium; 1990. 251 pp. (Proceedings of the Congress of the International Comparative Literature Association 12: 1.) [†Relationship to comparative literature.]

[1772] Lynn, Steven. "A Passage into Critical Theory." 99-113 in Moran, Charles, ed.; Penfield, Elizabeth F., ed. *Conversations: Contemporary Critical Theory and the Teaching of Literature.* Urbana: Nat. Council of Teachers of Eng.; 1990. viii, 237 pp. [†Applied to Gill, Brendan: *Here at the* New Yorker.]

[1773] Meregalli, Franco. "Über die literarhistorische Epocheneinteilung." 106-113 in Baasner, Frank, ed. *Literaturgeschichtsschreibung in Italien und Deutschland: Traditionen und aktuelle Probleme.* Tübingen: Niemeyer; 1989. viii, 197 pp. [†Role of periodization.]

[1774] Petronio, Giuseppe. "Geschichtlichkeit der Literatur und Literaturgeschichte." 133-144 in Baasner, Frank, ed. *Literaturgeschichtsschreibung in Italien und Deutschland: Traditionen und aktuelle Probleme.* Tübingen: Niemeyer; 1989. viii, 197 pp.

[1775] Schulz-Buschhaus, Ulrich. "De Sanctis und Croce: Geschichte oder Enzyklopädie der Literatur." 145-157 in Baasner, Frank, ed. *Literaturgeschichtsschreibung in Italien und Deutschland: Traditionen und aktuelle Probleme.* Tübingen: Niemeyer; 1989. viii, 197 pp. [†Theories of De Sanctis, Francesco; Croce, Benedetto.]

[1776] Stock, Brian. "Historical Worlds, Literary History." 44-57 in Cohen, Ralph, ed. *The Future of Literary Theory.* New York: Routledge; 1989. xx, 445 pp. [†Relationship to medieval studies.]

[1777] Syndram, Karl Ulrich. "Das Problem der nationalen Literaturgeschichtsschreibung als Gegenstand der komparatistischen Imagologie." 36-42 in Bauer, Roger, ed.; Fokkema, Douwe, ed.; Graat, Michael de, asst. ed.; Kaiser, Gerhard, asst.; Rinner, Fridrun, asst.; Wertheimer, Jürgen, asst. *Proceedings of the XIIth Congress of the International Comparative Literature Association/Actes du XIIe congrès de l'Association Internationale de Littérature Comparée: München 1988 Munich, IV: Space and Boundaries of Literature/Espace et frontières de la littérature.* Munich: Iudicium; 1990. 651 pp. (Proceedings of the Congress of the International Comparative Literature Association 12: 4.) [†Relationship to national literature.]

[1778] Szili, Joseph. "Permanence and Change of Literature Concepts." 247-252 in Valdés, Mario J., ed. *Toward a Theory of Comparative Literature: Selected Papers Presented in the Division of Theory of Literature at the XIth International Comparative Literature Congress.* New York: Peter Lang; 1990. 275 pp. (Proceedings of the International Comparative Literature Association 11: 3.) [†Role of concept.]

[1779] Titzmann, Michael; Ormrod, John, tr. "Outline of a Systematics of Literary Science and Literary History." 317-323 in Bauer, Roger, ed.; Fokkema, Douwe, ed.; Graat, Michael de, asst. ed.; Fischer-Lichte, Erika, asst.; Garstin, Marguerite, asst.; Ibsch, Elrud, asst.; Stackelberg, Jürgen von, asst. *Proceedings of the XIIth Congress of the International Comparative Literature Association/Actes du XIIe congrès de l'Association Internationale de Littérature Comparée: München 1988 Munich, V: Space and Boundaries in Literary Theory and Criticism/Espace et frontières dans la critique et la théorie littéraire; Space and Boundaries in the Teaching of General and Comparative Literature/Espace et frontières dans l'enseignement de la littérature générale et comparée.* Munich: Iudicium; 1990. 415 pp. (Proceedings of the Congress of the International Comparative Literature Association 12: 5.)

[1780] Träger, Claus. "Entwicklungsformationen und Periodisierung der Literatur." 56-62 in Bauer, Roger, ed.; Fokkema, Douwe, ed.; Graat, Michael de, asst. ed.; Kaiser, Gerhard, asst.; Rinner, Fridrun, asst.; Wertheimer, Jürgen, asst. *Proceedings of the XIIth Congress of the International Comparative Literature Association/Actes du XIIe congrès de l'Association Internationale de Littérature Comparée: München 1988 Munich, IV: Space and Boundaries of Literature/Espace et frontières de la littérature.* Munich: Iudicium; 1990. 651 pp. (Proceedings of the Congress of the International Comparative Literature Association 12: 4.) [†Role of periodization.]

[1781] Vosskamp, Wilhelm. "Theorien und Probleme gegenwärtiger Literaturgeschichtsschreibung." 166-174 in Baasner, Frank, ed. *Literaturgeschichtsschreibung in Italien und Deutschland: Traditionen und aktuelle Probleme.* Tübingen: Niemeyer; 1989. viii, 197 pp.

[1782] Wyss, Ulrich. "Die Literatur und ihr Schatten." 175-197 in Baasner, Frank, ed. *Literaturgeschichtsschreibung in Italien und Deutschland: Traditionen und aktuelle Probleme.* Tübingen: Niemeyer; 1989. viii, 197 pp.

Bibliography

[1783] Woudhuysen, H. R. "Reference, Literary History, and Bibliography." *YWES.* 1987; 68: 1-11. [†And research tools.]

MARXIST LITERARY THEORY AND CRITICISM

[1784] Bennett, Tony. *Outside Literature.* London: Routledge; 1990. x, 310 pp.

[1785] Danius, Sara. "En amerikansk marxist: Fredric Jameson." *OB.* 1989; 4: 70-73. [†Theories of Jameson, Fredric.]

[1786] Eagleton, Terry. "Marxism and the Future of Criticism." 177-180 in Wood, David, ed.; Levinas, Emmanuel, fwd.; Allison, David, tr. of fwd. *Writing the Future.* London: Routledge; 1990. x, 213 pp. (Warwick Studies in Philosophy and Literature.) [†Relationship to utopianism.]

[1787] Goldstein, Philip. *The Politics of Literary Theory: An Introduction to Marxist Criticism.* Tallahassee: Florida State UP; 1990. 242 pp.

[1788] Higgins, John. "Critical Resources: Raymond Williams 1921-1988." *Pretexts.* 1989 Winter; 1(1): 79-91. [†Role of Williams, Raymond.]

[1789] Kim, Jongsoon. "A Study of Fredric Jameson's *The Political Unconscious: Narrative as a Socially Symbolic Act.*" *JELL.* 1989 Spring; 35(1): 29-39. [†Narrative as political discourse; relationship to interpretation. Treatment in Jameson, Fredric: *The Political Unconscious.*]

[1790] Klein, Alfred. "Fortsetzungslinien: Beobachtungen zur Entfaltung des Berliner Realismuskonzepts von Georg Lukács im Moskauer Exil." *WB.* 1990; 36(9): 1465-1491. [†On realism. Theories of Lukács, György.]

[1791] Ovejero Lucas, Félix. "Notas sobre diez años de marxismo analítico (entre el fracaso de la teoría y la esperanza de la moral)." *Arbor.* 1989 Oct.; 134(526): 97-122.

[1792] Petrey, Sandy. "L'Histoire dans 'Le Roman historique'." 41-62 in Thomson, Clive, ed. *Georg Lukács et la théorie littéraire contemporaine.* Montreal: Assn. des Professeurs de Fr. des Univ. & Collèges Can.; 1983. 164 pp. [†Relationship to history. Theories of Lukács, György: *Der historische Roman.*]

[1793] Sarkany, Stéphane. "Le Concept de 'révolution' chez Lukács ou la critique française post-structuraliste peut-elle réserver une place à l'esthétique lukácsienne? (Quelques données et éléments de réflexion)." 83-98 in Thomson, Clive, ed. *Georg Lukács et la théorie littéraire contemporaine.* Montreal: Assn. des Professeurs de Fr. des Univ. & Collèges Can.; 1983. 164 pp. [†Role of revolution; relationship to poststructuralism in France. Theories of Lukács, György.]

[1794] Teschke, Holger. "'Arbeit ist Hoffnung'." *SiTZ.* 1989 Sept.; 27(111): 238-240.

SEE SUBJECT INDEX FOR CROSS-REFERENCES

NARRATIVE THEORY

[1795] Adam, Jean-Michel. "L'Analyse linguistique du récit: Rhétorique, poétique et pragmatique textuelle." *ZFSL*. 1990; 100: 7-24. [†Linguistic analysis of *récit*.]

[1796] Bell, Michael. "How Primordial Is Narrative?" 172-198 in Nash, Cristopher, ed. *Narrative in Culture: The Uses of Storytelling in the Sciences, Philosophy, and Literature*. London: Routledge; 1990. xvi, 228 pp. (Warwick Studies in Philosophy and Literature.

[1797] Bessière, Jean, ed. *Fiction, texte, narratologie, genre*. New York: Peter Lang; 1989. 238 pp. [†And semiotic literary theory and criticism.]

[1798] Britton, Bruce K., ed.; Pellegrini, A. D., ed. *Narrative Thought and Narrative Language*. Pub. of Cognitive Studies Group & Inst. for Behavioral Research at Univ. of Georgia. Hillsdale, NJ: Erlbaum; 1990. viii, 278 pp. [Incl. pref.]

[1799] Chafe, Wallace. "Some Things That Narratives Tell Us about the Mind." 79-98 in Britton, Bruce K., ed.; Pellegrini, A. D., ed. *Narrative Thought and Narrative Language*. Hillsdale, NJ: Erlbaum; 1990. viii, 278 pp. [†Application in linguistics; anthropology; psychology.]

[1800] Cornis-Pope, Marcel. "Poststructuralist Narratology and Critical Writing: *A Figure in the Carpet* Textshop." *JNT*. 1990 Spring; 20(2): 245-265. [†On reading; interpretation; study example: James, Henry, Jr.: "The Figure in the Carpet." Pedagogical approach.]

[1801] Doležel, Lubomír. "Two Narratologies: Propp and Vodička." 13-27 in Eimermacher, Karl, ed.; Grzybek, Peter, ed.; Witte, Georg, ed. *Issues in Slavic Literary and Cultural Theory*. Bochum: Brockmeyer; 1989. 631 pp. (Evolutionary Cultural Semiotics 21.) [†On thematic structure; relationship to formalism; structuralism. Theories of Propp, Vladimir Iakovlevich compared to Vodička, Felix.]

[1802] Gelley, Alexander. "Premises for a Theory of Description." 77-88 in Bessière, Jean, ed. *Fiction, texte, narratologie, genre*. New York: Peter Lang; 1989. 238 pp. [†On description; relationship to reference.]

[1803] Genette, Gérard; Öberg, Johan, tr. "Gérard Genettes palimpsester." *OB*. 1990; 3: 18-36.

[1804] Green, Jennifer M. "Stories in an Exhibition: Narrative and Nineteenth-Century Photographic Documentary." *JNT*. 1990 Spring; 20(2): 147-166. [Illus. †Applied to documentary photography; study example: photographs (1855) by Fenton, Roger.]

[1805] Hardee, A. Maynor, ed.; Henry, Freeman G., ed. "Narratology and Narrative." *FLS*. 1990; 17. [Spec. iss. †Applied to French literature (1800-1999).]

[1806] Hunt, Peter, ed. "Narrative Theory." *CLAQ*. 1990 Summer; 15(2): 46-57. [Spec. sect.; incl. introd. †Applied to literature for children.]

[1807] Jackson, Bernard S. "Narrative Theories and Legal Discourse." 23-50 in Nash, Cristopher, ed. *Narrative in Culture: The Uses of Storytelling in the Sciences, Philosophy, and Literature*. London: Routledge; 1990. xvi, 228 pp. (Warwick Studies in Philosophy and Literature.) [†Applied to legal discourse.]

[1808] Loriggio, Francesco. "The Dynamics of Space: The Literary Voyage and Narratology." 355-361 in Bauer, Roger, ed.; Fokkema, Douwe, ed.; Graat, Michael de, ed.; Boening, John, ed.; Gillespie, Gerald, ed.; Moog-Grünewald, Maria, ed.; Nemoianu, Virgil, ed.; Ricapito, Joseph, ed.; Schmeling, Manfred, ed.; Thüsen, Joachim von der, ed.; Uhlig, Claus, ed. *Proceedings of the XIIth Congress of the International Comparative Literature Association/Actes du XIIe congrès de l'Association Internationale de Littérature Comparée: München 1988 Munich, II: Space and Boundaries in Literature/Espace et frontières dans la littérature*. Munich: Iudicium; 1990. 606 pp. (Proceedings of the Congress of the International Comparative Literature Association 12: 2.) [†Relationship to space; voyage.]

[1809] Martin, Wallace. *Recent Theories of Narrative*. Ithaca: Cornell UP; 1987. 242 pp. [Rpt. of 1986 ed.]

[1810] Martonyi, Eva. "Structure narrative et structure archétypique." 53-63 in Bessière, Jean, ed. *Fiction, texte, narratologie, genre*. New York: Peter Lang; 1989. 238 pp. [†On archetypal structure.]

[1811] Myers, Greg. "Making a Discovery: Narratives of Split Genes." 102-126 in Nash, Cristopher, ed. *Narrative in Culture: The Uses of Storytelling in the Sciences, Philosophy, and Literature*. London: Routledge; 1990. xvi, 228 pp. (Warwick Studies in Philosophy and Literature.) [†Applied to biology. Treatment in Watson, James D.: *The Double Helix*.]

[1812] Olson, David R. "Thinking about Narrative." 99-111 in Britton, Bruce K., ed.; Pellegrini, A. D., ed. *Narrative Thought and Narrative Language*. Hillsdale, NJ: Erlbaum; 1990. viii, 278 pp.

[1813] Pavarini, Stefano. "Su alcuni recenti contributi di teoria narrativa." *LeS*. 1990 Dec.; 24(4): 507-531.

[1814] Pimentel-Anduiza, Luz Aurora. "Metaphoric Narration: The Role of Metaphor in Narrative Discourse." 43-51 in Bessière, Jean, ed. *Fiction, texte, narratologie, genre*. New York: Peter Lang; 1989. 238 pp. [See also 1986 Bibliog. II.1648. †Metaphor.]

[1815] Prince, Gerald. "On Narratology: Past, Present, Future." *FLS*. 1990; 17: 1-14.

[1816] Reiner, Richard. "Narratology: Science, Protoscience, Prescience?" *DS/SD*. 1988 Winter; 1(1): 69-85. [†Relationship to semiotics.]

[1817] Ron, Moshe. "The Restricted Abyss: Nine Problems in the Theory of *mise en abyme*." *PoT*. 1987; 8(2): 417-438. [†*Mise en abyme*. Theories of Dällenbach, Lucien: *Le Récit spéculaire*; Bal, Mieke.]

[1818] Seager, Dennis L. "An Ecosystem Theory of Metadiegetic Narrative." *DAI*. 1990 Feb.; 50(8): 2481A-2482A. [†Intercalated narrative; study example: Cervantes Saavedra, Miguel de: *Quijote*; Sterne, Laurence: *Tristram Shandy*; Cortázar, Julio: *Rayuela*. Dissertation abstract.]

[1819] Seemann, Klaus-Dieter. "Theory of Medieval Narration: A Critical Essay on Slavic Contributions." 179-191 in Eimermacher, Karl, ed.; Grzybek, Peter, ed.; Witte, Georg, ed. *Issues in Slavic Literary and Cultural Theory*. Bochum: Brockmeyer; 1989. 631 pp. (Evolutionary Cultural Semiotics 21.) [†Applied to literature of Middle Ages. Application of theories of Likhachëv, Dmitriĭ Sergeevich: *Poètika drevnerusskoĭ literatury*.]

[1820] Siaflekis, Zacharias I. "Frontières du texte littéraire et espace de la lecture." 91-97 in Bauer, Roger, ed.; Fokkema, Douwe, ed.; Graat, Michael de, asst. ed.; Fischer-Lichte, Erika, asst.; Garstin, Marguerite, asst.; Ibsch, Elrud, asst.; Stackelberg, Jürgen von, asst. *Proceedings of the XIIth Congress of the International Comparative Literature Association/Actes du XIIe congrès de l'Association Internationale de Littérature Comparée: München 1988 Munich, V: Space and Boundaries in Literary Theory and Criticism/Espace et frontières dans la critique et la théorie littéraire; Space and Boundaries in the Teaching of General and Comparative Literature/Espace et frontières dans l'enseignement de la littérature générale et comparée*. Munich: Iudicium; 1990. 415 pp. (Proceedings of the Congress of the International Comparative Literature Association 12: 5.) [†Intertextuality; hypertextuality; relationship to reader.]

[1821] Sturgess, Philip. "Narrativity and Double Logics." *Neophil*. 1990 Apr.; 74(2): 161-177. [†Theories of Culler, Jonathan; Miller, J. Hillis.]

[1822] Suvin, Darko. "The Chronotope, Possible Worlds, and Narrativity." 33-41 in Bessière, Jean, ed. *Fiction, texte, narratologie, genre*. New York: Peter Lang; 1989. 238 pp.

[1823] Sweeney, S. E. "Locked Rooms: Detective Fiction, Narrative Theory, and Self-Reflexivity." 1-14 in Walker, Ronald G., ed.; Frazer, June M., ed.; Anderson, David R., afterword. *The Cunning Craft: Original Essays on Detective Fiction and Contemporary Literary Theory*. Macomb: Western Illinois Univ.; 1990. vii, 203 pp. (Essays in Literature.) [†Self-reflexiveness; study example: detective fiction.]

[1824] Szegedy-Maszák, Mihály. "Spatial Metaphors in Narratology." 98-104 in Bauer, Roger, ed.; Fokkema, Douwe, ed.; Graat, Michael de, asst. ed.; Fischer-Lichte, Erika, asst.; Garstin, Marguerite, asst.; Ibsch, Elrud, asst.; Stackelberg, Jürgen von, asst. *Proceedings of the XIIth Congress of the International Comparative Literature Association/Actes du XIIe congrès de l'Association Internationale de Littérature Comparée: München 1988 Munich, V: Space and Boundaries in Literary Theory and Criticism/Espace et frontières dans la critique et la théorie littéraire; Space and Boundaries in the Teaching of General and Comparative Literature/Espace et frontières dans l'enseignement de la littérature générale et comparée*. Munich: Iudicium; 1990. 415 pp. (Proceedings of the Congress of the International Comparative Literature Association 12: 5.) [†Spatial metaphor.]

[1825] Walkup, James. "Narrative in Psychoanalysis: Truth? Consequences?" 237-267 in Britton, Bruce K., ed.; Pellegrini, A. D., ed. *Narrative Thought and Narrative Language*. Hillsdale, NJ: Erlbaum; 1990. viii, 278 pp. [†Applied to psychoanalysis.]

[1826] White, Eric Charles. "Contemporary Cosmology and Narrative Theory." 91-112 in Peterfreund, Stuart, ed. *Literature and Science: Theory & Practice*. Boston: Northeastern UP; 1990. vi, 248 pp. [†Applied to cosmology.]

Bibliography

[1827] Starr, William T. "Narratology: A Bibliography." *FLS*. 1990; 17: 143-152. [†Applied to French literature (1500-1999).]

NEW CRITICISM

[1828] Firchow, Peter Ederly. "The New Criticism...*und kein Ende?* Or, The Boundaries of the New Criticism." 51-58 in Bauer, Roger, ed.; Fokkema, Douwe, ed.; Graat, Michael de, asst. ed.; Fischer-Lichte, Erika, asst.; Garstin, Marguerite, asst.; Ibsch, Elrud, asst.; Stackelberg, Jürgen von, asst. *Proceedings of the XIIth Congress of the International Comparative Literature Association/Actes du XIIe congrès de l'Association Internationale de Littérature Comparée: München 1988 Munich, V: Space and Boundaries in Literary Theory and Criticism/Espace et frontières dans la critique et la théorie littéraire; Space and Boundaries in the Teaching of General and Comparative Literature/Espace et frontières dans l'enseignement de la littérature générale et comparée*. Munich: Iudicium; 1990. 415 pp. (Proceedings of the Congress of the International Comparative Literature Association 12: 5.)

[1829] Schlanger, Judith. "Autour du renouvellement critique." *O&C*. 1990; 15(2): 13-21.

[1830] Snyder, Howard R. "The Emergence of a Contextualist Theory of Language: A Historical and Comparative Review." *DAI*. 1990 Feb.; 50(8): 2436A-2437A. [†1900-1999. Compared to reader-response theory and criticism; contextualist criticism. Dissertation abstract.]

Bibliography

[1831] Walsh, John Michael. *Cleanth Brooks: An Annotated Bibliography*. New York: Garland; 1990. xl, 438 pp. (GRLH 1208; Bibliographies of Modern Critics and Critical Schools 14.) [†Theories of Brooks, Cleanth. (1933-1989).]

NEW HISTORICISM

[1832] Bhabha, Homi K. "Articulating the Archaic: Notes on Colonial Nonsense." 203-218 in Collier, Peter, ed.; Geyer-Ryan, Helga, ed. *Literary Theory Today*. Ithaca: Cornell UP; 1990. xii, 249 pp. [†Relationship to colonialism.]

[1833] Chvatík, Květoslav. "Literatur und Kunst als historisches Prozess." 503-532 in Eimermacher, Karl, ed.; Grzybek, Peter, ed.; Witte, Georg, ed. *Issues in Slavic Literary and Cultural Theory*. Bochum: Brockmeyer; 1989. 631 pp. (Evolutionary Cultural Semiotics 21.)

[1834] Endre, Bojtár. "The Literary Trend." 493-502 in Eimermacher, Karl, ed.; Grzybek, Peter, ed.; Witte, Georg, ed. *Issues in Slavic Literary and Cultural Theory*. Bochum: Brockmeyer; 1989. 631 pp. (Evolutionary Cultural Semiotics 21.)

NEW HISTORICISM

[1835] Greenblatt, Stephen. "Resonance and Wonder." 74-90 in Collier, Peter, ed.; Geyer-Ryan, Helga, ed. *Literary Theory Today*. Ithaca: Cornell UP; 1990. xii, 249 pp.

[1836] Hacking, Ian; Hollinger, David, reply. "Two Kinds of 'New Historicism' for Philosophers." *NLH*. 1990 Winter; 21(2): 343-376. [Incl. rejoinder. †Relationship to philosophy. Theories of Locke, John; Rorty, Richard; James, William.]

[1837] Hunt, Lynn. "History Beyond Social Theory." 95-111 in Carroll, David, ed. *The States of "Theory": History, Art, and Critical Discourse*. New York: Columbia UP; 1990. x, 316 pp. (Irvine Studies in the Humanities.)

[1838] Lehan, Richard. "The Theoretical Limits of the New Historicism." *NLH*. 1990 Spring; 21(3): 533-553. [†Relationship to poststructuralism; novel.]

[1839] Levinson, Marjorie. "The New Historicism: Back to the Future." 18-63 in Levinson, Marjorie, ed. *Rethinking Historicism: Critical Readings in Romantic History*. Oxford: Blackwell; 1989. vi, 149 pp. [†Applied to Romantic studies.]

[1840] Levinson, Marjorie, ed. *Rethinking Historicism: Critical Readings in Romantic History*. Oxford: Blackwell; 1989. vi, 149 pp. [Incl. introd.]

[1841] Nancy, Jean-Luc. "Finite History." 149-172 in Carroll, David, ed. *The States of "Theory": History, Art, and Critical Discourse*. New York: Columbia UP; 1990. x, 316 pp. (Irvine Studies in the Humanities.)

[1842] Peters, Jochen-Ulrich. "Literaturgeschichte als Funktionsgeschichte: Überlegungen zur genese und literarischen Evolution des russischen Realismus." 533-549 in Eimermacher, Karl, ed.; Grzybek, Peter, ed.; Witte, Georg, ed. *Issues in Slavic Literary and Cultural Theory*. Bochum: Brockmeyer; 1989. 631 pp. (Evolutionary Cultural Semiotics 21.) [†Applied to Russian fiction (1800-1899); relationship to realism.]

[1843] Porter, Carolyn. "Are We Being Historical Yet?" 27-62 in Carroll, David, ed. *The States of "Theory": History, Art, and Critical Discourse*. New York: Columbia UP; 1990. x, 316 pp. (Irvine Studies in the Humanities.)

[1844] Porter, Carolyn; Fraden, Rena, reply. "History and Literature: 'After the New Historicism'." *NLH*. 1990 Winter; 21(2): 253-281. [Incl. rejoinder. †Role of history; relationship to New Criticism; formalism.]

[1845] Robinson, Forrest G. "The New Historicism and the Old West." *WAL*. 1990 Aug.; 25(2): 103-123. [†Relationship to Western American literature.]

[1846] Ross, Marlon B. "Contingent Predilections: The Newest Historicisms and the Question of Method." *CentR*. 1990 Fall; 34(4): 485-538. [†Theories of Greenblatt, Stephen J. compared to McGann, Jerome J.]

[1847] Veeser, Harold. "The New Historicism: Political Commitment and the Post-Modern Critic." 152-168 in Harasym, Sarah, ed. *The Post-Colonial Critic: Interviews, Strategies, Dialogues: Gayatri Chakravorty Spivak*. New York: Routledge; 1990. viii, 168 pp. [†Theories of Spivak, Gayatri Chakravorty. Includes interview.]

[1848] Ziegler, Heide. "Directions in German American Studies: The Challenge of the 'New Historicism'." 356-368 in Freese, Peter, ed. *Germany and German Thought in American Literature and Cultural Criticism*. Essen: Blaue Eule; 1990. (Arbeiten zur Amerikanistik 6.)

PHILOSOPHICAL LITERARY THEORY AND CRITICISM

[1849] Anderson, Charles. "Literature and Medicine: Why Should the Physician Read ... or Write?" 33-58 in Peterfreund, Stuart, ed. *Literature and Science: Theory & Practice*. Boston: Northeastern UP; 1990. vi, 248 pp. [†Relationship to doctor.]

[1850] Davenport, Edward. "The Devils of Positivism." 17-31 in Peterfreund, Stuart, ed. *Literature and Science: Theory & Practice*. Boston: Northeastern UP; 1990. vi, 248 pp. [†Positivism.]

[1851] Davies, Paul. "Experience and Distance: Heidegger, Blanchot, Levinas." *DAI*. 1990 July; 51(1): 180A. [†Theories of Heidegger, Martin; Blanchot, Maurice; Levinas, Emmanuel. Dissertation abstract.]

[1852] Herman, Luc, ed.; Humbeeck, Kris, ed.; Lernout, Geert, ed. *(Dis)continuities: Essays on Paul de Man*. Amsterdam: Rodopi; 1989. 239 pp. (PmdnS 2.) [Incl. introd. †Role of de Man, Paul.]

[1853] Kristeva, Julia. "Identification and the Real." 167-176 in Collier, Peter, ed.; Geyer-Ryan, Helga, ed. *Literary Theory Today*. Ithaca: Cornell UP; 1990. xii, 249 pp.

[1854] Makkreel, Rudolf A. "Traditional Historicism, Contemporary Interpretations of Historicity, and the History of Philosophy." *NLH*. 1990 Autumn; 21(4): 977-991. [†History; relationship to culture. Theories of Kant, Immanuel compared to Dilthey, Wilhelm.]

[1855] Nussbaum, Martha. "Perceptive Equilibrium: Literary Theory and Ethical Theory." 58-85 in Cohen, Ralph, ed. *The Future of Literary Theory*. New York: Routledge; 1989. xx, 445 pp. [†Relationship to ethics.]

[1856] Spanos, William V. "Heidegger, Nazism, and the Repressive Hypothesis: The American Appropriation of the Question." *BoundaryII*. 1990 Summer; 17(2): 199-280. [†Theories of Heidegger, Martin; relationship to Nazism.]

Bibliography

[1857] Racevskis, Karlis. "Bibliographie." *BSAPLF*. 1989 Fall; 1(3): 31-40. [†(1984-1986).]

POSTMODERNIST LITERARY THEORY AND CRITICISM

[1858] Altieri, Charles. "The Powers and the Limits of Oppositional Postmodernism." *AmLH*. 1990 Fall; 2(3): 443-481. [†Relationship to visual arts.]

[1859] Behler, Ernst. *Irony and the Discourse of Modernity*. Seattle: U of Washington P; 1990. xiii, 154 pp. [†Relationship to irony; modernity.]

[1860] Buuren, Maarten van. "Literatuur als tekst." *Spektator*. 1989 May; 18(5): 354-355. [†Theories of Ricœur, Paul.]

[1861] Flax, Jane. *Thinking Fragments: Psychoanalysis, Feminism, and Postmodernism in the Contemporary West*. Berkeley: U of California P; 1990. ix, 277 pp. [†Relationship to psychoanalysis; feminism.]

[1862] Folch-Serra, Mireya. "A Postmodern Conversation." *QQ*. 1988 Autumn; 95(3): 618-640. [†Review article.]

[1863] Hawthorn, Geoffrey. "The Post-Modern Condition: The End of Politics?" 17-34 in Harasym, Sarah, ed. *The Post-Colonial Critic: Interviews, Strategies, Dialogues: Gayatri Chakravorty Spivak*. New York: Routledge; 1990. viii, 168 pp. [†Theories of Spivak, Gayatri Chakravorty. Includes interview.]

[1864] Heilman, Robert B. "Post-Tomorrow and Tomorrow and Tomorrow: An Aspect of the Humanistic Tongue." *SR*. 1988 Fall; 96(4): 703-713.

[1865] Irrlitz, Gerd. "Postmoderne-Philosophie, ein ästhetisches Konzept." *WB*. 1990; 36(3): 357-380.

[1866] Kaplan, E. Ann. "Feminism/Oedipus/Postmodernism: The Case of MTV." 30-44 in Kaplan, E. Ann, ed. *Postmodernism and Its Discontents: Theories, Practices*. London: Verso; 1988. xi, 249 pp. (Haymarket Series.) [†Relationship to feminism; television.]

[1867] Kaplan, E. Ann, ed. *Postmodernism and Its Discontents: Theories, Practices*. London: Verso; 1988. xi, 249 pp. (Haymarket Series.) [Incl. introd.]

[1868] Kee, James M. "'Postmodern' Thinking and the Status of the Religious." *R&L*. 1990 Summer-Autumn; 22(2-3): 47-60. [†Relationship to religion. Theories of Culler, Jonathan; Heidegger, Martin.]

[1869] Norris, Christopher. *What's Wrong with Postmodernism: Critical Theory and the Ends of Philosophy*. Baltimore: Johns Hopkins UP; 1990. vii, 287 pp.

[1870] Schleifer, Ronald. *Rhetoric and Death: The Language of Modernism and Postmodern Discourse Theory*. Urbana: U of Illinois P; 1990. viii, 252 pp. [†Rhetoric; relationship to death.]

[1871] Thiher, Allen. "Postmodernism's Evolution as Seen by Ihab Hassan." *ConL*. 1990 Summer; 31(2): 236-239. [On Hassan, Ihab. *The Postmodern Turn: Essays in Postmodern Theory and Culture*. †Review article.]

[1872] Tölölyan, Khachig. "The Second Time as Farce: Postmodernism without Consequences." *AmLH*. 1990 Winter; 2(4): 756-771. [†Review article.]

[1873] Welsch, Wolfgang. "Die Geburt der postmodernen Philosophie aus dem Geist der modernen Kunst." *PJGG*. 1990; 97(1): 15-37. [†Role of philosophy; relationship to modern art.]

POSTSTRUCTURALIST LITERARY THEORY AND CRITICISM

[1874] Brown, Larry Avis. "Contemporary Poetics and Dramatic Theory: Structuralist and Post-Structuralist Approaches." *DAI*. 1990 Jan.; 50(7): 1851A. [†Applied to drama. Dissertation abstract.]

[1875] Cain, William E. "Criticism and the Complexities of the Canon." *CentR*. 1990 Winter; 34(1): 6-16. [†Relationship to canon.]

[1876] Clark, Suzanne; Hulley, Kathleen. "An Interview with Julia Kristeva: Cultural Strangeness and the Subject in Crisis." *Discourse*. 1990-1991 Fall-Winter; 13(1): 149-180. [†Interview with Kristeva, Julia.]

[1877] Colapietro, Vincent M.; Stuhr, John J., reply. "The Vanishing Subject of Contemporary Discourse: A Pragmatic Response." *JP*. 1990 Nov.; 87(11): 644-657. [†And structuralist literary theory and criticism. Relationship to pragmatism. Theories of Derrida, Jacques compared to Dewey, John.]

[1878] Gemünden, Gerd. "'Der Unterschied Liegt in der Differenz': On Hermeneutics, Deconstruction, and Their Compatibility." *NGC*. 1989 Fall; 48: 176-192. [On Frank, Manfred. *What Is Neostructuralism?* †Relationship to hermeneutics; structuralism. Review article.]

[1879] Gleason, Barbara. "Epistemologies of Composition." *DAI*. 1990 July; 51(1): 19A. [†Application in teaching of writing; relationship to epistemology. Application of theories of Derrida, Jacques; Husserl, Edmund. Dissertation abstract.]

[1880] Ivbulis, Viktors. "Daudzveidība bez vienības: Mazliet par Rietumu visjaunāko literatūrzinātni." *Karogs*. 1990; 1: 154-166.

[1881] Jeffrey, David Lyle. "Mistakenly 'Logocentric': Centering Poetic Language in a Scriptural Tradition." *R&L*. 1990 Summer-Autumn; 22(2-3): 33-46. [†Nihilism; logocentrism; relationship to Christianity.]

[1882] Kujundzic, Dragon. "Laughter as Otherness in Bakhtin and Derrida." *DS/SD*. 1990 Spring-Summer; 3(1-2): 271-293. [†Role of otherness; relationship to laughter. Theories of Bakhtin, Mikhail Mikhaĭlovich compared to Derrida, Jacques.]

[1883] Martens, Gunter. "Was ist ein Text? Ansätze zur Bestimmung eines Leitbegriffs der Textphilologie." *Poetica*. 1989; 21(1-2): 1-25. [†On text.]

[1884] Morrison, Paul. "Paul de Man: Resistance and Collaboration." *Representations*. 1990 Fall; 32: 50-74. [†Role of subversion; relationship to ideology of liberalism. Theories of de Man, Paul; Derrida, Jacques.]

[1885] Poster, Mark. "Foucault and Data Bases." *Discourse*. 1990 Spring-Summer; 12(2): 110-127. [†On speech; writing; relationship to electronic language; surveillance. Theories of Foucault, Michel.]

[1886] Racevskis, Karlis. "The Critique of Poststructuralism and the Revival of Eurocentric Thought." *W&D*. 1987 Spring; 5(1 [9]): 65-72. [†Relationship to European philosophy.]

[1887] Selden, Raman. "From Persona to the Split Subject." *CCrit*. 1990; 12: 57-70. [†Role of subjectivity; the self; relationship to humanism; New Criticism. Application of theories of Lacan, Jacques.]

SEE SUBJECT INDEX FOR CROSS-REFERENCES

[1888]   Spivak, Gayatri Chakravorty. "Poststructuralism, Marginality, Postcoloniality and Value." 219-244 in Collier, Peter, ed.; Geyer-Ryan, Helga, ed. *Literary Theory Today*. Ithaca: Cornell UP; 1990. xii, 249 pp. [†Relationship to colonialism; marginality.]

[1889]   Tompkins, Jane. "A Short Course in Post-Structuralism." 19-37 in Moran, Charles, ed.; Penfield, Elizabeth F., ed. *Conversations: Contemporary Critical Theory and the Teaching of Literature*. Urbana: Nat. Council of Teachers of Eng.; 1990. viii, 237 pp

[1890]   Young, Robert. *White Mythologies: Writing History and the West*. London: Routledge; 1990. viii, 232 pp. [†And Marxist literary theory and criticism; relationship to history.]

PSYCHOANALYTIC LITERARY THEORY AND CRITICISM

[1891]   Cacheiro, Maximino. "Freud e a Literatura." *Grial*. 1990 Oct.-Dec.; 28(108): 506-509. [†Theories of Freud, Sigmund.]

[1892]   Feldstein, Richard, ed.; Sussman, Henry, ed. *Psychoanalysis and ...*. New York: Routledge; 1990. viii, 224 pp. [Incl. introd.]

[1893]   Flieger, Jerry Aline. "The Female Subject: (What) Does Woman Want?" 54-63 in Feldstein, Richard, ed.; Sussman, Henry, ed. *Psychoanalysis and ...*. New York: Routledge; 1990. viii, 224 pp. [†Relationship to feminism.]

[1894]   Forrester, John. "'... A Perfect Likeness of the Past' (Freud): Dreaming of the Future." 98-105 in Wood, David, ed.; Levinas, Emmanuel, fwd.; Allison, David, tr. of fwd. *Writing the Future*. London: Routledge; 1990. x, 213 pp. (Warwick Studies in Philosophy and Literature.) [†Role of dream; relationship to the future. Theories of Freud, Sigmund.]

[1895]   Gallop, Jane. "Why Does Freud Giggle When the Women Leave the Room?" 49-53 in Feldstein, Richard, ed.; Sussman, Henry, ed. *Psychoanalysis and ...*. New York: Routledge; 1990. viii, 224 pp. [†Relationship to feminism. Theories of Freud, Sigmund: *Der Witz und seine Beziehung zum Unbewussten*.]

[1896]   Gardner, Sebastian. "Psychoanalysis and the Story of Time." 81-97 in Wood, David, ed.; Levinas, Emmanuel, fwd.; Allison, David, tr. of fwd. *Writing the Future*. London: Routledge; 1990. x, 213 pp. (Warwick Studies in Philosophy and Literature.) [†On life as narrative; relationship to time. Theories of Freud, Sigmund; Sartre, Jean-Paul; Rorty, Richard.]

[1897]   Hell, Victor. "Théories psychanalytiques de la culture, langages, création poétique." 155-162 in Valdés, Mario J., ed. *Toward a Theory of Comparative Literature: Selected Papers Presented in the Division of Theory of Literature at the XIth International Comparative Literature Congress*. New York: Peter Lang; 1990. 275 pp. (Proceedings of the International Comparative Literature Association 11: 3.) [†Theories of Prinzhorn, Hans.]

[1898]   Hogan, Patrick. "What's Wrong with the Psychoanalysis of Literature?" *ChildL*. 1990; 18: 135-140. [†Relationship to literature for children.]

[1899]   Holland, Norman N. "I-ing Lacan." 87-108 in Hogan, Patrick Colm, ed.; Pandit, Lalita, ed. *Criticism and Lacan: Essays and Dialogue on Language, Structure, and the Unconscious*. Athens: U of Georgia P; 1990. 296 pp. [†Theories of Lacan, Jacques.]

[1900]   ——. "[Jacques Lacan]." *Psychoanalytic Psychology*. 1990; 7(1): 139-149. [On Benvenuto, Bice; Kennedy, Roger. *The Works of Jacques Lacan: An Introduction*. †Relationship to language. Theories of Lacan, Jacques. Review article.]

[1901]   Jacobs, Karen. "Two Mirrors Facing: Freud, Blanchot, and the Logic of Invisibility." *QPar*. 1990 Fall; 4(1): 21-46. [†Relationship to Oedipus; Orpheus. Theories of Freud, Sigmund; Blanchot, Maurice.]

[1902]   Kassai, Georges. "Le Style et ses rapports avec l'inconscient." *RSH*. 1986 Jan.-Mar.; 72(201 [1]): 79-89. [†Style; relationship to the unconscious.]

[1903]   Knoepflmacher, U. C. "The Doubtful Marriage: A Critical Fantasy." *ChildL*. 1990; 18: 131-134. [†On literature for children.]

[1904]   Muckley, Peter A. "The Radicalness of These Differences: Reading 'The Purloined Letter'." *UMSE*. 1990; 8: 227-242. [†Applied to Poe, Edgar Allan: "The Purloined Letter."]

[1905]   Nelson, Cary. "Psychoanalysis as an Intervention in Contemporary Theory." 11-20 in Feldstein, Richard, ed.; Sussman, Henry, ed. *Psychoanalysis and ...*. New York: Routledge; 1990. viii, 224 pp. [†Relationship to politics.]

[1906]   O'Hara, Daniel T. "Mask Plays: Theory, Cultural Studies, and the Fascist Imagination." *BoundaryII*. 1990 Summer; 17(2): 129-154. [†On fascism. Treatment in Theweleit, Klaus: *Männerphantasien*; relationship to theories of Heidegger, Martin: *Einführung in die Metaphysik*.]

[1907]   Park, Chan-Bu. "Transferential Structure of Reading: An Essay on Psychoanalysis and Literary Criticism." *JELL*. 1989 Spring; 35(1): 41-56. [†On reading; relationship to transference. Application of theories of Jung, Carl Gustav; Lacan, Jacques.]

[1908]   Phillips, Jerry; Wojcik-Andrews, Ian. "Notes toward a Marxist Critical Practice." *ChildL*. 1990; 18: 127-130. [†And Marxist literary theory and criticism. On literature for children.]

[1909]   Rashkin, Esther. "Tools for a New Psychoanalytic Literary Criticism: The Work of Abraham and Torok." *Diacritics*. 1988 Winter; 18(4): 31-52. [On Abraham, Nicolas; Torok, Maria. *The Wolfman's Magic Word: A Cryptonymy*; Abraham, Nicolas; Torok, Maria. *L'Ecorce et le noyau*; & Abraham, Nicolas. "The Phantom of Hamlet or the Sixth Act: Preceded by the Intermission of Truth". †Role of Oedipus complex. Theories of Abraham, Nicolas and Torok, Maria compared to Freud, Sigmund; Lacan, Jacques. Review article.]

[1910]   Ross, Andrew. "The Politics of Impossibility." 113-125 in Feldstein, Richard, ed.; Sussman, Henry, ed. *Psychoanalysis and ...*. New York: Routledge; 1990. viii, 224 pp. [†Relationship to poststructuralism.]

[1911]   Salvaggio, Ruth. "Psychoanalysis and Deconstruction and Women." 151-160 in Feldstein, Richard, ed.; Sussman, Henry, ed. *Psychoanalysis and ...*. New York: Routledge; 1990. viii, 224 pp. [†Relationship to deconstructionism; feminist literary theory and criticism.]

[1912]   Schafer, Roy. "The Sense of an Answer: Ambiguities of Interpretation in Clinical and Applied Psychoanalysis." 188-207 in Cohen, Ralph, ed. *The Future of Literary Theory*. New York: Routledge; 1989. xx, 445 pp. [†On ambiguity of language; relationship to psychoanalysis.]

[1913]   Silvaggio, Ruth. "The Case of Two Cultures: Psychoanalytic Theories of Science and Literature." 54-65 in Barr, Marleen S., ed.; Feldstein, Richard, ed. *Discontented Discourses: Feminism/Textual Intervention/Psychoanalysis*. Urbana: U of Illinois P; 1989. 250 pp. [†Relationship to science.]

[1914]   Sussman, Henry. "Psychoanalysis Modern and Post-Modern." 129-150 in Feldstein, Richard, ed.; Sussman, Henry, ed. *Psychoanalysis and ...*. New York: Routledge; 1990. viii, 224 pp.

[1915]   Weber, Samuel. "Psychoanalysis, Literary Criticism, and the Problem of Authority." 21-32 in Feldstein, Richard, ed.; Sussman, Henry, ed. *Psychoanalysis and ...*. New York: Routledge; 1990. viii, 224 pp. [†Relationship to authority.]

[1916]   Zizek, Slavoj. "The Limits of the Semiotic Approach to Psychoanalysis." 89-110 in Feldstein, Richard, ed.; Sussman, Henry, ed. *Psychoanalysis and ...*. New York: Routledge; 1990. viii, 224 pp. [†Relationship to semiotics. Application of theories of Lacan, Jacques.]

PSYCHOLOGICAL LITERARY THEORY AND CRITICISM

[1917]   Worthington, Pepper, introd. "Special Issue: The Psychological Approach to Literature." *MOR*. 1989 Spring; 3. [Spec. iss.]

READER-RESPONSE THEORY AND CRITICISM

[1918]   Beers, Terry. "Reading Reading Constraints: Conventions, Schemata, and Literary Interpretation." *Diacritics*. 1988 Winter; 18(4): 82-93. [On 1982 Bibliog. I. 5568 (IV.933). †Role of reader; relationship to American fiction. Theories of Mailloux, Steven compared to Fish, Stanley; Culler, Jonathan. Review article.]

[1919]   Cohen, Tova. "Simultaneous Reading in Hebrew Poetry: An Interpretive Strategy." 128-139 in Spolsky, Ellen, ed. *The Uses of Adversity: Failure and Accommodation in Reader Response*. Lewisburg, PA: Bucknell UP; 1990. 216 pp. [†On interpretive communities; study example: Hebrew language poetry (1800-1899). Application of theories of Fish, Stanley.]

[1920]   Comley, Nancy R. "Reading and Writing Genders." 179-192 in Henricksen, Bruce, ed.; Morgan, Thais E., ed. *Reorientations: Critical Theories & Pedagogies*. Urbana: U of Illinois P; 1990. x, 275 pp. [†Role of gender. Pedagogical approach.]

[1921]   Cronin, Frank C. "Textuality, Reader-Response Theory, and the English Classroom." *EngR*. 1989; 40(1): 29-31. [†Relationship to textuality.]

[1922]   Ferraresi, Mauro. "Il lettore liminare: Per una semiotica dell'invenzione." *Versus*. 1989 Jan.-May; 52-53: 99-111. [†Relationship to inference by reader.]

[1923]   Ferraresi, Mauro, ed.; Pugliatti, Paola, ed. "Il lettore: Modelli, processi ed effetti dell'interpretazione." *Versus*. 1989 Jan.-May; 52-53. [Spec. iss.; incl. introd.]

[1924]   Fisch, Harold. "Prophet versus Audience." 114-127 in Spolsky, Ellen, ed. *The Uses of Adversity: Failure and Accommodation in Reader Response*. Lewisburg, PA: Bucknell UP; 1990. 216 pp. [†Applied to Bible.]

[1925]   Flynn, Elizabeth A. "The Classroom as Interpretive Community: Teaching Reader-Response Theory and Composition Theory to Preprofessional Undergraduates." 193-215 in Henricksen, Bruce, ed.; Morgan, Thais E., ed. *Reorientations: Critical Theories & Pedagogies*. Urbana: U of Illinois P; 1990. x, 275 pp. [†On interpretive communities. Pedagogical approach.]

[1926]   Gandelman, Claude. "Master Text and Slave Text: A Hegelian Theory of Writing." 90-98 in Spolsky, Ellen, ed. *The Uses of Adversity: Failure and Accommodation in Reader Response*. Lewisburg, PA: Bucknell UP; 1990. 216 pp. [†On dialectic. Application of theories of Hegel, Georg Wilhelm Friedrich.]

[1927]   Hirsch, E. D., Jr. "Author as Reader and Reader as Author: Reflections on the Limits of Accommodation." 36-48 in Spolsky, Ellen, ed. *The Uses of Adversity: Failure and Accommodation in Reader Response*. Lewisburg, PA: Bucknell UP; 1990. 216 pp. [†Role of authorial intention; relationship to reader.]

[1928]   Jehlen, Myra. "Literature and Authority." 7-18 in Moran, Charles, ed.; Penfield, Elizabeth F., ed. *Conversations: Contemporary Critical Theory and the Teaching of Literature*. Urbana: Nat. Council of Teachers of Eng.; 1990. viii, 237 pp. [†And poststructuralist literary theory and criticism. Applied to teaching of literature; study example: Clemens, Samuel: *The Adventures of Huckleberry Finn*; Douglass, Frederick: *Narrative of the Life of Frederick Douglass*.]

[1929]   Mailloux, Steven. "The Turns of Reader-Response Criticism." 38-54 in Moran, Charles, ed.; Penfield, Elizabeth F., ed. *Conversations: Contemporary Critical Theory and the Teaching of Literature*. Urbana: Nat. Council of Teachers of Eng.; 1990. viii, 237 pp

[1930]   Mamardašvili, Merabs; Treile, Jolanta, tr. "Literatūrkritika kā lasišanas akts." *Grāmata*. 1990 Nov.; 11: 33-36.

[1931]   Michael, John. "Fish Shticks: Rhetorical Questions in Stanley Fish's *Doing What Comes Naturally*." *Diacritics*. 1990 Summer; 20(2): 54-74. [On 1989 Bibliog. IV.2710. †Theories of Fish, Stanley. Review article.]

[1932]   Petöfi, János S. "Readers and Reader Models: Some Basic Questions of Interpretation Theory." *Versus*. 1989 Jan.-May; 52-53: 43-52. [†Relationship to reader.]

[1933] Prince, Gerald. "On Textual Readers and Evaluators." *Versus.* 1989 Jan.-May; 52-53: 113-120. [†Reader in narrative.]

[1934] Prodi, Giorgio. "L'interpretazione come cambiamento dell'interprete." *Versus.* 1989 Jan.-May; 52-53: 21-41. [†Relationship to interpreter.]

[1935] Rojtman, Betty. "Bible Reading: The Hermeneutic Narrative." 101-113 in Spolsky, Ellen, ed. *The Uses of Adversity: Failure and Accommodation in Reader Response.* Lewisburg, PA: Bucknell UP; 1990. 216 pp. [†Applied to Bible.]

[1936] Schulte-Sasse, Jochen. "L'Evaluation en littérature." 287-307 in Angenot, Marc, ed.; Bessière, Jean, ed.; Fokkema, Douwe, ed.; Kushner, Eva, ed. *Théorie littéraire.* Paris: PU de France; 1989. 395 pp.

[1937] Spolsky, Ellen. "The Uses of Adversity: The Literary Text and the Audience That Doesn't Understand." 17-35 in Spolsky, Ellen, ed. *The Uses of Adversity: Failure and Accommodation in Reader Response.* Lewisburg, PA: Bucknell UP; 1990. 216 pp. [†Role of audience.]

[1938] Spolsky, Ellen, ed. *The Uses of Adversity: Failure and Accommodation in Reader Response.* Pub. Assisted by Lechter Inst. Lewisburg, PA: Bucknell UP; 1990. 216 pp. [Incl. introd.]

[1939] Sternberg, Meir. "Time and Reader." 49-89 in Spolsky, Ellen, ed. *The Uses of Adversity: Failure and Accommodation in Reader Response.* Lewisburg, PA: Bucknell UP; 1990. 216 pp. [†Role of time; difference in generations; relationship to reading.]

[1940] Wyatt, Jean. *Reconstructing Desire: The Role of the Unconscious in Women's Reading and Writing.* Chapel Hill: U of North Carolina P; 1990. x, 271 pp. [†And feminist literary theory and criticism. Relationship to the unconscious of women. Theories of Freud, Sigmund; Lacan, Jacques.]

RECEPTION THEORY

[1941] Conforti, Pina. "Per una teoria sociologico-communicativa della letteratura: Il contributo dell'estetica della ricezione." *SCr.* 1990 Sept.; 5(3 [64]): 379-396. [†Role of sociology of communication.]

[1942] de Castell, Suzanne. "Teaching the Textbook: Teacher/Text Authority and the Problem of Interpretation." *L&E.* 1990 Spring; 2(1): 75-90. [†Applied to textbook.]

[1943] Dove, George N. "The Detection Formula and the Act of Reading." 25-37 in Walker, Ronald G., ed.; Frazer, June M., ed.; Anderson, David R., afterword. *The Cunning Craft: Original Essays on Detective Fiction and Contemporary Literary Theory.* Macomb: Western Illinois Univ.; 1990. vii, 203 pp. (Essays in Literature.) [†Applied to detective fiction. Theories of Iser, Wolfgang: *Der Akt des Lesens.*]

[1944] Grana, Gianni. "Literaturwissenschaft und/oder Literaturgeschichte? Die Mythisierung der 'Rezeption'." 60-84 in Baasner, Frank, ed. *Literaturgeschichtsschreibung in Italien und Deutschland: Traditionen und aktuelle Probleme.* Tübingen: Niemeyer; 1989. viii, 197 pp. [†Treatment in German criticism; Italian criticism.]

[1945] Horn, András. "Über die zweifache subjektive Bedingtheit des literarästhetischen Genusses." *OL.* 1990; 45(1): 1-29. [†Role of aesthetics. Theories of Jauss, Hans Robert; Iser, Wolfgang.]

[1946] Ibsch, Elrud. "La Réception littéraire." 249-271 in Angenot, Marc, ed.; Bessière, Jean, ed.; Fokkema, Douwe, ed.; Kushner, Eva, ed. *Théorie littéraire.* Paris: PU de France; 1989. 395 pp. [†In Germany; United States.]

[1947] Jauss, Hans Robert. "The Theory of Reception: A Retrospective of Its Unrecognized Prehistory." 53-73 in Collier, Peter, ed.; Geyer-Ryan, Helga, ed. *Literary Theory Today.* Ithaca: Cornell UP; 1990. xii, 249 pp.

[1948] Robillard, Monic. "La Disparition élocutoire et le génie critique." *O&C.* 1990; 15(2): 77-90. [†Creativity; relationship to genius.]

[1949] Senardi, Fulvio. "Dall'estetica della ricezione all'ermeneutica letteraria: Riflessioni su H. R. Jauss." *Problemi.* 1990 Jan.-Apr.; 87: 17-46. [†Theories of Jauss, Hans Robert.]

[1950] Wünsch, Marianne; Ormrod, John, tr. "The Status and Significance of Reception Studies in Literary History." 324-330 in Bauer, Roger, ed.; Fokkema, Douwe, ed.; Graat, Michael de, asst. ed.; Fischer-Lichte, Erika, asst.; Garstin, Marguerite, asst.; Ibsch, Elrud, asst.; Stackelberg, Jürgen von, asst. *Proceedings of the XIIth Congress of the International Comparative Literature Association/Actes du XIIe congrès de l'Association Internationale de Littérature Comparée: München 1988 Munich, V: Space and Boundaries in Literary Theory and Criticism/Espace et frontières dans la critique et la théorie littéraire; Space and Boundaries in the Teaching of General and Comparative Literature/Espace et frontières dans l'enseignement de la littérature générale et comparée.* Munich: Iudicium; 1990. 415 pp. (Proceedings of the Congress of the International Comparative Literature Association 12: 5.) [†Relationship to literary history.]

RHETORICAL CRITICISM

[1951] Brock, Bernard L., ed.; Scott, Robert L., ed.; Chesebro, James W., ed. *Methods of Rhetorical Criticism: A Twentieth-Century Perspective.* Detroit: Wayne State UP; 1989. 518 pp. [3rd rev. ed.]

[1952] Hernadi, Paul, ed. *The Rhetoric of Interpretation and the Interpretation of Rhetoric.* Durham: Duke UP; 1989. xiii, 228 pp. [Rpt. from *Poetics Today.* 1988; 9(2).]

[1953] Kibédi Varga, Aron. "Rhétorique et production du texte." 219-234 in Angenot, Marc, ed.; Bessière, Jean, ed.; Fokkema, Douwe, ed.; Kushner, Eva, ed. *Théorie littéraire.* Paris: PU de France; 1989. 395 pp. [†Relationship to genre.]

Bibliography

[1954] "Eugene E. White: A Bibliography." 421-423 in Benson, Thomas W., ed.; Perry, Lewis, fwd. *American Rhetoric: Context and Criticism.* Carbondale: Southern Illinois UP; 1989. x, 427 pp. [†Of scholarship by White, Eugene Edmond.]

SEMIOTIC LITERARY THEORY AND CRITICISM

[1955] Alexandrescu, Sorin. "Aperçu sur la sociosémiotique." *RSH.* 1986 Jan.-Mar.; 72(201 [1]): 15-20. [†Sociosemiotics.]

[1956] Bal, Mieke. "Visual Poetics: Reading with the Other Art." 135-150 in Kreiswirth, Martin, ed.; Cheetham, Mark A., ed. *Theory between the Disciplines: Authority/Vision/Politics.* Ann Arbor: U of Michigan P; 1990. xii, 257 pp. [†Poetics; relationship to the visual.]

[1957] Bayer, Udo. "'Der Zipfel einer Welt': Übergänge zwischen Objektthematik und ästhetischer Eigenrealität." *Semiosis.* 1989; 14(3-4 [55-56]): 47-57. [Eng. sum. †Theories of Bense, Max.]

[1958] Bertrand, Marc. "La Sémiose affranchie: De l'usage proprement poétique du signe." *RSH.* 1986 Jan.-Mar.; 72(201 [1]): 129-139. [†Relationship to poetry.]

[1959] Boklund-Lagopoulou, Karin. "Materialism and Semiotics in Contemporary Critical Theory." *Yearbook of English Studies* (Greece). 1989; 1: 277-296. [†Relationship to Marxist literary theory and criticism. Theories of Kristeva, Julia; Lacan, Jacques.]

[1960] Boler, John F. "Isomorphism: Reflections on Similitude and Form in Medieval Sign Theory." *Livstegn.* 1989; 7(2): 72-90. [†Isomorphism; similarity. Theories of Augustine, Saint; Thomas Aquinas, Saint; Peirce, Charles Sanders.]

[1961] Burg, Peter. "Peirce und Jakobson: Zur Kritik des Iconismus in der Kunsttheorie und der Modernen Poetik." 279-290 in Eimermacher, Karl, ed.; Grzybek, Peter, ed.; Witte, Georg, ed. *Issues in Slavic Literary and Cultural Theory.* Bochum: Brockmeyer; 1989. 631 pp. (Evolutionary Cultural Semiotics 21.) [†Theories of Peirce, Charles Sanders compared to Jakobson, Roman Osipovich.]

[1962] Chang, Han-liang. "Towards a Poetics of the Script." 112-115 in Bauer, Roger, ed.; Fokkema, Douwe, ed.; Graat, Michael de, asst. ed.; Fischer-Lichte, Erika, asst.; Garstin, Marguerite, asst.; Ibsch, Elrud, asst.; Stackelberg, Jürgen von, asst. *Proceedings of the XIIth Congress of the International Comparative Literature Association/Actes du XIIe congrès de l'Association Internationale de Littérature Comparée: München 1988 Munich, V: Space and Boundaries in Literary Theory and Criticism/Espace et frontières dans la critique et la théorie littéraire; Space and Boundaries in the Teaching of General and Comparative Literature/Espace et frontières dans l'enseignement de la littérature générale et comparée.* Munich: Iudicium; 1990. 415 pp. (Proceedings of the Congress of the International Comparative Literature Association 12: 5.) [†Writing systems; relationship to poetics.]

[1963] Corti, Maria. "Towards a Typology of Semiotic Criticism in Italy." *QI.* 1990 Fall; 11(2): 299-308. [†In Italy.]

[1964] Danesi, Marcel. "The Semiotics of the Circus: A Note on the Italian Version of Bouissac's Analysis of Nonsense." *QI.* 1990 Fall; 11(2): 309-313. [†Treatment of nonsense in Italian language translation of Bouissac, Paul: *Cirque et culture.*]

[1965] Danow, David K. "Dialogism: Perspectives and Delimitations." *CASS.* 1988; 22(1-4): 43-50. [†On dialogism.]

[1966] Díaz Arenas, Angel; Bobes Naves, María del Carmen, vol. I introd.; Villanueva, Darío, vol. II introd. *Teoría y práctica semiótica, I: Revisión interdisciplinaria; II: Aproximación pragmática a la obra de Camilo José Cela.* Kassel: Reichenberger; 1990. xvi, 1-217(vol. I) + xiv, 219-414(vol. II) pp.

[1967] Eimermacher, Karl. "'Semiotik der Analyse' und 'Semiotik des Textes': Fortsetzung eines Dauergespräches." *WSlA.* 1989; 23: 23-31.

[1968] Eimermacher, Karl, ed.; Grzybek, Peter, ed.; Witte, Georg, ed. *Issues in Slavic Literary and Cultural Theory.* Bochum: Brockmeyer; 1989. 631 pp. (Evolutionary Cultural Semiotics 21.)

[1969] Eng, Jan van der. "Expressive, Referential, and Phatic Aspects of the Aesthetic Function." *CASS.* 1988; 22(1-4): 51-56. [†Aesthetics.]

[1970] Feijter, F. J. M. de. "Over Michael Riffaterre: 'Semiotics of Poetry'." *Spektator.* 1987 Sept.; 17(1): 51-59. [†Intertextuality. Theories of Riffaterre, Michael: *Semiotics of Poetry.*]

[1971] Fleischer, Michael. "Über die Fruchtbarkeit einer Dauerkrise: Die sowejeticshe Semiotik und die Theoriebildung." 41-58 in Eimermacher, Karl, ed.; Grzybek, Peter, ed.; Witte, Georg, ed. *Issues in Slavic Literary and Cultural Theory.* Bochum: Brockmeyer; 1989. 631 pp. (Evolutionary Cultural Semiotics 21.) [†Relationship to cybernetics; information theory. Theories of Saussure, Ferdinand de; Peirce, Charles Sanders; Bense, Max.]

[1972] Gasparov, B. M. "Tartuskaia shkola 1960-kh godov kak semioticheskiĭ fenomen." *WSlA.* 1989; 23: 7-21. [†By Tartu School (1960-1969).]

[1973] Ginsburg, Ruth. "Karneval und Fasten: Excess und Mangel in der Sprache des Körpers." *Poetica.* 1989; 21(1-2): 26-42. [†The carnivalesque; study example: Kafka, Franz: *Ein Hungerkünstler.* Application of theories of Bakhtin, Mikhail Mikhaĭlovich.]

[1974] Giroud, Jean-Claude; Panier, Louis. "Sémiotique du discours religieux." *RSH.* 1986 Jan.-Mar.; 72(201 [1]): 119-128. [†Relationship to religious literature.]

[1975] Grivel, Charles. "Vingt-deux thèses préparatoires dur la doxa, le réel et le vrai." *RSH.* 1986 Jan.-Mar.; 72(201 [1]): 49-55. [†*Doxa.*]

[1976] Grübel, Rainer. "Zum Entwurf des ästhetischen Wertes in den Theorien von Michail Bachtin, Jan Mukařovský und Roman Ingarden." 59-92 in Eimermacher, Karl, ed.; Grzybek, Peter, ed.; Witte, Georg, ed. *Issues in Slavic Literary and Cultural Theory.* Bochum: Brockmeyer; 1989. 631 pp. (Evolutionary Cultural Semiotics 21.)

SEE SUBJECT INDEX FOR CROSS-REFERENCES

[†Theories of Bakhtin, Mikhail Mikhaĭlovich compared to Ingarden, Roman; Mukařovský, Jan.]

[1977] Grygar, Mojimir. "On the Semiotic Interpretation of the Historical Avant-Garde." *CASS*. 1988; 22(1-4): 211-230. [†Relationship to avant-garde.]

[1978] Grygar, Mojmír. "Das 'gegenstandslose' Zeichen: Zum Problem der vergleichenden Kunstsemiotik." 321-347 in Eimermacher, Karl, ed.; Grzybek, Peter, ed.; Witte, Georg, ed. *Issues in Slavic Literary and Cultural Theory*. Bochum: Brockmeyer; 1989. 631 pp. (Evolutionary Cultural Semiotics 21.)

[1979] ——. "'Tupý smysl' a 'nezáměrnost': Poznámky k semiotice R. Barthesa a J. Mukařovského." 173-202 in Grygar, Mojmír, ed. *Czech Studies: Literature, Language, Culture/České studie: Literatura, Jazyk, Kultura*. Amsterdam: Rodopi; 1990. 336 pp. [†Theories of Barthes, Roland; Mukařovský, Jan.]

[1980] Haidu, Peter. "The Semiotics of Alterity: A Comparison with Hermeneutics." *NLH*. 1990 Spring; 21(3): 671-691. [†Role of otherness in literature of Middle Ages; relationship to hermeneutics. Theories of Jauss, Hans Robert; Gadamer, Hans-Georg.]

[1981] Harshav, Benjamin. "Literariness Revisited." 93-106 in Eimermacher, Karl, ed.; Grzybek, Peter, ed.; Witte, Georg, ed. *Issues in Slavic Literary and Cultural Theory*. Bochum: Brockmeyer; 1989. 631 pp. (Evolutionary Cultural Semiotics 21.) [†Relationship to reference.]

[1982] Helbo, André. "Evidences et stratégies de l'analyse théâtrale." *RSH*. 1986 Jan.-Mar.; 72(201 [1]): 141-145. [†Applied to theater.]

[1983] Hoek, Leo H., ed. "Sémiotique et discours littéraire." *RSH*. 1986 Jan.-Mar.; 72(201 [1]). [Spec. iss.; incl. introd.]

[1984] Imbert, Patrick. "Ceci est mon corps/ceci n'est pas une pipe." *Degrés*. 1989 Spring; 57: e1-e21. [†Applied to discourse of mass media; advertising.]

[1985] Kevelson, Roberta. "Peirce's Students on the Science of Value: Marquaid and Ladd-Franklin on Aspects of Esthetics in Form and Color." *CASS*. 1988; 22(1-4): 57-75. [†Aesthetics of color; form. Theories of Marquand, Allan; Ladd-Franklin, Christine; relationship to Peirce, Charles Sanders.]

[1986] Kibédi Varga, A. "Rhétorique et sémiotique." *RSH*. 1986 Jan.-Mar.; 72(201 [1]): 105-118. [†Relationship to rhetoric.]

[1987] Kloepfer, Rolf. "Narrative Kooperation-Semiotische Anmerkungen zum ästhetischen Genuss." *ZFSL*. 1990; 100: 138-153. [†Aesthetics.]

[1988] Koch, Walter A. "Evolution of Culture as the Evolution of Stereotypes: Following Some Ideas by V. V. Ivanov and V. N. Toporov." *CASS*. 1988; 22(1-4): 77-100. [†On stereotypes. Theories of Ivanov, Viacheslav Vsevolodovich; Toporov, Vladimir Nikolaevich.]

[1989] Lachmann, Renate. "Concepts of Intertextuality." 391-399 in Eimermacher, Karl, ed.; Grzybek, Peter, ed.; Witte, Georg, ed. *Issues in Slavic Literary and Cultural Theory*. Bochum: Brockmeyer; 1989. 631 pp. (Evolutionary Cultural Semiotics 21.) [†Intertextuality.]

[1990] Larsen, Svend Erik. "Manet, Picasso, and the Spectator: Identity or Iconicity?" *Livstegn*. 1989; 7(2): 99-113. [†Iconicity; metaphor. Theories of Bühler, Karl.]

[1991] Lefkovitz, Lori H. "The Subject of Writing within the Margins." 165-178 in Henricksen, Bruce, ed.; Morgan, Thais E., ed. *Reorientations: Critical Theories & Pedagogies*. Urbana: U of Illinois P; 1990. x, 275 pp. [†Relationship to pedagogy.]

[1992] Măgureanu, Anca. "Le Sujet en pragmatique." *CREL*. 1989; 1: 28-37. [†And pragmatics; relationship to subject; subjectivity.]

[1993] Markiewicz, Henryk. "Some Remarks about the Iconicity of Literary Signs." 401-409 in Eimermacher, Karl, ed.; Grzybek, Peter, ed.; Witte, Georg, ed. *Issues in Slavic Literary and Cultural Theory*. Bochum: Brockmeyer; 1989. 631 pp. (Evolutionary Cultural Semiotics 21.) [†Iconicity.]

[1994] Pelc, Jerzy. "Natural versus Conventional Signs." *CASS*. 1988; 22(1-4): 115-123. [†Sign.]

[1995] Penas Ibáñez, Beatriz. "Los límites del texto estético literario." 157-166 in Sección Departamental de Logroño, introd. *Actas de las I jornadas de lengua y literatura inglesa y norteamericana*. Logroño: Pubs. del Colegio Univ. de Logroño; 1990. 178 pp.

[1996] Posner, Roland. "The Epistemological Status of Semiotics and the Tasks of a Semiotic Handbook: Eight Theses." *CASS*. 1988; 22(1-4): 125-130. [†Theories of Posner, Roland.]

[1997] ——. "The Place of Iconicity in Communication: Abstract." *Livstegn*. 1989; 7(2): 92-97. [†Iconicity.]

[1998] Réthoré, Joëlle. "Conditions de l'approche sémiotique du texte littéraire." 437-450 in Deledalle, Gérard, ed. *Semiotics and Pragmatics*. Amsterdam: Benjamins; 1989. 467 pp. (FoS 18.)

[1999] Rogers, Robert. "Freud and the Semiotics of Repetition." *PoT*. 1987; 8(3-4): 579-590. [†Repetition. Relationship to theories of Freud, Sigmund: *Jenseits des Lustprinzips*.]

[2000] Schmid, Herta. "Das 'Drei-Phasen-Modell' des tschechischen literaturwissenschaftlichen Strukturalismus." 107-152 in Eimermacher, Karl, ed.; Grzybek, Peter, ed.; Witte, Georg, ed. *Issues in Slavic Literary and Cultural Theory*. Bochum: Brockmeyer; 1989. 631 pp. [†Relationship to structuralism. Theories of Mukařovský, Jan.]

[2001] Schwarz, Wolfgang Friedrich. "Some Remarks on the Development, Poetic Range and Operational Disposition of Mukařovský's Term 'Semantic Gesture'." 153-178 in Eimermacher, Karl, ed.; Grzybek, Peter, ed.; Witte, Georg, ed. *Issues in Slavic Literary and Cultural Theory*. Bochum: Brockmeyer; 1989. 631 pp. (Evolutionary Cultural Semiotics 21.) [†Relationship to semantics. Theories of Mukařovský, Jan.]

[2002] Shavit, Zohar. "The Entrance of a New Model into the System: The Law of Transformation." 593-600 in Eimermacher, Karl, ed.; Grzybek, Peter, ed.; Witte, Georg, ed. *Issues in Slavic Literary and Cultural Theory*. Bochum: Brockmeyer; 1989. 631 pp. (Evolutionary Cultural Semiotics 21.)

[2003] Shukman, Ann. "Semiotics of Culture and the Influence of M. M. Bakhtin." 193-207 in Eimermacher, Karl, ed.; Grzybek, Peter, ed.; Witte, Georg, ed. *Issues in Slavic Literary and Cultural Theory*. Bochum: Brockmeyer; 1989. 631 pp. (Evolutionary Cultural Semiotics 21.) [†Theories of Bakhtin, Mikhail Mikhaĭlovich compared to Lotman, Iuriĭ Mikhaĭlovich.]

[2004] Singh, Gurbhagat. "Towards International Poetics." 209-217 in Valdés, Mario J., ed. *Toward a Theory of Comparative Literature: Selected Papers Presented in the Division of Theory of Literature at the XIth International Comparative Literature Congress*. New York: Peter Lang; 1990. 275 pp. (Proceedings of the International Comparative Literature Association 11: 3.) [†And psychoanalytic literary theory and criticism; role of signifier; relationship to desire.]

[2005] Vedel, Kjerstin. "Øjets semiotik: Et resume af 'Øjets umulige rejse'." *Prépub*. 1990 Jan.; 120: 23-38. [†Theories of Bataille, Georges.]

[2006] Winner, Irene Portis. "Segmentation and Reconstruction of Ethnic Culture Texts: Narration, Montage, and the Interpenetration of the Visual and Verbal Spheres." 411-431 in Eimermacher, Karl, ed.; Grzybek, Peter, ed.; Witte, Georg, ed. *Issues in Slavic Literary and Cultural Theory*. Bochum: Brockmeyer; 1989. 631 pp. (Evolutionary Cultural Semiotics 21.) [†Relationship to ethnicity.]

[2007] Winner, Thomas. "Otakar Zich as a Precursor of Prague Literary Structuralism and Semiotics: With Special Reference to Dramaturgy." 227-242 in Eimermacher, Karl, ed.; Grzybek, Peter, ed.; Witte, Georg, ed. *Issues in Slavic Literary and Cultural Theory*. Bochum: Brockmeyer; 1989. 631 pp. (Evolutionary Cultural Semiotics 21.) [†Relationship to structuralism compared to formalism. Theories of Mukařovský, Jan compared to Zich, Otakar.]

[2008] Zima, Pierre V. "Pour une sémiotique sociocritique." *RSH*. 1986 Jan.-Mar.; 72(201 [1]): 21-34. [†Sociosemiotics.]

SOCIALIST REALIST LITERARY THEORY AND CRITICISM

[2009] Boĭtar, Endre. "Kak mozhno stat' realistom sotsializma?" *CASS*. 1988; 22(1-4): 317-327. [†Theories of Andrzejewski, Jerzy; Miłosz, Czesław.]

SOCIOLOGICAL LITERARY THEORY AND CRITICISM

[2010] Adamson, Walter. "The Problem of Cultural Self-Representation." 50-58 in Harasym, Sarah, ed. *The Post-Colonial Critic: Interviews, Strategies, Dialogues: Gayatri Chakravorty Spivak*. New York: Routledge; 1990. viii, 168 pp. [†Theories of Spivak, Gayatri Chakravorty. Includes interview.]

[2011] Angenot, Marc. "Littérature et discours social, la fonction interdiscursive des formes littéraires: Hypothèses de recherche." 99-107 in Valdés, Mario J., ed. *Toward a Theory of Comparative Literature: Selected Papers Presented in the Division of Theory of Literature at the XIth International Comparative Literature Congress*. New York: Peter Lang; 1990. 275 pp. (Proceedings of the International Comparative Literature Association 11: 3.) [†Role of social discourse.]

[2012] ——. "Social Discourse Analysis: Outlines of a Research Project." *DS/SD*. 1988 Winter; 1(1): 1-21. [†Role of social discourse; relationship to semiotics; ideology; textuality.]

[2013] Bhatnagar, Rashmi. "The Post-Colonial Critic." 67-74 in Harasym, Sarah, ed. *The Post-Colonial Critic: Interviews, Strategies, Dialogues: Gayatri Chakravorty Spivak*. New York: Routledge; 1990. viii, 168 pp. [†Theories of Spivak, Gayatri Chakravorty. Includes interview.]

[2014] Cros, Edmond. "Sociologie de la littérature." 127-149 in Angenot, Marc, ed.; Bessière, Jean, ed.; Fokkema, Douwe, ed.; Kushner, Eva, ed. *Théorie littéraire*. Paris: PU de France; 1989. 395 pp.

[2015] Cros, Edmond, ed. "Theories and Perspectives, III." *Sociocriticism*. 1989; 5(1 [9]). [Spec. iss.]

[2016] Dienst, Richard. "Negotiating the Structures of Violence." 138-151 in Harasym, Sarah, ed. *The Post-Colonial Critic: Interviews, Strategies, Dialogues: Gayatri Chakravorty Spivak*. New York: Routledge; 1990. viii, 168 pp. [†Theories of Spivak, Gayatri Chakravorty. Includes interview.]

[2017] Furuland, Lars. "'Kärlek och halm i träskorna är svåra att dölja': En litteraturforskare inför folkminnena." *SLSF*. 1989; 112(315): 25-35. [Eng. sum. †Relationship to folk literature.]

[2018] Gunew, Sneja. "Questions of Multi-Culturalism." 59-66 in Harasym, Sarah, ed. *The Post-Colonial Critic: Interviews, Strategies, Dialogues: Gayatri Chakravorty Spivak*. New York: Routledge; 1990. viii, 168 pp. [†Theories of Spivak, Gayatri Chakravorty. Includes interview.]

[2019] Harasym, Sarah. "Practical Politics of the Open End." 95-112 in Harasym, Sarah, ed. *The Post-Colonial Critic: Interviews, Strategies, Dialogues: Gayatri Chakravorty Spivak*. New York: Routledge; 1990. viii, 168 pp. [†Theories of Spivak, Gayatri Chakravorty. Includes interview.]

[2020] Link, Jürgen. "Interdiscours, système du symbolisme collectif, littérature: Thèses à propos d'une théorie générative du discours et de la littérature." *Sociocriticism*. 1989; 5(1 [9]): 39-53. [†Intertextuality.]

[2021] Malcuzynski, M.-Pierrette. "Mikhail Bakhtin and the Sociocritical Practice." *DS/SD*. 1990 Spring-Summer; 3(1-2): 83-97. [†Relationship to dialogism. Theories of Bakhtin, Mikhail Mikhaĭlovich.]

[2022] Scherber, Peter. "'Literary Life' as a Topic of Literary History." 571-592 in Eimermacher, Karl, ed.; Grzybek, Peter, ed.; Witte, Georg, ed. *Issues in Slavic Literary and Cultural Theory*. Bochum: Brockmeyer; 1989. 631 pp. (Evolutionary Cultural Semiotics 21.)

STRUCTURALIST LITERARY THEORY AND CRITICISM

[2023] Aguirre Beltrán, Gonzalo. "Derrumbe de paradigmas." *PH*. 1990 Apr.-June; 74: 5-25.

[2024] Avalle, D'Arco Silvio. "Dallo strutturalismo alla semiologia: Questioni terminologiche." *SCr*. 1990 Sept.; 5(3 [64]): 295-314. [†Relationship to semiotics.]

[2025] Faryno, Jerzy. "Position of Text in the Structure of the Literary Work." 291-319 in Eimermacher, Karl, ed.; Grzybek, Peter, ed.; Witte, Georg, ed. *Issues in Slavic Literary and Cultural Theory*. Bochum: Brockmeyer; 1989. 631 pp. (Evolutionary Cultural Semiotics 21.) [†And linguistic literary theory and criticism.]

[2026] Freundlieb, Dieter. "From Structuralism to Post-Structuralism: Was the Structuralist Project beyond Redemption?" *PoeticsJ*. 1989 June; 18(3): 271-298. [†Compared to poststructuralist literary theory and criticism. Role of theories of Saussure, Ferdinand de in theories of Culler, Jonathan.]

[2027] Grzybek, Peter. "Invariant Meaning Structures in Texts: Proverb and Fable." 349-389 in Eimermacher, Karl, ed.; Grzybek, Peter, ed.; Witte, Georg, ed. *Issues in Slavic Literary and Cultural Theory*. Bochum: Brockmeyer; 1989. 631 pp. (Evolutionary Cultural Semiotics 21.) [†Applied to proverb; fable. Theories of Jakobson, Roman Osipovich.]

[2028] Merrell, Floyd. *Estructuralismo y proceso estructurante: Teoría y análisis de Al filo del agua, "La cuesta de las comadres" y "Las ruinas circulares"*. Kassel: Reichenberger; 1990. 245 pp. (PSem 15.) [†Study example: Yáñez, Agustín: *Al filo del agua*; Rulfo, Juan: "La cuesta de las comadres"; Borges, Jorge Luis: "Las ruinas circulares."]

[2029] Rudenev, Vadim. "V poiskakh utrachenova strukturalizma." *Daugava*. 1990 July; 7(157): 115-121. [†Theories of Barthes, Roland.]

[2030] Rudnev, Vadim. "Strukturnaia poètika i motyvnyï analiz." *Daugava*. 1990 Jan.; 1 [151]: 99-101.

[2031] Schmid, Wolf. "Ebenen der Erzählperspektive." 433-449 in Eimermacher, Karl, ed.; Grzybek, Peter, ed.; Witte, Georg, ed. *Issues in Slavic Literary and Cultural Theory*. Bochum: Brockmeyer; 1989. 631 pp. (Evolutionary Cultural Semiotics 21.) [†On subject; plot.]

[2032] Suchanek, Lucjan. "Dialogue, the Other's Word, and the Poetic Text." 451-461 in Eimermacher, Karl, ed.; Grzybek, Peter, ed.; Witte, Georg, ed. *Issues in Slavic Literary and Cultural Theory*. Bochum: Brockmeyer; 1989. 631 pp. (Evolutionary Cultural Semiotics 21.) [†On dialogue. Theories of Bakhtin, Mikhail Mikhaĭlovich; Buber, Martin.]

[2033] Szegedy-Maszák, Mihály. "Le Texte comme structure et communication." 183-219 in Angenot, Marc, ed.; Bessière, Jean, ed.; Fokkema, Douwe, ed.; Kushner, Eva, ed. *Théorie littéraire*. Paris: PU de France; 1989. 395 pp.

[2034] Tschumi, Raymond. "La littérature comme chiffre et comme trace." 219-225 in Valdés, Mario J., ed. *Toward a Theory of Comparative Literature: Selected Papers Presented in the Division of Theory of Literature at the XIth International Comparative Literature Congress*. New York: Peter Lang; 1990. 275 pp. (Proceedings of the International Comparative Literature Association 11: 3.) [†And poststructuralist literary theory and criticism; relationship to hermeneutics.]

[2035] Wight, Doris T. "'Structuralism Is Dead,' but Why Did the Structuralists Give Up? Jonathan Culler's 'Poetics of the Lyre.'" *Ball State University Forum*. 1989 Summer; 30(3): 53-59. [†Theories of Culler, Jonathan: *Structuralist Poetics*.]

Genres

[2036] Butterfield, Ardis. "Medieval Genres and Modern Genre Theory." *Paragraph*. 1990 July; 13(2): 184-201. [†Genre theory; relationship to literature of Middle Ages.]

[2037] Cohen, Ralph. "Do Postmodern Genres Exist?" 11-27 in Perloff, Marjorie, ed.; Davis, Robert Con, fwd.; Schleifer, Ronald, fwd. *Postmodern Genres*. Norman: U of Oklahoma P; 1989. xx, 276 pp. (Oklahoma Project for Discourse and Theory.) [See also 1988 bibliog. IV.2144. †Relationship to Postmodernism.]

[2038] Fowler, Alastair. "The Future of Genre Theory: Functions and Constructional Types." 291-303 in Cohen, Ralph, ed. *The Future of Literary Theory*. New York: Routledge; 1989. xx, 445 pp. [†Genre theory.]

[2039] Gerhart, Mary. "The Dilemma of the Text: How to 'Belong' to a Genre." *PoeticsJ*. 1989 Oct.; 18(4-5): 355-373. [†Genre theory.]

[2040] Głowiński, Michał. "Les Genres littéraires." 81-94 in Angenot, Marc, ed.; Bessière, Jean, ed.; Fokkema, Douwe, ed.; Kushner, Eva, ed. *Théorie littéraire*. Paris: PU de France; 1989. 395 pp.

[2041] Harries, Elizabeth W. "The 'Space' of the Fragment: Problems of Space, Time, and Genre." 482-487 in Bauer, Roger, ed.; Fokkema, Douwe, ed.; Graat, Michael de, asst. ed.; Kaiser, Gerhard, asst.; Rinner, Fridrun, asst.; Wertheimer, Jürgen, asst. *Proceedings of the XIIth Congress of the International Comparative Literature Association/Actes du XIIe congrès de l'Association Internationale de Littérature Comparée: München 1988 Munich, IV: Space and Boundaries of Literature/Espace et frontières de la littérature*. Munich: Iudicium; 1990. 651 pp. (Proceedings of the Congress of the International Comparative Literature Association 12: 4.) [†Role of space in fragment.]

[2042] Kuon, Peter. "Gattungsgeschichte, Literaturgeschichte, ästhetische Erfahrung: Zur Aktualität Benedetto Croces in Deutschland (und anderswo)." 85-105 in Baasner, Frank, ed. *Literaturgeschichtsschreibung in Italien und Deutschland: Traditionen und aktuelle Probleme*. Tübingen: Niemeyer; 1989. viii, 197 pp. [†Theories of Croce, Benedetto; reception in Germany.]

[2043] Naveh, Hannah. *HaVidui, HaGenre, UBehinato*. Tel Aviv: Papyrus, Tel Aviv Univ.; 1988. 257 pp.

[2044] Perloff, Marjorie, ed.; Davis, Robert Con, fwd.; Schleifer, Ronald, fwd. *Postmodern Genres*. Norman: U of Oklahoma P; 1989. xx, 276 pp. (Oklahoma Project for Discourse and Theory.) [Incl. introd.]

[2045] Schaeffer, Jean-Marie. "Literary Genres and Textual Genericity." 167-187 in Cohen, Ralph, ed. *The Future of Literary Theory*. New York: Routledge; 1989. xx, 445 pp. [†Genre theory.]

AUTOBIOGRAPHY

[2046] Carson, Josephine. "The Narrowing Field: Memoirs of an Autobiography Writing Group." *ABSt*. 1989 Summer; 5(1): 48-65. [†Relationship to psychotherapy.]

[2047] Chandler, Marilyn R. "A Healing Art: Therapeutic Dimensions of Autobiography." *ABSt*. 1989 Summer; 5(1): 4-14. [†Relationship to psychotherapy.]

[2048] Chandler, Marilyn R., ed. "The Therapeutic Dimension of Autobiography." *ABSt*. 1989 Summer; 5(1). [Spec. iss.; incl. introd. †Relationship to psychotherapy.]

[2049] Feldman, Yael S. "New Psychoanalytic Models for the Theory of Comparative Study of Autobiography." 125-133 in Valdés, Mario J., ed. *Toward a Theory of Comparative Literature: Selected Papers Presented in the Division of Theory of Literature at the XIth International Comparative Literature Congress*. New York: Peter Lang; 1990. 275 pp. (Proceedings of the International Comparative Literature Association 11: 3.) [†Treatment in psychoanalytic theory.]

[2050] Griffin, Charles J. G. "The Rhetoric of Form in Conversion Narratives." *QJS*. 1990 May; 76(2): 152-163. [†Syllogistic form; qualitative form in spiritual autobiography; study example: Colson, Charles W.: *Born Again*.]

[2051] Niggl, Gunter, ed. *Die Autobiographie: Zu Form und Geschichte einer literarischen Gattung*. Darmstadt: Wiss. Buchgesell.; 1989. 592 pp. (WdF 565.) [Incl. introd. †Anthology of criticism.]

[2052] Peterson, Linda H. "Female Autobiographer, Narrative Duplicity." *SLitI*. 1990 Fall; 23(2): 165-176. [†By women writers. 1700-1899. Treatment of the self; relationship to duplicity in narrative.]

[2053] Smith, Sidonie. "Construing Truth in Lying Mouths: Truthtelling in Women's Autobiography." *SLitI*. 1990 Fall; 23(2): 145-163. [†By women writers. Treatment of the self; relationship to truth. Feminist approach.]

[2054] Tilkin, Françoise. *Quand la folie se racontait: Récit et antipsychiatrie*. Amsterdam: Rodopi; 1990. 416 pp. (FauxT 47.) [†And biography. Treatment of madness; relationship to psychiatry.]

[2055] Woodcock, John. "The Therapeutic Journals of Joanna Field and Etty Hillesum." *ABSt*. 1989 Summer; 5(1): 15-25. [†Relationship to psychotherapy; study example: Milner, Marion Blackett: *A Life of One's Own*; Hillesum, Etty: *Het verstoorde leven*.]

BIOGRAPHY

[2056] Alvarez, María Antonia. "Leon Edel: La nueva biografía literaria." *Epos*. 1990; 6: 425-435. [†Theories of Edel, Leon.]

[2057] Babcock, Barbara Allen. "Reconstructing the Person: The Case of Clara Shortridge Foltz." *Biography*. 1989 Winter; 12(1): 5-16.

[2058] Manis, Jerome G. "Great Little Persons." *Biography*. 1989 Winter; 12(1): 17-28.

[2059] Sisk, John P. "Biography without End." *AR*. 1990 Fall; 48(4): 449-459.

[2060] Torbacke, Jarl. "Biografin som problem för den generaliserande historikern." *PHT*. 1989; 85(3-4): 105-109. [†Application of theories of Gramsci, Antonio; relationship to history.]

Bibliography

[2061] Wachter, Phyllis E. "Bibliography of Works about Life-Writing for the Latter 1980s." *Biography*. 1988 Fall; 11(4): 316-325. 1989 Fall; 12(4): 320-327. [†(1985-1988).]

DRAMA

[2062] "Drama i teror." *Izraz*. 1990 Apr.; 34(4). [Spec. iss. †Treatment of terrorism.]

[2063] Astington, John H., ed. "Contemporary Theatre and Political Crisis." *MD*. 1990 Mar.; 33(1). [Spec. iss. †1900-1999. Relationship to politics.]

[2064] Barr, Richard Lewis. "Spectatorial Stages: Perspectival Communities in the Modern Theatre." *DAI*. 1990 Mar.; 50(9): 2892A. [†And theater. Role of spectator; relationship to perspective. Dissertation abstract.]

[2065] Bennett, Benjamin. *Theater as Problem: Modern Drama and Its Place in Literature*. Ithaca: Cornell UP; 1990. x, 272 pp. [†Drama theory.]

[2066] Burwick, Frederick. "Romantic Drama: From Optics to Illusion." 167-208 in Peterfreund, Stuart, ed. *Literature and Science: Theory & Practice*. Boston: Northeastern UP; 1990. vi, 248 pp. [†Romantic period. Staging.]

[2067] Courtney, Richard. *Drama and Intelligence: A Cognitive Theory*. Montreal: McGill-Queen's UP; 1990. 190 pp. [†Relationship to cognition.]

[2068] Dal, Meri Kerin; Meseldžija, Biljana, tr. "Državni terorizam i dramske protivmere." *Izraz*. 1990 Apr.; 34(4): 494-504. [†1900-1999. Treatment of terrorism; relationship to government.]

[2069] Džeruld, Denijel C.; Meseldžija, Biljana, tr. "Terorizam i drama, istorijski pogled." *Izraz*. 1990 Apr.; 34(4): 423-451. [†Treatment of terrorism.]

[2070] Hartigan, Karelisa, ed. *Text and Presentation*. Lanham, MD: UP of America; 1989. x, 168 pp. (CDCP 9.)

[2071] Helbo, André; Pérez Botero, Luis, tr. "El texto semiótico: El ojo, la voz, la escena." *Dispositio*. 1988; 13(33-35): 81-90. [†Role of the visual; relationship to the verbal; staging.]

[2072] Hristić, Jovan; Gantar, Jure, tr. "Teoretična vprašanja, praktični odgovori." *Sodobnost*. 1989; 37(8-9): 835-842. [†And theater.]

[2073] Kalan, Filip. "O presoji igralčeve stvarilnosti." *Sodobnost*. 1988; 36(1): 39-50. [†And theater. Treatment of reality in performance.]

[2074] Klaić, Dragan. "Drmske aporije političkog nasilja." *Izraz*. 1990 Apr.; 34(4): 453-460. [†Treatment of violence; terrorism.]

[2075] Klein, Holger M. "Exploring Place and Space in Drama and in Fiction." 174-181 in Bauer, Roger, ed.; Fokkema, Douwe, ed.; Graat, Michael de, asst. ed.; Aldridge, A. Owen, asst.; Higonnet, Margaret, asst.; Klein, Holger M., asst.; Meisami, Julie Scott, asst.; Rigney, Ann, asst.; Ronen, Ruth, asst.; Sondrup, Steven P., asst.; Templeton, Joan, asst.; Walker, Janet A., asst. *Proceedings of the XIIth Congress of the International Comparative Literature Association/Actes du XIIe congrès de l'Association Internationale de Littérature Comparée: München 1988 Munich, III: Space and Boundaries in Literature (Continuation)/Espace et frontières dans la littérature (suite)*. Munich: Iudicium; 1990. 509 pp. (Proceedings of the Congress of the International Comparative Literature Association 12: 3.) [†And fiction. Treatment of space; place.]

[2076] Komar, Michał. "Bestiarium współczesne rozszerzone o polaków." *DialogW*. 1990 Dec.; 35(12 [411]): 82-86. [†1900-1999. Treatment of Poles.]

[2077] Kowzan, Tadeusz. "Théâtre comme spatialisation de la littérature: Question des frontières." 119-124 in Bauer, Roger, ed.; Fokkema, Douwe, ed.; Graat, Michael de, asst. ed.; Fischer-Lichte, Erika, asst.; Garstin, Marguerite, asst.; Ibsch, Elrud, asst.; Stackelberg, Jürgen von, asst. *Proceedings of the XIIth Congress of the International Comparative Literature Association/Actes du XIIe congrès de l'Association Internationale de Littérature Comparée: München 1988 Munich, V: Space and Boundaries in Literary Theory and Criticism/Espace et frontières dans la critique et la théorie littéraire; Space and Boundaries in the Teaching of General and Comparative Literature/Espace et frontières dans l'enseignement de la littérature générale et comparée*. Munich: Iudicium; 1990. 415 pp. (Proceedings of the Congress of the International Comparative Literature Association 12: 5.) [†And theater. Spatial form.]

[2078] Krause, Carol Wright Kathleen. "The Playwright in Process and Production." *DAI*. 1990 May; 50(11): 3417A. [†Role of dramatists. Dissertation abstract.]

[2079] Maár, Judit. "Aspects de l'analyse sémantique des textes dramatiques et narratifs." *SCr*. 1990 May; 5(2 [63]): 235-247. [†And narrative. Semantic analysis.]

[2080] MacDonald, Erik Lars. "The Politics of Style: Textuality in Post-Structuralist Theatre." *DAI*. 1990 Apr.; 50(10): 3108A. [†Textuality; relationship to poststructuralism. Dissertation abstract.]

[2081] Mango, Achille. "'Que los sueños, sueños son'." 129-137 in Dolfi, Laura, ed. *L'imposible/possible di Federico García Lorca*. Naples: Edizioni Scientifiche Italiane; 1989. 333 pp. (Pubblicazioni dell'Università degli Studi di Salerno 27.) [†Relationship to dream.]

[2082] Misailović, Milenko. "Svest i dramaturgija." *Izraz*. 1990 Jan.; 34(1): 82-89.

[2083] Murray, Edward. *Varieties of Dramatic Structure: A Study of Theory and Practice*. Lanham, MD: UP of America; 1990. xiii, 143 pp. [†Dramatic structure.]

[2084] Norris, Joe. "Some Authorities as Co-Authors in a Collective Creation Production." *DAI*. 1990 May; 50(11): 3417A. [†Collaboration in writing; theatrical production. Dissertation abstract.]

[2085] Or, Džon; Meseldžija, Biljana, tr. "Terorizam kao društvena drama i dramski oblik." *Izraz*. 1990 Apr.; 34(4): 481-493. [†Treatment of terrorism. Sociological approach.]

[2086] Pavis, Patrice. "Del texto a la puesta en escena: La travesía histórica." *Dispositio*. 1988; 13(33-35): 29-50. [†Role of text; relationship to theatrical production. Semiotic approach.]

[2087] Rädle, Fidel. "Das Alte Testament im Drama der Jesuiten." 239-252 in Link, Franz, ed. *Paradeigmata: Literarische Typologie des Alten Testaments, I: Von den Anfängen bis zum 19. Jahrhundert; II: 20. Jahrhundert*. Berlin: Duncker & Humblot; 1989. 945 pp. (Schriften zur Literaturwissenschaft 5.) [†By Jesuit dramatists. 1500-1799. Sources in Old Testament.]

[2088] Redmond, James, ed. *Drama and Philosophy*. Cambridge: Cambridge UP; 1990. xiii, 227 pp. (ThD 12.)

[2089] Redmond, James, pref. *Women in Theatre*. Cambridge: Cambridge UP; 1989. 297 pp. (ThD 11.) [†Role of women.]

[2090] Richardson, Brian. "Point of View in Drama: Diegetic Monologue, Unreliable Narrators, and the Author's Voice on Stage." *CompD*. 1988 Fall; 22(3): 193-214. [†Point of view.]

[2091] ——. "'Time Is Out of Joint': Narrative Models and the Temporality of the Drama." *PoT*. 1987; 8(2): 299-309. [†As narrative; relationship to temporality.]

[2092] Stapele, Peter van. "The Analysis of Deixis as a Basis for Discourse Analysis of Dramatic Texts." II: 333-348 in Halliday, M. A. K., ed.; Gibbons, John, ed.; Nicholas, Howard, ed. *Learning, Keeping, and Using Language: Selected Papers from the 8th World Congress of Applied Linguistics, Sydney, 16-21 August 1987, I & II*. Amsterdam: Benjamins; 1990. xx, 508 + xv, 489 pp. [†Deixis; relationship to audience response.]

[2093] Štromajer, Igor. "Homo theatralis." *Sodobnost*. 1989; 37(2): 190-193. [†And theater.]

[2094] Udodov, A. B. "O polifonizme v drame." *FN*. 1990; 6: 22-30. [†Relationship to polyphony. Application of theories of Bakhtin, Mikhail Mikhaĭlovich.]

[2095] Yarrow, Ralph. "He Was Never Entirely Himself: Forms of Consciousness in Theatre." *NewComp*. 1990 Spring; 9: 28-40.

Bibliography

[2096] "Drame o teroru i terorizmu." *Izraz*. 1990 Apr.; 34(4): 540-541. [†Treatment of terrorism.]

[2097] Carpenter, Charles A. "Modern Drama Studies: An Annual Bibliography." *MD*. 1990 June; 33(2): 155-305. [Monog. iss.]

[2098] Gray, John, ed. *Black Theatre and Performance: A Pan-African Bibliography*. New York: Greenwood; 1990. xv, 414 pp. (Bibliographies and Indexes in Afro-American and African Studies 25.) [†By black dramatists. And theater.]

Comic drama

[2099] Issacharoff, Michael; Guitart, María, tr. "El discurso cómico y la referencia." *Dispositio*. 1988; 13(33-35): 71-80. [†Referentiality; relationship to semiotics.]

Historical drama

[2100] Lindenberger, Herbert. "Experiencing History." *SS*. 1990 Winter; 62(1): 7-23. [†1700-1999.]

Theater of the absurd

[2101] Mileto, Thales de. "Gato Alucinado na Cristaleira." *RdT*. 1985 July-Sept.; 455: 31-37.

Tragic drama

[2102] Schumacher, Ernst. "Noch einmal: Die Marxisten und die Tragödie." *WB*. 1990; 36(4): 562-579. [†Marxist approach.]

Tragicomedy

[2103] Argullol, Rafael. "Da Traxicomedia Moderna." *Grial*. 1990 Apr.-June; 28(106): 154-164. [†Relationship to Modernism.]

FICTION

[2104] Abbele, Francesca Morino. "Il bambino e la narrazione." *Cristallo*. 1990 Aug.; 32(2): 31-40. [†For children. Treatment of the marvelous; adventure.]

[2105] Assmann, Aleida. "Fiktion als Differenz." *Poetica*. 1989; 21(3-4): 239-260. [†1900-1999. Relationship to reality.]

[2106] Bange, P. "L'Analyse pragmatique des récits littéraires." 339-349 in Deledalle, Gérard, ed. *Semiotics and Pragmatics*. Amsterdam: Benjamins; 1989. 467 pp. (FoS 18.)

[2107] Barrera-Vidal, Albert. "Comics, Fumetti, Bande Dessinée—Semiotik und Didaktik eines Massenmediums." *NsM*. 1986 Aug.; 39(3): 166-173. [†Comic strip.]

[2108] Bosmajian, Hamida. "Conventions of Image and Form in Nuclear War Narratives for Young Readers." *PLL*. 1990 Winter; 26(1): 73-89. [†Image; form; relationship to literary conventions. Treatment of nuclear war.]

[2109] Brooks, Peter. "The Tale vs. the Novel." 303-310 in Spilka, Mark, ed.; McCracken-Flesher, Caroline, ed. *Why the Novel Matters: A Postmodern Perplex*. Bloomington: Indiana UP; 1990. xi, 388 pp.

[2110] Caenepeel, Mimo. "Aspect, Temporal Ordering and Perspective in Narrative Fiction." *DAI*. 1990 Dec.; 51(6): 2007A. [†Perspective; relationship to temporal relations. Dissertation abstract.]

[2111] Campos, Ruby Reyna C. "Patterns of Social Behavior Endorsed in Children's Stories: A Socio-Pragmatic Approach." *SLRJ*. 1989 June; 20(1): 80-91. [†For children. Treatment of morality; relationship to social behavior.]

[2112] Campra, Rosalba. "La lectura de los textos de ficción." *Escritura*. 1987 Jan.-Dec.; 12(23-24): 59-72.

[2113] Chamberlain, Daniel Frank. *Narrative Perspective in Fiction: A Phenomenological Mediation of Reader, Text, and World*. Toronto: U of Toronto P; 1990. 266 pp. (UTFS 59.) [†Point of view. Hermeneutic approach. Application of theories of Gadamer, Hans-Georg; Merleau-Ponty, Maurice; Ricœur, Paul.]

[2114] Chatman, Seymour. *Coming to Terms: The Rhetoric of Narrative in Fiction and Film*. Ithaca: Cornell UP; 1990. ix, 240 pp. [†And film. Narratological approach.]

[2115] Cooney, Barbara. "Narrating Chaucer, Grimm, New England, and Cooney." 25-31 in Otten, Charlotte F., ed.; Schmidt, Gary D., ed. *The Voice of the Narrator in Children's Literature: Insights from Writers and Critics*. New York: Greenwood; 1989. xviii, 414 pp. (CSWL 28.) [Illus. †For children. Narrative voice. Interview with Schmidt, Gary D.]

[2116] Currie, Gregory. *The Nature of Fiction*. Cambridge: Cambridge UP; 1990. xii, 222 pp. [†Role of writer; relationship to reader; text. Philosophical approach.]

[2117] Doležel, Lubomír. "Fictional Reference: Mimesis and Possible Worlds." 109-124 in Valdés, Mario J., ed. *Toward a Theory of Comparative Literature: Selected Papers Presented in the Division of Theory of Literature at the XIth International Comparative Literature Congress*. New York: Peter Lang; 1990. 275 pp. (Proceedings of the International Comparative Literature Association 11: 3.) [†Fictionality; relationship to mimesis.]

[2118] Doloughan, Fiona Joy. "'Great Expectations' and 'Lost Illusions': Systematic Disillusionment as a Mode of Literary Realism." *DAI*. 1990 Apr.; 50(10): 3220A. [†1800-1999. Realism; relationship to disillusionment. Dissertation abstract.]

[2119] Doty, William G. "Contextual Fictions That Bridge Our Worlds: A Whole New Poetry." *L&T*. 1990 Mar.; 4(1): 104-129. [†Relationship to religion: myth; poststructuralist literary theory and criticism.]

[2120] Easley, Rex Burton. "Common Ground: Fiction-Writing and Composition." *DAI*. 1990 Feb.; 50(8): 2412A. [†Relationship to composition. Dissertation abstract.]

[2121]   Eckstein, Barbara J. *The Language of Fiction in a World of Pain: Reading Politics as Paradox.* Philadelphia: U of Pennsylvania P; 1990. ix, 210 pp. (New Cultural Studies.) [†Treatment of politics.]

[2122]   Eco, Umberto. "Small Worlds." *Versus.* 1989 Jan.-May; 52-53: 53-70. [†Application of possible worlds semantics.

[2123]   Ellerby, Janet Mason. "Repetition and Redemption." *DAI.* 1990 Apr.; 50(10): 3224A. [†As autobiography. Repetition by narrator. Dissertation abstract.]

[2124]   Embree, Ainslie T. "Imagining India: English-Language Fiction Set in Post-Independence India." 71-84 in Winks, Robin W., ed.; Rush, James R., ed. *Asia in Western Fiction.* Honolulu: U of Hawaii P; 1990. x, 229 pp. [†English language literature. 1900-1999. Treatment of India.]

[2125]   Fernández, Graciela Beatriz. "El problema de la referencia en los textos de ficción." *EFil.* 1989; 24: 111-118. [†Reference.]

[2126]   Fisher, Leonard Everett. "Finding the Narrative Voice through Dramatically Resolved Form." 32-39 in Otten, Charlotte F., ed.; Schmidt, Gary D., ed. *The Voice of the Narrator in Children's Literature: Insights from Writers and Critics.* New York: Greenwood; 1989. xviii, 414 pp. (CSWL 28.) [Illus. †For children. English language literature. 1900-1999.]

[2127]   Francoeur, Louise. "Le Statut pragmatique du texte de fiction." 397-406 in Deledalle, Gérard, ed. *Semiotics and Pragmatics.* Amsterdam: Benjamins; 1989. 467 pp. (FoS 18.)

[2128]   Godard, Barbara; Berberović, Jesenka, tr.; Neretljak, Edina, tr. "'Samonastavite': Feministkinje (iznova) stvaraju pripovijesti." *Izraz.* 1990 Feb.-Mar.; 34(2-3): 258-273. [†By feminist writers.]

[2129]   Greene, Gayle. "Feminist Fiction, Feminist Form." *Frontiers.* 1990; 11(2-3): 82-88. [†1900-1999. Treatment of feminism.]

[2130]   Grodal, Torben Kragh. "Kognition, emotion og neurale modeller." *KuKl.* 1990; 17(4): 93-111. [†Relationship to reception theory. Psychoanalytic approach.]

[2131]   Hambly, Gavin R. G. "Muslims in English-Language Fiction." 35-52 in Winks, Robin W., ed.; Rush, James R., ed. *Asia in Western Fiction.* Honolulu: U of Hawaii P; 1990. x, 229 pp. [†English language literature. 1800-1999. Treatment of Islam; Moslems.]

[2132]   Henke, Suzette A. "The Ideology of Female (Re)Production: The Spinster in Twentieth-Century Literature." *W&D.* 1988 Spring-Fall; 6(1-2 [11-12]): 167-183. [†1900-1999. Treatment of spinster; relationship to marginality.]

[2133]   Imbert, Patrick. "'L'Espace' de la démolition." 72-76 in Bauer, Roger, ed.; Fokkema, Douwe, ed.; Graat, Michael de, asst. ed.; Fischer-Lichte, Erika, asst.; Garstin, Marguerite, asst.; Ibsch, Elrud, asst.; Stackelberg, Jürgen von, asst. *Proceedings of the XIIth Congress of the International Comparative Literature Association/Actes du XIIe congrès de l'Association Internationale de Littérature Comparée: München 1988 Munich, V: Space and Boundaries in Literary Theory and Criticism/Espace et frontières dans la critique et la théorie littéraire; Space and Boundaries in the Teaching of General and Comparative Literature/Espace et frontières dans l'enseignement de la littérature générale et comparée.* Munich: Iudicium; 1990. 415 pp. (Proceedings of the Congress of the International Comparative Literature Association 12: 5.) [†Role of space.]

[2134]   Kasics, Kaspar. *Literatur und Fiktion: Zur Theorie und Geschichte der literarischen Kommunikation.* Heidelberg: Winter; 1990. 163 pp. (RSieg 94.)

[2135]   Langford, Larry L. "The Ethics of Mimesis: Postmodernism and the Possibility of History." *DAI.* 1990 June; 50(12): 3947A. [†Mimesis; relationship to historiography; Postmodernism. Dissertation abstract.]

[2136]   Maguire, Gregory. "Themes in English Language: Fantastic Literature for Children, 1938-1988." *DAI.* 1990 Dec.; 51(6): 2013A. [†For children (1938-1988). English language literature. Role of the fantastic. Dissertation abstract.]

[2137]   Marshall, Brenda K. "Fiction and Theory of the Postmodern Moment." *DAI.* 1990 Sept.; 51(3): 840A. [†1900-1999. Relationship to Postmodernism. Dissertation abstract.]

[2138]   Martin, Charles Gaines. "The Deministrelization of Black Figures in Fiction." *DAI.* 1990 May; 50(11): 3579A. [†1800-1999. Treatment of African Americans as minstrels. Dissertation abstract.]

[2139]   Masseron, Caroline. "L'Elaboration d'un texte long: L'Exemple du genre fantastique en 4ᵉ." *Pratiques.* 1990 June; 66: 3-56. [†Role of the fantastic; relationship to teaching of writing.]

[2140]   Miller, Luree. "The Himalayas in Fact and Fiction." 85-99 in Winks, Robin W., ed.; Rush, James R., ed. *Asia in Western Fiction.* Honolulu: U of Hawaii P; 1990. x, 229 pp. [†English language literature. 1900-1999. Treatment of Himalayas.]

[2141]   Montandon, Alain. "Espaces et frontières dans l'imaginaire du merveilleux." 384-391 in Bauer, Roger, ed.; Fokkema, Douwe, ed.; Graat, Michael de, ed.; Boening, John, ed.; Gillespie, Gerald, ed.; Moog-Grünewald, Maria, ed.; Nemoianu, Virgil, ed.; Ricapito, Joseph, ed.; Schmeling, Manfred, ed.; Thüsen, Joachim von der, ed.; Uhlig, Claus, ed. *Proceedings of the XIIth Congress of the International Comparative Literature Association/Actes du XIIe congrès de l'Association Internationale de Littérature Comparée: München 1988 Munich, II: Space and Boundaries in Literature/Espace et frontières dans la littérature.* Munich: Iudicium; 1990. 606 pp. (Proceedings of the Congress of the International Comparative Literature Association 12: 2.) [†Treatment of space; relationship to the fantastic.]

[2142]   Montulet, Norma. "De waarheid over Sherlock Holmes: Over fictionaliteit en referentie." *Spektator.* 1988 Nov.; 18(2): 83-95. [†Nonreferential language; relationship to truth compared to fictionality.]

[2143]   Mooij, J. J. A. "Fictionality and the Speech Act Theory." 15-22 in Bessière, Jean, ed. *Fiction, texte, narratologie, genre.* New York: Peter Lang; 1989. 238 pp. [†Fictionality. Application of speech act theory.]

[2144]   Morsy, Faten I. "The Frame-Narrative and Short Fiction: A Continuum from 'One Thousand and One Nights' to Borges." *DAI.* 1990 Nov.; 51(5): 1605A. [†Interpretive frame. Sources in *The Thousand and One Nights.* Dissertation abstract.]

[2145]   Nøjgaard, Morten. "Esthétique de l'admiration: Le Désir occulté de fiction." *RevR.* 1990; 25(2): 376-390. [†Relationship to desire; reader. Psychoanalytic approach.]

[2146]   Pascal, Roy. "Narrative Fictions and Reality: A Comment on Frank Kermode's *The Sense of an Ending.*" 65-75 in Spilka, Mark, ed.; McCracken-Flesher, Caroline, ed. *Why the Novel Matters: A Postmodern Perplex.* Bloomington: Indiana UP; 1990. xi, 388 pp. [†Theories of Kermode, Frank: *The Sense of an Ending.*]

[2147]   Pezzotta, Alberto. "Il racconto omodiegetico in terza persona." *SCr.* 1990 Sept.; 5(3 [64]): 397-405. [†Third person narration. Application of theories of Genette, Gérard.]

[2148]   Richardson, Miles. "Point of View in Anthropological Discourse." 31-39 in Dennis, Philip, ed.; Aycock, Wendell, ed. *Literature and Anthropology.* Lubbock: Texas Tech UP; 1989. ix, 227 pp. (SCLit 20.) [†Narrator; point of view; relationship to story; study example: Sandars, Nancy Katharine: *The Epic of Gilgamesh.* Anthropological approach.]

[2149]   Rubio Montaner, Pilar. "Primacía de la focalización en la instancia narrativa." *RL.* 1990 Jan.-June; 52(103): 47-66. [†Focalization; relationship to narrative voice.]

[2150]   Schmeling, Manfred. "Erzählort und Erzählmodus in moderner Literatur." 66-71 in Bauer, Roger, ed.; Fokkema, Douwe, ed.; Graat, Michael de, asst. ed.; Fischer-Lichte, Erika, asst.; Garstin, Marguerite, asst.; Ibsch, Elrud, asst.; Stackelberg, Jürgen von, asst. *Proceedings of the XIIth Congress of the International Comparative Literature Association/Actes du XIIe congrès de l'Association Internationale de Littérature Comparée: München 1988 Munich, V: Space and Boundaries in Literary Theory and Criticism/Espace et frontières dans la critique et la théorie littéraire; Space and Boundaries in the Teaching of General and Comparative Literature/Espace et frontières dans l'enseignement de la littérature générale et comparée.* Munich: Iudicium; 1990. 415 pp. (Proceedings of the Congress of the International Comparative Literature Association 12: 5.) [†Narrative technique; relationship to spatiality.]

[2151]   Smetak, Jacqueline R. "So Long, Mom: The Politics of Nuclear Holocaust Fiction." *PLL.* 1990 Winter; 26(1): 41-59. [†Treatment of politics; relationship to nuclear war.]

[2152]   Sorapure, Madeleine. "Assuming Authority: Self-Conscious Authorship in Contemporary Fiction." *DAI.* 1990 Sept.; 51(3): 841A. [†Self-consciousness; relationship to authorship.]

[2153]   Spence, Jonathan D. "Chinese Fictions in the Twentieth Century." 100-116 in Winks, Robin W., ed.; Rush, James R., ed. *Asia in Western Fiction.* Honolulu: U of Hawaii P; 1990. x, 229 pp. [†Treatment of China.]

[2154]   Tomasi, John. "Plato's *Statesmen* Story: The Birth of Fiction Reconceived." *P&L.* 1990 Oct.; 14(2): 348-358. [†Sources in Plato.]

[2155]   Turnbull, C. Mary. "Hong Kong: Fragrant Harbour, City of Sin and Death." 117-136 in Winks, Robin W., ed.; Rush, James R., ed. *Asia in Western Fiction.* Honolulu: U of Hawaii P; 1990. x, 229 pp. [†1900-1999. Treatment of Hong Kong.]

[2156]   Varsava, Jerry A. *Contingent Meanings: Postmodern Fiction, Mimesis, and the Reader.* Tallahassee: Florida State UP; 1990. xiii, 233 pp. [†Mimesis; relationship to reader; Postmodernism.]

[2157]   Weimann, Robert. "Text, Author-Function and Society: Towards a Sociology of Representation and Appropriation in Modern Narrative." 91-106 in Collier, Peter, ed.; Geyer-Ryan, Helga, ed. *Literary Theory Today.* Ithaca: Cornell UP; 1990. xii, 249 pp. [†Representation. Sociological approach.]

[2158]   Winks, Robin W., ed.; Rush, James R., ed. *Asia in Western Fiction.* Honolulu: U of Hawaii P; 1990. x, 229 pp. [Incl. introd. & prev. pub. material. †Treatment of Asia.]

[2159]   Yacobi, Tamar. "Narrative Structure and Fictional Mediation." *PoT.* 1987; 8(2): 335-372. [†Narrator as mediator between writer and reader.]

Crime fiction

[2160]   Thompson, Jon Francis. "Modernism's Illegitimate Progeny: Fictions of Crime and the Experience of Modernity." *DAI.* 1990 Oct.; 51(4): 1223A. [†Relationship to Postmodernism. Dissertation abstract.]

Detective fiction

[2161]   Schnedecker, Catherine. "Comment reconnaître un policier?" *Pratiques.* 1989 June; 62: 53-69. [†Application of text linguistics.]

Fantasy fiction

[2162]   Lehnert-Rodiek, Gertrud. "Zur Funktion der Raum-Zeit-Korrelation in phantastischer Literatur." 398-404 in Bauer, Roger, ed.; Fokkema, Douwe, ed.; Graat, Michael de, ed.; Boening, John, ed.; Gillespie, Gerald, ed.; Moog-Grünewald, Maria, ed.; Nemoianu, Virgil, ed.; Ricapito, Joseph, ed.; Schmeling, Manfred, ed.; Thüsen, Joachim von der, ed.; Uhlig, Claus, ed. *Proceedings of the XIIth Congress of the International Comparative Literature Association/Actes du XIIe congrès de l'Association Internationale de Littérature Comparée: München 1988 Munich, II: Space and Boundaries in Literature/Espace et frontières dans la littérature.* Munich: Iudicium; 1990. 606 pp. (Proceedings of the Congress of the International Comparative Literature Association 12: 2.) [†Role of spatiotemporal relations.]

Fantasy fiction/Bibliography

[2163]   Barron, Neil, ed.; Bishop, Michael, introd. *Fantasy Literature: A Reader's Guide.* New York: Garland; 1990. xxvii, 586 pp. (GRLH 874.) [Incl. pref.]

Gothic fiction/Bibliography

[2164] Barron, Neil, ed. & pref.; Bishop, Michael, introd. *Horror Literature: A Reader's Guide.* New York: Garland; 1990. xxvii, 596 pp. (GRLH 1220.) [†And horror fiction. (1762-1988).]

Horror fiction

[2165] Bridgstock, Martin. "The Twilit Fringe—Anthropology and Modern Horror Fiction." *JPC.* 1989 Winter; 23(3): 115-123. [†1900-1999. Relationship to anthropology.]

Märchen

[2166] Zipes, Jack. "Fairy Tale as Myth/Myth as Fairy Tale." 107-110 in Gannon, Susan R., ed.; Thompson, Ruth Anne, ed. *Cross-Culturalism in Children's Literature: Selected Papers from the Children's Literature Association, Carleton University, Ottawa, Canada, May 14-17, 1987.* New York: Pace Univ.; 1988. i, 116 pp. [†For children. As myth.]

Modernist fiction

[2167] Hayman, David. *Re-Forming the Narrative: Toward a Mechanics of Modernist Fiction.* Urbana: U of Illinois P; 1987. xii, 219 pp. [†Narrative technique.]

Popular fiction

[2168] Milojković, Andjelka. "'Masovna' književnost—poetika stvarnosti—da ili ne?" *Slavia.* 1990; 59(4): 414-421. [†Relationship to realism.]

[2169] Roberts, Thomas J. *An Aesthetics of Junk Fiction.* Athens: U of Georgia P; 1990. x, 284 pp.

Postmodernist fiction

[2170] Musschoot, Anne Marie. "The Challenge of Postmodernism: Representation—Historiography—Metafiction." *DC.* 1990 Summer; 41: 3-15. [†Metafiction.]

[2171] Olsen, Lance. "Making Stew with What You Got: Postmodern Humor in Barth, Nabokov, and Everybody Else." *Thalia.* 1988 Spring-Summer; 10(1): 23-29. [†Humor.]

Science fiction

[2172] Allman, John. "Motherless Creation: Motifs in Science Fiction." *NDQ.* 1990 Spring; 58(2): 124-132. [†1900-1999. Treatment of monsters; motherhood.]

[2173] Benford, Gregory. "SF, Rhetoric and Realities." *Foundation.* 1989-1990 Winter; 47: 43-45. [†Role of aesthetics; relationship to science.]

[2174] Borgmeier, Raimund. "Objectives and Methods in the Analysis of Science Fiction: The Case of *Science-Fiction Studies.*" *SFS.* 1990 Nov.; 17(3 [52]): 383-391. [Fr. sum. †Treatment in criticism in *Science-Fiction Studies.*]

[2175] Bozzetto, Roger; Evans, Arthur, ed. & tr. "Kepler's *Somnium*: Or, Science Fiction's Missing Link." *SFS.* 1990 Nov.; 17(3 [52]): 370-382. [Fr. sum. †Sources in Kepler, Johann: *Somnium, seu Opus Posthumum de Astronomia Lunari.*]

[2176] Dalgaard, Niels. "Science fiction skal tages alvorligt." *Samtiden.* 1990; 1: 60-64.

[2177] Grant, Richard. "The Profession of Science Fiction, 41: Git Along, Little Robot." *Foundation.* 1989-1990 Winter; 47: 55-66. [†Role of consciousness.]

[2178] Guthke, Karl S. "Are We Alone? The Idea of Extraterrestrial Intelligence in Literature and Philosophy from Copernicus to H. G. Wells." 91-104 in Berghahn, Klaus L., ed.; Grimm, Reinhold, ed.; Kreuzer, Helmut, ed. *Utopian Vision, Technological Innovation and Poetic Imagination.* Heidelberg: Winter; 1990. 130 pp. (RSieg 91.) [†Treatment of extraterrestrial life.]

[2179] Guthke, Karl S.; Atkins, Helen, tr. *The Last Frontier: Imagining Other Worlds, from the Copernican Revolution to Modern Science Fiction.* Ithaca: Cornell UP; 1990. xii, 402 pp. [Tr. of 1983 Bibliog. IV.2904.]

[2180] Hollinger, Veronica. "Feminist Science Fiction: Breaking Up the Subject." *Extrapolation.* 1990 Fall; 31(3): 229-239. [†By feminist writers. Subjectivity; relationship to humanism; Postmodernism.]

[2181] Jameson, Fredric. "Critical Agendas." *SFS.* 1990 Mar.; 17(1 [50]): 93-102. [On Slusser, George E., ed.; Rabkin, Eric. S., ed. *Aliens: The Anthropology of Science Fiction*; Slusser, George E., ed.; Greenland, Colin, ed.; Rabkin, Eric S. ed. *Storm Warnings: Science Fiction Confronts the Future*; & Del Buffa, Giuseppa Saccaro, ed.; Lewis, Arthur, ed. *Utopie per gli anni Ottanta: Studi interdisciplinari sui temi, la storia, i progetti.* †Review article.]

[2182] Moskowitz, Sam. "The Origins of Science Fiction Fandom: A Reconstruction." *Foundation.* 1990 Spring; 48: 5-25. [†1800-1999. Role of periodicals; relationship to fans in United States. Publishing history.]

[2183] Schafer, William J. "On Being Read by Science Fiction." *NER.* 1990 Summer; 12(4): 387-394.

[2184] Westfahl, Gary; Aldiss, Brian, reply; Stableford, Brian, reply; James, Edward, reply. "On the True History of Science Fiction." *Foundation.* 1989-1990 Winter; 47: 5-33. [†Theories of Gernsback, Hugo.]

Utopian fiction

[2185] Dietz, Frank. "The Image of Medicine in Utopian and Dystopian Fiction." 115-126 in Clarke, Bruce, ed.; Aycock, Wendell, ed. *The Body and the Text: Comparative Essays in Literature and Medicine.* Lubbock: Texas Tech UP; 1990. ix, 221 pp. (SCLit 22.) [†And dystopian fiction. 1500-1999. Treatment of medicine.]

[2186] Hadomi, Lea. *Bein Tikva LeSafek: Sippur HaUtopia.* Tel Aviv: HaKibbutz HaMeuchad; 1989. 208 pp.

NOVEL

[2187] Armstrong, Nancy. "The Rise of Feminine Authority in the Novel." 94-112 in Spilka, Mark, ed.; McCracken-Flesher, Caroline, ed. *Why the Novel Matters: A Postmodern Perplex.* Bloomington: Indiana UP; 1990. xi, 388 pp. [†Authority of women.]

[2188] Benczik, Vilmos. "Preskaŭ cent romanoj." *Revuo Orienta.* 1990 June; 71(6): 233-235. [†Esperanto language literature.]

[2189] Bialostosky, Don H. "Booth's Rhetoric, Bakhtin's Dialogics and the Future of Novel Criticism." 22-29 in Spilka, Mark, ed.; McCracken-Flesher, Caroline, ed. *Why the Novel Matters: A Postmodern Perplex.* Bloomington: Indiana UP; 1990. xi, 388 pp. [†Theories of Booth, Wayne Clayson: *The Rhetoric of Fiction* compared to Bakhtin, Mikhail Mikhaĭlovich: *Problemy poétiki Dostoevskogo.*]

[2190] Brady, Patrick. "Unknown Spaces, Far Frontiers: The New World as Anti-Paradise from *Moll Flanders* to *Riders in the Chariot.*" 53-58 in Bauer, Roger, ed.; Fokkema, Douwe, ed.; Graat, Michael de, ed.; Boening, John, ed.; Gillespie, Gerald, ed.; Moog-Grünewald, Maria, ed.; Nemoianu, Virgil, ed.; Ricapito, Joseph, ed.; Schmeling, Manfred, ed.; Thüsen, Joachim von der, ed.; Uhlig, Claus, ed. *Proceedings of the XIIth Congress of the International Comparative Literature Association/Actes du XIIe congrès de l'Association Internationale de Littérature Comparée: München 1988 Munich, II: Space and Boundaries in Literature/Espace et frontières dans la littérature.* Munich: Iudicium; 1990. 606 pp. (Proceedings of the Congress of the International Comparative Literature Association 12: 2.) [†Treatment of New World; relationship to exile; prison.]

[2191] Brennan, Joseph G. "Retort and Bell Jar: Closed Space and Hermetic Transformation in Modernist and Postmodernist Novels." 195-200 in Bauer, Roger, ed.; Fokkema, Douwe, ed.; Graat, Michael de, ed.; Boening, John, ed.; Gillespie, Gerald, ed.; Moog-Grünewald, Maria, ed.; Nemoianu, Virgil, ed.; Ricapito, Joseph, ed.; Schmeling, Manfred, ed.; Thüsen, Joachim von der, ed.; Uhlig, Claus, ed. *Proceedings of the XIIth Congress of the International Comparative Literature Association/Actes du XIIe congrès de l'Association Internationale de Littérature Comparée: München 1988 Munich, II: Space and Boundaries in Literature/Espace et frontières dans la littérature.* Munich: Iudicium; 1990. 606 pp. (Proceedings of the Congress of the International Comparative Literature Association 12: 2.) [†Treatment of enclosure; relationship to Modernism; Postmodernism.]

[2192] Clere, Sarah V. "Great Literature: Not for Adults Only." *MOR.* 1990 Spring; 4: 29-34. [†For children.]

[2193] Cohan, Steven. "Figures beyond the Text: A Theory of Readable Character in the Novel." 113-136 in Spilka, Mark, ed.; McCracken-Flesher, Caroline, ed. *Why the Novel Matters: A Postmodern Perplex.* Bloomington: Indiana UP; 1990. xi, 388 pp. [†Characterization.]

[2194] Duyfhuizen, Bernard. "Mimesis, Authority, and Belief in Narrative Poetics: Toward a Transmission Theory for a Poetics of Fiction." 29-35 in Spilka, Mark, ed.; McCracken-Flesher, Caroline, ed. *Why the Novel Matters: A Postmodern Perplex.* Bloomington: Indiana UP; 1990. xi, 388 pp. [†Relationship to narrative theory.]

[2195] Ebert, Martina. "The Interaction of Subjectivity and Ideology in the Novel." *DAI.* 1990 Apr.; 50(10): 3220A-3221A. [†Subjectivity; relationship to ideology. Dissertation abstract.]

[2196] Enckell, Barbro. "Hjälten, hjältinnan och jag: Det ljuvliga i att läsa adertonhundratalsromaner." *Horisont.* 1990; 37(4): 22-28. [†Treatment of heroine.]

[2197] Epstein, Joseph. "Educated by Novels." *Commentary.* 1989 Aug.; 88(2): 33-39. [On Alter, Robert. *The Pleasures of Reading* & Booth, Wayne C. *The Company We Keep.* †Role of ideology; relationship to treatment in criticism. Review article.]

[2198] Gold, Joseph. "The Function of Fiction: A Biological Model." 270-279 in Spilka, Mark, ed.; McCracken-Flesher, Caroline, ed. *Why the Novel Matters: A Postmodern Perplex.* Bloomington: Indiana UP; 1990. xi, 388 pp. [†Relationship to therapy for reader.]

[2199] Hunter, J. Paul. "Robert Boyle and the Epistemology of the Novel." *ECF.* 1990 July; 2(4): 275-291. [†Relationship to knowledge; epistemology. Theories of Boyle, Robert: *The Christian Virtuoso; Occasional Reflections on Several Subjects.*]

[2200] Jakob, Michael. "Idylle und Roman: ein Vergleich." *Arcadia.* 1989; 24(1): 1-12. [†Treatment of love. Sources in Theocritus: *Idylls.*]

[2201] Jørgensen, Kathrine Sørensen Ravn. "Pour une nouvelle typologie du roman." *CEBAL: Copenhagen School of Economics and Business Administration. Language Department Publications.* 1985; 7: 83-101.

[2202] Kahan, Phyllis. "The Heartbeat of a Novel." *AR.* 1988 Summer; 46(3): 374-382.

[2203] Kaitting, Mary Lou. "Le Seuil interdit." 256-260 in Bauer, Roger, ed.; Fokkema, Douwe, ed.; Graat, Michael de, ed.; Boening, John, ed.; Gillespie, Gerald, ed.; Moog-Grünewald, Maria, ed.; Nemoianu, Virgil, ed.; Ricapito, Joseph, ed.; Schmeling, Manfred, ed.; Thüsen, Joachim von der, ed.; Uhlig, Claus, ed. *Proceedings of the XIIth Congress of the International Comparative Literature Association/Actes du XIIe congrès de l'Association Internationale de Littérature Comparée: München 1988 Munich, II: Space and Boundaries in Literature/Espace et frontières dans la littérature.* Munich: Iudicium; 1990. 606 pp. (Proceedings of the Congress of the International Comparative Literature Association 12: 2.) [†And film. Treatment of threshold; relationship to the sacred; the profane.]

[2204] Kamačo, Georgo. "Originalaj romanoj en Esperanto: Panoramo kaj perspektivoj." *Fonto.* 1990 Feb.; 10(110): 5-11. [See also *Hungara Vivo.* 1989; 24(5): 191-193. †Esperanto language literature.]

[2205] Kaufmann, David Barry. "Answers from the Whirlwind: Chaos, Closure, and the Ends of Narrative." *DAI.* 1990 Dec.; 51(6): 2025A. [†Closure; study example: Richardson, Samuel: *Pamela*; Burney, Frances: *Evelina*; Austen, Jane: *Mansfield Park.* Dissertation abstract.]

[2206] Komar, Kathleen L. "Of Curves and Caves and Culture: Uses of Space by Contemporary Women Writers." 494-499 in Bauer, Roger, ed.; Fokkema, Douwe, ed.; Graat, Michael de, asst. ed.; Aldridge, A. Owen, asst.; Higonnet, Margaret, asst.; Klein, Holger M., asst.; Meisami, Julie Scott, asst.; Rigney, Ann, asst.; Ronen, Ruth, asst.; Sondrup, Steven P., asst.; Templeton, Joan, asst.; Walker, Janet A., asst. *Proceedings of the XIIth Congress of the International Comparative Literature Association/Actes du XIIe congrès de l'Association Internationale de Littérature Comparée: München 1988 Munich, III: Space and Boundaries in Literature (Continuation)/Espace et frontières dans la littérature (suite)*. Munich: Iudicium; 1990. 509 pp. (Proceedings of the Congress of the International Comparative Literature Association 12: 3.) [†By women novelists. Treatment of space.]

[2207] Leps, Marie-Christine. "Discursive Displacements: The Example of Nineteenth-Century Realism." 231-236 in Bauer, Roger, ed.; Fokkema, Douwe, ed.; Graat, Michael de, asst. ed.; Fischer-Lichte, Erika, asst.; Garstin, Marguerite, asst.; Ibsch, Elrud, asst.; Stackelberg, Jürgen von, asst. *Proceedings of the XIIth Congress of the International Comparative Literature Association/Actes du XIIe congrès de l'Association Internationale de Littérature Comparée: München 1988 Munich, V: Space and Boundaries in Literary Theory and Criticism/Espace et frontières dans la critique et la théorie littéraire; Space and Boundaries in the Teaching of General and Comparative Literature/Espace et frontières dans l'enseignement de la littérature générale et comparée*. Munich: Iudicium; 1990. 415 pp. (Proceedings of the Congress of the International Comparative Literature Association 12: 5.) [†1800-1899. Realism.

[2208] Lodge, David. "The Novel Now: Theories and Practices." 143-156 in Spilka, Mark, ed.; McCracken-Flesher, Caroline, ed. *Why the Novel Matters: A Postmodern Perplex*. Bloomington: Indiana UP; 1990. xi, 388 pp. [†Treatment in postmodernist literary theory and criticism.]

[2209] Miller, Nancy K. "Feminist Writing and the History of the Novel." 328-339 in Spilka, Mark, ed.; McCracken-Flesher, Caroline, ed. *Why the Novel Matters: A Postmodern Perplex*. Bloomington: Indiana UP; 1990. xi, 388 pp. [†Treatment in feminist literary theory and criticism.]

[2210] Palmer, R. Burton. "Languages and Power in the Novel: Mapping the Monologic." *SLitI*. 1990 Spring; 23(1): 99-127. [†Monologism. Theories of Bakhtin, Mikhail Mikhaïlovich.]

[2211] Pearce, Richard. "The Present and Future States of Novel Criticism: Our Two-Headed Profession." 35-39 in Spilka, Mark, ed.; McCracken-Flesher, Caroline, ed. *Why the Novel Matters: A Postmodern Perplex*. Bloomington: Indiana UP; 1990. xi, 388 pp. [†Treatment in postmodernist literary theory and criticism.]

[2212] Petruso, Thomas Francesco. "Characterization in the Novel since Proust and Joyce." *DAI*. 1990 Nov.; 51(5): 1605A. [†Characterization. Dissertation abstract.]

[2213] Radner, Hilary. "Extra-Curricular Activities: Women Writers and the Readerly Text." 251-267 in Broe, Mary Lynn, ed.; Ingram, Angela, ed. *Women's Writing in Exile*. Chapel Hill: U of North Carolina P; 1989. xii, 442 pp. [†By women novelists. 1900-1999. Treatment of exile in academia. Application of theories of Barthes, Roland: *S/Z*.]

[2214] Roof, Judith. "The Match in the Crocus: Representations of Lesbian Sexuality." 100-116 in Barr, Marleen S., ed.; Feldstein, Richard, ed. *Discontented Discourses: Feminism/Textual Intervention/Psychoanalysis*. Urbana: U of Illinois P; 1989. 250 pp. [†1900-1999. Treatment of lesbianism. Feminist approach.]

[2215] Sabatini, Arthur J. "Performance Novels: Notes toward an Extension of Bakhtin's Theories of Genre and the Novel." *DS/SD*. 1990 Spring-Summer; 3(1-2): 135-145. [†Relationship to the real; performance. Theories of Bakhtin, Mikhail Mikhaïlovich.]

[2216] Scholes, Robert. "The Novel as Ethical Paradigm?" 206-214 in Spilka, Mark, ed.; McCracken-Flesher, Caroline, ed. *Why the Novel Matters: A Postmodern Perplex*. Bloomington: Indiana UP; 1990. xi, 388 pp. [†Role of ethics.]

[2217] Schwartz, Murray. "Beyond Fantasy: The Novel as Play." 280-283 in Spilka, Mark, ed.; McCracken-Flesher, Caroline, ed. *Why the Novel Matters: A Postmodern Perplex*. Bloomington: Indiana UP; 1990. xi, 388 pp. [†Role of play.]

[2218] Schwarz, Daniel R. "The Case for a Humanistic Poetics." 39-61 in Spilka, Mark, ed.; McCracken-Flesher, Caroline, ed. *Why the Novel Matters: A Postmodern Perplex*. Bloomington: Indiana UP; 1990. xi, 388 pp. [†Treatment in criticism.]

[2219] ———. "The Ethics of Reading: The Case for Pluralistic and Transactional Reading." 215-236 in Spilka, Mark, ed.; McCracken-Flesher, Caroline, ed. *Why the Novel Matters: A Postmodern Perplex*. Bloomington: Indiana UP; 1990. xi, 388 pp. [†Rhetoric; relationship to narrative theory.]

[2220] Singer, Alan. "The Voice of History/The Subject of the Novel." 191-197 in Spilka, Mark, ed.; McCracken-Flesher, Caroline, ed. *Why the Novel Matters: A Postmodern Perplex*. Bloomington: Indiana UP; 1990. xi, 388 pp.

[2221] Škulj, Jola. "The Modern Novel: The Concept of Spatialization (Frank) and the Dialogic Principle (Bakhtin)." 43-50 in Bauer, Roger, ed.; Fokkema, Douwe, ed.; Graat, Michael de, asst. ed.; Fischer-Lichte, Erika, asst.; Garstin, Marguerite, asst.; Ibsch, Elrud, asst.; Stackelberg, Jürgen von, asst. *Proceedings of the XIIth Congress of the International Comparative Literature Association/Actes du XIIe congrès de l'Association Internationale de Littérature Comparée: München 1988 Munich, V: Space and Boundaries in Literary Theory and Criticism/Espace et frontières dans la critique et la théorie littéraire; Space and Boundaries in the Teaching of General and Comparative Literature/Espace et frontières dans l'enseignement de la littérature générale et comparée*. Munich: Iudicium; 1990. 415 pp. (Proceedings of the Congress of the International Comparative Literature Association 12: 5.) [†Spatial form compared to dialogism. Theories of Frank, Joseph compared to Bakhtin, Mikhail Mikhaïlovich.]

[2222] Spacks, Patricia. "The Novel as Ethical Paradigm." 199-206 in Spilka, Mark, ed.; McCracken-Flesher, Caroline, ed. *Why the Novel Matters: A Postmodern Perplex*. Bloomington: Indiana UP; 1990. xi, 388 pp. [†Role of ethics.]

[2223] Spilka, Mark. "Still towards a Poetics of Fiction? No—and Then Again Yes." 15-22 in Spilka, Mark, ed.; McCracken-Flesher, Caroline, ed. *Why the Novel Matters: A Postmodern Perplex*. Bloomington: Indiana UP; 1990. xi, 388 pp. [†Relationship to narrative theory.]

[2224] Spilka, Mark, ed.; McCracken-Flesher, Caroline, ed. *Why the Novel Matters: A Postmodern Perplex*. Bloomington: Indiana UP; 1990. xi, 388 pp. [Incl. introd.]

[2225] Suleiman, Susan Rubin. "Playing and Modernity." 284-292 in Spilka, Mark, ed.; McCracken-Flesher, Caroline, ed. *Why the Novel Matters: A Postmodern Perplex*. Bloomington: Indiana UP; 1990. xi, 388 pp. [†Relationship to therapy for reader.]

[2226] Tölölyan, Khachig. "Discoursing with Culture: The Novel as Interlocutor." 246-256 in Spilka, Mark, ed.; McCracken-Flesher, Caroline, ed. *Why the Novel Matters: A Postmodern Perplex*. Bloomington: Indiana UP; 1990. xi, 388 pp.

[2227] Torgovnick, Marianna. "The Present and Future States of Novel Criticism: A Hopeful Overview." 12-15 in Spilka, Mark, ed.; McCracken-Flesher, Caroline, ed. *Why the Novel Matters: A Postmodern Perplex*. Bloomington: Indiana UP; 1990. xi, 388 pp.

[2228] Vargas Llosa, Mario. "Historicismo y ficción." *Suplemento Literario La Nación* (Buenos Aires). 1990 Feb. 4: 1. [†1900-1999. Relationship to history.]

[2229] Walker, Janet A. "On the Applicability of the Term 'Novel' to Modern Non-Western Long Fiction." *YCGL*. 1988; 37: 47-68.

[2230] West, Catherine Jones. "La Mise en jeu de l'autorité dans la préface de roman." *DAI*. 1990 Apr.; 50(10): 3219A. [†Authorial voice in preface. Dissertation abstract.]

Popular romance novel

[2231] Bettinotti, Julia. "Répétition et invention dans le roman d'amour: L'Evolution des collections Harlequin." 201-208 in Constans, Ellen, ed. *Le Roman sentimental*. Limoges: Univ. de Limoges; 1990. 426 pp. (Travaux et Mémoires.) [†Plot in Harlequin Romances.]

[2232] Giet, Sylvette. "Un Récit sentimental en images: Le Roman-dessiné." 81-92 in Constans, Ellen, ed. *Le Roman sentimental*. Limoges: Univ. de Limoges; 1990. 426 pp. (Travaux et Mémoires.) [†Plot. Sources in film of Hollywood.]

[2233] Houel, Annik. "L'Amant Harlequin." 277-283 in Constans, Ellen, ed. *Le Roman sentimental*. Limoges: Univ. de Limoges; 1990. 426 pp. (Travaux et Mémoires.) [†Treatment of love; relationship to stereotypes; study example: Harlequin Romances.]

[2234] Moffitt, Mary Anne Smeltzer. "Understanding Middle-Class Adolescent Leisure: A Cultural Studies Approach to Romance Novel Reading." *DAI*. 1990 Oct.; 51(4): 1035A. [†Relationship to adolescents and leisure. Dissertation abstract.]

[2235] Noizet, Pascale. "Naissance du roman d'amour de grande consommation: Harlequin à la recherche de ses aïeux." 95-100 in Constans, Ellen, ed. *Le Roman sentimental*. Limoges: Univ. de Limoges; 1990. 426 pp. (Travaux et Mémoires.) [†Study example: Harlequin Romances. Sources in Ohnet, Georges; Richardson, Samuel; Austen, Jane.]

[2236] Péquignot, Bruno. "Le Roman sentimental, un objet pour quelle sociologie?" 185-198 in Constans, Ellen, ed. *Le Roman sentimental*. Limoges: Univ. de Limoges; 1990. 426 pp. (Travaux et Mémoires.) [†Relationship to women; ideology; treatment in sociological literary theory and criticism.]

[2237] Raabe, Juliette. "Impossibles rêves d'amour." 239-251 in Constans, Ellen, ed. *Le Roman sentimental*. Limoges: Univ. de Limoges; 1990. 426 pp. (Travaux et Mémoires.) [†Treatment of love; relationship to myth; legend.]

Bildungsroman

[2238] Redfield, Marc. "The Politics of Reception: Aesthetic Ideology and the *Bildungsroman*." *DAI*. 1990 Oct.; 51(4): 1222A. [†Relationship to aesthetics. Dissertation abstract.]

Detective novel

[2239] Bauer, Stefan. "Das wahrscheinliche Unwahrscheinliche: Realitätsansprüche in der Kriminalliteratur." *Arcadia*. 1989; 24(3): 284-296. [†Realism.]

[2240] Christianson, Scott R. "A Heap of Broken Images: Hardboiled Detective Fiction and the Discourse(s) of Modernity." 135-148 in Walker, Ronald G., ed.; Frazer, June M., ed.; Anderson, David R., afterword. *The Cunning Craft: Original Essays on Detective Fiction and Contemporary Literary Theory*. Macomb: Western Illinois Univ.; 1990. vii, 203 pp. (Essays in Literature.) [†Hard-boiled detective novel. Relationship to Modernism; study example: Chandler, Raymond; Eliot, T. S.: *The Waste Land*.]

[2241] Hilfer, Tony. *The Crime Novel: A Deviant Genre*. Austin: U of Texas P; 1990. xiv, 180 pp.

Dystopian novel

[2242] Barclay, Michael W. "Utopia/Dystopia/Atopia: A Dissertation on Psychopathology and Utopian Thinking." *DAI*. 1990 Dec.; 51(6): 3111B. [†1900-1999. Influence on theories of psychology. Dissertation abstract.]

Modernist novel

[2243] Krysinski, Wladimir. "Bakhtin and the Evolution of the Post-Dostoevskian Novel." *DS/SD*. 1990 Spring-Summer; 3(1-2): 109-134. [†Dialogue; relationship to Dostoevskiĭ, Fëdor Mikhaĭlovich: *Zapiski iz podpol'ia*. Application of theories of Bakhtin, Mikhail Mikhaĭlovich.]

Roman à thèse

[2244] Robin, Régine. "Le réalisme socialiste devant la théorie littéraire." 181-193 in Valdés, Mario J., ed. *Toward a Theory of Comparative Literature: Selected Papers Presented in the Division of Theory of Literature at the XIth International Comparative Literature Congress.* New York: Peter Lang; 1990. 275 pp. (Proceedings of the International Comparative Literature Association 11: 3.) [†Relationship to socialist realism.]

Sentimental novel

[2245] Constans, Ellen, ed. *Le Roman sentimental.* Actes du Colloque des 14-16 mars 1989. Limoges: Univ. de Limoges; 1990. 426 pp. (Travaux et Mémoires.) [†And popular romance novel.]

[2246] Reuter, Yves. "Le Roman sentimental: Système des personnages et circulation sociale de la thématique amoureuse." 209-223 in Constans, Ellen, ed. *Le Roman sentimental.* Limoges: Univ. de Limoges; 1990. 426 pp. (Travaux et Mémoires.) [†Characterization; plot. Treatment of love.]

[2247] Robert, Raymonde. "Jalons pour une étude du traitement des topoi romanesques dans le roman sentimental." 13-27 in Constans, Ellen, ed. *Le Roman sentimental.* Limoges: Univ. de Limoges; 1990. 426 pp. (Travaux et Mémoires.) [†Treatment of seduction.]

[2248] Robine, Nicole. "La Réception du roman sentimental: Enquête auprès des lecteurs." 327-340 in Constans, Ellen, ed. *Le Roman sentimental.* Limoges: Univ. de Limoges; 1990. 426 pp. (Travaux et Mémoires.) [†Reception study. Sociological approach.]

[2249] Weil, Françoise. "La Lecture du roman sentimental dans les bibliothèques publiques: L'Exemple de Dijon." 317-325 in Constans, Ellen, ed. *Le Roman sentimental.* Limoges: Univ. de Limoges; 1990. 426 pp. (Travaux et Mémoires.) [†Reception study: reception in France: Dijon.]

Social novel

[2250] Grimm, Reinhold R. "Der romantische Sozialroman als Paradigma des Art Social." 85-124 in Claeys, Gregory, ed.; Glage, Liselotte, ed. *Radikalismus in Literatur und Gesellschaft des 19. Jahrhunderts.* Frankfurt: Peter Lang; 1987. 316 pp. (Aspekte der Englischen Geistes- und Kulturgeschichte/Aspects of English Intellectual, Cultural, and Literary History 11.)

War novel

[2251] Fréris, Georges. "L'Espace réel et imaginaire dans le roman de guerre." 228-233 in Bauer, Roger, ed.; Fokkema, Douwe, ed.; Graat, Michael de, asst. ed.; Aldridge, A. Owen, asst.; Higonnet, Margaret, asst.; Klein, Holger M., asst.; Meisami, Julie Scott, asst.; Rigney, Ann, asst.; Ronen, Ruth, asst.; Sondrup, Steven P., asst.; Templeton, Joan, asst.; Walker, Janet A., asst. *Proceedings of the XIIth Congress of the International Comparative Literature Association/Actes du XIIe congrès de l'Association Internationale de Littérature Comparée: München 1988 Munich, III: Space and Boundaries in Literature (Continuation)/Espace et frontières dans la littérature (suite).* Munich: Iudicium; 1990. 509 pp. (Proceedings of the Congress of the International Comparative Literature Association 12: 3.) [†Treatment of space.]

POETRY

[2252] Antin, David. "The Stranger at the Door." 229-247 in Perloff, Marjorie, ed.; Davis, Robert Con, fwd.; Schleifer, Ronald, fwd. *Postmodern Genres.* Norman: U of Oklahoma P; 1989. xx, 276 pp. (Oklahoma Project for Discourse and Theory.) [See also 1988 Bibliog. IV.2467.]

[2253] Atkinson, David W. "Fullness and Silence: Poetry and the Sacred Word." 189-204 in Blodgett, E. D., ed.; Coward, H. G., ed. *Silence, the Word and the Sacred.* Waterloo: Wilfrid Laurier UP for Calgary Inst. for the Humanities; 1989. xii, 226 pp. [†Treatment of the sacred.]

[2254] Barrento, João. "Die Zeit als Ort: Das erzählerische Paradigma im zeitgenössischen Gedicht." 57-61 in Bauer, Roger, ed.; Fokkema, Douwe, ed.; Graat, Michael de, asst. ed.; Aldridge, A. Owen, asst.; Higonnet, Margaret, asst.; Klein, Holger M., asst.; Meisami, Julie Scott, asst.; Rigney, Ann, asst.; Ronen, Ruth, asst.; Sondrup, Steven P., asst.; Templeton, Joan, asst.; Walker, Janet A., asst. *Proceedings of the XIIth Congress of the International Comparative Literature Association/Actes du XIIe congrès de l'Association Internationale de Littérature Comparée: München 1988 Munich, III: Space and Boundaries in Literature (Continuation)/Espace et frontières dans la littérature (suite).* Munich: Iudicium; 1990. 509 pp. (Proceedings of the Congress of the International Comparative Literature Association 12: 3.) [†Narrative time; relationship to Postmodernism.]

[2255] Bedient, Calvin. "Kristeva and Poetry as Shattered Signification." *CritI.* 1990 Summer; 16(4): 807-829. [†Treatment of the chora; relationship to representation. Theories of Kristeva, Julia: *Révolution du langage poétique*.]

[2256] Berge, Claude; Larsen, Kevin S., tr. "Matemática e Literatura: Algunas Novas Interferências/Mathematics and Literature: Some New Interferences." *Ometeca.* 1989-1990; 1(2)-2(1): 144-164. [†Relationship to mathematics.]

[2257] Bernhart, Walter. "Setting a Poem: The Composer's Choice for or against Interpretation." *YCGL.* 1988; 37: 32-46. [†Relationship to musical setting.]

[2258] Blaser, Robin. "Poetry and Positivisms: High-Muck-a-Muck or 'Spiritual Ketchup'." 21-50 in Blodgett, E. D., ed.; Coward, H. G., ed. *Silence, the Word and the Sacred.* Waterloo: Wilfrid Laurier UP for Calgary Inst. for the Humanities; 1989. xii, 226 pp.

[2259] Blodgett, E. D. "Sublations: Silence in Poetic and Sacred Discourse." 207-220 in Blodgett, E. D., ed.; Coward, H. G., ed. *Silence, the Word and the Sacred.* Waterloo: Wilfrid Laurier UP for Calgary Inst. for the Humanities; 1989. xii, 226 pp. [†Treatment of the sacred.]

[2260] Carr, Timothy. "La lingvo, la poet' kaj la cetero …." *LFoiro.* 1990 Oct.; 21(127): 10-18. [†Esperanto language literature.]

[2261] Chapman, Michael. "The Voice of Poetry, IX: Poetry and City." *CRUX.* 1989 May; 23(2): 8-19. [†City poetry.]

[2262] ——. "The Voice of Poetry, V: Poetry and Nature." *CRUX.* 1988 Apr.; 22(2): 41-50. [†Treatment of nature.]

[2263] ——. "The Voice of Poetry, VI: Poetry and Science." *CRUX.* 1988 Jan.; 22(1): 15-24. [†Relationship to science. Theories of Snow, C. P.]

[2264] Clampitt, Amy. "What Comes Up Out of the Ground: On Budenz, Heaney, Ashbery, and Others." 263-268 in McCorkle, James, ed. *Conversant Essays: Contemporary Poets on Poetry.* Detroit: Wayne State UP; 1990. 588 pp.

[2265] Deguy, Michel. "Motifs pour une poétique émotive." *FSSA.* 1990; 19: 1-10.

[2266] Dishon, Yehudit, ed.; Hazan, Ephraim, ed. *Pirkei Shira: From the Hidden Treasures of Jewish Poetry.* Jerusalem: Bar Ilan Univ. & Missgav Yerushalayim; 1990. 166 pp. [†By Jewish poets.]

[2267] Esteban, Claude; Asiain, Aurelio, tr. "Crítica de la razón poética: Las palabras de la preocupación." *Vuelta.* 1990 Sept.; 14(166): 9-13. [†Poetic language.]

[2268] Fjodorov, Aleksandr. "Al tempo fluanta vertikale." *Gazeto.* 1990 Dec.; 6(1 [31]): 15-20. [On 1988 Bib. IV.2538. †Esperanto language literature. Structuralist approach. Review article.]

[2269] Friggieri, Oliver. "Eternal and Contemporary Poetic Themes." *Boletim: Centro de Letras e Ciências Humanas.* 1990 Jan.-June; 18: 21-27.

[2270] Greenberg, Mark L. "Eighteenth-Century Poetry Represents Moments of Scientific Discovery: Appropriation and Generic Transformation." 115-137 in Peterfreund, Stuart, ed. *Literature and Science: Theory & Practice.* Boston: Northeastern UP; 1990. vi, 248 pp. [†1700-1799. Relationship to science.]

[2271] Hazen, Edith P., ed.; Fryer, Deborah J., ed. *The Columbia Granger's Index to Poetry.* New York: Columbia UP; 1990. xxviii, 2082 pp. [9th rev. ed. †Index.]

[2272] Jaggi, Satya Dev. "The Language of Poetry with Special Reference to the Critical Writings of I. A. Richards." *DAI.* 1990 Nov.; 51(5): 1601A. [†Poetic language. Application of theories of Richards, I. A. Dissertation abstract.]

[2273] Jaskoski, Helen. "Poetry Therapy: A Problem of Definition." *American Journal of Social Psychiatry.* 1987 Spring; 7(2): 125-127. [†As therapy; relationship to psychiatry.]

[2274] Jung, Willi. "Über Grundlagen und Methoden der Gedichtinterpretation—eine bibliographische Dokumentation." *NS.* 1990 Apr.; 89(2): 199-216. [†Includes bibliography.]

[2275] Jurado Valencia, Fabio. "Lenguaje y poesía." *GlottaC.* 1989 Sept.-Dec.; 4(3): 40-45. [†Poetic language. Interview with García Maffla, Jaime.]

[2276] Konstantinović, Radivoje. "Kontekst u pesnichkom prevodu." *Mostovi.* 1987 Oct.-Dec.; 18(4 [72]): 450-452. [†On translation.]

[2277] Krieger, Murray. "The Semiotic Desire for the Natural Sign: Poetic Uses and Political Abuses." 221-253 in Carroll, David, ed. *The States of "Theory": History, Art, and Critical Discourse.* New York: Columbia UP; 1990. x, 316 pp. (Irvine Studies in the Humanities.) [†Rhetoric compared to political discourse. Semiotic approach.]

[2278] Landa, Josu. "Meditaciones sobre poesía y verdad." *Osamayor.* 1990 Winter; 2(3): 12-33. [†Relationship to truth.]

[2279] Laurent Catrice, Nicole. "El decir y el no-decir en la poesía." *Gaceta de Cuba.* 1990 June: 10-11. [†Poetic language.]

[2280] Long, Kris. "Memstarigi." *Gazeto.* 1990 Mar. 15; 5(3 [27]): 13-19. [†Esperanto language literature.]

[2281] ——. "Sub dubnub' … aŭ pretere?" *LFoiro.* 1990 Oct.; 21(127): 40-42. [†Esperanto language literature.]

[2282] Mills-Courts, Karen. *Poetry as Epitaph: Representation and Poetic Language.* Baton Rouge: Louisiana State UP; 1990. x, 326 pp. [†As epitaph; relationship to representation.]

[2283] Monaghan, Patricia. "'She Want It All': The Sun Goddess in Contemporary Women's Poetry." *Frontiers.* 1990; 11(2-3): 21-25. [†By women poets. Treatment of sun goddess.]

[2284] Mooij, J. J. A. "Sculpture as an Emblem of Poetry." 508-513 in Bauer, Roger, ed.; Fokkema, Douwe, ed.; Graat, Michael de, asst. ed.; Kaiser, Gerhard, asst.; Rinner, Fridrun, asst.; Wertheimer, Jürgen, asst. *Proceedings of the XIIth Congress of the International Comparative Literature Association/Actes du XIIe congrès de l'Association Internationale de Littérature Comparée: München 1988 Munich, IV: Space and Boundaries of Literature/Espace et frontières de la littérature.* Munich: Iudicium; 1990. 651 pp. (Proceedings of the Congress of the International Comparative Literature Association 12: 4.) [†1800-1999. Treatment of sculpture.]

[2285] Nims, John Frederick. *Poems in Translation: Sappho to Valéry.* Fayetteville: U of Arkansas P; 1990. xviii, 415 pp. [Rev. & enl. ed.; introd., 1-18. †Multilingual anthology.]

[2286] Oliver, Douglas. "Ah, Desire." *Talisman.* 1990 Fall; 5: 3-7. [†Relationship to desire.]

[2287] Parisot, J.; Cart, Th. *Esperanto verstarado kaj rimado, laŭ verkoj de d-ro Zamenhof kaj aliaj aŭtoroj.* Saarbrucken: Iltis; 1990. 41 pp. [Rpt. of 2nd ed., 1909. †Esperanto language literature. Prosody; rhyme.]

[2288] Paz, Octavio. "La otra voz: Poesía y fin de siglo." *Vuelta.* 1990 Nov.; 14(168): 13-17. [†Relationship to modernity.]

[2289] Ramos, Oscar Gerardo. "La poesía, ministerio del hombre." *BAC.* 1984 Apr.-June; 34(144): 102-109.

[2290] Richter, David H. "Dialogism and Poetry." *SLitI*. 1990 Spring; 23(1): 9-27. [†Dialogism. Application of theories of Bakhtin, Mikhail Mikhaĭlovich.]

[2291] Santos, Fernando Brandão dos. "O Canto dos Helenos." *RDLet*. 1989; 29: 97-102. [Eng. sum. †Relationship to tragedy. Sources in Ancient Greek literature.

[2292] Schenck, Celeste M. "Exiled by Genre: Modernism, Canonicity, and the Politics of Exclusion." 225-250 in Broe, Mary Lynn, ed.; Ingram, Angela, ed. *Women's Writing in Exile*. Chapel Hill: U of North Carolina P; 1989. xii, 442 pp. [†By women poets. 1900-1999. Treatment of exile.]

[2293] Segarra Montaner, Marta. "El ritmo, un descubrimiento antropológico y poético." 529-534 in Menchacatorre, Félix, ed. *Ensayos de literatura europea e hispanoamericana*. San Sebastián: Univ. del País Vasco; 1990. xvi, 605 pp. [†Rhythm.]

[2294] Shapir, Maksim. "Metrum et rhythmus sub specie semiotical." *Daugava*. 1990 Oct.; 10(160): 63-82. [†Rhythm; meter; relationship to semantics. Theories of Tomashevskiĭ, Boris Viktorovich.]

[2295] Smith, Gerard Michael. "Sound Foundations: Music, Language and Poetry." *DAI*. 1990 Feb.; 50(8): 2298A. [†Sound; relationship to music. Dissertation abstract.]

[2296] Spinner, Bettye Tyson. "A Study of Academic and Nonacademic Experiences That Promote and Sustain Adult Interest in the Reading and Writing of Poetry." *DAI*. 1990 Aug.; 51(2): 439A. [†Dissertation abstract.]

[2297] Steele, Timothy. *Missing Measures: Modern Poetry and the Revolt against Meter*. Fayetteville: U of Arkansas P; 1990. x, 340 pp. [†Meter.]

[2298] Strydom, Leon. "The Function of Inter-Stanzaic Space: A Logical Analysis." 491-496 in Bauer, Roger, ed.; Fokkema, Douwe, ed.; Graat, Michael de, asst. ed.; Kaiser, Gerhard, asst.; Rinner, Fridrun, asst.; Wertheimer, Jürgen, asst. *Proceedings of the XIIth Congress of the International Comparative Literature Association/Actes du XIe congrès de l'Association Internationale de Littérature Comparée: München 1988 Munich, IV: Space and Boundaries of Literature/Espace et frontières de la littérature*. Munich: Iudicium; 1990. 651 pp. (Proceedings of the Congress of the International Comparative Literature Association 12: 4.) [†Stanzas; relationship to spatial form.]

[2299] Vaughn, M. Lynn. "The Experience of Writing Poetry: An Heuristic Investigation." *DAI*. 1990 Dec.; 51(6): 3116B. [†Creative process. Psychological approach. Dissertation abstract.]

[2300] Walker, Noojin; Walker, Martha Fulton. *The Twain Meet: The Physical Sciences and Poetry*. New York: Peter Lang; 1989. 303 pp. (GenL 23.) [†Relationship to science.]

[2301] Warren, Russelle, ed.; Depew, Chauncey M., introd.; Miller, J. Wesley, ed. *The Lawyer's Alcove: Poems by the Lawyer, for the Lawyer and about the Lawyer*. Buffalo: Hein; 1990. [Rev. ed. †Relationship to law.]

[2302] Weiss, David. "Refusing to Name the Animals." *GettR*. 1990 Winter; 3(1): 233-241. [†Naming.]

[2303] Weller, Suzanne Currier. "La Sémiologie musicale dans la poésie." *DAI*. 1990 July; 51(1): 161A. [†Relationship to music. Semiotic approach. Application of theories of Saussure, Ferdinand de. Dissertation abstract.]

[2304] Wishbow, Nina Ann. "Studies of Creativity in Poets." *DAI*. 1990 Aug.; 51(2): 491A. [†Relationship to creativity. Dissertation abstract.]

Concrete poetry

[2305] Vos, Eric. "On Concrete Poetry and a 'Classification of the Visual in Literature'." *Restant*. 1990; 18(1): 241-280. [†Relationship to the visual. Application of theories of Stevenson, Charles Leslie.]

Epic poetry

[2306] Bakker, Egbert J. "Homerus als orale poezie." *Lampas: Tijdschrift voor Nederlandse Classici*. 1990 Nov.-Dec.; 23(4-5): 384-405. [†Hexameter in oral poetry. Sources in Homer. Application of theories of Parry, Milman.]

[2307] Hainsworth, J. B., ed.; Hatto, A. T., gen. ed. *Traditions of Heroic and Epic Poetry, II: Characteristics and Techniques*. London: Mod. Humanities Research Assn.; 1989. vii, 319 pp. (Publications of the Modern Humanities Research Association 13.) [Incl. introd.]

[2308] Hatto, A. T. "Towards an Anatomy of Heroic/Epic Poetry." 145-306 in Hainsworth, J. B., ed.; Hatto, A. T., gen. ed. *Traditions of Heroic and Epic Poetry, II: Characteristics and Techniques*. London: Mod. Humanities Research Assn.; 1989. vii, 319 pp. (Publications of the Modern Humanities Research Association 13.)

Lyric poetry

[2309] García Berrio, Antonio. "La Lecture lyrique." *Versus*. 1989 Jan.-May; 52-53: 71-80. [†Application of reader-response theory and criticism.]

[2310] Miller, Paul Allen. "Lyric Texts and Lyric Consciousness." *DAI*. 1990 Mar.; 50(9): 2890A.

[2311] Villegas, Juan. "Para una historia diversificada de la lírica." *TCrit*. 1988 July-Dec.; 14(39): 3-11.

Lyrics

[2312] Wilhelm, James J., ed. *Lyrics of the Middle Ages: An Anthology*. New York: Garland; 1990. xix, 341 pp. (GRLH 1268.) [Illus. †Middle Ages. Anthology.]

Pastoral poetry

[2313] Downing, Gregory Marshall. "Pastoral in Early Christianity from the Gospels to Theodolus: A Sample of an Analytic History of Pastoralism in Culture." *DAI*. 1990 Mar.; 50(9): 2888A. [†Relationship to culture. Dissertation abstract.]

Postmodernist poetry

[2314] Davidson, Michael. "Palimtexts: Postmodern Poetry and the Material Text." 75-95 in Perloff, Marjorie, ed.; Davis, Robert Con, fwd.; Schleifer, Ronald, fwd. *Postmodern Genres*. Norman: U of Oklahoma P; 1989. xx, 276 pp. (Oklahoma Project for Discourse and Theory.) [See also 1988 Bibliog. IV.2597. †Intertextuality.]

PROSE

[2315] Rubio Tovar, Joaquín. "Síntoma y justificación del prólogo." *RO*. 1990 May; 108: 97-109. [†Preface.]

[2316] Winterowd, W. Ross. "Reading (and Rehabilitating) the Literature of Fact." *RhetRev*. 1989 Fall; 8(1): 44-59. [†Relationship to *belles-lettres*.]

Autobiographical prose

[2317] Heinzelman, Susan Sage. "Women's Petty Treason: Feminism, Narrative, and the Law." *JNT*. 1990 Spring; 20(2): 89-106. [†And fiction; representation of women; legal discourse (1700-1899).]

Devotional literature

[2318] Beeck, F. J. van. "A Note on Two Liturgical Greetings and the People's Reply." *Ephemerides Liturgicae* (Rome). 1989 Nov.-Dec.; 103(6): 519-522. [Lat. sum. †Treatment of liturgical formulas. Sources in Chrysostom, John: *De Sancta Pentecoste*; Theodore of Mopsuestia: *Homiliae Catecheticae*; Pseudo-Epiphanius of Salamis: *Homilia in Diuini Corporis Sepulturam*.]

[2319] Foley, Edward. "The *Libri Ordinarii*: An Introduction." *Ephemerides Liturgicae* (Rome). 1988 Mar.-Apr.; 102(2): 129-137. [Lat. sum. †Liturgical literature.]

[2320] Gibert Tarruel, Jordi. "L'uso della *Liturgia Horarum* romana nelle comunità monastiche e contemplative." *Ephemerides Liturgicae* (Rome). 1990 Nov.-Dec.; 104(6): 415-461. [Lat. sum.]

[2321] Ramis, Gabriel. "La bendición de las viudas en las liturgias occidentales." *Ephemerides Liturgicae* (Rome). 1990 Mar.-June; 104(2-3): 159-175. [Lat. sum. †Treatment of blessing of widow. Sources in Hippolytus: *Traditio Apostolica*.]

Diary

[2322] Cardinal, Roger. "Unlocking the Diary." *CCrit*. 1990; 12: 71-87. [†Role of writing; relationship to the self.]

Essay

[2323] Atkins, G. Douglas. "The Return of/to the Essay." *ADEB*. 1990 Fall; 96: 11-18.

[2324] Faery, Rebecca Blevins. "On the Possibilities of the Essay: A Meditation." *IowaR*. 1990 Spring-Summer; 20(2): 19-27.

[2325] Hardison, O. B., Jr. "Binding Proteus: An Essay on the Essay." *SR*. 1988 Fall; 96(4): 610-632.

[2326] Klaus, Carl H. "On Virginia Woolf on the Essay." *IowaR*. 1990 Spring-Summer; 20(2): 28-34. [†Treatment in Woolf, Virginia: "The Modern Essay."]

Historiography

[2327] Foresta, Gaetano. "Il mondo epico, esotico, favoloso nei cronisti del nuovo mondo." *Prometeo*. 1989 Jan.-Mar.; 9(33): 11-25. [†Treatment of New World.]

[2328] Hutcheon, Linda. "'The Pastime of Past Time': Fiction, History, Historiographic Metafiction." 54-74 in Perloff, Marjorie, ed.; Davis, Robert Con, fwd.; Schleifer, Ronald, fwd. *Postmodern Genres*. Norman: U of Oklahoma P; 1989. xx, 276 pp. (Oklahoma Project for Discourse and Theory.) [See also 1988 Bibliog. IV.2376. †1900-1999. Compared to metafiction.]

[2329] Jacques, T. Carlos. "The Primacy of Narrative in Historical Understanding." *ClioI*. 1990 Spring; 19(3): 197-214. [†Narrative.]

[2330] Kemp, Anthony Maynard Francis. "The Estrangement of the Past: Reformation Historiography and the Origins of Modern Historical Consciousness." *DAI*. 1990 Apr.; 50(10): 3221A. [†Dissertation abstract.]

[2331] Levine, Robert M. "Historical Writing and Visual Imagery: Photographs as Documents." *Restant*. 1990; 18(1): 45-72. [Illus. †Use of photographs as documentation; relationship to visual imagery.]

[2332] Ostrowski, Donald. "A Metahistorical Analysis: Hayden White and Four Narratives of 'Russian' History." *ClioI*. 1990 Spring; 19(3): 215-236. [†Relationship to Russian history. Narrative. Theories of White, Hayden V.: *Metahistory*.]

[2333] Stern, Laurent; Fain, Haskell, reply. "Narrative versus Description in Historiography." *NLH*. 1990 Spring; 21(3): 555-577. [Incl. rejoinder. †Narrative.]

Letters

[2334] Ivask, Ivar. "The Letter: A Dying Art?" *WLT*. 1990 Spring; 64(2): 213-214. [†By European writers.]

[2335] Moriarty, Catherine, comp. *The Voice of the Middle Ages in Personal Letters 1100-1500*. New York: Peter Bedrick; 1990. 331 pp. [†Middle Ages. Anthology.]

Philosophical prose

[2336] Berni, Stefano. "La filosofia come genere di racconto." *Ponte*. 1990 Nov.; 46(11): 103-111. [†Relationship to narrative.]

Preface

[2337] Dunn, Walter Kevin. "'To the Gentle Reader': Prefatory Rhetoric in the Renaissance." *DAI*. 1990 May; 50(11): 3578A. [†Renaissance. Dissertation abstract.]

Religious prose

[2338] Link-Salinger, Ruth, ed. *Of Scholars, Savants, and Their Texts: Studies in Philosophy and Religious Thought.* Essays in Honor of Arthur Hyman. New York: Peter Lang; 1989. 263 pp. [†Festschrift for Hyman, Arthur.]

Scientific prose

[2339] Goldbort, Robert Charles. "Scientific Writing and the College Curriculum." *DAI.* 1990 Jan.; 50(7): 2041A-2042A. [†Role in pedagogy. Dissertation abstract.]

[2340] Harré, Rom. "Some Narrative Conventions of Scientific Discourse." 81-101 in Nash, Cristopher, ed. *Narrative in Culture: The Uses of Storytelling in the Sciences, Philosophy, and Literature.* London: Routledge; 1990. xvi, 228 pp. (Warwick Studies in Philosophy and Literature.) [†Narrative conventions.]

SHORT STORY

[2341] Fitzgerald, Sheila, ed. *Short Story Criticism, II: Excerpts from Criticism of the Works of Short Fiction Writers.* Detroit: Gale; 1989. xiii, 477 pp. [Illus. †Treatment in criticism.]

[2342] Goldberg, Lea. *Omanut HaSippur: Iyunim BeTzurot HaSippur HaKatzar VeToldotav.* Tel Aviv: Sifriat Poalim; 1988. 230 pp.

[2343] Lubbers, Klaus. *Typologie der Short Story.* Darmstadt: Wiss. Buchgesell.; 1989. viii, 216 pp. (IdF 25.) [Rpt. of 1979 ed.]

[2344] Theille, Anthony. "Method and Characterization of Teaching Modern Short Stories." *DAI.* 1990 Nov.; 51(5): 1610A. [†Role of schema theory in teaching. Psycholinguistic approach. Dissertation abstract.]

[2345] Wheeler, David, ed.; Friedman, Bruce Jay, fwd. *No, but I Saw the Movie: The Best Short Stories Ever Made into Film.* New York: Penguin; 1989. 412 pp. [†Relationship to film adaptation. Edition.]

Figures of speech

[2346] Arrington, Phillip K. "Content(ious) Forms: Trope and the Study of Composition." 149-167 in Ronald, Kate, ed.; Roskelly, Hephzibah, ed. *Farther Along: Transforming Dichotomies in Rhetoric and Composition.* Portsmouth, NH: Boynton/Cook; 1990. x, 208 pp. [†Relationship to teaching of writing.]

[2347] Bowers, John Waite. "Dating 'A Figure of Thought'." *M&SA.* 1990; 5(4): 249-250. [†Treatment in Lakoff, George.]

[2348] Murphy, James J. *Topos* and *Figura:* Historical Cause and Effect?" 239-253 in Bursill-Hall, G. L., ed.; Ebbesen, Sten, ed.; Koerner, Konrad, ed. *De Ortu Grammaticae: Studies in Medieval Grammar and Linguistic Theory in Memory of Jan Pinborg.* Amsterdam: Benjamins; 1990. x, 372 pp. (SHL 43.) [†And topos.]

[2349] Nilsen, Don L. "Discourse Tendency: A Study in Extended Tropes." *RSQ.* 1989 Summer; 19(3): 263-272.

[2350] Purcell, William M. "Tropes, *Transsumptio, Assumptio,* and the Redirection of Studies in Metaphor." *M&SA.* 1990; 5(1): 35-53. [†Relationship to *transsumptio; assumptio.*]

[2351] Schraw, Gregory John. "Salience, Relevance, and Similarity." *DAI.* 1990 Dec.; 51(6): 1962A. [†Comparison. Dissertation abstract.]

IMAGERY

[2352] László, János. "Images of Social Categories vs. Images of Literary and Non-Literary Objects." *PoeticsJ.* 1990 June; 19(3): 277-291. [†Relationship to cognitive processes of reader; study example: Móricz, Zsigmond: "Barbárok"; newspaper article.]

IRONY

[2353] Fetzer, John Francis. "Romantic Irony." 19-36 in Hoffmeister, Gerhart, ed. *European Romanticism: Literary Cross-Currents, Modes, and Models.* Detroit: Wayne State UP; 1990. 369 pp.

[2354] Rougé, Bertrand. "L'Ironie, ou la double représentation." *Lendemains.* 1988; 13(50): 34-40. [Ger. sum. †Semiotic approach.]

[2355] Serper, Arié. "Le Concept d'ironie, de Platon au Moyen Age." *CAIEF.* 1986 May; 38: 7-25.

[2356] Yaari, Monique. "Ironic Architecture: The Puzzles of Multiple (En)Coding." *Restant.* 1990; 18(1): 335-384. [Illus. †Relationship to architecture. Semiotic approach.]

METAPHOR

[2357] Black, Max. *Perplexities: Rational Choice, the Prisoner's Dilemma, Metaphor, Poetic Ambiguity, and Other Puzzles.* Ithaca: Cornell UP; 1990. ix, 201 pp.

[2358] Briosi, Sandro. "Due voci per un dizionario di retorica." *QI.* 1990 Fall; 11(2): 290-298. [†And metonymy.]

[2359] Couser, G. Thomas. "Seeing through Metaphor: Teaching Figurative Literacy." *RSQ.* 1990 Spring; 20(2): 143-153.

[2360] Gibb, Heather; Wales, Robert. "Metaphor or Simile: Psychological Determinants of the Differential Use of Each Sentence Form." *M&SA.* 1990; 5(4): 199-213. [†Compared to simile. Psychological approach.]

[2361] Gordon, Paul. "The Enigma of Aristotelian Metaphor: A Deconstructive Analysis." *M&SA.* 1990; 5(2): 83-90. [†Relationship to enigma; epiphora. Theories of Aristotle; treatment in Derrida, Jacques.]

[2362] Hayles, N. Katherine. "Self-Reflexive Metaphors in Maxwell's Demon and Shannon's Choice: Finding the Passages." 209-237 in Peterfreund, Stuart, ed. *Literature and Science: Theory & Practice.* Boston: Northeastern UP; 1990. vi, 248 pp. [†Relationship to self-reflexiveness. Theories of Maxwell, James Clerk; Shannon, Claude Elwood.]

[2363] Kennedy, John M. "Metaphor: Its Intellectual Basis." *M&SA.* 1990; 5(2): 115-123. [†Theories of Olson, David R.]

[2364] Khatena, Joe; Khatena, Nelly. "Metaphor Motifs and Creative Imagination in Art." *M&SA.* 1990; 5(1): 21-34. [†And analogy.]

[2365] Losse, Deborah N. "Sampling the Book: Beginning Metaphors and Their Poetic Function." *Neophil.* 1990 Apr.; 74(2): 192-201.

[2366] Parker, Patricia. "Metaphor and Catachresis." 60-73 in Bender, John, ed.; Wellbery, David E., ed. *The Ends of Rhetoric: History, Theory, Practice.* Stanford: Stanford UP; 1990. xiv, 238 pp. [†And catachresis. Theories of Quintilianus.]

[2367] Read, Stephen J.; Cesa, Ian L.; Jones, David K.; Collins, Nancy L. "When Is the Federal Budget Like a Baby? Metaphor in Political Rhetoric." *M&SA.* 1990; 5(3): 125-149. [†Use in political discourse; relationship to persuasion; inference.]

[2368] Shen, Yeshayahu. "Symmetric and Asymmetric Comparisons." *PoeticsJ.* 1989 Dec.; 18(6): 517-536. [†Compared to literal meaning; comparison.]

[2369] Thomas, Jean-Jacques. "Metaphor: The Image and the Formula." *PoT.* 1987; 8(3-4): 479-501. [†As image; formula.]

[2370] Utaker, Arild. "Metaforen som sammenligning." *Livstegn.* 1989; 7(2): 178-186. [†Relationship to iconicity.]

[2371] Van Besien, Fred. "Metaphor and Simile." *Interface.* 1990; 4(2): 85-106. [†Compared to simile.]

[2372] Waggoner, John E. "Interaction Theories of Metaphor: Psychological Perspectives." *M&SA.* 1990; 5(2): 91-108. [†Psychological approach. Theories of Black, Max.]

[2373] Weimar, Klaus. "Vom barocken Sinn der Metapher." *MLN.* 1990 Apr.; 105(3): 453-471. [†Relationship to the Baroque.]

[2374] Wheeler, Cathy J. "A Question with No Answer: Or, Reality as Literalism and as Metaphor." *M&SA.* 1990; 5(1): 55-61. [†Relationship to nonmetaphorical concept. Theories of Johnson, Mark Leonard.]

[2375] Whitson, Steve. "'Sanitized for Your Protection': On the Hygiene of Metaphors." *RSQ.* 1989 Summer; 19(3): 253-262. [†Relationship to rhetorical criticism.]

SYMBOL

[2376] Foster, Stephen William. "Symbolism and the Problem of Postmodern Representation." 117-137 in Ashley, Kathleen M., ed. *Victor Turner and the Construction of Cultural Criticism.* Bloomington: Indiana UP; 1990. xxii, 185 pp. (Between Literature and Anthropology.)

[2377] Hopper, Stanley. "The Word as Symbol in Sacred Experience." 83-109 in Blodgett, E. D., ed.; Coward, H. G., ed. *Silence, the Word and the Sacred.* Waterloo: Wilfrid Laurier UP for Calgary Inst. for the Humanities; 1989. xii, 226 pp. [†Relationship to the sacred.]

[2378] Todorov, Tzvetan; Porter, Catherine, tr. *Theories of the Symbol.* Ithaca: Cornell UP; 1987. 302 pp. [Tr. of 1977 Bibliog. III.8658.]

Literary forms

ALLEGORY

[2379] Grodal, Torben Kragh. "Allegori eller software?" *KuKl.* 1990; 17(4): 134-140. [Replies to Østergaard, below.]

[2380] Holmgaard, Jørgen. "Allegorikernes litani—et svar." *KuKl.* 1990; 17(4): 126-134. [Rejoinder to Østergaard, below.]

[2381] Østergaard, Claus Bratt. "Læsningens allegorier." *KuKl.* 1990; 17(4): 112-126. [Replies to 1989 Bibliog. IV.1478; see also Grodal, above & Holmgaard, above.]

ANECDOTE

[2382] Rudenev, Vadim. "Pragmatika anekdota." *Daugava.* 1990 July; 6(156): 99-102. [†Theories of Freud, Sigmund.]

DIALOGUE

[2383] Bessonnat, Daniel. "Paroles de personnages: Problèmes, activités d'apprentissage." *Pratiques.* 1990 Mar.; 65: 7-35. [Cont. from Coltier, D.; Bessonnat, Daniel. "Apprendre à rédiger des paroles de personnages." *Pratiques.* 64: 5-38. †In narrative. Compared to dramatic dialogue; relationship to teaching of writing.]

[2384] Swearingen, C. Jan. "The Narration of Dialogue and Narration within Dialogue: The Transition from Story to Logic." 173-197 in Britton, Bruce K., ed.; Pellegrini, A. D., ed. *Narrative Thought and Narrative Language.* Hillsdale, NJ: Erlbaum; 1990. viii, 278 pp. [†Relationship to narration.]

EMBLEM

[2385] Bath, Michael. "What Is the Corpus?" 5-20 in Daly, Peter M., ed. *The Index of Emblem Art Symposium.* New York: AMS; 1990. xiv, 184 pp. (AMSSE 6.) [†Relationship to genre; canon.]

[2386] Daly, Peter M. "A Preliminary Model for an Index of Emblem Art: A Discussion Paper." 139-145 in Daly, Peter M., ed. *The Index of Emblem Art Symposium.* New York: AMS; 1990. xiv, 184 pp. (AMSSE 6.) [†Indexing.]

[2387] ——. "A Rationale for an Index of Emblem Art." 1-4 in Daly, Peter M., ed. *The Index of Emblem Art Symposium.* New York: AMS; 1990. xiv, 184 pp. (AMSSE 6.) [†Indexing.

[2388] ——. "A Revised Model for an Index of Emblem Art." 155-165 in Daly, Peter M., ed. *The Index of Emblem Art Symposium.* New York: AMS; 1990. xiv, 184 pp. (AMSSE 6.) [†Indexing.]

[2389] Daly, Peter M., ed. *The Index of Emblem Art Symposium.* Papers from the McGill Symposium "An Index of Emblem Art". New York: AMS; 1990. xiv, 184 pp. (AMSSE 6.) [†Indexing.]

[2390] Drewer, Lois. "What Can Be Learned from the Procedures of the Index of Christian Art." 121-138 in Daly, Peter M., ed. *The Index of Emblem Art Symposium.* New York: AMS; 1990. xiv, 184 pp. (AMSSE 6.) [Incl. discussion. †In index.]

[2391] Fowler, Kenneth. "Round Table Discussion: 'Ways and Means to Create the Index of Emblem Art'." 153-154 in Daly, Peter M., ed. *The Index of Emblem Art Symposium.* New York: AMS; 1990. xiv, 184 pp. (AMSSE 6.) [†Indexing.]

[2392] Landwehr, John. "A Bouquet of Bookish Emblems." 447-458 in Croiset van Uchelen, Ton, ed.; Horst, Koert van der, ed.; Schilder, Günter, ed.; Hesselink, Sebastiaan S., fwd. Theatrum Orbis Librorum: Liber Amicorum *Presented to Nico Israel on the Occasion of His Seventieth Birthday.* Utrecht: HES; 1989. xii, 518 pp. [†Treatment of book; printing; book collectors.]

[2393] Manning, John. "Incorporating an Historical Dimension into the Index of Emblem Art." 37-62 in Daly, Peter M., ed. *The Index of Emblem Art Symposium.* New York: AMS; 1990. xiv, 184 pp. (AMSSE 6.) [Illus. †Indexing; relationship to history.]

[2394] Moseley, Charles. *A Century of Emblems: An Introductory Anthology.* Hants: Scolar; 1989. x, 321 pp. [†Of Renaissance (1531-1647). Anthology.]

[2395] Rosenfield, Myra Nan. "The Needs of the Architectural Historian in Using the Index of Emblem Art." 89-106 in Daly, Peter M., ed. *The Index of Emblem Art Symposium.* New York: AMS; 1990. xiv, 184 pp. (AMSSE 6.) [†Imagery of architecture in index.]

[2396] Russell, Daniel S. "The Needs of the Literary Historian." 107-119 in Daly, Peter M., ed. *The Index of Emblem Art Symposium.* New York: AMS; 1990. xiv, 184 pp. (AMSSE 6.) [Incl. discussion. †Relationship to literary history.]

[2397] Scholz, Bernhard F. "The *Res Picta* and the *Res Significans* of an Emblem, and the Indexer's Eye: Notes on the Basis of an Index of Emblem Art." 63-88 in Daly, Peter M., ed. *The Index of Emblem Art Symposium.* New York: AMS; 1990. xiv, 184 pp. (AMSSE 6.) [Illus. †Relationship to illustration. Indexing.]

[2398] Young, Alan R. "The Place of Imprese in an Index of Emblem Art." 21-35 in Daly, Peter M., ed. *The Index of Emblem Art Symposium.* New York: AMS; 1990. xiv, 184 pp. (AMSSE 6.) [Illus. †Relationship to *impresa.* Indexing.]

HUMOR

[2399] Bauer, Dale M. "The Joke Cure: Spectacle and Subversive Humor." *W&D.* 1989 Spring; 7(1 [13]): 91-101. [†Relationship to feminism; study example: McTiernan, John: *Die Hard.*]

[2400] Clark, John R. "Addenda on Black Humor." *NConL.* 1990 Jan.; 20(1): 12. [†Black humor.]

[2401] Daemmrich, Ingrid G. "The Cyclical Seasons of Humor in Literature." *Humor.* 1990; 3(4): 415-434. [†Relationship to seasons of the year.]

[2402] Gloss, Teresa Guerra. "Humour in Literature: Three Levels." *DAI.* 1990 Apr.; 50(10): 3221A. [†Dissertation abstract.]

[2403] Schüsseler, Matti. *Unbeschwert aufgeklärt: Scherzhafte Literatur im 18. Jahrhundert.* Tübingen: Niemeyer; 1990. 180 pp. (SzDL 109.) [†1700-1799. Role of jokes; pun; relationship to aesthetics.]

[2404] Tarozzi-Goldsmith, Marcella Fausta. "Nonrepresentational Forms of the Comic: Humor, Irony, and Jokes." *DAI.* 1990 Jan.; 50(7): 2091A. [†And irony; jokes. Psychoanalytic approach. Dissertation abstract.]

MYTH

[2405] Buck, Dorothy Cecelia. "The Journey of the Swan Maiden: A Verse Narrative Retelling of an Ancient Myth." *DAI.* 1990 Sept.; 51(3): 887A-888A. [†Of swan maiden. Dissertation abstract.]

[2406] Dourado, Autran. "Proposições sobre Mito." *MGSL.* 1988 Feb. 20; 22(1094): 5.

[2407] Lange, N. R. M. de. "Judaísmo y cristianismo: Mitos antiguos y diálogo moderno." *MEAH.* 1990; 39(2): 5-29. [†Relationship to Judaism; Christianity.]

[2408] Risco, Antón. "Para un Estudio dos Mitos Actuais, II: Civilización e Barbarie." *Grial.* 1990 Oct.-Dec.; 28(108): 510-519. [†Relationship to Postmodernism.]

[2409] Siganos, André. "Le Minotaure et la signification: De l'animalité comme lieu de transit." 225-232 in Bessière, Jean, ed. *Fiction, texte, narratologie, genre.* New York: Peter Lang; 1989. 238 pp. [†Treatment of labyrinth; monsters.]

[2410] Stewart, Robert Scott. "The Epistemological Function of Platonic Myth." *P&R.* 1989; 22(4): 260-280. [†Relationship to dialectic. Role in Plato.]

[2411] Tinkle, Theresa. "Saturn of the Several Faces: A Survey of the Medieval Mythographic Traditions." *Viator.* 1987; 18: 289-307. [†Middle Ages.]

PARODY

[2412] Gobin, Pierre. "Preliminaries: Towards a Study of the *Parodying* Activity." 36-47 in Thomson, Clive, ed. *Essays on Parody.* Toronto: Victoria Univ.; 1986. 103 pp.

(Monographs, Working Papers and Prepublications of The Toronto Semiotic Circle 4.)

[2413] Hambidge, Joan. "Die parodie as stylfiguur." *TvL.* 1989 Nov.; 27(4): 54-60.

[2414] Karrer, Wolfgang; Wall, Anthony, tr. "Parody, Travesty, and Pastiche qua Communication Processes." 1-35 in Thomson, Clive, ed. *Essays on Parody.* Toronto: Victoria Univ.; 1986. 103 pp. (Monographs, Working Papers and Prepublications of The Toronto Semiotic Circle 4.) [Incl. tr. introd. †And travesty; pastiche; relationship to social relations; psychology. Application of communication theory.]

[2415] Lubich, Frederick Alfred. "The Parody of Romanticism: Quixotic Reflections in the Romantic Novel." 309-329 in Hoffmeister, Gerhart, ed. *European Romanticism: Literary Cross-Currents, Modes, and Models.* Detroit: Wayne State UP; 1990. 369 pp. [†Romanticism.]

[2416] Thomson, Clive, ed. *Essays on Parody.* Toronto: Victoria Univ.; 1986. 103 pp. (Monographs, Working Papers and Prepublications of The Toronto Semiotic Circle 4.) [Incl. pref.]

RHETORIC

[2417] Asensi, Manuel. "Retórica logográfica y psicagogías de la retórica." *RL.* 1990 Jan.-June; 52(103): 5-46. [†1900-1999. Relationship to structuralism; hermeneutics; deconstructionism.]

[2418] Bazerman, Charles, introd.; Geisler, Cheryl, conclusion; Jarratt, Susan C., conclusion. "What Are We Doing as a Research Community?" *RhetRev.* 1989 Spring; 7(2): 223-292. [Spec. sect., 223-292.]

[2419] Bender, John; Wellbery, David E. "Rhetoricality: On the Modernist Return of Rhetoric." 3-39 in Bender, John, ed.; Wellbery, David E., ed. *The Ends of Rhetoric: History, Theory, Practice.* Stanford: Stanford UP; 1990. xiv, 238 pp. [†Relationship to Modernism.]

[2420] Bender, John, ed.; Wellbery, David E., ed. *The Ends of Rhetoric: History, Theory, Practice.* Stanford: Stanford UP; 1990. xiv, 238 pp. [Incl. pref.]

[2421] Benson, Thomas W., ed.; Perry, Lewis, fwd. *American Rhetoric: Context and Criticism.* Carbondale: Southern Illinois UP; 1989. x, 427 pp. [Incl. introd.]

[2422] Berquist, Goodwin. "The Rhetorical Travels of Robert T. Oliver." *RhetRev.* 1990 Fall; 9(1): 173-183. [†Treatment in Oliver, Robert Tarbell.]

[2423] Bessière, Jean. "Rhétoricité et littérature: Figures de la discordance, figures du partage de Roland Barthes à Paul de Man." *LFr.* 1988 Sept.; 79: 37-50. [†And figures of speech. Theories of Barthes, Roland; de Man, Paul.]

[2424] Bineham, Jeffery L. "The Cartesian Anxiety in Epistemic Rhetoric: An Assessment of the Literature." *P&R.* 1990; 23(1): 43-62. [†Epistemic rhetoric.]

[2425] Bliese, John. "Richard M. Weaver and the Rhetoric of a Lost Cause." *RSQ.* 1989 Fall; 19(4): 313-325. [†Figuration; verisimilitude. Treatment in Weaver, Richard M.]

[2426] Borch-Jacobsen, Mikkel. "Analytic Speech: From Restricted to General Rhetoric." 127-139 in Bender, John, ed.; Wellbery, David E., ed. *The Ends of Rhetoric: History, Theory, Practice.* Stanford: Stanford UP; 1990. xiv, 238 pp.

[2427] Borutti, Silvana. "Epistémologie et questionnement: Le Modèle en tant que forme de l'interrogation scientifique." *RIPh.* 1990; 44(3 [174]): 370-393. [†Role of question; metaphor; image in scientific language; relationship to epistemology. Theories of Meyer, Michel; Kant, Immanuel.]

[2428] Broaddus, Dorothy C. "The Demons of Old and New Rhetoric." 183-195 in Ronald, Kate, ed.; Roskelly, Hephzibah, ed. *Farther Along: Transforming Dichotomies in Rhetoric and Composition.* Portsmouth, NH: Boynton/Cook; 1990. x, 208 pp.

[2429] Brummett, Barry. "Perfection and the Bomb: Nuclear Weapons, Teleology, and Motives." *JC.* 1989 Winter; 39(1): 85-95. [See also Cherwitz & Hikins, below. †Relationship to public discourse on nuclear weapons. Application of theories of Burke, Kenneth.]

[2430] ——. "The Reported Demise of Epistemic Rhetoric: A Eulogy for Epistemic Rhetoric." *QJS.* 1990 Feb.; 76(1): 69-72. [†(1967-1989). Relationship to epistemology.]

[2431] Campbell, Jonathan Lee. "The Relevant Communication of Rhetorical Arguments." *DAI.* 1990 Dec.; 51(6): 2001A. [†Argumentation; relationship to relevance.]

[2432] Carrilho, Manuel Maria. "Problématicité, rationalité et interrogativité." *RIPh.* 1990; 44(3 [174]): 309-328. [†Role of question in argumentation.]

[2433] Carter, Michael. "*Stasis* and *Kairos*: Principles of Social Construction in Classical Rhetoric." *RhetRev.* 1988 Fall; 7(1): 97-112. [†*Stasis*; *kairos*; treatment in Classical rhetoric; relationship to social construction.]

[2434] Cherwitz, Richard A.; Hikins, James W. "Burying the Undertaker: A Eulogy for the Eulogists of Rhetorical Epistemology." *QJS.* 1990 Feb.; 76(1): 73-77. [Replies to Brummett, above. †Relationship to epistemology.]

[2435] Claussen, Regina. "Zeichen und Ideologie: Vom ideologiekritischen Wert der Rhetorik." *Semiosis.* 1989; 14(3-4 [55-56]): 39-46. [Eng. sum. †Relationship to ideology. Treatment in Peirce, Charles Sanders; Bense, Max.]

[2436] Coe, Richard M. "Defining Rhetoric—and Us." *JAC.* 1990; 10(1): 39-52. [†Treatment in Burke, Kenneth.]

[2437] Conners, Patricia E. "The History of Intuition and Its Role in the Composing Process." *RSQ.* 1990 Winter; 20(1): 71-78. [†Role of intuition; relationship to creative process.]

[2438] Connors, Robert J. "Rhetorical History as a Component of Composition Studies." *RhetRev.* 1989 Spring; 7(2): 230-240. [†Relationship to teaching of writing.]

SEE SUBJECT INDEX FOR CROSS-REFERENCES

[2439] Consigny, Scott. "Dialectical, Rhetorical, and Aristotelian Rhetoric." *P&R*. 1989; 22(4): 281-287. [†Treatment in Aristotle.]

[2440] Corbett, Edward P. J. *Classical Rhetoric for the Modern Student*. NY: Oxford UP; 1990. xiv, 591 pp. [3rd ed.]

[2441] Corder, Jim W. "Hunting for *Ethos* Where They Say It Can't Be Found." *RhetRev*. 1989 Spring; 7(2): 299-316. [†Ethos; relationship to poststructuralist literary theory and criticism.]

[2442] Crosswhite, James. "Universality in Rhetoric: Perelman's Universal Audience." *P&R*. 1989; 22(3): 157-173. [†Rhetorical theory; relationship to universal audience. Theories of Perelman, Chaim.]

[2443] Crowley, Sharon. "A Plea for the Revival of Sophistry." *RhetRev*. 1989 Spring; 7(2): 318-334. [†Sophistry; relationship to epistemology; scientific discourse.]

[2444] Crusius, Timothy W. "Reflections on *A Pragmatic Theory of Rhetoric*." *JAC*. 1990; 10(1): 53-72. [On Beale, Walter H. *A Pragmatic Theory of Rhetoric*. †Review article.]

[2445] D'Angelo, Frank J. "Tropics of Arrangement: A Theory of *Dispositio*." *JAC*. 1990; 10(1): 101-109.

[2446] Enos, Theresa, prol.; Brown, Stuart C., introd.; Berlin, James A.; Berthoff, Ann E.; Booth, Wayne C.; Corder, Jim W.; Murphy, James J.; Young, Richard. "Professing the New Rhetorics." *RhetRev*. 1990 Fall; 9(1): 5-35. [†Round table discussion.]

[2447] Fafner, Jörgen. "Retorikkens brændpunkt." *NorskIrrn*. 1990; 14(1): 14-25.

[2448] Faigley, Lester. "The Study of Writing and the Study of Language." *RhetRev*. 1989 Spring; 7(2): 240-256. [†Relationship to linguistic theory; ideology.]

[2449] Farrell, Thomas B. "From the Parthenon to the Bassinet: Death and Rebirth along the Epistemic Trail." *QJS*. 1990 Feb.; 76(1): 78-84. [Replies to Brummett, above & Cherwitz and Hikins, above. †Relationship to epistemology.]

[2450] Garver, Eugene. "Essentially Contested Concepts: The Ethics and Tactics of Argument." *P&R*. 1990; 23(4): 251-270. [†Essentially contested concept; relationship to argumentation.]

[2451] Goodwin, David. "*Controversiae Meta-Asystatae* and the New Rhetoric." *RSQ*. 1989 Summer; 19(3): 205-216. [†Stasis. Relationship to theories of Perelman, Chaim; Burke, Kenneth.]

[2452] Greene, Stuart. "Toward a Dialectical Theory of Composing." *RhetRev*. 1990 Fall; 9(1): 149-172. [†Social construction; relationship to teaching of writing. Theories of Bruffee, Kenneth A.]

[2453] Gross, Alan G. *The Rhetoric of Science*. Cambridge: Harvard UP; 1990. vi, 248 pp. [†Relationship to scientific prose.]

[2454] Gustainis, J. Justin. "Demagoguery and Political Rhetoric: A Review of the Literature." *RSQ*. 1990 Spring; 20(2): 155-161. [†Relationship to demagoguery.]

[2455] Harris, R. Allen. "Assent, Dissent, and Rhetoric in Science." *RSQ*. 1990 Winter; 20(1): 13-37. [†Relationship to science; knowledge.]

[2456] Haswell, Richard H. "No Title: A Response to Sam Meyer." *JAC*. 1990 Fall; 10(2): 396-399. [Replies to 1988 Bibliog. IV.2741; see also Meyer, Sam, below. †Relationship to work title.]

[2457] Jacquette, Dale. "Epistemic Blood from Logical Turnips." *P&R*. 1989; 22(3): 203-211. [Rejoinder to Sorensen, below. †Slippery slope argument; relationship to fallacy.]

[2458] Jamieson, Kathleen Hall. "The Cunning Rhetor, the Complicitous Audience, the Conned Censor, and the Critic." *ComM*. 1990 Mar.; 57(1): 73-78. [†And allegory.]

[2459] Johnson, Ralph H. "Acceptance Is Not Enough: A Critique of Hamblin." *P&R*. 1990; 23(4): 271-287. [†Argumentation. Theories of Hamblin, Charles Leonard.]

[2460] Kahn, Victoria. "Rhetoric and the Law." *Diacritics*. 1989 Summer; 19(2): 21-34. [†Relationship to law.]

[2461] Karis, Bill. "Conflict in Collaboration: A Burkean Perspective." *RhetRev*. 1989 Fall; 8(1): 113-126. [†Relationship to dialectic; collaboration. Theories of Burke, Kenneth compared to Rogers, Carl Ransom.]

[2462] Kent, Thomas. "Paralogic Hermeneutics and the Possibilities of Rhetoric." *RhetRev*. 1989 Fall; 8(1): 24-42. [†Paralogism; relationship to dialogism. Sources in sophistry. Theories of Davidson, Donald; Derrida, Jacques; Bakhtin, Mikhail Mikhailovich.]

[2463] Kravinsky, Zell. "A Table of Rhetorical Elements." *DAI*. 1990 Jan.; 50(7): 2064A-2065A. [†Dissertation abstract.]

[2464] Lassner, Phyllis. "Feminist Responses to Rogerian Argument." *RhetRev*. 1990 Spring; 8(2): 220-232. [†Argumentation; relationship to feminism. Theories of Rogers, Carl Ransom.]

[2465] Lausberg, Heinrich; Arens, Arnold, fwd. *Handbuch der literarischen Rhetorik: Eine Grundlegung der Literaturwissenschaft*. Stuttgart: Steiner; 1990. 983 pp. [3rd ed.]

[2466] Lunsford, Andrea A.; Ede, Lisa. "Rhetoric in a New Key: Women and Collaboration." *RhetRev*. 1990 Spring; 8(2): 234-241. [†Relationship to collaboration in writing; women.]

[2467] Lyne, John; Howe, Henry F. "The Rhetoric of Expertise: E. O. Wilson and Sociobiology." *QJS*. 1990 May; 76(2): 134-151. [†In Wilson, Edward Osborne: *On Human Nature*; relationship to discourse framing.]

[2468] Mao, LuMing. "Persuasion, Cooperation and Diversity of Rhetorics." *RSQ*. 1990 Spring; 20(2): 131-142. [†Persuasion.]

[2469] Marmo, Costantino. "From Analogical Points of View: On the Use of Analogy in Ancient Greek Medical Texts." *Versus*. 1988 May-Dec.; 50-51: 19-37. [†Analogy in medical prose.]

[2470] McClellan, William. "The Dialogic Other: Bakhtin's Theory of Rhetoric." *DS/SD*. 1990 Spring-Summer; 3(1-2): 233-249. [†Relationship to otherness. Theories of Bakhtin, Mikhail Mikhailovich.]

[2471] McClish, Glen. "Some Less-Acknowledged Links: Rhetorical Theory, Interpersonal Communication, and the Tradition of the Liberal Arts." *RSQ*. 1990 Spring; 20(2): 105-118. [†Dialectic; relationship to rhetorical theory; interpersonal communication.]

[2472] Meyer, Michel; Jung, Christophe, tr. "Die Figuren des Menschlichen." *RIPh*. 1990; 44(3 [174]): 448-470.

[2473] Meyer, Sam. "Let's Continue to Take It from the Top: A Response to Richard Haswell." *JAC*. 1990 Fall; 10(2): 400-402. [Rejoinder to Haswell, above. †Relationship to work title.]

[2474] Miller, Thomas P. "Where Did College English Studies Come From?" *RhetRev*. 1990 Fall; 9(1): 50-69. [†History of rhetoric in England; Scotland; United States (1650-1799).]

[2475] Mowery, Diane; Duffy, Eve. "The Power of Language to Efface and Desensitize." *RSQ*. 1990 Spring; 20(2): 163-171.

[2476] Murphy, James J., prol.; Berlin, James; Connors, Robert J.; Crowley, Sharon; Enos, Richard Leo; Vitanza, Victor J.; Jarratt, Susan C.; Johnson, Nan; Swearingen, Jan. "The Politics of Historiography." *RhetRev*. 1988 Fall; 7(1): 5-49. [†Relationship to historiography.]

[2477] Nesselroth, Peter W. "Rhetoric and the Psychoanalytic Meaning of Literary Form." 163-172 in Valdés, Mario J., ed. *Toward a Theory of Comparative Literature: Selected Papers Presented in the Division of Theory of Literature at the XIth International Comparative Literature Congress*. New York: Peter Lang; 1990. 275 pp. (Proceedings of the International Comparative Literature Association 11: 3.) [†Relationship to figures of speech; psychoanalytic literary theory and criticism.]

[2478] Ochs, Donovan J. "Cicero and Philosophic *Inventio*." *RSQ*. 1989 Summer; 19(3): 217-227. [†Inventio; relationship to philosophical language. Treatment in Cicero.]

[2479] Porter, James E. "*Diviso* as Em-/De-Powering Topic: A Basis for Argument in Rhetoric and Composition." *RhetRev*. 1990 Spring; 8(2): 191-205. [†Diviso.]

[2480] Ramoni, Marco. "La scoperta impossibile: Astuzie e poteri del discorso scientifico in Aristotele." *Versus*. 1989 Sept.-Dec.; 54: 27-42. [†Argumentation in scientific language. Theories of Aristotle compared to Plato.]

[2481] Reynolds, John Frederick. "Concepts of Memory in Contemporary Composition." *RSQ*. 1989 Summer; 19(3): 245-252. [†Role of *memoria*; relationship to writing.]

[2482] Ronald, Kate. "A Reexamination of Personal and Public Discourse in Classical Rhetoric." *RhetRev*. 1990 Fall; 9(1): 36-48. [†Ethos; relationship to discourse.]

[2483] Ronald, Kate, ed.; Roskelly, Hephzibah, ed. *Farther Along: Transforming Dichotomies in Rhetoric and Composition*. Portsmouth, NH: Boynton/Cook; 1990. x, 208 pp.

[2484] Ryan, Charlton. "Theories of Rhetorical Invention, 1960-1987: A Critique of Theory and Practice." *DAI*. 1990 Dec.; 51(6): 2008A. [†Theories of invention (1960-1987). Dissertation abstract.]

[2485] Schiappa, Edward. "History and Neo-Sophistic Criticism: A Reply to Poulakos." *P&R*. 1990; 23(4): 307-315. [Rejoinder to Poulakos, John. "Interpreting Sophistical Rhetoric: A Response to Schiappa." *Philos. & Rhetoric*. 1990; 23(3): 218-228. †Relationship to Sophists.]

[2486] Schriver, Karen A. "Theory Building in Rhetoric and Composition: The Role of Empirical Scholarship." *RhetRev*. 1989 Spring; 7(2): 272-288. [†Rhetorical theory; relationship to teaching of writing. On empirical approach.]

[2487] Sennett, Richard. "The Rhetoric of Ethnic Identity." 191-206 in Bender, John, ed.; Wellbery, David E., ed. *The Ends of Rhetoric: History, Theory, Practice*. Stanford: Stanford UP; 1990. xiv, 238 pp. [†Relationship to ethnic identity.]

[2488] Shenk, Robert. "The Ancient Rhetorical *Suasoria* versus the Modern Technical Case." *RhetRev*. 1988 Fall; 7(1): 113-127. [†Suasoria; relationship to technical writing.]

[2489] Short, Bryan C. "The Temporality of Rhetoric." *RhetRev*. 1989 Spring; 7(2): 367-379. [†Future perfect tense in argumentation; relationship to psychoanalytic literary theory and criticism. Theories of Aristotle; Lacan, Jacques; Derrida, Jacques.]

[2490] Sipiora, Philip; Atwill, Jane. "Rhetoric and Cultural Explanation: A Discussion with Gayatri Chakravorty Spivak." *JAC*. 1990 Fall; 10(2): 293-304. [†Relationship to culture studies. Interview with Spivak, Gayatri Chakravorty.]

[2491] Smith, Robert E., III. "Reconsidering Richard Rorty." *RSQ*. 1989 Fall; 19(4): 349-364. [†Treatment in Rorty, Richard.]

[2492] Sorensen, Roy A. "Slipping off the Slippery Slope: A Reply to Professor Jacquette." *P&R*. 1989; 22(3): 195-202. [Replies to Jacquette, above. †Slippery slope argument; relationship to fallacy.]

[2493] Sperber, Dan; Wilson, Deirdre. "Retórica y pertinencia." *RO*. 1990 Dec.; 115: 5-26.

[2494] ——. "Rhetoric and Relevance." 140-155 in Bender, John, ed.; Wellbery, David E., ed. *The Ends of Rhetoric: History, Theory, Practice*. Stanford: Stanford UP; 1990. xiv, 238 pp.

[2495] Suber, Peter. "A Case Study in *Ad Hominem* Arguments: Fichte's *Science of Knowledge*." *P&R*. 1990; 23(1): 12-42. [†Ad hominem argument. In Fichte, Johann Gottlieb: *Wissenschaftslehre*.]

[2496] Sullivan, Dale L. "Attitudes toward Imitation: Classical Culture and the Modern Temper." *RhetRev*. 1989 Fall; 8(1): 5-21. [†Imitation.]

[2497] Trimbur, John. "Essayist Literacy and the Rhetoric of Deproduction." *RhetRev*. 1990 Fall; 9(1): 72-86. [†Essayist literacy.]

[2498] Weir, Vickie Elaine Ricks. "Revisioning Traditions through Rhetoric: Studies in Gertrude Buck's Social Theory of Discourse." *DAI*. 1990 Mar.; 50(9): 2876A. [†Treatment in Buck, Gertrude: *The Metaphor*. Dissertation abstract.

[2499] Whitson, Steve. "The Phaedrus Complex." *Pre/Text*. 1988 Spring-Summer; 9(1-2): 9-25. [†Treatment in Plato: *Phaidros*; *Gorgias*; relationship to philosophy; psychoanalysis.]

[2500] Zappen, James P. "Francis Bacon and the Historiography of Scientific Rhetoric." *RhetRev*. 1989 Fall; 8(1): 74-88. [†Scientific rhetoric. Treatment in Bacon, Francis.]

Bibliography

[2501] Payne, Melinda A.; Ratchford, Suzanne M.; Wooley, Lillian N. "Richard M. Weaver: A Bibliographical Essay." *RSQ*. 1989 Fall; 19(4): 327-332. [†Treatment in Weaver, Richard M.]

SATIRE

[2502] Knight, Charles A. "The Images of Nations in Eighteenth-Century Satire." *ECS*. 1989 Summer; 22(4): 489-511. [†1700-1799. Relationship to nationalism.]

[2503] ———. "Imagination's Cerberus: Satire and the Metaphor of Genre." *PQ*. 1990 Spring; 69(2): 131-151. [†As genre; relationship to metaphor. Sources in Diomedes.]

TRAGEDY

[2504] Gould, Thomas. "The Ancient Quarrel between Poetry and Philosophy." 1-19 in Redmond, James, ed. *Drama and Philosophy*. Cambridge: Cambridge UP; 1990. xiii, 227 pp. (ThD 12.) [†Role of pathos. Sources in Plato; Aristotle.]

[2505] Steiner, George. "Literary Forms: A Note on Absolute Tragedy." *L&T*. 1990 July; 4(2): 147-156.

[2506] Sutherland, Stewart R. "Christianity and Tragedy." *L&T*. 1990 July; 4(2): 157-168. [†Relationship to Christianity.]

[2507] Walker, Steven F. "Les Mythes dans la tragédie: Nouvelles perspectives jungiennes." 87-96 in Valdés, Mario J., ed. *Toward a Theory of Comparative Literature: Selected Papers Presented in the Division of Theory of Literature at the XIth International Comparative Literature Congress*. New York: Peter Lang; 1990. 275 pp. (Proceedings of the International Comparative Literature Association 11: 3.) [†Relationship to myth. Application of theories of Jung, Carl Gustav.]

TRANSLATION

[2508] Alexieva, Bistra. "Creativity in Simultaneous Interpretation." *Babel*. 1990; 36(1): 1-6. [Fr. sum. †Role of creativity in simultaneous translation.]

[2509] Allison, David B. "The *Différance* of Translation." 177-190 in Silverman, Hugh J., ed.; Aylesworth, Gary E., ed. *The Textual Sublime: Deconstruction and Its Differences*. Albany: State U of New York P; 1990. 274 pp. (Contemporary Studies in Philosophy and Literature 1.) [†English language translation of theories of deconstructionism from French language (Modern).]

[2510] Auld, William. "Prozaj tradukoj en Esperanto." *Fonto*. 1990 Jan.; 10(109): 5-16. [†Esperanto language translation.]

[2511] Bassnett, Susan. "Beyond Translation." *NewComp*. 1989 Autumn; 8: 1-98. [Spec. sect.; incl. introd.]

[2512] Beekman, E. M. "Scio/Nescio: Reflections on Translation." 35-48 in Westerweel, Bart, ed.; D'haen, Theo, ed. *Something Understood: Studies in Anglo-Dutch Literary Translation*. Amsterdam: Rodopi; 1990. 335 pp. (DQR: Studies in Literature 5.)

[2513] Bellm, Dan. "Words Fail: The Unbearable Toughness of Translating." *Village Voice Literary Supplement*. 1990 Feb.; 82: 19-20. [†On English language translation.]

[2514] Berlind, Bruce. "A Conference Call on Translating Poetry." *TRev*. 1990; 32-33: 3-6. [†Of poetry.]

[2515] Blair, Dorothy S. "More Thoughts on Milan Kundera and the Art of the Translation." *Professional Translator & Interpreter*. 1990; 3: 23-24.

[2516] Brulard, I. "La Traduction comme miroir d'un changement dans l'approche du sens à la Renaissance." *CdIL*. 1990; 16(1): 13-21. [†Of Bible during Renaissance.]

[2517] Bühler, Hildegund. "Didaktische Aspekte des literarischen Übersetzens." *DU*. 1990 Feb.; 42(1): 23-28. [†Pedagogical approach.]

[2518] Celt, Sandra. "Thought for Food." *Language International: The Magazine for the Language Professions*. 1990 Aug.; 2(4): 21-25. [†Of poetry.]

[2519] Chen, Dianxing. "Khudozhest' vennost' perevoda i kachestva perevodchika kak khudozhnika." *Waiguoyu*. 1990 Apr.; 2(66): 58-62. [In Chin.]

[2520] Chevallaz, Georges-André. "Traduction." *EdL*. 1989 Oct.-Dec.; 4: 113-115.

[2521] Fischer, Michael M. J.; Abedi, Mehdi. "Translating Qur'anic Dialogics: Islamic Poetics and Politics for Muslims and for Us." *TrP*. 1990; 5: 111-129. [†Of dialogue of Koran; relationship to oral tradition.]

[2522] Frank, Armin Paul. "Systems and Histories in the Study of Literary Translations: A Few Distinctions." 41-63 in Bauer, Roger, ed.; Fokkema, Douwe, ed.; Graat, Michael de, asst. ed.; Wimmer, Ruprecht, asst.; Goppel, Thomas, greeting. *Proceedings of the XIIth Congress of the International Comparative Literature Association/Actes du XIIe congrès de l'Association Internationale de Littérature Comparée: München 1988 Munich, I: Plenary Sessions/Séances plénières; Colloquium Munich/Colloque Munich*. Munich: Iudicium; 1990. 251 pp. (Proceedings of the Congress of the International Comparative Literature Association 12: 1.)

[2523] ———. "'Translation as System' and *Übersetzungskultur*: On Histories and Systems in the Study of Literary Translation." *NewComp*. 1989 Autumn; 8: 85-98. [†Relationship to literary history.]

[2524] Graham, Joseph F. "Around and about Babel." 167-176 in Silverman, Hugh J., ed.; Aylesworth, Gary E., ed. *The Textual Sublime: Deconstruction and Its Differences*. Albany: State U of New York P; 1990. 274 pp. (Contemporary Studies in Philosophy and Literature 1.) [†English language translation of theories of deconstructionism from French language (Modern).]

[2525] Handke, Peter; Goldschmidt, Georges-Arthur; Lenschen, H.; Lenschen, W. "Discussion entre Peter Handke, Georges-Arthur Goldschmidt et le public." *EdL*. 1989 Oct.-Dec.; 4: 35-52. [†Round table discussion.]

[2526] Hoeksema, Thomas; Babin, Pierre, tr. *Esperanto et traduction littéraire*. Rotterdam: Universala Esperanto-Asocio; 1984. 40 pp. (DLE 16F.) [Tr. of 1982 Bibliog. III.8209. †Esperanto language translation. Interview with Tonkin, Humphrey.]

[2527] Janićijević, Jovan. "Recepciona merila vrednovanja književnih prevoda." *Mostovi*. 1987 Oct.-Dec.; 18(4 [72]): 442-446.

[2528] Jindra, Miroslav. "Translating 'Classical' Novels: Problems of 'Modernization' and 'Archaization'." 363-366 in Bauer, Roger, ed.; Fokkema, Douwe, ed.; Graat, Michael de, asst. ed.; Fischer-Lichte, Erika, asst.; Garstin, Marguerite, asst.; Ibsch, Elrud, asst.; Stackelberg, Jürgen von, asst. *Proceedings of the XIIth Congress of the International Comparative Literature Association/Actes du XIIe congrès de l'Association Internationale de Littérature Comparée: München 1988 Munich, V: Space and Boundaries in Literary Theory and Criticism/Espace et frontières dans la critique et la théorie littéraire; Space and Boundaries in the Teaching of General and Comparative Literature/Espace et frontières dans l'enseignement de la littérature générale et comparée*. Munich: Iudicium; 1990. 415 pp. (Proceedings of the Congress of the International Comparative Literature Association 12: 5.)

[2529] Jones, Francis R. "On Aboriginal Sufferance: A Process Model of Poetic Translating." *Target*. 1989; 1(2): 183-199. [Fr. sum. †Of poetry.]

[2530] Jonson, Ann-Marie; Pitsis, Alexandra. "Lost in the Transformation." *Meanjin*. 1989 Summer; 48(4): 685-688.

[2531] Jordan, Albert. "Translation and Intercultural Understanding." *BACLA*. 1989 Fall; 11(2): 51-55. [Fr. sum.]

[2532] Kingscott, Geoffrey. "The Translation of Names and Titles." *Language International: The Magazine for the Language Professions*. 1990 Dec.; 2(6): 13-21. [†Of names; work title; forms of address.]

[2533] Lambert, José. "La Traduction." 151-159 in Angenot, Marc, ed.; Bessière, Jean, ed.; Fokkema, Douwe, ed.; Kushner, Eva, ed. *Théorie littéraire*. Paris: PU de France; 1989. 395 pp.

[2534] Lambert, José, ed.; Lefevere, André, ed.; Stackelberg, Jürgen von, ed.; Wertheimer, Jürgen, ed. "Groupe de travail: Intégration de l'étranger: Fonction de la traduction en histoire littéraire/Workshop: Assimilating the Foreign: The Function of Translation in Literary History." 331-410 in Bauer, Roger, ed.; Fokkema, Douwe, ed.; Graat, Michael de, asst. ed.; Fischer-Lichte, Erika, asst.; Garstin, Marguerite, asst.; Ibsch, Elrud, asst.; Stackelberg, Jürgen von, asst. *Proceedings of the XIIth Congress of the International Comparative Literature Association/Actes du XIIe congrès de l'Association Internationale de Littérature Comparée: München 1988 Munich, V: Space and Boundaries in Literary Theory and Criticism/Espace et frontières dans la critique et la théorie littéraire; Space and Boundaries in the Teaching of General and Comparative Literature/Espace et frontières dans l'enseignement de la littérature générale et comparée*. Munich: Iudicium; 1990. 415 pp. (Proceedings of the Congress of the International Comparative Literature Association 12: 5.) [Spec. sect.; incl. introd.]

[2535] Leavey, John P., Jr. "Bold Counsels and Carpenters: Pagan Translation." *TrP*. 1990; 5: 69-82. [†Relationship to untranslatability; untranslatability of poetic language; study example: Rimbaud, Arthur: *Une Saison en enfer*; *Illuminations*. Application of theories of Gadamer, Hans-Georg.]

[2536] ———. "Lations, Cor, Trans, Re, &c." 191-202 in Silverman, Hugh J., ed.; Aylesworth, Gary E., ed. *The Textual Sublime: Deconstruction and Its Differences*. Albany: State U of New York P; 1990. 274 pp. (Contemporary Studies in Philosophy and Literature 1.) [†English language translation of theories of deconstructionism from French language (Modern).]

[2537] Lefevere, André. "Jenseits von Gut und Schlecht—zu einer Genealogie des Übersetzens." 406-410 in Bauer, Roger, ed.; Fokkema, Douwe, ed.; Graat, Michael de, asst. ed.; Fischer-Lichte, Erika, asst.; Garstin, Marguerite, asst.; Ibsch, Elrud, asst.; Stackelberg, Jürgen von, asst. *Proceedings of the XIIth Congress of the International Comparative Literature Association/Actes du XIIe congrès de l'Association Internationale de Littérature Comparée: München 1988 Munich, V: Space and Boundaries in Literary Theory and Criticism/Espace et frontières dans la critique et la théorie littéraire; Space and Boundaries in the Teaching of General and Comparative Literature/Espace et frontières dans l'enseignement de la littérature générale et comparée*. Munich: Iudicium; 1990. 415 pp. (Proceedings of the Congress of the International Comparative Literature Association 12: 5.)

[2538] Li, Miqing. "Styles of Translation." *Waiguoyu*. 1990 Apr.; 2(66): 51-57, 62. [In Chin.]

[2539] Marcus, James. "Foreign Exchange: How Books Break the Language Barrier." *Village Voice Literary Supplement*. 1990 Feb.; 82: 13-17. [†On English language translation.]

[2540] Meschonnic, Henri. "Sur l'importance d'une poétique de la traduction." *EdL*. 1989 Oct.-Dec.; 4: 5-16. [†Poetics.]

[2541] Mohanty, Panchanan. "Macrolinguistic Prerequisites to Literary Translation." *IJL*. 1988 Jan.-June; 15(1): 30-37. [†Linguistic approach.]

[2542] Musy, Gilbert. "La Traduction littéraire 'assistée par ordinateur'." *EdL*. 1989 Oct.-Dec.; 4: 85-88. [†Application of computer.]

[2543] Nelson, Ralph. "Confessions of a Translator." *TRev*. 1990; 32-33: 39-40. [†Of poetry.]

[2544] Newman, Aryeh. "Translation Universals—Perspectives and Explorations." *TrP*. 1987; 3: 69-83. [†Relationship to universals of language; study example: Bible.]

[2545] Newmark, Peter. "Paragraphs on Translation, V: Translation as a Weapon; VI: The Universal and the Cultural in Translation; VII-IX." *Linguist*. 1990; 29(1): 6-10. 1990; 29(2): 48-51. 1990; 29(3): 82-84. 1990; 29(4): 118-121. 1990; 29(5): 152-154. [Cont. from 1989 Bibliog. III.3618 (IV.2780).]

[2546] Norst, Marlene J. "Children's Literature in Translation." *Meanjin*. 1989 Summer; 48(4): 747-757. [†Translation of fiction for children.]

[2547] Pedersen, Ellen M. "The Bull's Horns: A Prolegomenon to a Rationalist Poetic of Translation." *StHum*. 1990 June; 17(1): 63-74. [†Of science fiction.]

[2548] Perricone, Christopher. "Translation, Art, and Culture." *ClioI*. 1989 Fall; 19(1): 1-16.

[2549] Poltermann, Andreas. "Schulkanon und literarische Avantgarde: Zwei Beispiele zur Funktion der literarischen Übersetzung in der Zielliteratur." 203-212 in Bauer, Roger, ed.; Fokkema, Douwe, ed.; Graat, Michael de, asst. ed.; Fischer-Lichte, Erika, asst.; Garstin, Marguerite, asst.; Ibsch, Elrud, asst.; Stackelberg, Jürgen von, asst. *Proceedings of the XIIth Congress of the International Comparative Literature Association/Actes du XIIe congrès de l'Association Internationale de Littérature Comparée: München 1988 Munich, V: Space and Boundaries in Literary Theory and Criticism/Espace et frontières dans la critique et la théorie littéraire; Space and Boundaries in the Teaching of General and Comparative Literature/Espace et frontières dans l'enseignement de la littérature générale et comparée*. Munich: Iudicium; 1990. 415 pp. (Proceedings of the Congress of the International Comparative Literature Association 12: 5.) [†Role in canon of target literature; relationship to secondary education in Germany.]

[2550] Rayor, Diane J. "Translating Fragments." *TRev*. 1990; 32-33: 15-18. [†English language translation of Sappho.]

[2551] Reid, Helene. "Literature on the Screen: Subtitle Translating for Public Broadcasting." 97-107 in Westerweel, Bart, ed.; D'haen, Theo, ed. *Something Understood: Studies in Anglo-Dutch Literary Translation*. Amsterdam: Rodopi; 1990. 335 pp. (DQR: Studies in Literature 5.) [†Of subtitles.]

[2552] Ross, Stephen David. "Translation as Transgression." *TrP*. 1990; 5: 25-42. [†As transgression; relationship to representation.]

[2553] Sanfelice Galli Zugaro, Annamaria. "Libri e computer nel golfo." *EdL*. 1989 Oct.-Dec.; 4: 107-109. [†Role of Collegio Europeo dei Traduttori Letterari in Italy: Procida.]

[2554] Schmidt, Dennis J., ed. "Hermeneutics and the Poetic Motion." *TrP*. 1990; 5. [Spec. iss.; incl. introd.]

[2555] Schmidt, Lawrence K. "The Exemplary Status of Translating." *TrP*. 1990; 5: 83-92. [†Relationship to hermeneutics. Application of theories of Gadamer, Hans-Georg.]

[2556] Schogt, H. G. "Langue étrangère et dialecte et leurs rapports avec le texte principal: Un Problème de traduction." *Contrastes*. 1988 Dec.; 17: 21-38.

[2557] St. Germain, Sheryl, ed. "Poetry in Translation." *TRev*. 1990; 32-33: 1-2. [Spec. sect.; introd., 1-3. †Of poetry.]

[2558] Stackelberg, Jürgen von. "Übersetzungen aus zweiter Hand und eklektisches Übersetzen." 359-362 in Bauer, Roger, ed.; Fokkema, Douwe, ed.; Graat, Michael de, asst. ed.; Fischer-Lichte, Erika, asst.; Garstin, Marguerite, asst.; Ibsch, Elrud, asst.; Stackelberg, Jürgen von, asst. *Proceedings of the XIIth Congress of the International Comparative Literature Association/Actes du XIIe congrès de l'Association Internationale de Littérature Comparée: München 1988 Munich, V: Space and Boundaries in Literary Theory and Criticism/Espace et frontières dans la critique et la théorie littéraire; Space and Boundaries in the Teaching of General and Comparative Literature/Espace et frontières dans l'enseignement de la littérature générale et comparée*. Munich: Iudicium; 1990. 415 pp. (Proceedings of the Congress of the International Comparative Literature Association 12: 5.) [†Relationship to literary history.]

[2559] Sturrock, John. "Writing between the Lines: The Language of Translation." *NLH*. 1990 Autumn; 21(4): 993-1013.

[2560] Toper, P. "Zum Begriff des Übersetzens in der Literaturgeschichte: Einige aktuelle Fragen." 367-374 in Bauer, Roger, ed.; Fokkema, Douwe, ed.; Graat, Michael de, asst. ed.; Fischer-Lichte, Erika, asst.; Garstin, Marguerite, asst.; Ibsch, Elrud, asst.; Stackelberg, Jürgen von, asst. *Proceedings of the XIIth Congress of the International Comparative Literature Association/Actes du XIIe congrès de l'Association Internationale de Littérature Comparée: München 1988 Munich, V: Space and Boundaries in Literary Theory and Criticism/Espace et frontières dans la critique et la théorie littéraire; Space and Boundaries in the Teaching of General and Comparative Literature/Espace et frontières dans l'enseignement de la littérature générale et comparée*. Munich: Iudicium; 1990. 415 pp. (Proceedings of the Congress of the International Comparative Literature Association 12: 5.) [†Relationship to literary history.]

[2561] Van Hoof, Henri. "Traduction biblique et genèse linguistique." *Babel*. 1990; 36(1): 38-43. [Eng. sum. †Of Bible; relationship to language change.]

[2562] Weaver, William; Covi, Giovanna, ed.; Rose, Marilyn Gaddis, ed. "A Conversation on Translation with William Weaver." *TrP*. 1987; 3: 84-91. [†Round table discussion.]

[2563] Weber, Markus. "Dramatic Communication and the Translation of Drama." *BCILA*. 1990 Oct.; 52: 99-114. [†Of drama.]

[2564] Woodsworth, Judith. "Traducteurs et écrivains: Vers une redéfinition de la traduction littéraire." *TTR*. 1988; 1(1): 115-125. [†Creative process.]

[2565] Yuill, W. E. "'Wovon man nicht sprechen kann ...': The Translator and the Cultural Interface." *GL&L*. 1990 July; 43(4): 343-355.

[2566] Zhang, Jing. "Remarks in Poem Translation." *Waiguoyu*. 1990 Dec.; 6(70): 63-65, 78. [In Chin. †Of poetry.]

Translation theory

[2567] Calero, Francisco. "La teoría de la traducción del maestro Baltasar Céspedes." *Epos*. 1990; 6: 455-462. [†1500-1599. Theories of Céspedes, Baltasar de.]

[2568] Harris, R. Thomas. "Is Translation Possible?" *Diogenes*. 1990 Spring; 149: 105-121.

[2569] Hrdlička, Milan; Kvapil, Dušan, tr. "O problemima kritike prevoda." *Mostovi*. 1988 Jan.-Mar.; 19(1 [73]): 37-41.

[2570] Hulst, J.; Kievit, K.; Loos, E. "Kinds of Translation: From Chasm to Cline." 83-96 in Westerweel, Bart, ed.; D'haen, Theo, ed. *Something Understood: Studies in Anglo-Dutch Literary Translation*. Amsterdam: Rodopi; 1990. 335 pp. (DQR: Studies in Literature 5.)

[2571] Lönker, Fred. "Der fremde Sinn: Überlegungen zu den Übersetzungskonzeptionen Schleiermachers und Benjamins." 345-352 in Bauer, Roger, ed.; Fokkema, Douwe, ed.; Graat, Michael de, asst. ed.; Fischer-Lichte, Erika, asst.; Garstin, Marguerite, asst.; Ibsch, Elrud, asst.; Stackelberg, Jürgen von, asst. *Proceedings of the XIIth Congress of the International Comparative Literature Association/Actes du XIIe congrès de l'Association Internationale de Littérature Comparée: München 1988 Munich, V: Space and Boundaries in Literary Theory and Criticism/Espace et frontières dans la critique et la théorie littéraire; Space and Boundaries in the Teaching of General and Comparative Literature/Espace et frontières dans l'enseignement de la littérature générale et comparée*. Munich: Iudicium; 1990. 415 pp. (Proceedings of the Congress of the International Comparative Literature Association 12: 5.) [†Theories of Schleiermacher, Friedrich Daniel Ernst; Benjamin, Walter.]

[2572] Nida, Eugene A. "Theories of Translation." *Waiguoyu*. 1989 Dec.; 6(64): 2-8.

[2573] Tirumalesh, K. V. "Translation as Literature Three." *LCrit*. 1990; 25(3): 1-12.

[2574] Turk, Horst. "The Question of Translatability: Benjamin, Quine, Derrida." *TrP*. 1990; 5: 43-56. [†Theories of Quine, W. V. O.; Derrida, Jacques; Benjamin, Walter.]

[2575] ——. "Zur Methode der Übersetzungsanalyse." 334-344 in Bauer, Roger, ed.; Fokkema, Douwe, ed.; Graat, Michael de, asst. ed.; Fischer-Lichte, Erika, asst.; Garstin, Marguerite, asst.; Ibsch, Elrud, asst.; Stackelberg, Jürgen von, asst. *Proceedings of the XIIth Congress of the International Comparative Literature Association/Actes du XIIe congrès de l'Association Internationale de Littérature Comparée: München 1988 Munich, V: Space and Boundaries in Literary Theory and Criticism/Espace et frontières dans la critique et la théorie littéraire; Space and Boundaries in the Teaching of General and Comparative Literature/Espace et frontières dans l'enseignement de la littérature générale et comparée*. Munich: Iudicium; 1990. 415 pp. (Proceedings of the Congress of the International Comparative Literature Association 12: 5.) [†Role of interpretation; reference; relationship to analysis of target text.]

[2576] Wilss, Wolfram; Norton, Roger C., tr. "Cognitive Aspects of the Translation Process." *L&C*. 1990; 10(1): 19-36.

Professional topics

[2577] Cayton, Mary Kupiec. "What Happens When Things Go Wrong: Women and Writing Blocks." *JAC*. 1990 Fall; 10(2): 321-337. [†Role of writers's block; relationship to women in academia.]

[2578] Dolinar, Darko. "O literarnoznanstvenih in literarnozgodovinskih metodah." *JiS*. 1990-1991 Oct.-Nov.; 36(1-2): 1-9. [Eng. sum. †Research methods (literature).]

[2579] Kaylor, Noel Harold, Jr. "Teaching Diversity of Medieval Thought in Undergraduate Courses." *ArthI*. 1989 Fall; 4(1): 32-42.

[2580] Klein, Julie Thompson. *Interdisciplinarity: History, Theory, and Practice*. Detroit: Wayne State UP; 1990. 331 pp. [†Interdisciplinary studies.]

[2581] Lynch, Michael. "Last Onsets: Teaching with AIDS." *Profession*. 1990: 32-36.

[2582] Marius, Richard. "On Academic Discourse." *ADEB*. 1990 Fall; 96: 4-7. [†Academic discourse.]

[2583] Sheppard, Jocelyn; Hartman, Donald K. "Novels as PhD Dissertations." *AWP Chronicle*. 1989 Dec.; 22(3): 1, 3-4.

[2584] Simon, Eckehard. "The Case for Medieval Philology." 16-20 in Ziolkowski, Jan, ed. *On Philology*. University Park: Penn State UP; 1990. 78 pp. [†Role of philology (1880-1940) in medieval studies.]

[2585] Steeves, Edna. "Getting Published." *EdN*. 1990 Fall; 9(2): 10-13.

[2586] Torgovnick, Marianna. "Experimental Critical Writing." *ADEB*. 1990 Fall; 96: 8-10. [See also *Profession*. 1990: 25-27. †Role of experimental writing; relationship to academic prose.]

[2587] Weintraub, Stanley. "Curiosity and Motivation in Scholarship." *JGE*. 1986; 38(3): 159-166.

CENSORSHIP

[2588] Aust, Hugo. "Gottes rote Tinte: Zur Rechtfertigung der Zensur in der Restaurationszeit." *Nestroyana*. 1989-1990; 9(1-2): 35-48. [†In Austria and Germany. Relationship to restoration (ca. 1815).]

[2589] Gordimer, Nadine. "La censura y sus consecuencias." *Suplemento Literario La Nación* (Buenos Aires). 1990 Dec. 23: 1-2. [†In South Africa. 1900-1999.]

[2590] Maryniak, Irena. "How Society Censors Its Writers." *IonC.* 1990 June-July; 19(6): 8. [†In U.S.S.R. Interview with Golodnyĭ, Mikhail.

[2591] Sauerland, Karol. "Zensur im realen Sozialismus." *GR.* 1990 Summer; 65(3): 130-131. [†In East Germany; Poland. Relationship to socialism.]

[2592] Scriven, Michael. "Les Intellectuels et les médias: De la censure à l'autocensure." *FBS.* 1990 Spring; 9: 77-85. [†In France (1940-1989).]

COMPARATIVE LITERATURE

[2593] Balakian, Anna. "Literary Theory and Comparative Literature." 17-24 in Valdés, Mario J., ed. *Toward a Theory of Comparative Literature: Selected Papers Presented in the Division of Theory of Literature at the XIth International Comparative Literature Congress.* New York: Peter Lang; 1990. 275 pp. (Proceedings of the International Comparative Literature Association 11: 3.) [†Relationship to literary theory and criticism.]

[2594] ——. "Theoretical Assumptions of Interartifactuality." 53-65 in Jost, François, ed.; Friedman, Melvin J., asst. ed. *Aesthetics and the Literature of Ideas: Essays in Honor of A. Owen Aldridge.* Newark: U of Delaware P; 1990. 290 pp.

[2595] Bauer, Roger. "Origines et métamorphoses de la littérature comparée." 21-27 in Bauer, Roger, ed.; Fokkema, Douwe, ed.; Graat, Michael de, asst. ed.; Wimmer, Ruprecht, asst.; Goppel, Thomas, greeting. *Proceedings of the XIIth Congress of the International Comparative Literature Association/Actes du XIIe congrès de l'Association Internationale de Littérature Comparée: München 1988 Munich, I: Plenary Sessions/Séances plénières; Colloquium Munich/Colloque Munich.* Munich: Iudicium; 1990. 251 pp. (Proceedings of the Congress of the International Comparative Literature Association 12: 1.)

[2596] Ceserani, Remo. "Gli studi comparati in Italia." *Belfagor.* 1990 May 31; 45(3 [267]): 311-318. [†In Italy.]

[2597] Claudon, Francis. "La Littérature comparée et les arts." *Neohelicon.* 1989; 16(1): 259-284.

[2598] Farinelli, Arturo; Weisstein, Ulrich, introd.; Friedman, Miriam, tr. "Literary Influences and the Pride of Nations." *YCGL.* 1987; 36: 69-74. [Tr. of excerpts from "Gl'influssi letterari e l'insuperbire delle nazioni" in *Mélanges d'histoire littéraire générale et comparée.* Paris: Champion; 1930.]

[2599] Firchow, Peter. "The Nature and Uses of Imagology." 135-142 in Valdés, Mario J., ed. *Toward a Theory of Comparative Literature: Selected Papers Presented in the Division of Theory of Literature at the XIth International Comparative Literature Congress.* New York: Peter Lang; 1990. 275 pp. (Proceedings of the International Comparative Literature Association 11: 3.) [†Role of imagology; relationship to literary studies.]

[2600] Fokkema, D.; Muliarchik, A. S., tr. "Problemy sravnitel'nogo izucheniia literatur." *IAN.* 1989 Sept.-Oct.; 48(5): 460-463. [Incl. introd.]

[2601] Fokkema, Douwe. "On Theory and Criticism in Literary Studies: The International Point of View: Presidential Address." 111-119 in Bauer, Roger, ed.; Fokkema, Douwe, ed.; Graat, Michael de, asst. ed.; Wimmer, Ruprecht, asst.; Goppel, Thomas, greeting. *Proceedings of the XIIth Congress of the International Comparative Literature Association/Actes du XIIe congrès de l'Association Internationale de Littérature Comparée: München 1988 Munich, I: Plenary Sessions/Séances plénières; Colloquium Munich/Colloque Munich.* Munich: Iudicium; 1990. 251 pp. (Proceedings of the Congress of the International Comparative Literature Association 12: 1.) [†And literary studies; relationship to literary theory and criticism.]

[2602] Gillespie, Gerald. "Elitist Dilemmas: Cultural Cross-Currents and Prospects of Comparative Studies on the National and Global Level." *Journal of Intercultural Studies* (Kansai Univ.). 1987; 14: 116-123.

[2603] ——. "Newer Trends of Comparative Studies in the West." 17-34 in Mohan, Chandra, ed. *Aspects of Comparative Literature: Current Approaches.* New Delhi: India Pubs. & Distributors; 1989. xviii, 300 pp. [†In Europe; United States. Role of literary theory and criticism.]

[2604] ——. "Temporal Axes in the Teaching of Comparative and General Literature in the United States." *Neohelicon.* 1985; 12(1): 123-130. [†At American universities. Literature of Middle Ages; Renaissance.]

[2605] Grève, Claude de. "'Comparative Reception': A New Approach to 'Rezeptionsästhetik'." 233-240 in Jost, François, ed.; Friedman, Melvin J., asst. ed. *Aesthetics and the Literature of Ideas: Essays in Honor of A. Owen Aldridge.* Newark: U of Delaware P; 1990. 290 pp. [†Relationship to reception theory.]

[2606] Grintser, P. A. "Sravnitel'noe literaturovedenie i istoricheskaia poėtika." *IAN.* 1990 Mar.-Apr.; 49(2): 99-107.

[2607] Kaufman, Eva. "Weltliteratur des 20. Jahrhunderts in der Lehrerausbildung." 213-218 in Bauer, Roger, ed.; Fokkema, Douwe, ed.; Graat, Michael de, asst. ed.; Fischer-Lichte, Erika, asst.; Garstin, Marguerite, asst.; Ibsch, Elrud, asst.; Stackelberg, Jürgen von, asst. *Proceedings of the XIIth Congress of the International Comparative Literature Association/Actes du XIIe congrès de l'Association Internationale de Littérature Comparée: München 1988 Munich, V: Space and Boundaries in Literary Theory and Criticism/Espace et frontières dans la critique et la théorie littéraire; Space and Boundaries in the Teaching of General and Comparative Literature/Espace et frontières dans l'enseignement de la littérature générale et comparée.* Munich: Iudicium; 1990. 415 pp. (Proceedings of the Congress of the International Comparative Literature Association 12: 5.) [†World literature; relationship to teacher training in East Germany.]

[2608] Lambert, José. "'Weltliteratur' et les études littéraires actuelles: Comment construire des schémas comparatistes?" 28-35 in Bauer, Roger, ed.; Fokkema, Douwe, ed.; Graat, Michael de, asst. ed.; Kaiser, Gerhard, asst.; Rinner, Fridrun, asst.; Wertheimer, Jürgen, asst. *Proceedings of the XIIth Congress of the International Comparative Literature Association/Actes du XIIe congrès de l'Association Internationale de Littérature Comparée: München 1988 Munich, IV: Space and Boundaries of Literature/Espace et frontières de la littérature.* Munich: Iudicium; 1990. 651 pp. (Proceedings of the Congress of the International Comparative Literature Association 12: 4.) [†World literature; relationship to national literature.]

[2609] Laurette, Pierre. "Universalité et comparabilité." 51-60 in Angenot, Marc, ed.; Bessière, Jean, ed.; Fokkema, Douwe, ed.; Kushner, Eva, ed. *Théorie littéraire.* Paris: PU de France; 1989. 395 pp.

[2610] Lawall, Sarah. "World Literature, Comparative Literature, Teaching Literature." 219-224 in Bauer, Roger, ed.; Fokkema, Douwe, ed.; Graat, Michael de, asst. ed.; Fischer-Lichte, Erika, asst.; Garstin, Marguerite, asst.; Ibsch, Elrud, asst.; Stackelberg, Jürgen von, asst. *Proceedings of the XIIth Congress of the International Comparative Literature Association/Actes du XIIe congrès de l'Association Internationale de Littérature Comparée: München 1988 Munich, V: Space and Boundaries in Literary Theory and Criticism/Espace et frontières dans la critique et la théorie littéraire; Space and Boundaries in the Teaching of General and Comparative Literature/Espace et frontières dans l'enseignement de la littérature générale et comparée.* Munich: Iudicium; 1990. 415 pp. (Proceedings of the Congress of the International Comparative Literature Association 12: 5.) [†Relationship to world literature.]

[2611] Marino, Adrian. "Spiritul comparatist modern." *RITL.* 1989-1990; 37-38(3-4): 66-72.

[2612] Miner, Earl. *Comparative Poetics: An Intercultural Essay on Theories of Literature.* Princeton: Princeton UP; 1990. xi, 259 pp. [†Role of poetics.]

[2613] ——. "Etudes comparées interculturelles." 161-179 in Angenot, Marc, ed.; Bessière, Jean, ed.; Fokkema, Douwe, ed.; Kushner, Eva, ed. *Théorie littéraire.* Paris: PU de France; 1989. 395 pp. [†Study example: Asian literature.]

[2614] ——. "Possible Canons of Literary Transmittal and Appropriation." *YCGL.* 1988; 37: 109-112.

[2615] Mohan, Chandra, ed. *Aspects of Comparative Literature: Current Approaches.* New Delhi: India Pubs. & Distributors; 1989. xviii, 300 pp.

[2616] Nalivaĭko, D. S. "Dominanty natsional'nykh kul'tur i mezhnatsional'nye literaturnye obshcheniia." *IAN.* 1990 Mar.-Apr.; 49(2): 108-118. [†World literature; relationship to national literature.]

[2617] Nyirö, Lajos. "L'Aspect empirique et théorique des recherches en littérature comparée." 67-75 in Valdés, Mario J., ed. *Toward a Theory of Comparative Literature: Selected Papers Presented in the Division of Theory of Literature at the XIth International Comparative Literature Congress.* New York: Peter Lang; 1990. 275 pp. (Proceedings of the International Comparative Literature Association 11: 3.) [†Relationship to empiricism; literary theory.]

[2618] Remak, Henry H. H. "Between Scylla and Charybdis: Quality Judgment in Comparative Literature." 21-33 in Jost, François, ed.; Friedman, Melvin J., asst. ed. *Aesthetics and the Literature of Ideas: Essays in Honor of A. Owen Aldridge.* Newark: U of Delaware P; 1990. 290 pp. [†Aesthetic judgment.]

[2619] Rinner, Fridrun. "Y a-t-il une théorie propre à la littérature comparée." 173-180 in Valdés, Mario J., ed. *Toward a Theory of Comparative Literature: Selected Papers Presented in the Division of Theory of Literature at the XIth International Comparative Literature Congress.* New York: Peter Lang; 1990. 275 pp. (Proceedings of the International Comparative Literature Association 11: 3.)

[2620] Savater, Fernando. "La república de los intelectuales." *Suplemento Literario La Nación* (Buenos Aires). 1990 Dec. 2: 1-2. [†1900-1999.]

[2621] Schipper, Mineke. "Towards an Intercultural Comparative Study of Critical Texts." 195-208 in Valdés, Mario J., ed. *Toward a Theory of Comparative Literature: Selected Papers Presented in the Division of Theory of Literature at the XIth International Comparative Literature Congress.* New York: Peter Lang; 1990. 275 pp. (Proceedings of the International Comparative Literature Association 11: 3.) [†Relationship to study of criticism.]

[2622] Segers, Rien T. "Over de wending van de comparatistische steven: Pleidooi voor een communicatieve benadering." *FdL.* 1990 Sept.; 31(3): 189-202.

[2623] Strelka, Joseph. "On German *Geistesgeschichte* and Its Impact on Comparative Literature." 44-52 in Jost, François, ed.; Friedman, Melvin J., asst. ed. *Aesthetics and the Literature of Ideas: Essays in Honor of A. Owen Aldridge.* Newark: U of Delaware P; 1990. 290 pp. [†Sources in history of ideas. Role of Gundolf, Friedrich: *Shakespeare und der deutsche Geist*; Unger, Rudolf: *Hamann und die Aufklärung.*]

[2624] Strutz, Janez. "Casarsa, Mat(t)erada, Vogrče/Rinkenberg: Ali medregionalnost in literatura—koncept regionalnega težišča celovške komparativistike." *PKn.* 1990; 13(1): 1-14. [Ger. sum. †1900-1999. At Universität für Bildungswissenschaften Klagenfurt; relationship to regionalism.]

[2625] Tatlow, Antony. "The Context of Comparative Literature." *Chinese/Foreign Comparative Literature Bulletin.* 1990 Mar. 1; 1: 2-5.

[2626] Vajdová, Libuša. "Les Modes d'organisation des littératures nationales dans le processus interlittéraire." 19-27 in Bauer, Roger, ed.; Fokkema, Douwe, ed.; Graat, Michael de, asst. ed.; Kaiser, Gerhard, asst.; Rinner, Fridrun, asst.; Wertheimer, Jürgen, asst. *Proceedings of the XIIth Congress of the International Comparative Literature Association/Actes du XIIe congrès de l'Association Internationale de Littérature Comparée: München 1988 Munich, IV: Space and Boundaries of Literature/Espace et frontières de la littérature.* Munich: Iudicium; 1990. 651 pp. (Proceedings of the Congress of the International Comparative Literature Association 12: 4.) [†National literature; relationship to world literature.]

[2627] Valdés, Mario J., ed. *Toward a Theory of Comparative Literature: Selected Papers Presented in the Division of Theory of Literature at the XIth International Comparative Literature Congress.* New York: Peter Lang; 1990. 275 pp. (Proceedings of the International Comparative Literature Association 11: 3.) [Incl. introd. †Relationship to literary theory and criticism.]

[2628] Walzel, Oskar; Hooper, Kent, tr.; Weisstein, Ulrich, ed. "The Mutual Illumination of the Arts: A Contribution to the Appreciation of Art History." *YCGL*. 1988; 37: 12-31. [Incl. introd. †Relationship to art history.

[2629] Wang, Zhiliang. "Anatomy of Comparative Studies in China." 245-250 in Bauer, Roger, ed.; Fokkema, Douwe, ed.; Graat, Michael de, asst. ed.; Fischer-Lichte, Erika, asst.; Garstin, Marguerite, asst.; Ibsch, Elrud, asst.; Stackelberg, Jürgen von, asst. *Proceedings of the XIIth Congress of the International Comparative Literature Association/Actes du XIIe congrès de l'Association Internationale de Littérature Comparée: München 1988 Munich, V: Space and Boundaries in Literary Theory and Criticism/Espace et frontières dans la critique et la théorie littéraire; Space and Boundaries in the Teaching of General and Comparative Literature/Espace et frontières dans l'enseignement de la littérature générale et comparée.* Munich: Iudicium; 1990. 415 pp. (Proceedings of the Congress of the International Comparative Literature Association 12: 5.) [†Relationship to Chinese literature.]

[2630] Weimann, Robert. "Toward a Social History of Representation." 253-275 in Valdés, Mario J., ed. *Toward a Theory of Comparative Literature: Selected Papers Presented in the Division of Theory of Literature at the XIth International Comparative Literature Congress.* New York: Peter Lang; 1990. 275 pp. (Proceedings of the International Comparative Literature Association 11: 3.) [†Relationship to literary theory and criticism.]

[2631] Weisstein, Ulrich. "*Lasciate ogni speranza*: Comparative Literature in Search of Lost Definitions." *YCGL*. 1988; 37: 98-108.

[2632] Wellek, René. "The New Nihilism in Literary Studies." 77-85 in Jost, François, ed.; Friedman, Melvin J., asst. ed. *Aesthetics and the Literature of Ideas: Essays in Honor of A. Owen Aldridge.* Newark: U of Delaware P; 1990. 290 pp. [†Relationship to nihilism.]

[2633] Yuan, Heh-Hsiang. "Two Assumptions: A Rapprochement of Chinese-Western Literary Ideas." 34-43 in Jost, François, ed.; Friedman, Melvin J., asst. ed. *Aesthetics and the Literature of Ideas: Essays in Honor of A. Owen Aldridge.* Newark: U of Delaware P; 1990. 290 pp. [†Chinese literature compared to Western literature.]

Bibliography

[2634] Cohen, Selma Jeanne, comp.; Barricelli, Jean-Pierre, comp.; Clüver, Claus, comp. & ed.; Faris, Wendy, comp.; Kelly, James R., comp.; Reynolds, John J., comp.; Scher, Steven P., comp.; Wallace, Robert K., comp.; Flanigan, C. Clifford, ed. "1988 Bibliography on the Relations of Literature and Other Arts." *YCGL*. 1988; 37: 224-272. [†(1988).]

[2635] Leerssen, Joseph Th., ed. "Bibliography of Comparative Literature in Britain and Ireland." *CCrit*. 1990; 12: 303-323. [†In Great Britain; Ireland. (1987).]

[2636] Weisstein, Ulrich. "Horst Frenz: Selected Bibliography, 1938-1984." *YCGL*. 1987; 36: 64-66. [†Theories of Frenz, Horst. (1938-1984).]

COMPUTER-ASSISTED RESEARCH

[2637] Corns, Thomas N., introd. "Literary Criticism and Computing." *L&LC*. 1990; 5(3): 219-249. [Spec. sect.]

[2638] Davidson, T. T. L. "Teaching with the Oxford Concordance Program." *L&LC*. 1990; 5(1): 80-85. [†Oxford Concordance program; application in teaching of literature.]

[2639] Deegan, Marilyn, introd. "[Computers and Language]." *L&LC*. 1990; 5(1): 36-93. [Spec. sect. †Application of information technology.]

[2640] Hockey, Susan, introd. "Papers from the Literature Workshop, Conference on Computers and Teaching in the Humanities, April 1990." *L&LC*. 1990; 5(4): 303-321. [Spec. sect.]

[2641] Hunter, Lynette. "Fact—Information—Data—Knowledge: Databases as a Way of Organizing Knowledge." *L&LC*. 1990; 5(1): 49-57. [†Application of database; relationship to humanities.]

[2642] Ide, Nancy M. "The Course in Methods of Literary Research: Integrating Computational Tools and Methodology." *LRN*. 1987 Spring-Summer; 12(2-3): 107-110. [†Pedagogical approach.]

[2643] Jackson, H. "OCP and the Computer Analysis of Texts: The Birmingham Polytechnic Experience." *L&LC*. 1990; 5(1): 86-88. [†Oxford Concordance program; application in teaching of literature.]

[2644] Kammer, Manfred. "WordCruncher: Problems of Multilingual Usage." *L&LC*. 1989; 4(2): 135-140. [†Application of WordCruncher computer program.]

[2645] Leslie, Michael. "The Hartlib Papers Project: Text Retrieval with Large Datasets." *L&LC*. 1990; 5(1): 58-69. [†Hartlib Papers Project; relationship to publishing by Hartlib, Samuel.]

[2646] Miall, D. S. *Personal Librarian*: A Tool for the Literature Classroom." *L&LC*. 1990; 5(1): 19-23. [†Personal Librarian computer program.]

[2647] Potter, Rosanne G., ed. *Literary Computing and Literary Criticism: Theoretical and Practical Essays on Theme and Rhetoric.* Philadelphia: U of Pennsylvania P; 1989. xxix, 276 pp. [Incl. bibliog.; prev. pub. essays. †Relationship to literary theory and criticism.]

[2648] Schanze, H. "A European Perspective for the PC Age." *L&LC*. 1990; 5(2): 171-173.

[2649] Schanze, Helmut, introd. "[Full Text Retrieval Systems]." *L&LC*. 1989; 4(2): 106-145. [Spec. sect. †On full text retrieval system.]

[2650] Smith, F. J.; Devine, K. "BIRD, QUILL and MicroBIRD: A Successful Family of Text Retrieval Systems." *L&LC*. 1989; 4(2): 115-120. [†BIRD retrieval system; QUILL retrieval system.]

Bibliography

[2651] Pellen, René, comp.; Pradines, Jacques, comp. "L'Informatique et les humanités: Bibliographie 1986-1989, d'après quelques périodiques spécialisées." *L&LC*. 1990; 5(1): 24-35. [†Relationship to humanities.]

HUMANITIES

[2652] Adler, Robert; Allgood, Myralyn; Brown, Diane; Coleman, Charlotte. "Summer Immersion Institutes: A Consortium Approach." 7-11 in Fernández Jiménez, Juan, ed.; Labrador Herraiz, José J., ed.; Valdivieso, L. Teresa, ed.; Morón Arroyo, Ciriaco, pref. *Estudios en homenaje a Enrique Ruiz-Fornells.* Erie, PA: Asociación de Licenciados & Doctores Españoles en Estados Unidos; 1990. xxvi, 706 pp. (Homenajes 1.) [†Second language teaching.]

[2653] Anderson, Vivienne Melluish. "Rhetoric and Cultural Conservatism: An Historical Examination." *DAI*. 1990 Mar.; 50(9): 2875A. [†Rhetoric; relationship to cultural conservatism; study example: Isocrates; Erasmus, Desiderius; Weaver, Richard M. Dissertation abstract.]

[2654] Arac, Jonathan. "Tradition, Discipline, and Trouble." *Profession*. 1990: 12-17. [†Relationship to tradition. Application of theories of Benjamin, Walter; Williams, Raymond.]

[2655] Armstrong, Paul B. "The English Coalition and the English Major." *ADEB*. 1990 Fall; 96: 30-33. [†On English Coalition Conference (1987).]

[2656] Arnold, Judy; Howard, Benjamin S. "The Structuralist Community College Student in a Post-Structuralist Age." 211-222 in Moran, Charles, ed.; Penfield, Elizabeth F., ed. *Conversations: Contemporary Critical Theory and the Teaching of Literature.* Urbana: Nat. Council of Teachers of Eng.; 1990. viii, 237 pp.

[2657] Baird, Rebecca L. Russell; Zordani, Bob. "An Interview with Catharine Stimpson." *W&D*. 1990 Spring; 8(1 [15]): 7-15. [†Multicultural education; relationship to literacy; feminism. Interview with Stimpson, Catharine R.]

[2658] Baker-Smith, Dominic. "A Renaissance Perspective." 5-14 in Westerweel, Bart, ed.; D'haen, Theo, ed. *Something Understood: Studies in Anglo-Dutch Literary Translation.* Amsterdam: Rodopi; 1990. 335 pp. (DQR: Studies in Literature 5.) [†Literary studies of Renaissance in Great Britain; Netherlands (1950-1990).]

[2659] Bal, Mieke. "Literatuurwetenschap Interdisciplinair." *Spektator*. 1989 May; 18(5): 336-339. [†Role of interdisciplinary studies in literary studies.]

[2660] Bednar, Lucy. "Enhancing Metalinguistic Awareness in the Literature Classroom: A Case Study Approach." *DAI*. 1990 Dec.; 51(6): 1935A. [†Teaching of literature; relationship to metalinguistic awareness. Dissertation abstract.]

[2661] Birnbaum, Milton. "Reopening the Cave of Illusion." *ModA*. 1988 Winter; 32(1): 9-13. [†In United States. Theories of Bloom, Allan David: *The Closing of the American Mind*; relationship to the past; democracy; reality.]

[2662] Blitz, Michael; Hurlbert, C. Mark. "Literacy Demands and Institutional Autobiography." *W&D*. 1989 Spring; 7(1 [13]): 7-33. [†Role of literacy.]

[2663] Britt, Suzanne. "The Philosophic Mind." *MOR*. 1990 Spring; 4: 71-76. [†Teaching of literature.]

[2664] Brothers, Barbara. "Is There a Hierarchy in This Class? Or, On Composing a Course without a Text." *ADEB*. 1990 Winter; 97: 26-30. [†Teaching of literature.]

[2665] Brown, Gillian. "Walking and Talking." *CritQ*. 1990 Winter; 32(4): 34-38. [†Treatment in *Cox Report on National Curriculum*.]

[2666] Burgan, Mary. "Academic Careers in the Nineties: Images and Realities." *ADEB*. 1990 Fall; 96: 19-24.

[2667] Burt, E. S., ed.; Vanpée, Janie, ed. "Reading the Archive: On Texts and Institutions." *YFS*. 1990; 77. [Spec. iss.; incl. pref. †On French literature; relationship to dissemination in universities.]

[2668] Cappelletti, Vincenzo, ed. "Lingua e cultura italiana negli Stati Uniti: La presenza e l'immagine." *Veltro*. 1989 Sept.-Dec.; 33(5-6). [Spec. iss. †On Italian studies; relationship to teaching in United States.]

[2669] Caprio, Anthony. "Translation Training within Reach: Program and Curriculum Development." *Selecta*. 1988; 9: 49-54. [†Teaching of translation at American universities.]

[2670] Carpenter, Mary Wilson. "Eco, Oedipus, and the 'View' of the University." *Diacritics*. 1990 Spring; 20(1): 77-85. [†On ageism; sexism in universities. Theories of Eco, Umberto; Derrida, Jacques.]

[2671] Chabot, C. Barry. "Going Beyond the English Coalition Report." *ADEB*. 1990 Fall; 96: 38-41. [†On English Coalition Conference (1987).]

[2672] Chambers, Ross. "Irony and the Canon." *Profession*. 1990: 18-24. [†Role of irony; relationship to canon in teaching of literature.]

[2673] Cheney, Lynne V. *Tyrannical Machines: A Report on Educational Practices Gone Wrong and Our Best Hopes for Setting Them Right.* Washington, DC: Nat. Endowment for the Humanities; 1990. 64 pp.

[2674] Clausen, Christopher. "'Canon,' Theme, and Code." *SWR*. 1990 Spring; 75(2): 264-279. [†Canon.]

[2675] ——. "Plantation Politics: The English Coalition and Its Report." *ADEB*. 1990 Fall; 96: 34-37. [†On English Coalition Conference (1987).]

[2676] Cohen, Ralph, ed. "Papers from the Commonwealth Center for Literary and Cultural Change." *NLH*. 1990 Autumn; 21(4). [Spec. iss.; incl. introd.]

[2677] Comprone, Joseph J. "The Literacies of Science and the Humanities: The Monologic and Dialogic Traditions." 52-70 in Ronald, Kate, ed.; Roskelly, Hephzibah, ed. *Farther Along: Transforming Dichotomies in Rhetoric and Composition.* Portsmouth, NH: Boynton/Cook; 1990. x, 208 pp. [†Relationship to literacy; science. Theories of Hirsch, Eric Donald; Bakhtin, Mikhail Mikhaïlovich.]

[2678] Côté, Paul Raymond. "From Principles to Pragmatics: Teaching Translation in the Classroom." *FR*. 1990 Feb.; 63(3): 433-443. [†Teaching of translation.]

[2679] Craige, Betty Jean. *Reconnection: Dualism to Holism in Literary Study*. Athens: U of Georgia P; 1988. xii, 153 pp. [†Role of dualism; holism; relationship to canon in literary studies. Theories of Descartes, René.]

[2680] Craven, Jerry. "The Lipstick on the Glass: Teaching Expository Writing through Creative Fiction." *CCTEP*. 1990 Sept.; 55: 67-74. [†Teaching of writing; relationship to fiction compared to prose.]

[2681] Crowley, Sharon. "Jacques Derrida on Teaching and Rhetoric: A Response." *JAC*. 1990 Fall; 10(2): 393-396. [Replies to Olson, below. †Application of deconstructionism. Theories of Derrida, Jacques.]

[2682] Dasenbrock, Reed Way. "What to Teach When the Canon Closes Down: Toward a New Essentialism." 63-76 in Henricksen, Bruce, ed.; Morgan, Thais E., ed. *Reorientations: Critical Theories & Pedagogics*. Urbana: U of Illinois P; 1990. x, 275 pp. [†Canon.]

[2683] Davies, Gordon K. "The Future of the Humanities in Virginia Higher Education." *NLH*. 1990 Autumn; 21(4): 863-866. [†In Virginia.]

[2684] Davis, Charles G. "Shifting Models of the University: Academia Slouches toward the Millennium." *ADEB*. 1990 Winter; 97: 43-46. [†Curriculum; relationship to marketplace.]

[2685] Davis, Lennard J., ed.; Mirabella, M. Bella, ed. *Left Politics and the Literary Profession*. New York: Columbia UP; 1990. xii, 316 pp. (Social Foundations of Aesthetic Forms.) [Incl. introd. †Relationship to left-wing politics.]

[2686] Davis, Robert Con. "A Manifesto for Oppositional Pedagogy: Freire, Bourdieu, Merod, and Graff." 248-267 in Henricksen, Bruce, ed.; Morgan, Thais E., ed. *Reorientations: Critical Theories & Pedagogics*. Urbana: U of Illinois P; 1990. x, 275 pp. [†Pedagogy. Theories of Freire, Paulo; Bourdieu, Pierre; Merod, Jim; Graff, Gerald.]

[2687] DeLotto, Jeffrey. "Imitating Poetic Models in Prose: Or, The Old Cumberland Professor." *CCTEP*. 1990 Sept.; 55: 23-32. [†Teaching of writing; relationship to imitation of poetry.]

[2688] Dendinger, Lloyd N. "Teaching Literature in the Post-Structuralist Era: A Classroom Teacher's Agenda." 164-178 in Moran, Charles, ed.; Penfield, Elizabeth F., ed. *Conversations: Contemporary Critical Theory and the Teaching of Literature*. Urbana: Nat. Council of Teachers of Eng.; 1990. viii, 237 pp. [†Teaching of literature; relationship to poststructuralism.]

[2689] Denham, Robert D. "The English Coalition Conference: A Pocketful of Wye." *ADEB*. 1990 Fall; 96: 26-29. [†On English Coalition Conference (1987).]

[2690] Dewar, Kenneth C. "Hilda Neatby and the Ends of Education." *QQ*. 1990 Summer; 97(1): 36-51. [†Theories of Neatby, Hilda Marion Ada: *So Little for the Mind*.]

[2691] D'haen, Theo. "Gone with the Shield of Achilles? English and American Literature at Dutch Universities." 23-34 in Westerweel, Bart, ed.; D'haen, Theo, ed. *Something Understood: Studies in Anglo-Dutch Literary Translation*. Amsterdam: Rodopi; 1990. 335 pp. (DQR: Studies in Literature 5.) [†Role of English departments in Netherlandic universities.]

[2692] Diaz, Olga. "Didactique littéraire." *Glottodidactica*. 1990; 20: 71-76. [†Teaching of literature.]

[2693] Doan, Laura L.; Town, Caren J. "'Don't Take That Class': Teaching Theory in the Small University." *ADEB*. 1990 Winter; 97: 31-36. [†Teaching of literary theory.]

[2694] Donaldson, Ian. "The Future of Research in the Humanities." *AUMLA*. 1990 May; 73: 5-23. [†Role of research.]

[2695] Dunn, Richard J. "Teaching Assistance, Not Teaching Assistants." *ADEB*. 1990 Winter; 97: 47-50. [†Training of teaching assistants.]

[2696] During, Simon. "Professing the Popular." *Meanjin*. 1990 Spring; 49(3): 481-491. [†Role of popular culture; relationship to teaching of literature.]

[2697] Elbow, Peter. *What Is English?* New York: Mod. Lang. Assn. of Amer.; 1990. Urbana: Nat. Council of Teachers of Eng.; 1990. viii, 271 pp. [†Role of English departments; language arts.]

[2698] Fenstermaker, John J. "'Literature' and 'Student Writing' Are Both Texts'." *LRN*. 1987 Spring-Summer; 12(2-3): 99-106. [†Role of literary theory and criticism in English studies.]

[2699] Flannery, Kathryn T. "Concepts of Culture: Cultural Literacy/Cultural Politics." 86-100 in Ronald, Kate, ed.; Roskelly, Hephzibah, ed. *Farther Along: Transforming Dichotomies in Rhetoric and Composition*. Portsmouth, NH: Boynton/Cook; 1990. x, 208 pp. [†Cultural knowledge. Theories of Hirsch, Eric Donald.]

[2700] Flowers, Betty S. "The Moral Imagination: Taking Literature to Heart." *ADEB*. 1990 Spring; 95: 18-20. [†Teaching of literature.]

[2701] Foehr, Regina Paxton. "Using the Simple to Teach the Complex: Teaching College Students to Interpret Complex Literature and to Write Literary Analysis Essays through Fairy Tales and Children's Stories." *DAI*. 1990 Mar.; 50(9): 2885A. [†Use of *Märchen*; literature for children in teaching of literature. Dissertation abstract.]

[2702] Fong, Bobby. "Local Canons: Professing Literature at the Small Liberal Arts College." 200-210 in Moran, Charles, ed.; Penfield, Elizabeth F., ed. *Conversations: Contemporary Critical Theory and the Teaching of Literature*. Urbana: Nat. Council of Teachers of Eng.; 1990. viii, 237 pp. [†Canon.]

[2703] Fontaine, Sheryl I. "The Unfinished Story of the Interpretive Community." *RhetRev*. 1988 Fall; 7(1): 86-96. [†Role of academic discourse; relationship to interpretive communities; social construction.]

[2704] Foster, Dennis A. "Interpretation and Betrayal: Talking with Authority." 35-48 in Donahue, Patricia, ed.; Quandahl, Ellen, ed. *Reclaiming Pedagogy: The Rhetoric of the Classroom*. Carbondale: Southern Illinois UP; 1989. ix, 179 pp. [†On teaching of reading; teaching of writing; relationship to authority.]

[2705] France, Alan W. "Self, Society, and Text in Rhetoric and Composition Theory since 1970." *DAI*. 1990 Mar.; 50(9): 2875A. [†On teaching of writing; relationship to cultural context. Dissertation abstract.]

[2706] Franklin, Phyllis. "The Academy and the Public." *SAQ*. 1990 Winter; 89(1): 207-215.

[2707] ——. "Waiting for the Barbarians." *MLS*. 1990 Winter; 20(1): 3-10.

[2708] Frith, Simon. "The 'Cox Report' and the University." *CritQ*. 1990 Winter; 32(4): 68-76. [†Treatment in *Cox Report on National Curriculum*.]

[2709] Frye, Charles. "Black Studies as an Educational Enterprise: A Prognosis." *Proteus*. 1990 Spring; 7(1): 20-24. [†African American studies.]

[2710] Gates, Henry Louis, Jr. "Canon Confidential: A Sam Slade Caper." *New York Times Book Review*. 1990 Mar. 25: 1, 36. [†Canon.]

[2711] Gaudard, F.-C. "Didactique et texte littéraire: Essai de théorisation d'une expérience pédagogique." *RevPL*. 1990; 95-97: 153-158. [†Role of teaching of literature in teaching of language.]

[2712] Gaudiano, Franco. "Imparare a scrivere." *Vita e Pensiero: Mensile di Cultura dell' Universita '1 Cattolica*. 1990 Apr.; 73(4): 273-280. [†In United States. Creative writing workshops.]

[2713] Gebhardt, Richard C. "Fiction Writing in Literature Classes." *RhetRev*. 1988 Fall; 7(1): 150-155. [†Role of writing of fiction in teaching of literature.]

[2714] Giroux, Henry A. "Liberal Arts Education and the Struggle for Public Life: Dreaming about Democracy." *SAQ*. 1990 Winter; 89(1): 113-138.

[2715] Gless, Darryl J., ed.; Smith, Barbara Herrnstein, ed. "The Politics of Liberal Education." *SAQ*. 1990 Winter; 89(1). [Spec. iss. †Relationship to canon.]

[2716] Graff, Gerald. "How to Deal with the Humanities Crisis: Organize It." *ADEB*. 1990 Spring; 95: 4-10.

[2717] ——. "Other Voices, Other Rooms: Organizing and Teaching the Humanities Conflict." *NLH*. 1990 Autumn; 21(4): 817-839. [†Teaching of literature; relationship to canon.]

[2718] ——. "Teach the Conflicts." *SAQ*. 1990 Winter; 89(1): 51-67. [†Canon.]

[2719] Grendler, Paul F., ed. "Education in the Renaissance and Reformation." *RenQ*. 1990 Winter; 43(4): 774-824. [Spec. sect. †In Europe. 1400-1599.]

[2720] Griffin, Gail. "Alma Mater." *Profession*. 1990: 37-42. [†Role of women in academia; study example: Stone, Lucinda Hinsdale.]

[2721] Haggard, Frank E. "Hiring and Mentoring New Faculty Members." *ADEB*. 1990 Spring; 95: 25-28. [†On tenure of faculty in English departments.]

[2722] Hallo, William W. "Assyriology and the Canon." *ASch*. 1990 Winter; 59(1): 105-108. [†Canon.]

[2723] Harrison, Frank R., III. "Values, Epistemology, and High-Tech." *ModA*. 1989 Summer; 32(3): 231-237. [†Relationship to vocation; technology.]

[2724] Hentzi, Gary. "The Literature of Cultural Crossing and the Project of Cultural Studies." *CritT*. 1990; 7(1): 19-27. [†Role of culture studies; relationship to cross-cultural communication.]

[2725] Herron, Jerry. "The Genrification of Desire and Posthistorical Pastiche." *SubStance*. 1987; 16(1 [52]): 45-58.

[2726] Hollow, John. "Renewal in Interesting Times: A Hope." *ADEB*. 1990 Spring; 95: 29-32. [†Role of curriculum in English studies.]

[2727] Huber, Bettina J. "Incorporating Minorities into English Programs: The Challenge of the Nineties." *ADEB*. 1990 Spring; 95: 38-44. [Incl. tables. †Role of minorities in English departments.]

[2728] ——. "Women in the Modern Languages, 1970-1990." *Profession*. 1990: 58-73. [Incl. tables. †Role of women.]

[2729] Humm, Maggie. "'An Experimental Collage, and Adventurous College': Feminism in Brazil." *Fiction International*. 1990 Fall; 19(1): 64-70. [†Role of feminism; relationship to women's studies in Brazil.]

[2730] Iandoli, Louis J. "CALL and the Profession: The Current State." *FR*. 1990 Dec.; 64(2): 261-272. [†Role of computer-assisted language learning in French language learning.]

[2731] James, Dorothy. "The Aftermath of Funding: Making It Work and Making It Last." *Profession*. 1990: 43-47. [†Role of funding.]

[2732] Jasen, Patricia. "Arnoldian Humanism, English Studies, and the Canadian University." *QQ*. 1988 Autumn; 95(3): 550-566. [†Role of English studies at Canadian universities. Application of theories of Arnold, Matthew: *Culture and Anarchy*.]

[2733] Jenson, Robert W. "Hope, the Gospel, and the Liberal Arts." 91-98 in Jones, Dennis M., ed. *A Humanist's Legacy: Essays in Honor of John Christian Bale*. Decorah, IA: Luther Coll.; 1990. 100 pp. [†Relationship to Christianity.]

[2734] Kampf, Louis. "Annals of Academic Life: An Exemplary Tale." 305-311 in Davis, Lennard J., ed.; Mirabella, M. Bella, ed. *Left Politics and the Literary Profession*. New York: Columbia UP; 1990. xii, 316 pp. (Social Foundations of Aesthetic Forms.) [†Relationship to left-wing politics.]

[2735] Kaplan, Alice Yaeger. "Working in the Archives." *YFS*. 1990; 77: 103-116. [†Archives.]

[2736] Kaplan, Carey; Rose, Ellen Cronan. *The Canon and the Common Reader*. Knoxville: U of Tennessee P; 1990. xix, 206 pp. [†Role of women writers; relationship to reader; canon. Feminist approach.]

[2737] Kennedy, George A. "Classics and Canons." *SAQ*. 1990 Winter; 89(1): 217-225.

SEE SUBJECT INDEX FOR CROSS-REFERENCES

[2738] Kidd, Sunnie D.; Kidd, James W. *Experiential Method: Qualitative Research in the Humanities Using Metaphysics and Phenomenology.* New York: Peter Lang; 1990. 154 pp. (American University Studies V: Philosophy 90.) [†Role of metaphysics; phenomenology.]

[2739] Kitzhaber, Albert R.; Gage, John T., introd. *Rhetoric in American Colleges, 1850-1900.* Dallas: Southern Methodist UP; 1990. xxv, 290 pp. (SMU Studies in Composition and Rhetoric.) [†Rhetoric.

[2740] Kort, Melissa Sue. "No More Band-Aids: Adult Learning and Faculty Development." *ADEB.* 1990 Spring; 95: 21-24. [†Faculty development in English departments.]

[2741] Kraemer, Don. "No Exit: A Play of Literacy and Gender." *JAC.* 1990 Fall; 10(2): 305-319. [†Academic discourse; literacy as language games; relationship to gender.]

[2742] Kristeller, Paul Oskar. "The Curriculum of the Italian Universities from the Middle Ages to the Renaissance." *PPMRC.* 1984; 9: 1-16. [†Curriculum at Italian universities (1100-1599).]

[2743] Kronik, John W. "On Men Mentoring Women: Then and Now." *Profession.* 1990: 52-57. [†Role of men teachers as mentor to female student.]

[2744] Kuklick, Bruce. "The Emergence of the Humanities." *SAQ.* 1990 Winter; 89(1): 195-206.

[2745] Laan, Nico. "Het belang van letterenstudie in historisch perspectief." *Spektator.* 1988 July; 17(6): 469-487. [†Literary studies.]

[2746] LaCapra, Dominick. "Culture and Ideology: From Geertz to Marx." *PoT.* 1988; 9(2): 377-394. [†Relationship to ideology; culture. Theories of Geertz, Clifford.]

[2747] Lambropoulos, Vassilis. "A Didactic Proposal." *JMGS.* 1990 May; 8(1): 81-84. [†Modern Greek studies.]

[2748] Landow, George P. "Changing Texts, Changing Readers: Hypertext in Literary Education, Criticism, and Scholarship." 133-161 in Henricksen, Bruce, ed.; Morgan, Thais E., ed. *Reorientations: Critical Theories & Pedagogies.* Urbana: U of Illinois P; 1990. x, 275 pp. [†Canon.]

[2749] Lanham, Richard A. "The Extraordinary Convergence: Democracy, Technology, Theory, and the University Curriculum." *SAQ.* 1990 Winter; 89(1): 27-50.

[2750] Laurence, David, introd.; Olsen, Stephen, introd. "The English Coalition Conference Report: Seven Responses." *ADEB.* 1990 Fall; 96: 25-49. [Spec. sect. †On English Coalition Conference (1987).]

[2751] Lauter, Paul. "Canon Theory and Emergent Practice." 127-146 in Davis, Lennard J., ed.; Mirabella, M. Bella, ed. *Left Politics and the Literary Profession.* New York: Columbia UP; 1990. xii, 316 pp. (Social Foundations of Aesthetic Forms.) [†Canon.]

[2752] Leddy, Michael. "'The One Thing Needful': The Argument of E. D. Hirsch's *Cultural Literacy.*" *W&D.* 1987 Spring; 5(1 [9]): 73-83. [†On Hirsch, Eric Donald: *Cultural Literacy.*]

[2753] Lefkowitz, Mary R. "Should Women Receive a Separate Education?" *NLH.* 1990 Autumn; 21(4): 799-815. [†Role of women's studies.]

[2754] Lewis, Magda Gere. "The Challenge of Feminist Pedagogy." *QQ.* 1989 Spring; 96(1): 117-130. [†Role of women; relationship to feminism. Review article.]

[2755] Lipking, Lawrence. "Teaching America." *ADEB.* 1990 Spring; 95: 11-13. [See also *Profession.* 1990: 8-11. †Relationship to canon.]

[2756] Lunsford, Andrea; Ede, Lisa. *Singular Texts/Plural Authors: Perspectives on Collaborative Writing.* Carbondale: Southern Illinois UP; 1990. xii, 285 pp. [†Teaching of writing.]

[2757] Lunsford, Andrea A., ed.; Moglen, Helene, ed.; Slevin, James, ed. *The Right to Literacy.* New York: Mod. Lang. Assn. of Amer.; 1990. 306 pp. [†Literacy.]

[2758] Lunsford, Andrea, ed.; Moglen, Helene, ed.; Slevin, James F., ed. *The Future of Doctoral Studies in English.* New York: Mod. Lang. Assn. of Amer.; 1989. xii, 179 pp. [Incl. introd. †English departments.]

[2759] Lyon, John. "Oncological Argument." *ModA.* 1988 Winter; 32(1): 30-34. [†In United States. Relationship to nihilism. Theories of Bloom, Allan David: *The Closing of the American Mind.*]

[2760] MacCabe, Colin. "Language, Literature, Identity: Reflections on the Cox Report." *CritQ.* 1990 Winter; 32(4): 7-13. [†Treatment in *Cox Report on National Curriculum.*]

[2761] Marcuse, Michael J., ed. "The Bibliography and Methods Course." *LRN.* 1987 Spring-Summer; 12(2-3). [Spec. iss.; incl. introd. †Research.]

[2762] Marius, Richard. "On Academic Discourse." *Profession.* 1990: 28-31. [†Role of academic discourse.]

[2763] Marshall, Donald G. "At Home on Babel Tower: Or, Why Should Children Learn a Second Language?" *ADFLB.* 1990 Winter; 21(2): 5-11. [†Second language learning.]

[2764] Martin, Jay. "Name-Dropping or Dropping Names? Modes of Legitimation in the Humanities." 19-34 in Kreiswirth, Martin, ed.; Cheetham, Mark A., ed. *Theory between the Disciplines: Authority/Vision/Politics.* Ann Arbor: U of Michigan P; 1990. xii, 257 pp.

[2765] McKay, Nellie Y. "Literature and Politics: Black Feminist Scholars Reshaping Literary Education in the White University, 1970-1986." 84-102 in Davis, Lennard J., ed.; Mirabella, M. Bella, ed. *Left Politics and the Literary Profession.* New York: Columbia UP; 1990. xii, 316 pp. (Social Foundations of Aesthetic Forms.) [†Role of African American women; relationship to feminism.]

[2766] McLeod, Susan H. "Cultural Literacy, Curricular Reform, and Freshman Composition." *RhetRev.* 1990 Spring; 8(2): 270-278. [†Cultural knowledge.]

[2767] Meriwether, Doris H. "The English Coalition Conference: 'Plain Living and High Thinking'." *ADEB.* 1990 Fall; 96: 45-46. [†On English Coalition Conference (1987).]

[2768] Michaels, Lloyd. "Reclaiming the Realm of Pleasure: A Response to the English Coalition Report." *ADEB.* 1990 Fall; 96: 42-44. [†On English Coalition Conference (1987).]

[2769] Miller, J. Hillis. "Face to Face: Plato's *Protagoras* as a Model for Collective Research in the Humanities." 281-295 in Carroll, David, ed. *The States of "Theory": History, Art, and Critical Discourse.* New York: Columbia UP; 1990. x, 316 pp. (Irvine Studies in the Humanities.) [†Application of theories of Plato: *Protagoras.*]

[2770] Miller, Jane. "Who Is Reading?" *CIEFLB.* 1989 Dec.; 1(2): 68-84. [†Literacy; relationship to teaching of literature.]

[2771] Miller, R. H. "New Directions in the Graduate Research Course." *LRN.* 1987 Spring-Summer; 12(2-3): 111-114. [†Relationship to literary theory and criticism. Pedagogical approach.]

[2772] Minnich, Elizabeth Kamarck. "From Ivory Tower to Tower of Babel?" *SAQ.* 1990 Winter; 89(1): 181-194.

[2773] Molnar, Thomas. "Adding to Organized Misunderstanding." *ModA.* 1988 Winter; 32(1): 35-38. [†In United States. Relationship to culture. Theories of Bloom, Allan David: *The Closing of the American Mind.*]

[2774] Montgomery, Marion. "Wanted: A Better Reason as Guide." *ModA.* 1988 Winter; 32(1): 39-44. [†Cultural knowledge; intellectualism; relationship to theories of Bloom, Allan David: *The Closing of the American Mind.*]

[2775] Myers, David Gershom. "Educating Writers: The Beginnings of 'Creative Writing' in the American University." *DAI.* 1990 May; 50(11): 3592A. [†Creative writing at American universities. Dissertation abstract.]

[2776] Nauert, Charles G., Jr. "Humanist Infiltration into the Academic World: Some Studies of Northern Universities." *RenQ.* 1990 Winter; 43(4): 799-812. [†In Europe. 1400-1599.]

[2777] Neel, Jasper. "'Where Have You Come from, Reb Derissa, and Where Are You Going?': Gary Olson's Interview with Jacques Derrida." *JAC.* 1990 Fall; 10(2): 387-392. [†Application of deconstructionism; relationship to rhetoric; logic. Theories of Derrida, Jacques.]

[2778] Ohmann, Richard. "The Function of English at the Present Time." 36-52 in Davis, Lennard J., ed.; Mirabella, M. Bella, ed. *Left Politics and the Literary Profession.* New York: Columbia UP; 1990. xii, 316 pp. (Social Foundations of Aesthetic Forms.) [†English departments.]

[2779] Olson, Rex. "Derrida (f)or Us? Composition and the Taking of Text." *Pre/Text.* 1988 Spring-Summer; 9(1-2): 27-60. [See also Crowley, above. †Composition studies in English departments. Application of theories of Derrida, Jacques.]

[2780] O'Malley, Susan Gushee. "What Has Happened to the Seeds of the Flower Children?" 299-304 in Davis, Lennard J., ed.; Mirabella, M. Bella, ed. *Left Politics and the Literary Profession.* New York: Columbia UP; 1990. xii, 316 pp. (Social Foundations of Aesthetic Forms.) [†Relationship to left-wing politics (1960-1969).]

[2781] Owens, Derek Vincent. "Resisting Writings (and the Boundaries of Composition)." *DAI.* 1990 June; 50(12): 3938A. [†Teaching of writing. Dissertation abstract.]

[2782] Panichas, George A. "The Liberal Tone—an Editorial." *ModA.* 1988 Spring; 32(2): 98-101. [†Canon; pedagogy in United States; relationship to liberalism compared to conservatism.]

[2783] Paranjape, Makarand. "The Invasion of 'Theory'—an Indian Response." *Quest.* 1990 May-June; 81: 151-161. [†In India. Role of literary theory and criticism; Western culture.]

[2784] Parker, Michael. "The Canon Debate: The Real Issue Is Inclusion." *MOR.* 1990 Spring; 4: 19-25. [†Role of canon.]

[2785] Parr, James A. "Method as Medium and Message: Technique and Its Discontents: A Teacher of Literature in a Language Department Looks at Theory." *ADFLB.* 1990 Winter; 21(2): 25-29. [†Role of literary theory and criticism.]

[2786] Paz Haro, María. "Las lenguas de España en la universidad norteamericana." 312-319 in Fernández Jiménez, Juan, ed.; Labrador Herraiz, José, ed.; Valdivieso, L. Teresa, ed.; Morón Arroyo, Ciriaco, pref. *Estudios en homenaje a Enrique Ruiz-Fornells.* Erie, PA: Asociación de Licenciados & Doctores Españoles en Estados Unidos; 1990. xxvi, 706 pp. (Homenajes 1.) [†Role of Modern Language Association of America.]

[2787] Pinsker, Sanford. "Revisionist Thought, Academic Power, and the Aging American Intellectual." *GettR.* 1990 Spring; 3(2): 417-426.

[2788] Pratt, Mary Louise. "Humanities for the Future: Reflections on the Western Culture Debate at Stanford." *SAQ.* 1990 Winter; 89(1): 7-25. [†Canon.]

[2789] Proctor, Robert E. "The *Studia Humanitatis*: Contemporary Scholarship and Renaissance Ideals." *RenQ.* 1990 Winter; 43(4): 813-818. [†1300-1599. Relationship to humanism; role of Petrarca, Francesco.]

[2790] Raymond, James C. "Authority, Desire, and Canons: Tendentious Meditations on Cultural Literacy." 76-86 in Moran, Charles, ed.; Penfield, Elizabeth F., ed. *Conversations: Contemporary Critical Theory and the Teaching of Literature.* Urbana: Nat. Council of Teachers of Eng.; 1990. viii, 237 pp. [†Canon.]

[2791] Regnery, Henry, fwd.; Panichas, George A., pref. "A Symposium on Allan Bloom's *The Closing of the American Mind.*" *ModA.* 1988 Winter; 32(1). [Spec. iss. †In United States. Theories of Bloom, Allan David: *The Closing of the American Mind.*]

[2792] Rich, Robert. "Somewhere Off the Coast of Academia." 291-294 in Davis, Lennard J., ed.; Mirabella, M. Bella, ed. *Left Politics and the Literary Profession.* New

[2792] York: Columbia UP; 1990. xii, 316 pp. (Social Foundations of Aesthetic Forms.) [†Relationship to left-wing politics.]

[2793] Robinson, Lillian S. "Canon Fathers and Myth Universe." 147-161 in Davis, Lennard J., ed.; Mirabella, M. Bella, ed. *Left Politics and the Literary Profession.* New York: Columbia UP; 1990. xii, 316 pp. (Social Foundations of Aesthetic Forms.) [†Canon; relationship to feminist literary theory and criticism.]

[2794] ——. "Some Historical Refractions." 295-298 in Davis, Lennard J., ed.; Mirabella, M. Bella, ed. *Left Politics and the Literary Profession.* New York: Columbia UP; 1990. xii, 316 pp. (Social Foundations of Aesthetic Forms.) [†Relationship to left-wing politics.]

[2795] Ronald, Kate. "On the Outside Looking In: Students' Analyses of Professional Discourse Communities." *RhetRev.* 1988 Fall; 7(1): 130-149. [†Writing across the curriculum; relationship to professional discourse; discourse community.]

[2796] Rorty, Richard. "Two Cheers for the Cultural Left." *SAQ.* 1990 Winter; 89(1): 227-234.

[2797] Rose, Shirley K. "Reading Representative Anecdotes of Literacy Practice: Or, 'See Dick and Jane Read and Write!'." *RhetRev.* 1990 Spring; 8(2): 244-259. [†Literacy; relationship to gender.]

[2798] Rosen, Robert C. "Politics and Literature, Then and Now." 287-290 in Davis, Lennard J., ed.; Mirabella, M. Bella, ed. *Left Politics and the Literary Profession.* New York: Columbia UP; 1990. xii, 316 pp. (Social Foundations of Aesthetic Forms.) [†Relationship to left-wing politics (1970-1990).]

[2799] Rothblatt, Sheldon. "A Long Apocrypha of Inquiries: The Humanities and Humanity." *Mosaic.* 1990 Winter; 23(1): 1-14. [†Relationship to humanity.]

[2800] Rowe, John Carlos. "The Ethics of Professional Letters: Eleven Theses." *Profession.* 1990: 48-51. [†On peer review; letters of recommendation; relationship to teaching; research.]

[2801] Sachs, Murray. "The Foreign Language Curriculum and the Orality-Literacy Question." *ADFLB.* 1989 Jan.; 20(2): 70-75. [†Teaching of literature; relationship to orality.]

[2802] Samuel, Raphael. "The Return of History." *LRB.* 1990 June 14; 12(11): 9-10, 12. [†In England. Educational reform; relationship to history.]

[2803] Schaefer, William D. *Education without Compromise: From Chaos to Coherence in Higher Education.* San Francisco: Jossey-Bass; 1990. xx, 155 pp. (Jossey-Bass Higher Education Series.)

[2804] Scholes, Robert. "Toward a Curriculum in Textual Studies." 95-112 in Henricksen, Bruce, ed.; Morgan, Thais E., ed. *Reorientations: Critical Theories & Pedagogies.* Urbana: U of Illinois P; 1990. x, 275 pp.

[2805] Seaton, James. "Cultural Conservatism, Political Radicalism." *JACult.* 1989 Fall; 12(3): 1-10. [†Cultural knowledge. Theories of Hirsch, Eric Donald: *Cultural Literacy*; Bloom, Allan David: *The Closing of the American Mind.*]

[2806] Sedgwick, Eve Kosofsky. "Pedagogy in the Context of an Antihomophobic Project." *SAQ.* 1990 Winter; 89(1): 139-156. [†Relationship to homosexuality. Pedagogical approach.]

[2807] Short, Mick. "Discourse Analysis in Stylistics and Literature Instruction." *ARAL.* 1990; 11: 181-195. [†Application of discourse analysis in teaching of literature.]

[2808] Silber, Ellen S. "Academic Alliances in Foreign Languages and Literatures: A Collaborative Vision for Our Future." *FR.* 1990 May; 63(6): 987-995. [†Role of academic alliances.]

[2809] Smith, Barbara Herrnstein. "Cult-Lit: Hirsch, Literacy, and the 'National Culture'." *SAQ.* 1990 Winter; 89(1): 69-88. [†Theories of Hirsch, Eric Donald: *Cultural Literacy.*]

[2810] Sosnoski, James J. "Literary Study in a Post-Modern Era: Rereading Its History." *W&D.* 1987 Spring; 5(1 [9]): 7-33. [†Role of literary studies; relationship to Postmodernism.]

[2811] Spivak, Gayatri Chakravorty. "The Making of Americans, the Teaching of English, and the Future of Culture Studies." *NLH.* 1990 Autumn; 21(4): 781-798. [†Role of politics; relationship to culture studies.]

[2812] Steinfeld, Torill. "'Norsk' som forsknings- og studiefag." *Norsklrrn.* 1990; 14(3): 52-56. [†On Norwegian studies.]

[2813] Stewart, Donald C. "Collaborative Learning and Composition: Boon or Bane?" *RhetRev.* 1988 Fall; 7(1): 58-83. [†Role of collaborative learning; relationship to teaching of writing.]

[2814] Stewart, Joan Hinde. "Gender in the Prism-House of Language." *ADFLB.* 1989 April; 20(3): 49-53. [†Teaching of literature; relationship to feminism.]

[2815] Stimpson, Catharine R. "What Am I Doing When I Do Women's Studies in 1990?" 55-83 in Davis, Lennard J., ed.; Mirabella, M. Bella, ed. *Left Politics and the Literary Profession.* New York: Columbia UP; 1990. xii, 316 pp. (Social Foundations of Aesthetic Forms.) [†Women's studies.]

[2816] Swaffar, Janet K. "Reading and Cultural Literacy." *JGE.* 1986; 38(2): 70-84. [†Relationship to cultural knowledge.]

[2817] Turner, Roy. "Friends and Enemies of the Canon." *QQ.* 1990 Summer; 97(2): 236-249. [†Canon; relationship to culture; art.]

[2818] Ulmer, Gregory L. "Textshop for an Experimental Humanities." 113-132 in Henricksen, Bruce, ed.; Morgan, Thais E., ed. *Reorientations: Critical Theories & Pedagogies.* Urbana: U of Illinois P; 1990. x, 275 pp.

[2819] Waller, Gary. "Knowing the Subject: Critiquing the Self, Critiquing the Culture." *ADEB.* 1990 Spring; 95: 14-17. [†English studies.]

[2820] Ward, Adrienne Marie, comp. *A Guide to Professional Organizations for Teachers of Language and Literature in the United States and Canada.* New York: Mod. Lang. Assn. of Amer.; 1990. vi, 104 pp.

[2821] Weber, Samuel. "The Vaulted Eye: Remarks on Knowledge and Professionalism." *YFS.* 1990; 77: 44-60. [†Professionalism.]

[2822] Welch, Kathleen E. "Electrifying Classical Rhetoric: Ancient Media, Modern Technology, and Contemporary Composition." *JAC.* 1990; 10(1): 22-38. [†Relationship to orality. Treatment in Ong, Walter J.; Havelock, Eric Alfred.]

[2823] Wood, P. B. "Enlightenment and Academe: The University in the Eighteenth Century." *QQ.* 1990 Spring; 97(1): 23-35. [†1700-1799. Pedagogy in England compared to France; relationship to philosophy. Review article.]

[2824] Yeakey, Carol Camp. "Social Change through the Humanities: An Essay on the Politics of Literacy and Culture in American Society." *NLH.* 1990 Autumn; 21(4): 841-862. [†On cultural knowledge. Theories of Bloom, Allan David; Hirsch, Eric Donald.]

[2825] Ziolkowski, Theodore. "The Shape of the PhD: Present, Past, and Future." *ADEB.* 1990 Winter; 97: 12-17. [†Doctoral programs in English departments.]

RESEARCH TOOLS

[2826] Beller, Manfred. "A New Direction in English and German Literary Definitions." *YCGL.* 1988; 37: 166-170. [On Daemmrich, Horst S.; Daemmrich, Ingrid. *Themes & Motifs in Western Literature: A Handbook* & Daemmrich, Horst S.; Daemmrich, Ingrid. *Themen und Motive in der Literatur: Ein Handbuch.* †Review article.]

[2827] Harner, James L. "Literary Reference Works: Some Desiderata." *SchP.* 1990 Apr.; 21(3): 171-183.

[2828] Irizarry, Estelle. "An Archive of Modern Hispanic Texts: A Quixotic Venture?" *L&LC.* 1990; 5(3): 209-214. [†Relationship to Spanish language literature (1900-1999). On electronic publishing.]

[2829] Neal, Gordon. "CONSTRUE: The Evolution of a Study Aid for Literary Texts." *L&LC.* 1990; 5(4): 319-321. [†Application of CONSTRUE.]

[2830] Stebelman, Scott. "Teaching Manuscript and Archival Resources." *LRN.* 1987 Winter; 12(1): 24-34. [†Role of manuscripts; archives.]

Themes and figures

ABNORMALITY

[2832] Holden, Lynn Rosemary. "A Motif-Index of Abnormalities, Deformities and Disabilities of the Human Form in Traditional Narrative." *DAI.* 1990 Apr.; 50(10): 3219A. [†Dissertation abstract of motif index.]

ALEXANDRIA

[2833] Bleicher, Thomas. "Alexandria: Fokus interkultureller Literatur." 88-96 in Bauer, Roger, ed.; Fokkema, Douwe, ed.; Graat, Michael de, asst. ed.; Kaiser, Gerhard, asst.; Rinner, Fridrun, asst.; Wertheimer, Jürgen, asst. *Proceedings of the XIIth Congress of the International Comparative Literature Association/Actes du XIIe congrès de l'Association Internationale de Littérature Comparée: München 1988 Munich, IV: Space and Boundaries of Literature/Espace et frontières de la littérature.* Munich: Iudicium; 1990. 651 pp. (Proceedings of the Congress of the International Comparative Literature Association 12: 4.)

ARTHUR, KING

[2834] Lagorio, Valerie M., ed.; Day, Mildred Leake, ed. *King Arthur through the Ages, I.* New York: Garland; 1990. xv, 327 pp. (GRLH 1269.)

[2835] ——. *King Arthur through the Ages, II.* New York: Garland; 1990. xvi, 335 pp. (GRLH 1301.)

[2836] Roberts, Ruth M. "Arthuriana, Alive and Well at Memphis State." *UMSE.* 1990; 8: 249-253. [On 1988 Bibliog. IV.3074, 1987 Bibliog. I.508, & 1984 Bibliog. I.5317. †Review article.]

BLACK AFRICANS

[2837] Droixhe, Daniel, ed.; Kiefer, Klaus H., ed.; Riesz, János, introd. *Images de l'Africain de l'antiquité au XXe siècle/Images of the African from Antiquity to the 20th Century/Bilder des Afrikaners von der Antike bis zur Gegenwart.* Frankfurt: Peter Lang; 1987. 222 pp. (Bayreuther Beiträge zur Literaturwissenschaft 10.) [Incl. pref. & fwd.]

CANNIBALISM

[2838] Kilgour, Maggie. *From Communion to Cannibalism: An Anatomy of Metaphors of Incorporation.* Princeton: Princeton UP; 1990. xi, 310 pp. [†Relationship to Eucharist (sacrament of); incorporation.]

CHARACTERS

[2839] Harris, Laurie Lanzen. *Characters in 20th-Century Literature.* Detroit: Gale; 1990. xii, 480 pp.

CHILDREN

[2840] Vriend, G. de. "Een exclusieve kinderwereld in de jeugdliteratuur." *Spektator*. 1989 May; 18(5): 393-395.

CHRIST

[2841] Lobell, Leona Michele. "The Lamb of God: The Sacred Made Visible." *DAI*. 1990 Nov.; 51(5): 1604A. [†As metaphor. Dissertation abstract.]

[2842] Niemeyer, Gerhart. "A Christian Sheen on a Secular World." *ModA*. 1987 Summer-Fall; 31(3-4): 355-361. [†Relationship to secularity.]

CHRISTIANITY

[2843] Schmidinger, Heinrich M. "Ironie und Christentum." *PJGG*. 1990; 97(2): 277-296. [†Relationship to irony.]

DEFEAT

[2844] Brulotte, Gaétan. "Défaite et littérature." *En Vrac*. 1990 Winter; 42: 18-20. [†Relationship to triumph.]

DEVIL

[2845] Gillespie, Gerald. "The Devil's Art." 77-95 in Hoffmeister, Gerhart, ed. *European Romanticism: Literary Cross-Currents, Modes, and Models*. Detroit: Wayne State UP; 1990. 369 pp.

DON JUAN

[2846] Gnüg, Hiltrud. "The Dandy and the Don Juan Type." 229-246 in Hoffmeister, Gerhart, ed. *European Romanticism: Literary Cross-Currents, Modes, and Models*. Detroit: Wayne State UP; 1990. 369 pp. [†And dandy.]

DREAM

[2847] Rudenev, Vadim. "Kultura i son." *Daugava*. 1990 Mar.; 3(153): 121-124. [†Theories of Freud, Sigmund.]

ECONOMIC VALUE

[2848] Turner, Frederick. "The Meaning of Value: An Economics for the Future." *NLH*. 1990 Spring; 21(3): 747-765.

EMOTIONS

[2849] Woodward, Kathleen, ed.; Mueller, Roswitha, ed. "A Special Issue on the Emotions." *Discourse*. 1990-1991 Fall-Winter; 13(1). [Spec. iss.; incl. introd.]

EXILE

[2850] Broe, Mary Lynn, ed.; Ingram, Angela, ed. *Women's Writing in Exile*. Chapel Hill: U of North Carolina P; 1989. xii, 442 pp. [Incl. introd. †Treatment in women writers.]

[2851] Edwards, Robert. "Exile, Self, and Society." 15-31 in Lagos-Pope, María-Inés, ed. *Exile in Literature*. Lewisburg, PA: Bucknell UP; 1988. 139 pp.

[2852] Guillén, Claudio. "The Sun and the Self: Notes on Some Responses to Exile." 261-282 in Jost, François, ed.; Friedman, Melvin J., asst. ed. *Aesthetics and the Literature of Ideas: Essays in Honor of A. Owen Aldridge*. Newark: U of Delaware P; 1990. 290 pp.

[2853] Lagos-Pope, María-Inés, ed. *Exile in Literature*. Lewisburg, PA: Bucknell UP; 1988. 139 pp.

EXISTENCE

[2854] Angelet, Christian. "Le Thème primitiviste de l'existence en confusion: Du philosophique au rhétorique." 38-45 in Bauer, Roger, ed.; Fokkema, Douwe, ed.; Graat, Michael de, ed.; Boening, John, ed.; Gillespie, Gerald, ed.; Moog-Grünewald, Maria, ed.; Nemoianu, Virgil, ed.; Ricapito, Joseph, ed.; Schmeling, Manfred, ed.; Thüsen, Joachim von der, ed.; Uhlig, Claus, ed. *Proceedings of the XIIth Congress of the International Comparative Literature Association/Actes du XIIe congrès de l'Association Internationale de Littérature Comparée: München 1988 Munich, II: Space and Boundaries in Literature/Espace et frontières dans la littérature*. Munich: Iudicium; 1990. 606 pp. (Proceedings of the Congress of the International Comparative Literature Association 12: 2.) [†1700-1799.]

THE FANTASTIC

[2855] Porter, Laurence M. "Redefining the Fantastic." *CRR*. 1989; 8: 1-12. [†Genre study.]

FAUST

[2856] Brown, Jane K. "Faust." 181-196 in Hoffmeister, Gerhart, ed. *European Romanticism: Literary Cross-Currents, Modes, and Models*. Detroit: Wayne State UP; 1990. 369 pp.

[2857] Green, Marcia. "The Demonic Pact: The Faust Myth in Music and Literature." 124-129 in Barricelli, Jean-Pierre, ed.; Gibaldi, Joseph, ed.; Lauter, Estella, ed. *Teaching Literature and Other Arts*. New York: Mod. Lang. Assn. of Amer.; 1990. vi, 183 pp. (Options for Teaching 10.) [†Includes treatment in music. Pedagogical approach.]

FEMME FATALE

[2858] Kurth-Voigt, Lieselotte E. "'La Belle Dame sans Merci': The Revenant as Femme Fatale in Romantic Poetry." 247-267 in Hoffmeister, Gerhart, ed. *European Ro-* manticism: Literary Cross-Currents, Modes, and Models*. Detroit: Wayne State UP; 1990. 369 pp. [†In Romantic poetry.]

FLOOD

[2859] Goetsch, Paul. "Die Sintfluterzählung in der modernen englischsprachigen Literatur." 651-684 in Link, Franz, ed. *Paradeigmata: Literarische Typologie des Alten Testaments, I: Von den Anfängen bis zum 19. Jahrhundert; II: 20. Jahrhundert*. Berlin: Duncker & Humblot; 1989. 945 pp. (Schriften zur Literaturwissenschaft 5.) [†English language literature. 1900-1999.]

FLOWERS

[2860] Sartiliot, Claudette. "Herbarium, Verbarium: The Discourse of Flowers." *Diacritics*. 1988 Winter; 18(4): 68-81. [†Relationship to theories of Hegel, Georg Wilhelm Friedrich: *Grundlinien der Philosophie des Rechts*; Freud, Sigmund: *Die Traumdeutung*; Derrida, Jacques: *Glas*. Review article.]

FRANKENSTEIN (FIGURE)

[2861] Roberston-Griffith, Olivia Pauline. "Frankenstein as the Permeative Myth of the Twentieth Century." *DAI*. 1990 Oct.; 51(4): 1222A-1223A. [†Dissertation abstract.]

GOD

[2862] Engelstad, Carl Fredrik. "Gud som litteræer mulighet." *Kirke og Kultur*. 1990; 95(5): 391-404.

[2863] Feiss, Hugh, O.S.B. "The Grace of Passion and the Compassion of God: Soundings in the Christian Tradition." *ABR*. 1990 June; 41(2): 141-156.

THE GROTESQUE

[2864] Burwick, Frederick. "The Grotesque in the Romantic Movement." 37-57 in Hoffmeister, Gerhart, ed. *European Romanticism: Literary Cross-Currents, Modes, and Models*. Detroit: Wayne State UP; 1990. 369 pp.

HIROSHIMA

[2865] Dorsey, John T. "Literature Related to the Atomic Bomb: From Hiroshima to the End of the World." 252-260 in Jost, François, ed.; Friedman, Melvin J., asst. ed. *Aesthetics and the Literature of Ideas: Essays in Honor of A. Owen Aldridge*. Newark: U of Delaware P; 1990. 290 pp. [†And nuclear age.]

HISTORY

[2866] Steinmetz, Horst. *Literatur und Geschichte: Vier Versuche*. Munich: Iudicium; 1988. 142 pp. (Literatur und Geschichte.)

THE HOLOCAUST

[2867] Braham, L. Randolph, ed. *Reflections of the Holocaust in Art and Literature*. New York: Columbia UP; 1990. vii, 166 pp. [Incl. introd.]

[2868] Fine, Ellen S. "Women Writers and the Holocaust: Strategies for Survival." 79-95 in Braham, L. Randolph, ed. *Reflections of the Holocaust in Art and Literature*. New York: Columbia UP; 1990. vii, 166 pp. [†Treatment in women writers.]

[2869] Langer, Lawrence L. "Fictional Facts and Factual Fictions: History in Holocaust Literature." 117-129 in Braham, L. Randolph, ed. *Reflections of the Holocaust in Art and Literature*. New York: Columbia UP; 1990. vii, 166 pp. [†Relationship to history; fictionality.]

[2870] Pinsker, Sanford, ed.; Fischel, Jack, ed. *Holocaust Studies Annual, 1990: General Essays*. New York: Garland; 1990. viii, 154 pp. (Garland Reference Library of Social Science 631.) [Incl. pref.]

[2871] Sungolowsky, Joseph. "Holocaust and Autobiography: Wiesel, Friedländer, Pisar." 131-146 in Braham, L. Randolph, ed. *Reflections of the Holocaust in Art and Literature*. New York: Columbia UP; 1990. vii, 166 pp. [†Discusses problem of emotional involvement in holocaust autobiography.]

HORIZON

[2872] Koschorke, Albrecht. "Der Horizont als Symbol der Überschreitung und Grenze: Zum Wandel eines literarischen Motivs zwischen Aufklärung und Realismus." 250-255 in Bauer, Roger, ed.; Fokkema, Douwe, ed.; Graat, Michael de, ed.; Boening, John, ed.; Gillespie, Gerald, ed.; Moog-Grünewald, Maria, ed.; Nemoianu, Virgil, ed.; Ricapito, Joseph, ed.; Schmeling, Manfred, ed.; Thüsen, Joachim von der, ed.; Uhlig, Claus, ed. *Proceedings of the XIIth Congress of the International Comparative Literature Association/Actes du XIIe congrès de l'Association Internationale de Littérature Comparée: München 1988 Munich, II: Space and Boundaries in Literature/Espace et frontières dans la littérature*. Munich: Iudicium; 1990. 606 pp. (Proceedings of the Congress of the International Comparative Literature Association 12: 2.) [†Relationship to literature of Enlightenment; Realist movement.]

HUMAN BODY

[2873] Geitner, Ursula. "Die 'Beredsamkeit des Leibes': Zur Unterscheidung von Bewusstsein und Kommunikation im 18. Jahrhundert." *Das Achtzehnte Jahrhundert*. 1990; 14(2): 181-195. [†1700-1799. Review article.]

[2874] Käuser, Andreas. "Anthropologie und Ästhetik im 18. Jahrhundert: Besprechung einiger Neuerscheinungen." *Das Achtzehnte Jahrhundert*. 1990; 14(2): 196-206. [†Relationship to aesthetics. Review article.]

[2875] Niestroj, Brigitte H. E. "Der Körper im 18. Jahrhundert: Essays zur historischen Anthropologie." *Das Achtzehnte Jahrhundert*. 1990; 14(2): 153-158. [†1700-1799. Relationship to history; politics.]

[2876] Porter, Roy. "Barely Touching: A Social Perspective on Mind and Body." 45-80 in Rousseau, G. S., ed.; Porter, Roy, introd. *The Languages of Psyche: Mind and Body in Enlightenment Thought.* Berkeley: U of California P; 1990. xix, 480 pp. (Publications from the Clark Library Professorship 12.) [†Relationship to mind.]

[2877] Schmid, Pia. "Zur Geschichte des weiblichen Körpers im 18. Jahrhundert: Besprechung einschlägiger Neuerscheinungen." *Das Achtzehnte Jahrhundert.* 1990; 14(2): 159-180. [†Of women. 1700-1799. Review article.

HYSTERIA

[2878] Diamond, Elin. "Realism and Hysteria: Toward a Feminist Mimesis." *Discourse.* 1990-1991 Fall-Winter; 13(1): 59-92. [†Relationship to realism; study example: Ibsen, Henrik: *Hedda Gabler; Rosmersholm; Fruen fra havet.* Feminist approach. Compared to theories of Freud, Sigmund.]

THE INDIGENOUS

[2879] King, Thomas, ed.; Calver, Cheryl, ed.; Hoy, Helen, ed. *The Native in Literature.* Oakville, Ont.: ECW; 1987. 232 pp. [Incl. introd. †1900-1999.]

INSOMNIA

[2880] Fontana, Ernest L. "Literary Insomnia." *NOR.* 1990 Summer; 17(2): 38-42.

JEANNE D'ARC, SAINT (1412-1431)

[2881] Margolis, Nadia. *Joan of Arc in History, Literature, and Film.* New York: Garland; 1990. xvii, 406 pp. (GRLH 1224.)

JEWS

[2882] Malachi, Zvi. "Dmut HaYehudi BeSifrut HaGoyim." *Mahut.* 1989; 1: 28-36.

LABYRINTH

[2883] Doob, Penelope Reed. *The Idea of Labyrinth from Classical Antiquity through the Middle Ages.* Ithaca: Cornell UP; 1990. xvii, 355 pp. [†Middle Ages.]

LESBIANS

[2884] Engelbrecht, Penelope J. "'Lifting Belly Is a Language': The Postmodern Lesbian Subject." *FSt.* 1990 Spring; 16(1): 85-114. [†1900-1999. Relationship to Postmodernism.]

LORELEI

[2885] Tunner, Erika. "The Lore Lay—a Fairy Tale from Ancient Times?" 269-286 in Hoffmeister, Gerhart, ed. *European Romanticism: Literary Cross-Currents, Modes, and Models.* Detroit: Wayne State UP; 1990. 369 pp. [†As *Märchen.* Source study.]

LOVE

[2886] Kaiser, Marita. "Passionierte Liebe als exklusives Refugium." *Das Achtzehnte Jahrhundert.* 1990; 14(2): 207-214. [†Review article.]

[2887] Ôhashi, Kenzaburô. "Bungaku ni Miru 'Ai' no Shudai, I(10 gatsu), II & III." *EigoS.* n.d.; 135: 340-341, 384-385, 431-432.

MACHINES

[2888] Cohen, Alexander Joseph. "The Machine as Literary Assemblage." *DAI.* 1990 June; 50(12): 3941A. [†Dissertation abstract.]

MADNESS

[2889] Felman, Shoshana; Evans, Martha Noel, tr.; Massumi, Brian, tr. *Writing and Madness (Literature/Philosophy/Psychoanalysis).* Ithaca: Cornell UP; 1985. 255 pp. [Tr. of *La Folie et la chose littéraire.*]

MELANCHOLY

[2890] Pinto do Amaral, Fernando. "En la órbita de Saturno: Un punto de vista sobre la melancolía y su relación con cierta literatura." *RO.* 1990 Oct.; 113: 73-94.

MERLIN

[2891] Goodrich, Peter, ed. *The Romance of Merlin: An Anthology.* Garland: New York; 1990. xix, 417 pp. (GRLH 867.) [†Anthology.]

MISOGYNY

[2892] Bloch, R. Howard, ed.; Ferguson, Frances, ed. *Misogyny, Misandry, and Misanthropy.* Berkeley: U of California P; 1989. xvii, 235 pp. [Incl. introd.; see also 1987 Bibliog. IV.29. †And misanthropy.]

MORALITY

[2893] Eldridge, Richard. "[Critical Discussions]." *P&L.* 1990 Oct.; 14(2): 387-394. [On Kekes, John. *Moral Tradition and Individuality.* †Review article.]

MOTIVATION

[2894] Doležel, Lubomír. "Pour une thématique de la motivation." *SCr.* 1989 May; 4(2 [60]): 193-207. [†Psychoanalytic approach.]

MOURNING

[2895] Woodward, Kathleen. "Freud and Barthes: Theorizing Mourning, Sustaining Grief." *Discourse.* 1990-1991 Fall-Winter; 13(1): 93-110. [†Theories of Freud, Sigmund; Barthes, Roland.]

NARCISSISM

[2896] Bann, Stephen. "René Girard and the Revisionist View of Narcissism." *CCrit.* 1990; 12: 89-104. [Illus. †Application of theories of Girard, René; Freud, Sigmund.]

NATIVE AMERICANS

[2897] Monkman, Leslie. "Visions and Revisions: Contemporary Writers and Exploration Accounts of Indigenous Peoples." 80-98 in King, Thomas, ed.; Calver, Cheryl, ed.; Hoy, Helen, ed. *The Native in Literature.* Oakville, Ont.: ECW; 1987. 232 pp.

NUCLEAR WAR

[2898] Sullivan, Alvin, ed.; Kittrell, Jean, ed.; Scheik, William J., introd. "[Nuclear Criticism]." *PLL.* 1990 Winter; 26(1). [Spec. iss.]

[2899] Zins, Daniel L. "Exploding the Canon: Nuclear Criticism in the English Department." *PLL.* 1990 Winter; 26(1): 13-40.

OKLAHOMA

[2900] Ivask, Ivar. "Literature in, from, and about Oklahoma." *WLT.* 1990 Summer; 64(3): 381-389. [Incl. photographs.]

ORPHANS

[2901] Oxley, Brian. "Orphans and Bastards in the New World Novel." 419-430 in Davis, Geoffrey V., ed.; Maes-Jelinek, Hena, ed. *Crisis and Creativity in the New Literatures in English: Cross/Cultures.* Amsterdam: Rodopi; 1990. xii, 529 pp. (Readings in the Post/Colonial Literatures in English 1.) [†And bastard. In novel of New World.]

PEGASUS

[2902] Markus, Helmut. "'The Old Horse Dies Slow': Beobachtungen zu Typus und Variation des Pegasusmotive." 377-399 in Müllenbrock, Heinz-Joachim, ed.; Klein, Alfons, ed. *Motive and Themen in englischsprachiger Literatur als Indikatoren literaturgeschichtlicher Prozesse.* Tübingen: Niemeyer; 1990. ix, 418 pp.

PHYSICAL IMPAIRMENTS

[2903] De Felice, Robert J. "The Crippled Body Speaks." *DAI.* 1990 Sept.; 51(3): 840A-841A. [†Dissertation abstract.]

PROPHECY

[2904] Kugel, James L., ed.; Nagu, Gregory, fwd. *Poetry and Prophecy: The Beginnings of a Literary Tradition.* Ithaca: Cornell UP; 1990. ix, 251 pp. (Myth and Poetics.)

REALITY

[2905] Forrester, John. "Lying on the Couch." 145-165 in Lawson, Hilary, ed.; Appignanesi, Lisa, ed. *Dismantling Truth: Reality in the Post-Modern World.* New York: St. Martin's; 1989. xxviii, 180 pp. [†And truth. Relationship to representation in narrative.]

[2906] Lawson, Hilary, ed.; Appignanesi, Lisa, ed. *Dismantling Truth: Reality in the Post-Modern World.* Based on a ser. of papers presented at conf. at ICA & related materials. New York: St. Martin's; 1989. xxviii, 180 pp. [Incl. introd. & pref.]

[2907] Newton-Smith, W. H. "Rationality, Truth and the New Fuzzies." 23-42 in Lawson, Hilary, ed.; Appignanesi, Lisa, ed. *Dismantling Truth: Reality in the Post-Modern World.* New York: St. Martin's; 1989. xxviii, 180 pp. [†And truth.]

[2908] Woolgar, Steve. "The Ideology of Representation and the Role of the Agent." 131-144 in Lawson, Hilary, ed.; Appignanesi, Lisa, ed. *Dismantling Truth: Reality in the Post-Modern World.* New York: St. Martin's; 1989. xxviii, 180 pp. [†And truth. Relationship to representation.]

RELIGION

[2909] Jasper, David, ed.; Wright, T. R., ed. *The Critical Spirit and the Will to Believe: Essays in Nineteenth-Century Literature and Religion.* New York: St. Martin's; 1989. xii; 239 pp. [†1800-1899.]

THE SACRED

[2910] Bond, Ronald B. "God's 'Back Parts': Silence and the Accommodating Word." 169-187 in Blodgett, E. D., ed.; Coward, H. G., ed. *Silence, the Word and the Sacred.* Waterloo: Wilfrid Laurier UP for Calgary Inst. for the Humanities; 1989. xii, 226 pp.

[2911] Coward, Harold G. "The Spiritual Power of Oral and Written Scripture." 111-137 in Blodgett, E. D., ed.; Coward, H. G., ed. *Silence, the Word and the Sacred.* Waterloo: Wilfrid Laurier UP for Calgary Inst. for the Humanities; 1989. xii, 226 pp.

[2912] Dumais, Monique. "Le Sacre et l'autre parole selon une voix féministe." 149-162 in Blodgett, E. D., ed.; Coward, H. G., ed. *Silence, the Word and the Sacred.* Waterloo: Wilfrid Laurier UP for Calgary Inst. for the Humanities; 1989. xii, 226 pp.

[2913] Goa, David. "The Word That Transfigures." 163-168 in Blodgett, E. D., ed.; Coward, H. G., ed. *Silence, the Word and the Sacred.* Waterloo: Wilfrid Laurier UP for Calgary Inst. for the Humanities; 1989. xii, 226 pp. [†Relationship to Christianity.]

[2914] Jones, D. G. "Notes on a Poetics of the Sacred." 67-82 in Blodgett, E. D., ed.; Coward, H. G., ed. *Silence, the Word and the Sacred.* Waterloo: Wilfrid Laurier UP for Calgary Inst. for the Humanities; 1989. xii, 226 pp. [†Linguistic approach; deconstructionist approach.]

SEE SUBJECT INDEX FOR CROSS-REFERENCES

THE SELF

[2915] Gillespie, Gerald. "Here Comes Everybody / Nobody: Self as Overly Edited Palimpsest." *NewComp.* 1990 Spring; 9: 3-15.

[2916] Shaffer, E. S., ed. "Representations of the Self." *CCrit.* 1990; 12. [Spec. iss.; incl. introd.

SENTIMENTALITY

[2917] Solomon, Robert C. "In Defense of Sentimentality." *P&L.* 1990 Oct.; 14(2): 305-323.

SEX

[2918] Paglia, Camille. *Sexual Personae: Art and Decadence from Nefertiti to Emily Dickinson.* New Haven: Yale UP; 1990. xiv, 718 pp.

SPACE

[2919] Becker, Claudia. "Zur Interiorisierung der Raumsymbolik in der Literatur der Moderne." 281-287 in Bauer, Roger, ed.; Fokkema, Douwe, ed.; Graat, Michael de, asst. ed.; Aldridge, A. Owen, asst.; Higonnet, Margaret, asst.; Klein, Holger M., asst.; Meisami, Julie Scott, asst.; Rigney, Ann, asst.; Ronen, Ruth, asst.; Sondrup, Steven P., asst.; Templeton, Joan, asst.; Walker, Janet A., asst. *Proceedings of the XIIth Congress of the International Comparative Literature Association / Actes du XIIe congrès de l'Association Internationale de Littérature Comparée: München 1988 Munich, III: Space and Boundaries in Literature (Continuation) / Espace et frontières dans la littérature (suite).* Munich: Iudicium; 1990. 509 pp. (Proceedings of the Congress of the International Comparative Literature Association 12: 3.) [†As symbol in Modernism.]

SPANISH CIVIL WAR

[2920] Monteath, Peter. "The Spanish Civil War and the Aesthetics of Reportage." 69-85 in Bevan, David, ed. *Literature and War.* Amsterdam: Rodopi; 1990. 209 pp. (RPML 3.) [†Use of reportage.]

SPARTACUS (D. 71 B.C.)

[2921] Hooff, Anton J. L. van. "'I am Spartacus, I am Spartacus': De gebruiksgeschiedenis van een antieke rebel." *Lampas: Tijdschrift voor Nederlandse Classici.* 1990 Jan.; 23(1): 89-117. [Eng. sum.]

THE SUBLIME

[2922] Chadwick, Vernon Davis. "Seizing Moments: Striking the Fundamental Mood of Academic Assignments in the Time of the Sublime: Longinus, Kant, Shelley, Heidegger, Derrida." *DAI.* 1990 May; 50(11): 3578A. [†Theories of Heidegger, Martin: *Sein und Zeit.* Dissertation abstract.]

[2923] Freeman, Barbara Claire. "Conjunctions: Studies in Twentieth Century Women's Literature and the Sublime." *DAI.* 1990 Mar.; 50(9): 2888A. [†And sexual difference; treatment in women writers (1900-1999). Dissertation abstract.]

TEACHER

[2924] Singer, Armand E., ed.; Spleth, Janice S., ed.; Luchok, John, ed. "Special Issue Devoted to the Teacher in Nineteenth- and Twentieth-Century Literature and Film." *WVUPP.* 1990; 36. [Spec. iss.; incl. pref.]

TIME

[2925] Felt, James W., S.J. "Faces of Time." *Thought.* 1987 Dec.; 62(247): 414-422.

TRANSGRESSION

[2926] Stallybrass, Peter; White, Allon. *The Politics and Poetics of Transgression.* Ithaca: Cornell UP; 1989. xi, 228 pp. [Rpt. of 1986 ed. †As the carnivalesque; relationship to social hierarchy. Application of theories of Bakhtin, Mikhail Mikhaïlovich; Elias, Norbert; Douglas, Mary.]

TROILUS

[2927] Boitani, Piero. "Eros and Thanatos: Cressida, Troilus, and the Modern Age." 281-305 in Boitani, Piero, ed. *The European Tragedy of Troilus.* Oxford: Clarendon; 1989. xiii, 316 pp. [†And Cressida; study example: opera; Morley, Christopher: *The Trojan Horse;* Wolf, Christa: *Kassandra.*]

TUBERCULOSIS

[2928] Latimer, Dan. "Erotic Susceptibility and Tuberculosis: Literary Images of a Pathology." *MLN.* 1990 Dec.; 105(5): 1016-1031.

UNDERWORLD

[2929] Williams, Rosalind. *Notes on the Underground: An Essay on Technology, Society, and the Imagination.* Cambridge: MIT Press; 1990. 265 pp. [†Relationship to technology; society; imagination.]

UTOPIA

[2930] Berghahn, Klaus L., ed.; Grimm, Reinhold, ed.; Kreuzer, Helmut, ed. *Utopian Vision, Technological Innovation and Poetic Imagination.* Heidelberg: Winter; 1990. 130 pp. (RSieg 91.) [Incl. pref.; illus.]

UTOPIANISM

[2931] Suvin, Darko. "Locus, Horizon, and Orientation: The Concept of Possible Worlds as a Key to Utopian Studies." *DS/SD.* 1988 Winter; 1(1): 87-108. [†Relationship to literary studies. Semiotic approach. Theories of Bloch, Ernst.]

VIRGIN MARY

[2932] Kent, John. "A Renovation of Images: Nineteenth-Century Protestant 'Lives of Jesus' and Roman Catholic Alleged Appearances of the Blessed Virgin Mary." 37-52 in Jasper, David, ed.; Wright, T. R., ed. *The Critical Spirit and the Will to Believe: Essays in Nineteenth-Century Literature and Religion.* New York: St. Martin's; 1989. xii; 239 pp.

WAR

[2933] Bevan, David, ed. *Literature and War.* Amsterdam: Rodopi; 1990. 209 pp. (RPML 3.) [Incl. introd. †1900-1999.]

[2934] Knibb, James. "Literary Strategies of War, Strategies of Literary War." 7-24 in Bevan, David, ed. *Literature and War.* Amsterdam: Rodopi; 1990. 209 pp. (RPML 3.)

WITCH

[2935] Olivieri, Mario. "L'*immagine* della strega." *GliA.* 1990 Jan.-June; 14: 33-111. [†Sociohistorical approach.]

WOMEN

Bibliography

[2936] Budge, Alice; Didur, Pam. "Women and War: A Selected Bibliography." *Mosaic.* 1990 Summer; 23(3): 151-173. [†Relationship to war. (1974-1989).]

WOMEN DETECTIVES

[2937] Marchino, Lois A. "The Female Sleuth in Academe." *JPC.* 1989 Winter; 23(3): 89-100. [†1900-1999. In academia.]

Subject Index

ABDRASHITOV, VADIM
  General literature. Film.
    Interview with ABDRASHITOV, VADIM. 462.
ABNORMALITY
See also classified section: 2832.
ABOLITION OF SLAVERY
See also related term: Slavery.
ABORTION
  General literature. Film.
    Treatment of sexuality; ABORTION in Scott, Ridley: *Alien.* 296.
ABRAHAM, NICOLAS (D. 1957)
  Literary theory and criticism. Psychoanalytic literary theory and criticism.
    Role of Oedipus complex. Theories of ABRAHAM, NICOLAS and Torok, Maria compared to Freud, Sigmund; Lacan, Jacques. Review article. 1909.
ABRAHAM LINCOLN BATTALION
See also related term: Spanish Civil War.
  General literature. Film. Film genres: documentary film.
    Treatment of ABRAHAM LINCOLN BATTALION in Buckner, Noel and Dore, Mary and Paskin, David and Sills, Sam: *The Good Fight.* 748.
ABSTINENCE
  General literature. Middle Ages.
    Treatment of marriage; relationship to ABSTINENCE from sexual intercourse. 66.
ABSTRACTION
  Literary movements.
    Modernism. ABSTRACTION; logic in language; relationship to Postmodernism. 1016.
THE ABSURD
See also related term: Theater of the absurd.
  General literature. Theater.
    Treatment of THE ABSURD; secularity; relationship to Postmodernism. 949.
ACADEMIA
  Genres. Novel by women novelists. 1900-1999.
    Treatment of exile in ACADEMIA. Application of theories of Barthes, Roland: *S/Z.* 2213.
  Literary theory and criticism.
    On crisis of literary theory in ACADEMIA. Review article. 1330.
  Literary theory and criticism. Feminist literary theory and criticism.
    Role in ACADEMIA. 1669.
  Professional topics.
    Role of writers's block; relationship to women in ACADEMIA. 2577.
  Professional topics. Humanities.
    Role of women in ACADEMIA; study example: Stone, Lucinda Hinsdale. 2720.
  Themes and figures. Women detectives. 1900-1999.
    In ACADEMIA. 2937.
ACADEMIC ALLIANCES
  Professional topics. Humanities.
    Role of ACADEMIC ALLIANCES. 2808.
ACADEMIC COSTUME
See also related term: Academia.
ACADEMIC DISCIPLINES
See also narrower term: Social sciences.
See also related term: Academia.
ACADEMIC DISCOURSE
  Professional topics.
    ACADEMIC DISCOURSE. 2582.
  Professional topics. Humanities.
    ACADEMIC DISCOURSE; literacy as language games; relationship to gender. 2741.
    Role of ACADEMIC DISCOURSE. 2762.
    ——; relationship to interpretive communities; social construction. 2703.
ACADEMIC PROSE
  Professional topics.
    Role of experimental writing; relationship to ACADEMIC PROSE. 2586.
ACADEMIC SETTING
See also related term: Academia.
THE ACADEMY
  Literary theory and criticism.
    In THE ACADEMY; relationship to rhetoric. Study example: de Man, Paul. 1354.
ACADEMY AWARDS
Use: Academy of Motion Picture Arts and Sciences awards.

ACADEMY OF MOTION PICTURE ARTS AND SCIENCES
See also related term: Academy of Motion Picture Arts and Sciences awards.
ACADEMY OF MOTION PICTURE ARTS AND SCIENCES AWARDS
Used for: Academy Awards.
  General literature. Film.
    ACADEMY OF MOTION PICTURE ARTS AND SCIENCES AWARDS. 327.
ACCENTUAL PATTERN
See also related term: Prosody.
ACCONCI, VITO (1940-)—STUDY EXAMPLE
  Literary movements.
    Postmodernism. Study example: ACCONCI, VITO. 1021.
ACID-FREE PAPER
See also related term: Book preservation.
ACTING
See also related terms: Actors; Theater.
  General literature. Theater.
    ACTING. Phenomenological approach. Dissertation abstract. 963.
    ——. Theories of Silvera, Frank. Dissertation abstract. 973.
    Role of ACTING; relationship to celebrity. Semiotic approach. Application of theories of Prague School of Linguistics. 959.
ACTING OUT
See also related term: Psychoanalysis.
ACTORS
See also narrower term: Film star.
See also related terms: Acting; Film; Performance art; Theater.
  General literature. Film in Hollywood (1933).
    Role of ACTORS as workers; relationship to subjectivity. Dissertation abstract. 293.
  General literature. Theater.
    Role of ACTORS. Semiotic approach. Application of theories of Greimas, Algirdas Julien. Dissertation abstract. 964.
ACTRESSES
See also narrower term: Film star.
See also related terms: Acting; Actors.
ACTUALITY
See also related term: Reality.
AD HOMINEM ARGUMENT
  Literary forms. Rhetoric.
    AD HOMINEM ARGUMENT. In Fichte, Johann Gottlieb: *Wissenschaftslehre.* 2495.
ADAGE
See also related term: Proverb.
ADAMS, HENRY BROOKS (1838-1918)—STUDY EXAMPLE
  General literature.
    Relationship to order; chaos; study example: ADAMS, HENRY BROOKS: *The Education of Henry Adams;* Lessing, Doris: *The Golden Notebook;* Lem, Stanisław. 96.
ADAPTATION
See also narrower terms: Dramatic adaptation; Film adaptation; Musical adaptation; Radio adaptation; Television adaptation; Theatrical adaptation.
  General literature.
    ADAPTATION into art. Pedagogical approach. 135.
ADDRESS
  Literary forms. Translation.
    Of names; work title; forms of ADDRESS. 2532.
ADDRESS SHIFT
See also related term: Address.
ADDRESSEE
See also related terms: Address; Communication.
ADJANI, ISABELLE (1955-)
  General literature. Film.
    Role of ADJANI, ISABELLE; relationship to politics. 548.
ADLER, MORTIMER JEROME (1902-)
  Literary theory and criticism.
    Theories of ADLER, MORTIMER JEROME: *How to Read a Book;* Pound, Ezra: *ABC of Reading.* 1477.
ADOLESCENCE
See also related term: Adolescents.
ADOLESCENT FEMALES
  General literature. Film in United States (1920-1970).
    Treatment of ADOLESCENT FEMALES. Dissertation abstract. 568.

ADOLESCENTS
Used for: Young people.
See also narrower term: Adolescent females.
  Genres. Novel. Popular romance novel.
    Relationship to ADOLESCENTS and leisure. Dissertation abstract. 2234.

ADOLESCENTS—AS AUDIENCE
  General literature for ADOLESCENTS.
    Relationship to nuclear age. 123.

ADORNO, THEODOR W. (1903-1969)
Used for: Wiesengrund, Theodor.
  General literature. Film.
    Cinematic technique; relationship to judgment. Theories of Heidegger, Martin; ADORNO, THEODOR W. 656.
  Literary movements.
    Modernism. Theories of ADORNO, THEODOR W.; Marx, Karl. 1011.
    Postmodernism. Theories of ADORNO, THEODOR W. 1060.
  Literary theory and criticism.
    Relationship to metaphysics. Theories of ADORNO, THEODOR W. 1570.
  Literary theory and criticism. Deconstructionism.
    Relationship to aesthetics. Theories of ADORNO, THEODOR W. 1645.

ADULT-CHILD RELATIONS
See also related term: Children.
  General literature for children.
    Treatment of ADULT-CHILD RELATIONS. Reader-response approach. 99.

ADULTERY
See also related term: Marriage.

ADULTS
See also narrower term: Young adults.
See also related term: Adult-child relations.

ADVANCE ORGANIZER
See also related term: Reading.

ADVENTURE
  Genres. Fiction for children.
    Treatment of the marvelous; ADVENTURE. 2104.

ADVENTURE FICTION
See also narrower terms: Detective fiction; Science fiction.
See also related terms: Adventure; Fantasy.

ADVENTURE NOVEL
See also related terms: Adventure; Penny dreadful.

ADVENTURER
See also related term: Adventure.

ADVERTISEMENT
See also related term: Advertising.

ADVERTISERS
  General literature. Television in Italy.
    Role of ADVERTISERS. 878.

ADVERTISING
  General literature. Film.
    Role of film star; relationship to ADVERTISING. 344.
  General literature. Television.
    ADVERTISING; relationship to myth. Dissertation abstract. 907.
    Role of ADVERTISING as entertainment. 889, 915.
  Literary theory and criticism. Semiotic literary theory and criticism.
    Applied to discourse of mass media; ADVERTISING. 1984.

ADVERTISING LANGUAGE
See also related term: Advertising.

ÆLFGIFU, QUEEN OF ENGLAND
Use: Emma, Queen of England (d. 1052).

AESTHETIC DEVICE
  Literary theory and criticism.
    Role of laughter as AESTHETIC DEVICE; relationship to truth. Theories of Bakhtin, Mikhail Mikhaĭlovich. 1499.

AESTHETIC EXPERIENCE
See also related term: Aesthetics.

AESTHETIC FORM
See also related term: Aesthetics.

AESTHETIC JUDGMENT
See also related term: Aesthetics.
  Professional topics. Comparative literature.
    AESTHETIC JUDGMENT. 2618.

AESTHETIC MYSTICISM MOVEMENT
Use: Hermetism.

AESTHETIC PERCEPTION
See also related term: Aesthetics.

AESTHETIC THEORY
See also related term: Aesthetics.

AESTHETIC VALUES
See also related term: Aesthetics.

AESTHETICISM
See also related term: Aesthetics.

AESTHETICS
Used for: Esthetics.
See also related term: Aesthetic judgment.
  General literature.
    AESTHETICS. 36.
    Relationship to AESTHETICS. 63.
  General literature. Film in black Africa.
    AESTHETICS. 372.
  Genres. Fiction. Science fiction.
    Role of AESTHETICS; relationship to science. 2173.
  Genres. Novel. *Bildungsroman.*
    Relationship to AESTHETICS. Dissertation abstract. 2238.
  Literary forms. Humor. 1700-1799.
    Role of jokes; pun; relationship to AESTHETICS. 2403.
  Literary movements.
    Postmodernism. Relationship to ethics; AESTHETICS. 1065.
    Romanticism. AESTHETICS. 1078.
  Literary theory and criticism.
    AESTHETICS. 1343.
    ——; relationship to anarchism. Theories of Reszler, André. 1559.
    ——; relationship to bourgeois society; politics; hegemony. 1386.
    ——; relationship to language. Review article. 1547.
    And AESTHETICS; critical methodology. Bibliography (1988-1989). 1581.
    On reading; relationship to AESTHETICS. Theories of Jauss, Hans Robert: *Aesthetische Erfahrung und literarische Hermeneutik* compared to Barthes, Roland: *Le Plaisir du texte.* 1361.
    Relationship to AESTHETICS of Romanticism. Theories of de Man, Paul. 1352.
    Role of AESTHETICS; relationship to German philosophy. 1387.
    Role of imagination; AESTHETICS. 1436.
  Literary theory and criticism. Deconstructionism.
    Relationship to AESTHETICS. Theories of Adorno, Theodor W. 1645.
    ——. Theories of Hartman, Geoffrey H. Review article. 1585.
  Literary theory and criticism. Hermeneutics.
    Relationship to AESTHETICS. 1717.
  Literary theory and criticism. Reception theory.
    Role of AESTHETICS. Theories of Jauss, Hans Robert; Iser, Wolfgang. 1945.
  Literary theory and criticism. Semiotic literary theory and criticism.
    AESTHETICS. 1969, 1987.
    —— of color; form. Theories of Marquand, Allan; Ladd-Franklin, Christine; relationship to Peirce, Charles Sanders. 1985.
  Themes and figures. Human body.
    Relationship to AESTHETICS. Review article. 2874.

AFER, PUBLIUS TERENTIUS
Use: Terence (ca. 195-159/8 B.C.).

AFFECT
See also related term: Emotions.
  Literary theory and criticism.
    Role of AFFECT; relationship to form; content. 1413.

AFFECTION
See also related term: Love.

AFFECTIVE DEVELOPMENT
See also related terms: Affect; Emotions.

AFRICA
See also related term: Black Africa.
  Bibliographical. Publishing. Marketing in AFRICA of French language literature. 1303.
  General literature. Film.
    Treatment of AFRICA in Rouch, Jean Pierre. 554, 555, 556, 557, 662.

AFRICAN AMERICAN COMMUNITY
See also related term: African Americans.
  General literature. Film.
    Treatment of AFRICAN AMERICAN COMMUNITY in Lee, Spike: *She's Gotta Have It; School Daze; Do the Right Thing.* 521.

AFRICAN AMERICAN CRITICS
  Literary theory and criticism. Feminist literary theory and criticism.
    And criticism by AFRICAN AMERICAN CRITICS. 1694.

AFRICAN AMERICAN EXPERIENCE
See also related term: African Americans.

AFRICAN AMERICAN FEMINISM
  Literary theory and criticism. Feminist literary theory and criticism.
    Relationship to AFRICAN AMERICAN FEMINISM. 1705.

AFRICAN AMERICAN FILMMAKERS
  General literature. Film by AFRICAN AMERICAN FILMMAKERS.
    On Lee, Spike: *Do the Right Thing.* Interview. 543.

AFRICAN AMERICAN NEIGHBORHOODS
  General literature. Film in Chicago (1905-1928).
    Relationship to exhibition in AFRICAN AMERICAN NEIGHBORHOODS. 281.

SEE CLASSIFIED SEQUENCE FOR ADDITIONAL ENTRIES

AFRICAN AMERICAN SOLDIERS
   General literature. Film. Film genres: war film.
      Treatment of AFRICAN AMERICAN SOLDIERS; relationship to Vietnam War. 782.

AFRICAN AMERICAN STUDIES
   Professional topics. Humanities.
      AFRICAN AMERICAN STUDIES. 2709.

AFRICAN AMERICAN WOMEN
   Professional topics. Humanities.
      Role of AFRICAN AMERICAN WOMEN; relationship to feminism. 2765.

AFRICAN AMERICANS
See also narrower terms: African American soldiers; African American women.
See also related term: African American community.
   General literature. Film.
      Representation of AFRICAN AMERICANS; slavery. Dissertation abstract. 361.
   Genres. Fiction. 1800-1999.
      Treatment of AFRICAN AMERICANS as minstrels. Dissertation abstract. 2138.

AFRICANS
See also narrower term: Black Africans.

AFTERLIFE
See also related term: Death.

AGEISM
   Professional topics. Humanities.
      On AGEISM; sexism in universities. Theories of Eco, Umberto; Derrida, Jacques. 2670.

ALBION
See also related term: England.

ALCIATI, ANDREA (1492-1550)
   Bibliographical. Printing. Latin language literature. 1500-1599.
      Of monomachia against ALCIATI, ANDREA. 1160.

ALDRIDGE, ALFRED OWEN (1915-)
   General literature.
      Festschrift for ALDRIDGE, ALFRED OWEN. 108.

ALEXANDRIA
See also classified section: 2833.

ALF LAYLAH WA-LAYLAH
Use: The Thousand and One Nights.

ALGORITHM
See also related term: Computer.

ALIEN BEINGS
See also related term: Extraterrestrial life.

ALIEN WORLDS
See also related term: Extraterrestrial life.

ALIYAH
See also related term: Jews.

ALLEGORICAL POETRY
See also related term: Allegory.

ALLEGORY
See also classified section: 2379 ff.
See also narrower term: Fable.
   Literary forms. Rhetoric.
      And ALLEGORY. 2458.
   Literary movements.
      Modernism. Narrative; relationship to ALLEGORY. Treatment in de Man, Paul. 1006.
   Literary theory and criticism. Deconstructionism.
      Authority of writer; relationship to reader; ALLEGORY. Treatment in de Man, Paul: "Rhetoric of Temporality." 1589.

ALLEN, DONALD MERRIAM (1912-)
   Bibliographical. Publishing in United States.
      By Grove Press. Interview with ALLEN, DONALD MERRIAM. 1242.

ALLEN, HEYWOOD
Use: Allen, Woody (1935-).

ALLEN, WOODY (1935-)
Used for: Allen, Heywood; Konigsberg, Allen Stewart.
   General literature. Film.
      Treatment of betrayal in ALLEN, WOODY: *Crimes and Misdemeanors* compared to Matt, Peter von: *Liebesverrat: Die Treulosen in der Literatur.* 528.
      Treatment of female characters; phallocentrism in ALLEN, WOODY. Feminist approach. 332.
      Treatment of Jewish identity in ALLEN, WOODY. 487.
      Treatment of schlemiel in ALLEN, WOODY. 531.

ALLITERATION
See also related term: Rhyme.

ALLOCUTION
See also related term: Address.

ALLUSION
See also narrower term: Classical allusion.

ALPHABET
See also related term: Writing systems.

ALPHABETIZATION
See also related term: Dictionary.

ALTERITY
Use: Otherness.

ALTERNATIVE FILM
   General literature. Film: ALTERNATIVE FILM by women filmmakers for women. 310.

ALTERNATIVE TELEVISION
   General literature. Television: ALTERNATIVE TELEVISION in United States. 857.

ALTMAN, ROBERT (1925-)
   General literature. Film. Film genres: American Western film.
      Treatment of frontier in ALTMAN, ROBERT: *McCabe and Mrs. Miller.* 788.

AMBIGUITY
   General literature. Film.
      Narrative form; AMBIGUITY; relationship to melodrama in Weir, Peter: *Picnic at Hanging Rock.* 512.
   Literary theory and criticism. Linguistic literary theory and criticism.
      Role of AMBIGUITY; indeterminacy. 1746.
   Literary theory and criticism. Psychoanalytic literary theory and criticism.
      On AMBIGUITY of language; relationship to psychoanalysis. 1912.

AMBIGUITY DETECTION
See also related term: Ambiguity.

AMERICA
See also related terms: American culture; American dream; American myth; United States.

AMERICAN BIOGRAPH COMPANY
   General literature. Film.
      And screenplay; film review; relationship to AMERICAN BIOGRAPH COMPANY; study example: Woods, Frank E.; Griffith, D. W. 229.

AMERICAN COUNCIL ON THE TEACHING OF FOREIGN LANGUAGES
See also related term: Teaching of language.

AMERICAN CRITICS
See also narrower term: African American critics.

AMERICAN CULTURE
   Literary theory and criticism.
      On American literature; AMERICAN CULTURE; relationship to Native Americans. Review article. 1458.

AMERICAN DREAM
   General literature. Film.
      Treatment of dancer; relationship to play; AMERICAN DREAM. 258.

AMERICAN EXPERIENCE
See also related term: American culture.

AMERICAN FICTION
   General literature. Film in United States (1975-1987).
      And AMERICAN FICTION. Treatment of journalists. Application of theories of Lowenthal, Leo. Dissertation abstract. 439.
   Literary theory and criticism. Reader-response theory and criticism.
      Role of reader; relationship to AMERICAN FICTION. Theories of Mailloux, Steven compared to Fish, Stanley; Culler, Jonathan. Review article. 1918.

AMERICAN FILM
See also narrower term: American Western film.

AMERICAN INDIANS
Use: Native Americans.

AMERICAN LITERARY TRADITION
See also related term: American literature.

AMERICAN LITERATURE
   General literature. Film.
      And AMERICAN LITERATURE. Treatment of Mormons in Western United States. 459.
      And English literature; AMERICAN LITERATURE; popular fiction. 389.
   Literary movements.
      Aesthetic movement. Relationship to European literature; AMERICAN LITERATURE. 987.
   Literary theory and criticism.
      On AMERICAN LITERATURE; American culture; relationship to Native Americans. Review article. 1458.

AMERICAN MYTH
   General literature. Film in United States (1930-1990).
      Treatment of AMERICAN MYTH. 503.

AMERICAN SOLDIERS
See also narrower term: African American soldiers.

AMERICAN SOUTH
Use: Southern United States.

AMERICAN UNIVERSITIES
  Professional topics. Comparative literature at AMERICAN UNIVERSITIES.
    Literature of Middle Ages; Renaissance. 2604.
  Professional topics. Humanities.
    Creative writing at AMERICAN UNIVERSITIES. Dissertation abstract. 2775.
    Teaching of translation at AMERICAN UNIVERSITIES. 2669.

AMERICAN WEST
Use: Western United States.

AMERICAN WESTERN FILM
Used for: Western film.
  General literature. Film. Film genres: AMERICAN WESTERN FILM.
    Reminiscence. 759.
    Treatment of frontier in Altman, Robert: *McCabe and Mrs. Miller*. 788.
    Treatment of nuclear family. 801.
  General literature. Film. Film genres: AMERICAN WESTERN FILM (1947-1957).
    Treatment of patriarchy in Zinnemann, Fred: *High Noon* compared to Mann, Anthony: *The Tin Star*. 786.

AMERICANS
See also narrower terms: African Americans; Native Americans.

AMERINDIANS
Use: Native Americans.

AMORALITY
See also related term: Morality.

AMSTERDAM
  Bibliographical. Printing. Binding in AMSTERDAM. 1600-1699.
    By Magnus, Albert. 1201.
  Bibliographical. Printing. Typography in AMSTERDAM. 1600-1799.
    Role of Dijk, Christoffel van; Kis, Miklós; relationship to typefaces in Armenian language. 1228.
  Bibliographical. Printing in AMSTERDAM. 1600-1699.
    By Blaeu, Joan. 1163.

AMUSEMENT PARK
  General literature. Film in Chicago (1906-1908).
    And nickelodeon; AMUSEMENT PARK as cultural space; relationship to sexuality of women. 536.

ANACHRONY
See also related term: Temporality.

ANALOGY
See also narrower terms: Metaphor; Simile.
  Figures of speech. Metaphor.
    And ANALOGY. 2364.
  Literary forms. Rhetoric.
    ANALOGY in medical prose. 2469.

ANALYSIS
  Literary forms. Translation. Translation theory.
    Role of interpretation; reference; relationship to ANALYSIS of target text. 2575.

ANALYTICAL BIBLIOGRAPHY
See also classified section: 1119.

ANAPHORA
See also related term: Reference.

ANAPHORA (STYLE)
See also related term: Repetition.

ANAPHORAL PRAYER
See also related term: Eucharist (sacrament of).

ANARCHISM
  General literature. 1800-1899: *fin de siècle.*
    Relationship to ANARCHISM. 201.
  Literary movements.
    Avant-garde. Relationship to ANARCHISM. 990.
    ——. Relationship to mass culture; ANARCHISM. Treatment in criticism. 993.
  Literary theory and criticism.
    Aesthetics; relationship to ANARCHISM. Theories of Reszler, André. 1559.

ANARCHISTS
See also related term: Anarchism.

ANARCHY
See also related term: Anarchism.

ANATOMICAL IMAGERY
See also related term: Human body.

ANATOMICAL METAPHOR
See also related term: Human body.

ANATOMY
See also related term: Human body.

ANATOMY (SATIRE)
See also related term: Menippean satire.

ANCIENT GREEK LITERATURE
Used for: Classical Greek literature.

ANCIENT GREEK LITERATURE—AS SOURCE
  Genres. Poetry.
    Relationship to tragedy. Sources in ANCIENT GREEK LITERATURE. 2291.

ANCIENT GREEK PHILOSOPHY
See also related term: Sophists.

ANDERSON, LAURIE (1947-)
  General literature. Theater.
    Visual imagery; relationship to text; Postmodernism in performance art by ANDERSON, LAURIE. 958.

ANDROCENTRISM
See also related term: Masculinity.

ANDRZEJEWSKI, JERZY (1909-1983)
  Literary theory and criticism. Socialist realist literary theory and criticism.
    Theories of ANDRZEJEWSKI, JERZY; Miłosz, Czesław. 2009.

ANECDOTE
See also classified section: 2382.
See also related term: Jokes.

ANGEL MALO
  General literature. Television: soap opera.
    On *ANGEL MALO*. 923.

ANGÉLIQUE, PIERRE
Use: Bataille, Georges (1897-1962).

ANGLO-AMERICAN CATALOGUING RULES II (1988)
  Bibliographical.
    Archival standards in documentary editing; use of *ANGLO-AMERICAN CATALOGUING RULES II*. 1116.

ANIMAL IMAGERY
See also related term: Animals.

ANIMAL LANGUAGE
See also related term: Animals.

ANIMAL SPIRITS
See also related term: Animals.

ANIMAL SYMBOLISM
See also related term: Animals.

ANIMALS
  General literature. Film.
    Treatment of ANIMALS; relationship to sympathy; sentimentality in Annaud, Jean-Jacques: *L'Ours* compared to Disney, Walt. 262.

ANIMATED FILM
See also related term: Cartoons.
  General literature. Film. Film genres: ANIMATED FILM.
    Spatiality. 762.
  General literature. Film. Film genres: ANIMATED FILM in France.
    Biography of Cohl, Emile. 754.

ANNAUD, JEAN-JACQUES
  General literature. Film.
    Treatment of animals; relationship to sympathy; sentimentality in ANNAUD, JEAN-JACQUES: *L'Ours* compared to Disney, Walt. 262.
  General literature. Film. Film adaptation.
    Of Eco, Umberto: *Il nome della rosa* by ANNAUD, JEAN-JACQUES. 675.

ANOMALIES
See also related term: Abnormality.

ANSWER
See also related term: Question.

ANTAGONIST
See also related term: Protagonist.

ANTECEDENT
See also related term: Reference.

ANTHROPOLOGICAL APPROACH
See also related term: Anthropology.
Documents applying specific approaches are so numerous that access to them is provided only in the electronic versions of the *Bibliography*.

ANTHROPOLOGY
  General literature.
    Fictionality; relationship to ANTHROPOLOGY. 101.
    Relationship to ANTHROPOLOGY. 8, 55.
  Genres. Fiction. Horror fiction. 1900-1999.
    Relationship to ANTHROPOLOGY. 2165.
  Literary theory and criticism. Deconstructionism.
    Role of hierarchy; self-reflexiveness; relationship to philosophy; ANTHROPOLOGY. Theories of Derrida, Jacques; Dumont, Louis. 1599.
  Literary theory and criticism. Narrative theory.
    Application in linguistics; ANTHROPOLOGY; psychology. 1799.

ANTHROPOPHAGY
Use: Cannibalism.

ANTI-INTELLECTUALISM
See also related term: Intellectualism.

ANTI-NAZISM
See also related term: Nazism.

ANTI-SEMITISM
See also related term: Jews.
　Literary movements.
　　Enlightenment. Role of ANTI-SEMITISM; racism; relationship to medicine.
　　1000.
　Literary theory and criticism.
　　By de Man, Paul; relationship to ANTI-SEMITISM. 1463.
　Literary theory and criticism. Deconstructionism.
　　Theories of de Man, Paul; relationship to ANTI-SEMITISM. 1630.

ANTIFASCISM
See also related term: Fascism.

ANTIFEMINISM
See also related term: Feminism.

ANTIMODERNISM
　Literary movements.
　　Modernism. ANTIMODERNISM. 1010.

ANTINATIONALISM
See also related term: Nationalism.

ANTINOMIANISM
See also related term: Faith.

ANTINOMY
　General literature. Film. Film adaptation.
　　Treatment of ANTINOMY; relationship to human nature in Scott, Ridley: *Blade Runner* as film adaptation of Dick, Philip K.: *Do Androids Dream of Electric Sheep?* 720.

ANTIPASTORALISM
See also related term: Pastoralism.

ANTIREALISM
See also related terms: The absurd; Fantasy; Realism; Surrealism.

ANTISLAVERY LITERATURE
See also related term: Slavery.

ANTITOTALITARIANISM
See also related term: Totalitarianism.

ANTIUTOPIA
Use: Dystopia.

ANTIUTOPIAN FICTION
Use: Dystopian fiction.

ANTIUTOPIAN NOVEL
Use: Dystopian novel.

ANTIWAR NOVEL
See also related term: War novel.

ANTONIONI, MICHELANGELO (1912-)
　General literature. Film.
　　Treatment of protagonist; relationship to myth of Oedipus in ANTONIONI, MICHELANGELO: *Identificazione di una donna.* 514.

ANXIETY
　Literary movements.
　　Enlightenment. Role of medicine; relationship to fear; ANXIETY. 998.

APHORISM
See also related term: Proverb.

THE APOCALYPSE
See also related term: Apocalyptic literature.
　Literary theory and criticism.
　　Role of THE APOCALYPSE; relationship to time. Theories of Levinas, Emmanuel: *Totalité et infini.* 1567.
　Literary theory and criticism. Deconstructionism.
　　Relationship to THE APOCALYPSE. Theories of Derrida, Jacques. 1610.

APOCALYPTIC IMAGERY
See also related term: The apocalypse.

APOCALYPTIC LITERATURE
See also related term: The apocalypse.
　General literature.
　　APOCALYPTIC LITERATURE; relationship to Dead Sea scrolls. 207.

APOCALYPTIC MOVEMENT
See also related term: Apocalyptic literature.

APOCALYPTIC VISION
See also related term: The apocalypse.

APOCRYPHA
See also related term: Old Testament.

APOLITICISM
See also related term: Politics.

APOLOGETICS
See also related term: Argumentation.

APOLOGIZING
See also related term: Speech acts.

APOLOGUE
Use: Fable.

APPARATUSES
See also narrower terms: Camera; Computer.
See also related term: Machines.

APPLIED LINGUISTICS
See also related term: Teaching of language.

APPRENTICESHIP NOVEL
Use: Bildungsroman.

APTITUDE
See also related term: Cognition.

THE ARABIAN NIGHTS ENTERTAINMENTS
Use: The Thousand and One Nights.

ARABIC LANGUAGE LITERATURE
　Bibliographical. Printing. History of printing.
　　Of ARABIC LANGUAGE LITERATURE in Malta by English Church Missionary Society (1825-1845). Dissertation abstract. 1194.

L'ARBRE
　Bibliographical. Publishing. History of publishing in France (1941-1948).
　　By L'ARBRE. 1280.

ARCAND, DENYS (1941-)
　General literature. Film.
　　On ARCAND, DENYS: *Jésus de Montréal.* 564.

ARCHETYPAL APPROACH
See also related term: Archetypes.
Documents applying specific approaches are so numerous that access to them is provided only in the electronic versions of the *Bibliography*.

ARCHETYPAL STRUCTURE
　Literary theory and criticism. Narrative theory.
　　On ARCHETYPAL STRUCTURE. 1810.

ARCHETYPES
See also related terms: Figures; Myth.
　General literature. Film. Film genres: horror film.
　　Treatment of ARCHETYPES of monsters carrying beautiful woman. 752.

ARCHITECTS
See also related term: Architecture.

ARCHITECTURAL IMAGERY
See also related term: Architecture.

ARCHITECTURAL METAPHOR
See also related term: Architecture.

ARCHITECTURAL PLANS
See also related term: Architecture.

ARCHITECTURAL SYMBOLISM
See also related term: Architecture.

ARCHITECTURE
　Figures of speech. Irony.
　　Relationship to ARCHITECTURE. Semiotic approach. 2356.
　General literature.
　　Spatial form; composition compared to ARCHITECTURE. Pedagogical approach. 65.
　Literary forms. Emblem.
　　Imagery of ARCHITECTURE in index. 2395.
　Literary movements.
　　Postmodernism. Relationship to ARCHITECTURE. 1071.
　　——. Relationship to ARCHITECTURE. Theories of Derrida, Jacques; Kant, Immanuel. 1028.

ARCHIVAL STANDARDS
　Bibliographical.
　　ARCHIVAL STANDARDS in documentary editing; use of *Anglo-American Cataloguing Rules II.* 1116.

ARCHIVE MANAGEMENT
See also related term: Archives.

ARCHIVES
　General literature. Film.
　　Treatment of the Holocaust. Catalogue of ARCHIVES in Israel; relationship to Steven Spielberg Jewish Film Archive. 584.
　General literature. Film in France.
　　Role of Cinémathèque universitaire; relationship to ARCHIVES. 257.
　Professional topics. Humanities.
　　ARCHIVES. 2735.
　Professional topics. Research tools.
　　Role of manuscripts; ARCHIVES. 2830.

AREAL APPROACH
Documents applying specific approaches are so numerous that access to them is provided only in the electronic versions of the *Bibliography*.

ARENBERG FAMILY
Bibliographical. 1400-1599.
Book collecting in Netherlands by ARENBERG FAMILY; relationship to Bibliothèque Royale Albert Iᵉʳ. 1089.

ARGENTINA
General literature. Film in ARGENTINA (1930-1939). 474.

ARGUMENT
See also related term: Argumentation.

ARGUMENTATION
Literary forms. Rhetoric.
ARGUMENTATION. Theories of Hamblin, Charles Leonard. 2459.
——; relationship to feminism. Theories of Rogers, Carl Ransom. 2464.
——; relationship to relevance. 2431.
—— in scientific language. Theories of Aristotle compared to Plato. 2480.
Essentially contested concept; relationship to ARGUMENTATION. 2450.
Future perfect tense in ARGUMENTATION; relationship to psychoanalytic literary theory and criticism. Theories of Aristotle; Lacan, Jacques; Derrida, Jacques. 2489.
Role of question in ARGUMENTATION. 2432.

ARGUMENTATION THEORY
See also related term: Argumentation.

ARIAS POLO, ARTURO
General literature. Film in Cuba.
Interview with ARIAS POLO, ARTURO. 392.

ARISTOCRACY
General literature. Film.
Treatment of ARISTOCRACY; relationship to Third Reich in Baky, Josef von: *Münchhausen*; Kästner, Erich: *Baron Münchhausen*. 291.

ARISTOCRATS
See also related term: Aristocracy.

ARISTOTLE (384-322 B.C.)
Figures of speech. Metaphor.
Relationship to enigma; epiphora. Theories of ARISTOTLE; treatment in Derrida, Jacques. 2361.
Literary forms. Rhetoric.
Argumentation in scientific language. Theories of ARISTOTLE compared to Plato. 2480.
Future perfect tense in argumentation; relationship to psychoanalytic literary theory and criticism. Theories of ARISTOTLE; Lacan, Jacques; Derrida, Jacques. 2489.
Treatment in ARISTOTLE. 2439.
Literary theory and criticism.
Mimesis. Theories of ARISTOTLE. 1358.

ARISTOTLE (384-322 B.C.)—AS SOURCE
Literary forms. Tragedy.
Role of pathos. Sources in Plato; ARISTOTLE. 2504.

ARMAGEDDON
See also related term: The apocalypse.

ARMENIAN EXILES
See also related term: Exile.

ARMENIAN LANGUAGE
Bibliographical. Printing. Typography in Amsterdam. 1600-1799.
Role of Dijk, Christoffel van; Kis, Miklós; relationship to typefaces in ARMENIAN LANGUAGE. 1228.

ARMY
See also narrower term: Soviet army.

ARNHEIM, RUDOLF (1904-)
General literature. Film. Film theory and criticism (1918-1933).
Theories of ARNHEIM, RUDOLF; relationship to Gestalt theory. 833.

ARNOLD, MATTHEW (1822-1888)
Professional topics. Humanities.
Role of English studies at Canadian universities. Application of theories of ARNOLD, MATTHEW: *Culture and Anarchy*. 2732.

ARS MORIENDI
See also related term: Death.

ARS POETICA
See also related term: Poetry.

ART
See also narrower term: Modern art.
See also related terms: Art history; Artist; Arts.
General literature.
Adaptation into ART. Pedagogical approach. 135.
And ART. Pedagogical approach. 13, 59.
——. Role of space. 47.
—— in Western world. Pedagogical approach. 138.
Relationship to ART. Bibliography (1987). 217.
——. Pedagogical approach. 43, 92.
Literary theory and criticism. Deconstructionism.
Relationship to ART. 1637.

Professional topics. Humanities.
Canon; relationship to culture; ART. 2817.

ART COLLECTING
See also related term: Art.

ART CRITICISM
See also related terms: Art; Literary theory and criticism.

ART HISTORY
See also related term: Art.
Literary theory and criticism.
Relationship to ART HISTORY. 1451.
Professional topics. Comparative literature.
Relationship to ART HISTORY. 2628.

ART MOVEMENTS
See also narrower term: Primitivism.
See also related terms: Art; Arts.

ART THERAPY
General literature by patient with cancer.
Relationship to ART THERAPY. Treatment of mourning; creativity. Psychoanalytic approach. Dissertation abstract. 62.

ARTHUR, KING
See also classified section: 2834 ff.
Used for: King Arthur.
See also related term: Arthurian legend.

General literature. Film. 1900-1999.
Treatment of ARTHUR in Boorman, John: *Excalibur*; Rohmer, Eric: *Perceval le Gallois*; Romero, George A.: *Knightriders*. 438.

ARTHURIAN LEGEND
See also related term: Arthur, King.
General literature. Film.
Treatment of ARTHURIAN LEGEND. 387.

ARTHURIAN TRADITION
See also related term: Arthur, King.

ARTICULATORY LOOP
See also related term: Memory.

ARTIFACTS
See also related term: Invention.

ARTIFICIAL INTELLIGENCE
See also related term: Computer.

ARTIST
See also related terms: Art; Arts.
General literature. Film.
Treatment of ARTIST; relationship to desire in Mizoguchi Kenji. 329.
——; relationship to mass media in Unruh, Fritz von: *Phaea*. 378.
—— in Mizoguchi Kenji. Dissertation abstract. 328.

ARTISTS
See also related term: Artist.

ARTISTS IN EXILE
See also related term: Exile.

ARTS
See also narrower terms: Architecture; Drama; Music; Painting; Photography; Sculpture; Visual arts.
See also related terms: Art; Artist.
General literature.
Relationship to ARTS. Pedagogical approach. 14.

ARTWORK
See also related term: Art.

ARTZT, CHARLES
Bibliographical. Printing in Western United States. 1800-1899.
Role of ARTZT, CHARLES; relationship to Western Lever Printing Press. 1159.

ASHBY, HAL (1936-1988)
General literature. Film.
Treatment of masculinity; relationship to love; war in ASHBY, HAL: *Coming Home*; Scott, Tony: *Top Gun*. 301.
General literature. Film and television.
Melodrama. Treatment of Vietnam War in ASHBY, HAL: *Coming Home*; *China Beach*. 485.

ASIA
General literature. Film in ASIA. 449.
Genres. Fiction.
Treatment of ASIA. 2158.

ASIAN LITERATURE—STUDY EXAMPLE
Professional topics. Comparative literature.
Study example: ASIAN LITERATURE. 2613.

ASKOL'DOV, ALEKSANDR
General literature. Film.
Role of censorship; relationship to ASKOL'DOV, ALEKSANDR: *Kommissar*. 598.

ASOR ROSA, ALBERTO
Used for: Rosa, Alberto Asor.
> **Literary theory and criticism. Hermeneutics.**
>> Application of theories of ASOR ROSA, ALBERTO. 1714.

ASPHAUG, MARTIN
> **General literature. Film.**
>> On ASPHAUG, MARTIN: *En håndfull tid.* 401.

ASQUITH, ANTHONY (1902-1968)
> **General literature. Film.**
>> Use of sound in ASQUITH, ANTHONY: *A Cottage on Dartmoor*; relationship to film history. 590.

ASSONANCE
See also related term: Rhyme.

ASSUMPTIO
> **Figures of speech.**
>> Relationship to *transsumptio*; ASSUMPTIO. 2350.

ASSUMPTION (FEAST OF)
See also related term: Virgin Mary.

ASTROLOGY
See also related term: Astronomy.

ASTRONOMICAL IMAGERY
See also related term: Astronomy.

ASTRONOMICAL METAPHOR
See also related term: Astronomy.

ASTRONOMY
> **Literary movements.**
>> Romanticism. Poetic language; relationship to synecdoche compared to language of ASTRONOMY. Application of theories of Newton, Sir Isaac compared to Herschel, Sir William. 1077.

ATHELING, WILLIAM
Use: Pound, Ezra (1885-1972).

ATOMIC AGE
Use: Nuclear age.

ATROCITIES
See also narrower term: Massacre.

ATTITUDES
See also narrower terms: Disenchantment; Subjectivity.
See also related term: Emotions.
> **General literature. Film.**
>> ATTITUDES of college students. Pedagogical approach. Dissertation abstract. 422.

ATTRIBUTION OF PRINTING
See also related term: Printing.

AUCH, LORD
Use: Bataille, Georges (1897-1962).

AUDIENCE
See also narrower term: Universal audience.
See also related terms: Audience response; Spectator.
> **General literature. Film.**
>> On Robbe-Grillet, Alain: *L'Immortelle* compared to novel; relationship to AUDIENCE. Narratological approach. 507.
>> Role of AUDIENCE in film history; relationship to exhibition. Reception study. 225.
> **General literature. Theater.**
>> Language; relationship to AUDIENCE. 928.
>> Social function; role of AUDIENCE. Semiotic approach. 932.
> **Literary theory and criticism. Reader-response theory and criticism.**
>> Role of AUDIENCE. 1937.

AUDIENCE ENTRAPMENT
See also related term: Audience.

AUDIENCE PARTICIPATION
See also related term: Audience.

AUDIENCE RESPONSE
See also related term: Audience.
> **General literature. Theater.**
>> Illusion; relationship to AUDIENCE RESPONSE. 935.
> **Genres. Drama.**
>> Deixis; relationship to AUDIENCE RESPONSE. 2092.

AUDIENCE STUDY
See also related term: Audience.

AUDIODISK
See also related term: Recordings.

AUDIOTAPE
See also related term: Recordings.

AUDITORY PERCEPTION
See also related term: The aural.

AUERBACH, ERICH (1892-1957)
> **Literary theory and criticism.**
>> Mimesis; realism; style. Theories of AUERBACH, ERICH: *Mimesis.* 1528.
>> Representation; relationship to historicity. Treatment in AUERBACH, ERICH: *Mimesis*; de Man, Paul. 1382.

AUGUSTINE, SAINT (354-430)
Used for: Augustinus, Aurelius.
> **Literary theory and criticism. Semiotic literary theory and criticism.**
>> Isomorphism; similarity. Theories of AUGUSTINE, SAINT; Thomas Aquinas, Saint; Peirce, Charles Sanders. 1960.

AUGUSTINUS, AURELIUS
Use: Augustine, Saint (354-430).

THE AURAL
> **General literature. Theater.**
>> Treatment in performance theory; relationship to THE AURAL; the visual. 941.

AUSTIN, J. L. (1911-1960)
> **Literary theory and criticism.**
>> Role of referent; relationship to realism; study example: Zola, Emile. Application of theories of AUSTIN, J. L. Review article. 1533.
> **Literary theory and criticism. Deconstructionism.**
>> Theories of de Man, Paul: *Allegories of Reading*; relationship to AUSTIN, J. L. 1593.
> **Literary theory and criticism. Linguistic literary theory and criticism.**
>> Relationship to speech act theory. Theories of AUSTIN, J. L. 1740.

AUSTRALIA
> **Bibliographical. Publishing. Book trade in AUSTRALIA (1989).**
>> Relationship to copyright law. 1290.
> **General literature. Film. Film theory and criticism in AUSTRALIA.**
>> Female spectator. 825.
> **Literary movements.**
>> Postmodernism compared to Modernism. Relationship to popular culture; militarism in AUSTRALIA. 1051.

AUSTRALIAN BROADCASTING COMMISSION
See also related term: Radio.

AUSTRIA
> **Professional topics. Censorship in AUSTRIA and Germany.**
>> Relationship to restoration (ca. 1815). 2588.

AUTHOR
Use: Writer.

AUTHORIAL INTENTION
> **Literary theory and criticism. Reader-response theory and criticism.**
>> Role of AUTHORIAL INTENTION; relationship to reader. 1927.

AUTHORIAL VOICE
See also related terms: Narrative voice; Polyphony.
> **Genres. Novel.**
>> AUTHORIAL VOICE in preface. Dissertation abstract. 2230.

AUTHORITY
> **General literature.**
>> AUTHORITY in discourse; relationship to community. Dissertation abstract. 144.
> **Genres. Novel.**
>> AUTHORITY of women. 2187.
> **Literary movements.**
>> Postmodernism. Relationship to AUTHORITY; truth. 1022.
> **Literary theory and criticism. Deconstructionism.**
>> AUTHORITY of writer; relationship to reader; allegory. Treatment in de Man, Paul: "Rhetoric of Temporality." 1589.
> **Literary theory and criticism. Psychoanalytic literary theory and criticism.**
>> Relationship to AUTHORITY. 1915.
> **Professional topics. Humanities.**
>> On teaching of reading; teaching of writing; relationship to AUTHORITY. 2704.

AUTHORITY FIGURES
See also related term: Authority.

AUTHORSHIP
> **General literature. Film in Hollywood.**
>> Narrative; relationship to AUTHORSHIP in Hitchcock, Alfred: *North by Northwest*; role of screenplay by Lehman, Ernest Paul. Dissertation abstract. 581.
> **Genres. Fiction.**
>> Self-consciousness; relationship to AUTHORSHIP. 2152.
> **Literary theory and criticism.**
>> Role of AUTHORSHIP. 1430.

AUTOBIOGRAPHICAL DISCOURSE
See also related term: Autobiography.

AUTOBIOGRAPHICAL FICTION
See also related term: Autobiography.

AUTOBIOGRAPHICAL LITERATURE
See also narrower term: Autobiographical prose.
See also related term: Autobiography.

AUTOBIOGRAPHICAL NOVEL
See also related term: Autobiography.

AUTOBIOGRAPHICAL POETRY
See also related term: Autobiography.

AUTOBIOGRAPHICAL PROSE
See also classified section: 2317.

AUTOBIOGRAPHY
See also classified section: 2046 ff.
See also narrower term: Spiritual autobiography.
See also related terms: Biography; Diary; Letters.

General literature.
Role of narrative; relationship to meaning; language; AUTOBIOGRAPHY. Psychological approach. 34.

General literature. Film.
Cinematic technique; relationship to AUTOBIOGRAPHY in Fellini, Federico: *La dolce vita.* 636.

General literature. Film. Film adaptation.
Role of AUTOBIOGRAPHY in film adaptation of Döblin, Alfred: *Berlin Alexanderplatz* by Fassbinder, Rainer Werner. 701.

Genres. Fiction as AUTOBIOGRAPHY.
Repetition by narrator. Dissertation abstract. 2123.

AUTOEROTICISM
See also related term: Sex.

AUTOMATED ANALYSIS
See also related term: Computer.

AUTOMATIC TEXT GENERATION
See also related terms: Computer; Text.

AUTOMATIC TEXT PROCESSING
See also related term: Computer.

AUTOSEMANTICS
See also related term: Text linguistics.

AVANT-GARDE
See also related term: Avant-garde film.

General literature.
Feminist literature. Treatment of gender; relationship to politics; AVANT-GARDE. 198.

Literary theory and criticism. Semiotic literary theory and criticism.
Relationship to AVANT-GARDE. 1977.

AVANT-GARDE ARTISTS
See also related term: Avant-garde.

AVANT-GARDE DRAMA
See also related term: Avant-garde.

AVANT-GARDE FICTION
See also related term: Avant-garde.

AVANT-GARDE FILM
See also related term: Avant-garde.

General literature. Film. Film genres: AVANT-GARDE FILM.
Role of Buñuel, Luis. Dissertation abstract. 799.
Treatment of objects in Buñuel, Luis. 798.

General literature. Film. Film genres: AVANT-GARDE FILM and video art.
Relationship to feminism. 787.

General literature. Film. Film genres: AVANT-GARDE FILM in U.S.S.R. 758.

AVANT-GARDE PAINTING
See also related term: Avant-garde.

AVANT-GARDE POETRY
See also related term: Avant-garde.

AVANT-GARDE THEATER
See also related term: Avant-garde.

AVANT-GARDE WRITERS
See also related term: Avant-garde.

AVILDSEN, JOHN GUILBERT (1936-)
General literature.
Treatment of criminal in AVILDSEN, JOHN GUILBERT: *Save the Tiger.* 605.

BABEL', ISAAK ÈMMANUILOVICH (1894-1941)
General literature. Film.
Screenplay by BABEL', ISAAK ÈMMANUILOVICH. 390.

BACON, FRANCIS (1561-1626)
Literary forms. Rhetoric.
Scientific rhetoric. Treatment in BACON, FRANCIS. 2500.

BACON, LLOYD (1890-1955)
General literature. Film (1930-1939).
Treatment of working women in Beaumont, Harry: *Our Blushing Brides* compared to BACON, LLOYD: *Marked Woman.* 384.

BAER, KARL ERNST VON (1792-1876)
Used for: Bėr, Karl Maksimovich.

Bibliographical. Publishing. Book trade.
By BAER, KARL ERNST VON in St. Petersburg. 1292.

BAKHTIN, MIKHAIL MIKHAĬLOVICH (1895-1975)
General literature. Film in China.
Treatment of human body; relationship to ideology in Chang I-mo: *Hung kao-liang.* Application of theories of Jameson, Fredric; BAKHTIN, MIKHAIL MIKHAĬLOVICH. 661.

General literature. Theater.
Relationship to laughter; popular culture. Theories of BAKHTIN, MIKHAIL MIKHAĬLOVICH; Eco, Umberto; Fo, Dario. 943.

Genres. Drama.
Relationship to polyphony. Application of theories of BAKHTIN, MIKHAIL MIKHAĬLOVICH. 2094.

Genres. Novel.
Monologism. Theories of BAKHTIN, MIKHAIL MIKHAĬLOVICH. 2210.
Relationship to the real; performance. Theories of BAKHTIN, MIKHAIL MIKHAĬLOVICH. 2215.
Spatial form compared to dialogism. Theories of Frank, Joseph compared to BAKHTIN, MIKHAIL MIKHAĬLOVICH. 2221.
Theories of Booth, Wayne Clayson: *The Rhetoric of Fiction* compared to BAKHTIN, MIKHAIL MIKHAĬLOVICH: *Problemy poétiki Dostoevskogo.* 2189.

Genres. Novel. Modernist novel.
Dialogue; relationship to Dostoevskiĭ, Fëdor Mikhaĭlovich: *Zapiski iz podpol'ia.* Application of theories of BAKHTIN, MIKHAIL MIKHAĬLOVICH. 2243.

Genres. Poetry.
Dialogism. Application of theories of BAKHTIN, MIKHAIL MIKHAĬLOVICH. 2290.

Literary forms. Rhetoric.
Paralogism; relationship to dialogism. Sources in sophistry. Theories of Davidson, Donald; Derrida, Jacques; BAKHTIN, MIKHAIL MIKHAĬLOVICH. 2462.
Relationship to otherness. Theories of BAKHTIN, MIKHAIL MIKHAĬLOVICH. 2470.

Literary movements.
Postmodernism. Role of the carnivalesque; kitsch; relationship to bicentennial of French Revolution in Paris (1989). Application of theories of BAKHTIN, MIKHAIL MIKHAĬLOVICH. 1057.

Literary theory and criticism.
And fiction. Theories of BAKHTIN, MIKHAIL MIKHAĬLOVICH. 1472.
Chronotope. Theories of BAKHTIN, MIKHAIL MIKHAĬLOVICH. 1569.
Dialogism; relationship to context; politics in novel. Theories of BAKHTIN, MIKHAIL MIKHAĬLOVICH. 1531.
Dialogue. Theories of BAKHTIN, MIKHAIL MIKHAĬLOVICH. 1437.
———; relationship to intersubjectivity. Theories of BAKHTIN, MIKHAIL MIKHAĬLOVICH compared to Piaget, Jean; Freud, Sigmund. 1384.
Menippean satire. Theories of BAKHTIN, MIKHAIL MIKHAĬLOVICH. 1331.
On dialogism. Theories of BAKHTIN, MIKHAIL MIKHAĬLOVICH. 1322.
On heteroglossia; relationship to society. Theories of BAKHTIN, MIKHAIL MIKHAĬLOVICH. 1429.
On novel; relationship to language. Theories of BAKHTIN, MIKHAIL MIKHAĬLOVICH. 1372.
———; relationship to language; society. Theories of BAKHTIN, MIKHAIL MIKHAĬLOVICH. 1319.
Otherness; relationship to identity in Europe. Theories of BAKHTIN, MIKHAIL MIKHAĬLOVICH. 1508.
Quasi-direct discourse; relationship to psychotherapy. Theories of BAKHTIN, MIKHAIL MIKHAĬLOVICH. 1397.
Relationship to film. Theories of BAKHTIN, MIKHAIL MIKHAĬLOVICH. Review article. 1385.
Role of BAKHTIN, MIKHAIL MIKHAĬLOVICH. 1485.
———; relationship to Russian Orthodox Church. 1393.
——— compared to de Man, Paul. 1520.
Role of laughter as aesthetic device; relationship to truth. Theories of BAKHTIN, MIKHAIL MIKHAĬLOVICH. 1499.
Role of politics; relationship to theories of BAKHTIN, MIKHAIL MIKHAĬLOVICH. Review article. 1392.
Role of the carnivalesque; relationship to Middle Ages. Theories of BAKHTIN, MIKHAIL MIKHAĬLOVICH. 1487.
Text; relationship to liturgy of Russian Orthodox Church. Relationship to theories of BAKHTIN, MIKHAIL MIKHAĬLOVICH; Florenskiĭ, Pavel Aleksandrovich: *Stolp i utverzhdenie istiny;* Kedrov, Konstantin Aleksandrovich: *Poéticheskiĭ kosmos.* 1558.
Theories of BAKHTIN, MIKHAIL MIKHAĬLOVICH. 1312, 1313, 1431, 1484, 1504.
———; relationship to Freud, Sigmund. 1507.
———; relationship to Prague School of Linguistics. 1404.
———: *Problemy poetiki Dostoevkogo* compared to Vinogradov, Viktor Vladimirovich: *O khudozhestvennoĭ proze.* 1345.
Theories of Mukařovský, Jan; Vodička, Felix; BAKHTIN, MIKHAIL MIKHAĬLOVICH. 1509.

Literary theory and criticism. Feminist literary theory and criticism.
Dialogism; relationship to difference; otherness. Application of theories of BAKHTIN, MIKHAIL MIKHAĬLOVICH. 1676.

Literary theory and criticism. Linguistic literary theory and criticism.
Chronotope; relationship to otherness. Theories of BAKHTIN, MIKHAIL MIKHAĬLOVICH compared to Welby, Victoria, Lady. 1753.
Theories of BAKHTIN, MIKHAIL MIKHAĬLOVICH. 1752.
——— compared to Lotman, Iuriĭ Mikhaĭlovich. 1755.

Literary theory and criticism. Poststructuralist literary theory and criticism.
Role of otherness; relationship to laughter. Theories of BAKHTIN, MIKHAIL MIKHAĬLOVICH compared to Derrida, Jacques. 1882.

SEE CLASSIFIED SEQUENCE FOR ADDITIONAL ENTRIES

Literary theory and criticism. Semiotic literary theory and criticism.
The carnivalesque; study example: Kafka, Franz: *Ein Hungerkünstler*. Application of theories of BAKHTIN, MIKHAIL MIKHAĬLOVICH. 1973.
Theories of BAKHTIN, MIKHAIL MIKHAĬLOVICH compared to Ingarden, Roman; Mukařovský, Jan. 1976
—— compared to Lotman, Iuriĭ Mikhaĭlovich. 2003.
Literary theory and criticism. Sociological literary theory and criticism.
Relationship to dialogism. Theories of BAKHTIN, MIKHAIL MIKHAĬLOVICH. 2021.
Literary theory and criticism. Structuralist literary theory and criticism.
On dialogue. Theories of BAKHTIN, MIKHAIL MIKHAĬLOVICH; Buber, Martin. 2032.
Professional topics. Humanities.
Relationship to literacy; science. Theories of Hirsch, Eric Donald; BAKHTIN, MIKHAIL MIKHAĬLOVICH. 2677.
Themes and figures. Transgression.
As the carnivalesque; relationship to social hierarchy. Application of theories of BAKHTIN, MIKHAIL MIKHAĬLOVICH; Elias, Norbert; Douglas, Mary. 2926.

BAKY, JOSEF VON (1902-1966)
General literature. Film.
Role of fantasy; relationship to masculinity in BAKY, JOSEF VON: *Münchhausen*. 539.
Treatment of aristocracy; relationship to Third Reich in BAKY, JOSEF VON: *Münchhausen*; Kästner, Erich: *Baron Münchhausen*. 291.

BAL, MIEKE (1946-)
Literary theory and criticism. Narrative theory.
Mise en abyme. Theories of Dällenbach, Lucien: *Le Récit spéculaire*; BAL, MIEKE. 1817.

BALBI, GIOVANNI (D. 1298)
Used for: Jean de Gênes.
Bibliographical. Printing in Germany. 1400-1499.
Of BALBI, GIOVANNI: *Catholicon*. 1168, 1177.

BALKAN STATES
See also narrower terms: Bulgaria; Romania; Yugoslavia.

BALTHASAR, HANS URS VON (1905-)
Literary theory and criticism. 1800-1899.
Faith. Theories of BALTHASAR, HANS URS VON. 1365.

BALTIC LITERATURE
See also narrower term: Latvian literature.

BALTIC STATES
See also narrower terms: Estonia; Latvia; Lithuania.

BAR MITZVAH
See also related term: Judaism.

BARBARY
See also related term: Morocco.

THE BAROQUE
Figures of speech. Metaphor.
Relationship to THE BAROQUE. 2373.

BAROQUE ART
See also related term: The Baroque.

BAROQUE DRAMA
See also related term: The Baroque.

BAROQUE LITERATURE
See also related term: The Baroque.

BAROQUE MUSIC
See also related term: The Baroque.

BAROQUE POETRY
See also related term: The Baroque.

BAROQUE THEATER
See also related term: The Baroque.

BARTHES, ROLAND (1915-1980)
General literature. Film in Italy (1945-1950).
Theories of BARTHES, ROLAND. 311.
Genres. Novel by women novelists. 1900-1999.
Treatment of exile in academia. Application of theories of BARTHES, ROLAND: *S/Z*. 2213.
Literary forms. Rhetoric.
And figures of speech. Theories of BARTHES, ROLAND; de Man, Paul. 2423.
Literary theory and criticism.
On BARTHES, ROLAND: *Ecrire la lecture*. 1552.
On reading; relationship to aesthetics. Theories of Jauss, Hans Robert: *Aesthetische Erfahrung und literarische Hermeneutik* compared to BARTHES, ROLAND: *Le Plaisir du texte*. 1361.
Relationship to text. Theories of BARTHES, ROLAND. 1560.
Role of text; relationship to cultural context. Theories of BARTHES, ROLAND. 1488.
Subjectivity in BARTHES, ROLAND; Foucault, Michel; Derrida, Jacques. Dissertation abstract. 1344.
Theories of BARTHES, ROLAND. 1375.
——: *Mythologies*. 1389.

Literary theory and criticism. Semiotic literary theory and criticism.
Theories of BARTHES, ROLAND; Mukařovský, Jan. 1979.
Literary theory and criticism. Structuralist literary theory and criticism.
Theories of BARTHES, ROLAND. 2029.
Themes and figures. Mourning.
Theories of Freud, Sigmund; BARTHES, ROLAND. 2895.

BASEBALL
General literature. Film (1929-1984).
Treatment of BASEBALL in United States. Dissertation abstract. 319.

BASEBALL PLAYERS
See also related term: Baseball.

BASKERVILLE, JOHN (1706-1775)
Bibliographical. Printing. 1700-1799.
Marbling by BASKERVILLE, JOHN. 1178.

BASQUES
General literature. Film. Film genres: documentary film.
Treatment of BASQUES in United States in Bordagaray, Stanley George, Jr.: *Amerikanuak: The Basques of the American West*. 816.

BASTARD
Themes and figures. Orphans and BASTARD.
In novel of New World. 2901.

BAT MITZVAH
See also related term: Judaism.

BATAILLE, GEORGES (1897-1962)
Used for: Angélique, Pierre; Auch, Lord.
Literary theory and criticism. Semiotic literary theory and criticism.
Theories of BATAILLE, GEORGES. 2005.

BATTLES
See also related term: War.

BAYER, HERBERT (1900-1985)
Bibliographical. Printing. Typography. 1900-1999.
Book design by BAYER, HERBERT. Dissertation abstract. 1222.

BAZIN, ANDRÉ (1918-1958)
General literature. Film. Film theory and criticism.
Spectator. Theories of BAZIN, ANDRÉ; Comolli, Jean-Louis. 819.
General literature. Film on wide-screen.
CinemaScope; relationship to ideology. Application of theories of BAZIN, ANDRÉ. 593.
Mise en scène. Application of theories of BAZIN, ANDRÉ. 265.

BBC
Use: British Broadcasting Corporation.

BEAST EPIC
See also related terms: Fable; Satire.

BEAT GENERATION
General literature. Film.
Treatment of BEAT GENERATION. 639.
General literature. Film. 1900-1999.
Treatment of BEAT GENERATION in Forman, Janet: *The Beat Generation: An American Dream*. 430.

BEATLES
See also related term: McCartney, Paul (1942-).

BEAUMONT, HARRY (1888-1966)
General literature. Film (1930-1939).
Treatment of working women in BEAUMONT, HARRY: *Our Blushing Brides* compared to Bacon, Lloyd: *Marked Woman*. 384.

BEAUTIFUL WOMAN
General literature. Film. Film genres: horror film.
Treatment of archetypes of monsters carrying BEAUTIFUL WOMAN. 752.

BECOMING
See also related term: Existence.

BEGRIFFSGESCHICHTE
See also related terms: History of ideas; Philology.

BEHAVIOR PATTERNS
See also related term: Social behavior.

BEHAVIORAL SCIENCE
See also related term: Social sciences.

BEING
See also related term: Existence.

BELGIUM
See also narrower term: Brabant.

BELIEFS
See also related term: Faith.

BELL, DANIEL (1919-)
Literary movements.
Postmodernism. Relationship to religion; politics. Application of theories of BELL, DANIEL; Jameson, Fredric. 1055.

BELLES-LETTRES
   Genres. Prose.
      Relationship to *BELLES-LETTRES*. 2316.

BELLOCCHIO, MARCO (1939-)
   General literature. Film. Film adaptation.
      Of Pirandello, Luigi: *Enrico IV* by BELLOCCHIO, MARCO. 710.

BELORUSSIAN LITERATURE
   General literature. Film.
      Relationship to BELORUSSIAN LITERATURE. 588.

BEMPORAD, ENRICO (1868-1944)
   Bibliographical. Publishing in Florence (1890-1920).
      By BEMPORAD, ENRICO; relationship to Gabinetto Vieusseux; *Nuova Antologia*. 1252.

BENJAMIN, WALTER (1892-1940)
Used for: Holz, Detlev.
   General literature. Film. Film genres: silent film in United States and Russian S. F.S.R.
      Melodrama; relationship to temporality. Theories of BENJAMIN, WALTER. 757.
   Literary forms. Translation. Translation theory.
      Theories of Quine, W. V. O.; Derrida, Jacques; BENJAMIN, WALTER. 2574. Theories of Schleiermacher, Friedrich Daniel Ernst; BENJAMIN, WALTER. 2571.
   Literary theory and criticism.
      Theories of BENJAMIN, WALTER; Larsen, Peter. 1549.
   Professional topics. Humanities.
      Relationship to tradition. Application of theories of BENJAMIN, WALTER; Williams, Raymond. 2654.

BENSE, MAX (1910-)
   Literary forms. Rhetoric.
      Relationship to ideology. Treatment in Peirce, Charles Sanders; BENSE, MAX. 2435.
   Literary theory and criticism. Semiotic literary theory and criticism.
      Relationship to cybernetics; information theory. Theories of Saussure, Ferdinand de; Peirce, Charles Sanders; BENSE, MAX. 1971. Theories of BENSE, MAX. 1957.

BENSON, LAURA
   General literature. Film.
      On Resnais, Alain: *I Want to Go Home*. Interview with BENSON, LAURA; Leterrier, Catherine; van Damme, Charlie; Laureux, Jean-Claude. 609.

BÉR, KARL MAKSIMOVICH
Use: Baer, Karl Ernst von (1792-1876).

BEREAVEMENT
See also related term: Mourning.

BERGFILM
Use: Mountain film.

BERTOLUCCI, BERNARDO (1940-)
   General literature. Film.
      Role of Italian identity in BERTOLUCCI, BERNARDO: *The Last Emperor*. 481.

BESTIALITY
See also related term: Sexuality.

BESTSELLERS
See also related terms: Book trade; Popular culture.

BETRAYAL
   General literature. Film.
      Treatment of BETRAYAL in Allen, Woody: *Crimes and Misdemeanors* compared to Matt, Peter von: *Liebesverrat: Die Treulosen in der Literatur*. 528.

BETTELHEIM, BRUNO (1903-1990)
   General literature for children.
      Sources in *Märchen*. Theories of BETTELHEIM, BRUNO: *The Uses of Enchantment*. 195.

BHATT, MAHESH
   General literature. Film.
      On BHATT, MAHESH: *Arth*. 619.

BIBLE
See also narrower terms: Gutenberg Bible; Old Testament.
   Literary forms. Translation.
      Of BIBLE; relationship to language change. 2561.
      Literary forms. Translation of BIBLE during Renaissance. 2516.
   Literary theory and criticism.
      Treatment of BIBLE. Theories of Hügel, Friedrich, Freiherr von. 1523.
   Literary theory and criticism. Reader-response theory and criticism.
      Applied to BIBLE. 1924, 1935.

BIBLE—STUDY EXAMPLE
   Literary forms. Translation.
      Relationship to universals of language; study example: BIBLE. 2544.

BIBLICAL ALLEGORY
See also related term: Bible.

BIBLICAL ALLUSION
See also related term: Bible.

BIBLICAL EXEGESIS
See also related term: Bible.

BIBLICAL IMAGERY
See also related term: Bible.

BIBLICAL POETRY
See also related term: Bible.

BIBLICAL SCHOLARSHIP
See also related term: Bible.

BIBLICAL SYMBOLISM
See also related term: Bible.

BIBLICAL TYPOLOGY
See also related term: Bible.

BIBLICISM
See also related term: Bible.

BIBLIOGRAPHER
See also related term: Bibliography.
   Bibliographical. 1900-1999.
      Role of Nowell-Smith, Simon Harcourt; Trevanion, Michael as BIBLIOGRAPHER; relationship to book collecting. 1094.

BIBLIOGRAPHICAL
See also classified section: 1083 ff.
See also narrower terms: Analytical bibliography; Manuscripts; Printing; Publishing; Textual criticism.

BIBLIOGRAPHICAL APPROACH
See also related term: Bibliographical.
Documents applying specific approaches are so numerous that access to them is provided only in the electronic versions of the *Bibliography*.

BIBLIOGRAPHICAL FEATURES
See also narrower terms: Binding; Editions; Fragment; Illustration; Paper; Watermarks.
See also related term: Analytical bibliography.

BIBLIOGRAPHICAL HISTORY
See also related term: Bibliography.

BIBLIOGRAPHICAL SERVICES
See also related term: Bibliographical.

BIBLIOGRAPHY
See also narrower term: Analytical bibliography.
See also related term: Bibliographer.
   Bibliographical. Printing in Canada.
      And BIBLIOGRAPHY. Role of Tremaine, Marie. Reminiscence. 1189.

BIBLIOPHILE
See also related term: Book collecting.

BIBLIOTECA VALLICELLIANA
   Bibliographical. Manuscripts.
      In uncial in BIBLIOTECA VALLICELLIANA. 1126.
   Bibliographical. Manuscripts. Manuscript collections.
      Of Statius in BIBLIOTECA VALLICELLIANA. 1143.

BIBLIOTHÈQUE ROYALE ALBERT Iᵉʳ
   Bibliographical. 1400-1599.
      Book collecting in Netherlands by Arenberg family; relationship to BIBLIOTHÈQUE ROYALE ALBERT Iᵉʳ. 1089.

BIBLIOTHERAPY
   General literature for children; young adults.
      Role of BIBLIOTHERAPY. 208.

BIDEN, EDMUND PRESTON
Use: Sturges, Preston (1898-1959).

BIESTKENS, NICOLAES, THE ELDER (D. 1585)
   Bibliographical. Printing (1559-1583).
      By BIESTKENS, NICOLAES, THE ELDER; relationship to Gailliart, Willem. 1156.

BILDUNG
See also related term: Bildungsroman.

BILDUNGSROMAN
See also classified section: 2238.
Used for: Apprenticeship novel; *Erziehungsroman*.

BILLINGTON, JAMES H. (1929-)
   Bibliographical.
      Libraries. Interview with BILLINGTON, JAMES H. 1100.

BINARY OPPOSITION
   Literary theory and criticism. Linguistic literary theory and criticism.
      Role of BINARY OPPOSITION. 1751.

BINDING
See also classified section: 1198 ff.
Used for: Bookbinding.
See also related term: Printing.

BIOGRAPHICAL APPROACH
Documents applying specific approaches are so numerous that access to them is provided only in the electronic versions of the *Bibliography*.

BIOGRAPHICAL DICTIONARY
See also related term: Biography.

BIOGRAPHICAL FICTION
See also related term: Biography.

BIOGRAPHICAL POETRY
See also related term: Biography.

BIOGRAPHY
See also classified section: 2056 ff.
See also narrower term: Hagiography.
See also related term: Autobiography.
   Genres. Autobiography and BIOGRAPHY.
      Treatment of madness; relationship to psychiatry. 2054.

BIOLOGICAL IMAGERY
See also related term: Biology.

BIOLOGY
   General literature. Theater.
      Role of BIOLOGY; human body; relationship to performance. 957.
   Literary theory and criticism. Narrative theory.
      Applied to BIOLOGY. Treatment in Watson, James D.: *The Double Helix*. 1811.

BIOTECHNOLOGY
See also related term: Biology.

BIRD RETRIEVAL SYSTEM
   Professional topics. Computer-assisted research.
      BIRD RETRIEVAL SYSTEM; QUILL retrieval system. 2650.

BLACK, MAX (1909-1988)
   Figures of speech. Metaphor.
      Psychological approach. Theories of BLACK, MAX. 2372.

BLACK AFRICA
See also related term: Africa.
   General literature. Film in BLACK AFRICA. 370, 373.
      Aesthetics. 372.
      Production; relationship to neocolonialism. 369.
      Relationship to urban areas. 368.
      Role of film industry. 364.
   General literature. Film in urban areas of BLACK AFRICA. 362.

BLACK AFRICAN CULTURE
See also related term: Black Africa.

BLACK AFRICANS
See also classified section: 2837.
   General literature. Film by BLACK AFRICANS.
      Relationship to oral tradition. Dissertation abstract. 618.

BLACK DRAMATISTS
   Genres. Drama by BLACK DRAMATISTS.
      And theater. Bibliography. 2098.

BLACK HUMOR
See also related term: Satire.

BLACK LIFE
See also related term: African Americans.

BLACK-WHITE RELATIONS
See also related term: Racism.

BLACK WOMEN
See also narrower term: African American women.
   General literature. Television.
      Role of BLACK WOMEN. 875.

BLACKS
See also narrower terms: African Americans; Black women.

BLAEU, JOAN (1596-1673)
Used for: Blaeu, Johannes Willenszoon.
   Bibliographical. Printing in Amsterdam. 1600-1699.
      By BLAEU, JOAN. 1163.

BLAEU, JOHANNES WILLENSZOON
Use: Blaeu, Joan (1596-1673).

BLANCHOT, MAURICE (1907-)
   Literary theory and criticism. Philosophical literary theory and criticism.
      Theories of Heidegger, Martin; BLANCHOT, MAURICE; Levinas, Emmanuel. Dissertation abstract. 1851.
   Literary theory and criticism. Psychoanalytic literary theory and criticism.
      Relationship to Oedipus; Orpheus. Theories of Freud, Sigmund; BLANCHOT, MAURICE. 1901.

BLESSING
   Genres. Prose. Devotional literature.
      Treatment of BLESSING of widow. Sources in Hippolytus: *Traditio Apostolica*. 2321.

BLOCH, ERNST (1885-1977)
   Literary theory and criticism. Hermeneutics.
      Relationship to the future; circularity. Theories of Heidegger, Martin; BLOCH, ERNST; Hegel, Georg Wilhelm Friedrich. 1727.
   Themes and figures. Utopianism.
      Relationship to literary studies. Semiotic approach. Theories of BLOCH, ERNST. 2931.

BLOOM, ALLAN DAVID (1930-)
   Professional topics. Humanities.
      Cultural knowledge. Theories of Hirsch, Eric Donald: *Cultural Literacy*; BLOOM, ALLAN DAVID: *The Closing of the American Mind*. 2805.
      ——; intellectualism; relationship to theories of BLOOM, ALLAN DAVID: *The Closing of the American Mind*. 2774.
      On cultural knowledge. Theories of BLOOM, ALLAN DAVID; Hirsch, Eric Donald. 2824.
   Professional topics. Humanities in United States.
      Relationship to culture. Theories of BLOOM, ALLAN DAVID: *The Closing of the American Mind*. 2773.
      Relationship to nihilism. Theories of BLOOM, ALLAN DAVID: *The Closing of the American Mind*. 2759.
      Theories of BLOOM, ALLAN DAVID: *The Closing of the American Mind*. 2791.
      ——: *The Closing of the American Mind*; relationship to the past; democracy; reality. 2661.

BLOT, JEAN-YVES
   General literature.
      Sign. Theories of BLOT, JEAN-YVES: *La Méduse, chronique d'un naufrage ordinaire*. 111.

BODLEY HEAD
   Bibliographical. Publishing in England (1889-1900).
      By BODLEY HEAD. 1267.

BODY
Use: Human body.

BODY MOVEMENT
See also related terms: Human body; Nonverbal communication.

BODY POSTURE
See also related term: Human body.

BOGAJEWICZ, JUREK
   General literature. Film.
      On BOGAJEWICZ, JUREK: *Anna*. 324.

BOGOMILS
See also related term: Gnosticism.

BOND, JAMES (CHARACTER)
   General literature. Film. Film genres: spy film.
      Role of BOND, JAMES (CHARACTER) compared to film by Hitchcock, Alfred. 776.

BONDAGE
See also related term: Slavery.

BOOK
See also narrower terms: Incunabula; Picture books; Rare books; Textbook.
See also related terms: Book auction; Book collecting; Book design; Book trade.
   Bibliographical. Latin language literature. 700-799.
      Donation of BOOK to Chiesa di San Clemente. Treatment in epigraph. 1111.
   Literary forms. Emblem.
      Treatment of BOOK; printing; book collectors. 2392.
   Literary theory and criticism. Hermeneutics and linguistic literary theory and criticism. Middle Ages.
      Applied to BOOK; relationship to myth; study example: Chaucer, Geoffrey; Dante. 1719.

BOOK AUCTION
See also related term: Book.
   Bibliographical. Publishing. Book trade in Stockholm (1782-1801).
      BOOK AUCTION. Dissertation abstract. 1284.

BOOK BURNING
See also related term: Book.

BOOK COLLECTING
See also related terms: Book; Book collectors.
   Bibliographical. 1400-1599.
      BOOK COLLECTING in Netherlands by Arenberg family; relationship to Bibliothèque Royale Albert Ier. 1089.
   Bibliographical. 1700-1799.
      BOOK COLLECTING by Hellier, Samuel. 1114.
      —— by Rawlinson, Richard. 1092.
   Bibliographical. 1900-1999.
      Role of Nowell-Smith, Simon Harcourt; Trevanion, Michael as bibliographer; relationship to BOOK COLLECTING. 1094.

BOOK COLLECTION
See also related terms: Book collecting; Book collectors.

BOOK COLLECTORS
See also related term: Book collecting.
   Bibliographical.
      Handbook for BOOK COLLECTORS. 1101.

Literary forms. Emblem.
Treatment of book; printing; BOOK COLLECTORS. 2392.

BOOK DESIGN
See also related term: Book.
Bibliographical. Printing.
BOOK DESIGN by Whitman, Sarah Wyman. 1172.
Bibliographical. Printing. Typography. 1900-1999.
BOOK DESIGN by Bayer, Herbert. Dissertation abstract. 1222.

BOOK DISTRIBUTION
Bibliographical. Publishing in France.
BOOK DISTRIBUTION; libraries; relationship to social class. 1259.

BOOK FAIR
Bibliographical. Publishing. Book trade.
BOOK FAIR. Theories of Weidhaas, Peter. 1299.

BOOK INDUSTRY
Use: Book trade.

BOOK MARKET
See also related terms: Book; Book trade; Publishing.

BOOK OF THE MONTH CLUB
Bibliographical. Publishing. Book trade.
Role of BOOK OF THE MONTH CLUB. 1295.

BOOK PLATES
See also related term: Book collecting.

BOOK PRESERVATION
Bibliographical.
Role of curator-conservator relations; relationship to BOOK PRESERVATION; rare books. 1104.
Role of deacidification; relationship to BOOK PRESERVATION. 1088.

BOOK PRODUCTION
See also related terms: Book; Printing.

BOOK REVIEW
See also related term: Book.

BOOK TRADE
See also classified section: 1283 ff.
Used for: Book industry.
See also narrower term: Rare book trade.
See also related terms: Book; Publishing.

BOOKBINDERS
See also related term: Binding.

BOOKBINDING
Use: Binding.

BOOKSELLERS
See also related term: Publishing.

BOORMAN, JOHN (1933-)
General literature. Film.
Treatment of women in BOORMAN, JOHN: Excalibur compared to Malory, Sir Thomas: Le Morte Darthur. 469.
General literature. Film. 1900-1999.
Treatment of Arthur (character) in BOORMAN, JOHN: Excalibur; Rohmer, Eric: Perceval le Gallois; Romero, George A.: Knightriders. 438.

BOOTH, WAYNE CLAYSON (1921-)
Genres. Novel.
Theories of BOOTH, WAYNE CLAYSON: The Rhetoric of Fiction compared to Bakhtin, Mikhail Mikhaĭlovich: Problemy poétiki Dostoevskogo. 2189.
Literary theory and criticism.
Theories of BOOTH, WAYNE CLAYSON: The Rhetoric of Fiction. 1530.

BORDAGARAY, STANLEY GEORGE, JR.
General literature. Film. Film genres: documentary film.
Treatment of Basques in United States in BORDAGARAY, STANLEY GEORGE, JR.: Amerikanuak: The Basques of the American West. 816.

BORDER
See also related term: Boundary.

BOUCOURECHLIEV, ANDRÉ (1925-)
General literature.
Role of text in musical composition. Interview with BOUCOURECHLIEV, ANDRÉ. 68.

BOUISSAC, PAUL (1934-)
Literary theory and criticism. Semiotic literary theory and criticism.
Treatment of nonsense in Italian language translation of BOUISSAC, PAUL: Cirque et culture. 1964.

BOUNDARY
General literature.
Treatment of space; BOUNDARY. 17.

BOUNDARY 2
Literary theory and criticism in BOUNDARY 2.
Relationship to Postmodernism. Interview with Spanos, William V. 1332.

BOUNDARY CROSSING
Use: Transgression.

BOURDIEU, PIERRE (1930-)
General literature. Television.
Role of cultural dominance; relationship to commercialism; popular culture. Application of theories of BOURDIEU, PIERRE. 867.
Literary theory and criticism.
Theories of BOURDIEU, PIERRE: La Distinction: Critique sociale du jugement. Review article. 1566.
Professional topics. Humanities.
Pedagogy. Theories of Freire, Paulo; BOURDIEU, PIERRE; Merod, Jim; Graff, Gerald. 2686.

THE BOURGEOIS
See also related terms: Bourgeois society; Bourgeoisie.

BOURGEOIS SOCIETY
Literary theory and criticism.
Aesthetics; relationship to BOURGEOIS SOCIETY; politics; hegemony. 1386.

BOURGEOISIE
Literary movements.
Enlightenment. Role of psychology; relationship to BOURGEOISIE; rhetoric. 999.

BOWLES, SALLY (CHARACTER)
General literature. Film and theater.
Treatment of BOWLES, SALLY (CHARACTER); relationship to spectator. Feminist approach. Dissertation abstract. 501.

BOYLE, ROBERT (1627-1691)
Genres. Novel.
Relationship to knowledge; epistemology. Theories of BOYLE, ROBERT: The Christian Virtuoso; Occasional Reflections on Several Subjects. 2199.

BRABANT
Bibliographical. Printing. Binding in BRABANT. 1400-1599. 1209.

BRAUN, MARIA (CHARACTER)
General literature. Film.
Treatment of BRAUN, MARIA (CHARACTER) in Fassbinder, Rainer Werner: Die Ehe der Maria Braun; relationship to Faust in Goethe, Johann Wolfgang von: Faust. 613.

BRAZIL
General literature. Television: soap opera in BRAZIL. 846.
General literature. Television and radio in BRAZIL. 864.
Professional topics. Humanities.
Role of feminism; relationship to women's studies in BRAZIL. 2729.

BRD
Use: West Germany.

BRECHT, BERTOLT (1898-1956)
General literature. Film.
Collaboration between BRECHT, BERTOLT and Eisler, Hanns. Dissertation abstract. 305.

BREIGUTU, BJØRN
General literature. Film.
By BREIGUTU, BJØRN. 403.

BRESSON, ROBERT (1907-)
General literature. Film.
By BRESSON, ROBERT. 571.

BRETT, EDWIN JOHN (1828-1895)
Bibliographical. Publishing in England (1850-1900).
By BRETT, EDWIN JOHN of pulp fiction; penny dreadful. 1266.

BRIDE
See also related term: Marriage.

BRIEFMALER
Bibliographical. Printing. Typography. 1500-1699.
Role of Kress, Georg as BRIEFMALER. 1229.

BRITAIN
Use: Great Britain.

BRITISH BROADCASTING CORPORATION
Used for: BBC.
See also related terms: Radio; Television.
General literature. Television.
Scene design in television adaptation of Shakespeare, William by BRITISH BROADCASTING CORPORATION (1978-1985). Dissertation abstract. 917.

BRITISH COLUMBIA
Bibliographical. Publishing in Canada: BRITISH COLUMBIA. 1237.

BRITISH FILM INSTITUTE
General literature. Film in Great Britain.
Role of BRITISH FILM INSTITUTE. 284, 464.

BRITISH LIBRARY
Bibliographical. Manuscripts. Illuminated manuscripts. 1400-1499.
BRITISH LIBRARY: MS Additional 54782. 1142.
Bibliographical. Manuscripts. Manuscript collections.
In BRITISH LIBRARY. Review article. 1149.

SEE CLASSIFIED SEQUENCE FOR ADDITIONAL ENTRIES

CANADA

Bibliographical. Printing in CANADA and United States. 1800-1899.

BROOK, PETER (1925-)
  General literature. Theater.
    Role of BROOK, PETER; Suzuki Tadashi. 939.

BROOKS, CLEANTH (1906-)
  Literary theory and criticism. New Criticism.
    Theories of BROOKS, CLEANTH. Bibliography (1933-1989). 1831.

BROTHEL
  See also related term: Prostitute.

BROWN, STEVENS (CHARACTER)
  General literature. Film. Film adaptation.
    Treatment of BROWN, STEVENS (CHARACTER) in film adaptation of Hébert, Anne: *Les Fous de Bassan* by Simoneau, Yves. 734.

BRÜCKNER, JUTTA
  General literature. Film.
    Treatment of the self; female identity in Sanders-Brahms, Helma: *Deutschland, bleiche Mutter*; BRÜCKNER, JUTTA: *Hungerjahre* compared to Wolf, Christa: *Kindheitsmuster*; Rehmann, Ruth: *Der Mann auf der Kanzel.* Dissertation abstract. 431.

BRUFFEE, KENNETH A. (1934-)
  Literary forms. Rhetoric.
    Social construction; relationship to teaching of writing. Theories of BRUFFEE, KENNETH A. 2452.

BUBER, MARTIN (1878-1965)
  Literary theory and criticism. Structuralist literary theory and criticism.
    On dialogue. Theories of Bakhtin, Mikhail Mikhaĭlovich; BUBER, MARTIN. 2032.

BUCK, GERTRUDE (1871-1922)
  Literary forms. Rhetoric.
    Treatment in BUCK, GERTRUDE: *The Metaphor.* Dissertation abstract. 2498.

BUCKNER, NOEL
  General literature. Film. Film genres: documentary film.
    Treatment of Abraham Lincoln Battalion in BUCKNER, NOEL and Dore, Mary and Paskin, David and Sills, Sam: *The Good Fight.* 748.

BÜHLER, KARL (1879-1963)
  Literary theory and criticism. Semiotic literary theory and criticism.
    Iconicity; metaphor. Theories of BÜHLER, KARL. 1990.

BULGARIA
  General literature. Film in BULGARIA. 599.

BUNDESREPUBLIK DEUTSCHLAND
  Use: West Germany.

BUÑUEL, LUIS (1900-1983)
  General literature. Film.
    By BUÑUEL, LUIS. Sources in Pérez Galdós, Benito. 341.
    Treatment of female characters; relationship to feminism in BUÑUEL, LUIS. 393.
  General literature. Film. Film adaptation.
    Treatment of objects as sign in film adaptation by BUÑUEL, LUIS. Dissertation abstract. 719.
  General literature. Film. Film genres: avant-garde film.
    Role of BUÑUEL, LUIS. Dissertation abstract. 799.
    Treatment of objects in BUÑUEL, LUIS. 798.

BURIAL
  See also related term: Death.

BURIAL RITES
  See also related term: Death.

BURIAL SITES
  See also related term: Death.

BURKE, KENNETH (1897-)
  Literary forms. Rhetoric.
    Relationship to dialectic; collaboration. Theories of BURKE, KENNETH compared to Rogers, Carl Ransom. 2461.
    Relationship to public discourse on nuclear weapons. Application of theories of BURKE, KENNETH. 2429.
    Stasis. Relationship to theories of Perelman, Chaim; BURKE, KENNETH. 2451.
    Treatment in BURKE, KENNETH. 2436.
  Literary theory and criticism.
    Theories of BURKE, KENNETH; Trilling, Lionel. Review article. 1329.

BURLESQUE
  See also related terms: Satire; Vaudeville.
  General literature. Theater: popular theater.
    Role of BURLESQUE; relationship to sexuality; female body. 926.

BURNS, AMY STECHLER
  General literature. Film. Film genres: documentary film.
    Treatment of Shakers in Burns, Ken and BURNS, AMY STECHLER. 811.

BURNS, KEN
  General literature. Film. Film genres: documentary film.
    Treatment of Shakers in BURNS, KEN and Burns, Amy Stechler. 811.

BURNS AND ALLEN
  Use: The George Burns and Gracie Allen Show.

BURTON, TIM
  General literature. Film.
    Treatment of racism in Lee, Spike: *Do the Right Thing* compared to BURTON, TIM: *Batman*; *Batman: The Dark Knight* by Miller, Frank. 550.

BURY STYLE
  Bibliographical. Manuscripts. Illuminated manuscripts. 1400-1499.
    BURY STYLE in Fitzwilliam Museum: MS 3-1979. 1141.

BUSH, DOUGLAS (1896-1983)
  Used for: Bush, John Nash Douglas.

BUSH, DOUGLAS (1896-1983)—STUDY EXAMPLE
  Literary theory and criticism. Literary history.
    Study example: BUSH, DOUGLAS: *English Literature in the Earlier Seventeenth Century.* 1763.

BUSH, JOHN NASH DOUGLAS
  Use: Bush, Douglas (1896-1983).

BUSINESS
  Used for: Commerce.
  See also narrower term: Marketing.
  See also related term: Commercialism.
  Bibliographical. Publishing.
    On English language translation as BUSINESS. 1247.

BUSINESS MEETING
  See also related term: Business.

BUSINESS NAMES
  See also related term: Business.

BUSINESS RELATIONS
  See also related term: Business.

CABRERA INFANTE, GUILLERMO (1929-)
  Used for: Cain, Guillermo.
  General literature. Film.
    And film theory and criticism; role of CABRERA INFANTE, GUILLERMO. 379.

CAGNEY, JAMES (1899-1986)
  General literature. Film. Film by independent filmmakers.
    Relationship to film studios; role of CAGNEY, JAMES (1941-1948). Film history. 374.

CAIN, GUILLERMO
  Use: Cabrera Infante, Guillermo (1929-).

CALIFORNIA
  See also narrower term: Hollywood.

CALL
  Use: Computer-assisted language learning.

CALLIGRAPHY
  See also related term: Writing systems.

CAMELOT
  See also related term: Arthurian legend.

CAMERA
  See also related term: Photography.
  General literature. Film.
    Use of CAMERA in Gehr, Ernie: *Morning*; *Serene Velocity*; *Eureka.* 470.

CAMERON, JAMES
  General literature. Film.
    Narrative technique in CAMERON, JAMES: *The Terminator.* Application of theories of Genette, Gérard. 479.
  General literature. Film. Film genres: horror film.
    On CAMERON, JAMES: *Aliens.* Feminist approach. 764.
  General literature. Film. Film genres: science fiction film.
    Treatment of time travel; primal scene; dystopia in CAMERON, JAMES: *The Terminator.* 792.

CAMOUFLAGE
  General literature. Theater.
    Scenography; relationship to CAMOUFLAGE; war. Dissertation abstract. 951.

CAMUS, MARIO
  General literature. Film. Film adaptation.
    Of Cela Trulock, Camilo José: *La familia de Pascual Duarte* by Franco, Ricardo compared to adaptation of Delibes, Miguel: *Los santos inocentes* by CAMUS, MARIO. Dissertation abstract. 729.
    Of Delibes, Miguel: *Los santos inocentes* by CAMUS, MARIO. 739.
    ——: *Los santos inocentes* by CAMUS, MARIO. Reception study: reception in France. 684.

CANADA
  See also narrower terms: British Columbia; Montreal; Quebec.
  Bibliographical. Printing. History of printing in CANADA. 1700-1899. 1197.
  Bibliographical. Printing. History of printing in CANADA (1751-1800). 1196.
  Bibliographical. Printing in CANADA.
    And bibliography. Role of Tremaine, Marie. Reminiscence. 1189.
  Bibliographical. Printing in CANADA. 1700-1899. 1173.
  Bibliographical. Printing in CANADA and United States. 1800-1899.
    Role of Mackenzie, William Lyon. 1186.

Bibliographical. Printing in CANADA and United States. 1800-1899.

Role of Mackenzie, William Lyon; relationship to politics. 1174.
Bibliographical. Publishing and printing in CANADA.
Bibliography. 1275.
Bibliographical. Publishing in CANADA (1905-1921).
Role of Macmillan Company of Canada. 1271.
General literature. Film. Film theory and criticism in CANADA.
Female spectator. 820.
General literature. Film in CANADA. 645.
General literature. Television in CANADA. 847.
Literary theory and criticism in CANADA.
Review article. 1539.
Role of theme; relationship to ethnic literature. 1473.

CANADIAN EXPERIENCE
See also related term: Canada.

CANADIAN OPERA COMPANY
See also related term: Opera.

CANADIAN UNIVERSITIES
Professional topics. Humanities.
Role of English studies at CANADIAN UNIVERSITIES. Application of theories of Arnold, Matthew: *Culture and Anarchy.* 2732.

CANCER
General literature by patient with CANCER.
Relationship to art therapy. Treatment of mourning; creativity. Psychoanalytic approach. Dissertation abstract. 62.

CANNIBALISM
See also classified section: 2838.
Used for: Anthropophagy.

CANON
Bibliographical.
Role of library collection; relationship to CANON. Collection study of collection at Harry Ransom Humanities Research Center at University of Texas at Austin. 1112.
Literary forms. Emblem.
Relationship to genre; CANON. 2385.
Literary forms. Translation.
Role in CANON of target literature; relationship to secondary education in Germany. 2549.
Literary theory and criticism.
Interpretive communities; relationship to CANON. Treatment in Fish, Stanley: *Is There a Text in This Class?* 1496.
Relationship to CANON. 1521.
——. Interview with Kermode, Frank. 1445.
Role of CANON. Empirical approach. 1381.
Literary theory and criticism. Literary history.
Relationship to CANON. 1762.
Literary theory and criticism. Poststructuralist literary theory and criticism.
Relationship to CANON. 1875.
Professional topics. Humanities.
CANON. 2674, 2682, 2702, 2710, 2718, 2722, 2748, 2751, 2788, 2790.
——; pedagogy in United States; relationship to liberalism compared to conservatism. 2782.
——; relationship to culture; art. 2817.
——; relationship to feminist literary theory and criticism. 2793.
Relationship to CANON. 2715, 2755.
Role of CANON. 2784.
Role of dualism; holism; relationship to CANON in literary studies. Theories of Descartes, René. 2679.
Role of irony; relationship to CANON in teaching of literature. 2672.
Role of women writers; relationship to reader; CANON. Feminist approach. 2736.
Teaching of literature; relationship to CANON. 2717.

CANTILLATION
See also related term: Liturgy.

CANTO
See also related term: Prosody.

CANUDO, RICCIOTTO (1879-1923)
General literature. Film. Film theory and criticism.
Theories of CANUDO, RICCIOTTO. 821.

CANUTE I, KING OF ENGLAND (995?-1035)
Used for: Cnut; Knut.
Bibliographical. Manuscripts. Illuminated manuscripts in England. 900-1099.
Patronage by CANUTE I, KING OF ENGLAND; Emma, Queen of England. 1139.

CAPRA, FRANK (1897-)
General literature. Film.
By Ford, John; CAPRA, FRANK; Coppola, Francis Ford; Scorsese, Martin. 456.

CARIBBEAN
See also narrower term: Cuba.

CARICATURE
See also related terms: Burlesque; Satire.

CARLOVINGIAN PERIOD
Use: Carolingian period.

CARNALITY
See also related term: Sexuality.

THE CARNIVALESQUE
Literary movements.
Postmodernism. Role of THE CARNIVALESQUE; kitsch; relationship to bicentennial of French Revolution in Paris (1989). Application of theories of Bakhtin, Mikhail Mikhaïlovich. 1057.
Literary theory and criticism.
Role of THE CARNIVALESQUE; relationship to Middle Ages. Theories of Bakhtin, Mikhail Mikhaïlovich. 1487.
Literary theory and criticism. Semiotic literary theory and criticism.
THE CARNIVALESQUE; study example: Kafka, Franz: *Ein Hungerkünstler.* Application of theories of Bakhtin, Mikhail Mikhaïlovich. 1973.
Themes and figures. Transgression.
As THE CARNIVALESQUE; relationship to social hierarchy. Application of theories of Bakhtin, Mikhail Mikhaïlovich; Elias, Norbert; Douglas, Mary. 2926.

CAROLINE MINUSCULE
Bibliographical. Manuscripts.
Use of CAROLINE MINUSCULE. Role of scribe. 1128.

CAROLINGIAN PERIOD
Used for: Carlovingian period.
Bibliographical. Manuscripts. CAROLINGIAN PERIOD. 1130.

CARPENTIER, ALEJO (1904-1980)
Used for: Jacqueline.
General literature. Film.
Edition of film review (1951-1959) by CARPENTIER, ALEJO. 540.

CARRADINE, DAVID (1936-)
General literature. Film.
Treatment of Vietnam War in CARRADINE, DAVID: *Americana.* 246.

CARRION, LOUIS (1547-1595)
Bibliographical. Manuscripts. Manuscript editing.
Manuscript collation of Valerius Flaccus, Gaius: *Argonautica* by CARRION, LOUIS. 1151.

CARROLL, NOEL E. (1947-)
General literature. Film. Film theory and criticism.
Relationship to phenomenology. Theories of CARROLL, NOEL E. 839.

CARTOONS
See also related term: Animated film.
General literature. Film. Film adaptation.
Treatment of Scrooge, Ebenezer (character) in Dickens, Charles: *A Christmas Carol* compared to television adaptation; theatrical production; CARTOONS. 686.

CASANOVA
See also related term: Don Juan.

CASTE SYSTEM
See also related term: Social class.

CASTING
See also related term: Theatrical production.

CASTS
See also related term: Theatrical production.

CASUISTRY
See also related term: Ethics.

CATACHRESIS
Figures of speech. Metaphor and CATACHRESIS.
Theories of Quintilianus. 2366.

CATAPHORA
See also related term: Reference.

CATASTROPHE
General literature. Theater.
On CATASTROPHE as theater. 981.

CATECHISM
General literature for children.
Didacticism; relationship to CATECHISM. 54.

CATES, GILBERT (1934-)
General literature. Film.
Treatment of homosexuality in Ray, Nicholas: *Rebel without a Cause* compared to CATES, GILBERT: *Consenting Adult.* 283.

CATHEDRAL
See also related term: Church.

CAVANI, LILIANA (1936-)
General literature. Film.
By CAVANI, LILIANA: *Francesco.* Interview. 482.
Narrative; relationship to history in CAVANI, LILIANA: *Interno berlinese.* 483.
Treatment of feminism in CAVANI, LILIANA: *Il portiere di notte.* 600.

CAVELL, STANLEY LOUIS (1926-)
Literary movements.
Postmodernism. Relationship to philosophy. Theories of Rorty, Richard; Derrida, Jacques; CAVELL, STANLEY LOUIS. 1041.

SEE CLASSIFIED SEQUENCE FOR ADDITIONAL ENTRIES

Literary theory and criticism.
Skepticism; relationship to ethics. Theories of CAVELL, STANLEY LOUIS: *The Claim of Reason* compared to Levinas, Emmanuel: *Totalité et infini*; *Autrement qu'être*. 1341.

CELEBRITY
General literature. Theater.
Role of acting; relationship to CELEBRITY. Semiotic approach. Application of theories of Prague School of Linguistics. 959.

CENSORSHIP
See also classified section: 2588 ff.
General literature. Film.
On Rossellini, Roberto: *Il miracolo*; relationship to CENSORSHIP. 323.
Role of CENSORSHIP; relationship to Askol'dov, Aleksandr: *Kommissar*. 598.
—— in Fleming, Victor: *Gone with the Wind*; relationship to Lewton, Val; Selznick, David O. 495.
Role of Goebbels, Joseph in CENSORSHIP of Lang, Fritz: *Das Testament des Dr. Mabuse*. 640.
General literature. Film in Great Britain (1909-1972).
Role of CENSORSHIP. Review article. 395.

CENSORSHIP TRIAL
See also related term: Censorship.

CENTRAL AFRICA
See also narrower term: Niger.

CENTRAL EUROPE
See also narrower terms: Austria; Czechoslovakia; Germany; Hungary; Poland.
General literature. Television.
Role of image; representation; relationship to revolution in CENTRAL EUROPE (1989). 896.

CENTRAL EUROPEAN LITERATURE
See also narrower terms: French literature; German literature; Polish literature.

CENTRAL FRANCE
See also narrower terms: Dijon; Lyon.

CENTRAL ITALY
See also narrower terms: Florence; Rome.

CÉSPEDES, BALTASAR DE (D. 1615)
Literary forms. Translation. Translation theory. 1500-1599.
Theories of CÉSPEDES, BALTASAR DE. 2567.

CHAGALL, MARC (1887-1985)
General literature. Film.
Treatment of childhood; nostalgia; relationship to homeland in Tarkovskiĭ, Andreĭ A.: *Ivanovo detstvo*; *Nostalghia*; *Offret* compared to Brodskiĭ, Iosif Aleksandrovich; CHAGALL, MARC. 551.

CHAMBERS, WHITTAKER (1901-1961)
Literary movements.
Modernism. Treatment in CHAMBERS, WHITTAKER; Voegelin, Eric; relationship to religion; politics. 1012.

CHANG I-MO
Used for: Zhang Yimou.
General literature. Film in China.
Treatment of human body; relationship to ideology in CHANG I-MO: *Hung kao-liang*. Application of theories of Jameson, Fredric; Bakhtin, Mikhail Mikhaĭlovich. 661.

CHAOS
See also related term: Chaos theory.
General literature.
Relationship to order; CHAOS; study example: Adams, Henry Brooks: *The Education of Henry Adams*; Lessing, Doris: *The Golden Notebook*; Lem, Stanisław. 96.

CHAOS THEORY
See also related term: Chaos.
Literary theory and criticism.
Applied to literature for children; relationship to CHAOS THEORY. 1500.
Literary theory and criticism. Deconstructionism.
Relationship to CHAOS THEORY. Review article. 1590.

CHAPLIN, CHARLES SPENCER (1889-1977)
Used for: Chaplin, Charlie.
General literature. Film.
Role of CHAPLIN, CHARLES SPENCER. Reception study: reception in Germany (1918-1933). 377.
——. Review article. 490.

CHAPLIN, CHARLIE
Use: Chaplin, Charles Spencer (1889-1977).

CHAPTER TITLE
See also related term: Work title.

CHARACTER
See also related term: Characterization.

CHARACTER DEVELOPMENT
See also related term: Characters.

CHARACTER NAMES
See also related term: Characters.

CHARACTER RELATIONS
See also related term: Characters.

CHARACTER TYPES
See also related term: Characterization.

CHARACTERIZATION
General literature.
CHARACTERIZATION. 72.
General literature. Film.
CHARACTERIZATION; relationship to obsession in Huston, John. 657.
—— in Spielberg, Steven: *Indiana Jones: The Last Crusade*. 454.
Genres. Novel.
CHARACTERIZATION. 2193.
——. Dissertation abstract. 2212.
Genres. Novel. Sentimental novel.
CHARACTERIZATION; plot. Treatment of love. 2246.

CHARACTERS
See also classified section: 2839.
See also narrower terms: Female characters; Stock characters.

CHARITY
See also related term: Donation.

CHASTITY
See also related term: Sexuality.

CHEERS
General literature. Television.
Role of culture in *CHEERS*. 876.

CHEMISE BINDING
Bibliographical. Printing. Binding.
CHEMISE BINDING; wrapper binding. 1207.

CH'EN K'AI-KO
Used for: Chen Kaige.
General literature. Film in China.
Treatment of reform in CH'EN K'AI-KO: *Huang t'u-ti*; *Ta yueh ping*; *Hai-tzu wang*. 288.

CHEN KAIGE
Use: Ch'en K'ai-ko.

CHIAROSCURO
See also related term: Painting.

CHICAGO
General literature. Film in CHICAGO (1905-1928).
Relationship to exhibition in African American neighborhoods. 281.
General literature. Film in CHICAGO (1906-1908).
And nickelodeon; amusement park as cultural space; relationship to sexuality of women. 536.

CHIESA DI SAN CLEMENTE
Bibliographical. Latin language literature. 700-799.
Donation of book to CHIESA DI SAN CLEMENTE. Treatment in epigraph. 1111.

CHILD DEVELOPMENT
See also narrower term: Primal scene.

CHILD LABOR
See also related term: Children.

CHILD REARING
See also related term: Children.

CHILDHOOD
See also related term: Children.
General literature. Film.
Treatment of CHILDHOOD; nostalgia; relationship to homeland in Tarkovskiĭ, Andreĭ A.: *Ivanovo detstvo*; *Nostalghia*; *Offret* compared to Brodskiĭ, Iosif Aleksandrovich; Chagall, Marc. 551.

CHILDREN
See also classified section: 2840.
See also narrower term: Orphans.
See also related terms: Adult-child relations; Childhood.
General literature. Film.
Treatment of CHILDREN in Truffaut, François: *Les Quatre Cents Coups*; *L'Enfant sauvage*; *L'Argent de poche*. Theories of Freud, Sigmund. 298.

CHILDREN—AS AUDIENCE
Bibliographical. Printing. Illustration.
In Latvian literature for CHILDREN. 1216.
Bibliographical. Publishing. Marketing.
Of literature for CHILDREN; relationship to reading preference. Dissertation abstract. 1304.
General literature. Film for CHILDREN (1920-1939).
Relationship to ethnography. Reception study. 314.
General literature for CHILDREN. 45, 77, 81, 82.
Bibliography (1988). 215.
Didacticism; relationship to catechism. 54.
Humor. 100, 199.
Illustration. 3.
——; relationship to comprehension. Semiotic approach. 89.

Illustration; relationship to realism. 23.
Psychoanalytic approach. Dissertation abstract. 151
Relationship to visual arts. 98.
Sources in *Märchen*. Theories of Bettelheim, Bruno: *The Uses of Enchantment.* 195.
Study example: Ségur, Sophie, comtesse de. Feminist approach. Dissertation abstract. 122.
Treatment in criticism. 187.
Treatment of adult-child relations. Reader-response approach. 99.
Treatment of science; technology. Reference guide. 113.
Use of code in picture books. 141.

General literature for CHILDREN. English language literature. 1900-1999.
Narrative voice. 202.
———. Treatment of Middle Ages. 116.

General literature for CHILDREN; young adults.
Role of bibliotherapy. 208.

General literature for CHILDREN (1900-1948). Hebrew language literature. 157.

Genres. Fiction. *Märchen* for CHILDREN.
As myth. 2166.

Genres. Fiction for CHILDREN.
Narrative voice. Interview with Schmidt, Gary D. 2115.
Treatment of morality; relationship to social behavior. 2111.
Treatment of the marvelous; adventure. 2104.

Genres. Fiction for CHILDREN. English language literature. 1900-1999. 2126.

Genres. Fiction for CHILDREN (1938-1988). English language literature.
Role of the fantastic. Dissertation abstract. 2136.

Genres. Novel for CHILDREN. 2192.

Literary forms. Translation.
Translation of fiction for CHILDREN. 2546.

Literary theory and criticism.
Applied to literature for CHILDREN; relationship to chaos theory. 1500.

Literary theory and criticism. Narrative theory.
Applied to literature for CHILDREN. 1806.

Literary theory and criticism. Psychoanalytic literary theory and criticism.
On literature for CHILDREN. 1903.
Relationship to literature for CHILDREN. 1898.

Literary theory and criticism. Psychoanalytic literary theory and criticism and Marxist literary theory and criticism.
On literature for CHILDREN. 1908.

Professional topics. Humanities.
Use of *Märchen*; literature for CHILDREN in teaching of literature. Dissertation abstract. 2701.

CHILDREN'S MUSEUMS
See also related term: Children.

CHILDREN'S SPEECH
See also related term: Children.

CHILE
General literature. Film in CHILE.
Role of Ruiz, Raúl. Sources in Borges, Jorge Luis. 520.

CHINA
Bibliographical. Publishing. Book trade.
And libraries in CHINA. 1286.

General literature. Film in CHINA. 527.
Relationship to massacre in Tiananmen Square. 585.
Role of Fifth Generation. 509.
Treatment of cultural change; relationship to Fifth Generation. 413.
Treatment of human body; relationship to ideology in Chang I-mo: *Hung kao-liang*. Application of theories of Jameson, Fredric; Bakhtin, Mikhail Mikhaïlovich. 661.
Treatment of reform in Ch'en K'ai-ko: *Huang t'u-ti; Ta yueh ping; Hai-tzu wang.* 288.

General literature. Film in CHINA (1930-1939).
Treatment of the Left. 255.

Genres. Fiction.
Treatment of CHINA. 2153.

CHINA BEACH
General literature. Film and television.
Melodrama. Treatment of Vietnam War in Ashby, Hal: *Coming Home; CHINA BEACH.* 485.

General literature. Television.
Treatment of women in *CHINA BEACH.* 871.

CHINESE FICTION
General literature. Film. Film adaptation.
Of CHINESE FICTION. Dissertation abstract. 705.

CHINESE LITERATURE

Professional topics. Comparative literature.
CHINESE LITERATURE compared to Western literature. 2633.
Relationship to CHINESE LITERATURE. 2629.

CHODOROW, NANCY (1944-)
Literary theory and criticism. Feminist literary theory and criticism (1968-1979).
Sources in Beauvoir, Simone de: *Le Deuxième Sexe.* Application of theories of CHODOROW, NANCY: *The Reproduction of Mothering.* Dissertation abstract. 1681.

CHOLAKOV, GEORGI
General literature. Film. Film genres: documentary film.
On CHOLAKOV, GEORGI and Ovcharov, Svetoslav: *Stefan Stambolov—süzidateliat i süsipateliat.* Interview. 779.

CHOPRA, JOYCE
General literature. Film. Film adaptation.
Treatment of violence against women in CHOPRA, JOYCE: *Smooth Talk* as film adaptation of Oates, Joyce Carol: "Where Are You Going, Where Have You Been?" 685.

THE CHORA
See also related term: Poetic language.
Genres. Poetry.
Treatment of THE CHORA; relationship to representation. Theories of Kristeva, Julia: *Révolution du langage poétique.* 2255.

CHOREOGRAPHER
See also related term: Dance.

CHOREOGRAPHY
See also related term: Dance.

CHRIST
See also classified section: 2841 ff.
Used for: Jesus Christ.
See also related term: Passion of Christ.
General literature. Film.
Treatment of CHRIST in Rossellini, Roberto: *Messia* compared to Scorsese, Martin: *The Last Temptation of Christ.* 629.

CHRISTIAN CHURCH
See also related term: Christianity.

CHRISTIAN COMMUNITY
See also related term: Christianity.

CHRISTIAN DOCTRINE
See also narrower term: Gnosticism.
See also related term: Christianity.

CHRISTIAN EXISTENTIALISM
See also related term: Christianity.

CHRISTIAN HUMANISM
See also related term: Christianity.

CHRISTIAN IMAGERY
See also related term: Christianity.

CHRISTIAN SCHOLARS
General literature.
Role of CHRISTIAN SCHOLARS. Interview with Ong, Walter J. 37.

CHRISTIAN THEOLOGY
See also related term: Christianity.

CHRISTIAN VALUES
See also related term: Christianity.

CHRISTIANITY
See also classified section: 2843.
General literature. Film.
Treatment of God; CHRISTIANITY in Kieslowski, Krzysztof: *Dekalog.* 434.
Literary forms. Myth.
Relationship to Judaism; CHRISTIANITY. 2407.
Literary forms. Tragedy.
Relationship to CHRISTIANITY. 2506.
Literary theory and criticism.
Poetics; relationship to CHRISTIANITY; redemption. 1390.
Literary theory and criticism. Poststructuralist literary theory and criticism.
Nihilism; logocentrism; relationship to CHRISTIANITY. 1881.
Professional topics. Humanities.
Relationship to CHRISTIANITY. 2733.
Themes and figures. The sacred.
Relationship to CHRISTIANITY. 2913.

CHRISTIANS
See also narrower term: Mormons.

CHRISTOCENTRISM
See also related term: Christ.

CHRISTOLOGY
See also related term: Christ.

CHRONICLE
See also narrower term: Diary.
See also related term: Biography.

CHRONOTOPE
See also related terms: Narrative conventions; Temporal structure.

Literary theory and criticism.
CHRONOTOPE. Theories of Bakhtin, Mikhail Mikhaïlovich. 1569.
Literary theory and criticism. Linguistic literary theory and criticism.
CHRONOTOPE; relationship to otherness. Theories of Bakhtin, Mikhail Mikhaïlovich compared to Welby, Victoria, Lady. 1753.

CHRYSOSTOM, JOHN (CA. 347-407)
Used for: Joannes Chrysostom.

CHRYSOSTOM, JOHN (CA. 347-407)—AS SOURCE
Genres. Prose. Devotional literature.
Treatment of liturgical formulas. Sources in CHRYSOSTOM, JOHN: *De Sancta Pentecoste*; Theodore of Mopsuestia: *Homiliae Catecheticae*; Pseudo-Epiphanius of Salamis: *Homilia in Diuini Corporis Sepulturam*. 2318.

CHURCH
Literary movements.
Romanticism. Treatment of stained-glass window of CHURCH as metaphor for epiphany. 1079.

CHURCH ARCHITECTURE
See also related term: Church.

CHURCH NAMES
See also related term: Church.

CHURCH POLITICS
See also related term: Church.

CICERO (106-43 B.C.)
Literary forms. Rhetoric.
Inventio; relationship to philosophical language. Treatment in CICERO. 2478.

CIMINO, MICHAEL (1943-)
General literature. Film.
Role of historical context in CIMINO, MICHAEL: *The Deer Hunter*. 267.

CINEMA
Use: Film.

CINÉMA VÉRITÉ
General literature. Film. Film genres: documentary film for television.
CINÉMA VÉRITÉ in film by Drew Associates. Dissertation abstract. 768.

CINEMASCOPE
General literature. Film on wide-screen.
CINEMASCOPE. 235.
——; relationship to ideology. Application of theories of Bazin, André. 593.
—— compared to Cinerama. 242.

CINÉMATHÈQUE UNIVERSITAIRE
General literature. Film in France.
Role of CINÉMATHÈQUE UNIVERSITAIRE; relationship to archives. 257.

CINEMATIC TECHNIQUE
Used for: Film technique.
See also narrower term: Voice-over narration.
See also related term: Film.
General literature. Film.
CINEMATIC TECHNIQUE; relationship to autobiography in Fellini, Federico: *La dolce vita*. 636.
——; relationship to judgment. Theories of Heidegger, Martin; Adorno, Theodor W. 656.
—— in Herzog, Werner: *Aguirre, der Zorn Gottes* compared to Valle-Inclán, Ramón María del: *Tirano Banderas*. 440.
—— in Tourneur, Jacques: *Cat People*. Psychoanalytic approach. 452.

CINEMATOGRAPHER
See also related term: Camera.

CINERAMA
General literature. Film on wide-screen.
CinemaScope compared to CINERAMA. 242.

CIRCULARITY
Literary theory and criticism. Hermeneutics.
Relationship to the future; CIRCULARITY. Theories of Heidegger, Martin; Bloch, Ernst; Hegel, Georg Wilhelm Friedrich. 1727.

CIRCULATION
See also related terms: Printing; Publishing.

CIRCUS
General literature. Theater.
CIRCUS on television. Semiotic approach. 931.

CIRCUS ACTS
See also related term: Circus.

CIRCUS IMAGERY
See also related term: Circus.

CIRCUS PERFORMERS
See also related term: Circus.

CITATION
See also related term: Quotation.

CITIES
Use: Urban areas.

CITY
See also related term: Urban areas.

CITY IMAGERY
See also related term: City poetry.

CITY POETRY
Used for: Urban poetry.
Genres. Poetry: CITY POETRY. 2261.

CITYSCAPE
See also related term: City poetry.

CIVIL RIGHTS MOVEMENT
See also related term: African Americans.

CIVILIZATION
See also related term: Culture.

CIXOUS, HÉLÈNE (1937-)
Literary theory and criticism. Feminist literary theory and criticism.
Theories of CIXOUS, HÉLÈNE. 1661.

CLARKE, SHIRLEY (1925-)
General literature. Film. Film adaptation.
Narrative technique in film adaptation of Miller, Warren: *The Cool World* by CLARKE, SHIRLEY. 700.

CLASS
Use: Social class.

CLASS CONFLICT
See also related term: Social class.

CLASS REVOLUTION
See also related term: Social class.

CLASS STRUGGLE
See also related term: Social class.

CLASSICAL ALLUSION
See also related term: Classical literature.
General literature. Film. Film adaptation.
CLASSICAL ALLUSION in film adaptation of Lindsay, Joan: *Picnic at Hanging Rock* by Weir, Peter. 703.

CLASSICAL CULTURE
See also related term: Classical allusion.

CLASSICAL DRAMA—AS SOURCE
General literature. Theater.
Sources in CLASSICAL DRAMA. 980.

CLASSICAL GREEK LITERATURE
Use: Ancient Greek literature.

CLASSICAL HISTORY
See also related term: Classical allusion.

CLASSICAL LITERATURE
See also narrower terms: Ancient Greek literature; Classical drama.
See also related term: Classical allusion.
General literature.
Relationship to CLASSICAL LITERATURE. Bibliography (1987). 219.

CLASSICAL MYTH
See also related term: Classical allusion.

CLASSICAL RHETORIC
Literary forms. Rhetoric.
Stasis; *kairos*; treatment in CLASSICAL RHETORIC; relationship to social construction. 2433.

CLASSROOM INTERACTION
See also narrower term: Student-teacher interaction.

CLAYTON, JACK (1921-)
General literature. Film. Film adaptation.
Of Braine, John: *Room at the Top* by CLAYTON, JACK. 715.

CLIMAX
See also related term: Crisis.

CLOCK
See also related term: Time.

CLOSE, GLENN (1947-)
General literature. Film.
On Frears, Stephen: *Dangerous Liaisons*. Interview with CLOSE, GLENN. 466.

CLOSURE
General literature.
On written language; relationship to narrative voice; CLOSURE; oral tradition. 159.
Genres. Novel.
CLOSURE; study example: Richardson, Samuel: *Pamela*; Burney, Frances: *Evelina*; Austen, Jane: *Mansfield Park*. Dissertation abstract. 2205.
Literary movements.
Postmodernism. And pedagogy; relationship to CLOSURE; crisis. 1039.

CLOTHING
See also narrower term: Costume.

CNUT
Use: Canute I, King of England (995?-1035).

COCTEAU, JEAN (1889-1963)
  General literature. Film.
    On COCTEAU, JEAN: *La Belle et la bête* compared to McKinley, Robin: *Beauty*; romance novel; folk tale. 375.

CODE
  General literature for children.
    Use of CODE in picture books. 141.

CODICOLOGY
See also classified section: 1134 ff.
See also related term: Manuscripts.

COGNITION
See also related terms: Cognitive processes; Cognitive representation; Memory; Schema theory.
  Genres. Drama.
    Relationship to COGNITION. 2067.

COGNITIVE ABILITIES
See also related term: Cognition.

COGNITIVE ASSESSMENT
See also related term: Cognition.

COGNITIVE CONTROL
See also related term: Cognition.

COGNITIVE DEVELOPMENT
See also related terms: Cognition; Cognitive processes.

COGNITIVE EFFICIENCY
See also related terms: Cognition; Cognitive processes.

COGNITIVE GRAMMAR
See also related term: Cognition.

COGNITIVE PROCESSES
See also narrower term: Memory.
See also related term: Cognition.
  Figures of speech. Imagery.
    Relationship to COGNITIVE PROCESSES of reader; study example: Móricz, Zsigmond: "Barbárok"; newspaper article. 2352.
  General literature.
    Narrative; relationship to COGNITIVE PROCESSES. 71.

COGNITIVE PROCESSING
See also related terms: Cognition; Cognitive processes.

COGNITIVE PSYCHOLOGY
See also related terms: Cognition; Cognitive processes.

COGNITIVE REPRESENTATION
Used for: Mental representation.
See also related term: Cognition.
  General literature. Television.
    Imagery; relationship to COGNITIVE REPRESENTATION; Postmodernism. Application of theories of Jameson, Fredric. 920.

COGNITIVE STRATEGIES
See also related term: Cognition.

COGNITIVE STYLE
See also related terms: Cognition; Cognitive processes.

COHERENCE
  Literary theory and criticism. Hermeneutics.
    Relationship to context; COHERENCE. 1721.

COHL, EMILE (1857-1938)
  General literature. Film. Film genres: animated film in France.
    Biography of COHL, EMILE. 754.

COITAL IMAGERY
See also related term: Sexual intercourse.

COITUS
Use: Sexual intercourse.

COLD WAR
  General literature. Film.
    Relationship to COLD WAR; technology. 435.
  General literature. Television in United States (1960-1975).
    Imagery of COLD WAR in treatment of Vietnam War. Dissertation abstract. 921.

COLE, GEORGE WATSON (1850-1939)
  Bibliographical.
    Theories of COLE, GEORGE WATSON. 1091.

COLE, TRISTAN DE VERE
  General literature. Film.
    On COLE, TRISTAN DE VERE: *Dykket*. 381.

COLLABORATION
  General literature. Film.
    COLLABORATION between Brecht, Bertolt and Eisler, Hanns. Dissertation abstract. 305.
    Role of COLLABORATION in Cukor, George: *Holiday*; relationship to studio system in Hollywood (1935-1939). 499.

General literature. Film. Film genres: documentary film.
    COLLABORATION. Dissertation abstract. 775.
  General literature. Theater.
    COLLABORATION in women's theater groups; relationship to rhetoric; politics. Feminist approach. 983.
  Genres. Drama.
    COLLABORATION in writing; theatrical production. Dissertation abstract. 2084.
  Literary forms. Rhetoric.
    Relationship to COLLABORATION in writing; women. 2466.
    Relationship to dialectic; COLLABORATION. Theories of Burke, Kenneth compared to Rogers, Carl Ransom. 2461.
  Literary theory and criticism. Feminist literary theory and criticism.
    Relationship to COLLABORATION in writing. 1652.

COLLABORATIVE LEARNING
  Professional topics. Humanities.
    Role of COLLABORATIVE LEARNING; relationship to teaching of writing. 2813.

COLLATING
See also narrower term: Manuscript collation.
See also related term: Textual criticism.

COLLECTING
See also narrower term: Book collecting.
  Bibliographical. Manuscripts. Illuminated manuscripts. 1400-1499.
    COLLECTING by Edward IV, King of England; Henry VII, King of England. 1137.

COLLECTION STUDY
  Bibliographical.
    COLLECTION STUDY of collection at Library of Congress. 1113.
    Role of library collection; relationship to canon. COLLECTION STUDY of collection at Harry Ransom Humanities Research Center at University of Texas at Austin. 1112.

COLLECTIONS
See also narrower terms: Library collection; Personal collections.
See also related term: Collection study.

COLLECTIVE CHARACTER
See also related term: Characterization.

COLLECTIVE STRUGGLE
  General literature. Film. Film genres: political film in Hollywood (1970-1987).
    Treatment of working class; relationship to violence; COLLECTIVE STRUGGLE. Dissertation abstract. 778.

COLLECTIVE UNCONSCIOUS
See also related term: Memoria.

COLLECTORS
See also narrower term: Book collectors.
See also related term: Collecting.

COLLEGE STUDENTS
  General literature.
    Role of the self in interpretation by COLLEGE STUDENTS. Pedagogical approach. Dissertation abstract. 41.
  General literature. Film.
    Attitudes of COLLEGE STUDENTS. Pedagogical approach. Dissertation abstract. 422.

COLLEGES
See also related term: Universities.

COLLEGIO EUROPEO DEI TRADUTTORI LETTERARI
  Literary forms. Translation.
    Role of COLLEGIO EUROPEO DEI TRADUTTORI LETTERARI in Italy: Procida. 2553.

COLONIAL RULE
See also related term: Colonialism.

COLONIAL WRITERS
See also related term: Postcolonial writers.

COLONIALISM
See also related terms: Neocolonialism; Postcolonialism.
  General literature. English language literature. 1900-1999.
    Relationship to COLONIALISM. 110.
  General literature. Film.
    Treatment of sexism; COLONIALISM. 541.
  Literary theory and criticism. New Historicism.
    Relationship to COLONIALISM. 1832.
  Literary theory and criticism. Poststructuralist literary theory and criticism.
    Relationship to COLONIALISM; marginality. 1888.

COLOPHONS
See also related term: Publishing.

COLOR
  Literary theory and criticism. Semiotic literary theory and criticism.
    Aesthetics of COLOR; form. Theories of Marquand, Allan; Ladd-Franklin, Christine; relationship to Peirce, Charles Sanders. 1985.

SEE CLASSIFIED SEQUENCE FOR ADDITIONAL ENTRIES

COLOR IMAGERY
See also related term: Color.

COLOR NAMING
See also related term: Color.

COLOR SYMBOLISM
See also related term: Color.

COLORADO
General literature. Film by independent filmmakers in COLORADO (1897-1928).
Film history. 632.

COLORIZATION
General literature. Film.
Role of COLORIZATION. 222.

COLSON, CHARLES W. (1931-)—STUDY EXAMPLE
Genres. Autobiography.
Syllogistic form; qualitative form in spiritual autobiography; study example: COLSON, CHARLES W.: *Born Again.* 2050.

COMBAT
See also related term: War.

COMEDIA
See also related terms: Comic drama; Tragicomedy.

COMEDY
See also narrower term: Burlesque.
See also related terms: Comic drama; Satire; Tragicomedy.

COMIC BOOK
See also related term: Comic strip.
Bibliographical. Publishing.
Of COMIC BOOK; relationship to cultural criticism. 1251.

COMIC BOOK CHARACTER
See also related term: Comic book.

COMIC DRAMA
See also classified section: 2099.
See also narrower terms: Pantomime; Situation comedy.
See also related terms: Tragicomedy; Vaudeville.

COMIC FILM
General literature. Film. Film genres: COMIC FILM.
Dissertation abstract. 806.
General literature. Film. Film genres: COMIC FILM in U.S.S.R. 794.
General literature. Film. Film genres: COMIC FILM in United States.
Relationship to vaudeville. Dissertation abstract. 774.

COMIC STRIP
See also related term: Comic book.
General literature. Film.
And COMIC STRIP; theater; relationship to popular culture (1895-1903). 230.
Genres. Fiction: COMIC STRIP. 2107.

COMIN DA TRINO
Bibliographical. Printing. Typography. 1500-1599.
By COMIN DA TRINO of Latin language literature. 1230.

COMMAND
See also related term: Speech acts.

COMMERCE
Use: Business.

COMMERCIALISM
See also related term: Business.
General literature. Film in India in Hindi language.
Role of COMMERCIALISM. 623.
General literature. Television.
Role of cultural dominance; relationship to COMMERCIALISM; popular culture. Application of theories of Bourdieu, Pierre. 867.

COMMERCIALIZATION
See also related terms: Business; Commercialism.

COMMUNICATION
See also narrower terms: Cross-cultural communication; Interpersonal communication; Nonverbal communication.
See also related term: Communication theory.
General literature.
COMMUNICATION in ethnic text. 212.
Literary theory and criticism. Linguistic literary theory and criticism.
On COMMUNICATION; relationship to reader response. 1750.
Relationship to COMMUNICATION. 1736.
Literary theory and criticism. Reception theory.
Role of sociology of COMMUNICATION. 1941.

COMMUNICATION AIDS
See also related term: Communication.

COMMUNICATION APPREHENSION
See also related term: Communication.

COMMUNICATION ASSESSMENT
See also related term: Communication.

COMMUNICATION BARRIERS
See also related term: Communication.

COMMUNICATION BREAKDOWN
See also related term: Communication.

COMMUNICATION DISORDERS
See also related term: Communication.

COMMUNICATION GOAL
See also related term: Communication.

COMMUNICATION RULES
See also related term: Communication.

COMMUNICATION SKILLS
See also related term: Communication.

COMMUNICATION TECHNOLOGY
See also related term: Communication.

COMMUNICATION THEORY
See also related terms: Communication; Information theory.

COMMUNICATION THEORY—APPLICATION
Literary forms. Parody.
And travesty; pastiche; relationship to social relations; psychology. Application of COMMUNICATION THEORY. 2414.

COMMUNICATIVE ACTS
See also related term: Communication.

COMMUNICATIVE APPROACH
Documents applying specific approaches are so numerous that access to them is provided only in the electronic versions of the *Bibliography.*

COMMUNICATIVE BEHAVIOR
See also related term: Communication.

COMMUNICATIVE COMPETENCE
See also related term: Communication.

COMMUNICATIVE DEVELOPMENT
See also related term: Communication.

COMMUNICATIVE FUNCTION
See also related term: Communication.

COMMUNICATIVE STRATEGY
See also related term: Communication.

COMMUNICATIVE STYLE
See also related term: Communication.

COMMUNISM
See also related terms: Communist Party; Marxism.

COMMUNIST PARTY
Bibliographical. Publishing (1917-1940).
By COMMUNIST PARTY in Lithuania. 1273.

COMMUNISTS
See also related term: Communist Party.

COMMUNITY
See also narrower term: African American community.
See also related term: Society.
General literature.
Authority in discourse; relationship to COMMUNITY. Dissertation abstract. 144.

COMOLLI, JEAN-LOUIS
General literature. Film. Film theory and criticism.
Spectator. Theories of Bazin, André; COMOLLI, JEAN-LOUIS. 819.

COMPARATIVE APPROACH
Documents applying specific approaches are so numerous that access to them is provided only in the electronic versions of the *Bibliography.*

COMPARATIVE LITERATURE
See also classified section: 2593 ff.
Literary theory and criticism.
Role of typology; relationship to COMPARATIVE LITERATURE. 1548.
Literary theory and criticism. Literary history.
Relationship to COMPARATIVE LITERATURE. 1771.
Role in COMPARATIVE LITERATURE. 1770.

COMPARISON
Figures of speech.
COMPARISON. Dissertation abstract. 2351.
Figures of speech. Metaphor.
Compared to literal meaning; COMPARISON. 2368.

COMPLAINING
See also related term: Speech acts.

COMPLIMENTING
See also related term: Speech acts.

COMPOSITE BOOKS
Bibliographical. Printing.
COMPOSITE BOOKS. 1169.

COMPOSITION
See also related term: Writing.

General literature.
Spatial form; COMPOSITION compared to architecture. Pedagogical approach. 65.
Genres. Fiction.
Relationship to COMPOSITION. Dissertation abstract. 2120.

COMPOSITION STUDIES
Professional topics. Humanities.
COMPOSITION STUDIES in English departments. Application of theories of Derrida, Jacques. 2779.

COMPOSITOR
See also related term: Printing.

COMPREHENSION
See also related term: Understanding.
General literature for children.
Illustration; relationship to COMPREHENSION. Semiotic approach. 89.

COMPREHENSION STRATEGIES
See also related term: Comprehension.

COMPUTATIONAL LINGUISTICS
See also related term: Computer.

COMPUTER
See also related term: Computer-assisted research.

COMPUTER—APPLICATION
General literature.
Role of topos; relationship to application of COMPUTER. 120.
Literary forms. Translation.
Application of COMPUTER. 2542.
Literary theory and criticism.
On meaning; relationship to application of COMPUTER. 1360.

COMPUTER-ASSISTED INSTRUCTION
See also narrower term: Computer-assisted language learning.
See also related term: Computer.

COMPUTER-ASSISTED LANGUAGE LEARNING
Used for: CALL.
Professional topics. Humanities.
Role of COMPUTER-ASSISTED LANGUAGE LEARNING in French language learning. 2730.

COMPUTER-ASSISTED RESEARCH
See also classified section: 2637 ff.
See also related term: Computer.

COMPUTER ASSISTED TOOLS FOR SEPTUAGINT STUDIES (CATSS)
See also related term: Computer-assisted research.

COMPUTER-GENERATED LITERATURE
See also related term: Computer.

COMPUTER-HUMAN DIALOGUE
See also related term: Computer.

COMPUTER MANUAL
See also related term: Computer.

COMPUTER NETWORKS
See also related term: Computer.

COMPUTER PROCESSABLE LANGUAGES
See also related term: Computer.

COMPUTER PROGRAMS
See also narrower term: Oxford Concordance program.

COMPUTER SCIENCE
See also related term: Computer.

COMPUTER SCREEN
See also related term: Computer.

COMPUTER TECHNOLOGY
See also related term: Computer.

CONCEPT
Literary theory and criticism. Literary history.
Role of CONCEPT. 1778.

CONCEPTUAL DEVELOPMENT
See also related term: Cognition.

CONCRETE POETRY
See also classified section: 2305.

CONCURRENT PERFECTING
Bibliographical. Printing.
CONCURRENT PERFECTING by Walker & Greig in Edinburgh (1817-1822). 1176.

CONFESSION
General literature.
CONFESSION in narrative. 74.

CONFESSIONAL MODE
See also related term: Confession.

CONFESSOR
See also related term: Confession.

CONFIDENCE GAME
General literature. Film.
Treatment of psychoanalysis; CONFIDENCE GAME; relationship to male-female relations in Mamet, David: House of Games. 622.

CONFIGURATIONISM (PSYCHOLOGY)
Use: Gestalt theory.

CONNECTIVITY
See also related term: Coherence.

CONNOTATION
See also related term: Meaning.

CONSCIOUSNESS
See also narrower term: Self-consciousness.
See also related terms: Mind; The unconscious.
Genres. Fiction. Science fiction.
Role of CONSCIOUSNESS. 2177.
Literary theory and criticism. Deconstructionism.
Role of time; CONSCIOUSNESS. Treatment in Derrida, Jacques: La Voix et le phénomène; relationship to Husserl, Edmund. Dissertation abstract. 1582.

CONSECRATION
See also related terms: Eucharist (sacrament of); Liturgy.

CONSERVATISM
Professional topics. Humanities.
Canon; pedagogy in United States; relationship to liberalism compared to CONSERVATISM. 2782.

CONSONANCE
See also related term: Rhyme.

CONSTRUCTIVISM
Literary theory and criticism.
Relationship to CONSTRUCTIVISM; empiricism. 1526.

CONSTRUE—APPLICATION
Professional topics. Research tools.
Application of CONSTRUE. 2829.

CONSUMER
See also related term: Consumerism.

CONSUMER SOCIETY
See also related term: Consumerism.

CONSUMERISM
General literature. Film.
Treatment of women; relationship to CONSUMERISM. Film history. 382.

CONSUMPTION
See also related term: Consumerism.

CONTE DE FÉES
See also related term: Märchen.

CONTENT
Literary theory and criticism.
Role of affect; relationship to form; CONTENT. 1413.

CONTEXT
See also narrower term: Cultural context.
See also related term: Interpretive frame.
Literary theory and criticism.
Dialogism; relationship to CONTEXT; politics in novel. Theories of Bakhtin, Mikhail Mikhaĭlovich. 1531.
Literary theory and criticism. Hermeneutics.
Relationship to CONTEXT; coherence. 1721.

CONTEXTUAL APPROACH
Documents applying specific approaches are so numerous that access to them is provided only in the electronic versions of the Bibliography.

CONTEXTUAL REFERENCE
See also related term: Context.

CONTEXTUALIST CRITICISM
Literary theory and criticism. New Criticism. 1900-1999.
Compared to reader-response theory and criticism; CONTEXTUALIST CRITICISM. Dissertation abstract. 1830.

CONTRADICTION
See also related term: Antinomy.

CONVENTIONS
See also narrower terms: Linguistic conventions; Literary conventions.

CONVERSATION
See also related term: Dialogue.

CONVERSATION THEORY
See also related term: Communication theory.

COOK, DAVID BRUCE (1946-)
Literary movements.
Postmodernism. Treatment in Kroker, Arthur and COOK, DAVID BRUCE: The Postmodern Scene: Excremental Culture and Hyper-Aesthetics. 1046.

COOPER, MERIAN C. (1894-1973)
  General literature. Film.
    Intertextuality in COOPER, MERIAN C.: *King Kong*. 572.

COPPOLA, FRANCIS FORD (1939-)
  General literature. Film.
    By Ford, John; Capra, Frank; COPPOLA, FRANCIS FORD; Scorsese, Martin. 456.
    Narrative structure. Treatment of Vietnam War in COPPOLA, FRANCIS FORD: *Apocalypse Now*. Application of theories of Lévi-Strauss, Claude. 644.
    On COPPOLA, FRANCIS FORD: *Apocalypse Now*. Sources in Conrad, Joseph: "Heart of Darkness." 348.
    ——: *One from the Heart*. 342.
    Postmodernism in COPPOLA, FRANCIS FORD; Lucas, George; DePalma, Brian; Spielberg, Steven; Scorsese, Martin. Dissertation abstract. 630.
  General literature. Film. Film adaptation.
    On COPPOLA, FRANCIS FORD: *Apocalypse Now* as film adaptation of Conrad, Joseph: "Heart of Darkness." 718.

COPY TEXT
See also related terms: Editions; Textual criticism.

COPYRIGHT
See also related term: Copyright law.
  Bibliographical. Printing. Typography in Venice (ca. 1500).
    Italics by Manuzio, Aldo; relationship to COPYRIGHT. 1225.
  Bibliographical. Publishing in England. 1700-1799.
    Role of scribe; relationship to COPYRIGHT. 1255.

COPYRIGHT LAW
See also related term: Copyright.
  Bibliographical. Manuscripts.
    Unpublished manuscripts; relationship to COPYRIGHT LAW. 1124.
  Bibliographical. Publishing. Book trade in Australia (1989).
    Relationship to COPYRIGHT LAW. 1290.

CORPORATION
See also related term: Business.

CORPOREALITY
See also related terms: Human body; Spirituality.

CORPUS CHRISTI (FEAST OF)
See also related term: Eucharist (sacrament of).

CORRESPONDENCE
Use: Letters.

COSMATOS, GEORGE PAN (1941-)
  General literature. Film.
    Role of pastoralism in Kotcheff, Ted: *First Blood* compared to COSMATOS, GEORGE PAN: *Rambo II*; Mulcahy, Russell: *Rambo III*. 273.

COSMOGONY
See also related term: Astronomy.

COSMOLOGY
  Literary theory and criticism. Narrative theory.
    Applied to COSMOLOGY. 1826.

COSTA-GAVRAS, CONSTANTIN (1933-)
Used for: Gavras, Constantin.
  General literature. Film.
    Interview with COSTA-GAVRAS, CONSTANTIN. 307.

COSTUME
  General literature. Film.
    COSTUME by Plunkett, Walter in Fleming, Victor: *Gone with the Wind*; relationship to Selznick, David O. 346.

COSTUME DESIGN
See also related term: Costume.

COSTUME TERMS
See also related term: Costume.

COTTA, JOHANN FRIEDRICH, BARON VON COTTENDORF (1764-1832)
  Bibliographical. Publishing.
    Biography of COTTA, JOHANN FRIEDRICH, BARON VON COTTENDORF. 1253.
  Bibliographical. Publishing in Germany. 1700-1799.
    By COTTA, JOHANN FRIEDRICH, BARON VON COTTENDORF. 1254.

COUÉISM
See also related term: Psychotherapy.

COUNTERCULTURE
See also related term: Culture.
  Literary movements.
    Avant-garde. Relationship to COUNTERCULTURE. 992.

COUNTERHISTORY
See also related term: History.

COUNTERREVOLUTION
See also related term: Revolution.

COUNTERSUBLIME
See also related term: The sublime.

COURT
See also narrower term: Royal court.

COURTLY LIFE
See also related term: Royal court.

COX REPORT ON NATIONAL CURRICULUM
  Professional topics. Humanities.
    Treatment in *COX REPORT ON NATIONAL CURRICULUM*. 2665, 2708, 2760.

CRAIG, EDWARD GORDON (1872-1966)
Used for: Craig, Gordon.
  General literature. Theater.
    Marionettes; relationship to performance theory. Theories of CRAIG, EDWARD GORDON: "The Actor and the Über-marionette"; Meïerkhol'd, Vsevolod Emil'evich; Schlemmer, Oskar; Kleist, Heinrich von: "Über das Marionettentheater." Dissertation abstract. 962.

CRAIG, GORDON
Use: Craig, Edward Gordon (1872-1966).

CRAIG, STUART
  General literature. Film.
    On Frears, Stephen: *Dangerous Liaisons*. Interview with CRAIG, STUART. 468.

CRAVEN, WES (1940-)
  General literature. Film.
    Interview with CRAVEN, WES. 233.

CREATIVE PROCESS
See also related term: Creativity.
  General literature.
    CREATIVE PROCESS. 53, 94.
  General literature. Film.
    Screenplay by Fuchs, Daniel. CREATIVE PROCESS. 340.
  Genres. Poetry.
    CREATIVE PROCESS. Psychological approach. Dissertation abstract. 2299.
  Literary forms. Rhetoric.
    Role of intuition; relationship to CREATIVE PROCESS. 2437.
  Literary forms. Translation.
    CREATIVE PROCESS. 2564.

CREATIVE WRITING
  Professional topics. Humanities.
    CREATIVE WRITING at American universities. Dissertation abstract. 2775.

CREATIVE WRITING PROGRAMS
See also related term: Creative writing.

CREATIVE WRITING WORKSHOPS
  Professional topics. Humanities in United States.
    CREATIVE WRITING WORKSHOPS. 2712.

CREATIVITY
See also related terms: Creative process; Imagination; Invention.
  General literature.
    And science. CREATIVITY. 6.
    Role of CREATIVITY; relationship to novelty. Psychological approach. 133.
  General literature by patient with cancer.
    Relationship to art therapy. Treatment of mourning; CREATIVITY. Psychoanalytic approach. Dissertation abstract. 62.
  Genres. Poetry.
    Relationship to CREATIVITY. Dissertation abstract. 2304.
  Literary forms. Translation.
    Role of CREATIVITY in simultaneous translation. 2508.
  Literary theory and criticism. Reception theory.
    CREATIVITY; relationship to genius. 1948.

CREATOR
See also narrower terms: Artist; Writer.
See also related terms: Creativity; God; Invention.

CREOLE GENESIS
See also related term: Creole languages.

CREOLE LANGUAGES
See also: entries under headings for specific creole languages.
  General literature in CREOLE LANGUAGES.
    Application of polysystem theory. 121.

CREOLIZATION
See also related term: Creole languages.

CRESSIDA
Used for: Criseyde.
  Themes and figures. Troilus.
    And CRESSIDA; study example: opera; Morley, Christopher: *The Trojan Horse*; Wolf, Christa: *Kassandra*. 2927.

CRILE, GEORGE
  General literature. Television.
    Treatment of deception of the public; relationship to Vietnam War in CRILE, GEORGE: *The Uncounted Enemy: A Vietnam Deception*. 910.

CRIME
See also related term: Criminal.

CRIME FICTION
See also classified section: 2160.
See also related term: Detective fiction.

CRIME NOVEL
See also related term: Detective novel.

CRIMINAL
Used for: Lawbreaker.
  General literature. Film.
    Treatment of CRIMINAL in Avildsen, John Guilbert: *Save the Tiger.* 605.

CRIMINAL PERSONALITY
See also related term: Criminal.

CRISEYDE
Use: Cressida.

CRISIS
  Literary movements.
    Postmodernism. And pedagogy; relationship to closure; CRISIS. 1039.
  Literary theory and criticism.
    On CRISIS of literary theory in academia. Review article. 1330.

CRISIS IMAGERY
See also related term: Crisis.

CRITICAL BIBLIOGRAPHY
Use: Textual criticism.

CRITICAL EDITING
Use: Textual editing.

CRITICAL EDITION
See also related term: Textual criticism.
  Bibliographical. Publishing. Editing.
    Role of format for CRITICAL EDITION. Application of EDMAC; TEX. 1301.

CRITICAL JUDGMENT
See also related term: Literary theory and criticism.
  Literary movements.
    Romanticism. Theories of imagination; inspiration; relationship to rationality; CRITICAL JUDGMENT. 1074.

CRITICAL METHODOLOGY
  Literary theory and criticism.
    And aesthetics; CRITICAL METHODOLOGY. Bibliography (1988-1989). 1581.

CRITICISM
Used as a genre for works of criticism. See also: "literary theory and criticism."
  General literature. Television.
    Role of entertainment; relationship to CRITICISM. 874.
  Literary movements.
    Avant-garde. Relationship to mass culture; anarchism. Treatment in CRITICISM. 993.
  Professional topics. Comparative literature.
    Relationship to study of CRITICISM. 2621.

CRITICS
See also narrower term: Men critics.

CROCE, BENEDETTO (1866-1952)
  Genres.
    Theories of CROCE, BENEDETTO; reception in Germany. 2042.
  Literary theory and criticism. Literary history.
    Theories of De Sanctis, Francesco; CROCE, BENEDETTO. 1775.

CRONENBERG, DAVID (1948-)
  General literature. Film. Film genres: horror film.
    Treatment of women; womb; relationship to the grotesque; hysteria of men in CRONENBERG, DAVID: *Dead Ringers.* Application of theories of Freud, Sigmund. 756.

CROSLAND, ALAN (1894-1936)
  General literature. Film.
    Use of sound in CROSLAND, ALAN: *The Jazz Singer* compared to use of Vitaphone in short film. 653.

CROSS-CULTURAL COMMUNICATION
Used for: Intercultural communication.
  Professional topics. Humanities.
    Role of culture studies; relationship to CROSS-CULTURAL COMMUNICATION. 2724.

CROSS-CULTURAL CONFLICT
See also related term: Culture.

CROSS-CULTURAL CONTACT
See also related term: Culture.

CROSS-CULTURAL RELATIONS
See also related term: Culture.

CROSS-DISCIPLINARY WRITING
Use: Writing across the curriculum.

CRUCIFIXION OF CHRIST
See also related term: Christ.

CUBA
  General literature. Film in CUBA.
    Interview with Arias Polo, Arturo. 392.
    —— with Váldes, Oscar. 510.
  General literature. Film in CUBA (1980-1989). 497.

CUBAN EXILES
See also related term: Exile.

CUKOR, GEORGE (1899-1983)
  General literature. Film.
    Role of collaboration in CUKOR, GEORGE: *Holiday*; relationship to studio system in Hollywood (1935-1939). 499.

CULLER, JONATHAN (1944-)
  Literary theory and criticism. Narrative theory.
    Theories of CULLER, JONATHAN; Miller, J. Hillis. 1821.
  Literary theory and criticism. Postmodernist literary theory and criticism.
    Relationship to religion. Theories of CULLER, JONATHAN; Heidegger, Martin. 1868.
  Literary theory and criticism. Reader-response theory and criticism.
    Role of reader; relationship to American fiction. Theories of Mailloux, Steven compared to Fish, Stanley; CULLER, JONATHAN. Review article. 1918.
  Literary theory and criticism. Structuralist literary theory and criticism.
    Compared to poststructuralist literary theory and criticism. Role of theories of Saussure, Ferdinand de in theories of CULLER, JONATHAN. 2026.
    Theories of CULLER, JONATHAN: *Structuralist Poetics.* 2035.

CULTS
  Bibliographical. Manuscripts. Illuminated manuscripts. 1300-1399.
    Relationship to CULTS of John the Baptist, Saint; John the Apostle, Saint. 1138.

CULTURAL ADAPTATION
See also related term: Culture.

CULTURAL ALIENATION
See also related term: Culture.

CULTURAL AUTHENTICITY
See also related term: Culture.

CULTURAL CHANGE
See also related term: Culture.
  General literature. Film in China.
    Treatment of CULTURAL CHANGE; relationship to Fifth Generation. 413.

CULTURAL CONSERVATISM
  Professional topics. Humanities.
    Rhetoric; relationship to CULTURAL CONSERVATISM; study example: Isocrates; Erasmus, Desiderius; Weaver, Richard M. Dissertation abstract. 2653.

CULTURAL CONTEXT
See also related term: Culture.
  Literary theory and criticism.
    Role of CULTURAL CONTEXT in interpretation. 1502.
    Role of text; relationship to CULTURAL CONTEXT. Theories of Barthes, Roland. 1488.
  Professional topics. Humanities.
    On teaching of writing; relationship to CULTURAL CONTEXT. Dissertation abstract. 2705.

CULTURAL CRITICISM
  Bibliographical. Publishing.
    Of comic book; relationship to CULTURAL CRITICISM. 1251.
  Literary theory and criticism.
    CULTURAL CRITICISM. Theories of Turner, Victor Witter. 1310.
    ——; relationship to teaching of writing. 1326.
    Relationship to CULTURAL CRITICISM. Application of theories of Propp, Vladimir Iakovlevich. 1391.

CULTURAL DIFFERENCES
See also related term: Culture.

CULTURAL DOMINANCE
See also related term: Culture.
  General literature. Television.
    Role of CULTURAL DOMINANCE; relationship to commercialism; popular culture. Application of theories of Bourdieu, Pierre. 867.

CULTURAL HISTORY
See also related term: Culture.
  General literature.
    Relationship to CULTURAL HISTORY; historiography. Sources in Herodotus. 184.

CULTURAL HOMOGENEITY
See also related term: Culture.

CULTURAL IDENTITY
See also related term: Culture.
  General literature. Film.
    Role of exile; relationship to CULTURAL IDENTITY; study example: Ruiz, Raúl: *Les Trois Couronnes du matelot*; Solanas, Fernando E.: *Tangos—L'Exil de Gardel.* 526.
  General literature. Television in Europe.
    Role of CULTURAL IDENTITY. 900.

SEE CLASSIFIED SEQUENCE FOR ADDITIONAL ENTRIES

CULTURAL INTEGRATION
See also related term: Culture.

CULTURAL KNOWLEDGE
Used for: Cultural literacy.
See also related term: Culture.
  Professional topics. Humanities.
    CULTURAL KNOWLEDGE. 2766.
    ——. Theories of Hirsch, Eric Donald. 2699.
    ——. Theories of Hirsch, Eric Donald: *Cultural Literacy*; Bloom, Allan David: *The Closing of the American Mind*. 2805.
    ——; intellectualism; relationship to theories of Bloom, Allan David: *The Closing of the American Mind*. 2774.
    On CULTURAL KNOWLEDGE. Theories of Bloom, Allan David; Hirsch, Eric Donald. 2824.
    Relationship to CULTURAL KNOWLEDGE. 2816.

CULTURAL LITERACY
Use: Cultural knowledge.

CULTURAL PATTERNS
See also related term: Culture.

CULTURAL PHENOMENA
See also narrower terms: Arts; Cultural change; Cultural identity; Religion.
See also related term: Culture.

CULTURAL PLURALISM
See also related terms: Culture; Minorities.

CULTURAL POLICY
See also related term: Culture.

CULTURAL SPACE
  General literature. Film in Chicago (1906-1908).
    And nickelodeon; amusement park as CULTURAL SPACE; relationship to sexuality of women. 536.

CULTURAL TRADITION
See also related term: Culture.

CULTURAL VALUES
See also related term: Culture.

CULTURE
See also narrower terms: Mass culture; National culture; Popular culture; Western culture.
See also related terms: Counterculture; Cultural change; Cultural context; Cultural dominance; Cultural history; Cultural identity; Cultural knowledge; Institution.
See also: entries for culture in specific countries by consulting the index under the adjectival form of the country.
  General literature.
    Language; relationship to CULTURE. 80.
    Text; relationship to CULTURE. 73.
  General literature. 1800-1999.
    Role of gender; relationship to CULTURE. 190.
  General literature. Television.
    Role of CULTURE in *Cheers*. 876.
  Genres. Poetry. Pastoral poetry.
    Relationship to CULTURE. Dissertation abstract. 2313.
  Literary theory and criticism. Feminist literary theory and criticism.
    Role of women; relationship to writing; CULTURE. 1708.
  Literary theory and criticism. Philosophical literary theory and criticism.
    History; relationship to CULTURE. Theories of Kant, Immanuel compared to Dilthey, Wilhelm. 1854.
  Professional topics. Humanities.
    Canon; relationship to CULTURE; art. 2817.
    Relationship to ideology; CULTURE. Theories of Geertz, Clifford. 2746.
  Professional topics. Humanities in United States.
    Relationship to CULTURE. Theories of Bloom, Allan David: *The Closing of the American Mind*. 2773.

CULTURE STUDIES
  General literature. Television.
    Relationship to CULTURE STUDIES. Review article. 863.
  Literary forms. Rhetoric.
    Relationship to CULTURE STUDIES. Interview with Spivak, Gayatri Chakravorty. 2490.
  Literary theory and criticism.
    Relationship to CULTURE STUDIES. Theories of Thompson, Edward Palmer; Hobsbawm, Eric J. 1335.
  Professional topics. Humanities.
    Role of CULTURE STUDIES; relationship to cross-cultural communication. 2724.
    Role of politics; relationship to CULTURE STUDIES. 2811.

A CURRENT AFFAIR—STUDY EXAMPLE
  General literature. Television.
    Tabloid television; study example: *A CURRENT AFFAIR*. 869.

CURRENT EVENTS
See also related term: News.

CURRICULUM
  Professional topics. Humanities.
    CURRICULUM; relationship to marketplace. 2684.
    —— at Italian universities (1100-1599). 2742.
    Role of CURRICULUM in English studies. 2726.

CURTIZ, MICHAEL (1888-1962)
  General literature. Film.
    Role of myth; genre; relationship to history in CURTIZ, MICHAEL: *The Charge of the Light Brigade*. 587.
    Role of politics; myth in CURTIZ, MICHAEL: *Casablanca*. Psychoanalytic approach. 343.

CYBERNETICS
  General literature. Film. Film adaptation.
    Treatment of CYBERNETICS in Scott, Ridley: *Blade Runner* as film adaptation of Dick, Philip K.: *Do Androids Dream of Electric Sheep?* 733.
  Literary theory and criticism. Semiotic literary theory and criticism.
    Relationship to CYBERNETICS; information theory. Theories of Saussure, Ferdinand de; Peirce, Charles Sanders; Bense, Max. 1971.

CZECH CRITICISM
See also narrower term: Prague School of Linguistics.

CZECHOSLOVAKIA
  Bibliographical. Printing in CZECHOSLOVAKIA. 1500-1599.
    By Had, Jan. 1157.
  Bibliographical in CZECHOSLOVAKIA. 1108.

DACIA
See also related term: Romania.

DÄLLENBACH, LUCIEN
  Literary theory and criticism. Narrative theory.
    Mise en abyme. Theories of DÄLLENBACH, LUCIEN: *Le Récit spéculaire*; Bal, Mieke. 1817.

DANCE
See also related term: Dancer.
  Literary movements.
    Postmodernism. Role of DANCE. 1049.

DANCE IMAGERY
See also related term: Dance.

DANCE METAPHOR
See also related term: Dance.

DANCE MUSIC
See also related term: Dance.

DANCE NOTATION
See also related term: Dance.

DANCE SYMBOLISM
See also related term: Dance.

DANCER
See also related terms: Dance; Performance art.
  General literature. Film.
    Treatment of DANCER; relationship to play; American dream. 258.

DANDY
  Themes and figures. Don Juan and DANDY. 2846.

DANGER
See also related terms: Crisis; Fear.

DARK AGES
Use: Middle Ages.

DARWIN, CHARLES ROBERT (1809-1882)
  General literature. Theater.
    Representation of nature in theatrical production; relationship to Realist movement and Naturalism. Theories of DARWIN, CHARLES ROBERT; Le Brun, Charles. 960.

DATA BASE
Use: Database.

DATA PROCESSING
See also related term: Computer.

DATABASE
Used for: Data base.

DATABASE—APPLICATION
  Professional topics. Computer-assisted research.
    Application of DATABASE; relationship to humanities. 2641.

DAVENPORT, TOM
  General literature. Film. Film genres: documentary film.
    Treatment of gospel music in DAVENPORT, TOM: *A Singing Stream*. 808.

DAVIDSON, DONALD (1917-)
  Literary forms. Rhetoric.
    Paralogism; relationship to dialogism. Sources in sophistry. Theories of DAVIDSON, DONALD; Derrida, Jacques; Bakhtin, Mikhail Mikhaïlovich. 2462.

DBASE III+—APPLICATION
  Bibliographical. Manuscripts. Manuscript collections.
    Application of DBASE III+. 1144.

DDR
Use: East Germany.

DE MAN, PAUL (1919-1983)
Literary forms. Rhetoric.
And figures of speech. Theories of Barthes, Roland; DE MAN, PAUL. 2423.
Literary movements.
Modernism. Narrative; relationship to allegory. Treatment in DE MAN, PAUL. 1006.
Romanticism. Treatment in DE MAN, PAUL. 1080.
Literary theory and criticism.
By DE MAN, PAUL. Review article. 1394.
——; relationship to anti-Semitism. 1463.
——; relationship to history. Sources in Schiller, Johann Christoph Friedrich von; Kant, Immanuel. 1515.
——; relationship to history; politics. Review article. 1490.
Relationship to aesthetics of Romanticism. Theories of DE MAN, PAUL. 1352.
Representation; relationship to historicity. Treatment in Auerbach, Erich: *Mimesis*; DE MAN, PAUL. 1382.
Role of Bakhtin, Mikhail Mikhaïlovich compared to DE MAN, PAUL. 1520.
Role of DE MAN, PAUL. 1369, 1440, 1545.
——; relationship to fascism. Treatment in Derrida, Jacques: "Like the Sound of the Sea Deep within a Shell." 1546.
——; relationship to humanism. Review article. 1516.
——; relationship to theology. 1424.
——: *Confessions.* 1374.
Role of intention. Theories of DE MAN, PAUL. 1364.
Role of textuality. Treatment in DE MAN, PAUL; relationship to Empson, William. 1428.
Theories of DE MAN, PAUL. 1353, 1376, 1427.
——; relationship to Kierkegaard, Søren. 1494.
Literary theory and criticism. Deconstructionism.
Authority of writer; relationship to reader; allegory. Treatment in DE MAN, PAUL: "Rhetoric of Temporality." 1589.
Relationship to literary history. Theories of DE MAN, PAUL. 1615.
Relationship to Nazism. Theories of Heidegger, Martin; DE MAN, PAUL; Derrida, Jacques. 1612.
Role of DE MAN, PAUL. 1643.
Role of writing; relationship to politics. Theories of DE MAN, PAUL. 1631.
Theories of DE MAN, PAUL. Review article. 1605.
——; relationship to anti-Semitism. 1630.
——; relationship to Nazism. 1613.
——: *Allegories of Reading*; relationship to Austin, J. L. 1593.
——: "Rhetoric of Temporality"; *Allegories of Reading*. Review article. 1626.
——: "The Epistemology of Metaphor." 1638.
Theories of Derrida, Jacques; relationship to DE MAN, PAUL. 1609.
Literary theory and criticism. Linguistic literary theory and criticism.
Theories of DE MAN, PAUL; relationship to Heidegger, Martin. 1756.
Literary theory and criticism. Philosophical literary theory and criticism.
Role of DE MAN, PAUL. 1852.
Literary theory and criticism. Poststructuralist literary theory and criticism.
Role of subversion; relationship to ideology of liberalism. Theories of DE MAN, PAUL; Derrida, Jacques. 1884.

DE MAN, PAUL (1919-1983)—STUDY EXAMPLE
Literary theory and criticism.
In the Academy; relationship to rhetoric. Study example: DE MAN, PAUL. 1354.
Literary theory and criticism. Deconstructionism.
Role of discipleship. Study example: DE MAN, PAUL; Johnson, Barbara. 1583.

DE PALMA, BRIAN
Use: DePalma, Brian (1940-).

DE SANCTIS, FRANCESCO (1817-1883)
Literary theory and criticism. Literary history.
Theories of DE SANCTIS, FRANCESCO; Croce, Benedetto. 1775.

DE SICA, VITTORIO (1901-1974)
General literature. Film.
Iterative narrative in Ford, John: *How Green Was My Valley* compared to Stevens, George Cooper: *A Place in the Sun*; DE SICA, VITTORIO: *Umberto D.*; Olmi, Ermanno: *Il posto*. Application of theories of Genette, Gérard. 425.

DEACIDIFICATION
Bibliographical.
Role of DEACIDIFICATION; relationship to book preservation. 1088.

DEAD SEA SCROLLS
Used for: Qumran scrolls.
General literature.
Apocalyptic literature; relationship to DEAD SEA SCROLLS. 207.

DEATH
General literature. Film.
Treatment of DEATH. Dissertation abstract. 562.
General literature. Television.
Treatment of DEATH in news. 892.
Literary theory and criticism.
Role of DEATH in time. Theories of Heidegger, Martin compared to Levinas, Emmanuel. 1351.

Literary theory and criticism. Postmodernist literary theory and criticism.
Rhetoric; relationship to DEATH. 1870.

DEATH IMAGERY
See also related term: Death.

DEATH SCENE
See also related term: Death.

DEATHBED
See also related term: Death.

DEATHBED REPENTANCE
See also related term: Death.

DECEPTION
General literature. Television.
Treatment of DECEPTION of the public; relationship to Vietnam War in Crile, George: *The Uncounted Enemy: A Vietnam Deception*. 910.

DECLAMATION
See also narrower term: Suasoria.

DECONSTRUCTION
Literary theory and criticism. Hermeneutics and DECONSTRUCTION.
Relationship to religion. Theories of Steiner, George. 1728.

DECONSTRUCTIONISM
See also classified section: 1582 ff.
Used for: Deconstructionist criticism.
Bibliographical. Textual criticism.
Role of text compared to role in DECONSTRUCTIONISM. 1121.
Literary forms. Rhetoric. 1900-1999.
Relationship to structuralism; hermeneutics; DECONSTRUCTIONISM. 2417.
Literary forms. Translation.
English language translation of theories of DECONSTRUCTIONISM from French language (Modern). 2509, 2524, 2536.
Literary theory and criticism. Feminist literary theory and criticism.
Style; image; relationship to ideology compared to DECONSTRUCTIONISM. 1699.
Literary theory and criticism. Feminist literary theory and criticism and DECONSTRUCTIONISM. 1665.
Literary theory and criticism. Hermeneutics.
Role of subjectivity; relationship to DECONSTRUCTIONISM; humanism. Theories of Hegel, Georg Wilhelm Friedrich compared to Heidegger, Martin; Marx, Karl; Freud, Sigmund. 1716.
Literary theory and criticism. Psychoanalytic literary theory and criticism.
Relationship to DECONSTRUCTIONISM; feminist literary theory and criticism. 1911.

DECONSTRUCTIONISM—APPLICATION
Professional topics. Humanities.
Application of DECONSTRUCTIONISM. Theories of Derrida, Jacques. 2681.
——; relationship to rhetoric; logic. Theories of Derrida, Jacques. 2777.

DECONSTRUCTIONIST APPROACH
See also related term: Deconstructionism.
Documents applying specific approaches are so numerous that access to them is provided only in the electronic versions of the *Bibliography*.

DECONSTRUCTIONIST CRITICISM
Use: Deconstructionism.

DECREOLIZATION
See also related term: Creole languages.

DEFEAT
See also classified section: 2844.

DEFORMITY
See also related terms: Abnormality; Physical impairments.

DEICTIC PRONOUN
See also related term: Deixis.

DEIXIS
Genres. Drama.
DEIXIS; relationship to audience response. 2092.

DELBECQ, JEAN BAPTISTE (1776-1840)
Bibliographical. Printing. Illustration.
On woodcuts of Passion of Christ by DELBECQ, JEAN BAPTISTE and Schreiber, Wilhelm Ludwig. 1211.

DELFT
Bibliographical. Printing in DELFT (1450-1475). Illustration.
In Psalter. 1218.

DELUGE
Use: Flood.

DELUSION
See also related term: Madness.

DELVAUX, ANDRÉ (1926-)
General literature. Film. Film adaptation.
Of Yourcenar, Marguerite: *L'Œuvre au noir* by DELVAUX, ANDRÉ. 696.

SEE CLASSIFIED SEQUENCE FOR ADDITIONAL ENTRIES

DEMAGOGUERY
Literary forms. Rhetoric.
Relationship to DEMAGOGUERY. 2454.

DEMILLE, CECIL B. (1881-1959)
General literature. Film.
Role of religious groups; relationship to DEMILLE, CECIL B.: *King of Kings*. 478.

DEMISE
See also related term: Death.

DEMIURGE
See also related term: God.

DEMOCRACY
Professional topics. Humanities in United States.
Theories of Bloom, Allan David: *The Closing of the American Mind*; relationship to the past; DEMOCRACY; reality. 2661.

DEMOTT, JOEL
General literature. Film.
Treatment of social class; sexuality in DEMOTT, JOEL: *Demon Lover Diary*. 663.

DÉNARRÉ
General literature.
Topos; relationship to *DÉNARRÉ*. 173.

DENIAL
General literature. Film.
Treatment of DENIAL of human body in Siegel, Don: *Invasion of the Body Snatchers*; Kaufman, Philip: *Invasion of the Body Snatchers*. 442.

DENOUEMENT
General literature. Film. Film adaptation.
DENOUEMENT in film adaptation of Laclos, Pierre Ambroise François Choderlos de: *Les Liaisons dangereuses*. 732.

DEPALMA, BRIAN (1940-)
Used for: De Palma, Brian.
General literature. Film.
Postmodernism in Coppola, Francis Ford; Lucas, George; DEPALMA, BRIAN; Spielberg, Steven; Scorsese, Martin. Dissertation abstract. 630.
Role of misogyny in DEPALMA, BRIAN. 472.
Treatment of female figures in DEPALMA, BRIAN: *Body Double*; Lynch, David: *Blue Velvet* compared to Acker, Kathy: *Don Quixote, Which Was a Dream*. 356.

DEPRESSION
Literary theory and criticism.
Treatment of DEPRESSION. Theories of Kristeva, Julia: *Soleil noir, dépression et mélancolie*. 1447.

DEPTH PSYCHOLOGY
See also related term: The unconscious.

DERRIDA, JACQUES (1930-)
Figures of speech. Metaphor.
Relationship to enigma; epiphora. Theories of Aristotle; treatment in DERRIDA, JACQUES. 2361.
General literature. Film. Film theory and criticism.
Theories of DERRIDA, JACQUES. 822.
Literary forms. Rhetoric.
Future perfect tense in argumentation; relationship to psychoanalytic literary theory and criticism. Theories of Aristotle; Lacan, Jacques; DERRIDA, JACQUES. 2489.
Paralogism; relationship to dialogism. Sources in sophistry. Theories of Davidson, Donald; DERRIDA, JACQUES; Bakhtin, Mikhail Mikhaïlovich. 2462.
Literary forms. Translation. Translation theory.
Theories of Quine, W. V. O.; DERRIDA, JACQUES; Benjamin, Walter. 2574.
Literary movements.
Postmodernism. Relationship to architecture. Theories of DERRIDA, JACQUES; Kant, Immanuel. 1028.
——. Relationship to philosophy. Theories of Rorty, Richard; DERRIDA, JACQUES; Cavell, Stanley Louis. 1041.
Literary theory and criticism.
Indeterminacy; relationship to the future. Theories of DERRIDA, JACQUES compared to Kant, Immanuel; Rousseau, Jean-Jacques. 1317.
Interpretation. Theories of Hegel, Georg Wilhelm Friedrich; DERRIDA, JACQUES. Dissertation abstract. 1371.
Role of de Man, Paul; relationship to fascism. Treatment in DERRIDA, JACQUES: "Like the Sound of the Sea Deep within a Shell." 1546.
Role of text. Theories of Foucault, Michel: "Qu'est-ce qu'un auteur?"; *Folie et déraison*; DERRIDA, JACQUES: "La Pharmacie de Platon." 1555.
Subjectivity in Barthes, Roland; Foucault, Michel; DERRIDA, JACQUES. Dissertation abstract. 1344.
Theories of Lévi-Strauss, Claude; DERRIDA, JACQUES. 1421.
Literary theory and criticism. Deconstructionism.
And rhetorical criticism. Includes interview with DERRIDA, JACQUES. 1625.
Applied to Husserl, Edmund: *Erfahrung und Urteil*. On preface by DERRIDA, JACQUES. 1587.
Latvian language translation of excerpt from DERRIDA, JACQUES: *De la grammatologie*. 1628.
Parodic play; relationship to reason. Theories of DERRIDA, JACQUES compared to Levinas, Emmanuel. 1606.

Pathos. Theories of Nietzsche, Friedrich Wilhelm in theories of DERRIDA, JACQUES. 1586.
Philosophical language; relationship to poetic language. Treatment in Habermas, Jürgen; relationship to theories of DERRIDA, JACQUES. 1639.
Relationship to generative anthropology. Theories of DERRIDA, JACQUES. 1621.
Relationship to metaphysics. Theories of DERRIDA, JACQUES. 1629.
Relationship to mysticism; transgression. Theories of DERRIDA, JACQUES compared to Eckhart, Meister. 1592.
Relationship to Nazism. Theories of Heidegger, Martin; de Man, Paul; DERRIDA, JACQUES. 1612.
Relationship to the apocalypse. Theories of DERRIDA, JACQUES. 1610.
Relationship to violence. Treatment in DERRIDA, JACQUES compared to Levinas, Emmanuel. 1646.
Role of DERRIDA, JACQUES. 1619.
Role of Heidegger, Martin: *Zur Seinsfrage* in theories of DERRIDA, JACQUES. 1632.
Role of hierarchy; self-reflexiveness; relationship to philosophy; anthropology. Theories of DERRIDA, JACQUES; Dumont, Louis. 1599.
Role of language; relationship to technology. Theories of DERRIDA, JACQUES: *De la grammatologie* compared to Heidegger, Martin: "Die Frage nach der Technik." 1584.
Role of time; consciousness. Treatment in DERRIDA, JACQUES: *La Voix et le phénomène*; relationship to Husserl, Edmund. Dissertation abstract. 1582.
Sign; representation. Treatment in DERRIDA, JACQUES: *De la grammatologie* compared to Hegel, Georg Wilhelm Friedrich. 1594.
Theories of DERRIDA, JACQUES. 1600, 1622, 1633, 1640.
——. Review article. 1635.
——; relationship to de Man, Paul. 1609.
——; relationship to Heidegger, Martin. 1595, 1597, 1644.
——; relationship to Nietzsche, Friedrich Wilhelm. 1647.
——; Simmel, Georg. 1642.
——: *De la grammatologie* compared to Saussure, Ferdinand de: *Cours de linguistique générale*. 1588.
—— compared to Freud, Sigmund. 1618.
Theories of Descartes, René; relationship to theories of DERRIDA, JACQUES: "Cogito et histoire de la folie" compared to theories of Foucault, Michel. 1616.
Theories of Foucault, Michel: *Folie et déraison*; relationship to theories of DERRIDA, JACQUES. 1603.
Theories of Kant, Immanuel: *Kritik der Urteilskraft* in theories of DERRIDA, JACQUES: "Parergon." 1608.
Theories of Plato: *Pharmakon* in theories of DERRIDA, JACQUES. 1591.
Theories of Sartre, Jean-Paul; Hegel, Georg Wilhelm Friedrich; relationship to theories of DERRIDA, JACQUES. 1614.
Literary theory and criticism. Poststructuralist literary theory and criticism.
Application in teaching of writing; relationship to epistemology. Application of theories of DERRIDA, JACQUES; Husserl, Edmund. Dissertation abstract. 1879.
Role of otherness; relationship to laughter. Theories of Bakhtin, Mikhail Mikhaïlovich compared to DERRIDA, JACQUES. 1882.
Role of subversion; relationship to ideology of liberalism. Theories of de Man, Paul; DERRIDA, JACQUES. 1884.
Literary theory and criticism. Poststructuralist literary theory and criticism and structuralist literary theory and criticism.
Relationship to pragmatism. Theories of DERRIDA, JACQUES compared to Dewey, John. 1877.
Professional topics. Humanities.
Application of deconstructionism. Theories of DERRIDA, JACQUES. 2681.
——; relationship to rhetoric; logic. Theories of DERRIDA, JACQUES. 2777.
Composition studies in English departments. Application of theories of DERRIDA, JACQUES. 2779.
On ageism; sexism in universities. Theories of Eco, Umberto; DERRIDA, JACQUES. 2670.
Themes and figures. Flowers.
Relationship to theories of Hegel, Georg Wilhelm Friedrich: *Grundlinien der Philosophie des Rechts*; Freud, Sigmund: *Die Traumdeutung*; DERRIDA, JACQUES: *Glas*. Review article. 2860.

DESCARTES, RENÉ (1596-1650)
Professional topics. Humanities.
Role of dualism; holism; relationship to canon in literary studies. Theories of DESCARTES, RENÉ. 2679.

DESCRIPTION
Literary theory and criticism. Narrative theory.
On DESCRIPTION; relationship to reference. 1802.

DESIGNING WOMEN
General literature. Television.
Treatment of ordination of women in *DESIGNING WOMEN*. 904.

DESIRE
General literature. Film.
Treatment of artist; relationship to DESIRE in Mizoguchi Kenji. 329.
Treatment of DESIRE in Seidelman, Susan: *Desperately Seeking Susan*. Psychoanalytic approach. 249.
Genres. Fiction.
Relationship to DESIRE; reader. Psychoanalytic approach. 2145.
Genres. Poetry.
Relationship to DESIRE. 2286.

DESIRE

Literary theory and criticism. Semiotic literary theory and criticism.

Literary theory and criticism. Semiotic literary theory and criticism.
And psychoanalytic literary theory and criticism; role of signifier; relationship to DESIRE. 2004.

DESKTOP PUBLISHING
Bibliographical. Publishing. 1900-1999.
DESKTOP PUBLISHING. 1244.

DESPAIR
See also related term: Depression.

DETECTION
General literature. Film.
Treatment of DETECTION in Welles, Orson: *Citizen Kane* compared to Hampton, Christopher: *Able's Will.* 358.

DETECTIVE
See also narrower terms: Private eye; Women detectives.
See also related terms: Detection; Detective fiction.

DETECTIVE FICTION
See also classified section: 2161.
Used for: Who-done-it fiction.
See also narrower terms: Detective novel; Hard-boiled detective fiction.
See also related term: Crime fiction.
Literary theory and criticism.
Applied to DETECTIVE FICTION. 1563.
Literary theory and criticism. Reception theory.
Applied to DETECTIVE FICTION. Theories of Iser, Wolfgang: *Der Akt des Lesens.* 1943.

DETECTIVE FICTION—STUDY EXAMPLE
Literary theory and criticism. Narrative theory.
Self-reflexiveness; study example: DETECTIVE FICTION. 1823.

DETECTIVE FILM
General literature. Film. Film genres: DETECTIVE FILM.
And television; hard-boiled detective fiction. Treatment of private eye. Reference guide. 751.

DETECTIVE MAGAZINES
See also related term: Detective fiction.

DETECTIVE NOVEL
See also classified section: 2239 ff.

DETERMINISM
General literature.
Relationship to DETERMINISM; uncertainty. 192.

DEUTSCHE DEMOKRATISCHE REPUBLIK
Use: East Germany.

DEVELOPMENT OF LANGUAGE
See also related term: Cognition.

DEVICE
See also related term: Emblem.

DEVIL
See also classified section: 2845.

DEVIL IMAGERY
See also related term: Devil.

DEVOTIONAL LITERATURE
See also classified section: 2318 ff.
See also related term: Religion.

DEWAREEN
General literature. Television in Pakistan (1985-1989).
Treatment of gender; relationship to Pakistani society in *DEWAREEN*; *Tanhaiyan.* Dissertation abstract. 919.

DEWEY, JOHN (1859-1952)
Literary theory and criticism. Poststructuralist literary theory and criticism and structuralist literary theory and criticism.
Relationship to pragmatism. Theories of Derrida, Jacques compared to DEWEY, JOHN. 1877.

DIACHRONIC APPROACH
Documents applying specific approaches are so numerous that access to them is provided only in the electronic versions of the *Bibliography.*

DIAGNOSIS
See also related term: Medicine.

DIALECTIC
See also related term: Rhetoric.
Literary forms. Myth.
Relationship to DIALECTIC. Role in Plato. 2410.
Literary forms. Rhetoric.
DIALECTIC; relationship to rhetorical theory; interpersonal communication. 2471.
Relationship to DIALECTIC; collaboration. Theories of Burke, Kenneth compared to Rogers, Carl Ransom. 2461.
Literary theory and criticism. Reader-response theory and criticism.
On DIALECTIC. Application of theories of Hegel, Georg Wilhelm Friedrich. 1926.

DIALECTICS
General literature. Film.
DIALECTICS of narration. Dissertation abstract. 423.

DIALOGISM
Genres. Novel.
Spatial form compared to DIALOGISM. Theories of Frank, Joseph compared to Bakhtin, Mikhail Mikhaĭlovich. 2221.
Genres. Poetry.
DIALOGISM. Application of theories of Bakhtin, Mikhail Mikhaĭlovich. 2290.
Literary forms. Rhetoric.
Paralogism; relationship to DIALOGISM. Sources in sophistry. Theories of Davidson, Donald; Derrida, Jacques; Bakhtin, Mikhail Mikhaĭlovich. 2462.
Literary theory and criticism.
DIALOGISM; relationship to context; politics in novel. Theories of Bakhtin, Mikhail Mikhaĭlovich. 1531.
On DIALOGISM. Theories of Bakhtin, Mikhail Mikhaĭlovich. 1322.
Literary theory and criticism. Feminist literary theory and criticism.
DIALOGISM; relationship to difference; otherness. Application of theories of Bakhtin, Mikhail Mikhaĭlovich. 1676.
Literary theory and criticism. Semiotic literary theory and criticism.
On DIALOGISM. 1965.
Literary theory and criticism. Sociological literary theory and criticism.
Relationship to DIALOGISM. Theories of Bakhtin, Mikhail Mikhaĭlovich. 2021.

DIALOGUE
See also classified section: 2383 ff.
Genres. Novel. Modernist novel.
DIALOGUE; relationship to Dostoevskiĭ, Fëdor Mikhaĭlovich: *Zapiski iz podpol'ia.* Application of theories of Bakhtin, Mikhail Mikhaĭlovich. 2243.
Literary forms. Translation.
Of DIALOGUE of Koran; relationship to oral tradition. 2521.
Literary theory and criticism.
DIALOGUE. Theories of Bakhtin, Mikhail Mikhaĭlovich. 1437.
———; relationship to intersubjectivity. Theories of Bakhtin, Mikhail Mikhaĭlovich compared to Piaget, Jean; Freud, Sigmund. 1384.
Literary theory and criticism. Structuralist literary theory and criticism.
On DIALOGUE. Theories of Bakhtin, Mikhail Mikhaĭlovich; Buber, Martin. 2032.

DIALOGUE MARKING
See also related term: Dialogue.

DIALOGUE PROCESSES
See also related term: Dialogue.

DIALOGUE STRUCTURE
See also related term: Dialogue.

DIARY
See also classified section: 2322.
Used for: Journal.
See also related term: Autobiography.

DIARY FORM
See also related term: Diary.

DIARY NOVEL
See also related term: Diary.

DIATHESIS
See also related term: Voice.

DICTAMEN
See also related term: Letters.

DICTATORSHIP
See also related term: Fascism.

DICTIONARY
Bibliographical. Printing. Illustration.
Of DICTIONARY. 1214.

DIDACTIC HYMN
See also related term: Didacticism.

DIDACTIC LITERATURE
See also related term: Didacticism.

DIDACTIC NOVEL
See also related term: Didacticism.

DIDACTICISM
General literature.
Relationship to DIDACTICISM. 39.
General literature for children.
DIDACTICISM; relationship to catechism. 54.

DIEGESIS
See also related term: Mimesis.

DIFFERENCE
Literary theory and criticism. Deconstructionism.
Role of DIFFERENCE. 1604.
Literary theory and criticism. Feminist literary theory and criticism.
Dialogism; relationship to DIFFERENCE; otherness. Application of theories of Bakhtin, Mikhail Mikhaĭlovich. 1676.

SEE CLASSIFIED SEQUENCE FOR ADDITIONAL ENTRIES

DOCTOR

General literature. Film in United States (1930-1939).

Literary theory and criticism. Reader-response theory and criticism.
Role of time; DIFFERENCE in generations; relationship to reading. 1939.

DIJK, CHRISTOFFEL VAN
Bibliographical. Printing. Typography in Amsterdam. 1600-1799.
Role of DIJK, CHRISTOFFEL VAN; Kis, Miklós; relationship to typefaces in Armenian language. 1228.

DIJON
Genres. Novel. Sentimental novel.
Reception study: reception in France: DIJON. 2249.

DILTHEY, WILHELM (1833-1911)
Used for: Hoffner, Wilhelm.
Literary theory and criticism. Philosophical literary theory and criticism.
History; relationship to culture. Theories of Kant, Immanuel compared to DILTHEY, WILHELM. 1854.

DIME NOVEL
See also related term: Penny dreadful.

DIMENSION PICTURES—STUDY EXAMPLE
General literature. Film by independent filmmakers (1970-1979).
Study example: DIMENSION PICTURES. 458.

DIOMEDES—AS SOURCE
Literary forms. Satire.
As genre; relationship to metaphor. Sources in DIOMEDES. 2503.

DIRECT DISCOURSE
See also narrower term: Dialogue.

DIRECTING
See also related terms: Director; Film; Theatrical production.

DIRECTOR
General literature. Theater.
Role of DIRECTOR; spectator. 929.

DISAGREEING
See also related term: Speech acts.

DISAMBIGUATION
See also related term: Ambiguity.

DISASTER
See also related term: Catastrophe.

DISCIPLESHIP
Literary theory and criticism. Deconstructionism.
Role of DISCIPLESHIP. Study example: de Man, Paul; Johnson, Barbara. 1583.

DISCOURSE
See also narrower terms: Academic discourse; Legal discourse; Political discourse; Professional discourse; Scientific discourse.
See also related term: Discourse analysis.
General literature.
Authority in DISCOURSE; relationship to community. Dissertation abstract. 144.
DISCOURSE. 104.
General literature. Television: music television.
DISCOURSE; relationship to power compared to masque for royal court of Jacobean period. 858.
General literature. Theater.
Relationship to DISCOURSE. Semiotic approach. Theories of Ubersfeld, Anne. 937.
Literary forms. Rhetoric.
Ethos; relationship to DISCOURSE. 2482.
Literary theory and criticism.
Relationship to DISCOURSE. Application of theories of Foucault, Michel; relationship to Nietzsche, Friedrich Wilhelm. 1544.
Literary theory and criticism. Semiotic literary theory and criticism.
Applied to DISCOURSE of mass media; advertising. 1984.

DISCOURSE ANALYSIS
See also related term: Discourse.
Literary theory and criticism.
Relationship to DISCOURSE ANALYSIS. 1455.
Literary theory and criticism. Feminist literary theory and criticism.
Relationship to DISCOURSE ANALYSIS. Theories of Lacan, Jacques; Kristeva, Julia. 1670.
Literary theory and criticism. Linguistic literary theory and criticism.
On DISCOURSE ANALYSIS. 1735.

DISCOURSE ANALYSIS—APPLICATION
Professional topics. Humanities.
Application of DISCOURSE ANALYSIS in teaching of literature. 2807.

DISCOURSE COMMUNITY
See also related terms: Teaching of writing; Writing across the curriculum.
Professional topics. Humanities.
Writing across the curriculum; relationship to professional discourse; DISCOURSE COMMUNITY. 2795.

DISCOURSE FRAMING
Literary forms. Rhetoric.
In Wilson, Edward Osborne: *On Human Nature*; relationship to DISCOURSE FRAMING. 2467.

DISCOURSE GRAMMAR
See also related term: Discourse analysis.

DISCOURSE PATTERNS
See also related term: Discourse.

DISCOURSE REPRESENTATION THEORY
See also related term: Discourse.

DISCOURSE STRATEGIES
See also related terms: Discourse; Discourse analysis.

DISCOURSE STRUCTURE
See also related terms: Discourse; Discourse analysis.

DISCOURSE TYPES
See also related terms: Discourse; Discourse analysis.

DISEASES
See also narrower terms: Cancer; Tuberculosis.
See also related term: Physical impairments.

DISENCHANTMENT
General literature.
Relationship to DISENCHANTMENT. 70.

DISFIGURED BODY
See also related term: Human body.

DISILLUSIONMENT
Genres. Fiction. 1800-1999.
Realism; relationship to DISILLUSIONMENT. Dissertation abstract. 2118.

DISNEY, WALT (1901-1966)
Used for: Yensid, Retlaw.
General literature. Film.
Naming of dwarf in DISNEY, WALT: *Snow White and the Seven Dwarfs*; relationship to Tolkien, J. R. R. 659.
On DISNEY, WALT: *Fantasia*. 652.
Treatment of animals; relationship to sympathy; sentimentality in Annaud, Jean-Jacques: *L'Ours* compared to DISNEY, WALT. 262.

DISORDER
General literature. Television.
Treatment of DISORDER in housekeeping by women in *Roseanne* compared to *Married ... with Children*. 912.

DISTANCE
General literature. Film. Film adaptation.
Of Shakespeare, William; relationship to formality; DISTANCE. 690.

DISTRIBUTION
See also related term: Publishing.

DIVIDED SELF
General literature. Film.
Treatment of DIVIDED SELF in Ray, Satyajit compared to Wells, H. G.; Rushdie, Salman. 505.

DIVINE GRACE
See also related term: God.

DIVINE JUDGMENT
See also related term: God.

DIVINE JUSTICE
See also related term: God.

DIVINE LOVE
See also related term: God.

DIVINE PROVIDENCE
See also related term: God.

DIVINE PUNISHMENT
See also related term: God.

DIVINE WILL
See also related term: God.

DIVISION
See also related term: Rhetoric.

DIVISO
Literary forms. Rhetoric.
DIVISO. 2479.

DIVORCE
See also related term: Marriage.

DMYTRYK, EDWARD (1908-)
General literature. Film. Film genres: *film noir*.
Nonverbal communication in Garnett, Tay: *The Postman Always Rings Twice*; Hawks, Howard: *The Big Sleep*; DMYTRYK, EDWARD: *Murder, My Sweet* compared to remakes by Rafelson, Bob; Winner, Michael; Richards, Dick. Dissertation abstract. 767.

DOCTOR
Used for: Physician.
See also narrower term: Psychiatrist.
General literature. Film in United States (1930-1939).
Treatment of DOCTOR. Includes filmography. 646.

Literary theory and criticism. Philosophical literary theory and criticism.
Relationship to DOCTOR. 1849.

DOCTOR-PATIENT RELATIONS
See also related term: Doctor.

DOCTOR WHO
General literature. Television.
On *DOCTOR WHO*; relationship to science fiction. Application of theories of Propp, Vladimir Iakovlevich. Dissertation abstract. 891.

DOCTORAL PROGRAMS
Professional topics. Humanities.
DOCTORAL PROGRAMS in English departments. 2825.

DOCTRINES
See also related term: Ideology.

DOCUDRAMA
See also related term: Television.
General literature. Film. Film genres: DOCUDRAMA.
On Hudson, Hugh: *Chariots of Fire.* 790.
General literature. Television: DOCUDRAMA.
Role of memory; relationship to fact. 849.
General literature. Television: DOCUDRAMA and movie of the week.
Treatment of social problems. 881.

DOCUMENTARY EDITING
Bibliographical.
Archival standards in DOCUMENTARY EDITING; use of *Anglo-American Cataloguing Rules II.* 1116.

DOCUMENTARY FILM
General literature. Film. Film genres: DOCUMENTARY FILM.
By Ophüls, Marcel. Includes interview. 791.
Collaboration. Dissertation abstract. 775.
Interview with Martín, Paolo. 747.
On Cholakov, Georgi and Ovcharov, Svetoslav: *Stefan Stambolov—sŭzidateliat i sŭsipateliat.* Interview. 779.
On Moore, Michael: *Roger and Me.* 750.
Relationship to *film noir* in Huston, John: *Let There Be Light.* 761.
Representation. Dissertation abstract. 793.
Role of Thomas, Dylan: *Deaths and Entrances* in Eldridge, John: *Wales—Green Mountain Black Mountain; Our Country.* 765.
Treatment of Abraham Lincoln Battalion in Buckner, Noel and Dore, Mary and Paskin, David and Sills, Sam: *The Good Fight.* 748.
Treatment of Basques in United States in Bordagaray, Stanley George, Jr.: *Amerikanuak: The Basques of the American West.* 816.
Treatment of gospel music in Davenport, Tom: *A Singing Stream.* 808.
Treatment of Shakers in Burns, Ken and Burns, Amy Stechler. 811.
General literature. Film. Film genres: DOCUMENTARY FILM (1970-1985) by women filmmakers.
Treatment of women. Dissertation abstract. 784.
General literature. Film. Film genres: DOCUMENTARY FILM for television.
Cinéma vérité in film by Drew Associates. Dissertation abstract. 768.
General literature. Film. Film genres: DOCUMENTARY FILM in Germany during Third Reich. 795.
General literature. Film. Film genres: DOCUMENTARY FILM in Israel.
Interview with Gitai, Amos. 800.
General literature. Film. Film genres: DOCUMENTARY FILM in Turkey.
Dissertation abstract. 815.
General literature. Film. Film genres: DOCUMENTARY FILM in U.S.S.R.
Treatment of youth; relationship to *glasnost'.* 770.

DOCUMENTARY PHOTOGRAPHY
Literary theory and criticism. Narrative theory.
Applied to DOCUMENTARY PHOTOGRAPHY; study example: photographs (1855) by Fenton, Roger. 1804.

DOCUMENTARY TELEVISION
See also related terms: Docudrama; Documentary film; Television.

DOCUMENTATION
Genres. Prose. Historiography.
Use of photographs as DOCUMENTATION; relationship to visual imagery. 2331.

DOLCE STIL NUOVO
See also related term: Lyric poetry.

DOM JUAN (CHARACTER)
See also related term: Don Juan.

DON JUAN
See also classified section: 2846.
General literature. Film.
Treatment of DON JUAN. 582.

DON JUANISM
See also related term: Libertinism.

DONATION
Bibliographical. Latin language literature. 700-799.
DONATION of book to Chiesa di San Clemente. Treatment in epigraph. 1111.

DONNADIEU, MARGUERITE
Use: Duras, Marguerite (1914-).

DOOR
See also related term: Threshold.

DOPPELGÄNGER
Use: The double.

DORE, MARY
General literature. Film. Film genres: documentary film.
Treatment of Abraham Lincoln Battalion in Buckner, Noel and DORE, MARY and Paskin, David and Sills, Sam: *The Good Fight.* 748.

DORPELLI, GIULIAN
Use: Pirandello, Luigi (1867-1936).

THE DOUBLE
Used for: Doppelgänger.
General literature. Film.
Treatment of THE DOUBLE in Fassbinder, Rainer Werner. 612.

DOUGLAS, MARY (1921-)
Themes and figures. Transgression.
As the carnivalesque; relationship to social hierarchy. Application of theories of Bakhtin, Mikhail Mikhaïlovich; Elias, Norbert; DOUGLAS, MARY. 2926.

DOWRY
See also related term: Marriage.

DOXA
Literary theory and criticism. Semiotic literary theory and criticism.
DOXA. 1975.

DRAMA
See also classified section: 2062 ff.
See also narrower terms: Classical drama; Comic drama; Historical drama; Melodrama; Social drama; Television drama; Theater of the absurd; Tragic drama; Tragicomedy.
See also related terms: Drama theory; Dramatic adaptation; Dramatic structure; Dramatists; Performance; Theater.
See also: entries for drama in specific countries by consulting the index under the adjectival form of the country.
General literature. Film. Film adaptation.
And television in Great Britain (1959-1963). Realism; relationship to working class life in film adaptation; television adaptation of DRAMA; fiction. 711.
General literature. Theater.
And DRAMA. 946, 971.
——. Bibliography of feminist literary theory and criticism. 986.
Literary forms. Translation.
Of DRAMA. 2563.
Literary theory and criticism. Feminist literary theory and criticism.
Relationship to DRAMA. 1653.
Literary theory and criticism. Poststructuralist literary theory and criticism.
Applied to DRAMA. Dissertation abstract. 1874.

DRAMA THEORY
See also related term: Drama.
Genres. Drama.
DRAMA THEORY. 2065.

DRAMATIC ADAPTATION
See also related terms: Drama; Theatrical adaptation.
General literature. Film. Film adaptation.
And DRAMATIC ADAPTATION of Laclos, Pierre Ambroise François Choderlos de: *Les Liaisons dangereuses.* 708.
Of Puig, Manuel: *El beso de la mujer araña* compared to DRAMATIC ADAPTATION. 678.

DRAMATIC BEGINNING
See also related term: Drama.

DRAMATIC CONVENTIONS
See also related term: Drama.

DRAMATIC CYCLE
See also related term: Drama.

DRAMATIC DIALOGUE
Literary forms. Dialogue in narrative.
Compared to DRAMATIC DIALOGUE; relationship to teaching of writing. 2383.

DRAMATIC FORM
See also related terms: Drama; Dramatic structure.

DRAMATIC IRONY
Use: Irony.

DRAMATIC STRUCTURE
See also related term: Drama.
Genres. Drama.
DRAMATIC STRUCTURE. 2083.

DRAMATIC TECHNIQUE
See also related term: Drama.

DRAMATIC TENSION
See also related term: Drama.

DRAMATISM
See also related term: Drama.

DRAMATISTS
Used for: Playwrights.
See also narrower terms: Black dramatists; Jesuit dramatists.
See also related term: Drama.
  Genres. Drama.
    Role of DRAMATISTS. Dissertation abstract. 2078.
DRAMATURG
See also related term: Drama.
DRAMATURGY
See also related term: Drama.
DREAM
See also classified section: 2847.
See also related term: Dream imagery.
  General literature. Film.
    Treatment of DREAM; relationship to initiation in Fleming, Victor: *The Wizard of Oz* compared to Lynch, David: *Blue Velvet.* Psychoanalytic approach. 453.
  Genres. Drama.
    Relationship to DREAM. 2081.
  Literary theory and criticism. Psychoanalytic literary theory and criticism.
    Role of DREAM; relationship to the future. Theories of Freud, Sigmund. 1894.
DREAM ALLEGORY
See also related term: Dream.
DREAM BOOK
See also related term: Dream.
DREAM IMAGERY
See also related term: Dream.
  General literature. Film.
    DREAM IMAGERY in Tarkovskiĭ, Andreĭ A.: *Zerkalo; Stalker.* 522.
DREAM SYMBOLISM
See also related term: Dream.
DREAM VISION
See also related term: Dream.
DREAM WORLD
See also related term: Dream.
DREAMER
See also related term: Dream.
DREAMING
See also related term: Dream.
DREW ASSOCIATES
  General literature. Film. Film genres: documentary film for television.
    Cinéma vérité in film by DREW ASSOCIATES. Dissertation abstract. 768.
DREYER, ERICH
  Bibliographical. Printing. Illustration in Germany. 1900-1999.
    By DREYER, ERICH; Wendt, Max of three-dimensional pictures. 1217.
DREYFUSS, RANDY (1956-)
  General literature. Film.
    Treatment in Medved, Harry and DREYFUSS, RANDY: *The Fifty Worst Films of All Time.* 560.
DUAL CODING
See also related term: Memory.
DUAL CODING THEORY
See also related terms: Cognition; Memory.
DUALISM
  Professional topics. Humanities.
    Role of DUALISM; holism; relationship to canon in literary studies. Theories of Descartes, René. 2679.
DUBBING
  General literature. Film. Film adaptation.
    Role of DUBBING in Spanish language translation in film adaptation of Queneau, Raymond: *Zazie dans le métro.* 728.
  General literature. Television.
    Subtitles; DUBBING. 883.
DULAC, GERMAINE (1882-1942)
Used for: Saisset-Schneider, Charlotte-Elisabeth-Germaine.
  General literature. Film in France by women filmmakers.
    Feminism in DULAC, GERMAINE; Epstein, Marie; Varda, Agnès. 336.
DUMONT, LOUIS (1911-)
  Literary theory and criticism. Deconstructionism.
    Role of hierarchy; self-reflexiveness; relationship to philosophy; anthropology. Theories of Derrida, Jacques; DUMONT, LOUIS. 1599.
DUPLICITY
  Genres. Autobiography by women writers. 1700-1899.
    Treatment of the self; relationship to DUPLICITY in narrative. 2052.
DURAS, MARGUERITE (1914-)
Used for: Donnadieu, Marguerite.
  General literature. Film.
    By DURAS, MARGUERITE; relationship to feminism; psychoanalysis. Dissertation abstract. 561.

Narrative distance; narrative voice in DURAS, MARGUERITE. Dissertation abstract. 602.
Subjectivity in DURAS, MARGUERITE. Narratological approach. Dissertation abstract. 353.
Voice-over narration in DURAS, MARGUERITE: *India Song.* 263.
  General literature. Film. Film adaptation.
    Treatment of gender in DURAS, MARGUERITE: *Le Navire Night* compared to prose version. 676.
DWARF
  General literature. Film.
    Naming of DWARF in Disney, Walt: *Snow White and the Seven Dwarfs*; relationship to Tolkien, J. R. R. 659.
DYING
See also related term: Death.
DYSLEXIA
See also related term: Reading.
DYSTOPIA
Used for: Antiutopia.
See also related terms: Dystopian fiction; Dystopian novel; Utopia.
  General literature. Film. Film genres: science fiction film.
    Treatment of time travel; primal scene; DYSTOPIA in Cameron, James: *The Terminator.* 792.
DYSTOPIAN FICTION
Used for: Antiutopian fiction.
See also narrower term: Dystopian novel.
See also related terms: Dystopia; Utopia; Utopian fiction.
  Genres. Fiction. Utopian fiction and DYSTOPIAN FICTION. 1500-1999.
    Treatment of medicine. 2185.
DYSTOPIAN NOVEL
See also classified section: 2242.
Used for: Antiutopian novel.
See also related terms: Dystopia; Utopia.
EAST ASIA
See also narrower terms: China; Japan; Korea.
EAST ASIAN LITERATURE
See also narrower term: Chinese literature.
EAST GERMANY
Used for: DDR; Deutsche Demokratische Republik; GDR; German Democratic Republic.
  General literature. Film. Film theory and criticism in EAST GERMANY.
    And television theory; relationship to socialism. 832.
  General literature. Film in EAST GERMANY. 278.
  Professional topics. Censorship in EAST GERMANY; Poland.
    Relationship to socialism. 2591.
  Professional topics. Comparative literature.
    World literature; relationship to teacher training in EAST GERMANY. 2607.
EASTER PLAY
See also related term: Passion play.
EASTERN EUROPEAN FILMMAKERS
See also narrower terms: Hungarian filmmakers; Polish filmmakers; Yugoslavian filmmakers.
  General literature. Film by EASTERN EUROPEAN FILMMAKERS in United States; Europe. 523.
EASTERN ORTHODOX CHURCH
See also narrower term: Russian Orthodox Church.
EASTERN WORLD
See also related term: Western world.
EATON, REBECCA (1947-)
  General literature. Television.
    On *Mystery* (television program). Interview with EATON, REBECCA. 897.
ECCLESIASTICAL PROSE
Use: Religious prose.
ECCLESIOLOGY
See also related term: Church.
ECHO
See also related terms: Intertextuality; Repetition.
ECO, UMBERTO (1932-)
  General literature. Theater.
    Relationship to laughter; popular culture. Theories of Bakhtin, Mikhail Mikhaĭlovich; ECO, UMBERTO; Fo, Dario. 943.
  Professional topics. Humanities.
    On ageism; sexism in universities. Theories of ECO, UMBERTO; Derrida, Jacques. 2670.
ECOFEMINISM
  Literary theory and criticism. Feminist literary theory and criticism.
    Relationship to ECOFEMINISM. 1685.
ECONOMIC CHANGE
See also related term: Economics.

ECONOMIC DEPRESSION
See also related term: Economics.

ECONOMIC FACTORS
See also related term: Economics.

ECONOMIC FORECASTING
See also related term: Economics.

ECONOMIC GROWTH
See also related term: Economics.

ECONOMIC SYSTEM
See also narrower term: Socialism.
See also related term: Economics.

ECONOMIC THEORY
See also related term: Economics.

ECONOMIC VALUE
See also classified section: 2848.
Used for: Value.

ECONOMICS
  General literature. Film.
    Treatment of sexual identity; relationship to ECONOMICS in Fassbinder, Rainer Werner: *Die Ehe der Maria Braun.* 385.
  Literary theory and criticism.
    Applied to ECONOMICS. 1476.

ECONOMIST
See also related term: Economics.

ECONOMY
See also related term: Economics.

ÉCRITURE FÉMININE
See also related term: Women writers.
  Literary theory and criticism. Feminist literary theory and criticism.
    Role of *ÉCRITURE FÉMININE.* 1664.

EDEL, LEON (1907-)
  Genres. Biography.
    Theories of EDEL, LEON. 2056.

EDINBURGH
  Bibliographical. Printing.
    Concurrent perfecting by Walker & Greig in EDINBURGH (1817-1822). 1176.

EDITALIA
Used for: Edizioni d'Italia.
  Bibliographical. Publishing.
    By EDITALIA. 1249.

EDITING
See also classified section: 1300 ff.
See also narrower term: Manuscript editing.
See also related term: Publishing.

EDITIONS
  Bibliographical. Printing (1503-1767).
    Of EDITIONS of Terence. Bibliography. 1190.

EDITOR
See also related terms: Editing; Publishing.

EDIZIONI D'ITALIA
Use: Editalia.

EDMAC—APPLICATION
  Bibliographical. Publishing. Editing.
    Role of format for critical edition. Application of EDMAC; TEX. 1301.

EDUCATION
See also narrower terms: Multicultural education; Secondary education.
See also related terms: Curriculum; Educational reform; Literacy; Research; Teaching.

EDUCATIONAL INSTITUTIONS
See also narrower term: Universities.

EDUCATIONAL REFORM
  Professional topics. Humanities in England.
    EDUCATIONAL REFORM; relationship to history. 2802.

EDWALL, ALLAN
  General literature. Film in Norway.
    Interview with EDWALL, ALLAN. 583.

EDWARD IV, KING OF ENGLAND (1442-1483)
  Bibliographical. Manuscripts. Illuminated manuscripts. 1400-1499.
    Collecting by EDWARD IV, KING OF ENGLAND; Henry VII, King of England. 1137.

EGO
See also related term: Psychoanalytic theory.

EGYPT
See also narrower term: Alexandria.

EIFFEL TOWER
See also related term: Paris.

EINAUDI
  Bibliographical. Publishing by EINAUDI (1935-1956).
    Treatment in Turi, Gabriele: *Casa Einaudi: Libri uomini idee oltre il fascismo.* 1234.

EISLER, HANNS (1898-1962)
  General literature. Film.
    Collaboration between Brecht, Bertolt and EISLER, HANNS. Dissertation abstract. 305.

ĖĬZENSHTEĬN, SERGEĬ MIKHAĬLOVICH (1898-1948)
  General literature. Film.
    On ĖĬZENSHTEĬN, SERGEĬ MIKHAĬLOVICH: *Rezhissura.* 359.
    Role of ĖĬZENSHTEĬN, SERGEĬ MIKHAĬLOVICH; relationship to Joyce, James. 641.
    Treatment of Russian history in ĖĬZENSHTEĬN, SERGEĬ MIKHAĬLOVICH: *Ivan Groznyĭ.* Sources in Shakespeare, William. 290.
  General literature. Film and theater.
    Role of ĖĬZENSHTEĬN, SERGEĬ MIKHAĬLOVICH. 441.

THE ELDERLY
See also related term: Ageism.

ELDRIDGE, JOHN (1917-)
  General literature. Film. Film genres: documentary film.
    Role of Thomas, Dylan: *Deaths and Entrances* in ELDRIDGE, JOHN: *Wales—Green Mountain Black Mountain; Our Country.* 765.

ELECTRA
See also related term: Oedipus complex.

ELECTRA COMPLEX
See also related term: Oedipus complex.

ELECTRONIC LANGUAGE
  Literary theory and criticism. Poststructuralist literary theory and criticism.
    On speech; writing; relationship to ELECTRONIC LANGUAGE; surveillance. Theories of Foucault, Michel. 1885.

ELECTRONIC PUBLISHING
  Bibliographical. Publishing.
    ELECTRONIC PUBLISHING. 1236.
  Professional topics. Research tools.
    Relationship to Spanish language literature (1900-1999). On ELECTRONIC PUBLISHING. 2828.

ELIAS, NORBERT (1897-)
  Themes and figures. Transgression.
    As the carnivalesque; relationship to social hierarchy. Application of theories of Bakhtin, Mikhail Mikhaĭlovich; ELIAS, NORBERT; Douglas, Mary. 2926.

ELITE CULTURE
See also related term: Mass culture.

ELLUL, JACQUES (1912-)
  Literary theory and criticism. Hermeneutics.
    Relationship to visual perception. Theories of ELLUL, JACQUES. 1723.

EMANCIPATION OF WOMEN
See also related terms: Feminism; Women.

EMBEDDED NARRATIVE
Use: Intercalated narrative.

EMBLEM
See also classified section: 2385 ff.
See also related term: Impresa.

EMBLEM BOOK
See also related term: Emblem.

EMBLEMATIC IMAGERY
See also related term: Emblem.

EMIC APPROACH
Documents applying specific approaches are so numerous that access to them is provided only in the electronic versions of the *Bibliography.*

EMMA, QUEEN OF ENGLAND (D. 1052)
Used for: Ælfgifu, Queen of England.
  Bibliographical. Manuscripts. Illuminated manuscripts in England. 900-1099.
    Patronage by Canute I, King of England; EMMA, QUEEN OF ENGLAND. 1139.

EMOTION RECOGNITION
See also related term: Emotions.

EMOTION TERMS
See also related term: Emotions.

EMOTIONAL DISORDERS
See also related term: Emotions.

EMOTIONALISM
See also related term: Emotions.

EMOTIONS
See also classified section: 2849.
See also narrower terms: Anxiety; Desire; Disenchantment; Fear; Love; Melancholy; Nostalgia; Obsession.
See also related terms: Affect; Attitudes.

SEE CLASSIFIED SEQUENCE FOR ADDITIONAL ENTRIES

EMPIRICAL APPROACH
See also related term: Empiricism.
Documents applying specific approaches are so numerous that access to them is provided only in the electronic versions of the *Bibliography*.

EMPIRICISM
See also related term: Positivism.
Literary theory and criticism.
Relationship to Constructivism; EMPIRICISM. 1526.
Relationship to EMPIRICISM. 1327.
Role of EMPIRICISM. 1311.
——; relationship to genre classification. 1433.
Literary theory and criticism in United States compared to Germany.
Relationship to EMPIRICISM. 1434.
Professional topics. Comparative literature.
Relationship to EMPIRICISM; literary theory. 2617.

EMPLOTMENT
See also related term: Plot.
General literature. Theater.
EMPLOTMENT; relationship to narrative. Feminist approach. Dissertation abstract. 974.

EMPLOYER-EMPLOYEE RELATIONS
See also related term: Workers.

EMPSON, WILLIAM (1906-1984)
Literary theory and criticism.
Role of textuality. Treatment in de Man, Paul; relationship to EMPSON, WILLIAM. 1428.

ENCLOSURE
Genres. Novel.
Treatment of ENCLOSURE; relationship to Modernism; Postmodernism. 2191.

ENCODING
See also related terms: Cognition; Memory.

ENCODING DEFICIT
See also related terms: Cognition; Memory.

END OF THE WORLD
See also related term: The apocalypse.

ENDING
See also related terms: Closure; Denouement.

ENDRESEN, SIGVE
General literature. Film.
On ENDRESEN, SIGVE: *For harde livet*. 457.

ENGLAND
See also narrower term: London.
Bibliographical. Manuscripts. Illuminated manuscripts in ENGLAND. 900-1099.
Patronage by Canute I, King of England; Emma, Queen of England. 1139.
Bibliographical. Manuscripts. Illuminated manuscripts in ENGLAND. 1000-1199. 1140.
Bibliographical. Manuscripts in ENGLAND. 400-1099 Old English period. 1133.
Bibliographical. Printing. Binding in ENGLAND. 1300-1499.
Study example: *Speculum Humanae Salvationis*; *Meditaciones de Passione Christi*. 1203.
Bibliographical. Printing. Binding in ENGLAND. 1400-1499.
Of Georges d'Esclavonie: *Le Château de virginité*. 1204.
Bibliographical. Printing. History of printing in ENGLAND. 1500-1699. 1195.
Bibliographical. Printing. Typography in ENGLAND. 1500-1699.
Role of font analysis. 1232.
Bibliographical. Printing in ENGLAND. 1800-1899. 1166.
Bibliographical. Printing in ENGLAND (ca. 1510).
Of *Short-Title Catalogue*: No. 14077c41 by Faques, Richard. 1171.
Bibliographical. Publishing. History of publishing in ENGLAND. 1700-1799.
Of English novel. 1278.
Bibliographical. Publishing. History of publishing in ENGLAND (1790-1860).
Relationship to popular culture. Dissertation abstract. 1276.
Bibliographical. Publishing in ENGLAND.
Relationship to law reports; printing. Application of Justus Project. 1272.
Bibliographical. Publishing in ENGLAND. 1700-1799.
Role of scribe; relationship to copyright. 1255.
Bibliographical. Publishing in ENGLAND (1850-1900).
By Brett, Edwin John of pulp fiction; penny dreadful. 1266.
Bibliographical. Publishing in ENGLAND (1889-1900).
By Bodley Head. 1267.
General literature. Film. Film adaptation (1920-1984).
Of women writers in ENGLAND and United States. Handbook. 697.
General literature. Film. Film genres: war film in ENGLAND during World War II.
Treatment of hero. 814.
Literary forms. Rhetoric.
History of rhetoric in ENGLAND; Scotland; United States (1650-1799). 2474.
Professional topics. Humanities. 1700-1799.
Pedagogy in ENGLAND compared to France; relationship to philosophy. Review article. 2823.

Professional topics. Humanities in ENGLAND.
Educational reform; relationship to history. 2802.

ENGLISH CHURCH MISSIONARY SOCIETY
Bibliographical. Printing. History of printing.
Of Arabic language literature in Malta by ENGLISH CHURCH MISSIONARY SOCIETY (1825-1845). Dissertation abstract. 1194.

ENGLISH COALITION CONFERENCE
Professional topics. Humanities.
On ENGLISH COALITION CONFERENCE (1987). 2655, 2671, 2675, 2689, 2750, 2767, 2768.

ENGLISH DEPARTMENTS
See also related term: English studies.
Professional topics. Humanities.
Composition studies in ENGLISH DEPARTMENTS. Application of theories of Derrida, Jacques. 2779.
Doctoral programs in ENGLISH DEPARTMENTS. 2825.
ENGLISH DEPARTMENTS. 2758, 2778.
Faculty development in ENGLISH DEPARTMENTS. 2740.
On tenure of faculty in ENGLISH DEPARTMENTS. 2721.
Role of ENGLISH DEPARTMENTS; language arts. 2697.
—— in Netherlandic universities. 2691.
Role of minorities in ENGLISH DEPARTMENTS. 2727.

ENGLISH DRAMA
General literature. Film.
On Rice, Tim: *Jesus Christ Superstar*; relationship to ENGLISH DRAMA (1100-1499). Pedagogical approach. 380.

ENGLISH LANGUAGE LITERATURE
General literature. ENGLISH LANGUAGE LITERATURE. 1900-1999.
Relationship to colonialism. 110.
General literature. Film. ENGLISH LANGUAGE LITERATURE; German language literature.
Treatment of prostitute. Dissertation abstract. 597.
General literature by postcolonial writers. ENGLISH LANGUAGE LITERATURE. 1900-1999. 51.
Relationship to marginality. 86.
Treatment of oppression. 95.
General literature by women writers. ENGLISH LANGUAGE LITERATURE.
Handbook. 28.
General literature for children. ENGLISH LANGUAGE LITERATURE. 1900-1999.
Narrative voice. 202.
——. Treatment of Middle Ages. 116.
Genres. Fiction. ENGLISH LANGUAGE LITERATURE. 1800-1999.
Treatment of Islam; Moslems. 2131.
Genres. Fiction. ENGLISH LANGUAGE LITERATURE. 1900-1999.
Treatment of Himalayas. 2140.
Treatment of India. 2124.
Genres. Fiction for children. ENGLISH LANGUAGE LITERATURE. 1900-1999. 2126.
Genres. Fiction for children (1938-1988). ENGLISH LANGUAGE LITERATURE.
Role of the fantastic. Dissertation abstract. 2136.
Themes and figures. Flood. ENGLISH LANGUAGE LITERATURE. 1900-1999. 2859.

ENGLISH LANGUAGE TRANSLATION
Bibliographical. Publishing.
On ENGLISH LANGUAGE TRANSLATION as business. 1247.
Literary forms. Translation.
ENGLISH LANGUAGE TRANSLATION of Sappho. 2550.
—— of theories of deconstructionism from French language (Modern). 2509, 2524, 2536.
On ENGLISH LANGUAGE TRANSLATION. 2513, 2539.
Literary theory and criticism. Feminist literary theory and criticism.
On ENGLISH LANGUAGE TRANSLATION of Irigaray, Luce: *Ce sexe qui n'en est pas un*. 1688.

ENGLISH LITERATURE
General literature. Film.
And ENGLISH LITERATURE; American literature; popular fiction. 389.

ENGLISH NOVEL
Bibliographical. Publishing. History of publishing in England. 1700-1799.
Of ENGLISH NOVEL. 1278.
General literature. Television: soap opera.
Treatment of family; sexuality; patriarchy compared to ENGLISH NOVEL (1700-1799). 909.

ENGLISH STUDIES
See also related term: English departments.
Literary movements.
Aesthetic movement. Relationship to ENGLISH STUDIES. 988.
Literary theory and criticism.
Relationship to ENGLISH STUDIES. 1538.
Professional topics. Humanities.
ENGLISH STUDIES. 2819.

Role of curriculum in ENGLISH STUDIES. 2726.

Role of ENGLISH STUDIES at Canadian universities. Application of theories of Arnold, Matthew: *Culture and Anarchy.* 2732

Role of literary theory and criticism in ENGLISH STUDIES. 2698.

ENGLISH WOMEN
See also narrower term: English women writers.

ENGLISH WOMEN WRITERS
Bibliographical. Publishing. Book trade. 1900-1999.
Rare book trade; relationship to ENGLISH WOMEN WRITERS (1600-1799). 1294.

ENGLISH WRITERS
See also narrower term: English women writers.

ENIGMA
Figures of speech. Metaphor.
Relationship to ENIGMA; epiphora. Theories of Aristotle; treatment in Derrida, Jacques. 2361.

ENLIGHTENMENT
See also: entries under headings for Enlightenment in specific countries by consulting the index under the adjectival form of the country.
Themes and figures. Horizon.
Relationship to literature of ENLIGHTENMENT; Realist movement. 2872.

ENSLAVEMENT
See also related term: Slavery.

ENTERTAINMENT
General literature. 1900-1999.
As ENTERTAINMENT. 75.
General literature. Television.
Role of advertising as ENTERTAINMENT. 889, 915.
Role of ENTERTAINMENT; relationship to criticism. 874.
——; relationship to mass media studies. 914.
General literature. Television in Great Britain and West Germany.
Relationship to ENTERTAINMENT. 856.

ENTERTAINMENT INDUSTRY
See also related term: Entertainment.

ENTERTAINMENTS
See also related term: Entertainment.

ENVIRONMENT
See also related terms: Nature; Setting.

EPIC FILM
General literature. Film. Film genres: EPIC FILM.
Treatment of history. 807.

EPIC POETRY
See also classified section: 2306 ff.
Used for: Heroic poetry.

EPIGRAPH
Bibliographical. Latin language literature. 700-799.
Donation of book to Chiesa di San Clemente. Treatment in EPIGRAPH. 1111.

EPIPHANY
Literary movements.
Romanticism. Treatment of stained-glass window of church as metaphor for EPIPHANY. 1079.

EPIPHORA
Figures of speech. Metaphor.
Relationship to enigma; EPIPHORA. Theories of Aristotle; treatment in Derrida, Jacques. 2361.

EPISTEMIC RHETORIC
Literary forms. Rhetoric.
EPISTEMIC RHETORIC. 2424.

EPISTEMOLOGY
Used for: Gnoseology.
See also narrower term: Empiricism.
See also related term: Knowledge.
General literature.
Role of fictionality in narrative; relationship to logic; EPISTEMOLOGY. 119.
Genres. Novel.
Relationship to knowledge; EPISTEMOLOGY. Theories of Boyle, Robert: *The Christian Virtuoso; Occasional Reflections on Several Subjects.* 2199.
Literary forms. Rhetoric.
Relationship to EPISTEMOLOGY. 2434, 2449.
Role of question; metaphor; image in scientific language; relationship to EPISTEMOLOGY. Theories of Meyer, Michel; Kant, Immanuel. 2427.
Sophistry; relationship to EPISTEMOLOGY; scientific discourse. 2443.
Literary forms. Rhetoric (1967-1989).
Relationship to EPISTEMOLOGY. 2430.
Literary theory and criticism.
Relationship to EPISTEMOLOGY of Positivism. Application of theories of Foucault, Michel; Habermas, Jürgen; Lyotard, Jean François. 1401.
Literary theory and criticism. Feminist literary theory and criticism.
On neologism; relationship to EPISTEMOLOGY. 1701.

Literary theory and criticism. Linguistic literary theory and criticism.
Compared to semiotic literary theory and criticism; relationship to EPISTEMOLOGY; scientific method. 1742.
Literary theory and criticism. Poststructuralist literary theory and criticism.
Application in teaching of writing; relationship to EPISTEMOLOGY. Application of theories of Derrida, Jacques; Husserl, Edmund. Dissertation abstract. 1879.

EPISTLE
See also related term: Letters.

EPISTOLARY FORM
See also related term: Letters.

EPISTOLARY STYLE
See also related term: Letters.

EPITAPH
Genres. Poetry.
As EPITAPH; relationship to representation. 2282.

ÉPSHTEĬN, MIKHAIL SEMENOVICH
Use: Golodnyĭ, Mikhail (1903-1949).

EPSTEIN, MARIE (1899-)
General literature. Film in France by women filmmakers.
Feminism in Dulac, Germaine; EPSTEIN, MARIE; Varda, Agnès. 336.

ERASMUS, DESIDERIUS (1469-1536)—STUDY EXAMPLE
Professional topics. Humanities.
Rhetoric; relationship to cultural conservatism; study example: Isocrates; ERASMUS, DESIDERIUS; Weaver, Richard M. Dissertation abstract. 2653.

ERMETICI
Use: Hermetism.

ERMETISMO
Use: Hermetism.

EROTIC LITERATURE
Literary theory and criticism.
Narrator; narratee in EROTIC LITERATURE. Theories of Genette, Gérard. 1340.

EROTICA
See also narrower term: Erotic literature.
See also related term: Sexuality.

EROTICISM
See also related term: Erotic literature.

ERZIEHUNGSROMAN
Use: Bildungsroman.

ESCAPE LITERATURE
See also narrower term: Fantasy fiction.

ESCHENBURG, JOHANN JOACHIM (1743-1820)
Used for: Urinus, August Friedrich.
Bibliographical. 1700-1799.
Treatment in ESCHENBURG, JOHANN JOACHIM: "Grundriss einer Anleitung zur Bücherkunde." 1095.

ESCLAVONIE, GEORGES D'
Use: Georges d'Esclavonie.

ESPERANTO LANGUAGE LITERATURE
General literature. ESPERANTO LANGUAGE LITERATURE. 58, 67, 93, 136, 154, 174, 180.
General literature. Theater. ESPERANTO LANGUAGE LITERATURE. 930.
Genres. Novel. ESPERANTO LANGUAGE LITERATURE. 2188, 2204.
Genres. Poetry. ESPERANTO LANGUAGE LITERATURE. 2260, 2280, 2281.
Prosody; rhyme. 2287.
Structuralist approach. Review article. 2268.

ESPERANTO LANGUAGE TRANSLATION
Literary forms. Translation.
ESPERANTO LANGUAGE TRANSLATION. 2510.
——. Interview with Tonkin, Humphrey. 2526.

ESSAY
See also classified section: 2323 ff.

ESSAYIST LITERACY
Literary forms. Rhetoric.
ESSAYIST LITERACY. 2497.

ESSENTIALLY CONTESTED CONCEPT
Literary forms. Rhetoric.
ESSENTIALLY CONTESTED CONCEPT; relationship to argumentation. 2450.

ESTHETICS
Use: Aesthetics.

ESTIENNE, GOMMAR
Bibliographical. Printing. Binding in France. 1500-1599.
By ESTIENNE, GOMMAR. 1205.

ESTONIA
Bibliographical. Publishing. History of publishing.
In ESTONIA. 1279.

SEE CLASSIFIED SEQUENCE FOR ADDITIONAL ENTRIES

ETERNAL FEMININE
See also related term: Femininity.

ETERNITY
See also related term: Time.

ETHICAL ACTION
See also related term: Ethics.

ETHICS
Used for: Moral law.
  Genres. Novel.
    Role of ETHICS. 2216, 2222.
  Literary movements.
    Postmodernism. Relationship to ETHICS; aesthetics. 1065.
  Literary theory and criticism.
    Relationship to ETHICS. 1524.
    ——. Role of theories of Sartre, Jean-Paul: *L'Etre et le néant; Cahiers pour une morale.* 1457.
    Role of reader; relationship to ETHICS. 1565.
    Role of the other; language; relationship to ETHICS; religion. Theories of Levinas, Emmanuel; Marion, Jean-Luc. 1577.
    Skepticism; relationship to ETHICS. Theories of Cavell, Stanley Louis: *The Claim of Reason* compared to Levinas, Emmanuel: *Totalité et infini; Autrement qu'être.* 1341.
  Literary theory and criticism. Feminist literary theory and criticism.
    And psychoanalytic literary theory and criticism; role of ETHICS; relationship to sexual difference. Theories of Foucault, Michel; Irigaray, Luce. 1677.
    Relationship to ETHICS; historiography. 1687.
  Literary theory and criticism. Philosophical literary theory and criticism.
    Relationship to ETHICS. 1855.

ETHNIC GROUPS
See also related terms: Ethnic identity; Ethnic literature; Minorities; Religious groups.

ETHNIC IDENTITY
See also narrower term: Jewish identity.
See also related terms: Ethnicity; National identity.
See also: entries for specific ethnic identities by consulting the index under the adjectival form of the country or area.
  Literary forms. Rhetoric.
    Relationship to ETHNIC IDENTITY. 2487.

ETHNIC LITERATURE
  Literary theory and criticism in Canada.
    Role of theme; relationship to ETHNIC LITERATURE. 1473.

ETHNIC TEXT
  General literature.
    Communication in ETHNIC TEXT. 212.

ETHNICITY
See also related term: Ethnic identity.
  Literary theory and criticism. Semiotic literary theory and criticism.
    Relationship to ETHNICITY. 2006.

ETHNOCENTRISM
See also related term: Ethnicity.

ETHNOGRAPHIC APPROACH
See also related term: Ethnography.
Documents applying specific approaches are so numerous that access to them is provided only in the electronic versions of the *Bibliography.*

ETHNOGRAPHIC FILM
See also related term: Ethnography.

ETHNOGRAPHIC TERMS
See also related term: Ethnography.

ETHNOGRAPHY
  General literature. Film for children (1920-1939).
    Relationship to ETHNOGRAPHY. Reception study. 314.
  General literature. Film in New Zealand.
    Treatment of tourism; ETHNOGRAPHY; relationship to Maori in McDonald, James. 264.

ETHNOLINGUISTIC APPROACH
Documents applying specific approaches are so numerous that access to them is provided only in the electronic versions of the *Bibliography.*

ETHNOLOGICAL APPROACH
Documents applying specific approaches are so numerous that access to them is provided only in the electronic versions of the *Bibliography.*

ETHOS
  Literary forms. Rhetoric.
    ETHOS; relationship to discourse. 2482.
    ——; relationship to poststructuralist literary theory and criticism. 2441.

ETIC APPROACH
Documents applying specific approaches are so numerous that access to them is provided only in the electronic versions of the *Bibliography.*

ETYMOLOGICAL APPROACH
Documents applying specific approaches are so numerous that access to them is provided only in the electronic versions of the *Bibliography.*

EUCHARIST (SACRAMENT OF)
Used for: Holy Communion; Holy Eucharist.
  Themes and figures. Cannibalism.
    Relationship to EUCHARIST (SACRAMENT OF); incorporation. 2838.

EUPHONY
See also related term: Sound.

EUROPE
See also narrower terms: Central Europe; Great Britain; Ireland.
  Bibliographical. Printing. History of printing in EUROPE. Middle Ages.
    And universities; relationship to modernity. 1193.
  General literature. Film by Eastern European filmmakers in United States; EUROPE. 523.
  General literature. Television and radio in EUROPE.
    Role of translator; interpreter. 886.
  General literature. Television in EUROPE.
    Role of cultural identity. 900.
  Literary theory and criticism.
    Otherness; relationship to identity in EUROPE. Theories of Bakhtin, Mikhail Mikhaïlovich. 1508.
  Professional topics. Comparative literature in EUROPE; United States.
    Role of literary theory and criticism. 2603.
  Professional topics. Humanities in EUROPE. 1400-1599. 2719, 2776.

EUROPEAN AMERICANS
See also narrower term: Italian Americans.

EUROPEAN FILMMAKERS
See also narrower term: Eastern European filmmakers.

EUROPEAN LITERARY TRADITION
See also related term: European literature.

EUROPEAN LITERATURE
  General literature. 1900-1999.
    World literature; relationship to EUROPEAN LITERATURE. 131.
  Literary movements.
    Aesthetic movement. Relationship to EUROPEAN LITERATURE; American literature. 987.

EUROPEAN PHILOSOPHY
  Literary theory and criticism. Poststructuralist literary theory and criticism.
    Relationship to EUROPEAN PHILOSOPHY. 1886.

EUROPEAN WRITERS
  Genres. Prose. Letters by EUROPEAN WRITERS. 2334.

EURYDICE
See also related term: Orpheus.

EVANGELISM
  General literature. Television in United States.
    Role of EVANGELISM. 873.

EVANGELIST
See also related term: Evangelism.

EVERGREEN REVIEW
  Bibliographical. Publishing in United States.
    By Grove Press; relationship to *EVERGREEN REVIEW.* 1250, 1274.
    ——; relationship to *EVERGREEN REVIEW;* jazz music. 1248.

EVIL
  General literature. Film.
    Treatment of EVIL at Journées Cinématographiques de Carthage in Tunis (1988). 367.

EVTUSHENKO, EVGENIĬ ALEKSANDROVICH (1933-)
  General literature. Film.
    On EVTUSHENKO, EVGENIĬ ALEKSANDROVICH: *Pokhorony Stalina.* Interview. 221.

EXCHANGE
  General literature. Film. Film adaptation.
    Treatment of identity; relationship to substitution; EXCHANGE in film adaptation of Döblin, Alfred: *Berlin Alexanderplatz* by Fassbinder, Rainer Werner. 694.

EXECUTION
See also related term: Death.

EXHIBITION
  Bibliographical.
    Role of library exhibition catalogues; relationship to EXHIBITION of rare books and manuscripts. 1097.
  General literature. Film.
    Role of audience in film history; relationship to EXHIBITION. Reception study. 225.
  General literature. Film in Chicago (1905-1928).
    Relationship to EXHIBITION in African American neighborhoods. 281.

EXILE
See also classified section: 2850 ff.
  General literature. Film.
    By Kieslowski, Krzysztof; relationship to EXILE. 295.

Role of EXILE; relationship to cultural identity; study example: Ruiz, Raúl: *Les Trois Couronnes du matelot*; Solanas, Fernando E.: *Tangos—L'Exil de Gardel*. 526.

Genres. Novel.
Treatment of New World; relationship to EXILE; prison. 2190.

Genres. Novel by women novelists. 1900-1999.
Treatment of EXILE in academia. Application of theories of Barthes, Roland: *S/Z*. 2213.

Genres. Poetry by women poets. 1900-1999.
Treatment of EXILE. 2292.

EXISTENCE
See also classified section: 2854.

EXISTENCE OF GOD
See also related term: God.

EXISTENTIAL CRISIS
See also related term: Existentialism.

EXISTENTIAL FREEDOM
See also related term: Existentialism.

EXISTENTIAL PESSIMISM
See also related term: Existentialism.

EXISTENTIALISM
See also related term: Theater of the absurd.
General literature.
Relationship to EXISTENTIALISM. 182.

EXPANSIONISM
See also related term: Imperialism.

EXPATRIATION
See also related term: Exile.

EXPEDITION
General literature. Film.
Treatment of EXPEDITION in Herzog, Werner: *Aguirre, der Zorn Gottes*. Dissertation abstract. 545.

EXPERIMENTAL APPROACH
Documents applying specific approaches are so numerous that access to them is provided only in the electronic versions of the *Bibliography*.

EXPERIMENTAL WRITING
Professional topics.
Role of EXPERIMENTAL WRITING; relationship to academic prose. 2586.

EXPERIMENTS
See also related term: Research.

EXPORTATION
Bibliographical. Publishing in Quebec.
EXPORTATION. 1269.

EXTENDED FAMILY
See also related term: Nuclear family.

EXTRATERRESTRIAL LIFE
Genres. Fiction. Science fiction.
Treatment of EXTRATERRESTRIAL LIFE. 2178.

EXTRATEXTUALITY
General literature.
Text; relationship to EXTRATEXTUALITY. Dissertation abstract. 126.

EYE MOVEMENT
See also related term: Reading.

FABIAN SOCIETY
See also related term: Socialism.

FABLE
Used for: Apologue.
Literary theory and criticism. Structuralist literary theory and criticism.
Applied to proverb; FABLE. Theories of Jakobson, Roman Osipovich. 2027.

FABLIAU
See also related term: Satire.

FACHBIBLIOTHEK FÜR THEATERWISSENSCHAFT
General literature. Theater.
Role of FACHBIBLIOTHEK FÜR THEATERWISSENSCHAFT at Universität Wien. 967.

FACSIMILE
Bibliographical. Printing. Illustration. Middle Ages.
Of FACSIMILE of Gutenberg Bible. 1213.

FACT
See also narrower term: Historical fact.
See also related terms: Reality; Truth.
General literature. Television: docudrama.
Role of memory; relationship to FACT. 849.

FACULTY
Professional topics. Humanities.
On tenure of FACULTY in English departments. 2721.

FACULTY DEVELOPMENT
Professional topics. Humanities.
FACULTY DEVELOPMENT in English departments. 2740.

FAIRY TALE
Use: Märchen.

FAITH
See also related terms: God; Religion.
Literary theory and criticism. 1800-1899.
FAITH. Theories of Balthasar, Hans Urs von. 1365.

FALLACY
Literary forms. Rhetoric.
Slippery slope argument; relationship to FALLACY. 2457, 2492.

FAMILY
See also narrower terms: Mother; Nuclear family.
See also related term: Society.
General literature. Film and television in United States (1954-1963).
Treatment of FAMILY. Dissertation abstract. 446.

General literature. Television: soap opera.
Treatment of FAMILY; sexuality; patriarchy compared to English novel (1700-1799). 909.

FAMILY GROUPS
See also related term: Family.

FAMILY INTERACTION
See also related term: Family.

FAMILY LIFE
See also related term: Family.

FAMILY RELATIONS
See also related term: Family.

FAMILY RITES
See also related term: Family.

FAMILY STRUCTURE
See also related term: Family.

FAN MAGAZINES
General literature. Film. Film genres: horror film.
Relationship to FAN MAGAZINES. 802.

FANCY
See also related terms: Fantasy; Imagination.

FANS
General literature. Film.
Role of song by FANS; relationship to Meyer, Nicholas: *Star Trek II: The Wrath of Khan*. 409.

General literature. Film. Film genres: science fiction film.
And television; relationship to women as FANS. Ethnography. Dissertation abstract. 746.

Genres. Fiction. Science fiction. 1800-1999.
Role of periodicals; relationship to FANS in United States. Publishing history. 2182.

THE FANTASTIC
See also classified section: 2855.
Genres. Fiction.
Role of THE FANTASTIC; relationship to teaching of writing. 2139.
Treatment of space; relationship to THE FANTASTIC. 2141.
Genres. Fiction for children (1938-1988). English language literature.
Role of THE FANTASTIC. Dissertation abstract. 2136.

FANTASY
See also related terms: Fantasy fiction; Science fiction; Utopian fiction.
General literature. Film.
Role of FANTASY; relationship to masculinity in Baky, Josef von: *Münchhausen*. 539.

FANTASY FICTION
See also classified section: 2162 ff.
See also related term: Fantasy.

FANTASY NOVEL
See also related term: Fantasy.

FAQUES, RICHARD (FL. 1509-1530)
Bibliographical. Printing in England (ca. 1510).
Of *Short-Title Catalogue*: No. 14077c41 by FAQUES, RICHARD. 1171.

FARCE
See also related term: Burlesque.

FASCISM
General literature. Film.
Mise en scène; narrative; relationship to FASCISM in Lang, Fritz: *Siegfried*; *Kriemhilds Rache*. 376.
Literary theory and criticism.
Relationship to FASCISM. 1350.
——; Romanticism. Theories of Lovejoy, Arthur Oncken; Spitzer, Leo. 1564.
Role of de Man, Paul; relationship to FASCISM. Treatment in Derrida, Jacques: "Like the Sound of the Sea Deep within a Shell." 1546.

SEE CLASSIFIED SEQUENCE FOR ADDITIONAL ENTRIES

FEMINISM

General literature. Film. Film theory and criticism in Great Britain.

Literary theory and criticism. Psychoanalytic literary theory and criticism.
On FASCISM. Treatment in Theweleit, Klaus: *Männerphantasien*; relationship to theories of Heidegger, Martin: *Einführung in die Metaphysik*. 1906.

FASHION
Literary movements.
Postmodernism. Relationship to FASHION. 1034.

FASSBINDER, RAINER WERNER (1946-1982)
General literature. Film.
By FASSBINDER, RAINER WERNER. 575.
——. Reception study: reception in United States. 617.
On FASSBINDER, RAINER WERNER: *Berlin Alexanderplatz*; relationship to television in West Germany. Dissertation abstract. 574.
Role of FASSBINDER, RAINER WERNER. 611.
Treatment of Braun, Maria (character) in FASSBINDER, RAINER WERNER: *Die Ehe der Maria Braun*; relationship to Faust in Goethe, Johann Wolfgang von: *Faust*. 613.
Treatment of sexual identity; relationship to economics in FASSBINDER, RAINER WERNER: *Die Ehe der Maria Braun*. 385.
Treatment of the double in FASSBINDER, RAINER WERNER. 612.
General literature. Film. Film adaptation.
Modernism in film adaptation of Döblin, Alfred: *Berlin Alexanderplatz* by FASSBINDER, RAINER WERNER. 680.
Role of autobiography in film adaptation of Döblin, Alfred: *Berlin Alexanderplatz* by FASSBINDER, RAINER WERNER. 701.
Treatment of identity; relationship to substitution; exchange in film adaptation of Döblin, Alfred: *Berlin Alexanderplatz* by FASSBINDER, RAINER WERNER. 694.
General literature. Film. Film genres.
Melodrama in FASSBINDER, RAINER WERNER. 804.
General literature. Film. Film theory and criticism.
Feminist film theory and criticism and psychoanalytic film theory and criticism; applied to FASSBINDER, RAINER WERNER: *Angst essen Seele auf*. 831.

FATALISM
General literature. Film.
Treatment of prophecy; FATALISM in Hawks, Howard: *Scarface*. 274.

FATHERHOOD
See also related term: Motherhood.

FATHERLAND
See also related term: Homeland.

FAUST
See also classified section: 2856 ff.
General literature. Film.
Treatment of Braun, Maria (character) in Fassbinder, Rainer Werner: *Die Ehe der Maria Braun*; relationship to FAUST in Goethe, Johann Wolfgang von: *Faust*. 613.
General literature. Film. Film adaptation.
Treatment of FAUST. Dissertation abstract. 731.

FEAR
Literary movements.
Enlightenment. Role of medicine; relationship to FEAR; anxiety. 998.

FELLINI, FEDERICO (1920-)
General literature. Film.
By FELLINI, FEDERICO. 450.
Cinematic technique; relationship to autobiography in FELLINI, FEDERICO: *La dolce vita*. 636.
Representation; relationship to signification in FELLINI, FEDERICO. 276.
Role of FELLINI, FEDERICO; Pirandello, Luigi. Dissertation abstract. 347.
Treatment of gaze of female protagonist in FELLINI, FEDERICO: *Giulietta degli spiriti*. 635.

FEMALE BODY
General literature. Film.
Narrative discourse. Treatment of FEMALE BODY in Rainer, Yvonne: *The Man Who Envied Women*. 350.
General literature. Theater: popular theater.
Role of burlesque; relationship to sexuality; FEMALE BODY. 926.

FEMALE CHARACTERS
Used for: Women characters.
See also narrower term: Female protagonist.
See also related term: Women.
General literature. Film.
Treatment of FEMALE CHARACTERS; phallocentrism in Allen, Woody. Feminist approach. 332.
——; relationship to feminism in Buñuel, Luis. 393.

FEMALE FIGURES
See also narrower terms: Beautiful woman; *Femme fatale*; Heroine; Lesbians; Mother; Prostitute; Spinster; Superwoman; Swan maiden; Widow; Women detectives.
See also related term: Women.
General literature. Film.
Treatment of FEMALE FIGURES in DePalma, Brian: *Body Double*; Lynch, David: *Blue Velvet* compared to Acker, Kathy: *Don Quixote, Which Was a Dream*. 356.

FEMALE IDENTITY
See also related term: Women.

General literature. Film.
Treatment of the self; FEMALE IDENTITY in Sanders-Brahms, Helma: *Deutschland, bleiche Mutter*; Brückner, Jutta: *Hungerjahre* compared to Wolf, Christa: *Kindheitsmuster*; Rehmann, Ruth: *Der Mann auf der Kanzel*. Dissertation abstract. 431.

FEMALE IMAGERY
See also related term: Women.

FEMALE IMPERSONATION
General literature.
Treatment of FEMALE IMPERSONATION; relationship to feminism; poststructuralism. Dissertation abstract. 204.

FEMALE INITIATION
See also related term: Women.

FEMALE-MALE RELATIONS
Use: Male-female relations.

FEMALE PERSONA
See also related term: Female identity.

FEMALE POINT OF VIEW
See also related term: Women.
General literature. Film.
Treatment of nuclear war; relationship to FEMALE POINT OF VIEW in Littman, Lynne: *Testament* compared to McCloy, Helen: *The Last Day*; Merril, Judith: *Shadow on the Hearth*. 271.

FEMALE PROTAGONIST
See also related term: Heroine.
General literature. Film.
Treatment of gaze of FEMALE PROTAGONIST in Fellini, Federico: *Giulietta degli spiriti*. 635.

FEMALE SELF
See also related terms: Female identity; Women.

FEMALE SPECTATOR
General literature. Film.
FEMALE SPECTATOR. 251.
——; relationship to magazines for women. 515.
General literature. Film. Film theory and criticism.
Sign; relationship to FEMALE SPECTATOR; feminist literary theory and criticism; semiotic literary theory and criticism. 840.
General literature. Film. Film theory and criticism in Australia.
FEMALE SPECTATOR. 825.
General literature. Film. Film theory and criticism in Canada.
FEMALE SPECTATOR. 820.
General literature. Film. Film theory and criticism in Great Britain.
Relationship to feminism; FEMALE SPECTATOR. 836.

FEMALE STUDENT
Professional topics. Humanities.
Role of men teachers as mentor to FEMALE STUDENT. 2743.

FEMALE VOICE
See also related term: Narrative voice.

THE FEMININE
Use: Femininity.

FEMININITY
Used for: The feminine.
See also related term: Women.
General literature. Film.
Treatment of FEMININITY; relationship to masquerade in Tourneur, Jacques: *Anne of the Indies*. 411.
General literature. Television.
Treatment of FEMININITY; narcissism in *Moonlighting* as television adaptation of Shakespeare, William: *The Taming of the Shrew*. Feminist approach. 908.

FEMINISM
General literature.
Treatment of female impersonation; relationship to FEMINISM; poststructuralism. Dissertation abstract. 204.
Treatment of FEMINISM; hysteria. Psychoanalytic approach. Theories of Freud, Sigmund. 24.
Writing; relationship to FEMINISM. 61.
General literature. Film.
As pornography; relationship to FEMINISM. Review article. 280.
By Duras, Marguerite; relationship to FEMINISM; psychoanalysis. Dissertation abstract. 561.
FEMINISM; relationship to film history. 524.
Relationship to FEMINISM. 405.
Treatment of female characters; relationship to FEMINISM in Buñuel, Luis. 393.
Treatment of FEMINISM in Cavani, Liliana: *Il portiere di notte*. 600.
General literature. Film. Film genres: avant-garde film and video art.
Relationship to FEMINISM. 787.
General literature. Film. Film theory and criticism.
Relationship to FEMINISM in Italy. 823.
General literature. Film. Film theory and criticism in Great Britain.
Relationship to FEMINISM; female spectator. 836.

General literature. Film by women filmmakers.
Relationship to FEMINISM. 486.

General literature. Film in France by women filmmakers.
FEMINISM in Dulac, Germaine; Epstein, Marie; Varda, Agnès. 336.
Role of FEMINISM. Review article. 625.

General literature. Television.
Treatment of women in home; relationship to FEMINISM. 906.

General literature by women writers.
Relationship to FEMINISM; utopia. 107.

Genres. Fiction. 1900-1999.
Treatment of FEMINISM. 2129.

Literary forms. Humor.
Relationship to FEMINISM; study example: McTiernan, John: *Die Hard.* 2399.

Literary forms. Rhetoric.
Argumentation; relationship to FEMINISM. Theories of Rogers, Carl Ransom. 2464.

Literary theory and criticism. Postmodernist literary theory and criticism.
Relationship to FEMINISM; television. 1866.
Relationship to psychoanalysis; FEMINISM. 1861.

Literary theory and criticism. Psychoanalytic literary theory and criticism.
Relationship to FEMINISM. 1893.
——. Theories of Freud, Sigmund: *Der Witz und seine Beziehung zum Unbewussten.* 1895.

Professional topics. Humanities.
Multicultural education; relationship to literacy; FEMINISM. Interview with Stimpson, Catharine R. 2657.
Role of African American women; relationship to FEMINISM. 2765.
Role of FEMINISM; relationship to women's studies in Brazil. 2729.
Role of women; relationship to FEMINISM. Review article. 2754.
Teaching of literature; relationship to FEMINISM. 2814.

FEMINIST
See also narrower term: Feminist writers.
See also related term: Feminism.

FEMINIST APPROACH
See also related terms: Feminism; Feminist literary theory and criticism; Women; Women writers.
Documents applying specific approaches are so numerous that access to them is provided only in the electronic versions of the *Bibliography.*

FEMINIST CRITICISM
Use: Feminist literary theory and criticism.

FEMINIST FILM THEORY AND CRITICISM
General literature. Film. Film theory and criticism.
FEMINIST FILM THEORY AND CRITICISM and psychoanalytic film theory and criticism; applied to Fassbinder, Rainer Werner: *Angst essen Seele auf.* 831.
General literature. Film. Film theory and criticism: FEMINIST FILM THEORY AND CRITICISM. 827.
Applied to Vidor, King: *Duel in the Sun.* 835.
Psychoanalytic approach. 826.

FEMINIST LITERARY THEORY AND CRITICISM
See also classified section: 1648 ff.
Used for: Feminist criticism.
General literature. Film. Film theory and criticism.
Sign; relationship to female spectator; FEMINIST LITERARY THEORY AND CRITICISM; semiotic literary theory and criticism. 840.
General literature. Theater.
And drama. Bibliography of FEMINIST LITERARY THEORY AND CRITICISM. 986.
Genres. Novel.
Treatment in FEMINIST LITERARY THEORY AND CRITICISM. 2209.
Literary theory and criticism. Psychoanalytic literary theory and criticism.
Relationship to deconstructionism; FEMINIST LITERARY THEORY AND CRITICISM. 1911.
Literary theory and criticism. Reader-response theory and criticism and FEMINIST LITERARY THEORY AND CRITICISM.
Relationship to the unconscious of women. Theories of Freud, Sigmund; Lacan, Jacques. 1940.
Professional topics. Humanities.
Canon; relationship to FEMINIST LITERARY THEORY AND CRITICISM. 2793.

FEMINIST LITERATURE
General literature.
FEMINIST LITERATURE. Treatment of gender; relationship to politics; avant-garde. 198.

FEMINIST STUDIES
Literary theory and criticism. Feminist literary theory and criticism.
Role of *FEMINIST STUDIES; Frontiers; Signs.* Dissertation abstract. 1693.

FEMINIST WRITERS
Genres. Fiction. Science fiction by FEMINIST WRITERS.
Subjectivity; relationship to humanism; Postmodernism. 2180.
Genres. Fiction by FEMINIST WRITERS. 2128.

FEMME FATALE
See also classified section: 2858.

FENTON, ROGER (1819-1869)
Literary theory and criticism. Narrative theory.
Applied to documentary photography; study example: photographs (1855) by FENTON, ROGER. 1804.

FESTIVALS
See also narrower term: Masquerade.

FESTSCHRIFT
Bibliographical. Publishing. 1900-1999.
Of FESTSCHRIFT. 1245.

FETISH
See also related term: Fetishism.

FETISHISM
General literature. Film.
Treatment of women; relationship to sexuality; FETISHISM in Sternberg, Josef von: *Der blaue Engel.* 579.

FEUILLETON
See also related term: Newspapers.

FICHTE, JOHANN GOTTLIEB (1762-1814)
Literary forms. Rhetoric.
Ad hominem argument. In FICHTE, JOHANN GOTTLIEB: *Wissenschaftslehre.* 2495.

FICTION
See also classified section: 2104 ff.
Used for: Prose fiction.
See also narrower terms: Dystopian fiction; Fantasy fiction; Modernist fiction; Novel; Popular fiction; Postmodernist fiction; Pulp fiction; Science fiction.
See also related terms: Metafiction; Prose.
See also: entries for fiction in specific countries by consulting the index under the adjectival form of the country.
General literature.
Narrative; relationship to FICTION; scientific discourse. 153.
General literature. Film.
And FICTION. Treatment of Middle East. 234.
General literature. Film. Film adaptation.
And television in Great Britain (1959-1963). Realism; relationship to working class life in film adaptation; television adaptation of drama; FICTION. 711.
Treatment of reality; relationship to FICTION in film adaptation of Fowles, John: *The French Lieutenant's Woman* by Reisz, Karel. 712.
Genres. Prose. Autobiographical prose.
And FICTION; representation of women; legal discourse (1700-1899). 2317.
Literary forms. Translation.
Translation of FICTION for children. 2546.
Literary theory and criticism.
And FICTION. Theories of Bakhtin, Mikhail Mikhaĭlovich. 1472.
FICTION. 1425.
Role of narrative; relationship to subject in FICTION. 1491.
Professional topics. Humanities.
Role of writing of FICTION in teaching of literature. 2713.
Teaching of writing; relationship to FICTION compared to prose. 2680.

FICTIONAL CONVENTIONS
See also related term: Fiction.

FICTIONALITY
General literature.
FICTIONALITY; relationship to anthropology. 101.
Role of FICTIONALITY in narrative; relationship to logic; epistemology. 119.
Genres. Fiction.
FICTIONALITY. Application of speech act theory. 2143.
——; relationship to mimesis. 2117.
Themes and figures. The Holocaust.
Relationship to history; FICTIONALITY. 2869.

FIDEISM
See also related term: Faith.

FIELD, JOANNA
Use: Milner, Marion Blackett (1900-).

FIELDWORK
See also related term: Collecting.

FIFTH GENERATION
General literature. Film in China.
Role of FIFTH GENERATION. 509.
Treatment of cultural change; relationship to FIFTH GENERATION. 413.

FIGURATION
See also related terms: Figures; Imagery; Symbolism.
Literary forms. Rhetoric.
FIGURATION; verisimilitude. Treatment in Weaver, Richard M. 2425.
Literary theory and criticism.
FIGURATION; relationship to literal meaning; study example: scientific language; philosophical language (1630-1800). Review article. 1506.

FIGURATIVE LANGUAGE
See also narrower term: Figures of speech.

SEE CLASSIFIED SEQUENCE FOR ADDITIONAL ENTRIES

FISH, STANLEY (1938-)

Literary theory and criticism. Linguistic literary theory and criticism.

FIGURES
See also narrower terms: Adolescents; Bastard; Criminal; The double; Female figures; The individual; Intellectuals; The other; Patient; Schlemiel; Television viewer.
See also related terms: Archetypes; Figuration.
 General literature.
  FIGURES; relationship to rhetoric; semiotics. 176.

FIGURES OF SPEECH
See also classified section: 2346 ff.
Used for: Rhetorical devices; Rhetorical figures; Tropes (rhetoric).
See also narrower terms: Analogy; Imagery; Irony; Metaphor; Metonymy; Simile; Symbol; Synecdoche; Synesthesia.
 Literary forms. Rhetoric.
  And FIGURES OF SPEECH. Theories of Barthes, Roland; de Man, Paul. 2423.
  Relationship to FIGURES OF SPEECH; psychoanalytic literary theory and criticism. 2477.

FILM
Used for: Cinema.
See also narrower terms: Animated film; Avant-garde film; Comic film; Detective film; Documentary film; Epic film; *Film noir*; Horror film; Mountain film; Musical film; Political film; Science fiction film; Serial film; Short film; Silent film; Spy film; War film.
See also related terms: Actors; Cinematic technique; Film adaptation; Film genres; Film industry; Film review; Film star; Film studies; Film theory and criticism; Popular culture.
 General literature. 1900-1999.
  Relationship to FILM; recordings. 115.
 General literature. Film.
  On Kluge, Alexander and Schamoni, Peter: *Brutalität im Stein*; relationship to FILM during Third Reich. 538.
 General literature. Television and FILM.
  Relationship to mass culture. 855.
 Genres. Fiction.
  And FILM. Narratological approach. 2114.
 Genres. Novel.
  And FILM. Treatment of threshold; relationship to the sacred; the profane. 2203.
 Literary theory and criticism.
  Relationship to FILM. Theories of Bakhtin, Mikhail Mikhaĭlovich. Review article. 1385.

FILM—AS SOURCE
 Genres. Novel. Popular romance novel.
  Plot. Sources in FILM of Hollywood. 2232.

FILM ADAPTATION
See also classified section: 672 ff.
See also related terms: Film; Screenplay.
 General literature. Film. Film adaptation.
  And television in Great Britain (1959-1963). Realism; relationship to working class life in FILM ADAPTATION; television adaptation of drama; fiction. 711.
 Genres. Short story.
  Relationship to FILM ADAPTATION. Edition. 2345.

FILM ARCHIVES
See also narrower term: Steven Spielberg Jewish Film Archive.
See also related term: Film.

FILM CONVENTIONS
See also related term: Film.

FILM CRITICISM
Use: Film theory and criticism.

FILM EDUCATION
 General literature. Film.
  FILM EDUCATION (1930-1939). 404.

FILM FESTIVAL
See also related term: Film.

FILM GENRES
See also classified section: 744 ff.
See also related term: Film.

FILM HISTORY
 General literature. Film.
  By Lang, Fritz; relationship to independent filmmakers; film studios. FILM HISTORY. 252.
  Feminism; relationship to FILM HISTORY. 524.
  Language. FILM HISTORY. 275.
  Role of audience in FILM HISTORY; relationship to exhibition. Reception study. 225.
  Treatment of women; relationship to consumerism. FILM HISTORY. 382.
  Use of sound in Asquith, Anthony: *A Cottage on Dartmoor*; relationship to FILM HISTORY. 590.
 General literature. Film. Film theory and criticism.
  Relationship to FILM HISTORY. 830.
 General literature. Film. Film theory and criticism: FILM HISTORY. 829.
 General literature. Film. Film theory and criticism: FILM HISTORY in United States; Germany.
  Review article. 838.

General literature. Film by independent filmmakers.
  FILM HISTORY. 254.
  Relationship to film industry; study example: United Artists Corporation. FILM HISTORY. 232.
  Relationship to film studios; role of Cagney, James (1941-1948). FILM HISTORY. 374.
 General literature. Film by independent filmmakers in Colorado (1897-1928).
  FILM HISTORY. 632.

FILM INDUSTRY
See also related terms: Film; Star system; Vitagraph Company of America; Vitaphone.
 General literature. Film by independent filmmakers.
  Relationship to FILM INDUSTRY; study example: United Artists Corporation. Film history. 232.
 General literature. Film in black Africa.
  Role of FILM INDUSTRY. 364.

FILM METAPHOR
See also related term: Film.

FILM NOIR
 General literature. Film. Film genres: documentary film.
  Relationship to *FILM NOIR* in Huston, John: *Let There Be Light*. 761.
 General literature. Film. Film genres: *FILM NOIR*. 771.
  Nonverbal communication in Garnett, Tay: *The Postman Always Rings Twice*; Hawks, Howard: *The Big Sleep*; Dmytryk, Edward: *Murder, My Sweet* compared to remakes by Rafelson, Bob; Winner, Michael; Richards, Dick. Dissertation abstract. 767.
  Realism. Dissertation abstract. 797.
 General literature. Film and television.
  On Lynch, David: *Twin Peaks*; *Blue Velvet*; Scorsese, Martin: *GoodFellas*; relationship to *FILM NOIR*. 396.

FILM PRIZES
See also narrower term: Academy of Motion Picture Arts and Sciences awards.

FILM REVIEW
See also related term: Film.
 General literature. Film.
  And screenplay; FILM REVIEW; relationship to American Biograph Company; study example: Woods, Frank E.; Griffith, D. W. 229.
  Edition of FILM REVIEW (1951-1959) by Carpentier, Alejo. 540.

FILM STAR
Used for: Movie star.
See also related terms: Film; Star system.
 General literature. Film.
  Role of FILM STAR; relationship to advertising. 344.

FILM STUDIES
See also related term: Film.
 General literature. Television in Great Britain.
  Role of quality; relationship to television studies; FILM STUDIES. 860.

FILM STUDIOS
 General literature. Film.
  By Lang, Fritz; relationship to independent filmmakers; FILM STUDIOS. Film history. 252.
 General literature. Film by independent filmmakers.
  Relationship to FILM STUDIOS; role of Cagney, James (1941-1948). Film history. 374.

FILM TECHNIQUE
Use: Cinematic technique.

FILM TERMS
See also related term: Film.

FILM THEORY AND CRITICISM
See also classified section: 818 ff.
Used for: Film criticism.
See also related term: Film.
 General literature. Film.
  And FILM THEORY AND CRITICISM. 309.
  ——; role of Cabrera Infante, Guillermo. 379.

FILMMAKERS
See also narrower terms: African American filmmakers; Women filmmakers.
See also related term: Film.

FILMMAKING
See also related term: Film.

FIN DE SIÈCLE
 General literature. 1800-1899: *FIN DE SIÈCLE*.
  Relationship to anarchism. 201.

FISH, STANLEY (1938-)
 Literary theory and criticism.
  Interpretive communities; relationship to canon. Treatment in FISH, STANLEY: *Is There a Text in This Class?* 1496.
 Literary theory and criticism. Linguistic literary theory and criticism.
  Stylistics; relationship to linguistic conventions. Theories of FISH, STANLEY. 1754.

Literary theory and criticism. Reader-response theory and criticism.
On interpretive communities; study example: Hebrew language poetry (1800-1899). Application of theories of FISH, STANLEY. 1919.
Role of reader; relationship to American fiction. Theories of Mailloux, Steven compared to FISH, STANLEY; Culler, Jonathan. Review article. 1918
Theories of FISH, STANLEY. Review article. 1931.

FISH, STANLEY (1938-)—STUDY EXAMPLE
Literary movements.
Postmodernism. Relationship to paranoia; study example: FISH, STANLEY: *Is There a Text in This Class?* Application of theories of Shapiro, David. 1026.

FITZWILLIAM MUSEUM
Bibliographical. Manuscripts. Illuminated manuscripts. 1400-1499.
Bury style in FITZWILLIAM MUSEUM: MS 3-1979. 1141.

FLACCUS, GAIUS VALERIUS
Use: Valerius Flaccus, Gaius (d. ca. 95 A.D.).

FLEMING, VICTOR (1883-1949)
General literature. Film.
Costume by Plunkett, Walter in FLEMING, VICTOR: *Gone with the Wind*; relationship to Selznick, David O. 346.
On FLEMING, VICTOR: *Gone with the Wind*. 607.
Role of censorship in FLEMING, VICTOR: *Gone with the Wind*; relationship to Lewton, Val; Selznick, David O. 495.
Treatment of dream; relationship to initiation in FLEMING, VICTOR: *The Wizard of Oz* compared to Lynch, David: *Blue Velvet*. Psychoanalytic approach. 453.

FLOOD
See also classified section: 2859.
Used for: Deluge.

FLORENCE
Bibliographical. Publishing in FLORENCE (1890-1920).
By Bemporad, Enrico; relationship to Gabinetto Vieusseux; *Nuova Antologia*. 1252.

FLORENSKIĬ, PAVEL ALEKSANDROVICH (1882-1943)
Literary theory and criticism.
Text; relationship to liturgy of Russian Orthodox Church. Relationship to theories of Bakhtin, Mikhail Mikhaĭlovich; FLORENSKIĬ, PAVEL ALEKSANDROVICH: *Stolp i utverzhdenie istiny*; Kedrov, Konstantin Aleksandrovich: *Poéticheskiĭ kosmos*. 1558.

FLOWER IMAGERY
See also related term: Flowers.

FLOWER NAMES
See also related term: Flowers.

FLOWER SYMBOLISM
See also related term: Flowers.

FLOWERS
See also classified section: 2860.

FO, DARIO (1926-)
General literature. Theater.
Relationship to laughter; popular culture. Theories of Bakhtin, Mikhail Mikhaĭlovich; Eco, Umberto; FO, DARIO. 943.

FOCALIZATION
General literature. Film.
Narrative technique; relationship to suture; FOCALIZATION compared to Joyce, James: *A Portrait of the Artist as a Young Man*. 334.
Genres. Fiction.
FOCALIZATION; relationship to narrative voice. 2149.

FOLK BELIEF SYSTEMS
See also narrower term: Religion.

FOLK CRAFT
See also narrower terms: Architecture; Costume.

FOLK HISTORIES
See also related terms: Jokes; Legend; Myth.

FOLK LITERATURE
Literary theory and criticism. Sociological literary theory and criticism.
Relationship to FOLK LITERATURE. 2017.

FOLK MUSIC
See also narrower terms: Gospel music; Jazz music.

FOLK NARRATIVE
See also narrower terms: Anecdote; Folk tale; Jokes; Legend; Myth.

FOLK POETRY
See also narrower terms: Epic poetry; Folk song; Oral poetry.

FOLK SONG
See also: entries for folk song in specific countries by consulting the index under the adjectival form of the country.
General literature. Film in India.
Role of FOLK SONG. 231.

FOLK SONG DUELS
See also related term: Folk song.

FOLK SPEECH PLAY
See also narrower terms: Names; Proverb.

FOLK TALE
See also narrower terms: Fable; *Märchen*.
See also related term: Myth.
See also: entries for folk tale in specific countries by consulting the index under the adjectival form of the country.
General literature. Film.
On Cocteau, Jean: *La Belle et la bête* compared to McKinley, Robin: *Beauty*; romance novel; FOLK TALE. 375.
General literature. Film. Film adaptation.
Of Lorenzini, Carlo: *Le avventure di Pinocchio* compared to FOLK TALE. 673.

FOLKLORE
See also narrower term: Folk literature.

FONT ANALYSIS
Bibliographical. Printing. Typography in England. 1500-1699.
Role of FONT ANALYSIS. 1232.

FOOD
See also related term: Vegetarianism.

FORD, JOHN (1895-1973)
General literature. Film.
By FORD, JOHN; Capra, Frank; Coppola, Francis Ford; Scorsese, Martin. 456.
Iterative narrative in FORD, JOHN: *How Green Was My Valley* compared to Stevens, George Cooper: *A Place in the Sun*; De Sica, Vittorio: *Umberto D.*; Olmi, Ermanno: *Il posto*. Application of theories of Genette, Gérard. 425.
Treatment of hero in FORD, JOHN: *Fort Apache*. 643.

FOREIGN LANGUAGE LEARNING
Use: Second language learning.

FOREIGN LANGUAGE PUBLISHING
Bibliographical. Printing and publishing.
In Mažoji Lietuva (1524-1939); relationship to FOREIGN LANGUAGE PUBLISHING. 1170.

FOREWORD
Use: Preface.

FORGETTING
See also related term: Memory.

FORGIVENESS
General literature. Television.
Treatment of FORGIVENESS in *Hill Street Blues*. Sources in religion. 865.

FORM
See also narrower terms: Narrative form; Spatial form.
See also related term: Structure.
Genres. Fiction.
Image; FORM; relationship to literary conventions. Treatment of nuclear war. 2108.
Literary theory and criticism.
Role of affect; relationship to FORM; content. 1413.
Literary theory and criticism. Semiotic literary theory and criticism.
Aesthetics of color; FORM. Theories of Marquand, Allan; Ladd-Franklin, Christine; relationship to Peirce, Charles Sanders. 1985.

FORMALISM
Literary theory and criticism. Narrative theory.
On thematic structure; relationship to FORMALISM; structuralism. Theories of Propp, Vladimir Iakovlevich compared to Vodička, Felix. 1801.
Literary theory and criticism. New Historicism.
Role of history; relationship to New Criticism; FORMALISM. 1844.
Literary theory and criticism. Semiotic literary theory and criticism.
Relationship to structuralism compared to FORMALISM. Theories of Mukařovský, Jan compared to Zich, Otakar. 2007.

FORMALIST APPROACH
See also related term: Formalist literary theory and criticism.
Documents applying specific approaches are so numerous that access to them is provided only in the electronic versions of the *Bibliography*.

FORMALIST CRITICISM
Use: Formalist literary theory and criticism.

FORMALIST LITERARY THEORY AND CRITICISM
See also classified section: 1710.
Used for: Formalist criticism.

FORMALITY
General literature. Film. Film adaptation.
Of Shakespeare, William; relationship to FORMALITY; distance. 690.

FORMAN, JANET
General literature. Film. 1900-1999.
Treatment of Beat Generation in FORMAN, JANET: *The Beat Generation: An American Dream*. 430.

FORMAN, MILOŠ (1932-)
General literature. Film.
On FORMAN, MILOŠ: *Amadeus*. 448.
——: *Valmont*. Interview. 429.
Treatment of rebel in FORMAN, MILOŠ. 637.

FRENCH LANGUAGE LITERATURE

Bibliographical. Publishing. Marketing in Africa of FRENCH LANGUAGE LITERATURE.

General literature. Film. Film adaptation.
Of Laclos, Pierre Ambroise François Choderlos de: *Les Liaisons dangereuses* by FORMAN, MILOŠ; Frears, Stephen; relationship to Hampton, Christopher: *Les Liaisons dangereuses*. 707.
Of Shaffer, Peter: *Amadeus* by FORMAN, MILOŠ. 682

FORMAT

Bibliographical. Publishing. Editing.
Role of FORMAT for critical edition. Application of EDMAC; TEX. 1301.

FORMULA

Figures of speech. Metaphor.
As image; FORMULA. 2369.

FORMULAIC EXPRESSIONS
See also related term: Formula.

FORTUNOFF VIDEO ARCHIVE FOR HOLOCAUST TESTIMONIES
See also related term: The Holocaust.

FOUCAULT, MICHEL (1926-1984)

Literary theory and criticism.
On similarity. Treatment in FOUCAULT, MICHEL: *Ceci n'est pas une pipe* compared to Magritte, René. 1468.
Political criticism. Theories of FOUCAULT, MICHEL; Said, Edward W. 1370.
Relationship to discourse. Application of theories of FOUCAULT, MICHEL; relationship to Nietzsche, Friedrich Wilhelm. 1544.
Relationship to epistemology of Positivism. Application of theories of FOUCAULT, MICHEL; Habermas, Jürgen; Lyotard, Jean François. 1401.
Role of text. Theories of FOUCAULT, MICHEL: "Qu'est-ce qu'un auteur?"; *Folie et déraison*; Derrida, Jacques: "La Pharmacie de Platon." 1555.
Subjectivity in Barthes, Roland; FOUCAULT, MICHEL; Derrida, Jacques. Dissertation abstract. 1344.
Theories of FOUCAULT, MICHEL. 1320, 1396.
Writing. Theories of FOUCAULT, MICHEL. 1441.

Literary theory and criticism. Deconstructionism.
Theories of Descartes, René; relationship to theories of Derrida, Jacques: "Cogito et histoire de la folie" compared to theories of FOUCAULT, MICHEL. 1616.
Theories of FOUCAULT, MICHEL: *Folie et déraison*; relationship to theories of Derrida, Jacques. 1603.

Literary theory and criticism. Feminist literary theory and criticism.
And psychoanalytic literary theory and criticism; role of ethics; relationship to sexual difference. Theories of FOUCAULT, MICHEL; Irigaray, Luce. 1677.
Relationship to humanism. Theories of Nussbaum, Martha Craven: *The Fragility of Goodness: Luck and Ethics in Greek Tragedy and Philosophy*; Gilligan, Carol: *In a Different Voice* compared to FOUCAULT, MICHEL. 1700.

Literary theory and criticism. Poststructuralist literary theory and criticism.
On speech; writing; relationship to electronic language; surveillance. Theories of FOUCAULT, MICHEL. 1885.

FRAGMENT

General literature.
FRAGMENT. 127.

Genres.
Role of space in FRAGMENT. 2041.

FRAME
Use: Interpretive frame.

FRAME SEMANTICS
See also related term: Frame theory.

FRAME STRUCTURE
See also related term: Frame theory.

FRAME THEORY—APPLICATION

General literature. Theater.
Relationship to spectator. Application of reception theory; FRAME THEORY. 936.

FRAMING
See also related term: Intercalated narrative.

General literature.
FRAMING; relationship to style; ideology. Dissertation abstract. 128.

FRAMPTON, HOLLIS (1936-)

General literature. Film.
Subjectivity in FRAMPTON, HOLLIS: *(nostalgia)*; *Zorns Lemma*. 580.

FRANCE

Bibliographical. Printing. Binding in FRANCE. 1500-1599.
By Estienne, Gommar. 1205.

Bibliographical. Publishing. History of publishing.
In FRANCE. 1277.

Bibliographical. Publishing. History of publishing in FRANCE. 1800-1899.
1281.

Bibliographical. Publishing. History of publishing in FRANCE (1941-1948).
By L'Arbre. 1280.

Bibliographical. Publishing in FRANCE.
Book distribution; libraries; relationship to social class. 1259.

Bibliographical. Publishing in United States; FRANCE.
By Grove Press; Olympia Press. Interview with Girodias, Maurice. 1243.

General literature. Film. Film adaptation.
Of Delibes, Miguel: *Los santos inocentes* by Camus, Mario. Reception study: reception in FRANCE. 684.

General literature. Film. Film genres: animated film in FRANCE.
Biography of Cohl, Emile. 754.

General literature. Film. Film genres: melodrama in FRANCE (1905-1907).
By Pathé Frères. 744.

General literature. Film in FRANCE.
Role of Cinémathèque universitaire; relationship to archives. 257.
Sources in Pirandello, Luigi. 650.

General literature. Film in FRANCE (1930-1939).
For women. Realism; relationship to melodrama. 626.

General literature. Film in FRANCE by women filmmakers.
Feminism in Dulac, Germaine; Epstein, Marie; Varda, Agnès. 336.
Role of feminism. Review article. 625.

Literary theory and criticism. Marxist literary theory and criticism.
Role of revolution; relationship to poststructuralism in FRANCE. Theories of Lukács, György. 1793.

Professional topics. Censorship.
In FRANCE (1940-1989). 2592.

Professional topics. Humanities. 1700-1799.
Pedagogy in England compared to FRANCE; relationship to philosophy. Review article. 2823.

FRANCE-LIVRE

Bibliographical. Publishing. Book trade in Quebec (1944-1946).
Includes catalogue of books by FRANCE-LIVRE. 1287.

***FRANCESCA DA RIMINI* (1908)**

General literature. Film. Film adaptation.
Of Shakespeare, William: *Julius Caesar* compared to *FRANCESCA DA RIMINI* by Vitagraph Company of America as film adaptation of Dante: *La Divina Commedia: Inferno*. Reception study. 738.

FRANCO, RICARDO

General literature. Film. Film adaptation.
Of Cela Trulock, Camilo José: *La familia de Pascual Duarte* by FRANCO, RICARDO compared to adaptation of Delibes, Miguel: *Los santos inocentes* by Camus, Mario. Dissertation abstract. 729.

FRANK, JOSEPH (1916-)

Genres. Novel.
Spatial form compared to dialogism. Theories of FRANK, JOSEPH compared to Bakhtin, Mikhail Mikhaïlovich. 2221.

FRANKENSTEIN (FIGURE)
See also classified section: 2861.

FREARS, STEPHEN (1931-)

General literature. Film.
On FREARS, STEPHEN: *Dangerous Liaisons*. Interview. 467.
——: *Dangerous Liaisons*. Interview with Close, Glenn. 466.
——: *Dangerous Liaisons*. Interview with Craig, Stuart. 468.
——: *Dangerous Liaisons*. Interview with Hampton, Christopher. 465.

General literature. Film. Film adaptation.
Of Laclos, Pierre Ambroise François Choderlos de: *Les Liaisons dangereuses* by Forman, Miloš; FREARS, STEPHEN; relationship to Hampton, Christopher: *Les Liaisons dangereuses*. 707.

FRED HACHEE

General literature. Television in Netherlands.
Role of Postmodernism in *Sjef van Oekel*; *FRED HACHEE*. 852.

FREE INDIRECT DISCOURSE
See also related term: Point of view.

FREEDMAN, JERROLD

General literature. Film. Film adaptation.
Of Wright, Richard: *Native Son* by FREEDMAN, JERROLD. 683.

FREEDOM OF EXPRESSION
See also related term: Censorship.

FREĬDENBERG, OL'GA MIKHAĬLOVNA (1890-1955)
Used for: Freudenberg, Ol'ga.

Literary theory and criticism.
Theories of FREĬDENBERG, OL'GA MIKHAĬLOVNA. 1505.

FREIRE, PAULO (1921-)
Used for: Neves Freire, Paulo Reglus.

Professional topics. Humanities.
Pedagogy. Theories of FREIRE, PAULO; Bourdieu, Pierre; Merod, Jim; Graff, Gerald. 2686.

FRENCH LANGUAGE LEARNING

Professional topics. Humanities.
Role of computer-assisted language learning in FRENCH LANGUAGE LEARNING. 2730.

FRENCH LANGUAGE LITERATURE

Bibliographical. Publishing. Marketing in Africa of FRENCH LANGUAGE LITERATURE. 1303.

FRENCH LANGUAGE (MODERN)

Literary forms. Translation.
English language translation of theories of deconstructionism from FRENCH LANGUAGE (MODERN). 2509, 2524, 2536.

FRENCH LANGUAGE TEACHING
See also related term: French language learning.

FRENCH LITERARY HISTORY
See also related term: French literature.

FRENCH LITERARY TRADITION
See also related term: French literature.

FRENCH LITERATURE

General literature. Film.
Relationship to FRENCH LITERATURE (1900-1999). 428.

Literary theory and criticism. Narrative theory.
Applied to FRENCH LITERATURE (1500-1999). Bibliography. 1827.
—— (1800-1999). 1805.

Professional topics. Humanities.
On FRENCH LITERATURE; relationship to dissemination in universities. 2667.

FRENCH NOVEL

General literature. Film. Film adaptation.
Of FRENCH NOVEL (1930-1939). 672.

FRENCH POETS

Literary theory and criticism. 1800-1999.
Role of FRENCH POETS; Russian poets; German poets. 1349.

FRENCH REVOLUTION

Bibliographical. Printing. Paper.
Watermarks (1789-1799); relationship to FRENCH REVOLUTION. 1221.

General literature. Film. Film adaptation.
Treatment of FRENCH REVOLUTION in film adaptation of Hofmann, Fritz: "Treffen in Travers" by Knauf, Thomas; Gwisdek, Michael. 737.

General literature. Theater. 1900-1999.
Treatment of FRENCH REVOLUTION. 950.

Literary movements.
Postmodernism. Role of the carnivalesque; kitsch; relationship to bicentennial of FRENCH REVOLUTION in Paris (1989). Application of theories of Bakhtin, Mikhail Mikhaĭlovich. 1057.

FRENZ, HORST (1912-)

Professional topics. Comparative literature.
Theories of FRENZ, HORST. Bibliography (1938-1984). 2636.

FREUD, SIGMUND (1856-1939)

General literature.
Treatment of feminism; hysteria. Psychoanalytic approach. Theories of FREUD, SIGMUND. 24.

General literature. Film.
Treatment of children in Truffaut, François: *Les Quatre Cents Coups*; *L'Enfant sauvage*; *L'Argent de poche*. Theories of FREUD, SIGMUND. 298.

General literature. Film. Film genres: horror film.
Treatment of women; womb; relationship to the grotesque; hysteria of men in Cronenberg, David: *Dead Ringers*. Application of theories of FREUD, SIGMUND. 756.

Literary forms. Anecdote.
Theories of FREUD, SIGMUND. 2382.

Literary theory and criticism.
Dialogue; relationship to intersubjectivity. Theories of Bakhtin, Mikhail Mikhaĭlovich compared to Piaget, Jean; FREUD, SIGMUND. 1384.
Theories of Bakhtin, Mikhail Mikhaĭlovich; relationship to FREUD, SIGMUND. 1507.
Theories of Kristeva, Julia; relationship to FREUD, SIGMUND. 1503.

Literary theory and criticism. Deconstructionism.
Theories of Derrida, Jacques compared to FREUD, SIGMUND. 1618.

Literary theory and criticism. Feminist literary theory and criticism.
And gay studies. Theories of FREUD, SIGMUND. 1706.

Literary theory and criticism. Hermeneutics.
Role of subjectivity; relationship to deconstructionism; humanism. Theories of Hegel, Georg Wilhelm Friedrich compared to Heidegger, Martin; Marx, Karl; FREUD, SIGMUND. 1716.

Literary theory and criticism. Psychoanalytic literary theory and criticism.
On life as narrative; relationship to time. Theories of FREUD, SIGMUND; Sartre, Jean-Paul; Rorty, Richard. 1896.
Relationship to feminism. Theories of FREUD, SIGMUND: *Der Witz und seine Beziehung zum Unbewussten*. 1895.
Relationship to Oedipus; Orpheus. Theories of FREUD, SIGMUND; Blanchot, Maurice. 1901.
Role of dream; relationship to the future. Theories of FREUD, SIGMUND. 1894.
Role of Oedipus complex. Theories of Abraham, Nicolas and Torok, Maria compared to FREUD, SIGMUND; Lacan, Jacques. Review article. 1909.
Theories of FREUD, SIGMUND. 1891.

Literary theory and criticism. Reader-response theory and criticism and feminist literary theory and criticism.
Relationship to the unconscious of women. Theories of FREUD, SIGMUND; Lacan, Jacques. 1940.

Literary theory and criticism. Semiotic literary theory and criticism.
Repetition. Relationship to theories of FREUD, SIGMUND: *Jenseits des Lustprinzips*. 1999.

Themes and figures. Dream.
Theories of FREUD, SIGMUND. 2847.

Themes and figures. Flowers.
Relationship to theories of Hegel, Georg Wilhelm Friedrich: *Grundlinien der Philosophie des Rechts*; FREUD, SIGMUND: *Die Traumdeutung*; Derrida, Jacques: *Glas*. Review article. 2860.

Themes and figures. Hysteria.
Relationship to realism; study example: Ibsen, Henrik: *Hedda Gabler*; *Rosmersholm*; *Fruen fra havet*. Feminist approach. Compared to theories of FREUD, SIGMUND. 2878.

Themes and figures. Mourning.
Theories of FREUD, SIGMUND; Barthes, Roland. 2895.

Themes and figures. Narcissism.
Application of theories of Girard, René; FREUD, SIGMUND. 2896.

FREUDENBERG, OL'GA
Use: Freĭdenberg, Ol'ga Mikhaĭlovna (1890-1955).

FRG
Use: West Germany.

FRIGIDITY
See also related term: Sexuality.

FRIULI-VENEZIA GIULIA

Bibliographical. Printing. Typography in FRIULI-VENEZIA GIULIA. 1500-1599. 1223.

FRONTIER

General literature. Film. Film genres: American Western film.
Treatment of FRONTIER in Altman, Robert: *McCabe and Mrs. Miller*. 788.

FRONTIERS

Literary theory and criticism. Feminist literary theory and criticism.
Role of *Feminist Studies*; *FRONTIERS*; *Signs*. Dissertation abstract. 1693.

FRYE, NORTHROP (1912-)

Literary theory and criticism.
Theories of FRYE, NORTHROP. 1362, 1416.

FSL
See also related term: French language learning.

FUCHS, DANIEL (1909-)

General literature. Film.
Screenplay by FUCHS, DANIEL. Creative process. 340.

FULL TEXT RETRIEVAL SYSTEM

Professional topics. Computer-assisted research.
On FULL TEXT RETRIEVAL SYSTEM. 2649.

FUNCTIONAL APPROACH
Documents applying specific approaches are so numerous that access to them is provided only in the electronic versions of the *Bibliography*.

FUNCTIONAL-COMMUNICATIVE APPROACH
Documents applying specific approaches are so numerous that access to them is provided only in the electronic versions of the *Bibliography*.

FUNDING

Professional topics. Humanities.
Role of FUNDING. 2731.

THE FUTURE

Literary theory and criticism.
Indeterminacy; relationship to THE FUTURE. Theories of Derrida, Jacques compared to Kant, Immanuel; Rousseau, Jean-Jacques. 1317.
On memory; relationship to THE FUTURE. Theories of Heidegger, Martin; Sartre, Jean-Paul. 1454.
On writing of history; relationship to THE FUTURE; nuclear war. 1540.
Role of THE FUTURE; time. 1575.

Literary theory and criticism. Hermeneutics.
Relationship to THE FUTURE; circularity. Theories of Heidegger, Martin; Bloch, Ernst; Hegel, Georg Wilhelm Friedrich. 1727.

Literary theory and criticism. Psychoanalytic literary theory and criticism.
Role of dream; relationship to THE FUTURE. Theories of Freud, Sigmund. 1894.

FUTURE PERFECT TENSE

Literary forms. Rhetoric.
FUTURE PERFECT TENSE in argumentation; relationship to psychoanalytic literary theory and criticism. Theories of Aristotle; Lacan, Jacques; Derrida, Jacques. 2489.

GABINETTO VIEUSSEUX

Bibliographical. Publishing in Florence (1890-1920).
By Bemporad, Enrico; relationship to GABINETTO VIEUSSEUX; *Nuova Antologia*. 1252.

GADAMER, HANS-GEORG (1900-)

Genres. Fiction.
Point of view. Hermeneutic approach. Application of theories of GADAMER, HANS-GEORG; Merleau-Ponty, Maurice; Ricœur, Paul. 2113.

SEE CLASSIFIED SEQUENCE FOR ADDITIONAL ENTRIES

Literary forms. Translation.
Relationship to hermeneutics. Application of theories of GADAMER, HANS-GEORG. 2555.
Relationship to understanding; untranslatability of poetic language; study example: Rimbaud, Arthur: *Une Saison en enfer*; *Illuminations*. Application of theories of GADAMER, HANS-GEORG. 2535

Literary theory and criticism. Hermeneutics.
Compared to pragmatics. Theories of GADAMER, HANS-GEORG. 1715.
Relationship to rhetoric. Theories of GADAMER, HANS-GEORG. 1733.

Literary theory and criticism. Semiotic literary theory and criticism.
Role of otherness in literature of Middle Ages; relationship to hermeneutics. Theories of Jauss, Hans Robert; GADAMER, HANS-GEORG. 1980.

GAILLIART, WILLEM
Bibliographical. Printing (1559-1583).
By Biestkens, Nicolaes, the Elder; relationship to GAILLIART, WILLEM. 1156.

GALICIA (SPAIN)
Bibliographical. Publishing. Book trade in GALICIA (SPAIN). 1296.

GALLOP, JANE (1952-)
Literary theory and criticism. Feminist literary theory and criticism.
Relationship to psychoanalysis. Theories of Mitchell, Juliet; GALLOP, JANE. 1658.

GAME SHOW
General literature. Television: GAME SHOW; quiz show. 870.

GAMES
See also narrower term: Language games.

GAPS
Literary theory and criticism.
Role of GAPS. 1532.

GARCÍA MAFFLA, JAIME (1944-)
Genres. Poetry.
Poetic language. Interview with GARCÍA MAFFLA, JAIME. 2275.

GARNETT, TAY (1894-1977)
General literature. Film. Film genres: *film noir.*
Nonverbal communication in GARNETT, TAY: *The Postman Always Rings Twice*; Hawks, Howard: *The Big Sleep*; Dmytryk, Edward: *Murder, My Sweet* compared to remakes by Rafelson, Bob; Winner, Michael; Richards, Dick. Dissertation abstract. 767.

GATES, HENRY LOUIS, JR. (1950-)
Literary theory and criticism.
Relationship to signification. Theories of GATES, HENRY LOUIS, JR.: *The Signifying Monkey*. 1342.

GAVRAS, CONSTANTIN
Use: Costa-Gavras, Constantin (1933-).

GAY STUDIES
Literary theory and criticism.
Relationship to homosexuality; GAY STUDIES. 1356.

Literary theory and criticism. Feminist literary theory and criticism.
And GAY STUDIES. Theories of Freud, Sigmund. 1706.

GAZE
General literature. Film.
Treatment of GAZE of female protagonist in Fellini, Federico: *Giulietta degli spiriti*. 635.

GDR
Use: East Germany.

GEERTZ, CLIFFORD (1926-)
Professional topics. Humanities.
Relationship to ideology; culture. Theories of GEERTZ, CLIFFORD. 2746.

GEHR, ERNIE (1943-)
General literature. Film.
Use of camera in GEHR, ERNIE: *Morning*; *Serene Velocity*; *Eureka*. 470.

GENDER
See also related terms: Sex roles; Sexism; Sexuality.
General literature.
Feminist literature. Treatment of GENDER; relationship to politics; avant-garde. 198.

General literature. 1800-1999.
Role of GENDER; relationship to culture. 190.

General literature. Film. Film adaptation.
Role of GENDER compared to theatrical adaptation of Brontë, Charlotte: *Jane Eyre*. 721.
Treatment of GENDER in Duras, Marguerite: *Le Navire Night* compared to prose version. 676.

General literature. Television in Pakistan (1985-1989).
Treatment of GENDER; relationship to Pakistani society in *Dewareen*; *Tanhaiyan*. Dissertation abstract. 919.

General literature by women writers.
Poetics; relationship to GENDER. 35.

Literary theory and criticism. Feminist literary theory and criticism.
Subjectivity; relationship to GENDER. Treatment in Irigaray, Luce. 1697.

Literary theory and criticism. Reader-response theory and criticism.
Role of GENDER. Pedagogical approach. 1920.

Professional topics. Humanities.
Academic discourse; literacy as language games; relationship to GENDER. 2741.
Literacy; relationship to GENDER. 2797.

GENDER CHARACTERISTICS
See also related term: Gender.

GENDER RELATIONS
Use: Male-female relations.

GENDER ROLES
Use: Sex roles.

GENERAL LITERATURE
See also classified section: 1 ff.

GENERATION EFFECT
See also related term: Memory.

GENERATIONS
Literary theory and criticism. Reader-response theory and criticism.
Role of time; difference in GENERATIONS; relationship to reading. 1939.

GENERATIVE ANTHROPOLOGY
General literature.
Relationship to GENERATIVE ANTHROPOLOGY. 83.

Literary theory and criticism. Deconstructionism.
Relationship to GENERATIVE ANTHROPOLOGY. Theories of Derrida, Jacques. 1621.

GENERATIVE APPROACH
Documents applying specific approaches are so numerous that access to them is provided only in the electronic versions of the *Bibliography*.

GENERATIVE GRAMMAR
Use: Transformational-generative grammar.

GENERATIVE METRICAL THEORY
See also related term: Transformational-generative grammar.

GENETTE, GÉRARD (1930-)
General literature. Film.
Iterative narrative in Ford, John: *How Green Was My Valley* compared to Stevens, George Cooper: *A Place in the Sun*; De Sica, Vittorio: *Umberto D.*; Olmi, Ermanno: *Il posto*. Application of theories of GENETTE, GÉRARD. 425.
Narrative technique in Cameron, James: *The Terminator*. Application of theories of GENETTE, GÉRARD. 479.

Genres. Fiction.
Third person narration. Application of theories of GENETTE, GÉRARD. 2147.

Literary theory and criticism.
Narrator; narratee in erotic literature. Theories of GENETTE, GÉRARD. 1340.

GENIUS
General literature. Film.
Treatment of GENIUS of women; relationship to Nazism in Pabst, Georg Wilhelm: *Komödianten*. 570.

Literary theory and criticism. Reception theory.
Creativity; relationship to GENIUS. 1948.

GENRE
See also related terms: Genre classification; Genre study; Genre theory; Genres.
General literature.
Role of history; relationship to GENRE; values; institution. 124.

General literature. Film.
Role of myth; GENRE; relationship to history in Curtiz, Michael: *The Charge of the Light Brigade*. 587.

General literature. Television.
Role of GENRE; relationship to television adaptation of Shakespeare, William: *Twelfth Night* compared to theatrical production. 905.

General literature. Television: music video.
Role of music; relationship to GENRE. 916.

Literary forms. Emblem.
Relationship to GENRE; canon. 2385.

Literary forms. Satire.
As GENRE; relationship to metaphor. Sources in Diomedes. 2503.

Literary theory and criticism. Rhetorical criticism.
Relationship to GENRE. 1953.

GENRE ANALYSIS
See also related terms: Discourse analysis; Discourse community; Genre; Text linguistics.

GENRE CLASSIFICATION
See also related term: Genre.
Literary theory and criticism.
Role of empiricism; relationship to GENRE CLASSIFICATION. 1433.

GENRE CONVENTIONS
See also related term: Genre.

GENRE NAMES
See also related term: Genre.

GENRE STUDY
See also related term: Genre.

Themes and figures. The fantastic.
GENRE STUDY. 2855.

GENRE THEORY
See also related term: Genre.

Genres.
GENRE THEORY. 2038, 2039, 2045.
——; relationship to literature of Middle Ages. 2036.

GENRES
See also classified section: 2036 ff.
See also narrower terms: Autobiography; Biography; Drama; Fiction; Letters; Novel; Periodicals; Poetry; Prose; Short story; Social novel.
See also related term: Genre.

GEOLINGUISTIC APPROACH
Documents applying specific approaches are so numerous that access to them is provided only in the electronic versions of the *Bibliography*.

THE GEORGE BURNS AND GRACIE ALLEN SHOW
Used for: Burns and Allen.

General literature. Television: situation comedy.
Self-reflexiveness in *THE GEORGE BURNS AND GRACIE ALLEN SHOW*; *I Love Lucy*; *The Jack Benny Show*. 868.

GEORGES D'ESCLAVONIE
Used for: Esclavonie, Georges d'.

Bibliographical. Printing. Binding in England. 1400-1499.
Of GEORGES D'ESCLAVONIE: *Le Château de virginité*. 1204.

GEORGIAN S.S.R.
General literature. Film in GEORGIAN S.S.R.
Treatment of youth. 289.

GERMAN CRITICISM
Literary theory and criticism. Reception theory.
Treatment in GERMAN CRITICISM; Italian criticism. 1944.

GERMAN CULTURE
See also related term: Germans.

GERMAN DEMOCRATIC REPUBLIC
Use: East Germany.

GERMAN LANGUAGE LITERATURE
General literature. Film. English language literature; GERMAN LANGUAGE LITERATURE.
Treatment of prostitute. Dissertation abstract. 597.

GERMAN LITERATURE
General literature. Film in Germany.
And GERMAN LITERATURE. Treatment of World War I; World War II. 432.

GERMAN PHILOSOPHY
Literary theory and criticism.
Role of aesthetics; relationship to GERMAN PHILOSOPHY. 1387.

GERMAN POETS
Literary theory and criticism. 1800-1999.
Role of French poets; Russian poets; GERMAN POETS. 1349.

GERMAN WRITERS
See also narrower term: German poets.

GERMANS
General literature. Film (1945-1989).
Treatment of GERMANS. Bibliography. 670.

GERMANY
See also narrower terms: East Germany; West Germany.
Bibliographical. Printing. Illustration in GERMANY. 1900-1999.
By Dreyer, Erich; Wendt, Max of three-dimensional pictures. 1217.
Bibliographical. Printing in GERMANY. 1400-1499.
Of Balbi, Giovanni: *Catholicon*. 1168, 1177.
Of Latin language literature by Schöffer family. 1183.
Bibliographical. Publishing in GERMANY. 1700-1799.
By Cotta, Johann Friedrich, Baron von Cottendorf. 1254.
General literature. Film.
Role of Chaplin, Charles Spencer. Reception study: reception in GERMANY (1918-1933). 377.
General literature. Film. Film genres: documentary film in GERMANY during Third Reich. 795.
General literature. Film. Film genres: war film in GERMANY (1950-1959). 769.
General literature. Film. Film genres in GERMANY.
Mountain film; relationship to modernity; Nazism. 796.
General literature. Film. Film theory and criticism: film history in United States; GERMANY.
Review article. 838.
General literature. Film. Film theory and criticism in GERMANY (1912-1933, 1945-1988). 837.
General literature. Film in GERMANY.
And German literature. Treatment of World War I; World War II. 432.
Relationship to the Left in Weimar Republic. 504.
Role of Pommer, Erich. Dissertation abstract. 386.

Theme; relationship to symbolism. 525.
General literature. Film in GERMANY (1910-1914). Film genres.
Melodrama; social drama. 803.
General literature. Film in GERMANY (1918-1933). 241.
Treatment of homosexuals. 325.
Genres.
Theories of Croce, Benedetto; reception in GERMANY. 2042.
Literary forms. Translation.
Role in canon of target literature; relationship to secondary education in GERMANY. 2549.
Literary theory and criticism. Literary history in GERMANY; Italy. 1761.
Literary theory and criticism. Reception theory in GERMANY; United States. 1946.
Literary theory and criticism in United States compared to GERMANY.
Relationship to empiricism. 1434.
Professional topics. Censorship in Austria and GERMANY.
Relationship to restoration (ca. 1815). 2588.

GERNSBACK, HUGO (1884-1967)
Genres. Fiction. Science fiction.
Theories of GERNSBACK, HUGO. 2184.

GESTALT THEORY
Used for: Configurationism (psychology).
General literature. Film. Film theory and criticism (1918-1933).
Theories of Arnheim, Rudolf; relationship to GESTALT THEORY. 833.

GESTURE
See also related term: Nonverbal communication.

GHETTO
See also related term: Urban areas.

GHOST STORY
See also related term: Gothic fiction.

GIFT
See also related term: Donation.

GILBERT, LEWIS (1920-)
General literature. Film.
Treatment of student-teacher interaction in GILBERT, LEWIS: *Educating Rita* compared to Spark, Muriel: *The Prime of Miss Jean Brodie*; Shaw, George Bernard: *Pygmalion*; Ionesco, Eugène: *La Leçon*. 268.

GILBERT, SANDRA M. (1936-)
Literary theory and criticism. Feminist literary theory and criticism.
On transvestism; study example: Joyce, James: *Ulysses*. Treatment in GILBERT, SANDRA M.; Gubar, Susan. 1655.

GILL, BRENDAN (1914-)
Literary theory and criticism. Literary history.
Applied to GILL, BRENDAN: *Here at the* New Yorker. 1772.

GILLIGAN, CAROL (1936-)
Literary theory and criticism. Feminist literary theory and criticism.
Relationship to humanism. Theories of Nussbaum, Martha Craven: *The Fragility of Goodness: Luck and Ethics in Greek Tragedy and Philosophy*; GILLIGAN, CAROL: *In a Different Voice* compared to Foucault, Michel. 1700.

GIRARD, RENÉ (1923-)
Themes and figures. Narcissism.
Application of theories of GIRARD, RENÉ; Freud, Sigmund. 2896.

GIRDLEBOOKS
Bibliographical. Printing. Binding. 1500-1599.
Of Latin language literature in GIRDLEBOOKS. 1208.

GIRLS
See also related term: Adolescent females.

GIRODIAS, MAURICE (1919-)
Used for: Kahane, Maurice.
Bibliographical. Publishing in United States; France.
By Grove Press; Olympia Press. Interview with GIRODIAS, MAURICE. 1243.

GITAI, AMOS
General literature. Film. Film genres: documentary film in Israel.
Interview with GITAI, AMOS. 800.

GIULLARI
See also related term: Minstrels.

GLAMOUR
General literature. Television: music television.
Treatment of men; women; GLAMOUR; sexuality. 885.

GLASNOST'
See also related term: Perestroïka.
General literature. Film. Film genres: documentary film in U.S.S.R.
Treatment of youth; relationship to *GLASNOST'*. 770.

GNOSEOLOGY
Use: Epistemology.

GNOSIS
See also related term: Gnosticism.

GNOSTICISM
    Literary movements.
        Modernism. Relationship to GNOSTICISM. 1013.

GOD
See also classified section: 2862 ff.
See also related terms: Faith; Religion.
    General literature. Film.
        Treatment of GOD; Christianity in Kieslowski, Krzysztof: *Dekalog.* 434.

GODARD, JEAN-LUC (1930-)
Used for: Lucas, Hans.
    General literature. Film.
        On GODARD, JEAN-LUC: *Prénom Carmen.* 300.
        Treatment of postcards in GODARD, JEAN-LUC: *Les Carabiniers* compared to Simon, Claude: *Histoire.* 451.

GODDESS
See also narrower term: Sun goddess.

GOEBBELS, JOSEPH (1897-1945)
Used for: Goebbels, Paul Joseph.
    General literature. Film.
        Role of GOEBBELS, JOSEPH in censorship of Lang, Fritz: *Das Testament des Dr. Mabuse.* 640.

GOEBBELS, PAUL JOSEPH
Use: Goebbels, Joseph (1897-1945).

GOLODNYĬ, MIKHAIL (1903-1949)
Used for: Ėpshteĭn, Mikhail Semenovich.
    Professional topics. Censorship in U.S.S.R.
        Interview with GOLODNYĬ, MIKHAIL. 2590.

GOSKINO
    General literature. Film in U.S.S.R.
        Role of *perestroĭka*; relationship to GOSKINO. 443.

GOSPEL MUSIC
    General literature. Film. Film genres: documentary film.
        Treatment of GOSPEL MUSIC in Davenport, Tom: *A Singing Stream.* 808.

GOSPEL SONG
See also related term: Gospel music.

GOTHIC CONVENTIONS
See also related term: Gothic fiction.

GOTHIC FICTION
See also classified section: 2164.
See also related term: Gothicism.

GOTHICISM
See also related term: Gothic fiction.
    General literature.
        GOTHICISM. 134.
    General literature. Film.
        Treatment of GOTHICISM in Kubrick, Stanley compared to Faulkner, William: "A Rose for Emily"; *As I Lay Dying; Sanctuary;* Pynchon, Thomas: *V.; Gravity's Rainbow; The Crying of Lot 49.* Dissertation abstract. 330.

GOTLAND
See also narrower term: Visby.

GOVERNMENT
See also related terms: Political science; Politics.
    Genres. Drama. 1900-1999.
        Treatment of terrorism; relationship to GOVERNMENT. 2068.

GOVERNMENT FUNDING
See also related term: Government.

GOVERNMENT OFFICIALS
See also related term: Government.

GOVERNMENT PROGRAMS
See also related term: Government.

GOVERNMENT REGULATION
See also related term: Government.

GOVERNMENT SUBSIDIES
    General literature. Theater.
        Role in society; relationship to GOVERNMENT SUBSIDIES. 953.

GRAFF, GERALD (1937-)
    Professional topics. Humanities.
        Pedagogy. Theories of Freire, Paulo; Bourdieu, Pierre; Merod, Jim; GRAFF, GERALD. 2686.

GRAMSCI, ANTONIO (1891-1937)
    Genres. Biography.
        Application of theories of GRAMSCI, ANTONIO; relationship to history. 2060.

GRAPH THEORY—APPLICATION
    Bibliographical. Manuscripts. Manuscript editing.
        Stemma. Application of GRAPH THEORY. 1150.

GRAPHEME
See also related term: Writing systems.

GRAPHIC FORM
See also related term: Typography.

GREAT BRITAIN
Used for: Britain.
See also narrower terms: England; Scotland.
    Bibliographical.
        In GREAT BRITAIN; United States. Bibliography. 1117.
    General literature. Film. Film adaptation.
        And television in GREAT BRITAIN (1959-1963). Realism; relationship to working class life in film adaptation; television adaptation of drama; fiction. 711.
    General literature. Film. Film genres: horror film in GREAT BRITAIN (1956-1973).
        Relationship to national culture. Dissertation abstract. 772.
    General literature. Film. Film theory and criticism in GREAT BRITAIN.
        Relationship to feminism; female spectator. 836.
    General literature. Film in GREAT BRITAIN.
        Role of British Film Institute. 284, 464.
    General literature. Film in GREAT BRITAIN (1909-1972).
        Role of censorship. Review article. 395.
    General literature. Television in GREAT BRITAIN.
        Role of quality; relationship to television studies; film studies. 860.
        Role of television workshop. 894.
    General literature. Television in GREAT BRITAIN and West Germany.
        Relationship to entertainment. 856.
    Professional topics. Comparative literature in GREAT BRITAIN; Ireland.
        Bibliography (1987). 2635.
    Professional topics. Humanities.
        Literary studies of Renaissance in GREAT BRITAIN; Netherlands (1950-1990). 2658.

GREAT PATRIOTIC WAR (USSR)
Use: World War II.

GREEK LITERATURE
See also narrower term: Ancient Greek literature.

GREEK SAINTS
    Bibliographical. Manuscripts.
        Relationship to hagiography of GREEK SAINTS. 1131.

GREENAWAY, PETER (1942-)
    General literature. Film.
        On GREENAWAY, PETER: *The Cook, the Thief, His Wife and Her Lover.* 559.
        Treatment of twins in GREENAWAY, PETER: *A Zed and Two Noughts* compared to Barth, John: "Petition"; Calvino, Italo: *Il visconte dimezzato;* Schwob, Marcel: *Les Sans-Gueules.* Feminist approach. 437.

GREENBLATT, STEPHEN J. (1943-)
    Literary theory and criticism. New Historicism.
        Theories of GREENBLATT, STEPHEN J. compared to McGann, Jerome J. 1846.

GREIMAS, ALGIRDAS JULIEN (1917-)
    General literature. Theater.
        Role of actors. Semiotic approach. Application of theories of GREIMAS, ALGIRDAS JULIEN. Dissertation abstract. 964.

GRIFFITH, D. W. (1875-1948)
    General literature. Film.
        Role of GRIFFITH, D. W. 463.

GRIFFITH, D. W. (1875-1948)—STUDY EXAMPLE
    General literature. Film.
        And screenplay; film review; relationship to American Biograph Company; study example: Woods, Frank E.; GRIFFITH, D. W. 229.

GRIGOR'EV, APOLLON ALEKSANDROVICH (1822-1864)
    Literary theory and criticism. 1800-1899.
        Role of Hennequin, Emile: *La Critique scientifique;* Scherer, Wilhelm: *Geschichte der deutschen Literatur;* GRIGOR'EV, APOLLON ALEKSANDROVICH. Sources in Positivism. Dissertation abstract. 1465.

THE GROTESQUE
See also classified section: 2864.
    General literature. Film. Film genres: horror film.
        Treatment of women; womb; relationship to THE GROTESQUE; hysteria of men in Cronenberg, David: *Dead Ringers.* Application of theories of Freud, Sigmund. 756.

GROTESQUE IMAGERY
See also related term: The grotesque.

GROUP FOR RESEARCH INTO THE INSTITUTIONALIZATION AND PROFESSIONALIZATION OF LITERARY STUDIES
    Literary theory and criticism.
        Role of GROUP FOR RESEARCH INTO THE INSTITUTIONALIZATION AND PROFESSIONALIZATION OF LITERARY STUDIES. 1367.

GROVE PRESS
    Bibliographical. Publishing in United States.
        By GROVE PRESS. 1233, 1235, 1257, 1264.
        ——. Interview (1981) with Rosset, Barnet Lee, Jr. 1256.
        ——. Interview with Allen, Donald Merriam. 1242.
        ——; relationship to *Evergreen Review.* 1250, 1274.

By GROVE PRESS; relationship to *Evergreen Review*; jazz music. 1248.
——; role of Rosset, Barnet Lee, Jr. 1241

Bibliographical. Publishing in United States; France.
By GROVE PRESS; Olympia Press. Interview with Girodias, Maurice. 1243.

GRUMBACH, JEAN-PIERRE
Use: Melville, Jean-Pierre (1917-1973).

GUBAR, SUSAN (1944-)
Literary theory and criticism. Feminist literary theory and criticism.
On transvestism; study example: Joyce, James: *Ulysses.* Treatment in Gilbert, Sandra M.; GUBAR, SUSAN. 1655.

GUNDELFINGER, FRIEDRICH
Use: Gundolf, Friedrich (1880-1931).

GUNDOLF, FRIEDRICH (1880-1931)
Used for: Gundelfinger, Friedrich.
Professional topics. Comparative literature.
Sources in history of ideas. Role of GUNDOLF, FRIEDRICH: *Shakespeare und der deutsche Geist*; Unger, Rudolf: *Hamann und die Aufklärung.* 2623.

GUNN, BILL (1929-1989)
Used for: Gunn, William Harrison.
General literature. Film.
Role of GUNN, BILL. Index. 651.

GUNN, WILLIAM HARRISON
Use: Gunn, Bill (1929-1989).

GUTENBERG BIBLE
Bibliographical. Printing. Illustration. Middle Ages.
Of facsimile of GUTENBERG BIBLE. 1213.

GWISDEK, MICHAEL
General literature. Film. Film adaptation.
Treatment of French Revolution in film adaptation of Hofmann, Fritz: "Treffen in Travers" by Knauf, Thomas; GWISDEK, MICHAEL. 737.

GYPSIES
General literature.
Treatment of GYPSIES. 161.

HABERMAS, JÜRGEN (1929-)
Literary theory and criticism.
Pedagogical approach. Theories of Nietzsche, Friedrich Wilhelm; HABERMAS, JÜRGEN. 1450.
Relationship to epistemology of Positivism. Application of theories of Foucault, Michel; HABERMAS, JÜRGEN; Lyotard, Jean François. 1401.
Literary theory and criticism. Deconstructionism.
Philosophical language; relationship to poetic language. Treatment in HABERMAS, JÜRGEN; relationship to theories of Derrida, Jacques. 1639.
Literary theory and criticism. Hermeneutics.
Applied to narrative in psychoanalysis. Application of theories of HABERMAS, JÜRGEN. 1711.

HAD, JAN (D. 1543)
Bibliographical. Printing in Czechoslovakia. 1500-1599.
By HAD, JAN. 1157.

HAGIOGRAPHY
Used for: Saints' lives.
Bibliographical. Manuscripts.
Relationship to HAGIOGRAPHY of Greek saints. 1131.

HAMARTIA
See also related term: Tragedy.

HAMBLIN, CHARLES LEONARD (1922-)
Literary forms. Rhetoric.
Argumentation. Theories of HAMBLIN, CHARLES LEONARD. 2459.

HAMPTON, CHRISTOPHER (1946-)
General literature. Film.
On Frears, Stephen: *Dangerous Liaisons.* Interview with HAMPTON, CHRISTOPHER. 465.

HAND-PRINTED BOOKS
See also related term: Printing.

HANDKE, PETER (1942-)
General literature. Film. Film adaptation.
Treatment of male-female relations in film adaptation of Duras, Marguerite: *La Maladie de la mort* by HANDKE, PETER. 724.

HANDWRITING
See also narrower terms: Caroline minuscule; Uncial.
See also related term: Writing systems.

HARD-BOILED DETECTIVE
See also related term: Hard-boiled detective fiction.

HARD-BOILED DETECTIVE FICTION
General literature. Film. Film genres: detective film.
And television; HARD-BOILED DETECTIVE FICTION. Treatment of private eye. Reference guide. 751.

HARD-BOILED DETECTIVE NOVEL
Genres. Novel. Detective novel: HARD-BOILED DETECTIVE NOVEL.
Relationship to Modernism; study example: Chandler, Raymond; Eliot, T. S.: *The Waste Land.* 2240.

HARLEQUIN ROMANCES
Genres. Novel. Popular romance novel.
Plot in HARLEQUIN ROMANCES. 2231.

HARLEQUIN ROMANCES—STUDY EXAMPLE
Genres. Novel. Popular romance novel.
Study example: HARLEQUIN ROMANCES. Sources in Ohnet, Georges; Richardson, Samuel; Austen, Jane. 2235.
Treatment of love; relationship to stereotypes; study example: HARLEQUIN ROMANCES. 2233.

HARLOT
Use: Prostitute.

HARRY RANSOM HUMANITIES RESEARCH CENTER
Used for: Humanities Research Center.
Bibliographical.
Catalogue of incunabula in David Jackson McWilliams Collection at HARRY RANSOM HUMANITIES RESEARCH CENTER. 1087.
Role of library collection; relationship to canon. Collection study of collection at HARRY RANSOM HUMANITIES RESEARCH CENTER at University of Texas at Austin. 1112.

HARTLIB, SAMUEL (1600-1662)
Professional topics. Computer-assisted research.
Hartlib Papers Project; relationship to publishing by HARTLIB, SAMUEL. 2645.

HARTLIB PAPERS PROJECT
Professional topics. Computer-assisted research.
HARTLIB PAPERS PROJECT; relationship to publishing by Hartlib, Samuel. 2645.

HARTMAN, GEOFFREY H. (1929-)
Literary theory and criticism.
Interview with HARTMAN, GEOFFREY H. 1336.
Literary theory and criticism. Deconstructionism.
Relationship to aesthetics. Theories of HARTMAN, GEOFFREY H. Review article. 1585.

HARVARD THEATRE COLLECTION
General literature. Theater.
Role of HARVARD THEATRE COLLECTION. 952.

HATRED
See also narrower terms: Misanthropy; Misogyny.

HAVELOCK, ERIC ALFRED (1903-1988)
Professional topics. Humanities.
Relationship to orality. Treatment in Ong, Walter J.; HAVELOCK, ERIC ALFRED. 2822.

HAWKS, HOWARD (1896-1977)
General literature. Film.
Treatment of power in HAWKS, HOWARD: *Scarface.* 224.
Treatment of prophecy; fatalism in HAWKS, HOWARD: *Scarface.* 274.
General literature. Film. Film genres: *film noir.*
Nonverbal communication in Garnett, Tay: *The Postman Always Rings Twice*; HAWKS, HOWARD: *The Big Sleep*; Dmytryk, Edward: *Murder, My Sweet* compared to remakes by Rafelson, Bob; Winner, Michael; Richards, Dick. Dissertation abstract. 767.

HAYES, JOHN MICHAEL (1919-)
General literature. Film. Film adaptation.
Of Hellman, Lillian: *The Children's Hour* by Wyler, William; role of HAYES, JOHN MICHAEL. 726.

HEALERS
See also related term: Doctor.

HEBREW LANGUAGE LITERATURE
General literature for children (1900-1948). HEBREW LANGUAGE LITERATURE. 157.

HEBREW LANGUAGE POETRY—STUDY EXAMPLE
Literary theory and criticism. Reader-response theory and criticism.
On interpretive communities; study example: HEBREW LANGUAGE POETRY (1800-1899). Application of theories of Fish, Stanley. 1919.

HECKSCHER, WILHELM SEBASTIAN (1904-)
General literature.
And visual arts. Festschrift for HECKSCHER, WILHELM SEBASTIAN. 186.

HEGEL, GEORG WILHELM FRIEDRICH (1770-1831)
Literary theory and criticism.
Interpretation. Theories of HEGEL, GEORG WILHELM FRIEDRICH; Derrida, Jacques. Dissertation abstract. 1371.
Literary theory and criticism. Deconstructionism.
Sign; representation. Treatment in Derrida, Jacques: *De la grammatologie* compared to HEGEL, GEORG WILHELM FRIEDRICH. 1594.
Theories of Sartre, Jean-Paul; HEGEL, GEORG WILHELM FRIEDRICH; relationship to theories of Derrida, Jacques. 1614.

SEE CLASSIFIED SEQUENCE FOR ADDITIONAL ENTRIES

Literary theory and criticism. Hermeneutics.
Relationship to the future; circularity. Theories of Heidegger, Martin; Bloch, Ernst; HEGEL, GEORG WILHELM FRIEDRICH. 1727.
Role of subjectivity; relationship to deconstructionism; humanism. Theories of HEGEL, GEORG WILHELM FRIEDRICH compared to Heidegger, Martin; Marx, Karl; Freud, Sigmund. 1716

Literary theory and criticism. Reader-response theory and criticism.
On dialectic. Application of theories of HEGEL, GEORG WILHELM FRIEDRICH. 1926.

Themes and figures. Flowers.
Relationship to theories of HEGEL, GEORG WILHELM FRIEDRICH: *Grundlinien der Philosophie des Rechts*; Freud, Sigmund: *Die Traumdeutung*; Derrida, Jacques: *Glas*. Review article. 2860.

HEGEMONY
Literary theory and criticism.
Aesthetics; relationship to bourgeois society; politics; HEGEMONY. 1386.

HEIDEGGER, MARTIN (1889-1976)
General literature. Film.
Cinematic technique; relationship to judgment. Theories of HEIDEGGER, MARTIN; Adorno, Theodor W. 656.

General literature. Film. Film theory and criticism.
Spatiotemporal relations; relationship to phenomenology. Application of theories of HEIDEGGER, MARTIN; Merleau-Ponty, Maurice. Dissertation abstract. 834.

Literary theory and criticism.
On memory; relationship to the future. Theories of HEIDEGGER, MARTIN; Sartre, Jean-Paul. 1454.
Role of death in time. Theories of HEIDEGGER, MARTIN compared to Levinas, Emmanuel. 1351.

Literary theory and criticism. Deconstructionism.
Relationship to Nazism. Theories of HEIDEGGER, MARTIN; de Man, Paul; Derrida, Jacques. 1612.
Role of HEIDEGGER, MARTIN: *Zur Seinsfrage* in theories of Derrida, Jacques. 1632.
Role of language; relationship to technology. Theories of Derrida, Jacques: *De la grammatologie* compared to HEIDEGGER, MARTIN: "Die Frage nach der Technik." 1584.
Theories of Derrida, Jacques; relationship to HEIDEGGER, MARTIN. 1595, 1597, 1644.

Literary theory and criticism. Hermeneutics.
Relationship to postmodernist literary theory and criticism. Theories of HEIDEGGER, MARTIN. 1732.
Relationship to the future; circularity. Theories of HEIDEGGER, MARTIN; Bloch, Ernst; Hegel, Georg Wilhelm Friedrich. 1727.
Role of subjectivity; relationship to deconstructionism; humanism. Theories of Hegel, Georg Wilhelm Friedrich compared to HEIDEGGER, MARTIN; Marx, Karl; Freud, Sigmund. 1716.

Literary theory and criticism. Linguistic literary theory and criticism.
Theories of de Man, Paul; relationship to HEIDEGGER, MARTIN. 1756.

Literary theory and criticism. Philosophical literary theory and criticism.
Theories of HEIDEGGER, MARTIN; Blanchot, Maurice; Levinas, Emmanuel. Dissertation abstract. 1851.
——; relationship to Nazism. 1856.

Literary theory and criticism. Postmodernist literary theory and criticism.
Relationship to religion. Theories of Culler, Jonathan; HEIDEGGER, MARTIN. 1868.

Literary theory and criticism. Psychoanalytic literary theory and criticism.
On fascism. Treatment in Theweleit, Klaus: *Männerphantasien*; relationship to theories of HEIDEGGER, MARTIN: *Einführung in die Metaphysik.* 1906.

Themes and figures. The sublime.
Theories of HEIDEGGER, MARTIN: *Sein und Zeit*. Dissertation abstract. 2922.

HEIMATKUNST
See also related term: Homeland.

HELL
See also related term: Underworld.

HELLIER, SAMUEL (1738-1784)
Bibliographical. 1700-1799.
Book collecting by HELLIER, SAMUEL. 1114.

HENNEQUIN, EMILE (1859-1888)
Literary theory and criticism. 1800-1899.
Role of HENNEQUIN, EMILE: *La Critique scientifique*; Scherer, Wilhelm: *Geschichte der deutschen Literatur*; Grigor'ev, Apollon Aleksandrovich. Sources in Positivism. Dissertation abstract. 1465.

HENRY, PIERRE (1927-)
General literature.
Role of text in musical adaptation. Interview with HENRY, PIERRE. 69.

HENRY BRADSHAW SOCIETY
Bibliographical. Publishing.
Of liturgical books by HENRY BRADSHAW SOCIETY (1891-1900). 1270.

HENRY VII, KING OF ENGLAND (1456-1509)
Used for: Richmond, Henry Tudor, Earl of; Tudor, Henry, Earl of Richmond.
Bibliographical. Manuscripts. Illuminated manuscripts. 1400-1499.
Collecting by Edward IV, King of England; HENRY VII, KING OF ENGLAND. 1137.

HERALDIC IMAGERY
See also related term: Heraldry.

HERALDRY
Bibliographical. Printing. 1500-1599.
Relationship to HERALDRY. 1180.

HERMENEUTIC APPROACH
Documents applying specific approaches are so numerous that access to them is provided only in the electronic versions of the *Bibliography*.

HERMENEUTIC CRITICISM
Use: Hermeneutics.

HERMENEUTICS
See also classified section: 1711 ff.
Used for: Hermeneutic criticism.
General literature.
Relationship to science; HERMENEUTICS. 185.

Literary forms. Rhetoric. 1900-1999.
Relationship to structuralism; HERMENEUTICS; deconstructionism. 2417.

Literary forms. Translation.
Relationship to HERMENEUTICS. Application of theories of Gadamer, Hans-Georg. 2555.

Literary theory and criticism. Deconstructionism.
Relationship to semiotic literary theory and criticism; HERMENEUTICS. 1617.

Literary theory and criticism. Deconstructionism and HERMENEUTICS.
Role of the individual; relationship to transcendence. 1636.

Literary theory and criticism. HERMENEUTICS.
Applied to narrative in psychoanalysis. Application of theories of Habermas, Jürgen. 1711.

Literary theory and criticism. Literary history.
Relationship to periodization; HERMENEUTICS. 1760.

Literary theory and criticism. Poststructuralist literary theory and criticism.
Relationship to HERMENEUTICS; structuralism. Review article. 1878.

Literary theory and criticism. Semiotic literary theory and criticism.
Role of otherness in literature of Middle Ages; relationship to HERMENEUTICS. Theories of Jauss, Hans Robert; Gadamer, Hans-Georg. 1980.

Literary theory and criticism. Structuralist literary theory and criticism.
And poststructuralist literary theory and criticism; relationship to HERMENEUTICS. 2034.

HERMETIC POETRY
See also related term: Hermetism.

HERMETICISM
Use: Hermetism.

HERMETISM
Used for: Aesthetic Mysticism movement; *Ermetici*; *Ermetismo*; Hermeticism; Literary Asceticism movement.
Literary movements.
HERMETISM. Review article. 1003.

HERO
See also related terms: Heroine; Protagonist.
General literature. Film.
Treatment of HERO. 335.
—— in Ford, John: *Fort Apache*. 643.
—— of Vietnam War; relationship to mythification. 333.
General literature. Film. Film genres: war film (1940-1955).
Treatment of HERO. 780.
General literature. Film. Film genres: war film in England during World War II.
Treatment of HERO. 814.
General literature. Radio and television.
Treatment of Lone Ranger as HERO. 845.

HERODOTUS (484-406 B.C.)—AS SOURCE
General literature.
Relationship to cultural history; historiography. Sources in HERODOTUS. 184.

HEROIC POETRY
Use: Epic poetry.

HEROINE
See also related terms: Female protagonist; Hero.
General literature. Film. Film genres: melodrama.
Treatment of HEROINE. 805.
Genres. Novel.
Treatment of HEROINE. 2196.

HEROISM
See also related terms: Hero; Heroine.

HERSCHEL, SIR WILLIAM (1738-1822)
Literary movements.
Romanticism. Poetic language; relationship to synecdoche compared to language of astronomy. Application of theories of Newton, Sir Isaac compared to HERSCHEL, SIR WILLIAM. 1077.

HERZOG, WERNER (1942-)
General literature. Film.
Cinematic technique in HERZOG, WERNER: *Aguirre, der Zorn Gottes* compared to Valle-Inclán, Ramón María del: *Tirano Banderas*. 440.

Treatment of expedition in HERZOG, WERNER: *Aguirre, der Zorn Gottes*. Dissertation abstract. 545.

HETEROGLOSSIA
  Literary theory and criticism.
    On HETEROGLOSSIA; relationship to society. Theories of Bakhtin, Mikhail Mikhaïlovich. 1429.

HEXAMETER
  Genres. Poetry. Epic poetry.
    HEXAMETER in oral poetry. Sources in Homer. Application of theories of Parry, Milman. 2306.

HIERARCHY
See also narrower term: Social hierarchy.
  Literary theory and criticism. Deconstructionism.
    Role of HIERARCHY; self-reflexiveness; relationship to philosophy; anthropology. Theories of Derrida, Jacques; Dumont, Louis. 1599.

HILL STREET BLUES
  General literature. Television.
    Treatment of forgiveness in *HILL STREET BLUES*. Sources in religion. 865.

HILLESUM, ESTHER
Use: Hillesum, Etty (1914-1943).

HILLESUM, ETTY (1914-1943)
Used for: Hillesum, Esther.

HILLESUM, ETTY (1914-1943)—STUDY EXAMPLE
  Genres. Autobiography.
    Relationship to psychotherapy; study example: Milner, Marion Blackett: *A Life of One's Own*; HILLESUM, ETTY: *Het verstoorde leven*. 2055.

HIMALAYAS
  Genres. Fiction. English language literature. 1900-1999.
    Treatment of HIMALAYAS. 2140.

HINDI LANGUAGE
  General literature. Film. Film genres: melodrama in India in HINDI LANGUAGE (1950-1959). 809.
  General literature. Film in India in HINDI LANGUAGE.
    Role of commercialism. 623.

HIPPOLYTUS (D. 235)—AS SOURCE
  Genres. Prose. Devotional literature.
    Treatment of blessing of widow. Sources in HIPPOLYTUS: *Traditio Apostolica*. 2321.

HIROSHIMA
See also classified section: 2865.

HIRSCH, ERIC DONALD (1928-)
  Literary theory and criticism.
    On Kripke, Saul A.: *Naming and Necessity*. Treatment in HIRSCH, ERIC DONALD. 1541.
  Literary theory and criticism. Hermeneutics.
    Theories of HIRSCH, ERIC DONALD applied to theology. Dissertation abstract. 1729.
  Professional topics. Humanities.
    Cultural knowledge. Theories of HIRSCH, ERIC DONALD. 2699.
    ——. Theories of HIRSCH, ERIC DONALD: *Cultural Literacy*; Bloom, Allan David: *The Closing of the American Mind*. 2805.
    On cultural knowledge. Theories of Bloom, Allan David; HIRSCH, ERIC DONALD. 2824.
    On HIRSCH, ERIC DONALD: *Cultural Literacy*. 2752.
    Relationship to literacy; science. Theories of HIRSCH, ERIC DONALD; Bakhtin, Mikhail Mikhaïlovich. 2677.
    Theories of HIRSCH, ERIC DONALD: *Cultural Literacy*. 2809.

HISTORIC PRESERVATION
See also related term: History.

HISTORICAL APPROACH
See also related terms: History; History of ideas.
Documents applying specific approaches are so numerous that access to them is provided only in the electronic versions of the *Bibliography*.

HISTORICAL CONSCIOUSNESS
See also related terms: Historiography; History; The past.
  Literary theory and criticism. Feminist literary theory and criticism.
    Relationship to HISTORICAL CONSCIOUSNESS. 1662.

HISTORICAL CONTEXT
  General literature. Film.
    Role of HISTORICAL CONTEXT in Cimino, Michael: *The Deer Hunter*. 267.

HISTORICAL CRITICISM
Use: New Historicism.

HISTORICAL DISCOURSE
  Literary theory and criticism.
    Applied to HISTORICAL DISCOURSE. 1318.

HISTORICAL DRAMA
See also classified section: 2100.
Used for: History play.

HISTORICAL EVENTS
See also narrower terms: Revolution; War.

HISTORICAL FACT
See also related terms: Historicity; History.
  General literature. Film.
    Treatment of Vietnam War; relationship to HISTORICAL FACT in Stone, Oliver: *Platoon* compared to Herr, Michael: *Dispatches*. 542.

HISTORICAL PROSE
See also related term: History.

HISTORICAL SETTING
See also related term: Historical consciousness.

HISTORICISTS
See also related term: History.

HISTORICITY
See also related terms: Historical fact; Historiography; History.
  Literary theory and criticism.
    Representation; relationship to HISTORICITY. Treatment in Auerbach, Erich: *Mimesis*; de Man, Paul. 1382.

HISTORIOGRAPHY
See also classified section: 2327 ff.
See also related terms: Historical consciousness; Historicity.
  General literature.
    Relationship to cultural history; HISTORIOGRAPHY. Sources in Herodotus. 184.
  Genres. Fiction.
    Mimesis; relationship to HISTORIOGRAPHY; Postmodernism. Dissertation abstract. 2135.
  Literary forms. Rhetoric.
    Relationship to HISTORIOGRAPHY. 2476.
  Literary theory and criticism.
    Relationship to HISTORIOGRAPHY. 1572.
  Literary theory and criticism. Feminist literary theory and criticism.
    Relationship to ethics; HISTORIOGRAPHY. 1687.
    Relationship to history of women; HISTORIOGRAPHY. 1690.

HISTORY
See also classified section: 2866.
See also narrower terms: Art history; Cultural history; Film history; History of ideas; History of rhetoric; Theater history.
See also related terms: Historical consciousness; Historical fact; Historicity; The past.
See also: entries for history of specific countries by consulting the index under the adjectival form of the country.
  General literature.
    Narrative; relationship to HISTORY. 52.
    Relationship to HISTORY. 2, 117, 183.
    ——. Theories of Thierry, Augustin; Michelet, Jules. 91.
    Role of HISTORY; relationship to genre; values; institution. 124.
  General literature. Film.
    Narrative; relationship to HISTORY in Cavani, Liliana: *Interno berlinese*. 483.
    Role of myth; genre; relationship to HISTORY in Curtiz, Michael: *The Charge of the Light Brigade*. 587.
    Treatment of HISTORY; relationship to postmodernist literary theory and criticism. 408.
    ——; relationship to war; television. 513.
  General literature. Film. Film genres: epic film.
    Treatment of HISTORY. 807.
  Genres. Biography.
    Application of theories of Gramsci, Antonio; relationship to HISTORY. 2060.
  Genres. Novel. 1900-1999.
    Relationship to HISTORY. 2228.
  Literary forms. Emblem.
    Indexing; relationship to HISTORY. 2393.
  Literary movements.
    Postmodernism. Relationship to HISTORY. 1027.
    ——. Relationship to HISTORY. Theories of Owens, Craig; Jameson, Fredric. 1023.
  Literary theory and criticism.
    By de Man, Paul; relationship to HISTORY. Sources in Schiller, Johann Christoph Friedrich von; Kant, Immanuel. 1515.
    ——; relationship to HISTORY; politics. Review article. 1490.
    On writing of HISTORY; relationship to the future; nuclear war. 1540.
    Relationship to HISTORY. 1355, 1439.
    ——. Review article. 1406.
  Literary theory and criticism. Feminist literary theory and criticism.
    Relationship to HISTORY of women; historiography. 1690.
  Literary theory and criticism. Marxist literary theory and criticism.
    Relationship to HISTORY. Theories of Lukács, György: *Der historische Roman*. 1792.
  Literary theory and criticism. New Historicism.
    Role of HISTORY; relationship to New Criticism; formalism. 1844.
  Literary theory and criticism. Philosophical literary theory and criticism.
    HISTORY; relationship to culture. Theories of Kant, Immanuel compared to Dilthey, Wilhelm. 1854.

Literary theory and criticism. Poststructuralist literary theory and criticism.
And Marxist literary theory and criticism; relationship to HISTORY. 1890.

Professional topics. Humanities in England.
Educational reform; relationship to HISTORY. 2802.

Themes and figures. Human body. 1700-1799.
Relationship to HISTORY; politics. 2875.

Themes and figures. The Holocaust.
Relationship to HISTORY; fictionality. 2869.

HISTORY AND STUDY OF FOLKLORE
See also narrower term: Archives.
See also related term: Folk literature.

HISTORY OF BOOKS
See also related terms: Bibliographical; Printing; Publishing.

HISTORY OF FOLKLORE
See also related term: Archives.

HISTORY OF IDEAS
See also related term: Philosophy.

HISTORY OF IDEAS—AS SOURCE
Professional topics. Comparative literature.
Sources in HISTORY OF IDEAS. Role of Gundolf, Friedrich: *Shakespeare und der deutsche Geist*; Unger, Rudolf: *Hamann und die Aufklärung.* 2623.

HISTORY OF PHILOSOPHY
See also related term: Philosophy.

HISTORY OF PRINTING
See also classified section: 1191 ff.
See also related term: Printing.

HISTORY OF PUBLISHING
See also classified section: 1276 ff.
See also related term: Publishing.

HISTORY OF RHETORIC
See also related term: Rhetoric.

Literary forms. Rhetoric.
HISTORY OF RHETORIC in England; Scotland; United States (1650-1799). 2474.

HISTORY OF SCIENCE
See also related term: Science.

HISTORY PLAY
Use: Historical drama.

HITCHCOCK, ALFRED (1899-1981)
General literature. Film.
On HITCHCOCK, ALFRED: *Rope.* 494.
Role of the other in HITCHCOCK, ALFRED. 664.
Treatment of mother; relationship to Nazism in postwar period in HITCHCOCK, ALFRED: *Notorious.* Application of theories of Jung, Carl Gustav. 244.
Treatment of Titanic; relationship to HITCHCOCK, ALFRED; Selznick, David O. 567.

General literature. Film. Film genres: spy film.
Role of Bond, James (character) compared to film by HITCHCOCK, ALFRED. 776.

General literature. Film in Hollywood.
Narrative; relationship to authorship in HITCHCOCK, ALFRED: *North by Northwest*; role of screenplay by Lehman, Ernest Paul. Dissertation abstract. 581.

HITCHCOCK, ALFRED (1899-1981)—STUDY EXAMPLE
General literature. Film.
Treatment of psychiatrist; study example: Wiene, Robert: *Das Kabinett des Doktor Caligari*; Robson, Mark: *Home of the Brave*; HITCHCOCK, ALFRED: *Psycho*; Meyer, Russ: *The Immoral Mr. Teas.* 569.

HOBSBAWM, ERIC J. (1917-)
Used for: Hobsbawn, Eric; Newton, Francis.
Literary theory and criticism.
Relationship to culture studies. Theories of Thompson, Edward Palmer; HOBSBAWM, ERIC J. 1335.

HOBSBAWN, ERIC
Use: Hobsbawm, Eric J. (1917-).

HOFFNER, WILHELM
Use: Dilthey, Wilhelm (1833-1911).

HOGGART, RICHARD (1918-)
General literature. Television.
Role of temporality. Theories of HOGGART, RICHARD. 850.

HOLISM
Professional topics. Humanities.
Role of dualism; HOLISM; relationship to canon in literary studies. Theories of Descartes, René. 2679.

HOLLAND
Use: Netherlands.

HOLLYWOOD
General literature. Film.
Role of collaboration in Cukor, George: *Holiday*; relationship to studio system in HOLLYWOOD (1935-1939). 499.

General literature. Film. Film adaptation by filmmakers in HOLLYWOOD. 704.

General literature. Film. Film genres: political film in HOLLYWOOD (1970-1987).
Treatment of working class; relationship to violence; collective struggle. Dissertation abstract. 778.

General literature. Film by Yugoslavian filmmakers.
Relationship to HOLLYWOOD. 397.

General literature. Film in HOLLYWOOD.
Narrative; relationship to authorship in Hitchcock, Alfred: *North by Northwest*; role of screenplay by Lehman, Ernest Paul. Dissertation abstract. 581. Reception study: reception in Yugoslavia. 517.

General literature. Film in HOLLYWOOD (1930-1939).
Style; relationship to semiotics; ideology. Dissertation abstract. 302.

General literature. Film in HOLLYWOOD (1933).
Role of actors as workers; relationship to subjectivity. Dissertation abstract. 293.

General literature. Film in HOLLYWOOD by women filmmakers. 248.

Genres. Novel. Popular romance novel.
Plot. Sources in film of HOLLYWOOD. 2232.

HOLLYWOOD FILM
General literature. Film.
Treatment of stock characters in HOLLYWOOD FILM. 320.

THE HOLOCAUST
See also classified section: 2867 ff.
General literature. Film.
Treatment of THE HOLOCAUST. Catalogue of archives in Israel; relationship to Steven Spielberg Jewish Film Archive. 584.

General literature. Film in United States (1970-1989).
Treatment of THE HOLOCAUST. 270.

Literary theory and criticism.
Relationship to the other; THE HOLOCAUST; Judaism. Theories of Levinas, Emmanuel; Perelman, Chaim: *The New Rhetoric*; Rosenzweig, Franz. 1420.

HOLY COMMUNION
Use: Eucharist (sacrament of).

HOLY EUCHARIST
Use: Eucharist (sacrament of).

HOLY FAMILY
See also narrower terms: Christ; Virgin Mary.

HOLZ, DETLEV
Use: Benjamin, Walter (1892-1940).

HOME
General literature. Film.
Treatment of loss of humanism; HOME in Tarkovskiĭ, Andreĭ A.: *Nostalghia.* 477.

General literature. Television.
Treatment of women in HOME; relationship to feminism. 906.

HOME VIDEO
General literature. Television: HOME VIDEO in Italy. 880.

HOMELAND
General literature. Film.
Treatment of childhood; nostalgia; relationship to HOMELAND in Tarkovskiĭ, Andreĭ A.: *Ivanovo detstvo; Nostalghia; Offret* compared to Brodskiĭ, Iosif Aleksandrovich; Chagall, Marc. 551.

HOMELESSNESS
See also related term: Home.

HOMER—AS SOURCE
Genres. Poetry. Epic poetry.
Hexameter in oral poetry. Sources in HOMER. Application of theories of Parry, Milman. 2306.

HOMOEROTICISM
Use: Homosexuality.

HOMOPHOBIA
See also related term: Homosexuality.

HOMOSEXUALITY
Used for: Homoeroticism.
See also narrower term: Lesbianism.
See also related terms: Homosexuals; Lesbians.
General literature. Film.
Treatment of HOMOSEXUALITY in Ophüls, Max: *Letter from an Unknown Woman* compared to James, Henry, Jr.: "The Beast in the Jungle." 285.
Treatment of transvestism; HOMOSEXUALITY in Waters, John: *Pink Flamingos; Polyester.* 502.

General literature. Theater.
Treatment of HOMOSEXUALITY. 942.

Literary theory and criticism.
Relationship to HOMOSEXUALITY; gay studies. 1356.

Professional topics. Humanities.
Relationship to HOMOSEXUALITY. Pedagogical approach. 2806.

HOMOSEXUALS
See also related terms: Homosexuality; Lesbians.

General literature. Film in Germany (1918-1933).
Treatment of HOMOSEXUALS. 325.

HONG KONG
Genres. Fiction. 1900-1999.
Treatment of HONG KONG. 2155.

HORIZON
See also classified section: 2872.

HORROR FICTION
See also classified section: 2165.
Used for: Terror fiction.
See also narrower term: Gothic fiction.
Genres. Fiction. Gothic fiction and HORROR FICTION.
Bibliography (1762-1988). 2164.

HORROR FILM
General literature. Film. Film genres.
HORROR FILM. 766.
General literature. Film. Film genres: HORROR FILM.
On Cameron, James: *Aliens*. Feminist approach. 764.
Relationship to fan magazines. 802.
Review article. 755.
Treatment of archetypes of monsters carrying beautiful woman. 752.
Treatment of women; womb; relationship to the grotesque; hysteria of men in Cronenberg, David: *Dead Ringers*. Application of theories of Freud, Sigmund. 756.
General literature. Film. Film genres: HORROR FILM in Great Britain (1956-1973).
Relationship to national culture. Dissertation abstract. 772.

HOUSEKEEPING
General literature. Television.
Treatment of disorder in HOUSEKEEPING by women in *Roseanne* compared to *Married ... with Children*. 912.

HOWE, IRVING (1920-)
Literary theory and criticism.
Interview with HOWE, IRVING. 1346.

HUDSON, HUGH
General literature. Film.
On HUDSON, HUGH: *Chariots of Fire*; relationship to teaching. 473.
General literature. Film. Film genres: docudrama.
On HUDSON, HUGH: *Chariots of Fire*. 790.

HÜGEL, FRIEDRICH, FREIHERR VON (1852-1925)
Used for: Von Hügel, Friedrich, Baron of the Holy Roman Empire.
Literary theory and criticism.
Treatment of Bible. Theories of HÜGEL, FRIEDRICH, FREIHERR VON. 1523.

HUMAN BEHAVIOR
See also narrower terms: Anti-Semitism; Betrayal; Deception; Forgiveness; Mourning; Persuasion; Sacrifice; Terrorism; Transgression.

HUMAN BODY
See also classified section: 2873 ff.
Used for: Body.
See also narrower term: Female body.
General literature. Film.
Treatment of denial of HUMAN BODY in Siegel, Don: *Invasion of the Body Snatchers*; Kaufman, Philip: *Invasion of the Body Snatchers*. 442.
General literature. Film in China.
Treatment of HUMAN BODY; relationship to ideology in Chang I-mo: *Hung kao-liang*. Application of theories of Jameson, Fredric; Bakhtin, Mikhail Mikhaïlovich. 661.
General literature. Theater.
Role of biology; HUMAN BODY; relationship to performance. 957.
Literary theory and criticism.
Poetics; relationship to HUMAN BODY; society. Dissertation abstract. 1510.

HUMAN DEVELOPMENTAL PERIODS
See also narrower terms: Childhood; Youth.

HUMAN NATURE
General literature. Film. Film adaptation.
Treatment of antinomy; relationship to HUMAN NATURE in Scott, Ridley: *Blade Runner* as film adaptation of Dick, Philip K.: *Do Androids Dream of Electric Sheep?* 720.

HUMAN QUALITIES
See also related term: Emotions.

HUMAN RACE
See also related term: Humanity.

HUMAN RELATIONS
See also narrower terms: Adult-child relations; Discipleship; Male-female relations; Social relations.

HUMANISM
Bibliographical. Manuscripts. Renaissance; HUMANISM. 1129.
General literature.
Treatment of nonhuman figures; relationship to HUMANISM. Dissertation abstract. 130.

General literature. Film.
Treatment of loss of HUMANISM; home in Tarkovskiĭ, Andreĭ A.: *Nostalghia*. 477.
Genres. Fiction. Science fiction by feminist writers.
Subjectivity; relationship to HUMANISM; Postmodernism. 2180.
Literary theory and criticism.
Role of de Man, Paul; relationship to HUMANISM. Review article. 1516.
Literary theory and criticism. Feminist literary theory and criticism.
Relationship to HUMANISM. Theories of Nussbaum, Martha Craven: *The Fragility of Goodness: Luck and Ethics in Greek Tragedy and Philosophy*; Gilligan, Carol: *In a Different Voice* compared to Foucault, Michel. 1700.
Literary theory and criticism. Hermeneutics.
Role of HUMANISM. 1713.
Role of subjectivity; relationship to deconstructionism; HUMANISM. Theories of Hegel, Georg Wilhelm Friedrich compared to Heidegger, Martin; Marx, Karl; Freud, Sigmund. 1716.
Literary theory and criticism. Poststructuralist literary theory and criticism.
Role of subjectivity; the self; relationship to HUMANISM; New Criticism. Application of theories of Lacan, Jacques. 1887.
Professional topics. Humanities. 1300-1599.
Relationship to HUMANISM; role of Petrarca, Francesco. 2789.

HUMANISTS
See also related terms: Humanism; Humanities.

HUMANITIES
See also classified section: 2652 ff.
See also narrower terms: History of ideas; Literature; Theology.
Professional topics. Computer-assisted research.
Application of database; relationship to HUMANITIES. 2641.
Relationship to HUMANITIES. Bibliography. 2651.

HUMANITIES RESEARCH CENTER
Use: Harry Ransom Humanities Research Center.

HUMANITY
Professional topics. Humanities.
Relationship to HUMANITY. 2799.

HUMOR
See also classified section: 2399 ff.
General literature for children.
HUMOR. 100, 199.
Genres. Fiction. Postmodernist fiction.
HUMOR. 2171.

HUMOR THEORY
See also related term: Humor.

HUNGARIAN FILMMAKERS
General literature. Film by HUNGARIAN FILMMAKERS. 534.

HUNGARY
Bibliographical. Printing in HUNGARY. 1400-1499. 1158.

HUSSERL, EDMUND (1859-1938)
Literary theory and criticism. Deconstructionism.
Applied to HUSSERL, EDMUND: *Erfahrung und Urteil*. On preface by Derrida, Jacques. 1587.
Role of time; consciousness. Treatment in Derrida, Jacques: *La Voix et le phénomène*; relationship to HUSSERL, EDMUND. Dissertation abstract. 1582.
Literary theory and criticism. Poststructuralist literary theory and criticism.
Application in teaching of writing; relationship to epistemology. Application of theories of Derrida, Jacques; HUSSERL, EDMUND. Dissertation abstract. 1879.

HUSTON, JOHN (1906-1987)
General literature. Film.
By HUSTON, JOHN. 304, 357.
Characterization; relationship to obsession in HUSTON, JOHN. 657.
Irony; relationship to sentimentality in HUSTON, JOHN: *Prizzi's Honor*. 331.
On HUSTON, JOHN: *The Misfits*. 272.
Treatment of women in HUSTON, JOHN. 388.
General literature. Film. Film adaptation.
Of Joyce, James: "The Dead" by HUSTON, JOHN. 681, 699.
——: *Ulysses*; *A Portrait of the Artist as a Young Man* by Strick, Joseph compared to HUSTON, JOHN: *The Dead*; Pearce, Michael: *James Joyce's Women*. 722.
General literature. Film. Film genres: documentary film.
Relationship to *film noir* in HUSTON, JOHN: *Let There Be Light*. 761.

HUTCHEON, LINDA (1947-)
Literary movements.
Postmodernism. Relationship to politics. Theories of HUTCHEON, LINDA. 1067.

HYMAN, ARTHUR (1921-)
Genres. Prose. Religious prose.
Festschrift for HYMAN, ARTHUR. 2338.

HYPERMNESIA
See also related term: Memory.

HYPERTEXTUALITY
See also related term: Intertextuality.

SEE CLASSIFIED SEQUENCE FOR ADDITIONAL ENTRIES

Literary theory and criticism. Narrative theory.
Intertextuality; HYPERTEXTUALITY; relationship to reader. 1820.

HYSTERIA
See also classified section: 2878.
General literature.
Treatment of feminism; HYSTERIA. Psychoanalytic approach. Theories of Freud, Sigmund. 24.
General literature. Film. Film genres: horror film.
Treatment of women; womb; relationship to the grotesque; HYSTERIA of men in Cronenberg, David: *Dead Ringers.* Application of theories of Freud, Sigmund. 756.

I LOVE LUCY
General literature. Television: situation comedy.
Self-reflexiveness in *The George Burns and Gracie Allen Show*; *I LOVE LUCY*; *The Jack Benny Show.* 868.

IBERIAN PENINSULA
See also narrower term: Spain.

ICONICITY
Figures of speech. Metaphor.
Relationship to ICONICITY. 2370.
Literary theory and criticism. Linguistic literary theory and criticism.
ICONICITY of poetic language. Structuralist approach. Compared to treatment in Pater, W. de and Langendonck, W. van: "Natuurlijkheid van de taal en iconiciteit." 1739.
Literary theory and criticism. Semiotic literary theory and criticism.
ICONICITY. 1993, 1997.
——; metaphor. Theories of Bühler, Karl. 1990.

IDEA
See also related term: Concept.

IDENTITY
See also narrower terms: Cultural identity; Ethnic identity; Female identity; National identity; Self-identity; Sexual identity.
See also: entries for nationalities in specific countries by consulting the index under the adjectival form of the country or area.
General literature. Film. Film adaptation.
Treatment of IDENTITY; relationship to substitution; exchange in film adaptation of Döblin, Alfred: *Berlin Alexanderplatz* by Fassbinder, Rainer Werner. 694.
Literary theory and criticism.
Otherness; relationship to IDENTITY in Europe. Theories of Bakhtin, Mikhail Mikhaïlovich. 1508.
Relationship to IDENTITY. Theories of Novitz, David. 1536.

IDENTITY CRISIS
See also related term: Identity.

IDEOLOGY
General literature.
Framing; relationship to style; IDEOLOGY. Dissertation abstract. 128.
General literature. Film in China.
Treatment of human body; relationship to IDEOLOGY in Chang I-mo: *Hung kao-liang.* Application of theories of Jameson, Fredric; Bakhtin, Mikhail Mikhaïlovich. 661.
General literature. Film in Hollywood (1930-1939).
Style; relationship to semiotics; IDEOLOGY. Dissertation abstract. 302.
General literature. Film on wide-screen.
CinemaScope; relationship to IDEOLOGY. Application of theories of Bazin, André. 593.
General literature. Television.
Role of representation; relationship to social discourse; IDEOLOGY; study example: inauguration (1981) of Reagan, Ronald. 866.
General literature. Television: situation comedy.
Role of IDEOLOGY. 899.
Genres. Novel.
Role of IDEOLOGY; relationship to treatment in criticism. Review article. 2197.
Subjectivity; relationship to IDEOLOGY. Dissertation abstract. 2195.
Genres. Novel. Popular romance novel.
Relationship to women; IDEOLOGY; treatment in sociological literary theory and criticism. 2236.
Literary forms. Rhetoric.
Relationship to IDEOLOGY. Treatment in Peirce, Charles Sanders; Bense, Max. 2435.
Relationship to linguistic theory; IDEOLOGY. 2448.
Literary theory and criticism.
Relationship to politics; IDEOLOGY. 1471.
Literary theory and criticism. Feminist literary theory and criticism.
Style; image; relationship to IDEOLOGY compared to deconstructionism. 1699.
Literary theory and criticism. Poststructuralist literary theory and criticism.
Role of subversion; relationship to IDEOLOGY of liberalism. Theories of de Man, Paul; Derrida, Jacques. 1884.
Literary theory and criticism. Sociological literary theory and criticism.
Role of social discourse; relationship to semiotics; IDEOLOGY; textuality. 2012.
Professional topics. Humanities.
Relationship to IDEOLOGY; culture. Theories of Geertz, Clifford. 2746.

IDO LANGUAGE POETRY
General literature.
IDO LANGUAGE POETRY. 38.

IDYLL
See also related term: Pastoral poetry.
ILLINOIS
See also narrower term: Chicago.
ILLITERACY
See also related term: Literacy.
ILLOCUTIONARY FORCE
See also related term: Speech acts.
ILLUMINATED MANUSCRIPTS
See also classified section: 1136 ff.
Used for: Manuscript illumination.
ILLUSION
See also related term: Reality.
General literature. Theater.
ILLUSION; relationship to audience response. 935.
ILLUSTRATED BOOKS
See also narrower term: Picture books.
See also related term: Illustration.
ILLUSTRATION
See also classified section: 1210 ff.
Used for: Pictures.
See also related terms: Picture books; Printing.
Bibliographical. Printing. Binding.
And ILLUSTRATION in Sweden (1989). 1206.
General literature.
ILLUSTRATION by Rudakov, Konstantin Ivanovich. 206.
—— in Poland (1700-1899). 209.
General literature for children.
ILLUSTRATION. 3.
——; relationship to comprehension. Semiotic approach. 89.
——; relationship to realism. 23.
Literary forms. Emblem.
Relationship to ILLUSTRATION. Indexing. 2397.

ILLUSTRATORS
See also related term: Illustration.

IMAGE
Figures of speech. Metaphor.
As IMAGE; formula. 2369.
General literature. Television.
Role of IMAGE; representation; relationship to revolution in Central Europe (1989). 896.
Genres. Fiction.
IMAGE; form; relationship to literary conventions. Treatment of nuclear war. 2108.
Literary forms. Rhetoric.
Role of question; metaphor; IMAGE in scientific language; relationship to epistemology. Theories of Meyer, Michel; Kant, Immanuel. 2427.
Literary theory and criticism. Feminist literary theory and criticism.
Style; IMAGE; relationship to ideology compared to deconstructionism. 1699.
Literary theory and criticism. Linguistic literary theory and criticism.
Poetic language; relationship to mental model; IMAGE; rhythm. 1757.

IMAGERY
See also classified section: 2352.
See also narrower terms: Dream imagery; Visual imagery.
See also related term: Figuration.
General literature.
Language; relationship to IMAGERY in painting by Turner, Joseph Mallord William. 168.
General literature. Film.
IMAGERY. 416.
—— in Lynch, David: *Blue Velvet* compared to Dante: *La Divina Commedia.* 535.
General literature. Film and video art; music video.
Role of sexuality; relationship to Postmodernism. IMAGERY. 601.
General literature. Television.
IMAGERY; relationship to cognitive representation; Postmodernism. Application of theories of Jameson, Fredric. 920.
General literature. Television in United States (1960-1975).
IMAGERY of Cold War in treatment of Vietnam War. Dissertation abstract. 921.
Literary forms. Emblem.
IMAGERY of architecture in index. 2395.

THE IMAGINARY
See also related term: Imagination.

IMAGINARY BIOGRAPHY
General literature. Film.
On Truffaut, François: *Les Quatre Cents Coups* as IMAGINARY BIOGRAPHY. 577.

IMAGINATION
See also related terms: Creativity; Invention.
Literary movements.
Romanticism. Theories of IMAGINATION; inspiration; relationship to rationality; critical judgment. 1074.

Literary theory and criticism.
Relationship to IMAGINATION. 1579.
Role of IMAGINATION; aesthetics. 1436

Themes and figures. Underworld.
Relationship to technology; society; IMAGINATION. 2929.

IMAGO
See also related term: Psychoanalytic theory.

IMAGOLOGY
Professional topics. Comparative literature.
Role of IMAGOLOGY; relationship to literary studies. 2599.

IMITATION
Literary forms. Rhetoric.
IMITATION. 2496.

Professional topics. Humanities.
Teaching of writing; relationship to IMITATION of poetry. 2687.

IMMERSION PROGRAM
See also related terms: Second language learning; Teaching of language.

IMMORAL BEHAVIOR
See also related term: Morality.

IMPERIALISM
General literature. Film in United States.
Relationship to spectacle; IMPERIALISM. 546.

IMPERSONATION
See also narrower term: Female impersonation.

General literature. Theater.
IMPERSONATION in solo performance. Dissertation abstract. 944.

IMPLIED AUTHOR
See also related term: Authorial voice.

IMPLIED READER
See also related term: Narratee.

IMPOTENCE
See also related term: Sexuality.

IMPRESA
See also related term: Emblem.

Literary forms. Emblem.
Relationship to *IMPRESA*. Indexing. 2398.

INAUGURATION—STUDY EXAMPLE
General literature. Television.
Role of representation; relationship to social discourse; ideology; study example: INAUGURATION (1981) of Reagan, Ronald. 866.

INCEST
See also related term: Sexuality.

INCORPORATION
Themes and figures. Cannibalism.
Relationship to Eucharist (sacrament of); INCORPORATION. 2838.

INCUNABULA
Bibliographical.
Catalogue of INCUNABULA in David Jackson McWilliams Collection at Harry Ransom Humanities Research Center. 1087.

INDEPENDENT FILMMAKERS
General literature. Film.
By Lang, Fritz; relationship to INDEPENDENT FILMMAKERS; film studios. Film history. 252.

General literature. Film by INDEPENDENT FILMMAKERS.
Film history. 254.
Relationship to film industry; study example: United Artists Corporation. Film history. 232.
Relationship to film studios; role of Cagney, James (1941-1948). Film history. 374.

General literature. Film by INDEPENDENT FILMMAKERS (1970-1979).
Study example: Dimension Pictures. 458.

General literature. Film by INDEPENDENT FILMMAKERS in Colorado (1897-1928).
Film history. 632.

INDETERMINACY
Literary theory and criticism.
INDETERMINACY; relationship to the future. Theories of Derrida, Jacques compared to Kant, Immanuel; Rousseau, Jean-Jacques. 1317.

Literary theory and criticism. Linguistic literary theory and criticism.
Role of ambiguity; INDETERMINACY. 1746.

INDEXING
Literary forms. Emblem.
INDEXING. 2386, 2387, 2388, 2389, 2391.
——; relationship to history. 2393.
Relationship to illustration. INDEXING. 2397.
Relationship to *impresa*. INDEXING. 2398.

INDIA
General literature. Film. Film genres: melodrama in INDIA in Hindi language (1950-1959). 809.
General literature. Film in INDIA.
Repetition. 620.
Role of folk song. 231.

General literature. Film in INDIA in Hindi language.
Role of commercialism. 623.

Genres. Fiction. English language literature. 1900-1999.
Treatment of INDIA. 2124.

Literary theory and criticism in INDIA. 1512.

Professional topics. Humanities in INDIA.
Role of literary theory and criticism; Western culture. 2783.

INDIANS (AMERICA)
Use: Native Americans.

THE INDIGENOUS
See also classified section: 2879.

THE INDIVIDUAL
See also related term: The self.

Literary theory and criticism. Deconstructionism and hermeneutics.
Role of THE INDIVIDUAL; relationship to transcendence. 1636.

INDIVIDUAL WILL
See also related term: The individual.

INDIVIDUALISM
See also related term: The individual.

INDONESIA
General literature. Film in INDONESIA.
Treatment of revolution. 563.

INDUSTRIAL THEATER
General literature. Theater: INDUSTRIAL THEATER.
Dissertation abstract. 956.

INFERENCE
Figures of speech. Metaphor.
Use in political discourse; relationship to persuasion; INFERENCE. 2367.
Literary theory and criticism. Reader-response theory and criticism.
Relationship to INFERENCE by reader. 1922.

INFORMATION
See also related terms: Communication theory; Information theory; Knowledge.

INFORMATION RETRIEVAL SYSTEM
See also related term: Database.

INFORMATION SCIENCE
See also related term: Information theory.

INFORMATION TECHNOLOGY—APPLICATION
Professional topics. Computer-assisted research.
Application of INFORMATION TECHNOLOGY. 2639.

INFORMATION THEORY
See also related term: Communication theory.

Literary theory and criticism. Semiotic literary theory and criticism.
Relationship to cybernetics; INFORMATION THEORY. Theories of Saussure, Ferdinand de; Peirce, Charles Sanders; Bense, Max. 1971.

INGARDEN, ROMAN (1893-1970)
Literary theory and criticism. Semiotic literary theory and criticism.
Theories of Bakhtin, Mikhail Mikhaïlovich compared to INGARDEN, ROMAN; Mukařovský, Jan. 1976.

INHABITED WORLDS
See also related term: Extraterrestrial life.

INITIALS (BIBLIOGRAPHICAL)
See also related terms: Manuscripts; Typography.

INITIALS (NAMES)
See also related term: Names.

INITIATION
General literature. Film.
Treatment of dream; relationship to INITIATION in Fleming, Victor: *The Wizard of Oz* compared to Lynch, David: *Blue Velvet*. Psychoanalytic approach. 453.

INITIATION RITES
See also related term: Initiation.

THE INSANE
See also related term: Madness.

INSANITY
Use: Madness.

INSISTING
See also related term: Speech acts.

INSOMNIA
See also classified section: 2880.
Used for: Sleeplessness.

SEE CLASSIFIED SEQUENCE FOR ADDITIONAL ENTRIES

INSPIRATION
Literary movements.
Romanticism. Theories of imagination; INSPIRATION; relationship to rationality; critical judgment. 1074.

INSTITUTION
See also related term: Culture.
General literature.
Role of history; relationship to genre; values; INSTITUTION. 124.
Literary theory and criticism.
On literature as INSTITUTION. 1492.

INTELLECT
See also related term: Intellectuals.

INTELLECTUAL HISTORY
See also related term: History of ideas.

INTELLECTUAL LIFE
See also related term: Intellectuals.

INTELLECTUALISM
See also related term: Intellectuals.
Professional topics. Humanities.
Cultural knowledge; INTELLECTUALISM; relationship to theories of Bloom, Allan David: *The Closing of the American Mind.* 2774.

INTELLECTUALITY
See also related term: Intellectualism.

INTELLECTUALS
See also related term: Intellectualism.
General literature.
Role of INTELLECTUALS; relationship to politics (1945-1990). 163.

INTELLIGENCE
See also related term: Knowledge.

INTENSIONALITY
Literary theory and criticism. Linguistic literary theory and criticism.
Relationship to semantics; INTENSIONALITY of narrative. 1734.

INTENTION
Literary theory and criticism.
Role of INTENTION. Theories of de Man, Paul. 1364.

INTENTIONALITY
See also related term: Intention.

INTERCALATED NARRATIVE
Used for: Embedded narrative; Metadiegetic narrative.
See also related term: Framing.
Literary theory and criticism. Narrative theory.
INTERCALATED NARRATIVE; study example: Cervantes Saavedra, Miguel de: *Quijote*; Sterne, Laurence: *Tristram Shandy*; Cortázar, Julio: *Rayuela.* Dissertation abstract. 1818.

INTERCULTURAL COMMUNICATION
Use: Cross-cultural communication.

INTERDISCIPLINARY STUDIES
See also narrower terms: African American studies; English studies; Medieval studies; Norwegian studies; Romantic studies; Theater studies; Women's studies.
Professional topics.
INTERDISCIPLINARY STUDIES. 2580.
Professional topics. Humanities.
Role of INTERDISCIPLINARY STUDIES in literary studies. 2659.

INTERETHNIC COMMUNICATION
See also related term: Cross-cultural communication.

INTERLANGUAGE
See also related term: Second language learning.

INTERLANGUAGE DEVELOPMENT
See also related term: Second language learning.

INTERNATIONAL BRIGADES
See also narrower term: Abraham Lincoln Battalion.
See also related term: Spanish Civil War.

INTERNATIONAL COMMUNICATION
See also related term: Cross-cultural communication.

INTERNATIONAL INFORMATION CENTRE FOR TERMINOLOGY
See also related term: Terminology.

INTERPERSONAL COMMUNICATION
Literary forms. Rhetoric.
Dialectic; relationship to rhetorical theory; INTERPERSONAL COMMUNICATION. 2471.

INTERPOLATION
See also related term: Intercalated narrative.

INTERPRETATION
See also related terms: Interpreter; Textual analysis.
General literature.
Role of the self in INTERPRETATION by college students. Pedagogical approach. Dissertation abstract. 41.

Literary forms. Translation. Translation theory.
Role of INTERPRETATION; reference; relationship to analysis of target text. 2575.
Literary theory and criticism.
Applied to Midrash; relationship to INTERPRETATION; intertextuality. 1334.
INTERPRETATION. Dissertation abstract. 1551.
———. Theories of Hegel, Georg Wilhelm Friedrich; Derrida, Jacques. Dissertation abstract. 1371.
———; relationship to truth. 1414.
On INTERPRETATION. 1309.
Role of cultural context in INTERPRETATION. 1502.
Role of INTERPRETATION; relationship to politics; social criticism. Review article. 1379.
Literary theory and criticism. Marxist literary theory and criticism.
Narrative as political discourse; relationship to INTERPRETATION. Treatment in Jameson, Fredric: *The Political Unconscious.* 1789.
Literary theory and criticism. Narrative theory.
On reading; INTERPRETATION; study example: James, Henry, Jr.: "The Figure in the Carpet." Pedagogical approach. 1800.

INTERPRETER
See also related terms: Interpretation; Simultaneous translation; Translator.
General literature. Television and radio in Europe.
Role of translator; INTERPRETER. 886.
Literary theory and criticism. Reader-response theory and criticism.
Relationship to INTERPRETER. 1934.

INTERPRETING
See also related term: Translation.

INTERPRETIVE COMMUNITIES
Literary theory and criticism.
INTERPRETIVE COMMUNITIES; relationship to canon. Treatment in Fish, Stanley: *Is There a Text in This Class?* 1496.
Role of INTERPRETIVE COMMUNITIES. 1443.
Literary theory and criticism. Reader-response theory and criticism.
On INTERPRETIVE COMMUNITIES. Pedagogical approach. 1925.
———; study example: Hebrew language poetry (1800-1899). Application of theories of Fish, Stanley. 1919.
Professional topics. Humanities.
Role of academic discourse; relationship to INTERPRETIVE COMMUNITIES; social construction. 2703.

INTERPRETIVE CONVENTIONS
Literary theory and criticism.
Role of INTERPRETIVE CONVENTIONS in language. Review article. 1495.

INTERPRETIVE FRAME
Used for: Frame.
See also related term: Context.
Genres. Fiction.
INTERPRETIVE FRAME. Sources in *The Thousand and One Nights.* Dissertation abstract. 2144.

INTERROGATIVE ADJECTIVE
See also related term: Question.

INTERROGATIVE CLAUSE
See also related term: Question.

INTERROGATIVE MOOD
See also related term: Question.

INTERROGATIVE PARTICLE
See also related term: Question.

INTERROGATIVE PRONOUN
See also related term: Question.

INTERROGATIVE SENTENCE
See also related term: Question.

INTERRUPTED SPEECH
See also related term: Interruption.

INTERRUPTION
General literature.
On reading; relationship to INTERRUPTION. 29.

INTERSUBJECTIVITY
See also related term: Subjectivity.
Literary theory and criticism.
Dialogue; relationship to INTERSUBJECTIVITY. Theories of Bakhtin, Mikhail Mikhaïlovich compared to Piaget, Jean; Freud, Sigmund. 1384.

INTERTEXTUAL APPROACH
See also related term: Intertextuality.
Documents applying specific approaches are so numerous that access to them is provided only in the electronic versions of the *Bibliography.*

INTERTEXTUALITY
See also related term: Hypertextuality.
General literature.
INTERTEXTUALITY in Midrash. 30.
General literature. Film.
INTERTEXTUALITY in Cooper, Merian C.: *King Kong.* 572.

—— relationship to painting in Robbe-Grillet, Alain: *L'Eden et après*; *La Belle Captive*. 591.

Genres. Poetry. Postmodernist poetry.
INTERTEXTUALITY. 2314.

Literary movements.
Postmodernism. Role of writer; relationship to reader; INTERTEXTUALITY. 1040.

Literary theory and criticism.
Applied to Midrash; relationship to interpretation; INTERTEXTUALITY. 1334. INTERTEXTUALITY. 1338, 1442, 1446.

Literary theory and criticism. Narrative theory.
INTERTEXTUALITY; hypertextuality; relationship to reader. 1820.

Literary theory and criticism. Semiotic literary theory and criticism.
INTERTEXTUALITY. 1989.
——. Theories of Riffaterre, Michael: *Semiotics of Poetry*. 1970.

Literary theory and criticism. Sociological literary theory and criticism.
INTERTEXTUALITY. 2020.

INTRAHISTORIA
See also related term: History.

INTRIGUE
See also related term: Deception.

INTUITION
Literary forms. Rhetoric.
Role of INTUITION; relationship to creative process. 2437.

INVECTIVE
See also related term: Satire.

INVENTIO
Literary forms. Rhetoric.
INVENTIO; relationship to philosophical language. Treatment in Cicero. 2478.

INVENTION
See also related terms: Creativity; Imagination.
Literary forms. Rhetoric.
Theories of INVENTION (1960-1987). Dissertation abstract. 2484.

INVENTOR
See also related term: Invention.

IRELAND
Professional topics. Comparative literature in Great Britain; IRELAND.
Bibliography (1987). 2635.

IRIGARAY, LUCE (1939-)
Literary theory and criticism. Feminist literary theory and criticism.
And psychoanalytic literary theory and criticism; role of ethics; relationship to sexual difference. Theories of Foucault, Michel; IRIGARAY, LUCE. 1677.
On English language translation of IRIGARAY, LUCE: *Ce sexe qui n'en est pas un*. 1688.
Subjectivity; relationship to gender. Treatment in IRIGARAY, LUCE. 1697.

IRONY
See also classified section: 2353 ff.
Used for: Dramatic irony.
See also narrower term: Romantic irony.
General literature. Film.
IRONY; relationship to sentimentality in Huston, John: *Prizzi's Honor*. 331.
Literary forms. Humor.
And IRONY; jokes. Psychoanalytic approach. Dissertation abstract. 2404.
Literary theory and criticism. Postmodernist literary theory and criticism.
Relationship to IRONY; modernity. 1859.
Professional topics. Humanities.
Role of IRONY; relationship to canon in teaching of literature. 2672.
Themes and figures. Christianity.
Relationship to IRONY. 2843.

IRRATIONALITY
See also related term: Madness.
General literature. Film.
Narrative technique; relationship to IRRATIONALITY in Lynch, David: *Blue Velvet*. 519.

ISER, WOLFGANG (1926-)
Literary theory and criticism. Reception theory.
Applied to detective fiction. Theories of ISER, WOLFGANG: *Der Akt des Lesens*. 1943.
Role of aesthetics. Theories of Jauss, Hans Robert; ISER, WOLFGANG. 1945.

ISKUSSTVO KINO
General literature. Film.
Treatment in *ISKUSSTVO KINO*. 228.

ISLAM
See also related term: Moslems.
Genres. Fiction. English language literature. 1800-1999.
Treatment of ISLAM; Moslems. 2131.

ISOCRATES (436-338 B.C.)—STUDY EXAMPLE
Professional topics. Humanities.
Rhetoric; relationship to cultural conservatism; study example: ISOCRATES; Erasmus, Desiderius; Weaver, Richard M. Dissertation abstract. 2653.

ISOMORPHISM
Literary theory and criticism. Semiotic literary theory and criticism.
ISOMORPHISM; similarity. Theories of Augustine, Saint; Thomas Aquinas, Saint; Peirce, Charles Sanders. 1960.

ISRAEL
General literature. Film.
Treatment of the Holocaust. Catalogue of archives in ISRAEL; relationship to Steven Spielberg Jewish Film Archive. 584.
General literature. Film. Film genres: documentary film in ISRAEL.
Interview with Gitai, Amos. 800.

ISRAEL, NICO (1919-)
Bibliographical.
Festschrift for ISRAEL, NICO. 1090.

ISRAELI HISTORY
General literature. Film.
Treatment of ISRAELI HISTORY. 266.

ITALIAN AMERICAN EXPERIENCE
See also related term: Italian Americans.

ITALIAN AMERICANS
General literature. Film.
Treatment of ITALIAN AMERICANS. 227.

ITALIAN CRITICISM
Literary theory and criticism. Reception theory.
Treatment in German criticism; ITALIAN CRITICISM. 1944.

ITALIAN IDENTITY
General literature. Film.
Role of ITALIAN IDENTITY in Bertolucci, Bernardo: *The Last Emperor*. 481.

ITALIAN LANGUAGE TRANSLATION
Literary theory and criticism. Semiotic literary theory and criticism.
Treatment of nonsense in ITALIAN LANGUAGE TRANSLATION of Bouissac, Paul: *Cirque et culture*. 1964.

ITALIAN STUDIES
Professional topics. Humanities.
On ITALIAN STUDIES; relationship to teaching in United States. 2668.

ITALIAN UNIVERSITIES
Professional topics. Humanities.
Curriculum at ITALIAN UNIVERSITIES (1100-1599). 2742.

ITALICS
Bibliographical. Printing. Typography in Venice (ca. 1500).
ITALICS by Manuzio, Aldo; relationship to copyright. 1225.

ITALY
Bibliographical. Analytical bibliography in ITALY. 1800-1899. 1119.
Bibliographical. Printing in ITALY. 1500-1599. 1165, 1179.
Bibliographical in ITALY. 1900-1999. 1093.
General literature. Film. Film theory and criticism.
Relationship to feminism in ITALY. 823.
General literature. Film in ITALY.
Neorealism. 338.
Role of Magnani, Anna. 500.
General literature. Film in ITALY (1945-1950).
Theories of Barthes, Roland. 311.
General literature. Television: home video in ITALY. 880.
General literature. Television in ITALY.
Role of advertisers. 878.
Literary theory and criticism. Feminist literary theory and criticism.
In ITALY. 1680.
Literary theory and criticism. Literary history in Germany; ITALY. 1761.
Literary theory and criticism. Semiotic literary theory and criticism.
In ITALY. 1963.
Professional topics. Comparative literature in ITALY. 2596.

ITERATION
Use: Repetition.

ITERATIVE NARRATIVE
General literature. Film.
ITERATIVE NARRATIVE in Ford, John: *How Green Was My Valley* compared to Stevens, George Cooper: *A Place in the Sun*; De Sica, Vittorio: *Umberto D.*; Olmi, Ermanno: *Il posto*. Application of theories of Genette, Gérard. 425.

IVANOV, VIACHESLAV VSEVOLODOVICH
Literary theory and criticism. Semiotic literary theory and criticism.
On stereotypes. Theories of IVANOV, VIACHESLAV VSEVOLODOVICH; Toporov, Vladimir Nikolaevich. 1988.

THE JACK BENNY SHOW
General literature. Television: situation comedy.
Self-reflexiveness in *The George Burns and Gracie Allen Show*; *I Love Lucy*; *THE JACK BENNY SHOW*. 868.

JACOBEAN PERIOD
General literature. Television: music television.
Discourse; relationship to power compared to masque for royal court of JACOBEAN PERIOD. 858.

SEE CLASSIFIED SEQUENCE FOR ADDITIONAL ENTRIES

JACQUELINE
Use: Carpentier, Alejo (1904-1980).

JAKOBSON, ROMAN OSIPOVICH (1896-1982)
Literary theory and criticism. Semiotic literary theory and criticism.
Theories of Peirce, Charles Sanders compared to JAKOBSON, ROMAN OSIPOVICH. 1961.
Literary theory and criticism. Structuralist literary theory and criticism.
Applied to proverb; fable. Theories of JAKOBSON, ROMAN OSIPOVICH. 2027.

JAMES, WILLIAM (1842-1910)
Literary theory and criticism.
Relationship to Modernism. Theories of Santayana, George; Royce, Josiah; JAMES, WILLIAM. 1466.
Literary theory and criticism. New Historicism.
Relationship to philosophy. Theories of Locke, John; Rorty, Richard; JAMES, WILLIAM. 1836.

JAMESON, FREDRIC (1934-)
General literature. Film in China.
Treatment of human body; relationship to ideology in Chang I-mo: *Hung kao-liang.* Application of theories of JAMESON, FREDRIC; Bakhtin, Mikhail Mikhaĭlovich. 661.
General literature. Television.
Imagery; relationship to cognitive representation; Postmodernism. Application of theories of JAMESON, FREDRIC. 920.
Literary movements.
Postmodernism. Relationship to history. Theories of Owens, Craig; JAMESON, FREDRIC. 1023.
——. Relationship to religion; politics. Application of theories of Bell, Daniel; JAMESON, FREDRIC. 1055.
Literary theory and criticism. Marxist literary theory and criticism.
Narrative as political discourse; relationship to interpretation. Treatment in JAMESON, FREDRIC: *The Political Unconscious.* 1789.
Theories of JAMESON, FREDRIC. 1785.

JAPAN
See also narrower term: Hiroshima.
General literature. Film.
Treatment of JAPAN in Scott, Ridley: *Black Rain.* 322.

JAUSS, HANS ROBERT (1921-)
Literary theory and criticism.
On reading; relationship to aesthetics. Theories of JAUSS, HANS ROBERT: *Aesthetische Erfahrung und literarische Hermeneutik* compared to Barthes, Roland: *Le Plaisir du texte.* 1361.
Literary theory and criticism. Reception theory.
Role of aesthetics. Theories of JAUSS, HANS ROBERT; Iser, Wolfgang. 1945. Theories of JAUSS, HANS ROBERT. 1949.
Literary theory and criticism. Semiotic literary theory and criticism.
Role of otherness in literature of Middle Ages; relationship to hermeneutics. Theories of JAUSS, HANS ROBERT; Gadamer, Hans-Georg. 1980.

JAZZ MUSIC
Bibliographical. Publishing in United States.
By Grove Press; relationship to *Evergreen Review;* JAZZ MUSIC. 1248.

JAZZ MUSICIAN
See also related term: Jazz music.

JEAN DE GÊNES
Use: Balbi, Giovanni (d. 1298).

JEANNE D'ARC, SAINT (1412-1431)
See also classified section: 2881.
General literature. Film.
Treatment of JEANNE D'ARC, SAINT. Dissertation abstract. 261.

JEHOVAH
See also related term: God.

JEST
See also related term: Jokes.

JESUIT DRAMATISTS
Genres. Drama by JESUIT DRAMATISTS. 1500-1799.
Sources in Old Testament. 2087.

JESUS CHRIST
Use: Christ.

JEWISH CHARACTERS
See also related term: Jews.

JEWISH EXPERIENCE
See also related term: Judaism.

JEWISH-GENTILE RELATIONS
See also related term: Jews.

JEWISH HISTORY
See also related terms: Jews; Judaism.

JEWISH IDENTITY
See also related terms: Jews; Judaism.
General literature. Film.
Treatment of JEWISH IDENTITY in Allen, Woody. 487.

JEWISH POETS
Genres. Poetry by JEWISH POETS. 2266.

JEWISH WRITERS
See also narrower term: Jewish poets.

JEWS
See also classified section: 2882.
See also related terms: Anti-Semitism; Jewish identity; Judaism.

JOANNES CHRYSOSTOM
Use: Chrysostom, John (ca. 347-407).

JOCASTA
See also related term: Oedipus.

JOHN OF LANCASTER, DUKE OF BEDFORD (1389-1435)
Bibliographical. Manuscripts. Manuscript collections. 1400-1499.
Of JOHN OF LANCASTER, DUKE OF BEDFORD. 1148.

JOHN RYLANDS UNIVERSITY LIBRARY OF MANCHESTER
Bibliographical. Printing.
By private presses. Checklist of collection at JOHN RYLANDS UNIVERSITY LIBRARY OF MANCHESTER. 1181.

JOHN THE APOSTLE, SAINT (D. 99 A.D.)
Used for: John the Divine, Saint; John the Evangelist (d. 99 A.D.).
Bibliographical. Manuscripts. Illuminated manuscripts. 1300-1399.
Relationship to cults of John the Baptist, Saint; JOHN THE APOSTLE, SAINT. 1138.

JOHN THE BAPTIST, SAINT (6 B.C.-32 A.D.)
Bibliographical. Manuscripts. Illuminated manuscripts. 1300-1399.
Relationship to cults of JOHN THE BAPTIST, SAINT; John the Apostle, Saint. 1138.

JOHN THE DIVINE, SAINT
Use: John the Apostle, Saint (d. 99 A.D.).

JOHN THE EVANGELIST (D. 99 A.D.)
Use: John the Apostle, Saint (d. 99 A.D.).

JOHNSON, BARBARA (1947-)—STUDY EXAMPLE
Literary theory and criticism. Deconstructionism.
Role of discipleship. Study example: de Man, Paul; JOHNSON, BARBARA. 1583.

JOHNSON, MARK LEONARD (1949-)
Figures of speech. Metaphor.
Relationship to nonmetaphorical concept. Theories of JOHNSON, MARK LEONARD. 2374.

JOKES
See also related term: Anecdote.
Literary forms. Humor.
And irony; JOKES. Psychoanalytic approach. Dissertation abstract. 2404.
Literary forms. Humor. 1700-1799.
Role of JOKES; pun; relationship to aesthetics. 2403.

JOU, LOUIS (1881-1968)
Bibliographical. Printing. Typography. 1900-1999.
By JOU, LOUIS. 1226.

JOURNAL
Use: Diary.

JOURNALISTS
General literature. Film in United States (1975-1987).
And American fiction. Treatment of JOURNALISTS. Application of theories of Lowenthal, Leo. Dissertation abstract. 439.

JOURNÉES CINÉMATOGRAPHIQUES DE CARTHAGE
General literature. Film.
Treatment of evil at JOURNÉES CINÉMATOGRAPHIQUES DE CARTHAGE in Tunis (1988). 367.

JOURNEY
See also related terms: Expedition; Voyage.

JUDAISM
See also related terms: Jewish identity; Jews.
Literary forms. Myth.
Relationship to JUDAISM; Christianity. 2407.
Literary theory and criticism.
Relationship to the other; the Holocaust; JUDAISM. Theories of Levinas, Emmanuel; Perelman, Chaim: *The New Rhetoric;* Rosenzweig, Franz. 1420.

JUDGMENT
General literature. Film.
Cinematic technique; relationship to JUDGMENT. Theories of Heidegger, Martin; Adorno, Theodor W. 656.

JUNG, CARL GUSTAV (1875-1961)
General literature. Film.
Treatment of mother; relationship to Nazism in postwar period in Hitchcock, Alfred: *Notorious.* Application of theories of JUNG, CARL GUSTAV. 244.
Literary forms. Tragedy.
Relationship to myth. Application of theories of JUNG, CARL GUSTAV. 2507.

JUNG, CARL GUSTAV (1875-1961)

Literary theory and criticism. Psychoanalytic literary theory and criticism.

Literary theory and criticism. Psychoanalytic literary theory and criticism.
On reading; relationship to transference. Application of theories of JUNG, CARL GUSTAV; Lacan, Jacques. 1907.

JUSTUS PROJECT—APPLICATION
Bibliographical. Publishing in England.
Relationship to law reports; printing. Application of JUSTUS PROJECT. 1272.

JUTRA, CLAUDE (1930-1986?)
General literature. Film.
On JUTRA, CLAUDE: *Mon oncle Antoine*. Pedagogical approach. 628.

KAHANE, MAURICE
Use: Girodias, Maurice (1919-).

KAIROS
See also related term: Time.
Literary forms. Rhetoric.
Stasis; *KAIROS*; treatment in Classical rhetoric; relationship to social construction. 2433.

KANT, IMMANUEL (1724-1804)
Literary forms. Rhetoric.
Role of question; metaphor; image in scientific language; relationship to epistemology. Theories of Meyer, Michel; KANT, IMMANUEL. 2427.
Literary movements.
Postmodernism. Relationship to architecture. Theories of Derrida, Jacques; KANT, IMMANUEL. 1028.
Literary theory and criticism.
Indeterminacy; relationship to the future. Theories of Derrida, Jacques compared to KANT, IMMANUEL; Rousseau, Jean-Jacques. 1317.
Literary theory and criticism. Deconstructionism.
Theories of KANT, IMMANUEL: *Kritik der Urteilskraft* in theories of Derrida, Jacques: "Parergon." 1608.
Literary theory and criticism. Philosophical literary theory and criticism.
History; relationship to culture. Theories of KANT, IMMANUEL compared to Dilthey, Wilhelm. 1854.

KANT, IMMANUEL (1724-1804)—AS SOURCE
Literary theory and criticism.
Semiotic idealism. Sources in KANT, IMMANUEL; Saussure, Ferdinand de. 1402.

KASDAN, LAWRENCE (1949-)
General literature. Film.
Treatment of Vietnam War; male-female relations in KASDAN, LAWRENCE: *The Big Chill* compared to Mason, Bobbie Ann: *In Country*. 239.

KAUFMAN, PHILIP (1936-)
General literature. Film.
Treatment of denial of human body in Siegel, Don: *Invasion of the Body Snatchers*; KAUFMAN, PHILIP: *Invasion of the Body Snatchers*. 442.

KAURISMÄKI, AKI
General literature. Film in Norway.
Interview with KAURISMÄKI, AKI and Kaurismäki, Mika. 461.

KAURISMÄKI, MIKA
General literature. Film in Norway.
Interview with Kaurismäki, Aki and KAURISMÄKI, MIKA. 461.

KEDROV, KONSTANTIN ALEKSANDROVICH
Literary theory and criticism.
Text; relationship to liturgy of Russian Orthodox Church. Relationship to theories of Bakhtin, Mikhail Mikhaïlovich; Florenskiĭ, Pavel Aleksandrovich: *Stolp i utverzhdenie istiny*; KEDROV, KONSTANTIN ALEKSANDROVICH: *Poéticheskiĭ kosmos*. 1558.

KELLAM, LAURENCE (CA. 1563-1611/13)
Bibliographical. Publishing. Book trade.
Trademark of KELLAM, LAURENCE. 1297.

KENOSIS
See also related term: Christ.

KENTUCKY
See also narrower term: Lexington (Kentucky).

KERMODE, FRANK (1919-)
Genres. Fiction.
Theories of KERMODE, FRANK: *The Sense of an Ending*. 2146.
Literary theory and criticism.
Relationship to canon. Interview with KERMODE, FRANK. 1445.
Theories of KERMODE, FRANK: *The Sense of an Ending*. 1529.

KIERKEGAARD, SØREN (1813-1855)
Literary theory and criticism.
Theories of de Man, Paul; relationship to KIERKEGAARD, SØREN. 1494.

KIESLOWSKI, KRZYSZTOF (1941-)
General literature. Film.
By KIESLOWSKI, KRZYSZTOF. 606.
——; relationship to exile. 295.
On KIESLOWSKI, KRZYSZTOF: *Dekalog*. 260.
Treatment of God; Christianity in KIESLOWSKI, KRZYSZTOF: *Dekalog*. 434.

KING ARTHUR
Use: Arthur, King.

KIS, MIKLÓS
Bibliographical. Printing. Typography in Amsterdam. 1600-1799.
Role of Dijk, Christoffel van; KIS, MIKLÓS; relationship to typefaces in Armenian language. 1228.

KITSCH
Literary movements.
Postmodernism. Role of the carnivalesque; KITSCH; relationship to bicentennial of French Revolution in Paris (1989). Application of theories of Bakhtin, Mikhail Mikhaïlovich. 1057.

KLEIST, BERND HEINRICH WILHELM VON
Use: Kleist, Heinrich von (1777-1811).

KLEIST, HEINRICH VON (1777-1811)
Used for: Kleist, Bernd Heinrich Wilhelm von.
General literature. Theater.
Marionettes; relationship to performance theory. Theories of Craig, Edward Gordon: "The Actor and the Über-marionette"; Meĭerkhol'd, Vsevolod Émil'evich; Schlemmer, Oskar; KLEIST, HEINRICH VON: "Über das Marionettentheater." Dissertation abstract. 962.

KLUGE, ALEXANDER (1932-)
General literature. Film.
By KLUGE, ALEXANDER. 383.
On KLUGE, ALEXANDER and Schamoni, Peter: *Brutalität im Stein*; relationship to film during Third Reich. 538.

KNAUF, THOMAS
General literature. Film. Film adaptation.
Treatment of French Revolution in film adaptation of Hofmann, Fritz: "Treffen in Travers" by KNAUF, THOMAS; Gwisdek, Michael. 737.

KNOWLEDGE
See also narrower term: Cultural knowledge.
See also related term: Epistemology.
Genres. Novel.
Relationship to KNOWLEDGE; epistemology. Theories of Boyle, Robert: *The Christian Virtuoso*; *Occasional Reflections on Several Subjects*. 2199.
Literary forms. Rhetoric.
Relationship to science; KNOWLEDGE. 2455.

KNOWLEDGE REPRESENTATION
See also related term: Knowledge.

KNOWLEDGE STRUCTURE
See also related term: Knowledge.

KNUT
Use: Canute I, King of England (995?-1035).

KOFMAN, SARAH (1934-)
Literary theory and criticism. Feminist literary theory and criticism.
Theories of KOFMAN, SARAH. 1691.

KOMMUNISTISCHE PARTEI DEUTSCHLANDS
See also related term: Communist Party.

KONCHALOVSKIĬ, ANDREĬ SERGEEVICH
Use: Mikhalkov-Konchalovskiĭ, Andreĭ Sergeevich (1937-).

KONIGSBERG, ALLEN STEWART
Use: Allen, Woody (1935-).

KORAN
Used for: Qur'ān.
Literary forms. Translation.
Of dialogue of KORAN; relationship to oral tradition. 2521.

KOREA
General literature. Film in KOREA (1987-1988).
Dissertation abstract. 412.

KOTCHEFF, TED (1931-)
Used for: Kotcheff, William Theodore.
General literature. Film.
Role of pastoralism in KOTCHEFF, TED: *First Blood* compared to Cosmatos, George Pan: *Rambo II*; Mulcahy, Russell: *Rambo III*. 273.

KOTCHEFF, WILLIAM THEODORE
Use: Kotcheff, Ted (1931-).

KOZINTSEV, GRIGORIĬ MIKHAĬLOVICH (1905-1973)
General literature. Film.
On KOZINTSEV, GRIGORIĬ MIKHAĬLOVICH and Trauberg, Leonid Zakharovich: *Odna*. 614.

KRESS, GEORG (FL. 1606-1621)
Bibliographical. Printing. Typography. 1500-1699.
Role of KRESS, GEORG as *Briefmaler*. 1229.

KRIPKE, SAUL A. (1940-)
Literary theory and criticism.
On KRIPKE, SAUL A.: *Naming and Necessity*. Treatment in Hirsch, Eric Donald. 1541.

KRISTEVA, JULIA (1941-)
Genres. Poetry.
Treatment of the chora; relationship to representation. Theories of KRISTEVA, JULIA: *Révolution du langage poétique*. 2255.

SEE CLASSIFIED SEQUENCE FOR ADDITIONAL ENTRIES

Literary movements.
Avant-garde. Role of women. Interview with KRISTEVA, JULIA. 995.
Literary theory and criticism.
Theories of KRISTEVA, JULIA. 1543.
——; relationship to Freud, Sigmund. 1503.
Treatment of depression. Theories of KRISTEVA, JULIA: *Soleil noir, dépression et mélancolie*. 1447.
Literary theory and criticism. Feminist literary theory and criticism.
Relationship to discourse analysis. Theories of Lacan, Jacques; KRISTEVA, JULIA. 1670.
Literary theory and criticism. Poststructuralist literary theory and criticism.
Interview with KRISTEVA, JULIA. 1876.
Literary theory and criticism. Semiotic literary theory and criticism.
Relationship to Marxist literary theory and criticism. Theories of KRISTEVA, JULIA; Lacan, Jacques. 1959.

KROKER, ARTHUR (1945-)
Literary movements.
Postmodernism. Treatment in KROKER, ARTHUR and Cook, David Bruce: *The Postmodern Scene: Excremental Culture and Hyper-Aesthetics*. 1046.

KRUITWAGEN, BONAVENTURA (B. 1874)
Used for: Kruitwagen, Frans Joseph.
Bibliographical. Printing.
Of letters (1461); relationship to Neuhausen. Theories of KRUITWAGEN, BONAVENTURA. 1188.

KRUITWAGEN, FRANS JOSEPH
Use: Kruitwagen, Bonaventura (b. 1874).

KUBRICK, STANLEY (1928-)
General literature. Film.
Treatment of Gothicism in KUBRICK, STANLEY compared to Faulkner, William: "A Rose for Emily"; *As I Lay Dying*; *Sanctuary*; Pynchon, Thomas: *V.*; *Gravity's Rainbow*; *The Crying of Lot 49*. Dissertation abstract. 330.

KULTUR OG KLASSE
Literary theory and criticism.
In *KULTUR OG KLASSE*. 1305.

KÜNSTLERROMAN
See also related term: Bildungsroman.

KUNSTMÄRCHEN
See also related term: Märchen.

LABORERS
Use: Workers.

LABYRINTH
See also classified section: 2883.
Used for: Maze.
Literary forms. Myth.
Treatment of LABYRINTH; monsters. 2409.

LABYRINTH POEM
See also related term: Labyrinth.

LACAN, JACQUES (1901-1981)
General literature. Film.
Role of Lennon, John and McCartney, Paul in Webb, Peter: *Give My Regards to Broad Street*. Application of theories of LACAN, JACQUES. 603.
Literary forms. Rhetoric.
Future perfect tense in argumentation; relationship to psychoanalytic literary theory and criticism. Theories of Aristotle; LACAN, JACQUES; Derrida, Jacques. 2489.
Literary theory and criticism.
Theories of LACAN, JACQUES. 1405.
Literary theory and criticism. Feminist literary theory and criticism.
Relationship to discourse analysis. Theories of LACAN, JACQUES; Kristeva, Julia. 1670.
Literary theory and criticism. Poststructuralist literary theory and criticism.
Role of subjectivity; the self; relationship to humanism; New Criticism. Application of theories of LACAN, JACQUES. 1887.
Literary theory and criticism. Psychoanalytic literary theory and criticism.
On reading; relationship to transference. Application of theories of Jung, Carl Gustav; LACAN, JACQUES. 1907.
Relationship to language. Theories of LACAN, JACQUES. Review article. 1900.
Relationship to semiotics. Application of theories of LACAN, JACQUES. 1916.
Role of Oedipus complex. Theories of Abraham, Nicolas and Torok, Maria compared to Freud, Sigmund; LACAN, JACQUES. Review article. 1909.
Theories of LACAN, JACQUES. 1899.
Literary theory and criticism. Reader-response theory and criticism and feminist literary theory and criticism.
Relationship to the unconscious of women. Theories of Freud, Sigmund; LACAN, JACQUES. 1940.
Literary theory and criticism. Semiotic literary theory and criticism.
Relationship to Marxist literary theory and criticism. Theories of Kristeva, Julia; LACAN, JACQUES. 1959.

LADD-FRANKLIN, CHRISTINE (1847-1930)
Literary theory and criticism. Semiotic literary theory and criticism.
Aesthetics of color; form. Theories of Marquand, Allan; LADD-FRANKLIN, CHRISTINE; relationship to Peirce, Charles Sanders. 1985.

LAKOFF, GEORGE (1941-)
Figures of speech.
Treatment in LAKOFF, GEORGE. 2347.

LANDSCAPE
See also related term: Nature.

LANG, FRITZ (1890-1976)
General literature. Film.
By LANG, FRITZ; Pabst, Georg Wilhelm. Psychoanalytic approach. 250.
——; relationship to independent filmmakers; film studios. Film history. 252.
Mise en scène; narrative; relationship to fascism in LANG, FRITZ: *Siegfried*; *Kriemhilds Rache*. 376.
Role of Goebbels, Joseph in censorship of LANG, FRITZ: *Das Testament des Dr. Mabuse*. 640.
Role of Vernon, Howard in Melville, Jean-Pierre: *Le Silence de la mer*; LANG, FRITZ: *Die tausend Augen des Dr. Mabuse*. Includes discussion with Vernon. 345.

LANGENDONCK, W. VAN
Literary theory and criticism. Linguistic literary theory and criticism.
Iconicity of poetic language. Structuralist approach. Compared to treatment in Pater, W. de and LANGENDONCK, W. VAN: "Natuurlijkheid van de taal en iconiciteit." 1739.

LANGUAGE
See also narrower terms: Literary language; Metalanguage; Nonreferential language; Philosophical language; Poetic language; Scientific language.
Bibliographical. Printing. Illustration.
Visual imagery; LANGUAGE; relationship to signifier. 1212.
General literature.
LANGUAGE; relationship to culture. 80.
——; relationship to imagery in painting by Turner, Joseph Mallord William. 168.
Role of narrative; relationship to meaning; LANGUAGE; autobiography. Psychological approach. 34.
General literature. Film.
LANGUAGE. Film history. 275.
Treatment of Vietnam War; relationship to LANGUAGE. 589.
General literature. Theater.
LANGUAGE; relationship to audience. 928.
Literary movements.
Modernism. Abstraction; logic in LANGUAGE; relationship to Postmodernism. 1016.
Postmodernism. Relationship to LANGUAGE. 1053.
——. Use of LANGUAGE. Application of theories of Nietzsche, Friedrich Wilhelm. 1063.
Romanticism. Poetic language; relationship to synecdoche compared to LANGUAGE of astronomy. Application of theories of Newton, Sir Isaac compared to Herschel, Sir William. 1077.
Literary theory and criticism.
Aesthetics; relationship to LANGUAGE. Review article. 1547.
LANGUAGE. 1363.
On novel; relationship to LANGUAGE. Theories of Bakhtin, Mikhail Mikhaĭlovich. 1372.
——; relationship to LANGUAGE; society. Theories of Bakhtin, Mikhail Mikhaĭlovich. 1319.
Role of interpretive conventions in LANGUAGE. Review article. 1495.
Role of the other; LANGUAGE; relationship to ethics; religion. Theories of Levinas, Emmanuel; Marion, Jean-Luc. 1577.
Literary theory and criticism. Deconstructionism.
Role of LANGUAGE; relationship to technology. Theories of Derrida, Jacques: *De la grammatologie* compared to Heidegger, Martin: "Die Frage nach der Technik." 1584.
Literary theory and criticism. Psychoanalytic literary theory and criticism.
On ambiguity of LANGUAGE; relationship to psychoanalysis. 1912.
Relationship to LANGUAGE. Theories of Lacan, Jacques. Review article. 1900.

LANGUAGE ARTS
Professional topics. Humanities.
Role of English departments; LANGUAGE ARTS. 2697.

LANGUAGE CHANGE
Literary forms. Translation.
Of Bible; relationship to LANGUAGE CHANGE. 2561.

LANGUAGE CONTACT
See also related term: Creole languages.

LANGUAGE DECAY
See also related term: Language change.

LANGUAGE GAMES
Professional topics. Humanities.
Academic discourse; literacy as LANGUAGE GAMES; relationship to gender. 2741.

LANGUAGE INTERACTION
See also related terms: Creole languages; Translation.

LANGUAGE LABORATORY
See also related term: Teaching of language.

LANGUAGE LEARNING
Use: Second language learning.

LANGUAGE MIXING
See also related term: Creole languages.

LANGUAGES FOR SPECIAL PURPOSES
See also related terms: Second language learning; Second language teaching.

***LANGUE/PAROLE* DISTINCTION**
See also related term: Language.

LARSEN, PETER (1943-)
　Literary theory and criticism.
　　Theories of Benjamin, Walter; LARSEN, PETER. 1549.

LAST JUDGMENT
See also related term: The apocalypse.

LAST RITES
See also related term: Death.

LATIN AMERICA
　Bibliographical. Publishing. Book trade in LATIN AMERICA and Spain. 1298.
　General literature. Film in LATIN AMERICA. 476.

LATIN LANGUAGE LITERATURE
　Bibliographical. LATIN LANGUAGE LITERATURE. 700-799.
　　Donation of book to Chiesa di San Clemente. Treatment in epigraph. 1111.
　Bibliographical. Manuscripts. Codicology. LATIN LANGUAGE LITERATURE. 1134, 1135.
　Bibliographical. Manuscripts. LATIN LANGUAGE LITERATURE. 1125.
　Bibliographical. Printing. Binding. 1500-1599.
　　Of LATIN LANGUAGE LITERATURE in girdlebooks. 1208.
　Bibliographical. Printing. LATIN LANGUAGE LITERATURE. 1500-1599.
　　Of monomachia against Alciati, Andrea. 1160.
　Bibliographical. Printing. Typography. 1500-1599.
　　By Comin da Trino of LATIN LANGUAGE LITERATURE. 1230.
　Bibliographical. Printing in Germany. 1400-1499.
　　Of LATIN LANGUAGE LITERATURE by Schöffer family. 1183.
　Literary theory and criticism. Middle Ages.
　　Relationship to textual criticism; LATIN LANGUAGE LITERATURE. Review article. 1576.

LATVIA
　Bibliographical. Publishing. Book trade in LATVIA. 1288.

LATVIAN LITERATURE
　Bibliographical. Printing. Illustration.
　　In LATVIAN LITERATURE for children. 1216.

LAUD
See also related term: Liturgy.

LAUGHTER
　General literature. Theater.
　　Relationship to LAUGHTER; popular culture. Theories of Bakhtin, Mikhail Mikhaïlovich; Eco, Umberto; Fo, Dario. 943.
　Literary theory and criticism.
　　Role of LAUGHTER as aesthetic device; relationship to truth. Theories of Bakhtin, Mikhail Mikhaïlovich. 1499.
　Literary theory and criticism. Poststructuralist literary theory and criticism.
　　Role of otherness; relationship to LAUGHTER. Theories of Bakhtin, Mikhail Mikhaïlovich compared to Derrida, Jacques. 1882.

LAUREUX, JEAN-CLAUDE
　General literature. Film.
　　On Resnais, Alain: *I Want to Go Home*. Interview with Benson, Laura; Leterrier, Catherine; van Damme, Charlie; LAUREUX, JEAN-CLAUDE. 609.

LAW
Used for: Legislation.
See also related term: Legal discourse.
　General literature.
　　Relationship to LAW. 170.
　General literature. Television.
　　Treatment of LAW; relationship to style in *Miami Vice*. 913.
　Genres. Poetry.
　　Relationship to LAW. 2301.
　Literary forms. Rhetoric.
　　Relationship to LAW. 2460.

LAW REPORTS
　Bibliographical. Publishing in England.
　　Relationship to LAW REPORTS; printing. Application of Justus Project. 1272.

LAWBREAKER
Use: Criminal.

LE BRUN, CHARLES (1619-1690)
　General literature. Theater.
　　Representation of nature in theatrical production; relationship to Realist movement and Naturalism. Theories of Darwin, Charles Robert; LE BRUN, CHARLES. 960.

LEARNING
See also narrower term: Second language learning.

LEE, SPIKE
　General literature. Film.
　　On LEE, SPIKE: *Do the Right Thing*. 586.
　　Treatment of African American community in LEE, SPIKE: *She's Gotta Have It*; *School Daze*; *Do the Right Thing*. 521.
　　Treatment of racism in LEE, SPIKE: *Do the Right Thing* compared to Burton, Tim: *Batman*; *Batman: The Dark Knight* by Miller, Frank. 550.
　General literature. Film by African American filmmakers.
　　On LEE, SPIKE: *Do the Right Thing*. Interview. 543.

THE LEFT
See also related term: Left-wing politics.
　General literature. Film in China (1930-1939).
　　Treatment of THE LEFT. 255.
　General literature. Film in Germany.
　　Relationship to THE LEFT in Weimar Republic. 504.

LEFT-WING POLITICS
Used for: Leftist politics.
See also related term: The Left.
　Professional topics. Humanities.
　　Relationship to LEFT-WING POLITICS. 2685, 2734, 2792, 2794.
　　—— (1960-1969). 2780.
　　—— (1970-1990). 2798.

LEFT-WING WRITERS
See also related term: Left-wing politics.

LEFTIST POLITICS
Use: Left-wing politics.

LEGAL CASES
See also related term: Law.

LEGAL DISCOURSE
See also related term: Law.
　Genres. Prose. Autobiographical prose.
　　And fiction; representation of women; LEGAL DISCOURSE (1700-1899). 2317.
　Literary theory and criticism. Narrative theory.
　　Applied to LEGAL DISCOURSE. 1807.

LEGAL HISTORY
See also related term: Law.

LEGAL LANGUAGE
See also related term: Legal discourse.

LEGAL SYSTEM
See also related term: Law.

LEGAL THEORY
See also related term: Law.

LEGEND
See also narrower term: Arthurian legend.
See also: entries for legends of specific countries, areas, or peoples by consulting the index under the adjectival form of the country, area, or people.
　Genres. Novel. Popular romance novel.
　　Treatment of love; relationship to myth; LEGEND. 2237.

LEGEND TRIPS
See also related term: Legend.

LEGENDARY FIGURES
See also narrower terms: Arthur, King; Cressida; Faust; Merlin; Oedipus.

LEGISLATION
Use: Law.

LEHMAN, ERNEST PAUL (1915-)
　General literature. Film in Hollywood.
　　Narrative; relationship to authorship in Hitchcock, Alfred: *North by Northwest*; role of screenplay by LEHMAN, ERNEST PAUL. Dissertation abstract. 581.

LEISURE
　Genres. Novel. Popular romance novel.
　　Relationship to adolescents and LEISURE. Dissertation abstract. 2234.

LEITMOTIFS
See also related term: Theme.

LEM, STANISŁAW (1921-)—STUDY EXAMPLE
　General literature.
　　Relationship to order; chaos; study example: Adams, Henry Brooks: *The Education of Henry Adams*; Lessing, Doris: *The Golden Notebook*; LEM, STANISŁAW. 96.

LENINGRAD
See also related term: St. Petersburg.

LENNON, JOHN (1940-1980)
　General literature. Film.
　　Role of LENNON, JOHN and McCartney, Paul in Webb, Peter: *Give My Regards to Broad Street*. Application of theories of Lacan, Jacques. 603.

LENZ, SIEGFRIED (1926-)
　General literature. Film.
　　On LENZ, SIEGFRIED: *Ein Kriegsende*. 654.

SEE CLASSIFIED SEQUENCE FOR ADDITIONAL ENTRIES

LIFE

Literary theory and criticism. Psychoanalytic literary theory and criticism.

LESBIANISM
See also related term: Lesbians.
  Genres. Novel. 1900-1999.
    Treatment of LESBIANISM. Feminist approach. 2214.
LESBIANS
See also classified section: 2884.
See also related terms: Homosexuality; Homosexuals; Lesbianism.
  Themes and figures. LESBIANS. 1900-1999.
    Relationship to Postmodernism. 2884.
LESSING, DORIS (1919-)
Used for: Somers, Jane.
LESSING, DORIS (1919-)—STUDY EXAMPLE
  General literature.
    Relationship to order; chaos; study example: Adams, Henry Brooks: *The Education of Henry Adams*; LESSING, DORIS: *The Golden Notebook*; Lem, Stanisław. 96.
LETERRIER, CATHERINE
  General literature. Film.
    On Resnais, Alain: *I Want to Go Home*. Interview with Benson, Laura; LETERRIER, CATHERINE; van Damme, Charlie; Laureux, Jean-Claude. 609.
LETTER RECOGNITION
See also related term: Reading.
LETTER WRITING
See also related term: Letters.
LETTERS
See also classified section: 2334 ff.
Used for: Correspondence.
See also narrower term: Letters of recommendation.
See also related term: Autobiography.
  Bibliographical. Printing.
    Of LETTERS (1461); relationship to Neuhausen. Theories of Kruitwagen, Bonaventura. 1188.
LETTERS OF RECOMMENDATION
  Professional topics. Humanities.
    On peer review; LETTERS OF RECOMMENDATION; relationship to teaching; research. 2800.
LÉVI-STRAUSS, CLAUDE (1908-)
  General literature. Film.
    Narrative structure. Treatment of Vietnam War in Coppola, Francis Ford: *Apocalypse Now*. Application of theories of LÉVI-STRAUSS, CLAUDE. 644.
  Literary theory and criticism.
    Theories of LÉVI-STRAUSS, CLAUDE; Derrida, Jacques. 1421.
LEVINAS, EMMANUEL (1905-)
  Literary theory and criticism.
    Relationship to the other; the Holocaust; Judaism. Theories of LEVINAS, EMMANUEL; Perelman, Chaim: *The New Rhetoric*; Rosenzweig, Franz. 1420.
    Role of death in time. Theories of Heidegger, Martin compared to LEVINAS, EMMANUEL. 1351.
    Role of the apocalypse; relationship to time. Theories of LEVINAS, EMMANUEL: *Totalité et infini*. 1567.
    Role of the other; language; relationship to ethics; religion. Theories of LEVINAS, EMMANUEL; Marion, Jean-Luc. 1577.
    Skepticism; relationship to ethics. Theories of Cavell, Stanley Louis: *The Claim of Reason* compared to LEVINAS, EMMANUEL: *Totalité et infini*; *Autrement qu'être*. 1341.
  Literary theory and criticism. Deconstructionism.
    Parodic play; relationship to reason. Theories of Derrida, Jacques compared to LEVINAS, EMMANUEL. 1606.
    Relationship to violence. Treatment in Derrida, Jacques compared to LEVINAS, EMMANUEL. 1646.
  Literary theory and criticism. Philosophical literary theory and criticism.
    Theories of Heidegger, Martin; Blanchot, Maurice; LEVINAS, EMMANUEL. Dissertation abstract. 1851.
LÉVY, BERNARD-HENRI (1948-)
  Literary theory and criticism.
    Interview with LÉVY, BERNARD-HENRI. 1537.
LEWTON, VAL (1904-1951)
  General literature. Film.
    Role of censorship in Fleming, Victor: *Gone with the Wind*; relationship to LEWTON, VAL; Selznick, David O. 495.
LEXICAL APPROACH
Documents applying specific approaches are so numerous that access to them is provided only in the electronic versions of the *Bibliography*.
LEXICAL DERIVATION
See also related term: Word.
LEXICAL ENTRY
See also related term: Dictionary.
LEXICAL MEANING
See also related terms: Semantics; Word.
LEXICAL RETRIEVAL
See also related term: Word.

LEXICOGRAPHY
See also related terms: Dictionary; Word.
LEXICOLOGY
See also related terms: Terminology; Word.
LEXICON
See also related term: Word.
LEXICOSTATISTICAL APPROACH
Documents applying specific approaches are so numerous that access to them is provided only in the electronic versions of the *Bibliography*.
LEXINGTON (KENTUCKY)
  General literature. Film in United States: LEXINGTON (KENTUCKY) (1897-1906). 634.
LIBERAL ARTS
See also narrower term: Humanities.
LIBERALISM
  Literary theory and criticism. Poststructuralist literary theory and criticism.
    Role of subversion; relationship to ideology of LIBERALISM. Theories of de Man, Paul; Derrida, Jacques. 1884.
  Professional topics. Humanities.
    Canon; pedagogy in United States; relationship to LIBERALISM compared to conservatism. 2782.
LIBERALS
See also related term: Liberalism.
LIBERTINE (FIGURE)
See also narrower term: Don Juan.
See also related term: Libertinism.
LIBERTINES (GROUP)
See also related term: Libertinism.
LIBERTINISM
  General literature. Film. Film adaptation.
    Treatment of LIBERTINISM; women in film adaptation of Laclos, Pierre Ambroise François Choderlos de: *Les Liaisons dangereuses* by Vadim, Roger. 679.
LIBRARIANS
  Bibliographical.
    On training of LIBRARIANS about rare books; manuscripts. 1109.
LIBRARIES
See also narrower terms: Biblioteca Vallicelliana; Bibliothèque Royale Albert Iᵉr; British Library; John Rylands University Library of Manchester; Library of Congress; Personal library.
  Bibliographical.
    LIBRARIES. 1098.
    ——. Interview with Billington, James H. 1100.
    —— in Lithuania. Role of Vladimirovas, Levas. 1105.
    —— in Lithuania (1941-1942); relationship to Soviet army. 1110.
    Relationship to LIBRARIES; publishing in Lithuania. Treatment in Vladimirovas, Levas. Bibliography. 1118.
  Bibliographical. Publishing. Book trade.
    And LIBRARIES in China. 1286.
  Bibliographical. Publishing in France.
    Book distribution; LIBRARIES; relationship to social class. 1259.
LIBRARY COLLECTION
  Bibliographical.
    Role of LIBRARY COLLECTION; relationship to canon. Collection study of collection at Harry Ransom Humanities Research Center at University of Texas at Austin. 1112.
    ——; relationship to mail-order catalogue. 1107.
    Role of online catalogs; relationship to LIBRARY COLLECTION. 1103.
LIBRARY EXHIBITION CATALOGUES
  Bibliographical.
    Relationship to LIBRARY EXHIBITION CATALOGUES. 1086.
    Role of LIBRARY EXHIBITION CATALOGUES; relationship to exhibition of rare books and manuscripts. 1097.
  Bibliographical. Printing.
    Of LIBRARY EXHIBITION CATALOGUES. 1153.
LIBRARY OF CONGRESS
  Bibliographical.
    Collection study of collection at LIBRARY OF CONGRESS. 1113.
LIBRETTIST
See also related term: Dramatists.
LIBRETTO
See also related terms: Lyrics; Opera.
LIEB, FRITZ (B. 1892)
  Bibliographical.
    Personal library of LIEB, FRITZ; relationship to Russian literature; Slavic literature. 1099.
LIFE
See also narrower terms: Extraterrestrial life; Working class life.
  Literary theory and criticism. Psychoanalytic literary theory and criticism.
    On LIFE as narrative; relationship to time. Theories of Freud, Sigmund; Sartre, Jean-Paul; Rorty, Richard. 1896.

LIFE CYCLE
See also related term: Life.

LIGHTING
See also related term: Staging.

LIKHACHËV, DMITRIĬ SERGEEVICH (1906-)
Literary theory and criticism. Narrative theory.
Applied to literature of Middle Ages. Application of theories of LIKHACHËV, DMITRIĬ SERGEEVICH: *Poétika drevnerusskoĭ literatury.* 1819.

LIMITS
See also related terms: Boundary; Transcendence.

LINGUISTIC ANALYSIS
See also narrower term: Semantic analysis.
Literary theory and criticism. Narrative theory.
LINGUISTIC ANALYSIS of *récit.* 1795.

LINGUISTIC APPROACH
Documents applying specific approaches are so numerous that access to them is provided only in the electronic versions of the *Bibliography.*

LINGUISTIC AWARENESS
See also narrower term: Metalinguistic awareness.

LINGUISTIC CONVENTIONS
Literary theory and criticism. Linguistic literary theory and criticism.
Stylistics; relationship to LINGUISTIC CONVENTIONS. Theories of Fish, Stanley. 1754.

LINGUISTIC FIELDWORK
See also related term: Linguistics.

LINGUISTIC INNOVATION
See also related term: Neologism.

LINGUISTIC LITERARY CRITICISM
Use: Linguistic literary theory and criticism.

LINGUISTIC LITERARY THEORY AND CRITICISM
See also classified section: 1734 ff.
Used for: Linguistic literary criticism.
Literary theory and criticism. Hermeneutics and LINGUISTIC LITERARY THEORY AND CRITICISM. Middle Ages.
Applied to book; relationship to myth; study example: Chaucer, Geoffrey; Dante. 1719.
Literary theory and criticism. Structuralist literary theory and criticism.
And LINGUISTIC LITERARY THEORY AND CRITICISM. 2025.

LINGUISTIC REPRESENTATION
Literary movements.
Postmodernism. LINGUISTIC REPRESENTATION; relationship to philosophy; psychology. 1045.

LINGUISTIC SCHOOLS
See also narrower term: Prague School of Linguistics.

LINGUISTIC THEORY
See also narrower terms: Frame theory; Transformational-generative grammar.
Literary forms. Rhetoric.
Relationship to LINGUISTIC THEORY; ideology. 2448.

LINGUISTICS
See also narrower term: Text linguistics.
See also: entries for linguistics in specific countries by consulting the index under the adjectival form of the country.
Literary theory and criticism. Narrative theory.
Application in LINGUISTICS; anthropology; psychology. 1799.

LINGUISTS
See also related term: Linguistics.

LITERACY
See also related term: Reading.
Bibliographical. Printing. History of printing.
Relationship to LITERACY. 1192.
Professional topics. Humanities.
Academic discourse; LITERACY as language games; relationship to gender. 2741.
LITERACY. 2757.
——; relationship to gender. 2797.
——; relationship to teaching of literature. 2770.
Multicultural education; relationship to LITERACY; feminism. Interview with Stimpson, Catharine R. 2657.
Relationship to LITERACY; science. Theories of Hirsch, Eric Donald; Bakhtin, Mikhail Mikhaĭlovich. 2677.
Role of LITERACY. 2662.

LITERACY DEVELOPMENT
See also related term: Literacy.

LITERAL MEANING
Figures of speech. Metaphor.
Compared to LITERAL MEANING; comparison. 2368.
Literary theory and criticism.
Figuration; relationship to LITERAL MEANING; study example: scientific language; philosophical language (1630-1800). Review article. 1506.

LITERARINESS
Literary theory and criticism.
On LITERARINESS; relationship to literary conventions. 1368.
Literary theory and criticism. Formalist literary theory and criticism.
LITERARINESS. 1710.

LITERARY ASCETICISM MOVEMENT
Use: Hermetism.

LITERARY CONVENTIONS
See also narrower term: Narrative conventions.
Genres. Fiction.
Image; form; relationship to LITERARY CONVENTIONS. Treatment of nuclear war. 2108.
Literary theory and criticism.
On literariness; relationship to LITERARY CONVENTIONS. 1368.

LITERARY CRITICISM
Use: Literary theory and criticism.

LITERARY FORMS
See also classified section: 2379 ff.
See also narrower terms: Allegory; Dialogue; Emblem; Epigraph; Epitaph; Fable; Fantasy; Humor; Myth; Parody; Pastiche; Proverb; Rhetoric; Romance; Satire; Tragedy; Translation.

LITERARY GROUPS
See also narrower term: Beat Generation.

LITERARY HISTORY
See also classified section: 1760 ff.
Bibliographical.
On personal collections (1600-1799); relationship to LITERARY HISTORY. Treatment in criticism (1975-1988). 1084.
General literature. Theater.
Theater history; relationship to LITERARY HISTORY. 955.
Literary forms. Emblem.
Relationship to LITERARY HISTORY. 2396.
Literary forms. Translation.
Relationship to LITERARY HISTORY. 2523, 2558, 2560.
Literary theory and criticism. Deconstructionism.
Relationship to LITERARY HISTORY. Theories of de Man, Paul. 1615.
Literary theory and criticism. Reception theory.
Relationship to LITERARY HISTORY. 1950.

LITERARY LANGUAGE
General literature.
LITERARY LANGUAGE compared to spoken language. 140.

LITERARY MARKETPLACE
See also related term: Marketing.

LITERARY MOVEMENTS
See also classified section: 987 ff.
See also narrower terms: Avant-garde; The Baroque; Constructivism; Enlightenment; Formalism; Hermetism; Humanism; Modernism; Naturalism; New Criticism; Postmodernism; Poststructuralism; Realist movement; Regionalism; Romanticism; Socialist realism; Structuralism; Surrealism.

LITERARY PERIODS
See also narrower terms: *Fin de siècle*; Romantic period.

LITERARY PRIZES
See also narrower terms: Neustadt International Prize for Literature; Nobel Prize in Literature.

LITERARY PRODUCTION
See also related term: Publishing.

LITERARY REPUTATION
See also related term: Reception study.

LITERARY SCHOOLS
See also related term: Literary movements.

LITERARY STUDIES
Professional topics. Comparative literature.
And LITERARY STUDIES; relationship to literary theory and criticism. 2601.
Role of imagology; relationship to LITERARY STUDIES. 2599.
Professional topics. Humanities.
LITERARY STUDIES. 2745.
—— of Renaissance in Great Britain; Netherlands (1950-1990). 2658.
Role of dualism; holism; relationship to canon in LITERARY STUDIES. Theories of Descartes, René. 2679.
Role of interdisciplinary studies in LITERARY STUDIES. 2659.
Role of LITERARY STUDIES; relationship to Postmodernism. 2810.
Themes and figures. Utopianism.
Relationship to LITERARY STUDIES. Semiotic approach. Theories of Bloch, Ernst. 2931.

LITERARY TERMS
General literature.
Dictionary of LITERARY TERMS. 11.

LITERARY THEORY
Use: Literary theory and criticism.

SEE CLASSIFIED SEQUENCE FOR ADDITIONAL ENTRIES

LITERARY THEORY AND CRITICISM
See also classified section: 1305 ff.
Used for: Literary criticism; Literary theory.
See also narrower terms: Contextualist criticism; Cultural criticism; Deconstructionism; Feminist literary theory and criticism; Formalist literary theory and criticism; Genre study; Genre theory; Hermeneutics; Interpretive communities; Linguistic literary theory and criticism; Literary history; Marxist literary theory and criticism; Narrative theory; New Criticism; New Historicism; Philosophical literary theory and criticism; Poetics; Political criticism; Postmodernist literary theory and criticism; Poststructuralist literary theory and criticism; Psychoanalytic literary theory and criticism; Psychological literary theory and criticism; Reader-response theory and criticism; Reception theory; Rhetorical criticism; Rhetorical theory; Semiotic literary theory and criticism; Socialist realist literary theory and criticism; Sociological literary theory and criticism; Structuralist literary theory and criticism.
See also related term: Critical judgment.
See also: entries for literary theory and criticism in specific countries by consulting the index under the adjectival form of the country.

Professional topics. Comparative literature.
And literary studies; relationship to LITERARY THEORY AND CRITICISM. 2601.
Relationship to LITERARY THEORY AND CRITICISM. 2593, 2627, 2630.

Professional topics. Comparative literature in Europe; United States.
Role of LITERARY THEORY AND CRITICISM. 2603.

Professional topics. Computer-assisted research.
Relationship to LITERARY THEORY AND CRITICISM. 2647.

Professional topics. Humanities.
Relationship to LITERARY THEORY AND CRITICISM. Pedagogical approach. 2771.
Role of LITERARY THEORY AND CRITICISM. 2785.
—— in English studies. 2698.

Professional topics. Humanities in India.
Role of LITERARY THEORY AND CRITICISM; Western culture. 2783.

LITERARY VALUE
Literary theory and criticism.
Role of LITERARY VALUE. 1388.

LITERATURE
See also narrower terms: Apocalyptic literature; *Belles-lettres*; Classical literature; Erotic literature; Ethnic literature; Folk literature; National literature; Popular literature; Religious literature; Western literature; World literature.
See also: entries under national literature headings, e.g., English literature, German literature, etc.

Literary theory and criticism.
On LITERATURE as institution. 1492.
—— as system. 1525.

Literary theory and criticism. Narrative theory.
Applied to LITERATURE of Middle Ages. Application of theories of Likhachëv, Dmitriĭ Sergeevich: *Poétika drevnerusskoĭ literatury.* 1819.

LITERATURE OF THE BRITISH ISLES
See also narrower term: English literature.

LITERATURES OF EAST EUROPE, CENTRAL ASIA, AND SIBERIA
See also narrower terms: Belorussian literature; Russian literature.

LITHOGRAPHY
Bibliographical. Printing. Typography in Middle East. 1500-1999.
Use of LITHOGRAPHY. 1231.

LITHUANIA
Bibliographical.
Libraries in LITHUANIA. Role of Vladimirovas, Levas. 1105.
—— in LITHUANIA (1941-1942); relationship to Soviet army. 1110.
Relationship to libraries; publishing in LITHUANIA. Treatment in Vladimirovas, Levas. Bibliography. 1118.

Bibliographical. Publishing. History of publishing.
In LITHUANIA. 1282.

Bibliographical. Publishing (1917-1940).
By Communist Party in LITHUANIA. 1273.

Bibliographical. Publishing in LITHUANIA. 1500-1799. 1258.

LITTMAN, LYNNE (1941-)
General literature. Film.
Treatment of nuclear war; relationship to female point of view in LITTMAN, LYNNE: *Testament* compared to McCloy, Helen: *The Last Day*; Merril, Judith: *Shadow on the Hearth.* 271.

LITURGICAL BOOKS
Bibliographical. Publishing.
Of LITURGICAL BOOKS by Henry Bradshaw Society (1891-1900). 1270.

LITURGICAL DRAMA
See also related term: Liturgy.

LITURGICAL FORMULAS
Genres. Prose. Devotional literature.
Treatment of LITURGICAL FORMULAS. Sources in Chrysostom, John: *De Sancta Pentecoste*; Theodore of Mopsuestia: *Homiliae Catecheticae*; Pseudo-Epiphanius of Salamis: *Homilia in Diuini Corporis Sepulturam.* 2318.

LITURGICAL LITERATURE
Genres. Prose. Devotional literature.
LITURGICAL LITERATURE. 2319.

LITURGICAL POETRY
See also related term: Liturgy.

LITURGY
Literary theory and criticism.
Text; relationship to LITURGY of Russian Orthodox Church. Relationship to theories of Bakhtin, Mikhail Mikhaĭlovich; Florenskiĭ, Pavel Aleksandrovich: *Stolp i utverzhdenie istiny*; Kedrov, Konstantin Aleksandrovich: *Poéticheskiĭ kosmos.* 1558.

THE LIVING
See also related term: Life.

LIVING DEATH
See also related terms: Death; Life.

LOCAL COLOR
See also related terms: Realism; Regionalism.

LOCALIZATION
See also related term: Regionalism.

LOCKE, JOHN (1632-1704)
Literary theory and criticism. New Historicism.
Relationship to philosophy. Theories of LOCKE, JOHN; Rorty, Richard; James, William. 1836.

LOGIC
See also narrower terms: Dialectic; Paralogism.
General literature.
Role of fictionality in narrative; relationship to LOGIC; epistemology. 119.
Literary movements.
Modernism. Abstraction; LOGIC in language; relationship to Postmodernism. 1016.
Professional topics. Humanities.
Application of deconstructionism; relationship to rhetoric; LOGIC. Theories of Derrida, Jacques. 2777.

LOGIC TEXTBOOK
Bibliographical. Printing in Salamanca. Middle Ages.
Of LOGIC TEXTBOOK. 1167.

LOGICAL POSITIVISM
See also related term: Empiricism.

LOGOCENTRISM
Literary theory and criticism. Poststructuralist literary theory and criticism.
Nihilism; LOGOCENTRISM; relationship to Christianity. 1881.

LOGOS
Literary movements.
Postmodernism. Relationship to LOGOS. 1020.

LONDON
Bibliographical. Printing. Binding in LONDON. 1400-1499.
By Scales Binder. 1202.
Bibliographical. Printing. Binding in LONDON. 1800-1899.
By Williams, John. 1199.
Bibliographical. Publishing in LONDON. 1700-1799.
Role of Noble, Francis; Noble, John. 1260.

LONE RANGER
General literature. Radio and television.
Treatment of LONE RANGER as hero. 845.

LOOKING
See also related term: Gaze.

LORELEI
See also classified section: 2885.

LOSING
See also related term: Loss.

LOSS
General literature. Film.
Treatment of LOSS of humanism; home in Tarkovskiĭ, Andreĭ A.: *Nostalghia.* 477.

LOTMAN, IURIĬ MIKHAĬLOVICH (1922-)
Literary theory and criticism. Linguistic literary theory and criticism.
Theories of Bakhtin, Mikhail Mikhaĭlovich compared to LOTMAN, IURIĬ MIKHAĬLOVICH. 1755.
Literary theory and criticism. Semiotic literary theory and criticism.
Theories of Bakhtin, Mikhail Mikhaĭlovich compared to LOTMAN, IURIĬ MIKHAĬLOVICH. 2003.

LOVE
See also classified section: 2886 ff.
General literature.
Relationship to moral philosophy; LOVE. 155.
General literature. Film.
Treatment of masculinity; relationship to LOVE; war in Ashby, Hal: *Coming Home*; Scott, Tony: *Top Gun.* 301.

Genres. Novel.
   Treatment of LOVE. Sources in Theocritus: *Idylls.* 2200.
Genres. Novel. Popular romance novel.
   Treatment of LOVE; relationship to myth; legend. 2237.
   ——; relationship to stereotypes; study example: Harlequin Romances. 2233.
Genres. Novel. Sentimental novel.
   Characterization; plot. Treatment of LOVE. 2246.

LOVE AFFAIR
See also related term: Love.

LOVE LETTERS
See also related term: Love.

LOVE POETRY
See also related term: Love.

LOVE POTION
See also related term: Love.

LOVE TRIANGLE
See also related terms: Love; Sexuality.

LOVEJOY, ARTHUR ONCKEN (1873-1962)
Literary theory and criticism.
   Relationship to fascism; Romanticism. Theories of LOVEJOY, ARTHUR ONCK-EN; Spitzer, Leo. 1564.

LOVER
See also related term: Love.

LOVESICKNESS
See also related term: Love.

LOW COUNTRIES
See also narrower term: Netherlands.

LOWENTHAL, LEO (1900-)
General literature. Film in United States (1975-1987).
   And American fiction. Treatment of journalists. Application of theories of LOWENTHAL, LEO. Dissertation abstract. 439.

LUCAS, GEORGE (1944-)
General literature. Film.
   Postmodernism in Coppola, Francis Ford; LUCAS, GEORGE; DePalma, Brian; Spielberg, Steven; Scorsese, Martin. Dissertation abstract. 630.
General literature. Film. Film genres: science fiction film.
   Treatment of totalitarianism in LUCAS, GEORGE: *THX-1138* compared to Plato: *Politeia.* 753.

LUCAS, HANS
Use: Godard, Jean-Luc (1930-).

LUKÁCS, GYÖRGY (1885-1971)
Literary theory and criticism.
   Realism. Theories of LUKÁCS, GYÖRGY. 1307.
   Theories of LUKÁCS, GYÖRGY. 1554, 1561.
Literary theory and criticism. Marxist literary theory and criticism.
   On realism. Theories of LUKÁCS, GYÖRGY. 1790.
   Relationship to history. Theories of LUKÁCS, GYÖRGY: *Der historische Roman.* 1792.
   Role of revolution; relationship to poststructuralism in France. Theories of LUKÁCS, GYÖRGY. 1793.

LUXURY
General literature. Television: serial drama.
   Representation of LUXURY; relationship to television viewer. 898.

LYING (SPEECH ACT)
See also related term: Speech acts.

LYKKE-SEEST, PETER (1868-1948)
General literature. Film.
   By LYKKE-SEEST, PETER. 402.

LYNCH, DAVID (1947-)
General literature. Film.
   Imagery in LYNCH, DAVID: *Blue Velvet* compared to Dante: *La Divina Commedia.* 535.
   Narrative; relationship to Postmodernism in LYNCH, DAVID: *Blue Velvet.* 460.
   Narrative technique; relationship to irrationality in LYNCH, DAVID: *Blue Velvet.* 519.
   Treatment of dream; relationship to initiation in Fleming, Victor: *The Wizard of Oz* compared to LYNCH, DAVID: *Blue Velvet.* Psychoanalytic approach. 453.
   Treatment of female figures in DePalma, Brian: *Body Double*; LYNCH, DAVID: *Blue Velvet* compared to Acker, Kathy: *Don Quixote, Which Was a Dream.* 356.
General literature. Film and television.
   On LYNCH, DAVID: *Twin Peaks*; *Blue Velvet*; Scorsese, Martin: *GoodFellas*; relationship to *film noir.* 396.

LYON
Bibliographical. Printing in LYON and Paris (1470-1485).
   Relationship to Jean de Vignay: *La Légende dorée.* 1161.

LYOTARD, JEAN FRANÇOIS (1924-)
Literary theory and criticism.
   Relationship to epistemology of Positivism. Application of theories of Foucault, Michel; Habermas, Jürgen; LYOTARD, JEAN FRANÇOIS. 1401.

LYRIC POETRY
See also classified section: 2309 ff.
See also narrower term: Emblem.
See also related term: Song.

LYRICS
See also classified section: 2312.
Used for: Song lyrics.
See also related term: Song.

MACH, ERNST (1838-1916)
General literature.
   Relationship to science. Application of theories of MACH, ERNST: *Erkenntnis und Irrtum*; Vaihinger, Hans. 145.

MACHIAVELLI, NICCOLÒ (1469-1527)
Literary theory and criticism.
   Relationship to MACHIAVELLI, NICCOLÒ: *Discorsi.* 1464.

MACHINE TRANSLATION
See also related term: Computer.

MACHINES
See also classified section: 2888.
See also related term: Technology.

MACHISMO
See also related term: Masculinity.

MACKENZIE, WILLIAM LYON (1795-1861)
Used for: Swift, Patrick.
Bibliographical. Printing in Canada and United States. 1800-1899.
   Role of MACKENZIE, WILLIAM LYON. 1186.
   ——; relationship to politics. 1174.

MACMILLAN COMPANY OF CANADA
Bibliographical. Publishing in Canada (1905-1921).
   Role of MACMILLAN COMPANY OF CANADA. 1271.

MADHOUSE
See also related term: Madness.

MADNESS
See also classified section: 2889.
Used for: Insanity.
See also related term: Irrationality.
Genres. Autobiography and biography.
   Treatment of MADNESS; relationship to psychiatry. 2054.

MADONNA
See also related term: Virgin Mary.

MAGAZINES
General literature. Film.
   Female spectator; relationship to MAGAZINES for women. 515.

MAGNANI, ANNA (1905-1973)
General literature. Film in Italy.
   Role of MAGNANI, ANNA. 500.

MAGNUS, ALBERT (1642-1689)
Bibliographical. Printing. Binding in Amsterdam. 1600-1699.
   By MAGNUS, ALBERT. 1201.

MAGRITTE, RENÉ (1898-1967)
Literary theory and criticism.
   On similarity. Treatment in Foucault, Michel: *Ceci n'est pas une pipe* compared to MAGRITTE, RENÉ. 1468.

MAHESH YOGI, MAHARISHI
Used for: Yogi, Mahesh, Maharishi.
Literary theory and criticism. Deconstructionism.
   Compared to science. Application of theories of MAHESH YOGI, MAHARISHI. 1607.

MAIL-ORDER CATALOGUE
Bibliographical.
   Role of library collection; relationship to MAIL-ORDER CATALOGUE. 1107.

MAILLOUX, STEVEN (1950-)
Literary theory and criticism. Reader-response theory and criticism.
   Role of reader; relationship to American fiction. Theories of MAILLOUX, STEVEN compared to Fish, Stanley; Culler, Jonathan. Review article. 1918.

MAKAVEJEV, DUŠAN (1932-)
General literature. Film.
   By MAKAVEJEV, DUŠAN. 352.
   On MAKAVEJEV, DUŠAN: *Sweet Movie.* 608.

MALE CHAUVINISM
See also related term: Men.

MALE-FEMALE RELATIONS
Used for: Female-male relations; Gender relations.
General literature. Film.
   Treatment of psychoanalysis; confidence game; relationship to MALE-FEMALE RELATIONS in Mamet, David: *House of Games.* 622.
   Treatment of Vietnam War; MALE-FEMALE RELATIONS in Kasdan, Lawrence: *The Big Chill* compared to Mason, Bobbie Ann: *In Country.* 239.

SEE CLASSIFIED SEQUENCE FOR ADDITIONAL ENTRIES

General literature. Film. Film adaptation.
Treatment of MALE-FEMALE RELATIONS in film adaptation of Duras, Marguerite: *La Maladie de la mort* by Handke, Peter. 724.

MALE FIGURES
See also narrower terms: Dandy; Homosexuals.
See also related term: Men.

MALE IDENTITY
See also related term: Men.

MALE IMAGERY
See also related term: Men.

MALE POINT OF VIEW
See also related term: Men.

MALE VOICE
See also related term: Narrative voice.

MALLE, LOUIS (1932-)
General literature. Film.
By MALLE, LOUIS. Interview. 313.

MALTA
Bibliographical. Printing. History of printing.
Of Arabic language literature in MALTA by English Church Missionary Society (1825-1845). Dissertation abstract. 1194.

MAMET, DAVID (1947-)
General literature. Film.
Treatment of psychoanalysis; confidence game; relationship to male-female relations in MAMET, DAVID: *House of Games*. 622.

MAMOULIAN, ROUBEN (1897-1987)
General literature. Film and theater in United States.
Role of MAMOULIAN, ROUBEN. Dissertation abstract. 594.

MANHOOD
See also related terms: Masculinity; Men.

MANN, ANTHONY (1906-1967)
General literature. Film. Film genres: American Western film (1947-1957).
Treatment of patriarchy in Zinnemann, Fred: *High Noon* compared to MANN, ANTHONY: *The Tin Star*. 786.

MANUSCRIPT COLLATION
Bibliographical. Manuscripts. Manuscript editing.
MANUSCRIPT COLLATION of Valerius Flaccus, Gaius: *Argonautica* by Carrion, Louis. 1151.

MANUSCRIPT COLLECTIONS
See also classified section: 1143 ff.
See also related term: Manuscripts.

MANUSCRIPT EDITING
See also classified section: 1150 ff.
See also related term: Manuscripts.

MANUSCRIPT ILLUMINATION
Use: Illuminated manuscripts.

MANUSCRIPT PRESERVATION
See also related term: Book preservation.

MANUSCRIPT STUDY
See also related term: Manuscripts.

MANUSCRIPT TRADITION
See also related term: Manuscripts.

MANUSCRIPT VARIANTS
See also related term: Manuscripts.

MANUSCRIPTS
See also classified section: 1123 ff.
See also narrower terms: Illuminated manuscripts; Unpublished manuscripts.
See also related terms: Codicology; Manuscript collections; Manuscript editing; Stemma; Uncial.
Bibliographical.
On training of librarians about rare books; MANUSCRIPTS. 1109.
Role of library exhibition catalogues; relationship to exhibition of rare books and MANUSCRIPTS. 1097.
Professional topics. Research tools.
Role of MANUSCRIPTS; archives. 2830.

MANUZIO, ALDO (1547-1597)
Bibliographical. Printing. Typography in Venice (ca. 1500).
Italics by MANUZIO, ALDO; relationship to copyright. 1225.

MAORI
General literature. Film in New Zealand.
Treatment of tourism; ethnography; relationship to MAORI in McDonald, James. 264.

MARBLING
Bibliographical. Printing. 1700-1799.
MARBLING by Baskerville, John. 1178.

MÄRCHEN
See also classified section: 2166.
Used for: Fairy tale; *Volksmärchen.*

General literature. Film. Film adaptation.
Use of proverb; *MÄRCHEN* in Jordan, Neil and Carter, Angela: *The Company of Wolves.* 702.
Professional topics. Humanities.
Use of *MÄRCHEN*; literature for children in teaching of literature. Dissertation abstract. 2701.
Themes and figures. Lorelei.
As *MÄRCHEN*. Source study. 2885.

MÄRCHEN—AS SOURCE
General literature for children.
Sources in *MÄRCHEN*. Theories of Bettelheim, Bruno: *The Uses of Enchantment*. 195.

MARGINAL LITERATURE
General literature.
MARGINAL LITERATURE. 44.

MARGINALITY
General literature.
MARGINALITY. 205.
General literature by postcolonial writers. English language literature. 1900-1999.
Relationship to MARGINALITY. 86.
Literary theory and criticism. Poststructuralist literary theory and criticism.
Relationship to colonialism; MARGINALITY. 1888.

MARIAN LITERATURE
See also related term: Virgin Mary.

MARIN, EDWIN L. (1899-1951)
General literature. Film. Film adaptation.
Of Conan Doyle, Sir Arthur: *A Study in Scarlet* by MARIN, EDWIN L. 736.

MARION, JEAN-LUC (1946-)
Literary theory and criticism.
Role of the other; language; relationship to ethics; religion. Theories of Levinas, Emmanuel; MARION, JEAN-LUC. 1577.

MARIONETTE COMPANIES
See also related term: Marionettes.

MARIONETTE THEATER
See also related term: Marionettes.

MARIONETTES
General literature. Theater.
MARIONETTES; relationship to performance theory. Theories of Craig, Edward Gordon: "The Actor and the Über-marionette"; Meïerkhol'd, Vsevolod Émil'evich; Schlemmer, Oskar; Kleist, Heinrich von: "Über das Marionettentheater." Dissertation abstract. 962.

MARKEDNESS
See also related term: Binary opposition.

MARKET
Use: Marketplace.

MARKETING
See also classified section: 1303 ff.
See also narrower term: Advertising.
See also related term: Publishing.
Bibliographical. Publishing. Book trade and MARKETING. 1285.

MARKETPLACE
Used for: Market.
Professional topics. Humanities.
Curriculum; relationship to MARKETPLACE. 2684.

MARQUAND, ALLAN (1853-1924)
Literary theory and criticism. Semiotic literary theory and criticism.
Aesthetics of color; form. Theories of MARQUAND, ALLAN; Ladd-Franklin, Christine; relationship to Peirce, Charles Sanders. 1985.

MARRIAGE
General literature. Film.
Treatment of women; relationship to MARRIAGE in Rapper, Irving: *Now, Voyager*. 286.
General literature. Middle Ages.
Treatment of MARRIAGE; relationship to abstinence from sexual intercourse. 66.

MARRIAGE CONTRACT
See also related term: Marriage.

MARRIAGE PROPOSAL
See also related term: Marriage.

MARRIED . . . WITH CHILDREN
General literature. Television.
Treatment of disorder in housekeeping by women in *Roseanne* compared to *MARRIED . . . WITH CHILDREN*. 912.

MARTÍN, PAOLO
General literature. Film. Film genres: documentary film.
Interview with MARTÍN, PAOLO. 747.

THE MARVELOUS
Genres. Fiction for children.
Treatment of THE MARVELOUS; adventure. 2104.

MARX, KARL (1818-1883)
  Literary movements.
    Modernism. Theories of Adorno, Theodor W.; MARX, KARL. 1011.
  Literary theory and criticism. Hermeneutics.
    Role of subjectivity; relationship to deconstructionism; humanism. Theories of Hegel, Georg Wilhelm Friedrich compared to Heidegger, Martin; MARX, KARL; Freud, Sigmund. 1716.

MARXISM
See also related term: Marxist literary theory and criticism.
  Literary movements.
    Postmodernism. Relationship to MARXISM. 1054.

MARXIST APPROACH
See also related terms: Marxism; Marxist literary theory and criticism.
Documents applying specific approaches are so numerous that access to them is provided only in the electronic versions of the *Bibliography*.

MARXIST CRITICISM
Use: Marxist literary theory and criticism.

MARXIST LITERARY THEORY AND CRITICISM
See also classified section: 1784 ff.
Used for: Marxist criticism.
See also related term: Marxism.
  Literary theory and criticism. Poststructuralist literary theory and criticism.
    And MARXIST LITERARY THEORY AND CRITICISM; relationship to history. 1890.
  Literary theory and criticism. Psychoanalytic literary theory and criticism and MARXIST LITERARY THEORY AND CRITICISM.
    On literature for children. 1908.
  Literary theory and criticism. Semiotic literary theory and criticism.
    Relationship to MARXIST LITERARY THEORY AND CRITICISM. Theories of Kristeva, Julia; Lacan, Jacques. 1959.

MARXIST THEORY
See also related terms: Dialectic; Marxism.

MASCULINITY
See also related term: Men.
  General literature. Film.
    Role of fantasy; relationship to MASCULINITY in Baky, Josef von: *Münchhausen.* 539.
    Treatment of MASCULINITY; relationship to love; war in Ashby, Hal: *Coming Home*; Scott, Tony: *Top Gun.* 301.

MASHAL
See also related term: Midrash.

MASQUE
  General literature. Television: music television.
    Discourse; relationship to power compared to MASQUE for royal court of Jacobean period. 858.

MASQUERADE
  General literature. Film.
    Treatment of femininity; relationship to MASQUERADE in Tourneur, Jacques: *Anne of the Indies.* 411.

MASS
See also related term: Eucharist (sacrament of).

MASS COMMUNICATION
Use: Mass media.

MASS CULTURE
  General literature. Television and film.
    Relationship to MASS CULTURE. 855.
  Literary movements.
    Avant-garde. Relationship to MASS CULTURE; anarchism. Treatment in criticism. 993.

MASS MEDIA
Used for: Mass communication; Media.
See also narrower terms: Periodicals; Radio; Television.
  General literature. Film.
    Treatment of artist; relationship to MASS MEDIA in Unruh, Fritz von: *Phaea.* 378.
  General literature. Television.
    And MASS MEDIA. Semiotic approach. 872.
  Literary theory and criticism. Semiotic literary theory and criticism.
    Applied to discourse of MASS MEDIA; advertising. 1984.

MASS MEDIA STUDIES
  General literature. Television.
    Role of entertainment; relationship to MASS MEDIA STUDIES. 914.

MASSACRE
  General literature. Film in China.
    Relationship to MASSACRE in Tiananmen Square. 585.

MASTER OF THE REVELS
See also related term: Censorship.

MATERIAL CULTURE
See also narrower term: Technology.

MATERNAL WOMAN
See also related term: Mother.

MATERNITY
Use: Motherhood.

MATHEMATICAL ABILITY
See also related term: Mathematics.

MATHEMATICAL APPROACH
See also related term: Mathematics.
Documents applying specific approaches are so numerous that access to them is provided only in the electronic versions of the *Bibliography*.

MATHEMATICAL IMAGERY
See also related term: Mathematics.

MATHEMATICAL LINGUISTICS
See also related term: Mathematics.

MATHEMATICAL THEORY
See also related term: Mathematics.
  Literary theory and criticism.
    Relationship to MATHEMATICAL THEORY. Treatment of writer; relationship to reader. 1347.

MATHEMATICS
See also related term: Mathematical theory.
  Genres. Poetry.
    Relationship to MATHEMATICS. 2256.

MATRICIDE
See also related term: Mother.

MATRIMONY (SACRAMENT OF)
See also related term: Marriage.

MATTHIESSEN, F. O. (1902-1950)
  Literary theory and criticism.
    Theories of MATTHIESSEN, F. O.; Trilling, Lionel. Review article. 1333.

MAXIM
See also related term: Proverb.

MAXWELL, JAMES CLERK (1831-1879)
  Figures of speech. Metaphor.
    Relationship to self-reflexiveness. Theories of MAXWELL, JAMES CLERK; Shannon, Claude Elwood. 2362.

MAY FOURTH MOVEMENT
See also related term: China.

MAZE
Use: Labyrinth.

MAŽOJI LIETUVA
  Bibliographical. Printing and publishing.
    In MAŽOJI LIETUVA (1524-1939); relationship to foreign language publishing. 1170.

MCCARTNEY, PAUL (1942-)
  General literature. Film.
    Role of Lennon, John and MCCARTNEY, PAUL in Webb, Peter: *Give My Regards to Broad Street.* Application of theories of Lacan, Jacques. 603.

MCDONALD, JAMES
  General literature. Film in New Zealand.
    Treatment of tourism; ethnography; relationship to Maori in MCDONALD, JAMES. 264.

MCGANN, JEROME J. (1937-)
  Literary theory and criticism. New Historicism.
    Theories of Greenblatt, Stephen J. compared to MCGANN, JEROME J. 1846.

MCNAUGHTON, JOHN
  General literature. Film.
    On MCNAUGHTON, JOHN: *Henry: Portrait of a Serial Killer.* 240.

MCTIERNAN, JOHN—STUDY EXAMPLE
  Literary forms. Humor.
    Relationship to feminism; study example: MCTIERNAN, JOHN: *Die Hard.* 2399.

DAVID JACKSON MCWILLIAMS COLLECTION
  Bibliographical.
    Catalogue of incunabula in DAVID JACKSON MCWILLIAMS COLLECTION at Harry Ransom Humanities Research Center. 1087.

MEANING
See also narrower term: Literal meaning.
See also related term: Semantics.
  General literature.
    Role of narrative; relationship to MEANING; language; autobiography. Psychological approach. 34.
  Literary theory and criticism.
    MEANING. 1511.
    On MEANING; relationship to application of computer. 1360.

MEANINGFULNESS
See also related term: Meaning.

MECHANIZATION
See also related term: Machines.

MEDIA
Use: Mass media.

MEDIATOR
Genres. Fiction.
Narrator as MEDIATOR between writer and reader. 2159.

MEDICAL EDUCATION
See also related term: Medicine.

MEDICAL IMAGERY
See also related term: Medicine.

MEDICAL PROSE
Literary forms. Rhetoric.
Analogy in MEDICAL PROSE. 2469.

MEDICAL SOCIETIES
See also narrower term: Svenska Läkaresällskapet.
See also related term: Medicine.

MEDICINE
General literature.
And MEDICINE. Pedagogical approach. 213.
Narrative; rhetoric; relationship to MEDICINE; study example: Percy, Walker: *Lancelot*; *The Moviegoer*. 143.
Relationship to MEDICINE. 42, 106.
Genres. Fiction. Utopian fiction and dystopian fiction. 1500-1999.
Treatment of MEDICINE. 2185.
Literary movements.
Enlightenment. Role of anti-Semitism; racism; relationship to MEDICINE. 1000.
——. Role of MEDICINE; relationship to fear; anxiety. 998.

MEDIEVAL PERIOD
Use: Middle Ages.

MEDIEVAL REVIVAL
See also related term: Middle Ages.

MEDIEVAL STUDIES
See also related term: Middle Ages.
Literary theory and criticism.
Relationship to MEDIEVAL STUDIES. 1534.
Literary theory and criticism. Literary history.
Relationship to MEDIEVAL STUDIES. 1776.
Professional topics.
Role of philology (1880-1940) in MEDIEVAL STUDIES. 2584.

MEDIEVALISM
See also related term: Middle Ages.

MEDVED, HARRY (1961-)
General literature. Film.
Treatment in MEDVED, HARRY and Dreyfuss, Randy: *The Fifty Worst Films of All Time*. 560.

MEÏERKHOL'D, VSEVOLOD ÉMIL'EVICH (1874-1940)
Used for: Meyerhold, Vsevolod Émil'evich.
General literature. Theater.
Marionettes; relationship to performance theory. Theories of Craig, Edward Gordon: "The Actor and the Über-marionette"; MEÏERKHOL'D, VSEVOLOD ÉMIL'EVICH; Schlemmer, Oskar; Kleist, Heinrich von: "Über das Marionettentheater." Dissertation abstract. 962.

MELANCHOLY
See also classified section: 2890.

MELODRAMA
See also related term: Soap opera.
General literature. Film.
Narrative form; ambiguity; relationship to MELODRAMA in Weir, Peter: *Picnic at Hanging Rock*. 512.
General literature. Film. Film genres.
MELODRAMA in Fassbinder, Rainer Werner. 804.
General literature. Film. Film genres: MELODRAMA. 810.
Treatment of heroine. 805.
General literature. Film. Film genres: MELODRAMA in France (1905-1907).
By Pathé Frères. 744.
General literature. Film. Film genres: MELODRAMA in India in Hindi language (1950-1959). 809.
General literature. Film. Film genres: silent film in United States and Russian S.F.S.R.
MELODRAMA; relationship to temporality. Theories of Benjamin, Walter. 757.
General literature. Film and television.
MELODRAMA. Treatment of Vietnam War in Ashby, Hal: *Coming Home*; *China Beach*. 485.
General literature. Film in France (1930-1939).
For women. Realism; relationship to MELODRAMA. 626.
General literature. Film in Germany (1910-1914). Film genres.
MELODRAMA; social drama. 803.

MELVILLE, JEAN-PIERRE (1917-1973)
Used for: Grumbach, Jean-Pierre.

General literature. Film.
Role of Vernon, Howard in MELVILLE, JEAN-PIERRE: *Le Silence de la mer*; Lang, Fritz: *Die tausend Augen des Dr. Mabuse*. Includes discussion with Vernon. 345.

MEMENTO MORI
See also related term: Death.

MEMOIR
See also related terms: Autobiography; Biography.

MEMORIA
See also related term: The unconscious.
Literary forms. Rhetoric.
Role of *MEMORIA*; relationship to writing. 2481.

MEMORY
See also related term: Cognition.
General literature. Film in West Germany.
Treatment of mourning; MEMORY; relationship to Third Reich; study example: Syberberg, Hans Jürgen: *Hitler, ein Film aus Deutschland*; Reitz, Edgar: *Heimat*. 566.
General literature. Television: docudrama.
Role of MEMORY; relationship to fact. 849.
Literary theory and criticism.
On MEMORY; relationship to the future. Theories of Heidegger, Martin; Sartre, Jean-Paul. 1454.

MEMORY ASSESSMENT
See also related term: Memory.

MEMORY DEFICIT
See also related term: Memory.

MEMORY DEVELOPMENT
See also related term: Memory.

MEMORY DISORDERS
See also related term: Memory.

MEMORY SPAN
See also related term: Memory.

MEMORY STRATEGIES
See also related term: Memory.

MEN
See also related term: Masculinity.
General literature. Film.
Relationship to subjectivity of MEN. Psychoanalytic approach. 578.
General literature. Film. Film genres: horror film.
Treatment of women; womb; relationship to the grotesque; hysteria of MEN in Cronenberg, David: *Dead Ringers*. Application of theories of Freud, Sigmund. 756.
General literature. Television: music television.
Treatment of MEN; women; glamour; sexuality. 885.

MEN CRITICS
Literary theory and criticism. Feminist literary theory and criticism by MEN CRITICS. 1656, 1657.

MEN TEACHERS
Professional topics. Humanities.
Role of MEN TEACHERS as mentor to female student. 2743.

MENIPPEAN SATIRE
Used for: Varronian satire.
Literary theory and criticism.
MENIPPEAN SATIRE. Theories of Bakhtin, Mikhail Mikhaïlovich. 1331.

MEN'S STUDIES
See also related term: Men.

MENTAL ILLNESS
See also related term: Madness.

MENTAL MODEL
Literary theory and criticism. Linguistic literary theory and criticism.
Poetic language; relationship to MENTAL MODEL; image; rhythm. 1757.

MENTAL REPRESENTATION
Use: Cognitive representation.

MENTOR
Professional topics. Humanities.
Role of men teachers as MENTOR to female student. 2743.

MERLEAU-PONTY, MAURICE (1908-1961)
General literature. Film. Film theory and criticism.
Spatiotemporal relations; relationship to phenomenology. Application of theories of Heidegger, Martin; MERLEAU-PONTY, MAURICE. Dissertation abstract. 834.
Genres. Fiction.
Point of view. Hermeneutic approach. Application of theories of Gadamer, Hans-Georg; MERLEAU-PONTY, MAURICE; Ricœur, Paul. 2113.

MERLIN
See also classified section: 2891.
Used for: Myrddhin.

MEROD, JIM (1942-)
  Professional topics. Humanities.
    Pedagogy. Theories of Freire, Paulo; Bourdieu, Pierre; MEROD, JIM; Graff, Gerald. 2686.

MESCHONNIC, HENRI (1932-)
  Literary theory and criticism.
    Poetics. Theories of MESCHONNIC, HENRI. 1556.

MESOAMERICA
See also related term: Mexico.

METACRITICISM
See also related term: Literary theory and criticism.

METADIEGETIC NARRATIVE
Use: Intercalated narrative.

METADRAMA
See also related term: Drama.

METAFICTION
See also related term: Fiction.
  Genres. Fiction. Postmodernist fiction.
    METAFICTION. 2170.
  Genres. Prose. Historiography. 1900-1999.
    Compared to METAFICTION. 2328.

METALANGUAGE
  Literary theory and criticism.
    Mimesis; speech acts; relationship to METALANGUAGE. 1383.

METALEPSIS
See also related term: Metonymy.

METALINGUISTIC AWARENESS
  Professional topics. Humanities.
    Teaching of literature; relationship to METALINGUISTIC AWARENESS. Dissertation abstract. 2660.

METALINGUISTICS
See also related term: Metalinguistic awareness.

METALITERATURE
See also narrower term: Metafiction.

METANOVEL
See also related term: Novel.

METAPHOR
See also classified section: 2357 ff.
See also narrower term: Spatial metaphor.
See also related terms: Metonymy; Synecdoche.
  Literary forms. Rhetoric.
    Role of question; METAPHOR; image in scientific language; relationship to epistemology. Theories of Meyer, Michel; Kant, Immanuel. 2427.
  Literary forms. Satire.
    As genre; relationship to METAPHOR. Sources in Diomedes. 2503.
  Literary movements.
    Romanticism. Treatment of stained-glass window of church as METAPHOR for epiphany. 1079.
  Literary theory and criticism. Linguistic literary theory and criticism.
    METAPHOR. 1738.
  Literary theory and criticism. Narrative theory.
    METAPHOR. 1814.
  Literary theory and criticism. Semiotic literary theory and criticism.
    Iconicity; METAPHOR. Theories of Bühler, Karl. 1990.
  Themes and figures. Christ.
    As METAPHOR. Dissertation abstract. 2841.

METAPHOR COMPREHENSION
See also related term: Metaphor.

METAPHYSICS
  Literary theory and criticism.
    Relationship to METAPHYSICS. Theories of Adorno, Theodor W. 1570.
  Literary theory and criticism. Deconstructionism.
    Relationship to METAPHYSICS. Theories of Derrida, Jacques. 1629.
  Professional topics. Humanities.
    Role of METAPHYSICS; phenomenology. 2738.

METAPOETRY
See also related term: Poetry.

METAPSYCHOLOGY
See also related term: Psychology.

METATHEATER
See also related term: Theater.

METER
See also narrower term: Hexameter.
See also related terms: Poetry; Prosody.
  Genres. Poetry.
    METER. 2297.
    Rhythm; METER; relationship to semantics. Theories of Tomashevskiĭ, Boris Viktorovich. 2294.

METONYMY
See also related term: Metaphor.
  Figures of speech. Metaphor.
    And METONYMY. 2358.

METRICAL ANALYSIS
See also related terms: Meter; Poetry.

METRICAL STRUCTURE
See also related term: Meter.

METRICAL THEORY
See also related term: Meter.

METRICS
See also related terms: Meter; Prosody.

METZ, CHRISTIAN
  General literature. Film.
    Style; relationship to realism in Rossellini, Roberto: *Roma, città aperta*. Application of theories of METZ, CHRISTIAN. 480.

MEXICO
  General literature. Film in MEXICO. 642.

MEXICO-UNITED STATES BORDER
See also related terms: Mexico; United States.

MEYER, MICHEL
  Literary forms. Rhetoric.
    Role of question; metaphor; image in scientific language; relationship to epistemology. Theories of MEYER, MICHEL; Kant, Immanuel. 2427.

MEYER, NICHOLAS
  General literature. Film.
    Role of song by fans; relationship to MEYER, NICHOLAS: *Star Trek II: The Wrath of Khan*. 409.

MEYER, RUSS (1923-)—STUDY EXAMPLE
  General literature. Film.
    Treatment of psychiatrist; study example: Wiene, Robert: *Das Kabinett des Doktor Caligari*; Robson, Mark: *Home of the Brave*; Hitchcock, Alfred: *Psycho*; MEYER, RUSS: *The Immoral Mr. Teas*. 569.

MEYERHOLD, VSEVOLOD ÉMIL'EVICH
Use: Meĭerkhol'd, Vsevolod Émil'evich (1874-1940).

MIAMI VICE
  General literature. Television.
    Role of sex roles in *MIAMI VICE*. 884.
    Treatment of law; relationship to style in *MIAMI VICE*. 913.

MICHELET, JULES (1798-1874)
  General literature.
    Relationship to history. Theories of Thierry, Augustin; MICHELET, JULES. 91.

MIDDLE AGES
Used for: Dark Ages; Medieval period.
See also related term: Medieval studies.
  Bibliographical. Printing. History of printing in Europe. MIDDLE AGES.
    And universities; relationship to modernity. 1193.
  Bibliographical. Printing. Illustration. MIDDLE AGES.
    Of facsimile of Gutenberg Bible. 1213.
    Of *Ordinarius Strigonienis*. 1210.
  Bibliographical. Printing in Salamanca. MIDDLE AGES.
    Of logic textbook. 1167.
  General literature.
    Role of women; relationship to history; literature in MIDDLE AGES. 105.
  General literature. MIDDLE AGES.
    Treatment of marriage; relationship to abstinence from sexual intercourse. 66.
  General literature. MIDDLE AGES and Renaissance.
    Treatment of women. Panel discussion. 150.
  General literature for children. English language literature. 1900-1999.
    Narrative voice. Treatment of MIDDLE AGES. 116.
  Genres.
    Genre theory; relationship to literature of MIDDLE AGES. 2036.
  Genres. Poetry. Lyrics. MIDDLE AGES.
    Anthology. 2312.
  Genres. Prose. Letters. MIDDLE AGES.
    Anthology. 2335.
  Literary forms. Myth. MIDDLE AGES. 2411.
  Literary theory and criticism.
    Role of the carnivalesque; relationship to MIDDLE AGES. Theories of Bakhtin, Mikhail Mikhaĭlovich. 1487.
  Literary theory and criticism. Hermeneutics and linguistic literary theory and criticism. MIDDLE AGES.
    Applied to book; relationship to myth; study example: Chaucer, Geoffrey; Dante. 1719.
  Literary theory and criticism. MIDDLE AGES.
    Relationship to textual criticism; Latin language literature. Review article. 1576.
  Literary theory and criticism. Narrative theory.
    Applied to literature of MIDDLE AGES. Application of theories of Likhachëv, Dmitriĭ Sergeevich: *Poétika drevnerusskoĭ literatury*. 1819.

SEE CLASSIFIED SEQUENCE FOR ADDITIONAL ENTRIES

Literary theory and criticism. Semiotic literary theory and criticism.
Role of otherness in literature of MIDDLE AGES; relationship to hermeneutics. Theories of Jauss, Hans Robert; Gadamer, Hans-Georg. 1980.
Professional topics. Comparative literature at American universities.
Literature of MIDDLE AGES; Renaissance. 2604.
Themes and figures. Labyrinth. MIDDLE AGES. 2883.

MIDDLE CLASS
See also related term: Bourgeoisie.

MIDDLE EAST
Bibliographical. Printing. Typography in MIDDLE EAST. 1500-1999.
Use of lithography. 1231.
General literature. Film.
And fiction. Treatment of MIDDLE EAST. 234.

MIDRASH
General literature.
Intertextuality in MIDRASH. 30.
Literary theory and criticism.
Applied to MIDRASH; relationship to interpretation; intertextuality. 1334.

MIKHALKOV-KONCHALOVSKIĬ, ANDREĬ SERGEEVICH (1937-)
Used for: Konchalovskiĭ, Andreĭ Sergeevich.
General literature. Film.
By MIKHALKOV-KONCHALOVSKIĬ, ANDREĬ SERGEEVICH. 410.

MIKHALKOV-KONCHALOVSKIĬ, NIKITA
General literature. Film.
By MIKHALKOV-KONCHALOVSKIĬ, NIKITA. 647, 648.

MILITARISM
General literature. Film. Film theory and criticism.
Perception in film; relationship to MILITARISM. Theories of Virilio, Paul: *Guerre et cinéma.* 841.
Literary movements.
Postmodernism compared to Modernism. Relationship to popular culture; MILITARISM in Australia. 1051.

MILITARY GROUPS
See also narrower term: Abraham Lincoln Battalion.

MILLER, J. HILLIS (1928-)
Literary theory and criticism. Deconstructionism.
Treatment in Norris, Christopher: *Deconstruction: Theory and Practice*; MILLER, J. HILLIS: "The Function of Rhetorical Study at the Present Time." 1602.
Literary theory and criticism. Narrative theory.
Theories of Culler, Jonathan; MILLER, J. HILLIS. 1821.

MILNER, MARION BLACKETT (1900-)
Used for: Field, Joanna.

MILNER, MARION BLACKETT (1900-)—STUDY EXAMPLE
Genres. Autobiography.
Relationship to psychotherapy; study example: MILNER, MARION BLACKETT: *A Life of One's Own*; Hillesum, Etty: *Het verstoorde leven.* 2055.

MIŁOSZ, CZESŁAW (1911-)
Used for: Syruc, J.
Literary theory and criticism. Socialist realist literary theory and criticism.
Theories of Andrzejewski, Jerzy; MIŁOSZ, CZESŁAW. 2009.

MIME
Use: Pantomime.

MIMESIS
Genres. Fiction.
Fictionality; relationship to MIMESIS. 2117.
MIMESIS; relationship to historiography; Postmodernism. Dissertation abstract. 2135.
——; relationship to reader; Postmodernism. 2156.
Literary theory and criticism.
MIMESIS. Theories of Aristotle. 1358.
——; realism; style. Theories of Auerbach, Erich: *Mimesis.* 1528.
——; speech acts; relationship to metalanguage. 1383.
Theories of MIMESIS; relationship to poetic language. Sources in Philodemus. 1432.

MIMIC
See also related term: Pantomime.

MIND
See also related term: Consciousness.
Themes and figures. Human body.
Relationship to MIND. 2876.

MINORITIES
See also related term: Religious groups.
Professional topics. Humanities.
Role of MINORITIES in English departments. 2727.

MINORITY CULTURE
See also related term: Minorities.

MINSTREL TRADITION
See also related term: Minstrels.

MINSTRELS
Genres. Fiction. 1800-1999.
Treatment of African Americans as MINSTRELS. Dissertation abstract. 2138.

MIRACLE PLAY
See also related term: Passion play.

MIRTH
See also related term: Laughter.

MISANDRY
See also related term: Misogyny.

MISANTHROPY
Themes and figures. Misogyny and MISANTHROPY. 2892.

MISE EN ABYME
See also related term: Self-reflexiveness.
Literary theory and criticism. Narrative theory.
MISE EN ABYME. Theories of Dällenbach, Lucien: *Le Récit spéculaire*; Bal, Mieke. 1817.

MISE EN SCÈNE
See also related term: Staging.
General literature. Film.
MISE EN SCÈNE; narrative; relationship to fascism in Lang, Fritz: *Siegfried*; *Kriemhilds Rache.* 376.
——; narrative in Velle, Gaston: *Tour du monde d'un policier.* 549.
General literature. Film on wide-screen.
MISE EN SCÈNE. Application of theories of Bazin, André. 265.

MISINTERPRETATION
See also related term: Interpretation.

MISOGAMY
See also related term: Marriage.

MISOGYNY
See also classified section: 2892.
See also related term: Women.
General literature. Film.
Role of MISOGYNY in DePalma, Brian. 472.

MISPRINT
See also related term: Printing.

MISQUOTATION
See also related term: Quotation.

MISUNDERSTANDING
See also related term: Understanding.

MITCHELL, JULIET (1940-)
Literary theory and criticism. Feminist literary theory and criticism.
Relationship to psychoanalysis. Theories of MITCHELL, JULIET; Gallop, Jane. 1658.

MIZOGUCHI KENJI (1898-1956)
General literature. Film.
Treatment of artist; relationship to desire in MIZOGUCHI KENJI. 329.
—— in MIZOGUCHI KENJI. Dissertation abstract. 328.
General literature. Film (1930-1939).
Narration in MIZOGUCHI KENJI. Dissertation abstract. 427.

MLA
Use: Modern Language Association of America.

MNEMONICS
See also related term: Memory.

MODERN ART
Literary theory and criticism. Postmodernist literary theory and criticism.
Role of philosophy; relationship to MODERN ART. 1873.

MODERN CULTURE
See also related term: Modernity.

MODERN GREEK STUDIES
Professional topics. Humanities.
MODERN GREEK STUDIES. 2747.

MODERN LANGUAGE ASSOCIATION OF AMERICA
Used for: MLA.
Professional topics. Humanities.
Role of MODERN LANGUAGE ASSOCIATION OF AMERICA. 2786.

MODERN LIFE
See also related term: Modernity.

MODERN SOCIETY
See also related term: Modernity.

MODERN WOMEN
See also related term: Modernity.

MODERNISM
See also narrower term: Surrealism.
See also related term: Postmodernism.
General literature. Film.
Silent film; relationship to MODERNISM. 529.

General literature. Film. Film adaptation.
MODERNISM in film adaptation of Döblin, Alfred: *Berlin Alexanderplatz* by Fassbinder, Rainer Werner. 680.
Genres. Drama. Tragicomedy.
Relationship to MODERNISM. 2103.
Genres. Novel.
Treatment of enclosure; relationship to MODERNISM; Postmodernism. 2191.
Genres. Novel. Detective novel: hard-boiled detective novel.
Relationship to MODERNISM; study example: Chandler, Raymond; Eliot, T. S.: *The Waste Land.* 2240.
Literary forms. Rhetoric.
Relationship to MODERNISM. 2419.
Literary movements.
Avant-garde and MODERNISM. 994.
MODERNISM. Relationship to primitivism. 1018.
Postmodernism compared to MODERNISM. Relationship to popular culture; militarism in Australia. 1051.
Literary theory and criticism.
Relationship to MODERNISM. Theories of Santayana, George; Royce, Josiah; James, William. 1466.
Themes and figures. Space.
As symbol in MODERNISM. 2919.

MODERNIST FICTION
See also classified section: 2167.
See also narrower term: Modernist novel.

MODERNIST NOVEL
See also classified section: 2243.

MODERNIST POETRY
See also related term: Postmodernist poetry.

MODERNITY
Bibliographical. Printing. History of printing in Europe. Middle Ages.
And universities; relationship to MODERNITY. 1193.
General literature. Film. Film genres in Germany.
Mountain film; relationship to MODERNITY; Nazism. 796.
Genres. Poetry.
Relationship to MODERNITY. 2288.
Literary theory and criticism. Postmodernist literary theory and criticism.
Relationship to irony; MODERNITY. 1859.

MOLDAVIA
See also related term: Romania.

MONASTERY
See also related term: Religious groups.

MONICELLI, MARIO (1915-)
General literature. Film.
By MONICELLI, MARIO. 256.

MONISM
See also related term: Dualism.

MONOLOGISM
Genres. Novel.
MONOLOGISM. Theories of Bakhtin, Mikhail Mikhaïlovich. 2210.

MONOLOGUE
See also related terms: Dialogue; *Récit.*

MONOMACHIA
Bibliographical. Printing. Latin language literature. 1500-1599.
Of MONOMACHIA against Alciati, Andrea. 1160.

MONOMYTH
See also related term: Myth.

MONSTERS
General literature. Film. Film genres: horror film.
Treatment of archetypes of MONSTERS carrying beautiful woman. 752.
Genres. Fiction. Science fiction. 1900-1999.
Treatment of MONSTERS; motherhood. 2172.
Literary forms. Myth.
Treatment of labyrinth; MONSTERS. 2409.

MONTREAL
Bibliographical. Publishing in MONTREAL (1911-1912).
Role of Publishers Press. 1265.

MOOD
See also related term: Emotions.

MOONLIGHTING
General literature. Television.
Treatment of femininity; narcissism in *MOONLIGHTING* as television adaptation of Shakespeare, William: *The Taming of the Shrew.* Feminist approach. 908.

MOORE, MICHAEL
General literature. Film. Film genres: documentary film.
On MOORE, MICHAEL: *Roger and Me.* 750.

MORAL CONFUSION
See also related term: Morality.

MORAL GROWTH
See also related term: Morality.

MORAL LAW
Use: Ethics.

MORAL PHILOSOPHERS
See also related term: Moral philosophy.

MORAL PHILOSOPHY
General literature.
Relationship to MORAL PHILOSOPHY; love. 155.

MORAL PURPOSE
See also related terms: Moral values; Morality.

MORAL REFORM
See also related term: Morality.

MORAL VALUES
General literature.
Treatment of women; relationship to MORAL VALUES. 112.

MORALISM
See also related term: Morality.

MORALITY
See also classified section: 2893.
Genres. Fiction for children.
Treatment of MORALITY; relationship to social behavior. 2111.

MORALITY PLAY
See also related term: Allegory.

MORALS
See also related term: Morality.

MORES
See also related term: Morality.

MORITA YOSHIMITSU (1950-)
General literature. Film. Film adaptation.
Of Natsume Sōseki: *Sorekara* by MORITA YOSHIMITSU. 717.

MORITURUS LYRIC
See also related term: Death.

MORLEY, CHRISTOPHER (1890-1957)—STUDY EXAMPLE
Themes and figures. Troilus.
And Cressida; study example: opera; MORLEY, CHRISTOPHER: *The Trojan Horse*; Wolf, Christa: *Kassandra.* 2927.

MORMONISM
See also related term: Mormons.

MORMONS
General literature. Film.
And American literature. Treatment of MORMONS in Western United States. 459.

MOROCCO
Bibliographical. Printing in MOROCCO (1865-1912).
Relationship to social change. Dissertation abstract. 1152.

MORPHEME ACQUISITION ORDER
See also related term: Second language learning.

MORPHOLOGICAL APPROACH
Documents applying specific approaches are so numerous that access to them is provided only in the electronic versions of the *Bibliography.*

MORRISSEY, PAUL
General literature. Film (1963-1988).
By Warhol, Andy; MORRISSEY, PAUL. Dissertation abstract. 493.

MORTALITY
See also narrower term: Death.

MOSHER, THOMAS BIRD (1852-1923)
Bibliographical. Publishing in United States. 1800-1899.
By MOSHER, THOMAS BIRD. 1238.

MOSLEMS
Used for: Muslems.
See also related term: Islam.
Genres. Fiction. English language literature. 1800-1999.
Treatment of Islam; MOSLEMS. 2131.

MOTHER
See also related term: Motherhood.
General literature. Film.
Treatment of MOTHER; relationship to Nazism in postwar period in Hitchcock, Alfred: *Notorious.* Application of theories of Jung, Carl Gustav. 244.

MOTHERHOOD
Used for: Maternity.
See also related term: Mother.
General literature. Film.
Treatment of MOTHERHOOD. Psycholanalytic approach. 418.
——; relationship to Postmodernism. 417.
Treatment of sexuality; relationship to MOTHERHOOD. 419.

SEE CLASSIFIED SEQUENCE FOR ADDITIONAL ENTRIES

Genres. Fiction. Science fiction. 1900-1999.
Treatment of monsters; MOTHERHOOD. 2172.

MOTHERING
See also related term: Motherhood.

MOTHERLAND
See also related term: Homeland.

MOTHERLESSNESS
See also related term: Mother.

MOTHER'S DAY
See also related term: Mother.

MOTIVATION
See also classified section: 2894.

MOTTO
See also related term: Impresa.

MOUNTAIN FILM
Used for: Bergfilm.
General literature. Film. Film genres in Germany.
MOUNTAIN FILM; relationship to modernity; Nazism. 796.

MOURNING
See also classified section: 2895.
General literature. Film in West Germany.
Treatment of MOURNING; memory; relationship to Third Reich; study example: Syberberg, Hans Jürgen: *Hitler, ein Film aus Deutschland*; Reitz, Edgar: *Heimat*. 566.
General literature by patient with cancer.
Relationship to art therapy. Treatment of MOURNING; creativity. Psychoanalytic approach. Dissertation abstract. 62.

MOVEMENTS
See also narrower term: Literary movements.

MOVIE OF THE WEEK
General literature. Television: docudrama and MOVIE OF THE WEEK.
Treatment of social problems. 881.

MOVIE STAR
Use: Film star.

MOVIEGOER
See also related term: Film.

MTV
Use: Music television.

MUKAŘOVSKÝ, JAN (1891-1975)
Literary theory and criticism.
Theories of MUKAŘOVSKÝ, JAN; Vodička, Felix; Bakhtin, Mikhail Mikhaïlovich. 1509.
Literary theory and criticism. Semiotic literary theory and criticism.
Relationship to semantics. Theories of MUKAŘOVSKÝ, JAN. 2001.
Relationship to structuralism. Theories of MUKAŘOVSKÝ, JAN. 2000.
—— compared to formalism. Theories of MUKAŘOVSKÝ, JAN compared to Zich, Otakar. 2007.
Theories of Bakhtin, Mikhail Mikhaïlovich compared to Ingarden, Roman; MUKAŘOVSKÝ, JAN. 1976.
Theories of Barthes, Roland; MUKAŘOVSKÝ, JAN. 1979.

MULCAHY, RUSSELL
General literature. Film.
Role of pastoralism in Kotcheff, Ted: *First Blood* compared to Cosmatos, George Pan: *Rambo II*; MULCAHY, RUSSELL: *Rambo III*. 273.

MULTICULTURAL EDUCATION
Professional topics. Humanities.
MULTICULTURAL EDUCATION; relationship to literacy; feminism. Interview with Stimpson, Catharine R. 2657.

MULTICULTURAL EDUCATION PROGRAM
See also related term: Multicultural education.

MULTICULTURALISM
See also related terms: Culture; Ethnicity; Minorities; Multicultural education.

MUNICH
Bibliographical. Printing in MUNICH (ca. 1900). 1162.

MUSEUM OF NEW MEXICO
Bibliographical. Manuscripts. Manuscript collections.
At MUSEUM OF NEW MEXICO. 1146.

MUSEUMS
See also narrower term: Museum of New Mexico.
See also related term: Archives.

MUSIC
See also narrower term: Rock and roll music.
See also related term: Musical composition.
General literature.
Relationship to MUSIC. 90.
——. Pedagogical approach. 193.
General literature. 1800-1899.
Relationship to MUSIC. 118.

General literature. Film.
Role of MUSIC. 433.
—— in Truffaut, François: *Les Quatre Cents Coups*. 508.
General literature. Television: music video.
Role of MUSIC; relationship to genre. 916.
General literature. Theater: opera.
Symbolism in word; MUSIC; staging. 938.
Genres. Poetry.
Relationship to MUSIC. Semiotic approach. Application of theories of Saussure, Ferdinand de. Dissertation abstract. 2303.
Sound; relationship to MUSIC. Dissertation abstract. 2295.
Themes and figures. Faust.
Includes treatment in MUSIC. Pedagogical approach. 2857.

MUSIC EDUCATION
See also related term: Music.

MUSIC TELEVISION
Used for: MTV.
General literature. Film. Film genres: musical film.
And music video; MUSIC TELEVISION. 745.
General literature. Television: MUSIC TELEVISION.
Discourse; relationship to power compared to masque for royal court of Jacobean period. 858.
Treatment of men; women; glamour; sexuality. 885.

MUSIC THEORY
See also related term: Music.

MUSIC VIDEO
Used for: Video record.
See also related term: Videotape.
General literature. Film. Film genres: musical film.
And MUSIC VIDEO; music television. 745.
General literature. Film and video art; MUSIC VIDEO.
Role of sexuality; relationship to Postmodernism. Imagery. 601.
General literature. Television.
MUSIC VIDEO as oral poetry. Dissertation abstract. 887.
General literature. Television: MUSIC VIDEO.
Role of music; relationship to genre. 916.

MUSICAL ADAPTATION
See also related term: Musical setting.
General literature.
Role of text in MUSICAL ADAPTATION. Interview with Henry, Pierre. 69.
General literature. Film. Film adaptation.
And MUSICAL ADAPTATION; radio adaptation; recordings of Poe, Edgar Allan. Catalogue. 735.

MUSICAL ALLUSION
See also related term: Music.

MUSICAL COMPOSITION
See also narrower term: Musical setting.
See also related term: Music.
General literature.
Role of text in MUSICAL COMPOSITION. 84.
—— in MUSICAL COMPOSITION. Interview with Boucourechliev, André. 68.

MUSICAL FILM
General literature. Film. Film genres: MUSICAL FILM.
And music video; music television. 745.
Review article. 777.
Role of Powell, Dick. 785.

MUSICAL IMAGERY
See also related term: Music.

MUSICAL METAPHOR
See also related term: Music.

MUSICAL SCALE
See also related term: Music.

MUSICAL SETTING
See also related term: Musical adaptation.
Genres. Poetry.
Relationship to MUSICAL SETTING. 2257.

MUSICAL STRUCTURE
See also related term: Music.

MUSICAL THEATER
General literature. Opera.
And operetta; MUSICAL THEATER. Plot. Index. 844.

MUSICALITY
See also related term: Music.

MUSICIAN
See also narrower term: Minstrels.

MUSICIANS IN EXILE
See also related term: Exile.

MUSLEMS
Use: Moslems.

MYRDDHIN
Use: Merlin.

MYSTERY FICTION
See also narrower terms: Detective fiction; Horror fiction.

MYSTERY NOVEL
See also related term: Penny dreadful.

MYSTERY PLAY
See also narrower term: Passion play.

MYSTERY **(TELEVISION PROGRAM)**
    General literature. Television.
        On *MYSTERY* (TELEVISION PROGRAM). Interview with Eaton, Rebecca. 897.

MYSTICAL EXPERIENCE
See also related term: Mysticism.

MYSTICISM
    Literary theory and criticism. Deconstructionism.
        Relationship to MYSTICISM; transgression. Theories of Derrida, Jacques compared to Eckhart, Meister. 1592.

MYSTICS
See also related term: Mysticism.

MYTH
See also classified section: 2405 ff.
See also related terms: Archetypes; Folk tale; Mythification.
See also: entries for myths of specific countries, areas, or peoples by consulting the index under the adjectival form of the country, area, or people.
    General literature. Film.
        Role of MYTH; genre; relationship to history in Curtiz, Michael: *The Charge of the Light Brigade.* 587.
        Role of politics; MYTH in Curtiz, Michael: *Casablanca.* Psychoanalytic approach. 343.
        Treatment of protagonist; relationship to MYTH of Oedipus in Antonioni, Michelangelo: *Identificazione di una donna.* 514.
    General literature. Television.
        Advertising; relationship to MYTH. Dissertation abstract. 907.
    Genres. Fiction.
        Relationship to religion; MYTH; poststructuralist literary theory and criticism. 2119.
    Genres. Fiction. *Märchen* **for children.**
        As MYTH. 2166.
    Genres. Novel. Popular romance novel.
        Treatment of love; relationship to MYTH; legend. 2237.
    Literary forms. Tragedy.
        Relationship to MYTH. Application of theories of Jung, Carl Gustav. 2507.
    Literary theory and criticism. Hermeneutics and linguistic literary theory and criticism. Middle Ages.
        Applied to book; relationship to MYTH; study example: Chaucer, Geoffrey; Dante. 1719.

MYTHIC HERO
See also related term: Myth.

MYTHICAL CREATURES
See also narrower terms: Monsters; Pegasus.

MYTHIFICATION
Used for: Mythologization.
See also related term: Myth.
    General literature. Film.
        Treatment of hero of Vietnam War; relationship to MYTHIFICATION. 333.

MYTHOGRAPHY
See also related term: Myth.

MYTHOLOGICAL FIGURES
See also narrower term: Orpheus.

MYTHOLOGIZATION
Use: Mythification.

MYTHOPOESIS
See also related terms: Myth; Mythification.

NAME CHANGE
See also related terms: Names; Naming.

NAMES
See also related term: Naming.
    Literary forms. Translation.
        Of NAMES; work title; forms of address. 2532.

NAMING
See also related term: Names.
    General literature. Film.
        NAMING of dwarf in Disney, Walt: *Snow White and the Seven Dwarfs*; relationship to Tolkien, J. R. R. 659.
    Genres. Poetry.
        NAMING. 2302.

NAMING DEFICIT
See also related term: Naming.

NARCISSISM
See also classified section: 2896.
    General literature. Television.
        Treatment of femininity; NARCISSISM in *Moonlighting* as television adaptation of Shakespeare, William: *The Taming of the Shrew.* Feminist approach. 908.
    Literary movements.
        Romanticism. Relationship to patriarchy; NARCISSISM. 1082.

NARCISSUS
See also related term: Narcissism.

NARRATEE
See also related terms: Narration; Narrator.
    General literature.
        Narrative; relationship to NARRATEE. 172.
    Literary theory and criticism.
        Narrator; NARRATEE in erotic literature. Theories of Genette, Gérard. 1340.

NARRATION
See also narrower term: Voice-over narration.
See also related terms: Narratee; Narrative; Narrative technique; Narrative theory; Narrative voice; Narrator; Point of view.
    General literature. Film.
        Dialectics of NARRATION. Dissertation abstract. 423.
        NARRATION in Renoir, Jean: *Le Crime de M. Lange.* 532.
    General literature. Film (1930-1939).
        NARRATION in Mizoguchi Kenji. Dissertation abstract. 427.
    Literary forms. Dialogue.
        Relationship to NARRATION. 2384.
    Literary theory and criticism.
        NARRATION. Theories of Ricœur, Paul: *Temps et récit.* 1408.

NARRATIVE
See also narrower terms: Intercalated narrative; Iterative narrative.
See also related terms: Narration; Narrative conventions; Narrative structure; Narrative technique.
    General literature.
        Confession in NARRATIVE. 74.
        NARRATIVE. 78.
        ——; relationship to cognitive processes. 71.
        ——; relationship to fiction; scientific discourse. 153.
        ——; relationship to history. 52.
        ——; relationship to narratee. 172.
        ——; rhetoric; relationship to medicine; study example: Percy, Walker: *Lancelot; The Moviegoer.* 143.
        Role of fictionality in NARRATIVE; relationship to logic; epistemology. 119.
        Role of NARRATIVE; relationship to meaning; language; autobiography. Psychological approach. 34.
        Temporality in NARRATIVE. 178.
    General literature. Film.
        Mise en scène; NARRATIVE; relationship to fascism in Lang, Fritz: *Siegfried; Kriemhilds Rache.* 376.
        ——; NARRATIVE in Velle, Gaston: *Tour du monde d'un policier.* 549.
        NARRATIVE. 321.
        ——; relationship to history in Cavani, Liliana: *Interno berlinese.* 483.
        ——; relationship to Postmodernism in Lynch, David: *Blue Velvet.* 460.
    General literature. Film in Hollywood.
        NARRATIVE; relationship to authorship in Hitchcock, Alfred: *North by Northwest*; role of screenplay by Lehman, Ernest Paul. Dissertation abstract. 581.
    General literature. Television.
        NARRATIVE. 879.
    General literature. Theater.
        Emplotment; relationship to NARRATIVE. Feminist approach. Dissertation abstract. 974.
    Genres. Autobiography by women writers. 1700-1899.
        Treatment of the self; relationship to duplicity in NARRATIVE. 2052.
    Genres. Drama.
        As NARRATIVE; relationship to temporality. 2091.
    Genres. Drama and NARRATIVE.
        Semantic analysis. 2079.
    Genres. Prose. Historiography.
        NARRATIVE. 2329, 2333.
        Relationship to Russian history. NARRATIVE. Theories of White, Hayden V.: *Metahistory.* 2332.
    Genres. Prose. Philosophical prose.
        Relationship to NARRATIVE. 2336.
    Literary forms. Dialogue in NARRATIVE.
        Compared to dramatic dialogue; relationship to teaching of writing. 2383.
    Literary movements.
        Modernism. NARRATIVE; relationship to allegory. Treatment in de Man, Paul. 1006.
    Literary theory and criticism.
        Role of NARRATIVE; relationship to subject in fiction. 1491.
    Literary theory and criticism. Hermeneutics.
        Applied to NARRATIVE in psychoanalysis. Application of theories of Habermas, Jürgen. 1711.
    Literary theory and criticism. Linguistic literary theory and criticism.
        Relationship to semantics; intensionality of NARRATIVE. 1734.

Literary theory and criticism. Marxist literary theory and criticism.
NARRATIVE as political discourse; relationship to interpretation. Treatment in Jameson, Fredric: *The Political Unconscious*. 1789.

Literary theory and criticism. Psychoanalytic literary theory and criticism.
On life as NARRATIVE; relationship to time. Theories of Freud, Sigmund; Sartre, Jean-Paul; Rorty, Richard. 1896.

Literary theory and criticism. Reader-response theory and criticism.
Reader in NARRATIVE. 1933.

Themes and figures. Reality and truth.
Relationship to representation in NARRATIVE. 2905.

NARRATIVE CONVENTIONS
See also related terms: Chronotope; Narrative.

Genres. Prose. Scientific prose.
NARRATIVE CONVENTIONS. 2340.

NARRATIVE DISCOURSE

General literature. Film.
NARRATIVE DISCOURSE. Treatment of female body in Rainer, Yvonne: *The Man Who Envied Women*. 350.

NARRATIVE DISTANCE

General literature. Film.
NARRATIVE DISTANCE; narrative voice in Duras, Marguerite. Dissertation abstract. 602.

NARRATIVE FORM
See also narrower terms: Qualitative form; Syllogistic form.

General literature. Film.
NARRATIVE FORM; ambiguity; relationship to melodrama in Weir, Peter: *Picnic at Hanging Rock*. 512.

NARRATIVE FRAME
See also related term: Framing.

NARRATIVE PATTERN
Use: Narrative structure.

NARRATIVE POETRY
See also narrower terms: Epic poetry; Romance.

NARRATIVE SKILLS
See also related term: Narrative.

NARRATIVE STRATEGY
Use: Narrative technique.

NARRATIVE STRUCTURE
Used for: Narrative pattern.
See also related term: Narrative.

General literature. Film.
NARRATIVE STRUCTURE. Treatment of Vietnam War in Coppola, Francis Ford: *Apocalypse Now*. Application of theories of Lévi-Strauss, Claude. 644.

NARRATIVE TECHNIQUE
Used for: Narrative strategy.
See also narrower term: Narrative voice.
See also related terms: Narration; Narrative.

General literature. Film.
NARRATIVE TECHNIQUE; relationship to irrationality in Lynch, David: *Blue Velvet*. 519.
——; relationship to suture; focalization compared to Joyce, James: *A Portrait of the Artist as a Young Man*. 334.
—— in Cameron, James: *The Terminator*. Application of theories of Genette, Gérard. 479.

General literature. Film. Film adaptation.
NARRATIVE TECHNIQUE in film adaptation of Miller, Warren: *The Cool World* by Clarke, Shirley. 700.

Genres. Fiction.
NARRATIVE TECHNIQUE; relationship to spatiality. 2150.

Genres. Fiction. Modernist fiction.
NARRATIVE TECHNIQUE. 2167.

NARRATIVE THEORY
See also classified section: 1795 ff.
See also related term: Narration.

Genres. Novel.
Relationship to NARRATIVE THEORY. 2194, 2223.
Rhetoric; relationship to NARRATIVE THEORY. 2219.

NARRATIVE TIME

Genres. Poetry.
NARRATIVE TIME; relationship to Postmodernism. 2254.

NARRATIVE TRADITION
See also related term: Narrative.

NARRATIVE UNITY
See also related term: Narrative.

NARRATIVE VOICE
See also related terms: Authorial voice; Narration; Narrator; Point of view; Voice-over narration.

General literature.
On written language; relationship to NARRATIVE VOICE; closure; oral tradition. 159.

General literature. Film.
Narrative distance; NARRATIVE VOICE in Duras, Marguerite. Dissertation abstract. 602.
NARRATIVE VOICE. Treatment of Vietnam War compared to Rabe, David: *Sticks and Bones*; *Streamers*; *The Basic Training of Pavlo Hummel*. 317.

General literature for children. English language literature. 1900-1999.
NARRATIVE VOICE. 202.
——. Treatment of Middle Ages. 116.

Genres. Fiction.
Focalization; relationship to NARRATIVE VOICE. 2149.

Genres. Fiction for children.
NARRATIVE VOICE. Interview with Schmidt, Gary D. 2115.

NARRATOR
See also related terms: Narratee; Narration; Narrative voice.

Genres. Fiction.
NARRATOR; point of view; relationship to story; study example: Sandars, Nancy Katharine: *The Epic of Gilgamesh*. Anthropological approach. 2148.
—— as mediator between writer and reader. 2159.

Genres. Fiction as autobiography.
Repetition by NARRATOR. Dissertation abstract. 2123.

Literary theory and criticism.
NARRATOR; narratee in erotic literature. Theories of Genette, Gérard. 1340.

NATHANS, JEREMY H.—STUDY EXAMPLE

Literary theory and criticism. Linguistic literary theory and criticism.
Applied to scientific discourse; study example: NATHANS, JEREMY H. 1743.

NATION
See also related terms: National culture; National identity; Nationalism.

NATIONAL BROADCASTING COMPANY
See also related term: Radio; Television.

General literature. Television.
Role of Weaver, Sylvester Laflin; relationship to NATIONAL BROADCASTING COMPANY. 882.

NATIONAL CULTURE

General literature. Film. Film genres: horror film in Great Britain (1956-1973).
Relationship to NATIONAL CULTURE. Dissertation abstract. 772.

NATIONAL FILM BOARD OF CANADA
See also related term: Film industry.

NATIONAL GROUPS
See also narrower terms: Basques; Germans.
See also related term: Minorities.

NATIONAL IDENTITY
See also: entries for nationalities in specific countries by consulting the index under the adjectival form of the country or area.
See also related terms: Ethnic identity; Nationalism.

General literature. Film.
Relationship to NATIONAL IDENTITY. 308, 394.

NATIONAL LANGUAGE
See also related term: National identity.

NATIONAL LITERATURE

Literary theory and criticism. Literary history.
Relationship to NATIONAL LITERATURE. 1777.

Professional topics. Comparative literature.
NATIONAL LITERATURE; relationship to world literature. 2626.
World literature; relationship to NATIONAL LITERATURE. 2608, 2616.

NATIONAL SOCIALISM
Use: Nazism.

NATIONALISM
See also: entries for nationalism in specific countries by consulting the index under the adjectival from of the country or area.
See also related terms: National identity; Politics.

Literary forms. Satire. 1700-1799.
Relationship to NATIONALISM. 2502.

NATIVE AMERICAN EXPERIENCE
See also related term: Native Americans.

NATIVE AMERICANS
See also classified section: 2897.
Used for: American Indians; Amerindians; Indians (America).
See also: entries under headings for specific groups of Native Americans.

Literary theory and criticism.
On American literature; American culture; relationship to NATIVE AMERICANS. Review article. 1458.

NATURAL LAW
See also related term: Nature.

NATURAL SCIENCES
See also narrower term: Biology.

NATURALISM

General literature. Theater.
Representation of nature in theatrical production; relationship to Realist movement and NATURALISM. Theories of Darwin, Charles Robert; Le Brun, Charles. 960.

NATURE

General literature. Theater.
Representation of NATURE in theatrical production; relationship to Realist movement and Naturalism. Theories of Darwin, Charles Robert; Le Brun, Charles. 960.
Role of theater theory applied to performance compared to science; quantum theory applied to NATURE. 968

Genres. Poetry.
Treatment of NATURE. 2262.

NATURE IMAGERY
See also related term: Nature.

NATURE POETRY
See also narrower term: Pastoral poetry.

NATURE SYMBOLISM
See also related term: Nature.

NAZI PERSECUTOR
See also related term: The Holocaust.

NAZISM
Used for: National Socialism.
See also related term: Third Reich.

General literature. Film.
Treatment of genius of women; relationship to NAZISM in Pabst, Georg Wilhelm: *Komödianten*. 570.
Treatment of mother; relationship to NAZISM in postwar period in Hitchcock, Alfred: *Notorious*. Application of theories of Jung, Carl Gustav. 244.
Treatment of sexuality; relationship to NAZISM in Rossellini, Roberto: *Roma, città aperta*; Visconti, Luchino: *Ossessione*. 349.

General literature. Film. Film genres in Germany.
Mountain film; relationship to modernity; NAZISM. 796.

Literary theory and criticism. Deconstructionism.
Relationship to NAZISM. Theories of Heidegger, Martin; de Man, Paul; Derrida, Jacques. 1612.
Theories of de Man, Paul; relationship to NAZISM. 1613.

Literary theory and criticism. Philosophical literary theory and criticism.
Theories of Heidegger, Martin; relationship to NAZISM. 1856.

NEATBY, HILDA MARION ADA (1904-1975)
Professional topics. Humanities.
Theories of NEATBY, HILDA MARION ADA: *So Little for the Mind*. 2690.

NECROPHILIA
See also related term: Sexuality.

NEGATIVE ANSWER
See also related term: Question.

NEOCOLONIALISM
See also related term: Colonialism.

General literature. Film in black Africa.
Production; relationship to NEOCOLONIALISM. 369.

NEOLOGISM
Literary theory and criticism. Feminist literary theory and criticism.
On NEOLOGISM; relationship to epistemology. 1701.

NEOREALISM
See also related term: Realist movement.

General literature. Film.
NEOREALISM. 312.

General literature. Film in Italy.
NEOREALISM. 338.

NETHERLANDIC UNIVERSITIES
Professional topics. Humanities.
Role of English departments in NETHERLANDIC UNIVERSITIES. 2691.

NETHERLANDS
Used for: Holland.
See also narrower terms: Amsterdam; Delft.

Bibliographical. 1400-1599.
Book collecting in NETHERLANDS by Arenberg family; relationship to Bibliothèque Royale Albert I^{r}r. 1089.

General literature. Television in NETHERLANDS.
Role of Postmodernism in *Sjef van Oekel*; *Fred Hachee*. 852.

Literary theory and criticism. Deconstructionism in NETHERLANDS.
Relationship to Postmodernism. 1611.

Professional topics. Humanities.
Literary studies of Renaissance in Great Britain; NETHERLANDS (1950-1990). 2658.

NEUHAUSEN
Bibliographical. Printing.
Of letters (1461); relationship to NEUHAUSEN. Theories of Kruitwagen, Bonaventura. 1188.

NEUROLINGUISTIC APPROACH
Documents applying specific approaches are so numerous that access to them is provided only in the electronic versions of the *Bibliography*.

NEUSTADT INTERNATIONAL PRIZE FOR LITERATURE
General literature.
NEUSTADT INTERNATIONAL PRIZE FOR LITERATURE (1990). 179.

NEVES FREIRE, PAULO REGLUS
Use: Freire, Paulo (1921-).

NEW CRITICISM
See also classified section: 1828 ff.

Literary theory and criticism. New Historicism.
Role of history; relationship to NEW CRITICISM; formalism. 1844.

Literary theory and criticism. Poststructuralist literary theory and criticism.
Role of subjectivity; the self; relationship to humanism; NEW CRITICISM. Application of theories of Lacan, Jacques. 1887.

NEW FORMALIST POETS
See also related term: Formalism.

NEW GERMAN CINEMA
See also related term: Film.

NEW HISTORICAL APPROACH
Documents applying specific approaches are so numerous that access to them is provided only in the electronic versions of the *Bibliography*.

NEW HISTORICAL LITERARY THEORY
Use: New Historicism.

NEW HISTORICISM
See also classified section: 1832 ff.
Used for: Historical criticism; New historical literary theory.

NEW HISTORICISM—APPLICATION
General literature. Theater.
Application of NEW HISTORICISM. 979.

NEW MAN
See also related term: Socialism.

NEW WORLD
Genres. Novel.
Treatment of NEW WORLD; relationship to exile; prison. 2190.

Genres. Prose. Historiography.
Treatment of NEW WORLD. 2327.

Themes and figures. Orphans and bastard.
In novel of NEW WORLD. 2901.

NEW ZEALAND
General literature. Film in NEW ZEALAND.
Treatment of tourism; ethnography; relationship to Maori in McDonald, James. 264.

NEWMARKET
Bibliographical. Printing in Ontario: NEWMARKET. 1800-1899. 1164.

NEWS
See also related term: Newspapers.

General literature. Television.
Treatment of death in NEWS. 892.

NEWS REPORTING
See also related term: News.

NEWSPAPER ARCHIVES
See also related term: Newspapers.

NEWSPAPER ARTICLE
Used for: Newspaper story.
See also related term: Newspapers.

NEWSPAPER ARTICLE—STUDY EXAMPLE
Figures of speech. Imagery.
Relationship to cognitive processes of reader; study example: Móricz, Zsigmond: "Barbárok"; NEWSPAPER ARTICLE. 2352.

NEWSPAPER EDITOR
See also related term: Newspapers.

NEWSPAPER HEADLINES
See also related term: Newspapers.

NEWSPAPER LANGUAGE
See also related term: Newspapers.

NEWSPAPER STORY
Use: Newspaper article.

NEWSPAPERS
See also related terms: News; Newspaper article.

General literature. Television.
Television criticism in NEWSPAPERS. Dissertation abstract. 890.

NEWTON, FRANCIS
Use: Hobsbawm, Eric J. (1917-).

NEWTON, SIR ISAAC (1642-1727)
Literary movements.
Romanticism. Poetic language; relationship to synecdoche compared to language of astronomy. Application of theories of NEWTON, SIR ISAAC compared to Herschel, Sir William. 1077.

SEE CLASSIFIED SEQUENCE FOR ADDITIONAL ENTRIES

NICKELODEON

General literature. Film in Chicago (1906-1908).
And NICKELODEON; amusement park as cultural space; relationship to sexuality of women. 536.

NIETZSCHE, FRIEDRICH WILHELM (1844-1900)

Literary movements.
Postmodernism. Relationship to NIETZSCHE, FRIEDRICH WILHELM. 1038.
——. Use of language. Application of theories of NIETZSCHE, FRIEDRICH WILHELM. 1063.

Literary theory and criticism.
Pedagogical approach. Theories of NIETZSCHE, FRIEDRICH WILHELM; Habermas, Jürgen. 1450.
Relationship to discourse. Application of theories of Foucault, Michel; relationship to NIETZSCHE, FRIEDRICH WILHELM. 1544.

Literary theory and criticism. Deconstructionism.
Pathos. Theories of NIETZSCHE, FRIEDRICH WILHELM in theories of Derrida, Jacques. 1586.
Theories of Derrida, Jacques; relationship to NIETZSCHE, FRIEDRICH WILHELM. 1647.

NIETZSCHE, FRIEDRICH WILHELM (1844-1900)—AS SOURCE

Literary movements.
Modernism and Postmodernism. Role of nihilism. Sources in NIETZSCHE, FRIEDRICH WILHELM. 1017.

NIGER

General literature. Film in NIGER. 371.

NIHILISM

General literature. Film.
Treatment of NIHILISM in Weir, Peter: *Dead Poets Society*. 400.
Treatment of Vietnam War; relationship to NIHILISM in Stone, Oliver: *Platoon*. 516.

Literary movements.
Modernism and Postmodernism. Role of NIHILISM. Sources in Nietzsche, Friedrich Wilhelm. 1017.

Literary theory and criticism. Poststructuralist literary theory and criticism.
NIHILISM; logocentrism; relationship to Christianity. 1881.

Professional topics. Comparative literature.
Relationship to NIHILISM. 2632.

Professional topics. Humanities in United States.
Relationship to NIHILISM. Theories of Bloom, Allan David: *The Closing of the American Mind*. 2759.

NIMSHAL

See also related term: Midrash.

NIVOLA

See also related term: Novel.

NOBEL PRIZE

See also narrower term: Nobel Prize in Literature.

NOBEL PRIZE IN LITERATURE

General literature by recipients of NOBEL PRIZE IN LITERATURE (1901-1988).
Biographical dictionary. 171.

NOBLE, FRANCIS

Bibliographical. Publishing in London. 1700-1799.
Role of NOBLE, FRANCIS; Noble, John. 1260.

NOBLE, JOHN

Bibliographical. Publishing in London. 1700-1799.
Role of Noble, Francis; NOBLE, JOHN. 1260.

NOMENCLATURE

Use: Terminology.

NONFICTION

See also related terms: Fact; Prose.

NONFICTION NOVEL

See also related terms: Fiction; Prose.

NONHUMAN FIGURES

General literature.
Treatment of NONHUMAN FIGURES; relationship to humanism. Dissertation abstract. 130.

NONMETAPHORICAL CONCEPT

Figures of speech. Metaphor.
Relationship to NONMETAPHORICAL CONCEPT. Theories of Johnson, Mark Leonard. 2374.

NONREFERENTIAL LANGUAGE

Genres. Fiction.
NONREFERENTIAL LANGUAGE; relationship to truth compared to fictionality. 2142.

NONSENSE

Literary theory and criticism. Semiotic literary theory and criticism.
Treatment of NONSENSE in Italian language translation of Bouissac, Paul: *Cirque et culture*. 1964.

NONVERBAL COMMUNICATION

General literature. Film. Film genres: *film noir*.
NONVERBAL COMMUNICATION in Garnett, Tay: *The Postman Always Rings Twice*; Hawks, Howard: *The Big Sleep*; Dmytryk, Edward: *Murder, My Sweet* compared to remakes by Rafelson, Bob; Winner, Michael; Richards, Dick. Dissertation abstract. 767.

NONVIOLENCE

See also related term: Violence.

NORRIS, CHRISTOPHER (1947-)

Literary theory and criticism. Deconstructionism.
Treatment in NORRIS, CHRISTOPHER: *Deconstruction: Theory and Practice*; Miller, J. Hillis: "The Function of Rhetorical Study at the Present Time." 1602.

NORTH AMERICA

See also narrower terms: Canada; Mexico; United States.

NORTHERN AFRICA

See also narrower term: Morocco.
See also related term: Middle East.

NORTHERN FRANCE

See also narrower term: Paris.

NORTHERN ITALY

See also narrower terms: Friuli-Venezia Giulia; Venice.

NORWAY

General literature. Film in NORWAY.
Interview with Edwall, Allan. 583.
—— with Kaurismäki, Aki and Kaurismäki, Mika. 461.

NORWEGIAN STUDIES

Professional topics. Humanities.
On NORWEGIAN STUDIES. 2812.

NOSTALGIA

See also related term: The past.

General literature. Film.
Treatment of childhood; NOSTALGIA; relationship to homeland in Tarkovskiĭ, Andreĭ A.: *Ivanovo detstvo*; *Nostalghia*; *Offret* compared to Brodskiĭ, Iosif Aleksandrovich; Chagall, Marc. 551.

NOVEL

See also classified section: 2187 ff.
See also narrower terms: Bildungsroman; Detective novel; Dystopian novel; Modernist novel; Penny dreadful; Popular romance novel; *Roman à thèse*; Romance novel; Sentimental novel; Social novel; War novel.
See also: entries for novel in specific countries by consulting the index under the adjectival form of the country.

Literary theory and criticism.
Dialogism; relationship to context; politics in NOVEL. Theories of Bakhtin, Mikhail Mikhaĭlovich. 1531.
On NOVEL; relationship to language. Theories of Bakhtin, Mikhail Mikhaĭlovich. 1372.
——; relationship to language; society. Theories of Bakhtin, Mikhail Mikhaĭlovich. 1319.

Literary theory and criticism. New Historicism.
Relationship to poststructuralism; NOVEL. 1838.

Themes and figures. Orphans and bastard.
In NOVEL of New World. 2901.

NOVEL FOR TELEVISION

See also related term: Television.

NOVELISTS

See also narrower term: Women novelists.
See also related term: Novel.

NOVELLA

See also related terms: Novel; Short story.

NOVELTY

General literature.
Role of creativity; relationship to NOVELTY. Psychological approach. 133.

NOVITZ, DAVID

Literary theory and criticism.
Relationship to identity. Theories of NOVITZ, DAVID. 1536.

NOWELL-SMITH, SIMON HARCOURT (1909-)

Bibliographical. 1900-1999.
Role of NOWELL-SMITH, SIMON HARCOURT; Trevanion, Michael as bibliographer; relationship to book collecting. 1094.

NUCLEAR AGE

Used for: Atomic age.
See also related term: Nuclear war.

General literature for adolescents.
Relationship to NUCLEAR AGE. 123.
Themes and figures. Hiroshima and NUCLEAR AGE. 2865.

NUCLEAR CRITICISM

See also related term: Nuclear war.

NUCLEAR DETERRENCE

See also related term: Nuclear war.

NUCLEAR DISASTER
See also related terms: Nuclear age; Nuclear war.

NUCLEAR ENERGY
See also related term: Nuclear age.

NUCLEAR FAMILY
  General literature. Film. Film genres: American Western film.
    Treatment of NUCLEAR FAMILY. 801.

NUCLEAR TESTING
See also related term: Nuclear war.

NUCLEAR WAR
See also classified section: 2898 ff.
See also related term: Nuclear age.
  General literature. Film.
    Treatment of NUCLEAR WAR; relationship to female point of view in Littman, Lynne: *Testament* compared to McCloy, Helen: *The Last Day*; Merril, Judith: *Shadow on the Hearth*. 271.
  Genres. Fiction.
    Image; form; relationship to literary conventions. Treatment of NUCLEAR WAR. 2108.
    Treatment of politics; relationship to NUCLEAR WAR. 2151.
  Literary theory and criticism.
    On writing of history; relationship to the future; NUCLEAR WAR. 1540.
    Relationship to NUCLEAR WAR. 1449.

NUCLEAR WEAPON
See also related term: Nuclear age.

  Literary forms. Rhetoric.
    Relationship to public discourse on NUCLEAR WEAPONS. Application of theories of Burke, Kenneth. 2429.

NUOVA ANTOLOGIA
  Bibliographical. Publishing in Florence (1890-1920).
    By Bemporad, Enrico; relationship to Gabinetto Vieusseux; *NUOVA ANTOLOGIA*. 1252.

NUSSBAUM, MARTHA CRAVEN (1947-)
  Literary theory and criticism. Feminist literary theory and criticism.
    Relationship to humanism. Theories of NUSSBAUM, MARTHA CRAVEN: *The Fragility of Goodness: Luck and Ethics in Greek Tragedy and Philosophy*; Gilligan, Carol: *In a Different Voice* compared to Foucault, Michel. 1700.

OBJECTIVITY
See also related term: Subjectivity.

OBJECTS
  General literature. Film. Film adaptation.
    Treatment of OBJECTS as sign in film adaptation by Buñuel, Luis. Dissertation abstract. 719.
  General literature. Film. Film genres: avant-garde film.
    Treatment of OBJECTS in Buñuel, Luis. 798.

OBJET D'ART
See also related term: Art.

OBSESSION
  General literature. Film.
    Characterization; relationship to OBSESSION in Huston, John. 657.

OCCUPATIONAL GROUPS
See also narrower terms: Journalists; Librarians.

OCEANIA
See also narrower terms: Australia; New Zealand.

OEDIPAL CONFLICT
See also related terms: Oedipus; Oedipus complex.

OEDIPUS
See also related term: Oedipus complex.
  General literature. Film.
    Treatment of protagonist; relationship to myth of OEDIPUS in Antonioni, Michelangelo: *Identificazione di una donna*. 514.
  Literary theory and criticism. Psychoanalytic literary theory and criticism.
    Relationship to OEDIPUS; Orpheus. Theories of Freud, Sigmund; Blanchot, Maurice. 1901.

OEDIPUS COMPLEX
See also related term: Oedipus.
  Literary theory and criticism. Psychoanalytic literary theory and criticism.
    Role of OEDIPUS COMPLEX. Theories of Abraham, Nicolas and Torok, Maria compared to Freud, Sigmund; Lacan, Jacques. Review article. 1909.

OERTEL, CURT
  General literature. Film. Film adaptation.
    Of Storm, Theodor: *Pole Poppenspäler* by OERTEL, CURT. 695.

OKLAHOMA
See also classified section: 2900.

OLD TESTAMENT
  Literary theory and criticism.
    On quotation in OLD TESTAMENT: Isaiah. Diachronic approach. Dissertation abstract. 1527.

OLD TESTAMENT—AS SOURCE
  General literature.
    Sources in OLD TESTAMENT. 125.
  Genres. Drama by Jesuit dramatists. 1500-1799.
    Sources in OLD TESTAMENT. 2087.

OLIVER, ROBERT TARBELL (1909-)
  Literary forms. Rhetoric.
    Treatment in OLIVER, ROBERT TARBELL. 2422.

OLMI, ERMANNO (1931-)
  General literature. Film.
    Iterative narrative in Ford, John: *How Green Was My Valley* compared to Stevens, George Cooper: *A Place in the Sun*; De Sica, Vittorio: *Umberto D.*; OLMI, ERMANNO: *Il posto*. Application of theories of Genette, Gérard. 425.

OLSON, DAVID R. (1935-)
  Figures of speech. Metaphor.
    Theories of OLSON, DAVID R. 2363.

OLYMPIA PRESS
  Bibliographical. Publishing in United States; France.
    By Grove Press; OLYMPIA PRESS. Interview with Girodias, Maurice. 1243.

OMNIPOTENCE
See also related term: God.

ONG, WALTER J. (1912-)
  General literature.
    Orality. Interview with ONG, WALTER J. 210.
    Role of Christian scholars. Interview with ONG, WALTER J. 37.
  Professional topics. Humanities.
    Relationship to orality. Treatment in ONG, WALTER J.; Havelock, Eric Alfred. 2822.

ONOMASTIC APPROACH
Documents applying specific approaches are so numerous that access to them is provided only in the electronic versions of the *Bibliography*.

ONTOLOGY
  Literary movements.
    Postmodernism. Relationship to ONTOLOGY. 1061.

OPENNESS
See also related term: Space.

OPERA
See also related term: Operetta.
  General literature. Theater: OPERA.
    Symbolism in word; music; staging. 938.

OPERA—STUDY EXAMPLE
  Themes and figures. Troilus.
    And Cressida; study example: OPERA; Morley, Christopher: *The Trojan Horse*; Wolf, Christa: *Kassandra*. 2927.

OPERETTA
See also related term: Opera.
  General literature. Opera.
    And OPERETTA; musical theater. Plot. Index. 844.

OPHÜLS, MARCEL (1927-)
  General literature. Film. Film genres: documentary film.
    By OPHÜLS, MARCEL. Includes interview. 791.

OPHÜLS, MAX (1902-1957)
  General literature. Film.
    Treatment of homosexuality in OPHÜLS, MAX: *Letter from an Unknown Woman* compared to James, Henry, Jr.: "The Beast in the Jungle." 285.

OPINIONS
See also related term: Attitudes.

OPPIZZONI, GAETANO
  Bibliographical. Manuscripts.
    In personal library of OPPIZZONI, GAETANO. 1132.

OPPOSITION
See also narrower term: Binary opposition.

THE OPPRESSED
See also related term: Oppression.

OPPRESSION
  General literature by postcolonial writers. English language literature. 1900-1999.
    Treatment of OPPRESSION. 95.

ORAL-FORMULAIC COMPOSITION
See also related term: Oral poetry.

ORAL LANGUAGE
Use: Spoken language.

ORAL LITERATURE
See also narrower term: Oral poetry.

ORAL POETRY
  General literature. Television.
    Music video as ORAL POETRY. Dissertation abstract. 887.

Genres. Poetry. Epic poetry.
Hexameter in ORAL POETRY. Sources in Homer. Application of theories of Parry, Milman. 2306.

ORAL STYLE
General literature.
ORAL STYLE. 109.

ORAL TRADITION
General literature.
Compared to ORAL TRADITION. 16.
On written language; relationship to narrative voice; closure; ORAL TRADITION. 159.
Performance of ORAL TRADITION. 152.
General literature. Film by black Africans.
Relationship to ORAL TRADITION. Dissertation abstract. 618.
Literary forms. Translation.
Of dialogue of Koran; relationship to ORAL TRADITION. 2521.

ORALITY
General literature.
ORALITY. 158.
——. Interview with Ong, Walter J. 210.
Professional topics. Humanities.
Relationship to ORALITY. Treatment in Ong, Walter J.; Havelock, Eric Alfred. 2822.
Teaching of literature; relationship to ORALITY. 2801.

ORDER
General literature.
Relationship to ORDER; chaos; study example: Adams, Henry Brooks: *The Education of Henry Adams*; Lessing, Doris: *The Golden Notebook*; Lem, Stanisław. 96.

ORDINARIUS STRIGONIENSIS
Bibliographical. Printing. Illustration. Middle Ages.
Of *ORDINARIUS STRIGONIENSIS*. 1210.

ORDINATION
General literature. Television.
Treatment of ORDINATION of women in *Designing Women*. 904.

ORGANICISM
Literary theory and criticism.
Relationship to ORGANICISM. 1456.

ORIGINALITY
See also related terms: Creativity; Invention.

ORPHANS
See also classified section: 2901.

ORPHEUS
Literary theory and criticism. Psychoanalytic literary theory and criticism.
Relationship to Oedipus; ORPHEUS. Theories of Freud, Sigmund; Blanchot, Maurice. 1901.

THE OTHER
See also related term: Otherness.
General literature. Film.
Role of THE OTHER in Hitchcock, Alfred. 664.
Literary theory and criticism.
Relationship to THE OTHER; the Holocaust; Judaism. Theories of Levinas, Emmanuel; Perelman, Chaim: *The New Rhetoric*; Rosenzweig, Franz. 1420.
Role of THE OTHER; language; relationship to ethics; religion. Theories of Levinas, Emmanuel; Marion, Jean-Luc. 1577.

OTHERNESS
Used for: Alterity.
See also related term: The other.
Literary forms. Rhetoric.
Relationship to OTHERNESS. Theories of Bakhtin, Mikhail Mikhaïlovich. 2470.
Literary theory and criticism.
OTHERNESS; relationship to identity in Europe. Theories of Bakhtin, Mikhail Mikhaïlovich. 1508.
Literary theory and criticism. Feminist literary theory and criticism.
Dialogism; relationship to difference; OTHERNESS. Application of theories of Bakhtin, Mikhail Mikhaïlovich. 1676.
Literary theory and criticism. Linguistic literary theory and criticism.
Chronotope; relationship to OTHERNESS. Theories of Bakhtin, Mikhail Mikhaïlovich compared to Welby, Victoria, Lady. 1753.
Literary theory and criticism. Poststructuralist literary theory and criticism.
Role of OTHERNESS; relationship to laughter. Theories of Bakhtin, Mikhail Mikhaïlovich compared to Derrida, Jacques. 1882.
Literary theory and criticism. Semiotic literary theory and criticism.
Role of OTHERNESS in literature of Middle Ages; relationship to hermeneutics. Theories of Jauss, Hans Robert; Gadamer, Hans-Georg. 1980.

OUSMANE SEMBÈNE
Use: Sembène Ousmane (1923-).

OVCHAROV, SVETOSLAV
General literature. Film. Film genres: documentary film.
On Cholakov, Georgi and OVCHAROV, SVETOSLAV: *Stefan Stambolov—süzidateliat i süsipateliat*. Interview. 779.

OWENS, CRAIG
Literary movements.
Postmodernism. Relationship to history. Theories of OWENS, CRAIG; Jameson, Fredric. 1023.

OXFORD CONCORDANCE PROGRAM
Professional topics. Computer-assisted research.
OXFORD CONCORDANCE PROGRAM; application in teaching of literature. 2638, 2643.

PABST, GEORG WILHELM (1885-1967)
General literature. Film.
By Lang, Fritz; PABST, GEORG WILHELM. Psychoanalytic approach. 250.
Treatment of genius of women; relationship to Nazism in PABST, GEORG WILHELM: *Komödianten*. 570.

PACIFIC NORTHWEST
See also narrower term: British Columbia.
See also related terms: Canada; United States.

PAINTING
General literature.
Language; relationship to imagery in PAINTING by Turner, Joseph Mallord William. 168.
Temporality; spatiality compared to PAINTING. Pedagogical approach. 196.
General literature. 1900-1999.
And PAINTING. Pedagogical approach. 50.
General literature. Film.
Intertextuality relationship to PAINTING in Robbe-Grillet, Alain: *L'Eden et après*; *La Belle Captive*. 591.

PAKISTAN
General literature. Television in PAKISTAN (1985-1989).
Treatment of gender; relationship to Pakistani society in *Dewareen*; *Tanhaiyan*. Dissertation abstract. 919.

PAKISTANI SOCIETY
General literature. Television in Pakistan (1985-1989).
Treatment of gender; relationship to PAKISTANI SOCIETY in *Dewareen*; *Tanhaiyan*. Dissertation abstract. 919.

PALEONTOLOGY
See also related term: Biology.

PANTISOCRACY
See also related term: Utopia.

PANTOMIME
Used for: Mime.
See also related term: Performance art.
General literature. Theater: PANTOMIME.
Dissertation abstract. 925.

PAPER
See also classified section: 1220 ff.
See also related term: Printing.

PARABLE
See also related term: Fable.

PARADJANOV, SERGHIEJ
Use: Paradzhanov, Sergeï (1924-1990).

PARADOX
See also related term: Antinomy.

PARADZHANOV, SERGEÏ (1924-1990)
Used for: Paradjanov, Serghiej.
General literature. Film.
On PARADZHANOV, SERGEÏ: *Saiat Nova*. 245.

PARALINGUISTICS
See also related term: Nonverbal communication.

PARALOGISM
Literary forms. Rhetoric.
PARALOGISM; relationship to dialogism. Sources in sophistry. Theories of Davidson, Donald; Derrida, Jacques; Bakhtin, Mikhail Mikhaïlovich. 2462.

PARANOIA
Literary movements.
Postmodernism. Relationship to PARANOIA; study example: Fish, Stanley: *Is There a Text in This Class?* Application of theories of Shapiro, David. 1026.

PARAPSYCHOLOGY
See also related term: Psychology.

PARATHEATER
General literature. Television in United States.
Wrestling as PARATHEATER. 877.

PARENT-ADOLESCENT COMMUNICATION
See also related term: Adolescents.

PARENT-CHILD RELATIONS
See also related term: Children.

PARENTAL FIGURES
See also narrower term: Mother.

PARENTHOOD
See also narrower term: Motherhood.
See also related term: Mother.

PARIS

Bibliographical. Printing in Lyon and PARIS (1470-1485).
Relationship to Jean de Vignay: *La Légende dorée.* 1161.

Literary movements.
Postmodernism. Role of the carnivalesque; kitsch; relationship to bicentennial of French Revolution in PARIS (1989). Application of theories of Bakhtin, Mikhail Mikhaïlovich. 1057.

PARODIC PLAY

Literary theory and criticism. Deconstructionism.
PARODIC PLAY; relationship to reason. Theories of Derrida, Jacques compared to Levinas, Emmanuel. 1606.

PARODY
See also classified section: 2412 ff.
See also related term: Pastiche.

General literature. Film.
PARODY. 414.

PARONOMASIA
Use: Pun.

PARRY, MILMAN (1902-1935)

Genres. Poetry. Epic poetry.
Hexameter in oral poetry. Sources in Homer. Application of theories of PARRY, MILMAN. 2306.

PARTON, DOLLY (1946-)

General literature. Film.
Interview with PARTON, DOLLY. 407.

PASCAL, BLAISE (1623-1662)

Literary theory and criticism.
Role of subject; relationship to representation. Application of theories of PASCAL, BLAISE; Piles, Roger de. 1470.

PASKIN, DAVID

General literature. Film. Film genres: documentary film.
Treatment of Abraham Lincoln Battalion in Buckner, Noel and Dore, Mary and PASKIN, DAVID and Sills, Sam: *The Good Fight.* 748.

PASOLINI, PIER PAOLO (1922-1975)

General literature. Film.
Signification. Treatment of passion in PASOLINI, PIER PAOLO: *Teorema.* 624.
Treatment of the sacred in PASOLINI, PIER PAOLO: *Teorema.* 287.

PASSION

General literature. Film.
Signification. Treatment of PASSION in Pasolini, Pier Paolo: *Teorema.* 624.

PASSION OF CHRIST
See also related term: Christ.

Bibliographical. Printing. Illustration.
On woodcuts of PASSION OF CHRIST by Delbecq, Jean Baptiste and Schreiber, Wilhelm Ludwig. 1211.

PASSION PLAY

General literature. Theater: PASSION PLAY.
Interview with Stephan, Brother. 972.

THE PAST
See also related terms: Historical consciousness; History; Nostalgia.

Professional topics. Humanities in United States.
Theories of Bloom, Allan David: *The Closing of the American Mind*; relationship to THE PAST; democracy; reality. 2661.

PASTICHE
See also related terms: Parody; Satire.

Literary forms. Parody.
And travesty; PASTICHE; relationship to social relations; psychology. Application of communication theory. 2414.

PASTORAL
See also related term: Pastoral poetry.

PASTORAL POETRY
See also classified section: 2313.

PASTORALISM

General literature. Film.
Role of PASTORALISM in Kotcheff, Ted: *First Blood* compared to Cosmatos, George Pan: *Rambo II*; Mulcahy, Russell: *Rambo III.* 273.

PATER, W. DE

Literary theory and criticism. Linguistic literary theory and criticism.
Iconicity of poetic language. Structuralist approach. Compared to treatment in PATER, W. DE and Langendonck, W. van: "Natuurlijkheid van de taal en iconiciteit." 1739.

PATHÉ FRÈRES

General literature. Film. Film genres: melodrama in France (1905-1907).
By PATHÉ FRÈRES. 744.

PATHOLOGY
See also related term: Medicine.

PATHOS

Literary forms. Tragedy.
Role of PATHOS. Sources in Plato; Aristotle. 2504.

Literary theory and criticism. Deconstructionism.
PATHOS. Theories of Nietzsche, Friedrich Wilhelm in theories of Derrida, Jacques. 1586.

PATIENT

General literature by PATIENT with cancer.
Relationship to art therapy. Treatment of mourning; creativity. Psychoanalytic approach. Dissertation abstract. 62.

PATRIARCHY

General literature. Film. Film genres: American Western film (1947-1957).
Treatment of PATRIARCHY in Zinnemann, Fred: *High Noon* compared to Mann, Anthony: *The Tin Star.* 786.

General literature. Television: soap opera.
Treatment of family; sexuality; PATRIARCHY compared to English novel (1700-1799). 909.

Literary movements.
Romanticism. Relationship to PATRIARCHY; narcissism. 1082.

PATRON
See also related term: Patronage.

PATRONAGE

Bibliographical. Manuscripts. Illuminated manuscripts in England. 900-1099.
PATRONAGE by Canute I, King of England; Emma, Queen of England. 1139.

PEACE
See also related term: War.

PEARCE, MICHAEL

General literature. Film. Film adaptation.
Of Joyce, James: *Ulysses; A Portrait of the Artist as a Young Man* by Strick, Joseph compared to Huston, John: *The Dead*; PEARCE, MICHAEL: *James Joyce's Women.* 722.

PEDAGOGICAL APPROACH
See also related term: Pedagogy.
Documents applying specific approaches are so numerous that access to them is provided only in the electronic versions of the *Bibliography.*

PEDAGOGICAL GRAMMAR
See also related terms: Pedagogy; Teaching of language.

PEDAGOGICAL TERMS
See also related term: Pedagogy.

PEDAGOGICAL TOOL

General literature. Film.
On Truffaut, François: *L'Argent de poche* as PEDAGOGICAL TOOL. 303.

PEDAGOGY
See also related term: Teaching.

Genres. Prose. Scientific prose.
Role in PEDAGOGY. Dissertation abstract. 2339.

Literary movements.
Postmodernism. And PEDAGOGY; relationship to closure; crisis. 1039.

Literary theory and criticism.
Relationship to PEDAGOGY. 1426.

Literary theory and criticism. Semiotic literary theory and criticism.
Relationship to PEDAGOGY. 1991.

Professional topics. Humanities.
Canon; PEDAGOGY in United States; relationship to liberalism compared to conservatism. 2782.
PEDAGOGY. Theories of Freire, Paulo; Bourdieu, Pierre; Merod, Jim; Graff, Gerald. 2686.

Professional topics. Humanities. 1700-1799.
PEDAGOGY in England compared to France; relationship to philosophy. Review article. 2823.

PEDERASTY
See also related term: Homosexuality.

PEDOPHILIA
See also related term: Sexuality.

PEER REVIEW

Professional topics. Humanities.
On PEER REVIEW; letters of recommendation; relationship to teaching; research. 2800.

PEGASUS
See also classified section: 2902.

PEIRCE, CHARLES SANDERS (1839-1914)

General literature. Film.
Speech acts. Application of theories of PEIRCE, CHARLES SANDERS. 277.

Literary forms. Rhetoric.
Relationship to ideology. Treatment in PEIRCE, CHARLES SANDERS; Bense, Max. 2435.

Literary theory and criticism. Semiotic literary theory and criticism.
Aesthetics of color; form. Theories of Marquand, Allan; Ladd-Franklin, Christine; relationship to PEIRCE, CHARLES SANDERS. 1985.
Isomorphism; similarity. Theories of Augustine, Saint; Thomas Aquinas, Saint; PEIRCE, CHARLES SANDERS. 1960.

SEE CLASSIFIED SEQUENCE FOR ADDITIONAL ENTRIES

Relationship to cybernetics; information theory. Theories of Saussure, Ferdinand de; PEIRCE, CHARLES SANDERS; Bense, Max. 1971.
Theories of PEIRCE, CHARLES SANDERS compared to Jakobson, Roman Osipovich. 1961

PEKING
See also narrower term: Tiananmen Square.

PENITENTIARY
Use: Prison.

PENNY DREADFUL
Bibliographical. Publishing in England (1850-1900).
By Brett, Edwin John of pulp fiction; PENNY DREADFUL. 1266.

PENTAGON
Use: United States Department of Defense.

PERCEPTION
See also narrower term: Visual perception.
General literature.
PERCEPTION compared to visual arts. Pedagogical approach. 40.
General literature. Film. Film theory and criticism.
PERCEPTION in film; relationship to militarism. Theories of Virilio, Paul: *Guerre et cinéma.* 841.

PERCEPTUAL PROCESSING
See also related term: Perception.

PERCY, WALKER (1916-1990)—STUDY EXAMPLE
General literature.
Narrative; rhetoric; relationship to medicine; study example: PERCY, WALKER: *Lancelot; The Moviegoer.* 143.

PERELMAN, CHAIM (1912-1984)
Literary forms. Rhetoric.
Rhetorical theory; relationship to universal audience. Theories of PERELMAN, CHAIM. 2442.
Stasis. Relationship to theories of PERELMAN, CHAIM; Burke, Kenneth. 2451.
Literary theory and criticism.
Relationship to the other; the Holocaust; Judaism. Theories of Levinas, Emmanuel; PERELMAN, CHAIM: *The New Rhetoric*; Rosenzweig, Franz. 1420.

PERESTROĬKA
See also related term: Glasnost'.
General literature. Film in U.S.S.R.
Relationship to *PERESTROĬKA.* 269.
Role of *PERESTROĬKA*; relationship to Goskino. 443.
General literature. Film in U.S.S.R. (1986-1989).
Relationship to *PERESTROĬKA.* 576.

PERFECT CULTURE
See also related term: Humanism.

PERFORMANCE
See also related terms: Drama; Theater.
General literature.
PERFORMANCE of oral tradition. 152.
General literature. Theater.
Role of biology; human body; relationship to PERFORMANCE. 957.
Role of theater theory applied to PERFORMANCE compared to science; quantum theory applied to nature. 968.
Genres. Drama.
And theater. Treatment of reality in PERFORMANCE. 2073.
Genres. Novel.
Relationship to the real; PERFORMANCE. Theories of Bakhtin, Mikhail Mikhaĭlovich. 2215.

PERFORMANCE ART
Used for: Performance theater.
See also related terms: Actors; Dancer; Pantomime.
General literature. Theater.
Visual imagery; relationship to text; Postmodernism in PERFORMANCE ART by Anderson, Laurie. 958.

PERFORMANCE STUDY
See also related terms: Performance; Theatrical production.

PERFORMANCE THEATER
Use: Performance art.

PERFORMANCE THEORY
General literature. Theater.
Marionettes; relationship to PERFORMANCE THEORY. Theories of Craig, Edward Gordon: "The Actor and the Über-marionette"; Meĭerkhol'd, Vsevolod Émil'evich; Schlemmer, Oskar; Kleist, Heinrich von: "Über das Marionettentheater." Dissertation abstract. 962.
Treatment in PERFORMANCE THEORY; relationship to the aural; the visual. 941.

PERFORMATIVE SENTENCE
See also related term: Speech acts.

PERFORMER
See also narrower terms: Actors; Dancer.
See also related terms: Performance; Performance art.

PERFORMING ARTS
See also narrower terms: Dance; Drama; Music; Opera; Theater.

PERIODICALS
See also narrower terms: Magazines; Newspapers.
See also: entries under titles of specific periodicals.
Genres. Fiction. Science fiction. 1800-1999.
Role of PERIODICALS; relationship to fans in United States. Publishing history. 2182.

PERIODIZATION
Literary theory and criticism. Literary history.
Relationship to PERIODIZATION; hermeneutics. 1760.
Role of PERIODIZATION. 1773, 1780.

PERSONA
See also related term: Point of view.

PERSONAL COLLECTIONS
Used for: Private collections.
Bibliographical.
On PERSONAL COLLECTIONS (1600-1799); relationship to literary history. Treatment in criticism (1975-1988). 1084.

PERSONAL IDENTITY
Use: Self-identity.

PERSONAL LIBRARIAN COMPUTER PROGRAM
Professional topics. Computer-assisted research.
PERSONAL LIBRARIAN COMPUTER PROGRAM. 2646.

PERSONAL LIBRARY
Used for: Private library.
Bibliographical.
PERSONAL LIBRARY of Lieb, Fritz; relationship to Russian literature; Slavic literature. 1099.

PERSPECTIVE
Genres. Drama.
And theater. Role of spectator; relationship to PERSPECTIVE. Dissertation abstract. 2064.
Genres. Fiction.
PERSPECTIVE; relationship to temporal relations. Dissertation abstract. 2110.

PERSPECTIVISM
Literary theory and criticism.
Relationship to PERSPECTIVISM. Review article. 1398.

PERSUASION
See also related term: Suasoria.
Figures of speech. Metaphor.
Use in political discourse; relationship to PERSUASION; inference. 2367.
Literary forms. Rhetoric.
PERSUASION. 2468.

PESHITTA
See also related term: Old Testament.

PESSIMISM
See also related term: Skepticism.

PETRUS (FL. 1470-1480)
Bibliographical. Manuscripts. Illuminated manuscripts in Venice; Rome. Renaissance.
Role of PETRUS. 1136.

PHALLOCENTRISM
General literature. Film.
Treatment of female characters; PHALLOCENTRISM in Allen, Woody. Feminist approach. 332.

PHARMACEUTICAL INDUSTRY
See also related term: Medicine.

PHENOMENOLOGICAL APPROACH
See also related term: Phenomenology.
Documents applying specific approaches are so numerous that access to them is provided only in the electronic versions of the *Bibliography*.

PHENOMENOLOGY
General literature. Film. Film theory and criticism.
Relationship to PHENOMENOLOGY. Theories of Carroll, Noel E. 839.
Spatiotemporal relations; relationship to PHENOMENOLOGY. Application of theories of Heidegger, Martin; Merleau-Ponty, Maurice. Dissertation abstract. 834.
Professional topics. Humanities.
Role of metaphysics; PHENOMENOLOGY. 2738.

PHILIPPE D'HARCOURT, BISHOP OF BAYEUX (D. 1163)
Bibliographical. Manuscripts. Manuscript collections. 1100-1199.
Of PHILIPPE D'HARCOURT, BISHOP OF BAYEUX. 1147.

PHILODEMUS (CA. 110-CA. 40 B.C.)—AS SOURCE
Literary theory and criticism.
Theories of mimesis; relationship to poetic language. Sources in PHILODEMUS. 1432.

PHILOLOGICAL APPROACH
See also related term: Philology.

Documents applying specific approaches are so numerous that access to them is provided only in the electronic versions of the *Bibliography*.

PHILOLOGY

    Literary theory and criticism.
        Especially textual criticism; relationship to PHILOLOGY. 1366.
        Relationship to PHILOLOGY. 1497, 1578.

    Professional topics.
        Role of PHILOLOGY (1880-1940) in medieval studies. 2584.

PHILOSOPHERS
See also narrower term: Sophists.

PHILOSOPHICAL APPROACH
See also related term: Philosophy.
Documents applying specific approaches are so numerous that access to them is provided only in the electronic versions of the *Bibliography*.

PHILOSOPHICAL LANGUAGE
See also related term: Philosophy.

    Literary forms. Rhetoric.
        Inventio; relationship to PHILOSOPHICAL LANGUAGE. Treatment in Cicero. 2478.

    Literary theory and criticism. Deconstructionism.
        PHILOSOPHICAL LANGUAGE; relationship to poetic language. Treatment in Habermas, Jürgen; relationship to theories of Derrida, Jacques. 1639.

PHILOSOPHICAL LANGUAGE—STUDY EXAMPLE

    Literary theory and criticism.
        Figuration; relationship to literal meaning; study example: scientific language; PHILOSOPHICAL LANGUAGE (1630-1800). Review article. 1506.

PHILOSOPHICAL LITERARY THEORY AND CRITICISM
See also classified section: 1849 ff.

PHILOSOPHICAL PROSE
See also classified section: 2336.

PHILOSOPHY
See also narrower terms: Cosmology; Determinism; Empiricism; Epistemology; Ethics; Existentialism; Holism; Humanism; Logic; Marxism; Metaphysics; Moral philosophy; Mysticism; Nihilism; Ontology; Organicism; Perspectivism; Positivism; Pragmatism; Primitivism; Skepticism.
See also related terms: History of ideas; Philosophical language.
See also: entries for philosophy in specific countries by consulting the index under the adjectival form of the country.

    Literary forms. Rhetoric.
        Treatment in Plato: *Phaidros*; *Gorgias*; relationship to PHILOSOPHY; psychoanalysis. 2499.

    Literary movements.
        Postmodernism. Linguistic representation; relationship to PHILOSOPHY; psychology. 1045.
        ——. Relationship to PHILOSOPHY. Theories of Rorty, Richard; Derrida, Jacques; Cavell, Stanley Louis. 1041.

    Literary theory and criticism.
        Relationship to PHILOSOPHY. 1323, 1542.

    Literary theory and criticism. Deconstructionism.
        Role of hierarchy; self-reflexiveness; relationship to PHILOSOPHY; anthropology. Theories of Derrida, Jacques; Dumont, Louis. 1599.

    Literary theory and criticism. New Historicism.
        Relationship to PHILOSOPHY. Theories of Locke, John; Rorty, Richard; James, William. 1836.

    Literary theory and criticism. Postmodernist literary theory and criticism.
        Role of PHILOSOPHY; relationship to modern art. 1873.

    Professional topics. Humanities. 1700-1799.
        Pedagogy in England compared to France; relationship to PHILOSOPHY. Review article. 2823.

PHILOSOPHY OF HISTORY
See also related term: History.

PHILOSOPHY OF LAW
See also related term: Law.

PHILOSOPHY OF SCIENCE
See also related term: Science.

PHONOGRAPH RECORDS
Use: Recordings.

PHONOLOGY
See also narrower term: Prosody.

PHOTOCOPIES
See also related term: Printing.

PHOTOGRAPHS
See also related term: Photography.

    Genres. Prose. Historiography.
        Use of PHOTOGRAPHS as documentation; relationship to visual imagery. 2331.

PHOTOGRAPHS—STUDY EXAMPLE

    Literary theory and criticism. Narrative theory.
        Applied to documentary photography; study example: PHOTOGRAPHS (1855) by Fenton, Roger. 1804.

PHOTOGRAPHY
See also related terms: Camera; Photographs.

    Literary movements.
        Postmodernism. Relationship to PHOTOGRAPHY. 1072.

THE PHYSICAL
See also related term: Human body.

PHYSICAL IMPAIRMENTS
See also classified section: 2903.

PHYSICIAN
Use: Doctor.

PHYSICS
See also related term: Quantum theory.

PIAGET, JEAN (1896-1980)

    Literary theory and criticism.
        Dialogue; relationship to intersubjectivity. Theories of Bakhtin, Mikhail Mikhaïlovich compared to PIAGET, JEAN; Freud, Sigmund. 1384.

PICHUL, VASILIĬ

    General literature. Film.
        Socialist realism in PICHUL, VASILIĬ: *Malen'kaia Vera*. 326.

PICTORIAL ART
See also related term: Visual arts.

PICTURE BOOKS
See also related term: Illustration.

    General literature for children.
        Use of code in PICTURE BOOKS. 141.

PICTURES
Use: Illustration.

PIDGIN LANGUAGES
See also related term: Creole languages.

PIDGINIZATION
See also related term: Creole languages.

PILES, ROGER DE (1635-1709)

    Literary theory and criticism.
        Role of subject; relationship to representation. Application of theories of Pascal, Blaise; PILES, ROGER DE. 1470.

PIRANDELLO, LUIGI (1867-1936)
Used for: Dorpelli, Giulian.

    General literature. Film.
        Role of Fellini, Federico; PIRANDELLO, LUIGI. Dissertation abstract. 347.

PLACE

    Genres. Drama and fiction.
        Treatment of space; PLACE. 2075.

PLAKHOV, ANDREĬ

    General literature. Film in U.S.S.R.
        Interview with PLAKHOV, ANDREĬ. 238.

PLANCTUS MARIAE
See also related term: Passion play.

PLANTIJN, CHRISTOPHE VAN
Use: Plantin, Christophe (1514-1589).

PLANTIN, CHRISTOPHE (1514-1589)
Used for: Plantijn, Christophe van.

    Bibliographical. Printing. Binding. 1500-1599.
        By PLANTIN, CHRISTOPHE. 1198.

PLATO (429-347 B.C.)

    Bibliographical. Manuscripts.
        Of PLATO. Catalogue. 1123.

    General literature. Film. Film genres: science fiction film.
        Treatment of totalitarianism in Lucas, George: *THX-1138* compared to PLATO: *Politeia*. 753.

    Literary forms. Myth.
        Relationship to dialectic. Role in PLATO. 2410.

    Literary forms. Rhetoric.
        Argumentation in scientific language. Theories of Aristotle compared to PLATO. 2480.
        Treatment in PLATO: *Phaidros*; *Gorgias*; relationship to philosophy; psychoanalysis. 2499.

    Literary theory and criticism. Deconstructionism.
        Theories of PLATO: *Pharmakon* in theories of Derrida, Jacques. 1591.

    Professional topics. Humanities.
        Application of theories of PLATO: *Prótagoras*. 2769.

PLATO (429-347 B.C.)—AS SOURCE

    Genres. Fiction.
        Sources in PLATO. 2154.

    Literary forms. Tragedy.
        Role of pathos. Sources in PLATO; Aristotle. 2504.

PLAY

    General literature. Film.
        Treatment of dancer; relationship to PLAY; American dream. 258.

    Genres. Novel.
        Role of PLAY. 2217.

PLAYBILL
See also related term: Theater.

PLAYWRIGHTS
Use: Dramatists.

PLIEVIER, THEODOR (1892-1955)
Used for: Plivier, Theodor.
  General literature. Film.
    Treatment of World War II; relationship to sacrifice in PLIEVIER, THEODOR: *Stalingrad.* 223.

PLIVIER, THEODOR
Use: Plievier, Theodor (1892-1955).

PLOT
See also related term: Emplotment.
  General literature. Opera.
    And operetta; musical theater. PLOT. Index. 844.
  Genres. Novel. Popular romance novel.
    PLOT. Sources in film of Hollywood. 2232.
    —— in Harlequin Romances. 2231.
  Genres. Novel. Sentimental novel.
    Characterization; PLOT. Treatment of love. 2246.
  Literary theory and criticism. Structuralist literary theory and criticism.
    On subject; PLOT. 2031.

PLUNKETT, WALTER (1902-1982)
  General literature. Film.
    Costume by PLUNKETT, WALTER in Fleming, Victor: *Gone with the Wind;* relationship to Selznick, David O. 346.

PLURALISM
See also related term: Dualism.

POETIC COMPETENCE
See also related term: Poetics.

POETIC CONVENTIONS
See also related term: Poetry.

POETIC CYCLE
See also related term: Poetry.

POETIC FORM
See also related term: Poetry.

POETIC LANGUAGE
See also related terms: The chora; Poetry.
  Genres. Poetry.
    POETIC LANGUAGE. 2267, 2279.
    ——. Application of theories of Richards, I. A. Dissertation abstract. 2272.
    ——. Interview with García Maffla, Jaime. 2275.
  Literary forms. Translation.
    Relationship to understanding; untranslatability of POETIC LANGUAGE; study example: Rimbaud, Arthur: *Une Saison en enfer; Illuminations.* Application of theories of Gadamer, Hans-Georg. 2535.
  Literary movements.
    Romanticism. POETIC LANGUAGE; relationship to synecdoche compared to language of astronomy. Application of theories of Newton, Sir Isaac compared to Herschel, Sir William. 1077.
  Literary theory and criticism.
    POETIC LANGUAGE. Dissertation abstract. 1448.
    Theories of mimesis; relationship to POETIC LANGUAGE. Sources in Philodemus. 1432.
  Literary theory and criticism. Deconstructionism.
    Philosophical language; relationship to POETIC LANGUAGE. Treatment in Habermas, Jürgen; relationship to theories of Derrida, Jacques. 1639.
  Literary theory and criticism. Linguistic literary theory and criticism.
    Iconicity of POETIC LANGUAGE. Structuralist approach. Compared to treatment in Pater, W. de and Langendonck, W. van: "Natuurlijkheid van de taal en iconiciteit." 1739.
    POETIC LANGUAGE; relationship to mental model; image; rhythm. 1757.

POETIC LINE
See also related term: Meter.

POETIC SPACE
Use: Space.

POETIC TECHNIQUE
See also narrower terms: Meter; Rhyme; Rhythm.
See also related term: Poetry.

POETIC TERMS
See also related term: Poetry.

POETIC THEORY
Use: Poetics.

POETICS
Used for: Poetic theory.
See also narrower terms: Constructivism; Prosody.
  General literature by women writers.
    POETICS; relationship to gender. 35.

Literary forms. Translation.
    POETICS. 2540.
  Literary theory and criticism.
    POETICS. Theories of Meschonnic, Henri. 1556.
    ——; relationship to Christianity; redemption. 1390.
    ——; relationship to human body; society. Dissertation abstract. 1510.
    Radicalism in POETICS; relationship to poetry. 1321.
  Literary theory and criticism. Literary history.
    POETICS. 1764.
  Literary theory and criticism. Semiotic literary theory and criticism.
    POETICS; relationship to the visual. 1956.
    Writing systems; relationship to POETICS. 1962.
  Professional topics. Comparative literature.
    Role of POETICS. 2612.

POETRY
See also classified section: 2252 ff.
See also narrower terms: City poetry; Concrete poetry; Epitaph; Hebrew language poetry; Ido language poetry; Lyric poetry; Oral poetry; Pastoral poetry; Postmodernist poetry; Romantic poetry.
See also related terms: Meter; Poetic language.
See also: entries for poetry in specific countries by consulting the index under the adjectival form of the country.
  Literary forms. Translation.
    Of POETRY. 2518, 2529, 2566.
  Literary movements. 1600-1699.
    Humanism. Role of POETRY; relationship to science. 1004.
  Literary theory and criticism.
    Radicalism in poetics; relationship to POETRY. 1321.
  Literary theory and criticism. Semiotic literary theory and criticism.
    Relationship to POETRY. 1958.
  Professional topics. Humanities.
    Teaching of writing; relationship to imitation of POETRY. 2687.

POETRY COLLECTIONS
See also related term: Poetry.

POETS
See also narrower terms: Jewish poets; Women poets.
See also related term: Poetry.

POINT OF VIEW
See also narrower term: Female point of view.
See also narrower terms: Narration; Narrative voice; Voice-over narration.
  Genres. Drama.
    POINT OF VIEW. 2090.
  Genres. Fiction.
    Narrator; POINT OF VIEW; relationship to story; study example: Sandars, Nancy Katharine: *The Epic of Gilgamesh.* Anthropological approach. 2148.
    POINT OF VIEW. Hermeneutic approach. Application of theories of Gadamer, Hans-Georg; Merleau-Ponty, Maurice; Ricœur, Paul. 2113.

POLAND
See also narrower term: Warsaw.
  Bibliographical in POLAND. 1085.
  General literature.
    Illustration in POLAND (1700-1899). 209.
  Professional topics. Censorship in East Germany; POLAND.
    Relationship to socialism. 2591.

POLANSKI, ROMAN (1933-)
  General literature. Film. Film adaptation.
    Of Shakespeare, William: *Macbeth* by POLANSKI, ROMAN. 688.

POLES
  Genres. Drama. 1900-1999.
    Treatment of POLES. 2076.

POLISH FILMMAKERS
  General literature. Film by POLISH FILMMAKERS. 360, 471.

POLISH LITERATURE
  Bibliographical.
    University libraries in United States; relationship to POLISH LITERATURE. 1115.
  Bibliographical. Publishing. Book trade (1918-1990).
    Of POLISH LITERATURE; Russian literature. 1291.

POLITICAL ALLEGORY
See also related term: Politics.

POLITICAL CAMPAIGN
See also related term: Politics.

POLITICAL CHANGE
See also related term: Politics.

POLITICAL CRITICISM
  Literary theory and criticism.
    POLITICAL CRITICISM. Theories of Foucault, Michel; Said, Edward W. 1370.

POLITICAL DISCOURSE
Used for: Political language.
See also related term: Politics.

Figures of speech. Metaphor.
Use in POLITICAL DISCOURSE; relationship to persuasion; inference. 2367.
Genres. Poetry.
Rhetoric compared to POLITICAL DISCOURSE. Semiotic approach. 2277.
Literary theory and criticism. Marxist literary theory and criticism.
Narrative as POLITICAL DISCOURSE; relationship to interpretation. Treatment in Jameson, Fredric: *The Political Unconscious.* 1789.

POLITICAL ESSAY
See also related term: Politics.

POLITICAL FICTION
See also related term: Politics.

POLITICAL FILM
General literature. Film. Film genres: POLITICAL FILM in Hollywood (1970-1987).
Treatment of working class; relationship to violence; collective struggle. Dissertation abstract. 778.

POLITICAL HERO
See also related term: Politics.

POLITICAL HISTORY
See also related term: Politics.

POLITICAL HUMOR
See also related term: Politics.

POLITICAL IDEOLOGIES
See also narrower terms: Anarchism; Aristocracy; Conservatism; Fascism; Imperialism; Liberalism; Marxism; Militarism; Nationalism; Nazism; Radicalism; Totalitarianism; Utopianism.

POLITICAL INDEPENDENCE
See also related term: Politics.

POLITICAL LANGUAGE
Use: Political discourse.

POLITICAL METAPHOR
See also related term: Politics.

POLITICAL PARTIES
See also narrower term: Communist Party.

POLITICAL PROPAGANDA
See also related term: Politics.

POLITICAL PROTEST
See also related term: Politics.

POLITICAL REFORM
See also related term: Politics.

POLITICAL RHETORIC
See also related terms: Political discourse; Politics.

POLITICAL SCIENCE
See also related terms: Government; Politics.
Literary movements.
Modernism. Relationship to POLITICAL SCIENCE; religion; publishing. 1019.

POLITICAL SPEECHES
See also related term: Politics.

POLITICAL SYMBOLISM
See also related term: Politics.

POLITICAL SYSTEMS
See also narrower term: Democracy.

POLITICAL THEATER
See also related term: Street theater.

POLITICS
See also narrower term: Left-wing politics.
See also related terms: Government; Nationalism; Political discourse; Political science.
See also: entries under headings for politics in specific countries by consulting the index under the adjectival form of the country.
Bibliographical. Printing in Canada and United States. 1800-1899.
Role of Mackenzie, William Lyon; relationship to POLITICS. 1174.
General literature.
Feminist literature. Treatment of gender; relationship to POLITICS; avant-garde. 198.
Role of intellectuals; relationship to POLITICS (1945-1990). 163.
General literature. Film.
Relationship to POLITICS. Interview with Stone, Oliver. 399.
Role of Adjani, Isabelle; relationship to POLITICS. 548.
Role of POLITICS; myth in Curtiz, Michael: *Casablanca.* Psychoanalytic approach. 343.
General literature. Film in United States.
Treatment of POLITICS. Bibliography: filmography. 666.
General literature. Theater.
Collaboration in women's theater groups; relationship to rhetoric; POLITICS. Feminist approach. 983.
Genres. Drama. 1900-1999.
Relationship to POLITICS. 2063.

Genres. Fiction.
Treatment of POLITICS. 2121.
——; relationship to nuclear war. 2151.
Literary movements.
Modernism. Treatment in Chambers, Whittaker; Voegelin, Eric; relationship to religion; POLITICS. 1012.
Postmodernism. Relationship to POLITICS. 1037, 1058.
——. Relationship to POLITICS. Theories of Hutcheon, Linda. 1067.
——. Relationship to religion; POLITICS. Application of theories of Bell, Daniel; Jameson, Fredric. 1055.
Literary theory and criticism.
Aesthetics; relationship to bourgeois society; POLITICS; hegemony. 1386.
By de Man, Paul; relationship to history; POLITICS. Review article. 1490.
Dialogism; relationship to context; POLITICS in novel. Theories of Bakhtin, Mikhail Mikhaïlovich. 1531.
Relationship to POLITICS. 1444.
——. Review article. 1486.
——; ideology. 1471.
Role of interpretation; relationship to POLITICS; social criticism. Review article. 1379.
Role of POLITICS; relationship to theories of Bakhtin, Mikhail Mikhaïlovich. Review article. 1392.
Literary theory and criticism. Deconstructionism.
Relationship to POLITICS. Review article. 1598.
Role of writing; relationship to POLITICS. Theories of de Man, Paul. 1631.
Literary theory and criticism. Psychoanalytic literary theory and criticism.
Relationship to POLITICS. 1905.
Professional topics. Humanities.
Role of POLITICS; relationship to culture studies. 2811.
Themes and figures. Human body. 1700-1799.
Relationship to history; POLITICS. 2875.

POLYPHONY
See also related term: Authorial voice.
Genres. Drama.
Relationship to POLYPHONY. Application of theories of Bakhtin, Mikhail Mikhaïlovich. 2094.

POLYSEMY
See also narrower term: Heteroglossia.
See also related terms: Meaning; Semantics.

POLYSYSTEM THEORY—APPLICATION
General literature in creole languages.
Application of POLYSYSTEM THEORY. 121.

POMMER, ERICH (1889-1966)
General literature. Film in Germany.
Role of POMMER, ERICH. Dissertation abstract. 386.

POPULAR CULTURE
See also related terms: Film; Television.
Bibliographical. Publishing. History of publishing in England (1790-1860).
Relationship to POPULAR CULTURE. Dissertation abstract. 1276.
General literature. Film.
And comic strip; theater; relationship to POPULAR CULTURE (1895-1903). 230.
Relationship to POPULAR CULTURE. Review article. 339.
General literature. Film in United States.
Relationship to POPULAR CULTURE. 294.
General literature. Television.
Role of cultural dominance; relationship to commercialism; POPULAR CULTURE. Application of theories of Bourdieu, Pierre. 867.
Television adaptation of Michener, James A.: *Space*; relationship to POPULAR CULTURE. 903.
General literature. Theater.
Relationship to laughter; POPULAR CULTURE. Theories of Bakhtin, Mikhail Mikhaïlovich; Eco, Umberto; Fo, Dario. 943.
Literary movements.
Postmodernism compared to Modernism. Relationship to POPULAR CULTURE; militarism in Australia. 1051.
Professional topics. Humanities.
Role of POPULAR CULTURE; relationship to teaching of literature. 2696.

POPULAR FICTION
See also classified section: 2168 ff.
See also narrower term: Harlequin Romances.
General literature. Film.
And English literature; American literature; POPULAR FICTION. 389.

POPULAR LITERATURE
See also narrower term: Popular fiction.
General literature.
And POPULAR LITERATURE. 1.

POPULAR MUSIC
See also related term: Popular culture.

POPULAR ROMANCE FICTION
See also narrower term: Popular romance novel.

SEE CLASSIFIED SEQUENCE FOR ADDITIONAL ENTRIES

POSTSTRUCTURALISM

Literary theory and criticism. Psychoanalytic literary theory and criticism.

POPULAR ROMANCE NOVEL
See also classified section: 2231 ff.
Used for: Romantic novel.
See also narrower term: Harlequin Romances.
   Genres. Novel. Sentimental novel and POPULAR ROMANCE NOVEL. 2245.

POPULAR SONG
See also related terms: Folk song; Music video.

POPULAR THEATER
  General literature. Theater: POPULAR THEATER.
    Role of burlesque; relationship to sexuality; female body. 926.

PORNOGRAPHIC LITERATURE
See also related term: Pornography.

PORNOGRAPHIC NOVEL
See also related term: Pornography.

PORNOGRAPHIC THEATER
See also related term: Pornography.

PORNOGRAPHY
  General literature. Film.
    As PORNOGRAPHY; relationship to feminism. Review article. 280.

POSITIONALITY
See also related terms: Feminism; Identity.

POSITIVISM
See also related term: Empiricism.
  Literary theory and criticism.
    Relationship to epistemology of POSITIVISM. Application of theories of Foucault, Michel; Habermas, Jürgen; Lyotard, Jean François. 1401.
  Literary theory and criticism. Philosophical literary theory and criticism. POSITIVISM. 1850.

POSITIVISM—AS SOURCE
  Literary theory and criticism. 1800-1899.
    Role of Hennequin, Emile: *La Critique scientifique*; Scherer, Wilhelm: *Geschichte der deutschen Literatur*; Grigor'ev, Apollon Aleksandrovich. Sources in POSITIVISM. Dissertation abstract. 1465.

POSNER, ROLAND (1942-)
  Literary theory and criticism. Semiotic literary theory and criticism.
    Theories of POSNER, ROLAND. 1996.

POSSIBLE WORLDS SEMANTICS—APPLICATION
  Genres. Fiction.
    Application of POSSIBLE WORLDS SEMANTICS. 2122.

POST, TED (1925-)
  General literature. Film. Film genres: war film.
    Treatment of Vietnam War in POST, TED: *Go Tell the Spartans*; Stone, Oliver: *Platoon*. 749.

POSTCARDS
  General literature. Film.
    Treatment of POSTCARDS in Godard, Jean-Luc: *Les Carabiniers* compared to Simon, Claude: *Histoire*. 451.

POSTCOLONIAL LITERATURE
  General literature.
    POSTCOLONIAL LITERATURE. 191.

POSTCOLONIAL PERIOD
See also related term: Postcolonialism.

POSTCOLONIAL WRITERS
  General literature by POSTCOLONIAL WRITERS. English language literature. 1900-1999. 51.
    Relationship to marginality. 86.
    Treatment of oppression. 95.

POSTCOLONIALISM
See also related term: Colonialism.
  Literary movements.
    Postmodernism. Relationship to POSTCOLONIALISM. 1052.
  Literary theory and criticism. Feminist literary theory and criticism.
    Relationship to POSTCOLONIALISM. 1651.

POSTMODERNISM
See also related term: Modernism.
  General literature. Film.
    Narrative; relationship to POSTMODERNISM in Lynch, David: *Blue Velvet*. 460.
    POSTMODERNISM in Coppola, Francis Ford; Lucas, George; DePalma, Brian; Spielberg, Steven; Scorsese, Martin. Dissertation abstract. 630.
    Relationship to POSTMODERNISM. 655.
    Treatment of motherhood; relationship to POSTMODERNISM. 417.
  General literature. Film and video art; music video.
    Role of sexuality; relationship to POSTMODERNISM. Imagery. 601.
  General literature. Television.
    Imagery; relationship to cognitive representation; POSTMODERNISM. Application of theories of Jameson, Fredric. 920.
    Relationship to POSTMODERNISM. 918.

General literature. Television in Netherlands.
    Role of POSTMODERNISM in *Sjef van Oekel*; *Fred Hachee*. 852.
General literature. Theater.
    Relationship to POSTMODERNISM. 977.
    Treatment of the absurd; secularity; relationship to POSTMODERNISM. 949.
    Visual imagery; relationship to text; POSTMODERNISM in performance art by Anderson, Laurie. 958.
Genres.
    Relationship to POSTMODERNISM. 2037.
Genres. Fiction.
    Mimesis; relationship to historiography; POSTMODERNISM. Dissertation abstract. 2135.
    ——; relationship to reader; POSTMODERNISM. 2156.
Genres. Fiction. 1900-1999.
    Relationship to POSTMODERNISM. Dissertation abstract. 2137.
Genres. Fiction. Crime fiction.
    Relationship to POSTMODERNISM. Dissertation abstract. 2160.
Genres. Fiction. Science fiction by feminist writers.
    Subjectivity; relationship to humanism; POSTMODERNISM. 2180.
Genres. Novel.
    Treatment of enclosure; relationship to Modernism; POSTMODERNISM. 2191.
Genres. Poetry.
    Narrative time; relationship to POSTMODERNISM. 2254.
Literary forms. Myth.
    Relationship to POSTMODERNISM. 2408.
Literary movements.
    Modernism. Abstraction; logic in language; relationship to POSTMODERNISM. 1016.
    —— and POSTMODERNISM. 1007.
    —— and POSTMODERNISM. Role of nihilism. Sources in Nietzsche, Friedrich Wilhelm. 1017.
    POSTMODERNISM. 1056.
Literary theory and criticism. Deconstructionism in Netherlands.
    Relationship to POSTMODERNISM. 1611.
Literary theory and criticism. Feminist literary theory and criticism.
    Relationship to POSTMODERNISM. 1666, 1678, 1707.
Literary theory and criticism in *Boundary 2*.
    Relationship to POSTMODERNISM. Interview with Spanos, William V. 1332.
Professional topics. Humanities.
    Role of literary studies; relationship to POSTMODERNISM. 2810.
Themes and figures. Lesbians. 1900-1999.
    Relationship to POSTMODERNISM. 2884.

POSTMODERNIST CRITICISM
Use: Postmodernist literary theory and criticism.

POSTMODERNIST FICTION
See also classified section: 2170 ff.

POSTMODERNIST LITERARY THEORY AND CRITICISM
See also classified section: 1858 ff.
Used for: Postmodernist criticism.
  General literature. Film.
    Treatment of history; relationship to POSTMODERNIST LITERARY THEORY AND CRITICISM. 408.
  General literature. Television.
    Treatment in POSTMODERNIST LITERARY THEORY AND CRITICISM. Review article. 853.
  Genres. Novel.
    Treatment in POSTMODERNIST LITERARY THEORY AND CRITICISM. 2208, 2211.
  Literary theory and criticism. Hermeneutics.
    Relationship to POSTMODERNIST LITERARY THEORY AND CRITICISM. Theories of Heidegger, Martin. 1732.

POSTMODERNIST POETRY
See also classified section: 2314.

POSTMODERNIST WRITERS
See also related term: Postmodernism.

POSTSTRUCTURALISM
See also related term: Structuralism.
  General literature.
    Treatment of female impersonation; relationship to feminism; POSTSTRUCTURALISM. Dissertation abstract. 204.
  Genres. Drama.
    Textuality; relationship to POSTSTRUCTURALISM. Dissertation abstract. 2080.
  Literary theory and criticism. Deconstructionism.
    Relationship to POSTSTRUCTURALISM. Terminology. 1620.
  Literary theory and criticism. Feminist literary theory and criticism.
    Role of writer; relationship to POSTSTRUCTURALISM. 1704.
  Literary theory and criticism. Marxist literary theory and criticism.
    Role of revolution; relationship to POSTSTRUCTURALISM in France. Theories of Lukács, György. 1793.
  Literary theory and criticism. New Historicism.
    Relationship to POSTSTRUCTURALISM; novel. 1838.
  Literary theory and criticism. Psychoanalytic literary theory and criticism.
    Relationship to POSTSTRUCTURALISM. 1910.

Professional topics. Humanities.
   Teaching of literature; relationship to POSTSTRUCTURALISM. 2688.

POSTSTRUCTURALIST APPROACH
See also related term: Poststructuralism.
Documents applying specific approaches are so numerous that access to them is provided only in the electronic versions of the *Bibliography.*

POSTSTRUCTURALIST CRITICISM
Use: Poststructuralist literary theory and criticism.

POSTSTRUCTURALIST LITERARY THEORY AND CRITICISM
See also classified section: 1874 ff.
Used for: Poststructuralist criticism.

   Genres. Fiction.
      Relationship to religion; myth; POSTSTRUCTURALIST LITERARY THEORY AND CRITICISM. 2119.
   Literary forms. Rhetoric.
      Ethos; relationship to POSTSTRUCTURALIST LITERARY THEORY AND CRITICISM. 2441.
   Literary theory and criticism. Deconstructionism and POSTSTRUCTURALIST LITERARY THEORY AND CRITICISM. 1641.
   Literary theory and criticism. Reader-response theory and criticism and POSTSTRUCTURALIST LITERARY THEORY AND CRITICISM.
      Applied to teaching of literature; study example: Clemens, Samuel: *The Adventures of Huckleberry Finn*; Douglass, Frederick: *Narrative of the Life of Frederick Douglass.* 1928.
   Literary theory and criticism. Structuralist literary theory and criticism.
      And POSTSTRUCTURALIST LITERARY THEORY AND CRITICISM; relationship to hermeneutics. 2034.
      Compared to POSTSTRUCTURALIST LITERARY THEORY AND CRITICISM. Role of theories of Saussure, Ferdinand de in theories of Culler, Jonathan. 2026.

POSTWAR PERIOD
   General literature. Film.
      Treatment of mother; relationship to Nazism in POSTWAR PERIOD in Hitchcock, Alfred: *Notorious.* Application of theories of Jung, Carl Gustav. 244.

POUND, EZRA (1885-1972)
Used for: Atheling, William; Venison, Alfred.
   Literary theory and criticism.
      Theories of Adler, Mortimer Jerome: *How to Read a Book*; POUND, EZRA: *ABC of Reading.* 1477.

POWELL, DICK (1904-1963)
   General literature. Film. Film genres: musical film.
      Role of POWELL, DICK. 785.

POWER
   General literature. Film.
      Treatment of POWER in Hawks, Howard: *Scarface.* 224.
   General literature. Television: music television.
      Discourse; relationship to POWER compared to masque for royal court of Jacobean period. 858.

POWER ELITES
See also related term: Power.

POWERLESSNESS
See also related term: Power.

PRAGMATIC APPROACH
See also related term: Pragmatics.
Documents applying specific approaches are so numerous that access to them is provided only in the electronic versions of the *Bibliography.*

PRAGMATIC CONSTRAINTS
See also related term: Pragmatics.

PRAGMATIC DEVELOPMENT
See also related term: Pragmatics.

PRAGMATICS

   Literary theory and criticism. Hermeneutics.
      Compared to PRAGMATICS. Theories of Gadamer, Hans-Georg. 1715.
   Literary theory and criticism. Semiotic literary theory and criticism.
      And PRAGMATICS; relationship to subject; subjectivity. 1992.

PRAGMATISM
   Literary theory and criticism. Poststructuralist literary theory and criticism and structuralist literary theory and criticism.
      Relationship to PRAGMATISM. Theories of Derrida, Jacques compared to Dewey, John. 1877.

PRAGUE SCHOOL OF LINGUISTICS
   General literature. Theater.
      Role of acting; relationship to celebrity. Semiotic approach. Application of theories of PRAGUE SCHOOL OF LINGUISTICS. 959.
   Literary theory and criticism.
      Theories of Bakhtin, Mikhail Mikhaĭlovich; relationship to PRAGUE SCHOOL OF LINGUISTICS. 1404.

PRAYER
See also related term: Devotional literature.

PREACHING
See also narrower term: Evangelism.
See also related term: Religion.

PREDICTION
See also related term: Prophecy.

PREFACE
See also classified section: 2337.
Used for: Foreword.
   Genres. Novel.
      Authorial voice in PREFACE. Dissertation abstract. 2230.
   Genres. Prose.
      PREFACE. 2315.
   Literary theory and criticism. Deconstructionism.
      Applied to Husserl, Edmund: *Erfahrung und Urteil.* On PREFACE by Derrida, Jacques. 1587.

PREGNANCY
See also related term: Abortion.

PRESERVATION
See also narrower term: Book preservation.

THE PRESS
See also related terms: News; Periodicals.

PRESSES
See also narrower term: Private presses.

PRIMAL SCENE
See also related term: Sexual intercourse.
   General literature. Film. Film genres: science fiction film.
      Treatment of time travel; PRIMAL SCENE; dystopia in Cameron, James: *The Terminator.* 792.

PRIMITIVISM
   Literary movements.
      Modernism. Relationship to PRIMITIVISM. 1018.

PRINTERS
See also related term: Printing.

PRINTING
See also classified section: 1152 ff.
See also narrower term: Lithography.
See also related terms: Binding; History of printing; Illustration; Paper; Publishing.
   Bibliographical. Publishing and PRINTING in Canada.
      Bibliography. 1275.
   Bibliographical. Publishing in England.
      Relationship to law reports; PRINTING. Application of Justus Project. 1272.
   Literary forms. Emblem.
      Treatment of book; PRINTING; book collectors. 2392.

PRINTING HISTORY
See also related terms: Editions; Publishing history.

PRINTING HOUSES
See also related term: Printing.

PRINZHORN, HANS (1886-1933)
   Literary theory and criticism. Psychoanalytic literary theory and criticism.
      Theories of PRINZHORN, HANS. 1897.

PRISON
Used for: Penitentiary.
   Genres. Novel.
      Treatment of New World; relationship to exile; PRISON. 2190.

PRISON CAMPS
See also related term: Prison.

PRISON IMAGERY
See also related term: Prison.

PRIVATE COLLECTIONS
Use: Personal collections.

PRIVATE EYE
   General literature. Film. Film genres: detective film.
      And television; hard-boiled detective fiction. Treatment of PRIVATE EYE. Reference guide. 751.

PRIVATE LIBRARY
Use: Personal library.

PRIVATE PRESSES
   Bibliographical. Printing.
      By PRIVATE PRESSES. Checklist of collection at John Rylands University Library of Manchester. 1181.

PROCIDA
   Literary forms. Translation.
      Role of Collegio Europeo dei Traduttori Letterari in Italy: PROCIDA. 2553.

PRODUCER
   General literature. Film.
      Role of Selznick, David O. as PRODUCER. 638.

PRODUCTION
See also narrower term: Theatrical production.

SEE CLASSIFIED SEQUENCE FOR ADDITIONAL ENTRIES

PSYCHOANALYSIS

Literary theory and criticism. Psychoanalytic literary theory and criticism.

General literature. Film in black Africa.
PRODUCTION; relationship to neocolonialism. 369.

THE PROFANE
Genres. Novel.
And film. Treatment of threshold; relationship to the sacred; THE PROFANE. 2203.

PROFESSIONAL DISCOURSE
Professional topics. Humanities.
Writing across the curriculum; relationship to PROFESSIONAL DISCOURSE; discourse community. 2795.

PROFESSIONAL FIGURES
See also narrower terms: Doctor; Teacher.
See also related term: Professionalism.

PROFESSIONAL TOPICS
See also classified section: 2577 ff.
See also narrower terms: Censorship; Comparative literature; Computer-assisted research; Research tools.

PROFESSIONALISM
Professional topics. Humanities.
PROFESSIONALISM. 2821.

PROFESSIONS
See also narrower terms: Law; Medicine.
See also related term: Professional discourse.

PROGRESSIVE EDUCATION
Literary theory and criticism.
Relationship to social sciences; PROGRESSIVE EDUCATION. 1574.

PROLEPSIS
See also related term: The future.

THE PROLETARIAT
Use: Working class.

PROMISING
See also related term: Speech acts.

PROPHECY
See also classified section: 2904.
General literature. Film.
Treatment of PROPHECY; fatalism in Hawks, Howard: *Scarface*. 274.

PROPHET
See also related term: Prophecy.

PROPP, VLADIMIR IAKOVLEVICH (1895-1970)
General literature. Television.
On *Doctor Who*; relationship to science fiction. Application of theories of PROPP, VLADIMIR IAKOVLEVICH. Dissertation abstract. 891.
Literary theory and criticism.
Relationship to cultural criticism. Application of theories of PROPP, VLADIMIR IAKOVLEVICH. 1391.
Literary theory and criticism. Narrative theory.
On thematic structure; relationship to formalism; structuralism. Theories of PROPP, VLADIMIR IAKOVLEVICH compared to Vodička, Felix. 1801.

PROSE
See also classified section: 2315 ff.
See also narrower terms: Academic prose; Autobiographical prose; Essay; Historiography; Philosophical prose; Religious prose; Reportage; Scientific prose.
See also related term: Fiction.
Professional topics. Humanities.
Teaching of writing; relationship to fiction compared to PROSE. 2680.

PROSE ADAPTATION
See also related term: Prose.

PROSE FICTION
Use: Fiction.

PROSODIC CHANGE
See also related term: Prosody.

PROSODIC DEVELOPMENT
See also related term: Prosody.

PROSODIC DISORDERS
See also related term: Prosody.

PROSODIC FEATURES
See also related term: Prosody.

PROSODIC INTERFERENCE
See also related term: Prosody.

PROSODIC PROCESSING
See also related term: Prosody.

PROSODIC RECONSTRUCTION
See also related term: Prosody.

PROSODIC STRUCTURE
See also related term: Prosody.

PROSODY

See also related terms: Meter; Rhyme; Rhythm; Stanzas.
Genres. Poetry. Esperanto language literature.
PROSODY; rhyme. 2287.

PROSTITUTE
Used for: Harlot; Whore.
General literature. Film. English language literature; German language literature.
Treatment of PROSTITUTE. Dissertation abstract. 597.

PROSTITUTION
See also related terms: Prostitute; Sexuality.

PROTAGONIST
See also narrower term: Female protagonist.
See also related term: Hero.
General literature. Film.
Treatment of PROTAGONIST; relationship to myth of Oedipus in Antonioni, Michelangelo: *Identificazione di una donna*. 514.

PROTESTANTS
See also narrower term: Shakers.

PROVERB
General literature. Film. Film adaptation.
Use of PROVERB; *Märchen* in Jordan, Neil and Carter, Angela: *The Company of Wolves*. 702.
Literary theory and criticism. Structuralist literary theory and criticism.
Applied to PROVERB; fable. Theories of Jakobson, Roman Osipovich. 2027.

PROVERBIAL EXPRESSION
See also related term: Proverb.

PROXEMICS
See also related term: Nonverbal communication.

PSALTER
Bibliographical. Printing in Delft (1450-1475). Illustration.
In PSALTER. 1218.

PSEUDO-EPIPHANIUS OF SALAMIS—AS SOURCE
Genres. Prose. Devotional literature.
Treatment of liturgical formulas. Sources in Chrysostom, John: *De Sancta Pentecoste*; Theodore of Mopsuestia: *Homiliae Catecheticae*; PSEUDO-EPIPHANIUS OF SALAMIS: *Homilia in Diuini Corporis Sepulturam*. 2318.

PSEUDOSCIENCE
See also related term: Science.

PSYCHIATRIC TERMS
See also related term: Psychiatry.

PSYCHIATRIST
General literature. Film.
Treatment of PSYCHIATRIST; study example: Wiene, Robert: *Das Kabinett des Doktor Caligari*; Robson, Mark: *Home of the Brave*; Hitchcock, Alfred: *Psycho*; Meyer, Russ: *The Immoral Mr. Teas*. 569.

PSYCHIATRY
See also related terms: Psychoanalysis; Psychology.
Genres. Autobiography and biography.
Treatment of madness; relationship to PSYCHIATRY. 2054.
Genres. Poetry.
As therapy; relationship to PSYCHIATRY. 2273.

PSYCHOACOUSTIC APPROACH
Documents applying specific approaches are so numerous that access to them is provided only in the electronic versions of the *Bibliography*.

PSYCHOANALYSIS
See also related terms: Psychiatry; Psychoanalytic literary theory and criticism; Psychoanalytic theory; Psychology.
General literature. Film.
By Duras, Marguerite; relationship to feminism; PSYCHOANALYSIS. Dissertation abstract. 561.
Relationship to PSYCHOANALYSIS. 355, 420.
Treatment of PSYCHOANALYSIS; confidence game; relationship to male-female relations in Mamet, David: *House of Games*. 622.
General literature. Film. Film theory and criticism.
Relationship to PSYCHOANALYSIS. Review article. 828.
Literary forms. Rhetoric.
Treatment in Plato: *Phaidros*; *Gorgias*; relationship to philosophy; PSYCHOANALYSIS. 2499.
Literary theory and criticism. Feminist literary theory and criticism.
Relationship to PSYCHOANALYSIS. 1672, 1686.
——. Theories of Mitchell, Juliet; Gallop, Jane. 1658.
Literary theory and criticism. Hermeneutics.
Applied to narrative in PSYCHOANALYSIS. Application of theories of Habermas, Jürgen. 1711.
Literary theory and criticism. Narrative theory.
Applied to PSYCHOANALYSIS. 1825.
Literary theory and criticism. Postmodernist literary theory and criticism.
Relationship to PSYCHOANALYSIS; feminism. 1861.
Literary theory and criticism. Psychoanalytic literary theory and criticism.
On ambiguity of language; relationship to PSYCHOANALYSIS. 1912.

PSYCHOANALYTIC APPROACH
See also related term: Psychoanalysis.
Documents applying specific approaches are so numerous that access to them is provided only in the electronic versions of the *Bibliography*.

PSYCHOANALYTIC CRITICISM
Use: Psychoanalytic literary theory and criticism.

PSYCHOANALYTIC FILM THEORY AND CRITICISM
General literature. Film. Film theory and criticism.
Feminist film theory and criticism and PSYCHOANALYTIC FILM THEORY AND CRITICISM; applied to Fassbinder, Rainer Werner: *Angst essen Seele auf.* 831.

PSYCHOANALYTIC LITERARY THEORY AND CRITICISM
See also classified section: 1891 ff.
Used for: Psychoanalytic criticism.
See also related term: Psychoanalysis.
General literature. Film.
Treatment of women; relationship to PSYCHOANALYTIC LITERARY THEORY AND CRITICISM. 633.
Literary forms. Rhetoric.
Future perfect tense in argumentation; relationship to PSYCHOANALYTIC LITERARY THEORY AND CRITICISM. Theories of Aristotle; Lacan, Jacques; Derrida, Jacques. 2489.
Relationship to figures of speech; PSYCHOANALYTIC LITERARY THEORY AND CRITICISM. 2477.
Literary theory and criticism. Feminist literary theory and criticism.
And PSYCHOANALYTIC LITERARY THEORY AND CRITICISM; role of ethics; relationship to sexual difference. Theories of Foucault, Michel; Irigaray, Luce. 1677.
Literary theory and criticism. Semiotic literary theory and criticism.
And PSYCHOANALYTIC LITERARY THEORY AND CRITICISM; role of signifier; relationship to desire. 2004.

PSYCHOANALYTIC THEORY
See also narrower term: Primal scene.
See also related terms: Psychoanalysis; Transference.
Genres. Autobiography.
Treatment in PSYCHOANALYTIC THEORY. 2049.

PSYCHOANALYTIC THERAPY
Use: Psychotherapy.

PSYCHOBIOGRAPHICAL APPROACH
Documents applying specific approaches are so numerous that access to them is provided only in the electronic versions of the *Bibliography*.

PSYCHOBIOLOGICAL APPROACH
Documents applying specific approaches are so numerous that access to them is provided only in the electronic versions of the *Bibliography*.

PSYCHODRAMA
See also related term: Psychotherapy.

PSYCHOLINGUISTIC APPROACH
Documents applying specific approaches are so numerous that access to them is provided only in the electronic versions of the *Bibliography*.

PSYCHOLINGUISTICS
See also related terms: Cognition; Memory; Reading; Second language learning.

PSYCHOLOGICAL APPROACH
See also related terms: Psychological literary theory and criticism; Psychology.
Documents applying specific approaches are so numerous that access to them is provided only in the electronic versions of the *Bibliography*.

PSYCHOLOGICAL CRITICISM
Use: Psychological literary theory and criticism.

PSYCHOLOGICAL DISORDERS
See also narrower term: Hysteria.

PSYCHOLOGICAL LITERARY THEORY AND CRITICISM
See also classified section: 1917.
Used for: Psychological criticism.

PSYCHOLOGICAL REALITY
See also related term: Cognition.

PSYCHOLOGICAL RESEARCH
See also related term: Psychology.

PSYCHOLOGICAL STATE
See also related term: Mind.

PSYCHOLOGICAL THEORY
See also narrower terms: Gestalt theory; Psychoanalytic theory.

PSYCHOLOGY
See also related terms: Psychiatry; Psychoanalysis; Psychotherapy; Social sciences.
General literature.
PSYCHOLOGY of writer. 88.
Genres. Novel. Dystopian novel. 1900-1999.
Influence on theories of PSYCHOLOGY. Dissertation abstract. 2242.
Literary forms. Parody.
And travesty; pastiche; relationship to social relations; PSYCHOLOGY. Application of communication theory. 2414.

Literary movements.
Enlightenment. Role of PSYCHOLOGY; relationship to bourgeoisie; rhetoric. 999.
Postmodernism. Linguistic representation; relationship to philosophy; PSYCHOLOGY. 1045.
Literary theory and criticism. Narrative theory.
Application in linguistics; anthropology; PSYCHOLOGY. 1799.

PSYCHOTHERAPIST
See also narrower term: Psychiatrist.

PSYCHOTHERAPY
Used for: Psychoanalytic therapy.
See also related term: Psychology.
Genres. Autobiography.
Relationship to PSYCHOTHERAPY. 2046, 2047, 2048.
——; study example: Milner, Marion Blackett: *A Life of One's Own*; Hillesum, Etty: *Het verstoorde leven.* 2055.
Literary theory and criticism.
Quasi-direct discourse; relationship to PSYCHOTHERAPY. Theories of Bakhtin, Mikhail Mikhaïlovich. 1397.

PTOLEMAISM
See also related term: Astronomy.

THE PUBLIC
General literature. Television.
Treatment of deception of THE PUBLIC; relationship to Vietnam War in Crile, George: *The Uncounted Enemy: A Vietnam Deception.* 910.

PUBLIC BROADCASTING SERVICE
See also related term: Television.

PUBLIC DISCOURSE
Literary forms. Rhetoric.
Relationship to PUBLIC DISCOURSE on nuclear weapons. Application of theories of Burke, Kenneth. 2429.

PUBLIC EVENTS
See also related term: The public.

PUBLIC OPINION
See also related term: The public.

PUBLIC SECTOR
See also related term: The public.

PUBLICATION
Use: Publishing.

PUBLICATION HISTORY
Use: Publishing history.

PUBLISHERS
See also narrower terms: Bodley Head; Editalia; Grove Press; Olympia Press; Small publishers; University presses.
See also related term: Publishing.

PUBLISHERS PRESS
Bibliographical. Publishing in Montreal (1911-1912).
Role of PUBLISHERS PRESS. 1265.

PUBLISHING
See also classified section: 1233 ff.
Used for: Publication.
See also narrower terms: Desktop publishing; Electronic publishing; Scholarly publishing.
See also related terms: Book trade; Editing; History of publishing; Marketing; Printing.
Bibliographical.
Relationship to libraries; PUBLISHING in Lithuania. Treatment in Vladimirovas, Levas. Bibliography. 1118.
Bibliographical. Printing and PUBLISHING.
In Mažoji Lietuva (1524-1939); relationship to foreign language publishing. 1170.
Literary movements.
Modernism. Relationship to political science; religion; PUBLISHING. 1019.
Professional topics. Computer-assisted research.
Hartlib Papers Project; relationship to PUBLISHING by Hartlib, Samuel. 2645.

PUBLISHING CONTRACTS
See also related term: Publishing.

PUBLISHING HISTORY
Used for: Publication history.
Genres. Fiction. Science fiction. 1800-1999.
Role of periodicals; relationship to fans in United States. PUBLISHING HISTORY. 2182.

PUBLISHING NEGOTIATIONS
See also related term: Publishing.

PULP FICTION
See also narrower term: Penny dreadful.
Bibliographical. Publishing in England (1850-1900).
By Brett, Edwin John of PULP FICTION; penny dreadful. 1266.

PULP MAGAZINES
See also related term: Pulp fiction.

PUN
Used for: Paronomasia.
  Literary forms. Humor. 1700-1799.
    Role of jokes; PUN; relationship to aesthetics. 2403.

PUNCTUATION
  Bibliographical. Printing (1400-1550).
    PUNCTUATION. 1182.

PUNCTUATION MARKS
See also related term: Punctuation.

PUPPETS
See also narrower term: Marionettes.

PYGMALION
  Literary theory and criticism. Deconstructionism.
    Relationship to PYGMALION. 1623.

QUALITATIVE FORM
  Genres. Autobiography.
    Syllogistic form; QUALITATIVE FORM in spiritual autobiography; study example: Colson, Charles W.: *Born Again.* 2050.

QUALITY
  General literature. Television in Great Britain.
    Role of QUALITY; relationship to television studies; film studies. 860.

QUANTAL RELATIONS
See also related term: Quantum theory.

QUANTITATIVE APPROACH
Documents applying specific approaches are so numerous that access to them is provided only in the electronic versions of the *Bibliography.*

QUANTUM MECHANICS
See also related term: Quantum theory.

QUANTUM THEORY
  General literature. Theater.
    Role of theater theory applied to performance compared to science; QUANTUM THEORY applied to nature. 968.

QUASI-DIRECT DISCOURSE
  Literary theory and criticism.
    QUASI-DIRECT DISCOURSE; relationship to psychotherapy. Theories of Bakhtin, Mikhail Mikhaĭlovich. 1397.

QUEBEC
  Bibliographical. Publishing. Book trade in QUEBEC. 1900-1999. 1293.
  Bibliographical. Publishing. Book trade in QUEBEC (1944-1946).
    Includes catalogue of books by France-Livre. 1287.
  Bibliographical. Publishing in QUEBEC.
    Exportation. 1269.
  Bibliographical. Publishing in QUEBEC. 1800-1999.
    Relationship to state. 1262.
  Literary theory and criticism. Feminist literary theory and criticism.
    In QUEBEC (1970-1980). 1683.

QUESTION
  Literary forms. Rhetoric.
    Role of QUESTION; metaphor; image in scientific language; relationship to epistemology. Theories of Meyer, Michel; Kant, Immanuel. 2427.
    —— in argumentation. 2432.

QUESTION ANSWERING
See also related term: Question.

QUILL RETRIEVAL SYSTEM
  Professional topics. Computer-assisted research.
    BIRD retrieval system; QUILL RETRIEVAL SYSTEM. 2650.

QUINE, W. V. O. (1908-)
  Literary forms. Translation. Translation theory.
    Theories of QUINE, W. V. O.; Derrida, Jacques; Benjamin, Walter. 2574.

QUINTILIAN
Use: Quintilianus (ca. 35-ca. 100).

QUINTILIANUS (CA. 35-CA. 100)
Used for: Quintilian.
  Figures of speech. Metaphor and catachresis.
    Theories of QUINTILIANUS. 2366.

QUIZ SHOW
  General literature. Television: game show; QUIZ SHOW. 870.

QUMRAN SCROLLS
Use: Dead Sea scrolls.

QUOTATION
  General literature.
    QUOTATION. Reference guide. 189.
  Literary theory and criticism.
    On QUOTATION in Old Testament: Isaiah. Diachronic approach. Dissertation abstract. 1527.

QUR'ÂN
Use: Koran.

RABBINIC LITERATURE
See also narrower term: Midrash.

RACIAL ATTITUDES
See also narrower terms: Anti-Semitism; Racism.

RACIAL GROUPS
See also related term: Minorities.

RACISM
  General literature. Film.
    Treatment of RACISM in Lee, Spike: *Do the Right Thing* compared to Burton, Tim: *Batman; Batman: The Dark Knight* by Miller, Frank. 550.
  Literary movements.
    Enlightenment. Role of anti-Semitism; RACISM; relationship to medicine. 1000.

RACIST LANGUAGE
See also related term: Racism.

RADICALISM
  Literary theory and criticism.
    RADICALISM in poetics; relationship to poetry. 1321.

RADIO
See also related terms: British Broadcasting Corporation; National Broadcasting Company; Radio adaptation; Radiodiffusion-Télévision Française.
  General literature. Television and RADIO in Brazil. 864.
  General literature. Television and RADIO in Europe.
    Role of translator; interpreter. 886.

RADIO ADAPTATION
See also related term: Radio.
  General literature. Film. Film adaptation.
    And musical adaptation; RADIO ADAPTATION; recordings of Poe, Edgar Allan. Catalogue. 735.

RADIO BROADCAST
See also related term: Radio.

RADIO DRAMA
See also related term: Radio.

RADIO PRODUCTION
See also related term: Radio.

RADIODIFFUSION-TÉLÉVISION FRANÇAISE
Used for: RTF.
See also related terms: Radio; Television.
  General literature. Television.
    Role of Touchard, Pierre-Aimé at RADIODIFFUSION-TÉLÉVISION FRANÇAISE. 859.

RAFELSON, BOB (1935-)
  General literature. Film. Film genres: *film noir.*
    Nonverbal communication in Garnett, Tay: *The Postman Always Rings Twice;* Hawks, Howard: *The Big Sleep;* Dmytryk, Edward: *Murder, My Sweet* compared to remakes by RAFELSON, BOB; Winner, Michael; Richards, Dick. Dissertation abstract. 767.

RAINER, YVONNE (1934-)
  General literature. Film.
    By RAINER, YVONNE. 354.
    Narrative discourse. Treatment of female body in RAINER, YVONNE: *The Man Who Envied Women.* 350.

RAMSTEN, LARS
  Bibliographical.
    On collection of RAMSTEN, LARS. 1106.

RAPPER, IRVING (1898-)
  General literature. Film.
    Treatment of women; relationship to marriage in RAPPER, IRVING: *Now, Voyager.* 286.

RARE BOOK TRADE
See also related term: Rare books.
  Bibliographical. Publishing. Book trade. 1900-1999.
    RARE BOOK TRADE; relationship to English women writers (1600-1799). 1294.

RARE BOOKS
See also related term: Rare book trade.
  Bibliographical.
    On training of librarians about RARE BOOKS; manuscripts. 1109.
    Role of curator-conservator relations; relationship to book preservation; RARE BOOKS. 1104.
    Role of library exhibition catalogues; relationship to exhibition of RARE BOOKS and manuscripts. 1097.

RATIONALITY
  Literary movements.
    Romanticism. Theories of imagination; inspiration; relationship to RATIONALITY; critical judgment. 1074.

RAWLINSON, RICHARD (1690-1755)
  Bibliographical. 1700-1799.
    Book collecting by RAWLINSON, RICHARD. 1092.

RAY, NICHOLAS (1911-)
  General literature. Film.
    Treatment of homosexuality in RAY, NICHOLAS: *Rebel without a Cause* compared to Cates, Gilbert: *Consenting Adult.* 283.

RAY, SATYAJIT (1922-)
Used for: Raya, Satyajit; Satyajit Ray.
  General literature. Film.
    Treatment of divided self in RAY, SATYAJIT compared to Wells, H. G.; Rushdie, Salman. 505.

RAYA, SATYAJIT
Use: Ray, Satyajit (1922-).

READABILITY
See also related term: Reading.

READER
See also narrower term: Narratee.
  Bibliographical. Textual criticism.
    Role of writer; READER. 1122.
  Figures of speech. Imagery.
    Relationship to cognitive processes of READER; study example: Móricz, Zsigmond: "Barbárok"; newspaper article. 2352.
  General literature.
    Relationship to READER. 9.
  Genres. Fiction.
    Mimesis; relationship to READER; Postmodernism. 2156.
    Narrator as mediator between writer and READER. 2159.
    Relationship to desire; READER. Psychoanalytic approach. 2145.
    Role of writer; relationship to READER; text. Philosophical approach. 2116.
  Genres. Novel.
    Relationship to therapy for READER. 2198, 2225.
  Literary movements.
    Postmodernism. Role of writer; relationship to READER; intertextuality. 1040.
  Literary theory and criticism.
    Relationship to mathematical theory. Treatment of writer; relationship to READER. 1347.
    Role of READER; relationship to ethics. 1565.
  Literary theory and criticism. Deconstructionism.
    Authority of writer; relationship to READER; allegory. Treatment in de Man, Paul: "Rhetoric of Temporality." 1589.
  Literary theory and criticism. Narrative theory.
    Intertextuality; hypertextuality; relationship to READER. 1820.
  Literary theory and criticism. Reader-response theory and criticism.
    READER in narrative. 1933.
    Relationship to inference by READER. 1922.
    Relationship to READER. 1932.
    Role of authorial intention; relationship to READER. 1927.
    Role of READER; relationship to American fiction. Theories of Mailloux, Steven compared to Fish, Stanley; Culler, Jonathan. Review article. 1918.
  Professional topics. Humanities.
    Role of women writers; relationship to READER; canon. Feminist approach. 2736.

READER RESPONSE
  Literary theory and criticism.
    On READER RESPONSE; study example: Schiller, Johann Christoph Friedrich von: "Eine grossmütige Handlung, aus der neusten Geschichte." 1306.
  Literary theory and criticism. Linguistic literary theory and criticism.
    On communication; relationship to READER RESPONSE. 1750.

READER-RESPONSE APPROACH
See also related terms: Reader response; Reader-response theory and criticism. Documents applying specific approaches are so numerous that access to them is provided only in the electronic versions of the *Bibliography.*

READER-RESPONSE CRITICISM
Use: Reader-response theory and criticism.

READER-RESPONSE THEORY AND CRITICISM
See also classified section: 1918 ff.
Used for: Reader-response criticism.
  Literary theory and criticism. Linguistic literary theory and criticism and READER-RESPONSE THEORY AND CRITICISM.
    Application of transformational-generative grammar. 1747.
  Literary theory and criticism. New Criticism. 1900-1999.
    Compared to READER-RESPONSE THEORY AND CRITICISM; contextualist criticism. Dissertation abstract. 1830.

READER-RESPONSE THEORY AND CRITICISM—APPLICATION
  Genres. Poetry. Lyric poetry.
    Application of READER-RESPONSE THEORY AND CRITICISM. 2309.

READING
See also related terms: Literacy; Teaching of reading.
  General literature.
    On READING; relationship to interruption. 29.
    Relationship to READING. 79.
    Role of the real; relationship to READING; textuality. 10.

  Literary theory and criticism.
    On READING; relationship to aesthetics. Theories of Jauss, Hans Robert: *Aesthetische Erfahrung und literarische Hermeneutik* compared to Barthes, Roland: *Le Plaisir du texte.* 1361.
  Literary theory and criticism. Narrative theory.
    On READING; interpretation; study example: James, Henry, Jr.: "The Figure in the Carpet." Pedagogical approach. 1800.
  Literary theory and criticism. Psychoanalytic literary theory and criticism.
    On READING; relationship to transference. Application of theories of Jung, Carl Gustav; Lacan, Jacques. 1907.
  Literary theory and criticism. Reader-response theory and criticism.
    Role of time; difference in generations; relationship to READING. 1939.

READING ACQUISITION
See also related term: Reading.

READING COMPETENCE
See also related term: Reading.

READING COMPREHENSION
See also related term: Reading.

READING DIFFICULTIES
See also related term: Reading.

READING DISABILITIES
See also related term: Reading.

READING PREFERENCE
  Bibliographical. Publishing. Marketing.
    Of literature for children; relationship to READING PREFERENCE. Dissertation abstract. 1304.

READING SPEED
See also related term: Reading.

READING STRATEGIES
See also related term: Reading.

REAGAN, RONALD (1911-)
  General literature. Television.
    Role of representation; relationship to social discourse; ideology; study example: inauguration (1981) of REAGAN, RONALD. 866.

THE REAL
  General literature.
    Role of THE REAL; relationship to reading; textuality. 10.
  Genres. Novel.
    Relationship to THE REAL; performance. Theories of Bakhtin, Mikhail Mikhaïlovich. 2215.

REALISM
See also related term: Realist movement.
  General literature. Film.
    Style; relationship to REALISM in Rossellini, Roberto: *Roma, città aperta.* Application of theories of Metz, Christian. 480.
  General literature. Film. Film adaptation.
    And television in Great Britain (1959-1963). REALISM; relationship to working class life in film adaptation; television adaptation of drama; fiction. 711.
  General literature. Film. Film genres: *film noir.*
    REALISM. Dissertation abstract. 797.
  General literature. Film in France (1930-1939).
    For women. REALISM; relationship to melodrama. 626.
  General literature for children.
    Illustration; relationship to REALISM. 23.
  Genres. Fiction. 1800-1999.
    REALISM; relationship to disillusionment. Dissertation abstract. 2118.
  Genres. Fiction. Popular fiction.
    Relationship to REALISM. 2168.
  Genres. Novel. 1800-1899.
    REALISM. 2207.
  Genres. Novel. Detective novel.
    REALISM. 2239.
  Literary theory and criticism.
    Mimesis; REALISM; style. Theories of Auerbach, Erich: *Mimesis.* 1528.
    REALISM. Theories of Lukács, György. 1307.
    Role of referent; relationship to REALISM; study example: Zola, Emile. Application of theories of Austin, J. L. Review article. 1533.
  Literary theory and criticism. Marxist literary theory and criticism.
    On REALISM. Theories of Lukács, György. 1790.
  Literary theory and criticism. New Historicism.
    Applied to Russian fiction (1800-1899); relationship to REALISM. 1842.
  Themes and figures. Hysteria.
    Relationship to REALISM; study example: Ibsen, Henrik: *Hedda Gabler; Rosmersholm; Fruen fra havet.* Feminist approach. Compared to theories of Freud, Sigmund. 2878.

REALIST MOVEMENT
See also related terms: Neorealism; Realism.
  General literature. Theater.
    Representation of nature in theatrical production; relationship to REALIST MOVEMENT and Naturalism. Theories of Darwin, Charles Robert; Le Brun, Charles. 960.

SEE CLASSIFIED SEQUENCE FOR ADDITIONAL ENTRIES

Themes and figures. Horizon.
Relationship to literature of Enlightenment; REALIST MOVEMENT. 2872.

REALITY
See also classified section: 2905 ff.
See also related terms: Fact; Illusion.
General literature. Film. Film adaptation.
Treatment of REALITY; relationship to fiction in film adaptation of Fowles, John: *The French Lieutenant's Woman* by Reisz, Karel. 712.
Genres. Drama.
And theater. Treatment of REALITY in performance. 2073.
Genres. Fiction. 1900-1999.
Relationship to REALITY. 2105.
Professional topics. Humanities in United States.
Theories of Bloom, Allan David: *The Closing of the American Mind*; relationship to the past; democracy; REALITY. 2661.

REASON
Literary theory and criticism. Deconstructionism.
Parodic play; relationship to REASON. Theories of Derrida, Jacques compared to Levinas, Emmanuel. 1606.

REBEL
General literature. Film.
Treatment of REBEL in Forman, Miloš. 637.

REBELLION
See also related terms: Rebel; Revolution.

RECALL DEFICIT
See also related term: Memory.

RECEPTION HISTORY
See also related term: Reception study.

RECEPTION STUDY
Used for: Reputation study.
General literature. Film.
By Fassbinder, Rainer Werner. RECEPTION STUDY: reception in United States. 617.
Role of audience in film history; relationship to exhibition. RECEPTION STUDY. 225.
Role of Chaplin, Charles Spencer. RECEPTION STUDY: reception in Germany (1918-1933). 377.
General literature. Film. Film adaptation.
Of Delibes, Miguel: *Los santos inocentes* by Camus, Mario. RECEPTION STUDY: reception in France. 684.
Of Shakespeare, William: *Julius Caesar* compared to *Francesca da Rimini* by Vitagraph Company of America as film adaptation of Dante: *La Divina Commedia: Inferno.* RECEPTION STUDY. 738.
On Stroheim, Erich von: *Greed* as film adaptation of Norris, Frank: *McTeague.* RECEPTION STUDY. 687.
General literature. Film for children (1920-1939).
Relationship to ethnography. RECEPTION STUDY. 314.
General literature. Film in Hollywood.
RECEPTION STUDY: reception in Yugoslavia. 517.
Genres. Novel. Sentimental novel.
RECEPTION STUDY. Sociological approach. 2248.
——: reception in France: Dijon. 2249.

RECEPTION THEORY
See also classified section: 1941 ff.
Genres. Fiction.
Relationship to RECEPTION THEORY. Psychoanalytic approach. 2130.
Professional topics. Comparative literature.
Relationship to RECEPTION THEORY. 2605.

RECEPTION THEORY—APPLICATION
General literature. Theater.
Relationship to spectator. Application of RECEPTION THEORY; frame theory. 936.

RÉCIT
Literary theory and criticism. Narrative theory.
Linguistic analysis of *RÉCIT.* 1795.

RECITATIVE
See also related term: Opera.

RECORDING COMPANIES
See also related term: Recordings.

RECORDINGS
Used for: Phonograph records.
General literature. 1900-1999.
Relationship to film; RECORDINGS. 115.
General literature. Film. Film adaptation.
And musical adaptation; radio adaptation; RECORDINGS of Poe, Edgar Allan. Catalogue. 735.

RECREATION
See also related term: Leisure.

REDEMPTION
General literature. 1800-1999.
Relationship to REDEMPTION. 25.

Literary theory and criticism.
Poetics; relationship to Christianity; REDEMPTION. 1390.

REDUNDANCY
See also related term: Repetition.

REED, SIR CAROL (1906-1976)
General literature. Film. Film adaptation.
Role of Selznick, David O. in film adaptation of Greene, Graham: *The Third Man* by REED, SIR CAROL. 677.

REFERENCE
See also related terms: Referent; Referentiality.
Genres. Fiction.
REFERENCE. 2125.
Literary forms. Translation. Translation theory.
Role of interpretation; REFERENCE; relationship to analysis of target text. 2575.
Literary theory and criticism. Narrative theory.
On description; relationship to REFERENCE. 1802.
Literary theory and criticism. Semiotic literary theory and criticism.
Relationship to REFERENCE. 1981.

REFERENCE BOOK
See also narrower term: Dictionary.

REFERENT
See also related term: Reference.
Literary theory and criticism.
Role of REFERENT; relationship to realism; study example: Zola, Emile. Application of theories of Austin, J. L. Review article. 1533.

REFERENTIAL COMMUNICATION
See also related term: Reference.

REFERENTIALITY
See also related term: Reference.
General literature. Theater.
Role of sign theory; REFERENTIALITY. 927.
Genres. Drama. Comic drama.
REFERENTIALITY; relationship to semiotics. 2099.

REFLEXIVITY
General literature. Television in United States.
REFLEXIVITY. Dissertation abstract. 861.

REFORM
See also narrower term: Educational reform.
General literature. Film in China.
Treatment of REFORM in Ch'en K'ai-ko: *Huang t'u-ti; Ta yueh ping; Hai-tzu wang.* 288.

REGIONAL NOVEL
See also related term: Regionalism.

REGIONALISM
General literature. Film in United States (1978-1988).
REGIONALISM. Dissertation abstract. 406.
Professional topics. Comparative literature. 1900-1999.
At Universität für Bildungswissenschaften Klagenfurt; relationship to REGIONALISM. 2624.

REISZ, KAREL (1926-)
General literature. Film. Film adaptation.
Treatment of reality; relationship to fiction in film adaptation of Fowles, John: *The French Lieutenant's Woman* by REISZ, KAREL. 712.

REITERATION
Use: Repetition.

REITZ, EDGAR—STUDY EXAMPLE
General literature. Film in West Germany.
Treatment of mourning; memory; relationship to Third Reich; study example: Syberberg, Hans Jürgen: *Hitler, ein Film aus Deutschland;* REITZ, EDGAR: *Heimat.* 566.

RELATIVES
See also related term: Family.

RELEVANCE
Literary forms. Rhetoric.
Argumentation; relationship to RELEVANCE. 2431.

RELIGION
See also classified section: 2909.
See also narrower terms: Christianity; Islam; Judaism.
See also related terms: Devotional literature; Faith; God; Theology.
Genres. Fiction.
Relationship to RELIGION; myth; poststructuralist literary theory and criticism. 2119.
Literary movements.
Modernism. Relationship to political science; RELIGION; publishing. 1019.
——. Treatment in Chambers, Whittaker; Voegelin, Eric; relationship to RELIGION; politics. 1012.
Postmodernism. Relationship to RELIGION; politics. Application of theories of Bell, Daniel; Jameson, Fredric. 1055.

Literary theory and criticism.
Role of the other; language; relationship to ethics; RELIGION. Theories of Levinas, Emmanuel; Marion, Jean-Luc. 1577.

Literary theory and criticism. Hermeneutics and deconstruction.
Relationship to RELIGION. Theories of Steiner, George. 1728.

Literary theory and criticism. Postmodernist literary theory and criticism.
Relationship to RELIGION. Theories of Culler, Jonathan; Heidegger, Martin. 1868.

RELIGION—AS SOURCE

General literature. Television.
Treatment of forgiveness in *Hill Street Blues*. Sources in RELIGION. 865.

RELIGIOUS ALLEGORY
See also related term: Religion.

RELIGIOUS ART
See also related term: Religion.

RELIGIOUS BELIEFS
See also narrower term: Fatalism.
See also related term: Religion.

RELIGIOUS CEREMONIES
See also narrower term: Liturgy.
See also related term: Religion.

RELIGIOUS CONFLICT
See also related term: Religion.

RELIGIOUS CONTROVERSY
See also related term: Religion.

RELIGIOUS CULTS
See also related term: Religion.

RELIGIOUS DENOMINATION
See also related term: Religion.

RELIGIOUS DOCTRINES
See also narrower term: Mysticism.

RELIGIOUS DRAMA
See also narrower term: Passion play.

RELIGIOUS ECSTASY
See also related term: Religion.

RELIGIOUS ETHNOLOGY
See also related term: Religion.

RELIGIOUS EXPERIENCE
See also related term: Religion.

RELIGIOUS FIGURES
See also narrower term: Virgin Mary.

RELIGIOUS FREEDOM
See also related term: Religion.

RELIGIOUS GROUPS
See also narrower terms: Jews; Moslems.
See also related term: Minorities.

General literature. Film.
Role of RELIGIOUS GROUPS; relationship to DeMille, Cecil B.: *King of Kings*. 478.

RELIGIOUS IMAGERY
See also related term: Religion.

RELIGIOUS LITERATURE
See also narrower terms: Devotional literature; Religious prose.

Literary theory and criticism. Semiotic literary theory and criticism.
Relationship to RELIGIOUS LITERATURE. 1974.

RELIGIOUS OBSERVANCES
See also related term: Religion.

RELIGIOUS ORDERS
See also related term: Religious groups.

RELIGIOUS PROSE
See also classified section: 2338.
Used for: Ecclesiastical prose; Theological prose.

RELIGIOUS REFORM
See also related term: Religion.

RELIGIOUS RITES
See also narrower term: Ordination.

RELIGIOUS SYMBOLISM
See also related term: Religion.

REMAKES

General literature. Film. Film genres: *film noir.*
Nonverbal communication in Garnett, Tay: *The Postman Always Rings Twice*; Hawks, Howard: *The Big Sleep*; Dmytryk, Edward: *Murder, My Sweet* compared to REMAKES by Rafelson, Bob; Winner, Michael; Richards, Dick. Dissertation abstract. 767.

RENAISSANCE
See also: entries under headings for Renaissance in specific countries by consulting the index under the adjectival form of the country.

Bibliographical. Manuscripts. Illuminated manuscripts in Venice; Rome. RENAISSANCE.
Role of Petrus. 1136.

Bibliographical. Manuscripts. RENAISSANCE; humanism. 1129.

General literature. Middle Ages and RENAISSANCE.
Treatment of women. Panel discussion. 150.

Genres. Prose. Preface. RENAISSANCE.
Dissertation abstract. 2337.

Literary forms. Emblem of RENAISSANCE (1531-1647).
Anthology. 2394.

Literary forms. Translation of Bible during RENAISSANCE. 2516.

Professional topics. Comparative literature at American universities.
Literature of Middle Ages; RENAISSANCE. 2604.

Professional topics. Humanities.
Literary studies of RENAISSANCE in Great Britain; Netherlands (1950-1990). 2658.

RENAISSANCE ART
See also related term: Renaissance.

RENOIR, JEAN (1894-1979)

General literature. Film.
Narration in RENOIR, JEAN: *Le Crime de M. Lange*. 532.
On RENOIR, JEAN: *La Marseillaise*. 627.

RENOU, JEAN-JOSEPH
Use: Rousseau, Jean-Jacques (1712-1778).

REPETITION
Used for: Iteration; Reiteration.

General literature. Film in India.
REPETITION. 620.

Genres. Fiction as autobiography.
REPETITION by narrator. Dissertation abstract. 2123.

Literary theory and criticism. Semiotic literary theory and criticism.
REPETITION. Relationship to theories of Freud, Sigmund: *Jenseits des Lustprinzips*. 1999.

REPORTAGE

Themes and figures. Spanish Civil War.
Use of REPORTAGE. 2920.

REPRESENTATION
See also narrower terms: Cognitive representation; Linguistic representation.

General literature. Film.
REPRESENTATION; relationship to signification in Fellini, Federico. 276.
—— in Tarkovskiĭ, Andreĭ A.: *Offret*. 445.
—— of African Americans; slavery. Dissertation abstract. 361.

General literature. Film. Film genres: documentary film.
REPRESENTATION. Dissertation abstract. 793.

General literature. Television.
Role of image; REPRESENTATION; relationship to revolution in Central Europe (1989). 896.
Role of REPRESENTATION; relationship to social discourse; ideology; study example: inauguration (1981) of Reagan, Ronald. 866.

General literature. Television: serial drama.
REPRESENTATION of luxury; relationship to television viewer. 898.

General literature. Theater.
REPRESENTATION of nature in theatrical production; relationship to Realist movement and Naturalism. Theories of Darwin, Charles Robert; Le Brun, Charles. 960.

Genres. Fiction.
REPRESENTATION. Sociological approach. 2157.

Genres. Poetry.
As epitaph; relationship to REPRESENTATION. 2282.
Treatment of the chora; relationship to REPRESENTATION. Theories of Kristeva, Julia: *Révolution du langage poétique*. 2255.

Genres. Prose. Autobiographical prose.
And fiction; REPRESENTATION of women; legal discourse (1700-1899). 2317.

Literary forms. Translation.
As transgression; relationship to REPRESENTATION. 2552.

Literary theory and criticism.
REPRESENTATION; relationship to historicity. Treatment in Auerbach, Erich: *Mimesis*; de Man, Paul. 1382.
Role of subject; relationship to REPRESENTATION. Application of theories of Pascal, Blaise; Piles, Roger de. 1470.

Literary theory and criticism. Deconstructionism.
Sign; REPRESENTATION. Treatment in Derrida, Jacques: *De la grammatologie* compared to Hegel, Georg Wilhelm Friedrich. 1594.

Themes and figures. Reality and truth.
Relationship to REPRESENTATION. 2908.
—— in narrative. 2905.

REPRINT EDITION
See also related term: Critical edition.

REPUBLIC OF LETTERS

General literature.
Role of REPUBLIC OF LETTERS. 132.

SEE CLASSIFIED SEQUENCE FOR ADDITIONAL ENTRIES

REPUTATION STUDY
Use: Reception study.

RESEARCH
See also related term: Research methods (literature).
    Professional topics. Humanities.
        On peer review; letters of recommendation; relationship to teaching; RESEARCH. 2800.
        RESEARCH. 2761.
        Role of RESEARCH. 2694.

RESEARCH CENTERS
See also narrower term: Harry Ransom Humanities Research Center.

RESEARCH METHODS (FOLKLORE)
See also related terms: Archives; Research.

RESEARCH METHODS (LINGUISTICS)
See also related term: Research.

RESEARCH METHODS (LITERATURE)
See also related term: Research.
    Professional topics.
        RESEARCH METHODS (LITERATURE). 2578.

RESEARCH TOOLS
See also classified section: 2826 ff.
    Literary theory and criticism. Literary history.
        And RESEARCH TOOLS. Bibliography. 1783.

RESEMBLANCE
Use: Similarity.

RESNAIS, ALAIN (1922-)
    General literature. Film.
        By RESNAIS, ALAIN. 306.
        On RESNAIS, ALAIN: *I Want to Go Home.* Interview with Benson, Laura; Leterrier, Catherine; van Damme, Charlie; Laureux, Jean-Claude. 609.
        Voice in RESNAIS, ALAIN: *L'Année dernière à Marienbad; Hiroshima mon amour.* 297.

RESTORATION
    Professional topics. Censorship in Austria and Germany.
        Relationship to RESTORATION (ca. 1815). 2588.

RESURRECTION OF CHRIST
See also related term: Christ.

RESZLER, ANDRÉ
    Literary theory and criticism.
        Aesthetics; relationship to anarchism. Theories of RESZLER, ANDRÉ. 1559.

REVIEWS
See also narrower term: Film review.
See also related term: Literary theory and criticism.

REVOLT
See also related term: Revolution.

REVOLUTION
See also narrower term: French Revolution.
See also related term: War.
    General literature. Film in Indonesia.
        Treatment of REVOLUTION. 563.
    General literature. Television.
        Role of image; representation; relationship to REVOLUTION in Central Europe (1989). 896.
    General literature. Theater.
        Treatment of REVOLUTION. 966.
    Literary theory and criticism. Marxist literary theory and criticism.
        Role of REVOLUTION; relationship to poststructuralism in France. Theories of Lukács, György. 1793.

RÉVOLUTION TRANQUILLE
See also related term: Quebec.

REVOLUTIONARIES
See also related terms: Rebel; Revolution.

RHETORIC
See also classified section: 2417 ff.
See also narrower terms: Classical rhetoric; Scientific rhetoric.
See also related terms: Dialectic; History of rhetoric; Rhetorical theory; Stylistics.
    General literature.
        Figures; relationship to RHETORIC; semiotics. 176.
        Narrative; RHETORIC; relationship to medicine; study example: Percy, Walker: *Lancelot; The Moviegoer.* 143.
    General literature. Film.
        RHETORIC in Weir, Peter: *Witness.* Dissertation abstract. 489.
    General literature. Theater.
        Collaboration on women's theater groups; relationship to RHETORIC; politics. Feminist approach. 983.
    Genres. Novel.
        RHETORIC; relationship to narrative theory. 2219.
    Genres. Poetry.
        RHETORIC compared to political discourse. Semiotic approach. 2277.

    Literary movements.
        Enlightenment. Role of psychology; relationship to bourgeoisie; RHETORIC. 999.
    Literary theory and criticism.
        In the Academy; relationship to RHETORIC. Study example: de Man, Paul. 1354.
    Literary theory and criticism. Hermeneutics.
        Relationship to RHETORIC. Theories of Gadamer, Hans-Georg. 1733.
    Literary theory and criticism. Postmodernist literary theory and criticism.
        RHETORIC; relationship to death. 1870.
    Literary theory and criticism. Semiotic literary theory and criticism.
        Relationship to RHETORIC. 1986.
    Professional topics. Humanities.
        Application of deconstructionism; relationship to RHETORIC; logic. Theories of Derrida, Jacques. 2777.
        RHETORIC. 2739.
        ——; relationship to cultural conservatism; study example: Isocrates; Erasmus, Desiderius; Weaver, Richard M. Dissertation abstract. 2653.

RHETORICAL APPROACH
See also related term: Rhetoric.
Documents applying specific approaches are so numerous that access to them is provided only in the electronic versions of the *Bibliography.*

RHETORICAL CRITICISM
See also classified section: 1951 ff.
    Figures of speech. Metaphor.
        Relationship to RHETORICAL CRITICISM. 2375.
    Literary theory and criticism. Deconstructionism.
        And RHETORICAL CRITICISM. Includes interview with Derrida, Jacques. 1625.

RHETORICAL DEVICES
Use: Figures of speech.

RHETORICAL FICTION
See also related term: Rhetoric.

RHETORICAL FIGURES
Use: Figures of speech.

RHETORICAL LITERARY THEORY
Use: Rhetorical theory.

RHETORICAL STRATEGY
See also related term: Rhetoric.

RHETORICAL TECHNIQUE
See also narrower term: Stasis.
See also related term: Rhetoric.

RHETORICAL THEORY
Used for: Rhetorical literary theory.
See also related term: Rhetoric.
    Literary forms. Rhetoric.
        Dialectic; relationship to RHETORICAL THEORY; interpersonal communication. 2471.
        RHETORICAL THEORY; relationship to teaching of writing. On empirical approach. 2486.
        ——; relationship to universal audience. Theories of Perelman, Chaim. 2442.

RHETORICAL TRADITION
See also related term: Rhetoric.

RHYME
See also related term: Prosody.
    Genres. Poetry. Esperanto language literature.
        Prosody; RHYME. 2287.

RHYTHM
See also related term: Prosody.
    Genres. Poetry.
        RHYTHM. 2293.
        ——; meter; relationship to semantics. Theories of Tomashevskiĭ, Boris Viktorovich. 2294.
    Literary theory and criticism. Linguistic literary theory and criticism.
        Poetic language; relationship to mental model; image; RHYTHM. 1757.

RHYTHM PERCEPTION
See also related term: Rhythm.

RHYTHMIC PATTERNS
See also related term: Rhythm.

RICE, TIM (1944-)
    General literature. Film.
        On RICE, TIM: *Jesus Christ Superstar;* relationship to English drama (1100-1499). Pedagogical approach. 380.

RICHARDS, DICK (1936-)
    General literature. Film. Film genres: *film noir.*
        Nonverbal communication in Garnett, Tay: *The Postman Always Rings Twice;* Hawks, Howard: *The Big Sleep;* Dmytryk, Edward: *Murder, My Sweet* compared to remakes by Rafelson, Bob; Winner, Michael; RICHARDS, DICK. Dissertation abstract. 767.

RICHARDS, I. A. (1893-1979)
    Genres. Poetry.
        Poetic language. Application of theories of RICHARDS, I. A. Dissertation abstract. 2272.

Literary theory and criticism.
Synesthesia. Theories of RICHARDS, I. A. Dissertation abstract. 1418.

RICHMOND, HENRY TUDOR, EARL OF
Use: Henry VII, King of England (1456-1509).

RICŒUR, PAUL (1913-)
Genres. Fiction.
Point of view. Hermeneutic approach. Application of theories of Gadamer, Hans-Georg; Merleau-Ponty, Maurice; RICŒUR, PAUL. 2113.
Literary theory and criticism.
Narration. Theories of RICŒUR, PAUL: *Temps et récit.* 1408.
Theories of RICŒUR, PAUL. 1423.
Literary theory and criticism. Hermeneutics.
Application of theories of RICŒUR, PAUL: *La Tâche de l'herméneutique.* 1726.

RIDDLES
See also related term: Proverb.

RIDICULE
See also related term: Satire.

RIFFATERRE, MICHAEL (1924-)
Literary theory and criticism. Semiotic literary theory and criticism.
Intertextuality. Theories of RIFFATERRE, MICHAEL: *Semiotics of Poetry.* 1970.

RISK
General literature.
Writer as profession; relationship to RISK. 33.

ROBBE-GRILLET, ALAIN (1922-)
General literature. Film.
By ROBBE-GRILLET, ALAIN. 547.
——: *La Belle Captive; L'Eden et après.* Sources in Surrealism. 337.
Intertextuality relationship to painting in ROBBE-GRILLET, ALAIN: *L'Eden et après; La Belle Captive.* 591.
On ROBBE-GRILLET, ALAIN: *L'Immortelle* compared to novel; relationship to audience. Narratological approach. 507.

ROBSON, MARK (1913-1978)—STUDY EXAMPLE
General literature. Film.
Treatment of psychiatrist; study example: Wiene, Robert: *Das Kabinett des Doktor Caligari;* ROBSON, MARK: *Home of the Brave;* Hitchcock, Alfred: *Psycho;* Meyer, Russ: *The Immoral Mr. Teas.* 569.

ROCK AND ROLL MUSIC
Used for: Rock music.
General literature. Film in United States. Film genres: war film.
Treatment of Vietnam War; relationship to ROCK AND ROLL MUSIC compared to Herr, Michael: *Dispatches.* 773.

ROCK AND ROLL MUSIC BANDS
See also related term: Rock and roll music.

ROCK MUSIC
Use: Rock and roll music.

ROGERS, CARL RANSOM (1902-1987)
Literary forms. Rhetoric.
Argumentation; relationship to feminism. Theories of ROGERS, CARL RANSOM. 2464.
Relationship to dialectic; collaboration. Theories of Burke, Kenneth compared to ROGERS, CARL RANSOM. 2461.

ROHMER, ERIC (1920-)
General literature. Film. 1900-1999.
Treatment of Arthur (character) in Boorman, John: *Excalibur;* ROHMER, ERIC: *Perceval le Gallois;* Romero, George A.: *Knightriders.* 438.

ROLES
See also narrower term: Sex roles.

ROMAN À THÈSE
See also classified section: 2244.

ROMAN-FEUILLETON
See also related term: Novel.

ROMANCE
Literary theory and criticism.
Relationship to ROMANCE. 1481.

ROMANCE FICTION
See also narrower term: Romance novel.

ROMANCE NOVEL
General literature. Film.
On Cocteau, Jean: *La Belle et la bête* compared to McKinley, Robin: *Beauty;* ROMANCE NOVEL; folk tale. 375.

ROMANIA
General literature. Film in ROMANIA. 533.

ROMANTIC
See also related term: Romance.

ROMANTIC IRONY
Literary movements.
Romanticism. ROMANTIC IRONY. 1076.

ROMANTIC NOVEL
Use: Popular romance novel.

ROMANTIC PERIOD
Genres. Drama. ROMANTIC PERIOD.
Staging. 2066.

ROMANTIC POETRY
See also related term: Romanticism.
Themes and figures. *Femme fatale.*
In ROMANTIC POETRY. 2858.

ROMANTIC STUDIES
See also related term: Romanticism.
Literary theory and criticism. New Historicism.
Applied to ROMANTIC STUDIES. 1839.

ROMANTICISM
See also related terms: Romantic poetry; Romantic studies.
See also: entries under headings for Romanticism in specific countries by consulting the index under the adjectival form of the country.
Literary forms. Parody.
ROMANTICISM. 2415.
Literary movements.
Postmodernism. Relationship to ROMANTICISM. 1050.
Literary theory and criticism.
Relationship to aesthetics of ROMANTICISM. Theories of de Man, Paul. 1352.
Relationship to fascism; ROMANTICISM. Theories of Lovejoy, Arthur Oncken; Spitzer, Leo. 1564.

ROME
Bibliographical. Manuscripts. Illuminated manuscripts in Venice; ROME. Renaissance.
Role of Petrus. 1136.

ROMERO, GEORGE A. (1939-)
General literature. Film. 1900-1999.
Treatment of Arthur (character) in Boorman, John: *Excalibur;* Rohmer, Eric: *Perceval le Gallois;* ROMERO, GEORGE A.: *Knightriders.* 438.

RORTY, RICHARD (1931-)
Literary forms. Rhetoric.
Treatment in RORTY, RICHARD. 2491.
Literary movements.
Postmodernism. Relationship to philosophy. Theories of RORTY, RICHARD; Derrida, Jacques; Cavell, Stanley Louis. 1041.
Literary theory and criticism. New Historicism.
Relationship to philosophy. Theories of Locke, John; RORTY, RICHARD; James, William. 1836.
Literary theory and criticism. Psychoanalytic literary theory and criticism.
On life as narrative; relationship to time. Theories of Freud, Sigmund; Sartre, Jean-Paul; RORTY, RICHARD. 1896.

ROSA, ALBERTO ASOR
Use: Asor Rosa, Alberto.

ROSEANNE
General literature. Television.
Treatment of disorder in housekeeping by women in *ROSEANNE* compared to *Married ... with Children.* 912.

ROSENZWEIG, FRANZ (1886-1929)
Literary theory and criticism.
Relationship to the other; the Holocaust; Judaism. Theories of Levinas, Emmanuel; Perelman, Chaim: *The New Rhetoric;* ROSENZWEIG, FRANZ. 1420.

ROSSELLINI, ROBERTO (1906-1977)
General literature. Film.
By ROSSELLINI, ROBERTO. 455.
——. Reminiscence. 552.
On ROSSELLINI, ROBERTO: *Il miracolo;* relationship to censorship. 323.
——: *Roma, città aperta.* 444.
Style; relationship to realism in ROSSELLINI, ROBERTO: *Roma, città aperta.* Application of theories of Metz, Christian. 480.
Treatment of Christ in ROSSELLINI, ROBERTO: *Messia* compared to Scorsese, Martin: *The Last Temptation of Christ.* 629.
Treatment of sexuality; relationship to Nazism in ROSSELLINI, ROBERTO: *Roma, città aperta;* Visconti, Luchino: *Ossessione.* 349.

ROSSET, BARNET LEE, JR. (1922-)
Used for: Rosset, Barney.
Bibliographical. Publishing in United States.
By Grove Press. Interview (1981) with ROSSET, BARNET LEE, JR. 1256.
——; role of ROSSET, BARNET LEE, JR. 1241.

ROSSET, BARNEY
Use: Rosset, Barnet Lee, Jr. (1922-).

ROSTOPCHINE, SOPHIE
Use: Ségur, Sophie, comtesse de (1799-1874).

ROUCH, JEAN PIERRE (1917-)
General literature. Film.
By ROUCH, JEAN PIERRE. 631.
——. Bibliography. 665.
Treatment of Africa in ROUCH, JEAN PIERRE. 554, 555, 556, 557, 662.

SEE CLASSIFIED SEQUENCE FOR ADDITIONAL ENTRIES

ROUND TABLE
See also related terms: Arthur, King; Arthurian legend.

ROUSSEAU, JEAN-JACQUES (1712-1778)
Used for: Renou, Jean-Joseph.
Literary theory and criticism.
Indeterminacy; relationship to the future. Theories of Derrida, Jacques compared to Kant, Immanuel; ROUSSEAU, JEAN-JACQUES. 1317.

ROYAL COURT—AS AUDIENCE
General literature. Television: music television.
Discourse; relationship to power compared to masque for ROYAL COURT of Jacobean period. 858.

ROYCE, JOSIAH (1855-1916)
Literary theory and criticism.
Relationship to Modernism. Theories of Santayana, George; ROYCE, JOSIAH; James, William. 1466.

RTF
Use: Radiodiffusion-Télévision Française.

RUDAKOV, KONSTANTIN IVANOVICH (1891-)
General literature.
Illustration by RUDAKOV, KONSTANTIN IVANOVICH. 206.

RUIZ, RAÚL (1941-)
General literature. Film in Chile.
Role of RUIZ, RAÚL. Sources in Borges, Jorge Luis. 520.

RUIZ, RAÚL (1941-)—STUDY EXAMPLE
General literature. Film.
Role of exile; relationship to cultural identity; study example: RUIZ, RAÚL: *Les Trois Couronnes du matelot*; Solanas, Fernando E.: *Tangos—L'Exil de Gardel.* 526.

RUIZ DE SANTAYANA Y BORRAIS, JORGE
Use: Santayana, George (1863-1952).

RUSSIAN EMPIRE
See also narrower term: St. Petersburg.
General literature. Film in RUSSIAN EMPIRE (1908-1919).
Film guide. 615.

RUSSIAN FICTION
Literary theory and criticism. New Historicism.
Applied to RUSSIAN FICTION (1800-1899); relationship to realism. 1842.

RUSSIAN HISTORY
General literature. Film.
Treatment of RUSSIAN HISTORY in Ėĭzenshteĭn, Sergeĭ Mikhaĭlovich: *Ivan Groznyĭ*. Sources in Shakespeare, William. 290.
Genres. Prose. Historiography.
Relationship to RUSSIAN HISTORY. Narrative. Theories of White, Hayden V.: *Metahistory*. 2332.

RUSSIAN LITERATURE
Bibliographical.
Personal library of Lieb, Fritz; relationship to RUSSIAN LITERATURE; Slavic literature. 1099.
Bibliographical. Publishing. Book trade (1918-1990).
Of Polish literature; RUSSIAN LITERATURE. 1291.

RUSSIAN ORTHODOX CHURCH
Literary theory and criticism.
Role of Bakhtin, Mikhail Mikhaĭlovich; relationship to RUSSIAN ORTHODOX CHURCH. 1393.
Text; relationship to liturgy of RUSSIAN ORTHODOX CHURCH. Relationship to theories of Bakhtin, Mikhail Mikhaĭlovich; Florenskiĭ, Pavel Aleksandrovich: *Stolp i utverzhdenie istiny*; Kedrov, Konstantin Aleksandrovich: *Poéticheskiĭ kosmos*. 1558.

RUSSIAN POETS
Literary theory and criticism. 1800-1999.
Role of French poets; RUSSIAN POETS; German poets. 1349.

RUSSIAN S.F.S.R.
General literature. Film. Film genres: silent film in United States and RUSSIAN S.F.S.R.
Melodrama; relationship to temporality. Theories of Benjamin, Walter. 757.

SABINE RIVER
See also related term: Texas.

SACRAMENTS
See also narrower term: Eucharist (sacrament of).

THE SACRED
See also classified section: 2910 ff.
Figures of speech. Symbol.
Relationship to THE SACRED. 2377.
General literature. Film.
Treatment of THE SACRED in Pasolini, Pier Paolo: *Teorema*. 287.
Genres. Novel.
And film. Treatment of threshold; relationship to THE SACRED; the profane. 2203.
Genres. Poetry.
Treatment of THE SACRED. 2253, 2259.

SACRIFICE
General literature. Film.
Treatment of World War II; relationship to SACRIFICE in Plievier, Theodor: *Stalingrad*. 223.

SACRIFICIAL CHILD
See also related term: Sacrifice.

SADISM
See also related term: Sexuality.

SADNESS
See also related term: Depression.

SADOMASOCHISM
See also related term: Sexuality.

SAGA
See also related terms: Legend; Myth.

SAGNER, OTTO (1920-)
Bibliographical.
Festschrift for SAGNER, OTTO. 1102.

SAID, EDWARD W. (1935-)
Literary theory and criticism.
Political criticism. Theories of Foucault, Michel; SAID, EDWARD W. 1370.

ST. PETERSBURG
Bibliographical. Publishing. Book trade.
By Baer, Karl Ernst von in ST. PETERSBURG. 1292.

SAINTS' LIVES
Use: Hagiography.

SAISSET-SCHNEIDER, CHARLOTTE-ELISABETH-GERMAINE
Use: Dulac, Germaine (1882-1942).

SALAMANCA
Bibliographical. Printing in SALAMANCA. Middle Ages.
Of logic textbook. 1167.

SALES ENCOUNTER
See also related term: Business.

SALVATION
See also related term: Faith.

SAMB, ABABACAR
Use: Samb-Makharam, Ababacar (1934-).

SAMB-MAKHARAM, ABABACAR (1934-)
Used for: Samb, Ababacar.
General literature. Film.
Interview with SAMB-MAKHARAM, ABABACAR. 365.

SANDARS, NANCY KATHARINE (1914-)—STUDY EXAMPLE
Genres. Fiction.
Narrator; point of view; relationship to story; study example: SANDARS, NANCY KATHARINE: *The Epic of Gilgamesh*. Anthropological approach. 2148.

SANDERS-BRAHMS, HELMA (1940-)
General literature. Film.
Treatment of the self; female identity in SANDERS-BRAHMS, HELMA: *Deutschland, bleiche Mutter*; Brückner, Jutta: *Hungerjahre* compared to Wolf, Christa: *Kindheitsmuster*; Rehmann, Ruth: *Der Mann auf der Kanzel*. Dissertation abstract. 431.

SANTAYANA, GEORGE (1863-1952)
Used for: Ruiz de Santayana y Borrais, Jorge.
Literary theory and criticism.
Relationship to Modernism. Theories of SANTAYANA, GEORGE; Royce, Josiah; James, William. 1466.

SAPPHO (B. CA. 625 B.C.)
Literary forms. Translation.
English language translation of SAPPHO. 2550.

SARDINIA
General literature. Film. Film adaptation.
Treatment of SARDINIA in film adaptation of Ledda, Gavino: *Padre padrone* by Taviani, Paolo and Taviani, Vittorio. 674.

SARTRE, JEAN-PAUL (1905-1980)
Literary theory and criticism.
On memory; relationship to the future. Theories of Heidegger, Martin; SARTRE, JEAN-PAUL. 1454.
Relationship to ethics. Role of theories of SARTRE, JEAN-PAUL: *L'Etre et le néant*; *Cahiers pour une morale*. 1457.
Literary theory and criticism. Deconstructionism.
Theories of SARTRE, JEAN-PAUL; Hegel, Georg Wilhelm Friedrich; relationship to theories of Derrida, Jacques. 1614.
Literary theory and criticism. Psychoanalytic literary theory and criticism.
On life as narrative; relationship to time. Theories of Freud, Sigmund; SARTRE, JEAN-PAUL; Rorty, Richard. 1896.

SATAN
See also related term: Devil.

SATIRE
See also classified section: 2502 ff.

See also narrower term: Menippean satire.
See also related terms: Burlesque; Pastiche.

SATIRICAL STRUCTURE
See also related term: Satire.

SATYAJIT RAY
Use: Ray, Satyajit (1922-).

SAURA, CARLOS (1932-)
General literature. Film.
Treatment of Spanish history in SAURA, CARLOS: *El jardín de las delicias.* Dissertation abstract. 573.

SAUSSURE, FERDINAND DE (1857-1913)
Genres. Poetry.
Relationship to music. Semiotic approach. Application of theories of SAUSSURE, FERDINAND DE. Dissertation abstract. 2303.
Literary theory and criticism. Deconstructionism.
Theories of Derrida, Jacques: *De la grammatologie* compared to SAUSSURE, FERDINAND DE: *Cours de linguistique générale.* 1588.
Literary theory and criticism. Semiotic literary theory and criticism.
Relationship to cybernetics; information theory. Theories of SAUSSURE, FERDINAND DE; Peirce, Charles Sanders; Bense, Max. 1971.
Literary theory and criticism. Structuralist literary theory and criticism.
Compared to poststructuralist literary theory and criticism. Role of theories of SAUSSURE, FERDINAND DE in theories of Culler, Jonathan. 2026.

SAUSSURE, FERDINAND DE (1857-1913)—AS SOURCE
Literary theory and criticism.
Semiotic idealism. Sources in Kant, Immanuel; SAUSSURE, FERDINAND DE. 1402.

SAYINGS
See also related term: Proverb.

SCALES BINDER (FL. 1456-1465)
Bibliographical. Printing. Binding in London. 1400-1499.
By SCALES BINDER. 1202.

SCANDINAVIA
See also narrower terms: Norway; Sweden.

SCANSION
See also related term: Meter.

SCENE DESIGN
Used for: Set design.
See also related terms: Scenography; Staging; Theater.
General literature. Film and television.
SCENE DESIGN by Solov'ev, Nikolaï. 616.
General literature. Television.
SCENE DESIGN in television adaptation of Shakespeare, William by British Broadcasting Corporation (1978-1985). Dissertation abstract. 917.

SCENERY
See also related terms: Mise en scène; Scene design.

SCENOGRAPHY
See also related term: Scene design.
General literature. Theater.
SCENOGRAPHY; relationship to camouflage; war. Dissertation abstract. 951.

SCEPTICISM
Use: Skepticism.

SCHAMONI, PETER
General literature. Film.
On Kluge, Alexander and SCHAMONI, PETER: *Brutalität im Stein*; relationship to film during Third Reich. 538.

SCHEMA
See also related term: Schema theory.

SCHEMA THEORY
See also related term: Cognition.
Genres. Short story.
Role of SCHEMA THEORY in teaching. Psycholinguistic approach. Dissertation abstract. 2344.

SCHERER, WILHELM (1841-1886)
Literary theory and criticism. 1800-1899.
Role of Hennequin, Emile: *La Critique scientifique*; SCHERER, WILHELM: *Geschichte der deutschen Literatur*; Grigor'ev, Apollon Aleksandrovich. Sources in Positivism. Dissertation abstract. 1465.

SCHLEIERMACHER, FRIEDRICH DANIEL ERNST (1768-1834)
Literary forms. Translation. Translation theory.
Theories of SCHLEIERMACHER, FRIEDRICH DANIEL ERNST; Benjamin, Walter. 2571.

SCHLEMIEL
General literature. Film.
Treatment of SCHLEMIEL in Allen, Woody. 531.

SCHLEMMER, OSKAR (1888-1943)
General literature. Theater.
Marionettes; relationship to performance theory. Theories of Craig, Edward Gordon: "The Actor and the Über-marionette"; Meïerkhol'd, Vsevolod Emil'evich;

SCHLEMMER, OSKAR; Kleist, Heinrich von: "Über das Marionettentheater." Dissertation abstract. 962.

SCHMIDT, GARY D.
Genres. Fiction for children.
Narrative voice. Interview with SCHMIDT, GARY D. 2115.

SCHÖFFER FAMILY
Bibliographical. Printing in Germany. 1400-1499.
Of Latin language literature by SCHÖFFER FAMILY. 1183.

SCHOLARLY ORGANIZATIONS
See also narrower term: Modern Language Association of America.

SCHOLARLY PUBLISHING
Bibliographical. Publishing.
SCHOLARLY PUBLISHING. 1261.

SCHOLARS
See also related term: Academia.

SCHOLARSHIP
See also narrower term: Literary studies.

SCHREIBER, WILHELM LUDWIG (1855-1932)
Bibliographical. Printing. Illustration.
On woodcuts of Passion of Christ by Delbecq, Jean Baptiste and SCHREIBER, WILHELM LUDWIG. 1211.

SCIENCE
See also related terms: Scientific discourse; Scientific method; Scientific prose; Scientific rhetoric; Technology.
General literature.
And SCIENCE. Creativity. 6.
Relationship to SCIENCE. 167.
——. Application of theories of Mach, Ernst: *Erkenntnis und Irrtum*; Vaihinger, Hans. 145.
——; hermeneutics. 185.
Treatment of SCIENCE. 166.
General literature. Theater.
Role of theater theory applied to performance compared to SCIENCE; quantum theory applied to nature. 968.
General literature for children.
Treatment of SCIENCE; technology. Reference guide. 113.
Genres. Fiction. Science fiction.
Role of aesthetics; relationship to SCIENCE. 2173.
Genres. Poetry.
Relationship to SCIENCE. 2300.
——. Theories of Snow, C. P. 2263.
Genres. Poetry. 1700-1799.
Relationship to SCIENCE. 2270.
Literary forms. Rhetoric.
Relationship to SCIENCE; knowledge. 2455.
Literary movements. 1600-1699.
Humanism. Role of poetry; relationship to SCIENCE. 1004.
Literary theory and criticism.
Compared to SCIENCE. 1475.
Literary theory and criticism. Deconstructionism.
Compared to SCIENCE. Application of theories of Mahesh Yogi, Maharishi. 1607.
Literary theory and criticism. Psychoanalytic literary theory and criticism.
Relationship to SCIENCE. 1913.
Professional topics. Humanities.
Relationship to literacy; SCIENCE. Theories of Hirsch, Eric Donald; Bakhtin, Mikhail Mikhaĭlovich. 2677.

SCIENCE FICTION
See also classified section: 2172 ff.
See also narrower term: Science fiction film.
See also related terms: Fantasy; Utopian fiction.
General literature. Television.
On *Doctor Who*; relationship to SCIENCE FICTION. Application of theories of Propp, Vladimir Iakovlevich. Dissertation abstract. 891.
Literary forms. Translation.
Of SCIENCE FICTION. 2547.

SCIENCE FICTION FILM
General literature. Film. Film genres: SCIENCE FICTION FILM.
And television; relationship to women as fans. Ethnography. Dissertation abstract. 746.
Treatment of time travel; primal scene; dystopia in Cameron, James: *The Terminator.* 792.
Treatment of totalitarianism in Lucas, George: *THX-1138* compared to Plato: *Politeia.* 753.
General literature. Film. Film genres: SCIENCE FICTION FILM in U.S.S.R. 783.

SCIENCE-FICTION STUDIES
Genres. Fiction. Science fiction.
Treatment in criticism in *SCIENCE-FICTION STUDIES.* 2174.

SCIENTIFIC APPROACH
See also related term: Scientific method.

Documents applying specific approaches are so numerous that access to them is provided only in the electronic versions of the *Bibliography*.

SCIENTIFIC DISCOURSE
See also related terms: Science; Scientific language.
 General literature.
  Narrative; relationship to fiction; SCIENTIFIC DISCOURSE. 153.
 Literary forms. Rhetoric.
  Sophistry; relationship to epistemology; SCIENTIFIC DISCOURSE. 2443.
 Literary theory and criticism. Linguistic literary theory and criticism.
  Applied to SCIENTIFIC DISCOURSE; study example: Nathans, Jeremy H. 1743.

SCIENTIFIC LANGUAGE
See also related terms: Scientific discourse; Scientific prose.
 Literary forms. Rhetoric.
  Argumentation in SCIENTIFIC LANGUAGE. Theories of Aristotle compared to Plato. 2480.
  Role of question; metaphor; image in SCIENTIFIC LANGUAGE; relationship to epistemology. Theories of Meyer, Michel; Kant, Immanuel. 2427.

SCIENTIFIC LANGUAGE—STUDY EXAMPLE
 Literary theory and criticism.
  Figuration; relationship to literal meaning; study example: SCIENTIFIC LANGUAGE; philosophical language (1630-1800). Review article. 1506.

SCIENTIFIC METHOD
See also related term: Science.
 Literary theory and criticism. Hermeneutics.
  Relationship to SCIENTIFIC METHOD. 1722.
 Literary theory and criticism. Linguistic literary theory and criticism.
  Compared to semiotic literary theory and criticism; relationship to epistemology; SCIENTIFIC METHOD. 1742.

SCIENTIFIC PROSE
See also classified section: 2339 ff.
See also narrower term: Medical prose.
See also related terms: Science; Scientific language.
 Literary forms. Rhetoric.
  Relationship to SCIENTIFIC PROSE. 2453.

SCIENTIFIC RHETORIC
See also related term: Science.
 Literary forms. Rhetoric.
  SCIENTIFIC RHETORIC. Treatment in Bacon, Francis. 2500.

SCIENTIFIC STYLE
See also related term: Scientific language.

SCIENTIFIC TERMS
See also related term: Scientific language.

SCIENTIFIC THEORY
See also narrower term: Quantum theory.
See also related term: Science.

SCORSESE, MARTIN (1942-)
 General literature. Film.
  By Ford, John; Capra, Frank; Coppola, Francis Ford; SCORSESE, MARTIN. 456.
  Postmodernism in Coppola, Francis Ford; Lucas, George; DePalma, Brian; Spielberg, Steven; SCORSESE, MARTIN. Dissertation abstract. 630.
  Treatment of Christ in Rossellini, Roberto: *Messia* compared to SCORSESE, MARTIN: *The Last Temptation of Christ*. 629.
 General literature. Film and television.
  On Lynch, David: *Twin Peaks*; *Blue Velvet*; SCORSESE, MARTIN: *GoodFellas*; relationship to *film noir*. 396.

SCOTLAND
See also narrower term: Edinburgh.
 Literary forms. Rhetoric.
  History of rhetoric in England; SCOTLAND; United States (1650-1799). 2474.

SCOTT, RIDLEY (1938-)
 General literature. Film.
  On SCOTT, RIDLEY: *Blade Runner*. Bibliography. 669.
  Treatment of Japan in SCOTT, RIDLEY: *Black Rain*. 322.
  Treatment of sexuality; abortion in SCOTT, RIDLEY: *Alien*. 296.
 General literature. Film. Film adaptation.
  Treatment of antinomy; relationship to human nature in SCOTT, RIDLEY: *Blade Runner* as film adaptation of Dick, Philip K.: *Do Androids Dream of Electric Sheep?* 720.
  Treatment of cybernetics in SCOTT, RIDLEY: *Blade Runner* as film adaptation of Dick, Philip K.: *Do Androids Dream of Electric Sheep?* 733.

SCOTT, TONY (1944-)
 General literature. Film.
  Treatment of masculinity; relationship to love; war in Ashby, Hal: *Coming Home*; SCOTT, TONY: *Top Gun*. 301.

SCREENPLAY
See also related term: Film adaptation.
 General literature. Film.
  And SCREENPLAY; film review; relationship to American Biograph Company; study example: Woods, Frank E.; Griffith, D. W. 229.
  Relationship to SCREENPLAY. Linguistic approach. 484.
  SCREENPLAY by Babel', Isaak Ėmmanuilovich. 390.

SCREENPLAY by Fuchs, Daniel. Creative process. 340.
 General literature. Film and television.
  Role of SCREENPLAY; television drama. Pedagogical approach. 621.
 General literature. Film in Hollywood.
  Narrative; relationship to authorship in Hitchcock, Alfred: *North by Northwest*; role of SCREENPLAY by Lehman, Ernest Paul. Dissertation abstract. 581.

SCREENWRITER
 General literature. Film.
  On Verga, Giovanni as SCREENWRITER. 660.

SCREENWRITING
See also related term: Screenwriter.

SCRIBE
 Bibliographical. Manuscripts.
  Use of Caroline minuscule. Role of SCRIBE. 1128.
 Bibliographical. Publishing in England. 1700-1799.
  Role of SCRIBE; relationship to copyright. 1255.

SCRIPTORIUM
See also related term: Manuscripts.

SCRIPTURE
See also related term: Bible.

SCROOGE, EBENEZER (CHARACTER)
 General literature. Film. Film adaptation.
  Treatment of SCROOGE, EBENEZER (CHARACTER) in Dickens, Charles: *A Christmas Carol* compared to television adaptation; theatrical production; cartoons. 686.

SCULPTURE
 Genres. Poetry. 1800-1999.
  Treatment of SCULPTURE. 2284.

SEASONS OF THE YEAR
 Literary forms. Humor.
  Relationship to SEASONS OF THE YEAR. 2401.

SECOND EMPIRE
See also related term: France.

SECOND LANGUAGE ACQUISITION
Use: Second language learning.

SECOND LANGUAGE COMPETENCE
See also related term: Second language learning.

SECOND LANGUAGE COMPREHENSION
See also related term: Second language learning.

SECOND LANGUAGE LEARNERS
See also related term: Second language learning.

SECOND LANGUAGE LEARNING
Used for: Foreign language learning; Language learning; Second language acquisition.
See also narrower term: Computer-assisted language learning.
See also related term: Second language teaching.
See also: entries under headings for the learning of specific languages, e.g., English language learning, French language learning, etc.
 Professional topics. Humanities.
  SECOND LANGUAGE LEARNING. 2763.

SECOND LANGUAGE TEACHING
See also related term: Second language learning.
 Professional topics. Humanities.
  SECOND LANGUAGE TEACHING. 2652.

SECOND SELF
See also related term: The double.

SECONDARY EDUCATION
 Literary forms. Translation.
  Role in canon of target literature; relationship to SECONDARY EDUCATION in Germany. 2549.

SECONDARY SCHOOL STUDENTS
See also related term: Secondary education.

SECTS
See also related term: Religious groups.

SECULARITY
 General literature. Theater.
  Treatment of the absurd; SECULARITY; relationship to Postmodernism. 949.
 Themes and figures. Christ.
  Relationship to SECULARITY. 2842.

SEDUCTION
 Genres. Novel. Sentimental novel.
  Treatment of SEDUCTION. 2247.

SÉGUR, SOPHIE, COMTESSE DE (1799-1874)
Used for: Rostopchine, Sophie.

SÉGUR, SOPHIE, COMTESSE DE (1799-1874)—STUDY EXAMPLE
 General literature for children.
  Study example: SÉGUR, SOPHIE, COMTESSE DE. Feminist approach. Dissertation abstract. 122.

SEIDELMAN, SUSAN (1952-)
General literature. Film.
Treatment of desire in SEIDELMAN, SUSAN: *Desperately Seeking Susan.* Psychoanalytic approach. 249.

THE SELF
See also classified section: 2915 ff.
See also narrower term: Divided self.
See also related term: The individual.
See also: entries under headings for related terms beginning with the prefix *self-*, e.g., *self-consciousness, self-image,* etc.
General literature.
Role of THE SELF in interpretation by college students. Pedagogical approach. Dissertation abstract. 41.
General literature. Film.
Treatment of THE SELF; female identity in Sanders-Brahms, Helma: *Deutschland, bleiche Mutter;* Brückner, Jutta: *Hungerjahre* compared to Wolf, Christa: *Kindheitsmuster;* Rehmann, Ruth: *Der Mann auf der Kanzel.* Dissertation abstract. 431.
Genres. Autobiography by women writers.
Treatment of THE SELF; relationship to truth. Feminist approach. 2053.
Genres. Autobiography by women writers. 1700-1899.
Treatment of THE SELF; relationship to duplicity in narrative. 2052.
Genres. Prose. Diary.
Role of writing; relationship to THE SELF. 2322.
Literary theory and criticism. Poststructuralist literary theory and criticism.
Role of subjectivity; THE SELF; relationship to humanism; New Criticism. Application of theories of Lacan, Jacques. 1887.

SELF-ANALYSIS
See also related term: Psychoanalysis.

SELF-CONCEPTION
Use: Self-identity.

SELF-CONSCIOUSNESS
Genres. Fiction.
SELF-CONSCIOUSNESS; relationship to authorship. 2152.

SELF-IDENTITY
Used for: Personal identity; Self-conception.
General literature. Film. Film theory and criticism.
Spectator; relationship to SELF-IDENTITY. Dissertation abstract. 842.

SELF-REFLEXIVENESS
See also related term: Mise en abyme.
Figures of speech. Metaphor.
Relationship to SELF-REFLEXIVENESS. Theories of Maxwell, James Clerk; Shannon, Claude Elwood. 2362.
General literature.
SELF-REFLEXIVENESS. 64.
General literature. Television: situation comedy.
SELF-REFLEXIVENESS in *The George Burns and Gracie Allen Show; I Love Lucy; The Jack Benny Show.* 868.
Literary theory and criticism. Deconstructionism.
Role of hierarchy; SELF-REFLEXIVENESS; relationship to philosophy; anthropology. Theories of Derrida, Jacques; Dumont, Louis. 1599.
Literary theory and criticism. Narrative theory.
SELF-REFLEXIVENESS; study example: detective fiction. 1823.

SELF-TRANSLATION
See also related term: Translator.

SELZNICK, DAVID O. (1902-1965)
General literature. Film.
Costume by Plunkett, Walter in Fleming, Victor: *Gone with the Wind;* relationship to SELZNICK, DAVID O. 346.
Role of censorship in Fleming, Victor: *Gone with the Wind;* relationship to Lewton, Val; SELZNICK, DAVID O. 495.
Role of SELZNICK, DAVID O. as producer. 638.
Treatment of Titanic; relationship to Hitchcock, Alfred; SELZNICK, DAVID O. 567.
General literature. Film. Film adaptation.
Role of SELZNICK, DAVID O. in film adaptation of Greene, Graham: *The Third Man* by Reed, Sir Carol. 677.

SEMANTIC ANALYSIS
Genres. Drama and narrative.
SEMANTIC ANALYSIS. 2079.

SEMANTIC APPROACH
Documents applying specific approaches are so numerous that access to them is provided only in the electronic versions of the *Bibliography.*

SEMANTIC ENCODING
See also related terms: Cognition; Memory.

SEMANTICS

See also narrower term: Possible worlds semantics.
See also related term: Meaning.
See also: entries under headings for related terms beginning with the modifier *semantic,* e.g., *semantic change, semantic features,* etc.

General literature.
Thematic structure; relationship to SEMANTICS. 175.
Genres. Poetry.
Rhythm; meter; relationship to SEMANTICS. Theories of Tomashevskiĭ, Boris Viktorovich. 2294.
Literary theory and criticism. Linguistic literary theory and criticism.
Relationship to SEMANTICS; intensionality of narrative. 1734.
Literary theory and criticism. Semiotic literary theory and criticism.
Relationship to SEMANTICS. Theories of Mukařovský, Jan. 2001.

SEMBÈNE OUSMANE (1923-)
Used for: Ousmane Sembène.
General literature. Film.
By SEMBÈNE OUSMANE. 366.

SEME
See also related term: Meaning.

SEMIOLOGY
Use: Semiotics.

SEMIOTIC ANALYSIS
See also related term: Semiotics.

SEMIOTIC APPROACH
See also related term: Semiotics.
Documents applying specific approaches are so numerous that access to them is provided only in the electronic versions of the *Bibliography.*

SEMIOTIC CRITICISM
Use: Semiotic literary theory and criticism.

SEMIOTIC IDEALISM
Literary theory and criticism.
SEMIOTIC IDEALISM. Sources in Kant, Immanuel; Saussure, Ferdinand de. 1402.

SEMIOTIC LITERARY THEORY AND CRITICISM
See also classified section: 1955 ff.
Used for: Semiotic criticism.
General literature. Film. Film theory and criticism.
Sign; relationship to female spectator; feminist literary theory and criticism; SEMIOTIC LITERARY THEORY AND CRITICISM. 840.
General literature. Television.
Relationship to SEMIOTIC LITERARY THEORY AND CRITICISM. 854.
Literary theory and criticism. Deconstructionism.
Relationship to SEMIOTIC LITERARY THEORY AND CRITICISM; hermeneutics. 1617.
Literary theory and criticism. Linguistic literary theory and criticism.
Compared to SEMIOTIC LITERARY THEORY AND CRITICISM; relationship to epistemology; scientific method. 1742.
Literary theory and criticism. Narrative theory and SEMIOTIC LITERARY THEORY AND CRITICISM. 1797.

SEMIOTIC SYSTEMS
See also related term: Semiotics.

SEMIOTICS
Used for: Semiology.
See also narrower terms: Pragmatics; Semantics.
See also related term: Sign theory.
General literature.
Figures; relationship to rhetoric; SEMIOTICS. 176.
General literature. Film in Hollywood (1930-1939).
Style; relationship to SEMIOTICS; ideology. Dissertation abstract. 302.
General literature. Theater.
Relationship to SEMIOTICS. 940.
Genres. Drama. Comic drama.
Referentiality; relationship to SEMIOTICS. 2099.
Literary theory and criticism. Narrative theory.
Relationship to SEMIOTICS. 1816.
Literary theory and criticism. Psychoanalytic literary theory and criticism.
Relationship to SEMIOTICS. Application of theories of Lacan, Jacques. 1916.
Literary theory and criticism. Sociological literary theory and criticism.
Role of social discourse; relationship to SEMIOTICS; ideology; textuality. 2012.
Literary theory and criticism. Structuralist literary theory and criticism.
Relationship to SEMIOTICS. 2024.

SEMIOTICS—APPLICATION
General literature. Theater.
Application of SEMIOTICS. 970.

SENATE
See also related term: Government.

SENSE ANALOGY
Use: Synesthesia.

SENTIMENT
See also related term: Sentimentality.

SENTIMENTAL FICTION
See also narrower term: Sentimental novel.

SENTIMENTAL NOVEL
See also classified section: 2245 ff.

SEE CLASSIFIED SEQUENCE FOR ADDITIONAL ENTRIES

SENTIMENTALISM
See also related terms: Sentimental novel; Sentimentality.

SENTIMENTALITY
See also classified section: 2917.

General literature. Film.
Irony; relationship to SENTIMENTALITY in Huston, John: *Prizzi's Honor*. 331.
Treatment of animals; relationship to sympathy; SENTIMENTALITY in Annaud, Jean-Jacques: *L'Ours* compared to Disney, Walt. 262.

SEQUEL FILMS
Use: Serial film.

SERIAL DRAMA
General literature. Television: SERIAL DRAMA.
Representation of luxury; relationship to television viewer. 898.

SERIAL FILM
Used for: Sequel films.
General literature. Film: SERIAL FILM.
Bibliography. 668.

SERIALIZATION
See also related term: Publishing.

SERIALS
See also narrower term: Periodicals.

SESSA, GIOVANNI BATTISTA (D. 1509?)
Bibliographical. Printing in Venice. 1500-1599.
Role of SESSA, GIOVANNI BATTISTA. 1154.

SET DESIGN
Use: Scene design.

SETTING
General literature.
Role of space; relationship to SETTING. 137.

SEX
See also classified section: 2918.
See also related terms: Sexism; Sexual intercourse; Sexuality.
General literature. Film. Film genres: war film.
Treatment of Vietnam War; relationship to SEX; violence. 760.

SEX DIFFERENCES
See also related terms: Gender; Sex roles; Sexism; Sexuality.

SEX-ROLE REVERSAL
See also related term: Sex roles.

SEX ROLES
Used for: Gender roles.
See also related terms: Gender; Sexuality.
General literature. Television.
Role of SEX ROLES in *Miami Vice*. 884.

SEXISM
See also related terms: Gender; Sex.
General literature. Film.
Treatment of SEXISM; colonialism. 541.
Professional topics. Humanities.
On ageism; SEXISM in universities. Theories of Eco, Umberto; Derrida, Jacques. 2670.

SEXUAL ALLUSION
See also related term: Sexuality.

SEXUAL DIFFERENCE
Literary theory and criticism. Feminist literary theory and criticism.
And psychoanalytic literary theory and criticism; role of ethics; relationship to SEXUAL DIFFERENCE. Theories of Foucault, Michel; Irigaray, Luce. 1677.
Themes and figures. The sublime.
And SEXUAL DIFFERENCE; treatment in women writers (1900-1999). Dissertation abstract. 2923.

SEXUAL DISCRIMINATION
See also related term: Sexism.

SEXUAL IDENTITY
General literature. Film.
Treatment of SEXUAL IDENTITY; relationship to economics in Fassbinder, Rainer Werner: *Die Ehe der Maria Braun*. 385.

SEXUAL IMAGERY
See also related term: Sexuality.

SEXUAL INTERCOURSE
Used for: Coitus.
See also related terms: Primal scene; Sex.
General literature. Middle Ages.
Treatment of marriage; relationship to abstinence from SEXUAL INTERCOURSE. 66.

SEXUAL NATURE
Use: Sexuality.

SEXUAL RELATIONS
See also related term: Sex roles.

SEXUAL STEREOTYPES
See also related term: Sex roles.

SEXUAL SYMBOLISM
See also related term: Sexuality.

SEXUALITY
Used for: Sexual nature.
See also narrower term: Homosexuality.
See also related terms: Gender; Sex; Sex roles.
See also: entries under headings for related terms beginning with the modifier *sexual*, e.g., *sexual behavior, sexual relations*, etc.
General literature. Film.
Treatment of SEXUALITY; abortion in Scott, Ridley: *Alien*. 296.
——; relationship to motherhood. 419.
——; relationship to Nazism in Rossellini, Roberto: *Roma, città aperta*; Visconti, Luchino: *Ossessione*. 349.
Treatment of social class; SEXUALITY in DeMott, Joel: *Demon Lover Diary*. 663.
Treatment of women; relationship to SEXUALITY; fetishism in Sternberg, Josef von: *Der blaue Engel*. 579.
General literature. Film and video art; music video.
Role of SEXUALITY; relationship to Postmodernism. Imagery. 601.
General literature. Film in Chicago (1906-1908).
And nickelodeon; amusement park as cultural space; relationship to SEXUALITY of women. 536.
General literature. Television: music television.
Treatment of men; women; glamour; SEXUALITY. 885.
General literature. Television: soap opera.
Treatment of family; SEXUALITY; patriarchy compared to English novel (1700-1799). 909.
General literature. Theater: popular theater.
Role of burlesque; relationship to SEXUALITY; female body. 926.

SFUMATO
See also related term: Painting.

SHAGGY DOG STORIES
See also related term: Jokes.

SHAKERS
General literature. Film. Film genres: documentary film.
Treatment of SHAKERS in Burns, Ken and Burns, Amy Stechler. 811.

SHANNON, CLAUDE ELWOOD (1916-)
Figures of speech. Metaphor.
Relationship to self-reflexiveness. Theories of Maxwell, James Clerk; SHANNON, CLAUDE ELWOOD. 2362.

SHAPIRO, DAVID (1947-)
Literary movements.
Postmodernism. Relationship to paranoia; study example: Fish, Stanley: *Is There a Text in This Class?* Application of theories of SHAPIRO, DAVID. 1026.

SHIPS
See also narrower term: Titanic.

SHIPWRECK
See also related term: Titanic.

SHORT FICTION
See also narrower term: Short story.

SHORT FILM
General literature. Film.
Use of sound in Crosland, Alan: *The Jazz Singer* compared to use of Vitaphone in SHORT FILM. 653.

SHORT STORY
See also classified section: 2341 ff.

SHORT STORY CYCLE
See also related term: Short story.

SHORT-TITLE CATALOGUE
Bibliographical. Printing in England (ca. 1510).
Of *SHORT-TITLE CATALOGUE*: No. 14077c41 by Faques, Richard. 1171.

SIEGEL, DON (1912-)
General literature. Film.
Treatment of denial of human body in SIEGEL, DON: *Invasion of the Body Snatchers*; Kaufman, Philip: *Invasion of the Body Snatchers*. 442.

SIGN
General literature.
SIGN. Theories of Blot, Jean-Yves: *La Méduse, chronique d'un naufrage ordinaire*. 111.
General literature. Film. Film adaptation.
Treatment of objects as SIGN in film adaptation by Buñuel, Luis. Dissertation abstract. 719.
General literature. Film. Film theory and criticism.
SIGN; relationship to female spectator; feminist literary theory and criticism; semiotic literary theory and criticism. 840.
Literary theory and criticism. Deconstructionism.
SIGN; representation. Treatment in Derrida, Jacques: *De la grammatologie* compared to Hegel, Georg Wilhelm Friedrich. 1594.

SIGN

Literary theory and criticism. Semiotic literary theory and criticism.

Literary theory and criticism. Semiotic literary theory and criticism.
   SIGN. 1994.

SIGN STRUCTURE
See also related term: Sign.

SIGN THEORY
See also related term: Semiotics.

   General literature. Theater.
      Role of SIGN THEORY; referentiality. 927.

SIGNATURES
See also related term: Printing.

SIGNIFICATION
   General literature. Film.
      Representation; relationship to SIGNIFICATION in Fellini, Federico. 276.
      SIGNIFICATION. Treatment of passion in Pasolini, Pier Paolo: *Teorema.* 624.

   Literary theory and criticism.
      Relationship to SIGNIFICATION. Theories of Gates, Henry Louis, Jr.: *The Signifying Monkey.* 1342.

SIGNIFIER
   Bibliographical. Printing. Illustration.
      Visual imagery; language; relationship to SIGNIFIER. 1212.

   Literary theory and criticism. Semiotic literary theory and criticism.
      And psychoanalytic literary theory and criticism; role of SIGNIFIER; relationship to desire. 2004.

SIGNS
   Literary theory and criticism. Feminist literary theory and criticism.
      Role of *Feminist Studies; Frontiers; SIGNS.* Dissertation abstract. 1693.

SILENT FILM
   General literature. Film.
      SILENT FILM; relationship to Modernism. 529.

   General literature. Film. Film genres: SILENT FILM in United States and Russian S.F.S.R.
      Melodrama; relationship to temporality. Theories of Benjamin, Walter. 757.

SILLS, SAM
   General literature. Film. Film genres: documentary film.
      Treatment of Abraham Lincoln Battalion in Buckner, Noel and Dore, Mary and Paskin, David and SILLS, SAM: *The Good Fight.* 748.

SILVERA, FRANK (1914-1970)
   General literature. Theater.
      Acting. Theories of SILVERA, FRANK. Dissertation abstract. 973.

SIMILARITY
Used for: Resemblance.

   Literary theory and criticism.
      On SIMILARITY. Treatment in Foucault, Michel: *Ceci n'est pas une pipe* compared to Magritte, René. 1468.

   Literary theory and criticism. Semiotic literary theory and criticism.
      Isomorphism; SIMILARITY. Theories of Augustine, Saint; Thomas Aquinas, Saint; Peirce, Charles Sanders. 1960.

SIMILE
   Figures of speech. Metaphor.
      Compared to SIMILE. 2371.
      ——. Psychological approach. 2360.

SIMMEL, GEORG (1858-1918)
   Literary theory and criticism. Deconstructionism.
      Theories of Derrida, Jacques; SIMMEL, GEORG. 1642.

SIMONEAU, YVES
   General literature. Film. Film adaptation.
      Treatment of Brown, Stevens (character) in film adaptation of Hébert, Anne: *Les Fous de Bassan* by SIMONEAU, YVES. 734.

SIMONY
See also related term: Religion.

SIMULTANEOUS INTERPRETING
Use: Simultaneous translation.

SIMULTANEOUS TRANSLATION
Used for: Simultaneous interpreting.
See also related term: Interpreter.

   Literary forms. Translation.
      Role of creativity in SIMULTANEOUS TRANSLATION. 2508.

SIN
See also related term: Transgression.

SINGING
See also related term: Song.

SINGSPIEL
See also related term: Opera.

SINN FEIN
See also related term: Ireland.

SIREN
See also narrower term: Lorelei.

SITUATION COMEDY
See also related terms: Television; Television drama.

   General literature. Television: SITUATION COMEDY.
      Role of ideology. 899.
      Self-reflexiveness in *The George Burns and Gracie Allen Show; I Love Lucy; The Jack Benny Show.* 868.

   General literature. Television: SITUATION COMEDY (1980-1985).
      Treatment of women as superwoman. 888.

SJEF VAN OEKEL
   General literature. Television in Netherlands.
      Role of Postmodernism in *SJEF VAN OEKEL; Fred Hachee.* 852.

SKAZKA
See also related term: Märchen.

SKEPTICISM
Used for: Scepticism.

   Literary theory and criticism.
      SKEPTICISM; relationship to ethics. Theories of Cavell, Stanley Louis: *The Claim of Reason* compared to Levinas, Emmanuel: *Totalité et infini; Autrement qu'être.* 1341.

SKOLIMOWSKI, JERZY (1938-)
   General literature. Film.
      On SKOLIMOWSKI, JERZY: *The Lightship* compared to Conrad, Joseph: *Victory.* 292.

SKY
See also related term: Horizon.

SLAVE NARRATIVE
See also related terms: Slavery

SLAVE TRADE
See also related term: Slavery.

SLAVERY
   General literature. Film.
      Representation of African Americans; SLAVERY. Dissertation abstract. 361.

SLAVES
See also related term: Slavery.

SLAVIC LITERATURE
   Bibliographical.
      Personal library of Lieb, Fritz; relationship to Russian literature; SLAVIC LITERATURE. 1099.

SLAVOPHILES
See also related term: Russian history.

SLEEP
See also related term: Insomnia.

SLEEPLESSNESS
Use: Insomnia.

SLIPPERY SLOPE ARGUMENT
   Literary forms. Rhetoric.
      SLIPPERY SLOPE ARGUMENT; relationship to fallacy. 2457, 2492.

SLUMS
See also related term: Urban areas.

SMALL PUBLISHERS
   Bibliographical. Publishing.
      By SMALL PUBLISHERS. 1246.

SNOW, C. P. (1905-1980)
   Genres. Poetry.
      Relationship to science. Theories of SNOW, C. P. 2263.

SOAP OPERA
See also related term: Melodrama.

   General literature. Television: SOAP OPERA.
      On *Angel Malo.* 923.
      Treatment of family; sexuality; patriarchy compared to English novel (1700-1799). 909.

   General literature. Television: SOAP OPERA in Brazil. 846.

SOCIAL BEHAVIOR
   Genres. Fiction for children.
      Treatment of morality; relationship to SOCIAL BEHAVIOR. 2111.

SOCIAL CHANGE
   Bibliographical. Printing in Morocco (1865-1912).
      Relationship to SOCIAL CHANGE. Dissertation abstract. 1152.

SOCIAL CLASS
Used for: Class.
See also narrower terms: Bourgeoisie; Working class.

   Bibliographical. Publishing in France.
      Book distribution; libraries; relationship to SOCIAL CLASS. 1259.

   General literature. Film.
      Treatment of SOCIAL CLASS; sexuality in DeMott, Joel: *Demon Lover Diary.* 663.

SOCIAL CONFLICT
See also related term: Society.

SOCIAL CONSTRUCTION

Literary forms. Rhetoric.
SOCIAL CONSTRUCTION; relationship to teaching of writing. Theories of Bruffee, Kenneth A. 2452.
Stasis; kairos; treatment in Classical rhetoric; relationship to SOCIAL CONSTRUCTION. 2433

Professional topics. Humanities.
Role of academic discourse; relationship to interpretive communities; SOCIAL CONSTRUCTION. 2703.

SOCIAL CRITICISM

Literary theory and criticism.
Role of interpretation; relationship to politics; SOCIAL CRITICISM. Review article. 1379.

SOCIAL DISCOURSE

General literature. Television.
Role of representation; relationship to SOCIAL DISCOURSE; ideology; study example: inauguration (1981) of Reagan, Ronald. 866.

Literary theory and criticism. Sociological literary theory and criticism.
Role of SOCIAL DISCOURSE. 2011.
——; relationship to semiotics; ideology; textuality. 2012.

SOCIAL DRAMA

General literature. Film in Germany (1910-1914). Film genres.
Melodrama; SOCIAL DRAMA. 803.

SOCIAL FUNCTION

General literature. Theater.
SOCIAL FUNCTION; role of audience. Semiotic approach. 932.

SOCIAL HIERARCHY

See also related term: Society.

Themes and figures. Transgression.
As the carnivalesque; relationship to SOCIAL HIERARCHY. Application of theories of Bakhtin, Mikhail Mikhaïlovich; Elias, Norbert; Douglas, Mary. 2926.

SOCIAL HISTORY

See also related term: Society.

SOCIAL IDEOLOGIES

See also related term: Society.

SOCIAL INSTITUTIONS

See also related term: Social behavior.

SOCIAL INTERACTION

See also related term: Social relations.

SOCIAL ISSUES

Use: Social problems.

SOCIAL NOVEL

See also classified section: 2250.

SOCIAL ORDER

See also related term: Society.

SOCIAL PHENOMENA

See also narrower terms: Social behavior; Social problems.

SOCIAL PROBLEMS

Used for: Social issues.
See also related term: Society.

General literature. Television: docudrama and movie of the week.
Treatment of SOCIAL PROBLEMS. 881.

SOCIAL REFORM

See also related term: Society.

SOCIAL RELATIONS

Literary forms. Parody.
And travesty; pastiche; relationship to SOCIAL RELATIONS; psychology. Application of communication theory. 2414.

SOCIAL SCIENCES

See also narrower terms: Anthropology; Economics; History; Political science; Sociology.
See also related term: Psychology.

Literary theory and criticism.
Relationship to SOCIAL SCIENCES; progressive education. 1574.

SOCIAL STRUCTURE

See also related term: Society.

SOCIALISM

General literature. Film. Film theory and criticism in East Germany.
And television theory; relationship to SOCIALISM. 832.

Professional topics. Censorship in East Germany; Poland.
Relationship to SOCIALISM. 2591.

SOCIALIST COUNTRIES

See also related term: Socialism.

SOCIALIST REALISM

General literature. Film.
SOCIALIST REALISM in Pichul, Vasiliĭ: *Malen'kaia Vera.* 326.

Genres. Novel. *Roman à thèse.*
Relationship to SOCIALIST REALISM. 2244.

SOCIALIST REALIST CRITICISM

Use: Socialist realist literary theory and criticism.

SOCIALIST REALIST LITERARY THEORY AND CRITICISM

See also classified section: 2009.
Used for: Socialist realist criticism.

SOCIALIST REALIST NOVEL

See also related term: Socialist realism.

SOCIALIST REALISTS

See also related term: Socialist realism.

SOCIALIST WRITERS

See also related term: Socialism.

SOCIETY

See also narrower terms: Bourgeois society; Patriarchy; Utopia.
See also related terms: Community; Family; Social hierarchy; Social problems.
See also: entries under headings for society in specific countries by consulting the index under the adjectival form of the country.

General literature. Theater.
Role in SOCIETY; relationship to government subsidies. 953.

Literary theory and criticism.
On heteroglossia; relationship to SOCIETY. Theories of Bakhtin, Mikhail Mikhaïlovich. 1429.
On novel; relationship to language; SOCIETY. Theories of Bakhtin, Mikhail Mikhaïlovich. 1319.
Poetics; relationship to human body; SOCIETY. Dissertation abstract. 1510.

Themes and figures. Underworld.
Relationship to technology; SOCIETY; imagination. 2929.

SOCIOCRITICISM

Use: Sociological literary theory and criticism.

SOCIOCULTURAL APPROACH

Documents applying specific approaches are so numerous that access to them is provided only in the electronic versions of the *Bibliography.*

SOCIOECONOMIC APPROACH

Documents applying specific approaches are so numerous that access to them is provided only in the electronic versions of the *Bibliography.*

SOCIOECONOMICS

See also related terms: Economics; Sociology.

SOCIOHISTORICAL APPROACH

Documents applying specific approaches are so numerous that access to them is provided only in the electronic versions of the *Bibliography.*

SOCIOLINGUISTIC APPROACH

Documents applying specific approaches are so numerous that access to them is provided only in the electronic versions of the *Bibliography.*

SOCIOLOGICAL APPROACH

See also related terms: Marxist literary theory and criticism; Sociological literary theory and criticism; Sociology.
Documents applying specific approaches are so numerous that access to them is provided only in the electronic versions of the *Bibliography.*

SOCIOLOGICAL CRITICISM

Use: Sociological literary theory and criticism.

SOCIOLOGICAL LITERARY THEORY AND CRITICISM

See also classified section: 2010 ff.
Used for: Sociocriticism; Sociological criticism.

Genres. Novel. Popular romance novel.
Relationship to women; ideology; treatment in SOCIOLOGICAL LITERARY THEORY AND CRITICISM. 2236.

SOCIOLOGY

Literary theory and criticism. Reception theory.
Role of SOCIOLOGY of communication. 1941.

SOCIOPOLITICAL APPROACH

Documents applying specific approaches are so numerous that access to them is provided only in the electronic versions of the *Bibliography.*

SOCIOPSYCHOLOGICAL APPROACH

Documents applying specific approaches are so numerous that access to them is provided only in the electronic versions of the *Bibliography.*

SOCIOSEMIOTICS

Literary theory and criticism. Semiotic literary theory and criticism.
SOCIOSEMIOTICS. 1955, 2008.

SOLANAS, FERNANDO E. (1936-)

General literature. Film.
Interview with SOLANAS, FERNANDO E. 279.

SOLANAS, FERNANDO E. (1936-)—STUDY EXAMPLE

General literature. Film.
Role of exile; relationship to cultural identity; study example: Ruiz, Raúl: *Les Trois Couronnes du matelot;* SOLANAS, FERNANDO E.: *Tangos—L'Exil de Gardel.* 526.

SOLECISM

See also related term: Linguistic conventions.

SOLO PERFORMANCE
General literature. Theater.
Impersonation in SOLO PERFORMANCE. Dissertation abstract. 944.

SOLOV'EV, NIKOLAĬ (1910-1976)
General literature. Film and television.
Scene design by SOLOV'EV, NIKOLAĬ. 616.

SOLUM, OLA
General literature. Film.
On SOLUM, OLA: *Landstrykere*. 604.

SOMERS, JANE
Use: Lessing, Doris (1919-).

SONG
See also narrower term: Folk song.
See also related terms: Lyric poetry; Lyrics.
General literature. Film.
Role of SONG by fans; relationship to Meyer, Nicholas: *Star Trek II: The Wrath of Khan*. 409.

SONG FESTIVALS
See also related term: Song.

SONG LYRICS
Use: Lyrics.

SOPHISM
Use: Sophistry.

SOPHISTRY
Used for: Sophism.
Literary forms. Rhetoric.
SOPHISTRY; relationship to epistemology; scientific discourse. 2443.

SOPHISTRY—AS SOURCE
Literary forms. Rhetoric.
Paralogism; relationship to dialogism. Sources in SOPHISTRY. Theories of Davidson, Donald; Derrida, Jacques; Bakhtin, Mikhail Mikhaĭlovich. 2462.

SOPHISTS
Literary forms. Rhetoric.
Relationship to SOPHISTS. 2485.

SORCERESS
See also related term: Witch.

SOUND
General literature. Film.
Use of SOUND in Asquith, Anthony: *A Cottage on Dartmoor*; relationship to film history. 590.
—— in Crosland, Alan: *The Jazz Singer* compared to use of Vitaphone in short film. 653.
Genres. Poetry.
SOUND; relationship to music. Dissertation abstract. 2295.

SOUND IMAGERY
See also related term: Sound.

SOUND RECORDING TECHNOLOGY
See also narrower term: Vitaphone.
See also related term: Recordings.

SOUND SYMBOLISM
See also related term: Sound.

SOUTH AFRICA
Professional topics. Censorship in SOUTH AFRICA. 1900-1999. 2589.

SOUTH AMERICA
See also narrower terms: Argentina; Brazil; Chile; Venezuela.

SOUTH ASIA
See also narrower terms: Himalayas; India; Pakistan.

SOUTH CENTRAL UNITED STATES
See also narrower terms: Oklahoma; Texas.

SOUTHEAST ASIA
See also narrower term: Indonesia.

SOUTHEASTERN UNITED STATES
See also narrower term: Virginia.

SOUTHERN AFRICA
See also narrower term: South Africa.

SOUTHERN AMERICAN CULTURE
See also related term: Southern United States.

SOUTHERN AMERICAN LITERATURE
See also related term: Southern United States.

SOUTHERN EUROPE
See also narrower terms: France; Italy; Malta; Spain.

SOUTHERN ITALY
See also narrower term: Sardinia.

SOUTHERN UNITED STATES
Used for: American South.
General literature. Film.
Treatment of women in SOUTHERN UNITED STATES. 488.

SOUTHWESTERN UNITED STATES
See also narrower term: Colorado.

SOVIET ARMY
Bibliographical.
Libraries in Lithuania (1941-1942); relationship to SOVIET ARMY. 1110.

SOVIET POETS
See also narrower term: Constructivism.

SOVIET UNION
Use: U.S.S.R.

SPACE
See also classified section: 2919.
Used for: Poetic space.
See also related term: Spatial metaphor.
General literature.
And art. Role of SPACE. 47.
Role of SPACE. 19, 20.
——. Feminist approach. 97.
——; relationship to setting. 137.
Treatment of SPACE; boundary. 17.
General literature. Theater.
Role of SPACE. 975.
Genres.
Role of SPACE in fragment. 2041.
Genres. Drama and fiction.
Treatment of SPACE; place. 2075.
Genres. Fiction.
Role of SPACE. 2133.
Treatment of SPACE; relationship to the fantastic. 2141.
Genres. Novel. War novel.
Treatment of SPACE. 2251.
Genres. Novel by women novelists.
Treatment of SPACE. 2206.
Literary theory and criticism. Narrative theory.
Relationship to SPACE; voyage. 1808.

SPAIN
See also narrower terms: Galicia (Spain); Salamanca.
Bibliographical. Publishing. Book trade in Latin America and SPAIN. 1298.
General literature. Film in SPAIN. 475, 498.
General literature. Film in SPAIN (1896-1920). 491.

SPANISH CIVIL WAR
See also classified section: 2920.
See also related term: Abraham Lincoln Battalion.
General literature. Film. Film adaptation.
Treatment of SPANISH CIVIL WAR in film adaptation of Spanish novel (1900-1999). 689.

SPANISH HISTORY
General literature. Film.
Treatment of SPANISH HISTORY in Saura, Carlos: *El jardín de las delicias*. Dissertation abstract. 573.

SPANISH LANGUAGE LITERATURE
Professional topics. Research tools.
Relationship to SPANISH LANGUAGE LITERATURE (1900-1999). On electronic publishing. 2828.

SPANISH LANGUAGE TRANSLATION
General literature. Film. Film adaptation.
Role of dubbing in SPANISH LANGUAGE TRANSLATION in film adaptation of Queneau, Raymond: *Zazie dans le métro*. 728.

SPANISH NOVEL
General literature. Film. Film adaptation.
Treatment of Spanish Civil War in film adaptation of SPANISH NOVEL (1900-1999). 689.

SPANOS, WILLIAM V. (1925-)
Literary theory and criticism in *Boundary 2*.
Relationship to Postmodernism. Interview with SPANOS, WILLIAM V. 1332.

SPARTACUS (D. 71 B.C.)
See also classified section: 2921.

SPATIAL FORM
See also related term: Spatiality.
General literature.
SPATIAL FORM; composition compared to architecture. Pedagogical approach. 65.
Genres. Drama.
And theater. SPATIAL FORM. 2077.
Genres. Novel.
SPATIAL FORM compared to dialogism. Theories of Frank, Joseph compared to Bakhtin, Mikhail Mikhaĭlovich. 2221.
Genres. Poetry.
Stanzas; relationship to SPATIAL FORM. 2298.
Literary theory and criticism.
SPATIAL FORM; relationship to temporal structure. 1493.

SEE CLASSIFIED SEQUENCE FOR ADDITIONAL ENTRIES

SPATIAL METAPHOR
See also related term: Space.
 Literary theory and criticism. Feminist literary theory and criticism.
  SPATIAL METAPHOR. 1679.
 Literary theory and criticism. Narrative theory.
  SPATIAL METAPHOR. 1824.

SPATIAL RELATIONS
See also related term: Spatiotemporal relations.

SPATIAL SYMBOLISM
See also related term: Space.

SPATIALITY
See also related term: Spatial form.
 General literature.
  Temporality; SPATIALITY compared to painting. Pedagogical approach. 196.
 General literature. Film. Film genres: animated film.
  SPATIALITY. 762.
 Genres. Fiction.
  Narrative technique; relationship to SPATIALITY. 2150.

SPATIOTEMPORAL RELATIONS
See also related term: Temporal relations.
 General literature. Film. Film theory and criticism.
  SPATIOTEMPORAL RELATIONS; relationship to phenomenology. Application of theories of Heidegger, Martin; Merleau-Ponty, Maurice. Dissertation abstract. 834.
 Genres. Fiction. Fantasy fiction.
  Role of SPATIOTEMPORAL RELATIONS. 2162.

SPECTACLE
 General literature. Film in United States.
  Relationship to SPECTACLE; imperialism. 546.

SPECTATOR
See also related term: Audience.
 General literature. Film. Film theory and criticism.
  SPECTATOR. Theories of Bazin, André; Comolli, Jean-Louis. 819.
  ——; relationship to self-identity. Dissertation abstract. 842.
 General literature. Film and theater.
  Treatment of Bowles, Sally (character); relationship to SPECTATOR. Feminist approach. Dissertation abstract. 501.
 General literature. Theater.
  Relationship to SPECTATOR. Application of reception theory; frame theory. 936.
  Role of director; SPECTATOR. 929.
 Genres. Drama.
  And theater. Role of SPECTATOR; relationship to perspective. Dissertation abstract. 2064.

SPEECH
See also related term: Spoken language.
See also: entries under headings for related terms beginning with the modifier *speech*, e.g., *speech perception, speech rate*, etc.
 Literary theory and criticism. Poststructuralist literary theory and criticism.
  On SPEECH; writing; relationship to electronic language; surveillance. Theories of Foucault, Michel. 1885.

SPEECH ACT THEORY
See also related term: Speech acts.
 Literary theory and criticism.
  SPEECH ACT THEORY. 1417.
 Literary theory and criticism. Linguistic literary theory and criticism.
  Relationship to SPEECH ACT THEORY. Theories of Austin, J. L. 1740.

SPEECH ACT THEORY—APPLICATION
 Genres. Fiction.
  Fictionality. Application of SPEECH ACT THEORY. 2143.

SPEECH ACTS
See also related term: Speech act theory.
 General literature. Film.
  SPEECH ACTS. Application of theories of Peirce, Charles Sanders. 277.
 Literary theory and criticism.
  Mimesis; SPEECH ACTS; relationship to metalanguage. 1383.

SPEECH COMMUNITY
See also related term: Discourse community.

SPEECH UNDERSTANDING
See also related term: Computer.

SPIELBERG, STEVEN (1947-)
 General literature. Film.
  Characterization in SPIELBERG, STEVEN: *Indiana Jones: The Last Crusade.* 454.
  Postmodernism in Coppola, Francis Ford; Lucas, George; DePalma, Brian; SPIELBERG, STEVEN; Scorsese, Martin. Dissertation abstract. 630.

SPIELBERG JEWISH FILM ARCHIVE
Use: Steven Spielberg Jewish Film Archive.

SPINSTER
 Genres. Fiction. 1900-1999.
  Treatment of SPINSTER; relationship to marginality. 2132.

SPIRITUAL AUTOBIOGRAPHY
 Genres. Autobiography.
  Syllogistic form; qualitative form in SPIRITUAL AUTOBIOGRAPHY; study example: Colson, Charles W.: *Born Again.* 2050.

SPIRITUALITY
 General literature. Film.
  Treatment of SPIRITUALITY in Tarkovskiĭ, Andreĭ A. 421.

SPITZER, LEO (1887-1960)
 Literary theory and criticism.
  Relationship to fascism; Romanticism. Theories of Lovejoy, Arthur Oncken; SPITZER, LEO. 1564.

SPIVAK, GAYATRI CHAKRAVORTY (1942-)
 Literary forms. Rhetoric.
  Relationship to culture studies. Interview with SPIVAK, GAYATRI CHAKRAVORTY. 2490.
 Literary theory and criticism.
  Theories of SPIVAK, GAYATRI CHAKRAVORTY. 1422.
 Literary theory and criticism. Feminist literary theory and criticism.
  Theories of SPIVAK, GAYATRI CHAKRAVORTY. Includes interview. 1675.
 Literary theory and criticism. Linguistic literary theory and criticism.
  Theories of SPIVAK, GAYATRI CHAKRAVORTY. Includes interview. 1748, 1749.
 Literary theory and criticism. New Historicism.
  Theories of SPIVAK, GAYATRI CHAKRAVORTY. Includes interview. 1847.
 Literary theory and criticism. Postmodernist literary theory and criticism.
  Theories of SPIVAK, GAYATRI CHAKRAVORTY. Includes interview. 1863.
 Literary theory and criticism. Sociological literary theory and criticism.
  Theories of SPIVAK, GAYATRI CHAKRAVORTY. Includes interview. 2010, 2013, 2016, 2018, 2019.

SPOKEN LANGUAGE
Used for: Oral language.
See also related term: Speech.
 General literature.
  Literary language compared to SPOKEN LANGUAGE. 140.

SPORTS
See also narrower terms: Baseball; Wrestling.

SPY FILM
 General literature. Film. Film genres: SPY FILM.
  Role of Bond, James (character) compared to film by Hitchcock, Alfred. 776.
 General literature. Film. Film genres: SPY FILM in United States.
  Encyclopedia. 781.

STAGE DESIGN
See also related term: Staging.

STAGE DIRECTIONS
See also related terms: Staging; Theatrical production.

STAGE MANAGER
See also related term: Theatrical production.

STAGE PRODUCTION
Use: Theatrical production.

STAGE PROPS
See also related terms: Mise en scène; Staging.

STAGING
See also related terms: Mise en scène; Scene design; Theater; Theatrical production.
 General literature. Theater: opera.
  Symbolism in word; music; STAGING. 938.
 Genres. Drama.
  Role of the visual; relationship to the verbal; STAGING. 2071.
 Genres. Drama. Romantic period.
  STAGING. 2066.

STAINED-GLASS WINDOW
 Literary movements.
  Romanticism. Treatment of STAINED-GLASS WINDOW of church as metaphor for epiphany. 1079.

STANZAS
See also related term: Prosody.
 Genres. Poetry.
  STANZAS; relationship to spatial form. 2298.

STAR SYSTEM
See also related terms: Film industry; Film star.
 General literature. Film in United States (1907-1922).
  Role of STAR SYSTEM. 315.

STARVATION
See also related term: Death.

STASIS
Used for: Status (rhetoric).
 Literary forms. Rhetoric.
  STASIS. Relationship to theories of Perelman, Chaim; Burke, Kenneth. 2451.
  ——; *kairos;* treatment in Classical rhetoric; relationship to social construction. 2433.

STATE
Bibliographical. Publishing in Quebec. 1800-1999.
Relationship to STATE. 1262.

STATISTICAL APPROACH
Documents applying specific approaches are so numerous that access to them is provided only in the electronic versions of the *Bibliography*.

STATIUS (61-96)
Bibliographical. Manuscripts. Manuscript collections.
Of STATIUS in Biblioteca Vallicelliana. 1143.

STATUS (RHETORIC)
Use: Stasis.

STEINER, GEORGE (1929-)
Literary theory and criticism. Hermeneutics and deconstruction.
Relationship to religion. Theories of STEINER, GEORGE. 1728.

STEMMA
See also related term: Manuscripts.
Bibliographical. Manuscripts. Manuscript editing.
STEMMA. Application of graph theory. 1150.

STEPHAN, BROTHER
General literature. Theater: passion play.
Interview with STEPHAN, BROTHER. 972.

STEREOTYPES
Genres. Novel. Popular romance novel.
Treatment of love; relationship to STEREOTYPES; study example: Harlequin Romances. 2233.
Literary theory and criticism. Semiotic literary theory and criticism.
On STEREOTYPES. Theories of Ivanov, Viacheslav Vsevolodovich; Toporov, Vladimir Nikolaevich. 1988.

STERNBERG, JONAS
Use: Sternberg, Josef von (1894-1969).

STERNBERG, JOSEF VON (1894-1969)
Used for: Sternberg, Jonas; Von Sternberg, Josef.
General literature. Film.
Treatment of women; relationship to sexuality; fetishism in STERNBERG, JOSEF VON: *Der blaue Engel*. 579.

STEVEN SPIELBERG JEWISH FILM ARCHIVE
Used for: Spielberg Jewish Film Archive.
General literature. Film.
Treatment of the Holocaust. Catalogue of archives in Israel; relationship to STEVEN SPIELBERG JEWISH FILM ARCHIVE. 584.

STEVENS, GEORGE COOPER (1904-1975)
General literature. Film.
Iterative narrative in Ford, John: *How Green Was My Valley* compared to STEVENS, GEORGE COOPER: *A Place in the Sun*; De Sica, Vittorio: *Umberto D.*; Olmi, Ermanno: *Il posto*. Application of theories of Genette, Gérard. 425.

STEVENSON, CHARLES LESLIE (1908-1979)
Genres. Poetry. Concrete poetry.
Relationship to the visual. Application of theories of STEVENSON, CHARLES LESLIE. 2305.

STIMPSON, CATHARINE R. (1936-)
Professional topics. Humanities.
Multicultural education; relationship to literacy; feminism. Interview with STIMPSON, CATHARINE R. 2657.

STOCK CHARACTERS
General literature. Film.
Treatment of STOCK CHARACTERS in Hollywood film. 320.

STOCKHOLM
Bibliographical. Publishing. Book trade in STOCKHOLM (1782-1801).
Book auction. Dissertation abstract. 1284.

STONE, LUCINDA HINSDALE (1814-1900)—STUDY EXAMPLE
Professional topics. Humanities.
Role of women in academia; study example: STONE, LUCINDA HINSDALE. 2720.

STONE, OLIVER (1946-)
General literature. Film.
Relationship to politics. Interview with STONE, OLIVER. 399.
Treatment of Vietnam War; relationship to historical fact in STONE, OLIVER: *Platoon* compared to Herr, Michael: *Dispatches*. 542.
——; relationship to nihilism in STONE, OLIVER: *Platoon*. 516.
General literature. Film. Film adaptation.
Of Kovic, Ron: *Born on the Fourth of July* by STONE, OLIVER. 709.
General literature. Film. Film genres: war film.
Treatment of Vietnam War in Post, Ted: *Go Tell the Spartans*; STONE, OLIVER: *Platoon*. 749.

STORY
Genres. Fiction.
Narrator; point of view; relationship to STORY; study example: Sandars, Nancy Katharine: *The Epic of Gilgamesh*. Anthropological approach. 2148.

STORY STRUCTURE
See also related term: Story.

STORYTELLING
General literature.
Relationship to STORYTELLING. 60.

STORYTELLING BEHAVIOR
See also related term: Storytelling.

STRATIFICATIONAL APPROACH
Documents applying specific approaches are so numerous that access to them is provided only in the electronic versions of the *Bibliography*.

STRATIFICATIONAL GRAMMAR
See also related term: Linguistic analysis.

STREAM-OF-CONSCIOUSNESS FICTION
See also related term: Consciousness.

STREET THEATER
General literature. Theater.
STREET THEATER. 924, 947, 948.

STRICK, JOSEPH (1923-)
General literature. Film. Film adaptation.
Of Joyce, James: *Ulysses*; *A Portrait of the Artist as a Young Man* by STRICK, JOSEPH compared to Huston, John: *The Dead*; Pearce, Michael: *James Joyce's Women*. 722.

STROHEIM, ERICH VON (1885-1957)
Used for: Von Stroheim, Erich.
General literature. Film. Film adaptation.
On STROHEIM, ERICH VON: *Greed* as film adaptation of Norris, Frank: *McTeague*. Reception study. 687.

STRUCTURAL ELEMENTS
See also narrower terms: Denouement; Epiphany; Formula; Plot; Preface.

STRUCTURAL UNITY
See also related term: Structure.

STRUCTURALISM
See also related terms: Poststructuralism; Structuralist literary theory and criticism.
Literary forms. Rhetoric. 1900-1999.
Relationship to STRUCTURALISM; hermeneutics; deconstructionism. 2417.
Literary theory and criticism. Narrative theory.
On thematic structure; relationship to formalism; STRUCTURALISM. Theories of Propp, Vladimir Iakovlevich compared to Vodička, Felix. 1801.
Literary theory and criticism. Poststructuralist literary theory and criticism.
Relationship to hermeneutics; STRUCTURALISM. Review article. 1878.
Literary theory and criticism. Semiotic literary theory and criticism.
Relationship to STRUCTURALISM. Theories of Mukařovský, Jan. 2000.
—— compared to formalism. Theories of Mukařovský, Jan compared to Zich, Otakar. 2007.

STRUCTURALIST APPROACH
See also related terms: Prague School of Linguistics; Structuralism.
Documents applying specific approaches are so numerous that access to them is provided only in the electronic versions of the *Bibliography*.

STRUCTURALIST CRITICISM
Use: Structuralist literary theory and criticism.

STRUCTURALIST CRITICS
See also related term: Structuralism.

STRUCTURALIST LITERARY THEORY AND CRITICISM
See also classified section: 2023 ff.
Used for: Structuralist criticism.
See also related term: Structuralism.
Literary theory and criticism. Poststructuralist literary theory and criticism and STRUCTURALIST LITERARY THEORY AND CRITICISM.
Relationship to pragmatism. Theories of Derrida, Jacques compared to Dewey, John. 1877.

STRUCTURE
See also narrower terms: Dramatic structure; Narrative structure; Temporal structure; Thematic structure.
See also related term: Form.
General literature.
Role of word; relationship to STRUCTURE. 156.

STUART WORTLEY, VICTORIA ALEXANDRINA MARIA LOUISA
Use: Welby, Victoria, Lady (1837-1912).

STUDENT-TEACHER INTERACTION
Used for: Teacher-student interaction.
See also related term: Teacher.
General literature. Film.
Treatment of STUDENT-TEACHER INTERACTION in Gilbert, Lewis: *Educating Rita* compared to Spark, Muriel: *The Prime of Miss Jean Brodie*; Shaw, George Bernard: *Pygmalion*; Ionesco, Eugène: *La Leçon*. 268.

STUDENTS
See also narrower term: College students.
See also related term: Student-teacher interaction.

STUDIO AUDIENCE
General literature. Television.
Role of STUDIO AUDIENCE. 922.

SEE CLASSIFIED SEQUENCE FOR ADDITIONAL ENTRIES

STUDIO SYSTEM
  General literature. Film.
    Role of collaboration in Cukor, George: *Holiday*; relationship to STUDIO SYS-TEM in Hollywood (1935-1939). 499.

STURGES, PRESTON (1898-1959)
Used for: Biden, Edmund Preston.
  General literature. Film.
    By STURGES, PRESTON. 596.

STURM UND DRANG
See also related term: Romanticism.

STYLE
See also narrower terms: Gothicism; Oral style.
See also related term: Stylistics.
  General literature.
    Framing; relationship to STYLE; ideology. Dissertation abstract. 128.
  General literature. Film.
    STYLE; relationship to realism in Rossellini, Roberto: *Roma, città aperta*. Applica-tion of theories of Metz, Christian. 480.
  General literature. Film in Hollywood (1930-1939).
    STYLE; relationship to semiotics; ideology. Dissertation abstract. 302.
  General literature. Television.
    Treatment of law; relationship to STYLE in *Miami Vice*. 913.
  Literary theory and criticism.
    Mimesis; realism; STYLE. Theories of Auerbach, Erich: *Mimesis*. 1528.
  Literary theory and criticism. Feminist literary theory and criticism.
    STYLE; image; relationship to ideology compared to deconstructionism. 1699.
  Literary theory and criticism. Linguistic literary theory and criticism.
    On STYLE. Application of text linguistics. 1759.
    STYLE. 1745.
  Literary theory and criticism. Psychoanalytic literary theory and criticism.
    STYLE; relationship to the unconscious. 1902.

STYLISTIC ANALYSIS
See also related term: Stylistics.

STYLISTIC APPROACH
See also related term: Stylistics.
Documents applying specific approaches are so numerous that access to them is provided only in the electronic versions of the *Bibliography*.

STYLISTICS

See also related terms: Rhetoric; Style.
  Literary theory and criticism. Linguistic literary theory and criticism.
    STYLISTICS; relationship to linguistic conventions. Theories of Fish, Stanley. 1754.

STYLOMETRIC ANALYSIS
See also related term: Stylistics.

SUASORIA
See also related term: Persuasion.
  Literary forms. Rhetoric.
    SUASORIA; relationship to technical writing. 2488.

THE SUBCONSCIOUS
See also related term: Psychoanalytic theory.

SUBCULTURE
See also related term: Culture.

SUBJECT
  Literary theory and criticism.
    Role of narrative; relationship to SUBJECT in fiction. 1491.
    Role of SUBJECT; relationship to representation. Application of theories of Pas-cal, Blaise; Piles, Roger de. 1470.
  Literary theory and criticism. Semiotic literary theory and criticism.
    And pragmatics; relationship to SUBJECT; subjectivity. 1992.
  Literary theory and criticism. Structuralist literary theory and criticism.
    On SUBJECT; plot. 2031.

SUBJECT INVERSION
See also related term: Subject.

SUBJECT MARKING
See also related term: Subject.

SUBJECT-OBJECT RELATIONS
See also related term: Subjectivity.

SUBJECT OMISSION
See also related term: Subject.

SUBJECT PRONOUN
See also related term: Subject.

SUBJECT RAISING RULE
See also related term: Subject.

SUBJECTIVITY
See also related term: Intersubjectivity.
  General literature. Film.
    Relationship to SUBJECTIVITY of men. Psychoanalytic approach. 578.

SUBJECTIVITY in Duras, Marguerite. Narratological approach. Dissertation ab-stract. 353.
—— in Frampton, Hollis: *(nostalgia)*; *Zorns Lemma*. 580.
  General literature. Film in Hollywood (1933).
    Role of actors as workers; relationship to SUBJECTIVITY. Dissertation abstract. 293.
  Genres. Fiction. Science fiction by feminist writers.
    SUBJECTIVITY; relationship to humanism; Postmodernism. 2180.
  Genres. Novel.
    SUBJECTIVITY; relationship to ideology. Dissertation abstract. 2195.
  Literary theory and criticism.
    On SUBJECTIVITY. 1460.
    SUBJECTIVITY in Barthes, Roland; Foucault, Michel; Derrida, Jacques. Disser-tation abstract. 1344.
    Textuality; SUBJECTIVITY. 1411.
  Literary theory and criticism. Feminist literary theory and criticism.
    SUBJECTIVITY; relationship to gender. Treatment in Irigaray, Luce. 1697.
  Literary theory and criticism. Hermeneutics.
    Role of SUBJECTIVITY; relationship to deconstructionism; humanism. Theories of Hegel, Georg Wilhelm Friedrich compared to Heidegger, Martin; Marx, Karl; Freud, Sigmund. 1716.
  Literary theory and criticism. Poststructuralist literary theory and criticism.
    Role of SUBJECTIVITY; the self; relationship to humanism; New Criticism. Ap-plication of theories of Lacan, Jacques. 1887.
  Literary theory and criticism. Semiotic literary theory and criticism.
    And pragmatics; relationship to subject; SUBJECTIVITY. 1992.

SUBJECTLESS SENTENCE
See also related term: Subject.

SUBLIMATION
See also related term: Sexuality.

THE SUBLIME
See also classified section: 2922 ff.

SUBSTITUTION
  General literature. Film. Film adaptation.
    Treatment of identity; relationship to SUBSTITUTION; exchange in film adapta-tion of Döblin, Alfred: *Berlin Alexanderplatz* by Fassbinder, Rainer Werner. 694.

SUBTITLES
  General literature. Television.
    SUBTITLES; dubbing. 883.
  Literary forms. Translation.
    Of SUBTITLES. 2551.

SUBVERSION
  Literary theory and criticism. Poststructuralist literary theory and criticism.
    Role of SUBVERSION; relationship to ideology of liberalism. Theories of de Man, Paul; Derrida, Jacques. 1884.

SUN
See also related term: Sun goddess.

SUN GODDESS
  Genres. Poetry by women poets.
    Treatment of SUN GODDESS. 2283.

SUPERNATURAL FIGURES
See also narrower terms: Devil; God; Witch.

SUPERWOMAN
  General literature. Television: situation comedy (1980-1985).
    Treatment of women as SUPERWOMAN. 888.

SURREALISM—AS SOURCE
  General literature. Film.
    By Robbe-Grillet, Alain: *La Belle Captive*; *L'Eden et après*. Sources in SURREAL-ISM. 337.

SURREALIST POETRY
See also related term: Surrealism.

SURREALIST WRITERS
See also related term: Surrealism.

SURVEILLANCE
  Literary theory and criticism. Poststructuralist literary theory and criticism.
    On speech; writing; relationship to electronic language; SURVEILLANCE. Theo-ries of Foucault, Michel. 1885.

SUSPENSE
See also related term: Plot.

SUTURE
  General literature. Film.
    Narrative technique; relationship to SUTURE; focalization compared to Joyce, James: *A Portrait of the Artist as a Young Man*. 334.

SUZUKI TADASHI (1939-)
  General literature. Theater.
    Role of Brook, Peter; SUZUKI TADASHI. 939.

SVENSKA LÄKARESÄLLSKAPET
  Bibliographical.
    Role of library of SVENSKA LÄKARESÄLLSKAPET. 1096.

SWAN
See also related term: Swan maiden.

SWAN MAIDEN
Literary forms. Myth.
Of SWAN MAIDEN. Dissertation abstract. 2405.

SWEDEN
See also narrower terms: Stockholm; Visby.
Bibliographical. Printing. Binding.
And illustration in SWEDEN (1989). 1206.

SWIFT, PATRICK
Use: Mackenzie, William Lyon (1795-1861).

SWITZERLAND
See also narrower term: Neuhausen.

SYBERBERG, HANS JÜRGEN (1935-)—STUDY EXAMPLE
General literature. Film in West Germany.
Treatment of mourning; memory; relationship to Third Reich; study example: SYBERBERG, HANS JÜRGEN: *Hitler, ein Film aus Deutschland*; Reitz, Edgar: *Heimat*. 566.

SYLLABARY
See also related term: Writing systems.

SYLLABUS
See also related terms: Curriculum; Teaching.

SYLLOGISM
See also related term: Rhetoric.

SYLLOGISTIC FORM
Genres. Autobiography.
SYLLOGISTIC FORM; qualitative form in spiritual autobiography; study example: Colson, Charles W.: *Born Again*. 2050.

SYMBOL
See also classified section: 2376 ff.
See also related term: Symbolism.
Themes and figures. Space.
As SYMBOL in Modernism. 2919.

SYMBOLISM
See also related terms: Figuration; Symbol.
General literature. Film in Germany.
Theme; relationship to SYMBOLISM. 525.
General literature. Theater: opera.
SYMBOLISM in word; music; staging. 938.

SYMBOLIST MOVEMENT
See also related terms: Symbol; Symbolism.

SYMPATHY
General literature. Film.
Treatment of animals; relationship to SYMPATHY; sentimentality in Annaud, Jean-Jacques: *L'Ours* compared to Disney, Walt. 262.

SYNAESTHESIA
Use: Synesthesia.

SYNCHRONIC APPROACH
Documents applying specific approaches are so numerous that access to them is provided only in the electronic versions of the *Bibliography*.

SYNECDOCHE
See also related term: Metaphor.
Literary movements.
Romanticism. Poetic language; relationship to SYNECDOCHE compared to language of astronomy. Application of theories of Newton, Sir Isaac compared to Herschel, Sir William. 1077.

SYNESTHESIA
Used for: Sense analogy; Synaesthesia.
Literary theory and criticism.
SYNESTHESIA. Theories of Richards, I. A. Dissertation abstract. 1418.

SYNTACTIC APPROACH
Documents applying specific approaches are so numerous that access to them is provided only in the electronic versions of the *Bibliography*.

SYNTACTIC CATEGORIES
See also narrower term: Subject.

SYNTAX
See also related term: Voice.

SYRUC, J.
Use: Miłosz, Czesław (1911-).

SYSTEM
Literary theory and criticism.
On literature as SYSTEM. 1525.

SZONDI, PETER (1929-1971)
Literary theory and criticism. Hermeneutics.
Theories of SZONDI, PETER. 1712.

TABLOID TELEVISION
General literature. Television.
TABLOID TELEVISION; study example: *A Current Affair*. 869.

TAGMEMICS
See also related term: Linguistic analysis.

TALE
See also narrower term: Folk tale.
See also related terms: *Märchen*; Short story.

TALK SHOW
See also related terms: Radio; Television.

TALL TALE
See also related terms: Folk tale; Jokes; Legend; Myth.

TANHAIYAN
General literature. Television in Pakistan (1985-1989).
Treatment of gender; relationship to Pakistani society in *Dewareen*; *TANHAIYAN*. Dissertation abstract. 919.

TARGET LITERATURE
Literary forms. Translation.
Role in canon of TARGET LITERATURE; relationship to secondary education in Germany. 2549.

TARGET TEXT
Literary forms. Translation. Translation theory.
Role of interpretation; reference; relationship to analysis of TARGET TEXT. 2575.

TARKOVSKIĬ, ANDREĬ A. (1932-1986)
General literature. Film.
Dream imagery in TARKOVSKIĬ, ANDREĬ A.: *Zerkalo*; *Stalker*. 522.
On TARKOVSKIĬ, ANDREĬ A.: *Offret*; relationship to Josephson, Erland: *En natt i den svenska sommaren*. 592.
Representation in TARKOVSKIĬ, ANDREĬ A.: *Offret*. 445.
Treatment of childhood; nostalgia; relationship to homeland in TARKOVSKIĬ, ANDREĬ A.: *Ivanovo detstvo*; *Nostalghia*; *Offret* compared to Brodskiĭ, Iosif Aleksandrovich; Chagall, Marc. 551.
Treatment of loss of humanism; home in TARKOVSKIĬ, ANDREĬ A.: *Nostalghia*. 477.
Treatment of spirituality in TARKOVSKIĬ, ANDREĬ A. 421.

TARTU SCHOOL
Literary theory and criticism. Semiotic literary theory and criticism by TARTU SCHOOL (1960-1969). 1972.

TATI, JACQUES (1907-1982)
General literature. Film.
On TATI, JACQUES: *Parade*. 610.

TAVIANI, PAOLO (1931-)
General literature. Film.
By TAVIANI, PAOLO and Taviani, Vittorio. 259.
General literature. Film. Film adaptation.
Treatment of Sardinia in film adaptation of Ledda, Gavino: *Padre padrone* by TAVIANI, PAOLO and Taviani, Vittorio. 674.

TAVIANI, VITTORIO (1929-)
General literature. Film.
By Taviani, Paolo and TAVIANI, VITTORIO. 259.
General literature. Film. Film adaptation.
Treatment of Sardinia in film adaptation of Ledda, Gavino: *Padre padrone* by Taviani, Paolo and TAVIANI, VITTORIO. 674.

TAXONOMIC APPROACH
See also related term: Linguistic analysis.
Documents applying specific approaches are so numerous that access to them is provided only in the electronic versions of the *Bibliography*.

TEACHER
See also classified section: 2924.
See also related terms: Student-teacher interaction; Teacher training.

TEACHER-STUDENT INTERACTION
Use: Student-teacher interaction.

TEACHER TRAINING
See also related terms: Teacher; Teaching.
Professional topics. Comparative literature.
World literature; relationship to TEACHER TRAINING in East Germany. 2607.

TEACHING
See also narrower terms: Teaching of language; Teaching of literature; Teaching of reading; Teaching of translation; Teaching of writing.
See also related terms: Pedagogy; Teacher training.
General literature.
On translation; relationship to TEACHING. 194.
General literature. Film.
On Hudson, Hugh: *Chariots of Fire*; relationship to TEACHING. 473.
Genres. Short story.
Role of schema theory in TEACHING. Psycholinguistic approach. Dissertation abstract. 2344.
Professional topics. Humanities.
On peer review; letters of recommendation; relationship to TEACHING; research. 2800.

SEE CLASSIFIED SEQUENCE FOR ADDITIONAL ENTRIES

TEACHING ASSISTANTS
Professional topics. Humanities.
Training of TEACHING ASSISTANTS. 2695.

TEACHING OF LANGUAGE
See also narrower term: Second language teaching.
See also: entries under headings for specific language teaching, e.g., English language teaching, French language teaching, etc.
Professional topics. Humanities.
Role of teaching of literature in TEACHING OF LANGUAGE. 2711.

TEACHING OF LITERARY THEORY
Professional topics. Humanities.
TEACHING OF LITERARY THEORY. 2693.

TEACHING OF LITERATURE
Literary theory and criticism.
Application in TEACHING OF LITERATURE. 1553.
Relationship to TEACHING OF LITERATURE. 1483.
——. Dissertation abstract. 1461.
Role in TEACHING OF LITERATURE. 1409.
Literary theory and criticism. Feminist literary theory and criticism.
Applied to TEACHING OF LITERATURE. 1689.
Literary theory and criticism. Reader-response theory and criticism and poststructuralist literary theory and criticism.
Applied to TEACHING OF LITERATURE; study example: Clemens, Samuel: *The Adventures of Huckleberry Finn*; Douglass, Frederick: *Narrative of the Life of Frederick Douglass*. 1928.
Professional topics. Computer-assisted research.
Oxford Concordance program; application in TEACHING OF LITERATURE. 2638, 2643.
Professional topics. Humanities.
Application of discourse analysis in TEACHING OF LITERATURE. 2807.
Literacy; relationship to TEACHING OF LITERATURE. 2770.
Role of irony; relationship to canon in TEACHING OF LITERATURE. 2672.
Role of popular culture; relationship to TEACHING OF LITERATURE. 2696.
Role of TEACHING OF LITERATURE in teaching of language. 2711.
Role of writing of fiction in TEACHING OF LITERATURE. 2713.
TEACHING OF LITERATURE. 2663, 2664, 2692, 2700.
——; relationship to canon. 2717.
——; relationship to feminism. 2814.
——; relationship to metalinguistic awareness. Dissertation abstract. 2660.
——; relationship to orality. 2801.
——; relationship to poststructuralism. 2688.
Use of *Märchen*; literature for children in TEACHING OF LITERATURE. Dissertation abstract. 2701.

TEACHING OF READING
See also related term: Reading.
Professional topics. Humanities.
On TEACHING OF READING; teaching of writing; relationship to authority. 2704.

TEACHING OF TRANSLATION
See also related term: Translation.
Professional topics. Humanities.
TEACHING OF TRANSLATION. 2678.
—— at American universities. 2669.

TEACHING OF WRITING
See also narrower term: Writing across the curriculum.
See also related terms: Discourse community; Writing.
Figures of speech.
Relationship to TEACHING OF WRITING. 2346.
Genres. Fiction.
Role of the fantastic; relationship to TEACHING OF WRITING. 2139.
Literary forms. Dialogue in narrative.
Compared to dramatic dialogue; relationship to TEACHING OF WRITING. 2383.
Literary forms. Rhetoric.
Relationship to TEACHING OF WRITING. 2438.
Rhetorical theory; relationship to TEACHING OF WRITING. On empirical approach. 2486.
Social construction; relationship to TEACHING OF WRITING. Theories of Bruffee, Kenneth A. 2452.
Literary theory and criticism.
Cultural criticism; relationship to TEACHING OF WRITING. 1326.
Literary theory and criticism. Poststructuralist literary theory and criticism.
Application in TEACHING OF WRITING; relationship to epistemology. Application of theories of Derrida, Jacques; Husserl, Edmund. Dissertation abstract. 1879.
Professional topics. Humanities.
On teaching of reading; TEACHING OF WRITING; relationship to authority. 2704.
On TEACHING OF WRITING; relationship to cultural context. Dissertation abstract. 2705.
Role of collaborative learning; relationship to TEACHING OF WRITING. 2813.
TEACHING OF WRITING. 2756.
——. Dissertation abstract. 2781.
——; relationship to fiction compared to prose. 2680.

TEACHING OF WRITING; relationship to imitation of poetry. 2687.
TECHNICAL LANGUAGE
See also related term: Technical writing.
TECHNICAL WRITING
Literary forms. Rhetoric.
Suasoria; relationship to TECHNICAL WRITING. 2488.
TECHNIQUE
See also narrower terms: Abstraction; Argumentation; Burlesque; Characterization; Description; Figuration; Focalization; Framing; Gaps; Hypertextuality; Intertextuality; Mimesis; *Mise en abyme*; Mythification; Narration; Narrative technique; Perspective; Point of view; Polyphony; Realism; Referentiality; Repetition; Satire; Setting; Style; Symbolism; Travesty; Verisimilitude.
See also related terms: Cinematic technique; Structure.
TECHNOLOGY
See also related terms: Machines; Science.
General literature. Film.
Relationship to Cold War; TECHNOLOGY. 435.
General literature for children.
Treatment of science; TECHNOLOGY. Reference guide. 113.
Literary theory and criticism. Deconstructionism.
Role of language; relationship to TECHNOLOGY. Theories of Derrida, Jacques: *De la grammatologie* compared to Heidegger, Martin: "Die Frage nach der Technik." 1584.
Professional topics. Humanities.
Relationship to vocation; TECHNOLOGY. 2723.
Themes and figures. Underworld.
Relationship to TECHNOLOGY; society; imagination. 2929.

TEENAGERS
See also related term: Adolescents.
TELENOVELA
See also related term: Soap opera.
TELEPLAY
Use: Television drama.
TELEVISION
See also related terms: British Broadcasting Corporation; Docudrama; National Broadcasting Company; Popular culture; Radiodiffusion-Télévision Française; Situation comedy; Television adaptation; Television drama; Television viewer.
General literature. Film.
On Fassbinder, Rainer Werner: *Berlin Alexanderplatz*; relationship to TELEVISION in West Germany. Dissertation abstract. 574.
Treatment of history; relationship to war; TELEVISION. 513.
General literature. Film. Film adaptation.
And TELEVISION in Great Britain (1959-1963). Realism; relationship to working class life in film adaptation; television adaptation of drama; fiction. 711.
General literature. Film. Film genres: detective film.
And TELEVISION; hard-boiled detective fiction. Treatment of private eye. Reference guide. 751.
General literature. Film. Film genres: documentary film for TELEVISION.
Cinéma vérité in film by Drew Associates. Dissertation abstract. 768.
General literature. Film. Film genres: science fiction film.
And TELEVISION; relationship to women as fans. Ethnography. Dissertation abstract. 746.
General literature. Film and TELEVISION.
Melodrama. Treatment of Vietnam War in Ashby, Hal: *Coming Home*; *China Beach*. 485.
On Lynch, David: *Twin Peaks*; *Blue Velvet*; Scorsese, Martin: *GoodFellas*; relationship to *film noir*. 396.
General literature. Film and TELEVISION (1980-1989).
Treatment of Texas compared to treatment in McMurtry, Larry. 565.
General literature. Film and TELEVISION in United States (1954-1963).
Treatment of family. Dissertation abstract. 446.
General literature. Radio and TELEVISION.
Treatment of Lone Ranger as hero. 845.
General literature. Theater.
Circus on TELEVISION. Semiotic approach. 931.
Literary theory and criticism. Postmodernist literary theory and criticism.
Relationship to feminism; TELEVISION. 1866.

TELEVISION ADAPTATION
See also related terms: Television; Television drama.
General literature. Film. Film adaptation.
And TELEVISION ADAPTATION of Wharton, Edith. 714.
And television in Great Britain (1959-1963). Realism; relationship to working class life in film adaptation; TELEVISION ADAPTATION of drama; fiction. 711.
Treatment of Scrooge, Ebenezer (character) in Dickens, Charles: *A Christmas Carol* compared to TELEVISION ADAPTATION; theatrical production; cartoons. 686.
General literature. Film. Film adaptation and TELEVISION ADAPTATION.
Role of videotape in criticism of adaptation of Shakespeare, William. Dissertation abstract. 725.
General literature. Television.
Role of genre; relationship to TELEVISION ADAPTATION of Shakespeare, William: *Twelfth Night* compared to theatrical production. 905.

TELEVISION ADAPTATION of Michener, James A.: *Space*; relationship to popular culture. 903.
—— of Waugh, Evelyn: *Brideshead Revisited*. Dissertation abstract. 848
Treatment of femininity; narcissism in *Moonlighting* as TELEVISION ADAPTATION of Shakespeare, William: *The Taming of the Shrew*. Feminist approach. 908.

TELEVISION COMMERCIALS
See also related term: Television.

TELEVISION CRITICISM
General literature. Television.
TELEVISION CRITICISM in newspapers. Dissertation abstract. 890.

TELEVISION DRAMA
Used for: Teleplay.
See also related terms: Situation comedy; Television; Television adaptation.
General literature. Film and television.
Role of screenplay; TELEVISION DRAMA. Pedagogical approach. 621.

TELEVISION INTERVIEW
See also related term: Television.

TELEVISION STUDIES
General literature. Television in Great Britain.
Role of quality; relationship to TELEVISION STUDIES; film studies. 860.

TELEVISION THEORY
General literature. Film. Film theory and criticism in East Germany.
And TELEVISION THEORY; relationship to socialism. 832.

TELEVISION VIEWER
See also related term: Television.
General literature. Television.
Relationship to TELEVISION VIEWER. 893.
General literature. Television: serial drama.
Representation of luxury; relationship to TELEVISION VIEWER. 898.

TELEVISION WORKSHOP
General literature. Television in Great Britain.
Role of TELEVISION WORKSHOP. 894.

TEMPLES
See also related term: Church.

TEMPO
See also related term: Rhythm.

TEMPORAL EXPRESSION
See also related term: Time.

TEMPORAL RELATIONS
See also related term: Spatiotemporal relations.
Genres. Fiction.
Perspective; relationship to TEMPORAL RELATIONS. Dissertation abstract. 2110.

TEMPORAL STRUCTURE
See also related terms: Chronotope; Temporality; Time.
Literary theory and criticism.
Spatial form; relationship to TEMPORAL STRUCTURE. 1493.

TEMPORAL TERMS
See also related term: Time.

TEMPORALITY
See also related terms: Temporal structure; Time.
General literature.
TEMPORALITY; spatiality compared to painting. Pedagogical approach. 196.
—— in narrative. 178.
General literature. Film. Film genres: silent film in United States and Russian S.F.S.R.
Melodrama; relationship to TEMPORALITY. Theories of Benjamin, Walter. 757.
General literature. Television.
Role of TEMPORALITY. Theories of Hoggart, Richard. 850.
Genres. Drama.
As narrative; relationship to TEMPORALITY. 2091.

TENURE
Professional topics. Humanities.
On TENURE of faculty in English departments. 2721.

TERATOLOGY
See also related term: Monsters.

TERENCE (CA. 195-159/8 B.C.)
Used for: Afer, Publius Terentius; Terentius Afer, Publius.
Bibliographical. Printing (1503-1767).
Of editions of TERENCE. Bibliography. 1190.

TERENTIUS AFER, PUBLIUS
Use: Terence (ca. 195-159/8 B.C.).

TERMINOLOGICAL DATABASE
See also related term: Terminology.

TERMINOLOGICAL DICTIONARY
See also related term: Terminology.

TERMINOLOGY
Used for: Nomenclature.

See also narrower term: Literary terms.
Literary theory and criticism.
Handbook of TERMINOLOGY. 1467.
TERMINOLOGY. 1395.
Literary theory and criticism. Deconstructionism.
Relationship to poststructuralism. TERMINOLOGY. 1620.

TERROR
See also related term: Fear.

TERROR FICTION
Use: Horror fiction.

TERRORISM
Genres. Drama.
Treatment of TERRORISM. 2062, 2069.
——. Bibliography. 2096.
——. Sociological approach. 2085.
Treatment of violence; TERRORISM. 2074.
Genres. Drama. 1900-1999.
Treatment of TERRORISM; relationship to government. 2068.

TERZA RIMA
See also related term: Rhyme.

TESSA, DELIO (1886-1939)
General literature. Film. Film theory and criticism.
Theories of TESSA, DELIO. 843.

TESTIMONIAL LITERATURE
See also related term: Social change.

TESTIMONIAL NOVEL
See also related terms: Social change; Social novel.

TESTIMONY
See also related term: Law.

TEX—APPLICATION
Bibliographical. Publishing. Editing.
Role of format for critical edition. Application of EDMAC; TEX. 1301.

TEXAS
General literature. Film and television (1980-1989).
Treatment of TEXAS compared to treatment in McMurtry, Larry. 565.

TEXT
See also related terms: Textual analysis; Textuality.
Bibliographical. Textual criticism.
Role of TEXT compared to role in deconstructionism. 1121.
General literature.
Role of TEXT in musical adaptation. Interview with Henry, Pierre. 69.
—— in musical composition. 84.
—— in musical composition. Interview with Boucourechliev, André. 68.
TEXT; relationship to culture. 73.
——; relationship to extratextuality. Dissertation abstract. 126.
General literature. Theater.
Relationship to TEXT. Semiotic approach. 978.
Visual imagery; relationship to TEXT; Postmodernism in performance art by Anderson, Laurie. 958.
Genres. Drama.
Role of TEXT; relationship to theatrical production. Semiotic approach. 2086.
Genres. Fiction.
Role of writer; relationship to reader; TEXT. Philosophical approach. 2116.
Literary theory and criticism.
Relationship to TEXT. Theories of Barthes, Roland. 1560.
Role of TEXT. Theories of Foucault, Michel: "Qu'est-ce qu'un auteur?"; *Folie et déraison*; Derrida, Jacques: "La Pharmacie de Platon." 1555.
——; relationship to cultural context. Theories of Barthes, Roland. 1488.
TEXT; relationship to liturgy of Russian Orthodox Church. Relationship to theories of Bakhtin, Mikhail Mikhaĭlovich; Florenskiĭ, Pavel Aleksandrovich: *Stolp i utverzhdenie istiny*; Kedrov, Konstantin Aleksandrovich: *Poėticheskiĭ kosmos*. 1558.
Literary theory and criticism. Poststructuralist literary theory and criticism.
On TEXT. 1883.

TEXT CONTRACTION
See also related term: Text.

TEXT INTERPRETATION
See also related terms: Text; Text linguistics.

TEXT LINGUISTICS—APPLICATION
Genres. Fiction. Detective fiction.
Application of TEXT LINGUISTICS. 2161.
Literary theory and criticism. Linguistic literary theory and criticism.
On style. Application of TEXT LINGUISTICS. 1759.

TEXT MEANING
See also related term: Text.

TEXT REPRESENTATION
See also related terms: Text; Text linguistics.

TEXT STRUCTURE
See also related term: Text.

TEXTBOOK
See also narrower term: Logic textbook.
  Literary theory and criticism. Reception theory.
    Applied to TEXTBOOK. 1942.

TEXTUAL ANALYSIS
Used for: Textual explication.
See also related terms: Interpretation; Text.
  General literature.
    TEXTUAL ANALYSIS. 142.

TEXTUAL BIBLIOGRAPHY
Use: Textual criticism.

TEXTUAL CRITICISM
See also classified section: 1120 ff.
Used for: Critical bibliography; Textual bibliography.
See also narrower term: Textual editing.
See also related term: Critical edition.
  Literary theory and criticism.
    Especially TEXTUAL CRITICISM; relationship to philology. 1366.
  Literary theory and criticism. Middle Ages.
    Relationship to TEXTUAL CRITICISM; Latin language literature. Review article.
    1576.

TEXTUAL EDITING
Used for: Critical editing; Textual emendation.
  Bibliographical. Textual criticism.
    TEXTUAL EDITING. 1120.

TEXTUAL EMENDATION
Use: Textual editing.

TEXTUAL EXPLICATION
Use: Textual analysis.

TEXTUAL REVISION
See also related term: Textual criticism.

TEXTUAL VARIANTS
See also related term: Textual criticism.

TEXTUALITY
See also related term: Text.
  General literature.
    Role of the real; relationship to reading; TEXTUALITY. 10.
  Genres. Drama.
    TEXTUALITY; relationship to poststructuralism. Dissertation abstract. 2080.
  Literary theory and criticism.
    Role of TEXTUALITY. Treatment in de Man, Paul; relationship to Empson, William. 1428.
    TEXTUALITY; subjectivity. 1411.
  Literary theory and criticism. Reader-response theory and criticism.
    Relationship to TEXTUALITY. 1921.
  Literary theory and criticism. Sociological literary theory and criticism.
    Role of social discourse; relationship to semiotics; ideology; TEXTUALITY. 2012.

THEATER
See also narrower terms: Musical theater; Opera; Performance art; Popular theater; Street theater; Theater of the absurd; Vaudeville.
See also related terms: Acting; Actors; Drama; Performance; Scene design; Staging; Theater history; Theater studies; Theater theory; Theatrical adaptation; Theatrical production.
See also: entries for theater in specific countries by consulting the index under the adjectival form of the country.
  General literature. Film.
    And comic strip; THEATER; relationship to popular culture (1895-1903). 230.
  General literature. Film and THEATER.
    Role of Ĕĭzenshteĭn, Sergeĭ Mikhaĭlovich. 441.
    Treatment of Bowles, Sally (character); relationship to spectator. Feminist approach. Dissertation abstract. 501.
  Genres. Drama.
    And THEATER. 2072, 2093.
    ——. Role of spectator; relationship to perspective. Dissertation abstract. 2064.
    ——. Spatial form. 2077.
    ——. Treatment of reality in performance. 2073.
  Genres. Drama by black dramatists.
    And THEATER. Bibliography. 2098.
  Literary theory and criticism. Semiotic literary theory and criticism.
    Applied to THEATER. 1982.

THEATER COMPANIES
See also related term: Theater.

THEATER CRITICISM
See also related terms: Literary theory and criticism; Theater.

THEATER CRITICS
See also related term: Theater.

THEATER HISTORY
See also related term: Theater.
  General literature. Theater.
    THEATER HISTORY; relationship to literary history. 955.

THEATER OF THE ABSURD
See also classified section: 2101.
See also related terms: The absurd; Existentialism.

THEATER STUDIES
See also related term: Theater.
  General literature. Theater.
    Role of THEATER STUDIES. 982.

THEATER TERMS
See also related term: Theater.

THEATER THEORY
Used for: Theatrical theory.
See also related term: Theater.
  General literature. Theater.
    Role of THEATER THEORY applied to performance compared to science; quantum theory applied to nature. 968.

THEATERS
See also related term: Theater.

THEATRICAL ADAPTATION
See also related terms: Dramatic adaptation; Theater.
  General literature. Film. Film adaptation.
    Role of gender compared to THEATRICAL ADAPTATION of Brontë, Charlotte: *Jane Eyre.* 721.

THEATRICAL CONVENTIONS
See also related term: Theater.

THEATRICAL IMAGERY
See also related term: Theater.

THEATRICAL METAPHOR
See also related term: Theater.

THEATRICAL PRODUCTION
Used for: Stage production.
See also related terms: Staging; Theater.
  General literature. Film. Film adaptation.
    Treatment of Scrooge, Ebenezer (character) in Dickens, Charles: *A Christmas Carol* compared to television adaptation; THEATRICAL PRODUCTION; cartoons. 686.
  General literature. Television.
    Role of genre; relationship to television adaptation of Shakespeare, William: *Twelfth Night* compared to THEATRICAL PRODUCTION. 905.
  General literature. Theater.
    Representation of nature in THEATRICAL PRODUCTION; relationship to Realist movement and Naturalism. Theories of Darwin, Charles Robert; Le Brun, Charles. 960.
  Genres. Drama.
    Collaboration in writing; THEATRICAL PRODUCTION. Dissertation abstract. 2084.
    Role of text; relationship to THEATRICAL PRODUCTION. Semiotic approach. 2086.

THEATRICAL THEORY
Use: Theater theory.

THEMATIC PROGRESSION
See also related term: Theme.

THEMATIC STRUCTURE
See also related term: Theme.
  General literature.
    THEMATIC STRUCTURE; relationship to semantics. 175.
  Literary theory and criticism. Narrative theory.
    On THEMATIC STRUCTURE; relationship to formalism; structuralism. Theories of Propp, Vladimir Iakovlevich compared to Vodička, Felix. 1801.

THEMATIC UNITY
See also related term: Theme.

THEMATIZATION
  General literature.
    THEMATIZATION. 31.

THEME
See also related term: Thematic structure.
  General literature. Film in Germany.
    THEME; relationship to symbolism. 525.
  Literary theory and criticism in Canada.
    Role of THEME; relationship to ethnic literature. 1473.

THEMES AND FIGURES
See also classified section: 2831 ff.
See also narrower term: Figures.

THEOCRITUS (CA. 310-250 B.C.)—AS SOURCE
  Genres. Novel.
    Treatment of love. Sources in THEOCRITUS: *Idylls.* 2200.

THEODORE OF MOPSUESTIA (350-429)—AS SOURCE
  Genres. Prose. Devotional literature.
    Treatment of liturgical formulas. Sources in Chrysostom, John: *De Sancta Pentecoste;* THEODORE OF MOPSUESTIA: *Homiliae Catecheticae;* Pseudo-Epiphanius of Salamis: *Homilia in Diuini Corporis Sepulturam.* 2318.

THEOLOGIANS
See also related term: Theology.

THEOLOGICAL APPROACH
Documents applying specific approaches are so numerous that access to them is provided only in the electronic versions of the *Bibliography*.

THEOLOGICAL PROSE
Use: Religious prose.

THEOLOGY
See also related term: Religion.
  Literary theory and criticism.
    Role of de Man, Paul; relationship to THEOLOGY. 1424.
  Literary theory and criticism. Hermeneutics.
    Theories of Hirsch, Eric Donald applied to THEOLOGY. Dissertation abstract. 1729.

THEORY
See also narrower terms: Feminism; Film theory and criticism; Mathematical theory.

THERAPY
See also narrower term: Psychotherapy.
  Genres. Novel.
    Relationship to THERAPY for reader. 2198, 2225.
  Genres. Poetry.
    As THERAPY; relationship to psychiatry. 2273.

THERMIDOR
See also related term: French Revolution.

THEWELEIT, KLAUS
  Literary theory and criticism. Psychoanalytic literary theory and criticism.
    On fascism. Treatment in THEWELEIT, KLAUS: *Männerphantasien*; relationship to theories of Heidegger, Martin: *Einführung in die Metaphysik*. 1906.

THIERRY, AUGUSTIN (1795-1856)
  General literature.
    Relationship to history. Theories of THIERRY, AUGUSTIN; Michelet, Jules. 91.

THIRD PERSON NARRATION
  Genres. Fiction.
    THIRD PERSON NARRATION. Application of theories of Genette, Gérard. 2147.

THIRD REICH
See also related term: Nazism.
  General literature. Film.
    On Kluge, Alexander and Schamoni, Peter: *Brutalität im Stein*; relationship to film during THIRD REICH. 538.
    Treatment of aristocracy; relationship to THIRD REICH in Baky, Josef von: *Münchhausen*; Kästner, Erich: *Baron Münchhausen*. 291.
  General literature. Film. Film genres: documentary film in Germany during THIRD REICH. 795.
  General literature. Film in West Germany.
    Treatment of mourning; memory; relationship to THIRD REICH; study example: Syberberg, Hans Jürgen: *Hitler, ein Film aus Deutschland*; Reitz, Edgar: *Heimat*. 566.

THIRD WORLD
See also related term: Third World literature.
  General literature in THIRD WORLD. 1900-1999.
    Marxist approach. 103.

THIRD WORLD LITERATURE
See also related term: Third World.
  Literary theory and criticism.
    Relationship to THIRD WORLD LITERATURE. 1478.

THIRD WORLD NOVEL
See also related term: Third World.

THOMAS AQUINAS, SAINT (1225?-1274)
  Literary theory and criticism. Semiotic literary theory and criticism.
    Isomorphism; similarity. Theories of Augustine, Saint; THOMAS AQUINAS, SAINT; Peirce, Charles Sanders. 1960.

THOMPSON, EDWARD PALMER (1924-)
  Literary theory and criticism.
    Relationship to culture studies. Theories of THOMPSON, EDWARD PALMER; Hobsbawm, Eric J. 1335.

THORNTON, LESLIE
  General literature. Film.
    On THORNTON, LESLIE: *Adynata*. 518.

THE THOUSAND AND ONE NIGHTS
Used for: Alf laylah wa-laylah; The Arabian Nights Entertainments.

THE THOUSAND AND ONE NIGHTS—AS SOURCE
  Genres. Fiction.
    Interpretive frame. Sources in *THE THOUSAND AND ONE NIGHTS*. Dissertation abstract. 2144.

THREE-DIMENSIONAL PICTURES
  Bibliographical. Printing. Illustration in Germany. 1900-1999.
    By Dreyer, Erich; Wendt, Max of THREE-DIMENSIONAL PICTURES. 1217.

THRESHOLD
  Genres. Novel.
    And film. Treatment of THRESHOLD; relationship to the sacred; the profane. 2203.

TIANANMEN SQUARE
  General literature. Film in China.
    Relationship to massacre in TIANANMEN SQUARE. 585.

TIME
See also classified section: 2925.
See also narrower terms: The future; Narrative time; The past.
See also related terms: Kairos; Temporal structure; Temporality; Time travel.
  Literary movements.
    Postmodernism. Relationship to TIME. 1069.
  Literary theory and criticism.
    Role of death in TIME. Theories of Heidegger, Martin compared to Levinas, Emmanuel. 1351.
    Role of the apocalypse; relationship to TIME. Theories of Levinas, Emmanuel: *Totalité et infini*. 1567.
    Role of the future; TIME. 1575.
  Literary theory and criticism. Deconstructionism.
    Role of TIME; consciousness. Treatment in Derrida, Jacques: *La Voix et le phénomène*; relationship to Husserl, Edmund. Dissertation abstract. 1582.
  Literary theory and criticism. Psychoanalytic literary theory and criticism.
    On life as narrative; relationship to TIME. Theories of Freud, Sigmund; Sartre, Jean-Paul; Rorty, Richard. 1896.
  Literary theory and criticism. Reader-response theory and criticism.
    Role of TIME; difference in generations; relationship to reading. 1939.

TIME TRAVEL
See also related term: Time.
  General literature. Film. Film genres: science fiction film.
    Treatment of TIME TRAVEL; primal scene; dystopia in Cameron, James: *The Terminator*. 792.

TIMELESSNESS
See also related term: Time.

TITANIC
  General literature. Film.
    Treatment of TITANIC; relationship to Hitchcock, Alfred; Selznick, David O. 567.

TITLES
See also narrower terms: Subtitles; Work title.

TOMASHEVSKIĬ, BORIS VIKTOROVICH (1890-1957)
  Genres. Poetry.
    Rhythm; meter; relationship to semantics. Theories of TOMASHEVSKIĬ, BORIS VIKTOROVICH. 2294.

TONKIN, HUMPHREY (1939-)
  Literary forms. Translation.
    Esperanto language translation. Interview with TONKIN, HUMPHREY. 2526.

TOPICS OF PROFESSIONAL INTEREST
See also related term: Teaching of language.

TOPOROV, VLADIMIR NIKOLAEVICH
  Literary theory and criticism. Semiotic literary theory and criticism.
    On stereotypes. Theories of Ivanov, Viacheslav Vsevolodovich; TOPOROV, VLADIMIR NIKOLAEVICH. 1988.

TOPOS
  Figures of speech.
    And TOPOS. 2348.
  General literature.
    Role of TOPOS; relationship to application of computer. 120.
    TOPOS. 49.
    ——; relationship to *dénarré*. 173.

TORAH
See also related term: Judaism.

TOROK, MARIA (1925-)
  Literary theory and criticism. Psychoanalytic literary theory and criticism.
    Role of Oedipus complex. Theories of Abraham, Nicolas and TOROK, MARIA compared to Freud, Sigmund; Lacan, Jacques. Review article. 1909.

TOTALITARIANISM
  General literature. Film. Film genres: science fiction film.
    Treatment of TOTALITARIANISM in Lucas, George: *THX-1138* compared to Plato: *Politeia*. 753.

TOUCHARD, PIERRE-AIMÉ (1903-1987)
  General literature. Television.
    Role of TOUCHARD, PIERRE-AIMÉ at Radiodiffusion-Télévision Française. 859.

TOURISM
  General literature. Film in New Zealand.
    Treatment of TOURISM; ethnography; relationship to Maori in McDonald, James. 264.

SEE CLASSIFIED SEQUENCE FOR ADDITIONAL ENTRIES

TOURNEUR, JACQUES (1904-)
   General literature. Film.
      Cinematic technique in TOURNEUR, JACQUES: *Cat People*. Psychoanalytic approach. 452.
      Role of TOURNEUR, JACQUES. 247
      Treatment of femininity; relationship to masquerade in TOURNEUR, JACQUES: *Anne of the Indies*. 411.

TRADE
See also narrower term: Book trade.
See also related term: Trademark.

TRADEMARK
   Bibliographical. Publishing. Book trade.
      TRADEMARK of Kellam, Laurence. 1297.

TRADITION
   Professional topics. Humanities.
      Relationship to TRADITION. Application of theories of Benjamin, Walter; Williams, Raymond. 2654.

TRADITIONALISM
See also related term: Tradition.

TRAGEDY
See also classified section: 2504 ff.
See also related terms: Tragic drama; Tragicomedy.
   Genres. Poetry.
      Relationship to TRAGEDY. Sources in Ancient Greek literature. 2291.

TRAGIC DRAMA
See also classified section: 2102.
See also related terms: Tragedy; Tragicomedy.

TRAGIC FALL
See also related term: Tragedy.

TRAGIC NOVEL
See also related term: Tragedy.

TRAGICOMEDY
See also classified section: 2103.
See also related terms: Comic drama; Tragedy; Tragic drama.

TRAIN
   General literature. Film.
      Treatment of TRAIN. Dissertation abstract. 426.

TRAIN IMAGERY
See also related term: Train.

TRAINING
   Bibliographical.
      On TRAINING of librarians about rare books; manuscripts. 1109.
   Professional topics. Humanities.
      TRAINING of teaching assistants. 2695.

TRAITOR
See also related term: Betrayal.

TRAMOYA
See also related term: Staging.

TRANSCENDENCE
   Literary theory and criticism. Deconstructionism and hermeneutics.
      Role of the individual; relationship to TRANSCENDENCE. 1636.

TRANSFERENCE
See also related term: Psychoanalytic theory.
   Literary theory and criticism. Psychoanalytic literary theory and criticism.
      On reading; relationship to TRANSFERENCE. Application of theories of Jung, Carl Gustav; Lacan, Jacques. 1907.

TRANSFORMATIONAL-GENERATIVE APPROACH
See also related term: Transformational-generative grammar.
Documents applying specific approaches are so numerous that access to them is provided only in the electronic versions of the *Bibliography*.

TRANSFORMATIONAL-GENERATIVE GRAMMAR
Used for: Generative grammar; Transformational grammar.

TRANSFORMATIONAL-GENERATIVE GRAMMAR—APPLICATION
   Literary theory and criticism. Linguistic literary theory and criticism and reader-response theory and criticism.
      Application of TRANSFORMATIONAL-GENERATIVE GRAMMAR. 1747.

TRANSFORMATIONAL GRAMMAR
Use: Transformational-generative grammar.

TRANSFORMATIONAL RULES
See also related term: Transformational-generative grammar.

TRANSGRESSION
See also classified section: 2926.
Used for: Boundary crossing.
   Literary forms. Translation.
      As TRANSGRESSION; relationship to representation. 2552.
   Literary theory and criticism. Deconstructionism.
      Relationship to mysticism; TRANSGRESSION. Theories of Derrida, Jacques compared to Eckhart, Meister. 1592.

TRANSLATION
See also classified section: 2508 ff.
See also narrower term: Simultaneous translation.
See also related terms: Teaching of translation; Translation theory; Translator.
See also: entries under headings for specific language translation, e.g., English language translation, French language translation, etc.
   General literature.
      On TRANSLATION; relationship to teaching. 194.
   Genres. Poetry.
      On TRANSLATION. 2276.

TRANSLATION EQUIVALENCE
See also related terms: Translation; Translation theory.

TRANSLATION ERRORS
See also related term: Translation.

TRANSLATION STYLE
See also related term: Translation.

TRANSLATION THEORY
See also classified section: 2567 ff.
See also related term: Translation.

TRANSLATOR
See also related terms: Interpreter; Translation.
   General literature. Television and radio in Europe.
      Role of TRANSLATOR; interpreter. 886.

TRANSMISSION
See also related term: Stemma.

TRANSSUMPTIO
   Figures of speech.
      Relationship to *TRANSSUMPTIO*; assumptio. 2350.

TRANSUBSTANTIATION
See also related term: Eucharist (sacrament of).

TRANSVESTISM
   General literature. Film.
      Treatment of TRANSVESTISM; homosexuality in Waters, John: *Pink Flamingos*; *Polyester*. 502.
   Literary theory and criticism. Feminist literary theory and criticism.
      On TRANSVESTISM; study example: Joyce, James: *Ulysses*. Treatment in Gilbert, Sandra M.; Gubar, Susan. 1655.

TRANSVESTITE
See also related term: Transvestism.

TRAUBERG, LEONID ZAKHAROVICH (1902-)
   General literature. Film.
      On Kozintsev, Grigoriĭ Mikhaĭlovich and TRAUBERG, LEONID ZAKHAROVICH: *Odna*. 614.

TRAVEL
See also related terms: Tourism; Voyage.

TRAVESTY
   Literary forms. Parody.
      And TRAVESTY; pastiche; relationship to social relations; psychology. Application of communication theory. 2414.

TREATISE
See also related term: Essay.

TREMAINE, MARIE (1902-1984)
   Bibliographical. Printing in Canada.
      And bibliography. Role of TREMAINE, MARIE. Reminiscence. 1189.

TREMENDISMO
See also related term: Spanish novel.

TREVANION, MICHAEL
   Bibliographical. 1900-1999.
      Role of Nowell-Smith, Simon Harcourt; TREVANION, MICHAEL as bibliographer; relationship to book collecting. 1094.

TRILLING, LIONEL (1905-1975)
   Literary theory and criticism.
      Theories of Burke, Kenneth; TRILLING, LIONEL. Review article. 1329.
      Theories of Matthiessen, F. O.; TRILLING, LIONEL. Review article. 1333.

TRIUMPH
Used for: Victory.
   Themes and figures. Defeat.
      Relationship to TRIUMPH. 2844.

TRIVIALLITERATUR
See also related term: Popular literature.

TROILUS
See also classified section: 2927.

TROPES (RHETORIC)
Use: Figures of speech.

TRUFFAUT, FRANÇOIS (1932-1984)
  General literature. Film.
    By TRUFFAUT, FRANÇOIS: *Tirez sur le pianiste*. 299.
    On TRUFFAUT, FRANÇOIS: *L'Argent de poche* as pedagogical tool. 303
    ——: *Les Quatre Cents Coups* as imaginary biography. 577.
    Role of music in TRUFFAUT, FRANÇOIS: *Les Quatre Cents Coups*. 508.
    Treatment of children in TRUFFAUT, FRANÇOIS: *Les Quatre Cents Coups*; *L'Enfant sauvage*; *L'Argent de poche*. Theories of Freud, Sigmund. 298.

TRUTH
See also related term: Fact.
  Genres. Autobiography by women writers.
    Treatment of the self; relationship to TRUTH. Feminist approach. 2053.
  Genres. Fiction.
    Nonreferential language; relationship to TRUTH compared to fictionality. 2142.
  Genres. Poetry.
    Relationship to TRUTH. 2278.
  Literary movements.
    Postmodernism. Relationship to authority; TRUTH. 1022.
  Literary theory and criticism.
    Interpretation; relationship to TRUTH. 1414.
    Role of laughter as aesthetic device; relationship to TRUTH. Theories of Bakhtin, Mikhail Mikhaĭlovich. 1499.
  Themes and figures. Reality and TRUTH. 2907.
    Relationship to representation. 2908.
    —— in narrative. 2905.

TSUKERMAN, SLAVA
  General literature. Film.
    On TSUKERMAN, SLAVA: *Liquid Sky*. Interview. 237.

TUBERCULOSIS
See also classified section: 2928.

TUDOR, HENRY, EARL OF RICHMOND
Use: Henry VII, King of England (1456-1509).

TUNIS
  General literature. Film.
    Treatment of evil at Journées Cinématographiques de Carthage in TUNIS (1988). 367.

TUNISIA
See also narrower term: Tunis.

TURI, GABRIELE
  Bibliographical. Publishing by Einaudi (1935-1956).
    Treatment in TURI, GABRIELE: *Casa Einaudi: Libri uomini idee oltre il fascismo*. 1234.

TURKEY
  General literature. Film. Film genres: documentary film in TURKEY.
    Dissertation abstract. 815.

TURNER, JOSEPH MALLORD WILLIAM (1775-1851)
  General literature.
    Language; relationship to imagery in painting by TURNER, JOSEPH MALLORD WILLIAM. 168.

TURNER, VICTOR WITTER (1920-1983)
  General literature.
    Influence on theories of TURNER, VICTOR WITTER. 203.
  Literary theory and criticism.
    Contributions of TURNER, VICTOR WITTER. 1474.
    Cultural criticism. Theories of TURNER, VICTOR WITTER. 1310.
    Relationship to theories of TURNER, VICTOR WITTER. 1557.
    Theories of TURNER, VICTOR WITTER. 1501, 1513.

TWINNING
See also related term: Twins.

TWINS
  General literature. Film.
    Treatment of TWINS in Greenaway, Peter: *A Zed and Two Noughts* compared to Barth, John: "Petition"; Calvino, Italo: *Il visconte dimezzato*; Schwob, Marcel: *Les Sans-Gueules*. Feminist approach. 437.

TYPE SIZE
  Bibliographical. Printing. Typography. 1400-1999.
    Role of TYPE SIZE. 1227.

TYPEFACES
  Bibliographical. Printing. Typography in Amsterdam. 1600-1799.
    Role of Dijk, Christoffel van; Kis, Miklós; relationship to TYPEFACES in Armenian language. 1228.

TYPOGRAPHICAL ERRORS
See also related term: Typography.

TYPOGRAPHY
See also classified section: 1222 ff.

TYPOLOGY
  Literary theory and criticism.
    Role of TYPOLOGY; relationship to comparative literature. 1548.

U.S.S.R.
Used for: Soviet Union.
See also narrower terms: Georgian S.S.R.; Russian S.F.S.R.
  General literature. Film. Film genres: avant-garde film in U.S.S.R. 758.
  General literature. Film. Film genres: comic film in U.S.S.R. 794.
  General literature. Film. Film genres: documentary film in U.S.S.R.
    Treatment of youth; relationship to *glasnost'*. 770.
  General literature. Film. Film genres: science fiction film in U.S.S.R. 783.
  General literature. Film in U.S.S.R. 398, 424.
    Interview with Plakhov, Andreĭ. 238.
    Relationship to *perestroĭka*. 269.
    Role of *perestroĭka*; relationship to Goskino. 443.
  General literature. Film in U.S.S.R. (1986-1989).
    Relationship to *perestroĭka*. 576.
  Professional topics. Censorship in U.S.S.R.
    Interview with Golodnyĭ, Mikhail. 2590.

UBERSFELD, ANNE
  General literature. Theater.
    Relationship to discourse. Semiotic approach. Theories of UBERSFELD, ANNE. 937.

UNCERTAINTY
  General literature.
    Relationship to determinism; UNCERTAINTY. 192.

UNCIAL
See also related term: Manuscripts.
  Bibliographical. Manuscripts.
    In UNCIAL in Biblioteca Vallicelliana. 1126.

THE UNCONSCIOUS
See also related terms: Consciousness; *Memoria*.
  Literary theory and criticism. Psychoanalytic literary theory and criticism.
    Style; relationship to THE UNCONSCIOUS. 1902.
  Literary theory and criticism. Reader-response theory and criticism and feminist literary theory and criticism.
    Relationship to THE UNCONSCIOUS of women. Theories of Freud, Sigmund; Lacan, Jacques. 1940.

UNDERSTANDING
See also related term: Comprehension.
  Literary forms. Translation.
    Relationship to UNDERSTANDING; untranslatability of poetic language; study example: Rimbaud, Arthur: *Une Saison en enfer*; *Illuminations*. Application of theories of Gadamer, Hans-Georg. 2535.

UNDERWORLD
See also classified section: 2929.

UNGER, RUDOLF (1876-1942)
  Professional topics. Comparative literature.
    Sources in history of ideas. Role of Gundolf, Friedrich: *Shakespeare und der deutsche Geist*; UNGER, RUDOLF: *Hamann und die Aufklärung*. 2623.

UNGNAD, HANS, BARON ZU SONNECK (1493-1564)
  Bibliographical. Printing. Illustration. 1500-1599.
    By UNGNAD, HANS, BARON ZU SONNECK. 1219.

UNIT-IDEA
See also related term: History of ideas.

UNITED ARTISTS CORPORATION—STUDY EXAMPLE
  General literature. Film by independent filmmakers.
    Relationship to film industry; study example: UNITED ARTISTS CORPORATION. Film history. 232.

UNITED STATES
See also narrower terms: Southern United States; Western United States.
See also: entries under individual states.
  Bibliographical.
    In Great Britain; UNITED STATES. Bibliography. 1117.
    University libraries in UNITED STATES; relationship to Polish literature. 1115.
  Bibliographical. Printing.
    In UNITED STATES (1649-1859). 1155.
  Bibliographical. Printing in Canada and UNITED STATES. 1800-1899.
    Role of Mackenzie, William Lyon. 1186.
    ——; relationship to politics. 1174.
  Bibliographical. Publishing in UNITED STATES. 1239, 1240.
    By Grove Press. 1233, 1235, 1257, 1264.
    ——. Interview (1981) with Rosset, Barnet Lee, Jr. 1256.
    ——. Interview with Allen, Donald Merriam. 1242.
    ——; relationship to *Evergreen Review*. 1250, 1274.
    ——; relationship to *Evergreen Review*; jazz music. 1248.
    ——; role of Rosset, Barnet Lee, Jr. 1241.
  Bibliographical. Publishing in UNITED STATES. 1800-1899.
    By Mosher, Thomas Bird. 1238.
  Bibliographical. Publishing in UNITED STATES; France.
    By Grove Press; Olympia Press. Interview with Girodias, Maurice. 1243.
  General literature. Film.
    By Fassbinder, Rainer Werner. Reception study: reception in UNITED STATES. 617.

SEE CLASSIFIED SEQUENCE FOR ADDITIONAL ENTRIES

General literature. Film. Film adaptation (1920-1984).
Of women writers in England and UNITED STATES. Handbook. 697.

General literature. Film. Film genres: comic film in UNITED STATES.
Relationship to vaudeville. Dissertation abstract. 774.

General literature. Film. Film genres: documentary film.
Treatment of Basques in UNITED STATES in Bordagaray, Stanley George, Jr.: *Amerikanuak: The Basques of the American West.* 816.

General literature. Film. Film genres: silent film in UNITED STATES and Russian S.F.S.R.
Melodrama; relationship to temporality. Theories of Benjamin, Walter. 757.

General literature. Film. Film genres: spy film in UNITED STATES.
Encyclopedia. 781.

General literature. Film. Film theory and criticism: film history in UNITED STATES; Germany.
Review article. 838.

General literature. Film (1929-1984).
Treatment of baseball in UNITED STATES. Dissertation abstract. 319.

General literature. Film and television in UNITED STATES (1954-1963).
Treatment of family. Dissertation abstract. 446.

General literature. Film and theater in UNITED STATES.
Role of Mamoulian, Rouben. Dissertation abstract. 594.

General literature. Film by Eastern European filmmakers in UNITED STATES; Europe. 523.

General literature. Film in UNITED STATES.
Dissertation abstract. 658.
Relationship to popular culture. 294.
Relationship to spectacle; imperialism. 546.
Treatment of politics. Bibliography: filmography. 666.
Treatment of Vietnam War compared to treatment in Wright, Stephen: *Meditations in Green.* 492.

General literature. Film in UNITED STATES. Film genres: war film.
Treatment of Vietnam War; relationship to rock and roll music compared to Herr, Michael: *Dispatches.* 773.

General literature. Film in UNITED STATES (1907-1922).
Role of star system. 315.

General literature. Film in UNITED STATES (1920-1970).
Treatment of adolescent females. Dissertation abstract. 568.

General literature. Film in UNITED STATES (1930-1939).
Treatment of doctor. Includes filmography. 646.

General literature. Film in UNITED STATES (1930-1990).
Treatment of American myth. 503.

General literature. Film in UNITED STATES (1970-1989).
Treatment of the Holocaust. 270.

General literature. Film in UNITED STATES (1975-1987).
And American fiction. Treatment of journalists. Application of theories of Lowenthal, Leo. Dissertation abstract. 439.

General literature. Film in UNITED STATES (1978-1988).
Regionalism. Dissertation abstract. 406.

General literature. Television: alternative television in UNITED STATES. 857.

General literature. Television in UNITED STATES.
Reflexivity. Dissertation abstract. 861.
Role of evangelism. 873.
Wrestling as paratheater. 877.

General literature. Television in UNITED STATES (1960-1975).
Imagery of Cold War in treatment of Vietnam War. Dissertation abstract. 921.

Genres. Fiction. Science fiction. 1800-1999.
Role of periodicals; relationship to fans in UNITED STATES. Publishing history. 2182.

Literary forms. Rhetoric.
History of rhetoric in England; Scotland; UNITED STATES (1650-1799). 2474.

Literary theory and criticism. Deconstructionism in UNITED STATES. 1601.

Literary theory and criticism. Reception theory in Germany; UNITED STATES. 1946.

Literary theory and criticism in UNITED STATES compared to Germany.
Relationship to empiricism. 1434.

Professional topics. Comparative literature in Europe; UNITED STATES.
Role of literary theory and criticism. 2603.

Professional topics. Humanities.
Canon; pedagogy in UNITED STATES; relationship to liberalism compared to conservatism. 2782.
On Italian studies; relationship to teaching in UNITED STATES. 2668.

Professional topics. Humanities in UNITED STATES.
Creative writing workshops. 2712.
Relationship to culture. Theories of Bloom, Allan David: *The Closing of the American Mind.* 2773.
Relationship to nihilism. Theories of Bloom, Allan David: *The Closing of the American Mind.* 2759.
Theories of Bloom, Allan David: *The Closing of the American Mind.* 2791.
——: *The Closing of the American Mind*; relationship to the past; democracy; reality. 2661.

UNITED STATES DEPARTMENT OF DEFENSE
Used for: Pentagon.

General literature. Film.
Treatment of war; role of UNITED STATES DEPARTMENT OF DEFENSE. 316.

UNITED STATES GOVERNMENT
See also narrower term: United States Department of Defense.

UNIVERSAL AUDIENCE
Literary forms. Rhetoric.
Rhetorical theory; relationship to UNIVERSAL AUDIENCE. Theories of Perelman, Chaim. 2442.

UNIVERSAL GRAMMAR
See also related term: Universals of language.

UNIVERSALITY
Literary theory and criticism.
Relationship to UNIVERSALITY. 1522.

UNIVERSALS OF LANGUAGE
Literary forms. Translation.
Relationship to UNIVERSALS OF LANGUAGE; study example: Bible. 2544.

UNIVERSITAH HA-'IVRET BI-YERUSHALAYIM
See also narrower term: Steven Spielberg Jewish Film Archive.

UNIVERSITÄT FÜR BILDUNGSWISSENSCHAFTEN KLAGENFURT
Professional topics. Comparative literature. 1900-1999.
At UNIVERSITÄT FÜR BILDUNGSWISSENSCHAFTEN KLAGENFURT; relationship to regionalism. 2624.

UNIVERSITÄT WIEN
General literature. Theater.
Role of Fachbibliothek für Theaterwissenschaft at UNIVERSITÄT WIEN. 967.

UNIVERSITIES
See also narrower terms: American universities; Canadian universities; University of Texas at Austin.
Bibliographical. Printing. History of printing in Europe. Middle Ages.
And UNIVERSITIES; relationship to modernity. 1193.
Literary theory and criticism.
Relationship to UNIVERSITIES. 1410.
Professional topics. Humanities.
On ageism; sexism in UNIVERSITIES. Theories of Eco, Umberto; Derrida, Jacques. 2670.
On French literature; relationship to dissemination in UNIVERSITIES. 2667.

UNIVERSITY LIBRARIES
Bibliographical.
UNIVERSITY LIBRARIES in United States; relationship to Polish literature. 1115.

UNIVERSITY LIFE
See also related terms: Academia; Universities.

UNIVERSITY OF MANCHESTER
See also related term: John Rylands University Library of Manchester.

UNIVERSITY OF TEXAS AT AUSTIN
See also narrower term: Harry Ransom Humanities Research Center.
Bibliographical.
Role of library collection; relationship to canon. Collection study of collection at Harry Ransom Humanities Research Center at UNIVERSITY OF TEXAS AT AUSTIN. 1112.

UNIVERSITY PRESSES
Bibliographical. Publishing. 1900-1999.
By UNIVERSITY PRESSES. 1268.

UNPUBLISHED MANUSCRIPTS
Bibliographical. Manuscripts.
UNPUBLISHED MANUSCRIPTS; relationship to copyright law. 1124.

UNRUH, FRITZ VON (1885-1970)
General literature. Film.
Treatment of artist; relationship to mass media in UNRUH, FRITZ VON: *Phaea.* 378.

UNTRANSLATABILITY
Literary forms. Translation.
Relationship to understanding; UNTRANSLATABILITY of poetic language; study example: Rimbaud, Arthur: *Une Saison en enfer; Illuminations.* Application of theories of Gadamer, Hans-Georg. 2535.

UPRISING
See also related term: Revolution.

URBAN AREAS
Used for: Cities.
General literature. Film in black Africa.
Relationship to URBAN AREAS. 368.
General literature. Film in URBAN AREAS of black Africa. 362.

URBAN CULTURE
See also related term: Urban areas.

URBAN DWELLERS
See also related term: Urban areas.

URBAN LANDSCAPE
See also related term: Urban areas.

URBAN POETRY
Use: City poetry.

URBAN SOCIETY
See also related term: Urban areas.

URBANIZATION
See also related term: Urban areas.

URINUS, AUGUST FRIEDRICH
Use: Eschenburg, Johann Joachim (1743-1820).

USER INTERFACE
See also related term: Computer.

UTOPIA
See also classified section: 2930.
See also related terms: Dystopia; Dystopian fiction; Dystopian novel; Utopian fiction; Utopianism.
  General literature by women writers.
    Relationship to feminism; UTOPIA. 107.

UTOPIAN FICTION
See also classified section: 2185 ff.
See also related terms: Dystopian fiction; Fantasy; Science fiction; Utopia.
  Genres. Fiction. UTOPIAN FICTION and dystopian fiction. 1500-1999.
    Treatment of medicine. 2185.

UTOPIAN LITERATURE
See also narrower term: Utopian fiction.
See also related term: Utopia.

UTOPIAN NOVEL
See also related term: Dystopian novel.

UTOPIANISM
See also classified section: 2931.
See also related term: Utopia.
  Literary theory and criticism. Marxist literary theory and criticism.
    Relationship to UTOPIANISM. 1786.

UTTERANCE
See also related term: Discourse.

VADIM, ROGER (1927-)
  General literature. Film. Film adaptation.
    Treatment of libertinism; women in film adaptation of Laclos, Pierre Ambroise François Choderlos de: *Les Liaisons dangereuses* by VADIM, ROGER. 679.

VAIHINGER, HANS (1852-1933)
  General literature.
    Relationship to science. Application of theories of Mach, Ernst: *Erkenntnis und Irrtum*; VAIHINGER, HANS. 145.

VÁLDES, OSCAR
  General literature. Film in Cuba.
    Interview with VÁLDES, OSCAR. 510.

VALERIUS FLACCUS, GAIUS (D. CA. 95 A.D.)
Used for: Flaccus, Gaius Valerius.
  Bibliographical. Manuscripts. Manuscript editing.
    Manuscript collation of VALERIUS FLACCUS, GAIUS: *Argonautica* by Carrion, Louis. 1151.

VALUE
Use: Economic value.

VALUES
See also narrower term: Moral values.
  General literature.
    Role of history; relationship to genre; VALUES; institution. 124.

VAN DAMME, CHARLIE
  General literature. Film.
    On Resnais, Alain: *I Want to Go Home*. Interview with Benson, Laura; Leterrier, Catherine; VAN DAMME, CHARLIE; Laureux, Jean-Claude. 609.

VARDA, AGNÈS (1928-)
  General literature. Film.
    On VARDA, AGNÈS: *Sans toit ni loi*. 649.
  General literature. Film in France by women filmmakers.
    Feminism in Dulac, Germaine; Epstein, Marie; VARDA, AGNÈS. 336.

VARIETY SHOW
Use: Vaudeville.

VARRONIAN SATIRE
Use: Menippean satire.

VAUDEVILLE
Used for: Variety show.
See also related terms: Burlesque; Comic drama.
  General literature. Film. Film genres: comic film in United States.
    Relationship to VAUDEVILLE. Dissertation abstract. 774.

VEGETABLES
See also related term: Vegetarianism.

VEGETARIANISM
  Literary theory and criticism. Feminist literary theory and criticism.
    Relationship to VEGETARIANISM. 1649.

VEHICLES
See also narrower term: Train.

VELLE, GASTON
  General literature. Film.
    Mise en scène; narrative in VELLE, GASTON: *Tour du monde d'un policier*. 549.

VENETIA
See also narrower term: Friuli-Venezia Giulia.

VENEZUELA
  General literature. Film in VENEZUELA. 496.

VENICE
  Bibliographical. Manuscripts. Illuminated manuscripts in VENICE; Rome. Renaissance.
    Role of Petrus. 1136.
  Bibliographical. Printing. Typography in VENICE (ca. 1500).
    Italics by Manuzio, Aldo; relationship to copyright. 1225.
  Bibliographical. Printing in VENICE. 1500-1599.
    Role of Sessa, Giovanni Battista. 1154.

VENISON, ALFRED
Use: Pound, Ezra (1885-1972).

VENNERØD, PETTER
  General literature. Film.
    On Wam, Svend and VENNERØD, PETTER: *Bryllupsfesten*. 226.

VERACITY
See also related term: Truth.

THE VERBAL
  General literature.
    Visual imagery; relationship to THE VERBAL. 57.
  Genres. Drama.
    Role of the visual; relationship to THE VERBAL; staging. 2071.

VERGANGENHEITSBEWÄLTIGUNG
See also related terms: The Holocaust; Nazism.

VERISIMILITUDE
Used for: Vraisemblance.
  Literary forms. Rhetoric.
    Figuration; VERISIMILITUDE. Treatment in Weaver, Richard M. 2425.

VERNON, HOWARD
  General literature. Film.
    Role of VERNON, HOWARD in Melville, Jean-Pierre: *Le Silence de la mer*; Lang, Fritz: *Die tausend Augen des Dr. Mabuse*. Includes discussion with Vernon. 345.

VERSE
See also related term: Folk song.

VERSIFICATION
See also related term: Prosody.

VICTORY
Use: Triumph.

VIDEO
Use: Videotape.

VIDEO ART
  General literature. Film. Film genres: avant-garde film and VIDEO ART.
    Relationship to feminism. 787.
  General literature. Film and VIDEO ART; music video.
    Role of sexuality; relationship to Postmodernism. Imagery. 601.
  General literature. Television.
    On VIDEO ART. 862.

VIDEO RECORD
Use: Music video.

VIDEOCASSETTE
Use: Videotape.

VIDEODISK
See also related term: Videotape.

VIDEOTAPE
Used for: Video; Videocassette.
See also related term: Music video.
  General literature. Film. Film adaptation and television adaptation.
    Role of VIDEOTAPE in criticism of adaptation of Shakespeare, William. Dissertation abstract. 725.

VIDEOTAPE RECORDER
See also related term: Videotape.

VIDOR, KING (1894/6-1982)
  General literature. Film. Film theory and criticism: feminist film theory and criticism.
    Applied to VIDOR, KING: *Duel in the Sun*. 835.

VIETNAM WAR
  General literature. Film.
    Narrative structure. Treatment of VIETNAM WAR in Coppola, Francis Ford: *Apocalypse Now*. Application of theories of Lévi-Strauss, Claude. 644.

SEE CLASSIFIED SEQUENCE FOR ADDITIONAL ENTRIES

Narrative voice. Treatment of VIETNAM WAR compared to Rabe, David: *Sticks and Bones*; *Streamers*; *The Basic Training of Pavlo Hummel*. 317.

Treatment of hero of VIETNAM WAR; relationship to mythification. 333

Treatment of VIETNAM WAR; male-female relations in Kasdan, Lawrence: *The Big Chill* compared to Mason, Bobbie Ann: *In Country*. 239.

——; relationship to historical fact in Stone, Oliver: *Platoon* compared to Herr, Michael: *Dispatches*. 542.

——; relationship to language. 589.

——; relationship to nihilism in Stone, Oliver: *Platoon*. 516.

—— in Carradine, David: *Americana*. 246.

General literature. Film. Film genres: war film.

Treatment of African American soldiers; relationship to VIETNAM WAR. 782.

Treatment of VIETNAM WAR. 763, 813.

——. Bibliography. 817.

——; relationship to sex; violence. 760.

—— in Post, Ted: *Go Tell the Spartans*; Stone, Oliver: *Platoon*. 749.

General literature. Film and television.

Melodrama. Treatment of VIETNAM WAR in Ashby, Hal: *Coming Home*; *China Beach*. 485.

General literature. Film in United States.

Treatment of VIETNAM WAR compared to treatment in Wright, Stephen: *Meditations in Green*. 492.

General literature. Film in United States. Film genres: war film.

Treatment of VIETNAM WAR; relationship to rock and roll music compared to Herr, Michael: *Dispatches*. 773.

General literature. Television.

Treatment of deception of the public; relationship to VIETNAM WAR in Crile, George: *The Uncounted Enemy: A Vietnam Deception*. 910.

General literature. Television in United States (1960-1975).

Imagery of Cold War in treatment of VIETNAM WAR. Dissertation abstract. 921.

VIEYRA, PAULIN SOUMANOU (1925-)

General literature. Film.

By VIEYRA, PAULIN SOUMANOU. 363.

VINOGRADOV, VIKTOR VLADIMIROVICH (1895-1969)

Literary theory and criticism.

Theories of Bakhtin, Mikhail Mikhaĭlovich: *Problemy poetiki Dostoevkogo* compared to VINOGRADOV, VIKTOR VLADIMIROVICH: *O khudozhestvennoĭ proze*. 1345.

VIOLENCE

General literature. Film. Film adaptation.

Treatment of VIOLENCE against women in Chopra, Joyce: *Smooth Talk* as film adaptation of Oates, Joyce Carol: "Where Are You Going, Where Have You Been?" 685.

General literature. Film. Film genres: political film in Hollywood (1970-1987).

Treatment of working class; relationship to VIOLENCE; collective struggle. Dissertation abstract. 778.

General literature. Film. Film genres: war film.

Treatment of Vietnam War; relationship to sex; VIOLENCE. 760.

Genres. Drama.

Treatment of VIOLENCE; terrorism. 2074.

Literary theory and criticism. Deconstructionism.

Relationship to VIOLENCE. Treatment in Derrida, Jacques compared to Levinas, Emmanuel. 1646.

VIRGIN MARY

See also classified section: 2932.

VIRGINIA

Professional topics. Humanities in VIRGINIA. 2683.

VIRGINITY

See also related term: Sexuality.

VIRILIO, PAUL (1932-)

General literature. Film. Film theory and criticism.

Perception in film; relationship to militarism. Theories of VIRILIO, PAUL: *Guerre et cinéma*. 841.

VISBY

Bibliographical. Publishing. Book trade in Sweden: VISBY (1909-1911). 1283.

VISCONTI, LUCHINO (1906-1976)

General literature. Film.

Treatment of sexuality; relationship to Nazism in Rossellini, Roberto: *Roma, città aperta*; VISCONTI, LUCHINO: *Ossessione*. 349.

General literature. Film. Film adaptation.

Of Tomasi di Lampedusa, Giuseppe: *Il gattopardo*; Mann, Thomas: *Der Tod in Venedig* by VISCONTI, LUCHINO. 742.

THE VISUAL

See also related term: Visual imagery.

General literature. Theater.

Treatment in performance theory; relationship to the aural; THE VISUAL. 941.

Genres. Drama.

Role of THE VISUAL; relationship to the verbal; staging. 2071.

Genres. Poetry. Concrete poetry.

Relationship to THE VISUAL. Application of theories of Stevenson, Charles Leslie. 2305.

Literary theory and criticism. Hermeneutics.

Relationship to THE VISUAL. 1724.

Literary theory and criticism. Semiotic literary theory and criticism.

Poetics; relationship to THE VISUAL. 1956.

VISUAL ARTS

General literature.

And VISUAL ARTS. Festschrift for Heckscher, Wilhelm Sebastian. 186.

——. Pedagogical approach. 139.

Perception compared to VISUAL ARTS. Pedagogical approach. 40.

Relationship to VISUAL ARTS. 165.

General literature for children.

Relationship to VISUAL ARTS. 98.

Literary theory and criticism. Postmodernist literary theory and criticism.

Relationship to VISUAL ARTS. 1858.

VISUAL IMAGERY

See also related term: The visual.

Bibliographical. Printing. Illustration.

VISUAL IMAGERY; language; relationship to signifier. 1212.

General literature.

VISUAL IMAGERY; relationship to the verbal. 57.

General literature. Theater.

VISUAL IMAGERY; relationship to text; Postmodernism in performance art by Anderson, Laurie. 958.

Genres. Prose. Historiography.

Use of photographs as documentation; relationship to VISUAL IMAGERY. 2331.

VISUAL METAPHOR

See also related term: The visual.

VISUAL PERCEPTION

Literary theory and criticism. Hermeneutics.

Relationship to VISUAL PERCEPTION. Theories of Ellul, Jacques. 1723.

VISUAL PROCESSING

See also related term: Visual perception.

VITAGRAPH COMPANY OF AMERICA

See also related term: Film industry.

General literature. Film adaptation.

Of Shakespeare, William: *Julius Caesar* by VITAGRAPH COMPANY OF AMERICA (1908). 723.

——: *Julius Caesar* compared to *Francesca da Rimini* by VITAGRAPH COMPANY OF AMERICA as film adaptation of Dante: *La Divina Commedia: Inferno*. Reception study. 738.

VITAPHONE

See also related term: Film industry.

General literature. Film.

Use of sound in Crosland, Alan: *The Jazz Singer* compared to use of VITAPHONE in short film. 653.

VIVISECTION

See also related term: Animals.

VLADIMIROVAS, LEVAS (1912-)

Bibliographical.

Libraries in Lithuania. Role of VLADIMIROVAS, LEVAS. 1105.

Relationship to libraries; publishing in Lithuania. Treatment in VLADIMIROVAS, LEVAS. Bibliography. 1118.

VOCABULARY

See also related terms: Dictionary; Terminology.

VOCABULARY ACQUISITION

See also related terms: Second language learning; Word.

VOCATION

Professional topics. Humanities.

Relationship to VOCATION; technology. 2723.

VODIČKA, FELIX (D. 1974)

Literary theory and criticism.

Theories of Mukařovský, Jan; VODIČKA, FELIX; Bakhtin, Mikhail Mikhaĭlovich. 1509.

Literary theory and criticism. Narrative theory.

On thematic structure; relationship to formalism; structuralism. Theories of Propp, Vladimir Iakovlevich compared to VODIČKA, FELIX. 1801.

VOEGELIN, ERIC (1901-1985)

Literary movements.

Modernism. Treatment in Chambers, Whittaker; VOEGELIN, ERIC; relationship to religion; politics. 1012.

VOICE

General literature. Film.

VOICE in Resnais, Alain: *L'Année dernière à Marienbad*; *Hiroshima mon amour*. 297.

VOICE-OVER NARRATION

See also related terms: Narrative voice; Point of view.

General literature. Film.

VOICE-OVER NARRATION in Duras, Marguerite: *India Song*. 263.

VOLKSMÄRCHEN

Use: Märchen.

VON HÜGEL, FRIEDRICH, BARON OF THE HOLY ROMAN EMPIRE
Use: Hügel, Friedrich, Freiherr von (1852-1925).

VON STERNBERG, JOSEF
Use: Sternberg, Josef von (1894-1969).

VON STROHEIM, ERICH
Use: Stroheim, Erich von (1885-1957).

VOYAGE
  Literary theory and criticism. Narrative theory.
    Relationship to space; VOYAGE. 1808.

VOYEURISM
See also related term: Sexuality.

VRAISEMBLANCE
Use: Verisimilitude.

WALKER & GREIG
  Bibliographical. Printing.
    Concurrent perfecting by WALKER & GREIG in Edinburgh (1817-1822). 1176.

WALZER, MICHAEL (1935-)
  Literary theory and criticism.
    Theories of WALZER, MICHAEL: *The Company of Critics*; *Interpretation and Social Criticism*. 1459.

WAM, SVEND
  General literature. Film.
    On WAM, SVEND and Vennerød, Petter: *Bryllupsfesten*. 226.

WAR
See also classified section: 2933 ff.
See also narrower terms: Nuclear war; Spanish Civil War; Vietnam War; World War I; World War II.
See also related terms: Revolution; War film.
  General literature. Film.
    Treatment of history; relationship to WAR; television. 513.
    Treatment of masculinity; relationship to love; WAR in Ashby, Hal: *Coming Home*; Scott, Tony: *Top Gun*. 301.
    Treatment of WAR; role of United States Department of Defense. 316.
  General literature. Theater.
    Scenography; relationship to camouflage; WAR. Dissertation abstract. 951.
  Themes and figures. Women; relationship to WAR.
    Bibliography (1974-1989). 2936.

WAR DANCE
See also related term: War.

WAR DEAD
See also related term: War.

WAR FICTION
See also narrower term: War novel.
See also related term: War.

WAR FILM
See also related term: War.
  General literature. Film. Film genres: WAR FILM.
    Treatment of African American soldiers; relationship to Vietnam War. 782.
    Treatment of Vietnam War. 763, 813.
    ——. Bibliography. 817.
    ——; relationship to sex; violence. 760.
    —— in Post, Ted: *Go Tell the Spartans*; Stone, Oliver: *Platoon*. 749.
  General literature. Film. Film genres: WAR FILM (1940-1955).
    Treatment of hero. 780.
  General literature. Film. Film genres: WAR FILM in England during World War II.
    Treatment of hero. 814.
  General literature. Film. Film genres: WAR FILM in Germany (1950-1959). 769.
  General literature. Film in United States. Film genres: WAR FILM.
    Treatment of Vietnam War; relationship to rock and roll music compared to Herr, Michael: *Dispatches*. 773.

WAR GAMES
See also related term: War.

WAR HERO
See also related term: War.

WAR IMAGERY
See also related term: War.

WAR NOVEL
See also classified section: 2251.

WAR POETRY
See also related term: War.

WAR RITES
See also related term: War.

WARFARE
See also related term: War.

WARHOL, ANDY (1928-1987)
Used for: Warhola, Andrew.

  General literature. Film (1963-1988).
    By WARHOL, ANDY; Morrissey, Paul. Dissertation abstract. 493.

WARHOLA, ANDREW
Use: Warhol, Andy (1928-1987).

WARSAW
  Bibliographical. Publishing. Book trade in WARSAW. 1700-1999. 1289.

WARSAW GHETTO
See also related term: Warsaw.

WATERMARKS
  Bibliographical. Printing. Paper.
    WATERMARKS (1789-1799); relationship to French Revolution. 1221.

WATERS, JOHN (1945-)
  General literature. Film.
    Treatment of transvestism; homosexuality in WATERS, JOHN: *Pink Flamingos*; *Polyester*. 502.

WATSON, JAMES D. (1928-)
  Literary theory and criticism. Narrative theory.
    Applied to biology. Treatment in WATSON, JAMES D.: *The Double Helix*. 1811.

WEAVER, PAT
Use: Weaver, Sylvester Laflin (1908-).

WEAVER, RICHARD M. (1910-1963)
  Literary forms. Rhetoric.
    Figuration; verisimilitude. Treatment in WEAVER, RICHARD M. 2425.
    Treatment in WEAVER, RICHARD M. Bibliography. 2501.

WEAVER, RICHARD M. (1910-1963)—STUDY EXAMPLE
  Professional topics. Humanities.
    Rhetoric; relationship to cultural conservatism; study example: Isocrates; Erasmus, Desiderius; WEAVER, RICHARD M. Dissertation abstract. 2653.

WEAVER, SYLVESTER LAFLIN (1908-)
Used for: Weaver, Pat.
  General literature. Television.
    Role of WEAVER, SYLVESTER LAFLIN; relationship to National Broadcasting Company. 882.

WEBB, PETER
  General literature. Film.
    Role of Lennon, John and McCartney, Paul in WEBB, PETER: *Give My Regards to Broad Street*. Application of theories of Lacan, Jacques. 603.

WEDDING
See also related term: Marriage.

WEIDHAAS, PETER
  Bibliographical. Publishing. Book trade.
    Book fair. Theories of WEIDHAAS, PETER. 1299.

WEIMAR REPUBLIC
  General literature. Film in Germany.
    Relationship to the Left in WEIMAR REPUBLIC. 504.

WEIR, PETER (1944-)
  General literature. Film.
    Narrative form; ambiguity; relationship to melodrama in WEIR, PETER: *Picnic at Hanging Rock*. 512.
    Rhetoric in WEIR, PETER: *Witness*. Dissertation abstract. 489.
    Treatment of nihilism in WEIR, PETER: *Dead Poets Society*. 400.
  General literature. Film. Film adaptation.
    Classical allusion in film adaptation of Lindsay, Joan: *Picnic at Hanging Rock* by WEIR, PETER. 703.

WELBY, VICTORIA, LADY (1837-1912)
Used for: Stuart Wortley, Victoria Alexandrina Maria Louisa; Welby-Gregory, Victoria Alexandrina Maria Louisa Stuart Wortley.
  Literary theory and criticism. Linguistic literary theory and criticism.
    Chronotope; relationship to otherness. Theories of Bakhtin, Mikhail Mikhaïlovich compared to WELBY, VICTORIA, LADY. 1753.

WELBY-GREGORY, VICTORIA ALEXANDRINA MARIA LOUISA STUART WORTLEY
Use: Welby, Victoria, Lady (1837-1912).

WELLEK, RENÉ (1903-)
  Literary theory and criticism.
    Interview with WELLEK, RENÉ. 1377.

WELLERISM
See also related term: Proverb.

WELLES, ORSON (1915-1985)
  General literature. Film.
    By WELLES, ORSON. 506.
    Treatment of detection in WELLES, ORSON: *Citizen Kane* compared to Hampton, Christopher: *Able's Will*. 358.

WENDERS, WIM (1945-)
  General literature. Film.
    Role of Handke, Peter in WENDERS, WIM: *Der Himmel über Berlin*. 236.

SEE CLASSIFIED SEQUENCE FOR ADDITIONAL ENTRIES

WENDT, MAX

Bibliographical. Printing. Illustration in Germany. 1900-1999.
By Dreyer, Erich; WENDT, MAX of three-dimensional pictures. 1217.

WEST GERMANY
Used for: BRD; Bundesrepublik Deutschland; FRG.
See also narrower term: Munich.

General literature. Film.
On Fassbinder, Rainer Werner: *Berlin Alexanderplatz*; relationship to television in WEST GERMANY. Dissertation abstract. 574.

General literature. Film in WEST GERMANY.
Treatment of mourning; memory; relationship to Third Reich; study example: Syberberg, Hans Jürgen: *Hitler, ein Film aus Deutschland*; Reitz, Edgar: *Heimat*. 566.

General literature. Television in Great Britain and WEST GERMANY.
Relationship to entertainment. 856.

General literature. Television in WEST GERMANY. 901.

WESTERN AMERICAN LITERATURE

Literary theory and criticism. New Historicism.
Relationship to WESTERN AMERICAN LITERATURE. 1845.

WESTERN ASIA
See also narrower terms: Israel; Turkey.
See also related term: Middle East.

WESTERN CULTURE

Professional topics. Humanities in India.
Role of literary theory and criticism; WESTERN CULTURE. 2783.

WESTERN FILM
Use: American Western film.

WESTERN LEVER PRINTING PRESS

Bibliographical. Printing in Western United States. 1800-1899.
Role of Artzt, Charles; relationship to WESTERN LEVER PRINTING PRESS. 1159.

WESTERN LITERATURE

Professional topics. Comparative literature.
Chinese literature compared to WESTERN LITERATURE. 2633.

WESTERN SLAVS
See also narrower term: Poles.

WESTERN UNITED STATES
Used for: American West.

Bibliographical. Printing in WESTERN UNITED STATES. 1800-1899.
Role of Artzt, Charles; relationship to Western Lever Printing Press. 1159.

General literature. Film.
And American literature. Treatment of Mormons in WESTERN UNITED STATES. 459.

WESTERN WORLD

General literature.
And art in WESTERN WORLD. Pedagogical approach. 138.

WHITE, EUGENE EDMOND (1919-)

Literary theory and criticism. Rhetorical criticism.
Bibliography of scholarship by WHITE, EUGENE EDMOND. 1954.

WHITE, HAYDEN V. (1928-)

Genres. Prose. Historiography.
Relationship to Russian history. Narrative. Theories of WHITE, HAYDEN V.: *Metahistory*. 2332.

WHITMAN, SARAH WYMAN (1842-1904)

Bibliographical. Printing.
Book design by WHITMAN, SARAH WYMAN. 1172.

WHO-DONE-IT FICTION
Use: Detective fiction.

WHORE
Use: Prostitute.

WIDE-SCREEN

General literature. Film on WIDE-SCREEN. 253.
CinemaScope. 235.
——; relationship to ideology. Application of theories of Bazin, André. 593.
—— compared to Cinerama. 242.
Mise en scène. Application of theories of Bazin, André. 265.

WIDOW

Genres. Prose. Devotional literature.
Treatment of blessing of WIDOW. Sources in Hippolytus: *Traditio Apostolica.* 2321.

WIENE, ROBERT (1881-1938)—STUDY EXAMPLE

General literature. Film.
Treatment of psychiatrist; study example: WIENE, ROBERT: *Das Kabinett des Doktor Caligari*; Robson, Mark: *Home of the Brave*; Hitchcock, Alfred: *Psycho*; Meyer, Russ: *The Immoral Mr. Teas*. 569.

WIESENGRUND, THEODOR
Use: Adorno, Theodor W. (1903-1969).

WILLIAMS, JOHN (FL. 1805)

Bibliographical. Printing. Binding in London. 1800-1899.
By WILLIAMS, JOHN. 1199.

WILLIAMS, RAYMOND (1921-)

Literary theory and criticism. Marxist literary theory and criticism.
Role of WILLIAMS, RAYMOND. 1788.

Professional topics. Humanities.
Relationship to tradition. Application of theories of Benjamin, Walter; WILLIAMS, RAYMOND. 2654.

WILSON, ADRIAN (1923-1988)

Bibliographical. Printing. 1900-1999.
Role of WILSON, ADRIAN. 1187.

WILSON, EDWARD OSBORNE (1929-)

Literary forms. Rhetoric.
In WILSON, EDWARD OSBORNE: *On Human Nature*; relationship to discourse framing. 2467.

WINNER, MICHAEL (1935-)

General literature. Film. Film genres: *film noir.*
Nonverbal communication in Garnett, Tay: *The Postman Always Rings Twice*; Hawks, Howard: *The Big Sleep*; Dmytryk, Edward: *Murder, My Sweet* compared to remakes by Rafelson, Bob; WINNER, MICHAEL; Richards, Dick. Dissertation abstract. 767.

WIRĀQAH
See also related term: Paper.

WISDOM
See also related term: Knowledge.

WITCH
See also classified section: 2935.

WITCHCRAFT
See also related term: Witch.

WOLF, CHRISTA (1929-)—STUDY EXAMPLE

Themes and figures. Troilus.
And Cressida; study example: opera; Morley, Christopher: *The Trojan Horse*; WOLF, CHRISTA: *Kassandra*. 2927.

WOMANHOOD
See also related terms: Femininity; Women.

WOMANISM
See also related term: Feminism.

WOMB

General literature. Film. Film genres: horror film.
Treatment of women; WOMB; relationship to the grotesque; hysteria of men in Cronenberg, David: *Dead Ringers*. Application of theories of Freud, Sigmund. 756.

WOMEN
See also classified section: 2936.
See also narrower terms: Adolescent females; Black women; Superwoman; Women filmmakers; Women writers; Working women.
See also related terms: Female characters; Female figures; Female identity; Female point of view; Femininity; Misogyny; Women's studies.

General literature.
Role of WOMEN; relationship to history; literature in Middle Ages. 105.
Treatment of WOMEN; relationship to moral values. 112.

General literature. Film.
Treatment of genius of WOMEN; relationship to Nazism in Pabst, Georg Wilhelm: *Komödianten*. 570.
Treatment of WOMEN; relationship to consumerism. Film history. 382.
——; relationship to marriage in Rapper, Irving: *Now, Voyager*. 286.
——; relationship to psychoanalytic literary theory and criticism. 633.
——; relationship to sexuality; fetishism in Sternberg, Josef von: *Der blaue Engel.* 579.
—— in Huston, John. 388.
—— in Southern United States. 488.

General literature. Film. Film adaptation.
Treatment of libertinism; WOMEN in film adaptation of Laclos, Pierre Ambroise François Choderlos de: *Les Liaisons dangereuses* by Vadim, Roger. 679.
Treatment of violence against WOMEN in Chopra, Joyce: *Smooth Talk* as film adaptation of Oates, Joyce Carol: "Where Are You Going, Where Have You Been?" 685.

General literature. Film. Film genres: documentary film (1970-1985) by women filmmakers.
Treatment of WOMEN. Dissertation abstract. 784.

General literature. Film. Film genres: horror film.
Treatment of WOMEN; womb; relationship to the grotesque; hysteria of men in Cronenberg, David: *Dead Ringers*. Application of theories of Freud, Sigmund. 756.

General literature. Film. Film genres: science fiction film.
And television; relationship to WOMEN as fans. Ethnography. Dissertation abstract. 746.

General literature. Film in Chicago (1906-1908).
And nickelodeon; amusement park as cultural space; relationship to sexuality of WOMEN. 536.

General literature. Middle Ages and Renaissance.
Treatment of WOMEN. Panel discussion. 150.

General literature. Television.
Treatment of disorder in housekeeping by WOMEN in *Roseanne* compared to *Married ... with Children*. 912.
Treatment of ordination of WOMEN in *Designing Women*. 904
Treatment of WOMEN in *China Beach*. 871.
—— in home; relationship to feminism. 906.

General literature. Television: music television.
Treatment of men; WOMEN; glamour; sexuality. 885.

General literature. Television: situation comedy (1980-1985).
Treatment of WOMEN as superwoman. 888.

Genres. Drama.
Role of WOMEN. 2089.

Genres. Novel.
Authority of WOMEN. 2187.

Genres. Novel. Popular romance novel.
Relationship to WOMEN; ideology; treatment in sociological literary theory and criticism. 2236.

Genres. Prose. Autobiographical prose.
And fiction; representation of WOMEN; legal discourse (1700-1899). 2317.

Literary forms. Rhetoric.
Relationship to collaboration in writing; WOMEN. 2466.

Literary movements.
Avant-garde. Role of WOMEN. 996.
——. Role of WOMEN. Interview with Kristeva, Julia. 995.

Literary theory and criticism. Feminist literary theory and criticism.
Relationship to history of WOMEN; historiography. 1690.
Role of WOMEN; relationship to writing; culture. 1708.

Literary theory and criticism. Reader-response theory and criticism and feminist literary theory and criticism.
Relationship to the unconscious of WOMEN. Theories of Freud, Sigmund; Lacan, Jacques. 1940.

Professional topics.
Role of writers's block; relationship to WOMEN in academia. 2577.

Professional topics. Humanities.
Role of WOMEN. 2728.
——; relationship to feminism. Review article. 2754.
—— in academia; study example: Stone, Lucinda Hinsdale. 2720.

Themes and figures. Human body of WOMEN. 1700-1799.
Review article. 2877.

WOMEN—AS AUDIENCE
General literature. Film.
Female spectator; relationship to magazines for WOMEN. 515.

General literature. Film: alternative film by women filmmakers for WOMEN. 310.

General literature. Film in France (1930-1939).
For WOMEN. Realism; relationship to melodrama. 626.

WOMEN CHARACTERS
Use: Female characters.

WOMEN DETECTIVES
See also classified section: 2937.
General literature. Television (1970-1979).
Treatment of WOMEN DETECTIVES. 911.

WOMEN FILMMAKERS
General literature. Film. Film genres: documentary film (1970-1985) by WOMEN FILMMAKERS.
Treatment of women. Dissertation abstract. 784.

General literature. Film: alternative film by WOMEN FILMMAKERS for women. 310.

General literature. Film by WOMEN FILMMAKERS.
Handbook. 436.
Relationship to feminism. 486.

General literature. Film in France by WOMEN FILMMAKERS.
Feminism in Dulac, Germaine; Epstein, Marie; Varda, Agnès. 336.
Role of feminism. Review article. 625.

General literature. Film in Hollywood by WOMEN FILMMAKERS. 248.

WOMEN MYSTICS
See also related term: Mysticism.

WOMEN NOVELISTS
Genres. Novel by WOMEN NOVELISTS.
Treatment of space. 2206.

Genres. Novel by WOMEN NOVELISTS. 1900-1999.
Treatment of exile in academia. Application of theories of Barthes, Roland: *S/Z*. 2213.

WOMEN POETS
Genres. Poetry by WOMEN POETS.
Treatment of sun goddess. 2283.

Genres. Poetry by WOMEN POETS. 1900-1999.
Treatment of exile. 2292.

WOMEN SAINTS
See also narrower term: Jeanne d'Arc, Saint (1412-1431).

WOMEN WORKERS
Use: Working women.

WOMEN WRITERS
See also narrower terms: Women novelists; Women poets; Women writers in exile.
See also related term: Écriture féminine.
General literature. Film. Film adaptation (1920-1984).
Of WOMEN WRITERS in England and United States. Handbook. 697.

General literature by WOMEN WRITERS. 4, 5, 102.
Poetics; relationship to gender. 35.
Relationship to feminism; utopia. 107.

General literature by WOMEN WRITERS. 1600-1699.
Includes biobibliographical information. 211.

General literature by WOMEN WRITERS. English language literature.
Handbook. 28.

Genres. Autobiography by WOMEN WRITERS.
Treatment of the self; relationship to truth. Feminist approach. 2053.

Genres. Autobiography by WOMEN WRITERS. 1700-1899.
Treatment of the self; relationship to duplicity in narrative. 2052.

Professional topics. Humanities.
Role of WOMEN WRITERS; relationship to reader; canon. Feminist approach. 2736.

Themes and figures. Exile.
Treatment in WOMEN WRITERS. 2850.

Themes and figures. The Holocaust.
Treatment in WOMEN WRITERS. 2868.

Themes and figures. The sublime.
And sexual difference; treatment in WOMEN WRITERS (1900-1999). Dissertation abstract. 2923.

WOMEN WRITERS IN EXILE
Literary movements.
Modernism. Relationship to WOMEN WRITERS IN EXILE. 1005.

WOMEN'S CULTURE
See also related term: Women.

WOMEN'S LIBERATION
See also related terms: Feminism; Women.

WOMEN'S RIGHTS
See also related term: Feminism.

WOMEN'S STUDIES
See also related term: Women.
Professional topics. Humanities.
Role of feminism; relationship to WOMEN'S STUDIES in Brazil. 2729.
Role of WOMEN'S STUDIES. 2753.
WOMEN'S STUDIES. 2815.

WOMEN'S THEATER GROUPS
General literature. Theater.
Collaboration in WOMEN'S THEATER GROUPS; relationship to rhetoric; politics. Feminist approach. 983.

WOODCUTS
Bibliographical. Printing. Illustration.
On WOODCUTS of Passion of Christ by Delbecq, Jean Baptiste and Schreiber, Wilhelm Ludwig. 1211.

WOODS, FRANK E. (1860?-1939)—STUDY EXAMPLE
General literature. Film.
And screenplay; film review; relationship to American Biograph Company; study example: WOODS, FRANK E.; Griffith, D. W. 229.

WOOLF, VIRGINIA (1882-1941)
Genres. Prose. Essay.
Treatment in WOOLF, VIRGINIA: "The Modern Essay." 2326.

WORD
See also: entries under headings for related terms beginning with the modifier *word*, e.g., *word association, word boundary*, etc.
General literature.
Role of WORD; relationship to structure. 156.
WORD. 160.
General literature. Theater: opera.
Symbolism in WORD; music; staging. 938.

WORD CHOICE
See also related term: Word.

WORD PLAY
See also narrower term: Pun.

WORDCRUNCHER COMPUTER PROGRAM—APPLICATION
Professional topics. Computer-assisted research.
Application of WORDCRUNCHER COMPUTER PROGRAM. 2644.

WORK TITLE
Literary forms. Rhetoric.
Relationship to WORK TITLE. 2456, 2473.
Literary forms. Translation.
Of names; WORK TITLE; forms of address. 2532.

WORKERS
Used for: Laborers.

See also related term: Working class.
General literature. Film in Hollywood (1933).
Role of actors as WORKERS; relationship to subjectivity. Dissertation abstract. 293.

WORKING CLASS
Used for: The proletariat.
See also related terms: Workers; Working class life.
General literature. Film. Film genres: political film in Hollywood (1970-1987).
Treatment of WORKING CLASS; relationship to violence; collective struggle. Dissertation abstract. 778.

WORKING CLASS LIFE
See also related term: Working class.
General literature. Film. Film adaptation.
And television in Great Britain (1959-1963). Realism; relationship to WORKING CLASS LIFE in film adaptation; television adaptation of drama; fiction. 711.

WORKING CLASS NOVEL
See also related term: Working class life.

WORKING CLASS WOMEN
See also related term: Working women.

WORKING WOMEN
Used for: Women workers.
General literature. Film (1930-1939).
Treatment of WORKING WOMEN in Beaumont, Harry: *Our Blushing Brides* compared to Bacon, Lloyd: *Marked Woman*. 384.

WORLD
See also narrower term: Western world.

WORLD LITERATURE
General literature. 1900-1999.
WORLD LITERATURE; relationship to European literature. 131.
Professional topics. Comparative literature.
National literature; relationship to WORLD LITERATURE. 2626.
Relationship to WORLD LITERATURE. 2610.
WORLD LITERATURE; relationship to national literature. 2608, 2616.
——; relationship to teacher training in East Germany. 2607.

WORLD WAR I
General literature. Film in Germany.
And German literature. Treatment of WORLD WAR I; World War II. 432.

WORLD WAR II
Used for: Great Patriotic War (USSR).
General literature. Film.
Treatment of WORLD WAR II; relationship to sacrifice in Plievier, Theodor: *Stalingrad*. 223.
General literature. Film. Film genres: war film in England during WORLD WAR II.
Treatment of hero. 814.
General literature. Film in Germany.
And German literature. Treatment of World War I; WORLD WAR II. 432.

WORLD ZIONIST ORGANIZATION
See also narrower term: Steven Spielberg Jewish Film Archive.

WORSHIP
See also related term: Liturgy.

WRAPPER BINDING
Bibliographical. Printing. Binding.
Chemise binding; WRAPPER BINDING. 1207.

WRESTLING
General literature. Television in United States.
WRESTLING as paratheater. 877.

WRITER
Used for: Author.
Bibliographical. Textual criticism.
Role of WRITER; reader. 1122.
General literature.
Psychology of WRITER. 88.
Role of WRITER. 15.
WRITER as profession; relationship to risk. 33.
Genres. Fiction.
Narrator as mediator between WRITER and reader. 2159.
Role of WRITER; relationship to reader; text. Philosophical approach. 2116.
Literary movements.
Postmodernism. Role of WRITER; relationship to reader; intertextuality. 1040.
Literary theory and criticism.
Of WRITER while living. 1571.
Relationship to mathematical theory. Treatment of WRITER; relationship to reader. 1347.
Literary theory and criticism. Deconstructionism.
Authority of WRITER; relationship to reader; allegory. Treatment in de Man, Paul: "Rhetoric of Temporality." 1589.
Literary theory and criticism. Feminist literary theory and criticism.
Role of WRITER; relationship to poststructuralism. 1704.

WRITERS
See also narrower terms: Dramatists; European writers; Feminist writers; Women writers.

WRITER'S BLOCK
Professional topics.
Role of WRITER'S BLOCK; relationship to women in academia. 2577.

WRITERS IN EXILE
See also narrower term: Women writers in exile.
See also related term: Exile.

WRITING
See also narrower term: Technical writing.
See also related terms: Composition; Teaching of writing; Written language.
General literature.
WRITING; relationship to feminism. 61.
Genres. Drama.
Collaboration in WRITING; theatrical production. Dissertation abstract. 2084.
Genres. Prose. Diary.
Role of WRITING; relationship to the self. 2322.
Literary forms. Rhetoric.
Relationship to collaboration in WRITING; women. 2466.
Role of *memoria*; relationship to WRITING. 2481.
Literary theory and criticism.
On WRITING of history; relationship to the future; nuclear war. 1540.
WRITING. Theories of Foucault, Michel. 1441.
Literary theory and criticism. Deconstructionism.
Role of WRITING; relationship to politics. Theories of de Man, Paul. 1631.
Literary theory and criticism. Feminist literary theory and criticism.
Relationship to collaboration in WRITING. 1652.
Role of women; relationship to WRITING; culture. 1708.
Literary theory and criticism. Poststructuralist literary theory and criticism.
On speech; WRITING; relationship to electronic language; surveillance. Theories of Foucault, Michel. 1885.
Professional topics. Humanities.
Role of WRITING of fiction in teaching of literature. 2713.

WRITING ACROSS THE CURRICULUM
Used for: Cross-disciplinary writing.
See also related term: Discourse community.
Professional topics. Humanities.
WRITING ACROSS THE CURRICULUM; relationship to professional discourse; discourse community. 2795.

WRITING DEVELOPMENT
See also related term: Writing.

WRITING SYSTEMS

See also related term: Written language.
Literary theory and criticism. Semiotic literary theory and criticism.
WRITING SYSTEMS; relationship to poetics. 1962.

WRITTEN LANGUAGE
See also related terms: Writing; Writing systems.
General literature.
On WRITTEN LANGUAGE; relationship to narrative voice; closure; oral tradition. 159.

WYLER, WILLIAM (1902-1981)
General literature. Film. Film adaptation.
Of Hellman, Lillian: *The Children's Hour* by WYLER, WILLIAM; role of Hayes, John Michael. 726.

YENSID, RETLAW
Use: Disney, Walt (1901-1966).

YESHIVA
See also related term: Judaism.

YIDDISH LANGUAGE LITERATURE
General literature. YIDDISH LANGUAGE LITERATURE. 27.

YOGI, MAHESH, MAHARISHI
Use: Mahesh Yogi, Maharishi.

YOUNG ADULTS—AS AUDIENCE
General literature for children; YOUNG ADULTS.
Role of bibliotherapy. 208.

YOUNG PEOPLE
Use: Adolescents.

YOUTH
General literature. Film. Film genres: documentary film in U.S.S.R.
Treatment of YOUTH; relationship to *glasnost'*. 770.
General literature. Film in Georgian S.S.R.
Treatment of YOUTH. 289.

YUGOSLAVIA
General literature. Film in Hollywood.
Reception study: reception in YUGOSLAVIA. 517.

YUGOSLAVIAN FILMMAKERS

General literature. Film by YUGOSLAVIAN FILMMAKERS.
Relationship to Hollywood. 397.

ZANUSSI, KRZYSZTOF (1939-)

General literature. Film.
Interview with ZANUSSI, KRZYSZTOF. 530.

ZAUM'
See also related terms: Neologism; Poetic language.

ZEFFIRELLI, FRANCO (1924-)

General literature. Film. Film adaptation.
Of Shakespeare, William: *Romeo and Juliet* by ZEFFIRELLI, FRANCO. Includes interview. 741.

ZHANG YIMOU
Use: Chang I-mo.

ZICH, OTAKAR (1879-1934)

Literary theory and criticism. Semiotic literary theory and criticism.
Relationship to structuralism compared to formalism. Theories of Mukařovský, Jan compared to ZICH, OTAKAR. 2007.

ZINNEMANN, FRED (1907-)

General literature. Film. Film genres: American Western film (1947-1957).
Treatment of patriarchy in ZINNEMANN, FRED: *High Noon* compared to Mann, Anthony: *The Tin Star*. 786.

ZIONISM
See also related term: Jews.

ZODIAC
See also related term: Astronomy.

ZOOLOGY
See also related term: Animals.

SEE CLASSIFIED SEQUENCE FOR ADDITIONAL ENTRIES

DOCUMENT AUTHOR INDEX

This index contains the names of all document authors, editors, illustrators, translators, etc., represented in the classified sequence. The name of the author, editor, and so on is listed first, followed by the entry number for the document listed.